TEXT IS PRINTED ON 10% POST
CONSUMER RECYCLED PAPER

# REGULATION OF FINANCIAL INSTITUTIONS

By

**Howell E. Jackson**

*Professor of Law*
*Harvard Law School*

and

**Edward L. Symons, Jr.**

*President, Dollins Symons Management, Inc.*
*(registered investment adviser)*
*Executive Vice President – Investments, Smithfield Trust Company*
*(state-chartered bank limited to trust powers)*

**AMERICAN CASEBOOK SERIES®**

WEST
GROUP

ST. PAUL, MINN., 1999

*To EVF, HVJ, & RHJ.*
        *HEJ*


*To my wife, Louise Quinn Symons,*
*and our children, Amy and Colin.*
        *ELS, Jr.*

# Preface

This casebook is experimental. Its goal is to provide the framework for an integrated law school course on the regulation of financial institutions, combining materials that traditionally have been covered in separate courses on banking law, insurance law, securities regulation, mutual funds, and pensions. There is no doubt that the financial services industry has become increasingly integrated in the past twenty years and that practitioners in the field must now be familiar with a number of different regulatory structures. Our premise in developing this book is that law school courses should be similarly broadened.

Another way in which this casebook is experimental is our intention to supplement it with materials made available to readers over the internet. These materials will include exercises on lending limits and professional responsibility, links to internet sites related to the regulation of financial institutions, readings on recent developments in the field, and various other academic materials. The address of this webpage, which will be available to the public by January 1999, is <http://cyber.harvard.edu/rfi/>. Professors interested in learning more about incorporating these internet materials into their teaching, should contact Howell Jackson at hjackson@law.harvard.edu.

Building as it does on past courses and casebooks, we have benefitted greatly from the work of those who have gone before us. For materials on banking law, we have incorporated elements of various editions of J.J. White and Ed Symons' banking law casebook, and have also profited from the extensive academic writings and thought-provoking teaching materials of Jonathan Macey and Geoffrey Miller. The treatises of Pauline Heller and Melanie Fein have also proved extremely useful in this area. In the insurance field, we are indebted to the work of Robert Keeton, Spencer Kimball, Alan Widiss, and especially Kenneth Abraham. In the field of securities regulation, various editions of the Jennings and Marsh casebook have been instructive as has the work of Don Langevoort, James Cox, and Robert Hillman and the writings of Thomas Hazen, David Lipton, Norman Poser, and David Ratner For investment company regulation, we have profited from the writings and guidance of Tamar Frankel, as well as from the suggestions of Cliff Kirsch. In pension law, we are indebted to John Langbein and Bruce Wolk's excellent casebook.

We are indebted to many people for their assistance and support in the production of this book. Professor Jackson expresses his thanks to Robert C. Pozen and John D. Hawke, Jr., for introducing him to the field and to Dean Robert C. Clark for generously supporting and encouraging his work on this book and related projects. Special thanks are also due to Susan Salvato and the staff of the Harvard Law School word processing department; to Jim Davis and Stephen Wagner for their careful editing of the manuscript; to Carol Igoe for her steadfast support of the entire production process; and to his many students and research assistants at Harvard Law School who contributed greatly to the book's development.

Former Professor Symons expresses two decades of thanks to former University of Pittsburgh School of Law Deans W. Edward Sell, John E. Murray, Jr. (now President of Duquesne University), and Mark A. Nordenberg (now Chancellor of the University of Pittsburgh) for their unwavering commitment to both teaching and scholarship. Ted Schroeder ('97) deserves special thanks for his research assistance, editing, and student's view of the materials. The law school's exceptional word processing center is lead by LuAnn Driscoll, and Karen Knochel, Carleen Mocello, Carolyn Rohan, and Barbara Salopek did their usual perfect job of manuscript preparation. And twenty-three years of students have provided both numerous ideas and much psychic income, all of which is greatly appreciated.

HOWELL E. JACKSON
EDWARD S. SYMONS, JR.

September 1998

# Summary of Contents

# Table of Contents

## PART III — INSURANCE INDUSTRY

## PART V — THE INVESTMENT COMPANY INDUSTRY

# PART VI — INTER-INDUSTRY COMPETITION

# Table of Cases and Regulatory Decisions

The principal cases and decisions are in bold type.  Cases and decisions that are cited or discussed in text are in roman type.  References are to pages.

# Table of Authorities

Authorities from which substantial extracts have been taken appear in bold type. Other authorities are in roman type. References are to pages.

# REGULATION OF
# FINANCIAL INSTITUTIONS

———————

# CHAPTER ONE

# THE BUSINESS OF FINANCIAL INSTITUTIONS

## Section 1. Introduction

This is a book about financial institutions and the ways these institutions are regulated in the United States. Most readers will already have a basic familiarity with these institutions. Banks and mutual funds, insurance companies and securities firms, all play prominent roles in our daily lives. These firms are the repository of much of our personal wealth, and they are the principal source of credit for most firms and individuals. In addition to this intermediation—that is, the linking of savers and borrowers—financial institutions offer numerous services essential to economic activity. Through check-writing and other payment services, financial institutions help us pay our bills. Insurance companies protect us against unexpected losses and expenses. And, many financial institutions serve as our advisors and agents in a variety of financial and other transactions. Less visible in daily life but equally important, financial institutions help implement a number of public policies. Depository institutions, for example, play a critical role in our country's monetary policy. Financial institutions also advance a wide range of social goals from income redistribution to civil rights initiatives, from consumer protection to credit allocation. The structure of our financial services industry even reflects a distinctly American vision of political economy.

The goal of this book is to take readers behind the familiar public facade of financial institutions and to examine the complex array of laws and regulatory structures that control almost every aspect of their operations. We explore a host of legal requirements applicable to a full range of financial institutions, considering how these rules have developed over time and what policies they were designed to advance. We regularly challenge the readers to evaluate our current legal structures critically. Do these regimes really advance the goals they were designed to address? Do the rules have any unintended and undesirable consequences? Might other legal structures better serve the public interest?

Where this book differs from prior efforts is its scope of coverage. In the past, commercial banks, savings and loan associations (also known as thrifts), insurance corporations, investment companies, and securities firms were considered separate industries with distinct products and discrete customer bases. Each industry had a unique system of regulation. Each was serviced by a specialized group of practitioners within the private bar. And each was the subject of a separate course of study within the law school curriculum. Over the past three decades, however, the lines between these categories of financial institutions have blurred. Today, what were once separate industries now compete in many arenas.  Commercial banks are major participants in the securities industry.  Brokerage houses as well as insurance firms have entered many fields that were traditionally the exclusive domains of banks and thrifts.  Computer technologies and increased financial sophistication have also given birth to numerous new products, such as securitized assets (e.g., bonds backed by mortgages and credit card receivables) and hybrid commodity/debt instruments (e.g., returns on savings accounts tied to the S&P 500 Index), which defy traditional systems of categorization.

This casebook responds to the changing landscape of the financial services industry by offering the first unified treatment of the field.  In contrast to prior texts that have focused on a single segment of the industry, we offer a trans-sectoral analysis, introducing readers to the major categories of financial intermediaries in the United States and the complex and highly idiosyncratic system of statutes, agencies, and regulations under which these institutions operate.  The first Part of the book covers depository institutions, such as commercial banks and savings and loan associations.  This Part provides an overview of the history and structure of depository institution regulation in the United States.  Using the regulation of depository institutions as a base, we then turn to insurance companies, broker-dealers, and investment companies.  In each area, we explore the history of that segment of the financial services industry and analyze regulatory problems and solutions unique to the segment.  The final section of the book examines a number of areas in which inter-sector competition has been particularly intense in the recent past and the jurisdictional fault-lines between sectors most hotly contested.

Of necessity, our analysis of many of the subjects will be skeletal.  The casebook is not intended to instill technical proficiency in all areas.  (Indeed, few practitioners or regulators would claim expertise in so many fields.)  We believe, however, that there are many advantages to adding breadth at the expense of some depth.  First, as a practical matter, lawyers in the financial services industry today cannot and do not limit themselves to a single field; they must have at least a general sense of neighboring fields in order to serve their clients effectively.  Second, as a pedagogical matter, there are numerous advantages of considering multiple sectors of the industry in a single course of study.  As is explored in numerous points throughout the book, the existence of related, but distinctive regulatory structures in each sector of the financial services industry poses a host of intriguing questions:  Does it make sense to have so many different legal rules and regulatory authorities for essentially similar economic functions?  Should the law of depository institutions be altered to resemble more closely our experiences in the securities field?  Should insurance firms be regulated like banks?  Of the many combinations of state and federal oversight that have evolved in this industry, which is the most sensible?  Finally, does it make sense to maintain distinctive regulatory structures for banking and insurance and securities firms, when the industry appears to be moving more and more towards consolidated financial services conglomerates, serving in one way or another the full range of financial services?

# Section 2.  Financial Intermediation and the Need for Regulation

Although this text is primarily concerned with laws and regulations, it is impossible to understand why these rules have developed or how the rules are likely to affect financial institutions without some appreciation of the business of financial intermediation.  We therefore begin our study by examining the economic role of financial intermediaries.  This role is outlined in the following excerpt by Dean Robert Clark.

---

## Robert C. Clark, The Federal Income Taxation of Financial Intermediaries
### 84 Yale L.J. 1603, 1605-13 (1975)

Financial intermediaries accumulate capital for reinvestment in debt or equity claims against ultimate investors such as nonfinancial business enterprises, governmental units, and purchasers of real property.  They are called intermediaries because they serve as middlemen between suppliers of capital–more particularly savers, investors, depositors, shareholders, policyholders, or beneficiaries–and investors in real assets.

Financial intermediaries may be grouped in two main classes according to their predominant source of funds.  One major class includes commercial banks, savings and loan associations, mutual savings banks, life insurance companies, fire and casualty insurance companies, mutual funds, real estate investment trusts, and public and private pension funds.  This class, which might be called "first order financial intermediaries," obtains most of its capital from individual households.  The other class, or "second order financial intermediaries," includes the Federal Reserve Banks, the Federal Home Loan Banks, finance companies, and many other institutions, and obtains funds directly from other financial entities, such as commercial banks, thrift institutions, and bank holding companies, and only indirectly from households and nonfinancial business enterprises. . . .

The enormous long term growth of financial intermediation is one of the most significant institutional facts about advanced economic systems as they have developed in this century.  The much studied and vigorously debated growth in the role of institutional investors in the stock markets is only one part of this movement, a part which for its own peculiar reasons has been highly publicized.  The role of financial intermediaries in the other major capital markets, such as the primary and secondary mortgage markets, the market for United States government securities, the market for corporate debt instruments, and the market for municipal securities, has been of equal or greater economic consequence.

The growth of financial intermediation is not accidental, nor is it a mere manifestation of the increasing complexity of our economic institutions.  The trend has its own economic logic.  Financial intermediaries offer several advantages to individual suppliers of capital:  putative financial expertise, economies of scale, and the ability to diversify and pool investments.

Intermediaries commonly advertise that their funds are managed by professional investment analysts, who might be thought to invest more wisely than the man in the street.  Intermediaries may realize economies of scale by allowing savers to share the costs of security analysis, portfolio management, and market transactions.  Diversification of financial assets allows savers or investors to reduce risk with no or little impairment of the expected return from their portfolios; intermediaries are a necessary means of achieving diversification because many individuals do not have enough money to diversify their investments successfully by themselves.  The pooling of assets by intermediaries enables the individual saver, who cannot accurately predict future contingencies affecting his need for money, to invest in relatively liquid claims against the intermediary, while the intermediary can reinvest those funds safely in less liquid and longer term claims against ultimate investors.  The reinvestment can be made with safety because of the law of large numbers:  what is a dramatic contingency to the individual is a small one to the intermediary, which is only concerned with the probabilities of overall net changes in the flow of funds to and from its suppliers of capital.  The pooling of assets is perhaps the basic reason for the growth of financial intermediaries.  It encourages capital formation and investment in longer term financial assets, and therefore suggests that intermediation has a beneficial effect on economic growth and stability.  Because of their importance to the economy in general and to the investment patterns of individuals in particular, financial intermediaries have been a subject of serious legislative concern. . . .

Financial intermediaries perform broadly similar economic functions.  They enable pooling and diversification of portfolio risk to take place more efficiently and on a larger scale.  By pooling their claims against assets, a group of individuals can take advantage of the law of large numbers, according to which contingencies unpredictable on an individual basis are quite predictable for large numbers.   In its simplest application, pooling enables financial intermediaries to accomplish liquidity intermediation.  Individuals often want to hold liquid assets because they cannot accurately predict future contingencies that will affect their need for cash, whereas users of capital, such as corporations, often want capital left with them for long periods of time.  An intermediary often issues relatively liquid claims against itself, that is, claims convertible to money within a short time at no or little sacrifice of their full value, and uses the proceeds to invest in fairly illiquid claims.  The intermediary can safely invest in illiquid claims, up to a point, because of the relative stability and predictability of the exercise of claims against itself that comes with large numbers of them.  Thus, the claim of even the smallest demand deposit accountholder at a commercial bank is, at any given time, quickly convertible into a fixed amount of currency or, indeed, usable as money itself.  Otherwise demand deposit accounts would not be as popular as they are.  Yet banks in turn do not simply make callable loans or invest in highly liquid securities on the strength of these assets, but make many business loans for which there is no significant secondary market, and which have substantial periods to maturity:  30, 60, and 90 day loans and even term loans for periods longer than a year.  Similarly, thrift institutions, whose individual depositors–or, more appropriately, "suppliers of capital"–hold savings deposits and time accounts that can be converted to cash on relatively short notice, make long term mortgage loans which are often not readily marketable.  Mutual fund shares are perhaps the ultimate in liquidity for the small investor who wishes to participate in the stock market, since he can always cash in his shares quickly for their net asset value.

. . . .

On the other hand, insurance companies and pension funds effect a different kind of intermediation between the time structures of the preferences for money of capital suppliers and capital users. In the absence of special legislation providing for cash surrender values and requiring that life insurance companies stand ready to make policy loans, a life insurance contract would be an illiquid investment. Yet a principal function of insurance (and of pension plans) is to provide money upon the happening of a predicted event or uncertain contingency that dramatically increases the capital supplier's need for money. Even if the policy were illiquid in general, it would become quickly convertible to cash without penalty at precisely the time when cash is needed to make up for a sudden though previously specified loss. A capital supplier who wanted to provide for beneficiaries in the event of his death by investing in a financial asset such as a long term commercial mortgage, and who had funds to invest in only one or two such assets, would be foolish to do so directly, even though his life expectancy might exactly equal the term of the mortgage loan. If he should die at a time other than the projected one, the need to convert the loan quickly into cash might entail a considerable sacrifice. Similar remarks can be made about fire and casualty insurance and about pension rights.

The other significant common economic function of financial intermediaries, their ability to provide diversification for public suppliers of capital, has been thoroughly discussed in the literature. It may be argued that financial intermediaries are not needed to provide pooling and investment diversification, because these functions can be served by the operation of ordinary corporations and the capital markets. As for pooling, if one looks only at the stock markets and the market for United States government securities, it might be thought that highly liquid assets are readily available for the buying without the help of intermediaries. This is true, of course, but the situation is not so fortunate in the markets for municipal securities and mortgage loans. As for investment diversification, it might be thought that corporations themselves could provide all of it that is needed; conglomerate mergers are routinely justified on the ground that they reduce risk to the shareholders. Why not allow conglomerates freely to diversify, so that even the smallest investor who can efficiently buy shares in only one public company can have the opportunity to buy shares in a widely diversified pool of business activities? Apart from serious doubts about the ability of managements to operate effectively conglomerate business empires, the answer is that diversification by this method will realize only a small portion of the possibilities for combining interests in different business activities. . . . The conglomeration of business activities by merger is in this sense a clumsy way of achieving the same end as putting together a diversified portfolio of securities.

---

As Dean Clark explains, financial institutions provide specialized services for borrowers and savers. The nature of these services, it is generally assumed, warrants a degree of regulatory control and oversight substantially more intrusive and expensive than the legal rules governing other business enterprises. The validity and robustness of this assumption warrant special attention. The vast majority of the legal rules covered in this text rest, either explicitly or implicitly, on the notion that financial intermediaries are special. In some areas, the institutions are thought to be special because they are so well-situated—or perhaps even indispensable—for effecting governmental programs such as monetary policy. More consistently, however, the principal justification for regulation in the field concerns the tendency of financial intermediaries to take excessive risks, if not severely restrained by governmental controls.

There are many reasons for our extensive regulation of financial institutions. Some concern the kinds of investors that place their funds in financial intermediaries and the limited capacity of these investors to protect themselves when dealing with a financial intermediary. The protection of public investors is not, however, the only reason for regulation in this field.

### 1. Protection of Public Investors

*a.) Collective Solution to Transaction Costs that Impede Self-Help.* A common explanation of risk-regulation in financial intermediaries proceeds on the assumption that public investors in financial intermediaries (that is, depositors, insurance policy-holders, and mutual fund shareholders) need some degree of protection from risk-taking in financial intermediaries. At a minimum, investors want to know the degree of risk associated with particular investments before they transfer their resources to an intermediary, and ideally also a sense of how those risks compare with the risks associated with other comparable investments. Equally important, once an investment is made, investors want assurances that the risk profile of their intermediary does not change in way that disadvantages the investor. Because their individual investments are small and the business of financial intermediation complex, public investors by themselves lack the expertise and incentives to demand appropriate information about the risk profile of financial intermediaries or to decipher that information or to monitor subsequent behavior on the part of an intermediary. The government, according to this line of reasoning, has a critical role to play in regulating and supervising the riskiness of financial intermediaries. In this view, much of our regulatory structure can be understood as a collective "best guess" regarding the form and content of advance disclosure of institutional risk-taking that most investors would demand before making an investment, as well as a continuing set of restrictions on institutional risk-taking reflecting a tradeoff between risk and return that most of the investing public would demand from financial intermediaries if the public had the time and expertise to police intermediaries directly.

*b.) Absolute Protection of Terms of Investment.* A second justification for risk regulation in financial intermediaries proceeds from a desire to offer complete or near-complete safety for members of the public who invest in financial intermediaries. People who make deposits in banks or purchase insurance contracts, it is sometimes said, expect (or should expect) to have those investments honored according to their literal terms. In other words, it is assumed, these investors don't want or expect to accept any degree of variation in return on their investments. Governmental regulation of intermediary operations ensures that the obligations of financial intermediaries are, in fact, honored according to their terms. Government insurance programs, such as those the Federal Deposit Insurance Corporation operates for depository institutions, also achieve this goal for insured depositors.

## 2. Elimination of Externalities from the Failure of Intermediaries

Other justifications for risk-regulation of financial intermediaries focus on possible externalities from risk-taking in financial intermediaries. In other words, these justifications proceed on the assumption that public investors may willingly and knowingly place their funds in high-risk intermediaries (presumably in return for the expectation of higher returns). Regulatory justifications that arise out of concerns over externalities are not directly concerned with the losses that a failed intermediary might impose on individuals who have invested funds in an intermediary, but rather with the costs that the intermediary's failure might impose on other members of society.

*a.) The Internalization of Social Losses.* The fiscal ramifications of financial intermediary failures are one sort of externality. The premise here is that the public fisc pays at least partially for intermediary failures, either through underfunded guarantee programs like the now-defunct Federal Savings and Loan Insurance Fund, or general welfare programs that have to support individuals who lose resources through intermediary mismanagement. To contain these public costs, the argument runs, the government must constrain risk-taking in intermediaries.

*b.) Systemic Costs of Intermediary Failures.* Another form of externality are systemic costs from financial failure, that is costs that are transmitted from failed institutions onto other unrelated participants in the economy. Irrational bank runs are perhaps the most common example of systemic costs, but there are other illustrations, including problems in clearing systems, disruption of capital underwriting, and unexpected contractions of the money supply. Because those injured by systemic costs have no easy way to prevent individual institutions from taking excessive risks and causing uncompensated losses to third parties, the government has another role in regulating financial institutions.

## 3. Other Considerations

While economic considerations often predominate in the regulation of financial institutions, other factors also contribute to legal systems in this field.

a.) *Redistributive Policies and Other Equitable Norms.* Though not inherent in the nature of financial intermediation, redistribution policies and other equitable norms are often factored into financial regulation. Policies of this sort are most apparent in the insurance field, where regulatory systems often restrict the kinds of classifications insurance companies can employ. (In the United States, for example, many states prohibit women from being charged lower automobile insurance premiums on the grounds that gender distinctions perpetuate illegitimate stereotypes.) Similarly, usury rules prohibit the charging of interest rates above certain levels. Legal requirements of this sort are not intended to preserve the solvency of financial intermediaries — indeed, at the margin, they probably impair solvency; rather, their purpose is to achieve various cross-subsidies through the financial system, typically advancing redistributive or other equitable norms.

b.) *Considerations of Political Economy.* A final set of justifications for regulation of financial intermediaries are considerations of political economy. The prevention of monopolies is, for example, a goal of many political systems, and antitrust norms are often built into financial regulatory systems. Political factors lead to other structural constraints on the financial services industry. It is, for example, not uncommon for countries to prohibit foreign participation in certain sectors of the financial services industry, and barriers to internal expansion of financial units also exist. In the United States, for example, the federal government for many years restricted the interstate expansion of banks. The justification for these structural restraints is, again, not to improve the performance of financial intermediaries, but rather to ensure that the industry comports with some broader political vision of appropriate financial structure.

---

Throughout this casebook, one of the questions to which we regularly return is how do these justifications for regulation differ across sectors of the industry? As Dean Clark suggests, the economic function of financial intermediaries are quite similar. But, do the different kinds of public claimants–from securities investors to bank depositors–face the same informational barriers and collective action problems? Or are some kinds of claims (perhaps insurance policy holders) better equipped to look out for themselves than other public claimants. Do all sectors of the industry present the same risks of systemic problems and other negative externalities? Or could our economy withstand the collapse of a portion of one sector (the mutual fund industry) more easily than some other sector (such as commercial banking)? And what about non-economic considerations? Are they generally applicable to the financial services industry or do some sectors of the industry better or more appropriate mechanisms for advancing broader social goals?

## Section 3.  Trends in the Growth of Financial Intermediation

This casebook deals principally with what Dean Clark refers to as "first order" financial intermediaries–commercial banks, insurance companies, and other institutions whose funds are primarily supplied by the general public. Table 1 summarizes the allocation of financial assets by financial intermediaries in 1995 and selected prior years. (Note that the data reported in this table represents gross assets in the financial services industry. It does not net out inter-sector investments. So, for example, a considerable fraction of private pension plan assets are invested with life insurance companies, but the table counts such assets for both private pension plans and insurance companies.)

As you review the table, note the relative sizes of the various sectors of the financial services industry. The structure of the financial services industry has changed significantly over the past forty-five years. Traditionally, commercial banks were this country's dominant financial institutions. Banks have, however, seen this dominance erode over the past few decades, as other intermediaries have gained in importance. In particular, pension plans and investment companies have grown dramatically over the past twenty years. Note also, the increasing importance of unregulated financial intermediaries.

# Table 1–Historical Data for Financial Institutions

### (Total Assets Measured in Millions of Current Dollars)

| | 1950 | 1960 | 1970 | 1980 | 1990 | 1995 |
|---|---|---|---|---|---|---|
| Depository Institutions | 200,592 | 368,590 | 832,771 | 2,341,700 | 4,913,300 | 5,827,400 |
| Commercial Banks | 166,792 | 256,322 | 570,167 | 1,481,700 | 3,338,600 | 4,501,100 |
| Thrift Institutions | 33,800 | 112,268 | 262,604 | 860,000 | 1,574,700 | 1,326,300 |
| S&Ls and Savings Banks | 32,800 | 106,568 | 244,804 | 792,400 | 1,357,700 | 1,016,200 |
| Credit Unions | 1,000 | 5,700 | 17,800 | 67,600 | 217,000 | 310,100 |
| Insurance Companies | 64,020 | 151,576 | 262,569 | 646,300 | 1,900,900 | 2,831,500 |
| Life Insurance Cos | 64,020 | 119,576 | 207,254 | 464,200 | 1,367,400 | 2,085,600 |
| Property-Casualty | n.a. | 32,000 | 55,315 | 182,100 | 533,500 | 745,900 |
| Pension Plans | n.a. | 51,700 | 172,300 | 701,000 | 2,431,300 | 3,933,900 |
| Private Plans | n.a. | 32,000 | 112,000 | 504,400 | 1,610,900 | 2,627,300 |
| State and Local Plans | n.a. | 19,700 | 60,300 | 196,600 | 820,400 | 1,306,600 |
| Security Brokers and Dealers | n.a. | n.a. | n.a. | 45,400 | 262,100 | 568,100 |
| Investment Companies | 3,402 | 19,467 | 51,624 | 146,100 | 1,154,600 | 2,717,800 |
| Mutual Funds | 2,530 | 17,383 | 47,600 | 138,200 | 1,101,700 | 2,598,100 |
| Money Market Funds | n.a. | n.a. | n.a. | 76,400 | 493,300 | 745,300 |
| Other Mutual Funds | 2,530 | 17,383 | 47,600 | 61,800 | 608,400 | 1,852,800 |
| Closed-End Companies | 872 | 2,084 | 4,024 | 7,900 | 52,900 | 119,700 |
| Bank Personal Trusts and Estates | n.a. | n.a. | n.a. | 244,800 | 522,100 | 740,000 |
| | | | | | | |
| ALL REGULATED INTERMEDIARIES | 268,014 | 591,333 | 1,319,264 | 4,125,300 | 11,184,300 | 16,618,700 |
| | | | | | | |
| Unregulated Intermediaries | 0 | 25,000 | 64,100 | 234,600 | 1,200,800 | 1,965,000 |
| Issuers of Asset-Backed Securities | 0 | 0 | 0 | 0 | 285,400 | 689,100 |
| Finance Companies | n.a. | 25,000 | 64,100 | 204,800 | 611,500 | 826,500 |
| Funding Corporations | n.a. | n.a. | n.a. | 13,700 | 254,700 | 415,300 |
| Mortgage Companies | n.a. | n.a. | n.a. | 16,100 | 49,200 | 34,100 |
| | | | | | | |
| TOTAL | $268,014 | $616,333 | $1,383,364 | $4,359,900 | $12,385,100 | $18,583,700 |

### (Measured in Percentage of Total Assets)

| | 1950 | 1960 | 1970 | 1980 | 1990 | 1995 |
|---|---|---|---|---|---|---|
| Depository Institutions | 74.84% | 59.80% | 60.20% | 53.71% | 39.67% | 31.36% |
| Commercial Banks | 62.23% | 41.59% | 41.22% | 33.98% | 26.96% | 24.22% |
| Thrift Institutions | 12.61% | 18.22% | 18.98% | 19.73% | 12.71% | 7.14% |
| S&Ls and Savings Banks | 12.24% | 17.29% | 17.70% | 18.17% | 10.96% | 5.47% |
| Credit Unions | 0.37% | 0.92% | 1.29% | 1.55% | 1.75% | 1.67% |
| Insurance Companies | 23.89% | 24.59% | 18.98% | 14.82% | 15.35% | 15.24% |
| Life Insurance Cos | 23.89% | 19.40% | 14.98% | 10.65% | 11.04% | 11.22% |
| Property-Casualty | n.a. | 5.19% | 4.00% | 4.18% | 4.31% | 4.01% |
| Pension Plans | n.a. | 8.39% | 12.46% | 16.08% | 19.63% | 21.17% |
| Private Plans | n.a. | 5.19% | 8.10% | 11.57% | 13.01% | 14.14% |
| State and Local Plans | n.a. | 3.20% | 4.36% | 4.51% | 6.62% | 7.03% |
| Security Brokers and Dealers | n.a. | n.a. | n.a. | 1.04% | 2.12% | 3.06% |
| Investment Companies | 1.27% | 3.16% | 3.73% | 3.35% | 9.32% | 14.62% |
| Mutual Funds | 0.94% | 2.82% | 3.44% | 3.17% | 8.90% | 13.98% |
| Money Market Funds | n.a. | n.a. | n.a. | 1.75% | 3.98% | 4.01 % |
| Other Mutual Funds | 0.94% | 2.82% | 3.44% | 1.42% | 4.91% | 9.97% |
| Closed-End Companies | 0.33% | 0.34% | 0.29% | 0.18% | 0.43% | 0.64% |
| Bank Personal Trusts and Estates | n.a. | n.a. | n.a. | 5.61% | 4.22% | 3.98% |
| | | | | | | |
| REGULATED INTERMEDIARIES | 100.00% | 95.94% | 95.37% | 94.62% | 90.30% | 89.43% |
| | | | | | | |
| Unregulated Intermediaries | 0.00% | 4.06% | 4.63% | 5.38% | 9.70% | 10.57% |
| Issuers of Asset-Backed Securities | n.a. | n.a. | n.a. | n.a. | 2.30% | 3.71% |
| Finance Companies | n.a. | 4.06% | 4.63% | 4.70% | 4.94% | 4.45% |
| Funding Corporations | n.a. | n.a. | n.a. | 0.31% | 2.06% | 2.23% |
| Mortgage Companies | n.a. | n.a. | n.a. | 0.37% | 0.40% | 0.18% |
| | | | | | | |
| TOTAL | 100.00% | 100.00% | 100.00% | 100.00% | 100.00% | 100.00% |

One of the issues we will consider in this book is the reason for the changing structure of the financial services industry.  To what extent do these changes reflect changing economic and social conditions?  To what extent has our regulatory structure contributed to these changes?  Does the existence of competing sectors within the financial services industry impede or enhance the regulatory process?

The apparent decline of depository institutions suggested by the table is a bit misleading.  Banks today generate substantial fee income from a variety of financial services which are not reflected in the assets measured by the table. Similarly, the apparent decline of life insurance companies is offset by the sale of investment vehicles such as variable annuities, which are categorized under investment companies. Nevertheless, the increase in securities assets since World War II is real, and reflects the long-term strength of the American economy, the increase in discretionary income, the favorable tax treatment of qualified retirement plans and annuities, and the increase in consumer awareness of the higher returns on equity investments since 1945.

What are the unregulated intermediaries?  Examples of issuers of asset-backed securities are government sponsored entities such as GNMA (Government National Mortgage Association) and FNMA (Federal National Mortgage Association - which is traded on the New York Stock Exchange). Examples of finance companies are Household Finance and Beneficial Finance. Examples of funding corporations are GMAC (General Motors Acceptance Corporation) and General Electric Credit. An example of a mortgage company is Countrywide Credit. These companies are not regulated because they avoid the activities which trigger regulation, such as taking deposits or insurance premiums, or selling investment instruments. Rather, they have found other ways in the capital markets to fund their activities.  Because these companies are not regulated as financial institutions, they avoid both the costs of specific regulations and the activity limits imposed on financial institutions. Yet they compete, particularly with depository institutions, in several financial institutions' activities, such as mortgages, and consumer and commercial loans.

# Section 4.  Financial Intermediaries, Corporate Finance, and the Problem of Hidden Motives

With such a large proportion of our national wealth tied up in the financial services industry, it will come as no surprise that the regulation of the field and the reform of that regulation is the subject of continuous and often contentious public debate.  The industry itself is, of course, directly concerned with the legal rules that govern its existence, as are the many other sectors of the economy that rely upon the industry for a variety of essential services.  Not disinterested either are the government officials who people the many regulatory agencies charged with the industry or the members of Congress and their staffs who gain prestige and power by overseeing the nation's financial services laws.

With so much money at stake and so many political forces at work, questions inevitably arise whether the legal rules in this field were really designed to advance their purported goals or whether these legal regimes have been subverted to advance hidden agendas.  Indeed, public-choice scholars, who are particularly sensitive to flaws in the operation of democratic institutions, have found numerous examples of "agency capture"— that is the phenomenon of an industry gaining excessive influence over regulatory authorities – in the American financial services industry.  In recognition of these concerns, we will periodically alert readers to the possibility that some, or even a large portion, of these regulations we are studying, have evolved to further not their purported goals but rather less legitimate interests, such as prerogatives of bureaucrats or the self-preservation of entrenched subsectors of the economy.  We will also consider whether inherent weaknesses of government oversight and industry self-regulation should somehow be factored into the design of regulatory structures in this field.

A prominent and provocative example of the public-choice critiques of financial regulation concerns restrictions on the investments of financial institutions.  As is explored in considerable detail later in this text, these rules are traditionally understood as an important means of limiting risk-taking of financial intermediaries.  In the following excerpt, Professor Roe views these restrictions through a different lens, that of a corporate law scholar primarily concerned with the development of legal tools for policing misconduct in corporate governance.  (As many students will recall from their corporate-law courses, individual shareholders of large public corporations are poorly equipped to provide effective oversight of corporate managers; among the first to identify this shortcoming were Professors Adolf A. Berle and Gardiner C. Means and their classic study — THE MODERN CORPORATION AND PRIVATE PROPERTY (1932)).  Professor Roe eyes large institutional investors as potentially valuable alternative mechanisms for corporate control for the "Berle-Means" corporation.

---

## Mark J. Roe, Strong Managers, Weak Owners 21-22, 149 (1994)

. . . . Fragmented securities markets are not the only way to move savings from households to the large firm.  There is at least one clear contender with the securities markets, namely, the powerful financial intermediary, which would move savings from people to firms and could take big blocks of stock, sit in boardrooms, and balance power with the CEO.  Enterprises could have obtained economies of scale and investors could have obtained diversification through large intermediaries that brought small investors and large firms together.  But American law and politics deliberately diminished the power of financial institutions in general, and often their power to hold the large equity blocks. . . . The origin of the modern corporation lies in technology, economics, and politics.

Although individuals rarely have enough money to hold a big, influential block of stock, institutions do.  The four dominant institutions are banks, insurance companies, mutual funds, and pension funds.  Respectively, they h[o]ld assets of $4.9 trillion, $2.3 trillion, $1.2 trillion, and $3.4 trillion [in 1993].

These four types of institutions, which hold nearly all of the corporate assets held by U.S. financial intermediaries, clearly could influence big firms.  But portfolio rules, antinetworking rules, and other fragmenting rules disable them from systematically having influential blocks. The following chapters show the detail, but these rules can be summarized:  Banks, the institution with the most money, have been barred from owning stock or operating nationally.  Mutual funds generally cannot own control blocks.  Insurers can put only a fragment of their investment portfolios into any one company's stock, and for most of this century the big insurers were banned from owning any stock at all.  Pension funds are less restricted, but they are fragmented; securities rules have made it hard for them to operate jointly to assert influence.  Private pension funds are under management control; they are not yet ready for a palace revolution in which they would assert control over their managerial bosses.

And we have just exhausted the major financial institutions in the United States; none can readily and without legal restraint control industrial companies.  That is the first step of my argument:  law has prohibited or raised the cost of institutional influence in industrial companies.

The second step is to examine the politics of corporate financial structure.  Many legal restraints had public-spirited backers; wise regulators, unburdened by politics, would adopt some of those rules.  But many key rules do not fit into this public-spirited mold, and even for those that do, wise regulators could have chosen alternatives, but politics helped lead them to choose as they did.  Examining financial regulation through the lens of the public choice literature reveals a complex and new political story, of law repeatedly foreclosing alternatives to the Berle-Means corporation.  [Upon] examin[ing] the affected groups' interests, popular ideology, and the preexisting pattern of political institutions . . . [,we] see how American politics deliberately fragmented financial institutions so that few institutions could focus their investments into powerful inside blocks of stock.  Different ways to develop corporate institutions are imaginable, but American politics cut their development paths off.

Opinion polls, show a popular mistrust of large financial institutions with accumulated power, a wariness of Wall Street's controlling industrial America.  Politicians responded to that distrust by restricting private accumulations of power by financial institutions.  Various interest groups also benefited from fragmentation; Congress and the administrative agencies also responded to them.

. . . The ideas of opinion leaders and political actors, and the content of major political investigations, lead us to speculate on a political explanation for corporate structure:  Main Street did not want to be controlled by Wall Street.  Laws discouraging and prohibiting control resulted.

Do not be deceived by the regulatory micro-detail[:]  A pattern is there.  Legislative history, popular ideology, the power of interest groups, and the views of opinion leaders reveal a consistent political story -- and hence one part of the foundation of the modern American corporation.  Politics never allowed financial institutions to become powerful enough to control operating firms; American politics preferred Berle-Means corporations to the alternative of concentrated institutional ownership, which it precluded.

\* \* \* \* \*

The historical evidence is that American ideology favored fragmentation, and politically powerful interest groups -- primarily small-town bankers in the past and managers today --

benefited from that ideology.  Political actors sometimes sincerely sought to implement public interest goals -- including at times the goal of fragmentation for its own sake, but frequently the more technical public interest goals could have been obtained through other means.

The political paradigm predicts that if a political system fragments intermediaries, the Berle-Means outcome is inevitable; if a political system does not fragment them, they could be organized differently than they are in the United States.  Differently organized intermediaries could then yield different governance structures at the top of the large firm.  The ideal experiment would be to rerun American history with changes in popular ideologies and interest group power to see if the large firm turns out differently.

That experiment is not yet possible, making us look to other economies to see if they have differently organized intermediaries and, consequently, differing corporate forms.  Although comparative work is full of pitfalls, it helps.  Even in Britain, the country most like the United States, we find that different financial histories yield slightly different structures; Britain has had weaker restrictions on some intermediaries, particularly insurers, and they have had a somewhat stronger role in corporate governance than their American counterparts have had.  But the strongest contrasts come from examining Germany and Japan.  Even a superficial glance at them reveals profound differences, which confirm the political paradigm.  After all, if economic evolution best explains how firms are organized, then we would expect the top of the large German or Japanese firm to resemble the top of the large American one.  But it does not; the German and Japanese firms have a flatter authority structure at the top.  The best explanation seems to lie not in differences of economic task but in differences in the organization of financial intermediaries.

The existence and persistence of the foreign structures casts doubt on the standard paradigm, which tends to see small, liquid holdings in well-developed securities markets as the best and highest, or at least essential, form of financial development and ownership, combining liquidity, diversification, and ownership rights with just the right proportion of trade-offs.  Germany and Japan are sometimes seen to be behind the United States in financial structures, but are seen as rapidly securitizing to catch up to the better-developed American financial markets.  But the persistence of the foreign ownership structures, and the nature of the forces threatening them -- many are political forces -- show that there is more than one evolutionary path . . .

---

In working through the balance of this book, readers should recall Professor Roe's critique.  Is it plausible that many of the restrictions imposed on financial intermediaries are in fact designed to protect management of operating companies from outside scrutiny?  Even if that were not the original purpose of these restrictions, is it possible that these considerations explain why the restrictions have not been liberalized over time?  Is Professor Roe correct in suggesting that the regulatory restrictions inposed on financial institutions in the United States reflect not just legitimate policy concerns, but also the self-interest of corporate managers and other special interest groups?  If so, which regulations should be relaxed and how far?  Finally, and perhaps most perplexingly, what should we make of the fact that financial intermediaries in other countries seem to perform different functions than their U.S. counterparts?  Professor Roe and others suggest that American financial intermediaries might well learn from their counterparts in Germany and Japan in taking a more active role in monitoring the the behavior of corporate management.  As our economy becomes more global, would we be well-advised to move towards emerging international standards of corporate governance, assuming such standards exist?  Or, are there some distinctly American aspects of our political economy that we should and can preserve?

---

### Problem 1-1

### The Unidentified Financial Institutions Exercise

As described above, the various classes of financial intermediaries perform economically similar functions.  As a matter of public perception, however, there is a substantial difference between categories of financial intermediaries.  Most people and most politicians perceive mutual funds, for example, in a very different light than commercial banks.  Insurance companies are thought to differ in material respects from thrift institutions.   Reality falls somewhere between economic theory and popular sensibilities.

As a step towards understanding the differences among the different classes of financial intermediaries to be touched upon in this course, work your way through the following exercise and try to address these questions:

1) Analyze as best you can the financial statements given for Unidentified Institution A.   How profitable was this institution in 1995?   Where did the institution's income come from?  What were its expenses?  How might management go about improving profitability?

2) Match the following financial statements of Unidentified Institution A and those of the other institutions provided on the following pages with the different types of financial institutions listed below.

3) If you have time, compare the relative profitability of these institutions.  Within the financial services industry, one important measure of profitability is return on assets (ROA), which is defined to be the ratio of net income to total assets.  How does ROA vary from institution to institution?  What other financial ratios offer a meaningful basis of comparison?

The institutions depicted in the following financial statements are:

1. *A Commercial Bank*:  Commercial banks are the most diversified and numerous of all United State financial institutions; they are intermediaries that attract funds largely through deposits and invest money in consumer and business loans, state and local government bonds, and United States governments.

2. *A Savings Bank*:  Savings banks traditionally have been organized in mutual (as opposed to stock) form.  Savings banks are primarily depository institutions that invest their funds in securities, bonds, and various other types of loans.

3.  *A Finance Company*:  Finance companies have traditionally supplied installment loans to consumers and various types of business credit.  In recent years, many finance companies, including the one in this exercise, have diversified into other areas of intermediation.

4.  *A Life Insurance Company*:  Life insurance companies accumulate savings for individuals and insure people against death, accidents, illness, and other misfortunes.

5.  *A Broker-Dealer*:  These companies underwrite and otherwise facilitate the issuance of securities and also promote the exchange of securities in the secondary markets.

6. *An Investment Company*:  Investment companies, which in certain forms are also known as mutual funds, offer individual and corporate investors pools of diversified marketable instruments, such as stocks or bonds, which are selected by professional money managers according to predetermined investment guidelines.

7. *A Money Market Mutual Fund*:  A money market mutual fund is a special form of investment company that limits itself to high-quality, short-term investments.

**Institution A**
**Balance Sheet as of October 31, 1997**

| Assets | $Million | % of Assets |
|---|---|---|
| Cash and Due From Banks | $15.08 | 1.37% |
| Short Term Investments | $32.14 | 2.93% |
| Investment Securities | $249.36 | 22.71% |
| Mortgage/Commercial Real Estate Loans | $561.25 | 51.12% |
| Commercial and Industrial Loans | $173.27 | 15.78% |
| Other Loans | $19.93 | 1.82% |
| Allowance for Possible Loan Losses | ($3.31) | -0.30% |
| **Total Loans** | **$751.45** | **68.44%** |
| Premises and Equipment | $28.28 | 2.58% |
| Other Assets | $21.90 | 1.99% |
| **Total Assets** | **$1,097.91** | **100.00%** |

| Liabilities and Surplus | $Million | % of Assets |
|---|---|---|
| Deposits | $984.40 | 89.66% |
| Other Liabilities | $21.09 | 1.92% |
| Retained Earnings | $92.361 | 8.41% |
| Unrealized Gain on Securities Available for Sale | $0.06 | 0.01% |
| **Total Liabilities and Surplus** | **$1097.91** | **100.00%** |

**Income Statement for Year Ending October 31, 1997**

| | $Million |
|---|---|
| Interest on Short-Term Investments and Investment Securities | $18.69 |
| Interest on Total Loans | $54.85 |
| Interest Expense on Deposits | ($40.25) |
| Provision for Possible Loan Losses | ($0.40) |
| **Net Income After Provision for Possible Losses** | **$33.32** |
| Non-Interest Income | $2.32 |
| Salaries and Benefits | ($12.98) |
| Office Occupancy and Equipment | ($4.54) |
| Other Expenses | ($7.32) |
| **Total Non-Interest Expense** | **($24.84)** |
| **Income Before Taxes** | **$10.80** |
| Taxes | $4.11 |
| **Net Income** | **$6.69** |

**Institution B**

**Balance Sheet as of December 31, 1997**

| Assets | $Million | % of Assets |
|---|---|---|
| Cash | $291.4 | 1.27% |
| Investment Securities | $1,723.8 | 7.52% |
| Home Equity Receivables | $6,953.1 | 30.32% |
| Visa/Mastercard Receivables | $4,105.0 | 17.90% |
| Other Receivables | $2,354.0 | 10.26% |
| Private Label | $3,365.2 | 14.67% |
| **Net Receivables** | **$17,667.8** | **77.04%** |
| Advances to parent Company and Affiliates | $10.5 | 0.05% |
| Acquired Intangibles | $1,734.2 | 7.56% |
| Properties and Equipment | $337.8 | 1.47% |
| Other Assets | $1,159.2 | 5.05% |
| **Total Assets** | **$22,934.7** | 100.00% |

| Liabilities and Shareholder's Equity | $Million | % of Assets |
|---|---|---|
| Commercial Paper, Bank and Other Borrowings | $4,962.0 | 21.64% |
| Insurance Policy and Claim Reserves | $1,057.1 | 4.61% |
| Senior and Senior Subordinate Debt | $12,022.0 | 52.42% |
| Other Liabilities | $862.2 | 3.76% |
| **Total Liabilities** | **$18,903.3** | 82.42% |
| Common Shareholders' Equity | $4,031.4 | 17.58% |
| **Total Liabilities and Shareholders' Equity** | **$22,934.7** | 100.00% |

**Institution B**

**Income Statement for Year Ending December 31, 1997**

|  | $Million |
|---|---|
| Interest and other Income from Securities | $22.1 |
| Finance Income from Receivables | $2,131.3 |
| Interest Expense | ($998.5) |
| Provision for Credit Losses on Receivables | ($801.1) |
| **Net Interest Margin** | **$1,154.9** |
| Securitization, Fee, and Other Income | $1,474.0 |
| Insurance Premiums and Contract Benefits | $175.1 |
| **Total Other Revenues** | **$1,758.1** |
| Salaries and Fringe Benefits | ($479.5) |
| Other Operating Expenses | ($681.2) |
| Policyholders' Benefits | ($165.2) |
| **Total Costs and Expenses** | **($1,326.2)** |
| **Income Before Taxes** | **$785.7** |
| Taxes | ($272.3) |
| **Net Income** | **$513.4** |

**Institution C**

**Balance Sheet as of December 31, 1997**

| Assets | $Million | % of Assets |
|---|---|---|
| Cash and Demand Balances Due From Banks | $1,304.4 | 6.48% |
| Money Market Assets | $678.9 | 3.37% |
| Portfolio Securities | $5,229.4 | 25.97% |
| Trading Account | $53.2 | 0.26% |
| Domestic Loans, Net of Unearned Income | $10,868.3 | 53.98% |
| Allowance for Possible Credit Losses | ($130.9) | 0.65% |
| Premises and Equipment | $314.6 | 1.56% |
| Customers' Liability on Acceptances | $46.5 | 0.23% |
| Other Assets | $1,769.1 | 8.79% |
| **Total Assets** | **$20,133.5** | **100.00%** |

| Liabilities and Shareholders' Equity | $Million | % of Assets |
|---|---|---|
| Deposits in Domestic Offices:  Interest bearing | $8,489.7 | 42.17% |
| Non-Interest bearing | $4,192.5 | 20.82% |
| Deposits in Foreign Offices:  Interest bearing | $1,731.4 | 8.60% |
| Non Interest bearing | $18.4 | 0.09% |
| Total Deposits | $14,432.0 | 71.68% |
| Federal Funds Purchased and Securities sold under Agreement | $2,451.9 | 12.18% |
| Short-Term Borrowings & Commercial Paper | $854.7 | 4.25% |
| Senior and Long-term Notes | $479.3 | 2.38% |
| Other Liabilities | $283.0 | 1.41% |
| **Total Liabilities** | **$18,500.9** | 91.89% |
| Stockholders' Equity | $1,632.6 | 8.11% |
| **Total Liabilities and Stockholders' Equity** | **$20,133.5** | 100.00% |

**Institution C**

**Income Statement for Year Ending December 31, 1997**

|  | $Million |
|---|---|
| Interest on Loans Including Fees | $927.1 |
| Interest on Money Market Assets | $44.1 |
| Interest on Portfolio Securities | $298.4 |
| **Total Interest Income** | **$1,269.6** |
| Interest Expense on Deposits | ($475.7) |
| Interest Expense on Short-term Borrowings and Commercial Paper | ($156.6) |
| Interest Expense on Senior and Long-term notes | ($66.4) |
| **Total Interest Expense** | **($698.7)** |
| Provision for Credit Losses | ($58.4) |
| **Net Interest Margin** | **$512.5** |
| Trust and Investment Management Fees | $133.7 |
| Trading Account, Foreign Exchange, Charge Card & Service Fees | $159.0 |
| Securities gains (losses) | $13.2 |
| Other Noninterest Income | $71.8 |
| **Total Other Revenues** | **$377.7** |
| Salaries, benefits & other compensation | ($372.1) |
| Net Occupancy and Equipment | ($104.7) |
| Deposit Insurance | ($3.0) |
| Other Expense | ($183.9) |
| **Total Noninterest Expenses** | **($663.7)** |
| **Income Before Taxes** | **$226.7** |
| Taxes | ($70.1) |
| **Net Income** | **$156.6** |

**Institution D**

**Balance Sheet as of December 31, 1997**

| Assets | $Million | % of Assets |
|---|---|---|
| Certificates of Deposits and Bank Notes | $1,621.7 | 23.10% |
| Commercial Paper and Corporate Notes | $4,353.8 | 62.00% |
| U.S. Government, Agency, & Instrumentality Obligations | $739.0 | 10.52% |
| Repurchase Agreements | $250.0 | 3.56% |
| Other Assets | $57.2 | 0.81% |
| **Total Assets** | **$7,021.7** | 100.00% |

| Liabilities and Shareholder's Equity | $Million | % of Assets |
|---|---|---|
| Payable for Investments Purchased | $79.2 | 1.13% |
| Other Liabilities | $2.1 | 0.03% |
| **Total Liabilities** | **$75.0** | **1.07%** |
| Shareholders Equity | $6,946.7 | 98.93% |
| **Total Liabilities and Shareholder Equity** | **$7,021.7** | 100.00% |

**Income Statement for year Ending December 31, 1997**

|  | $Million |
|---|---|
| Investment Income | $412.4 |
| Investment Advisory Fee | ($25.8) |
| Transfer Agent Fee | ($11.4) |
| Distribution Fees | ($8.2) |
| Printing and Shareholder Reports | ($0.3) |
| Trustees and Custodian Fees and Expenses | ($0.4) |
| Other Expenses | ($1.0) |
| **Total Expenses** | **($47.2)** |
| **Net Investment Income** | **$365.2** |
| Realized Gain on Investments | $0.2 |
| Change in Unrealized Appreciation on Investments | $0.3 |
| **Net Increase in Shareholders' Equity from Operations** | **$365.7** |

**Institution E**

**Balance Sheet as of December 31, 1997**

| Assets | $Million | % of Assets |
|---|---|---|
| Bonds | $93,970 | 36.21% |
| Stocks | $8,854 | 3.41% |
| Mortgage Loans | $16,004 | 6.17% |
| Investment Real Estate | $1,519 | 0.59% |
| Policy Loans | $6,827 | 2.63% |
| Cash and Short-term Investments | $15,742 | 6.07% |
| Other Invested Assets | $17,068 | 6.58% |
| Premiums Deferred and Uncollected | $5,994 | 2.31% |
| Investment Income Due and Accrued | $1,909 | 0.74% |
| Separate Account Assets | $74,046 | 28.54% |
| Other Assets | $17,549 | 6.76% |
| **Total Assets** | **$259,482** | **100.00%** |

| Liabilities and Shareholder's Equity | $Million | % of Assets |
|---|---|---|
| Reserves for Life and Health insurance and Annuities | $65,581 | 25.27% |
| Policyholders' Account Balances | $32,941 | 12.69% |
| Dividends due to Policyholders | $1,269 | 0.49% |
| Securities Sold under Agreements to Repurchase | $12,347 | 4.76% |
| Cash Collateral for Loaned Securities | $14,117 | 5.44% |
| Other Policy Liabilities | $6,659 | 2.57% |
| Short-term Debt | $6,774 | 2.61% |
| Long-term Debt | $4,273 | 1.65% |
| Liabilities Related to Separate Accounts | $73,658 | 28.39% |
| Other Liabilities | $22,146 | 8.53% |
| **Total Liabilities** | **$239,764** | **92.40%** |
| Surplus | $19,718 | 7.60% |
| **Total Liabilities and Surplus** | **$259,482** | **100.00%** |

**Institution E**

**Income Statement for Year Ending December 31, 1997**

|  | $Million |
|---|---|
| Premiums, annuity considerations and deposit funds | $18,534 |
| Consideration for supplementary contracts and dividend accumulations | $2,979 |
| **Net Investment Income** | **$12,050** |
| Other Income | $6,489 |
| **Total Income** | **$37,073** |
| Benefit Payment (other than dividends) | ($20,251) |
| Sales Practice Remediation Costs | ($1,640) |
| Insurance Expenses and Taxes | ($11,926) |
| Dividends to policyholders | ($2,429) |
| **Total Benefits and Expenses** | **($36,246)** |
| **Net Gain from Operations** | **$827** |
| Income Taxes | ($217) |
| **Net Income** | **$610** |

**Institution F**

**Balance Sheet as of December 31, 1997**

| Assets | $Billion | % of Assets |
|---|---|---|
| Cash and Interest-Bearing Equivalents | $17.3 | 5.91% |
| U.S. Government and Agency Securities | $9.8 | 3.35% |
| Foreign Government and Agency Securities | $9.7 | 3.31% |
| Corporate Debt | $32.5 | 11.10% |
| Options and Contractual Commitments | $21.2 | 7.24% |
| Equity Securities | $23.6 | 8.06% |
| Mortgage Loans/Collateralized Mortgage Securities | $7.3 | 2.49% |
| Other | $16.9 | 5.77% |
| Receivables | $145.4 | 49.66% |
| Property, Plant and Equipment | $2.1 | 0.72% |
| Other Assets, including Intangibles | $6.9 | 2.36% |
| **Total Assets** | **$292.8** | 100.00% |

| Liabilities and Shareholder's Equity | $Billion | % of Assets |
|---|---|---|
| Short-Term Borrowings | $44.9 | 15.33% |
| Payables under Repurchase Agreements | $77.9 | 26.61% |
| Trading Liabilities | $70.1 | 23.94% |
| Other | $47.8 | 16.33% |
| Long Term Borrowings | $43.1 | 14.72% |
| **Total Liabilities** | **$283.9** | **96.96%** |
| Redeemable Preferred Stock, Series A | $0.4 | 0.14% |
| Stockholders' Equity | $8.5 | 2.90% |
| **Total Liabilities and Stockholders' Equity** | **$292.8** | 100.00% |

**Institution F**

**Income Statement for Year Ending December 31, 1997**

|  | <u>$Million</u> |
|---|---|
| Revenues |  |
|   Interest and Dividends | $17.1 |
|   Principal Transactions | $3.8 |
|   Investment Banking | $2.7 |
|   Commissions | $4.7 |
|   Other | $3.5 |
| **Total Revenues** | **$31.8** |
| Interest Expense | ($16.1) |
| **Revenues, Net of Interest Expense** | **$15.7** |
| Non-Interest Expenses |  |
|   Compensation and Employee-Related | ($8.0) |
|   Other | ($4.6) |
| **Total Non-Interest Expenses** | **($12.6)** |
| **Income (Loss)** | **$3.1** |
| Income Tax Expense | ($1.2) |
| **Net Income (Loss)** | **$1.9** |

## Institution G

### Balance Sheet as of March 31, 1997

| Assets | $Million | % of Assets |
|---|---|---|
| Equity Securities | $33,909.4 | 85.21% |
| Corporate Notes | $2,029.9 | 5.10% |
| U.S. Treasury Obligations | $3,643.5 | 9.16% |
| Investment in Securities | $39,428.1 | 99.08% |
| Other Assets | $356.3 | 0.90% |
| Cash | $9.1 | 0.02% |
| **Total Assets** | **$39,793.5** | **100.00%** |

| Liabilities and Shareholder's Equity | $Million | % of Assets |
|---|---|---|
| Payable for Investments Purchased | $75.9 | 0.19% |
| **Total Liabilities** | **$75.9** | 0.19% |
| Shareholder Equity | $39,717.6 | 99.81% |
| **Total Liabilities and Shareholder Equity** | **$39,793.5** | **100.00%** |

### Income Statement for Year Ending March 31, 1997

| | $Million |
|---|---|
| Revenues | |
| Dividends | $600.5 |
| Interest | $279.1 |
| **Total Income** | **$879.6** |
| Basic Management Fee | ($90.4) |
| Distribution Expense | ($79.7) |
| Transfer Agent Fees | ($20.1) |
| Other Expenses | ($11.1) |
| Total Expenses | $201.30 |
| **Net Investment Income** | **$678.2** |
| Net Realized Gain on Investments | $3,800.2 |
| Net Unrealized Appreciation on Investments | $4,685.6 |
| **Net Increase in Shareholders Equity From Operations** | **$9,164.0** |

# CHAPTER TWO

# BANKING HISTORY, CHARTERING AND ANTITRUST

## Section 1. Development of the American Banking System

### A. Introduction

The traditional activities of banks are "deposit taking," "credit granting" and "credit exchange." Over the centuries, deposit taking has had numerous forms–taking gold and other precious metals for safekeeping as well as taking it for investment. Credit granting involves the ancient practice of lending money. Credit exchange is simply a general term for the various ways in which banks have facilitated the transfer of economic values among commercial ventures, such as issuing letters of credit.

These activities historically have caused banks to be deeply involved in the economic welfare of a country's people. As a consequence, governments from the earliest times have been concerned about those who engage in banking functions. Consider the following excerpt, which argues that banks have unique attributes that mandate special governmental oversight.

### E. Gerald Corrigan, Are Banks Special?
1982 Annual Report of Federal Reserve Bank of Minneapolis

Reduced to essentials, it would appear that there are three characteristics that distinguish banks from all other classes of institutions–both financial and nonfinancial. They are:

1. Banks offer transaction accounts.
2. Banks are the backup source of liquidity for all other institutions.
3. Banks are the transmission belt for monetary policy.

These three essential bank characteristics and the interrelationships between them are discussed below. Of necessity, the discussion treats each factor separately. However, it is clear that these essential characteristics are highly complementary and furthermore that it is the relationship among them that best captures the essence of what makes banks special.

## Issuance of Transaction Accounts

Only banks issue transaction accounts; that is, they incur liabilities payable on demand at par and are readily transferable by the owner to third parties.  The owner of a transaction account can demand and receive currency in the face amount deposited in the account; write a check in the full amount of the account; or, perhaps most importantly, the owner of the account can transfer the full amount of the account to a third party almost instantaneously by wire transfer.  The liquidity, mobility, and acceptability of bank issued transaction accounts permit our diverse economic and financial system to work with the relative ease and efficiency to which we are accustomed.  Moreover, in periods of financial stress, the capacity to quickly move transaction account balances to third parties takes on special significance by providing elements of flexibility and certainty in making and receiving payments that help to insure that financial disruptions do not spread.  Individual banks can also create these highly liquid and mobile balances through their lending function.  The capacity to "create" liabilities with these characteristics is vital to the ongoing needs of commerce, but it takes on special significance in periods of financial stress. . . .

Looked at in this perspective, the critical difference between banks and other classes of financial institutions rests with the capacity of banks to incur (and to create) liabilities that are payable on demand at par and that are readily transferable to third parties.  The resulting mismatch of the maturities of assets and liabilities makes banks particularly vulnerable to sudden drains on deposits that can jeopardize their solvency.  In practice, depositors–reinforced by the public policy safety net–have demonstrated tendencies to drain deposits from particular banks only when confronted with the reality or the perception of losses growing out of asset management problems and/or poor management of banking organizations.  Thus, while the deposit taking function of banks is what makes them unique, the integrity of that process depends upon the risks, real and perceived, associated with the lending and related activities of the banking system as a whole and its capacity to absorb shocks in the short run.

## Backup Sources of Liquidity

As discussed above, the fact that banks issue transaction deposits is the key factor that distinguishes them from other classes of financial and nonfinancial institutions.  However, experience also suggests that public confidence in the ability of banks to meet their deposit obligations is ultimately related to the quality of bank assets and to the overall financial condition of the bank.  This relationship takes on additional importance when it is recalled that banks can also create, through their lending activities, transaction deposits.  Indeed, in a very real way, banks are the primary source of liquidity for all other classes and sizes of institutions, both financial and nonfinancial. . . .

Looked at in this light, the ability of banks to fulfill their role as standby sources of liquidity and credit rests importantly on the quality and consistency of credit judgments made by banks.  This is particularly true in periods of stress when banks may be called on to supply credit to borrowers who, for one reason or another, temporarily do not have access to other sources of funds or to make the even more difficult decisions as to which borrowers are experiencing problems of a fundamental or irreparable nature.  It is in these particular circumstances that banks must be in a position to make rigorous, impartial, and objective credit decisions, because it is precisely in such circumstances that the potential for compromise in the impartiality of the credit decision making process is greatest and the potential for asset quality deterioration is the largest. It is in this light that considerations about the commingling of banking and other interests and concerns about the ownership and control of banks become compelling.

To summarize, virtually all other financial markets and other classes of institutions are directly or indirectly dependent on the banking system as their standby or backup source of credit and liquidity. Banks can fulfill this function for a variety of reasons, including their relative ease of access to deposit and nondeposit sources of funding. However, experience suggests that the capacity to provide this function or, more directly, to provide access to these markets and sources of funding—like the integrity of the deposit taking function—is ultimately related to the overall financial strength of banks and the quality of bank assets. This role of banks as a standby source of liquidity takes on special significance in periods of stress and in this light underscores the importance of rigorous and impartial credit judgments by banks. This, in turn, provides a particularly relevant context in which concerns about the commingling of banking and other interests should be evaluated.

Transmission Belt for Monetary Policy

As the preceding discussion suggests, there is a direct link between banks and the central bank arising in part from the central bank's lender of last resort function. More broadly, the fact that banks are subject to reserve requirements places the banking system in the unique position of being the "transmission belt" through which the actions and policies of the central bank have their effect on financial market conditions, money and credit creation, and economic conditions generally. To put it somewhat differently, the required reserves to the banking system have often been described as the fulcrum upon which the monetary authority operates monetary policy. The reserves in the banking system also serve the complementary purpose of providing the working balances which permit our highly efficient financial markets to function and to effect the orderly end-of-day settlement of the hundreds of billions of dollars of transactions that occur over the course of each business day.

Some have argued that neither monetary policy nor the payments mechanism are dependent on the relationship between reserves and the banking system. There have been, or are, schemes for conducting monetary policy and operating a payments mechanism that do not use bank reserves and the banking system in the way the U.S. system currently operates. However, it is also true that any of these alternative arrangements would entail major institutional changes and run the risk that they might not work as efficiently as the current framework or the possibility that they might not work at all. In short, to justify departure from the current arrangement the weight of evidence should be overwhelming that the current system is not working or that some alternative system would work decidedly better. . . .

As suggested above, these and other forces may already be working to introduce a larger margin of slack into the transmission belt. While the slack evident today is of manageable proportions, the future design of the banking and financial system must leave intact a strong yet adaptable mechanism through which monetary policy and the payments mechanism can function. This imperative underscores the case for attempting to segregate essential banking functions into an identifiable class of institutions and seeking to ensure that these institutions have the financial strength and vitality to perform their essential functions and to absorb changes in the credit market and economic conditions associated with periods of monetary restraint. . . .

## Comments and Questions

1. The discussion of banks as the transmission belt for monetary policy deserves some elaboration. The Federal Reserve is involved in the economic creation of money, as well as in the regulation of money and of banks. Control of the quantity of money is essential if its value is to be kept stable. If the money supply grows too rapidly, there is a fear of inflation. If the money supply grows too slowly, there is a fear of unemployment. The Federal Reserve tries to maintain equilibrium through the reserve requirements applied to banks and its own open market operations, both of which limit the amount of money that banks can create. Reserve requirements mandate that a bank can lend out only a percentage of the money it has on deposit, say 85 cents out of each dollar. Because of this, sooner or later the original new dollar deposited at a bank will stop creating money deposited in other banks, as the Federal Reserve raises or lowers reserve requirements. The Federal Reserve also increases and decreases the money supply through open-market operations, the purchase and sale of United States government securities. If the money supply is too large, the Federal Reserve sells government securities and receives money in exchange, which requires the buyer to take money out of the banking system. And the Federal Reserve can increase the money supply by buying government securities. Finally, the payments system is part of the transmission belt, as the banks' reserve accounts are used to net payments made each day through the banking system to settle monetary obligations among individuals and commercial entities. To what extent is the transmission belt harmed by, for example, the cash management accounts and money market mutual funds offered by broker-dealers?

2. Has Corrigan identified all the ways in which banks are special, or are there other characteristics of banks that make them unique and worthy of additional regulatory oversight? To what extent is Corrigan concerned about individuals who deposit their funds in banks? Should the government have a role in preventing these depositors from suffering losses? Is protecting people's "grocery money" deposited in banks different from protecting their other assets in insurance and securities?

3. To what extent is Corrigan concerned with competitive harms that can result when banks unfairly exploit the unique franchise they enjoy through federally insured deposits? Should we be more concerned about competitive injury? Should it matter if a bank tells its commercial loan customer that the bank would also like to manage the borrower's corporate profit sharing plan investments?

4. How distinctive are the characteristics that Corrigan identifies? Are they shared by other financial institutions covered in this book? Consider money market mutual funds and credit cards. Consider the ability of insurance companies and securities firms to provide liquidity to customers in times of stress. Consider the presence of large Wall Street government securities dealers. And what about other large corporate entities in the economy—do they too share some of the same characteristics, as significant players that are highly important in economic activity?

5. In short, what are the policy justifications underlying the extensive regulation of banks, and could those policies be implemented with less pervasive regulation?

---

The following historical overview is designed to give the reader a perspective of the evolution of banking and related financial institutions in the United States, and to yield some insight into the purpose for their regulation today. As you read the material, consider the extent to which the historical evolution of bank regulation in the United States is consistent with Corrigan's view of the specialness of banks.

## B.  European Origins of Banking in the United States

Commercial banks in various forms were familiar throughout Europe by the fifteenth century. The Bank of England, which was to become the model for the American banking system, was chartered in 1694. But the origins of banking and its regulation by government began even before that time.

The earliest "banks," which surfaced around the twelfth century, were involved in the very limited function of changing money. Over the next century or two other banking functions evolved. Banks began to receive objects of entrustment, the "depositor" of the object expecting return of the identical object on demand. Credit techniques began to develop. Banks loaned sums to merchants, often for a share of the merchant's profits. At first the funds loaned may have been the banker's. But eventually much of the funds loaned were those of depositors. Sometimes the return on funds deposited with the bank depended on the success of the particular venture in which the deposited funds had been invested. (Today, this would be called a form of investment banking.) At other times the rate of return to the bank depositor was fixed, and the return on the deposit and interest earned was dependent on the general success of all the banker's loans, investments and mercantile ventures. (Today, this would be akin to commercial banking.) Because of the increase in foreign commerce, bankers had agents in various locations. This, as well as the development of commerce in individual cities, resulted in the development of banks transferring payments among merchants and among depositors. In general, it is fair to say that much depositors' money was not loaned as we know it today, but was used as risk capital invested in mercantile ventures. Sometimes the bankers themselves were deeply involved in the actual operation of the mercantile venture, the forerunner of our current concept of merchant banking.

The interest of government in banks' activities heightened as deposit taking, of whatever form, became widespread. The accumulation of control of substantial assets was a notable force in society that was not to be left free to its own devices. As early as 1374 government regulation in the commercial centers of Italy prohibited banks from trading in certain speculative commodities and from otherwise investing more than one and a half times the amount they had invested in their own government's bonds.

From the earliest time banks resembled the various types of institutions that exist today.  There were institutions of special deposit (trust or pension funds), general deposit, commercial lending, and investment banking.  Banks became substantially involved in a broad range of mercantile and business activities, which often resulted in their supplying merchants with permanent capital, causing rather obvious problems when depositors sought to withdraw their credits.  While the development of negotiable commercial paper in the seventeenth century increased the liquidity of banks, it did not reduce the risk involved in the underlying commercial ventures to which the banks were heavily tied.  Certainly, regulation of banks was not uniform, but the importance of banks to the economic life of the various states and to their citizens caused continuous concern.  For example, it was thought that the First Bank of France might not have failed in 1720 if two mercantile schemes of the brilliant John Law had not been related to the bank.  Around the same time, much distrust of banking in England and the United States resulted from the speculative commercial ventures of the South Sea Company.

## C.  The First American Banks

The early history of the European origins of banking has had a substantial influence on banking in the United States.  The proposal to establish the Bank of England in 1694 made the existing merchant bankers, who were also commercial traders, apprehensive that the Bank of England might be a formidable competitor in the field of commercial trade.  To put the fears of the merchants to rest a clause was added to the bill forbidding the Bank of England to trade in "goods, wares or merchandise."  While some historians believe that the Bank of England would not have engaged in commerce in any case, this separation of the financial intermediation system from commerce continues to influence banking law in several regions of the world, particularly the United States.

While the then developing idea of the separation of banking and commerce did not guarantee the safety of deposits or necessarily achieve government purposes for stabilizing the economic life of a country, the early European experiences do suggest that the separation of banking and commerce could assist in achieving the safety and soundness desired.  Alexander Hamilton seemed to have this viewpoint, as evidenced by his adoption of much of the English experience in his preparation of banking legislation in the United States.

Earlier, before the birth of the United States as a nation, a lack of desire and need for banking institutions combined to prevent their effective formation in the colonial period.  Agrarian conservatism and distrust of corporations presented ideological obstacles while the willingness of merchant houses (private or unincorporated bankers) to discount notes and hold deposits provided viable alternatives to banking institutions.  Those  banks that did exist bore little resemblance to their present-day counterparts.  They  were organized by landowners who subscribed for mortgages on their land and in return received bank notes which constituted paper currency.  Publicly owned  banks also existed in the form of public loan offices.

In general, the early history of banking suggests that banks could best be identified by their various deposit taking activities. Having permitted that power to the banking sector, which resulted in a concentration of economic capital, governments then imposed various restrictions on their other activities. Often, these restrictions attempted to limit banks in various ways to credit granting and credit exchange, and to restrict their engagement or participation in commercial ventures. Certainly there have been exceptions, but the dominant theme has a substantial historical base.

The first incorporated bank in the United States was The Bank of North America, incorporated by the Continental Congress on December 31, 1781 and reincorporated by the Pennsylvania Assembly on April 1, 1782, due to doubts about the validity of the prior congressional charter. The principal powers of the bank were to issue notes with interest, to receive deposits, to loan money to both the government and the public, and to be the government's fiscal agent.

The Bank of North America enjoyed success insofar as the fiscal affairs of the Confederation in the business community were concerned. But agrarian opposition forced the 1785 repeal of its charter and limited the powers granted in its 1787 recharter. The agrarians were apparently motivated not so much by any act of the bank as by an anti-business animus. They believed that so powerful an institution as the Bank of North America contradicted the democratic ideal.

It is worth noting the substantially greater restrictions in the 1787 recharter of the Bank of North America. The 1787 charter expressly prohibited the bank, viewed as a creature of a central government, from trading in merchandise and from owning more real estate than was necessary for its place of business or for loan collateral.

This type of specific regulation steadily became more common in the early years of banking in the United States. Formation of a corporate, note issuing bank involved a specialized corporate enactment. As was common with corporations generally, bank charters were granted by individual acts of the legislature, and only the powers specifically granted could be exercised, although these powers were often generally worded. Individuals, however, could carry on any economic activity without limit (except issuance of notes intended to circulate as money), including engaging in the business of banking.

As the economy of the United States evolved, bank (or corporate) charters were sought to benefit agriculture, industrial and public improvement interests (such as canals, roads and waterworks). For example, under the direction of Aaron Burr, in 1799 a corporate charter was obtained for a corporation titled "the President and Directors of the Manhattan Company" under which the Bank of the Manhattan Company was subsequently established (later Chase Manhattan Bank). While the most discussed purpose of the chartered corporation was to provide Manhattan Island with wholesome water, its powers went well beyond that purpose. In effect, it was a charter for a corporation which could engage in any business enterprise and also be a bank. Work began immediately to establish a banking business, and within a year after the granting of the charter the corporation was also in the life insurance business. It was a one-corporation conglomerate.

This mixture of banking and commerce did not originate with Aaron Burr.  It is reminiscent of much of the experience in Europe and the United States at that time.  But as banking enterprises became more heavily involved in their commercial undertakings, experience gradually revealed that banking often could not be successfully combined with other commercial activities.  For example, if a canal venture were a business failure, so much of the bank's assets were lost that the bank could not redeem its notes and thus could not function as a bank.

Nevertheless, the organization of the Manhattan Company was indicative of the swelling tide of business enterprise in the United States.  Corporations chartered to serve one purpose were also given general powers sufficient to engage in banking.  Overall, the idea of uniting banking and business appeared to survive from the incorporation of the Manhattan Company in 1799 until the passage of the free banking law in New York in 1838.

Around 1800 three other types of credit institutions were emerging – unincorporated (or private) banks, mutual saving banks, and insurance companies.  The private banks tried to avoid an appearance of similarity to incorporated banks by eschewing bank note issuance, then considered to be the most important banking function because it involved putting money into circulation.  By remaining private banks (merchant banks) they were free to engage in any activity.  Private banks typically engaged in trade by importing for their own account and by extending credit for the importation of goods by others.  Either method involved short-term commercial activities.

Other companies or enterprises, often unincorporated, such as canal companies, issued their own note obligations that appeared to be money.  This activity was distinctly different from the note issuance that was intended to be permitted to banks, since bank notes were issued as obligations that were intended to be treated as money.  Generally the "restraint laws" of that time only prohibited individuals from issuing bank-like notes.  The laws did not identify deposit taking as the banking activity permitted only to banks, as is the case today.  As a consequence, if one was not incorporated one was not subject to other restrictions, and could do anything except note issuance.  But as a corollary, the later free banking statutes, which permitted note issuance, also prohibited commercial and industrial activities.  Therefore, by the time of the free banking acts in the late 1830s, typically one could choose banking or commerce, but not both.  Ultimately states began to prohibit the issuance of notes (meant to circulate as money) by unincorporated enterprises.  Nevertheless, it was difficult to distinguish between bank notes that were intended to circulate as money, and notes from other enterprises (today called commercial paper) that were not intended to serve as money.

During this period states continued to charter banks.  In 1814 Pennsylvania, through a single act, chartered 41 banks, each with an identical charter.  The act stated that no bank was to deal or trade in any manner in any merchandise, nor could any bank purchase any stock whatsoever, except for the stock of banks, government securities, and Pennsylvania internal improvement companies.  Further, these banks were not permitted to deal or trade in anything except bills of exchange, gold or silver, bullion, and the stock and treasury notes previously mentioned.

When the Second Bank of the United States' charter expired in 1836, Pennsylvania chartered the United States Bank of Pennsylvania. The charter given by Pennsylvania not only gave the bank broad powers but required it to invest in public works and to pay a large annual fee to Pennsylvania. There was hardly an enterprise in the United States that was not represented in the projects in which the bank had either made loans upon bonds or stocks or had directly invested. While it was thought that the stocks would go up in value, the exact opposite occurred. The United States Bank of Pennsylvania was the last nineteenth century incorporated bank that was prominently engaged in the function of dealing in stocks and bonds. The power to invest across a broad spectrum of business enterprise was part of the cause of the bank's demise, the investments often being illiquid and of declining value.

Legislatures in the early 1800s steadily increased the number of banks. Over the years this action resulted in the grant of so many individual charters that American banking eventually became much like it is today, a system generally committed to the "free" chartering of banks and free competition among them. The states, during these years, made an erratic but significant effort to limit the powers of banks in the charters they granted. The result intended was not always achieved. As noted, the charter of the Manhattan Company indicates that other corporate charters, by one means or another, could also, perhaps unintentionally, result in a grant of banking powers.

Many early banking charters simply granted the "usual" banking powers without further definition. Apparently, everyone knew what a bank did, for there had been numerous unincorporated private banks prior to banks receiving corporate charters. But banks, like other profit motivated enterprises, sought to do more. The eventual result was a more complete and somewhat limiting definition of the business of banking, based on a gradual realization that banks were important to the success of enterprise as well as the functioning of the economy. To accomplish consistently these two roles, banks needed powers that enabled them to assist in the functioning of the economy and in serving enterprise, but stopped them from becoming so involved in enterprise that they could be destroyed by it.

## D. The First and Second Banks of the United States

The First Bank of the United States was chartered in 1791. Its charter was prepared by Alexander Hamilton and patterned after the charter of the Bank of England. The charter was unusual in that it was much more detailed and restrictive than the early bank charters granted by the states. Like the recharter of the Bank of North America in 1787, the Bank of the United States was expressly forbidden from dealing or trading in commodities or goods.

Hamilton's enthusiasm was not greeted with universal appreciation. First, it was contrary to the agrarian interests which had debilitated the Bank of North America. Second, many, including Attorney General Edmund Randolph and Secretary of State Thomas Jefferson, held the Bank to be an unconstitutional extension of federal power;

even James Madison, co-author with Hamilton of the *Federalist*, denounced the bank as "condemned by the silence of the constitution."

Despite this opposition, history has generally judged the First Bank of the United States to have been a success, not only in terms of profit, but also in its method of operation. By the time its charter expired in 1811, it had acquired many of the functions of a central bank. It made substantial loans both to private business and to government. In concert with the Treasury it transferred money to state banks that required help, as in 1801 when $50,000 was deposited in the Bank of Columbia to stop a run by depositors. It circulated notes amounting to about $5 million, or about 20% of all the pocketbook money in the country. This circulation helped to provide a uniform currency for the country, but was self-defeating in that it added to the anti-Bank sentiment that prevented the Bank from being rechartered because the notes competed with the notes of state chartered banks.

During the lifetime of the First Bank of the United States from 1791 to 1811, the number of state banks increased so that by the early 1800s the country truly had a "dual banking system," i.e., some banks were chartered and regulated by the state of their incorporation while the Bank of the United States was federally chartered and regulated. No logic or plan seemed to support this development. State banks arose from the belief that they would aid business and commerce without the support of the distrusted federal bank. They were "commercial" banks, whose portfolios contained short-term loans to merchants that were secured by the goods of the borrower. From the establishment of the Bank of New York, the first modern state bank, in 1784 until 1809, the approximately 75 state banks continued without failure, although financial help from the Treasury and the Bank of the United States was at times necessary. From 1809 onward, however, failures were commonplace. Banks were established in areas with insufficient population or limited industry and commerce. Bank managers, inexperienced and unconstrained by regulatory agencies, exceeded traditionally conservative business practices. Failures increased after the expiration of the charter of the First Bank of the United States in 1811, as there was no central bank to bail adventurers out of their sinking financial exploits.

The dismal performance of state banks was most obvious during the War of 1812. Overissued bank notes depreciated rapidly and prices rose as no taxes were imposed to absorb the excess currency. By war's end, a return to dual banking was indicated, and the Second Bank of the United States was chartered in 1816.

The Second Bank was not to enjoy even the limited success of its predecessor. To the problems which had plagued the First Bank—foreign ownership, state bank antagonism, etc.—were added mismanagement ranging from poor judgment to fraud. Public opinion was so aroused against the Bank, that even when the Supreme Court upheld the institution's constitutionality and immunity from state taxation in *McCulloch v. Maryland*, 17 U.S. (4 Wheat.) 316 (1819), the state of Ohio, where anti-Bank feelings were particularly intense, continued to collect taxes against Bank branches in that state. By the time a second case was heard by the Supreme Court, however, the Bank was in the more capable hands of its third president, Nicholas Biddle, and the public furor over the Bank had subsided. In that case, *Osborn v. Bank of the United States*, 22 U.S. (9 Wheat.) 738 (1824), the Court affirmed the *McCulloch* decision.

Under Biddle, the Bank increasingly assumed the duties of a central bank, and it was during this period that the Bank most favorably influenced financial conditions. Biddle molded the Bank into the holder and protector of the country's specie (gold and silver) reserves, and shifted them between branches in response to need. He enlarged the previous practice of returning state bank notes for redemption in order to compel state banks towards conservative policies, though he refrained from redeeming the notes when he felt such a course would adversely affect the banking system.

The relative calm surrounding the Biddle administration was disrupted by the election of Andrew Jackson as President in 1828. Although the Bank had not been an election issue (indeed, Biddle had voted for Old Hickory), Jackson, upon ascending to the Presidency, led the movement to destroy the Bank.

Jackson was joined by state bankers, anti-Bank agrarians, states' rights politicians, and office seekers who wanted Jacksonians to staff the Bank. Lines were drawn, and, once again, the nation's banking structure was to be determined more by politics than by economic reasoning. The pro-Bank forces passed a recharter bill through Congress in early 1832, four years before the Bank's first charter was to expire. The pro-Bank strategy was to force Jackson to sign the bill, thus preserving the Bank, or to veto it, in which case Jackson would surely be defeated in the 1832 presidential election.

Jackson vetoed the bill. The veto turned the pro-Bank strategy into a Waterloo. Jackson was overwhelmingly reelected in 1832. By the end of the next year, Jackson had removed all government deposits from the Bank branches and redeposited them in state banks. The Second Bank of the United States expired with its charter in 1836.

## E. The Free Banking Acts

The demise of the Bank of the United States forecast a new era of growth for state banks. Encouraged by state governments, which viewed banking as an incentive to commerce and industry, state banks grew in numbers from 329 in 1829 to 606 in 1834. State banknote circulation more than doubled during the 1830s. Acceptance of state banknotes by the federal government as payment for public lands and the need for loans in money-scarce frontier areas provided further inducements to enter the field.

A major development of this period was "free banking," the forerunner of the national banking system. Free banking permitted incorporation of a bank by any group without any need for a special legislative act, similar to today's general business corporation laws. The New York Free Banking Act of 1838 was a principal source for the provisions of the National Bank Act in 1863 and for the banking laws of other states, including Michigan, which passed the first free banking act in 1837. Each group seeking to form a bank had to deposit securities with a state official from which the bank's depositors would be reimbursed if the bank failed. But the ability to reimburse was only as good as the securities deposited, and the amount raised upon their sale all too often was less than the value of outstanding notes of an insolvent bank.   Poor enforcement of collateral requirements, the absence of reserve requirements, and the establishment of more banks than a given area could support ("wildcat" banks) made the free banking system less secure in practice than in theory.   In some states, particularly Michigan where more than forty banks failed before the system was declared unconstitutional, the system is better characterized as a fiasco than a failure.  Here was another example where ideology replaced economic soundness.   Democratic spirit and laissez-faire capitalism had combined against what was seen as monopolistic practices of legislatively chartered banks to produce a system wherein anyone who so desired could start a bank which would fail a short time thereafter.  More accurately, the free banking experience varied from state to state, and its basic tenets were to become rooted in the National Bank Act some 25 years later.

## F.  The National Bank Act

The passage of the National Bank Act in 1863 was the next major historical event in the evolution of banking in the United States.  (From 1863 to 1874 the National Bank Act was known as the National Currency Act.  For purposes of simplicity all references will be to the "National Bank Act.")  The drafting of the National Bank Act drew heavily on the New York Act and the experiences derived from its operation.

The federal government was interested in enticing state chartered banks to convert to national charters under the National Bank Act in order to meet several federal concerns, such as:  (1) the development of a national currency, a uniform circulating medium replacing state bank notes as money; (2) the development of a market for federal bonds to finance the Civil War effort; and (3) the use of the national banks as federal depositories.  The Act passed the Senate by a single vote.  Probably its primary purpose was to provide money for a financially distraught and war-torn union.   Despite its precarious origins, the National Bank Act created the groundwork for the regulation of banks and relative stability of currency until the passage of the Federal Reserve Act in 1913.

The National Bank Act did not directly displace state banks, nor did it allow operation of a single bank on a national scale.  Rather, it codified free banking through federal, rather than state, charters.  The experience of free banking within the states allowed the Act to prescribe more stringent requirements for obtaining a national charter, including:  (1) the maintenance of a reserve against deposits, which reserves were kept either in the bank itself or in a New York City bank; (2) a sizable deposit in the form of United States bonds, which was to be kept with the Comptroller of the Currency—a new office created in the Treasury to oversee national banks—in return for which the bank received national bank notes equal to ninety percent, and later 100 percent, of the value of the deposited bonds; (3) limitations on the total issue of national bank notes; (4) allowance of real estate ownership only if necessary for the transaction of business or if acquired through foreclosure; (5) use of national banks as depositories for government funds other than customs duties; (6) adherence to specific capital requirements and loan restrictions in order to obtain and retain their charters; and (7) the maintenance of reserves proportional to liabilities.

Secretary of the Treasury Chase hoped that the state chartered banks would quickly convert to national status and that the resulting circulation of national bank notes would provide the nation with a uniform currency and drive state bank notes (and the banks themselves) out of operation.  But, primarily because national regulations were so much stricter than those of the states, the onrush of applicants for national charters did not materialize.  State bank notes still flooded the currency.  So, in March, 1865 Congress increased the tax on state bank notes from two to ten percent.  The evidence suggests that it was the hope of Chase, if not of Congress as a whole, that the ten percent surcharge would force all state banks to refrain from issuing their own notes, seek national charters, and circulate a uniform national currency.  By the time the Congressional action was challenged, Chase had left the Treasury and was quite handily sitting as Chief Justice of the United States Supreme Court, where he wrote the opinion upholding the constitutionality of the tax on state bank notes in *Veazie Bank v. Fenno*, 75 U.S. (8 Wall) 533 (1869), an interesting contrast to *McCulloch v. Maryland.*

The heavy tax made issuing bank notes unprofitable, and state banks increasingly converted to national charters.  By 1870 the number of national banks exceeded by five times the number of state banks, 1648 to 325, and the former held about seven times as much in assets.  But by 1890 state banks were again numerically dominant in the banking structure.  This paradox arose because, while state-bank notes had virtually disappeared, they were also less essential to the continued existence of state banks, for it was at this same time that the use of deposits as money (i.e., checking accounts) began to grow in the United States, giving state banks sufficient funds to continue their operations.

The national banking system suffered from certain defects.  The national note issue was inelastic; it was not geared to seasonal demand for or supply of money.  Thus, the system was unable to meet demands for cash in the panic years of 1873, 1893 and 1907.  Note issue depended upon the ability of issuing banks to secure the bills they obtained from the Treasury with government bonds, rather than upon business needs.

Yet the national banking system made contributions to the development of banking regulation.  The Office of the Comptroller of the Currency provided a central agency to supervise all national banks.  Supervision usually took the form of examining national banks and calling for periodic condition reports from the banks.  This combination of procedures allowed the Comptroller's office to suggest better operating methods, and thereby to reduce failures of national banks.  The national banking system also required a minimum capital for each national bank, and placed restrictions on loans extended and funds borrowed.

Shortly after the turn of the century, it became increasingly apparent that a federal system of bank chartering, supervision, and regulation would supplement, but not supersede, state banking.  Indeed, further attempts to attract banks to national status proved somewhat self-defeating.  The easing of national bank capital requirements permitted the formation of smaller, weaker banks, so that of the 23 banks which failed in

1905 alone, half were capitalized at $50,000 or less.  The dilemma of trying to compete with state banks also forced federal regulators to enforce regulations less ardently in order to match the lax requirements for state banks.

The defects in banking came to a head in the panic of 1907, which was precipitated by the New York banks' financing of stock market operations.  Congress responded by enacting the Aldrich-Vreeland Act in 1908.  The Act was primarily an emergency measure to permit a greater flow of national currency until the National Monetary Commission, organized under the provisions of the Act, could recommend a plan for a central bank.

## G.  The Federal Reserve System

Plans for a central bank reincarnated Jacksonian era fears of the banking industry.  Early plans for a national reserve association controlled by bankers met opposition on several grounds.  Agrarians objected to the private control aspects of the proposition, and they found support in the Democratic-controlled Congress which opposed a central bank controlled by bankers and issuing its own currency.  Anti-bank sentiment was bolstered by the investigations of the money trust by the Pujo committee, which were to culminate in the passage of the Clayton Act and the Federal Trade Commission Act.  Shortly after his inauguration, however, President Wilson called a special session of Congress to deal with banking reform and related problems.  Wilson supported greater government participation in the proposed system, and with changes made towards that end, the Federal Reserve Act was passed and signed into law in December, 1913.

The preamble of the Act as originally passed stated that its purpose was "To provide for the establishment of Federal reserve banks, to furnish an elastic currency, to afford means of rediscounting commercial paper, to establish a more effective supervision of banking in the United States, and for other purposes."

The Federal Reserve System is very different from the European style central bank, as it is not a body of totally centralized power, although over time it has moved in that direction.  Rather, power was deliberately decentralized, and to some extent privatized.  The seven member Board of Governors of the Federal Reserve System, appointed by the President, is a government entity.  But the twelve regional Federal Reserve Banks essentially are owned by the commercial banks in each federal reserve district.  National banks were compelled and state banks were allowed to become members of the Federal Reserve System and owners of the regional Federal Reserve Banks.  The Federal Reserve's Open Market Committee meets every six weeks to determine monetary and interest rate policy.  The membership of the Committee is the seven members of the Board of Governors in Washington plus the twelve presidents of the regional Federal Reserve Banks.  Only five of the twelve presidents vote on the Open Market Committee, those voting determined on an annual rotation basis.

The early years of the Federal Reserve system reflected the precarious nature of its passage through Congress. State banks seemed wary of the new regulatory body and only 37 of their number joined the System by 1916.  Twelve different districts had been established under the Federal Reserve Act, and the resulting diffusion of power prevented unity of control over the System's discount rate and manipulation of credit. Insufficient extensions of credit to farmers led to passage of the Federal Farm Loan Act in 1916. But from the start the System corrected many of the more important weaknesses of the national banking system including inelasticity of currency and concentration of reserves in a few cities, and supplied a medium for credit to which member banks could turn in emergencies.

The Federal Open Market Committee (FOMC) was originally intended as an agency through which the Federal Reserve banks could enter the market to increase their operating earnings and stimulate the establishment of discount markets. It has since become the chief arm of the Federal Reserve System for influencing the general credit and monetary situation of the country. For it is through the FOMC that the Federal Reserve buys or sells securities to create easier or tighter money conditions.

## H.  Trust Banking, Securities Activities, and Investment Banking

For most of the history of the United States, banking, securities, and insurance activities were not considered totally distinct or unrelated lines of business. In fact, there are numerous historical examples of affiliation between banks and other financial activities. Trust activities, as a form of securities activities, have been closely affiliated with banking at least since shortly after the Civil War. Other banks originated as insurance companies. Savings banks in New York and a few other states continue to sell life insurance today. These relations developed primarily because there is a functional relation among banking, securities and insurance activities. All take some form of deposits, either as general deposits, insurance premium deposits, or special deposits for investment purposes. All have as their primary activity the provision of money related services. All provide a form of investment opportunity. All are financial intermediaries between capital markets and other sectors of the economy. All are critical points of exchange for financing general commercial enterprises in our economy. All are acceptors of public assets and allocators of our capital resources to their most efficient use in our economy as a whole. Each is regulated with some concern for safety, soundness and economic neutrality. How the regulatory structure of these activities came to be is a major facet of the development of financial institutions in America.

In the early nineteenth century there was little need for separate securities firms, because there was little demand for large quantities of capital. As demand did increase, it first took the form of government bonds, next internal improvement bonds (e.g., roads and canals), and then railroad bonds and some stock. Banks, historically in the short-term financing business, naturally added longer-term financing (securities) as an activity. Such activities were the downfall of the United States Bank of Pennsylvania in 1841, which both sold securities to others and held them as its own assets, purchased with depositors' funds. There was much criticism of this risking of bank capital and deposits.

In response to the early problems which arose when commercial banking and securities activities were combined, the Free Banking Acts passed around 1840 generally limited incorporated banks to core banking activities, and banks were not thought to have the power to engage in other economic activities.  But then came the Civil War.  The federal government needed national banks to distribute government securities to finance the war.  The banks purchased, and either held or resold, the government securities.  The large volume of securities involved brought others into the business, and accelerated the specialization of enterprises in securities activities.  While commercial banks were in the securities business, the securities activities of both private banks (accepting deposits from corporations but not the general public) and stockbrokers (accepting no deposits) became more evident.

After the Civil War, trust companies began to appear.  Trust companies were not banks but were general corporations.  While they started out as true fiduciaries, managing estates which involved securities and other investments, they gradually broadened their activities into the general securities business and corporate accounts.  This occurred because their trust customers also had other financial matters to attend to, and it was natural that the trust companies desired to provide their customers with a full range of financial services.  State chartered banks, protesting the "unfair" competition, were given competitive trust powers—and thereafter trust companies were classified as banks for regulatory purposes.  National banks were not then given the broader securities or trust powers necessary to compete with state-chartered banks with trust powers, private banks and stockbrokers.

And so, national banks were not happy with the "unfair" competition of these institutions.  National banks were not completely barred, however, from the securities business.  Because they had to have some funds available upon the demand of depositors, they were allowed to invest some of their assets in liquid investments.  Consequently, banks had bond departments to handle these investments.  However, the private bankers and the state chartered institutions did not stop there.  As securities activities expanded in the late nineteenth century, these institutions began to underwrite securities and sell them to others, a true investment banking business.  Because national banks were not permitted this activity, in the very early twentieth century many of them began to establish affiliates to engage in securities activities.  Often the name of the securities affiliate was exactly or almost identical to that of the bank, and the same officers and directors served both institutions.

By 1930 the securities affiliates of national banks, which were underwriting over half of the new issues of securities in the United States, were replacing investment (private) bankers as the dominant force in securities activities.  The unregulated dealings between the banks and their securities affiliates were the basis of the scandals revealed in the 1930-33 Congressional hearings leading to the Banking and Securities Acts of 1933.

A related development in the late nineteenth and early twentieth century was the creation of trust departments within the banks themselves rather than as separate affiliates.  When state banks were given the same powers as trust companies, estate management became a separate department of the bank and became known as a trust department.

# I.   The Great Depression and the Federal Deposit Insurance Corporation

The 1920s was a period of great economic activity as well as the gathering of a great economic storm. From 1920 to 1928 the value of stocks traded on the New York Stock Exchange doubled, and by September 1929 it had almost doubled again. And yet during this same time there were signs of weakness in the United States economy. For example, the Federal Reserve System was unable to stem a rising tide of bank failures. Between 1921 and 1929, more than 5,700 banks suspended operations. The bank failures, coupled with branching and merger policies, and the ability of investors to get a better rate of return elsewhere than in banks, all contributed to such a decline in the number of banks that by 1934 there were 55.1 percent as many commercial banks as there had been in 1919.

The Great Depression, which began in the early 1930s, presented the banking system (both commercial and investment) with its most awesome challenge. The banking and securities regulatory structure that emerged from the Depression bore little resemblance to the relatively unregulated system known in 1929. Congressional reaction to the Depression established the pervasive government regulation that typifies the nation's current financial structure, and much of the remainder of this book will concern the effects of the decisions made during the Depression era.

In 1932 Congress enacted the Reconstruction Finance Corporation Act in an attempt to aid commercial banks, 5100 of which failed between 1930 and 1932. The RFC was empowered to make loans directly to banks and life insurance companies, and did, in fact, make some $2.9 billion worth of loans. Within this same period the Home Loan Bank system was established to support mortgages made by other financial institutions (savings and loan associations), and the Agriculture Credit Corporation was organized to make short-term loans to agriculture. As with the Banking Act of 1933, these emergency corporations, though altered in form, remain an integral part of the American financial structure today.

Next Congress passed the Banking Act of 1933. The Act authorized Federal Reserve banks to use government obligations, as well as commercial paper, as collateral for their note issues in an attempt to expand the currency and encourage economic activity. Equally if not more significant today, the 1933 Act, sometimes referred to as the Glass-Steagall Act, included four sections which generally required the separation of commercial and investment banking. Securities firms could not engage in or be affiliated with deposit taking, and banks that were members of the Federal Reserve could not participate in or be affiliated with securities firms.

These different measures could only give real aid to those institutions that held solid assets, i.e., those which needed it least. In February 1933, following a period of sporadic bank holidays in different states (in which many banks were closed to avoid runs on their deposits), the banking structure fell apart at its tattered seams. By Franklin D. Roosevelt's inauguration day almost all of the country's banks were closed. In his inaugural address, President Roosevelt suggested that the activities of bankers and the entire financial community were a major cause of the Depression. "Practices of the unscrupulous money changers stand indicted in the court of public opinion, rejected by the hearts and minds of men. . . . The money changers have fled from their high seats in the temple of our civilization. We may now restore that temple to the ancient truths."

The reopening of the banks under government examination began a series of governmental attempts to increase regulation and centralization of the banking industry. Reaction to the Depression became manifest in the recovery years through the integration of banking and fiscal policies.

The Banking Act of 1933 constituted the first step towards increasing the interrelationship of state and federal banking systems.  From a regulatory standpoint the most important provision of the Act was the establishment of the Federal Deposit Insurance Corporation (FDIC), through which the Federal government would insure deposits in qualified banks.  Insurance was first made available only to members of the Federal Reserve System, although nonmember state banks have long since been able to obtain insurance from the FDIC.  The Banking Act also prohibited the payment of interest on demand deposits (checking accounts), raised the minimum capital requirement for national banks, made mutual savings banks eligible for membership in the Federal Reserve System, and sought to divorce the functions of banking and investment institutions by requiring the separation of security affiliates from commercial banks, and allowing the Federal Reserve Board to forbid any member bank to use Reserve credit if it made undue use of credit for speculation purposes.  But the Act fell short of more radical proposals in that it did not require all banks to become members of the Federal Reserve System, thereby ensuring the perpetuation of the dual, federal and state, banking system.

With a strengthened Federal Reserve system, a neophyte FDIC, and an already powerful Comptroller of the Currency, the banking structure evolved from the Depression with a federal regulatory scheme designed to control as many banks as possible without annihilating the state banking systems.  Non-national banks were subject to Federal Reserve regulations if they joined that system, or FDIC control if they wished merely to have the safety of federal insurance.  These three agencies, assisted by several federal agencies that supervise or regulate other financial institutions, constitute the bulwark of federal banking regulation today.

In 1989 the FDIC was given the duty to insure the deposits of savings and loan associations as well as banks.  The legislation created two separate insurance funds:  the Bank Insurance Fund ("BIF"), and the Savings Association Insurance Fund ("SAIF").  Prior to the 1989 legislation deposit accounts in savings associations had been insured by a different federal institution, the Federal Savings and Loan Insurance Corporation (FSLIC).  The 1989 legislation provides for the assessment of deposit insurance premiums on depositary institutions in order to maintain a reserve ratio (assets in the insurance fund) of 1.25% of insured accounts.  Deposit amounts on which the assessment is based are determined from reports of condition made by the banks at least four times per year.

In 1996 Congress passed the Deposit Insurance Funds Act. The Act provides a method which requires both banks and savings and loan associations to share the costs of the savings and loan association failures in the 1980s and early 1990s, provides that banks and savings and loan associations will pay the same deposit insurance rates beginning in 2000, and provides for the merger of the BIF and the SAIF on January 1, 1999 if there are no savings and loan associations remaining in existence on that date. To that end, the Act provides for a Treasury Department study of a single charter for both banks and savings and loan associations.

## J. The Bank Holding Company Act

The question of the propriety of a bank being affiliated with investment and other business activities did not end with the Banking Act of 1933's separation of commercial and investment banking. Subsequently, two developments took place involving the affiliation of banks with various financial and nonfinancial activities.

One development was the formation of bank holding companies, designed to permit a bank to affiliate with other banks outside its normal geographic territory. The holding company format also enabled these same banks to affiliate with noninvestment banking activities (e.g., insurance, farming, petroleum, manufacturing) that might otherwise have been prohibited. A concern gradually developed that the ownership of several banks by a single bank holding company could create an undue concentration of financial resources, and the ownership by a bank holding company of nonbank enterprises could create undue connections between banking and commerce. As a consequence, the Bank Holding Company Act was passed in 1956, giving to the Board of Governors of the Federal Reserve System the power to regulate the concentration and geographic expansion of bank holding companies owning two or more banks and their affiliation with nonbanking, and particularly nonfinancial, activities. In 1970 the Act was amended to include bank holding companies owning only one bank.

## K. Banking Legislation in the 1980s and 1990s

Banking legislation in the 1980s initially took on a different tone, one of deregulation. In 1980 Congress lifted the limits on interest rates that financial institutions could pay and allowed savings associations to make a limited amount of consumer loans and investments in commercial real estate. At the same time, Congress raised the ceiling on federal deposit insurance from $40,000 to $100,000.

In 1982, Congress passed the Garn-St Germain Depository Institutions Act, in which Congress further eroded the barriers among the various types of financial institutions. Under that Act, savings associations could make nonresidential real property loans up to 40% of their assets, could make commercial loans up to 10% of their assets, could make consumer loans up to 30% of their assets, and could place up to 10% of their assets in lease financing. Finally, all depository institutions were given the power to offer money market deposit accounts, which are not limited as to interest rate payable or subject to reserve requirements, and which may be coupled with a checking account utilized to make third party payments.

Many savings associations took advantage of their new powers to make unsecured commercial loans and to invest in commercial real estate.  For reasons that will be discussed more fully in Chapter 5, savings associations suffered huge losses beginning in the mid-1980s, and began to fail by the hundreds.

In 1987, Congress concluded that the problem could be solved for approximately $10 billion and passed the Competitive Equality Banking Act of 1987 (CEBA).  While the Act in part sought to create more competitive equality among banks and savings associations, the legislation also put a moratorium on various deregulation efforts.  Rather, the primary objective of CEBA was to provide a period of regrouping, without substantial change in powers, and to replenish the financial resources of the Federal Savings and Loan Insurance Corporation.  The legislation suggested that Congress faced great uncertainty in trying to reconcile questions of deregulation of bank powers and geographic expansion with the increasing concern over the safety and soundness of banks and thrift institutions.  The Act was ineffective.  Bank failures continued to grow and the huge losses suffered by the thrift institutions could not be supported by FSLIC.

As a consequence, in 1989 Congress passed FIRREA, the Financial Institutions Reform, Recovery, and Enforcement Act.  The legislation totally reorganized the supervisory structure and powers of thrift institutions, replaced the Federal Home Loan Bank Board with the Office of Thrift Supervision (OTS), placed the thrift insurance fund under the administration of the FDIC, and gave the FDIC significantly enhanced regulatory enforcement powers.  The Act increased the likelihood of consolidation of the depository institutions industry, not only due to the closing of numerous failed thrifts, but also due to the authorization for bank holding companies to acquire savings and loan associations.  FIRREA placed the Office of Thrift Supervision under the Secretary of the Treasury, with the same degree of autonomy as the Comptroller of the Currency.  This new entity now has principal authority for the examination and regulation of federal and state savings associations.

The driving force behind FIRREA was the funding of the deposit insurance costs of the failed thrifts.  FIRREA established the Resolution Trust Corporation ("RTC") principally to keep the funding process off the federal budget.  The RTC in fact was managed by the FDIC which is the federal agency most experienced in financial institution receiverships.  The initial cost of resolving the failed institutions was funded through the Resolution Funding Corporation, a line of credit from the United States Treasury, and unsecured obligations issued by the RTC.  The initial authorized cost was $50 billion.  The expected cost to the United States taxpayers in early 1990 was estimated to be in excess of $300 billion, including interest costs.  The RTC was completely phased out by the end of 1995 and its duties assumed by the FDIC.

Congress passed the Federal Deposit Insurance Corporation Improvement Act of 1991 (FDICIA) to control the sometimes perverse incentives toward excessive risk-taking by troubled depository institutions, caused by the availability of the federal deposit insurance net for absorbing losses.  FDICIA created capital-based requirements for prompt corrective action, risk-based deposit insurance premiums, and least-cost resolution of failed institutions.  Under capital-based prompt corrective action, an institution falling below certain capital standards is faced with mandatory regulatory requirements to correct problems immediately. Risk-based deposit insurance premiums means that banks with riskier assets pay higher insurance premiums to the FDIC. Least-cost resolution requires the FDIC, for the first time, to use the least costly method of resolving a bank failure. Overall, these additions to federal regulatory policy seek to reduce the incentives of depository institutions in financial difficulty to take excessive risks and to reduce the ability of regulators to be too lenient when institutions are in difficulty.

The Riegle-Neal Interstate Banking and Branching Efficiency Act of 1994 dramatically reduced the geographic limitations on nationwide, interstate banking organizations. The Act allows a bank holding company to own separate bank subsidiaries in every state, regardless of state law. In addition, beginning June 1, 1997 it allows a single bank to acquire, by merger, branches in other states, unless a particular state opts out by passing legislation prior to June 1, 1997 that prohibits interstate branching in the state. The Act also establishes antitrust-type concentration limits on both the federal and state level for acquisitions structured as either interstate banking or interstate branching. The concentration limits are 10 percent of deposits nationwide, and 30 percent of deposits statewide, but states can alter the 30 percent limit by statute or regulation.

## L.  Structure of the Regulation of Banking Institutions in the United States Today

There are two general chartering authorities for banking institutions—the state and the federal governments. Thus we have state-chartered banks and national-chartered banks. A state-chartered bank is primarily regulated by each state's department of banking. A national bank is primarily regulated by the Office of the Comptroller of the Currency.

After this, matters become more complicated. All national banks located in the fifty states and the District of Columbia must be members of the Federal Reserve System and must be insured by the Federal Deposit Insurance Corporation. Consequently, they are subject to the regulations of both agencies. Virtually all state-chartered banks, in order to compete with national banks for deposit funds, also are insured by the Federal Deposit Insurance Corporation and thus subject to that agency's regulations, as well as to those of their state's banking department. State-chartered banks can also choose to become members of the Federal Reserve System. Consequently, we have three basic types of banking institutions: national banks; state-chartered member banks; and state-chartered nonmember banks. Similar structures exist for credit unions, savings banks and savings and loan associations.

The complications can be even greater. For example, suppose a bank holding company (BHC) owns one state-chartered nonmember bank and one national bank. The holding company is subject to the regulation of the Federal Reserve Board under the Bank Holding Company Act. The state-chartered bank is regulated by its state banking department and the FDIC. The national bank is regulated by the OCC. We hesitate to mention the regulatory authority of the Securities and Exchange Commission over securities issued by the BHC.

If one were writing on a clean slate, it is doubtful that such a regulatory structure would be designed.  Nevertheless, each element of the regulatory structure has come about at least partly because of historical needs of our society responded to by Congress and the evolution of the American banking system since the eighteenth century.

## M.  Savings Banks, Savings and Loan Associations, and Credit Unions

### 1.  Savings Banks

Savings banks in the United States, institutions only nominally reminiscent of commercial banks until recently, are of two types.  A stock savings bank has capital stock and is managed by a board of directors, similar to the organization of a commercial bank.  Historically more common, however, are the nation's mutual savings banks, which, until recently, differed greatly from commercial banks in form, function and geographical distribution.

Mutual savings banks differ radically from commercial banks in organization.  As their name implies, mutual savings banks have no stock or stockholders.  All distributed earnings from investments or interest on loans accrue for the theoretical benefit of depositors.  The depositors "own" the bank in the sense that when it is liquidated, they are entitled to receive an amount of the surplus (net assets minus debts including deposits) proportionate to the amount their deposits bear to the aggregate balance of all deposits.

Depositors retain the status of creditors of the bank, and they may, from a practical standpoint, withdraw their funds on demand, although the bank may in theory require previous notice.  Rather than a board of directors, a board of trustees decides policy for mutual savings banks.  Trustees are elected by past trustees (themselves) or a board of incorporators, and they in turn elect officers, establish bank policies, and supervise savings and investment operations.

Since 1978 some dramatic legislative changes have significantly altered the permissible activities and future prospects for savings banks.  Savings banks were given the power to offer negotiable orders of withdrawal—technically, the right to pay third parties out of a savings account—the result being the practical equivalent of a checking account on which interest is paid.  In 1978 Congress permitted savings banks to receive federal charters, thus establishing the same type of competition among regulators for savings bank charters as there historically has been for commercial banks.  Even more important, in 1982 Congress granted to federal mutual savings banks the power to convert to stock institutions.  At the same time, the 1982 legislation gave mutual savings banks substantially broader powers than have been historically available to them, such as noninterest bearing demand deposit accounts for business, commercial real estate loans, and a limited amount of business loans.  Several states have responded with similar legislation.

A final emerging development is that of savings banks and their affiliates expanding into "nonbanking" activities. Remember that many savings banks are state chartered institutions and are not members of the Federal Reserve. Consequently, depending on applicable state laws, some federal legislation, and perhaps the regulatory views of the FDIC as insurer, savings banks and their affiliates may have substantial uncharted territory to explore in their activities.

## 2. Savings and Loan Associations

Closely related to mutual savings banks in both history and function is another type of financial intermediary, the savings and loan association. Like savings banks, savings and loan associations are "thrift" organizations, and holders of time and savings deposits. But unlike mutual savings banks or commercial banks, the loan portfolio of a savings and loan association has been highly specialized in that its primary function has been to finance the purchase or construction of housing. In fact until the 1930s these institutions were commonly known as "building societies" or "building and loan associations."

While thrift institutions are gradually changing to the stock form, many of them are nonstock, mutual companies owned by the members who buy shares, as is the case with savings banks. The savers stand in a creditor relationship to the association, and borrowers from the association are its debtors. While the small, early building societies required active participation by members, the increase in numbers of depositors has made such participation virtually disappear. All earnings of the association are either distributed to savers as interest or added to reserves. But the actual supervision of association activities is undertaken by a board of directors, typically elected through the use of permanent proxies which are executed at the time deposit accounts are opened.

In recent years the structural convergence between mutual savings banks and savings and loan associations has been matched by a functional convergence. While financing construction and purchase of homes remains the primary function of the associations, and while, until 1982, they had been legally limited in their investments largely to home mortgages and United States government securities, federal law now permits federally chartered associations to make loans for college expenses and to invest in the general obligations of states, political subdivisions, and federal agencies. Federal law also permits Federal savings and loan associations to act as trustee for the funds of a qualified retirement plan trust invested in the association. And that is not all.

Just as with savings banks, savings and loan associations have seen a dramatic change in their powers and form in recent years. They, also, have been granted the power to convert from mutual to stock form and have been granted powers that enable them to compete much more directly with commercial banks for both deposits and uses of funds through non-residential real estate lending. Finally, savings and loan associations have been expanding into or affiliating with nonbanking activities even more than have savings banks.

While several provisions of FIRREA suggest that Congress would prefer to see savings associations continue to emphasize their home financing role, in fact other provisions suggest the continuing breakdown in distinctions between savings associations and banks. Of first importance is the Act's authorization for bank holding companies to acquire savings associations, an activity previously prohibited to them other than in the case of failing savings associations. Similarly, the creation of OTS within the same executive department as the Office of the Comptroller of the Currency increases the possibility of unification of administrative responsibility for both banks and thrifts, as does the unification of administrative responsibility of deposit insurance funds within the FDIC.

### 3. Credit Unions

Credit unions, another unique form of financial institution in the United States, are organizations of members who share common interest, often called a common bond (such as labor union members, employees of an employer, or ethnic fraternity members), pool their savings, and make consumer and possibly real estate loans to each other.

Today, credit unions may operate under a federal or state charter and are wholly owned by the members, similar to the mutual thrift institutions. Credit unions are governed internally by a series of committees, such as a committee on loan approvals. Credit unions are administered by officers, the most prominent being the treasurer who typically supervises the daily operations of the credit union. For many years, credit unions were viewed as a cross between savings and loan associations and mutual savings banks, though that view has changed somewhat in recent years as the role of credit unions has expanded to include many of the activities now conducted by commercial banks.

Several factors have combined to promote the success of credit unions. The most obvious advantage to credit unions is the tax-exempt status given to them by the federal government and most state governments. This special status, however, has been questioned as credit unions have become more homogenized with other types of financial institutions. Another advantage is low overhead, the result of office space and facilities frequently being provided by the employer or organization whose members belong to the credit union.

A primary area of litigation between banks and credit unions in recent years has been the National Credit Union Administration's liberal interpretation of the common bond requirement for credit union charters, which historically has been restricted to occupational or associational groups. One liberalization has been to allow multiple unrelated occupational groups to join together in a single credit union. A second liberalization has been to allow senior citizen organizations to charter a credit union, resulting in the American Association of Retired Persons operating a credit union for a few years before the members voted to cease operations. Such a loose common bond has always been questionable, as the group tends to have more of a client base for the services to be offered, rather than an independent membership bond. In 1998, the Supreme Court struck down the National Credit Union Administration's interpretation of the common bond requirement, see *National Credit Union Administration v. First National Bank & Trust Co.*, 118 S. Ct. 927 (1998), but shortly thereafter Congress enacted legislation largely reversing the Court's ruling. See *NCUA Issues Credit Union Membership Rule for Comment Amid Warnings from Bankers*, BNA Banking Daily, Sept.1, 1998.

Credit unions make most of their income through consumer loans, although some offer loans for real estate as well. The earnings on the loans are used to pay expenses and the net income is generally distributed to members in the form of dividends and interest. State-chartered credit unions typically are supervised by the state department of banking. The National Credit Union Administration oversees credit unions that are federally chartered. As with savings and loan associations and banks, both federal and state credit unions can take advantage of federal deposit insurance. The federal insurance programs insure all federal credit unions and permit insurance coverage for state-chartered credit unions as well.

Although credit unions have grown remarkably since World War II, their relative position in the financial community has recently been weakened as competitors have begun to pay higher rates of return and offer a broader range of financial services. Nevertheless, the strength of credit unions is evidenced by their position as the third largest short-term lender to consumers, behind commercial banks and finance companies.

# Section 2.  The Chartering Process

## A.  Introduction

A bank, like any other corporation, needs a charter issued by the appropriate government authority before it can commence doing business. That requirement is about the only similarity between the chartering process for banks and for general corporations. In the case of general corporations, state law chartering requirements typically consist of little more than filling out a standard form constituting articles of incorporation, filing the articles with the appropriate state authority, and paying the necessary fee. The charter application is routinely approved upon receipt, after which the corporation is authorized to do business. The chartering process for a bank, in contrast, can often take a year or more–and, even then, there is no guarantee that the application will be approved. Banks and other financial institutions are thought to be so important to our economic stability that their chartering, as well as their general regulation, is carefully scrutinized by governmental authorities.

A bank can seek either a state or national charter. We initially will look at the various factors that banks must consider in determining which charter to seek. We then will look at the chartering process for state and national banks–who makes the decision, how the decision is made, and the necessary procedural steps to be taken. Finally, it is possible for an existing bank to convert its charter from national to state, or vice versa. See 12 U.S.C.A. §§ 35, 214-214c.

## B.  State or National Charter?

### 1.    The Dual Banking System

The organizers of a bank may seek a charter under either state or federal law. The choice is part of the concept known as the "dual banking system." In addition to considering a federal or state bank charter, those seeking a charter can also consider a savings bank charter or a savings and loan association charter. We will focus, however, on seeking a commercial bank charter.

The theory of the dual banking system is to give both the state and the federal governments the power to charter banks and to supervise and regulate independently the banks they have chartered.  This is consistent with the historical democratic ideal of decentralizing the financial basis of our economy and providing for diverse decision making.  In a pure form, the dual banking system existed from the passage of the National Bank Act in 1863 until the passage of the Federal Reserve Act in 1913.  During that period banks choosing a state charter could operate almost unaffected by federal law.

A critical and somewhat contradictory facet of the dual banking system is the concept of competitive equality, which aims for equal treatment of banks, whether state or federally chartered.  But the primary thought is that the presence of two primary regulators reduces the likelihood of unimaginative and unresponsive regulation of the banking system that could occur were there a monopoly of regulation.  Duality forces both state and federal regulators to respond to new ideas.

Arthur Burns, a former chairman of the Federal Reserve Board, however, once called the dual banking system "competition in laxity."  History has shown more than one instance of a regulator offering greater powers or less regulation in order to encourage banks to convert from one form of charter to the other.  For example, in order to forestall conversions from state to national charter, a majority of state legislatures have enacted "wild card" statutes, under which powers granted to national banks automatically extend to state-chartered banks.  Some states have gone further, providing state-chartered banks with powers not available to national banks, such as operating a travel agency.

Over the years the federal government has gained increasing power over state-chartered banks.  Under the Federal Reserve Act, the Federal Reserve gained supervisory authority over state banks that chose to join the Federal Reserve System.  The federal government gained additional authority over state banks when it offered them membership in the Federal Deposit Insurance Corporation (beginning in 1933) and when it required all depository institutions to hold reserves against certain deposits with the Federal Reserve (beginning in 1980).

Today, the most important source of federal control of the substantive activities of state-chartered banks is found in 12 U.S.C.A. § 1831a.  The provision was enacted in 1991 in response to losses resulting from state-chartered, federally insured depository institutions, under powers granted by state law, investing as principal in activities such as real estate development.  While the FDIC has always had the power to prohibit activities of an insured, state-chartered bank that constituted unsafe or unsound practices, the 1991 legislation explicitly provides that such banks may not engage as principal in activities not permitted to national banks, absent FDIC approval.  The law, however, generally does not affect state bank powers as an agent, such as real estate agency or stock brokerage activities, that are  authorized by state law.

From the above discussion, one might conclude that state and national banks are essentially equal under state or federal law and that whether a bank has a state or national charter is a matter of indifference.  In many cases this may be true.  However, it almost certainly will be marginally more efficient for a given bank at a given time to be in one system than to be in the other, and an adviser to incorporators should be prepared to identify and investigate the factors that may make one form of doing business more desirable than the other.

### 2. Factors to Consider When Choosing Between State and National Charter

#### a. Availability of Charters

Several factors that affect the long- or short-term profitability of a proposed bank must be considered when choosing between a state or national charter. The initial question is, will a charter be available under the (a) national system, or (b) state system? Obviously, if a charter can be procured in only one of the systems, the research is ended and the question is answered. But because the state and the federal regulators are affected by one another's behavior, it is unlikely that a state commissioner of banking will long deny charters to applicants at a time when the Comptroller of the Currency is routinely granting national charters in that state.

#### b. Regulatory Considerations

Assuming that a charter appears to be available from either the state or federal banking regulator, one factor to consider is the various regulatory combinations applicable to each charter. In the case of a bank with a national charter, most regulatory supervision comes from a single regulator–the Comptroller of the Currency. A national bank's application to open a new branch, for example, is not reviewed by the Federal Reserve or the FDIC. Although a national bank must be a member of the Federal Reserve System and must have its deposits insured by the Federal Deposit Insurance Corporation, federal law makes clear that the Comptroller of the Currency is the primary regulator and examiner of national banks. Consequently, a national bank will have comparatively little conflict among various regulators.

The same cannot be said for a state-chartered bank. Although the general chartering and supervisory authority is the state banking department, virtually all state-chartered banks are also subject to regulation by the Federal Deposit Insurance Corporation, since, as a practical, competitive matter, it is necessary for state-chartered banks to have deposit insurance. This FDIC examination and supervisory control is independent of the state banking department. Thus, for a state-chartered bank dual approvals will frequently be required for charter amendment, branching, merger, and other changes in bank activities. This is hardly a dual banking system, with independent regulators. One can ask whether the FDIC, as primarily an insurer, should be expressly forbidden from ruling on branch applications and consumer affairs questions, for example, and be limited to regulating only for "safety." A probable FDIC response would be that such matters are within the scope of their safety concerns. Nevertheless, one advantage, perceived by many, of a state charter is that the state regulator will be more attentive to and flexible with the bank than the federal regulators, who are concerned with all fifty states and are often in distant locations.

Another function of both state and federal regulators is to approve or deny bank acquisitions. The circumstances of the transaction dictate who the deciding regulator will be. For example, if a national bank is going to acquire either a state or national bank through merger, the approving authority will be the Comptroller of the Currency. On the other hand, if the bank surviving the merger is a state-chartered nonmember bank, the approving authorities will be both the state banking department and the FDIC. For a state-chartered member bank, the approving authorities will be the state banking department and the Federal Reserve Board. While the same standards are theoretically applied by all three federal regulators, experience suggests that at times the results achieved can be substantially different from one regulator to another given substantially similar factual situations.

By the same token, other forms of acquisitions might yield different results depending on whether the bank is federally or state chartered. Thus, while some state banks may have the power to acquire subsidiaries which engage in real estate, insurance, travel agency services and other activities, a national bank could not make such acquisitions.

A third regulatory consideration is: to what extent may the states regulate the activities of federally chartered institutions? Does a state have authority to apply its own law (e.g., a consumer protection statute) for the protection and benefit of its citizens? Certainly, to the extent that there is direct conflict, state law is preempted, but absent that situation, what result? Must national banks comply with state laws requiring all banks to offer consumer "lifeline" checking accounts with maximum permissible monthly fees?

The answer is complex. National banks, of course, are subject to the National Bank Act and other relevant federal law. Similarly, state banks are subject to the applicable state banking code, the Federal Deposit Insurance Act, and federal laws that apply generally to deposit-taking institutions. Beyond the specific banking acts, however, both state and national banks are subject to state law such as contract, property and tort law. That is, national banks are subject to the law of the state in which they are located unless the state law expressly conflicts with federal law, frustrates the purpose for which national banks were created, or impairs their efficiency in discharging the duties imposed upon them by federal law. See for example, *National State Bank v. Long*, 630 F.2d 981 (3d Cir. 1980); *Joy v. North*, 692 F.2d 880 (2d Cir. 1982), *cert. denied*, 460 U.S. 1051 (1983). In addition, the Riegle-Neal Interstate Banking and Branching Efficiency Act of 1994 generally provides that national banks are subject to state laws covering consumer protection, fair lending, community reinvestment and intrastate branching, but that these laws are to be enforced by the Comptroller.

### c. Differences Between State and Federal Law

Overall, a comparison between the state and federal banking statutes should be made to discover the primary differences between state and national bank powers. Federal law may be more or less generous than state law in governing traditional banking activity, and that calculation will change as federal or state law changes. For example, the maximum amount of money which can be lent to one borrower may be different under state and federal law. One Iowa bank, on leaving the Federal Reserve, stated that it did so because its lending limit to one borrower under Iowa law would be almost twice its lending limit under federal law at that time. In Michigan, upon approval of two-thirds of its board of directors, a bank may loan 25 percent of its capital and surplus to any given borrower, while under federal law, the limit is 15 percent. M.C.L.A. § 487.496.

One should appreciate the continuous interplay between state and federal law. Generally, state and federal bank regulators try to dissuade banks under their jurisdiction from converting to the other system, through interpretation or amendment of existing law. In some cases where state banks have converted to national charters with loud complaints about legal limitations on their activity in the states of their incorporation, the regulators and legislatures of those states have changed their rules to bring them in line with the federal rules or to make them more generous. Federal law can be just as amenable to change designed to maintain the number of federally chartered banks. This willingness is illustrated by the Garn-St Germain Act of 1982, which increased the general lending limit for a loan to one borrower from 10 to 15 percent of a national bank's capital and surplus, and removed all loan to value ratio limits on real estate loans. But depository institution failures connected to real estate lending caused Congress in 1991 to authorize the OCC to reestablish loan to value ratios by regulation. The OCC responded with a regulation stated in general terms of diversification and prudence, accompanied with guidelines suggesting loan to value ratios that are liberal in historical context, such as 85 percent on improved property. See 12 C.F.R. Pt. 34, Subpt. D, App. A.

The Comptroller of the Currency, the Federal Reserve and the FDIC have one weapon that is not available to the states due to federal preemption. If a federal regulator can convince the Congress to enact a law that is binding not only on national banks and member banks, but also on insured banks, the national system need not adjust to the state law in order to retain its members; state banks would be subject to the federal law regardless of their affiliation. For example, for several years the Federal Reserve lobbied for Congressional approval of identical reserve requirements for most deposits, whether for member or nonmember banks. The legislation was finally enacted in 1980. As a result, state-chartered nonmember banks lost most of the competitive advantage of differing state law reserve requirements.

*Problem 2-1*

1. Suppose that Virginia passes a state law requiring all depository institutions to provide significantly greater security measures at ATM sites, including 24-hour video monitoring, stringent lighting standards, and enclosed ATM lobbies. Must national banks in Virginia comply with this state law? See 12 U.S.C.A. § 43.

2. Suppose that Massachusetts state-chartered banks have the power to engage in the travel agency business. Under § 1831a, can the FDIC prohibit an insured Massachusetts chartered bank from purchasing a block of ocean cruise trip packages that it intends to resell to customers? Would your answer be different if the activity were authorized to and engaged in by a wholly owned subsidiary of a Massachusetts bank?

## C.  The Approval Procedure for National Banks

The Office of the Comptroller of Currency, technically a bureau within the Treasury Department, was founded in 1863 to supervise the emerging national banking system. Today, the name of the office is an anachronism because the relation of the Comptroller to the currency has become purely ministerial.

The Comptroller is ultimately responsible for acting on charter applications which are presented by private parties who desire to form a national banking association.  The Comptroller must decide how many banks should enter the system and which banks will comprise that number.

It is beyond dispute today that the Comptroller has discretion to grant or deny a charter application so long as it does not act in an arbitrary or capricious manner. However, the Comptroller's view of its responsibilities in the chartering process has often changed since Hugh McCulloch was appointed the first Comptroller of the Currency in 1863.  Mr. McCulloch did not view himself bound to grant automatic approval of charter applications.  When he received an application, he insisted on three types of information: (1) a summary of the economic potential of the community in which the proposed bank would be located; (2) satisfactory references about the character and responsibility of the organizers; and (3) data on the current extent of banking facilities in the city of the proposed bank and in nearby communities.  With this information, Mr. McCulloch exercised what he believed to be his wide discretionary power in granting or denying the charter.

John Knox, the fourth Comptroller, believed that he had no discretionary power, but that he must grant a charter if the applicants had conformed to the legal requirements (i.e., proper application, sufficient capital, etc.).  Knox's view prevailed throughout the remainder of the 19th century.  A reading of 12 U.S.C.A. § 27 does suggest that if the charter applicant meets all the statutory requirements stated, the Comptroller must grant the charter.

The years between 1890 and 1900 saw the failure of approximately 1000 banks, and in 1908 Lawrence O. Murray, the new Comptroller, concluded that he had to change the automatic approval philosophy to avoid further "over-banking."  Murray believed that even though particular applicants had complied with the letter of the law, he had the discretion to deny them a charter because of his responsibilities to the stability of the overall banking system.

Since 1908 few have seriously challenged the proposition that the Comptroller has the discretion to consider the impact of the proposed bank on the banking system in deciding whether to grant a charter.  Overall, there have been periods in which this discretion has been liberally used to *grant* charters, and other periods when it has been liberally used to *deny* charters, so that the national banking system was effectively a closed club.

At least since the establishment of the FDIC in 1933, the 12 U.S.C.A. § 1816 factors, such as the "convenience and needs of the community," which are applicable to both national charter applications and deposit insurance applications, vest substantial discretion in the federal regulators.

The "automatic approval" policy of the 19th century has never completely returned although the position of James Saxon, who served as Comptroller of the Currency from 1961 to 1966, outlined below, still has some force.

Testimony of James Saxon, Hearings on the Conflict of Federal and State Banking Laws Before the House Committee on Banking and Currency, 88th Cong., 1st Sess., Vol. 1, at 274 (1963).

Our task in this Office has been to develop and apply standards of the *public* interest by which we could judge and act upon these private efforts to establish new banking facilities to serve our economy. I believe that it is fair to say, within the spirit of our private enterprise system, that a great deal of weight must be attached to decisions by our citizens to risk their capital in new enterprises.

Banking is a regulated industry, and there are sound considerations of the public interest which underlie our policy of restricting entry into this industry, and regulating the operating practices of banks. But we should not interpret the regulation of entry as a bar to entry. Controls over the formation of new banking institutions, and over the expansion of existing institutions, were not designed for the purpose of erecting an impenetrable barrier to new initiative in this industry. They were designed, instead, to provide a basis for judicious limitations conceived in terms of the public interest.

What are the standards by which the public interest in the expansion of banking facilities may properly be judged? There are two basic criteria which should be applied. Recognition must be accorded to the fact that our economy is a living and growing instrument, and that for its progress it requires the adequate provision of banking facilities. Our needs are ever changing, and our banking facilities must be attuned to these changing needs.

There is also a second consideration of coordinate importance, by which we must appraise private efforts to expand banking facilities. In the vast unregulated sector of our economy, we rely entirely upon private initiative to determine the desirability of undertaking new ventures. Indeed, through our anti-trust statutes, we endeavor to maintain conditions in which full freedom of entry will be sustained. There are some who believe that we could safely apply this policy to the industry of banking.

---

The impact of Saxon's philosophy on the granting of bank charters was significant. When Saxon took office in 1961 he publicized his willingness to receive more applications for charters. Between 1962 and 1964, 1134 applications were received, of which about half were approved. This three-year application total was more than had been submitted in the previous 20 years. Another surge of national bank charters occurred in the 1980s, with 928 national bank charters granted between 1980 and 1984. Subsequently, the number of new charters gradually decreased with 35 national banks being chartered in 1994.

Not only did Comptroller Saxon open the door for many new charters, he also welcomed and authorized many activities on the part of banks that had not previously been permitted. During his era, a number of banks switched from state to national charters in order to enjoy what seemed to be a much expanded area of business activity.

### 1. Policy Considerations

The Comptroller exercises discretion to grant or deny a charter according to his view of the impact of the proposed bank on the banking industry. The impact of the proposed bank in turn is measured by the policies which support the regulation of banks in general. The four most frequently cited policies that underlie the regulation of banks, and thus play a significant role in the decision to grant a charter are: (1) the prevention of bank failures; (2) the attainment of a competitive market; (3) the convenience and needs of the public; and (4) the preservation of "competitive equality" between state and national banks. Theoretically, the Comptroller measures the impact of the proposed bank in light of these policies and decides whether the granting of a charter is in the public interest.

Under 12 U.S.C.A. § 1816 and 12 C.F.R. § 5.20(c) the Comptroller must certify to the FDIC that consideration has been given to the following factors:

1. the bank's future earnings prospects;

2. the general character of its management;

3. the adequacy of its capital structure;

4. the convenience and needs of the community to be served by the bank;

5. the financial history and condition of the bank;

6. whether or not it has complied with all provisions of the National Bank Act and whether or not its corporate powers are consistent with the purposes of the Federal Deposit Insurance Act.

In general, it is difficult to ascertain exactly how the factors will be weighed in determining whether a charter will be granted.

### a. Prevention of Bank Failures

The policy of preventing bank failures is a reaction to the large number of bank failures in the late 19th and early 20th centuries. From 1890-1900, there were more than 1,000 bank failures, and from 1920-1930, 5,600 banks with two billion dollars of deposits failed, ultimately resulting in the loss of one billion dollars by depositors. These failures had a tremendous impact in this country and led to the realization that banks play a unique role in the economy. Banks in the United States deal almost exclusively with the assets of others. They are the custodians of the money supply and the administrators of much of the credit market. A bank failure, so the argument goes, has far-reaching disruptive effects, both economically and psychologically.

The experience of bank failures has lead some to hold that the major policy purpose of regulation is to protect existing banks from failure no matter how poorly those banks are performing their function. Most regulatory bodies and economists will not go that far, but the prevention of bank failures policy plays an important role in the chartering judgment.

One question to be considered is: What is more disruptive and damaging to a community, the bankruptcy of the local bank with deposits insured by the FDIC up to $100,000 per depositor, or the bankruptcy of the largest local employer? On the other hand, suppose the failing bank is one with national or international stature; will its failure cause ripple effects resulting in the failure of several other depository institutions? But is this question relevant to whether a charter should be granted to a new bank projecting $30 million in deposits after three years of operations?

### b. The Attainment of Competitive Banking Markets

To some extent, the attainment of a competitive banking system conflicts with the prevention of bank failures because efficient competitors can drive the less efficient out of business. In addition, there is no precise formula to determine exactly how much competition is too much or to tell when a new entrant should be excluded from the market. Yet, if every bank received an exclusive geographical franchise and no new entrants were permitted, the quality of services would surely decline and the price of those services would rise higher than they are under the current system. Therefore, the Comptroller may authorize new entrants to induce competition and to foster less expensive services of higher quality to the public.

Many banking markets, particularly in the large cities, are highly competitive. In those markets there is a continuing scramble for new accounts and, when money is not tight, for new debtors to whom the bank can make loans.

### c. "Convenience and Needs"

The third policy is the so-called convenience and needs test. Under this test the Comptroller must determine whether establishment of the proposed bank will satisfy the needs of, and be convenient to, the public. This policy is similar to that of maintenance of competitive markets, but can be distinguished in that the consideration of convenience and needs seeks not just to foster competition, but also to prevent bank failures which would be contrary to the public interest. The most generous characterization of the "needs" test is to describe it as a catch-all designed to reconcile the divergent tendencies of the first two policies. It is, however, an often used catch-all.

The "convenience and needs" test grants the Comptroller wide discretion in the chartering decision. This discretion is seldom successfully challenged. It has been recommended that the Comptroller's discretion be curbed by requiring either a concrete statement of general chartering policy, or by requiring explanatory decisions in charter cases, so as to build up a body of case law in the area. Kenneth Scott, *In Quest of Reason: The Licensing Decisions of the Federal Banking Agencies*, 42 U. CHI. L. REV. 235, 257-68, 294-95 (1975).

### d.  Competitive Equality

The policy of competitive equality, which resulted from the development of the dual banking system in the United States, seeks to insure the well-being of both the state and the national banking systems; it seeks to maintain their independence, but to grant neither an overpowering advantage over the other.

The attempt to maintain "competitive equality" has occasionally led to a "keep up with the Jones's" mentality.  From 1956 to 1960, when 168 national banks were chartered, 435 state banks were started.  In the three-year period of 1962-1965, when Comptroller Saxon granted 513 new charters, the state figure reached 502.  The state authorities were stimulated to greater liberality by the Comptroller's action.

In October, 1980, the Comptroller substantially modified its policy for chartering banks and elaborated its new policy at 12 C.F.R. § 5.20.  Under the new policy, the Comptroller appears to emphasize an evaluation of the group organizing the bank and its operating plan, rather than the previously stressed community, economic and competitive factors, which seem to be treated as benefits that will naturally accrue if the factors listed in 12 C.F.R. § 5.20(c) are favorable.  The changed emphasis is evident in the policy statement in 12 C.F.R. § 5.20(d), providing that the Comptroller is guided by the following principles: 1. the Comptroller has responsibility for maintaining a sound banking system; 2. the marketplace normally is the best regulator of economic activity; and 3. competition allows the marketplace to function and promotes a sound and more efficient banking system that better serves customers.  In effect, a group interested in starting a national bank in a market already highly competitive should have a better chance to obtain a charter under the new policy than under the old one.  Nevertheless, it still appears to be difficult to create a list of market factors that will be taken into account when the Comptroller rules on a charter application.  It seems to be left for speculation whether the specific market in which the intended bank will operate is an important element in appraising the relative strengths and weaknesses of the applicant.

Another question raised under the new regulation is whether independent bank organizers have the same chance to have their charters approved as bank holding companies have.  Overall, the changes raise the continuing questions of the Comptroller's extraordinary latitude to decide questions involving charter applications and the power of the Comptroller to effectively revoke the policies of his predecessors.

### Problem 2-2

There are five banks located on Main Street in Collegetown, USA.  It appears that they satisfy the banking needs of the community for general deposit and loan services.  A group of business owners in town want to start Sixth National Bank, which would concentrate on offering banking services to the students and employees at the College.  The organizers have plenty of capital and competent bank management personnel.  They do not intend to have Sixth National Bank offer any new or different services when compared to the five other banks in town.

1.   Under the policy articulated in § 5.20, will the bank organizers have to prove economic necessity or convenience and needs for the new bank charter to be granted?

2.   Would it be a significant factor in making the chartering decision if one of the existing banks was in financial trouble?

3.   Would it be a significant factor if the state banking commissioner had informally indicated a willingness to grant a new charter to another local group?   Should the Comptroller and the state banking authorities be required to coordinate their chartering decisions?

4.   Should it matter whether, of the five competitors, three are savings and loan associations and one is a credit union?

## Comments and Questions

1.   What chartering standards do you prefer?  Do you prefer the old emphasis on the market where the proposed bank is to operate, the new emphasis on the people filing the application and their plans for the bank, or something else?  Should it be enough in our free enterprise system if the organizers are willing to risk their own capital?  Or are responsibilities to the overall banking system and depositors also relevant, because bank charters continue to have a special attraction?  What is that special attraction?

2.   Should a bank be viewed more as a public utility, with specific societal obligations, perhaps including specified allocations of credit?

3.   Regulation § 5.20(d)(3)(iii) suggests that the minimum capital for a bank is $1,000,000, while experience suggests a number more like $3 to $5 million.  Should a local community group with $100,000 of capital be able to charter a neighborhood bank?

---

## 2.  The Comptroller's Discretion

It is essential to remember that state and federal regulators are not completely unfettered, and so must act within certain limits.  Yet while agency decisions are subject to judicial review, it typically is not de novo review.  Thus, the limits on agency discretion can be rather broad.  Consider the following case.

# Camp v. Pitts
## 411 U.S. 138 (1973)

PER CURIAM.

In its present posture this case presents a narrow, but substantial, question with respect to the proper procedure to be followed when a reviewing court determines that an administrative agency's stated justification for informal action does not provide an adequate basis for judicial review.

In 1967, respondents submitted an application to the Comptroller of the Currency for a certificate authorizing them to organize a new bank in Hartsville, South Carolina.  See 12 U.S.C. § 27; 12 CFR § 4.2 (1972).  On the basis of information received from a national bank examiner and from various interested parties, the Comptroller denied the application and notified respondents of his decision through a brief letter, which stated in part:  "(W)e have concluded that the factors in support of the establishment of a new National Bank in this area are not favorable." No formal hearings were required by the controlling statute or guaranteed by the applicable regulations, although the latter provided for hearings when requested and when granted at the discretion of the Comptroller.  Respondents did not request a formal hearing but asked for reconsideration.  That request was granted and a supplemental field examination was conducted, whereupon the Comptroller again denied the application, this time stating in a letter that "we were unable to reach a favorable conclusion as to the need factor," and explaining that conclusion to some extent.[2]  Respondents then brought an action in federal district court seeking review of the Comptroller's decision.  The entire administrative record was placed before the court, and, upon an examination of that record and of the two letters of explanation, the court granted summary judgment against respondents, holding that de novo review was not warranted in the circumstances and finding that "although the Comptroller may have erred, there is substantial basis for his determination, and . . . it was neither capricious nor arbitrary."  D.C., 329 F. Supp. 1302, 1308.  On appeal, the Court of Appeals did not reach the merits.  Rather, it held that the Comptroller's ruling was "unacceptable" because "its basis" was not stated with sufficient clarity to permit judicial review.  4 Cir., 463 F.2d 632, 633.  For the present, the Comptroller does not challenge this aspect of the court's decision.  He does, however, seek review here of the procedures that the Court of Appeals specifically ordered to be followed in the District Court on remand.  The court held that the case should be remanded "for a trial de novo before the District Court" because "the Comptroller has twice inadequately and inarticulately resolved the (respondents') presentation."  The court further specified that in the District Court, respondents "will open the trial with proof of their application and compliance with the statutory inquiries, and proffer of any other relevant evidence."  Then, "(t)estimony may . . . be adduced by the

---

[2]      The letter reads in part: "On each application we endeavor to develop the need and convenience factors in conjunction with all other banking factors and in this case we were unable to reach a favorable conclusion as to the need factor.  The record reflects that this market area is now served by the Peoples Bank with deposits of $7.2MM, The Bank of Hartsville with deposits of $12.8MM, The First Federal Savings and Loan Association with deposits of $5.4MM, The Mutual Savings and Loan Association with deposits of $8.2MM and the Sonoco Employees Credit Union with deposits of $6.5MM.  The aforementioned are as of December 31, 1968."

Comptroller or intervenors manifesting opposition, if any, to the new bank." On the basis of the record thus made, the District Court was instructed to make its own findings of fact and conclusions of law in order to determine "whether the (respondents) have shown by a preponderance of evidence that the Comptroller's ruling is capricious or an abuse of discretion." 463 F.2d, at 634.

We agree with the Comptroller that the trial procedures thus outlined by the Court of Appeals for the remand in this case are unwarranted under present law.

Unquestionably, the Comptroller's action is subject to judicial review under the Administrative Procedure Act (APA), 5 U.S.C. § 701. See *Association of Data Processing Service Organizations, Inc. v. Camp*, 397 U.S. 150, 156-158 (1970). But it is also clear that neither the National Bank Act nor the APA requires the Comptroller to hold a hearing or to make formal findings on the hearing record when passing on applications for new banking authorities. See 12 U.S.C. § 26; 5 U.S.C. § 557. Accordingly, the proper standard for judicial review of the Comptroller's adjudications is not the "substantial evidence" test which is appropriate when reviewing findings made on a hearing record, 5 U.S.C. § 706(2)(E). Nor was the reviewing court free to hold a de novo hearing under § 706(2)(F) and thereafter determine whether the agency action was "unwarranted by the facts." It is quite plain from our decision in *Citizens to Preserve Overton Park v. Volpe*, 401 U.S. 402 (1971), that de novo review is appropriate only where there are inadequate factfinding procedures in an adjudicatory proceeding, or where judicial proceedings are brought to enforce certain administrative actions. *Id.*, at 415. Neither situation applies here. The proceeding in the District Court was obviously not brought to enforce the Comptroller's decision, and the only deficiency suggested in agency action or proceedings is that the Comptroller inadequately explained his decision. As Overton Park demonstrates, however, that failure, if it occurred in this case, is not a deficiency in factfinding procedures such as to warrant the de novo hearing ordered in this case.

The appropriate standard for review was, accordingly, whether the Comptroller's adjudication was "arbitrary, capricious, an abuse of discretion, or otherwise not in accordance with law," as specified in 5 U.S.C. § 706(2)(A). In applying that standard, the focal point for judicial review should be the administrative record already in existence, not some new record made initially in the reviewing court. Respondents contend that the Court of Appeals did not envision a true de novo review and that, at most, all that was called for was the type of "plenary review" contemplated by *Overton Park, supra*, at 420. We cannot agree. The present remand instructions require the Comptroller and other parties to make an evidentiary record before the District Court "manifesting opposition, if any, to the new bank." The respondents were also to be afforded opportunities to support their application with "any other relevant evidence." These instructions seem to put aside the extensive administrative record already made and presented to the reviewing court.

If, as the Court of Appeals held and as the Comptroller does not now contest, there was such failure to explain administrative action as to frustrate effective judicial review, the remedy was not to hold a de novo hearing but, as contemplated by *Overton Park*, to obtain from the agency, either through affidavits or testimony, such additional explanation of the reasons for the agency decision as may prove necessary. We add a caveat, however. Unlike *Overton Park*, in the present case there was contemporaneous explanation of the agency decision. The explanation may have been curt, but it surely indicated the determinative reason for the final action taken: the finding that a new bank was an uneconomic venture in light of the banking needs and the banking services already available in the surrounding community.  The validity of the Comptroller's action must, therefore, stand or fall on the propriety of that finding, judged, of course, by the appropriate standard of review.  If that finding is not sustainable on the administrative record made, then the Comptroller's decision must be vacated and the matter remanded to him for further consideration.  See *SEC v. Chenery Corp.*, 318 U.S. 80 (1943).  It is in this context that the Court of Appeals should determine whether and to what extent, in the light of the administrative record, further explanation is necessary to a proper assessment of the agency's decision.

The petition for certiorari is granted, the judgment of the Court of Appeals is vacated, and the case is remanded for further proceedings consistent with this opinion.

## Comments and Questions

1.  Various administrative actions of the federal banking regulators are subject to the Administrative Procedure Act, 5 U.S.C.A. § 500 et seq., particularly the standards for judicial review there provided.  If a question of law is at issue, it is for the reviewing court to decide de novo.  Section 706 of 5 U.S.C.A. provides that: "to the extent necessary to decision and when presented, the reviewing court shall decide all relevant questions of law, interpret constitutional and statutory provisions, and determine the meaning or applicability of the terms of an agency action."

Nevertheless, a substantial body of judicial decision has developed under which the courts have shown great deference to the expertise of regulators in interpreting statutes the agencies have been designated by Congress to administer.  The Supreme Court has stated that "the construction of a statute by those charged with its administration is entitled to substantial deference." *United States v. Rutherford*, 442 U.S. 544, 553 (1979).

Current law governing judicial review of agencies' interpretations of statutes they administer is dominated by *Chevron U.S.A. Inc. v. Natural Resources Defense Council, Inc.*, 467 U.S. 837 (1984).  The Court stated:

When a court reviews an agency's construction of the statute it administers, it is confronted with two questions.  First, always, is the question of whether Congress has directly spoken to the precise question at issue.  If the intent of Congress is clear, that is the end of the matter; for the court, as well as the agency, must give effect to the unambiguously expressed intent of Congress.  If, however, the court determines Congress has not directly addressed the precise question at issue, the court does not simply impose its own construction on the statute, as would be necessary in the absence of an administrative interpretation.  Rather, if the statute is silent or ambiguous with respect to the specific issue, the question for the court is whether the agency's answer is based on a permissible construction of the statute.

The power of an administrative agency to administer a congressionally created . . . program necessarily requires the formulation of policy and the making of rules to fill any gap left, implicitly or explicitly, by Congress."  If Congress has explicitly left a gap for the agency to fill, there is an express delegation of authority to the agency to elucidate a specific provision of the statute by regulation.  Such legislative regulations are given controlling weight unless they are arbitrary, capricious, or manifestly contrary to the statute. Sometimes the legislative delegation to an agency on a particular question is implicit rather than explicit. In such a case, a court may not substitute its own construction of a statutory provision for a reasonable interpretation made by the administrator of an agency.

*Id.* at 842-44.

If the courts are to be the interpreter of the law, the *Chevron* concept of "substantial deference" is troublesome because it suggests complaisant acceptance of administrative action. A standard more consistent with the APA, while still recognizing the experience and knowledge of the regulators, could be a "dialogue" standard. Dialogue suggests a candid exchange of ideas and a willingness to learn from one another. While a court should respect and be closely attentive to an agency's interpretation of a statute, it should not necessarily defer to the agency, particularly if there is another interpretation which the court finds more consistent with the statutory language and intent. This dialogue standard would assure that the court ultimately determines the most appropriate interpretation, as required by the APA.

2. Most decisions of an administrative agency, however, are viewed as decisions of fact or application of settled law to the facts. For determinations of fact, the standard of judicial review is usually whether the agency action, finding or conclusion was "arbitrary or capricious." 5 U.S.C.A. § 706(2)(A).

Federal banking statutes and the Constitution do not usually require a hearing for such matters as chartering or branching applications. It is in these cases where there is no hearing that the arbitrary or capricious test is applied to questions of fact upon review by the court. The record reviewed by the court as the basis for the agency's action is all the information that was available to the agency—the entire agency file on the matter.

If a formal hearing is held by the regulator, then the standard of review for questions of fact is the substantial evidence test. In these cases the action of the agency rests on a closed, clearly defined adjudicatory record developed at the hearing, and § 706(2)(E) provides that the court can set aside an agency action and its conclusions if they are found to be "unsupported by substantial evidence."

The arbitrary or capricious standard and the substantial evidence standard are often regarded as being two different tests. This is said to be so because there is a different record of the administrative decision used for applying each test on appellate review. An examination of the case decisions suggests, however, that the two standards may actually be the same.

Under either standard, the essential question considered by the reviewing court is whether the agency decision is based on a *prima facie* case. A *prima facie* case exists if, from the record for administrative action, there is sufficient evidence for a reasonable person to conclude as the administrator did. If such sufficient evidence does not exist, then the agency's action is not justified, either because it is not based on substantial evidence (found in the closed record) or because it is arbitrary or capricious (based on all information available to the agency).

3.  A third area of judicial review of agency action involves interpretation of an agency's own regulations.  The most common articulation of the standard of review is that the agency interpretation is "of controlling weight unless it is plainly erroneous or inconsistent with the regulation."  *Bowles v. Seminole Rock & Sand Co.*, 325 U.S. 410, 414 (1945).

4.  Under the current state of the law, whatever the applicable standard of review, agency level determinations are rarely overturned upon judicial review.

5.  When an administrative hearing is held, what do people talk about?  Applications often say that the incorporators' principal purpose in establishing a proposed bank is to "serve the community."  In fact the purpose of opening a new bank is to make money.  Even if an opponent can point out inaccuracies in the various economic surveys submitted in support of an application, existing banks do not really believe that the applicant will fail to attract customers or is likely to fail.

6.  Suppose that you represent an existing bank.  An application has been filed for a new bank to be located in your town.  It is your judgment that the odds are 99 out of 100 that the proposed new bank will ultimately receive a charter and be profitable.  The president of the existing bank asks you to demand a hearing and present arguments in opposition to the new bank and to appeal any adverse determination.  Do you see any value or concerns in doing so?

# Section 3.  The Competing Policies of Dual Banking and Competitive Equality

A major theme of our discussion of the chartering process was the dual banking system—the idea that a bank can seek a charter under either state or federal law and so choose much of the banking law and the regulators under which it will operate.  At the same time, we briefly mentioned the competitive equality doctrine—the idea that banks with one type of charter should not be at a material competitive disadvantage to banks with the other type of charter.  Close consideration of these two policies reveals something of a contradiction.  On the one hand we envision a banking system in which state and national banks compete with each other—dual banking.  But we also strive to maintain "competitive equality" between state and national banks.  To what extent can the two policies coexist, or must one necessarily dominate the other?  Ultimately, do the policies serve any purpose today?

While Congress never intended the dual banking system when it enacted the National Bank Act in 1863, continuing concerns for substantial local control over banking have preserved it.  In 1863 the federal government wanted state chartered banks to convert to national charters in order to create a uniform national currency through national bank notes, as well as to create a structure for the sale of federal government bonds to finance the Civil War.  A ten percent tax on state bank notes was designed to force state banks to convert their charters and so destroy the state bank system.  But state banks discovered the checking account deposit system for money transfer as an alternative to state bank notes. And so, state banks survived and the dual banking system was created. States were then free to enact legislation providing what local bankers viewed as more desirable provisions on a variety of matters, such as permissible bank investments and branching. One result of the differing state and federal laws was regular claims of unfair competitive advantage of one type of bank charter over the other.

The consequence of the differing laws was the evolution of the competitive equality doctrine. An example is branch banking. Several states authorized bank branches, but the National Bank Act did not. After World War I state chartered banks began to grow rapidly. Congress responded in 1927, authorizing national banks to establish branches (in the same city as their home office), but only if state law granted the same power to state banks.

The particular example of competitive equality we consider in some detail involves the interest rate a bank may charge its customers. As we will see, the issue of permissible interest rates involves a complex of factors, including avoiding state laws disfavoring national banks, the supremacy clause of the Constitution, and the resulting preemption of state law by differing federal law.

In general, national banks are subject to state law, such as the Uniform Commercial Code. And state banks often are subject to federal law, such as the Federal Deposit Insurance Act. But under the Constitution, state law must give way to federal law if there is a conflict. The issue of conflict is easy if there is explicit federal statutory preemption of state power, or express regulatory preemption reasonably within the power of the federal regulatory agency. Finally, there can be implied preemption if state law is inconsistent with a federal law scheme.

Interest rates historically were governed solely by state law. With the National Bank Act came 12 U.S.C.A. § 85. Section 85 authorizes a national bank to charge interest at the rate allowed by the laws of the state where the bank is located (except that if a state provides a different rate for state banks, then that rate is allowed for national banks), or at one percent above the discount rate of its district Federal Reserve Bank, whichever is higher. In theory there is another possibility, but it never applies—if no interest rate is fixed by state law, then a national bank may charge seven percent.

The principal provision, providing interest rate parity between national and state banks, has been the source of extensive litigation for over 100 years. While the words of the provision suggest competitive equality, the judicial elaboration of the section contains an important additional facet, the concept of "most favored lender," which allows a national bank to charge the same rate as any competing lender in the state for a specified class of loans. See 12 C.F.R. § 7.4001.

In *Tiffany v. National Bank of Missouri*, 85 U.S. (18 Wall.) 409 (1873), a national bank had loaned money at nine percent, while the state statute provided an eight percent rate for state banks and a ten percent rate for other lenders. The Court held that the ten percent rate applied to the national bank's loan. At the time of the case there was great hostility to banks, especially in the West. The Court held that § 85 does not make the state bank rate the limit. The Act was designed to protect national banks from unfriendly state legislation, which could make their existence in a particular state impossible.  For example, a state might prescribe a rate of interest for state banks so low that banking could not be carried on except at a loss.  Consequently, the Court allowed national banks to charge the best state interest rate available to any competing lender.  This is so even though it may provide an advantage over state bank competitors that are limited to the rate allowed by state law to state banks.

At the time *Tiffany* was decided, banking was a distinctly local enterprise.  Today, however, it is commonplace for banks to make loans and issue credit cards nationwide, across state lines.  How does § 85 apply to loans made by a national bank headquartered in one state to borrowers in other states?  Does your understanding of competitive equality and most favored lender status as underlying policies help you answer the question as presented in the following case?

## Marquette National Bank v. First of Omaha Service Corp.
### 439 U.S. 299 (1978)

Mr. Justice BRENNAN delivered the opinion of the Court.

The question for decision is whether the National Bank Act, Rev. Stat. § 5197, as amended, 12 U.S.C. § 85, authorizes a national bank based in one State to charge its out-of-state credit-card customers an interest rate on unpaid balances allowed by its home State, when that rate is greater than that permitted by the State of the bank's nonresident customers.  The Minnesota Supreme Court held that the bank is allowed by § 85 to charge the higher rate.  *Minn.*, 262 N.W.2d 358 (1977).  We affirm.

I

The First National Bank of Omaha (Omaha Bank) is a national banking association with its charter address in Omaha, Neb.  Omaha Bank is a card-issuing member in the BankAmericard plan.  This plan enables cardholders to purchase goods and services from participating merchants and to obtain cash advances from participating banks throughout the United States and the world.  Omaha Bank has systematically sought to enroll in its BankAmericard program the residents, merchants, and banks of the nearby State of Minnesota.  The solicitation of Minnesota merchants and banks is carried on by respondent First of Omaha Service Corp. (Omaha Service Corp.), a wholly owned subsidiary of Omaha Bank.

Minnesota residents are obligated to pay Omaha Bank interest on the outstanding balances of their BankAmericards.  Nebraska law permits Omaha Bank to charge interest on the unpaid balances of cardholder accounts at a rate of 18% per year on the first $999.99, and 12% per year on amounts of $1,000 and over.  Minnesota law, however, fixes the permissible annual interest on such accounts at 12%.  To compensate for the reduced interest, Minnesota law permits banks to charge annual fees of up to $15 for the privilege of using a bank credit card.

The instant case began when petitioner Marquette National Bank of Minneapolis (Marquette) itself a national banking association enrolled in the BankAmericard plan, brought suit in the District Court of Hennepin County, Minn., to enjoin Omaha Bank and Omaha Service

Corp. from soliciting in Minnesota for Omaha Bank's BankAmericard program until such time as that program complied with Minnesota law. Marquette claimed to be losing customers to Omaha Bank because, unlike the Nebraska bank, Marquette was forced by the low rate of interest permissible under Minnesota law to charge a $10 annual fee for the use of its credit cards. App. 7a-15a, 45a-48a.

Marquette named as defendants Omaha Bank, Omaha Service Corp., which is organized under the laws of Nebraska but qualified to do business and doing business in Minnesota, and the Credit Bureau of St. Paul, Inc., a corporation organized under the laws of Minnesota having its principal office in St. Paul, Minn. Omaha Service Corp. participates in Omaha Bank's BankAmericard program by entering into agreements with banks and merchants necessary to the operation of the BankAmericard scheme. *Id.*, at 30a. At the time Marquette filed its complaint, Omaha Service Corp. had not yet entered into any such agreements in Minnesota, although it intended to do so. *Id.*, at 30a, 92a, 94a. For its services, Omaha Service Corp. receives a fee from Omaha Bank, but it does not itself extend credit or receive interest. *Id.*, at 94a, 97a-110a. It was alleged that the Credit Bureau of St. Paul, Inc., solicited prospective cardholders for Omaha Bank's BankAmericard program in Minnesota. *Id.*, at 9a, 30a. . . .

## II

In the present posture of this case Omaha Bank is no longer a party defendant. The federal question presented for decision is nevertheless the application of 12 U.S.C. § 85 to the operation of Omaha Bank's BankAmericard program. There is no allegation in petitioners' complaints that either Omaha Service Corp. or the Minnesota merchants and banks participating in the BankAmericard program are themselves extending credit in violation of Minn. Stat. § 48.185 (1978), and we therefore have no occasion to determine the application of the National Bank Act in such a case.

Omaha Bank is a national bank; it is an "instrumentalit[y]" of the federal government, created for a public purpose, and as such necessarily subject to the paramount authority of the United States." *Davis v. Elmira Savings Bank*, 161 U.S. 275, 283 (1896). The interest rate that Omaha Bank may charge in its BankAmericard program is thus governed by federal law. See *Farmers' & Mechanics' Nat. Bank v. Dearing*, 91 U.S. 29, 34 (1875). The provision of § 85 called into question states: "Any association may take, receive, reserve, and charge on any loan or discount made, or upon any notes, bills of exchange, or other evidences of debt, interest at the rate allowed by the laws of the State, Territory, or District *where the bank is located*, . . . and no more, except that where by the laws of any State a different rate is limited for banks organized under State laws, the rate so limited shall be allowed for associations organized or existing in any such State under this chapter." (Emphasis supplied.) Section 85 thus plainly provides that a national bank may charge interest "on any loan" at the rate allowed by the laws of the State in which the bank is "located." The question before us is therefore narrowed to whether Omaha Bank and its BankAmericard program are "located" in Nebraska and for that reason entitled to charge its Minnesota customers the rate of interest authorized by Nebraska law.

There is no question but that Omaha Bank itself, apart from its BankAmericard program, is located in Nebraska. Petitioners concede as much. See Brief for Petitioner in No. 77-1258, p. 3; Brief for Petitioner in No. 77-1265, pp. 3, 16, 33-34. The National Bank Act requires a national bank to state in its organization certificate "[t]he place where its operations of discount and deposit are to be carried on, designating the State, Territory, or district, and the particular county and city, town, or village." Rev. Stat. § 5134, 12 U.S.C. § 22. The charter address of Omaha Bank is in Omaha, Douglas County, Neb. The bank operates no branch banks in Minnesota, cf. *Seattle Trust & Savings Bank v. Bank of California*, 492 F.2d 48 (CA9 1974), nor apparently could it under federal law. See 12 U.S.C. § 36(c).

The State of Minnesota, however, contends that this conclusion must be altered if Omaha Bank's BankAmericard program is considered: "In the context of a national bank which systematically solicits Minnesota residents for credit cards to be used in transactions with Minnesota merchants the bank must be deemed to be 'located' in Minnesota for purposes of this credit card program." Reply Brief for Petitioner in No. 77-1258, p. 7.

We disagree. Section 85 was originally enacted as § 30 of the National Bank Act of 1864, 13 Stat. 108. The congressional debates surrounding the enactment of § 30 were conducted on the assumption that a national bank was "located" for purposes of the section in the State named in its organization certificate. See Cong. Globe, 38th Cong., 1st Sess., 2123-2127 (1864). Omaha Bank cannot be deprived of this location merely because it is extending credit to residents of a foreign State. Minnesota residents were always free to visit Nebraska and receive loans in that State. It has not been suggested that Minnesota usury laws would apply to such transactions. Although the convenience of modern mail permits Minnesota residents holding Omaha Bank's BankAmericards to receive loans without visiting Nebraska, credit on the use of their cards is nevertheless similarly extended by Omaha Bank in Nebraska by the bank's honoring of the sales drafts of participating Minnesota merchants and banks. Finance charges on the unpaid balances of cardholders are assessed by the bank in Omaha, Neb., and all payments on unpaid balances are remitted to the bank in Omaha, Neb. Furthermore, the bank issues its BankAmericards in Omaha, Neb., after credit assessments made by the bank in that city. App. 30a.

Nor can the fact that Omaha Bank's BankAmericards are used "in transactions with Minnesota merchants" be determinative of the bank's location for purposes of § 85. The bank's BankAmericard enables its holder "to purchase goods and services from participating merchants and obtain cash advances from participating banks throughout the United States and the world." Stipulation of Facts, App. 91a. Minnesota residents can thus use their Omaha Bank BankAmericards to purchase services in the State of New York or mail-order goods from the State of Michigan. If the location of the bank were to depend on the whereabouts of each credit-card transaction, the meaning of the term "located" would be so stretched as to throw into confusion the complex system of modern interstate banking. A national bank could never be certain whether its contacts with residents of foreign States were sufficient to alter its location for purposes of § 85. We do not choose to invite these difficulties by rendering so elastic the term "located." The mere fact that Omaha Bank has enrolled Minnesota residents, merchants, and banks in its BankAmericard program thus does not suffice to "locate" that bank in Minnesota for purposes of 12 U.S.C. § 85. See *Second Nat. Bank of Leavenworth v. Smoot*, 9 D.C. 371, 373 (1876).

## III

Since Omaha Bank and its BankAmericard program are "located" in Nebraska, the plain language of § 85 provides that the bank may charge "on any loan" the rate "allowed" by the State of Nebraska. Petitioners contend, however, that this reading of the statute violates the basic legislative intent of the National Bank Act. See *Train v. Colorado Public Interest Research Group*, 426 U.S. 1, 9-10 (1976). At the time Congress enacted § 30 of the National Bank Act of 1864, 13 Stat. 108, so petitioners' argument runs, it intended "to insure competitive equality between state and national banks in the charging of interest." Brief for Petitioner in No. 77-1265, p. 24. This policy could best be effectuated by limiting national banks to the rate of interest allowed by the States in which the banks were located. Since Congress in 1864 was addressing a financial system in which incorporated banks were "local institutions," it did not "contemplate a national bank soliciting customers and entering loan agreements outside of the state in which it was established." Brief for Petitioner in No. 77-1258, p. 17. Therefore to interpret § 85 to apply to interstate loans such as those involved in this case would not only enlarge impermissibly the original intent of Congress, but would also undercut the basic policy foundations of the statute by upsetting the competitive equality now existing between state and national banks.

We cannot accept petitioners' argument. Whatever policy of "competitive equality" has been discerned in other sections of the National Bank Act, *see, e.g.*, *First Nat. Bank v. Dickinson*, 396 U.S. 122, 131 (1969); *First Nat. Bank of Logan v. Walker Bank & Trust Co.*, 385 U.S. 252, 261-262 (1966), § 30 and its descendants have been interpreted for over a century to give "advantages to National banks over their State competitors." *Tiffany v. National Bank of Missouri*, 18 Wall. 409, 413 (1874). "National banks," it was said in *Tiffany*, "have been National favorites." The policy of competitive equality between state and national banks, however, is not truly at the core of this case. Instead, we are confronted by the inequalities that occur when a national bank applies the interest rates of its home State in its dealing with residents of a foreign State. These inequalities affect both national and state banks in the foreign State. Indeed, in the instant case Marquette is a national bank claiming to be injured by the unequal interest rates charged by another national bank. Whether the inequalities which thus occur when the interest rates of one State are "exported" into another violate the intent of Congress in enacting § 30 in part depends on whether Congress in 1864 was aware of the existence of a system of interstate banking in which such inequalities would seem a necessary part.

Close examination of the National Bank Act of 1864, its legislative history, and its historical context makes clear that, contrary to the suggestion of petitioners, Congress intended to facilitate what Representative Hooper termed a "national banking system." Cong. Globe, 38th Cong., 1st Sess., 1451 (1864). See also *Report of the Comptroller of the Currency* 4 (1864). Section 31 of the Act, for example, fully recognized the interstate nature of American banking by providing that three-fifths of the 15% of the aggregate amount of their notes in circulation that national banks were required to "have on hand, in lawful money" could

> "consist of balances due to an association available for the redemption of its circulating notes from associations approved by the comptroller of the currency, organized under this act, in the cities of Saint Louis, Louisville, Chicago, Detroit, Milwaukie [sic ], New Orleans, Cincinnati, Cleveland, Pittsburg, Baltimore, Philadelphia, Boston, New York, Albany, Leavenworth, San Francisco, and Washington City." 13 Stat. 108, 109.

The debates surrounding the enactment of this section portray a banking system of great regional interdependence.  Senator Chandler of Michigan, for example, noted:  "[T]he banking business of the Northwest is done upon bills of exchange.  The wool clip of Michigan, the wheat crop of Michigan, the hog crop of Iowa, are all purchased with drafts drawn chiefly upon [New York, Philadelphia, and Boston].  The wool clip is chiefly bought by drafts upon Boston.  I put in the three cities because it is convenient to the customer, to the broker, to the merchant, to be enabled to purchase a draft upon either one of these three places."  Cong. Globe, 38th Cong., 1st Sess., 2144 (1864).

*See also id.*, at 1343, 1376, 2143-2145, 2152, 2181-2182.  Similarly, the debates surrounding the enactment of § 41 of the Act, which provided that the shares of a national bank could be taxed as personal property "in the assessment of taxes imposed by or under state authority at the place where such bank is located, and not elsewhere," 13 Stat. 112, demonstrated a sensitive awareness of the possibilities of interstate ownership and control of national banks. *See, e.g.*, Cong. Globe, 38th Cong., 1st Sess., 1271, 1898-1899 (1864).

Although in the debates surrounding the enactment of § 30 there is no specific discussion of the impact of interstate loans, these debates occurred in the context of a developed interstate loan market.  As early as 1839 this Court had occasion to note:  "Money is frequently borrowed in one state, by a corporation created in another.  The numerous banks established by different states are in the constant habit of contracting and dealing with one another. . . .  These usages of commerce and trade have been so general and public, and have been practiced for so long a period of time, and so generally acquiesced in by the states, that the Court cannot overlook them . . . ." *Bank of Augusta v. Earle*, 13 Pet. 519, 590-591 (1839).  Examples of this interstate loan market have been noted by historians of American banking.  *See, e.g.*, 1 F. Redlich, *The Molding of American Banking* 49 (1968); 1 F. James, *The Growth of Chicago Banks* 546 (1938); Breckenridge, *Discount Rates in the United States*, 13 Pol. Sci. Q. 119, 136-138 (1898).  Evidence of this market is to be found in the numerous judicial decisions in cases arising out of interstate loan transactions.  *See, e.g.*, *Woodcock v. Campbell*, 2 Port. 456 (Ala. 1835); *Clarke v. Bank of Mississippi*, 10 Ark. 516 (1850); *Planters Bank v. Bass*, 2 La. Ann. 430 (1847); *Knox v. Bank of United States*, 27 Miss. 65 (1854); *Bard v. Poole*, 12 N.Y. 495 (1855); *Curtis v. Leavitt*, 15 N.Y. 9 (1857).  After passage of the National Bank Act of 1864, cases involving interstate loans begin to appear with some frequency in federal courts.  *See, e.g.*, In re *Wild*, 28 Fed. Cas. page 1211, No. 17,645 (S.D.N.Y. 1873); *Cadle v. Tracy*, 4 Fed. Cas. page 967, No. 2,279 (S.D.N.Y. 1873); *Farmers' Nat. Bank v. McElhinney*, 42 F. 801 (S.D. Iowa 1890); *Second Nat. Bank of Leavenworth v. Smoot*, 9 D.C. 371 (1876).

We cannot assume that Congress was oblivious to the existence of such common commercial transactions.  We find it implausible to conclude, therefore, that Congress meant through its silence to exempt interstate loans from the reach of § 30.  We would certainly be exceedingly reluctant to read such a hiatus into the regulatory scheme of § 30 in the absence of evidence of specific congressional intent.  Petitioners have adduced no such evidence.

Petitioners' final argument is that the "exportation" of interest rates, such as occurred in this case, will significantly impair the ability of States to enact effective usury laws.  This impairment, however, has always been implicit in the structure of the National Bank Act, since citizens of one State were free to visit a neighboring State to receive credit at foreign interest rates. Cf. Cong. Globe, 38th Cong., 1st Sess., 2123 (1864). This impairment may in fact be accentuated by the ease with which interstate credit is available by mail through the use of modern credit cards. But the protection of state usury laws is an issue of legislative policy, and any plea to alter § 85 to further that end is better addressed to the wisdom of Congress than to the judgment of this Court.

Affirmed.

## Comments and Questions

1. Recall the concerns for national banks expressed in *Tiffany*. Was the result in *Marquette* necessary to effectuate the policies of competitive equality and most favored lender? Or was First National Bank of Omaha allowed to charge an interest rate to Minnesota residents higher than could any lender in Minnesota under Minnesota law? Note the Court's acknowledgement that its approval of interest rate exportation would preempt state consumer protection policies.

2. Would a contrary result in *Marquette* have deprived First National Bank of Omaha of its location? Is Sears or Penney's deprived of its corporate location when the interest rate laws of the various states apply to their credit card receivables? For nonbank lenders, the applicable interest rate usually is determined by the billing address of each customer. In Interpretive Letter No. 686, September 11, 1995, the Comptroller determined that § 85 authorizes a Pennsylvania bank with branches in New Jersey to charge interest rates allowed by New Jersey for loans made from bank branch offices located in New Jersey. Consequently, the bank has two (and potentially 50) locations for § 85 purposes.

3. Section 92a authorizes the OCC to grant fiduciary powers to a national bank to the extent that such powers may be granted to competitive institutions by the law of the state where the national bank is located. In Interpretive Letter No. 695, December 8, 1995, the OCC opined that a national bank with fiduciary powers in one state can exercise fiduciary powers in another state, but only to the extent that fiduciary powers are authorized for state chartered institutions in the other state. Is this analysis consistent with the OCC's position in *Marquette*? Why or why not? Is the clause "when not in contravention of State or local law" in section 92a(a) and (b) significant to the differing treatment of state law applicable to interest charges and fiduciary powers, or is the clause simply another articulation of competitive equality? Do you think that a national bank should be authorized to export the law of a state granting expansive fiduciary powers to all other states?

---

The Supreme Court's decision in *Marquette* had significant ramifications for the supplying of consumer credit in this country. Consider the subsequent actions of the State of South Dakota and Citicorp described in the following order.

# In re Citibank (South Dakota), N.A.
## 67 Fed. Res. Bull. 181 (1981)

*Order Approving Acquisition of Bank*

Citicorp, New York, New York, a bank holding company within the meaning of the Bank Holding Company Act, has applied for the Board's approval under section 3(a)(3) of the Act (12 U.S.C. § 1842(a)(3)) to acquire all of the voting shares of Citibank (South Dakota), N.A., Sioux Falls, South Dakota ("Bank"), a proposed new bank.

Notice of the application, affording opportunity for interested persons to submit comments and views, has been given in accordance with section 3(b) of the Act.  The time for filing comments and views has expired, and the Board has considered the application and all comments received in light of the factors set forth in section 3(c) of the Act (12 U.S.C. § 1842(c)).

Citicorp, the largest banking organization in the state of New York, with total consolidated assets of $111 billion, operates through its two banking subsidiaries, Citibank, N.A., New York, New York ("Citibank"), and Citibank (New York State), N.A., Buffalo, New York ("Citibank-Buffalo"), 309 banking offices in New York state and 209 banking offices abroad.  Citicorp also engages in a wide variety of, nonbanking activities in 40 states.

Bank is a newly established bank organized by Citicorp to engage principally in nationwide consumer credit card lending activities currently conducted by Citibank-Buffalo.  In addition, Bank will engage in limited deposit-taking and commercial lending activities.  Citicorp proposes to relocate its credit card activities to South Dakota in light of the absence of that state of usury ceilings on consumer loan receivables.[2]

Section 3(d) of the Act (12 U.S.C. § 1842(d)) prohibits the Board from approving any application by a bank holding company to acquire any bank located outside of the state in which the operations of the bank holding company's banking subsidiaries are principally conducted unless such acquisition is "specifically authorized by the statute laws of the state in which such bank is located, by language to that effect and not merely by implication."  On March 12, 1980, South Dakota amended its banking laws to permit an out-of state bank holding company to acquire a single new bank located in the state.  The statute provides that such bank may have only a single banking office and that "such single banking office shall be operated in a manner and at a location which is not likely to attract customers from the general public in the state to the substantial detriment of existing banks in the state."  The South Dakota statute further provides that any acquisition under this provision must be approved by the South Dakota Banking Commission after consideration of the following factors:  (1) whether the convenience and benefit

---

[2]    South Dakota law permits commercial banks to charge rates of interest on consumer loan receivables as agreed by contract.  Until recently, New York law imposed usury ceilings on commercial bank credit card lending.  The Supreme Court, in *Marquette National Bank v. First of Omaha Serv. Corp.*, 439 U.S. 249 (1978), affirmed the right of a national bank to charge interest rates to out-of-state credit card customers at the rate permitted by the law of its home state.

to the public outweigh any adverse competitive effects; (2) whether the acquisition may result in undue concentration of resources or substantial lessening of competition; and (3) whether the location or proposed location of the banking office of the bank to be acquired is likely to attract the general public to the substantial detriment of existing banks.

Citicorp has asserted that Bank, in order to comply with South Dakota law, will not solicit or encourage personal or commercial deposits or loans from customers in South Dakota; however, Bank will not refuse such deposits or loans on an unsolicited basis. Bank will not have facilities to accept savings accounts, although it will have one teller primarily for the convenience of its employees. Moreover, Bank's proposed location is not designed to attract customers from the general public. The South Dakota Banking Commission, after a hearing on this matter approved the application of Citicorp to acquire Bank and found that the acquisition met the statutory requirements for approval under South Dakota law. In reviewing the above facts, the Board has determined that the proposed acquisition is in accord with South Dakota law and, furthermore, that the South Dakota statute specifically authorizes the acquisition of a bank chartered in South Dakota by an out-of-state bank holding company as required by section 3(d) of the Act.

In view of the limitations imposed upon the operations of banks acquired under the above-referenced South Dakota statute and the limited commercial lending and demand deposit-taking activities that Citicorp proposes for Bank, the Board has considered whether Bank will operate as a "bank within the meaning of section 2(c) of the Act (12 U.S.C. § 1841(c)). Section 2(c) defines "bank" to mean any institution that (1) accepts deposits that the depositor has a legal right to withdraw on demand, and (2) engages in the business of making commercial loans. The preliminary national bank charter granted to Bank authorizes Bank to engage in the full range of lending and deposit-taking activities permitted to national banks.

Citicorp has stated, both as part of its application and in hearings before the South Dakota Banking Commission and the Office of the Comptroller of the Currency, that Bank will accept demand deposits from credit card merchants, Citicorp subsidiaries, correspondent banks, and accounts resulting from Bank's overline lending activity. It appears to the Board that Bank's operations will satisfy the demand deposit taking requirement of section 2(c).

With respect to whether Bank will be deemed to be engaged in the business of making commercial loans, Citicorp states that Bank will purchase on a continuing basis participations in commercial loans made by Citibank, other bank and nonbank lenders, and also will make direct commercial loans in states other than South Dakota. Bank also will participate in overline loans offered by bank and nonbank financial institutions in South Dakota in accordance with the decision of the South Dakota Banking Commission approving Citicorp's application which sought to encourage Bank's participation in such loans. In light of the facts in this case and the Board's earlier rulings on this issue, the Board has determined that Bank's commercial lending activities warrant it being considered as engaged in the "business of making commercial loans" within the meaning of section 2(c) of the Act. In view of the purpose of the Bank Holding Company Act to "restrain undue concentration of commercial banking resources and to prevent possible abuses related to the control of commercial credit," the Board believes that the inclusion of Bank as a "bank" within the meaning of section 2(c) is in furtherance of the Act's purposes.

Accordingly, the Board is of the opinion that Bank should be regarded as a "bank" for purposes of the Act.

The proposed acquisition represents a transfer of Citicorp's existing credit card activities from Citibank Buffalo to Bank. The proposal is thus essentially an internal reorganization that will not alter the number of firms or the structure of the national market for bank credit card services. To the extent that Bank will purchase participations in commercial loans made by Citibank, the proposal may further be viewed as an internal reorganization of Citicorp's business without competitive effect. Because of the limitations imposed on Bank's operations by South Dakota law, Bank will not generally be in direct competition with local commercial banks in the state; however, Bank will engage de novo in providing some needed banking services in South Dakota, including overline banking services to other South Dakota banks, consistent with South Dakota law. To the extent that Bank will offer banking services as a new competitor in the market, the effect of the proposal will be procompetitive. Accordingly, the overall competitive effects of the proposal are consistent with approval.

The financial and managerial resources and future prospects of Citicorp, its subsidiaries and Bank are regarded as satisfactory. Bank's proposed overline lending activities should increase the availability of credit for South Dakota businesses and enhance the state's capital resources and access to out-of-state financing sources. Testimony at the administrative hearings on this matter by both South Dakota bankers and the Governor of South Dakota indicates that South Dakota is in need of capital; that need may in part be alleviated by Bank. Based upon the above facts and all the evidence of record in this matter, the Board finds that convenience and needs factors are positive and lend weight toward approval of the proposal.

On the basis of all the facts of record in this matter, it is the Board's judgment that approval of the application would be in the public interest and that the application should be approved. On the basis of the record, the application is approved for the reasons summarized above. The transaction shall not be made before the thirtieth calendar day following the effective date of this Order or later than three months after the effective date of this Order, unless such period is extended for good cause by the Board or by the Federal Reserve Bank of New York pursuant to delegated authority.

## Comments and Questions

1. Did Congress intend the National Bank Act to empower a bank's home state to overrule all of the lending laws of the credit card borrower's state? Did Congress authorize the law of all other states to be overruled by South Dakota or Delaware?

2. The position of the OCC is that while the definition of interest is governed by federal, not state, law, federal law looks to state law to establish the limits of what constitutes interest. Many states have amended their credit card laws to induce banks to locate their credit card operations in the state. An Arizona statute passed in 1989 is typical. First, it significantly expands the permissible fees and charges that may be contracted for on credit card accounts, to include such items as transaction charges for each separate purchase or loan; late payment or delinquency charges; returned check charges; stop payment charges; over-limit charges; and fees for providing invoices, checks, or other

documentary evidence. Second, the statute provides that all of the fees and charges in connection with the credit card account are deemed to be "interest" and "material to the determination of the interest rate." Do we now have 50 federal definitions of "interest"?

---

The high interest rates of the 1970s and early 1980s caused state interest rate laws, at times, to be a serious burden to lending institutions. It was in such an era that Congress enacted 12 U.S.C.A. § 1831d, governing interest rates permissible to federally insured state banks, effectively creating a § 85 for the benefit of state banks. Why was it necessary for Congress to pass a statute involving interest rates charged by state-chartered institutions? Why wasn't this simply a matter of local concern? Was Congress trying to avoid competitive disadvantage? And finally, what exactly is meant by the term "interest"?

## Greenwood Trust Co. v. Commonwealth of Massachusetts
971 F.2d 818 (1st Cir. 1992), *cert. denied*, 506 U.S. 1052 (1993)

SELYA, Circuit Judge.

This train wreck of a case arises out of a headlong collision between a state consumer-protection law and a federal banking law. It brings into sharp focus the tensions inherent in our federalist system while presenting a novel legal question: can a federally insured bank, chartered in Delaware, charge its Massachusetts credit-card customers a late fee on delinquent accounts, notwithstanding a Massachusetts statute explicitly prohibiting the practice? The district court answered this question in the negative, enforcing the state statute and granting partial summary judgment in appellees' favor. Because we believe that the lower court was on the wrong track, we reverse. Federal law has the right of way in this area.

### I.

### Background

The pertinent facts are largely undisputed. Plaintiff-appellant Greenwood Trust Company (Greenwood) is a Delaware banking corporation. Its deposits are insured by the Federal Deposit Insurance Corporation. Through a wholly owned subsidiary, Greenwood offers an open end credit card–the Discover Card–to customers nationwide. More than one hundred thousand of its cardholders live in Massachusetts.

The terms and conditions applicable to use of the Discover Card are spelled out in a Cardmember Agreement. The Agreement stipulates, *inter alia*, that the holder must make a minimum monthly payment, calculated by reference to the credit-card balance outstanding from time to time, on or before a designated due date. Failure to make this payment in a timeous fashion constitutes a default. If the default is not cured within twenty days, a ten-dollar late charge is automatically assessed.

On October 27, 1989, the Commonwealth of Massachusetts advised Greenwood that its imposition of late charges under such circumstances contravened state law. The Commonwealth threatened to take legal action. Greenwood promptly launched a preemptive strike, filing a complaint for declaratory and injunctive relief in the United States District Court for the District of Massachusetts.  The Commonwealth denied that federal law preempted the Massachusetts statute.  It also counterclaimed, seeking to bar Greenwood from assessing late charges and to collect restitutionary damages, together with civil penalties, referable to Greenwood's defiance of state law.

The district court adjudicated the parties' competing claims on cross-motions for summary judgment.  Discerning no federal preemption, the court ruled that Massachusetts law applied.  Since the court interpreted that law to forbid Greenwood's imposition of late charges upon cardholders who lived in Massachusetts, it denied Greenwood's motion and granted partial summary judgment in the Commonwealth's favor. . . .

## II.

### The Statutory Scheme

Two statutes lay at the heart of the dispute between these protagonists:  the state law that prohibits the imposition of late fees by credit-card issuers, viz., Mass. Gen. L. ch. 140, § 114B (1991) (Section 114B), and the federal law which arguably preempts the state statute, viz., Section 521 of the Depository Institutions Deregulation and Monetary Control Act of 1980 (DIDA) . . . . This case demands that we determine whether section 114B's immovable prohibition survives section 521's irresistible preemptive sweep.

The Massachusetts statute is straightforward.  It provides that:  "No creditor shall impose a delinquency charge, late charge, or similar charge on loans made pursuant to . . . an open end credit plan."  Mass. Gen. L. ch. 140, § 114B.

On the other hand, section 521 is equally uncompromising:  In order to prevent discrimination against State-chartered insured depository institutions, including insured savings banks, . . . with respect to interest rates, . . . such State bank[s] . . . may, notwithstanding any State constitution or statute which is hereby preempted for the purposes of this section, take, receive, reserve, and charge on any loan or discount made, or upon any note, bill of exchange, or other evidence of debt, interest at a rate of not more than 1 per centum in excess of the discount rate on ninety-day commercial paper in effect at the Federal Reserve bank in the Federal Reserve district where such State bank . . . is located or at the rate allowed by the laws of the State, territory, or district where the bank is located, whichever may be greater.

## III.

### A.  Preemption:  General Principles

In *Gibbons v. Ogden*, 22 U.S. (9 Wheat.) 1 (1824), Chief Justice Marshall declared that, under the rubric of the Supremacy Clause,[3] state laws which "interfere with, or are contrary to the laws of Congress, made in pursuance of the constitution," are preempted and, therefore,

---

[3]     The Supremacy Clause provides that:  This Constitution, and the Laws of the United States which shall be made in Pursuance thereof; and all Treaties made, or which shall be made, under the Authority of the United States, shall be the supreme Law of the Land; and the Judges in every State shall be bound thereby, any Thing in the Constitution or Laws of any State to the Contrary notwithstanding. U.S. Const., art. VI, cl. 2.

invalid. *Id.* 22 U.S. (9 Wheat.) at 211. This verity remains firmly embedded in our modern jurisprudence.

In placing constitutional theory into practice, the Court has generally distinguished between express and implied preemption. Express preemption occurs "when Congress has 'unmistakably . . . ordained' that its enactments alone are to regulate a [subject, and] state laws regulating that [subject] must fall." *Jones v. Rath Packing Co.*, 430 U.S. 519, 525 (1977) (quoting *Florida Lime & Avocado Growers, Inc. v. Paul*, 373 U.S. 132, 142 (1963)). . . .

Implied preemption can occur when Congress constructs a scheme of federal regulation "so pervasive as to make reasonable the inference that Congress left no room for the States to supplement it"; or when an "Act of Congress . . . touch[es] a field in which the federal interest is so dominant that the federal system will be assumed to preclude enforcement of state laws on the same subject"; or when the goals of, and obligations imposed by, the federal law make manifest a purpose to uproot state law. . . .

## B.

### The Track We Must Travel

We move now from the general to the particular. Section 521 boasts an express preemption clause. . . .

Our conclusion that the proper analysis in this case reduces to an inquiry into express preemption is unaffected by the fact that the inquiry requires us to interpret the terms "interest" and "interest rates" as they are employed in section 521. While uncertainty about the meaning of interstitial terms in the text of a federal statute may affect the scope of express preemption, it does not bear directly on the character of Congress's preemptory intent. See *Cipollone*, 112 S. Ct. at 2617-25 (plurality opinion); *id.* at 2625-31 ( Blackmun, J., concurring in part and dissenting in part); *Cable Television*, 954 F.2d at 98. In other words, so long as Congress's intent to effect preemption remains clear and manifest, uncertainty which pertains only to the contours of the ensuing preemption does not necessitate an alteration of a reviewing court's basic analytic approach.

## C.

### The Scope of Express Preemption under Section 521

We must still resolve the crucial question of *what* state laws are preempted. Put specifically, is a state law banning the imposition of late charges a law regulating "interest" within the purview of section 521? If so, chapter 140, § 114B is preempted. . . .

### 1.

The Commonwealth urges, and the lower court determined, *Greenwood Trust*, 776 F. Supp. at 36-38, that section 521's language plainly limits its preemptory impact to state laws that govern numerical interest rates, thereby leaving state laws regulating flat fees unscathed–even when, as here, such fees arise out of the extension and maintenance of credit. We are not persuaded that the plain meaning of "interest" and/or "interest rates" as used in section 521 requires so grudging an interpretation.

In the first place, we do not believe that the plain meaning of "interest" necessarily restricts the definition of the word to numerical percentage rates. Reference works typically define interest as "a charge for borrowed money[,] *generally* a percentage of the amount borrowed." *Webster's Ninth New Collegiate Dictionary* 630 (1989) (emphasis supplied); *see also Black's Law Dictionary* 812 (6th ed. 1990). Such definitions do not limit interest to numerical percentage rates, for they simply note that interest is often, but not always, expressed as a percentage. If the Commonwealth's circumscribed view of the word were accurate, there would be no basis for suggesting that exceptions exist.

Judicial opinions also tend to shy away from limiting the word "interest" to numerical percentage rates. Specifically, federal case law has long suggested that, in ordinary usage, interest may encompass late fees and kindred charges.[5] *See, e.g., Shoemaker v. United States*, 147 U.S. 282, 321 (1893) ("Interest accrues either by agreement of the debtor to allow it for the use of money, or, in the nature of damages, by reason of the failure of the debtor to pay the principal when due."); *Brown v. Hiatts*, 82 U.S. (15 Wall.) 177, 185 (1873) ("[i]nterest is the compensation allowed by law, or fixed by the parties, for the use or forbearance of money, or as damages for its detention").

Thus, the door is open to appellant's interpretation of the term. Suggesting that an additional fee attached to a delinquent, defaulted account is related to the creditor's cost of lending that money does no violence to language, to precedent, or, indeed, to logic. Default necessarily increases the creditor's cost of processing a loan. Therefore, a late fee is sufficiently related to the "use or forbearance of money, or . . . damages for its detention" that it can appropriately be classified as "interest."

In the second place, the use of words like "rate" in conjunction with the word "interest" does little to advance the Commonwealth's thesis. While there may exist support for the assertion that a flat fee is not included in the plain meaning of terms such as "rate" and "interest rates," section 521's preemptive reach cannot so easily be restricted to numerical percentage rates. Terms in an act whose meaning may appear plain outside the scheme of the statute can take on a different meaning when read in their proper context. . . .

Accordingly, we must move beyond the plain-meaning doctrine to determine the scope of express preemption under section 521.

2.

The preamble to section 521 states that the law was created "to prevent discrimination against State-chartered insured depository institutions, including insured savings banks." To understand the reference, we examine the historical context.

As the 1970s wound down, the Nation was caught in the throes of a devastating credit crunch. Interest rates soared. *See, e.g., United States v. Ven- Fuel, Inc.*, 758 F.2d 741, 764 n.20

---

[4]     Since we are interpreting the terms of a federal statute in a dispute between Massachusetts and a Delaware bank, we do not believe that definitions of interest emanating from courts in other states are relevant to our inquiry, except insofar as those cases purpose to interpret DIDA or its forebears. In any event, such state-law definitions go both ways. Compare, e.g., *Perry v. Stewart Title Co.*, 756 F.2d 1197, 1207-08 (5th Cir. 1985) (under Texas law, late charges are not a component of interest) with, e.g., *Swindell v. Federal Nat'l Mortgage Ass'n*, 330 N.C. 153, 409 S.E.2d 892, 894-95 (1991) (under North Carolina law, late charges are a component of interest).

(1st Cir. 1985) (cataloguing fluctuations in the prime rate from 1975 to 1983). Nevertheless, state lending institutions were constrained in the interest they could charge by state usury laws which often made loans economically unfeasible from a lender's coign of vantage. See *Gavey Properties/762 v. First Fin. Sav. & Loan*, 845 F.2d 519, 521 (5th Cir. 1988); *Bank of New York v. Hoyt*, 617 F. Supp. 1304, 1309 (D.R.I. 1985). National banks did not share this inhibition because they could charge whatever interest rates were allowed under the National Bank Act of 1864, ch. 106, 13 Stat. 99 (1864) (codified, as amended, in scattered sections of 12 U.S.C.) (the Bank Act), and specifically, those rates which were permitted under Bank Act § 85, 12 U.S.C. § 85 (1988), quoted *infra* note 7. Since section 85 authorized national banks to use interest rates set by reference to federal discount rates, state institutions were at an almost insuperable competitive disadvantage.

Congress tried to level the playing field between federally chartered and state-chartered banks when it enacted DIDA. See 126 Cong. Rec. 6,907 (1980) (section 521 will "allow[ ] competitive equity among financial institutions, and reaffirm[ ] the principle that institutions offering similar products should be subject to similar rules") (statement of Sen. Bumpers); 126 Cong. Rec. 6,900 (1980) (section 521 should "provide[ ] parity, or competitive equality, between national banks and State[-]chartered depository institutions on lending limits") (statement of Sen. Proxmire). To achieve this objective, Congress engrafted onto DIDA's bare bones, at several points, language taken from the Bank Act. Section 521, modeled on section 85 of the Bank Act, was the site of one such transplantation. The parallelism was not mere happenstance. To the exact contrary, Congress made a conscious choice to incorporate the Bank Act standard into DIDA. *See, e.g.*, 126 Cong. Rec. 6,907 (1980) (statement of Sen. Bumpers); 125 Cong. Rec. 30,655 (1979) (statement of Sen. Pryor); see also *Gavey*, 845 F.2d at 521.

The historical record clearly requires a court to read the parallel provisions of DIDA and the Bank Act *in pari materia*. It is, after all, a general rule that when Congress borrows language from one statute and incorporates it into a second statute, the language of the two acts should be interpreted the same way. . . .

While we believe that several principles inherent in section 85 were transfused into section 521, the critical item for present purposes is the principle of exportation. This principle, solidly embedded in the language and purpose of both acts, provides the mechanism whereby a bank may continue to use the favorable interest laws of its home state in certain transactions with out-of-state borrowers. See *Marquette Nat'l Bank v. First of Omaha Serv. Corp.*, 439 U.S. 299, 313-19 (1978); *Gavey*, 845 F.2d at 521. To the extent that a law or regulation enacted in the borrower's home state purposes to inhibit the bank's choice of an interest term under section 521, DIDA expressly preempts the state law's operation. . . .

We reach this conclusion mindful of the fact that the state statute here at issue visits two areas which are squarely within the ambit of the states' historic powers–banking and consumer protection. . . . When Congress has acted within its authority and its intent to displace state law is clear–preconditions which obtain here–preemption is not foreclosed by the fact that the federal statute intrudes into the range of subjects over which the states have traditionally exercised their police powers. See *Fidelity Fed. Sav. & Loan Ass'n v. De La Cuesta*, 458 U.S. 141, 153 (1982).

3.

To be sure, the impuissance of the Commonwealth's plain-meaning argument signifies only that the terms "interest" and "interest rates" as used in section 521 are susceptible to interpretation–not that the Commonwealth's interpretation of those terms is necessarily wrong or that the appellant's interpretation is necessarily correct. To like effect, our recognition of DIDA's ancestry, while illuminating, provides us with no definitive answer to the precise question at hand. Since DIDA's text and legislative history are, at bottom, inconclusive, we must look either to federal common law or to state law to give content to the terms in question.

In general, the words and phrases contained in a federal statute are defined by reference to federal law. There are two compelling reasons for adhering to this praxis. First, application of state-law definitions may threaten the policies or interests which a federal statute is designed to serve. See *United States v. Kimbell Foods, Inc.*, 440 U.S. 715, 728 (1979). Second, application of state-law definitions may disrupt Congress's desire for nationwide uniformity under a federal statute.

Resort to uniquely federal definitions is not, however, automatic. "Congress sometimes intends that a statutory term be given content by the application of state law." *Mississippi Band*, 490 U.S. at 43. In such instances, a federal court may properly use state law to fill the interstices within a federal legislative scheme. . . . This "does not mean that a State would be entitled to use [a statutory term] in a way entirely strange to those familiar with its ordinary usage, but at least to the extent that there are permissible variations in the ordinary concept [of that term] we [may] deem state law controlling." *De Sylva*, 351 U.S. at 581.

In this case, we need not decide whether federal or state law is the appropriate point of reference. Since both sources produce the same result, it would be a mere matter of form–and idle–to choose between them.

a.

Section 521 allows a state bank to charge interest "at the rate allowed by the laws of the State . . . where the bank is located." We think this is a fairly clear indication that, if a state-law definition of interest is applicable, it must emanate from Delaware law. We so hold, much bolstered by the recognition that section 85 "adopts the entire case law of [a state bank's home] state interpreting the state's limitations on usury; it does not merely incorporate the numerical rate adopted by the state." *First Nat'l Bank v. Nowlin*, 509 F.2d 872, 876 (8th Cir. 1975); accord *Roper v. Consurve, Inc.*, 777 F. Supp. 508, 510-11 (S.D. Miss. 1990), *aff'd*, 932 F.2d 965 (5th Cir.) (table), *cert. denied*, 181 (1991). Our conclusion is further fortified by the knowledge that several other federal tribunals, in addition to the *Nowlin* and *Roper* courts, have interpreted identical language in section 85 of the Bank Act as adopting definitions drawn from the law of the state where the bank is located.

Delaware law explicitly incorporates late charges into the definition of interest and allows lenders to assess such fees against credit-card customers. See Del. Code Ann. tit. 5, § 950 (1985 & Supp. 1990). Thus, were we to look to Delaware law for help in fathoming the meaning of "interest" and "interest rates," late charges would be included. In that event, section 114B's prohibition on late fees would be nullified by section 521's express preemption of state laws limiting exported interest rates.

### b.

Federal common law brings us to precisely the same result. Several courts, in analyzing the language of section 85 of the Bank Act, have had little trouble in construing the term "interest" to encompass a variety of lender-imposed fees and financial requirements which are independent of a numerical percentage rate. *See, e.g., American Timber & Trading Co. v. First Nat'l Bank*, 690 F.2d 781, 787-88 (9th Cir. 1982) (compensating balance requirement); *Fisher v. First Nat'l Bank*, 548 F.2d 255, 258-61 (8th Cir. 1977) (fee for cash advance); *Panos v. Smith*, 116 F.2d 445, 446-47 (6th Cir. 1940) (taxes and recording fees); *Cronkleton v. Hall*, 66 F.2d 384, 387 (8th Cir.) (bonus or commission paid to lender), *cert. denied*, 290 U.S. 685 (1933); *Nelson v. Citibank (South Dakota) N.A.*, 794 F. Supp. 312, 318 (D. Minn. 1992) (late fees). Fairly read, these opinions expand the scope of section 85 preemption–and, by implication, the scope of section 521 preemption–well beyond periodic percentage rates.

While we are aware that many of these cases involve the intrastate extension of loans by national banks rather than the exportation of interest rates, the analogy is persuasive. Furthermore, some of them do involve exportation. For example, *Fisher* concerned a credit-card cash advance fee charged by a Nebraska bank to a customer residing in Iowa. The court suggested that this fee was a component of the "rate of interest," making no distinction between the meaning of "interest" in intrastate, as opposed to interstate, transactions. *Fisher*, 548 F.2d at 258-61. For our part, we can discern no principled basis for such a distinction.

### 4.

It is, moreover, obvious that construing the terms "interest" and "interest rates" to include late charges fits most comfortably with the rationale undergirding section 521. DIDA was enacted in order to strike a competitive balance between state and national lending institutions by giving them equal power in charging interest rates. Allowing state banks to charge the same or similar fees in connection with the extension and maintenance of credit as national banks are allowed to charge ensures parity between the two types of institutions.

Such a construction also finds broad support in the rulings and informal opinion letters of the various agencies charged with interpreting the meaning of section 85 and section 521. *See, e.g.*, 12 C.F.R. § 7.7310(a) (1992) (ruling of the Comptroller of the Currency to the effect that all of a bank's home-state laws "material to the determination of the interest rate" are exportable); Letter by Robert B. Serino, Deputy Chief Counsel of the Office of the Comptroller of Currency, [1988-1989 Transfer Binder] Fed. Banking L. Rep. (CCH) ¶ 85,676 (Aug. 11, 1988) (concluding that, under Bank Act § 85, state-law prohibition of late charges may be preempted); Letter by Harry W. Quillian, Acting General Counsel of the Federal Home Loan Bank Board 3 (June 27, 1986) (similar; interpreting DIDA § 522).

We need not grease the rails. Given our conclusion that DIDA § 521 should be interpreted *in pari materia* with its direct lineal ancestor, section 85 of the Bank Act, and given, also, the litany of cases extending section 85 to a wide variety of fees and charges associated with the extension and maintenance of credit, we see no reason to define either the term "interest" or the term "interest rates," for purposes of section 521, in a manner that excludes late fees. . . .

Reversed.

## Comments and Questions

1. In light of *Greenwood Trust*, does the jurisdiction in which a borrower resides retain any meaningful control over the credit terms charged by out-of-state lenders? Could, for example, a borrower challenge an out-of-state lender's credit card fees based on a common law restriction against unreasonable liquidated damages terms? Would the common law governing liquidated damages in the lender's jurisdiction be relevant? All states have enacted the Uniform Commercial Code, which, at least for the sale of goods, establishes a rather uniform law of unconscionability. To the extent that unconscionability has become part of the common law of contracts of most states, has it been preempted by § 85?

2. While the Riegle-Neal Interstate Banking and Branch Efficiency Act of 1994 is principally concerned with the removal of interstate geographic restrictions on banks, it also contains some difficult language with respect to interest rate exportation. 12 U.S.C.A. § 36(f) was added to provide that any branch of an out-of state national bank is subject to state law with respect to consumer protection (and other matters) as if it were a branch of a host state bank. However, state law does not apply to the extent that it is preempted by federal law, or if the OCC determines that application of such law would have a discriminatory effect on the branch relative to host state banks. Finally, yet another section of the Act provides that 12 U.S.C.A. §§ 85 and 1831d are not to be affected. Are the sometimes conflicting policies of dual banking and competitive equality of any remaining value in resolving particular controversies?

3. As part of the dual banking system, the OCC has regularly preempted state law as applied to national banks. The Riegle-Neal Act in 12 U.S.C.A. § 43 establishes new procedures for bank regulatory agencies issuing preemption opinions, requiring publication of the question in the Federal Register and allowing interested parties not less than 30 days to comment.

4. Does it appear that the OCC both defers to state law when it chooses, and preempts state law when it chooses? Is the OCC trying to create uniformity within the banking industry, rather than competitive equality? Is the OCC trying to increase competition and so enhance banking services? Certainly competitive equality cannot mean that state and national banks must always compete on equal terms, and yet any action designed to gain competitive advantage appears to be contrary to the policy. Does this suggest that the dual banking system, at least in the eyes of the OCC with its federal preemption power, is a more powerful and pervasive policy than competitive equality?

5. Carefully consider the preemption analysis in *Greenwood Trust*. The court concluded that the 1980 law contained an express preemption relating to interest charged, but that the scope of preemption was unclear because of the lack of a statutory definition of interest. While several cases had included a variety of charges within the definition of interest, the court also recognized that the charges in question fell within two areas of law historically within state police powers–banking and consumer protection. Should preemption occur other than when either Congress intends federal law to occupy a given field or when state law actually conflicts with federal law?

6. The Supreme Court in *Smiley v. Citibank (South Dakota), N.A.,* 116 S. Ct. 1730 (1996), agreed with *Greenwood Trust* when it held that a national bank could export credit card late payment fees as part of the interest rate law of the state where it is located.

### Problem 2-3

A national bank located in Delaware uses Delaware law for purposes of determining the interest rate charged on its credit charge transactions throughout the United States. Delaware law does not provide for any interest rate limit whatsoever and further provides that all fees charged to credit card holders, wherever located, are part of the Delaware interest rate law. The list of items deemed material to the Delaware interest rate by state law include a variety of activities related only indirectly to credit extension, such as fees for account documentation (cancelled cash-advance checks or verification of purchase documents) and the charge for new packets of cash-advance checks.

The Delaware based national bank is, in fact, a credit card bank that is part of a much larger holding company with bank subsidiaries in 25 states, some of the banks having branches in multiple states. A customer of any of these affiliated full-service banks, upon applying for a credit card at any branch, receives an application form and ultimately a credit card from the Delaware based national bank.

Does § 85 allow the Delaware credit card bank to export its interest rates and related charges into other states even if it has a holding company affiliated bank located in the other state, or, alternatively, is the Delaware bank effectively located in the state where the bank affiliate or its branch is located? And, is there any limit to the state law definition of "interest"? Could a Delaware state chartered bank export more types of charges than could a national bank? See 12 C.F.R. § 7.4001.

### Problem 2-4

New Jersey law requires all banks offering checking accounts to offer low-cost checking accounts. The New Jersey state law requirements include that a bank cannot require an initial deposit of more than $50, or a minimum balance of more than $1 to keep an account open. Deposits and withdrawals must be free, and banks cannot charge more than $3 per month for the account.

While the National Bank Act encourages the provision of consumer checking accounts it certainly does not require them. Are national banks required to offer such accounts, or is the New Jersey law preempted? If the accounts are offered, are the charges interest and so limited by § 85? Do the policies of dual banking and competitive help your analysis of the problem?

# Section 4.  Bank Antitrust

## A.  Introduction

Anti-competitive, or economic concentration, concerns have historical origins in many aspects of U.S. banking regulation, and, as was suggested in section 1, have historical roots reaching to the earliest days of bank regulation in Europe.  Section 4(c)(8) of the Bank Holding Company Act provides that the Federal Reserve, in reviewing a bank holding company application to engage in an activity closely related to banking, must consider both the benefits of increased competition and the adverse effects of decreased or unfair competition.  The Bank Merger Act requires the regulators to consider the traditional antitrust standards, discussed in the next subsection, in every merger or acquisition of one bank by another.  And banks have long been faced with a host of geographic restrictions on expansion, which have had the effect of an indirect restriction on economic concentration by prohibiting mergers of banks in different markets.  But as the limits on geographic restrictions have lessened, the issue of economic concentration in bank mergers and acquisitions is more directly confronted by the antitrust laws.

## B.  Bank Mergers and Acquisitions

Banks, as well as other forms of business enterprise, prefer to avoid competition as much as possible.  As Adam Smith once put it in THE WEALTH OF NATIONS (1776), "People of the same trade seldom meet together, even for merriment and diversion, but the conversation ends in a conspiracy against the public, or in some contrivance to raise prices."  Smith saw a critical role for government in regulating the natural desire of businesses to enter into "treaties" with competitors that limited competition.  Government was to regulate business to assure competition.  Competition would then control selfishness and prices, and stimulate innovation.

Antitrust law is heavily based on economic theory and has engendered much controversy.  The proper balance between government regulation for the purpose of assuring maintenance of market forces, and government regulation that restricts productive and innovative activity, is not easy to determine.  Large mergers have given our society substantial benefits.  Without the efficiency of certain large manufacturing corporations we would not have our current standard of living.  And so, there are efficiencies in certain combinations that provide benefits, both economic and social, to our society.

It is the job of the antitrust laws to apply all of this to mergers and acquisitions.  While congressional enactments form the basis for antitrust, it is impossible to appreciate or understand the subject of antitrust simply by reading the statutes.  The statutes are at best broadly phrased as statements of basic antitrust policy that often appear to border on the nebulous.  As a consequence, the development of antitrust law has been left to the federal courts.  It has taken hundreds of cases to tell us what the general phrases of the antitrust statutes mean.  In this brief section, we will be able only to consider the antitrust laws in their most basic form as applied to the activities of depository institutions.

The Interstate Banking and Branching Efficiency Act of 1994 clearly suggests that we have heightened antitrust concerns where banks are involved. 12 U.S.C.A. § 1842(d)(2) provides for 10% national and 30% state insured deposits concentration limits, which suggest a belief that the results of a bank failure can be significantly different than the failure of the typical industrial concern. If large banks fail and the payment system fails, then all other facets of our economy are directly and immediately harmed. That risk is simply too great to our society.

Passage of the 1994 Act allowing interstate bank acquisitions has already stimulated additional bank merger and acquisition activity. Banking concentration can be examined on a number of levels. One level is nationwide concentration, which has been of interest because of a concern about the overall control of credit in the United States that dates back to the earliest times. The other area of concentration interest is at the local level. This is where most bank customers, particularly individuals and small businesses, find their financial services. To the extent that such customers are restricted to a local banking market, the preservation of competitive markets for local banking services is critical. For several decades, the percentage of total domestic deposits held by the one hundred largest banking organizations hovered at approximately 50%. At the end of 1993 that percentage was 64%, and these one hundred organizations held approximately 73% of all banking assets.

Before specifically discussing the antitrust laws applicable to bank mergers and acquisitions, two introductory points should be mentioned. First, in planning a bank merger or acquisition, it is often possible to select the regulator that will perform the primary antitrust review by altering the form of the acquisition, and by choosing between a state or national bank as the surviving institution. Other regulators may submit comments on the antitrust implications of the transaction, and the Justice Department has the power to file suit, but only the selected regulator has the power to disapprove the transaction.

The three major antitrust enactments applicable to banks are the Bank Merger Act, 12 U.S.C.A. § 1828(c), governing statutory mergers and purchase and assumption transactions between banks, the Bank Holding Company Act, 12 U.S.C.A. § 1842, governing mergers and acquisitions of a bank by a holding company, and the Change in Bank Control Act, 12 U.S.C.A. § 1817(j), which covers the acquisition of a bank by an individual. Which of the three statutes applies, and which federal regulator will review the transaction, again depends on the structure of the transaction. For example, if an individual buys control of a national bank, the individual must file with the Comptroller of the Currency for review under CBCA. If the bank being acquired is a state chartered bank, the CBCA filing must be with the FDIC. If the individual acquiring control forms a corporation to acquire the bank, then the acquisition will be governed by the Bank Holding Company Act and the filing must be with the Federal Reserve. If two banks are being merged, where the surviving bank is a national bank, approval must come from the Comptroller of the Currency under the Bank Merger Act, while if the surviving bank is a state chartered nonmember bank, approval under the Bank Merger Act must come from the FDIC. There are still other possibilities, but these examples make the point.

In theory, since the same antitrust standards are being applied in each case, the result should not vary among regulators.  But many bank antitrust practitioners believe that results can vary, and so frequently the structuring of the transaction is an important consideration.

The second introductory point is that there are a few notable differences between the general federal antitrust laws and the bank antitrust laws.  Read 12 U.S.C.A. § 1842(c).  In addition to the general antitrust provisions prohibiting mergers "whose effect in any section of the country may be substantially to lessen competition . . .," the statute also provides that such mergers may nevertheless be approved if the anticompetitive effects are "clearly outweighed" by the "convenience and needs of the community . . . ."  In addition, there is the somewhat mystifying § 1842(c)(2), which adds that "[i]n every case, the Board shall take into consideration the financial and managerial resources and future prospects of the company or companies and the banks concerned, and the convenience and needs of the community to be served."  Exactly what effect these and other variations from the general antitrust laws have in the consideration of bank mergers and other activities will be a topic for consideration.

There are many reasons why banks merge.  A bank may wish to expand its capital assets so it will have higher lending limits.  This might enable it better to compete for large industrial clients.  Or a bank may wish to realize economies of scale in the operation of various services.  A synergistic effect is most likely to occur where the merging banks have different strengths and weaknesses.  For example, one bank may have particularly good management resources that can be better used to exploit the competitive potential of the other bank, or one bank may have abundant trust funds while the other has a good investment management service.

Bank mergers, like many other banking activities, are regulated on both the state and federal levels.  Most states have laws specifically applicable to mergers resulting in state chartered banks; others control these mergers under more general laws of incorporation.  Most of these laws require certain procedures for stockholder approval and a final certification of the merger by the state banking authorities to protect the rights of dissenting shareholders, depositors, creditors, and the general public.  However, this section will deal only with the federal law of mergers.  In general, federal antitrust laws restricting bank mergers are grounded on the premise that competition, usually measured by the number of producers in a market, will eventually result in the lowest maintainable prices.

Most bank mergers involve either two banks or a bank and a bank holding company.  The standard for review under the BMA and BHCA are almost identical.  According to the BMA, the responsible agency shall not approve any merger transaction which would, in any part of the country, result in or increase the likelihood of a monopoly, substantially lessen competition, or in any other way restrain trade, unless the anticompetitive effects are outweighed by the convenience and needs of the community.  See 12 U.S.C.A. § 1828(c)(5).

Most of the language in § 1828(c)(5) was adopted from the basic antitrust statutes. Part (A) is nearly identical to section 2 of the Sherman Act (15 U.S.C.A. § 2). Part of (B), up to the clause beginning with "or which" is similar to section 7 of the Clayton Act (15 U.S.C.A. § 18), and the clause beginning with "or which" in part (B) is similar to section 1 of the Sherman Act (15 U.S.C.A. § 1). The embodiment of the language of the antitrust statutes brings into play all the case law surrounding those statutes, subject, of course, to the explicit "convenience and needs" exception in part (B).

The "Section 2 test," as evolved by the courts, focuses on monopolization. This could be found where the merged firm has "monopoly power" (generally well over 50% of the market). Lesser market power could still be attacked under section 2 where there is an "attempt" to monopolize, but this requires a showing of intent and a dangerous probability of success. In view of the lower standard of proof required under section 7 and section 1, it is not surprising that section 2 has seldom been used in merger cases.

The "Section 7 test" uses the language, "effect . . . may be substantially to lessen competition" and "to tend to create a monopoly," language which requires a lesser showing of market impact than section 2. In addition, the language extends to the probability of a future impact. This probability might be shown in a market with a trend toward concentration, or where the parties are potential competitors, even though the parties do not compete. An easier case under section 7 arises when the merger will eliminate significant existing competition between the merging parties, in what is typically called a horizontal or "in-market" merger.

In deciding bank merger cases under the antitrust laws the courts have tended to use market share figures as the primary consideration, and have not delved into all the economic subtleties of the competitive effects of each merger case. *Philadelphia National Bank v. United States*, 374 U.S. 321 (1963) is a leading case in this regard. Correspondingly, the Justice Department has issued "merger guidelines" that state in market share terms which mergers the Department will oppose. Of course, there is always room in the courts for economic considerations more complex than a set of market share figures. This is especially true where the market is difficult to define. Such considerations may include barriers to entry, rapid technological change, character of competition, and trends toward concentration. There is, however, a limit on the competence of the courts to integrate all of these secondary considerations. Also, many such phenomena exist only as temporary market conditions. Market shares, on the other hand, may be more indicative of a structural condition which will sooner or later manifest itself through specific anticompetitive effects. As a result, secondary considerations generally operate only as a basis for attack on a merger that looks harmless in market shares terms.

This emphasis on market shares has increased the importance of market definition. Defendants try desperately to show they are small fish in big ponds. Market definition is complex because of the requirement that it be analyzed in two dimensions: the product market and the geographic market. The product market (or "line of commerce") is generally said to include those products which are close substitutes with the product in question (in economic terms, those products with a high cross-elasticity of demand).

Sometimes, as in the *Philadelphia National Bank* case, the "product" is deemed to be a unique "cluster" of products and services called "commercial banking."

In the case of a horizontal or in-market merger, because a competitor in the market is eliminated and the market power of two firms is concentrated into the hands of one, the effect on competition is direct and obvious. The primary question is whether the effect is substantial enough to warrant prohibiting the merger.

The first step in analyzing a horizontal merger is to define the relevant product and geographic markets. Next, the market shares of the parties to the merger and the other firms in the market are determined. These figures help show the degree to which the market is already concentrated and the extent to which the merger will increase that concentration. Any more complex economic considerations should also be introduced at this point. Finally, the "convenience and needs" exception may be available.

The Department of Justice promulgated merger guidelines in 1968, again in 1982, and then revised the 1982 guidelines in 1984. The guidelines were further amended in 1992 for horizontal mergers. The guidelines focus primarily on the provisions of section 7 of the Clayton Act prohibiting mergers "where in any line of commerce in any section of the country, the effect of such acquisition may be substantially to lessen competition . . .." While the guidelines are not binding on the federal banking agencies, the agencies must be aware of them because the Department of Justice has the power to seek to enjoin any bank merger. The guidelines use a particular method of measuring market concentration, called the Herfindahl-Hirschman Index (HHI). The HHI is calculated by adding together the sum of the squares of the market shares of all the competing firms on the market. For example, a market with one firm controlling 50% of the deposits and five other firms each controlling 10% of the deposits would amount to an HHI of 3,000. The index is used both to determine industry concentration after the merger and the change in concentration brought about by the merger. In general, the larger the HHI and the change in it caused by the merger, the more likely that the market is concentrated and the more likely an objection to a merger will occur.

# In re Society Corp.
## 78 Fed. Res. Bull. 302 (1992)

*Order Approving the Acquisition of a Bank Holding Company*

Society Corporation, Cleveland, Ohio ("Society"), a bank holding company within the meaning of the Bank Holding Company Act (the "BHC Act"), has applied under section 3 of the BHC Act (12 U.S.C. § 1842) to merge with Ameritrust Corporation, Cleveland, Ohio ("Ameritrust"). . . .

*Competitive, Financial, Managerial and Supervisory Considerations*

Upon consummation of the transaction, Society would become the largest banking organization in Ohio, controlling deposits of $16.5 billion, representing 18.3 percent of the deposits in commercial banking organizations in the state; . . .

Society and Ameritrust compete directly in ten banking markets in Ohio and Indiana.[8] After considering the competition offered by thrift institutions,[9] the number of competitors remaining in the market, the increase in concentration, and the other facts of record, the Board has concluded that consummation of the proposal would not result in a significantly adverse effect on competition in the following banking markets: Akron, Canton, Cincinnati, Cleveland, Columbus and Youngstown-Warren in Ohio; and Elkhart-Niles-South Bend and Warsaw County in Indiana. Society has proposed divestitures to mitigate the anticompetitive effects of the proposed merger in the remaining banking markets of Ashtabula, Ohio, and Starke County, Indiana.[10]

In the Ashtabula banking market,[11] Society is the largest of ten depository institutions, with $186.8 million in deposits, which represents approximately 25.1 percent of the total deposits in depository institutions in the market ("market deposits"). Ameritrust is the third largest depository institution in the market, with $132.8 million in deposits, which represents approximately 17.9 percent of market deposits. Society has committed to divest four of the five Ameritrust branches in this market, representing approximately $105.0 million in market deposits, to a banking organization not currently operating in this market. With this divestiture,

---

[8]     Under the revised Department of Justice Merger Guidelines, 49 *Federal Register* 26,823 (June 29, 1984), a market in which the post-merger HHI is above 1800 is considered highly concentrated. In such markets, the Department is likely to challenge a merger that increases the HHI by more than 50 points. The Department has informed the Board that a bank merger or acquisition generally will not be challenged (in the absence of other factors indicating anticompetitive effects) unless the post-merger HHI is at least 1800 and the merger increases the HHI by 200 points. The Justice Department has stated that the higher than normal HHI thresholds for screening bank mergers for anticompetitive effects implicitly recognize the competitive effect of limited-purpose lenders and other non-depository financial entities.

[9]     The Board previously has indicated that thrift institutions have become, or have the potential to become, significant competitors of commercial banks. *WM Bancorp*, 76 *Federal Reserve Bulletin* 788 (1990); *First Union Corporation*, 76 *Federal Reserve Bulletin* 83 (1990); *Midwest Financial Group*, 75 *Federal Reserve Bulletin* 386 (1989). Thus, the Board has regularly included thrift deposits in the calculation of market share on a 50 percent weighted basis. *See e.g., First Hawaiian, Inc.*, 77 *Federal Reserve Bulletin* 52 (1991). In considering the competition offered by thrifts in all banking markets in this case, thrift deposits are weighted at 50 percent, unless otherwise noted. *See e.g., Ames National Corporation*, 78 *Federal Reserve Bulletin* 59 (1992); *Fleet/Norstar Financial Group Inc.*, 77 *Federal Reserve Bulletin* 750 (1990).

[10]     In each market in which Society has committed to divest branch offices to mitigate possible anticompetitive effects of this acquisition, Society has executed agreements that require consummation of these divestitures within 180 days of consummation of the proposal. If Society is unsuccessful in divesting these branches within 180 days of consummation, Society has committed to transfer these branches to an independent trustee with instructions to sell these branches promptly. *See e.g., United New Mexico Financial Corporation*, 77 *Federal Reserve Bulletin* 484, 485 (1991); *First Union Corporation*, 76 *Federal Reserve Bulletin* 83 (1990).

[11]     The Ashtabula banking market is approximated by Ashtabula County, Ohio.

the number of competitors in the Ashtabula banking market will not change following consummation of this proposal, and the HHI in this market would increase by 81 points to 1850.[12]

The Department of Justice ("Department") has indicated to the Board the Department's opinion that the proposal would have a significantly adverse competitive effect in Cuyahoga County and Lake County, Ohio.[14] The Department bases this conclusion on an analysis of the supply of and demand for credit to commercial customers, in particular small and medium-sized businesses, in these areas. The Department believes that the relevant product market for analyzing the competitive effects of this transaction is commercial loans other than commercial mortgage loans, and, that the relevant geographic markets consist of four counties, including Cuyahoga County and Lake County. The Department has stated its belief that the divestitures currently proposed by Applicant in Cuyahoga County do not appear to be sufficient to address the Department's concern regarding competition in that area. The Department has also indicated that it is continuing to discuss this matter with Applicant.

For the reasons explained in previous decisions and based on the record in this case, the Board believes that competitive analysis of this acquisition proposal should be based on the availability of the cluster of banking services to a range of customers in the local banking market. A recent study conducted by Board staff supports the conclusion that customers still seek to obtain this cluster of services. Based on this product market definition, the Board believes that the relevant geographic market is the Cleveland banking market.[17]

The Cleveland banking market is moderately concentrated, with 48 banking and thrift competitors in the market. Following consummation, the market would remain moderately concentrated with numerous competitors providing or poised to provide the cluster of banking products and services.[18] Furthermore, statistics relating to population per banking office, deposits per banking office, total banking assets and household income in the market, all indicate that Cleveland is an attractive market for entry. It is a major urban area, and includes the second largest city in Ohio. Seven banking organizations have entered the Cleveland banking market *de novo* since 1983, three of them in the last two years.

In considering the views of the Department, the Board notes that the Department has not provided the Board with evidence to support the Department's conclusions regarding the definition of the product market in this case. The Board also notes that, assuming the product market is defined by non-real estate commercial lending to small businesses, the Department does not indicate that it has taken into account competition in these products from nonbanking

---

[12] Following this proposed divestiture in the Ashtabula banking market, Society would remain the largest depository institution in the market, controlling approximately $214.6 million in deposits, representing approximately 28.9 percent of deposits in the market.

[14] The Department has indicated that, after taking into account the divestitures proposed in other markets, the transaction would not raise competitive concerns in other relevant banking markets.

[17] The Cleveland banking market is approximated by Cuyahoga, Geauga, Lake, and Lorain Counties, the northern third of Summit County, the northern two-thirds of Medina County, Aurora and Streetsboro townships in Portage County, and the City of Vermilion in Erie County, all in Ohio.

[18] With thrift deposits weighted at 50 percent, Society would control 34.4 percent of the market deposits, and the HHI would increase by 568 points to 1699 in the Cleveland market upon consummation of the proposal.

institutions, including finance companies, or the degree to which a variety of banking and nonbanking competitors supply other products, such as home equity loans and credit card loans, that may be effective substitutes for the products identified by the Department.  In light of the record before the Board, the Board believes that the appropriate product market is the cluster of banking products and services and the relevant geographic market is the Cleveland banking market as defined above.

Based on all of the facts of record in this case, and subject to the divestiture proposals made by Society, the Board concludes that consummation of this proposal would not have a significantly adverse effect on competition or the concentration of banking resources in any relevant banking market.  The Board has also sought comments from the Office of the Comptroller of the Currency ("OCC"), and the Federal Deposit Insurance Corporation ("FDIC") on the competitive effects of this proposal.  Neither the OCC nor the FDIC has provided any objection to consummation of this proposal or indicated that the proposal would have any significantly adverse competitive effects.

Based on the entire record, the Board also concludes that the financial and managerial resources, future prospects of Society, its subsidiary banks, and Ameritrust, and the supervisory factors in this case, are consistent with approval of this proposal.

By order of the Board of Governors, effective February 13, 1992.

*Dissenting Statement of Governor Angell*

I dissent from the Board's action in this case.  As I have indicated in previous cases, I believe that the structural measures used by the Board in analyzing bank acquisition proposals do not accurately reflect the competitive effects of these proposals.  In particular, I believe that these measures do not adequately account for the effect of these acquisitions on the availability and pricing of credit to small businesses.

I believe that the Board should focus particular attention on this aspect of the cluster of banking services in conducting its analysis of the competitive effects of bank acquisitions.  In this case, I agree with the conclusion expressed by the Department of Justice that this acquisition would have a significantly adverse effect on competition in the market for small business lending in these areas.

## Comments and Questions

1.  On March 13, 1992 the Department of Justice filed an antitrust suit to block the transaction.  The lawsuit was settled that very day, with Society agreeing to sell 28 Ameritrust branches to respond to the Department's competitive concerns.

2.  Everyone agrees that you have to define the product market before you can define the geographic market.  At the time of the *Philadelphia National Bank* case, product lines were fairly distinct—no one really competed with commercial banks.  Today, the product lines and competitors are increasingly blurred, with all types of depository institutions as well as many brokerage firms, finance companies, and others offering substantially similar deposit and loan services that once were the exclusive domain of banks.  Do you see how the product market definitions differ between the Federal Reserve Board and the

Department of Justice?  Do you see how this difference results in different geographical markets, concentration ratios, and ultimate conclusions?

3.  The Fed believed that the Department of Justice was incorrect when it failed to take into account competition in the small commercial loan market, particularly from finance companies which do a great deal of asset financing for business.  In addition, thrifts have the power to make commercial loans, as do companies such as Sears, General Electric, and General Motors.  It has been argued by the Justice Department that commercial finance companies do not provide the full array of lending services required by small businesses.  This is true in several aspects.  First, commercial finance companies typically limit themselves to asset-based financing, and do not make working capital loans.  Second, the finance companies' interest rates are much higher.  Third, they do not provide any other financial services.

4.  The cluster of banking services used by the Fed as the product market includes the typical variety of credit products and service products, such as checking accounts and trust administration, all combined together under the term "commercial banking."  The necessary implication of this view is that banks are assumed to compete only with other banks.  Perhaps this was true at the time of the *Philadelphia* decision.  But current conditions in the marketplace have substantially reduced the legal and economic barriers to entry into commercial banking product markets.  The result is that many nonbank providers of financial services exist in several of the same product markets as banks, because they offer reasonable substitutes for virtually all the traditional commercial bank products.  Do you see why this suggests that the cluster rule should be reexamined and the product-based antitrust analysis of the Department of Justice may be more consistent with competition theory?

5.  Other changes in market factors may potentially cause the Justice Department's views of product markets to be more amenable to mergers in the future.  First, as large banks lose the large corporate loan business to the commercial paper market, they will tend to redirect their lending capacity to small and medium sized businesses, thereby bringing more out-of-market competitors into any relatively concentrated markets.  Second, if small business commercial loans begin to be securitized and widely distributed, as have residential mortgages, this will again create a larger geographical market for the small business loan product.  As a result, these markets may become more national, and thus more competitive.

6.  The Federal Reserve and the Department of Justice also often reach different conclusions in defining the geographical market.  The Fed, by using the cluster of services product market, sees a large geographical area in which the cluster is offered and fairly consistent pricing exists.  Justice, however, focuses on how far customers are willing to travel for individual banking services.  The latter analysis can often result in a much smaller geographical area for product competition, as was true in *Society Corp.*

7.  Both the Federal Reserve and the Department of Justice use two initial screens to identify potentially anticompetitive mergers.  First, the postmerger HHI should be at least 1,800.  Second, the merger should produce a change in the HHI of at least 200.  But

the Fed and the Justice Department differ on the issues of both the relevant product market and the weight given to thrift deposits in judging competitive effects in the relevant geographical market.  The Federal Reserve typically gives thrift deposits 50% weight, while the Justice Department gives only 20% weight.  This means that where two banks are merging the Justice Department will tend to find a more concentrated market.  The reason for the difference is that the Department of Justice believes that thrifts do not compete with banks in one very important product line–commercial loans, particularly to small and mid-sized businesses.  One reason is that thrifts are restricted by law from investing more than 10% of their assets in commercial loans.

*Problem 2-5*

Utilizing the following table, determine whether the various mergers and acquisitions listed below will be accepted or challenged under the 1992 Department of Justice guidelines.

**Market Shares of Relevant Market**

| Institution | Deposits | Percentage | HHI |
|:-----------:|:--------:|:----------:|:-------:|
| A | 150 | 30.0 | 900.00 |
| B | 100 | 20.0 | 400.00 |
| C | 80 | 16.0 | 256.00 |
| D | 60 | 12.0 | 144.00 |
| E | 32 | 6.4 | 40.96 |
| F | 27 | 5.4 | 29.16 |
| G | 26 | 5.2 | 27.04 |
| H | 13 | 2.6 | 6.76 |
| I | 12 | 2.4 | 5.76 |
| Total | 500 | 100.00 | 1809.68 |

The four mergers or acquisitions to be considered are:

A.  Banks A and I;

B.  Two years after the AI merger, Banks AI and H;

C.  Banks B and E;

D.  Citicorp (which has no prior presence in this market) acquires Bank A.

*Problem 2-6*

For the following transactions, consider if you might reach different results depending on whether you utilize the Federal Reserve Board or the Department of Justice merger analysis methodology.

1. The Federal Reserve views the Washington, DC market as including both Washington, DC itself as well as the Maryland and Virginia suburbs. The largest consumer-retail bank in the Maryland suburbs wishes to merge with the largest consumer-retail bank in the Virginia suburbs. Would the Federal Reserve Board or the Department of Justice be more likely to conclude that these banks are in competition with each other?

2. Two banks, each with assets of $50 million, are located in Clymer, PA and are the only depository institutions in the town. They wish to merge. Might the Department of Justice object? Could the banks argue that the competitors for local retail deposits and consumer loans include Charles Schwab money market mutual funds accounts, Citicorp credit cards, certificates of deposits purchased throughout the United States from local newspaper ads, as well as automobile loans from GMAC and refrigerator loans from Sears?

3. Suppose that a commercial bank wishes to acquire the largest thrift in the local market. Is this merger more likely to be approved by the Justice Department or by the Federal Reserve Board?

———————

It is hard to foresee what the future might hold for the integration of financial services in the United States and its consequent effect on antitrust analysis. If commercial banks, securities firms, and insurance companies are allowed to affiliate with each other, it would appear that the analysis of product markets, geographical markets, and relevant competitors will change dramatically. With all the merger activity likely to occur, it should be recognized that small banks–those with less than $1 billion in assets–still account for a majority of all the banks in the United States, even if they hold far less than the majority of all banking assets. What this suggests is that small banks have not disappeared. There may be many reasons for this. One is that small banks may be best equipped to lend to local small businesses, as they have both the ability to monitor closely these firms and the organizational structure to be efficient in doing so. They may also be able to provide people with a higher level of personal service and lower turnover of personnel with whom customers must deal.

Overall, the analytical structure of antitrust applied to depository institution mergers is not particularly difficult. There are only a few policy issues, the most obvious being the appropriate product market definition. That question can be answered by determining whether there is any group of customers that is likely to face an increased risk of monopoly power resulting from the merger, and whether that monopoly power can be overcome by either new entry or responsive action by existing competitors. An additional but much more theoretical concern is whether the "convenience and needs" exception has any relevance. It was supposed to be utilized to give greater flexibility in dealing with anti-competitive bank mergers. But the Supreme Court in *United States v. Third National Bank in Nashville*, 390 U.S. 171 (1968), borrowed from the supposedly stricter "failing company" doctrine of general antitrust law and determined that there must be a "no less anti-competitive alternative purchaser" to satisfy the convenience and needs exception. The result is that bank antitrust law and general antitrust law are essentially identical.

*Problem 2-7*

Assume you are a legal advisor to the American Bankers Association ("ABA"). You have been asked to evaluate a Treasury Department proposal to consolidate anti-trust review of bank mergers in the Justice Department. Under the proposal, the federal banking agencies would no longer have jurisdiction to review competitive aspects of bank mergers; rather the Justice Department would evaluate these transactions in the same manner that the Department reviews mergers in other industries. Should the ABA support this proposal?

## C. Tie-Ins

The 1970 Tie-in Amendments to the Bank Holding Company Act make it illegal for a bank to condition an extension of credit by requiring that the customer obtain additional credit, property or service from the bank other than that related to and usually provided in connection with a loan. 12 U.S.C.A. § 1972. By regulation (12 C.F.R. § 225.7), the FRB has extended coverage of these rules to activities of BHCs. The statute reaches tie-ins to such services as correspondent banking, overline loans (those which are too large for one bank's lending limit and must be shared with other banks), and check clearing. Overall, while general antitrust law requires proof of a substantial lessening of competition for a tie-in to be illegal, § 1972 creates a per se standard applicable only to banking organizations.

Open questions of interpretation are the degree of compulsion required to constitute "condition or requirement" and the degree to which two services may be shown to be only a single service. There is language in the legislative history tending to show that "traditional banking practices" were to be excepted. An often cited example of such a practice is a "compensating balance" clause of a loan agreement which requires the borrower to maintain a certain level of deposits in the lending bank. Although the deposit effectively provides additional security to the bank, the arrangement clearly ties one service to another. Consider the following case.

# In re Fleet Financial Group
80 Fed. Res. Bull. 1134 (1994)

*Orders Approving an Exemption for the Anti-tying Provisions*

Fleet Financial Group, Inc., Providence, Rhode Island ("Fleet"), a bank holding company within the meaning of the Bank Holding Company Act, has requested that the Board permit its subsidiary banks to package and offer a discount on their products.  The discount would be available to customers who maintain a combined minimum balance in certain eligible Fleet products (which include securities brokerage accounts and mutual fund balances, as well as loan and deposit accounts).  Fleet seeks a Board interpretation that this arrangement is not covered by the anti-tying provisions of section 106 of the Bank Holding Company Act Amendments of 1970 (12 U.S.C. § 1972) or, if it is, an exemption from the statute permitting Fleet's subsidiary banks to offer such discounts.

The Fleet One Account provides a customer, for a $14 monthly fee, discounts and premiums on various Fleet services[1] so long as the customer maintains at least two accounts at Fleet.[2]  Under Fleet's proposal, a customer would be able to avoid the $14 fee by maintaining a $10,000 combined balance among the following eligible products:

(1) Deposits and certain loans at the Fleet bank at which the customer establishes the Fleet One Account;

(2) Credit card balances at Fleet Bank-NY;[3]

(3) Investment securities held at Fleet's brokerage subsidiary, Fleet Brokerage Securities, Providence, Rhode Island ("Fleet Brokerage"); and

---

[1]    These services include:

(1) A free checking account;

(2) A free credit card issued or maintained by Fleet Bank of New York, Albany, New York ("Fleet Bank-NY");

(3) A higher interest rate on money market savings;

(4) Discounted safe deposit box rental;

(5) Lower installment loan rates;

(6) No-fee traveler's checks;

(7) Discounts on equity line of credit or home equity loan closing costs; and

(8) Overdraft protection.

[2]    The customer could choose among the following accounts: checking, savings.  Galaxy Access (a sweep account), money market savings, Galaxy mutual funds, certificates of deposit, Fleet Brokerage accounts, and retirement accounts, as well as home equity, installment loans, credit card accounts, and cash reserve.  One of the two accounts must be a checking, savings or Galaxy Access account.

[3]    Fleet recently consolidated the credit card operations of the Fleet banks into Fleet Bank-NY.

(4) Shares held in one of the Galaxy Funds, a family of funds advised by Fleet Investment Advisors, a subsidiary of Fleet National Bank-RI, Providence, Rhode Island.

Fleet has represented that all products offered as part of these arrangements are separately available to customers at competitive prices.

Notice of this request, affording interested persons an opportunity to submit comments, has been published (59 *Federal Register* 9216 (1994)).  The time for filing comments has expired, and the Board received one comment, which supported Fleet's request.

*Background*

Fleet is the 13th largest banking organization in the nation, controlling deposits of $30.7 billion.  Fleet operates subsidiary banks in New York, Rhode Island, Connecticut, Maine, Massachusetts, and New Hampshire, and engages directly and through subsidiaries in a broad range of permissible nonbanking activities.

*Applicable Law*

Section 106 generally prohibits a bank from tying a product or service to another product or service offered by the bank or any of its affiliates.[5]  Violations of section 106 can be addressed by the Board through an enforcement action, by the Department of Justice through a request for an injunction, or by a customer or other party through an action for damages.  12 U.S.C. 1972, 1973 and 1975.

A bank engages in a tie for purposes of section 106 by:

(1) Offering a discount on a product or service (the "tying product") on the condition that the customer obtain some additional product or service (the "tied product") from the bank or from any of its affiliates; or

(2) Allowing the purchase of a product or service only if the customer purchases another product or service from the bank or from any of its affiliates.

Section 106 contains an explicit exception (the "statutory traditional bank product exception") that permits a bank to tie a product or service to a loan, discount, deposit, or trust service offered by that bank.  The Board has recently extended this exception by providing that a bank or any of its affiliates also may vary the consideration for a traditional bank product on condition that the customer obtain another traditional bank product from an affiliate (the "regulatory traditional bank product exception").

*Application of Section 106 to the Fleet One Account*

The two-product minimum requirement for the Fleet One Account and the combined-balance discount on that account appear to be covered by the terms of section 106. Although the two-account minimum requirement and the combined-balance discount are not conditioned on any *particular* product being purchased, the customer must purchase *some* product or products from a menu of eligible products in order to receive the Fleet One Account

---

[4]    Although section 106 applies only when a *bank* offers the tying product, the Board in 1971 extended the same restrictions to bank holding companies and their nonbank subsidiaries.  *See* 12 C.F.R. 225.7(a).

and the discount on that account.  Furthermore, the packaging of some of these products in the form proposed by Fleet does not appear to qualify for the statutory or regulatory traditional bank product exception.

On the other hand, the arrangement proposed by Fleet does not raise the types of anti-competitive concerns that section 106 was intended to address and provides benefits for customers.  Accordingly, to the extent that the Fleet proposal is prohibited by section 106, the Board has decided to grant an exemption to permit Fleet's subsidiary banks to offer the Fleet One Account and the combined-balance discount on that account.[6]  In this regard, the Board notes that the granting of an exemption, as opposed to an interpretation, will provide certainty as to the permissibility of the Fleet One Account under the anti-tying statute.

The Board has the authority to grant such an exemption so long as it is consistent with the purposes of section 106.  The Senate Report accompanying section 106 states that the Board should continue to allow appropriate traditional banking practices based on sound economic analysis.  The Board previously has granted exemptions where the proposal would not have anti-competitive effects and where there were benefits to the public such as lower costs to customers on banking services.

The Fleet One Account and the combined-balance discount that Fleet proposes to offer on that account are consistent with the type of banking relationships that section 106 recognized were important to preserve.  As noted, section 106 preserves such relationships through the statutory traditional bank product exception, which permits a bank to tie a product or service to a loan, discount, deposit, or trust service offered by that bank.  The legislative history of section 106 notes that this exception was intended to preserve a customer's ability to negotiate the price of multiple banking services with the bank on the basis of the customer's entire relationship with the bank.  Allowing the discounted Fleet One Account would serve the same purpose.

Moreover, under the statutory and regulatory traditional bank product exceptions, Fleet could offer a combined-balance discount on an account where all the products in the arrangement were traditional bank products (loans, discounts, deposits, and trust services), and Fleet could condition the Fleet One Account on a customer's maintaining two accounts at Fleet if all the relevant accounts were traditional bank products.  The requested exemption would simply permit Fleet to increase customer choice by adding a customer's securities brokerage account balance at Fleet Brokerage and shares of the Galaxy Funds to the menu of traditional bank products that count toward the minimum balance, and allow such non-traditional bank products to count toward the Fleet One Account's two account minimum.

Fleet's proposal is not only consistent with the statute's goal of preserving traditional banking relationships, but also its concerns about anti-competitive behavior.  Fleet includes all deposit accounts that a customer maintains at the Fleet bank offering the account in determining whether the customer has reached the minimum balance required to waive the Fleet One Account fee, and makes all deposit accounts at the bank eligible to satisfy the two-product requirement for

---

[5]     Fleet also argued that the counting of mutual fund shares towards the minimum balance was not covered by section 106 because mutual funds are not subsidiaries of bank holding companies and therefore not subject to section 106.  Because the Board granted Fleet an exemption, it was unnecessary to address this argument.

the Fleet One Account. Because a customer could qualify for the Fleet One Account and the discount on that account based solely on deposit balances and because Fleet will continue to offer customers all products involved in the arrangement separately and at competitive prices, there is no incentive for a customer to establish a brokerage account, or obtain any other product, that the customer does not want in order to obtain the Fleet One Account or a discount on that account.[10] For this reason, the Board has concluded that Fleet's proposed discount arrangement would not be coercive, anti-competitive, or otherwise inconsistent with the purposes of section 106. Moreover, approval of Fleet's proposal will provide Fleet's customers with greater choices and lower costs.

Fleet also demonstrated that the banking markets in which it operates are generally competitive and that no Fleet bank appears to have sufficient power in any of these markets to force a customer to purchase any tied product or service. The presence of other competitors in these banking markets lessens concerns that Fleet could use the Fleet One Account or a discount on that account to impair competition in other product markets.

*Conclusion*

For the reasons discussed above, the Board believes that the requested exemption is not contrary to the purposes of section 106, and that granting the exemption is consistent with the legislative authorization to permit exemptions for traditional banking services on the basis of sound economic analysis. The Board, however, reserves the right to terminate the exemption in the event that facts develop in the future that indicate that the tying arrangement is resulting in anti-competitive practices and thus would be inconsistent with the purpose of section 106.

Based on the above and all facts of record, and pursuant to its authority under section 106 of the Bank Holding Company Act Amendments of 1970 and the Bank Holding Company Act, the Board hereby grants an exemption to permit Fleet banks, to the extent that such activities are prohibited by section 106:

(1) To offer the "Fleet One Account" on the condition that a customer maintains two accounts at the Fleet bank and pays a monthly fee, and

(2) To offer a discount on the monthly fee charged for the Fleet One Account to a customer who maintains a combined minimum balance in certain eligible Fleet products.

This approval is based on the facts and circumstances presented by Fleet, and any material change in those facts or circumstances could result in a different outcome. The approval is subject to the conditions discussed above and the Board's authority to modify or terminate the exemption as set forth above and to all of the conditions that may be imposed by the Board in Regulation Y.

---

[10]  Under antitrust precedent, concerns over tying arrangements are substantially reduced where the buyer is free to take either product by itself even though the seller also may offer the two items as a unit at a single price. *Northern Pacific R. Co. v. United States*, 356 U.S. 1, 6 n.4 (1958).

## Comments and Questions

1. Section 1972 expressly authorizes the Federal Reserve to make exceptions to the anti-tying requirements of the statute. It was this authority that the Fed exercised in *Fleet*.

2. Beginning in 1993 the Federal Reserve Board took several actions to give banking organizations more flexibility in offering product combinations. Initially it allowed banking organizations to offer a discount on brokerage commissions to customers of traditional banking services in an affiliated bank. It subsequently allowed tying of banking services with nonbank affiliates, on the condition that all the products involved in the package were available separately for purchase. But that did not apply to products offered by an affiliated bank and also did not allow brokerage customers to receive discounted banking services. Then the Fleet Financial application followed, in which the Fed added mutual fund sales to the nontraditional services that may be packaged with traditional banking services. Subsequently it adopted the current regulation creating a general safe harbor for "combined-balance accounts" allowing computation of a combined minimum balance in products specified by the company, consequently allowing banks generally to engage in such activities without applying for a specific exemption to the Federal Reserve Board. Also, requiring that bank deposits count at least as much toward the minimum balance as nondeposit products is a way to protect community banks. This effectively prohibits large banks from limiting discounts to customers who use non-traditional products that may be viewed as more profitable by larger banks but may not be available at smaller banks.

3. Powerful remedy provisions for anti-tying violations are found in 12 U.S.C.A. §§ 1973, 1975, including temporary restraining orders and injunctions. Moreover, the provisions grant standing to sue to the government and to a private litigant "injured in his business or property," and allow treble damages for such injury. Because specific acts are forbidden, the plaintiff needs to show only the commission of such an act and need not prove a "substantial" foreclosure as required under the more general antitrust laws by *Fortner Enterprises v. U.S. Steel*, 394 U.S. 495 (1969).

### Problem 2-8

1. Anthony Forest Products applies to NationsBank for a letter of credit to back a bond issue of the company. The bank responds with a letter which states that before the Bank will issue any such letter of credit, the business relationship "must encompass the placement of business for the marketing of these bonds. We would not be in a position to offer a stand alone letter of credit. Our objective would be to become your primary and eventually exclusive bank." Is this an unlawful linking of a credit application to the other product of underwriting securities, which has a direct anti-competitive impact on those competitors in the securities markets who cannot offer federally insured money to lend?

2. Jones Brewing Company applies to South Hills National Bank for a $5 million loan. At lunch the bank's lending officer comments several times to the President of Jones Brewing that "we would really like to have the opportunity to be the investment

manager for your $25 million company pension plan." Is this a violation of the anti-tying provisions of federal banking law?

3. Roberts Rubbish Removal applies to Merrill Lynch for a $1 million working capital loan. Merrill Lynch responds in a letter which states that it is willing to make the loan on certain terms and conditions. Those terms and conditions are "based on the assumption" that Roberts agree to maintain "a substantial account relationship" with Merrill or otherwise "utilize substantial financial services offered" by Merrill. Is this letter a violation of federal law? If not, why not?

4. A bank offers free checking and discounts on loans to customers who invest in a mutual fund for which the bank is the investment adviser. Is this a violation of the anti-tying rules?

## D. Antitrust and Electronic Banking

Electronic banking comes in many forms: credit cards, debit cards, ATM systems, point of sale (POS) systems, and SMART (electronic money) cards. Many of these activities are structured as joint ventures. The best known examples of joint ventures are the Visa and Master Card networks. The generic question is whether a joint venture is pro-competitive or anti-competitive.

In theory, every bank could have its own ATM network and its own credit card network. But such networks require huge capital investments that are unrealistic for all but a few of the largest banks. As a consequence, many banks get together and form a joint venture. Antitrust claims can arise due to both underinclusiveness and overinclusiveness of participants in the joint venture. The basic argument for underinclusiveness is a claim of boycott. In general, a boycott or collective refusal to deal by independent parties who ordinarily are competitors often brings a claim of violation of section 1 of the Sherman Act. Like an agreement to fix prices, this type of agreement or collective refusal to deal is typically a per se violation, subjecting the violators to government action including criminal penalties and private treble damages.

On the other hand, if a joint venture includes all possible competitors it can become overinclusive and be detrimental to competition, since there are no competitors left. In the area of electronic banking, each of these claims has carried the day at one time or another. And so, the question of size is far more complex in the joint venture arena than in the typical merger. At some point the increased size of the network either ceases to result in significant increases in efficiency, or it is so dominant in a market that it is hard to find potential entrants of sufficient size to mount a competitive foray. At either point it would seem preferable to permit the network to exclude others, which would encourage the creation of competing networks.

Note the potentially conflicting legal mandates—limitations on cooperation among competitors and requirements that competitors be given access to an electronic banking system. On the one hand, if there are not strong economies of scale, a joint venture will raise antitrust problems if it continues to add members. On the other hand, if there are economies of scale, the joint venture looks like a "bottleneck monopoly" if it keeps people out.  In that case it appears to be hard for large, competing institutions both to have a joint venture and to keep others out.

We will principally consider the credit card market.  It is generally said that there are two levels of competition in the credit card market.  The first is at the network or system level where there are four major competitors–Visa, Master Card, American Express, and DISCOVER.  These network competitors offer services to their members, typically banks.  The second level of competition is at the issuer level, where there are thousands of competitors that issue credit cards.  These competitors include not only depository institutions but also such nonbank entities as General Motors and AT&T.

In terms of competition, there are two additional groups whose interests should be considered.  Those are the merchants who accept the cards as a form of payment, and consumers who use the cards as a form of payment.  Consider the following case.

## SCFC ILC, Inc. v. VISA USA, Inc.
### 36 F.3d 958 (10th Cir. 1994), *cert. denied*, 515 U.S. 1152 (1995).

JOHN P. MOORE, Circuit Judge.

Visa USA provides payment services to its 6,000 members which individually issue credit cards to consumers.  Sears, Roebuck and Company, a competitor offering its own credit card, the Discover Card, wanted to become a Visa USA member and also issue *Visa* cards.  The question presented by this case is whether Visa USA's refusal to admit Sears to its joint venture restrains trade in violation of section 1 of the Sherman Act, 15 U.S.C. § 1.  Rejecting Visa USA's legal and factual challenges to the jury's adverse verdict, the district court found the evidence of exclusion constituted antitrust injury and harm to competition.  *SCFC ILC, Inc. v. Visa U.S.A., Inc.*, 819 F. Supp. 956, 990 (D. Utah 1993).  We conclude, however, the exclusion does not trigger section 1 liability and reverse.

### I. Background

As set forth more extensively in the district court's order, the factual background of this dispute encompasses the history of the general purpose credit card industry.  What is known today "everywhere you want to be" as *Visa* has evolved over the last forty years from direct extensions of credit for a single purpose; for example, oil company or department store credit cards, to a "charge card which could be used for general purposes at a wide variety of retail establishments." *Id.* at 963 n.2.  The resulting card was offered without geographic restrictions under the neutral trademark, Visa.

Now, to its approximately 6,000 associates, Visa USA,[1] the umbrella organization, provides technology to process credit card transactions and regulates and coordinates the individual

---

[1]     In this opinion, Visa USA designates the joint venture named as the defendant.  We refer to its credit cards simply as Visa.

programs through rules and bylaws proposed by management and adopted by a board of directors (the Board).[2] The bylaws cover a range of issues: members' liability, termination, and confidentiality, to name a few. However, since its inception, each Visa USA member independently decides the terms and conditions of credit extensions, the number of cards issued, and the interest rates charged. That is, individual banks establish, operate, and promote their own credit card programs under the Visa aegis, while Visa USA serves as a clearinghouse for the ultimate transaction between issuer, consumer, and merchant. The fees members pay to Visa USA for its services vary according to a formula established by the association.

Any financial institution which is eligible for federal deposit insurance may become a Visa USA member. Among its current membership are Citicorp, Ford Motor Company, General Electric, and ITT. Although the membership was originally restricted to exclusively issuing Visa cards, a challenge to the bylaw prohibiting members from issuing MasterCard forced Visa USA to withdraw the rule. See *Worthen Bank & Trust Co. v. National BankAmericard, Inc.*, 345 F. Supp. 1309 (E.D. Ark. 1972), *rev'd*, 485 F.2d 119 (8th Cir. 1973), *cert. denied*, 415 U.S. 918 (1974). Consequently, Visa USA members now generally offer both Visa and MasterCard, a practice referred to in the industry as *duality*.

Prior to its entry into the general credit card arena, Sears[3] mustered a bankcard steering committee to investigate the alternatives of developing its own general purpose charge card or joining the Visa USA/MasterCard association. In 1985, Sears introduced the Discover Card, its own proprietary card, one "owned and distributed solely by a single business entity," 819 F. Supp. at 963 n.3., to be marketed and issued nationally. This entry was intended to compete with Visa, MasterCard, American Express, and Citibank's Diners' Club/Carte Blanche, the only other national proprietary cards. Despite Visa USA's aggressive efforts to thwart its new rival, *id.* at 963, Discover succeeded with such innovations as preapproved, no fee cards offering cash back bonuses to cardholders and deeper discounts to merchants. In fact, at the time of this litigation, Sears was the largest individual issuer of credit cards in terms of the number of cards distributed and the second largest, following Citicorp, in credit card receivables volume.[4] To compete with the Visa Gold Card and American Express Optima Card, Sears also introduced an upscale

---

[2] The Visa USA Board draws its members from twelve designated regions, each electing a representative, generally a bank's chief executive officer or chief operating officer. Based on a formula, larger regions may have a second board seat. Seven directors are elected nationally, and a separate seat is reserved for a director who represents small banks. Citicorp has its own seat on the board based on the rule of automatic appointment to any member with more than ten percent of the total volume of outstanding cards. MasterCard board members are not permitted to sit on the Visa USA board.

[3] Sears, Roebuck and Company is the parent corporation of Sears Consumer Financial Corporation and Dean Witter Financial Services Group, its wholly owned subsidiaries. Sears' counsel informed the court during oral argument that Dean Witter then owned plaintiff MountainWest. However, the designation Sears in this opinion collectivizes plaintiff bank and the Sears entities involved in the litigation.

[4] In 1991, approximately 24 million Discover cards had been issued, while Citicorp had approximately 21 million cards in the market.

Discover Card called Prime Issue. Another Sears' entity, Sears Payment Services (SPS), assists other companies in operating their credit card programs.

In 1988, Greenwood Trust Company, a Sears-owned Delaware bank which issues Discover Card, applied for membership in Visa USA, prompting the Board to adopt the bylaw which is the genesis of this antitrust litigation. The amendment to the Board rule, Bylaw 2.06, stated: Notwithstanding (a) above, if permitted by applicable law, the corporation shall not accept for membership any applicant which is issuing, directly or indirectly, Discover cards or American Express cards, or any other cards deemed competitive by the Board of Directors; an applicant shall be deemed to be issuing such cards if its parent, subsidiary or affiliate issues such cards. Subsequently, the Board denied Greenwood Trust's application to Visa USA.

In 1990, the Resolution Trust Corporation sold Sears the assets, including the Visa USA membership, of MountainWest Savings and Loan Association, a bankrupt savings and loan in Sandy, Utah. Sears then created a new entity, SCFC ILC, Inc., doing business as MountainWest Financial, by merging the Sandy bank with Basin Loans, a Utah Industrial Loan Company.

Through this vehicle, Sears was poised to inaugurate a national Visa program it dubbed the Prime Option card, a charge card featuring a two-tiered interest rate, 9.9% for the first two months and 15.9% thereafter. To this end, Sears moved Discover's top executives to Prime Option and ordered an initial printing of 1.5 million Prime Option Visa cards. However, upon inadvertently discovering the plan, Visa USA cancelled the printing and invoked Bylaw 2.06 to exclude Sears from the association. Sears then instituted this antitrust litigation.

## II. Fed. R. Civ. P. 50(b) Review

. . . Having stated its contrary view, but reluctant to substitute its judgment for that of the jury, the district court articulated those facts which it opined could become the basis for judgment: 1. Testimony of Sears' expert, Professor James Kearl, on the appropriateness of calculating Visa USA's market power by aggregating the individual market shares of Visa USA and MasterCard; and his conclusion that Visa USA exercised market power through its collective power to make rules; and testimony about the "presence of high profits." 2. Dean Witter's president, Phillip Purcell's testimony had Sears known that developing the Discover Card would disqualify it from Visa USA entry, it would not have placed a new proprietary card in the market. 3. Testimony that no new proprietary cards had been introduced in the relevant market since Bylaw 2.06 was enacted although memberships in Visa USA and MasterCard increased. 4. Testimony that Prime Option "would be a low-cost card which would be supported by powerful marketing and advertising strategies on a national level." 819 F. Supp. at 986-87. 5. Testimony by Sears' executives that Discover Card, in the face of Prime Option's entry, would remain an aggressive competitor. 6. Testimony that intersystem competition will not be harmed "because Prime Option Visa was designed to reach that part of the market that Discover does not reach." *Id.* at 987. 7. Testimony that "Sears would benefit significantly from issuing Prime Option Visa as opposed to Prime Option Discover or another separate proprietary card." *Id.*

This evidence, which the district court found sufficient to impose section 1 liability, however, must be placed in the specialized province of antitrust law and section 1. . . .

### III. Joint Ventures and Section I

Section 1 forbids agreements in restraint of trade.[5] Read costively, section 1 might prohibit "every conceivable contract or combination . . . anywhere in the whole field of human activity." *Standard Oil Co. of N.J. v. United States*, 221 U.S. 1, 60 (1911). However, "the 'rule of reason' limits the Act's literal words by forbidding only those arrangements the anticompetitive consequences of which outweigh their legitimate business justifications." *Clamp-All Corp. v. Cast Iron Soil Pipe Inst.*, 851 F.2d 478, 486 (1st Cir. 1988) (citing 7 *P. Areeda & D. Turner Antitrust Law* ¶ 1500, at 362-63 (1978)), *cert. denied*, 488 U.S. 1007 (1989). Hence, when we ask if a particular practice is "reasonable" or "unreasonable," or if the practice is "anticompetitive," we use these terms with special antitrust meaning reflecting the "Act's basic objectives, the protection of a competitive process that brings to consumers the benefits of lower prices, better products, and more efficient production methods." *Id.* at 486. In this lexicon, a practice ultimately judged anticompetitive is one which harms competition, not a particular competitor.

Of course, reasonability is of no consequence when certain practices, for example, price fixing, are entirely void of redeeming competitive rationales. These we deem *per se* illegal under section 1, no offsetting economic or efficiency justifications salvaging them. "This *per se* approach permits categorical judgments with respect to certain business practices that have proved to be predominantly anticompetitive." *Northwest Wholesale Stationers, Inc. v. Pacific Stationery & Printing Co.*, 472 U.S. 284, 289 (1985).

The sharp line between *per se* and rule of reason analysis, however, especially blurs under section 1 when the actors change. In the case of a joint venture, present here in the Visa USA association, competitive incentives between independent firms are intentionally restrained and their functions and operations integrated to achieve efficiencies and increase output. See Joseph F. Brodley, *Joint Ventures and Antitrust Policy*, 95 Harv. L. Rev. 1523, 1524 (1982). Although virtually any collaborative activity among business firms may be called a joint venture, joint ventures differ from mergers . . . .

> Indeed, the efficiencies created by joint ventures are similar to those resulting from mergers–risk-sharing, economies of scale, access to complementary resources and the elimination of duplication and waste. Joint ventures, however, differ from mergers in a critical way: because they are less integrated than mergers, *they allow their partners to continue to compete with each other in the relevant market.*

Thomas A. Piraino, Jr., *Beyond Per Se, Rule of Reason or Merger Analysis: A New Antitrust Standard for Joint Ventures*, 76 Minn. L. Rev. 1, 7 (1991). The whole becomes greater than the sum of its parts. However, at its center remains an agreement among competitors to eliminate competition in some way.

The Supreme Court has recognized this tension in its evolving treatment of allegedly anticompetitive agreements by joint ventures. In *Broadcast Music, Inc. v. Columbia Broadcasting, Inc.*, 441 U.S. 1 (1979) (BMI), the Court refused to condemn under a *per se*

---

[5]    In part, section 1 states, "Every contract, combination in the form of trust or otherwise, or conspiracy, in restraint of trade or commerce among the several States, or with foreign nations, is declared to be illegal."

analysis blanket licenses which amounted to price fixing among the participants.  The joint venture, the American Society of Composers, Authors and Publishers (ASCAP), was created as a clearinghouse through which individual music copyright owners licensed their compositions, and ASCAP then monitored the use of their work.  Virtually all participants in the copyright music market participated in ASCAP.  However, eschewing per se treatment, the Court acknowledged, "Joint ventures and other cooperative arrangements are also not usually unlawful, at least not as price-fixing schemes, where the agreement on price is necessary to market the product at all." *Id.* at 23.  Viewed in this light, the efficiency justification of increasing the aggregate output in the market rendered the agreement procompetitive.

In rejecting automatic *per se* treatment in these joint venture cases, the Court directs us instead to look at the challenged agreement to judge whether it represents the essential reason for the competitors' cooperation or reflects a matter merely ancillary to the venture's operation; whether it has the effect of decreasing output; and whether it affects price.  Underlying these cases is an effort to appreciate the economic reality of the particular business behavior to assure that the procompetitive goals, in fact, are neither undervalued nor mask a reduction in competition.  Key to the analysis of "the competitive significance of the restraint," NCAA, 468 U.S. at 103  (quoting *National Soc'y of Professional Eng'r v. United States*, 435 U.S. 679, 692 (1978)), is the Court's appreciation that the horizontal restraint may be essential to create the product in the first instance.  That understanding properly values the proprietary rights and incentives for innovation embodied by the joint venture as well as concerns about free-riding, "the diversion of value from a business rival's efforts without payment." *Chicago Professional Sports Ltd. Partnership v. NBA*, 961 F.2d 667, 675 (7th Cir.), *cert. denied*, 113 S. Ct. 409 (1992).

We do not read the Court's precedent involving joint ventures to imply any special treatment or differing antitrust analysis.  Indeed, aside from clarifying the inappropriateness of automatically invoking *per se* scrutiny of a joint venture's alleged antitrust violation, the Court has not articulated a different rule of reason approach.  Thus, under the Court's precedent, cooperative business activity in one setting may permit its participants to achieve market efficiencies or economies of scale, while in another, a similar activity might run afoul under rule of reason review.

Again, in the context of section 1, the focus of the procompetitive justifications for the business practice remains the ultimate consumer.  To be judged anticompetitive, the agreement must actually or potentially harm consumers. *Stamatakis Indus., Inc. v. King*, 965 F.2d 469 (7th Cir. 1992).  That concept cannot be overemphasized and is especially essential when a successful competitor alleges antitrust injury at the hands of a rival.  Indeed, "[w]henever producers invoke the antitrust laws and consumers are silent, this inquiry becomes especially pressing." *Chicago Professional Sports*, 961 F.2d at 670.

## IV.  Market Power

Rule of reason analysis first asks whether the offending competitor, here Visa USA, possesses market power in the relevant market where the alleged anticompetitive activity occurs.  The answer to that question may end the suit or permit an abbreviated rule of reason inquiry.

Broadly, market power is the ability to raise price by restricting output. . . . If market power is found, the court may then proceed under rule of reason analysis to assess the procompetitive justifications of the alleged anticompetitive conduct. *National Bancard Corp. (NaBanco) v. VISA, U.S.A.*, 779 F.2d 592, 603 (11th Cir.), *cert. denied*, 479 U.S. 923 (1986). . . .

## V. Issuer Market

This case illustrates both the utility and difficulties of the market power tool. In this lawsuit, Sears and Visa USA stipulated "the relevant market is the general purpose charge card market in the United States." 819 F. Supp. at 966. Presently, the only participants in this market are Visa USA, MasterCard, American Express, Citibank (Diners Club and Carte Blanche), and Sears (Discover Card). Competition among these five firms to place their individual credit cards into a consumer's pocket is called *intersystem*. "Interbrand competition is the competition among the manufacturers of the same generic product . . . and is the primary concern of antitrust law." *Continental T.V., Inc. v. GTE Sylvania Inc.*, 433 U.S. 36, 52 n.19 (1977).

In its complaint, Sears alleged the amendment to Bylaw 2.06 represented a concerted refusal to deal which unreasonably restrained trade in the general purpose charge card market. The parties agreed, and the testimony clearly established that in this relevant market competition occurs only at the issuer level. That is, to the extent that Visa USA is in the market, it operates in the *systems* market, not the *issuer* market. Its *members* issue cards, competing with each other to offer better terms or more attractive features for their individual credit card programs. This is *intrasystem* competition.

The issuer market, thus, remains atomistic, each issuer financial institution, bank, or other entity being independent from another.[11] Although Sears does not dispute this characterization of the market, it contends it attempted to launch its Prime Option program under the Visa aegis to "compete more effectively" at the issuer level. By offering multiple credit cards, Discover and Prime Option Visa, Sears contended it would then "strengthen competition."

If the general credit card issuer market is the relevant market, however, the evidence the district court relied upon to deny the Rule 50(b) motion belies Sears' contention and calls into question the definition of relevant market the court apparently adopted. First, the district court recounted the market shares of each intersystem competitor: "Visa was estimated to possess 45.6% of the nationwide general purpose charge card market; MasterCard, 26.4%; American Express, 20.5%; Discover Card, 5.5%; and Diners Club, 2.0%." 819 F. Supp. at 966 (footnote omitted). Within Visa USA's intersystem share, aggregated to include MasterCard issuers as well, the district court noted the evidence showed "in 1991 the ten largest issuers of Visa and MasterCard accounted for approximately 48% of the total Visa/MasterCard charge volume. The top-ten issuers were Citicorp, First Chicago, AT & T, Chase Manhattan, MBNA America, Bank of America, Nationsbank, Chemical Bank, Banc One, and Wells Fargo Bank. The largest issuer, Citicorp, accounted for approximately $42.5 billion in charge volume in 1991–representing approximately 15.8% of the Visa/MasterCard market and 11.4% of the entire general purpose charge card market." *Id.* at 966 n.8.

---

[11] Although approximately 6,000 financial institutions separately are issuers in the association, setting fees, interest rates, and other conditions, approximately 19,000 "participating members" offer cards under their own names and utilize the services of their issuing bank. Robert E. Litan, *Consumers, Competition, and Choice, The Impact of Price Controls on the Credit Card Industry*, March 1992.

While these raw figures may suggest Visa USA possesses market power in the intersystem market, the parties have established a different paradigm.  By their agreement, the context of this case was intended to focus on the issuance of credit cards as the relevant market.  Indeed, that is the market the district court defined for the jury.  To determine, therefore, whether Visa USA possesses market power, we must compare *issuers*, the point where both Sears and Visa USA agreed they compete.  At that level, testimony from both Sears and Visa experts established Discover Card is the second largest issuer preceded only by Citicorp in terms of charge volume, that is, what consumers owe on their credit cards.

Based on the district court's figures, Citicorp's charge volume represented about 15.8% of the Visa/MasterCard market share, aggregated at 72% of the general purpose credit card market.  If we compare issuers' charge volume, our calculations demonstrate Citicorp's is 21.9% in the relevant market, while that of Sears Discover Card is 5%.  Neither figure reflects *at the issuer* level that Visa USA through its members possesses market power.

Nevertheless, Sears' expert, Dr. James Kearl, upon whom the district court relied to conclude the evidence was sufficient to establish Visa USA's market power, explained he looked at the collective, aggregated shares of Visa and MasterCard, because "we have a collective rule, bylaw 2.06 . . .  I found that the collective share was very large, and as a consequence my conclusion was that the collective rule was *an exercise of market power*."  Dr. Kearl opined the association members

> have both incentive and the ability to exercise that market power.  They have the incentive because this market share was large and they want to protect that market share.  And they also had the incentive because since this is large, *if they can keep prices up or from falling they can make a lot of money*.

Second, despite the stipulation on the relevant market, "the market relevant to the legal issue before the court," *1993 Supplement*, at 535, the testimony reflects that Sears, in fact, sought to expand its competition not specifically in the general purpose credit card market but in a segment of that market represented by financial institutions or banks.  For example, Sears' executive, William O'Hara, stated, "We were trying to compete *in that segment* of the general purpose credit card market called the bank association segment."  Visa USA's witness, Richard Rosenberg, explained he voted for Bylaw 2.06, believing that because a non-bank like Dean Witter did not have to comply with certain requirements imposed on banks like the Community Reinvestment Act, Sears would have a competitive advantage over its bank rivals.

Indeed, albeit the stipulation, as the trial progressed, the "relevant market" devolved into *Visa USA's share* of the defined market.  Thus, the legal issue was transformed, equating exclusion from Visa USA to exclusion from the market. The evidence, however, does not support this mutation.  The district court recognized five active rivals presently compete at the intersystem level.  Of that market, for example, Citicorp represents 21.9%, American Express 20.5%, and Sears 5%.  At the issuer level, where intrasystem competition occurs, the court found, and the parties' experts agreed, the market is remarkably unconcentrated.[13]  Given the wide range of

---

[13]     Ironically, the district court rejected Visa USA's argument that the present market is highly concentrated, such that admitting Sears would constitute a violation of section 7 of the Clayton Act. After discussing the Herfindahl-Hirschman Index (HHI), which is used to determine market

interest rates and terms offered by various issuers and Sears' recognized intersystem strength, we are at a loss to find the evidence to support the district court's contrary conclusion.

From this standpoint, even if Visa USA possesses market power, Dr. Kearl's testimony that Visa USA exercised that market power in *its ability* to make collective rules misses the point in the context of joint ventures. "A joint venture made more efficient by ancillary restraints, is a fusion of the productive capacities of the members of the venture." *Rothery Storage*, 792 F.2d at 230. The very existence of a joint venture in the first instance is premised on a pooling of resources to affect competition in some manner and is made functional through some form of cooperative behavior or rule-making. However, the Court has made clear, as previously discussed, cooperative conduct alone is not prohibited.

Hence, it is not the rule-making *per se* that should be the focus of the market power analysis, but the effect of those rules–whether they increase price, decrease output, or otherwise capitalize on barriers to entry that potential rivals cannot overcome. Although Dr. Kearl testified "if they can keep prices up or from falling they can make a lot of money" to support his conclusion Visa USA possesses market power, there was no evidence that price had been increased, output had decreased, or other indicia of anticompetitive activity had occurred.

Thus, without any eye on effect, the very exercise of rule-making became the factual basis for rule of reason condemnation of Bylaw 2.06. Consequently, rule-making was not only divorced from its functional analysis but also from the facts of the case. "When an expert opinion is not supported by sufficient facts to validate it in the eyes of the law, or when indisputable record facts contradict or otherwise render the opinion unreasonable, it cannot support a jury's verdict." *Brooke Group, Ltd. v. Brown & Williamson Tobacco Corp.*, 113 S. Ct. 2578, 2598 (1993). In this complex area, the Court cautioned, "Expert testimony is useful as a guide to interpreting market facts, but it is not a substitute for them." *Id.*

We believe the evidence cited by the district court to conclude Visa USA possessed market power is insufficient as a matter of law. Although the district court did not end its rule of reason inquiry upon that finding, the conclusion set the path for its uncharted journey upon a landscape of speculation, conjecture, and theoretical harm. The consequence is the finding of liability based on tendentious and conclusory statements, none of which amounts to evidence of restraint of trade.

## VI. Efficiency Justifications

We therefore return to the two-step analysis previously discussed to assess the procompetitive justifications of Bylaw 2.06 to counteract Sears' allegation the restraint is unreasonable. Visa USA maintained it instituted Bylaw 2.06 to protect its property from intersystem competitors who otherwise would enjoy a free ride at this time of entry. Its general counsel, Bennett Katz, described technological advancements Visa USA achieved and incentives

---

concentration, the district court rejected Visa USA's aggregation of market shares, stating "the court agrees with Visa's expert Professor Schmalensee that each individual issuer of Visa and MasterCard cards should be included in the HHI analysis, resulting in a system HHI of below 500." *SCFC ILC, Inc. v. Visa U.S.A., Inc.*, 819 F. Supp. 956, 994 (D. Utah 1993). This figure represents an unconcentrated market.

for innovation to system-wide competition generated.  In a letter informing Sears of the Board's action, he stated, "As I indicated to you by phone, we believe that intersystem competition should be preserved and enhanced; membership by Greenwood Trust Co. would have the opposite effect."  Describing the industry as small, "we only have three basic competitors . . . Visa and MasterCard . . . American Express and Discover," Katz expressed concern about government regulation if the existing competition diminished or Visa USA became too large.[15]  In addition, there was testimony that after duality was permitted, MasterCard and Visa competed less aggressively, consumers regarding the two cards often as interchangeable.  Other witnesses expressed concern, for example, about Sears' threat to their own profits; the effect a big player like Sears would have on the many small banks that compete in the Visa USA association; and Sears' likely ability to become a Board member and privy to confidential information.

Against these justifications, Sears offered testimony about a two-stage strategy in which it had always planned to enter the market first with its Discover Card and then with a low-cost Visa card; that marketing the Prime Option card as a Discover Card program would not meet the objectives of "Sears' branding strategy," and that consumers would be harmed by being denied the opportunity to select a Prime Option Visa card from the possible choices in the general charge card market.  Broadly, Sears promised a low-cost, competitive alternative to the existing market's cards and elicited, through expert testimony, the prospect of other similarly situated potential intersystem competitors being excluded and discouraged from offering new rival cards because of Bylaw 2.06.

Most of this evidence relied upon by the district court is irrelevant to the central antitrust question posed, however.  First, intent to harm a rival, protect and maximize profits, or "do all the business if they can," *Ball Memorial Hosp.*, 784 F.2d at 1325, is neither actionable nor sanctioned by the antitrust laws.  "Competition, which is always deliberate, has never been a tort, intentional or otherwise."  *Olympia Equip. Leasing Co. v. Western Union Tel. Co.*, 797 F.2d 370, 379 (7th Cir. 1986), *cert. denied*, 480 U.S. 934 (1987).  "Most businessmen don't like their competitors or for that matter competition.  They want to make as much money as possible and getting a monopoly is one way of making a lot of money."  *Id.*  Thus, evidence that a Board member voted for Bylaw 2.06 to discourage price competition within Visa USA may reveal a mental state but is not an objective basis upon which section 1 liability may be found.  If Bylaw 2.06 is not "objectively anticompetitive the fact that it was motivated by hostility to competitors . . . is irrelevant."  *Id.* (citation omitted).

What we ask under section 1 is whether the alleged restraint is reasonably related to Visa USA's operation and no broader than necessary to effectuate the association's business.  *NaBanco*, 779 F.2d at 592, 601.  That is, is Bylaw 2.06 ancillary, "subordinate and collateral . . . [making] the main transaction more effective in accomplishing its purpose," which is to provide credit card services to its members?  *Rothery Storage*, 792 F.2d at 224.  If it is not ancillary, does it restrain trade in a manner which alters the structure of the general purpose credit card market and, thus, harms consumers?

---

[15]    In testimony, Katz explained, not only was Justice Department scrutiny a concern, but also "attorneys general around the country who had been looking at Visa and deciding whether it is too large."

We think the analysis in *Rothery Storage* helps us resolve this question. There, Atlas Van Lines adopted a new policy to prohibit any affiliated company from handling interstate hauling both under its own name as well as under the Atlas name. The policy was intended to prevent its affiliates from using Atlas equipment, facilities, and services for interstate hauling while independently negotiating contracts for their own accounts. Atlas announced the rule was necessary to prevent its agents from benefiting from a free ride, increasing Atlas' liability for interstate shipments while using Atlas' resources without any attendant return of revenue. "Atlas has required that any moving company doing business as its agent must not conduct independent interstate carrier operations. Thus, a carrier agent, in order to continue as an Atlas agent, must either abandon its independent interstate authority and operate only under Atlas' authority or create a new corporation (a 'carrier affiliate') to conduct interstate carriage separate from its operation as an Atlas agent. Atlas' agents may deal only with Atlas or other Atlas agents." *Id.* at 217.[17] Several Atlas carrier agents claimed the policy constituted a group boycott and filed a complaint under section 1.

After a thorough and well-reasoned analysis, the D.C. Circuit rejected plaintiffs' claim, based not simply on the evidence Atlas did not possess market power in the market for the interstate carriage of used household goods, but also on the conclusion the new rule was ancillary to Atlas' main enterprise, enhancing consumer welfare by creating efficiency. *Id.* at 223. What improved the company's efficiency, the court found, was the elimination of the free ride: The restraints preserve the efficiencies of the nationwide van line by eliminating the problem of the free ride. There is, on the other hand, no possibility that the restraints can suppress market competition and so decrease output. *Id.* at 229. This conclusion was built on the foundation of BMI, NCAA, and Northwest Wholesale Stationers.

Similarly, Visa USA urges its concern about protecting the property it has created over the years and preventing Sears and American Express,[18] successful rivals, from profiting by a free ride does not represent a refusal to deal or group boycott but is reasonably necessary to ensure the effective operation of its credit card services. It urges Bylaw 2.06 avoids "free-riding, an unlevel playing field, and the added costs that Sears would impose on VISA members by taking advantage of a brand and operating systems that it not only had done nothing to create but had chosen to compete against." Visa USA contends Sears does not need Visa USA to compete in the relevant market and cannot demonstrate it can only issue a low-cost card with Visa USA's help.

Sears urges the justification is pretext. "In this case, the issue is whether the selective exclusion imposed by Visa's Bylaw 2.06 is ancillary to Visa's legitimate purposes as an open industry association." Sears contends Visa USA is a network joint venture, one whose integrative efficiencies actually grow as its membership increases. To accept Visa USA's analogy to a research venture, one expending individual talent and resources in a small laboratory only to be forced to include rival researchers, Sears argues, is naive. It protests everyone gets into Visa USA except Sears itself. In support, Sears relies on the bulwarks of exclusionary conduct cases.

---

[17] That is, its interstate rivals can no longer compete in interstate hauling both as Atlas agents and as independent agents. The policy, then, is analogous to the rule at issue here.

[18] We note that American Express has never participated in this lawsuit.

We do not believe either precedent or policy compels Sears' position, however. . . .

Bylaw 2.06 did not alter the character of the general purpose credit card market or change any present pattern of distribution.  Nor did it bar Sears from access to this market.  There was no evidence Sears could only introduce a Prime Option card with Visa USA's help or that Visa USA's exclusion from its joint venture disabled Sears from developing its new card under the Discover mantle.  More importantly, there was no evidence the bylaw harms consumers, the focus of the alleged violation.  Indeed, the evidence established the current market in general purpose credit cards is structurally competitive, issuers targeting different consumer groups and consumer needs.  In this market, Sears already competes vigorously.  Surely, if its goal is to compete *more effectively* in that market, we do not believe this objective constitutes the proverbial sparrow the Sherman Act protects.  "[A] producer's loss is no concern of the antitrust laws, which protect consumers from suppliers rather than suppliers from each other." *Stamatakis Indus.*, 965 F.2d at 471.[20]

Given Visa USA's justification the bylaw is necessary to prevent free-riding in a market in which there was no evidence price was raised or output decreased or Sears needed Visa USA to develop the new card, we are left with a vast sea of commercial policy into which Sears would have us wade.  To impose liability on Visa USA for refusing to admit Sears or revise the bylaw to open its membership to intersystem rivals, we think, sucks the judiciary into an economic riptide of contrived market forces.  Whatever currents Sears imagines Visa USA has wrongly created, we believe can be better corrected by the marketplace itself.  The Sherman Act ultimately must protect competition, not a competitor, and were we tempted to collapse the distinction, we would distort its continuing viability to safeguard consumer welfare. . . .

We therefore REVERSE the district court's order holding Visa USA liable. . . .

---

[20]     Indeed, when the question becomes whether the restraint is reasonably necessary to achieve the joint venture's goals, "[e]xclusivity of venture membership will not generally be regarded as suspect."  1993 Supplement ¶ 1506, at 1115.  The Department of Justice has stated:  [S]electivity in the membership of a joint venture often enhances a joint venture's procompetitive potential.  Forcing joint ventures to open membership to all competitors (or to license the product of an R & D joint venture to all who seek licenses) would decrease the incentives to form joint ventures . . .  For example, the inability to exclude those who would bring little or nothing to the joint venture, or those who would fail to share fully in the risks, would decrease the efficiency of the joint venture and reduce the expected reward from successfully accomplishing the joint venture's mission.  An enforcement policy that denied a joint venture the ability to select its members might also encourage firms to forego risky endeavors in the hope of being able to gain access through antitrust litigation to the fruits of the successful endeavors of others.  Thus, the Department [of Justice] generally will be concerned about a joint venture's policy of excluding others only if (i) an excluded firm cannot compete in a related market or markets . . . in which the joint venture members are currently exercising market power without having access to the joint venture and (ii) there is no reasonable basis related to the efficient operation of the joint venture for excluding other firms.  Justice Department, International Operations Antitrust Enforcement Policy 42 (Nov. 10, 1988) (CCH Supp.) (quoted in 1993 Supplement ¶ 1506, at 1115).

## Comments and Questions

1. The court held that the "relevant market" for antitrust purposes is at the "issuer" level not the "system" level. Do you see that the analysis at the issuer level necessarily causes the conclusion that the market is not concentrated and that there is plenty of competition? The court went on to view the denial of membership to Dean Witter as procompetitive, stating that the decision eliminates a potential "free rider" on the Visa network. Do you agree or disagree with the result in the case? Why?

2. Isn't the real issue competition at the system level? If Dean Witter is barred from the Visa network because it also issues the competing Discover card, should Citicorp also be barred? Citicorp owns the much smaller but competing Carte Blanche and Diner's Club cards. Would barring Citicorp destroy Carte Blanche and Diner's Club, because they are so small?

3. Far more significant is that essentially all of Visa's members also offer the chief competitor, MasterCard. How can this be? Might it be that *SCFC* is right but the general duality historically allowed has been in error? Note that most members of Visa and MasterCard have great incentives to assure that the two networks and their products are nearly identical. Have merchants and consumers been the losers in this treaty between putative competitors? What competition might arise if Visa and MasterCard issuers were barred from duality? Would it reduce the interchange fees charged for transferring a credit card slip through a system? Would it generate other competition among networks in areas such as system and product innovations, annual fees, and merchant discounts?

4. Dean Witter argued that, if allowed to join Visa, it would charge lower annual fees, give more generous credit limits, and give lower interest rates. Wouldn't this bring welcomed price competition? Why would this be anticompetitive? Consider what happened when Discover created an additional network. It dramatically increased competition at the system or network level in terms of interchange fees, systems, and product innovation. And so, while there might be short term benefits to competition it appears that the long term detriments might well be greater.

### Problem 2-9

Five competing joint ventures are developing for the purpose of offering nationwide EFT (electronic funds transfer) services. You represent River of Cash, one of the five. It is a joint venture corporation formed to supply nationwide facilities to the banks that own stock in it. Since River of Cash is still in the planning stages, its management has a broad range of questions on which they seek your advice.

1. How should they best structure their entry into each market? They have been considering two possibilities. One is to seek out both or either the largest bank and the largest savings and loan association in each market and give those two institutions exclusive territorial rights, thereby denying access to the joint venture to any other financial institution in each applicable market. The second approach is to deny access only to the largest institution in each market if it has over 50 percent of the market, or otherwise to

the two largest institutions, and offer membership to all other financial institutions in the market.  In some markets this route could include as high as 80 percent of commercial bank deposits, although such an all-encompassing joint venture would be doubtful because of local competitive considerations in each market.  On the other hand, in some smaller markets both economies of scale and the amount of capital required to operate an EFT system might limit the number of the five competing joint ventures that would be interested in entering the market.

2.   Each ATM in a market would be owned by a single joint venture member institution.  In those markets where more than one institution was a member of the joint venture, River of Cash believes that it should have the authority to determine the location of any additional ATM facilities, in order to avoid ill-advised placements of ATMs.  This would ensure that the limited capital resources are applied most effectively to servicing the area, and avoid unnecessary competition between those who are supposed to be cooperating in the joint venture.  Finally, River of Cash wonders whether it should determine which services can be offered through the ATMs that are part of the joint venture.  Along these lines, for efficiency's sake and management simplicity, River of Cash would like to have agreement among the joint venturers on the following matters: Uniform design of the debit card; uniformity in advertising; and limitations on individual logos placed at the terminals.

### Problem 2-10

Electronic Payments Services, Inc. (EPS) is a joint venture of four major banking organizations.  They wish to acquire a substantial ATM network in Ohio currently owned by Ohio-based National City Corporation.  Two of the joint venture banks are based in Pennsylvania, and two are based in Ohio.  Upon purchase of the new Ohio ATM network, National City Corporation would become the fifth member of the joint venture.

Currently there are one hundred shared electronic fund transfer networks in the United States.  Seventeen of them have markets encompassing between two and five states, twenty-one have markets in between six and fifteen states, and four have markets encompassing more than fifteen states.  EPS has ATMs in seven states.

What are the relevant product and geographical markets?  If the acquisition is approved, EPS will have over 50% of the market in several major cities in Ohio, Kentucky, and Pennsylvania, and will have over 70% in some parts of Ohio.  Should Justice object to the acquisition?

One of the rules of the EPS ATM network is that if one bank in a holding company joins the network, then all affiliated banks of that holding company must also become members of the ATM network.  Is this a pro-competitive or anti-competitive rule?

# CHAPTER THREE

# THE REGULATION OF BANK ACTIVITIES

## Section 1.  Introduction

In many ways this is the most important chapter on bank regulation because it deals with our primary method for bank regulation—activities restrictions, or more generally, portfolio-shaping rules.  There are regulatory restrictions applicable to every sector of the balance sheet.  Asset restrictions include limits on the size of loans to one borrower and on the types of securities a bank can own.  Liability restrictions include controls on giving security for deposits.  And we will see that there are extensive capital requirements.

While similar portfolio-shaping rules apply to other sectors of the financial services industry, those sectors typically have alternative regulatory structures such as price regulation (insurance), disclosure regimes (broker-dealers), and fiduciary rules (mutual funds).  These alternative regulatory structures generally do not apply to depository institutions beyond a limited number of consumer protection laws.  Portfolio-shaping rules are the dominant regulatory structure for depository institutions.

What are the policy justifications for the portfolio-shaping regulatory restrictions on depository institutions?  First there is the historical political preference for a division between banking and commerce we discussed in Chapter 2, as well as some residual antitrust and economic concentration concerns.

In addition, there is public concern about financial intermediaries taking excessive risks.  There are many reasons why financial intermediaries might be thought particularly prone to excessive risk-taking.  Banks have the unique ability to acquire insured deposits at relatively low interest rates due to the backing of federal deposit insurance.  This creates two problems.  First, the high level of deposit liabilities that are withdrawable on demand by customers makes banks unusually susceptible to runs on their deposits, which is the source of funding for their assets (e.g., loans).  Second, the backing of deposits with federal insurance creates what is known as moral hazard, which means that much of the risk of loss is placed on federal deposit insurance while all of the reward of gain goes to management and shareholders.

Increased competition in the financial services industry has caused banks to seek expanded activities powers, which frequently have been granted.  Large banks in particular have an appetite for potentially high-risk activities such as financial derivatives, which are zero-sum (for every winner there is a loser) contractual instruments the value of which is derived from some underlying asset such as a stock index, interest rate, or currency exchange rate.  As we will see, the steady expansion of permissible activities, and the resulting lessening of the significance of portfolio-shaping rules on assets and liabilities, has tended to shift regulatory attention to capital adequacy requirements, in an attempt to have the banks assume the increased risk-taking.

A final basis for concern about risk-taking by banks is that they play a critical role in the creation and adjustment of the nation's money supply. Excessive risk-taking could disrupt the payments system and so the economic positions of businesses and individuals.

With these policy justifications in mind, we can classify the basic goals of regulation as follows: First, a stable system based on safety and soundness—protecting the stability of the financial intermediation system, thereby protecting depositors, other creditors, and the system for exchange of value in a complex economy. Second, a fair system which assures economic neutrality in the allocation of resources in our society, but occasionally requires banks to invest their assets in accord with statutory perceptions of the public interest. Third, a competitive system—protecting against undue concentration of economic, and therefore potentially political, power. And fourth, a cost contained system—reducing taxpayer risk by controlling the federal taxpayers' guarantee of the risks of bank activities in the form of federal deposit insurance.

In examining the materials that follow, the reader should question how well the specific regulations limiting and governing various bank activities serve the underlying policies and goals, and so their intended purposes. Are the regulations insufficiently or overly restrictive? Do the regulations prevent both banks and consumers from obtaining optimum returns on their investments, or are the risks of less regulation too great?

Intelligent consideration of these questions requires an understanding of traditional banking activities and of why banks have historically been limited to those activities. While history does help in understanding, it does not provide definitive answers. As circumstances change, reconsideration of society's needs becomes necessary. Prior to the Great Depression and the subsequent legislation of the early 1930s, a sense of undue restriction on bank activities existed. Since the late 1960s this sense of undue restriction has resurfaced. The laws designed in the 1930s to protect banks, depositors and the economy came to be viewed by many as unnecessary impediments to banks engaging in new, but arguably appropriate, activities.

In 1970, President Nixon appointed a commission to study the powers and regulation of the nation's financial institutions. The report of the Commission on Financial Structure and Regulation, known as the Hunt Commission (named after its chairman Reed O. Hunt), was released in late 1971. The Commission recommended drastic changes in the structure of the banking industry, including gradual elimination of ceilings on deposit interest rates; abolition of reserve requirements on certain categories of deposits, expansion of loan and investment powers; and encouragement, through tax credits, of investment in the housing market. In August, 1973, the President, in a message to Congress, urged implementation of several of the Commission's recommendations. Substantial banking legislation was passed in 1978, 1980, 1982, 1987, 1989, 1991 and 1994 implementing, revising or contradicting many of these proposals. Since 1980 the United States Treasury Department has generally supported the broadening of powers for all depository institutions (and, as will be examined in Chapter Four, the affiliation of these institutions with other nonbanking, financial activities).  The desirability of instituting such changes should, therefore, be considered in evaluating bank regulation.

A significant factor underlying the desire and support for broadening banking powers is the increased competition from other financial intermediaries, particularly insurance companies and securities firms.  These competitive pressures steadily increased during the 1980s and early 1990s with the development of major diversified financial services firms such as American Express, The Travelers, Merrill Lynch and General Electric Credit.  These firms have steadily expanded their nonbank activities across a virtually complete range of financial services.  Many of these institutions have also found ways to acquire a depository institution while continuing to operate their other activities free of the more costly regulatory restrictions that limit banks.

Other competitors have also appeared.  Both GMAC and Ford Motor Credit, as auto financing firms, have offered below market interest rates on auto loans.  Foreign banks have steadily increased their share of domestic loans in the United States and have come to be the most significant financial institutions in some areas, such as the issuance of letters of credit to serve as guarantees to enhance the bond ratings of both corporate and municipal issuers.

As a consequence of this increased competition, banks have constantly attempted to broaden their financial offerings to include activities in which their competitors are engaged.  Numerous examples of these attempts are illustrated through bank holding company activities, and through the powers granted to state chartered banks by their legislatures, such as South Dakota which passed a law permitting its banks to engage in "all facets of the insurance business."

The tension between statutory restrictions and competitive pressures on banks is historical.  The American banking system, originally modeled on the English system, has historically placed great emphasis on commercial, and more recently consumer, short-term loans made for the purpose of financing industry, trade, and retail purchases.  This type of lending is considered to be largely self-liquidating, because the continuing industry and trade activities produce funds to pay off the loans, as does the employment income of consumers.  The demand for credit in a growing country such as the United States, however, has produced several departures from the original ideas.  In the first half of the 19th century there were few financial institutions other than banks.  As the country became more industrialized there was a growing need for long-term credit for business.  This created the idea of long-term loans secured by fixed assets, such as industrial plants and railroads, and ultimately to more organized securities markets.

The line between permissible loans and impermissible securities as bank assets is not always easy to draw.  Even in the first half of the 19th century banks in various ways engaged in activities that today could be called the underwriting and distributing of securities—such as selling government and railroad bonds—as well as direct investment in various forms of securities.  In one sense, criticism of securities-like activities led to the statutory articulation of the concept of the business of banking, but in another sense this was partly reversed in the 1860s when the demand for credit to finance the Civil War set off another round of bank underwriting, this time of government securities as authorized by the National Bank Act.

Then, in 1902 the Comptroller of the Currency ruled that the National Bank Act prohibited national banks from underwriting and distributing equity securities. The banks effectively avoided this limitation by organizing state-chartered affiliates to carry on the securities business. Banks were interested in underwriting because large corporations began to develop, having the ability to raise long-term funds by selling securities rather than by borrowing from banks. Corporations were also able to cut back on short-term borrowings from banks by accumulating funds from earned income. These developments forced banks to seek alternative uses of their funds, whether making more small business loans and home mortgages, or purchasing investment securities.

Today, the distinctions between banks and other financial intermediaries has again begun to blur, much as it did prior to the 1930s. In the interim, both the Banking Act of 1933 and the Bank Holding Company Act of 1956 were passed, in large part to restrict banks to their traditional activities, principally by restraining their involvement in both securities activities and commercial enterprises. The Banking Act of 1933, in conjunction with the revisions added by the Banking Act of 1935, created what appeared to be two permanent provisions—(1) the establishment of federal deposit insurance, and (2) the separation of commercial banking from investment banking. The first provision still has significance today, while the second one has little. For a time the second provision stopped the ebb and flow of banks into a broader area of financial intermediation involving securities activities. But that was only temporary. Regulatory interpretations and court decisions have almost obliterated the apparent statutorily required separation. A related development was the passage of the Bank Holding Company Act of 1956, which to this day substantially separates banks and their affiliates from general commercial enterprises.

In 1987, Congress passed the Competitive Equality Banking Act (CEBA). This legislation was intended to give Congress greater control over the financial system by placing a moratorium on deregulation by the actions of state legislators, federal regulators, and judicial decisions. But the subsequent 1989 and 1991 legislation focused principally on dealing with the problems of regulating troubled and failed depository institutions. The Interstate Banking and Branching Efficiency Act of 1994 generally authorized both interstate mergers and branches for banks. Overall, Congress has failed to deal with a comprehensive reconsideration of the powers of banks and competing financial institutions, and so the difficult question of the proper scope of activities for banks and other financial institutions remains open to considerable discussion.

Financial intermediation, not just banking, is the engine of our economy. While at the end of World War II banks held almost 75% of financial assets, today they hold about 30%. Banks are not the dominant financial intermediary they once were. Securities firms, insurance companies, mutual funds, and pension and other qualified retirement plans are also major financial intermediaries. These other intermediaries have become increasingly relevant to how money is saved, invested, loaned, borrowed and circulated. Today, individuals tend to put more of their assets into mutual funds, insurance annuities, and qualified retirement plans, rather than bank deposits. In addition, corporations have greater capabilities today to acquire capital by building up cash surpluses, or by selling commercial paper, bonds, or common or preferred stock in the securities markets.

The traditional business of banking, taking deposits and making loans, is in some decline. We can say either that banking is becoming a new kind of business or that what we are watching is an evolution to an all-financial-intermediaries concept, described generically as financial institutions. Yet some form of taking deposits and lending will always exist. Whoever can attract money from households and nonfinancial business enterprises will have the ultimate ability to extend credit. For example, it is quite possible that when people begin to lose principal in something like a long-term bond mutual fund, which occurs when interest rates rise, the cycle may reverse and banks will find more people interested in making bank deposits, which guarantee the return of nominal principal.

How the activities of various financial institutions will evolve is unclear. Banks can be extremely powerful competitors in the securities and insurance fields. Banks, in their branching systems, have unmatched potential for the distribution of deposit, securities, insurance, and other financial products such as financial planning, tax preparation and real estate brokerage. More people have financial relationships with banks than with any other form of financial enterprise.

Compliance with bank regulations can be costly and so affect the flow of money. For example, there are regulatory requirements for frequent appraisals on real estate loans which impose a cost that is not imposed on investments in government securities. Therefore, if bank regulators engage in stringent regulation of bank lending, funds may be redirected to the purchase of government securities, which is a major source for the government to finance its deficits. On the other hand, if lending is encouraged by regulators in order to assist the private economy, then funds will tend to go to business loans and mortgages.

A more recent development is that banks have at times discouraged deposit growth and encouraged customers to invest in mutual funds affiliated with the bank. The consequence of this flow of funds is that money which formerly went into bank loans in the community is placed with mutual funds that tend to invest more heavily in debt and equity of larger companies, because only such companies can tap the securities markets in which the mutual funds invest their assets.

These developments can cause policy concerns. One is the concern for consumers who may not adequately comprehend the risk of moving money from insured bank accounts, which provide for return of principal, to higher yielding bond funds, where the share prices rise or fall inversely with interest rates. A second concern is the apparent diversion of funds to larger businesses. Should banks be regulated in a manner which will encourage them to serve their local markets by making small business loans? Small business loans have been viewed as one of the most effective engines for economic diversity and expansion.

When considering bank activities, one caveat is in order. Most of the rules that follow are federal law. This is partly because we have no room to summarize state laws on each topic, and partly because federal law often affects the scope of activities of state-chartered banks, either because they are members of the Federal Deposit Insurance Corporation (FDIC) or the Federal Reserve System, or because federal law is directly applicable to all depository institutions in certain instances. The reader should also note that the source of the specific federal law varies. Some rules have evolved from congressional determinations of proper bank activities. In other instances, however, Congress has delegated the authority to make specific regulations to administrative agencies, at most providing boundaries within which those bodies may operate. These agencies—the Board of Governors of the Federal Reserve System, the Comptroller of the Currency (OCC), the Office of Thrift Supervision (OTS), and the Board of Directors of the FDIC—have published the rules they have promulgated in Title 12 of the Code of Federal Regulations (12 C.F.R.). The regulations must be read with just as much care as the statutes. Note, however, that the regulations of each agency affect only those financial institutions within its jurisdiction.

## Section 2.  The Business of Banking

Before we undertake discussion of specific aspects of traditional banking activities and the portfolio-shaping rules, it is helpful to engage in a preliminary discussion of what it means to be a bank. Lawyers confront this problem in a variety of different context. One example are state statutes prohibiting any person from engaging in the "business of banking" unless that person is licensed under appropriate state or federal laws. See, e.g., Tex. Fin Code Ann. § 31.004(a)(West 1997). The logic of such statutes is that an entity should not be allowed to engage in the business of banking unless the entity is subject to a comprehensive system of regulation. Usually, it is clear when an entity enters the business of banking. On occasion, however, contested cases arise.

### Opinion of the Texas Attorney General
Opinion No. DM-329, 1995 WL 145055 (Mar. 9, 1995)

Ms. Catherine A. Ghiglieri
Commissioner, Texas Department of Banking
2601 North Lamar Boulevard
Austin, Texas  78705-4294

Dear Commissioner Ghiglieri:

On behalf of the Texas Department of Banking (the "department"), you ask about state and private university "debit card" programs. You generally describe such programs as follows: "[A] university accepts money from students (and sometimes from faculty and staff) and, in turn, issues a card to each . . . to be used for drawing against this account to obtain goods and services on campus." You state that the department is aware of at least three state universities that have established a debit card program: Texas A&M University, Stephen F. Austin State University, and Texas Tech University. You also inform us that Southern Methodist University, a private university, has such a program. In addition, we have received a brief from the University of Texas stating that it has several debit card programs.

[Y]ou ask whether an entity which issues debit cards acts as a bank and is required to obtain a bank charter. [Y]ou ask whether the foregoing entities are statutorily authorized to issue debit cards to students, faculty and staff. We have received briefs from all of the above universities arguing that their respective debit card programs do not amount to the sale of checks or unauthorized banking and that the institutions are authorized to issue such cards.

It is apparent from the briefs we have received that the universities' debit card programs vary. As we read your request, we understand that you are only interested in those debit card programs with the following features: A student, faculty member or staff person deposits a certain amount in an account with the university, and receives a card (or perhaps encoded information on a preexisting identification card) that identifies the account. The cardholder presents the card when making a purchase from a university vendor or, in some cases, third-party vendors operating concessions on campus pursuant to a contract with the university. When a purchase is made, the cashier uses the card to identify the account and determine whether the account balance is sufficient. After the purchase is made, the amount of the purchase is automatically deducted from the account. Because the purchase may not be made with the card if the account balance is insufficient, it is impossible to overdraw the account. We limit our discussion to the foregoing type of debit card program. We do not address "vend stripe" cards[1] or cards involving accounts with third parties. . . .

You . . . suggest that universities which issue debit cards are engaged in the unauthorized business of banking. We are not aware of a Texas statute which defines the term "bank" or "banking." You suggest that accepting deposits is the primary indicia of a bank. It is clear from Texas case law, however, that no one feature defines a bank.

Historically a bank merely served as a place for the safekeeping of the depositors' money and even now that is the primary function of a bank. 9 C.J.S., Banks and Banking, § 3, page 31. The term "bank" now by reason of the development and expansion of the banking business does not lend itself to an exact definition. 7 Am. Jur., Banks, § 2. Brenham Prod. Credit Ass'n v. Zeiss, 264 S.W.2d 95, 97 (Tex. 1953); see also Commercial Nat'l Bank v. First Nat'l Bank, 80 S.W. 601, 603 (Tex. 1904) (discussing activities of banks under federal law); V.T.C.S. art. 342-302 (listing powers of a state bank). Furthermore, authority from other jurisdictions suggests that an entity is not necessarily a bank just because it engages in certain acts that are typical of banks;

---

[1]    A person pays for a "vend stripe" card with a specific value. The card contains a magnetic (or "vend") stripe which is encoded with its value. Every time a purchase is made, the amount of the purchase is deducted from the card's value until the value of the card is exhausted.

We disagree with the contention of the University of Texas that vend stripe cards are indistinguishable from the type of debit card you ask about. A vend stripe card is like cash in that its value is inherent and no refund is available if it is lost or stolen. No money is held on deposit with the university.

rather one must look at the activities of the entity as a whole.  See, e.g., 9 C.J.S. Banks and Banking § 1, at 30 (1938) ("Banking is the business of receiving deposits payable on demand, discounting commercial paper, banking loans on collateral security, issuing notes payable on ..., collecting notes or drafts, buying and selling bills of exchange, negotiating loans, and dealing in negotiable securities. Exercise of all these functions is not necessary, nor does exercise of certain of them necessarily render a corporation a bank."); 10 Am. Jur. 2d Banks § 3, at 27 (1963) ("Carrying on a banking business does not mean the performance of a single disconnected banking business act[;] [i]t means conducting, prosecuting, and continuing business by performing progressively acts normally incident to the banking business"); see also Brenham Prod. Credit Ass'n, 264 S.W. 2d at 97 ("While ... the lending of money is one of the principal functions of a bank, nevertheless there are many agencies authorized by both state and federal governments to lend money, which are not banks nor considered as such").  We do not believe that a court would conclude that a university that offers a debit card program such as the one you describe among its many and various activities engages in banking.

You have submitted to this office an opinion issued by the Comptroller of Florida regarding whether the card program of a public university in that state constituted a banking activity.  The cards in that program could be used to pay for goods and services and to make cash withdrawals from automated teller machines ("ATMs") on and off campus operated by a private bank.  Relying in part on a federal appeals court decision holding that the payment of a cash withdrawal from an ATM constitutes payment of a check, Illinois ex rel. Lignoul v. Continental Illinois Nat'l Bank & Trust Co., 536 F.2d 176 (7th Cir.), cert. denied, 429 U.S. 871 (1976), the Comptroller of Florida concluded that the university paid checks by allowing cash withdrawals with its card at ATMs operated by a private bank.

We do not believe that this opinion supports your position that the kind of debit card program at issue here involves a sale of checks under the act or unauthorized banking.  First, Illinois ex rel. Lignoul dealt with whether a cash withdrawal from an ATM constituted "branch banking" within the meaning of the National Bank Act, 12 U.S.C. § 36(f).  We do not read that case to hold that an ATM withdrawal, or the use of any other card, necessarily constitutes payment of a check for purposes of section 3-104(3) of the Uniform Commercial Code.  Indeed, the primary case upon which Illinois ex rel. Lignoul relies clearly points out the difference between the Uniform Commercial Code's narrow definition of a check and the expansive definition of a branch bank in Section 36(f) of the National Bank Act.  See Independent Bankers Ass'n of America v. Smith, 534 F.2d 921, 942 (D.C. Cir. 1976).  Thus, although a cash withdrawal from an ATM may constitute payment of a check for purposes of the National Bank Act, it does not necessarily constitute a check for purposes of the Uniform Commercial Code or the common commercial understanding of the term.  Therefore, the Florida comptroller's opinion does not convince us that the debit card programs at issue here involve the sale of "checks" as that term is defined by the act.  We also believe that the Florida opinion is inapposite with respect to the question whether Texas universities that offer debit card programs engage in banking.  The type of debit card program you ask about does not permit cardholders to make cash withdrawals from their accounts much less allow them to make cash withdrawals from ATMs operated by a private bank.

This brings us to your [next] question, that is, whether a debit card program such as the one you describe exceeds the statutory authority of a state or private university.  Private universities, such as Southern Methodist University, are generally organized as nonprofit corporations. Their powers are set forth in their corporate charters and the Texas Non-Profit Corporation Act, V.T.C.S. arts. 1396-1.01 - 11.01. The Texas Non-Profit Corporation Act defines the powers of nonprofit corporations expansively: "each corporation shall have power ... [w]hether included in the foregoing or not, to have and exercise all powers necessary or appropriate to effect any or all of the purposes for which the corporation is organized." V.T.C.S. art. 1396- 2.02(15). For this reason, we believe that private universities are authorized to operate debit card programs, provided that the programs are consistent with the educational mission set forth in their corporate charters and do not . . . constitute unauthorized banking.

The state universities contend that their debit card programs are authorized by section 51.002 of the Education Code which provides that the governing board of certain institutions of higher education, including the state universities at issue here, "may retain control of [certain] sums of money collected at the institution, subject to Section 51.008 of this code." Educ. Code § 51.002. Included in that list are "students' voluntary deposits of money for safekeeping." Id. § 51.002(a)(8). Section 51.002, in essence, authorizes the institutions to hold such student monies locally rather than depositing them in the state treasury. We do not believe that this provision expressly authorizes debit card programs. At most, this language acknowledges the practice at many universities of holding student money for safekeeping. Furthermore, as you point out, this provision does not authorize public universities to retain the deposits of faculty and staff. For these reasons, we do not believe that section 51.002(a)(8) alone is a sufficient legal basis for the debit card programs you describe.

The University of Texas argues that its debit card programs are authorized by section 65.31 of the Education Code, which generally authorizes the board of regents to "govern, operate, support, and maintain" the University of Texas System, and its general power to offer benefits to its employees. There are similar provisions establishing the authority of the board of regents of Texas A&M University, see id. § 85.21, Stephen F. Austin State University, see id. §§ 101.11, .41, and Texas Tech University, see id. § 109.21. Although these provisions do not expressly authorize the state universities to operate debit card programs, it is possible that a court would conclude that such authority may be implied from the board of regents' general authority to govern the universities.

In past opinions, this office has concluded that state universities have broad authority to provide services and perform functions not expressly authorized by statute. See, e.g., Attorney General Opinions H-513 (1975) (food cooperative may be operated as student service or auxiliary enterprise of North Texas State University); WW-5 (1957) (Texas Tech authorized to operate educational television channel); Letter Advisory No. 6 (1973) (university may validly determine that public interest research activities constitute student services). In this case, provisions which broadly authorize state universities to provide student services, see Educ. Code § 54.503(b) (authorizing the governing board of an institution of higher education to charge and collect fees to cover cost of broad range of student services), and which recognize the authority of state universities to establish auxiliary enterprises, activities that are not strictly educational but that support the educational mission of the university, see Tex. Const. art. VII, § 17(f); Educ. Code s 61.003(14), may provide similar implied authority for debit card programs. In sum, although we have found no statute which expressly authorizes a state university to operate a debit card program, we believe that it is likely that a court would probably construe the broad powers of a board of regents to impliedly authorize a state university do to so.

Yours very truly,

Dan Morales
Attorney General of Texas

## Comments and Questions

1. How does this opinion determine whether or not the university in question was engaged in authorized banking? Why did the opinion reserve judgment on third-party providers of debit-card services? Does the opinion suggest that its answer would be different if a group of retailers got together and offered a similar debit card program? Should its answer be different?

2. The opinion does not discuss what the university did with the students' money. Would it make a difference to the opinion if the university was using the funds to make short-term loans to university employees or if it invested the funds in U.S. government notes or if it held the funds as cash in a safe in the office of the university president?

### Problem 3-1

Which, if any, of the following activities constitute the business of banking:

a. Benefit Finance Corporation specializes in making consumer loans. It raises most of its funds in the capital markets through the sale of commercial paper and other debt securities. Occasionally, it makes private placements of one-year notes to accredited investors (generally limited to individuals with a net worth of more than $1 million).

b. CyberScript is a new enterprise dedicated to facilitating anonymous purchases on the Internet. An individual opens accounts with CyberScript by making a deposit with a traditional check or credit card. The individual can then use his or her CyberCash account to make anonymous purchases through the Internet. The individual simply gives an Internet merchant the individual's CyberScript account number and password, and then the merchant gets its payment directly from CyberScript. CyberScript has agreed to keep all deposits in FDIC-insured accounts.

---

As mentioned above, once an entity is found to be engaged in the business of banking, the entity must obtain a charter as some sort of depository institution -- most commonly, a bank or a thrift -- from an appropriate state or federal agency. Through a combination of statutory requirements and administrative practices, these depository institutions are required to obtain federal deposit insurance. The chartering process thus begins a complex array of regulatory obligations — or portfolio shaping rules — which form of the core of the materials covered in this chapter. By crossing over into the business of banking — as interpreted in the opinion of the Texas Attorney General — an entity subjects itself to all that follows.  Do those activities defined in such threshold business-of-banking tests warrant so extensive a supervisory response?

---

Another important legal area requiring an interpretation of the business of banking is in defining the scope of permissible bank activities.  From the early days of the Republic, banks have been entities of limited powers.  The fact that bank powers are limited is well-understood; the precise nature of the limitation is not.  The confusion is due in part to the fact that bank powers are typically defined circularly to include "the business of banking." That phrase  can be found in banking lore since the earliest days of the United States, and that has been in the National Bank Act since the initial statute was enacted in 1863.  The critical statutory phrasing in 12 U.S.C.A. § 24(7) has changed little since then:

> [A] national banking association . . . shall have power . . . to exercise . . . all such incidental powers as shall be necessary to carry on *the business of banking*; by discounting and negotiating promissory notes, drafts, bills of exchange, and other evidences of debt; by receiving deposits; by buying and selling exchange, coin, and bullion; by loaning money on personal security; and by obtaining, issuing, and circulating notes according to the provisions of [this chapter].

Exactly what this clause means has been a matter of debate, particularly during the last 30 years.  To date, there has been no definitive elaboration of the powers of banks by either Congress or the Supreme Court.  There are various views of what is meant by the phrase "the business of banking."

The "narrow view" holds that a bank's powers are limited to those activities specifically enumerated in the phrases following "the business of banking" (i.e., "by discounting * * *").  Under this view, the specifically enumerated powers would delimit the general statement of the business of banking.  The "broad view" of the business of banking holds that the specifically enumerated activities following the "business of banking" phrase are simply examples of banking activities carried out in 1863, and that the generic phrase, the business of banking, is a separate grant of power, to be redefined as society's desires for financial services change.

All courts have begun their analysis of permissible bank powers with the assumption that the banking statutes constitute the full measure of a national bank's authority.  Under this assumption a bank has no powers except those expressly granted by the language of the statute or those incidental to carrying out the express powers.  The narrow view also has been founded on the additional rule of *expressio unius est exclusio alterius*, meaning that specifically enumerated powers control general powers.  No express power can be derived from the phrase "the business of banking;" rather, express powers can only be derived from the more specific clauses following the initial clause.  In other words, the express powers of banks are to be found only in the phrase following the preposition "by" in the quoted part of section 24(7).  The first clause is only to enable banks to engage in activities that are incidental to carrying out the powers expressly granted by the subsequent clauses.

For example, in *First National Bank v. Missouri*, 263 U.S. 640, 656-659 (1924), the Court stated:

> The extent of the powers of national banks is to be measured by the terms of the federal statutes relating to such associations, and they can rightfully exercise only such as are expressly granted or such incidental powers as are necessary to carry on the business for which they are established. * * * [A]n incidental power can avail neither to create powers which, expressly or by reasonable implication, are withheld nor to enlarge powers given; but only to carry into effect those which are granted.

In support of the narrow view it is argued that if, as argued by supporters of the broad view, the provision for engaging in the business of banking were itself an express power, then the subsequent more specific phrasing in section 24(7) would be superfluous language, contrary to the common statutory construction that a statute should be construed so as to give meaning to all words. Of course, interpretation does not address itself solely to the ordinary meaning of terms; history, experience, and other circumstantial evidence should also help to indicate the meaning that legislatures intended by the terms of their statutory expression. For example, there are numerous services offered by banks which would appear to be impermissible under the narrow view. Such activities as credit cards, the issuance of traveler's checks, and safe deposit boxes are nowhere expressly provided for in § 24(7). In fact, if you read all of § 24(7) you will see a limitation on the safe deposit power, without any express provision for engaging in that activity.

At the other extreme is the broad view of the business of banking. Proponents of this view believe the business of banking changes as society progresses, and virtually any financially related activity is potentially a part of the business of banking if it does not entail substantial risk to the bank. Any activity that is consistent with the mobilization of capital, the use of credit, or the provision of financial services to the public, and is not expressly prohibited by law, is within the scope of permissible bank powers. Supporters have suggested, for example, that it may be proper for a bank to operate a merchandise mart, in which a bank customer could purchase goods from a catalog and pay for the goods through the bank's debiting the customer's account for the price plus a bank commission.

*Curtis v. Leavitt*, 15 N.Y. 2 (1857), decided under the New York Free Banking Act from which § 24(7) was derived, is often cited by the proponents of the broad view. However, there are several opinions in the case; together they span an incredible 289 pages. Almost every judge issued a separate opinion. Therefore, it is rather easy to find something in the case to support any position. For example, Judge Paige reached the following conclusions in *Curtis* concerning the scope of the phrase, the business of banking.

> The restrictive clause in the charters granted previous to the 1838 act, in relation to trading in goods and stocks, was unnecessary. The chartered banks would not have possessed the power to trade in goods and stocks, had this restrictive clause been omitted. Their powers were restrained by the nature and purposes of their incorporation. They could only, in the absence of such restriction, have exercised the powers expressly granted, and such other

incidental powers as should be necessary to carry on the business of banking. *Curtis v. Leavitt*, 15 N.Y. 211-212 (1857).

Judge Paige discussed several factors that assisted him in deciding whether banks were permitted to engage in activities which had not been expressly permitted by statute. The factors can be summarized as (1) whether the activity is expressly prohibited, (2) whether the activity is inconsistent with the nature and objects of the bank, (3) whether the activity is necessary and usual in the operation of a bank, and (4) whether the activity enables a bank to accomplish its purposes. After considering these factors is it fair to suggest that some activities not expressed may be prohibited while other activities not expressed may be permitted? Can such a conclusion be reconciled with either the narrow or broad view?

The same bank that was at the center of the dispute in *Curtis v. Leavitt* was also at the center of the dispute in an earlier case, also involving interpretation of the business of banking under the New York Free Banking Act. In *Talmage v. Pell*, 7 N.Y. 328 (1852), Pell had borrowed $15,000 from the North American Trust and Banking Company to purchase some of its stock, and had given a mortgage as security for the loan. Shortly thereafter that same bank purchased on credit Ohio canal bonds. Subsequently the bank was unable to make the installment payments promised in payment of the bonds. Eventually the bank assigned to the state of Ohio various mortgages, including the one at suit, to secure payment for the canal bonds. The bank failed and went into receivership. As the suit was ultimately structured, Ohio was suing Pell to recover on the mortgage. The person appointed receiver of the bank also was a defendant and raised the defense that the assignment of the mortgage by the bank was void because under the New York Free Banking Act the bank did not have the power to purchase the Ohio bonds. The New York court agreed, holding that the bank had no power to purchase state "stocks," except when received as security for a loan or in payment of a debt. Consequently the assignment was void, and the receiver could reclaim the mortgage as an asset of the bank in receivership.

The same court decided both *Talmage v. Pell* and *Curtis v. Leavitt*, and thought they were consistent. How could this be? In *Talmage v. Pell* the bank had bought state "stocks" on credit, not with the intent to deposit them with the New York controller to back up the note issues of the bank, but rather to resell as a means of raising money to be used as capital in the bank. The bank had done this because it was unable to raise cash as capital. Unfortunately, it later turned out that the bank also was unable to sell the state stocks that had been bought on credit. The transaction in controversy in *Curtis v. Leavitt*, however, was different. In *Curtis v. Leavitt* the bank had issued bonds to be repaid in either five or seven years. These bonds were sold to raise money for the use of the bank. The difference was that in *Curtis* the bank received money to be used in its banking operations, while in *Talmage* the bank received securities, involving the type of investment-enterprise risk that had destroyed many banks prior to 1838. In *Curtis v. Leavitt*, the court held that the bonds were valid and enforceable securities of the bank. Put another way, the court said that the bank had the power to borrow money and to issue the promissory notes. In *Talmage* the court said that the bank did not have the power to deal in securities. The court believed that trading stocks was as far removed from the business of banking as ship building or general manufacturing.

This raises an interesting question. While certainly the New York Free Banking Act predecessor of section 24(7) did not say expressly that banks could trade in securities, it also did not say expressly that banks could borrow money. Proponents of the narrow view would tend to conclude that neither activity is permissible, while proponents of the broad view would conclude that both activities are permissible.

Consider a third view, a middle ground view. Examination of the historical development of the powers clause in § 24(7) suggests that there is a principled basis for elaborating the phrase the business of banking which is useful in determining what new and unforeseen financial activities should be permissible to banks, and what limits, if any, should be placed on such activities. Examination of the development of banking and the governing enactments reveals that the first clause of § 24(7), providing for "such incidental powers as shall be necessary to carry on the business of banking," is itself an express grant of a power to engage in the business of banking. This express power, however, does have limits founded on the historical development of banking.

The activities historically permitted to banks are deposit taking, credit granting and credit exchange activities. These activities take many forms. In 1863 only the most common forms of these activities were expressed in the subsequent clauses of section 24(7). Today, there are numerous forms of deposit taking that are not specifically enumerated in the subsequent clauses, yet are permitted to banks without a specific grant of power. For example, safe deposit activities always have been permitted to banks, yet they are not expressly named in the subsequent clauses. There are various types of credit activities also not specifically enumerated, such as letters of credit and credit cards. This suggests that the narrow view of the business of banking is inaccurate. But contrary to the broad view, the middle ground view of the business of banking as a substantive grant of power does not permit activities such as banks operating merchandise marts where all goods are sold on credit. A middle ground view is that such an activity is not deposit taking, credit granting or credit exchange and so, to be permitted, must be based on some *additional* express grant of power found elsewhere in the National Bank Act or other federal law.

How do we identify and delimit the scope of deposit taking, credit granting and credit exchange? There are principles which are central to understanding what is meant by the business of banking even though they are only incidentally expressed in the statutes. To some extent, we already have considered these principles. The first principle defining the business of banking is safety, soundness or absence of substantial risk to deposited funds and the monetary system. Thus, the 1982 repeal of 12 U.S.C.A. § 82, which had limited bank borrowings, enables banks under section 24(7) to engage in various "deposit" activities without a further specific grant of power. These activities are now controlled by the principle of safety and soundness delimiting all deposit taking activities. A second, correlative principle, controlling particularly the activities of credit granting and exchange, is one rarely discussed—economic neutrality in the allocation of economic resources. The reason that banks have been prohibited from owning stocks or taking equity interests in commercial enterprises, beyond considerations of safety and soundness, is to assure a high level of economic neutrality in the granting of credit to competing borrowers in our society. Banks are critical to the operation of the private competitive economic system. To the extent that bank activities go beyond credit granting and exchange, the private economic system could be critically skewed.

To summarize, the middle ground view suggests that the determination as to whether national banks have a particular power can be analyzed as follows:

1.  If the activity is encompassed within an express grant, such as negotiating promissory notes, it is permitted.

2. If the activity is encompassed within an express prohibition, such as engaging in lotteries or underwriting common stocks, it is not permitted.

3. If the activity is not expressly granted or prohibited, to be permissible the activity must be within the principled scope of the grant to engage in the business of banking, whether it is encompassed within deposit taking, credit granting, or credit exchange. In considering the third category it is helpful to analyze both the extent of economic risk involved and the extent to which the activity is an economically neutral allocation of monetary resources in our society. Even if an activity is generally within the powers of a national bank, its scope may be otherwise limited, so that its exercise does not violate the underlying principles.

These suggested limits on the business of banking apply only to the activities of banks, and are not to be taken as applicable in determining the limits of activities with which banks may be affiliated. That question is for separate inquiry and discussion in later chapters. In addition, the significance of the suggested limits on the business of banking is materially affected by the power of the regulator, under *Chevron*, to establish "reasonable" interpretations of the term, with the courts overruling the regulator only in extraordinary situations.

If you think that determining the application of these principles is easy, consider the case and problems that follow in this chapter.

## Arnold Tours, Inc. v. Camp
### 472 F.2d 427 (1st Cir. 1972)

HAMLEY, Circuit Judge.

This class action involves the authority of national banks to engage in the travel agency business. The plaintiffs are Arnold Tours, Inc., and forty-one other independent travel agents of Massachusetts engaged in the travel agency business.

One of the defendants is William B. Camp, Comptroller of the Currency (Comptroller), whose office has issued rulings and regulations to the effect that national banks may engage in that business. The other defendant is South Shore National Bank (South Shore), a national banking association chartered by the United States Government, with a principal place of business in Quincy, Massachusetts, and with twenty-seven branch offices throughout Massachusetts. South Shore has been engaged in the travel agency business, operating it as a department of the bank, since November, 1966, after having bought out the fourth largest travel bureau in New England. Plaintiffs asked for declaratory and injunctive relief, the effect of which would be to force South Shore out of the travel business. . . .

The parties are in agreement that if there is any statutory authority for national banks to engage in the travel agency business, it is to be found in the following language contained in 12 U.S.C. § 24, Seventh, a provision of the National Bank Act (Act): "Seventh. To exercise . . . all such incidental powers as shall be necessary to carry on the business of banking. . . ."

The Comptroller relied upon the quoted statutory words in his 1963 ruling that national banks could engage in the travel agency business. Thus, paragraph 7475 of the Comptroller's Manual for National Banks (1963), which is now codified as 12 C.F.R. § 7.7475, reads:

§ 7.7475 National banks acting as travel agents

Incident to those powers vested in them under 12 U.S.C. 24, national banks may provide travel services for their customers and receive compensation therefor. Such services may include the sale of trip insurance and the rental of automobiles as agent for a local rental service. In connection therewith, national banks may advertise, develop, and extend such travel services for the purpose of attracting customers to the bank.

In holding that 12 U.S.C. § 24, Seventh, did not authorize national banks to engage in the travel agency business the district court, in its opinion, first focused attention on the nature of South Shore's travel agency operation. The court relied upon the graphic description of a modern agency operation given by Charles F. Heartfield. Heartfield had served as vice-president of South Shore, in charge of its travel department, from November 1, 1966 to 1970. His description of a modern agency operation is set out in the margin.[4]

---

[4]     Heartfield said:

"A travel department is a functioning complete travel service bureau within the confines and control of the bank. It is a department store of travel- staffed by knowledgeable people-trained in the techniques of selling every mode of transportation-air, rail, steamship, U-drive car. It is a staff acquainted with thousands of hotels and resorts-proficient in the intricacies of foreign customs and regulations, health requirements and languages, accustomed with tipping customs, foreign exchange, conversant with foreign representatives and hotel managers, tour operators and tour guides, knowledgeable in the history and geography of our own great United States-as well as the rest of the shrinking world, constantly aware of changing tarriffs [sic] and schedules, well acquainted with over 60 airlines throughout the world, 40 domestic and international railroads, and numerous motorcoach lines, steamship companies, etc. They must be up-to-date in passport, visa and sailing permit information-"They must be specially trained and experienced in the preparation and planning of itineraries- "They must be ready to acquaint the traveler with climate conditions, wardrobe and packing suggestions-"They must have unlimited knowledge of foreign car purchases, U-drive-it regulations and costs-"They must be ready with shopping suggestions, and must be able to advise on travel accident and baggage insurance-"They must be able to arrange transfers and sightseeing, and must be aware of the proper assessments, head taxes, port taxes, and transportation taxes-"They must be knowledgeable in what to see and what to do-theatre tickets, ballet, opera, horse shows, yachting events-and -at their fingertips, a good travel staff has hundreds of tours, ranging from a week-end

The district court then observed that "To say that conduct of a business of the nature and type described by Mr. Heartfield is a sine qua non to the successful operation of a national bank is a self-refuting proposition, especially in view of the fact that on the defendants' own claim only 122 national banks out of the many hundreds if not thousands in existence were providing travel agency services in 1967."[5]

The Comptroller argues that the district court applied an erroneous legal standard in reviewing the Comptroller's construction of the "incidental powers" clause of the National Bank Act (12 U. S.C. § 24, Seventh), as indicated by the court's above-quoted use of the term sinc qua non.

We are in agreement with the Comptroller that a sine qua non standard would be an inappropriate measure of a national bank's incidental powers under 12 U.S.C. § 24, Seventh. While the pertinent language of that section refers to all such incidental powers "as shall be necessary to carry on the business of banking," we do not believe "necessary" was there used to connote that which is indispensable.

But we believe that, read in context with its entire opinion, the district court's reference to the concept of sine qua non was not intended to state the test for determining whether a particular bank activity is authorized as an incidental power. What seems to us to be a more reliable gauge of the district court's rationale is its discussion immediately following the sine qua non statement quoted in the margin.[6]

---

in New York to an African safari. A good travel agent's experience and interest lends the proper emphasis to his client's desires. He can put himself in the place of his customer. He must discover the traveler's budget and give him the most for his money-and here the bank's pay-later plan will be invaluable. The well-trained agent is able to decide whether his client should go by air or sea, or a combination of both,-which cruise will please his client the most-which hotel will satisfy his client's taste -whether a motor-coach or a chauffeur-driven sightseeing trip will be the answer to his client's wishes. There are escorted and independent tours-each has its own advantages. There are basic trips, charters, all-expense trips, and special flights. The agent's knowledge must encompass information on bike rentals in Bermuda to villa rentals on the Riviera to a houseboat in Kashmir.

"To sum it up-a good travel department is a personalized department store of travel."

[5]    At the end of 1965 there were 4,815 national banks; at the end of 1971 there were 4,587.

[6]    Immediately after its sine qua non references, the district court said:

I find that defendants' argument that because the bank may engage in selling letters of credit, travelers' checks and foreign currency, or make travel loans, it therefore should also be allowed to engage in the travel business, is a complete non sequitur. Selling travelers' checks or foreign currency, issuing letters of credit or making loans, are all financial transactions as they involve money or substitutes therefor, and all are obviously within the normal traditional range of monetary activities of a national bank. The difference between these activities and conducting a travel agency is just as great as the difference between these activities and running a mill, which was proscribed many many years ago in *Cockrill v. Abeles*, 86 F.2d 505 (8 Cir. 1898).

338 F. Supp. at 723.

The district court therein indicated that its chief concern was whether a travel agency business primarily involves the performance of financial transactions pertaining to money or substitutes therefor. If not, the court in effect ruled, that business was not within the normal and traditional range of the monetary activities of a national bank, and thus not encompassed by the "incidental powers" provision of 12 U.S.C. § 24, Seventh. It was on this basis that the district court distinguished the travel agency business from such approved "incidental powers" of national banks as those employed in selling travelers' checks or foreign currency, issuing letters of credit, or making travel loans.

But the Comptroller and South Shore do not agree that the "incidental powers" of national banks should even be restricted to the performance of financial transactions pertaining to money or substitutes therefor or that only such transactions lie within the normal traditional range of the activities of a national bank. The Comptroller and South Shore, for example, refer to *McCulloch v. Maryland*, 17 U.S. (4 Wheat.) 316, 4 L. Ed. 579 (1819), which upheld the constitutionality of the first Bank of the United States, as laying down the broad principle that the word "necessary" may include that which is convenient, or useful. . . .

The Comptroller and South Shore refer to the fact that the New York free banking law, enacted in 1838, contained an "incidental powers" provision almost identical with that contained in the National Bank Act, enacted in 1863; that, in 1857, a New York Court of Appeals in *Curtis v. Leavitt*, 15 N.Y. 9 (1857), gave the quoted words of the New York Act an expansive reading; and that those who sponsored the National Bank Act in Congress made it clear that the federal legislation was copied, almost word for word, from the earlier New York Act.

The essence of the New York decision in *Curtis* is distilled in these words in the opinion of the court:

> But necessity is a word of flexible meaning. There may be an absolute necessity, and a small necessity; and between these degrees there may be others depending on the ever varying exigencies of human affairs. It is plain that corporations, in executing their express powers, are not confined to means of such indispensable necessity that without them there could be no execution at all. . . .

15 N.Y. at 64.

We are in accord with these views and we are willing to assume that Congress entertained these views when it enacted the National Bank Act. But we do not find these views particularly helpful in determining whether the district court erred in holding that a national bank's incidental powers under 12 U.S.C. § 24, Seventh, are limited to the performance of financial transactions pertaining to money or substitutes therefor, and that the travel agency business falls outside the scope of such powers because it is not within the normal traditional range of the monetary activities of a national bank. It may be convenient and useful for a national bank to carry on any number of activities. But one of the critical questions here is whether a convenient and useful activity be within the incidental powers of a bank if it is not directly related to what 12 U.S.C. § 24, Seventh, refers to as "the business of banking."

The most reliable guides as to what is encompassed in the term "the business of banking" are the express powers of national banks as set out in the National Bank Act. And when one looks at past decisions it becomes apparent that the activities of national banks which have been held to be permissible under the "incidental powers" provision have been those which are directly related to one or another of a national bank's express powers.

Thus, in *Merchants' Bank v. State Bank*, 77 U.S. (10 Wall.) 604, 19 L. Ed. 1008 (1870), the Supreme Court held that national banks may, as an incidental power, engage in the practice of certifying checks. The Court there recognized the great similarity between the activity of certifying checks and the express power granted by the National Bank Act to discount and negotiate bills of exchange.

In *First National Bank v. National Exchange Bank*, 92 U.S. 122, 127, 23 L. Ed. 679 (1875), the Court held that the power to acquire stock in settlement of a claim arising out of a legitimate banking transaction is an incidental power of national banks. In *Wyman v. Wallace*, 201 U.S. 230, 243 (1906), the Court held that national banks may, as an incidental power, borrow money. The Court referred to a line of cases which trace back to *Auten v. United States Nat. Bank*, 174 U.S. 125, 141, 142 (1899), in which the Court had noted that a greater part of banking practice was "in strict sense borrowing" and that several of the express powers granted to banks created a debtor-creditor relationship.

In *Miller v. King*, 223 U.S. 505, 510-511 (1912), the Court held that national banks may, as an incidental power, collect a judgment on behalf of a depositor. Similarly, in *Clement National Bank v. Vermont*, 231 U.S. 120, 139-140 (1913), the Supreme Court held that national banks may, as an incidental power, pay taxes on behalf of depositors. As the Court there indicated, this activity is directly related to the express power of national banks to receive deposits.

In *First National Bank v. Hartford*, 273 U.S. 548, 559-560 (1927), the Court found that the sale of mortgages and other evidences of debt, acquired in the exercise of the express power to loan money and to discount and negotiate other evidences of debt, was permissible under the bank's incidental powers. In *Colorado Nat. Bank v. Bedford*, 310 U.S. 41, 49 (1940), the Court held that the operation of a safe deposit business was embraced within the bank's incidental powers because the operation of a safe deposit business is virtually identical to the express statutory authority of national banks to accept special deposits. 12 U.S.C. § 133.

Finally, in *Franklin Nat. Bank v. New York*, 347 U.S. 373, 375-377 (1957), the Court held that national banks were entitled to advertise the word "savings" because such advertising was incidental to the express power of such banks to receive time and savings deposits and to pay interest thereon.

In our opinion, these decisions amply demonstrate that a national bank's activity is authorized as an incidental power, "necessary to carry on the business of banking," within the meaning of 12 U.S.C. § 24, Seventh, if it is convenient or useful in connection with the performance of one of the bank's established activities pursuant to its express powers under the National Bank Act. If this connection between an incidental activity and an express power does not exist, the activity is not authorized as an incidental power.

This brings us to a consideration of the question of whether the operation of a travel agency business, such as that conducted by South Shore, may reasonably be said to be convenient or useful in connection with the performance of one of the bank's established activities in the exercise of its express powers.

While the Comptroller and South Shore do not concede that such a relationship between an incidental and an express power must exist, they suggest ways in which they believe a travel agency business is directly related to a national bank's normal banking operations. In presenting this view, they pursue two lines of argument. One of these is an effort to equate the basic functions performed by travel agencies with functions which have historically been performed by banks. The other is based on the premise that a substantial number of banks have, for a long time, been providing travel agency services.

With regard to the first of these contentions, defendants assert that the basic functions performed by travel agencies consist of: (1) procuring carrier passage and other travel accommodations by acting as agent for passengers and carriers, and (2) providing various informational services to the traveler. Defendants then assert that both of these "basic" travel agency functions are only particular applications of the broad agency and informational services which banks traditionally offer among their "congeries of services."

In our view this analysis unrealistically minimizes the basic functions of a travel agency business and unjustifiably exalts the agency and informational functions of national banks.

The operation of a travel agency in the United States today is a highly complex activity. Some of the aspects of that business are closely regulated under the supervision of the Civil Aeronautics Board, the Interstate Commerce Commission, and the Federal Maritime Commission. It is true that a travel agent acts as an agent for the traveler, but it also acts as an agent for carriers. A travel agency provides informational service for the traveler, but it also solicits travel business, advertises and in general promotes the interests of its carrier principals. More importantly, the agency and informational services a bank travel agency renders are pursuant to its own interest in making its travel department profitable, wholly apart from the bank's normal banking operations.

On the other hand, while national banks provide certain agency and informational services they are normally of a kind which are germane to the financial operations of the bank in the exercise of its express powers. There are, of course, instances in which banks have, as a convenience to their regular customers, and without additional compensation, obtained railroad, steamship or airline tickets for such customers, or provided information helpful to such customers in connection with their travels. But incidental good will service of this kind cannot reasonably be equated with the operation of a modern travel agency for profit. In short, there is a difference between supplying customers with financial and informational services helpful to their travel plans and developing a clientele which looks to the bank not as a source of general financial advice and support but as a travel management center.

The Comptroller asserts that one of the central purposes of the National Bank Act, enacted during the Civil War, was to serve as a unifying force to the nation and that the draftsmen of the Act contemplated that the Act would fulfill its unifying purpose by, among other things, facilitating interstate commerce and "facilitating travel."

As a reading of these documents demonstrates, the objective of establishing a "unifying force" and "facilitating travel" were viewed in those early years, not as being attainable through the operation of a banking travel service, but as being attainable through the establishment and circulation of a national currency. Prior to the National Currency Act of 1863, now also known as the National Bank Act, there was no national currency and financial transactions were largely conducted through the medium of bank notes issued by state banks. The establishment of a national currency provided a form of legal specie acceptable throughout the country, and it was this which provided the desired "unifying force" and assisted in "facilitating travel."

South Shore asserts that banks in the United States have been offering travel services to their customers since at least 1865, when the Security National Bank in Sheboygan, Wisconsin, formally established its bank travel department. According to South Shore, in the ensuing years of the nineteenth century and the period preceding World War I, numerous other banks began to offer travel services largely to accommodate the great number of immigrants arriving in this country. The travel service then rendered by banks involved assisting immigrants in remitting money to families in their native lands, obtaining steamship tickets for relatives, and transmitting these prepaid tickets to foreign addresses. Immigrants during this period made periodic trips "home" and needed travelers' checks, letters of credit, foreign currency and other banking assistance.

The limited and largely uncompensated services of this kind, rendered by banks during this period, bear very little resemblance to the functioning of a modern travel agency. Moreover, it was not until 1959 that the Comptroller of the Currency ruled that national banks could engage in a regular travel agency business. . . .

Despite the Comptroller's sanction, since 1959, of the operation of travel agency businesses by national banks, only one hundred twenty-two out of about four thousand seven hundred national banks were engaged in that business in 1967, when this action was brought. This is far from persuasive evidence that the operation of travel service departments is useful and convenient to the functioning of normal banking services under the express powers granted by the National Bank Act.

The Comptroller and South Shore urge us, on the authority of *Inland Waterways Corp. v. Young*, 309 U.S. 517, 524-525 (1940), and *Investment Co. Institute v. Camp*, 401 U.S. 617, 626-627 (1971), and other cases, to accord great weight to the Comptroller's construction, in 12 C.F.R. § 7.7475, of the "incidental powers" provision, 12 U.S.C. § 24, Seventh.

We fully recognize the principle to which defendants refer. But, as the Supreme Court said in *Zuber v. Allen*, 396 U.S. 168, at 192-193 (1969):

> While this Court has announced that it will accord great weight to a departmental construction of its own enabling legislation, especially a contemporaneous construction . . . it is only one input in the interpretational equation. . . .

"The Court may not, however, abdicate its ultimate responsibility to construe the language employed by Congress."

In view of the many considerations which lead to a contrary conclusion, as reviewed above, the lack of essential articulation supporting the Comptroller's 1963 ruling, issued without opinion or accompanying statement, and in the light of the lack of uniformity in the Comptroller's own interpretation of the statute, we conclude that the Comptroller's current interpretation, as embodied in 12 C.F.R. § 7.7475, is not entitled to dispositive deference. . . .

In our view the divestiture should be reasonably expeditious, but a limit should not be set which would be oppressive or inequitable. Our approval of the divestiture feature of the judgment is given with the qualification that the district court entertain and seriously consider any factual presentation South Shore wishes to make in the direction of lengthening the time for divestiture.

Subject to the qualification just stated, the judgment is affirmed.

## Comments and Questions

1. Is it fair to summarize *Arnold Tours* as follows: Authorization of what is permissible for a bank as an incidental power is limited to what is "necessary" to the business of banking. An activity is considered to be necessary to the business of banking if it is "convenient or useful" in the performance of a § 24(7) express power. And so, the activity must be convenient or useful to credit granting, deposit taking, or credit exchange. If an activity is not convenient or useful to a § 24(7) power, or is not granted as an express power by another statutory provision, then the activity cannot be permitted. If this is a fair summarization of *Arnold Tours*, which view is this—the narrow view, the broad view, or the middle ground view?

2. The importance of *Chevron* was evident in *NationsBank, N.A. v. VALIC*, 115 S. Ct. 810 (1995), where the Supreme Court held that the determination of the Comptroller was reasonable that national banks may serve as agents in the sale of insurance company annuities. A footnote stated "We expressly hold that the 'business of banking' is not limited to the enumerated powers in section 24 Seventh and that the Comptroller therefore has discretion to authorize activities beyond those specifically enumerated." The Court went on to say that "The exercise of the Comptroller's discretion, however, must be kept within reasonable bounds. Ventures distant from dealing in financial investment instruments—for example, operating a general travel agency—may exceed those bounds." 115 S. Ct. at 814 n.2. After *VALIC*, how broad is the Comptroller's discretion to authorize activities?

3. Subsequent to *Arnold Tours*, several decisions of the Comptroller show the overriding importance of *Chevron*. In 1985 the Office of the Comptroller of the Currency approved a proposal by a national bank to lease branch space to a local travel agency. Under the proposal, the lease rental would be based on a minimum rent charge as well as a percentage of the sales generated from the travel agency activity in the branch. As a condition to the approval, the OCC first required that the travel business be appropriately and separately identified so that the public understands it is not buying travel services from the bank. Also, there could be no tying involving the sale of travel agency services and the granting of credit or other banking services. OCC Interpretive Letter No. 342 (May 22, 1985).

4. In OCC Interpretive Letter No. 339 (May 16, 1985), the Comptroller approved an arrangement whereby a bank provided a travel tour operator with the names and addresses of bank customers who would receive tour and travel information, accompanied by a cover letter from the bank introducing them to the travel program. Both the sale of the list of customers, and the affiliation with the travel business program itself were viewed as legitimate promotional or marketing techniques, incidental to the business of banking.

5. In Alabama, a state chartered bank has the statutory power to own a travel agency. In OCC Interpretive Letter No. 399 (Oct. 29, 1987), the Comptroller approved an arrangement whereby an Alabama state chartered bank would form a travel agency as a subsidiary. The travel agency would then lease space at branches of national banks that were subsidiaries of the same bank holding company as the Alabama bank which owned the travel agency.

6. In *First National Bank of Eastern Arkansas v. Taylor*, 907 F.2d 775 (8th Cir.), *cert. denied*, 498 U.S. 972 (1990), the court held that offering debt cancellation contracts was within the business of banking, upholding an OCC regulation. A debt cancellation contract provides that in exchange for a fee paid by the borrower, the bank agrees to discharge the borrower's unpaid loan balance upon death. The test was whether the activity is "closely related to an express power and is useful in carrying out the business of banking." Debt cancellation contracts were found to be permissible because they are directly related to the power to make loans, and assist in controlling the risk to the parties of a credit transaction. (The *Taylor* decision is reproduced in Chapter Seven, Section 1.)

7. In Interpretive Letter No. 640, issued January 7, 1994, the Comptroller gave national banks the additional authority to provide debt cancellation contracts based on disability or unemployment of the borrower. Do you see a different level of risk, particularly with unemployment, than with the contingency of death? In other words, even though such a debt cancellation contract can be viewed as part of the provision of credit, it may, nevertheless, not be part of the business of banking, or incidental thereto, because it is so contrary to the policy of maintaining a safe and sound banking system.

---

National banks have been given some significant equity investment powers. Section 24(7) generally prohibits national banks from owning stock, "except as hereinafter provided or otherwise permitted by law." They may take "equity kickers" in loan transactions. 12 C.F.R. § 7.1006. National banks have the authority to buy convertible securities–securities that are convertible into stock–provided that they are not convertible at the option of the issuer. Under 15 U.S.C.A. § 682(b), national banks have the power to invest up to 5% of their capital and surplus in small business investment companies (SBICs). SBICs are a special creation of Congress designed to provide equity capital and long-term loans to small businesses. The program is run by the Small Business Administration and is designed to, through tax and other incentives, encourage persons to invest in small business.

There are various limitations on the investments of an SBIC. First, the enterprise must be a small business. While there are a variety of definitions depending on the type of business, the general standards are that the enterprise cannot have a net worth in excess of $18 million or average net after-tax income for the last two years in excess of $6 million. 13 C.F.R. § 121.802. Second, an SBIC cannot invest more than 20% of its capital and surplus in one enterprise. 15 U.S.C.A. § 686(a). Third, an SBIC cannot operate or exercise control over any enterprise in which it invests. Control is presumed if the SBIC (1) owns

50% or more of the voting securities of an enterprise with fewer than 50 shareholders, or (2) owns more than 25%, or a block of 20% (or more) which is as large as any other block, of the voting securities of an enterprise with 50 or more shareholders. Potential control through options and the like does not create a presumption of control.    13 C.F.R § 107.801.

### Problem 3-2

Diane Callahan has a Ph.D. in mathematics, and has worked for years as a theoretical mathematician on a consulting basis. Her hobby has been the stock market. Over the years she has developed stock market forecasting systems that have made her a millionaire. She decides that she wants to form her own investment advisory firm. This requires approximately $200,000 for the purchase of a state of the art computer, plus legal and accounting fees. She goes to X Bank seeking a fixed rate loan. The bank declines to lend her the money, even though they are convinced of the quality of her insight into the market, because she refuses to guarantee the loan personally, thereby subjecting her personal assets to the risk of the business.

However, the bank offers Diane the following deal. It will lend the money to Diane's corporation at a lower rate of interest than they would otherwise consider, and make up the difference by taking a 25 percent share of the business' profits for the five-year term of the loan. This 25 percent of profits may well reach a value of one million dollars. Is the transaction between Diane and the bank really a joint venture or general partnership agreement, in the sense that it is an agreement to share net profits and that repayment of the loan is contingent upon the profitability of Diane's business? May the bank and Diane enter into such a loan agreement, or is this really a venture capital purchase of securities? See 12 C.F.R. § 7.1006.

### Problem 3-3

Ventures Bank establishes a new SBIC with $5 million of capital and surplus. The SBIC enters into an agreement to exchange $1 million for 40% of the stock of Greenmore Stables, a horse breeding farm. The agreement of purchase provides the SBIC with the option to purchase the other 60% of the stock of Greenmore at 1.5 times book value, if the SBA's regulations are ever changed to permit the additional investment. Is this arrangement permissible?

---

State-chartered banks derive their powers from state law. Many states authorize their banks to conduct financial activities beyond those permitted to national banks under the National Bank Act, and even beyond those permitted to bank holding companies under the Bank Holding Company Act. Many of the statutes have conditions, such as that the activity must be conducted through a subsidiary, or is subject to individual regulatory approval, or is subject to a limited amount of investment. In overview, 30 states have authorized general insurance brokerage; 8 states have authorized insurance underwriting; 17 states have authorized general securities underwriting; 17 states have authorized general real estate brokerage; 26 states have authorized real estate development; a not quite identical list of 26 states have authorized real estate equity participation; and a few have authorized travel agencies. Since the FDIC is exposed to the risk of an insured bank's asset activities, it also has a regulatory concern.

*Problem 3-4*

North Carolina law provides banks with "leeway" investment authority. The law authorizes a state-chartered bank that is adequately capitalized to invest no more than 10% of its capital and surplus in any business enterprise located within the state. Venus Bank is an FDIC insured state-chartered bank located in North Carolina. It decides that it wishes to acquire Far Out Associates, a personality analysis firm located in North Carolina. Far Out engages in the business of offering professional services associated with the study and analysis of personality characteristics and their relationship to leadership effectiveness, personal development, and enhancement of leadership skills. What are the chances of Venus Bank getting the necessary regulatory approval from the North Carolina Department of Banking? How about FDIC approval? See 12 U.S.C.A. § 1831a(d). Would this activity, or any of the activities listed in the paragraph preceding this problem, be within the discretion of the OCC to authorize for national banks under *VALIC* (discussed in note 2 after *Arnold Tours*)?

# Section 3.  Lending Limits

## A.  Introduction

A look at the asset side of a typical bank balance sheet will reveal that the great majority of its assets are allocated between two classes: (1) various types of loans (the subject matter of this section and section 4), and (2) various types of fixed-income investment securities (the subject matter of section 5). These three sections, as a unit, seek to answer two questions: (1) can the bank engage in the activity (which frequently depends on how the transaction is classified among various types of generally permissible loans and securities), and if the answer is yes, (2) how large a loan or investment is permitted? We have developed a general answer to the first question in section 2, and so will begin this section with the principal focus on the second question.

Subject to numerous exceptions, a national bank may loan no more than 15% of its unimpaired capital stock and surplus to any one "person." 12 U.S.C.A. § 84. The term person is broadly defined in § 84(b)(2) to include any individual, business organization, trust, estate, government or similar entity or organization. The Comptroller is given the particular authority to "determine when a loan putatively made to a person shall for purposes of this section be attributed to another person," and so combine loans apparently made to different persons for the purpose of calculating the 15% lending limit.

12 U.S.C.A. § 84(d)(2). The Comptroller's rather extensive regulations governing loans are found at 12 C.F.R. Pt. 32.

The lending limit statute is important because it affects a large portion of a core activity of banks. Also, as we will see, violation of the lending limit can result in personal liability for bank officers, directors and employees.

When interpreting any statute it is helpful to identify the underlying policies. The primary policy of section 84 is risk reduction; a secondary policy is benefit spreading. Risk reduction aims to reduce the risk to the bank that would arise from loans concentrated with only a few borrowers. The goal is to safeguard the assets of the bank, and thus the bank's depositors, by limiting the bank's exposure to any one risk. Benefit spreading aims to spread a bank's loans among a large number of borrowers engaged in different activities in the community.

The argument has been made that risk reduction and benefit spreading compliment each other because concerns about concentration of credit risk will result in benefits being spread. The two policies, however, can yield differing results in determining appropriate lending limits. The idea of risk reduction suggests a loan limit dependent on the value of collateral securing the loan; therefore, loans can be permitted in excess of the general lending limit so long as the collateral is liquid and reasonably stable in value. See 12 U.S.C.A. § 84(c). The idea of benefit spreading, however, suggests an absolute loan limit to each person with few, if any, exceptions.

A similar problem arises with the question, later considered, of combining loans to separate borrowers. In determining whether different loans should be aggregated under the 15 percent limitation, and treated as loans to one person, should the regulator focus on the source of the collateral securing the loan (risk reduction), or the use to which the arguably separate loans will be put (benefit spreading)?

Finally, some argue that benefit spreading never occurs, because a loan greater than one bank's lending limit simply is participated (parts of the loan are sold to other banks, so that each bank assumes the risk of its part of the loan) among other banks. Any attempt to participate a loan, however, requires each participating bank to look independently at the creditworthiness and collateral of the transaction. And, even with loan participations, benefit spreading often will exist because a bank, limited in its ability to lend to a favored few, may be more likely to provide additional loans locally rather than elsewhere through purchasing participations.

## B. Obligations Governed by the Lending Limits

Banks engage in a variety of credit activities, not all of which are subject to the lending limits of § 84. Section 84 focuses on the risk exposure of a bank in terms of "loans and extensions of credit." This term is defined to include "all direct or indirect advances of funds to a person" who promises to repay the funds or pledges property as collateral. Consistent with the policy of risk reduction, the concept of extension of credit is broader than simply loans. A bank can be exposed to substantial risk without actually making a loan. Activities such as standby letters of credit and personal property leases are viewed as extensions of credit under § 84 because they expose the bank to essentially the same risk as a loan. For example, in a bank personal property lease transaction, the bank buys the property and the customer enters into a long-term lease of the property from the bank. The bank has virtually the same credit risk whether the bank-customer relation is loan or lease.

Banks engage in a variety of asset and liability management activities that are not always easily classified. First, not all engagements by a bank to extend credit are considered loans or extensions of credit subject to the lending limits. In theory, some credit risk, because it is too contingent, is not substantial enough to be subject to § 84 lending limits. Currently, documentary letters of credit based on transactions in goods (but not standby letters of credit, typically based on failure to perform) and most types of direct commitments to lend in the future are not considered a "contractual commitment to advance funds" subject to § 84. In addition, some credit risk transactions are subject to other limits, such as the limits applicable to bankers' acceptances under 12 U.S.C.A. § 372, and the limits on purchases of corporate bonds under section 24(7).

Another important distinction is between "loans and extensions of credit" and the purchase of assets. Most purchases of assets are not subject to § 84 lending limits, although they may be subject to other limits. The usual but not universal distinction between a purchase and a loan is whether the bank has unconditional, nonbreach recourse against the other party to the transaction. If the other party has a repayment obligation, the transaction is a loan. If the bank and customer have exchanged money for assets, and there has not been an unconditional promise by the customer to repay the money, then there has been a purchase of an asset. Banks "purchase" assets or "make" loans (which are also assets) for both short-term and long-term periods. Banks purchase assets when they purchase loans from other banks, federal and state government securities, or goods and services. A loan participation is both a purchase and a loan. It is a purchase from the selling bank, and a loan to the original borrower for the portion of the loan purchased. And finally, as will be discussed below, the Comptroller has not always ruled consistently when applying these various concepts of classification.

## Comments and Questions

1. It should be made clear that classifying a transaction as a loan or extension of credit, and so limiting its size, does not guarantee avoidance of subsequent disaster. Over the last 20 years the United States banking system has seen many examples of lawful loan transactions that resulted in bank failure. Depository institutions have suffered extensive losses in their credit relationships with real estate investment trusts, foreign country loans, energy loans, highly leveraged corporate buyout transactions, and real estate loans (again). In addition, depository institutions are subject to similar risks in off-balance sheet activities. For example, in September, 1993, off-balance sheet derivatives of banks were $12 trillion, which was more than three times the total assets of all banks. Although derivatives, such as interest rate swaps, are an off-balance sheet activity, and therefore less visible, they are not necessarily less risky than lending activities that have resulted in bank losses.

2. In general, banks can go far beyond adhering to the lending limits in seeking to reduce their risk exposure. They can make a very large number of small but high profit loans to many borrowers, instead of large loans (close to the lending limits) to a relatively small group of borrowers. Banks can accomplish this by making loans to customers who lack the bargaining power necessary to push rates to the lowest possible limit, such as medium and smaller sized businesses and consumers.

3. Lenders may have loan criteria that go beyond financial analysis, to include such considerations as the borrower's quality of management, commitment to the local community, employee turnover, and employee relations in general. It is not uncommon for these types of nontraditional loan criteria to be part of the final decision whether or not to make a loan.

4. On the other hand, there are ways by which a bank may lawfully concentrate its credit risk with a few customers. We will explore several examples in this chapter: a. traditional loan; b. loan secured by readily marketable collateral; c. loan secured by particular assets as provided for in § 84(c); d. issuance of bankers' acceptances for the same customer; e. purchase of corporate bonds issued by the same customer; f. issuance of documentary letters of credit for the same customer. Transactions (a), (b), and (c) are three types of loans each subject to different limits; transaction (d) is a separately categorized activity; transaction (e) is an investment security; and transaction (f) is none of the above and so subject to no limits.

## C. Computation of the Limit

For purposes of computing the lending limit, a bank's capital and surplus is defined as the sum of its Tier 1 and Tier 2 risk-based capital (essentially the capital accounts, examined in section 7) plus the balance of its loss reserves not included in Tier 2 capital for capital adequacy purposes. 12 C.F.R. § 32.2(b). This capital and surplus figure, derived from the bank's quarterly report of condition, is then multiplied by 15 percent to obtain the general lending limit for a single person from the particular national bank.

Section 84(a)(2) allows for an additional 10 percent to be loaned to the same borrower if the additional loan is fully secured by "readily marketable collateral," as defined in 12 C.F.R. § 32.2(m). The regulation requires that the collateral always maintain a value equal to at least 100 percent of the loan balance in excess of the general 15 percent limitation. If the collateral requirement is violated, section 32.6(c) requires that within thirty days either the collateral value be brought up to 100% or the collateral be sold.

Section 84(c) and 12 C.F.R. § 32.3 provide other important exceptions to the general 15 percent lending limit. One can understand these particular exceptions by remembering that the primary purposes of the statute are risk reduction and benefit spreading. Most of the § 84(c) exceptions are premised on the assumption that there is little risk in loans secured by particular types of collateral. A few of the exceptions are premised on the assumption that there is substantial benefit spreading in certain types of lending. See if you can compute the applicable lending limit for the various transactions in the following problem.

*Problem 3-5*

Roger Hammerstein is just a loan officer who can't say no. Examine the bank's consolidated statement of condition set out below, as well as the text of § 84 and Pt. 32, and make a decision: should the bank grant the following loans or is Roger Hammerstein off his carousel?

1. Mo van Onn, head of a large trucking firm, requested a loan of $34 million to purchase 375 new rigs. Van Onn agreed to give the bank a perfected security interest in the equipment. Can the bank make the loan? Is the existence of the collateral important to your answer? See § 84(a) and 12 C.F.R. §§ 32.2(m) and 32.3(b).

2. Betty Sootchatuah, president of Sootchatuah Tea Corporation, offered the bank a warehouse receipt for $55 million worth of Formosa Oolong tea in exchange for a loan of $80 million. Hammerstein recommends that the bank grant the loan. What advice would you give to the loan committee? See § 84(c) and 12 C.F.R. §§ 32.3(b)(1) and 32.2(n).

3. Suppose Betty offered as collateral $55 million worth of paintings by Picasso and Rubens, and several unset diamonds that have been valued by the president of the American Gemological Society to be worth an additional $55 million at wholesale?

4. Would Betty be better off if $55 million in IBM stock were her collateral? Would she be sufficiently better off to get the $80 million loan?

# CONSOLIDATED STATEMENT OF CONDITION
December 31, 1996

ASSETS

| | |
|---|---|
| Cash and Due from Banks ........................ | $1,027,982,743 |

Securities:

| | |
|---|---|
| U.S. Government ........................ | 172,697,255 |
| Federal Agency ........................ | 16,345,250 |
| Obligations of States and Political Subdivisions ........................ | 213,284,376 |
| Other ........................ | 12,572,302 |
| Trading Account ........................ | 61,979,557 |

Loans:

| | |
|---|---|
| Federal Funds Sold and Securities Purchased under Agreements to Resell ......... | 231,900,000 |
| Other Money Market ........................ | 536,599,490 |
| Other Loans ........................ | 1,607,839,442 |
| Direct Lease Financing ........................ | 13,547,381 |
| Buildings and Equipment ........................ | 66,637,655 |
| Other Assets ........................ | 49,169,391 |
| TOTAL ........................ | $4,010,554,842 |

LIABILITIES

Deposits:

| | |
|---|---|
| Demand ........................ | $ 874,983,331 |
| Savings ........................ | 583,568,421 |
| Other Time ........................ | 489,972,393 |
| Foreign Offices ........................ | 1,315,167,129 |
| Total Deposits ........................ | $3,263,691,274 |
| Federal Funds Purchased and Other Borrowings ........ | 448,653,654 |
| Accrued Taxes and Other Expenses ................. | 51,925,354 |
| Other Liabilities ........................ | 16,183,468 |
| Total Liabilities ........................ | $3,780,453,750 |
| Reserve for Possible Loan Losses ................... | $ 30,877,610 |

CAPITAL ACCOUNTS

| | |
|---|---|
| Subordinated Capital Notes—6 3/4% Due March 1, 2013 . | $ 30,000,000 |

Stockholder's Equity:

| | |
|---|---|
| Capital Stock ($20 Par Value) ................ | $ 60,000,000 |
| Surplus ........................ | 74,000,000 |
| Undivided Profits ........................ | 18,673,458 |
| Reserve for Contingencies ................... | 16,550,024 |
| Total Stockholder's Equity ........................ | $ 169,223,482 |
| TOTAL ........................ | $4,010,554,842 |

## D. Combining Loans to Separate Borrowers

A long-time concern of bank regulation has been that a person could avoid the lending limit by funneling a loan, to be used for his or her own benefit, through a different legal entity. In response, § 84(d)(2) grants the Comptroller the authority to determine when a loan putatively made to one person is to be attributed to another. Extensive regulations for combining loans to separate borrowers are at 12 C.F.R. § 32.5. The general rule, found at § 32.5(a), is that: "[l]oans or extensions of credit to one borrower will be attributed to another person and each person will be deemed a borrower . . . (1) when proceeds of a loan or extension of credit are to be used for the direct benefit of the other person . . . or (2) when a common enterprise is deemed to exist between the persons." The first test can be denominated the direct benefit test; the second, the common enterprise test. At the time of the following case, the single borrower lending limit was 10 percent rather than the current 15 percent of capital and surplus.

## del Junco v. Conover
### 682 F.2d 1338 (9th Cir. 1982)

FLETCHER, Circuit Judge:

In December 1979, a periodic examination by the Comptroller of the Currency ("Comptroller") of the Los Angeles National Bank ("Bank") disclosed a possible violation of the provisions of 12 U.S.C. § 84. Section 84 limits the amount that a bank can lend to a single borrower to 10% of the bank's capital stock. At issue was whether three of the Bank's loans were really to the same entity and whether, when added together, they exceeded the bank's legal lending limit.

The loans were to Rehbock Lewis ("Lewis"), President of Fame Furniture Co., Inc.; Fame Furniture Co., Inc. ("Fame"); and Ralph Ware ("Ware"), Treasurer of Fame. The chart below sets forth the date, borrower, and amount of each loan, as well as the legal lending limit of the bank at the time of each loan and the amount by which the loans, when aggregated, exceeded the legal lending limit:

| Date Granted | Borrower | Amount | Lending Limit | Excess Amount |
|---|---|---|---|---|
| 1/19/79 | Lewis | 225,000 | | |
| 5/9/79 | Fame | 225,000 | | |
| Subtotal | | 450,000 | 272,866 | 177,134 |
| 6/11/79 | Ware | 125,000 | | |
| Present Balance | | 575,000 | 277,108 | 297,892 |

The legality of the Lewis loan for $225,000 has never been at issue, as that loan did not exceed the legal lending limit of the bank when it was made. However, if the Lewis, Fame, and Ware loans could be aggregated, then the latter two loans would exceed the Bank's lending limit.

The Comptroller first requested the Directors of the Bank to indemnify the Bank for any losses sustained as a result of the two excess loans; the Directors refused. The Comptroller then began a formal cease and desist action against the Directors and the Bank by issuing a Notice of Charges. The Bank and Directors answered, and the Comptroller moved for summary judgment in an agency proceeding.

In the agency proceeding, the Bank and Directors admitted that they knew that the proceeds of the Fame and Lewis loans were to be used for the benefit of Fame. On these facts, the Administrative Law Judge (ALJ) ruled that it was proper to aggregate the Lewis and Fame loans so as to constitute a violation of 12 U.S.C. § 84. He also ruled, however, that an evidentiary hearing would be necessary to determine whether the proceeds of the Ware loan were actually used for the benefit of Fame, an element that had to be satisfied if the Ware loan could be added to the Fame loan. Such an evidentiary hearing was then held, and the ALJ determined that the Ware loan was used for the benefit of Fame. Accordingly, the ALJ recommended that the Comptroller issue a cease and desist order, that the Directors indemnify the Bank for the Fame and Ware loans, that the Bank recover costs of collection fees, and that the Bank recover attorneys' fees that it had paid for the Directors' defense. . . .

The Directors then moved this court to stay the Comptroller's final judgment. This court denied the motion without prejudice. Next, the Directors filed an identical motion with the Comptroller, who denied the motion. The Directors now appeal the final judgment of the Comptroller. . . .

## I. STANDARD OF REVIEW.

The parties agree that a "substantial evidence" standard applies to judicial review of administrative findings. The parties are correct. See 5 U.S.C. § 706(2)(E).

The Comptroller has broad discretion to fashion a remedy. See *Groos National Bank v. Comptroller of Currency*, 573 F.2d 889, 897 (5th Cir. 1978). "Substantial evidence is required for the Comptroller's findings, but once the Comptroller finds a violation he may, within his allowable discretion, fashion relief in such a form as to prevent future abuses." *Id.* Similarly, he has broad discretion to cure the effect of a violation.

In reviewing the order that actually issued, we consider whether the affirmative action taken by the Comptroller was appropriate to correct the condition resulting from the Directors' violation of the banking laws.[4]

---

[4]     The statutory grant of authority that allows the Comptroller to issue an order to cease and desist from a violation or practice states in part:

Such order may, by provisions which may be mandatory or otherwise, require the bank or its directors, officers, employees, agents, and other persons participating in the conduct of the affairs of such bank to cease and desist from the same, and, further, to take affirmative action to correct the conditions resulting from any such violation or practice.

12 U.S.C. § 1818(b)(1).

## II. THE COMPTROLLER'S FINDING IS SUPPORTED BY SUBSTANTIAL EVIDENCE

. . . The regulation that implements the lending statute provides that "(o)bligations of a corporation must be combined with any other extension of credit the proceeds of which are used for the benefit of the corporation." 12 C.F.R. § 7.1310(c)(3) (1981) (emphasis added). The issue presented by this regulation is whether there was substantial evidence to support a finding that the $125,000 loan to Ware, the Treasurer of Fame, was "used for the benefit of the corporation."

The Comptroller found:

> The hearing record clearly discloses the purpose and use of proceeds of the Ware loan. Mr. Ware, Fame's treasurer, testified that Fame's checking account at another bank was overdrawn. Accordingly, he and Mr. Lewis, Fame's president, went to the Bank to procure another loan. The Bank's vice president and senior lending officer, Mr. Jewett, informed Lewis and Ware that the Bank could not make an additional loan to Fame or to Mr. Lewis without violating the Bank's legal lending limit. Therefore, Mr. Ware's "name was used for the loan papers to borrow the money." Hearing Transcript 50-51. As agreed, the Bank put the Ware loan proceeds directly into Fame's corporate checking account. Hearing Transcript 51-52. *See also* Hearing Transcript 179-80, wherein Mr. Jewett testified that he knew the proceeds were "going to go through Mr. Ware to Fame." On these facts, the Comptroller agrees with the ALJ's finding and conclusion that the deposit of the Ware loan proceeds directly into Fame's corporate checking account shows that the proceeds were used for the benefit of Fame.

The evidence of the corporation's overdrawn account, the corporation's search for another loan, the action and knowledge of the Bank's lending officer, and the deposit of the loan proceeds directly into Fame's account is substantial enough to support the Comptroller's finding.

Thus, because sufficient evidence supported the finding that the Ware loan was for the benefit of Fame, that loan could be aggregated with other Fame loans to calculate whether an excess loan had been made. . . .

The Comptroller's decision and final order to cease and desist are affirmed.

### Comments and Questions

1. Should the court's analysis of the transactions in *del Junco v. Conover* be viewed as an application of the direct benefit test or of the common enterprise test?

2. Common enterprise is defined at § 32.5(c). In general, the determination of common enterprise depends upon all the facts and circumstances. The regulation, however, does provide three elaborations of common situations that ordinarily will be considered *per se* common enterprises. The first is where the expected source of repayment for each loan is the same for each borrower. The risk exposure in such a situation is self-evident. The second is where loans are made to persons who are related through common control. A common enterprise will be deemed to exist if the persons are engaged in interdependent businesses and there is substantial financial interdependence among them. The third *per se* situation of common enterprise is where separate persons

borrow from a bank for the purpose of acquiring a business enterprise in which those persons will own more than 50 percent of the voting securities.

3.   Should a pass-through from one person to another of borrowed funds always result in a combining of loans?  Suppose that both A and B are borrowers from one bank. B purchases goods from A and pays for them with the loan proceeds.  The transfer of loan proceeds from B to A certainly benefits A.  But the motivation for B taking a loan was to enable B to buy the goods, not to put A in funds.  Thus the benefit conferred upon A was incidental, not direct.  The purchase transaction should be viewed as separate from the loan.  B received present value for the funds transfer and so had its own source of repayment of the loan through the sale or use of the goods it purchased.

*Problem 3-6*

Jekyll, a respected physician, has received a $2.2 million loan commitment from the Second National Bank for the purpose of discovering a serum that will ensure the user everlasting youth and beauty.  So far, Jekyll has not requested any funds, but has agreed to repay the bank at an 8 percent interest rate for any loan he does receive.  Hyde, a part-time glass blower, supplies all the flasks for Jekyll's experiments.  But alas, Hyde has fallen on hard times, and even the $750,000 loan he just received from Second National, secured by a carload of handblown test tubes which was shipped last week, will not save Hyde from his current financial troubles.  Upon learning that Jekyll has access to a large sum of money, Hyde proposes that the two form a partnership to cut the cost of Jekyll's equipment.  Jekyll, whose business acumen parallels his scientific insight, agrees.  Hyde then mentions that if he could just pay off the $800,000 he owes his nonbank creditors, he could concentrate all his efforts on meeting Jekyll's needs.  Desirous of aiding his new partner, the good doctor volunteers to obtain the required sum and hastens to the bank. While at the bank, Jekyll thinks this is as good a time as any also to get funds for some new equipment.  He therefore receives a loan for $1.8 million.  You are an examiner from the Comptroller's office.  What will you do upon discovering the above transaction if Second National's balance sheet reads as set out below.  Consider 12 C.F.R. §§ 32.5(c) & (e); 32.2(f)(2) and (j)(1)(i).

## CONSOLIDATED BALANCE SHEET

| ASSETS | 1996 | 1995 |
|---|---|---|
| Cash and due from banks | $ 22,763,165 | $ 21,758,666 |
| Investment securities: | | |
|    U.S. Government | 11,954,145 | 15,912,897 |
|    U.S. Government agencies | 23,508,216 | 16,686,196 |
|    Public Housing Authority | 7,959,968 | 12,634,258 |
|    State and municipal | 14,278,964 | 16,390,283 |
|    Other | 270,000 | 255,000 |
|      **Total investment securities** | 57,971,293 | 61,878,634 |
| Federal funds sold and securities purchased | | |
|   under agreements to resell | 15,000,000 | 8,000,000 |
| Loans: | | |
|    Commercial and consumer | 57,935,939 | 56,355,060 |
|    Real estate mortgage | 46,390,051 | 44,421,497 |
|      **Total loans** | 104,325,990 | 100,776,557 |
| Bank premises and equipment | 3,916,010 | 3,793,351 |
| Accrued interest and other assets | 1,937,270 | 1,839,699 |
|      **TOTAL ASSETS** | $205,913,728 | $198,046,907 |

## LIABILITIES, RESERVE AND CAPITAL ACCOUNTS

| | 1996 | 1995 |
|---|---|---|
| Deposits: | | |
|    Demand | $ 72,916,662 | $ 73,254,404 |
|    Savings | 47,170,383 | 50,228,320 |
|    Time | 66,484,778 | 48,687,140 |
|      **Total deposits** | 185,571,823 | 172,169,864 |
| Federal funds purchased and securities | | |
|   sold under agreements to repurchase | -0- | 7,679,500 |
| Mortgage note payable | 1,222,227 | 1,272,736 |
| Unearned income | 2,184,488 | 2,220,718 |
| Accrued expenses and other liabilities | 1,936,655 | 1,666,266 |
|      **Total liabilities** | 191,915,193 | 185,009,084 |
| Reserve for possible loan losses | 1,633,428 | 1,543,843 |
| Capital accounts: | | |
|   Common stock–$10.00 par value: | | |
|      **1996**    **1995** | | |
|   Authorized  500,000  500,000 | | |
|   Outstanding  353,164  353,164 | 3,531,640 | 3,531,640 |
| Capital surplus | 4,968,360 | 4,968,360 |
| Retained earnings | 3,865,107 | 2,993,980 |
|      **Total capital accounts** | 12,365,107 | 11,493,980 |
| **TOTAL LIABILITIES, RESERVE, AND** | | |
|      **CAPITAL ACCOUNTS** | $205,913,728 | $198,046,907 |

*Problem 3-7*

In July, 1997 California National Bank, with a lending limit of $2 million, made a $1.4 million loan to Limited Partnership A for the purpose of purchasing a shopping center located in California. In August, 1997 the bank purchased from Texas National Bank a $1 million participation in a loan Texas National Bank had made to Limited Partnership B. The proceeds of the participation were used by B to purchase a horse breeding farm located in Texas. Sanctum Corporation is the general partner for both Limited Partnerships A nd B. In September, 1997 California National Bank made a $250,000 loan to Sanctum secured by a money market deposit account at the bank. In October, 1997 the bank approved a $1.25 million line of cedit to Sanctum, but no funds have been advanced against the line of credit. Should these four transactions be combined as loans or extensions of credit to one borrower? Would your answer be different if Limited Partnerships A and B were converted into corporations? See 12 U.S.C.A. § 84(c)(6); 12 C.F.R. §§ 32.2(f) and (*l*); 32.5(c) - (e).

## E.  Loans to Officers, Directors and Principal Shareholders

A particularly troublesome type of lending involves lending to individuals with special influence, typically called insiders.  There are three classifications of insiders–executive officers, directors, and principal (more than 10 percent) shareholders.  The General Accounting Office did a study of banks that failed during 1990 and 1991.  The study suggested that insider lending was a contributing factor in 175 of the 286 bank failures in those years.

Loans to insiders are governed by §§ 375a and 375b, and elaborated in 12 C.F.R. Pt. 215.  While §§ 375a and 375b, by their terms, apply only to member banks, § 1828(j)(2) provides that §§ 375a and 375b apply to all insured banks.  Section 375a applies only to executive officers of banks.  The lending restrictions of § 375b apply to insiders (and their related interests) whether affiliated with a bank, a bank holding company, or any subsidiary of either.  Exceptions can be made, however, for officers and directors of subsidiaries who do not participate in the bank's policy making functions.  And so, under § 375b insiders are, in effect, treated as having the same position with the bank as they actually have with the affiliated company.  Companies, political campaigns, or political committees affiliated with an insider, are typically considered to be "related interests."

The regulation under § 375b, 12 C.F.R. § 215.4, requires prior approval by the board of directors for loans to any insider aggregating more than the higher of $25,000 or 5% of bank capital and surplus, but not more than $500,000.  The effect of these limits is that there is always a lower limit of $25,000 for banks having total assets of approximately $7 million or less and an upper limit of $500,000 for banks having approximate total assets exceeding $140 million.  For banks in between those two limits, the amount would be 5% of capital and surplus.  Prior approval by the bank's directors is required for all loans to insiders exceeding $500,000 in the aggregate.

Loans to executive officers of banks are further regulated under § 375a and 12 C.F.R. § 215.5. Executive officers can receive loans in any otherwise permissible amount for the purposes of residential mortgages or education, and in any otherwise permissible amount for any other purpose if secured by a perfected security interest in government obligations or bank deposit accounts. Otherwise, loans to executive officers can be made only to the higher of $25,000 or 2.5 percent of bank capital and surplus, but not more than $100,000. The general purpose of these regulations is to control loans to individuals who have particular influence within a bank, and especially to control loans to those who have the power to obtain preferential or excessive credit that could threaten the financial stability of the bank.

One seemingly easy way around §§ 375a and 375b would be for banks to engage in reciprocal lending practices to each other's insiders. To some extent this may be possible. This type of activity, however, is limited by 12 U.S.C.A. § 1972(2) for banks with correspondent relationships. Banks with correspondent relationships may extend credit to officers of correspondent banks only on terms no more favorable than those prevailing for other customers. Nevertheless, correspondent banks are not limited by the more severe restrictions in §§ 375a and 375b applicable to their own insiders. In addition, there are no special limits on loans to insiders of another bank if there is no correspondent banking relation.

### Problem 3-8

1. Department stores often compensate their employees for traditionally low wages by allowing them sizeable discounts on store merchandise. Airlines permit employees and their families to ride free or at substantial discounts. These are but two examples of fringe benefits which give employees preferential treatment that persons not associated with the business do not generally receive. May banks do the same? For example, may banks make loans to all bank employees at 2% below the prime rate? May banks waive for all bank employees its ordinary service charges for checking accounts? See 12 C.F.R. § 215.4.

2. A bank director has a spouse who runs a business in his own right and they have a daughter who is a physician. Would the spouse's business or the daughter be considered a related interest of the director? Suppose further that the director is a co-signer on a loan to the daughter in the amount of $500,000, the director already has a loan outstanding for $500,000, and the lending limit for the bank is $1 million. Is this transaction permissible? See 12 C.F.R. § 215.2(g), (h), (m), and (n).

3. A bank director owns an auto leasing company. Can the bank lease several company cars for its officers from the director's company? Would it matter if the auto leasing company were owned by a spouse or child of the director? Even if a particular section of the federal banking laws does not prohibit the transaction, is there a question of potential breach of fiduciary duty by the bank's board of directors?

## Comments and Questions

1.  Exactly who is an executive officer? See 12 C.F.R. § 215.2(e)(1) and the accompanying footnote.

2.  In addition to the insider lending restrictions discussed above, there also is an aggregate limit on loans to insiders. Under § 375b(5) banks are only allowed to make aggregate loans to insiders up to 100% of the institution's capital and surplus. Banks with less than $100 million in deposits, however, may make loans to insiders in amounts up to 200% of the institution's capital and surplus, subject to certain conditions. First, the bank must be adequately capitalized and must have a CAMEL one or two supervision rating. Second, the bank's board of directors must adopt a resolution certifying that the higher insider lending limit is needed to avoid restricting credit or to help the bank attract directors. This requirement appears to restrict the increased limit to rural areas.

## F. Loans to Affiliates

In the past two decades a majority of banks have adopted the holding company form of organization. Most have acquired or created additional banks and nonbank affiliates engaged in such activities as mortgage banking, consumer finance, leasing, and securities activities. As a consequence, most banks are part of a highly complex organizational structure, with a parent bank holding company controlling numerous bank and nonbank affiliates. This has raised a major concern with financial transactions between affiliates within a holding company organization. Several banks have been damaged by such transactions. Probably the best known case involved the Hamilton Bank of Chattanooga, which failed after having purchased a large volume of low-quality mortgages from a distressed mortgage banking subsidiary of the parent holding company.

Affiliate transactions are governed by 12 U.S.C.A. § 371c, which was substantially amended in 1982, and § 371c-1 which was added in 1987. While §§ 371c and 371c-1 by their terms apply only to member banks, § 1828(j)(1) provides that both sections apply to all FDIC insured banks.

The sections are exceptionally complex, even though the underlying policy is not. Section 371c is designed to limit the access of non-bank affiliates to the assets of the bank, and to protect against preferential transactions between a bank and its affiliates.

The definition of affiliate is important. "Affiliate" includes the parent holding company, foreign bank subsidiaries of the bank, domestic and foreign bank subsidiaries of the holding company, non-bank subsidiaries of the holding company, any company controlled by the shareholders who control the bank, any company (such as a real estate investment trust) that is sponsored and advised by the bank, and any other company that the Federal Reserve determines has such relationship with the bank, or any subsidiary or affiliate, that may affect the relationship and make a transaction other than arms length.

The general limits of § 371c include: (1) quantitative limits that a bank's credit transactions with a single non-bank affiliate may not exceed 10% of the bank's capital and surplus, and the bank's transactions with all non-bank affiliates may not in the aggregate exceed 20% of capital and surplus; (2) transactions with non-bank affiliates must be fully secured by specified types of collateral; (3) a qualitative requirement that transactions with affiliates be carried out on terms and conditions consistent with safe and sound banking practices; and (4) a qualitative requirement that the transactions not include low-quality assets.

Of particular importance in applying these general rules is the § 371c(b)(7) definition of "covered transaction." Any covered transaction must meet all four of the above stated requirements. The term broadly includes the following: (1) loans to affiliates; (2) securities purchases from affiliates; (3) asset purchases from affiliates, except the purchase of real and personal property especially exempted by the Federal Reserve Board (the reason for the exemption is to enable the Board to permit a bank to purchase certain types of expensive property, such as a computer or a building, in cases where the purchase transaction does not violate the purposes of section 371c); (4) acceptance as collateral of securities issued by affiliates; and (5) guarantees on behalf of affiliates.

A significant exemption found in § 371c(d) is the authority to engage, without limit, in standard transfers of funds, loans, and other extensions of credit among affiliated domestic bank subsidiaries of the same holding company. In effect, the section treats separate bank subsidiaries like a branch banking system, allowing unlimited transactions among the bank subsidiaries (except for the purchase of low quality assets) while still requiring that every transaction be consistent with safe and sound banking practices. Consequently, it is possible to raise funds (e.g., attract deposits) in the most credit worthy bank subsidiary of a holding company to fund loans in another bank subsidiary. Similarly, under § 371c(b)(2)(A) a non-bank subsidiary of a bank generally is not an affiliate. Other complete exemptions from § 371c include transactions with any affiliates that are fully secured by government obligations or guaranteed by the United States or its agencies, and purchases from any affiliate of any asset "having a readily identifiable and publicly available market quotation and purchased at that market quotation."

Congress adopted § 371c-1 in 1987, possibly based on the assumption that commercial banks would become affiliated with securities firms. The section deals with conflict of interests between a bank and nonbank affiliate and covers numerous transactions, including the sale of securities or other assets to an affiliate, the payment of money or the furnishing of services to an affiliate, and any transactions in which an affiliate acts as an agent or broker or receives a fee for its services to the bank. Similar to § 371c, banks are not affiliates of other banks and so are free of the restrictions. Transactions with covered affiliates may be made only on terms and under circumstances that are substantially the same as those prevailing for comparable transactions involving non-affiliated enterprises. Consider the following problem.

*Problem 3-9*

1. Joan Jones is owner of 70% of the common stock of Jones Mortgage Banking, Inc. (JMB), and the owner of 25% of the voting common stock of First National Holding Company, which owns 100% of First National Bank. Ms. Jones serves as a director of First National Bank. She wants to know whether any loans by the bank to JMB are subject to the transactions with affiliates requirements, or any other special lending restrictions. See § 371c(b)(1).

2. Suppose that Ms. Jones owned only 40% of JMB. Alice Mitchell, an owner of 3% of JMB, but having no affiliation with First National Bank or its holding company, seeks a loan from First National Bank and wishes to offer as collateral her stock in JMB. Would this transaction be subject to the transactions with affiliates requirements? Consider §§ 375b; 371c(b)(7) and (c)(1).

3. First State Bank is a subsidiary of the same holding company as is First National Bank. Under state law First State Bank is authorized to and in fact owns a travel agency as a separate subsidiary of the bank. First National Bank wants to lease space in the lobby of three of its branches to the travel agency. Will this transaction be subject to the statutory limits on affiliate transactions? Consider §§ 371c(b)(2)(A), 371c-1(a) and (d)(1).

# Section 4.  Limits for Commercial and Real Estate Lending

## A.  Introduction

Loans are usually made and held by the same bank while investment securities are widely distributed to numerous, passive investors. But this and other differences between loans and investment securities are often difficult to discern. One example is a loan participation, where multiple banks or other lenders are owners of the same debt instrument, denominated a loan. Other common differences between loans and investment securities are that investment securities usually have what is known as a call (prepayment) protection, while loans usually do not. Call protection means that the debt cannot be repaid for a certain period of time, or if it can be repaid during that period of time it can only be repaid at a premium. Finally, today bank loans usually carry floating interest rates, while investment securities usually carry fixed interest rates.

Investment securities are a more common type of debt for large, established businesses, while loans are more commonly the form of debt issued by smaller, local businesses. Even the largest companies, however, may use loans rather than investment securities in order to achieve greater flexibility in the terms of borrowing. Banks are often willing to renegotiate the rate at which a loan is to be repaid, the various financial covenants, and the collateral requirements. The longest term bank loans are usually for no more than seven to ten years, while bonds can have longer maturities.

Historically, Congress has imposed few restrictions on the lending activities of national banks. Even under the Community Reinvestment Act, 12 U.S.C.A. §§ 2901-2907, while banks must serve the credit needs of their local community, they can still make loans outside that community. Just as there are no fixed geographic boundaries for bank lending activities, there are essentially no limits to the types or purposes of loans that banks can make for commercial, industrial, or consumer purposes. As we will discuss later in this section, restrictions on national banks' real estate lending activities have varied dramatically over time.

## B. Loan Participations

Small banks, in rural areas particularly, are faced with good customers whose credit requirements exceed what the bank itself may lend under § 84 and the exceptions thereto. One way for such a bank to service a good customer is to enter into a loan participation agreement. Under such an agreement the "lead" bank sells a portion of its customer's loan to one or more other banks, so that the portion retained by the lead bank is within the bank's lending limit. Note that the major purpose of loan participations is to maintain the risk reduction function of § 84, thus protecting the financial soundness of the lead bank, while also providing sufficient funds to meet the credit needs of the customer.

*Problem 3-10*

Does the following loan participation arrangement comply with the lending limits requirements of § 84 and 12 C.F.R. Pt. 32?

Bitty Bank has a lending limit of $1 million and its good customer Modern Office Supply Services (MOSS) requires a $5 million loan. Bitty Bank arranges a loan participation with its large correspondent bank, City Bank with City Bank taking the "overline" of $4 million. The loan participation agreement provides that the monthly payments made over the five-year term of the loan will first be utilized to pay interest to both Bitty and City Banks originally in the ratio of 1 to 4, and the funds remaining from each payment will be used to reduce the unpaid principal balance of the City Bank portion of the loan until it is repaid entirely. In addition, in the event of default, all proceeds recovered in default, and after payment of interest, will be utilized to pay City Bank before any funds are utilized to pay the $1 million principal loan made by Bitty Bank. See 12 C.F.R. § 32.2(j)(2)(vi).

---

Over the past several years the market for "non traditional" loan participations has increased to the point where it has become a multi-billion dollar business. Insurance companies, mutual funds, and other institutional investors are attracted to the higher yields and perceived safety of corporate loans. As a consequence, banks have been able to develop programs to market corporate loans to non-bank investors. This takes at least part of the transaction out of the normal scope of bank regulation and raises many questions that are present in the following case.

## Banco Espanol de Credito v. Security Pacific National Bank
### 973 F.2d 51 (2d Cir. 1992)

ALTIMARI, Circuit Judge:

. . . In 1988, Security Pacific extended a line of credit to Integrated permitting Integrated to obtain short-term unsecured loans from Security Pacific. Security Pacific subsequently made a series of short-term loans to Integrated. Security Pacific sold these loans, in whole or in part, to various institutional investors at differing interest rates. Resales of these loans were prohibited without Security Pacific's express written consent. The practice of selling loans to other institutions is known as "loan participation." Short-term loan participation permits a primary lender such as Security Pacific to spread its risk, while at the same time allowing a purchaser with excess cash to earn a higher return than that available on comparable money market instruments. Security Pacific, as manager of the loans, earned a fee equal to the difference between the interest paid by the debtor and the lower interest paid to the purchaser.

Security Pacific assumed no responsibility for the ability of Integrated to repay its loans. Indeed, each purchaser of loan participations was required to enter into a Master Participation Agreement ("MPA"), which contained a general disclaimer providing, in relevant part, that the purchaser "acknowledges that it has independently and without reliance upon Security [Pacific] and based upon such documents and information as the participant has deemed appropriate, made its own credit analysis."

In late 1988, Integrated began to encounter financial difficulties. In April 1989, Security Pacific refused a request by Integrated to extend further credit. Despite this refusal, Security Pacific continued to sell loan participations on Integrated's debt. Indeed, from mid-April through June 9, 1989, Security Pacific sold seventeen different loan participations to plaintiffs-appellants. Unable to obtain enough working capital, Integrated began defaulting on its loans on June 12, 1989. Integrated subsequently declared bankruptcy.

As a result of Integrated's default, two sets of investors, who had purchased the seventeen loan participations, initiated separate actions against Security Pacific in the United States District Court for the Southern District of New York. Contending that the loan participations were "securities" within the meaning of the Securities Act of 1933 ("the 1933 Act"), plaintiffs sought to rescind their purchase agreements by alleging that Security Pacific had failed to disclose to them material facts about Integrated's financial condition in violation of § 12(2) of the 1933 Act. 15 U.S.C. § 771(2). Plaintiffs also claimed that Security Pacific's failure to disclose constituted a breach of Security Pacific's implied and express contractual duties under its MPA's, and a breach of Security Pacific's duty to disclose material information based on superior knowledge. Based on these common law claims, plaintiffs sought to recover their investment plus unpaid interest. Plaintiffs in each of the two actions moved for partial summary judgment on the securities claim. Security Pacific cross-moved for summary judgment on all claims. The cases were consolidated for argument.

In ruling on these motions, the district court concluded that the loan participations were not "securities" within the meaning of the Securities Act of 1933, and that, therefore, plaintiffs could not assert a violation under § 12(2) of this Act. In addition, the district court held that the express disclaimer provisions in the MPA precluded plaintiffs' common law claims. Accordingly, the district court granted summary judgment to Security Pacific and dismissed the complaints. See *Banco Espanol de Credito v. Security Pacific National Bank*, 763 F. Supp. 36 (S.D.N.Y. 1991). Plaintiffs now appeal.

## DISCUSSION

Section 2(1) of the 1933 Act provides in pertinent part:

[U]nless the context otherwise requires–(1) the term "security" means any note . . . evidence of indebtedness, . . . investment contract, . . . or any certificate of interest or participation in . . . any of the foregoing.

15 U.S.C. § 77b(1). It is well-settled that certificates evidencing loans by commercial banks to their customers for use in the customers' current operations are not securities. *See, e.g., Reves v. Ernst & Young*, 494 U.S. 56, 65 (1990) (citing *Chemical Bank v. Arthur Andersen & Co.*, 726 F.2d 930, 939 (2d Cir.), *cert. denied*, 469 U.S. 884 (1984)). However, as the district court noted, a participation in an instrument might in some circumstances be considered a security even where the instrument itself is not. See *Banco Espanol de Credito*, 763 F. Supp. at 41.

With respect to loan participations, the district court reasoned that "because the plaintiffs . . . did not receive an undivided interest in a pool of loans, but rather purchased participation in a specific, identifiable short-term Integrated loan, the loan participation did not have an identity separate from the underlying loan." *Id*. at 42. Thus, Judge Pollack reasoned, because under *Chemical Bank* the loans to Integrated were not securities, the plaintiffs' purchase of discrete portions of these loans could not be considered securities.

On appeal, plaintiffs concede that traditional loan participations do not qualify as securities. Instead, plaintiffs contend that the peculiar nature of Security Pacific's loan participation program–which aimed at the sale of 100% of its loans through high speed telephonic sales and often pre-paid transactions–qualified these loan participations as securities. Specifically, plaintiffs argue that the loan participations sold by Security Pacific are more properly characterized as securities–in the nature of "notes"–as enumerated in § 2(1) of the 1933 Act.

In examining whether the loan participations could be considered "notes" which are also securities, the district court applied the "family resemblance" test set forth by the Supreme Court in *Reves*, 494 U.S. at 63-67. Under the family resemblance test, a note is presumed to be a security unless an examination of the note, based on four factors, reveals a strong resemblance between the note and one of a judicially-enumerated list of instruments that are not securities. *Id*. at 65. If the note in question is not sufficiently similar to one of these instruments, a court must then consider, using the same four factors, whether another category of non-security instruments should be added to the list. *Id*. at 67. The four *Reves* factors to be considered in this examination are: (1) the motivations that would prompt a reasonable buyer and seller to enter into the transaction; (2) the plan of distribution of the instrument; (3) the reasonable expectations of the investing public; and (4) whether some factor, such as the existence of another regulatory scheme, significantly reduces the risk of the instrument, thereby rendering application of the securities laws unnecessary. *Id*. at 66-67.

In addressing the first *Reves* factor, the district court found that Security Pacific was motivated by a desire to increase lines of credit to Integrated while diversifying Security Pacific's risk, that Integrated was motivated by a need for short-term credit at competitive rates to finance its current operations, and that the purchasers of the loan participations sought a short-term return on excess cash. Based on these findings, the district court concluded that "the overall motivation of the parties was the promotion of commercial purposes" rather than an investment in a business enterprise. *Banco Espanol de Credito*, 763 F. Supp. at 42-43.

Weighing the second *Reves* factor–the plan of distribution of the instrument–the district court observed that only institutional and corporate entities were solicited and that detailed individualized presentations were made by Security Pacific's sales personnel. The district court therefore concluded that the plan of distribution was "a limited solicitation to sophisticated financial or commercial institutions and not to the general public." *Id.* at 43. We agree.

The plan of distribution specifically prohibited resales of the loan participations without the express written permission of Security Pacific. This limitation worked to prevent the loan participations from being sold to the general public, thus limiting eligible buyers to those with the capacity to acquire information about the debtor. This limitation also distinguishes *Gary Plastic Packaging v. Merrill Lynch, Pierce, Fenner & Smith, Inc.*, 756 F.2d 230 (2d Cir. 1985), which involved a secondary market for the instruments traded in that case.

With regard to the third factor–the reasonable perception of the instrument by the investing public–the district court considered the expectations of the sophisticated purchasers who signed MPA's and determined that these institutions were given ample notice that the instruments were participations in loans and not investments in a business enterprise. *Id.*

Finally, the district court noted that the Office of the Comptroller of the Currency has issued specific policy guidelines addressing the sale of loan participations. Thus, the fourth factor–the existence of another regulatory scheme–indicated that application of the securities laws was unnecessary. *Id.*

Thus, under the *Reves* family resemblance analysis, as properly applied by the district court, we hold that the loan participations in the instant case are analogous to the enumerated category of loans issued by banks for commercial purposes and therefore do not satisfy the statutory definition of "notes" which are "securities." Since the loan participations do not meet the statutory definition of securities, plaintiffs may not maintain their action for relief under § 12(2) of the 1933 Act. . . .

Turning to plaintiffs' contractual and other common-law claims, we agree with the district court that the waiver provision in the MPA's signed by the loan participants specifically absolved Security Pacific of any responsibility to disclose information relating to Integrated's financial condition. Moreover, as an arms length transaction between sophisticated financial institutions, the law imposed no independent duty on Security Pacific to disclose information that plaintiffs could have discovered through their own efforts. *See, e.g., Aaron Ferer & Sons v. Chase Manhattan Bank*, 731 F.2d 112, 122 (2d Cir. 1984).

Based on the foregoing, and on Judge Pollack's well-reasoned opinion, we affirm the judgment of the district court.

## Comments and Questions

1. Putting aside the securities law issues for the moment, why isn't there a cause of action based on the common law of contracts? Why isn't the withholding of material, nonpublic information a violation of the obligation of good faith and fair dealing? To put it differently, one definition of a loan participation is a "transfer of risk from a party who lacks courage to one who lacks knowledge."

2. Turning to the securities law aspects of the case, the Securities and Exchange Commission, in a friend-of-the-court brief, argued that the loan participations were securities because they closely resemble commercial paper, which is admittedly subject to the federal securities laws. In addition, the SEC argued that Security Pacific had advertised its loan participations as competitive with commercial paper, had promoted sales with language and techniques used in the securities markets, and had conducted the loan participation activities from its trading department rather than its commercial loan department.

3. In the *Banco Espanol*, the Second Circuit applied a test the Supreme Court developed in Reves v. Ernst & Young, 494 U.S. 56 (1990). Consider the circuit's analysis of the second *Reves* factor, the plan of distribution of the instrument. While the majority opinion held that the bank's distribution plan was directed to sophisticated investors and not to the general public, should that be determinative? Or is the issue of sophistication of investors limited to the question of whether the securities have to be registered, not whether they are securities?

4. Consider the analysis of the fourth *Reves* factor, whether the existence of another regulatory regime reduces the risk of the instrument to the extent that there is no need to apply securities law. Is the OCC regulatory scheme sufficient to deal with issues of protection of investors? Note that the OCC regulation on banks' purchasing loan participations requires that each bank make an independent credit appraisal. For that to occur it would seem that the participants would require access to all material information in the lead bank's possession. Even if there were exculpatory provisions in the loan participation contract limiting the lead bank's liability and providing for an acknowledgment by the loan participant that it has made its own assessment of the credit worthiness of the borrower, would that be sufficient for the lead bank to avoid liability if the transaction were viewed as a security?

## C. Letters of Credit and Bankers' Acceptances

### 1. Rudiments of Letters of Credit

The commercial or documentary letter of credit is distinguished from the standby letter of credit in that the former is issued in connection with the direct purchase of merchandise or the presentation of title documents. The traditional purpose of the letter of credit is to facilitate trade, often international trade, by substituting the known credit worthiness of the bank for the credit worthiness of the buyer, which may be unknown to the seller. The letter of credit, in a sense, guarantees the exporter payment by the bank when specified documents are presented to the bank in accordance with the terms of the letter of credit.

To understand the commercial setting of letters of credit, it is first important to understand the three parties to a conventional letter of credit transaction and their obligations to one another. The three parties are the issuer of the letter of credit (typically a bank), the issuer's customer (typically a buyer of goods), and the beneficiary of the letter of credit (typically a seller of goods). Among these three parties there are three separate and distinct commercial agreements: (1) An underlying agreement for the sale of goods between the customer (buyer) and the beneficiary (seller) whereby the customer has an obligation to pay for the goods and the beneficiary agrees to obtain payment by drawing drafts under the letter of credit from the issuer (bank). (2) An agreement between the issuer and the customer whereby the issuer agrees to issue the letter of credit in favor of the beneficiary and the customer agrees to reimburse the issuer for payments made under the letter of credit. (3) The letter of credit itself, under which the issuer assumes the primary responsibility for paying the seller when drafts drawn under the letter of credit are accompanied by required documents.

Another important aspect is the level of risk assumed by the issuer. The issuer is well insulated from risk in a conventional letter of credit transaction for two reasons. First, if the issuer does pay on the letter of credit it immediately obtains documents of title representing the right to the underlying goods, having at least some value. Second, even absent substantial value in the goods, the issuer has a then-perfected claim against its customer for reimbursement—and the customer will typically have sufficient financial stability to perform its obligation to the issuer, even though the individual transaction was a failure.

An increasingly common business setting for the letter of credit has come to be known as the standby letter of credit. While both the three party and three agreement framework remain the same, the substance of two of the agreements changes. (1) The underlying agreement may be for the payment of a promissory note of the customer or for the performance of a contract by the customer. (2) The agreement between the issuer and the customer remains the same. (3) The letter of credit itself is critically different in its operative provisions. The issuer assumes the primary responsibility for paying drafts drawn under the letter of credit when accompanied simply by a writing stating that an event has occurred, such as nonpayment of a promissory note or noncompletion of construction of a building.

A standby letter of credit is riskier than a documentary letter of credit because the issuer exposes itself to a much greater likelihood of loss. The standby letter of credit will be utilized when the underlying transaction has *not* been properly performed–the promissory note has not been paid or the building has not been completed. And so, in return for paying out money, the issuer receives only the possibility of a judgment against its customer rather than the evidence of title to underlying goods. Furthermore, the very circumstances that caused the customer to be unable to perform its obligations on the underlying agreement will likely make it unable to perform its obligation to reimburse the issuer. As a result, the question faced by the issuer-bank is far more complex under a standby letter of credit. In a sense, it must predict the customer's performance, rather than predict the simpler obligation to pay.

Today, while letters of credit continue to be the prime financing medium in international trade, the domestic use of letters of credit has expanded greatly beyond traditional practice. Standby letters of credit are now used in numerous nonsale of goods transactions, in lieu of security deposits in government contracts, to guarantee performances under leases, construction contracts and managements contracts, and in aid of judicial proceedings. The only limits on their use in nonsale of goods transactions are the creative abilities of those who use them.

## 2. Rudiments of Bankers' Acceptances

The standby letter of credit can be viewed as a guarantee rather than as a commercial finance transaction: if the bank's customer doesn't pay, the bank will pay. Any authority that a national bank has to grant guarantees resides in the incidental powers clause of section 24(7), which grants powers "as shall be necessary to carry on the business of banking." The courts have not construed the powers clause to permit a national bank to guarantee another's obligation. Indeed, there are many early twentieth century cases that hold guarantee obligations by banks to be *ultra vires* and thus not enforceable. However, since the powers clause explicitly authorizes "discounting" and "negotiating" commercial paper, it contemplates and authorizes the making of commercial paper indorsements and similar contractual obligations, such as bankers' acceptances, that are effectively guarantees, but done in furtherance of a commercial finance transaction. Depending upon how one characterizes the obligation, one may similarly regard a bank's obligation on any letter of credit as no more than a guarantee that its customer will pay. But note the handling of commercial and standby letters of credit in 12 C.F.R. § 32.2(f), (j) and (p).

A bankers' acceptance is different from a letter of credit. A bankers' acceptance is created when a time draft (and typically other letter of credit documents such as the bill of lading for the goods sold) is presented to the bank by the exporter and the bank stamps the draft "accepted," thereby promising to pay the holder of the draft upon its maturity. And so, while a letter of credit is a contingent liability of the bank, a banker's acceptance creates a fixed liability. This distinguishes it from a commercial letter of credit, which is a contingent liability of the bank and is not reported on the bank's balance sheet.

Such trade acceptances have much to do with commercial letters of credit, but little to do with standby letters of credit. A bankers' acceptance that meets the criteria for eligibility for rediscount with a Federal Reserve Bank, as given in 12 U.S.C.A. § 372, is a marketable asset which the exporter can sell. Often, the accepting bank itself will discount the draft and remit cash to the exporter. Discounting occurs where the bank pays the exporter not the face value of the draft at maturity, but the reduced, current value–face value less the interest that could be earned on the reduced value until maturity. The bank then either holds the acceptance in its asset portfolio, in which case it is booked as a loan to its importer-customer, or sells the acceptance in a well established secondary market for such paper. In general, eligible acceptances are bankers' acceptances that meet all the requirements of 12 U.S.C.A. § 372 and are eligible for discount by a Federal Reserve Bank. Ineligible acceptances are bankers' acceptances that do not meet these requirements.

In general, an acceptance is eligible under § 372 if it (1) is used to finance a trade transaction involving exporting, importing or domestic shipment of goods or storage of readily marketable staples and (2) has a term to maturity at the time of discount of not more than six months sight (the time until actual payment). Section 372 also governs a bank's acceptance liabilities on an individual and aggregate basis and banks must report the volume of their acceptances outstanding.

The aggregate amount of eligible acceptances by an individual member bank cannot exceed 150 percent of the bank's capital and surplus, and up to 200 percent with the permission of the Federal Reserve. Eligible acceptances arising out of domestic transactions cannot exceed 50 percent of the aggregate acceptances permitted to the bank. However, any portion of an eligible acceptance created by a bank that is sold through participation agreements to another member bank need not be included in the calculation of the creating bank's aggregate limit on acceptances. Finally, unsecured eligible acceptances for one person are limited to 10 percent of the bank's capital stock and surplus. This limit may be exceeded if the bank is secured by documents of title representing the goods financed or by some other actual security growing out of the same transaction as the acceptance. No such regulation governs commercial letters of credit. Often a bankers' acceptance may be viewed as a product of a commercial letter of credit. *Any time draft accepted by a bank in fulfillment of its commitment on a letter of credit is a bankers' acceptance.*

### Problem 3-11

A national bank has a lending limit of $1.5 million. The bank approves a $4 million line of credit for a customer, and obtains a loan participation commitment in the "overline" portion from another bank. The line of credit is for asset-based financing of domestic and international trade. The line of credit may be used for letters of credit with up to 120-days sight, which would result in the creation of 120-day bankers' acceptances at the time the letters of credit are drawn upon. The beneficiaries of the letters of credit agree that they will receive payment at maturity, and not discount the bankers' acceptances.

The bank asks your advice in order to clarify the application of federal lending limit and bankers' acceptance law as the line of credit is utilized and acceptances are generated. First, suppose that the customer currently has a direct loan of $1.25 million from the bank and also has $2 million of commercial letters of credit outstanding. Is this permissible, or must the participation be implemented? Next, assume that all of the letters are drawn upon, giving rise to $2 million of 120-day acceptances. To what extent, if any, do the acceptances have to be participated? Would it matter if the bankers' acceptances were secured by the assets being purchased by the bank's customers? Would it matter if the bankers' acceptances are ineligible? What happens when the banker's acceptances are paid at maturity?

### Comments and Questions

1. While it is easy to distinguish commercial letters of credit from standby letters of credit, it is difficult to articulate a meaningful distinction between a standby letter of credit and a guarantee. One court decision found that a bank's standby obligation was not a guarantee, but a letter of credit, and therefore not *ultra vires*. *Barclay's Bank v. Mercantile National Bank*, 481 F.2d 1224 (5th Cir. 1973), *rehearing denied*, 481 F.2d 1403, *cert. dismissed*, 414 U.S. 1139 (1974). The "vast difference" that the court indorsed was that the "'issuer of a credit assumes a primary obligation to the beneficiary as opposed to a secondary liability under a guaranty.'" *Supra* at 1236, quoting Halls, The Uniform Commercial Code in Minnesota: Article 5–Letters of Credit, 50 Minn. L. Rev. 453 at 454 n. 3 (1966). Does that difference justify allowing banks to issue standby letters of credit but not guarantees, or does it arguably make guarantees safer, since there is an extra buffer (the bank's customer) between the bank and liability?

2. Subjecting standby letters of credit to the § 84 lending limit may not solve all of the problems. Consider the following problem.

### Problem 3-12

Weary Bank has decided to specialize in lending to commercial loan companies, *i.e.*, the bank does this by the use of something called documented discount notes. The loan company issues commercial paper and sells it in the commercial paper market accompanied by the standby letter of credit of the bank. The letter of credit promises that the bank will pay a holder of loan company commercial paper upon a certification by the holder that the loan company has defaulted. For any one loan company, the total of standby letters of credit does not exceed the bank's section 84 lending limit of $600,000.

Weary Bank has total assets of $50,000,000, with $35,000,000 out in loans. The bank also has outstanding $45,000,000 of standby letters of credit. Is such an aggregation of loans and letters of credit permissible? Should it be? Could the bank issue an equal amount of eligible acceptances?

Suppose that a depression comes which particularly affects customers of loan companies. Loan companies are not receiving loan payments from their customers and cannot pay off their commercial paper. Could the result be numerous simultaneous defaults and numerous demands on the bank's letters of credit? Is there any difference between this and a bank that concentrates its loans in a single line of business, such as petroleum exploration?

## D. Lease Transactions

Banks typically are in the business of lending money. For tax and other reasons it is common for users of goods to lease rather than to purchase goods such as airplanes, automobiles and ships. As part of the business of banking under § 24(7) banks have been allowed to finance not only the purchase, but also the long-term leasing of goods for periods approaching the useful life of the goods. Such long-term, or financing, leases are the functional equivalent of loans, as the lease payment terms provide for payment to the bank-lessor of the full value of the underlying goods plus the time-value of the money (interest) used by the bank to purchase the goods initially.

The Competitive Equality Banking Act of 1987 added § 24(10). It expressly empowers national banks to engage in an additional segment of the leasing market–the short-term lease of goods for a term that may not earn back the full cost of the goods, thus requiring the bank-lessor to sell or re-lease the item in order to recover the entire value of the bank's investment. The statute represents an additional power to engage in leasing transactions that may not be the functional equivalent of the power to lend money under § 24(7).

*Problem 3-13*

First National Bank wishes to expand its activities in accordance with the powers now allowed under 12 U.S.C.A. § 24(10). Please advise the bank whether it may engage in the following leasing activities. See 12 C.F.R. Pt. 23.

1. Suppose a bank with assets of $1 billion and a lending limit of $12 million has a customer that wishes to purchase a Boeing 747, with a useful life of 20 years, for $50 million. Rather than creating a loan participation, could the bank purchase the airplane for $50 million and then lease it to the customer for one year for $7 million? Could the bank lease the airplane to the customer for two years for $13.5 million? See 12 C.F.R. § 23.6.

2. In setting the lease rental price, is there any limitation on the percentage of the investment in the leased property that the bank may anticipate recovering from the residual value–the expected value of the equipment at resale after the termination of the lease–rather than from the lease payments? See 12 C.F.R. § 23.2(e).

3. If goods are owned but not under short-term lease, is there any timeframe before the bank is required to dispose of the property by sale or write-off of the remaining book value?

4. Can the bank use its bulk purchasing power in order to receive lower prices when purchasing numerous items of construction equipment, such as cranes and generators, to be leased over time to yet undetermined bank customers? See 12 C.F.R. § 23.4(a).

## E. Real Estate Lending and Ownership

Real estate has a special place in the history of bank powers. From the original passage of the National Bank Act in 1863 until 1913, national banks were prohibited from lending against real estate. From 1913 until 1982, there were a series of substantial regulatory limitations on real estate lending, particularly including loan-to-value ratios. From 1913 until 1974, federal law also took the position that, because real estate loans represented illiquid assets, such loans should be tied to the most stable bank deposit liabilities. Consequently, total real estate loans were limited to 25% of a bank's capital and surplus accounts or to 33% of its savings deposits. The Garn-St Germain Depository Institutions Act of 1982 removed the remaining statutory restrictions on national banks' real estate lending and made them subject only to terms, conditions and limitations as prescribed by the Comptroller. These regulations provided that real estate loans were limited only by the concept of safe and sound banking practices, and thus were essentially just as free of limits as are commercial, industrial, and consumer loans.

The banking industry has had many bad experiences with real estate lending. The 1975-76 collapse of real estate investment trusts, with substantial bank debt, brought on a major crisis and subsequent real estate loan problems. During the 1980s a variety of real estate lending problems occurred. In the early 1980s, oil prices dropped precipitously. Later, agricultural earnings declined and the price of agricultural land also declined. In the late 1980s there was a major downturn in the commercial real estate markets. At the same time, real estate lending as percentage of all banks loans had grown dramatically. In 1950, real estate loans were 8% of commercial bank assets. In 1980, the figure was 14.5%. By 1992 real estate loans were about 25% of total assets, and had replaced commercial and industrial loans as the largest sector of bank lending activity. Not only had the size of real estate loans changed but so had their makeup, as a higher percentage was based in construction and permanent financing for commercial real estate projects, while a lower percentage was in less risky mortgages for family residences.

Transactions of national banks involving real estate are governed primarily by five different sections of 12 U.S.C.A.: §§ 24(7), 29, 371, 371d and 1828(o). Section 24(7), in its elaboration of the business of banking, speaks of "loaning money on personal security." By negative implication, the section suggests that loaning money on real estate as security is not part of the business of banking. From 1913 until 1982, § 371 specially empowered banks to engage in real estate lending and provided numerous statutory restrictions on such lending. The Garn-St Germain Depository Institutions Act removed these restrictions.

But the Federal Deposit Insurance Corporation Improvement Act of 1991 added 12 U.S.C.A. § 1828(o), which requires the federal banking agencies to adopt uniform regulations prescribing standards for real estate lending, in order to reduce the risk to the deposit insurance funds. The rules that were established are quite general, simply requiring such items as loan portfolio diversification standards and prudent underwriting standards. However, accompanying the rules are interagency guidelines for real estate lending policies. See 12 C.F.R. Pt. 34, Subpart D, Appendix A. While these guidelines cut back on the complete removal of limitations enacted in 1982, they are still liberal in historical context. In particular, the guidelines establish supervisory loan-to-value limits as follows:

For raw land, a loan to value ratio of 65%;

For real estate developments loans, 75%;

For commercial construction, including condominiums, 80%;

For construction of 1 to 4 family residences, 85%;

For improved property, 85%.

Banks are allowed to have loans that are outside of these loan to value guidelines, and such loans are called exception loans. Total exception loans should not exceed 100% of an institution's total capital; exception loans for other than 1 to 4 family residences should not exceed 30% of total capital. Finally, the fact that a loan is within the LTV limits does not mean that the loan is automatically sound.

After loans, the second major aspect of national bank involvement in real estate transactions is ownership. Two sections apply. Section 29 initially provides for ownership of real estate necessary for the bank's accommodation in the transaction of its business. Otherwise, real estate not utilized as bank premises may only be owned by a national bank if it is allowed by the remainder of § 29. Such real estate is often referred to as OREO—other real estate owned. In addition to bank premises, under § 29 a national bank may own real estate only if it is mortgaged to the bank as security for debts previously contracted, conveyed to it in payment of debts previously contracted, purchased by it at sale under judgments, or purchased by it to secure debts due to the bank.

Section 371d limits bank investment in bank premises to 100 percent of the capital of the bank. The theory behind this provision is that only bank capital and not depositors' funds should be exposed to the risks of real estate speculation. To facilitate this goal, as well as to rechannel bank capital throughout the community and to prevent mass accumulation of real property by banks, no national bank may hold real estate obtained through mortgage foreclosure or the like for longer than five years. There are limited exceptions.

*Problem 3-14*

1. Halfbright has an unsecured $10,000 loan from Fulbright National Bank. Faced with business losses, Halfbright offers to give Fulbright a mortgage to some property he owns in Hartford worth $7,500. Fulbright agrees, and also insists that Halfbright pay a $500 prior lien on the property, held by Albright, so that Albright will not foreclose. Halfbright is unable to meet the obligation to Albright. To protect its own lien, Fulbright suggests to you, its chief legal advisor, that the bank pay the $500 due to Albright and take

an additional note and mortgage for that amount on a second, adjacent property owned by Halfbright in Hartford. The bank wants to know if these transactions violate § 29.

2. Halfbright's business has driven him to the brink of bankruptcy. Fulbright has purchased the Hartford properties to which it held the mortgages. After holding the properties for over four years, Fulbright decides to attract a larger share of the market by erecting a magnificent twenty-five story skyscraper at that location. The bank will maintain its offices on the first three floors of the structure. Other local banks claim that since Fulbright will be using such a minor portion of the edifice, it may not retain the land as necessary for the transaction of its business. Therefore, the bank will have to give up the property within the year. Again the officers of Fulbright rush to you for advice. What will you tell them? If you advise that they can build the building, could they do the same at their various branch locations? See 12 U.S.C.A. § 371d.

3. Fulbright issued a standby letter of credit to a borrower who was engaged in the development of a resort property and took a second mortgage on the property as security. The bank issued the standby letter of credit on the borrower's behalf to guarantee payment of another institution's construction real estate loan to the borrower. When the borrower defaulted, Fulbright was compelled to fund the letter of credit. The bank also has advanced funds to pay the operating expenses of the resort. Are the advances an additional loan to the borrower, subject to the § 84 lending limit, or are they an expenditure on OREO property subject to the separate provisions of § 29? Would it make a difference if Fulbright foreclosed on the resort property?

# Section 5.  Transactions in Money Market Instruments and Investment Securities

## A.  Introduction

Banks engage in a wide variety of credit granting activities in addition to traditional lending. These activities include the sale of federal funds (money loaned and borrowed between banks), and the purchase and sale of government and corporate bonds (investment securities).

These transactions can often be viewed as large credit transactions with virtually no regulatory limits, but with some risk, however small. It could be said that these transactions often are in the nature of loans, but are not viewed as loans for regulatory purposes.

## B.  Federal Funds

Federal funds activities are the borrowing and lending of commercial bank balances between banks, usually based on deposit balances at a Federal Reserve Bank or at a correspondent depository institution. Banks with excess funds on any particular day may lend those funds to other banks, typically as overnight loans. Such federal funds transactions are unsecured loans, *prima facie* subject to the lending limits of § 84. However, 12 C.F.R. § 32.2(j)(1)(vi) provides that only sales of federal funds with a maturity of more than one day are subject to the lending limit, consequently exempting overnight loans.

Funds may be borrowed simply to increase funds available for lending to customers, rather than for meeting reserve requirements. In addition, several banks borrow and lend funds on the same day, thus performing an intermediary role in the market. These banks channel funds from banks with a lesser need to banks with a greater need, frequently borrowing from smaller banks and lending to larger ones.

Some small banks intentionally accumulate large balances, selling the excess which is not needed for clearing checks or other purposes on a daily basis.

### Problem 3-15

Rural Bank has deposits of $28,000,000, capital and surplus of $3,000,000, and loans of $2,000,000. Most of its remaining assets are in federal funds, with $10,000,000 at Piggie Bank on an overnight basis. Is this a violation of § 84? See 12 C.F.R. § 32.2(j)(1)(vi). Suppose that while the funds are technically loaned on an overnight basis, in fact $10,000,000 has been at Piggie Bank for the last year and a half. Any different result? Would your answer be different if it were discovered that Piggie Bank had made long-term loans totaling $10,000,000 to three long-time customers of Rural Bank? In either case, what happens if Piggie Bank fails?

## C.  Bank Investments

Investments have been part of banking activities at least since the National Bank Act in 1863. Recall that one of the primary motivations for the enactment of the National Bank Act was to have the banks available to sell government securities to citizens of the United States. Today banks have an express power to engage in the purchase of such investment securities for their own portfolios under section 24(7).

Transactions in investment securities under § 24(7) are distinct and separate from loans under § 84. 12 C.F.R. § 32.1(c)(2). And so, transactions in investment securities are governed solely by § 24(7) and 12 C.F.R. Pt. 1. The rules apply not only to national banks but also to member banks, under 12 U.S.C.A. § 335.

To qualify as an investment security the instrument must be both marketable and of investment grade (not speculative). A security is marketable if it can be sold with reasonable promptness at a price which corresponds with its fair value. It is of investment grade and not speculative if it is so rated by a nationally recognized statistical rating organization. See 12 C.F.R. § 1.2 (d) - (g).

Investment securities are grouped into five categries, types I-V. Type I securities, U.S. treasury obligations and general obligations of state and municipal governments, are not subject to any restrictions on amount purchased, underwritten or dealt in.  Type II securities are obligations of certain federally created agencies and state housing, university and dormitory agencies.  Type III securities are investment securities that do not qualify as Type I, II, IV or V securities, such as municipal revenue bonds and corporate debt instruments.  A bank may not hold Type II or III securities of any one obligor in excess of 10% of capital and surplus.  Further, a bank may deal in and underwrite Type II, but not Type III, securities.  See 12 U.S.C.A. § 24 (7).

Type IV and V securities are derived from the Secondary Mortgage Market Enhancement Act of 1984 and the Riegle Community Development and Regulatory Improvement Act of 1994, which amended 12 U.S.C.A. 24(7) by removing quantitative limits on national banks' purchases of mortgage- and small business-related securities that are composed of a pool of loans to numerous obligors, subject to regulations issued by the Comptroller. Consequently, national banks now have broader authority to invest in certain mortgage and small business asset-backed securities sold in the secondary capital markets.

Until the last few decades, investment securities have fluctuated little in value because they ordinarily are only interest rate sensitive.  Consequently, they have been both a safe asset and a ready source with which to meet sudden and immediate demands for funds by customers.  It may be worthwhile to keep in mind the history and purposes of the investment securities power as you consider the following problem.

### Problem 3-16

A good customer of X Bank is Rollerskate Manufacturing Inc., which has reached its § 84 lending limit.  Rollerskate has tentatively worked out an arrangement with the local County Industrial Development Authority whereby the Industrial Development Authority will issue tax exempt industrial development bonds, whose proceeds will be utilized by the Authority to construct a manufacturing facility for Rollerskate in the industrial park.  The bonds are to be repaid from lease payments made by Rollerskate to the Authority.

The local Industrial Development Authority is a rather small entity.  In fact, X Bank negotiated the terms of the industrial development bonds directly with Rollerskate and intends to purchase the entire issue of bonds.  Rollerskate is an unrated company whose other securities are not traded publicly.  Is this a permissible bank activity involving Type I, II, or III investment securities?

Would it make any difference if one-third of the bonds were purchased by X Bank and the remainder by two other local banks?  Could the banks sell the bonds to local residents and, perhaps, make a local market in the bonds?  See 12 C.F.R. §§ 1.2, 1.3 and 32.1.  Should the loans to Rollerskate and the purchase of bonds from the Industrial Development Authority  be combined under 12 C.F.R. § 32.5?

## Comments & Questions

1.  Should there be a statutory limit on the percentage of assets that banks hold in investment securities, based on the argument that lending money in the private economy is a principal reason why banks have quasi-public charters and deposit insurance?

2.  Why do we allow banks to invest and deal in government securities?  If it is primarily to provide liquidity for deposit withdrawals and the increase and decrease in credit granting activities through economic cycles, do all such securities satisfy that purpose?

3.  Suppose that a bank holds a considerable portion of its assets in long-term state and local government bonds that have little credit quality risk.  Do you see any other risks that may be involved?

# Section 6.  Deposits, Deposit Insurance, and Other Forms of Guarantee For Deposits and Nondeposit Liabilities

## A.  Introduction

One of the central forces behind both bank stability and bank regulation is the Federal Deposit Insurance Corporation's backing of deposits up to $100,000. Consideration of the scope and consequences of deposit insurance raise many questions. Just how extensive is the FDIC guarantee?  Exactly what bank liabilities are covered by the guarantee?  If a bank liability is excluded, either from the definition of deposit or from insurance coverage of deposits because it is above $100,000, can the bank otherwise guarantee the liability by granting a perfected security interest, by entering into a trust arrangement, or by some other methodology?  Finally, what are the implications of the 1993 legislation (12 U.S.C.A. § 1821(d)(11)) providing for depositor preference over general, unsecured creditors in a bank failure?

The Great Depression resulted in a general collapse of the banking system and of public confidence in it, causing people to withhold their money from banks and causing banks to have great difficulty in engaging in the ordinary banking activities of using deposits to support loans and other commercial banking activities.  One significant response was the establishment of the federal deposit insurance system for depository institutions, as a way to restore public confidence and to restart the deposit system, so as to provide the funds necessary to encourage economic activity through bank lending.

Confidence was restored and the banking system was quite stable until the late 1970s. Permissible activities of banks were thought to be rather limited and traditional, and there was strict regulation of interest rates on deposits.  The situation began to change with legislation in 1980 and 1982 which eliminated federal ceilings on interest rates that banks could pay on deposits and allowed more diversified activities, particularly for savings and loan associations. State legislatures went even further in allowing state chartered savings and loan associations significantly expanded investment authorities, which ultimately led to substantial losses in commercial real estate and other activities. As depository institutions began to fail in the early 1980s, the concept of deposit insurance suddenly became important, as uninsured depositors, and other unsecured general creditors of failed institutions, were exposed to the possibility of substantial losses.

And so, it is important to understand both the extent to which bank liabilities are covered by deposit insurance and the other ways that bank creditors may otherwise gain security or guarantee.

## B. Deposits

The term "deposit" is defined in 12 U.S.C.A. § 1813(l). Consider the following case.

## Federal Deposit Insurance Corp. v. Philadelphia Gear Corp.
### 476 U.S. 426 (1986)

Justice O'CONNOR delivered the opinion of the Court.

We granted certiorari to consider whether a standby letter of credit backed by a contingent promissory note is insured as a "deposit" under the federal deposit insurance program. We hold that, in light of the longstanding interpretation of petitioner Federal Deposit Insurance Corporation (FDIC) that such a letter does not create a deposit and, in light of the fact that such a letter does not entrust any noncontingent assets to the bank, a standby letter of credit backed by a contingent promissory note does not give rise to an insured deposit.

I

Orion Manufacturing Corporation (Orion) was, at the time of the relevant transactions, a customer of respondent Philadelphia Gear Corporation (Philadelphia Gear). On Orion's application, the Penn Square Bank, N.A. (Penn Square) issued a letter of credit for the benefit of Philadelphia Gear in the amount of $145,200. The letter of credit provided that a draft drawn upon the letter of credit would be honored by Penn Square only if accompanied by Philadelphia Gear's "signed statement that [it had] invoiced Orion Manufacturing Corporation and that said invoices have remained unpaid for at least fifteen (15) days." App. 25. Because the letter of credit was intended to provide payment to the seller only if the buyer of the invoiced goods failed to make payment, the letter of credit was what is commonly referred to as a "standby" or "guaranty" letter of credit. *See, e.g.,* 12 CFR § 337.2(a), and n.1 (1985) (defining standby letters of credit and mentioning that they may "'guaranty' payment of a money obligation"). A conventional "commercial" letter of credit, in contrast, is one in which the seller obtains payment from the issuing bank without looking to the buyer for payment even in the first instance. See *ibid.* (distinguishing standby letters of credit from commercial letters of credit). . . .

On the same day that Penn Square issued the standby letter of credit, Orion executed an unsecured promissory note for $145,200 in favor of Penn Square. App. 27. The purpose of the note was listed as "Back up Letter of Credit." *Ibid.* Although the face of the note did not so indicate, both Orion and Penn Square understood that nothing would be considered due on the note, and no interest charged by Penn Square, unless Philadelphia Gear presented drafts on the standby letter of credit after nonpayment by Orion. 751 F.2d 1131, 1134 (CA10 1984). *See also* Tr. of Oral Arg. 32.

On July 5, 1982, Penn Square was declared insolvent. Petitioner FDIC was appointed its receiver. Shortly thereafter, Philadelphia Gear presented drafts on the standby letter of credit for payment of over $700,000 for goods delivered before Penn Square's insolvency. The FDIC returned the drafts unpaid. 751 F.2d at 1133-1134.

Philadelphia Gear sued the FDIC in the Western District of Oklahoma. Philadelphia Gear alleged that the standby letter of credit was an insured deposit under the definition of "deposit" set forth at 12 U.S.C. § 1813(l)(1), and that Philadelphia Gear was therefore entitled to $100,000 in deposit insurance from the FDIC. See 12 U.S.C. § 1821(a)(1) (setting forth $100,000 as the maximum amount generally insured by the FDIC for any single depositor at a given bank). . . .

As to the definition of "deposit," the Court of Appeals held that a standby letter of credit backed by a promissory note fell within the terms of 12 U.S.C. § 1813(l)(1)'s definition of "deposit," and was therefore insured. *Id.*, at 1134-1138. We granted the FDIC's petition for certiorari on this aspect of the Court of Appeals' ruling. 474 U.S. 918 (1985). We now reverse.

## II

Title 12 U.S.C. § 1813(l)(1) provides:

The term 'deposit' means–(1) the unpaid balance of money or its equivalent received or held by a bank in the usual course of business and for which it has given or is obligated to give credit, either conditionally or unconditionally, to a commercial . . . account, or which is evidenced by . . . a letter of credit or a traveler's check on which the bank is primarily liable: Provided, That, without limiting the generality of the term "money or its equivalent," any such account or instrument must be regarded as evidencing the receipt of the equivalent of money when credited or issued in exchange for checks or drafts or for a promissory note upon which the person obtaining any such credit or instrument is primarily or secondarily liable. . . .

Philadelphia Gear successfully argued before the Court of Appeals that the standby letter of credit backed by a contingent promissory note constituted a "deposit" under 12 U.S.C. § 1813(l)(1) because that letter was one on which the bank was primarily liable, and evidenced the receipt by the bank of "money or its equivalent" in the form of a promissory note upon which the person obtaining the credit was primarily or secondarily liable. The FDIC does not here dispute that the bank was primarily liable on the letter of credit. Brief for Petitioner 7, n.7. Nor does the FDIC contest the fact that the backup note executed by Orion is, at least in some sense, a "promissory note." See Tr. of Oral Arg. 7 (remarks of Mr. Rothfeld, representing the FDIC) ("It was labeled a note. It can be termed a note"). The FDIC argues rather that it has consistently interpreted § 1813(l)(1) not to include standby letters of credit backed only by a contingent promissory note because such a note represents no hard assets and thus does not constitute "money or its equivalent." Because the alleged "deposit" consists only of a *contingent* liability, asserts the FDIC, a standby letter of credit backed by a contingent promissory note does not give rise to a "deposit" that Congress intended the FDIC to insure. Under this theory, while the note here may have been labeled a promissory note on its face and may have been a promissory note under state law, it was not a promissory note for purposes of the federal law set forth in 12 U.S.C. § 1813(l)(1). . . .

The Court of Appeals quite properly looked first to the language of the statute. See *Florida Power & Light Co. v. Lorion*, 470 U.S. 729, 735 (1985); *United States v. Yermian*, 468 U.S. 63, 68 (1984). Finding the language of the proviso in § 1813(l)(1) sufficiently plain, the Court of Appeals looked no further. But as the FDIC points out, the terms "letter of credit" and "promissory note" as used in the statute have a federal definition, and the FDIC has developed and interpreted those definitions for many years within the framework of the complex statutory scheme that the FDIC administers. The FDIC's interpretation of whether a standby letter of credit backed by a contingent promissory note constitutes a "deposit" is consistent with Congress' desire to protect the hard earnings of individuals by providing for federal deposit insurance. Since the creation of the FDIC, Congress has expressed no dissatisfaction with the FDIC's interpretation of "deposit"; indeed, Congress in 1960 adopted the FDIC's regulatory definition as the statutory language. When we weigh all these factors together, we are constrained to conclude that the term "deposit" does not include a standby letter of credit backed by a contingent promissory note.

### A

. . . Congress' purpose in creating the FDIC was clear. Faced with virtual panic, Congress attempted to safeguard the hard earnings of individuals against the possibility that bank failures would deprive them of their savings. Congress passed the 1933 provisions "[i]n order to provide against a repetition of the present painful experience in which a vast sum of *assets and purchasing power* is 'tied up.'" S. Rep. No. 77, 73d Cong., 1st Sess., 12 (1933) (emphasis added). The focus of Congress was therefore upon ensuring that a deposit of "hard earnings" entrusted by individuals to a bank would not lead to a tangible loss in the event of a bank failure.

. . . [I]n light of the fact that instruments denominated "promissory notes" seem at the time to have been considered exclusively uncontingent, . . . it is unlikely that Congress would have had occasion to refer expressly to contingent notes such as the one before us here even if Congress had turned its attention to the definition of "deposit" when it first enacted the provision treating "money or its equivalent." . . . .

Congress' focus in providing for a system of deposit insurance–a system that has been continued to the present without modification to the basic definition of deposits that are "money or its equivalent"–was clearly a focus upon safeguarding the assets and "hard earnings" that businesses and individuals have entrusted to banks. Congress wanted to ensure that someone who put tangible assets into a bank could always get those assets back. The purpose behind the insurance of deposits in general, and especially in the section defining deposits as "money or its equivalent," therefore, is the protection of assets and hard earnings entrusted to a bank.

This purpose is not furthered by extending deposit insurance to cover a standby letter of credit backed by a contingent promissory note, which involves no such surrender of assets or hard earnings to the custody of the bank. Philadelphia Gear, which now seeks to collect deposit insurance, surrendered absolutely nothing to the bank. The letter of credit is for Philadelphia Gear's benefit, but the bank relied upon Orion to meet the obligations of the letter of credit and made no demands upon Philadelphia Gear. Nor, more importantly, did Orion surrender any assets unconditionally to the bank. The bank did not credit any account of Orion's in exchange for the promissory note, and did not treat its own assets as increased by its acceptance of the note. The bank could not have collected on the note from Orion unless Philadelphia Gear presented the unpaid invoices and a draft on the letter of credit. In the absence of a presentation by Philadelphia Gear of the unpaid invoices, the promissory note was a wholly contingent promise, and when Penn Square went into receivership, neither Orion nor Philadelphia Gear had lost anything except the ability to use Penn Square to reduce Philadelphia Gear's risk that Philadelphia Gear would go unpaid for a delivery of goods to Orion.

B

. . . . In 1960, Congress expanded the statutory definition of "deposit" in several categories, and also incorporated the regulatory definition that the FDIC had employed since 1935 into the statute that remains in force today. . . .

At no point did Congress disown its initial, clear desire to protect the hard assets of depositors. See *supra*, at 1935-1937. At no point did Congress criticize the FDIC's longstanding interpretation, see *infra*, at 1938-1939, that a standby letter of credit backed by a contingent promissory note is not a "deposit." In fact, Congress had reenacted the 1935 provisions in 1950 without changing the definition of "deposit" at all. Compare 49 Stat. 685-686 with 64 Stat. 874-875. When the statute giving rise to the longstanding interpretation has been reenacted without pertinent change, the "congressional failure to revise or repeal the agency's interpretation is persuasive evidence that the interpretation is the one intended by Congress." *NLRB v. Bell Aerospace*, 416 U.S. 267, 275 (1974). . . .

C

Although the FDIC does not argue that it has an express regulation excluding a standby letter of credit backed by a contingent promissory note from the definition of "deposit" in 12 U.S.C. § 1813(l)(1), that exclusion by the FDIC is nonetheless longstanding and consistent. At a meeting of FDIC and bank officials shortly after the FDIC's creation, a bank official asked whether a letter of credit issued by a charge against a customer's account was a deposit. The FDIC official replied:

"'If your letter of credit is issued by a charge against a depositor's account or for cash and the letter of credit is reflected on your books as a liability, you do have a deposit liability. If, on the other hand, you merely extend a line of credit to your customer, you will only show a contingent liability on your books. In that event no deposit liability has been created.'" Transcript as quoted in *FDIC v. Irving Trust Co.*, 137 F. Supp. 145, 161 (SDNY 1955).

Because Penn Square apparently never reflected the letter of credit here as a noncontingent liability, and because the interwoven financial instruments at issue here can be viewed most accurately as the extension of a line of credit by Penn Square to Orion, this transcript lends support to the FDIC's contention that its longstanding policy has been to exclude standby letters of credit backed by contingent promissory notes from 12 U.S.C. § 1813(l)(1)'s definition of "deposit."

The FDIC's contemporaneous understanding that standby letters of credit backed by contingent promissory notes do not generate a "deposit" for purposes of 12 U.S.C. § 1813(l)(1) has been fortified by its behavior over the following decades. The FDIC has asserted repeatedly that it has never charged deposit insurance premiums on standby letters of credit backed by contingent promissory notes, and Philadelphia Gear does not contest that assertion. . . .

Although the FDIC's interpretation of the relevant statute has not been reduced to a specific regulation, we conclude nevertheless that the FDIC's practice and belief that a standby letter of credit backed by a contingent promissory note does not create a "deposit" within the meaning of 12 U.S.C. § 1813(l)(1) are entitled in the circumstances of this case to the "considerable weight [that] should be accorded to an executive department's construction of a statutory scheme it is entrusted to administer." *Chevron U.S.A. Inc. v. Natural Resources Defense Council, Inc.*, 467 U.S. 837, 844 (1984). As we have stated above, the FDIC's interpretation here of a statutory definition adopted wholesale from the FDIC's own regulation is consistent with congressional purpose, and may certainly stand.

### III

Philadelphia Gear essentially seeks to have the FDIC guarantee the contingent credit extended to Orion, not assets entrusted to the bank by Philadelphia Gear or by Orion on Philadelphia Gear's behalf. With a standard "commercial" letter of credit, Orion would typically have unconditionally entrusted Penn Square with funds before Penn Square would have written the letter of credit, and thus Orion would have lost something if Penn Square became unable to honor its obligations. As the FDIC concedes, deposit insurance extends to such a letter of credit backed by an uncontingent promissory note. See Tr. of Oral Arg. 8 (statement of Mr. Rothfeld, representing the FDIC) ("If this note were a fully uncontingent negotiable note that were not limited by any side agreements, it would be a note backing a letter of credit within the meaning of the statute"). *See also id.* at 17-18. But here, with a standby letter of credit backed by a contingent promissory note, Penn Square was not in possession of any of Orion's or Philadelphia Gear's assets when it went into receivership. Nothing was ventured, and therefore no insurable deposit was lost. We believe that, whatever the relevant State's definition of "letter of credit" or "promissory note," Congress did not by using those phrases in 12 U.S.C. § 1813(l)(1) intend to protect with deposit insurance a standby letter of credit backed only by a contingent promissory note. We thus hold that such an arrangement does not give rise to a "deposit" under 12 U.S.C. § 1813(l)(1).

Accordingly, the judgment of the court below is reversed, and the case is remanded for further proceedings consistent with this opinion.

### Comments and Questions

1. 12 U.S.C.A. § 1813(l) defines deposits more broadly than a layperson might define the term. Isn't the language of the statute clear in determining that the beneficiary of a standby letter of credit holds a "deposit"?

2. How can the Court say that a standby letter of credit does not evidence money or its equivalent? The bank had issued a letter of credit and was primarily liable on it. While the Court agreed with this point, it went on to say that Orion had not given "money or its equivalent" to the bank. But hadn't Orion given Penn Square a promissory note and did not Philadelphia Gear sell assets in reliance?

3. Can you find anything about "hard earnings" in the statute? The source for this phrase is something the Supreme Court rarely pays attention to, legislative history from a discussion on the floor of the House of Representatives. What type of statutory interpretation methodology is this? Neither the statute nor any FDIC regulation contained such a suggestion.

4. On policy grounds, would "hard earnings" be an insufficient elaboration of "deposit"?

---

The term "insured deposit" is defined in 12 U.S.C.A. § 1813(m). Under 12 U.S.C.A. § 1821(a) the FDIC insures up to $100,000 of deposits held "in the same capacity and the same right." This phrase has often led the FDIC into the courts. The general, critical issue is whether various deposit accounts are in different categories of legal ownership, and so are entitled to separate deposit insurance within the $100,000 limit. Generally speaking, the FDIC recognizes several distinct categories of legal ownership: 1) individual; 2) joint; 3) a testamentary trust or revocable trust; 4) an irrevocable trust; 5) retirement and employee benefit accounts; 6) accounts held for another such as executor, custodian, or fiduciary; 7) business accounts; and 8) public unit accounts.

For 1), all individual ownership accounts of one person are added together. For 2), joint ownership accounts are separately insured from individual ownership accounts. For 3), testamentary or revocable trust accounts commonly involve Totten trust accounts or payable-on-death accounts. There are kinship restrictions on such accounts—they must include a relationship such as spouse, child or grandchild, and there must be an expressed indication of intention to have the account belong to the named beneficiary upon death of the grantor. For 4), an irrevocable trust is separate from any account of the grantor, trustee or beneficiary, if the trust is valid under state law and the account records indicate the existence of the trust and the beneficiary. For 5), all self-directed retirement accounts of a person are aggregated for insurance purposes. These include IRA accounts, Keogh accounts, self-directed defined contribution accounts and § 457 plan accounts. Other employee benefit plan accounts such as pension and profit sharing plans are viewed as separate accounts. For 6), accounts held for another are typically aggregated with the accounts of the other person. For example, the account of an executor is combined with that of the deceased owner, and the account of a guardian or custodian is added to any other account of that beneficiary. For 7), as for business accounts, there is separate insurance coverage for each entity that is engaged in an "independent activity," but divisions of one corporation are not separate. For 8), public unit accounts are usually treated separately for insurance coverage purposes if each account is either through a different custodian or for a different purpose. Consider the following problem.

*Problem 3-17*

Ozzie and Harriet, husband and wife, have a joint account with $75,000 in it at Fly-By-Night Bank of Michigan, a commercial bank insured by the FDIC. Ozzie has a separate checking account at the bank in his name alone, also with $75,000, and a savings account with $50,000. Ozzie also has a $75,000 account in his own name at the Detroit Savings Bank, which is also insured by the FDIC. Ozzie and Harriet have a 15-year old son, Ricky, who has amassed a small fortune of $25,000 by selling used editions of Gilbert's Law Outlines at discount prices. Ricky keeps his treasury in a separate account at Fly-By-Night. Harriet is settlor of a $100,000 irrevocable trust deposit at Fly-By-Night of which Ricky is beneficiary. Ozzie wins $100,000 in the Michigan lottery, and puts the proceeds in a certificate of deposit at Fly-by-Night as custodian for Ricky under the Uniform Gifts to Minor's Act, hoping that it will pay for a semester's tuition at Penn State University when Ricky is ready to attend college. Harriet's parents, Mickey and Matilda, sold their house for $220,000. Those funds are currently in their checking account at Fly-By-Night. Mickey and Matilda are moving into a retirement community which will charge them rent for an apartment at approximately $1,500 a month. Their plan was to use the checking account for their retirement household needs. Fly-By-Night closes its doors, never to reopen them. What will Ozzie, Harriet, Ricky, Mickey and Matilda receive from the FDIC?

## C. Brokered Deposits

The lifting of interest rates ceilings in the early 1980s created a new industry, the deposit brokerage industry. Individual banks were permitted to offer whatever interest rates they wished, and could pay a fee to brokers for obtaining deposits. Both Wall Street securities firms and other money brokers immediately began to move substantial funds in and out of various depository institutions as they chased the highest interest rates. This was done either by taking a large account and breaking it into $100,000 units, or taking small accounts and aggregating them. There was little concern about the long-term viability of the depository institutions because, so long as the deposits were in units of $100,000 or less, they were fully insured against loss. All that was required was compliance with the recordkeeping and disclosure standards.

The problem was a classic moral hazard risk transfer, with the weakest depository institutions typically offering the highest interest rates. In effect, the existence of the federal guarantee of deposit insurance resulted in deposits being directed to the firms having the greatest risk of loss. Since the loss would be covered by the FDIC, and not by the depositor, this risk shifting activity exposed the FDIC to substantial risk of loss.

The position of the FDIC was that such activity was not the purpose for which deposit insurance was developed; rather deposit insurance was to insure peoples' grocery money, the stable core deposits of local banks. Brokered deposits enabled banks that did not have the ability to generate core deposits to turn to volatile purchased funds to support their asset activities. Nevertheless, the FDIC lost the battle to treat brokered deposits as outside the purpose of deposit insurance. See *FAIC Securities, Inc. v. United*

*States*, 768 F.2d 352 (D.C. Cir. 1985). Several consequences became evident. First, it was clear that a large depositor through a deposit broker could receive 100% deposit insurance for all its funds at the highest rates available. Second, a multibank BHC could itself act as a deposit broker among its bank subsidiaries. For example, a BHC with ten bank subsidiaries could engage in unified advertising offering to deposit one million dollars among the 10 banks at $100,000 each, thus providing 100% FDIC deposit insurance. The *FAIC* decision was a "plain language" approach to statutory interpretation, in distinct contrast to *Philadelphia Gear*.

Beginning with FIRREA in 1989, Congress has authorized the FDIC to regulate brokered deposits. The limits on acceptance of brokered deposits are found in 12 U.S.C.A. § 1831f and 12 C.F.R. § 337.6. The term "deposit broker" is broadly defined, even to include an employee of one bank in a BHC system directing deposits to another bank in the same BHC family. Only well-capitalized institutions can take brokered deposits without restriction. Adequately capitalized institutions may get a waiver from the FDIC in order to accept brokered deposits, but even then cannot pay more than 0.75% above competing rates, as defined in 12 C.F.R. § 337.6(b). Under-capitalized institutions are prohibited from accepting brokered deposits.

## Comments and Questions

1.  Should prohibitions on brokered deposits apply to all banks? Similarly, should pension and profit sharing plan deposits be insured as a single plan deposit rather than for each individual beneficiary?

2.  Should deposit insurance only be available on "grocery money" accounts, or even be further restricted to one account per person regardless of the number of banks in which the person holds accounts?

## D.  New Deposit Products

The traditional types of deposits are monies received in the usual course of business for deposit in the following types of accounts: savings accounts, checking accounts, certificates of deposits, bank issued checks, money orders, and instruments for which the institution is primarily liable, such as commercial letters of credit. On the other side there are various account relationships offered by banks to attract funds that obviously are not deposits: mutual funds, bank stocks, subordinated obligations, and insurance annuities.

We know that banks are in competition for household savings, particularly with securities firms and insurance companies. The obvious competitive response is to create deposit products that combine the attractiveness of FDIC insurance with the additional benefits of securities or insurance products. If the purpose of deposit insurance is to provide security for "hard earnings" or savings, exactly what range of bank products should be considered deposits? Should hybrid products with some aspect of life insurance or stock investments be entitled to deposit insurance coverage? Consider the following problem.

*Problem 3-18*

In order to better compete with securities firms, Manufacturers and Traders Bank proposes a different type of certificate of deposit. The five year "stock index certificate of deposit" accumulates no interest, but promises a minimum value at maturity of at least the amount of deposited principal, plus a return equal to the performance of a stock market index. [The experience in the United States investment markets over the last 72 years is that the Standard and Poor's 500 Stock Index has an annual compound rate of return of 11.0%, while the highest yielding United States treasury securities over that same term have been 5-year notes which yield an annual compound rate of 5.3%.] Of course banks are not allowed to invest in equities, and they also need to have some profit margin. The bank pays for this equity-linked CD by using the interest foregone over the five years to purchase a call option or call option spread on the underlying stock index. The bank believes it can sell this as a product that can effectively compete with conservative mutual funds, with the additional value of a guaranteed return of deposited principal, plus deposit insurance. Is the stock index CD an insured deposit product?

## E. Security for Large Deposits and Non-deposit Bank Liabilities

A deposit is simply a form of borrowing by a bank from a depositor. When people borrow, they often give security for the funds borrowed. May a bank give security for a deposit? Read 12 U.S.C.A. § 90. It provides for the ability of national banks to pledge assets as security for the deposit of public monies, but otherwise generally prohibits banks from providing security for the typical private depositor. The justification is the supposed need to make public funds safe, as even a small municipality may have more than $1 million on deposit at the local bank. On the other hand, this means that the assets pledged to secure uninsured public deposits are not available to other unsecured general creditors, including unsecured private depositors. These uninsured and unsecured depositors can include local religious organizations and charities who often have deposits in excess of $100,000. They can also include people who happen to place the proceeds of a house sale in a deposit account shortly before failure, and farmers who have placed the proceeds of an annual crop or livestock sale in a deposit account for a short period of time. These people are prohibited from having any security.

The leading case in the area is *Texas & Pacific Railway Co. v. Pottoroff*, 291 U.S. 245 (1934). The case involved the question of whether a national bank had the power to pledge part of its assets to secure a private, nongovernment deposit. The court noted that the Comptroller of the Currency then disapproved of such pledges, and that there was little evidence that banks had traditionally made such pledges. Nevertheless, the railroad contended that the power to pledge was incidental to the power to engage in a deposit business and hence was permissible. The Court responded that the power to pledge assets was not necessary to deposit taking, and more important, a practice is not within the incidental powers of a bank merely because it is convenient in the performance of an express power. Finally, such a pledge would be inconsistent with many provisions of the National Bank Act designed to ensure the uniformity of treatment among depositors.

The pledge in *Pottoroff* would take general bank assets and limit their availability to a few depositors. This would clearly reduce the margin of safety for other depositors, thus violating the underlying principles of safety and economic neutrality. Where any general underlying principle of the business of banking is violated, it is not appropriate to conclude that the activity is a permissible incidental power. But if there is an express power to engage in the activity, it is permissible. Therefore, pledging of assets to secure public deposits is permissible as an express power.

Section 90 does not satisfy the desire of large, private depositors for some form of security. What, if anything, can be done? One possibility is to create a trust arrangement under 12 U.S.C.A. § 92a and 12 C.F.R. §§ 9.8 and 9.10(b) providing for collateralization of trust deposits. Under the statute and regulations, property held in trust accounts is not treated as part of the estate of the failed depository institution, and trust funds awaiting investment or distribution that are deposited with the commercial side of the bank are required to be collateralized. Thus, deposits of any size made in the form of a trust arrangement are fully secured against loss. Such a technique requires substantial administrative effort, in the form of an appropriate revocable trust agreement including a provision that the money can be held no longer than necessary to permit its investment or distribution, and in the form of maintaining separate books and records. As a consequence, this methodology may be realistic for various large commercial customers, but not for the typical household, farmer, religious organization or small charity. See *Comptroller of the Currency Trust Interpretive Letter No. 260* (May 14, 1991). In addition, such depositors have some difficulty utilizing the trust power exception for security because 12 U.S.C.A. § 92a(d) provides that "deposits of current funds subject to check" are prohibited from being received by bank trust departments.

In 1993 Congress passed a statute providing for depositor preference in case of bank failure. The statute (12 U.S.C.A. § 1821(d)(11)) provides that all depositors are given a preference in liquidation priority over almost all nondeposit liabilities of a failed bank. As a consequence, uninsured domestic depositors are now paid in full before junior creditors are paid. These junior creditors include unsecured nondeposit general creditors of the bank. They may be landlords, suppliers of goods and services, or unsecured creditors who have loaned money to the bank. But the 1993 statute may cause alert nondepositor creditors also to restructure their bank relations.

For example, banks are not prohibited generally from granting security interests. In 1989 FIRREA provided to participants in complex financial arrangements what amounts to the functional equivalent of insurance above $100,000 in a bank liquidation. Under 12 U.S.C.A. § 1821(e)(8)-(10) holders of "qualified financial contracts" (which contracts may be collateralized by perfected security interests in bank assets) have the power to terminate or liquidate the contracts, specifically including the power conferred under any security agreement to foreclose on bank assets held as collateral, thus rendering these contracts exempt from bank receivership powers. Foreclosure reduces the assets available both to the FDIC as insurer of deposits and to less sophisticated unsecured creditors.

Qualified financial contracts are highly complex. (Many of the contracts are more generically known as derivatives.) One example is an interest rate swap, which could work as follows. A bank is a borrower and pays interest on deposits which varies with market rates. A large portion of the bank's loan portfolio is in fixed rate mortgages. Therefore, the bank has a concern that deposit interest rates may rise and it may be at risk. At the same time, a consumer finance company has obtained its funds by issuing fixed rate bonds, but has loaned to customers based on variable interest rates. The risk to the finance company is that interest rates may drop and it may lose money. The two parties can insulate each other from interest rate risks by entering into an interest rate swap. The bank would agree to make periodic fixed amount payments to the finance company and the finance company would agree to make periodic variable rate payments to the bank. To get the two parties together usually requires a swap dealer, often a large commercial bank. The swap dealer must find parties whose needs are complementary to one another. Also, because the parties will not know each other, the swap dealer bank often will have to serve, in effect, as a guarantor in a way that substitutes its credit standing for that of the two swapped parties. Is the FDIC the guarantor of the guarantor? Are the provisions of § 1821(d) and (e) ineffective in dealing with the policy concerns?

### Problem 3-19

Medium National Bank recently has suffered numerous loan losses sufficient in amount to cause it to have no taxable income for this year and probably the next several years. Thus the bank has no real use for its large portfolio of tax-free municipal bonds, normally used to shelter taxable income. As a consequence, the bank would like to sell $100 million of its municipal bond portfolio to Big Brokerage Company, which intends to package the bonds as a tax-free municipal bond fund. Big Brokerage wishes to require in its bond purchase agreement that Medium Bank give Big Brokerage a security interest in $100 million of its assets, in case interest rates go up and the value of the bonds declines. Medium National Bank says this transaction clearly is permitted because, under § 24(7), banks are allowed to sell their assets and to borrow money. What do you think?

### Comments and Questions

1. It is probable that with the creation of depositor preference, nondepositor creditors quickly will realize that Congress wishes to shift the risk for bank failure more to them than to the FDIC. As a consequence, many nondeposit creditors will be willing to extend credit to banks only on a collateralized basis. The obvious effect of secured credit is that the creditors go from being a lower priority than either general depositors or the FDIC to a higher priority. What has § 1821(d) accomplished?

2. To the extent that large junior creditors are unsecured, is it now more likely that sophisticated nondeposit creditors will respond more quickly to any hint of troubling news about a large depository institution?

3. Would it help if banks were generally prohibited from giving any security to any depositor or any nondeposit creditor, other than a purchase money security interest? Would this help to implement the policy of having a cost-contained system by controlling the federal guarantee of risks of bank activities?

4. Certainly the federal deposit insurance system has prevented financial panic, but the question remains—what else has it brought? Has it permitted unsafe and even insolvent institutions to develop and continue at great costs to taxpayers and damage to the economy? We will consider this aspect of the question in more detail in Chapter Five.

# Section 7. Capital Adequacy

## A. In General

Capital regulation has received greatly increased attention over the past 15 years. Why is this so? Some say it is a symptom of regulatory inadequacy—the regulators have failed to enforce existing statutes and regulations to assure adequate safety and soundness in the portfolio activities of banks. Others say that as the portfolio-shaping limitations of the statutes and regulations have loosened, we rightly have become less confident in the efficacy of portfolio restrictions as a regulatory tool. In either case, capital regulation has become our residual regulatory structure.

Concern over bank capital adequacy as a way to protect both depositors and the banking system has a long history. In the nineteenth century Louisiana had a statute which required a certain level of capital against deposits, considered short-term credit to be for three months or less, and prohibited a bank from providing long-term credit in an amount greater than the capital provided by its shareholders. In the early 1900s state regulators developed a more generalized capital adequacy standard, which required a capital to total deposits ratio of 1 to 10. This ratio of capital to deposits was subsequently used by the Comptroller of the Currency.

In the late 1930s the banking regulators began to use a capital to assets ratio test rather than a capital to deposits test for the determination of capital adequacy. The change reflected the actual practice that banks sustained losses on their assets rather than on their deposits. Subsequently, discussion of appropriate capital adequacy levels shifted to a "qualitative analysis" of asset risk. Since some assets are riskier than others, the argument went, some banks should have higher capital ratios than others. Of course, there has always been the problem of trying to differentiate between "risk" assets and "riskless" assets; history has revealed that assets can shift categories with surprising quickness. An asset risk methodology was not implemented, and bank capital levels as a percentage of assets declined more than 50% from the inception of federal deposit insurance until about 1990. Overall, the existence of a federal safety net in the form of federal deposit insurance appears to be a material factor in explaining the historically low current capital ratios, and thus low risk buffer, that bank depositors are willing to accept.

As bank activities were perceived to be increasing in their level of complexity, diversity and risk, demands for adequate capital increased.  Risks involved in the activities of banks include prospective loan losses, expansion into more complex activities, sustained inflation, volatile interest rates, and growth in bank assets and liabilities far in excess of growth in the traditional bank capital accounts.  Such a level of growth often is caused by emphasis on "liability management" techniques, designed to attract deposits to finance loan demand and other asset activities, rather than limiting loans to locally obtainable deposits.

In the early 1980s, federal banking regulators began to establish quantitative capital adequacy standards.  In 1983, the Fifth Circuit decided the case of *First National Bank of Bellaire v. Comptroller of the Currency*, 697 F.2d 674 (5th Cir. 1983).  *Bellaire* involved review of a multifaceted regulatory cease and desist order.  The relevant aspect of the Comptroller's order required the bank to achieve a particular capital ratio in excess of that required by the Comptroller's published guidelines, because the Comptroller had concluded that the bank's established capital ratio was unsafe and unsound.  The opinion in *Bellaire* variously suggests that the Comptroller's conclusion was unreasonable, and that the circumstances did not warrant a cease and desist order because the capital position of the bank did not appear to threaten its financial stability.  The *Bellaire* court's overruling of the Comptroller's judgment as to what constitutes a safe and sound level of capital was a major factor in Congress enacting 12 U.S.C.A. § 3907 as part of the International Lending Supervision Act of 1983, effectively overruling *Bellaire*.  Also see 12 C.F.R. Pt. 3.

The statute requires federal bank regulatory agencies to establish minimum levels of capital for banks and bank holding companies.  It also empowers regulators to issue capital "directives" to individual banks, which are enforceable in federal district court in the same manner that final, administrative agency cease and desist orders can be enforced.  Thus the statute provides a specific grant of authority to establish levels of capital both for categories of institutions and for individual institutions.  The legislative history notes that Congress did not expect the agencies to have a single uniform capital ratio for all banks under all circumstances.  Rather Congress only expected that the general standards would be substantially uniform among the agencies, while banks with different characteristics could be treated differently than provided for by the general standards.

Today, banks and bank holding companies are required to meet minimum capital standards calculated on two bases—a simple "leverage" basis and a "risk-adjusted" basis.  The leverage standard is a ratio of balance sheet capital to assets—it specifies that a certain minimum amount of tier 1 capital (essentially common and most preferred stock balance sheet accounts) be held against the average assets shown on the balance sheet.  Leverage ratio requirements vary for both banks and bank holding companies depending on their examination ratings and other factors.

The level of leverage capital required depends on the regulator's overall risk assessment of each bank.  To measure overall risk, regulators use bank examiners' composite ratings not only of a bank's capital, but also of a bank's asset quality, management, earnings, and liquidity, which results in a CAMEL rating, an acronym from the five areas reviewed.  Composite CAMEL ratings range from 1 to 5, with 1 being the best and 5 being the worst. Under the new leverage capital rules, banks that have a CAMEL rating of 1 must have minimum tier 1 capital to assets (leverage) ratio of at least 3%. This rating generally applies only to banks and bank holding companies in very sound condition. Banks with a rating of less than 1 must have at least 4 to 5%, and perhaps more for banks with the worst ratings. The rules imply that the majority of banks will have minimum leverage ratios of at least 4 to 5%.

Under the old leverage formula, primary capital included all of the loan- and lease-loss reserves, but the current definition of tier 1 capital excludes such loss reserves. As a result, when failing banks increase their loss reserves, as is typically needed for growing expected losses, tier 1 capital is reduced because the required reduction in equity capital is not offset by the inclusion of the correlative increase in the loan loss reserve.

The risk-based capital standard is more complex. It incorporates both equity and other forms of capital and measures both balance sheet assets and off-balance sheet exposures (contingencies such as loan commitments, letters of credit, and swaps) on a risk-adjusted basis. The risk-based requirements are derived from an international agreement known as the Basle Accord negotiated by bank regulators from the major industrialized countries under the auspices of the Bank for International Settlements located in Basle, Switzerland.

Under the risk-based standard, risk weights are assigned to different asset categories. There are four risk weight categories: 0 percent, 20 percent, 50 percent, and 100 percent. Cash and United States government securities are given zero risk weight because they are considered to have no default risk; municipal securities, federal agency securities, and interbank obligations are given a 20% risk weight; first lien loans secured by residential real estate are assigned a 50% risk weight; other assets including most consumer and business loans are given a risk weight of 100%. For a complete list of asset risk weight categories, see 12 C.F.R. Pt. 3, App. A. In addition, credit equivalencies are assigned to off-balance sheet activities, which are risk weighted and added to the risk-adjusted assets on the balance sheet to arrive at total risk-weighted assets against which certain levels of capital must be held. In short, the more complex the on- and off-balance sheet activities of a bank, the more complex the computation of its risk-based capital.

All banks and bank holding companies are required to maintain tier 1 capital, as already defined, of at least 4% of risk-weighted assets. There is also a broader measure of capital, total capital, which combines tier 1 and tier 2 capital. Tier 2 capital primarily includes subordinated debt, mandatory convertible securities, and loss reserves of not more than 1.25% of risk-weighted assets. Banks and bank holding companies must maintain total capital of at least 8% of risk-weighted assets. The Federal Deposit Insurance Corporation Improvement Act of 1991 (FDICIA) required the additional development of interest rate risk regulations, which were finalized in 1995. Interest rate risk is the potential decrease in the value of fixed income assets due to rising interest rates. Interest rate fluctuations can also cause problems for a bank if there is a significant mismatch in the maturities of assets and liabilities in a bank due to either rising or falling rates.

Why do we have two systems for measuring capital adequacy? There are at least two reasons. The risk-based system described above principally focuses on credit risk from on- and off-balance sheet activities, rather than on interest rate risks and other noncredit risks. Continuation of the leverage ratio is intended to supplement the risk-based system by compensating for these gaps. Second, regulators believe that that continued use of both ratios is more effective in identifying potential failures than use of the risk-based standards alone.

Capital adequacy is closely related to a bank's exposure to regulatory sanctions, and so banks and bank holding companies have strong regulatory incentives to maintain capital levels in excess of the required minimum leverage and risk-based requirements. FDICIA added 12 U.S.C.A. § 1831o, which requires the regulators to establish specific capital "zones" for use in (1) determining eligibility for brokered deposits, (2) setting risk-based premiums for deposit insurance, and, most important, (3) taking prompt corrective regulatory action. Consequently, banks are assigned to capital adequacy groups as follows:

1. Well capitalized: the bank's tier 1 risk-based ratio is greater than 6%, total risk-based ratio is greater than 10%, and leverage ratio is greater than 5%.

2. Adequately capitalized: The bank is neither well capitalized nor under capitalized.

3. Undercapitalized: The bank's tier 1 risk-based ratio is less than 4%, total risk-based ratio is less than 8%, or leverage ratio is less than 4% (3% if the bank has a CAMEL rating of 1).

4. Significantly undercapitalized: The bank's tier 1 risk-based ratio is less than 3%, total risk-based ratio is less than 8%, or leverage ratio is less than 3%.

5. Critically undercapitalized: The bank's leverage ratio is less than 2%.

The last two categories are thought to encompass banks faced with a substantial risk of failure, and so requiring substantial regulatory action.

The difficulty of meeting the different capital requirements varies among banks. In general, smaller banks and bank holding companies tend to have higher risk-based capital ratios relative to their leverage ratios than do larger banks and bank holding companies for two reasons; (1) small banks rely more on permanent (common stock) capital as a source of equity, and (2) large banks typically have more off-balance sheet risk exposures. The small banks typically satisfy their total risk-based capital requirements with tier 1 capital and loss reserves. They generally do not issue subordinated debt or convertible bonds. This suggests, then, that for smaller institutions the leverage requirement may be more constraining. But the opposite is true for larger institutions.

The following case arose before the current capital definitions and ratios were developed. Primary capital was similar to the current Tier 1 capital. The bank's primary capital was below the required level.

## Federal Deposit Insurance Corporation v. Bank of Coushatta
930 F.2d 1122 (5th Cir.), cert. denied, 502 U.S. 857 (1991)

BARKSDALE, Circuit Judge:

The Federal Deposit Insurance Corporation issued a capital directive to the Bank of Coushatta and its directors (Board). After they failed to comply, the FDIC obtained an ex parte order from the district court to enforce the directive. The Bank and Board appeal from the order; they contend, pursuant to the Administrative Procedure Act (APA), 5 U.S.C. § 551, *et seq.*, and Fifth Amendment due process, that they were entitled to an agency hearing and judicial review in conjunction with issuance of the directive.

I.

Chartered by Louisiana,[1] the Bank is federally insured, subject to the Federal Deposit Insurance Act, 12 U.S.C. § 1811, *et seq.*, and FDIC rules and regulations. In July, 1989, it was operating under the FDIC capital forbearance program in an attempt to bring its capital to a minimum level. Under its second capital forbearance plan, the Bank had agreed to bring its primary capital ratio to 5.49% by year end. The FDIC determined that the Bank could not comply with the plan, because its loss classifications exceeded amounts projected for all of 1989. As a result, in July 1989, the FDIC issued a notice of intent, with preliminary findings of fact and conclusions of law, stating that the Bank's primary capital was lower than required by regulation and that the FDIC proposed to issue a capital directive requiring the Bank by December 31, 1989, to increase that capital by not less than $725,000 and to achieve ratios of primary and total capital to total assets of not less than 5.5% and 6.0% respectively.

Accompanying the notice was a letter to the Board, which discussed the financial condition of the Bank, the reasons for its deteriorating status, and the intent of a capital directive action.[2] Also enclosed was the report on the examination of the Bank conducted as of April 1989 by the FDIC and a state examiner.

Any response to the notice was due within 14 days after receipt and was to: "state any basis for relief from the proposed CAPITAL DIRECTIVE, and may seek modification of its terms, or seek other appropriate relief. Such response shall include any information, mitigating circumstances, documentation, or other relevant evidence which supports the Bank's position, and may include a plan for attaining the minimum capital requirement."

By only a 1 1/2 page letter in August 1989, the Board responded; it noted its efforts to find additional capital, its lack of financial capacity, and the weakened nature of the Louisiana economy, stating that "[t]he main reason for failure to achieve the goals in the Capital Forbearance Plan is loan losses and the deterioration of the parcels held as Other Real Estate."

---

[1]    The Louisiana Office of Financial Institutions submitted an amicus brief in support of appellants.

[2]    The Board was asked to both acknowledge receipt of the letter and "advise that the letter was made a part of the minutes of the Board." This, and similar facts, bear on its assertion that it is not a proper party to the district court enforcement proceeding from which this appeal lies. See note 5, *infra*.

The Board did not dispute any of the FDIC's classifications of assets or its calculations.  Nor did it submit any proposal for meeting the FDIC requirements, stating only that "[t]he Board believes it will have sufficient earning[s] to have a capital ratio in excess of 4% by year end, and will continue its efforts to find additional capital."  The Board acknowledged the "capital deficiency" and requested modification of the capital forbearance plan in lieu of a capital directive.

The FDIC issued the directive in September 1989, with supporting findings of fact and conclusions of law and a cover letter to the Board.  The Bank was directed (1) by December 31, 1989, to restore its ratio of primary capital to total assets to at least 5.5% and enhance that capital by at least $725,000; and (2) within 30 days, to submit a plan for achieving the capital level.  The directive stated that it was binding upon "the Bank [and] its directors," among others.

Because the Bank failed to comply, the FDIC filed a letter in May 1990, in the United States District Court in Louisiana, pursuant to 12 U.S.C. § 1818(i), requesting an order enforcing the directive against the Bank and Board.  Attached to the letter was a Petition for Enforcement of Administrative Order, stamped filed on June 14, 1990.  On July 13, 1990, the district court issued the requested ex parte order.  The Bank, its officers and directors were ordered to comply with the directive and to submit a report within 30 days "setting forth in detail the manner and form in which Respondent has complied with the provisions of this Order.  This Court shall retain jurisdiction . . . for the purpose of entertaining any petition which . . . [the FDIC] may make and entering further orders as may be necessary to enforce compliance with the terms of this Order."  The Bank and Board filed an appeal from that order and a motion for stay pending appeal; the district court and this court denied the stay.

## II.

The FDIC's authority to issue capital directives is one of its regulatory tools for dealing with troubled banks.  Most of these methods are set forth in 12 U.S.C. § 1818; however, authority for a directive is found in the International Lending Supervision Act of 1983 (ILSA), 12 U.S.C. § 3907, which provides in part:  (a)(1) Each appropriate Federal banking agency shall cause banking institutions to achieve and maintain adequate capital by establishing minimum levels of capital for such banking institutions and by using such other methods as the appropriate Federal banking agency *deems* appropriate.  (2) Each appropriate Federal banking agency shall have the authority to establish such minimum level of capital for a banking institution as the appropriate Federal banking agency, *in its discretion*, *deems* to be necessary or appropriate in light of the particular circumstances of the banking institution. (Emphasis added.)  Moreover, failure to maintain the requisite capital "may be *deemed* by the appropriate Federal banking agency, *in its discretion*, to constitute an unsafe and unsound practice. . . ."  12 U.S.C. § 3907(b)(1) (emphasis added).

If a bank fails to maintain the required capital, the agency may issue a directive: (B)(i) Such directive may require the banking institution to submit and adhere to a plan acceptable to the appropriate Federal banking agency describing the means and timing by which the banking institution shall achieve its required capital level. (ii) Any such directive issued pursuant to this paragraph . . . shall be enforceable under the provisions of Section 1818(i) . . . to the same extent as an effective and outstanding order issued pursuant to Section 1818(b) . . . which has become final.  12 U.S.C. §§ 3907(b)(2)(B)(i) and (ii).

The above referenced § 1818(b) governs cease-and-desist proceedings. Cease-and-desist orders are issued only after an agency hearing, §§ 1818(b)(1) and (h)(1), and "become effective at the expiration of thirty days after the service of such order . . . and shall remain effective and enforceable . . ., except to such extent as it is stayed, modified, terminated, or set aside by action of the agency or a reviewing court." 12 U.S.C. § 1818(b)(2). Such orders may be reviewed in a court of appeals within thirty days after service of the order. § 1818(h)(2). . . .

Accordingly, a capital directive may be enforced in the district court under § 1818(i). But, as also referenced above, the district court's jurisdiction is limited. "[S]ection 1818(i) . . . evinces a clear intention that [the] regulatory process is not to be disturbed by untimely judicial intervention, at least where there is no 'clear departure from statutory authority.'" *Groos Nat'l Bank v. Comptroller of Currency*, 573 F.2d 889, 895 (5th Cir. 1978) (citation omitted). Furthermore, the hearing requirements for cease-and-desist orders are not incorporated in the procedures for capital directives.

Section 3907 was enacted to provide "a stronger, unambiguous statutory directive to the regulators to strengthen banks' capital positions." H.R. Rep. No. 98-175, 98th Cong., 1st Sess. 45, *reprinted in* 1983 U.S. Code Cong. & Admin. News 1768, 1928.

The [Senate Banking and Finance] Committee's amendment explicitly makes failure to maintain established capital levels an "unsafe and unsound practice. . . ." The amendment requires regulators to demand that institutions below the required capital levels submit and adhere to an acceptable plan to achieve prescribed levels.

*Id.* at 1929.

Another congressional purpose behind § 3907 was in response to this court's decision in *First Nat'l Bank of Bellaire v. Comptroller of Currency*, 697 F.2d 674 (5th Cir. 1983), where the portion of a cease-and-desist order requiring a capital ratio was set aside as not being supported by substantial evidence. *Id.* at 684-87. Congress was concerned that *Bellaire* "clouded the authority of the bank regulatory agencies to exercise their *independent discretion* in establishing and requiring the maintenance of appropriate levels of capital." S. Rep. No. 98-122, 98th Cong., 1st Sess. 16 (emphasis added). "The Committee believes that establishing adequate levels of capital is properly left to the *expertise and discretion* of the agencies. Therefore, in order to clarify the authority of the banking agencies to establish adequate levels of capital requirements, to require the maintenance of those levels, and *to prevent the courts from disturbing such capital*, the Committee has provided a specific grant of authority to the banking agencies to establish levels of capital. . . ." *Id.* (emphasis added). . . .

The examination may lead to a capital directive being issued. But, the regulations require the FDIC to first issue a notice of its intention to issue the directive; and the notice must include detailed data, such as the current total capital ratio and the basis upon which the ratio is calculated. 12 C.F.R. § 325.6(c)(1). The bank has 14 days to respond, including explaining why the directive should not issue and seeking modification of its terms.

After the bank responds, the FDIC issues a decision, explaining its determination whether to issue a directive. The directive may order the bank to achieve the minimum capital requirement by a certain date; to submit a plan for achieving the minimum capital requirement; or to take other action necessary to achieve the minimum capital requirement; or a combination of the above. § 325.6(c)(3). If a directive is to be issued, it may be served upon the bank with the final determination. *Id.*

The regulations then allow enforcement, as described above, in the same manner as for a final cease-and-desist order. Moreover, "[i]n addition to enforcement of the directive, the FDIC may seek . . . penalties for violation of the directive against any bank, any officer, director, employee, agent, or other person participating in the conduct of the affairs of the bank, pursuant to 12 U.S.C. § 3909(d)." § 325.6(d)(1) (emphasis added).[5]

A.

In response to the contention that the district court ex parte proceedings deprived the Bank and Board of a right to judicial review under the APA, the FDIC asserts that the decision to issue a capital directive is not reviewable, because it is committed to agency discretion by law. Likewise, in denying a stay pending appeal, the district court held that "whether . . . to issue a capital directive is committed to the sole discretion of the FDIC and is, therefore, unreviewable under the [APA]. 5 U.S.C. § 701(a)(2)."

There is a presumption of reviewability. "[J]udicial review of a final agency action by an aggrieved person will not be cut off unless there is persuasive reason to believe that such was the purpose of Congress." *Abbott Laboratories v. Gardner*, 387 U.S. 136, 140 (1967); *see also Bowen v. Michigan Academy of Family Physicians*, 476 U.S. 667, 671 (1986) ("'Very rarely do statutes withhold judicial review.'") (quoting legislative history of APA).

The APA's provisions for judicial review of final agency actions are contained in 5 U.S.C. §§ 701-706. Section 702 provides: "A person suffering legal wrong because of agency action, or adversely affected or aggrieved by agency action within the meaning of a relevant statute, is entitled to judicial review thereof." Section 702, however, is limited by § 701(a). "[B]efore any review . . . may be had, a party must first clear the hurdle of § 701(a)." *Heckler v. Chaney*, 470 U.S. 821, 828 (1985). That section provides for judicial review, "except to the extent that–(1) statutes preclude judicial review; or (2) agency action is committed to agency discretion by law." 5 U.S.C. § 701(a). The distinction between subparts (1) and (2) in § 701(a) is that, "[t]he former applies when Congress has expressed an intent to preclude judicial review. The latter applies in different circumstances; even where Congress has not affirmatively precluded review, review is not to be had if the statute is drawn so that a court would have no meaningful

---

[5] Section 3907 only speaks to issuing a directive to "a banking institution." 12 U.S.C. § 3907(b)(2)(A). However, enforcement of the directive against only the "bank" would be meaningless. For example, a "bank" can not raise capital and otherwise seek to ensure that a capital directive is complied with; that is accomplished by its board and officers, among others. Accordingly, the district court's order was directed to the Bank and Board. They assert that there was no "indication that the individual defendants [the Board] would be named as parties in any litigation," because the Board members "were not parties to the capital directive." The Board was clearly on notice of the directive. Two cover letters, discussed *supra*, were addressed to it; and the response to the notice of intent was through the Board's counsel. Furthermore, the subsequently issued directive states, pursuant to the regulation described above, that it is "binding upon the Bank, its directors, officers, employees, agents, successors, assigns, and other persons participating in the affairs of the Bank."

standard against which to judge the agency's exercise of discretion. In such a case, the statute ("law") can be taken to have "committed" the decisionmaking to the agency's judgment absolutely." *Heckler*, 470 U.S. at 830.

In looking first to determine whether review is precluded under § 701(a)(1), we note that there is no statutory prohibition against it; but neither is there any procedure for it–unlike final cease-and-desist orders. Furthermore, no review is allowed in the district court enforcement proceeding; as discussed above, its jurisdiction is limited to the "power to order and require compliance." § 1818(i)(1).

As noted, § 3907 was enacted, in part, in response to judicial interference with capital requirements, as in *Bellaire*. Examination of the statutory scheme and its legislative history supports a congressional intention to preclude review. However, in the absence of an express prohibition, there is a "strong presumption that Congress did not mean to prohibit all judicial review of [the] decision." *Dunlop v. Bachowski*, 421 U.S. 560, 567 (1975). "[O]nly upon a showing of 'clear and convincing evidence' of a contrary legislative intent should the courts restrict access to judicial review." *Id.* (quoting *Abbott Labs*, 387 U.S. at 141). Because the standard for finding preclusion of review under § 701(a)(1) is a difficult hurdle to cross, we turn instead to the applicability, vel non, of § 701(a)(2) (agency action committed to its discretion).

In *Heckler*, the Supreme Court engaged in its first concentrated interpretation of § 701(a)(2) and noted that its construction was complicated by the "tension between a literal reading of § (a)(2), which exempts from judicial review those decisions committed to agency 'discretion,' and the primary scope of review prescribed by § 706(2)(A)–whether the agency's action was 'arbitrary, capricious, or an *abuse of discretion*.'" 470 U.S. at 829 (emphasis in original). Initially, the Court discussed *Citizens to Preserve Overton Park, Inc. v. Volpe*, 401 U.S. 402, (1971), where, in addressing whether an agency decision was subject to judicial review, it stated that the § 701(a)(2) exception was very narrow, to be applied only "in those rare instances where 'statutes are drawn in such broad terms that in a given case there is no law to apply.'" *Id.* at 410 (quoting S. Rep. No. 752, 79th Cong., 1st Sess., 26 (1945)). *Heckler* adopted the *Overton Park* reasoning and found it was not at odds with abuse of discretion review under § 706:

> [R]eview is not to be had if the statute is drawn so that a court would have no meaningful standard against which to judge the agency's exercise of discretion. In such a case, the statute . . . can be taken to have "committed" the decisionmaking to the agency's judgment absolutely. This construction avoids conflict with the "abuse of discretion" standard of review in § 706–if no judicially manageable standards are available for judging how and when an agency should exercise its discretion, then it is impossible to evaluate agency action for "abuse of discretion."

470 U.S. at 830. The reasoning in *Heckler* is helpful for our analysis; but, *Heckler* involved a refusal to take enforcement action. The Court held that such refusal was "generally committed to an agency's absolute discretion," because it "involves a complicated balancing of a number of factors which are peculiarly within its expertise." *Id.* at 831. The Court further noted that "when an agency *does* act to enforce, that action itself provides a focus for judicial review, inasmuch as the agency must have exercised its power in some manner. The action at least can be reviewed to determine whether the agency exceeded its statutory powers." *Id.* at 832 (emphasis in original).

In *Webster v. Doe*, 486 U.S. 592 (1988), the Court addressed § 701(a)(2) in the context of an agency's decision to act, thereby expanding its *Heckler* analysis.  In *Webster*, a discharged CIA employee contended that his termination violated the APA because it was, among other things, in violation of the procedures required by law and the CIA regulations.[6]  The statute in issue allowed termination of a CIA employee whenever the director "shall *deem* such termination necessary or advisable in the interests of the United States."  *Id.* at 600 (quoting § 102(c) of the National Security Act, 50 U.S.C. § 403(c)) (emphasis in original).  The Court first emphasized that § 701(a)(2) "requires careful examination of the statute on which the claim of agency illegality is based," *id.*, and held:

> This standard fairly exudes deference to the Director, and appears to us to foreclose the application of any meaningful judicial standard of review.  Short of permitting cross-examination of the Director concerning his views of the Nation's security and whether the discharged employee was inimical to those interests, we see no basis on which a reviewing court could properly assess an Agency termination decision.  The language of § 102(c) thus strongly suggests that its implementation was "committed to agency discretion by law."

> So too does the overall structure of the National Security Act.

*Id.*  In ruling, the Court relied on the legislative history of the National Security Act, which evidenced the Act's "extraordinary deference" to the CIA director and his decisions to terminate individual employees.  *Id.* at 601.

The FDIC contends that the legislative history and language of ILSA demonstrate that Congress likewise intended capital directives to be unreviewable.  Relying on *Webster*, it asserts that the repeated use of the word "deem" in the statute evidences deference and forecloses review.  Section 3907 uses the terms "deem" or "discretion" in almost every provision:  the FDIC may cause institutions to maintain adequate levels of capital by such methods as it "deems appropriate," § 3907(a)(1); it can establish minimum levels of capital which it "in its discretion, deems to be necessary or appropriate in light of the particular circumstances of the banking institution," § 3907(a)(2); the failure of a banking institution to maintain its capital "may be deemed by the appropriate Federal banking agency, in its discretion, to constitute an unsafe and unsound practice," § 3907(b)(1).[7]  And, the legislative history, discussed *supra*, also supports such a construction.  For example:  "The Committee believes that establishing adequate levels of capital is properly left to the *expertise and discretion* of the agencies . . . and to prevent the courts from disturbing such capital, the Committee has provided a specific grant of authority to the banking agencies to establish levels of capital. . . ."  S. Rep. No. 98-122 at 16 (emphasis added).

---

[6]    Several constitutional violations were also alleged, including Fifth Amendment procedural due process, as discussed *infra* in Part II.B.

[7]    As discussed *infra*, issuance of a capital directive is one of the least intrusive methods available to the FDIC when dealing with a troubled bank.  Its purpose is for prompt action, in order for banks to come into compliance before more drastic measures are required, such as issuance of a cease-and-desist order or termination of a bank's insured status.  See 12 U.S.C. § 1818(a)-(e).  These more drastic means provide for an APA hearing and judicial review.

The legislative history and language of the statute do not leave a court with a meaningful standard against which to judge the agency's exercise of its discretion. Accordingly, we conclude that even if review is not prohibited pursuant to § 702(a)(1), it is precluded pursuant to § 702(a)(2), because issuance of a directive is committed to the FDIC's discretion.

### B.

It is contended that the procedures for issuance of a capital directive violate Fifth Amendment due process and can be saved only by incorporation of APA hearing provisions. As discussed in *Webster*, even if agency action is committed to its discretion by law, judicial review of constitutional claims is still available, unless congressional intent to preclude such review is clear. *Id.* at 603. We do not find such intent. Moreover, the FDIC concedes that unreviewability does not extend to the issue of whether there is a "constitutional right to a full hearing on the record prior to issuance of a directive," and instead asserts that the procedures provide due process.

The Supreme Court "consistently has held that some form of hearing is required before an individual is finally deprived of a property interest." *Matthews v. Eldridge*, 424 U.S. 319, 333 (1976). . . . *Matthews* adopted a three factor test:

First, the private interest that will be affected by the official action; second, the risk of an erroneous deprivation of such interest through the procedures used, and the probable value, if any, of additional or substitute procedural safeguards; and finally, the Government's interest, including the function involved and the fiscal and administrative burdens that the additional or substitute procedural requirement would entail.

424 U.S. at 335.

### 1.

The Bank does not contend that the FDIC did not follow its procedures. Instead, it asserts that it is not allowed to dispute the underlying facts which make up the FDIC's determination that the Bank is not in compliance. However, the notice of intent states that the Bank could include "other relative evidence" which supported its position. The Bank could have responded to the notice with documentation that the FDIC's data was either in error or had changed. There is no limit on what a bank can say in its response. The Bank did not take full advantage of its opportunity to respond. Nor did it challenge any of the data provided it, including the report of examination. Needless to say, its failure to take such opportunity is not due to an inherent deficiency in the procedures.

Although the FDIC procedures do not involve a hearing, with testimony and examination before a neutral officer, they do allow notice and ample opportunity to respond before a directive issues. The directive issued in September 1989; enforcement was not sought until May 1990. Furthermore, under the regulations, once a directive has issued, a bank may request the FDIC to reconsider its terms and propose changes to any plan under which it is operating.

### 2.

We analyze the three *Matthews* factors against this procedural backdrop. First, the private interest affected is obviously substantial. For example, the directive requires a capital infusion of $725,000; and the regulations allow contempt sanctions for noncompliance.

Turning to the second factor, we find that the risk of an erroneous deprivation of the Bank's interests through the procedures described above is minimal. It had an opportunity to respond to the notice of intent, including to the examination report. The need for additional procedural safeguards is speculative. The Bank has not shown that evidence it could present at a hearing could not have been presented in response to the notice. While there is obvious advantage to the presence, and participation, of a neutral decision maker and examination of witnesses, especially cross-examination, it is not significant enough here to warrant a hearing prior to issuance of a directive. The decision to issue comes only after several deliberative steps and thorough documentation, including a bank examination, presentation of the examination report to a bank and consideration of any written response.

Third, the government's interest in having capital directives promptly implemented is significant. The benefits from a directive would be weakened greatly, if not lost, if additional procedures, including a hearing, were necessary. For example, if a hearing were required, the directive would be delayed; by the time the matter was resolved, a bank's financially troubled status, requiring issuance of a directive, may have deteriorated substantially.

The relationship of a capital directive to other regulatory tools the FDIC can employ in dealing with a troubled bank is relevant to this analysis. Other actions, such as a cease-and-desist order and termination of a bank's insured status, are much more intrusive. For example, a cease-and-desist order gives the FDIC authority "to place limitations on the activities or functions of an insured depository institution or any institution-affiliated party." 12 U.S.C. § 1818(b)(7). The institution may be required to restrict its growth; dispose of any loan or asset involved; rescind agreements or contracts; employ qualified officers or employees; or "take such other action as the banking agency determines to be appropriate." 12 U.S.C. § 1818(b)(6)(B)-(F). These actions provide for an APA evidentiary hearing and judicial review.

Therefore, we conclude that the capital directive procedures satisfy Fifth Amendment due process. . . . Accordingly, the order of the district court is AFFIRMED.

## Comments and Questions

1. Both regulatory and judicial decisions, as well as some legislation, have broadened the scope of permissible bank activities. As regulatory concerns arise, capital adequacy more commonly is the means of managing risk to the payments system, the insurance fund, and public confidence. And as *Coushatta* demonstrates, the capital directive is a virtually unchecked regulatory tool.

2. It is worth stepping back to reflect on the purposes of capital requirements. The primary function of bank capital is to provide a cushion against losses, enabling banks to survive in difficult economic times, primarily in order to protect both depositors and the stability of the payments system. We are interested in depositors and the payments system more than we are interested in the survival of individual depository institutions. But capital rules can never be sufficient to protect against all risk. Prudent management will always be an additional requirement. Would we be better served by relatively simple capital rules coupled with a sustained emphasis on the necessity of prudent management? Is such a judgment-based regulatory approach feasible?

3.   Capital adequacy issues become increasingly significant as American banks, securities firms and insurance companies tend to compete more with each other as well as with international financial institutions, such as the universal banks in Europe which act both as banks and as principals in securities and insurance. The issue is whether banks and other financial institutions should therefore be subject to exactly the same capital adequacy rules for purposes of having a "level playing field" and "harmonizing" international regulation of all financial institutions. Does the answer depend on whether one determines that bank, securities and insurance regulators are faced with implementing the same or different public policies and so have the same or different priorities? Securities firms have no depositors. Rather, their customers invest in publicly traded securities. Regulation focuses on protecting investors from fraud, malpractice, or negligence on the part of securities firms and issuers of securities. Securities firm customers are at some risk from the failure of a securities firm due to lack of capital. And securities firms involved in underwriting securities which suffer a lack of capital can affect primary securities markets. Similar comments can be made about insurance regulation. This brief discussion should suggest that a blind adherence to a "level playing field" and "harmonization" may not be based on a rational policy.

4.   Of course, the universal banks of Europe may prefer such across-the-board requirements. But the historic philosophy of the United States of separately regulating depository institutions, securities firms and insurance companies may make perfect sense both from competition policy and capital adequacy policy points of view. It may suggest that financial institutions, however denominated, should be required to place their securities markets activities and their nontrading activities in separate firms, subject to separate capital requirements for different public policy purposes. But the fact that there are separate securities, insurance and banking subsidiaries or affiliates does not necessarily mean that those entities would be subject to separate regulators. The principle of consolidated supervision in many countries allows a single regulator to regulate all subsidiaries within a group, regardless of their particular activities. Thus, it becomes clear that capital adequacy requirements may have a dramatic effect on corporate structure, regulatory structure, and competition policy.

5.   Probably much of the reason for needing regulatory capital requirements is the presence of federal deposit insurance. With deposit insurance, much market discipline is lost and moral hazard surfaces. Without deposit insurance, depositors would require a combination of higher interest rates paid on deposits and increased capital to offset increases in risk with the absence of insurance. And so, depositors would pressure bank managers to limit their risk taking. But deposit insurance substantially reduces the natural market pressures to limit risk taking by banks.

6.   In addition to protection of depositors and the payments system, a second purpose of capital is to play a role in minimizing the costs to the FDIC and taxpayers of resolving bank failures. To some people, this purpose suggests the special value of long-term, stable sources of capital such as common stock and subordinated debt. But experience suggests that regulators often fail to discipline troubled banks until the problems are out of control, and so more immediate marketplace discipline continues to

be necessary. One possible way to force market discipline on banks would be to require all banks to have short-term subordinated capital of at least 4 percent, which could not be paid at maturity if Tier 1 capital dropped below 4 percent. What do you think?

---

The following two problems ask you to apply your knowledge of the leverage and risk-based capital requirements to highly simplified bank financial statements. As you do these problems, ask yourself at least two questions: (1) How much differentiation for capital purposes should there be between different types of assets? For example, what difference, if any, should exist between money market instruments and commercial loans? (2) Should bank liabilities affect a bank's capital requirements more than they do, and if yes, what differentiations would you suggest?

### Problem 3-20

Bank A has the following assets: $200 million in United States government securities, $400 million in residential mortgages, and $800 million in business and consumer loans. Bank A's capital accounts consist solely of $65 million in paid-in capital for common stock and earned surplus. Does the bank meet the leverage ratio capital requirements?

If Bank A's balance sheet also shows $15 million in the loan loss reserve account, does the Bank meet the risk-based capital requirements?

### Problem 3-21

Consider the bank consolidated statement of condition set out in Problem 3-5 in section 3.C of this chapter. Does the bank meet the basic leverage ratio capital adequacy requirements? Suppose that, in addition to the assets listed in the statement of condition, the bank has $100 million of standby letters of credit and $200 million of long-term legally binding loan commitments to private corporations outstanding. Does the bank meet the risk-based capital adequacy requirements? In answering these questions assume that "trading accounts" represent government securities, and both "buildings and equipment" and "other assets" are risk weighted 100 percent.

Suppose the bank sold off $200 million dollars of commercial loans in participations of the sort described in the *Banco Espanol* case reproduced about in section 4.B of this Chapter. What effect would that transaction have on the bank's capital requirements? What if the bank agreed to buy back any of the loans that experiences credit problems? What if the bank agreed to buy back up to fifty percent of the loans sold? How about five percent? What if the bank simply offers the purchasers of the loans standard representations and warranties as to the quality of the loans?

## Comments and Questions

1. Do the risk-based capital standards create questionable incentives for bankers to put much of their money in assets that require little or no capital, such as single and multi-family residential mortgages (and related securities) and United States government securities? Is there an added cost to borrowers where banks must maintain 8% capital against most business and consumer loans? Is this sensible public policy? Is this an indirect approach to credit allocation?

2. Does it make sense that all bank consumer and business loans have the same risk-weight of 100%? Should loans have different capital requirements based on their level of risk? Which is riskier, a typical business loan or a leveraged buy-out loan? With equal risk-weighting, does it encourage banks to seek LBO loans that facially appear to be more profitable because they command higher interest rates?

3. Banks can manage the level of their capital by three principal methods. One is to increase their equity capital by selling additional stock, a second is to generate more earnings, and a third is to reduce or alter their assets. There are several ways to manipulate assets. One is to slow loan growth. Another is to exchange assets, such as commercial loans and residential mortgages, for zero risk assets. A third is to change assets into securities that can be sold to other investors. Securitization can be particularly attractive because it is a method whereby both assets can be reduced and earnings can be increased. The maintenance of the servicing rights on the securitied assets enable the depository institution to earn fees and maintain customer relationships, while at the same time transferring credit and interest rate risk. Are there any problems with this?

4. Current capital adequacy regulations have not captured all risks inherent in bank activities. (That is one reason for keeping the leverage ratio.) Precisely what risks are to be capitalized? Consider the following.

   a.  Credit risk, the risk of an individual borrower defaulting on obligations to the bank.

   b.  Concentration risk, the risk associated with either geographic or product type concentration in bank loans.

   c.  Liquidity risk, the potential for difficulties in meeting current liabilities out of current assets.

   d.  Operating risk, the losses resulting from mistakes and inefficiencies in bank operations, such as proper collateral control.

   e.  Country-transfer risk, the difficulty of receiving payments from foreign borrowers due to economic and political events in foreign countries.

   f.  Foreign exchange rate risk, fluctuations in exchange rates with respect to loans denominated in foreign currencies.

   g.  Fraud risk, a factor in a not insignificant number of depository institution failures.

It is really possible to develop capital standards to deal effectively with all these risks?

5. Similarly, the ability to effectively judge management capability, asset quality, and public confidence is exceptionally difficult. How do we regulate the common desire to engage in new activities that cannot be fully understood? In 1873, in *Lombard Street*, Walter Bagehot noted that "every great crisis reveals the excessive speculations of many houses which no one before expected, and which commonly indeed had not begun or had not carried very far those speculations, till they were tempted by the daily rise of price and the surrounding fever."

---

As the preceding material illustrate, the late 1980's and early 1990's saw a dramatic increase in capital requirements for depository institutions. The impact of these changes was most profound for federally-insured thrift institutions, many of whom had been allowed to operate for many years with little or no capital. The following case illustrates some of the conflicts that arose when Congress chose to change the structure of regulation in this area?

## United States v. Winstar
### 116 S. Ct. 2432 (July 1, 1996)

JUSTICE SOUTER announced the judgment of the Court and delivered an opinion, in which JUSTICE STEVENS and JUSTICE BREYER join, and in which JUSTICE O'CONNOR joins except as to Parts IV-A and IV-B.

### I

### A

The modern savings and loan industry traces its origins to the Great Depression, which brought default on 40 percent of the Nation's $20 billion in home mortgages and the failure of some 1700 of the nation's approximately 12,000 savings institutions. In the course of the debacle, Congress passed three statutes meant to stabilize the thrift industry. The Federal Home Loan Bank Act created the Federal Home Loan Bank Board (Bank Board), which was authorized to channel funds to thrifts for loans on houses and for preventing foreclosures on them. Next, the Home Owners' Loan Act of 1933 authorized the Bank Board to charter and regulate federal savings and loan associations. Finally, the National Housing Act created the Federal Savings and Loan Insurance Corporation (FSLIC), under the Bank Board's authority, with responsibility to insure thrift deposits and regulate all federally insured thrifts.

The resulting regulatory regime worked reasonably well until the combination of high interest rates and inflation in the late 1970's and early 1980's brought about a second crisis in the thrift industry. Many thrifts found themselves holding long-term, fixed-rate mortgages created when interest rates were low; when market rates rose, those institutions had to raise the rates they paid to depositors in order to attract funds. When the costs of short-term deposits overtook the revenues from long- term mortgages, some 435 thrifts failed between 1981 and 1983.

The first federal response to the rising tide of thrift failures was "extensive deregulation," including "a rapid expansion in the scope of permissible thrift investment powers and a similar expansion in a thrift's ability to compete for funds with other financial services providers."   Along with this deregulation came moves to weaken the requirement that thrifts maintain adequate capital reserves as a cushion against losses, see 12 CFR § 563.13 (1981), a requirement that one commentator described as "the most powerful source of discipline for financial institutions." The result was a drop in capital reserves required by the Bank Board from five to four percent of assets in November 1980, and to three percent in January of 1982;  at the same time, the Board developed new "regulatory accounting principles" (RAP) that in many instances replaced generally accepted accounting principles (GAAP) for purposes of determining compliance with its capital requirements.[2] According to the House Banking Committee, "[t]he use of various accounting gimmicks and reduced capital standards masked the worsening financial condition of the industry, and the FSLIC, and enabled many weak institutions to continue operating with an increasingly inadequate cushion to absorb future losses."   The reductions in required capital reserves, moreover, allowed thrifts to grow explosively without increasing their capital base, at the same time deregulation let them expand into new (and often riskier) fields of investment.

While the regulators tried to mitigate the squeeze on the thrift industry generally through deregulation, the multitude of already-failed savings and loans confronted FSLIC with deposit insurance liabilities that threatened to exhaust its insurance fund.  According to the General Accounting Office, FSLIC's total reserves declined from $6.46 billion in 1980 to $4.55 billion in 1985,  when the Bank Board estimated that it would take $15.8 billion to close all institutions deemed insolvent under generally accepted accounting principles.  By 1988, the year of the last transaction involved in this case, FSLIC was itself insolvent by over $50 billion.  And by early 1989, the GAO estimated that $85 billion would be needed to cover FSLIC's responsibilities and put it back on the road to fiscal health.  In the end, we now know, the cost was much more even than that.  See, e.g., Horowitz, The Continuing Thrift Bailout, Investor's Business Daily, Feb. 1, 1996, p. A1 (reporting an estimated $140 billion total public cost of the S & L crisis through 1995).

Realizing that FSLIC lacked the funds to liquidate all of the failing thrifts, the Bank Board chose to avoid the insurance liability by encouraging healthy thrifts and outside investors to take over ailing institutions in a series of "supervisory mergers."  Such transactions, in which the acquiring parties assumed the obligations of thrifts with liabilities that far outstripped their assets, were not intrinsically attractive to healthy institutions;  nor did FSLIC have sufficient cash to promote such acquisitions through direct subsidies alone, although cash contributions from FSLIC were often part of a transaction.  Instead, the principal inducement for these supervisory

---

[2]    "Regulatory and statutory accounting gimmicks included permitting thrifts to defer losses from the sale of assets with below market yields;  permitting the use of income capital certificates, authorized by Congress, in place of real capital;  letting qualifying mutual capital certificates be included as RAP capital;  allowing FSLIC members to exclude from liabilities in computing net worth, certain contra-asset accounts, including loans in process, unearned discounts, and deferred fees and credits;  and permitting the inclusion of net worth certificates, qualifying subordinated debentures and appraised equity capital as RAP net worth."   The result of these practices was that "[b]y 1984, the difference between RAP and GAAP net worth at S & L's stood at $9 billion," which meant "that the industry's capital position, or ... its cushion to absorb losses was overstated by $9 billion."

mergers was an understanding that the acquisitions would be subject to a particular accounting treatment that would help the acquiring institutions meet their reserve capital requirements imposed by federal regulations.

B

Under Generally Accepted Accounting Principles (GAAP) there are circumstances in which a business combination may be dealt with by the "purchase method" of accounting.   The critical aspect of that method for our purposes is that it permits the acquiring entity to designate the excess of the purchase price over the fair value of all identifiable assets acquired as an intangible asset called "goodwill."[3]   In the ordinary case, the recognition of goodwill as an asset makes sense:  a rational purchaser in a free market, after all, would not pay a price for a business in excess of the value of that business's assets unless there actually were some intangible "going concern" value that made up the difference.   For that reason, the purchase method is frequently used to account for acquisitions, and GAAP expressly contemplated its application to at least some transactions involving savings and loans.   Goodwill recognized under the purchase method as the result of an FSLIC-sponsored supervisory merger was generally referred to as "supervisory goodwill."

Recognition of goodwill under the purchase method was essential to supervisory merger transactions of the type at issue in this case.  Because FSLIC had insufficient funds to make up the difference between a failed thrift's liabilities and assets, the Bank Board had to offer a "cash substitute" to induce a healthy thrift to assume a failed thrift's obligations.  Former Bank Board Chairman Richard Pratt put it this way in testifying before Congress:

> "The Bank Board .... did not have sufficient resources to close all insolvent institutions, [but] at the same time, it had to consolidate the industry, move weaker institutions into stronger hands, and do everything possible to minimize losses during the transition period.  Goodwill was an indispensable tool in performing this task."

Supervisory goodwill was attractive to healthy thrifts for at least two reasons.  First, thrift regulators let the acquiring institutions count supervisory goodwill toward their reserve requirements under 12 CFR § 563.13 (1981).  This treatment was, of course, critical to make the transaction possible in the first place, because in most cases the institution resulting from the transaction would immediately have been insolvent under federal standards if goodwill had not counted toward regulatory net worth.  From the acquiring thrift's perspective, however, the treatment of supervisory goodwill as regulatory capital was attractive because it inflated the institution's reserves, thereby allowing the thrift to leverage more loans (and, it hoped, make more profits).

As we describe in more detail below, the accounting treatment to be accorded supervisory goodwill . . . was the subject of express arrangements between the regulators and the acquiring

---

[3]    See also Accounting Principles Board Opinion No. 17, ¶ 26, p. 339 (1970) (providing that "[i]ntangible assets acquired ... as part of an acquired company should ... be recorded at cost," which for unidentifiable intangible assets like goodwill is "measured by the difference between the cost of the ... enterprise acquired and the sum of the assigned costs of individual tangible and identifiable intangible assets acquired less liabilities assumed").

institutions. While the extent to which these arrangements constituted a departure from prior norms is less clear, an acquiring institution would reasonably have wanted to bargain for such treatment. Although GAAP demonstrably permitted the use of the purchase method in acquiring a thrift suffering no distress, the relevant thrift regulations did not explicitly state that intangible goodwill assets created by that method could be counted toward regulatory capital. Indeed, the rationale for recognizing goodwill stands on its head in a supervisory merger: ordinarily, goodwill is recognized as valuable because a rational purchaser would not pay more than assets are worth; here, however, the purchase is rational only because of the accounting treatment for the shortfall. In the end, of course, such reasoning circumvented the whole purpose of the reserve requirements, which was to protect depositors and the deposit insurance fund. As some in Congress later recognized, "[g]oodwill is not cash. It is a concept, and a shadowy one at that. When the Federal Government liquidates a failed thrift, goodwill is simply no good. It is valueless. That means, quite simply, that the taxpayer picks up the tab for the shortfall." 135 Cong. Rec. 11795 (1989) (Rep.Barnard). To those with the basic foresight to appreciate all this, then, it was not obvious that regulators would accept purchase accounting in determining compliance with regulatory criteria, and it was clearly prudent to get agreement on the matter.

C

Although the results of the forbearance policy, including the departures from GAAP, appear to have been mixed, it is relatively clear that the overall regulatory response of the early and mid-1980's was unsuccessful in resolving the crisis in the thrift industry. As a result, Congress enacted the Financial Institutions Reform, Recovery, and Enforcement Act of 1989 (FIRREA), with the objects of preventing the collapse of the industry, attacking the root causes of the crisis, and restoring public confidence.

FIRREA made enormous changes in the structure of federal thrift regulation by (1) abolishing FSLIC and transferring its functions to other agencies; (2) creating a new thrift deposit insurance fund under the Federal Deposit Insurance Corporation (FDIC); (3) replacing the Bank Board with the Office of Thrift Supervision (OTS), a Treasury Department office with responsibility for the regulation of all federally insured savings associations; and (4) establishing the Resolution Trust Corporation (RTC) to liquidate or otherwise dispose of certain closed thrifts and their assets. More importantly for the present case, FIRREA also obligated OTS to "prescribe and maintain uniformly applicable capital standards for savings associations" in accord with strict statutory requirements. 12 U.S.C. § 1464(t)(1)(A). In particular, the statute required thrifts to "maintain core capital in an amount not less than 3 percent of the savings association's total assets," and defined "core capital" to exclude "unidentifiable intangible assets," such as goodwill. Although the reform provided a "transition rule" permitting thrifts to count "qualifying supervisory goodwill" toward half the core capital requirement, this allowance was phased out by 1995. According to the House Report, these tougher capital requirements reflected a congressional judgment that "[t]o a considerable extent, the size of the thrift crisis resulted from the utilization of capital gimmicks that masked the inadequate capitalization of thrifts."

The impact of FIRREA's new capital requirements upon institutions that had acquired failed thrifts in exchange for supervisory goodwill was swift and severe. OTS promptly issued regulations implementing the new capital standards along with a bulletin noting that FIRREA "eliminates [capital and accounting] forbearances" previously granted to certain thrifts. OTS accordingly directed that "[a]ll savings associations presently operating with these forbearances ... should eliminate them in determining whether or not they comply with the new minimum regulatory capital standards." Despite the statute's limited exception intended to moderate transitional pains, many institutions immediately fell out of compliance with regulatory capital requirements, making them subject to seizure by thrift regulators.

II

In 1983, FSLIC solicited bids for the acquisition of Windom Federal Savings and Loan Association, a Minnesota-based thrift in danger of failing. At that time, the estimated cost to the Government of liquidating Windom was approximately $12 million. A group of private investors formed Winstar Corporation for the purpose of acquiring Windom and submitted a merger plan to FSLIC; it called for capital contributions of $2.8 million from Winstar and $5.6 million from FSLIC, as well as for recognition of supervisory goodwill to be amortized over a period of 35 years.

The Bank Board accepted the Winstar proposal and made an Assistance Agreement that incorporated, by an integration clause . . . , both the Board's resolution approving the merger and a forbearance letter issued on the date of the agreement. The forbearance letter provided that "[f]or purposes of reporting to the Board, the value of any intangible assets resulting from accounting for the merger in accordance with the purchase method may be amortized by [Winstar] over a period not to exceed 35 years by the straight-line method." Moreover, the Assistance Agreement itself contained an "Accounting Principles" section with the following provisions:

"Except as otherwise provided, any computations made for the purposes of this Agreement shall be governed by generally accepted accounting principles as applied on a going concern basis in the savings and loan industry, except that where such principles conflict with the terms of this Agreement, applicable regulations of the Bank Board or the [FSLIC], or any resolution or action of the Bank Board approving or adopted concurrently with this Agreement, then this Agreement, such regulations, or such resolution or action shall govern.... If there is a conflict between such regulations and the Bank Board's resolution or action, the Bank Board's resolution or action shall govern. For purposes of this section, the governing regulations and the accounting principles shall be those in effect on the Effective Date or as subsequently clarified, inter- preted, or amended by the Bank Board or the Financial Accounting Standards Board ("FASB"), respectively, or any successor organization to either." Id., at 108-109.

The Government emphasizes the last sentence of this clause, which provides that the relevant accounting principles may be "subsequently clarified ... or amended," as barring any inference that the Government assumed the risk of regulatory change. Its argument, however, ignores the preceding sentence providing that the Bank Board's resolutions and actions in connection with the merger must prevail over contrary regulations. If anything, then, the accounting principles clause tilts in favor of interpreting the contract to lock in the then-current regulatory treatment of supervisory goodwill.

In any event, we do not doubt the soundness of the Federal Circuit's finding that the overall "documentation in the Winstar transaction establishes an express agreement allowing Winstar to proceed with the merger plan approved by the Bank Board, including the recording of supervisory goodwill as a capital asset for regulatory capital purposes to be amortized over 35 years." . . . [T]he circumstances of the merger powerfully support this conclusion: The tangible net worth of the acquired institution was a negative $6.7 million, and the new Winstar thrift would have been out of compliance with regulatory capital standards from its very inception, without including goodwill in the relevant calculations. We thus accept the Court of Appeals's conclusion that "it was the intention of the parties to be bound by the accounting treatment for goodwill arising in the merger."

## III

The Government argues for reversal [of the Federal Circuit's ruling in favor of repondents], on the principle that "contracts that limit the government's future exercises of regulatory authority are strongly disfavored; such contracts will be recognized only rarely, and then only when the limitation on future regulatory authority is expressed in unmistakable terms." Hence, the Government says, the agreements between the Bank Board, FSLIC, and respondents should not be construed to waive Congress's authority to enact a subsequent bar to using supervisory goodwill and capital credits to meet regulatory capital requirements.

The argument mistakes the scope of the unmistakability doctrine. The thrifts do not claim that the Bank Board and FSLIC purported to bind Congress to ossify the law in conformity to the contracts; they seek no injunction against application of FIRREA's new capital requirements to them and no exemption from FIRREA's terms. They simply claim that the Government assumed the risk that subsequent changes in the law might prevent it from performing, and agreed to pay damages in the event that such failure to perform caused financial injury. The question, then, is not whether Congress could be constrained but whether the doctrine of unmistakability is applicable to any contract claim against the Government for breach occasioned by a subsequent act of Congress. The answer to this question is no.

## A

The unmistakability doctrine invoked by the Government was stated in Bowen v. Public Agencies Opposed to Social Security Entrapment: " '[S]overeign power ... governs all contracts subject to the sovereign's jurisdiction, and will remain intact unless surrendered in unmistakable terms.' " 477 U.S., at 52 (quoting Merrion v. Jicarilla Apache Tribe, 455 U.S. 130, 148 (1982)).

. . . [The] collective holding [of the Court's earlier unmistakability cases] is that a contract with a sovereign government will not be read to include an unstated term exempting the other contracting party from the application of a subsequent sovereign act (including an act of Congress), nor will an ambiguous term of a grant or contract be construed as a conveyance or surrender of sovereign power. The cases extending back into the 19th-century thus stand for a rule that applies when the Government is subject either to a claim that its contract has surrendered a sovereign power (e.g., to tax or control navigation), or to a claim that cannot be recognized without creating an exemption from the exercise of such a power (e.g., the equivalent of exemption from social security obligations). The application of the doctrine thus turns on whether enforcement of the contractual obligation alleged would block the exercise of a sovereign power of the Government.

The Government argues that enforcement of the contracts in this case would implicate the unmistakability principle. . . .  The Government's position is mistaken, however, for the complementary reasons that the contracts have not been construed as binding the Government's exercise of authority to modify banking regulation or of any other sovereign power, and there has been no demonstration that awarding damages for breach would be tantamount to any such limitation.

As construed by each of the courts that considered these contracts before they reached us, the agreements do not purport to bind the Congress from enacting regulatory measures, and respondents do not ask the courts to infer from silence any such limit on sovereign power . . . .  The contracts have been read as solely risk-shifting agreements and respondents seek nothing more than the benefit of promises by the Government to insure them against any losses arising from future regulatory change.  They seek no injunction against application of the law to them . . . and they acknowledge that the Bank Board and FSLIC could not bind Congress (and possibly could not even bind their future selves) not to change regulatory policy.

Nor do the damages respondents seek amount to exemption from the new law, in the manner of the compensation . . . .  Once general jurisdiction to make an award against the Government is conceded, a requirement to pay money supposes no surrender of sovereign power by a sovereign with the power to contract.  Even if the respondents were asking that the Government be required to make up any capital deficiency arising from the exclusion of goodwill . . . from the relevant calculations, such relief would hardly amount to an exemption from the capital requirements of FIRREA; after all, [any] respondent thrift still in operation[] would still be required to maintain adequate tangible capital reserves under FIRREA, and the purpose of the statute, the protection of the insurance fund, would be served.  Nor would such a damages award deprive the Government of money it would otherwise be entitled to receive (as a tax rebate would), since the capital requirements of FIRREA govern only the allocation of resources to a thrift and require no payments to the Government at all.

We recognize, of course, that while agreements to insure private parties against the costs of subsequent regulatory change do not directly impede the exercise of sovereign power, they may indirectly deter needed governmental regulation by raising its costs.  But all regulations have their costs, and Congress itself ex pressed a willingness to bear the costs at issue here when it authorized FSLIC to "guarantee [acquiring thrifts] against loss" that might occur as a result of a supervisory merger.  12 U.S.C. § 1729(f)(2) (1988 ed.) (repealed 1989).  Just as we have long recognized that the Constitution " 'bar[s] Government from forcing some people alone to bear public burdens which, in all fairness and justice, should be borne by the public as a whole,' " so we must reject the suggestion that the Government may simply shift costs of legislation onto its contractual partners who are adversely affected by the change in the law, when the Government has assumed the risk of such change.

The Government's position would not only thus represent a conceptual expansion of the unmistakability doctrine beyond its historical and practical warrant, but would place the doctrine at odds with the Government's own long-run interest as a reliable contracting partner in the myriad workaday transaction of its agencies.  Consider the procurement contracts that can be affected by congressional or executive scale-backs in federal regulatory or welfare activity;  or contracts to substitute private service-providers for the Government, which could be affected by a change in the official philosophy on privatization; or all the contracts to dispose of federal property, surplus or otherwise. If these contracts are made in reliance on the law of contract and without specific provision for default mechanisms, should all the private contractors be denied a remedy in damages unless they satisfy the unmistakability doctrine? The answer is obviously no because neither constitutional avoidance nor any apparent need to protect the Government from the consequences of standard operations could conceivably justify applying the doctrine. Injecting the opportunity for unmistakability litigation into every common contract action would, however, produce the untoward result of compromising the Government's practical capacity to make contracts, which we have held to be "of the essence of sovereignty" itself. From a practical standpoint, it would make an inroad on this power, by expanding the Government's opportunities for contractual abrogation, with the certain result of undermining the Government's credibility at the bargaining table and increasing the cost of its engagements. . . .

## B

The answer to the Government's unmistakability argument also meets its two related contentions on the score of ultra vires: that the Bank Board and FSLIC had no authority to bargain away Congress's power to change the law in the future, and that we should in any event find no such authority conferred without an express delegation to that effect. . . .

The first of these positions rests on the reserved powers doctrine, developed in the course of litigating claims that States had violated the Contract Clause. . . . The Government says that "[t]he logic of the doctrine ... applies equally to contracts alleged to have been made by the federal government." This may be so but is also beside the point, for the reason that the Government's ability to set capital requirements is not limited by the Bank Board's and FSLIC's promises to make good any losses arising from subsequent regulatory changes. The answer to the Government's contention that the State cannot barter away certain elements of its sovereign power is that a contract to adjust the risk of subsequent legislative change does not strip the Government of its legislative sovereignty. . . .

There is no question, conversely, that the Bank Board and FSLIC had ample statutory authority to do what the Court of Federal Claims and the Federal Circuit found they did do, that is, promise to permit respondents to count supervisory goodwill and capital credits toward regulatory capital and to pay respondents' damages if that performance became impossible. The organic statute creating FSLIC as an arm of the Bank Board, 12 U.S.C. § 1725(c) (1988 ed.) (repealed 1989), generally empowered it "[t]o make contracts," [FN36] and § 1729(f)(2), enacted in 1978, delegated more specific powers in the context of supervisory mergers:

"Whenever an insured institution is in default or, in the judgment of the Corporation, is in danger of default, the Corporation may, in order to facilitate a merger or consolidation of such insured institution with another insured institution ... guarantee such other insured institution against loss by reason of its merging or consolidating with or assuming the liabilities and purchasing the assets of such insured institution in or in danger of default." 12 U.S.C. § 1729(f)(2) (1976 ed. Supp. V) (repealed 1989).

Nor is there any reason to suppose that the breadth of this authority was not meant to extend to contracts governing treatment of regulatory capital. Congress specifically recognized FSLIC's authority to permit thrifts to count goodwill toward capital requirements when it modified the National Housing Act in 1987:

"No provision of this section shall affect the authority of the [FSLIC] to authorize insured institutions to utilize subordinated debt and goodwill in meeting reserve and other regulatory requirements." 12 U.S.C. § 1730h(d) (1988 ed.) (repealed 1989).

There is no serious question that FSLIC (and the Bank Board acting through it) was authorized to make the contracts in issue. . . .

We affirm the Federal Circuit's ruling that the United States is liable to respondents for breach of contract. Because the Court of Federal Claims has not yet determined the appropriate measure or amount of damages in this case, we remand for further proceedings consistent with our opinion.

It is so ordered.


### Comments and Questions

1. Why did federal regulatory authorities enter into the agreements that gave rise to this dispute? Could they have found buyers for the failed institutions without these commitments? Did they have another other options?

2. Drawing upon your knowledge of contract damages, how would you calculate the damages that the government owes the plaintiffs in these cases?


## B. Market Value Accounting

In the 1930s bank regulators used market values of bank investment portfolios to help determine bank solvency. There was a sharp economic down-turn, requiring an adjustment of market values, and a concern about the solvency of the nation's banks. Ultimately, the federal bank supervisory agencies established cost, rather than market value, as the basis for valuing good quality securities held by banks. But even after this 1938 change, cost was not used for lower-quality issues, or for long-term securities. It is also relevant that in 1938 banks held a very large portion of their assets in investment securities, rather than in loans.

In the 1980s, the dramatic difference in the status of an institution's capital depending on whether its assets were valued at cost or market again revealed the historic tension between the immediate truth of market value accounting and the traditional role of banks, consistent with cost value accounting, as holders of illiquid assets and as experts in assessing local credit quality.

Traditional cost value accounting of loans and investment securities obscured the full picture of the financial state of many banks and S&Ls until after they failed. The ultimate expense of the failures to the federal deposit insurance system was great, and began a return to market value accounting. Many institutions held long-term investment securities that had declined in value because of increased interest rates. In addition, banks held many loan assets, particularly fixed-rate residential mortgages, that had a market value far below their cost. To put it differently, depository institutions, particularly savings and loan associations, often had to pay more in interest on deposits than they received in interest on residential mortgages, creating a negative cash flow and a march toward insolvency. But this condition of troubled institutions often was disguised by accounting for the value of troubled assets in terms of hoped-for better conditions, rather than current market values.

While banks tend to value assets at cost, most other types of financial institutions use a complete system of market value accounting. This includes mortgage banks, investment banks, mutual funds, and pension funds. On the other hand, the accounting of insurance and finance companies is somewhere between the two other positions.

There are several benefits to market value accounting. First, it reveals the incremental economic changes in condition to depositors and investors, as well as to regulators. Second, it may help to reduce the future risk to taxpayers, as troubled depository institutions would likely be identified during earlier stages of decline. Third, it may make sense to have the same type of accounting for all types of financial institutions, particularly as affiliation among the different types continues to increase.

In fact, it would seem that market value accounting for financial assets would be easier to achieve than market value accounting for the assets of a manufacturing company. Most of the assets of financial institutions consist of different types of financial contracts which typically have various types of secondary markets available for valuing. Even in the absence of markets, financial values can be readily estimated from predicted cash flows.

Efforts to return to market value accounting were advocated by the Securities and Exchange Commission in the interest of full disclosure to investors, and by the Financial Accounting Standards Board in the interest of accurate accounting recognition of financial condition. The result of the efforts is one that falls short of a full blown market value standard requiring marking to market of all assets and all liabilities. But, to the extent market value accounting is used, it should improve the regulator's ability to evaluate the condition of banks and enable investors to identify incremental changes in market forces. In addition, it might also subject regulators to a form of market discipline.

But the arguments are not all on one side. Just as was true in the 1930s, if a bank has sufficient capital to withstand negative cashflows for a period of time, so long as low fixed interest rate assets are being paid on a current basis the underlying principal value is the same. The risk is interest rate risk, not credit risk. The problem can be avoided in a number of ways, such as emphasizing variable rate lending or securitization of assets. So long as there is not a risk of the institution failing to recover the principal value of assets before the capital accounts go below a certain minimum on a cost value accounting basis, perhaps the traditional role of the bank as manager of illiquid assets and analyst of local credit quality should be respected and cost value accounting allowed.

*Problem 3-22*

In the early 1980s, a bank in Oklahoma has a reasonably diversified portfolio of seemingly high quality fixed interest rate loans to retail firms in its community. The loans were relatively small and had individualized payment structures. These loans and similar loans by other banks are not traded in active markets. What valuation model should a bank accounting system use to estimate the potential certainty of expected cash flows of such loans, given our current knowledge of subsequent history that many similar loans defaulted because of a worldwide decline in the price of oil, a significant element of the economy in Oklahoma?

---

Ultimately, using market value accounting would largely place on the balance sheet what is already known to the banks themselves. Certainly it would discourage banks from investing in long-term securities, which may have a significant effect on the ability of the United States Treasury to sell the steady flow of bonds issued to finance the federal deficit, thus increasing the interest rates on such bonds in order to attract sufficient investors. And it could make it more difficult for local municipalities to sell long-term securities. So, what do you think of requiring financial institutions to adopt market value accounting?

## Section 8.  Community Reinvestment Act

The Community Reinvestment Act (CRA), 12 U.S.C.A. §§ 2901-2907, can be viewed as an exception to the general rule that banks can do business as they see fit (provided they comply with the basic portfolio shaping limitations we have considered). But the CRA exception to the general rule is more broad ranging than other federal consumer credit legislation.

CRA was passed in 1977 and is quite brief. The Act requires that in connection with the examination of a financial institution, the appropriate supervisory agency shall: 1) assess the institution's record of meeting the credit needs of its entire community, including low- and moderate-income neighborhoods, consistent with the safe and sound operation of such institutions; and 2) take this record into account in its evaluation of an application for a deposit facility by the institution.

This brief statement raises many points and questions. It suggests that an institution's lending activities must blanket the entire community, and not be targeted to particular areas or types of loans. It also suggests that enforcement for any violation of CRA can only take place in conjunction with the denial or conditioning of an application for a deposit facility, whether a branch, merger, or acquisition. Section 2901 uses the phrase "convenience and needs" of the community. This phrase, found both in the CRA and elsewhere in legislation involving bank regulation, is used to link the CRA with the existing regulatory system. In other words, CRA obligations stem from bank charters which state that banks should meet the convenience and needs of the communities they serve.

CRA is part of a larger group of statutes often encompassed by the catchall phrase "fair lending." The term "fair lending" typically includes the Fair Housing Act, the Equal Credit Opportunity Act, and the Home Mortgage Disclosure Act, as well as CRA. CRA is distinguished from the other acts in at least two important ways. One is that CRA applies only to depository institutions and not to all lenders. The other is that CRA goes beyond requirements of disclosure and nondiscrimination to create an affirmative obligation to engage in lending to meet community credit needs, particularly those of low- and moderate-income areas.

As a consequence, there is a substantial argument that CRA is a convenience and needs obligation that does not go to safety and soundness. If so, the major dilemma of CRA is that it may force sub-optimal loans on depository institutions—that CRA in fact conflicts with the fundamental tenets of safety and soundness.

The CRA statute was amended in 1989 by adding a new section requiring public disclosure of an institution's CRA rating, and further requiring the federal regulatory agencies to provide a written evaluation of each institution's performance, with a rating of outstanding, satisfactory, needs to improve, or substantial noncompliance. CRA contains no provision for an institution to challenge the regulator's CRA evaluation before public disclosure. CRA regulations are at 12 C.F.R. Pt. 25.

In March, 1989, the federal regulatory agencies issued a CRA policy statement which replaced a statement issued by them in 1980. The 1989 policy statement was reasonably specific about what constituted an effective CRA program. Each institution was required to define the community it served (referred to as its assessment area), determine the credit needs of each community, and take steps to help meet those needs through appropriate and prudent lending. In conjunction with the 1989 policy statement, the accompanying regulations elaborated an extensive, 12-factor test for evaluating an institution's CRA compliance. The factors utilized reflected an attempt to integrate the traditional "convenience and needs" standard of the statute into regulatory guidelines, linking CRA with the existing regulatory system. Regulators were to examine deposits, earnings, the bank's general performance record, the extent of advertising and marketing programs concerning credit services, evidence of discriminatory practices and discouragement of credit applications, and the degree of participation in community development and government insured programs. Compliance with the 12-factor test proved to be burdensome. Banks complained that meeting CRA requirements was not cost effective and had more to do with paper than performance, an argument which troubled community leaders as well as bankers.

New CRA regulations were made effective in 1995 with an emphasis on performance-based compliance. The 12-factor assessment test was replaced with a 3-prong test consisting of lending, service, and investment in the community.

The lending test is the most important and evaluates an institution's home mortgage, small business, small farm and consumer loans. Loans are analyzed for geographic and income level distribution, with particular emphasis on loans to both low- and moderate-income areas and individuals, as well as small farms and businesses. The service test focuses on whether the institution's facilities are accessible to all individuals in its assessment area. The investment test analyzes the institution's level of qualified investments (investments focusing on community development) and responsiveness to credit and community development needs.

The lending test is the most important of the three tests because the 1995 regulations require that a bank receive a rating of at least "low satisfactory" under that test before it can earn an overall rating of "satisfactory" or higher, and further provide that outstanding performance in lending weighs at least as much as lesser performance under the investment and service tests. See 12 C.F.R.  25.28. And so, under the 1995 regulations it appears that banks got what they asked for in two senses. First, the new tests are based on results rather than process or paper. And second, actual lending is the most important test. On the other hand, the banks may now have obligations they did not anticipate, as the lending and investment tests suggest that CRA compliance now requires actual loans and extensions of credit to low and moderate income communities regardless of credit risk. The naturally resulting economic costs would appear to be both fewer loans and extensions of credit by banks to other customers, and higher costs to those customers due to the greater scarcity of funds available to loan to them.

The 1995 regulations also established four different classifications of banks with varying regulatory obligations.  In addition to the general 3-prong test, there is a streamlined test for small banks (those with less than $250 million in assets), a specialized test for wholesale banks (those that specialize in activities such as credit cards, trusts, or international banking), and a strategic plan option available to any bank which believes that the standard 3-prong test is inappropriate for it.  A bank may devise its own strategic plan for CRA compliance, subject to community review and regulatory approval.

While an institution's CRA performance record is particularly relevant when making various applications to the regulators, CRA is also important as part of routine regulatory examinations.  Although institutions are not positively required by statute to comply with particular CRA standards, in fact a satisfactory examination record is important in order to avoid regulatory criticism during the application process.  Nevertheless, the application process remains the only method by which regulators can explicitly enforce CRA compliance.  This is not true for the other fair lending statutes.  Consider the following opinion of the Federal Reserve Board.

## In re Gore-Bronson Bancorp
### 78 Fed. Res. Bull. 784 (1992)

*Order Denying Acquisition of a Bank*

Gore-Bronson Bancorp, Inc., Prospect Heights, Illinois ("Gore-Bronson"), a bank holding company within the meaning of the Bank Holding Company Act ("BHC Act"), has applied for the Board's approval under section 3 of the BHC Act (12 U.S.C. § 1842) to acquire indirectly 96.3 percent of the voting shares of Water Tower Trust and Savings Bank ("Water Tower Bank"), from Water Tower Bancorporation ("Water Tower"), both of Chicago, Illinois.

Notice of the applications, affording interested persons an opportunity to submit comments, has been published (57 *Federal Register* 11,956 (1992)).  The time for filing comments has expired, and the Board has considered the applications and all comments received in light of the factors set forth in section 3(c) of the BHC Act.

Gore-Bronson is the 126th largest commercial banking organization in Illinois, controlling deposits of $152.9 million, representing less than 1 percent of the total deposits in commercial banking organizations in the state. Water Tower is the 92nd largest commercial banking organization in Illinois, controlling deposits of $188 million, representing less than 1 percent of the total deposits in commercial banking organizations in the state.

*Convenience and Needs Considerations*

In acting on an application under section 3 of the BHC Act, the Board must consider the convenience and needs of the communities to be served and take into account the records of the relevant depository institutions under the Community Reinvestment Act (12 U.S.C. § [2901] *et seq.*) ("CRA"). The CRA requires the federal financial supervisory agencies to encourage financial institutions to help meet the credit needs of the local communities in which they operate consistent with the safe and sound operation of such institutions. To accomplish this end, the CRA requires the appropriate federal supervisory authority to "assess the institution's record of meeting the credit needs of its entire community, including low- and moderate-income neighborhoods, consistent with the safe and sound operation of such institution," and to take this record into account in its evaluation of bank holding company applications.

The Board has carefully reviewed the CRA performance of Gore-Bronson, Water Tower, and their subsidiary banks, in light of the CRA, the Board's regulations, and the jointly issued Statement of the Federal Financial Supervisory Agencies Regarding the Community Reinvestment Act ("Agency CRA Statement"). The Agency CRA Statement indicates that decisions by agencies to allow financial institutions to expand will be made pursuant to an analysis of the institution's overall CRA performance and will be based on the actual record of performance of the institution.

*Record of Performance under the CRA*

A. CRA Performance Examinations

The Board has stated that a CRA examination is an important and often controlling factor in determining whether convenience and needs factors are consistent with approval of an expansionary proposal. Gore-Bronson controls two subsidiary banks, Irving Bank, Chicago, Illinois ("Irving Bank"), and Bronson-Gore Bank in Prospect Heights, Prospect Heights, Illinois ("B-G Bank"). Irving Bank, Gore-Bronson's largest subsidiary bank, has received two consecutive less than satisfactory CRA performance ratings from its primary federal supervisor, the Federal Deposit Insurance Corporation ("FDIC"), since its acquisition by Gore-Bronson.[6] B-G Bank's CRA performance rating from the FDIC has declined since its acquisition by

---

[6]     Irving Bank's CRA performance was rated "needs to improve" as of January 4, 1991, and again as of January 11, 1992.

Gore-Bronson to less than satisfactory.[7] Water Tower Bank also received a less than satisfactory rating in its most recent examination for CRA performance conducted by the FDIC.[8]

## B. CRA Performance Records of Gore-Bronson's Banks

*Irving Bank.* The FDIC examination of Irving Bank's CRA performance found that the bank does not have a fully implemented program to ascertain the credit needs of its community, and that only limited efforts are evident in ascertaining credit needs in low- and moderate-income areas within its community. In addition, Irving Bank's contact with community groups, civic officials and neighborhood organizations remain limited, though these types of contacts have increased since its last CRA evaluation.

While noting some increase in marketing activities, the FDIC examination concluded that the extent of advertising was limited and may not be effective in reaching the entire community, especially in some low- and moderate-income areas. For example, advertisements placed in church and community organization publications promoted the image of the bank but did not promote loan or deposit services. In addition, the examination found that, while the volume of bank officer calls had increased substantially, these calls are not evenly distributed throughout Irving Bank's delineated community. In the case of some of the bank's low- and moderate-income communities, a limited number or no calls were made. Overall, the FDIC examination characterized Irving Bank's record of extending credit within its delineated community as poor, and the extent of bank's community development lending as minimal.

*B-G Bank.* The FDIC examination of B-G Bank's CRA performance also found weaknesses in its ascertainment efforts. In this regard, minutes of meetings for B-G Bank's board do not indicate specific discussions of ascertainment efforts for the community's credit needs or discussions of overall CRA performance in terms of the types of credit extended. In addition, the record does not indicate that B-G Bank's board has undertaken a review of demographic data or geographic distribution of the bank's credit extensions. Overall, only approximately 28 percent of the bank's total loans were made within its delineate community.

B-G Bank's marketing efforts for consumer credit and home mortgage loans do not appear to target the bank's entire delineated community, which includes residents in low- and moderate-income areas.[9] The FDIC examination also found that B-G Bank was unable clearly to demonstrate reasonable efforts to meet the consumer and residential credit needs of it delineated community.

---

[7]    B-G Bank was rated "needs to improve" as of January 21, 1992.

[8]    Water Tower Bank was rated "needs to improve" as of June 6, 1990.

[9]    B-G Bank mailed questionnaires to its deposit customers in 1991 regarding bank services in general and offering to extend credit. Because a large portion of the bank's deposits were from businesses, however, the FDIC examination concluded that this ascertainment effort may not have had the effect of reaching all levels of the delineated community, including low- and moderate-income areas.

C. Additional CRA Considerations

Gore-Bronson maintains that the issues raised by these CRA performance records have been addressed by the steps initiated and to be initiated by B-G Bank and Irving Bank to improve their CRA-related activities. These steps include the introduction of VA and FHA lending programs, increased business calling programs and small business lending, increased contacts with community groups and government officials, and more comprehensive advertising efforts to reach low- and moderate-income consumers.

The Board previously has stated that when a banking organization files an application to expand its deposit-taking facilities, the organization should address its CRA responsibilities and have the necessary policies in place and working well. In addition, the Board has found commitments for future action to address CRA concerns to be appropriate considerations in the context of an application to expand deposit-taking facilities only where the applicant otherwise has a satisfactory CRA record, where the problems identified at the bank do not indicate chronic institutional deficiencies or a pattern of CRA deficiencies, and where the applicant takes immediate and effective action to address identified deficiencies in the CRA performance of its banks.

The record in this application indicates that Irving Bank and B-G Bank do not have a satisfactory record of performance in place, and have had deficiencies in CRA performance for some time. In the case of Irving Bank, these deficiencies have existed over a period of time encompassing two CRA performance examinations, and in the case of B-G Bank, its CRA performance has declined under Gore-Bronson's ownership.

Gore-Bronson has committed to take certain steps to address the CRA performance deficiencies of its subsidiary banks. Over time, these steps have the potential to remedy many of the deficiencies in the banks' CRA performance. Given the facts of this case, however, the Board does not believe that it is appropriate to rely on the future expectations or commitments for future action by Gore-Bronson. Accordingly, the Board does not believe that reliance on commitments for future action is appropriate in this case without a stronger showing of CRA performance.

The Board has carefully reviewed the CRA performance of Gore-Bronson, Water Tower, and their subsidiary banks in light of all the facts of record in this application. The Board notes that the FDIC, which is the primary federal supervisor for all the banks, has indicated its belief that the CRA records of B-G Bank and Irving Bank do not warrant approval of this application. Based on the record, and for the reasons discussed above, the Board concludes that CRA performance records of B-G Bank, Irving Bank, and Water Tower Bank weigh against approval of this application.

The Board has also considered Gore-Bronson's argument that the proposal will improve the financial condition of Water Tower Bank and consequently result in significant public benefits to the community. The Board notes, however, that Water Tower Bank has recently taken steps to improve its capital position and financial condition. In addition, as explained below, the Board does not believe that financial factors in this case support Gore-Bronson's claim that the proposal will substantially improve the financial condition of Water Tower Bank and result in substantial public benefits. Accordingly, the Board concludes that convenience and needs considerations are not consistent with approval of these applications at this time.

. . . Considerations relating to competitive, managerial resources,[12] and other factors required by the Board to be considered under the BHC Act do not lend sufficient weight to warrant approval of these applications.  Accordingly, the Board has determined that these applications should be, and hereby are, denied.

By order of the Board of Governors, effective August 13, 1992.

Voting for this action:  Chairman Greenspan and Governors Mullins, Angell, Kelley, LaWare, Lindsey, and Phillips.

### Comments and Questions

1.  Would Gore-Bronson fare better under the 1995 CRA regulations?  Why or why not?

2.  Was Gore-Bronson accused of discrimination in its lending activities?  Did it violate the Equal Credit Opportunity Act?  The Fair Housing Act and the Equal Credit Opportunity Act prohibit creditors from discriminating against loan applicants on such bases as race and gender.  But neither statute imposes an obligation on creditors to recruit status-based loan applicants.  If there is an affirmative duty to lend under CRA, does the statute require that banks depart from their traditional credit standards, adjust their pricing of loans, or revise the products they offer to meet community demands for bank services?  If so, can these goals be met without the bank sacrificing safety or soundness?

3.  Does every bank have to make consumer credit and home mortgage loans?  In 1977 depository institutions made over 80% of home mortgages.  Today they make approximately 45% of home mortgages.  While CRA applies only to depository institutions, only depository institutions have federal deposit insurance.  On the other hand, securities firms are aided by SIPC, the Securities Investors Protection Corporation.  Entities such as independent mortgage banks (which do not have bank charters) and insurance companies are heavily engaged in mortgage lending.  They make heavy use of government sponsored entities by selling loans to either the Federal National Mortgage Association or the Federal Home Loan Mortgage Corporation.  Should all non-depository financial institutions be subject to CRA to assure availability of their services to a broader spectrum of the population?

4.  A bank is allowed to define its own assessment area, subject to the requirements of 12 C.F.R. § 25.41, which says that generally a bank must include the geographic area where it has its main office, branches, and remote ATMs, or from where a majority of its loans are originated or purchased.  How should a multinational money center bank in New York City define its assessment area if only 5% of its deposits and loans come from noncorporate, New York City residents?

---

[12]    The Board has taken into account examination reports and other information regarding compliance with consumer lending laws from the FDIC and Gore-Bronson in reviewing considerations relating to the managerial resources factor.

5. Consider a radically different view of CRA. The Equal Credit Opportunity Act applies to all lenders, including insurance companies, mortgage bankers, and finance companies. CRA by its terms, does not appear to apply to race and gender; rather it is based largely on geography and individual economic status. And so we have one law, applicable to everyone, which says that discrimination is prohibited; and another law, applicable only to depository institutions, which suggests that a substantial amount of deposited funds should be loaned to low- and moderate-income areas and individuals. Why? Perhaps it is because CRA gives to people of lower economic status what federally guaranteed loans, such as the Farm Credit System, the Federal Home Loan Mortgage Corporation, the Federal National Mortgage Corporation, and the Small Business Administration, give to the rest of society—a special deal. In other words, people of poor economic circumstances simply are asking for the special, government supported deal that everybody else gets through various federal guarantee programs. The CRA low-income federal loan program is a price paid for deposit insurance.

*Problem 3-23*

You are counsel to Our Town National Bank. The board of directors presents you with several questions on which they desire your guidance.

1.    The Bank wants to concentrate its CRA lending in a few particular neighborhoods where it has extensive experience. What will happen if the Bank has little or no lending in certain low- and moderate-income areas (census tracts) within its community, but does have a strong overall record because of its historic work in particular neighborhoods? Does CRA require a bank to serve every low- and moderate-income area within its market? By the same token, does CRA require a bank to respond to all reasonable community group initiatives that have merit, even though the bank would prefer to engage in community development efforts focused in particular activities or targeted lending programs that concentrate on one area?

2. Current OCC real estate lending guidelines suggest a loan to value ratio which requires a minimum down payment of 15% for home mortgages. Few people in low- and moderate-income areas can afford a 15% down payment. Can the bank offer mortgages in these areas with only a 5% down payment for owner-occupied housing? How do you incorporate safety and soundness concerns in your opinion?

3. There is a great shortage of equity capital in the inner cities. Can the Bank take equity positions in nonbank enterprises as part of its lending to commercial enterprises in the inner city? The Bank believes that in this way it can allow for more affordable loan rates on the debt portion of high-risk financing, as it would be counterbalanced by the promise of big payoffs in the case of successful endeavors. How do you incorporate other policy concerns, such as economic neutrality and safety and soundness, in your guidance to the bank?

Some have said that CRA is a thinly disguised form of credit allocation. Credit allocation suggests an ability to determine that certain credit needs in society are entitled to preferential treatment. The argument against credit allocation is that it interferes with the economical flow of credit in our free market system, and is a major step away from a decentralized economic decision making economy to a centralized, planned allocation economy. What does this say about all government sponsored entities, such as the Federal National Mortgage Association and the Small Business Administration?

*Problem 3-24*

Congress passes a statute providing that the income tax rate applicable to banks will vary depending on the percentage of a bank's loans falling into each of three categories: (1) priority, (2) speculative and inflationary, and (3) neither. Among the uses designated priority are "normal operations of established business customers; essential and productive capital investment; low- and middle-income housing; small business and agriculture; and state and local governments." Among those classified as speculative and inflationary are: "purely financial activities–such as corporate acquisitions or the purchase of a company's own shares; loans for speculative purposes–such as purchasing securities or commodities other than in the ordinary course of business, excess inventory accumulation, or investing in land without well-defined plans for its useful development; and loans to foreigners or for foreign activities which divert loan funds away from U.S. customers."

How should the following loans be classified?

1. A loan to purchase 100 acres of land, the western third of which (according to the application) is to hold middle income housing, the central third of which is to remain "dormant," and the eastern third of which is to hold a shopping center and business offices.

2. A loan to a local supplier of heating oil for purposes of accumulating ten times more inventory than last year in expectation of expanded demand and diminished supply at a later date. Last year he could have sold almost all of what he wants to carry this year.

3. A loan to the heating oil supplier for the purpose of buying 400,000 boxes of paper clips (or 40 million clips). He has read that in two years the paper clip situation will parallel the oil crisis.

Who should make such classifications? Using what procedure? Is the statute a form of credit allocation and, if so, is it appropriate in light of the historic underlying policies of bank regulation we have considered?

---

As discussed above, the Community Reinvestment Act was originally enacted to prohibit red-lining practices of certain banks. Nowadays blatant red-lining is uncommon, but more subtle forms of discrimination may still persist. CRA proponents tend to believe that racial discrimination in lending practices is a widespread and substantial problem, justifying strong governmental responses such as the CRA. Opponents of the CRA, on the other hand, are less likely to perceive lending discrimination as a serious social problem. For them, the CRA represents a costly solution to a non-existence problem. The disagreement over the persistence of racial discrimination in lending markets is, in theory, susceptible to empirical investigation and resolution. The following excerpt summarizes some of the many recent studies of the subject. How does this analysis affect your understanding of the CRA?

## Douglas D. Evans & Lewis M. Segal, CRA and Fair Lending Regulations: Resulting Trends in Mortgage Lending
Economic Perspectives, Dec. 1996, at 19, 24-28

The CRA was introduced because redlining was believed to be a common practice by banks. The fair lending laws were passed because there was a perception that certain borrowing groups were not being treated equitably. However, there continues to be significant disagreement as to the extent of these problems.

Housing and mortgage discrimination has been a topical issue since the 1960s, when community groups argued that neighborhoods were deteriorating as a result of practices by mortgage originators. The originators were accused of using noneconomic criteria to limit funding to non-white applicants and/or non-white neighborhoods. Research in this area has intensified in recent years as amendments to HMDA reporting requirements have increased the availability of data used to compare lending patterns across race and ethnic groups, income groups, and geographic areas. However the data exclude many of the more relevant variables used in the credit evaluation process. The most meaningful studies of the role of race and neighborhood effects in mortgage lending incorporate information beyond HMDA data and evaluate discrimination based either on the neighborhood of the applicant or the characteristics of the individual applicant. These studies are divided into four classes: neighborhood redlining studies, application accept/reject studies, studies of default rates, and performance of institutions specializing in loans to low-income individuals or in low-income neighborhoods. Below, we summarize the studies to emphasize the ongoing controversies in this area of research.

### Redlining studies

Redlining is the practice of having the loan decision based on, or significantly influenced by, the location of the property without appropriate regard for the qualifications of the applicant or the value of the property. As a result, the neighborhood's financial needs are not adequately served and the region is unable to develop economically. Redlining studies typically take the neighborhood as the unit of observation, evaluating whether the aggregate supply of funds made available is related to the racial composition of the area.

Early analysis of differences in loan originations across markets found significant differences based on the racial composition of the neighborhood. However, these studies attributed all market differences to the race variable. . . .

Although improvements have been made in redlining studies, inherent methodological problems remain. First, in a number of redlining studies *the unit of observation may be too large.* To the extent redlining occurs, it could be for a relatively small area, such as two or three city blocks. In larger areas, such as metropolitan statistical areas (MSA), redlining may not be detectable in the aggregate data. Additionally, assuming some lenders redline and others do not, if borrowers eventually find the non-redlining lender, data at the broader level will imply that no redlining has occurred. The unit of observation should, therefore, be relatively small. There may also be a significant *omitted variable bias*. Exclusion of variables correlated with race may produce a significant coefficient for race even in the absence of discrimination. A standard criticism of redlining studies is that they inadequately account for demand factors. Thus, it is impossible to attribute differences in mortgage activity across markets to an inadequate supply of funding (redlining) or to a lower demand from potential borrowers. The creditworthiness of the applicant pool is also important since the riskiness of the loan will obviously be a determining factor in the underwriting decision. Additional variables to account for differences in borrower credit demand and creditworthiness that have been included in the recent studies are neighborhood average income, percent of owner-occupied houses, changes in property values, poverty and welfare rates, percent of housing units vacant, crime rates, wealth measures, mobility rates, average age of population and housing stock, total housing units, duration of residency, and the stock of conventional mortgages.

Typically, studies that have accounted for these market characteristics more comprehensively have reported a less significant impact of racial composition than that found in earlier studies. For example, when Holmes and Horvitz (1994) excluded measures of risk in their analysis of the Houston market, they found that the flow of mortgage credit was negatively associated with minority status, consistent with redlining. When the risk measure was included, minority status was not found to influence the flow of credit. Studies which employ a single-equation model to explain the amount of credit made available in a neighborhood will be mixing elements of both supply and demand for credit. Redlining will affect the supply loans. However, with the single-equation approach the supply and demand effects cannot be separated (Yezer, Phillips, and Trost, 1994). Arguing that the race variable represents discrimination requires that there be no demand-side effects. As mentioned above, a number of studies have shown this to be incorrect. Finally, *model specification* has been shown to drive some results (Horne, 1997). Concern with model specification argues that one should use a relatively flexible financial form which has the more commonly used alternative forms nested within it.

Some researchers have argued that the problems associated with the above credit flow type of redlining studies are too large to overcome and, as a result, these studies cannot adequately identify the role of racial composition of the neighborhood in loan decisions. An alternative approach, which addresses the problem of individuals eventually finding the non-redlining lender, is to directly survey individuals who were active in the mortgage market. Benston and Horsky (1992, 1979) surveyed home sellers and buyers to gather information on credit difficulties encountered in attempting to sell or purchase homes in several U.S. cities. Instead of viewing only the mortgages approved, the survey gathered information on individuals who requested credit but were unable to obtain it (for reasons such as redlining), in areas in which charges of redlining had been made and in control areas. If obtaining credit was a problem, additional information as to the reason for the problem was obtained—for example, unemployment, inadequate down payment, or location of the house. The survey explicitly asked home buyers if either a lending institution or real estate agent had stated or implied that obtaining a mortgage might be difficult because of the neighborhood in which the home was located. In both studies, the authors were unable to detect evidence of discrimination or unmet demand. The bottom line appears to be that there is little convincing evidence to suggest that redlining explains lending patterns in low-income neighborhoods.

### Accept/Reject studies

Given the above criticisms of credit flow studies, the availability of more detailed HMDA data since 1990, and a desire to more directly address the discrimination issue, recent research has taken a more microeconomic approach. Accept/reject studies take individual application data and evaluate the determinants of the lender's decision. They estimate a probability of rejection function based on various risk factors and include a race variable to account for discrimination. While these studies can also be used to test for redlining, their focus is on discrimination with respect to individual applicants.

Prior to the availability of HMDA data, Black et al. (1978) used special survey data to determine the economic variables important to the lending decision and whether personal variables such as race played a role. After accounting for economic variables and terms of the loans, they found that, although the personal characteristics did not significantly add to the power of their model in explaining the accept/denial decision, race was significant. Black applicants had a higher probability of denial at the 90 percent significance level.

In a well-publicized accept/reject study, Munnell et al. (1992) used HMDA data augmented with survey information about the creditworthiness of borrowers to analyze lending behavior in Boston. A variable to account for the racial composition of the market was not found to affect the lender's accept/reject decision, but applicant race was found to be statistically related to the decision. Minorities were rejected 56 percent more often than equally qualified whites.

The Boston study has been criticized for a number of reasons. First, as with the credit flow studies, there is the potential for omitted variable bias. If omitted variables are associated with the race variable, the coefficient on race will account for the true effect of race plus that of the omitted variable(s). The Boston study included several variables to account for borrower risk. However, not all risk factors could be captured, and some researchers argue that the race coefficient is actually capturing the riskiness of the applicant. Race would appear significant in an analysis which fails to account for wealth if, as has been shown elsewhere, minorities have lower levels of wealth. There was also little consideration of the characteristics of the property and credit history of the applicant. Second, the study has been criticized for data errors. These potential data errors include monthly incomes that are inconsistent with annual levels, negative interest rates, loan to value ratios exceeding one, loan to income ratios outside reasonable ranges, the inclusion of black applicant denials because of over-qualification for special lending programs, and a number of extreme outliers. Brown and Tootell (1995) and Munnell et al. (1996) contend that even after accounting for the data concerns, the fundamental result remains—minorities are more likely to be denied mortgages than similarly qualified whites.

Other follow-up studies have shown mixed results. Using data from Munnell et al. (1992), Zandi (1993) found no race effect, while Carr and Megbolugbe (1993) found the effect remains after "cleaning the data," as did Glennon and Stengel (1994). Using a model similar to that in Munnell et al. to evaluate the Boston and Philadelphia markets, Schill and Wachter (1993) found evidence consistent with redlining and discrimination. When variables are included to proxy for neighborhood risk, the neighborhood racial composition became insignificant, although racial status still significantly decreased the probability of acceptance. Stengel and Glennon (1995) also found that it is important to use bank-specific guidelines in the analysis to capture unique, but economically based, underwriting criteria. Using a more generic market model, for example, secondary market criteria, can lead to misleading results. Using cleansed data from Munnell et al. (1992), Hunter and Walker (1996) did not find evidence of discrimination via higher underwriting standards for all minorities. They contend that race matters only in the case of *marginally qualified* applications. Needless to say, there is little uniformity of view.

Yezer (1995) and Rosenblatt (1997) argue that fundamental problems in the use of accept/reject models to evaluate discrimination result from the informal prescreening of applicants. both applicants and lenders only want to proceed with applications that appear likely to qualify for a loan because denials are costly for both parties. Thus, during the initial lender-borrower contact, the lender and borrower decide whether the application warrants pursuing. Then, the formal application takes place, and denials occur only in those cases in which information not available in the initial contact affects the decision (for example, bad credit history). Therefore, denial may be as closely related to communication skills and cultural background as to economic variables. *Sophisticated* under qualified potential applicants will not reach the formal application process because they realize they will not be accepted, while *unsophisticated* candidates will follow through only to be denied. Thus, there is a significant selection bias problem in the formal application stage which may explain the race differentials. To support this view, Rosenblatt (1997) cites evidence that education levels are strongly predictive of credit approvals. The argument, therefore, is that the information in denial rate data may not be what researchers perceive it to be.

### Default rate studies

An alternative means of evaluating lender discrimination is to examine the default rates of borrowers thought to be discriminated against relative to other borrowers. Researchers have compared default rates across groups based on the theory that if minorities are overtly discriminated against, the average minority borrower should be of higher credit quality than the average nonminority borrower. This should be reflected in mortgage default rates and resulting loss rates; for minority loans, both should be lower. However, studies have not found evidence of lower default rates for minority holders of mortgages. In critiquing the Boston study, Becker (1993) cited data indicating the default rates were equal for white and minority sections of the Boston market, which was not consistent with overt discrimination. A more recent study by Berkovee et al. (1996) also tests for discrimination using default rates. Controlling for various loan, borrower, and property related characteristics, the authors evaluated the default rates and resulting losses for FHA-insured loans and found a higher likelihood of default on the part of black borrowers and higher loss rates. These results suggest that lenders, perhaps as a result of regulatory pressure, may have over-extended credit to minorities.

However, this line of research has also been criticized. First, if discrimination occurs, while the marginal minority borrower may be better qualified than the marginal white applicant, inferences about the average borrower cannot be made without making assumptions about the distribution of creditworthiness across the two groups of potential borrowers, for example, Ferguson and Peters (1995). The distributions could be significantly different. Additionally, minorities may also be treated differently once they are in default. Default studies typically use data on foreclosures. Bank forbearance in defaults favoring one of the two groups could bias the results.

### Performance studies

There are two general areas of research relating bank performance to the CRA and fair lending regulations. The first deals with the profitability associated with lending in low-income markets. If such lending is not profitable, regulation requiring it should adversely affect performance. The second area of research addresses the implications of mortgage discrimination on bank performance. If some banks are choosing to discriminate and forego profitable lending opportunities, other banks that do not discriminate should be able to exploit these opportunities.

During the debate prior to the enactment of the CRA, critics argued that economics was driving lending patterns and the CRA might either have no impact, but be costly to implement, or actually generate bad loans. From the banks' perspective it would be a tax and, if lending patterns did not change, it would be without benefits. If increased lending in the low-income market did occur, but was not as profitable as that in alternative markets, then the CRA would act as a tax and credit redistribution mechanism. The argument in favor of the CRA was that banks were foregoing profitable opportunities because of discriminatory behavior or market failure, and performance could be enchanced if they became more actively involved in this market (although performance could be adversely affected in the short run as start-up costs were incurred).

There have been a limited number of studies evaluating the effect on performance of lending in the low-income market. Canner and Passmore (1996) offered a number of testable ;hypotheses concerning the potential impact on profitability and the relationship between the extent of the bank's activity in this market and performance. They found no evidence of lower profitability at banks specializing in the low-income market, consistent with the view that once start-up cost are incurred, lending in this market can be just as profitable as in other markets. Beshouri and Glennon (1996) evaluated the relative performance of credit unions that specialize in the low-income market and found that while these specialized firms have greater return volatility, higher delinquency rates, charge-off rates, and operating costs, they are compensated for these differences and generate similar rates of return. Similarly, in analyzing the performance of low-income and minority lending, Malmquist, Phillips-Patrick, and Rossi (1997) found that while low-income lending was more costly, lenders were compensated with higher revenues, making profits similar for both low- and high-income lending. Finally, Esty (1995) evaluated the performance of Chicago's South Shore Bank, which has been held up as the model community development bank with the dual objectives of making a profit and aiding in the development of the local community. Esty's analysis found the economic return of the bank to be substandard. Shareholders, however, appeared to be willing to trade off the lower return for the social return received from community improvement. That is, the shareholders' objectives were apparently aligned with the dual objectives of the bank. In interviews with shareholders and employees, Lash and Mote (1994) found similar evidence of a willingness to trade off economic profit to emphasize the development objective. While the behavior of South Shore's management and shareholders may be admirable, if Esty's analysis is correct, it is not obvious that this model can be implemented across the entire industry.

The second performance-related area of research deals with the profit implications of discrimination. If an institution overtly discriminates, it will deliberately forego profitable leading opportunities. This implies that lenders that do not discriminate will be the beneficiaries of this behavior. Assuming that minority-owned banks do not discriminate against minorities, one might expect them to outperform the discriminating banks. Calomiris, Kahn, and Longhofer (1994) developed a model of *cultural affinity* to explain differences in minority denial rates. Their basic argument is that because of a general lack of familiarity with the culture of minority applicants, the typical white loan officer may not be as accommodating with these applicants as he would with a white applicant. For the minority applicant, the loan officer will rely more heavily on low-cost, objective information instead of making the extra effort, as with the white applicant, to obtain additional information to improve the chances of approval. There is some empirical support for this argument (see Hunter and Walker, 1996). Again, this implies that minority-owned banks should benefit, since they will not lack a cultural affinity with minority applicants.

If discriminatory banks forego profitable opportunities, *ceterus paribus*, minority-owned banks should have superior profitability, lower minority denial rates, and lower bad loans. However, the empirical evidence does not support this. A number of studies have found that minority-owned banks have lower profits (Bates and Bradford, 1980> Boorman and Kwast, 1974, and Brimmer, 1971). There is also evidence of higher loan losses at minority-owned banks (Kwast, 1981). Additionally, there is evidence that bank ownership shifts from white to black control result in fewer loans being generated (Dahl, 1996). Generally, there is evidence that minority-owned banks do not have particularly good performance or lending records and have relatively poor CRA ratings (Kwast and Black, 1983, Clair, 1988, and Black, Collins, and Cyree, 1997). This evidendce is not consistent with overt discrimination.

In summary, the findings for the various forms of discrimination are quite mixed. While some studies have found race to be a factor in loan decisions, the evidence is far from conclusive. Additionally, methodological problems bring into question the validity of many studies. Parties on either side of the issue frequently draw uncritically on the studies that align with their own position. Additional research is needed before we can draw meaningful conclusions. . .

# Section 9.  Trust Department Activities

## A.  Introduction

In addition to making loans and otherwise extending credit to customers, another significant activity of banks is providing fiduciary services, such as trust and estate administration. Trust department services have expanded over time. Fiduciary services are provided to affluent families, corporations, qualified retirement plans, governmental units, and others, and include a full range of investment portfolio management. Trust department activities are not within the general powers clause, section 24(7), because managing trust accounts is not within the activities of deposit taking, credit granting or credit exchange. Trust activities, rather, are an express power now found in 12 U.S.C.A. § 92a. See also 12 C.F.R. Pt. 9.

In the nineteenth century the National Bank Act was consistently interpreted to prohibit national banks from dealing in nongovernment securities. *Logan County National Bank v. Townsend,* 139 U.S. 67 (1891); *California National Bank v. Kennedy,* 167 U.S. 362 (1897). On the state level, however, first trust companies, and then banks, began to handle personal estates and corporate agency or fiduciary matters, steadily expanding to a full range of financial services, including investment banking. Trust activities were initially authorized for national banks in 1913, and have since grown to be a major segment of the commercial banking business in the United States.

Any profit making enterprise seeks to engage in profitable activities, and the growth of the capital markets in the United States generated an interest by banking institutions in the securities markets. From this there evolved both bank trust departments and separate securities affiliates. The Banking Act of 1933 largely separated commercial banking from investment banking, but allowed commercial banks to retain their fiduciary powers.

Today, bank trust departments are big business, but a limited number of banks account for most of the trust activity. Approximately 3,000 banks have trust powers. Of those banks, only about 500 are sufficiently large that they operate common trust funds. A common trust fund is the functional equivalent of a private mutual fund, as it invests the assets of multiple trusts and estates in a single account for reasons of administrative convenience. Of these 500 banks, fewer than 100 have common trust funds with more than $75 million in assets. As a whole, banks with trust powers manage over $4 trillion of assets, which annually generate over $400 billion in fee income and $25 billion in net profits.

The absence of trust powers, however, does not bar banks from engaging in investment activities. As we will discuss when examining the securities activities of financial institutions, many banks with or without trust powers have their own subsidiaries or BHC affiliates offering broker-dealer and registered investment advisory services, including their own mutual fund products.

Trust companies charge both for custodial services, where they simply maintain possession and control of assets, and for money management investment services. A common fee schedule on a $1 million account is 0.25% for custodial or bookkeeping services and 1% or more for money management investment services, including custodial services.

The critical statute when examining bank trust department powers, 12 U.S.C.A. § 92a, shows great deference to state law and the idea of competitive equality between national and state bank fiduciaries. The statute provides that the Comptroller cannot grant powers to national banks which exceed those permitted under state law for corporate fiduciaries with which a national bank may compete. But the Comptroller is also precluded by § 92a from approving some fiduciary activities even if they are permissible under state law. And even where the Comptroller is free to permit fiduciary activities commensurate with state law, the statute does not require the Comptroller to do so. The statute provides the Comptroller with discretion to adopt regulations concerning the appropriate exercise of fiduciary powers by national banks.

Examples of activities prohibited to national bank fiduciaries include § 92a(d), prohibiting accepting deposits in the trust department subject to check and requiring that deposits in the commercial side of the bank, of trust funds awaiting investment, be appropriately secured; and § 92a(c) requiring segregation of trust assets and the maintenance of separate books and records.

The enactment of the Interstate Banking and Branching Efficiency Act of 1994 raises additional concerns as bank trust activities become more interstate. Because of the deference of § 92a to state law, trust departments may have to deal with the variety of fiduciary laws found in the fifty states. As current law is written, it is not always possible for the OCC to preempt state fiduciary law. One particular problem may be fees that are allowed to be charged by fiduciaries in each state. On the other hand, it may well be that trust departments will be able to avoid many problems by writing trust instruments which designate the bank's home state as the law to which the trust is subject.

In this section we will first briefly identify the most typical trust services offered by a bank. Then we will consider the regulation of the operations of bank trust departments; we will review some of the problems relating to the administration of a trust generally; and we will consider some of the unique trust problems caused by the consolidation of a trust and a commercial department into a "full-service bank."

## B. Typical Trust Services

A bank trust department's activities can be divided into at least four types. The oldest and best known activity of a trust department is the personal trust business, utilized by individuals as an asset management tool as well as a means for protecting and passing on wealth through the planned investment of assets. As trustee, the bank takes title to the property and has power to manage it. The second area of activity is corporate trust services, such as dividend payment, stock issuance, municipal trusteeship for bond issues and, most important, corporate pension and profit sharing trust fund management. The third area of activity involves managing agency accounts. Here an individual places assets in a trust department account but retains all rights in and powers over the investments, rather than transferring ownership to a trust. The bank is given a limited power of attorney to direct investment of the account. While registration of the securities may be in the name of the bank, that is only for convenience. The fourth area of activities is pure custodial services. The trust department has neither title to nor investment discretion over the assets, and receives possession of the assets only as agent to perform the services specified in the custodial agreement, typically bookkeeping or recordkeeping services.

There are many differences between trust and agency roles, even though both trustees and agents are fiduciaries. A trustee has title to trust property, an agent does not, although the agent may have investment or management powers with respect to the property. An agent acts on behalf of a principal and is subject to the principal's control, while a trustee is not subject to the control of the beneficiary or settlor, at least in theory. Nevertheless, the trustee must deal with the trust property solely for the benefit of the beneficiary and in accordance with the terms of the trust. And so, while both agents and trustees are fiduciaries, their obligations, and thus their liabilities, may be significantly different.

## C. The Regulation of Trust Departments

### 1. Conflict of Interests

A trustee is a fiduciary subject to the law of trusts. When that trustee is also a bank, it is subject to further regulation *because* it is a bank. Banks generally are the only type of corporation which can be a trustee.

The trust departments of state banks are regulated in their operation by state banking law. These laws set conditions for establishing a trust and provide some general guidelines as to how the trust is to operate. Some additional understanding of the regulations applicable to trust services can be obtained by reviewing the excerpts from 12 C.F.R. Pt. 9 set out in the statutory supplement.

A fiduciary has a duty of loyalty which prohibits it from engaging in any transaction that creates a conflict of interests between the trustee and the trust or its beneficiaries. This is a difficult goal to obtain in a world where banks provide a multitude of financial services to a broad range of customers, in particular where banks operate a commercial as well as a trust department. One way to eliminate almost all conflicts of interests is to segregate completely commercial from trust banking. A few banks limit themselves to trust powers, but they typically are smaller and offer personal rather than corporate trust services.

The current structure of banks with both commercial and trust powers makes such a suggestion of complete separation unrealistic. Consequently, for a prohibited conflict of interests to arise between a full-service bank and its fiduciary responsibilities, there must be a real or serious possibility of conflict. Relationships cannot develop so that the bank is in a position where its own interests or an engagement it has with another customer operates to the detriment of the trust, at least without the explicit agreement of the trust or its beneficiaries.

Comptroller's regulation 12 C.F.R. § 9.12 covers this area. As the regulation indicates, serious difficulties can arise where the trust department engages in the purchase or sale of assets in transactions involving the trust, and the bank, bank insiders or customers.

*Problem 3-25*

Most states limit the amount of compensation that a trustee can receive for the management of assets.

1. Marvelous Bank & Trust Co. receives a trust account of $1 million. The interest paid on a 12-month time deposit at the Bank is 5% and the current prime lending rate is 8%. If the statutory fee schedule is 1% for the first $1 million of principal, do you see a way whereby the Bank can increase its "fee" on the trust management from $10,000 to $25,000? See generally 12 C.F.R. §§ 9.2, 9.10, 9.12 and 9.15.

2. Marvelous Bank and Trust Co. is the trustee of its own Discretionary Common Trust Fund (Equities). As trustee, Marvelous has lawfully invested the CTF assets in mutual funds which are managed by the registered investment adviser subsidiary of Marvelous' parent bank holding company. Can the assets in the CTF be subjected to both the investment management fees of the mutual funds and the trust management fees of Marvelous, which trust fees are limited by state law to 1%? See also 12 C.F.R. § 9.18(b)(9).

---

## 2. The Trust Department and the "Full-Service Bank"

Innumerable problems arise where the interests of trust beneficiaries and a bank's commercial customers intersect. In some circumstances, particularly with respect to federal securities law, it is often suggested that the commercial and trust departments of a bank should never interact. On the other hand, fiduciary law often suggests that a fiduciary has a duty to utilize knowledge available anywhere in the bank. Perhaps these problems can be solved at the inception of each fiduciary relationship, with each trust instrument providing that there is no duty to use information for the benefit of the trust that is subject to a duty of confidentiality to another customer, or, more generally, possessed by the bank outside the trust department. In other words, the parties to the trust instrument specifically agree to limit the scope of the fiduciary relationship.

### Overview

If $X$ corporation has a deposit account with the commercial department, the bank will be a depository; if $Y$ corporation has a loan outstanding, the bank is a creditor; if the bank holds shares of the two corporations in its trust department, the bank will be a stockholder. All of these relationships are normal, and usually they cause no problems. A problem may arise, however, when the bank deals with the single $XYZ$ corporation. The fact that the bank has business relationships with a firm whose shares the bank holds in trust may simply reflect a mutually advantageous arrangement—both have an interest in the success of the company, and they are able to work closely to achieve that end. Yet such a situation presents an inherent potential for conflict of interests. If the bank holds a large block of $XYZ$ stock, it may have the power to compel the corporation to do business with its commercial department. This power could come from control of the board or a threat to dump the stock at a critical time for the corporation. On the other hand, the bank's concern for maintaining good relations with $XYZ$, a large commercial customer, may interfere with the bank's fiduciary obligation to its beneficiaries to dispose of unproductive $XYZ$ stock or to vote the $XYZ$ stock it holds against the management on an issue crucial to the value of the trust investment.

Since the bank's position as a creditor may give it inside information about $XYZ$, there is a danger that this information might be used for investment purposes in violation of Rule 10b-5 under the Securities Exchange Act. And if information so acquired is *not* used for investment purposes, the bank may violate its fiduciary duty under the trust.

### Rule 10b-5 and Banks

Traditionally banks made unrestricted use of the information generated by all the resources of the bank—the trust department and the commercial department. This information flow was most helpful to the trust department in carrying out its fiduciary duty. Beneficiaries benefitted from the bank's investment decisions based on "inside information." This information flow within the bank was condoned by the courts, and in fact many courts implied that if the trust departments did *not* use this information, they would be in breach of their fiduciary duty. Thus, the bank was a recipient, a transmitter, and a user of inside information. Then Texas Gulf Sulphur, while digging for ore in Canada, discovered section 10b-5 of the Securities Exchange Act of 1934 and Rule 10b-5.

A bad omen for the banking industry was the Merrill Lynch case. Merrill Lynch had undertaken an investigation of Douglas Aircraft in anticipation of a public issuance of securities for Douglas. In the course of its investigation Merrill Lynch learned, somewhat in advance of the publication by Douglas of its quarterly figures, that earnings had declined significantly. This information was transmitted by Merrill Lynch to some of its investment advisory clients who then sold their Douglas stock before the bottom dropped out. The SEC imposed sanctions against Merrill Lynch, and the Second Circuit held that by their failure to disclose inside information to the investing public regarding Douglas, both Merrill Lynch and their clients who traded violated 10b-5.

In the SEC proceeding against Merrill Lynch the SEC published the following statement of policy.

### In re Merrill, Lynch, Pierce, Fenner & Smith
CCH Fed. Sec. L. Rep. ¶ 77,629, 83,351 (SEC 1968)

This Statement of Policy is adopted to provide more effective protection against disclosure of confidential information.

Material information obtained from a corporation by the Underwriting Division in connection with the consideration or negotiation of a public or private offering of its securities and which has not been disclosed by the corporation to the investing public, and conclusions based thereon, shall not be disclosed by any member of the Underwriting Division to anyone outside that Division except to

(a) senior executives of the firm and its Legal Department;

(b) lawyers, accountants and other persons directly involved with the underwriters in connection with the proposed offering;

(c) appropriate personnel of the Research Division whose views in connection with the proposed offering are to be sought by the Underwriting Division; and

(d) members of the buying departments of other firms who are prospective members of the underwriting group for the purpose of enabling such other firms to decide whether, the extent to which or the price at which, they will participate in the proposed offering.

Any employee of the firm who receives such information pursuant to the foregoing shall not disclose such information or any conclusions based thereon except as provided above for members of the Underwriting Division.

Material information, as used herein, refers to matters relating to a corporation which would be important to a reasonable investor in deciding whether he should buy, sell or hold securities of the corporation or which would be likely to have substantial market impact. Any such information which has not been disclosed by the corporation to the investing public, communicated in accordance herewith, shall be clearly identified as non-public information which is to be used by the recipient solely for the purpose of carrying out his responsibilities in connection with the proposed offering and which is not to be disclosed orally or in writing for any other purpose.

---

This policy has become known as "The Wall." As applied to a bank, it means that the bank is to establish a wall between its commercial and trust departments through which no material inside information is to pass. See if you can answer the following problem with the help of Mr. Arnold's guidelines and the SEC rule.

## Alvin L. Arnold, Guidelines for the Banker 'Insider' or 'Tippee'
### 86 Banking L.J. 319, 319-321 (1969)

The shock waves sent out by the decision of the Second Circuit Court of Appeals in the case of *S.E.C. v. Texas Gulf Sulphur* are still being felt in bankers' offices from coast to coast. Short of an absolute reversal by the U.S. Supreme Court, it seems clear that it's a new ball game for those who buy and sell stock on 'inside information.' We are many judicial decisions away from any real clear-cut rule for insider trading but certain tentative guidelines can be drawn for bank officials who, by the nature of their business, are privy to confidential corporate information.

*Access Test Defines 'Insider.'* Although the term 'insider' is broadly used to cover anyone who comes within the scope of Rule 10b-5 of the Securities and Exchange Commission, a more useful definition is the so-called *'access test.'* As stated by Professor Alan Bromberg of Southern Methodist University Law School, an insider is one who (a) has access to material, corporate information not publicly disclosed and which is intended to be confidential and (b) who makes unfair use of the information by buying or selling securities or transmitting the information to others who will do so.

When is information 'material'? The *objective* test says information is material when a 'reasonable investor or speculator' would act upon it. The *subjective* test says information is material by the very fact that it was acted upon. In other words, the subjective test practically eliminates any independent meaning of 'material.' Since no one knows which test the courts will follow, caution requires that the subjective test be used to measure liability.

*When May an Insider Trade?* Assuming that one is an insider and has in his possession material information, what can or cannot he do? The answer is he cannot buy or sell stock in the company until (1) the material information has been disclosed to the public and (2) enough time has elapsed to permit a reasonably wide dissemination of the news to investors. Here again, the guideline is necessarily vague. 'Disclosure' means, in general, publication in the press or transmission over the Dow-Jones 'broad tape' which is available in most brokerage offices. 'Elapsed time' is also a flexible concept–the impact of obviously good news will be absorbed rather quickly while more complicated information may have to be digested by investors before its impact is felt on the price of the stock.

*Who Is a Tippee?* A tippee is anyone who receives information from an insider or from another tippee. In theory, the information can be received tenth-hand and still make the tippee liable under Rule 10b-5. Professor Bromberg suggests several standards to determine if a tippee risks liability if he acts upon information he receives from a true insider.

*1. Specificity of Information:* The more specific the information, the more likely it is to result in violation if the tippee uses it or passes it along to another tippee. Another way of putting it is to say that very generalized information can hardly be material in deciding whether to buy or sell a security.

*2. Knowledge of Company Source:* The test here is whether the tippee knows that the information comes from a company source. He may, of course, believe that the information comes from a security analyst, from a broker, from a competitor or supplier of the company, etc. In general terms, the less likely it is that the tippee knows the information has come from the company or has reason to think it has come from the company, the less likely his action may be a violation of Rule 10b-5.

*3. Degree of Diffusion of Information:* This is related to whether the information has been publicly disclosed. (Of course, once public disclosure has occurred, anyone can trade or use the information.) Professor Bromberg's point is that as far as the tippee is concerned, a much lesser degree of public diffusion may relieve him from any liability than would relieve a trust insider. The real insider, under the *Texas Gulf Sulphur* case, is required to meet a very high standard of reasonable belief that public disclosure has in fact occurred. Presumably, a tippee would not have to meet the same high standard.

*4. Probability of Accuracy of Information:* This standard relates to preliminary information only, such as the results of a drill hole in *Texas Gulf Sulphur*. Here again, Professor Bromberg believes that the standard will be stricter for real insiders than for tippees. In other words, the highly improbable event may not be 'hard enough' information to prohibit trading by an insider before public disclosure. As it gets more probable, the real insider will have to refrain from acting until public disclosure occurs. On the other hand, a tippee (who probably can't judge the probability factor very well because he is not a real insider) will be subject to a much less strict standard.

*Problem 3-26*

The courts have not explored the implications of 10b-5 as it applies to a full-service bank. Yet, in some situations banks are clearly in danger of violating 10b-5:

1. Mr. Stanton is the chief lending officer of City National Bank. Mr. Salk of Salk Inc. comes to him with a secret formula for the cure of cancer and seeks a loan of $20 million. Stanton gets an analysis from a scientist and learns that the formula is indeed a cure for cancer. After closing the loan Stanton rushes to the cafeteria where he finds Ms. Bernbaum, the chief trust officer, having lunch with you—the bank's counsel. Stanton tells Bernbaum of this discovery and urges Bernbaum to go and buy as much Salk Inc. stock as she can. Since only Salk, the scientist and Stanton know of this discovery, Stanton is sure the stock is available at a reasonable price. Have you any words of advice for Stanton and Bernbaum?

2. Assume that you too knew of the discovery. You are discussing it with Stanton when Bernbaum comes over to join you for coffee. Before either Stanton or you say a word, Bernbaum says: "Say, I just saw Mr. Salk this morning. You know, I have a hunch that his firm is going places. I think I will sell our Microsoft stock in the Trust Department and buy Salk stock." What do you do now counsel?

3. Assume this time that you are at the water cooler with Ms. Bernbaum (lunch and coffee break both being finished), listening to her explain that she is about to sell the bank's vast holdings of Salk Inc., because she foresees imminent collapse for the firm. In fact, she says, she had even told her plans to Murat, a stockbroker, who that morning had, by coincidence, been named a director of a competing bank. At this point Mr. Stanton

comes over and relates the secret tale of Salk's amazing discovery. What do you advise: can your bank now *not* trade if it does not disclose?

4. Assume that six months later Mr. Stanton informs you the federal government has determined that Salk, Inc.'s secret formula is worthless. After this information becomes public knowledge a few weeks later, the value of Salk, Inc. stock collapses. Because of your impregnable wall, the trust department failed to sell any of the stock. The bank is sued by various trust beneficiaries in a Rule 10b-5 and breach of fiduciary duty action. What witnesses will you put on the stand to testify, to what and in what order, to prove that the wall was really impregnable and that there was no 10b-5 or fiduciary duty violation?

*Problem 3-27*

The heads of the commercial lending and trust departments come to you with the following question, seeking your advice.

They wish to breach "The Wall" that you have so elaborately constructed. The trust account managers have accumulated a variety of information on their customers, as have the commercial lending officers. The department heads wish to engage in the following activities: (1) swap customer lists, each informing the other about potential needs for trust or lending (or other commercial) services; (2) have both the commercial lending and trust account officers cross sell each other's services; (3) send out calling officers from both the commercial and trust side as a team; and (4) in general, permit trust and commercial lending officers to work together and share information in all ways, except that the Wall would prohibit a portfolio manager on the trust side from buying or selling stock on information he or she receives from the commercial side that is not available to the public. Are these activities permissible under 12 U.S.C.A. § 92a and rule 10b-5?

Could a Wall, or some internal bank policy, protect the bank in the following case?

---

# Jefferson National Bank v. Central National Bank
## 700 F.2d 1143 (7ᵗʰ Cir. 1983)

COFFEY, Circuit Judge.

This diversity action was brought by the corporate Personal Representative of the Estate of Philip Litner, Jefferson National Bank of Miami Beach, for the benefit of the beneficiaries under the decedent's will. The Personal Representative claims that the defendant corporate Trustee, "Central National Bank in Chicago," breached the fiduciary duty it owed to Mr. Philip Litner by failing to act prudently and conscientiously with the best interest of Philip paramount during the entire period the defendant acted as Trustee of the decedent's revocable *inter vivos* trust. * * * Following a jury trial in the district court, verdicts were returned in favor of the

Personal Representative * * *.  Actual damages were assessed against the Trustee in the amount of $394,475.40, while punitive damages were denied.  We AFFIRM.

## FACTS

On August 2, 1968, Philip Litner retired from his post as Chief Executive Officer of a subsidiary of Curtis Electro Corporation ("Curtis"), resigned as an officer of Curtis and sold all of his Curtis stock to the corporation.  Although its common stock was publicly traded, the Curtis Electro Corporation was controlled by members of the Litner family.  Philip's brothers and son were not only directors of the corporation but also occupied senior management positions.

Curtis agreed to purchase the stock of Philip Litner for $511,560.  At the time of sale, Philip Litner received a cash down payment of $148,352.40 and an unsecured promissory note of $363,207.60 for the remaining balance bearing interest at 5 percent and calling for payment of the principal in three installments:  one payment due on January 2, 1969; one on January 2, 1971; and the last payment due January 2, 1972.  Curtis made the first installment to Philip Litner, but failed to make the two remaining payments of $127,890 each.

William Purcell, a vice president of plaintiff-appellant "Central National Bank in Chicago" ("Central"), called on Philip Litner shortly after he sold his Curtis stock.  At this time, Mr. Purcell, responsible for the development of new trust business for Central, suggested to Philip that he consider establishing a "revocable living trust" for estate planning purposes.  Philip Litner expressed concerns regarding the administration of the trust and Purcell agreed that the Trustee would consult him (Philip) before making any investment decisions.  Mr. Purcell supported this agreement with a statement that the bank would not exercise investment control without Mr. Litner's permission.

Philip requested that Central supply Eli Fink (Philip's attorney) with a proposed trust agreement.  Mr. Fink and an attorney for Central negotiated the language to be contained in the agreement creating the *inter vivos* trust and on September 25, 1969, Philip Litner and a representative of Central signed the agreement designating Central as the Trustee of "Philip Litner Trust No. 1." ("Trust").  During his lifetime, Philip was to be the sole beneficiary of the Trust and upon his death new trusts were to be established for the benefit of his wife and children.  The initial Trust corpus consisted of Curtis Electro's promissory note of $255,780 and, in addition, other securities valued at approximately $220,000.

From September of 1969 until January of 1971, Central communicated with Philip Litner concerning Trust investments and on one occasion Mr. Litner gave Central written approval of an investment change.  Prior to January 17, 1971, there was limited discussion between Central and Philip Litner regarding the Curtis promissory note.

On January 17, 1971, Philip Litner suffered a severe stroke, was hospitalized for several weeks and thereafter was confined to a nursing home for temporary care.  The residuals of this stroke were rather severe in that Philip Litner was left partially paralyzed and no longer able to speak.  On or about January 25, 1971, Jerry Litner (Philip's son) contacted Central and informed the bank that his father had suffered a stroke and was in a coma.  The following month, Jerry Litner met with various officers of Central and advised them of his father's disability, reciting that his father could comprehend what was going on about him but was only able to communicate through physical gestures.  At this time, Jerry Litner expressed concern about how his father's increased medical, personal and living expenses would be paid. After discussion, an agreement was reached whereby the Trustee would make monthly disbursements to Betty (Philip's wife) and she, in turn, would take care of the expenses.

Because Curtis Electro suffered economic difficulties they were unable to make the January 2, 1971 note payment due to cash flow problems. In lieu thereof, Curtis executed a new two-year promissory note in the amount of $127,890 bearing interest at the prime rate. On or about March 15, 1971, Central, as Trustee, agreed to the substitution of a replacement note for the then due cash payment.

Subsequent to Jerry Litner's advising the Trustee of his father's condition, Central took no action to ascertain on its own the mental condition or competency of Philip Litner. Even though Philip was the sole beneficiary of the Trust, Central never communicated, or attempted to communicate, directly with him about the Trust for several years after his stroke. Instead of consulting with Philip, Trust matters were communicated to Jerry and Betty Litner. Monthly Trust statements were forwarded to Betty Litner and monthly Trust income payments were deposited in her bank account without obtaining Philip's approval. On several occasions between 1971 and 1973, investment recommendations for the Trust were also forwarded to Betty Litner and she indicated her approval of the same on Central's written consent forms.

As Curtis Electro's principal lender, Central entered into a commercial loan agreement which provided Curtis with an unsecured revolving line of credit in the amount of $1,500,000 for general business purposes. It should be noted that Philip Litner was personally aware of the Curtis loan agreement and of Central's position as principal commercial banker of Curtis at the time he designated the bank as Trustee. During the late 1960s and prior to August of 1972, pursuant to the revolving credit agreement, Central made unsecured loans to Curtis, the parent company, without taking collateral or obligating the subsidiaries in any way. The loan agreement with Central prohibited Curtis from pledging, mortgaging, encumbering or otherwise granting any security interest in any of Curtis' properties without the prior written approval of Central.

In 1970, Curtis lost in excess of $700,000 and, thereafter, was unable to meet its financial obligations as its economic well-being continued to deteriorate. At the September, 1971, meeting of the Curtis Board, attended by Jerry Litner and Michael Gaffigan, Curtis director and Central commercial loan officer, the payment of the third installment obligation on the Philip Litner note was discussed. The Curtis directors determined that due to the corporation's severe financial problems the payment could not be made and the Trustees should be contacted to negotiate a modification of the note obligation. Subsequently, Jerry Litner informed Bruce Duff, Central National's account administrator for the Trust, that Central would be contacted by Curtis concerning the company's cash flow problem vis-a-vis the January, 1972 note payment and urged him to "work out an arrangement" with the company.

Prior to being contacted by Curtis, Mr. Duff questioned Mr. Gaffigan regarding Curtis Electro Corporation's relationship with Central's Commercial Lending Department. Duff, the Litner Trust officer, was informed by Gaffigan that Curtis was a "good customer" of the bank and had been since 1968. On or about March 15, 1972, Central, acting as Trustee of the Litner Trust, and Curtis entered into a new repayment agreement and canceled the Curtis notes then held by the Trustee. The new repayment agreement provided for a five-year $255,780 unsecured note bearing an increased interest rate of seven and one-half percent. As a concession to Curtis, the monthly payments on the note were initially set at $2,000 per month and were to be increased during the term of the note.

On August 18, 1972, Central, again acting as Curtis' commercial lender, and Curtis Electro entered into an additional commercial loan agreement whereby, in contrast to the earlier agreements, each of the Curtis subsidiaries gave notes to Central for the entire amount then owed by Curtis, $1,900,000, and the bank obtained a security interest in the equipment of the subsidiaries. To further protect themselves as Curtis' banker, Central obtained a security interest in one hundred percent (100%) of the stock of the Curtis subsidiaries.

Late in June of 1973, Mr. Duff discovered that Curtis was in default on the March 15, 1972 promissory note. On several occasions Mr. Duff contacted Curtis regarding the default and Mr. William Robinson, Curtis' Chief Financial Officer, informed Duff that the company was in a "very deep cash crisis" and would be unable to make the regular monthly payments on the Trust's note. Two months later, in August of 1973, Duff received two checks from Curtis making the interest payments current on the note's then outstanding principal balance.

As Central was aware of Curtis' continuing severe financial problems, it now saw fit to protect itself as commercial banker by acquiring and perfecting security interests in additional collateral in conjunction with a September, 1973 business loan to one of Curtis' subsidiaries. Although this loan was repaid shortly thereafter, the additional collateral was retained and continued to secure loans Central had previously made to Curtis.

During December of 1973, Bruce Duff and members of the Special Assets Committee of Central's Trust Department discussed the advisability of retaining an attorney to initiate collection of the Curtis promissory note. Toward the end of that month, Mr. Duff contacted Attorney Fink (Philip's lawyer) and discussed with him the problems the Trust was having obtaining payment of the promissory note from Curtis.

The next month, on January 7, 1974, Duff informed Curtis that the Trust was considering retaining an attorney to commence litigation to collect the Curtis debt. Curtis management informed Duff that if a lawsuit were filed it would force Curtis into bankruptcy and, furthermore, all of Curtis' assets had previously been pledged to Central to secure its commercial loans.[13] Based on this information, Duff and Curtis then agreed the Trust would not file suit and Curtis would bring the interest payments up to a current status. Attorney Fink was advised by letter to take no legal action.

Three months later, on April 29, 1974, Curtis filed a Chapter 11 bankruptcy petition for reorganization. After the filing of the petition, Mr. Duff concluded that Central was facing a "potential conflict of interest" dilemma as Trustee, due to the problem existing between Curtis' secured and unsecured creditors. Mr. Duff informed the Litner family by letter of May 24, 1974 that it was the opinion of Central's top management that independent counsel should now be obtained by the Litner family to seek collection of the note as "vigorously as possible." Central stated that it did not recommend attempting the appointment of a successor trustee for the Litner Trust in view of the "questionable competency" of Philip Litner.

---

[13]    This was Mr. Duff's first notice of the fact that Curtis had granted Central's Commercial Lending Department numerous security interests to collateralize its commercial loans.

In the summer of 1974, Jerry Litner informed Bruce Duff that it was the opinion of the Litner family that Central should absorb any loss inuring to the Trust as a result of Curtis' insolvency. Mr. Duff replied that Central had not acted improperly and had only relied on his (Jerry Litner's) advice. In early August 1974, the Litner family contemplated filing an action on behalf of Philip Litner against Central as Trustee of the Litner Trust.

Prior to his death on September 5, 1976, Philip Litner revoked the Trust and ordered the Trust assets transferred to Jefferson National Bank of Miami ("Jefferson National"), the plaintiff-appellee herein. On May 1, 1978, Jefferson National, as Personal Representative of the Estate of Philip Litner, instituted the instant action and alleged, as noted above, that Central had breached the fiduciary relationship owed to Philip Litner while it acted as Trustee of the Litner Trust and sought recovery of actual and punitive damages. As referred to above, Central subsequently answered and filed a third-party complaint against Jerry Litner for reimbursement of any damages that might be recovered by Jefferson National. After a lengthy jury trial, judgment was entered in favor of Jefferson National in the amount of $394,475.40. The jury further determined there was no liability on the part of Jerry Litner and the trial court entered judgment accordingly. This appeal followed. . . .

## STANDARD OF CONDUCT

By statute, Illinois has outlined a so-called "Prudent Person Standard" against which the activities of trustees are generally measured. Trustees are expected to exercise the judgment and care which persons of prudence, discretion and intelligence would exercise in the management of their own personal affairs and under the circumstances then prevailing. Based on the voluminous record in this case, it is clear to this court that the jury had ample evidence to hold that Central failed to properly discharge its fiduciary obligations during its tenure as Trustee of the Philip Litner Trust.

Trustees are held to a high standard of conduct and must exercise the highest degree of fidelity and the utmost good faith in the administration of the trust. The trustee's primary responsibility is to the beneficiary. Especially where their individual interests are concerned, trustees' actions are governed by rules which exact of them the utmost good faith, honesty, integrity, faithfulness and fair dealing. The interests of the beneficiary must at all times remain paramount to the personal interests of the trustee. See *In Re Hartzell's Will*, 43 Ill. App. 2d 118, 192 N.E.2d 697, 706 (1963). *See also* Scott, *Trustee's Duty of Loyalty*, 49 Harv. L. Rev. 521 (1936). . . .

It is clear that Central, as Trustee of the Litner Trust, did not discharge its fiduciary duties as prudent individuals would manage their own affairs. On the other hand, Central, where its own dollars were involved as commercial banker of Curtis, did exactly what an astute investor holding an unsecured note of Curtis would do to protect their individual interest faced with the corporation's dismal financial situation. That prudent and intelligent individual would collateralize the debt just as Central did with their own commercial loan. If subsequently that collateral appeared to be insufficient, the self-interested creditor would demand additional security. This is the course of conduct Central followed in order to safeguard its financial interests vis-a-vis Curtis Electro Corporation. After Central had protected its own interests securing its commercial loans with all of the available assets of Curtis, Central (as Trustee) finally turned its attention to the best interest of the *cestui que* trust.

In its dealings with Curtis it is clear that Central at all times subordinated the interest of Philip Litner, the beneficiary, to that of its own commercial banking division. By the time Central clearly and unequivocally demonstrated to Eli Fink (Philip Litner's legal counsel) the need to take action to protect the Trust's interests regarding the Curtis notes, the hour was too late for the bank as Trustee to, at last, attempt to properly protect the beneficiary. We agree with the jury and affirm their verdict that Central is liable to the Estate of Philip Litner for the damages proximately caused by its significant breach of his trust.

## DAMAGES

Central contends that Judge McGarr improperly instructed the jury regarding two aspects of the damage issue: (A) the burden of proving the amount of damages proximately caused by Central's breach of trust; and (B) the imposition of pre-judgment interest. . . .

Central maintains that the trial court's jury instruction regarding the burden of proof of damages was erroneous and requires this court to reverse the judgment in favor of Jefferson National. The instruction complained of recited: "Plaintiff has the burden of proof on the issues of damages except that Central National Bank has the burden of proving that any part of the loss would have been incurred even if there had been no breach of trust." . . .

We agree with Central that the burden of proof was on Jefferson National to show that Central wrongfully caused the loss to the Trust but find Central's objection to Judge McGarr's jury instruction to be without merit. The judge correctly instructed the jury as to the plaintiff's burden of proof and a review of the record establishes without doubt that Jefferson National has met that burden. There is more than substantial and overwhelming evidence in the record to support Jefferson National's allegations that Central's conflict of interest, manifesting itself in the Trustee's failure to secure the payment of the Trust's promissory note, while encumbering the assets of Curtis as its commercial lender, was a proximate cause of the financial loss suffered by Philip Litner due to the unenforceability of the promissory note. A "proximate cause" need not be the only cause or the last or nearest cause of a loss. I.P.I.2d § 15.01 (1971).

The record clearly demonstrates that Central imprudently and improperly failed to perform its duties as Trustee of the Litner Trust. The wealth of such evidence easily overcomes any presumption that might have existed that Central had properly performed its duties while acting as the Trustee of the Philip Litner Trust. Central's actions in this case are replete with examples of the causal connection between Central's conflicting roles as Trustee and commercial lender and the unenforceability of the Curtis note. There is no doubt that at the time Curtis filed its bankruptcy petition the promissory note was virtually uncollectible.

We agree with the trial judge that once Jefferson National clearly demonstrated the breach of Central's duty and the resultant damage, the burden of proof switched to Central to prove in its defense that throughout the period of time involved the note was uncollectible or "worthless" through no fault of their own. The burden was on Central to prove that any attempt by the bank to collect or secure the Curtis' note during the time it was concurrently acting as Central's commercial lender would have been fruitless. See Estate of Stetson, 463 Pa. 64, 345 A.2d 679, 690 (1975). We need to look no further than the fact that Central itself in 1972 & 1973 obtained security interests in virtually all of Curtis' collateral to secure its commercial loans to find sufficient evidence to support the jury's implicit finding that the note was not uncollectible or unsecurable during the term of Central's trusteeship. . . .

Central's breach of its fiduciary duty proximately caused the Estate of Philip Litner to be deprived of the outstanding balance of the Curtis Promissory Note and all income that would have accrued thereon from early 1974 through the time of trial. It was within the province of the jury to determine that the prime rate accurately reflected the amount of income received by Central on monies properly attributable to and improperly denied to Philip Litner's Estate during the period at issue. A trustee who commits a breach of trust and incurs liability for a certain amount of money and the loss of income thereon is properly accountable not only for the return of the money but also interest actually received by him during that period. *Restatement (Second) of Trusts*, §§ 205 and 207 (1959). By its very definition, the prime rate is the interest rate at which a bank makes commercial loans and, therefore, was a proper award providing for full recovery of lost Trust income by the Estate of Philip Litner and preventing Central from profiting from its breach of trust. Accordingly, the judgment of the trial court is affirmed.

## Comments and Questions

1. Does *Jefferson National* suggest that a bank has an affirmative duty to obtain information from the commercial side of the bank to the extent necessary for the bank to make an informed judgment as trustee?

2. Would the trustee bank be in a better position if it had constructed a "Wall" between the trust and commercial departments which as a matter of bank policy restricted or prevented the flow of information? If not, is the trustee bank liable for a breach of the duty of loyalty in any case where the commercial and trust departments have adverse interests arising out of relations with a bank customer in addition to the trust beneficiary?

3. Considering that Phillip Litner knew of Central's status as principal lender to Curtis (and assuming that he told his lawyer of this), should his lawyer have recommended that he not enter into the trust agreement? While not true in this case, it is common that once a trustee of an irrevocable trust is appointed, it is nearly impossible for the settlor or beneficiaries to terminate the trustee. One solution to unforeseen disputes arising over management of a trust is for the settlor to have an escape clause in the original trust agreement, giving the beneficiaries the discretion to appoint a successor trustee, perhaps subject to court approval.

### Problem 3-28

Bank has a Wall between the commercial and trust departments. The bank is trustee of a trust which holds a 25% interest in a privately held company, Southwest Pipe. Southwest Pipe offers to buy back the stock from the trust. The trust department determines that it may be prudent to sell the stock, in order to diversify the investments of the trust. It proceeds to evaluate the worth of Southwest Pipe stock, which includes obtaining information from Southwest Pipe about the financial status of the company, including its liabilities. It turns out that one liability is a substantial loan from the commercial department of the Bank. It is evident that the higher the price paid by

Southwest Pipe to the trust to repurchase the stock the greater the impairment of Southwest Pipe's ability to repay the loan to the Banks.

Despite the Wall, the commercial and trust officers confer.  The commercial officer lets it be known that she does not want Southwest Pipe to pay too much for the stock because it could impair the company's ability to repay the bank's loan.  The trust department proceeds to sell the stock.  Beneficiaries sue and allege that the stock was sold at a price significantly below fair market value and that the Bank is liable for breach of its duty of loyalty in making the sale.

At trial, the trust officer testifies that he decided the trust had to sell the stock in order to diversify the trust assets, which had been 80 percent in Southwest Pipe stock, and the trust received in return what he thought was the highest price anyone could get for the stock. The commercial loan officer testifies that she had told the trust officer that the bank did not want any stock purchase to cost Southwest Pipe too much, because it could impair the company's ability to repay its loan to the bank.

What is the liability, if any, of the Bank?  Does the Wall between the trust and commercial departments neutralize any problems you see, or is there still a conflict between them?  Could the Comptroller of the Currency write a regulation preventing the flow of information between the trust department and the commercial department?  Is it unavoidable that some information would enter the knowledge of the trust department simply through obtaining basic information directly from Southwest Pipe?  Is the only solution that bank trust departments should never sell trust assets to bank customers?

---

State bank trust departments may also be subject to federal supervision.  Federal Reserve examiners oversee the operations of the trust departments of state member banks, and FDIC examiners perform the same function for trust departments of nonmember insured banks.  Also, the Internal Revenue Code, 26 U.S.C.A. §§ 584(a)(2) and 584(b), exempts "common trust funds" from taxation if such funds are operated in conformity with the rules and regulations of the Comptroller of Currency (a "common trust fund" is defined in Int. Rev. Code § 584(a)(1), as a fund maintained by a bank "exclusively for the collective investment and reinvestment of moneys contributed thereto by the bank in its capacity as a trustee, executor, administrator or guardian . . .").  The Comptroller's regulations governing common trust funds are found at 12 C.F.R. § 9.18.

Common trust funds are a substantial and important part of trust department activity.  They have significant securities law overtones.  The collective investment, or pooling, of trust funds in a common trust fund was first permitted in 1937.  The purpose of this authority is to enable banks to pool trust accounts already under their management, in order to diversify risk in individual portfolios and lessen the cost of administration.

While banks are permitted to advertise their individual trust services, they generally are prohibited from advertising the common trust fund itself as a separate service.  The reasons involve questions arising out of the separation of commercial and investment banking.  Advertising common trust funds would create an appearance of the sale of securities (proportionate shares in the common trust fund) rather than of trust services. The suggestion is that there is a difference between advertising a pooled fund and advertising general trust services which attract trust assets (that are subsequently pooled in a common trust fund as part of the trust administration).

Recently, common trust funds have become even more important. With the growth of corporate pension and profit sharing trusts has come what are known as collective investment funds for such plans. As with common trust funds, the idea is to enable banks to manage the assets efficiently and fulfill their trust responsibilities by pooling smaller pension funds, already under the bank's management, in order to reduce fees and obtain prudent diversification. Banks have been given permission to advertise their ability to invest pension trust funds collectively.

The general policy of the Comptroller for trust supervision is to keep absolute prohibitions to a minimum. Thus, no attempt has been made in 12 C.F.R. Pt. 9 to compile an all-inclusive list of restrictions and limitations. The Comptroller has concluded that no such listing is necessary in view of the fact that conformity to sound fiduciary principles is always required in the operations of trust departments.

*Problem 3-29*

Any bank that has both a commercial and trust side necessarily will face numerous conflicts of interests. Consider what policies or prohibitions, if any, ought to be established with respect to the following suggested trust department standards. See 12 C.F.R. §§ 9.12, 9.100.

(1) A trust department should be required to deposit all trust cash in a depository institution other than itself.

(2) Neither banks nor their customers may acquire any trust property from an estate or trust in the absence of either open competitive bidding or valuation by a court.

(3) A bank should not be allowed to invest trust assets in mutual funds for which the same bank serves as investment adviser.

(4) Do you have any other policies or prohibitions to suggest?

# CHAPTER FOUR

# REGULATION OF ORGANIZATIONAL STRUCTURE

---

## Section 1. Introduction

Virtually every aspect of the organizational structure surrounding a bank is regulated: bank branches principally under 12 U.S.C.A. § 36; bank subsidiaries principally under 12 U.S.C.A. § 24(7); and both parent bank holding companies and their nonbank subsidiaries under the Bank Holding Company Act, 12 U.S.C.A. §§ 1841-1850. While somewhat similar regulations exist for other types of financial institutions, particularly in the insurance field, the regulation of bank organizational structure is the most extensive.

We will start with branching, the simplest organizational method for geographical expansion. An interesting feature of United States banking regulation is that branching has traditionally been regulated at the state level, through federal statutory deference to state law. This has had important consequences for geographical expansion, whether de novo or through merger, by banks. See 12 U.S.C.A. § 36.

The preeminence of state law has presented some difficult questions of how far states can go in regulating branches before they infringe on national bank powers. Historically strict branching rules have also created pressure for banks to establish non-branch facilities (that either do not offer "core" banking activities, such as deposit taking, or are not "established" by a bank, such as shared ATM facilities).

In 1994 the Riegle-Neal Act sanctioned interstate branching by merger or acquisition, while still leaving substantial latitude at the state level, although the remaining state power remains vulnerable to the nonbranch expansion of the sort that existed before Riegle-Neal was enacted. See 12 U.S.C.A. § 1831u.

Our primary subject matter in this chapter will be the Bank Holding Company Act as well as the regulation of activities located outside the bank but within the corporate structure surrounding the bank. Bank holding companies (as well as chain banking) represent another organizational innovation that was developed to facilitate geographical expansion not possible at the bank level, due to either state law restrictions on intrastate branching or the ultimate limit of state borders on bank expansion. The BHCA both regulates geographical expansion of BHCs and creates a series of portfolio-shaping restrictions for bank holding companies and their nonbank subsidiaries that are similar to, but in theory less severe than, the restrictions imposed on banks and their subsidiaries. See 12 U.S.C.A. §§ 1841-1846. In response, the OCC has gradually elaborated an administrative law matrix regulating similar activities carried on in bank subsidiaries. As the barriers to geographical and activities expansion have eroded, the antitrust aspects of organizational expansion we discussed in Chapter 2 have become more relevant.

As complex organizational structures surrounding banks have proliferated, a concern has developed regarding the safety and soundness aspects of BHC regulation.  In contrast to the general corporate law doctrines of limited liability of shareholders and corporate separateness, a variety of regulatory initiatives have arisen that require BHC support for the safety and soundness of affiliated banks through statutory cross-guarantees and similar capital support mechanisms.  We will consider which, if any, of the regulatory approaches to intra-BHC financial obligations represents appropriate regulatory policy.  See 12 U.S.C.A. §§ 1815(e) and 1831o(e)(2), particularly subsection (E).

# Section 2.  Geographical Expansion of Banks

## A.  History

While businesses in the United States generally have been allowed to open offices wherever they please, historically that has not been true for banks.  Even though the restrictions on geographical expansion of banks have steadily lessened, particularly with the passage of the Riegle-Neal Interstate Banking and Branching Efficiency Act of 1994, it is worth briefly reviewing the origins of the restrictions.  The restrictions have had both intrastate and interstate characteristics.

Until 1994, the geographical limits in 12 U.S.C.A. § 36 provided that national bank branches could be located only within the state where the bank was headquartered, and only where state-chartered banks were authorized to locate branches.  At one time that meant anything from no branches to branches anywhere in the state, but today all but a few states allow branches state-wide.

Geographical restrictions developed for a variety of reasons.  In the nineteenth century, branching and geographical expansion were not substantial issues.  Both American society and the American economy were quite localized; consequently, so were the banks.  The ability to travel and communicate easily did not exist.  As a result, banks did not operate very far from their home localities.  The few that did were viewed as insignificant exceptions.  American society and the American economy began to change around 1900.  When expansionist activity began, protectionist sentiment followed, particularly among the smaller state-chartered institutions.  But state-chartered banks generally found, either through statutory silence or statutory permission, that they had the power to branch.  As society and the economy expanded geographically, so did the larger state-chartered banks.

National banks were not permitted to branch until 1927 when the National Bank Act was amended to permit national banks to branch within the cities or towns in which they were located if state-chartered banks in the state had the same authority.  In 1933 the Act was amended again to provide full equality for national banks to branch within the state as state-chartered banks could.  Note the historic deference of federal to state law, and the underlying concept of competitive equality between banks with state or national charters.

An additional historical theme for the geographical restrictions on banks has been concern about inordinate concentration of financial power and its perceived effect on political power. Until the 1980s, limits on economic concentration were an indirect result of the limits on geographical expansion of banks and bank holding companies. The limits on geographical expansion indirectly limited economic concentration by prohibiting mergers or affiliations of banks in different markets. But as the limits on geographical expansion lessened, the issue of economic concentration in banking had to be confronted more directly. We will see this issue surface in our discussion of the 1994 Act, as we did in our discussion of antitrust law.

In summary, it could be said that the historic restrictions on intrastate and interstate banking have been based on concerns about both concentration of economic power and a desire to focus bank activities on the development of local economies and close attention to local borrowers. But today, it is fair to say that if there is a public policy concern about local savings being drained from communities, the danger is as much related to non-bank financial institutions, such as securities firms and mutual funds with 800 telephone numbers, as it is to the steady growth of interstate banking. Our developed system of more than 10,000 separate depository institutions remains as a notable contrast to the highly concentrated banking systems of Canada, Japan, Germany, and most European countries.

Despite all the apparent limitations on geographical expansion, there steadily developed a large measure of interstate banking for most types of financial institution products. Banks were able to develop interstate (nonbranch) loan production offices, as well as shared ATM networks that were held not to be branches, as well as credit card banks which did not require a physical location in more than one state.

The Interstate Banking and Branching Efficiency Act of 1994 brought dramatic change. The Act contains an important distinction between interstate banking and interstate branching. Interstate banking allows bank holding companies to acquire separate banks in multiple states.

As for interstate branching, effective June 1, 1997, banks can merge with banks in any other state provided that the state has not "opted out" by enacting a law which expressly prohibits such branching. This, in effect, gives national banks the power to branch nationwide by merger, absent specific state prohibition, and works a substantial change in 12 U.S.C.A. § 36. By the end of 1996, 41 states (including Hawaii) has opted into interstate branching on or before June 1, 1997, while only one state, Texas, had opted out, but included a September 2, 1999 sunset in its opt out.

Before engaging in a closer analysis of the 1994 legislation and all its complexity, it is important to understand what level of bank activity constitutes a branch, thus subject to the geographical limitations and state controls that still exist.

## B. The Definition of Branch

A principal method of expansion for an existing bank is to "branch," that is, to open banking offices at new locations.  But what does this mean?  Certainly taking deposits is a branching activity.  12 U.S.C.A. § 36(j) makes evident that taking deposits, cashing checks or making loans results in the facility being classified as a branch.  The question has become more complex as electronic technology has made it economically feasible to communicate with customers at virtually any geographical location.  Obvious examples are automated teller machines and home computers.  Do such devices constitute branches?

An important case in determining the definition of branch is *First National Bank in Plant City v. Dickinson*, 396 U.S. 122 (1969).  In *Plant City*, a national bank established an armored car and shopping center receptacle service.  Branching was prohibited by Florida law.  The armored car service, at the customer's premises, both delivered cash in exchange for checks and received cash and checks for deposit.  Customers were given keys to the shopping center receptacle, which had a writing table and necessary forms for customers to leave deposits for the armored car to pick up.  The bank argued that neither the armored car nor the shopping center receptacle should be considered a branch since neither "received deposits."  In both cases the customer signed a contract which provided that the bank and the armored car were the agents of the customer and that the transmitted funds were not deemed to be a deposit until delivered into the bank's hands.  The Supreme Court rejected the contention of the bank and the Comptroller that these contractual relations precluded the armored car and shopping center facilities from constituting "branches."  The private contracts did not control the location of accepting the deposits for purposes of federal law.  Rather, the facilities gave the national bank a competitive advantage in attracting customers and providing the functional equivalent of deposit taking in a place away from authorized office locations.

Besides the three activities specifically enumerated in § 36(j), are there any other activities which, if engaged in, result in a facility being classified as a branch?  In *Clarke v. Securities Industry Association*, 479 U.S. 388 (1987), the Supreme Court held that facilities of a national bank which offered only discount brokerage services were not branches.  The Court said that only those facilities that carried on "core banking functions" would be considered branches.  The Court reconciled this holding with *Plant City* by stating that competitive equality was only necessary in regard to the core functions, not every incidental service.

So the question remains, what activities represent core banking functions?  In *St. Louis County National Bank v. Mercantile Trust Co.*, 548 F.2d 716 (8th Cir. 1976), *cert. denied*, 433 U.S. 909 (1977), the court held that the three activities listed in § 36(j) "are not the only indicia of branch banking," and that an office offering trust services was a branch.  The Supreme Court declined to consider the question in *Clarke*, leaving the scope of "core banking functions" unclear.  Can the branching issue be avoided entirely if the activity is engaged in by either an operating, wholly-owned subsidiary of a bank, or a non-bank subsidiary of a parent bank holding company?

*Problem 4-1*

X bank wants to know whether it can send a courier to a large customer who has just called the bank and has a $10 million check which it wishes to deposit as soon as possible. The customer is unable to release an employee to make the deposit and would like the bank courier to stop over, pick up the check and deposit slip, and carry them to the bank for deposit. Is this permissible or is this an illegal branching activity? If not illegal, may X bank expand this service by hiring a regular or part-time courier to pick up noncash deposits for customers? See 12 C.F.R. § 7.1012.

Could all the issues about branching by X bank be avoided by separately incorporating the courier service in a non-bank subsidiary of its parent bank holding company? See 12 C.F.R. § 225.28(b)(10).

---

And so, the first element of the definition of branch is that the facility must engage in "core banking functions." The second requirement is that the facility be "established by," i.e., owned or rented by, the bank. Thus, an automated teller machine (ATM) owned by a bank and made available to its customers typically is a branch because it can cash "checks" by dispensing cash, accept deposits, and, in effect, make loans against a prearranged line of credit.

The issue of whether an ATM is "established" by a bank has most commonly arisen in multi-bank shared ATM systems. In *Independent Bankers Assoc. v. Marine Midland Bank, N.A.*, 757 F.2d 453 (2d Cir. 1985), *cert. denied*, 476 U.S. 1186 (1986), Marine Midland paid a service fee to a grocery store which allowed its customers to use a shared ATM system in the store, a location where state law prohibited Marine from having a branch. The court held that since Marine did not own or rent the machine, therefore Marine had not established it, and consequently it was not a Marine branch. In fact, the ATM turned out not to be a branch of any bank.

Should whether or not a bank owns or rents an ATM be the deciding factor? In private property law, it is easy to turn a lease into a license. Is competitive equality a more relevant policy determinant? As a matter of both property law and policy-based statutory interpretation, is *Marine* different from *Plant City*? Surely it makes no difference to a customer whether or not its bank owns, rents or licenses the machine as long as the desired services are available. The Second Circuit acknowledged that the "owned or rented" standard was a somewhat arbitrary distinction but seemed untroubled by it. Should it have been? Suppose that a BHC has ownership of all ATMs used by customers of its multiple bank subsidiaries, and each bank subsidiary pays a transaction fee to the BHC for each use of the ATM by its customers. Would these ATMs constitute branches under *Marine*? Under *Plant City*? Does it make a difference whether the ATMs are available to competing banks, as are telephone and mail systems, and as was true in *Marine*? These questions are important, considering the fact that more than 50% of banking transactions now take place through ATMs, home banking, or other electronic delivery systems.   Is competitive equality the basis on which *Marine* and *Plant City* can be reconciled?

*Problem 4-2*

1.  First National Bank wants to develop an interstate electronic banking system focused on a shared network of ATMs owned in a fashion within the parameters of *Marine Midland.* Each ATM, however, would be located in a small, private office, with the ATM on a desk, along with a chair for the customer.  The customer, with the use of a bank card, could access any account he or she has in any participating bank located anywhere in the United States, and so make a deposit or withdrawal, take out a loan, or pay bills.  If some assistance is needed, the enhanced ATM would also permit voice and video communications between the customer and employees of his or her bank.  Does this proposed service constitute a branch?

2.  Cyber Bank creates a home page on the Internet enabling people to access multiple pages of information about its products and services.  Individuals with the appropriate home computer could fill out a loan application on one screen and write checks on another.  Would these Internet services be branches? See 12 C.F.R. § 7.1019.

---

At least conceptually, the first two prongs of what constitutes a branch are now clear. A facility must both engage in core banking activities and be established by the bank. However, some facilities might appear to be branches under these two criteria when in fact they are not.  As suggested in our discussion of *Plant City* and *Marine*, a third requirement for a branch is that it provide the bank with a competitive advantage in obtaining customers.  For example, banks have various back office facilities that process checks, but to which customers have no access.  See OCC Interpretive Letter No. 634 (July 23, 1993). Today, while technological advances have made the definition of "branch" less than clear, the definition may become less important as the barriers to interstate branching continue to erode.

## C.  Interstate Branching

Beginning June 1, 1997, the Riegle-Neal Act authorizes interstate branching through the consolidation or merger of banks located in different states.  The consolidating banks can be either already affiliated in an existing bank holding company system or currently independant banks that are merged.  The effect is to create a single national or state-chartered bank with interstate branches.  States are free to allow such interstate branching prior to the 1997 date by passing legislation "opting-in."  States may also opt-out if they enact appropriate legislation by June 1, 1997 expressly prohibiting interstate branching. If a state opts out, state or national banks with that state as their home state are prohibited from interstate branching.  Also, if a state opts out, out-of-state banks are prohibited from branching into that state. One potentially interesting question is whether a state can later change its opt-out decision.

The approval criteria for interstate mergers and branching are essentially identical to those for interstate banking (discussed later): concentration limits, adequate capital, and adequate management of the bank. See 12 U.S.C.A. § 1828(c). The statute defines adequately capitalized to mean "a level of capitalization which meets or exceeds all applicable federal regulatory capital standards." The term "adequately managed" is not defined but is left to the discretion of the banking agency. Finally, the banking agency cannot approve a merger if the bank and its affiliates will control more than 10% of the total amount of insured deposits in the United States. On the state level, a merger cannot be approved if the applicant has any presence in the state prior to the merger and would control 30% or more of the insured deposits in the state after the merger. States can raise or lower the 30% state deposit concentration limit. See 12 U.S.C.A. § 1831u(b).

While interstate branching by merger will be allowed automatically on June 1, 1997 except in states that pass contrary legislation, other methods of interstate branching can only be achieved if states expressly authorize such methodologies. The two most obvious additional methodologies are (1) de novo branching by a bank with no facilities in the host state (§ 36(g)), or (2) acquisition of one or more selected branches from an existing bank in the host state (§ 1831u(a)(4)).

Interstate branching may provide benefits beyond those of interstate banking (a BHC owning multiple banks). The most obvious is the convenience to bank customers in being able to deal with a bank as a single entity, wherever it is located in the United States. Other advantages suggested are the reduction of expenses, by consolidating various corporate bookkeeping and financial reporting obligations, by eliminating multiple management teams and boards of directors, and by the ability to move capital to where it is needed in the total banking organization.

The status of state-chartered banks requires special attention. If a state does nothing, national banks will be able to operate branches across state lines after June 1, 1997, but state banks will not. The suggestion is that if state banks are to remain competitive, the states will have to pass legislation either opting-out or authorizing state-chartered banks to branch interstate.

The idea of a state-chartered bank branching interstate creates numerous complications. If a national bank branches interstate, it still has to deal with only one regulator, the Comptroller of the Currency. This is due to federal preemption of much state law through the Supremacy Clause of the Constitution. Section 105 of the 1994 Act recognized this problem for state-chartered banks and authorized cooperative agreements among states. This section amends 12 U.S.C.A. § 1820 so that states can cooperatively create a methodology of home-state regulation for all activities of a state-chartered bank, except for four named activities, generally relating to consumer protection, which are reserved for host state regulation. In response, the Conference of State Bank Supervisors has adopted a plan for the states to implement such a methodology. Under this methodology, the home state of a state-chartered bank would have authority over applications for new branches, bank powers, and mergers, and would also use home-state law for general investment and corporate issues. But consultation with the host state amended the Riegle-Neal Act to clarify the allocation of supervisory responsibilities for and other issues related to state-banks that branch across interstate lines.

### Problem 4-3

1. Pelican National Bank, headquartered in Michigan, acquires by merger the Tern National Bank located in New Mexico. Subsequent to the merger, a lawsuit is brought in New Mexico against Pelican National Bank for damages previously caused by a breach of fiduciary duty by Tern National Bank's trust department. A final judgment of $10 million is rendered. Is Pelican National Bank liable for the judgment?

2. You are general counsel for the Vermont Department of Banking, and have an idea. Taking a page from Delaware corporation law, would it be possible for you to develop a Vermont banking law that would make Vermont the charter location of choice for state-chartered banks, allowing them various powers as well as unlimited interstate branching? Recall 12 U.S.C.A. § 1831a.

3. It is now 1998 and you are the attorney general for Vermont. Vermont did not pass any opt-in or opt-out legislation prior to June 1, 1997. New York National Bank wishes to branch de novo into Vermont. Can it do so? If not, could the bank achieve the same result by creating a national bank with its headquarters in Vermont, and after a "decent" interval merge the banks, or by buying a single branch from an existing bank?

---

Notwithstanding various actions of the states and the cooperative actions proposed by the Conference of State Bank Supervisors, the national bank charter may become the charter of choice. There are many reasons for such a view. First, a national bank is generally subject to federal banking law as well as the four areas where the states clearly can continue to regulate: CRA, fair lending, interstate branching, and consumer protection. See 12 U.S.C.A. § 36(f). But even these state laws are to be applied to national banks by the Comptroller of the Currency. On the other hand, state-chartered banks may be subject to all state law, which varies from state to state, such as "other real estate owned" holding periods, escheat laws, and lending limits. See 12 U.S.C.A. § 1831a(j).

Even if a state does opt-out of interstate branching, it may have difficulty keeping what looks like branching activity out of the state, even before June 1, 1997. Read 12 U.S.C.A. §§ 1828(r) and 1831u(a) and consider the following problem.

*Problem 4-4*

1. Big Bank Holding Company has a wholly-owned trust company subsidiary. While this subsidiary has a bank charter, it only engages in trust activities and does not take deposits or make loans. Management decides to locate an office of the trust company in Texas, which has opted-out of the interstate branching provisions. Can Texas bar this office of the trust company?

2. American Bank Holding Company has bank subsidiaries in 25 states, including Texas. It has subsidiaries in the contiguous states of New Mexico, Oklahoma, Arkansas, Missouri and Louisiana. American would like to integrate the activities of these banks by having each bank subsidiary, for the other affiliated banks, receive deposits, renew certificates of deposit and other time deposits, close loans, service loans and receive payments on loans as agent for one another. Can this occur, even though Texas has opted-out of interstate branching? Can the bank set up this agency structure without prior regulatory approval, including consideration of such factors as CRA?

# Section 3. Bank Holding Companies

Bank holding companies (as well as chain banks) represent another organizational innovation designed to facilitate geographical and activities expansion that historically was not possible at the bank level. In response to the innovation, the Bank Holding Company Act (BHCA), 12 U.S.C.A. §§ 1841-1850, recreates a series of restrictions at the holding company level that are similar to but generally less severe than the restrictions imposed at the bank level. We will discuss problems that arise in implementing the BHCA. For more complete treatment of the BHCA, see PAULINE B. HELLER & MELANIE FEIN, THE FEDERAL BANK HOLDING COMPANY ACT (rev. ed. 1997).

Bank holding companies (BHCs) are not a recent phenomena. They gradually developed from a form of multibranch banking by the First and Second Banks of the United States in which each branch of what was supposedly a unitary organization actually operated as an independent entity. Branches of both Banks, for example, had their own directors and presidents. By the late nineteenth century, individuals or associations controlled large groups of nominally separate banks, called "chain" banks. To form a chain of banks, the individuals or associations would purchase the controlling stock of several banks. Their majority interest in the bank stock allowed the shareholders to control the election of the board of directors of each bank and to determine the policies and activities of each bank in the "chain." While each bank seemed to be a separate independent entity, they actually operated under the control of a loosely organized common management. The chaining procedure reached such proportions that, in one instance, a single chain of 125 banks failed in 1926. By the 1920s the small, closely-held multiple-unit chains had given way to a holding company form replete with central management and assets in the hundreds of millions of dollars. While the chains connected primarily small, rural banks, the bank holding companies that developed before the Depression typically included at least one metropolitan bank to serve as a source of prestige, managerial talent, and commercial facilities for the smaller banks in the chain.

As an ordinary company, the BHC itself could not engage in banking.  Rather, the company would acquire a controlling interest in a bank or banks, and would thereafter supervise the activities of its subsidiaries.  BHCs have always been subject to state control through state incorporation laws and other statutes relating to businesses.  Notwithstanding the fact that bills designed to subject BHCs to federal regulation had been introduced in every session of Congress since 1933, the first comprehensive federal legislation was the Bank Holding Company Act of 1956.  Since then the growth and importance of BHCs have increased.  Aided by both the general broadening of banking activities and the permissive nature of the 1970 amendments to the 1956 Act, BHCs have multiplied in number, financial worth, and areas of activity.

As for BHC activities, just as national banks are prohibited by § 24(7) of the National Bank Act from owning general commercial enterprises, so § 1843 of the BHCA prohibits general commercial enterprises from owning banks.  Section 1843, however, does allow BHCs to control subsidiaries engaged in certain types of activities, particularly those that are "closely related to banking," and a "proper incident thereto."

## A.  General Definition and Control

The BHCA defines both "bank holding company" and "control" of a BHC in 12 U.S.C.A. § 1841(a).  "Control" is the relationship, between a company and either a bank or a BHC, which creates a bank holding company.  Control is an elusive concept to define, and the BHCA provides only general guidelines and a few elemental rules to help a company create or avoid a control relationship and BHC status.  You should become familiar with 12 U.S.C.A. § 1841(a), which establishes methods of direct control; § 1841(g), which defines methods of indirect control; and 12 C.F.R. § 225, which establishes conclusive and rebuttable presumptions of control.

The methods of control defined in § 1841(a)(2) apply to company relationships with both banks and nonbanks.  First, a company has control if it directly or indirectly controls or has the power to vote 25 percent of any class of voting securities of a bank or company, regardless of how small the class of securities may be in relation to the over-all capitalization of the bank or company.  Thus, a company may control 25 percent of a single issue of voting securities, but the percentage it holds of total voting securities may be so small that the shareholder-company has no direct influence in the affairs of the bank or the company.

Even if a company holds less than 25 percent of the bank or nonbank company stock, a control relationship may also exist if the company controls the election of a majority of a bank's directors or trustees.  Such a determination of actual control may be a difficult task.  The final and most crucial control section, 12 U.S.C.A. § 1841(a)(2)(C) allows the Board to find a control relationship if the company "directly or indirectly exercises a controlling influence over the management or policies of the bank or company."  The BHCA does not define "controlling influence," a term which is susceptible to such broad interpretation as to be nearly meaningless.  Section 1841(a)(3) does limit the scope of the preceding section somewhat by creating the rebuttable presumption that any company controlling less than five percent of the voting securities of any bank or BHC does not control that company. Indirect control of a company is defined in § 1841(g). Once a company meets one of the three tests of direct control or the definition of indirect control, it becomes a BHC and the controlled BHC, bank, or nonbank company becomes a "subsidiary" pursuant to § 1841(d).

To avoid some of the difficulties created by §§ 1841(a)(2) and (g)(2) of the BHCA, regulations establish conclusive (irrebuttable) and rebuttable presumptions of control. 12 C.F.R. §§ 225.2(e), 225.31. The conclusive presumptions merely reiterate the methods of control established by the BHCA but the rebuttable presumptions attempt to define precise circumstances under which a company may have a "controlling influence" over the management or policies of a bank or a BHC pursuant to section 1841(a)(2)(C). Once these circumstances exist, the company has the burden of proving noncontrol. While the conclusive presumptions provide clearcut rules, the rebuttable presumptions establish guidelines in an uncertain area where both the Federal Reserve and the companies have difficulties determining if a control relationship actually exists. The regulations put companies on notice that their investments in banks and BHCs which fall within this uncertain area may be subject to prior Board approval.

Structuring corporate transactions so as to avoid control relationships is often the responsibility of counsel. Consider the investment negotiated with the Federal Reserve Board's staff reported in the following announcement.

## In re Sumitomo Bank
### 73 Fed. Res. Bull. 24 (1987)

The Federal Reserve Board announced on November 19, 1986, that it had informed The Sumitomo Bank, Ltd., Osaka, Japan, that, with certain revisions, its proposed investment in Goldman, Sachs & Co., New York, New York, would be consistent with the Bank Holding Company Act. The Board reached this conclusion only after Sumitomo agreed to a number of changes to meet the Board's concerns about the investment as it was originally structured.

The investment, as originally proposed, took the form of a nonvoting $500 million limited partnership interest and subordinated debt, as an addition to an already existing subordinated debt investment of $100 million in that company.

The Board had to determine, under the Bank Holding Company Act, whether Sumitomo's role would be passive and noncontrolling and would not result in a situation in which Sumitomo had the power to exercise a controlling influence over the management or policies of Goldman, as well as whether it would adversely affect the safe and sound operation of banking organizations. In making these judgements, the Board has adopted policies and criteria for assessing particular proposed investments.

As relevant to the Sumitomo proposal, these criteria include consideration of whether the investment represents more than 25 percent of the total shareholders' equity; whether it contains restrictions limiting the target's freedom of action; whether it places the investor in the role of entrepreneur in the organization, promotion, or operation of the target firm; whether it results in significant intercompany ties; whether it provides for interlocking directors or management officials; or whether it allows for the extension of credit on favorable terms.

The Board found the original proposal inconsistent with these established policies and criteria. The points of inconsistency included the following:

• The total investment, including limited partnership equity and subordinated debt, would exceed 25 percent of Goldman's total equity.

• Sumitomo would have representation on the boards of directors of the subsidiaries of Goldman in Tokyo and London, and the name of the London subsidiary would reflect an affiliation with Sumitomo.

• Sumitomo would have a 50 percent voting interest in a London joint venture subsidiary and 12.5 percent in a Tokyo subsidiary.

• The investment was expected to result in an increased business relationship between the companies, at least in part through mutual referrals.

• Sumitomo employees could be transferred to Goldman as trainees and could be used to solicit business from Japanese companies.

Under this proposal business arrangements between the parties would have been complex and extensive. The Board was concerned that this combination of a significant equity investment and the maintenance of extensive business relationships would give the investor both the economic incentive and means to exercise or attempt to exercise a controlling influence over the management or policies of the target company. An investment operated in this framework cannot, as a practical matter, be expected to remain wholly passive, but contains within it that inherent potential–the power–for the exercise of an important influence, including from time to time a controlling influence, depending in part on the relative business success of the parties to the investment.

Aside from the control concerns expressed above, the Board believes that the proposed investment, even after compliance with the noncontrolling investment guidelines, has precedential implications for the Board's policies regarding the capital adequacy of bank holding companies and their obligation to serve as a continuing source of strength to subsidiary banks. The Board would expect that a U.S. bank holding company seeking to make an investment in such circumstances would be particularly strongly capitalized. Such an investment could not be given full weight in the evaluation of a bank holding company's capital adequacy or its continuing ability to serve as a source of financial strength to its subsidiary banks. To remedy the Board's concerns, Sumitomo has proposed the following changes in its proposed investment in Goldman, Sachs:

• Sumitomo's total investment in Goldman, Sachs, which will include both Sumitomo's partnership interests and all Sumitomo's subordinated debt, will not exceed 24.9 percent of Goldman, Sachs total partners' capital.

• Sumitomo will not acquire any stock in, or have any directors on the board of, any Goldman, Sachs affiliate, nor shall Sumitomo's name be used by an affiliate of Goldman, Sachs or vice versa.

• No present or former Sumitomo employees will be trainees of Goldman, Sachs, although Sumitomo reserves the right to seek relief from this condition under terms acceptable to the Board.

• Sumitomo and Goldman, Sachs will not increase the amount of business they currently do with each other as a result of the investment. Sumitomo will not solicit any business for Goldman, Sachs or vice versa. Nor will Sumitomo introduce Goldman, Sachs to customers, or vice versa, unless a customer specifically requests to be introduced, and any such business introduced at the request of customers will not exceed, in any year, 2½ percent of the consolidated gross revenues of the recipient of the introduction.

• Existing normal business relationships will be maintained on an arm's-length, nonexclusive basis, and there will be no advertising or marketing of each other's services.

• Subject to necessary internal approvals and as promptly as practical after the date of the closing of its investment in Goldman, Sachs, Sumitomo will enhance its capital position by an amount that will substantially offset the funds being invested in Goldman, Sachs.

• Sumitomo has reaffirmed its commitment that it will waive any right to select general partners under New York law and that the voting arrangements under the limited partnership agreement will provide that Sumitomo will not have the right to vote for or participate in the selection of Goldman's general partners or other management officials or vote for or direct other policies of Goldman.

The Board shall retain the authority to review regularly the investment to determine whether, under all the facts and circumstances, the investment is consistent with the requirements of no controlling influence and safe and sound banking practices. To address the possibility of a controlling influence developing in the future, the contract between Sumitomo and Goldman, Sachs will provide that the investment shall be terminated and promptly repaid in the event that the Board finds that Sumitomo has the power to exercise a controlling influence over Goldman unless the situation that resulted in such a finding is eliminated.

These changes have been reviewed by the Board, and the Board finds that the proposal, as modified, is consistent with the requirements of the Bank Holding Company Act.

The Board noted that considerable interest has focused on the proposal, in part because of perceived implications for administration of the Glass-Steagall Act. However, the only issue raised by the proposal concerns administration of the Bank Holding Company Act and, in particular, determination of whether the proposed transaction implies a controlling interest in a firm engaged in activities not permitted under that act, and its consequences for the capital strength of the bank holding company parent. A truly passive noncontrolling investment logically should not raise any Glass-Steagall issues.

Similarly, some question has been raised over whether U.S. banks would receive reciprocal treatment in Japan. While the Board has a continuing interest in encouraging open markets and fair treatment, this issue is also not relevant by law to the Board's consideration of this case. Under the policy of national treatment established by the Congress in the International Banking Act and the Bank Holding Company Act, the Board's evaluation of the investment is limited to the control question and to safety and soundness concerns.

## Comments and Questions

1.  How should the "controlling influence" test in § 1841(a)(2)(C) be interpreted? Should it be interpreted only to prohibit actual control, or should it be interpreted to preclude any arrangement that might implicate control?  How does the Federal Reserve interpret the statutory section?  Factors that might be relevant in determining control include the percentage of equity or total capital, including subordinated debt, the existence of any director interlock, and various commitments that the investment will be passive and non-entrepreneurial.

2.  Control relationships can also arise in unexpected ways.  In *Board of Governors v. DLG Financial Corp.*, 29 F.3d 993 (5th Cir. 1994), *cert. dismissed*, 513 U.S. 1140 (1995), DLG purchased two promissory notes that were secured by a pledge of bank stock.  The security agreement provided that if the notes defaulted, the security note holder could exercise all the voting rights of the pledged stock.  The notes actually went into default before their purchase, and the position of the Federal Reserve Board was that DLG Corporation, by acquiring the power to vote all of the stock of the bank, thus became a BHC.

*Problem 4-5*

Conglomerate Inc. holds 2% of the voting stock of First National Bank. Conglomerate has two subsidiaries, Tree Trimmers, Inc. and B & R Sales, Inc.  The directors of Conglomerate are considering the purchase of more of the bank's stock, but they do not want Conglomerate to become a BHC because its other business activities may be subject to review by the Federal Reserve and to restrictions under federal law.  The directors would like to create a relationship between Conglomerate and First National short of "control" as defined under the BHCA.  One of the directors of Conglomerate serves on the board of directors of the bank.  Tree Trimmers, Inc., holds 2% of the voting common stock of the bank and the wife of one of the directors of Conglomerate owns 10% of the non-voting preferred stock.  Conglomerate calls you and presents the following options.  Which ones would you suggest to avoid BHC status?  How can the other alternatives be changed to avoid a control relationship?  See § 1841(a)(5); (g)(1), (2)&(3); 12 C.F.R. § 225.31(d)(2).

1.  Conglomerate proposes to purchase twenty percent of the voting common stock and twenty-five percent of the nonvoting preferred stock of First National.

2.  Tree Trimmers will purchase twenty percent of the voting common stock of the bank.  Second National Bank, trustee of the pension trust of Conglomerate's employees, will purchase twenty percent of the voting common stock for the pension trust.  Second National Bank has the sole authority to vote the shares it holds, but in the past has always voted according to Conglomerate's wishes.

3.  Conglomerate will purchase two percent of the voting common stock and the ten members of the board of directors of B & R Sales, Inc. will each purchase two percent of the voting common stock of the bank.

## B.  Definition of Company

While the definition of a company in 12 U.S.C.A. § 1841(b) includes any corporation, partnership, business trust, association or similar organization, it still does not regulate individuals who control a bank or bank holding company.  A long (over twenty-five years) or perpetual trust may also be a company under the Act.

The more difficult questions usually arise where determining what types of relationships among individuals or business organizations may constitute a company.  For example, a group of linked partnerships ("linked" meaning that some individuals are in more than one of the partnerships), with each partnership owning less than 5 percent of the same bank, may or may not constitute a company.  Generally, the Federal Reserve is looking for relationships that rise to the level of a structured entity, of a group that evidences some legal formality in the group's internal relationship.

Because of the silence of the Bank Holding Company Act with respect to the acquisition of banks by individuals, in 1978 there was added to the federal law the Change in Bank Control Act, found at 12 U.S.C.A. § 1817(j).  This Act allows the "appropriate federal banking agency" to disapprove the acquisition of an insured depository institution by a person or group of persons.  But note that the Act does not limit ownership of other commercial enterprises by individuals who also own a bank.  Only "companies" are so limited in their affiliations by the BHCA.  And so, the regulatory consequences to an individual of being subject to review under the CBCA are much less severe than being subject to the BHCA.

*Problem 4-6*

1.  Six members of the Johnson family own 100 percent of the shares of both Johnson Wax Company and Racine National Bank.  All six individuals are both officers and directors of Johnson Wax Company, and directors of Racine National Bank.  Are the six family members (or Johnson Wax) a BHC?

2.  Six timber companies each acquire 4.5% of the voting stock of Oregon National Bank.  Do they constitute a company?  Would it change your opinion if either the same six timber companies also owned a logging joint venture in Oregon, or they each owned 4.5% of the voting stock of Montana National Bank?

## C.  What is a Bank?

This simple question has had an incredibly complex history under the often amended definition of bank in the BHCA, 12 U.S.C.A. § 1841(c).  Because of statutory amendments, from 1970 to 1987 corporations engaged in activities prohibited to BHC affiliates were nevertheless permitted to affiliate with institutions with bank charters which did not meet the definition of bank in the BHCA.  Neither having a bank charter nor the meaning of the phrase, "the business of banking," revealed the answer to what falls within the definition of bank under the BHCA.  And so, a deposit taking entity might have been a bank for purposes of the state and federal banking laws, but not for purposes of the BHCA.

When the BHCA was passed in 1956 a "bank" was sensibly defined as "any national banking institution or any state bank, savings bank, or trust company."  This could be called a chartering definition.  It was thought that the definition was adequate in scope to cover only organizations that needed to be included to accomplish the purposes of the Act.  However, the 1956 definition, by use of the term "savings bank" had covered a few companies that controlled two or more industrial banks, institutions not thought to be within the purposes of the BHCA.  In 1966 the definition was narrowed to include only "any institution that accepts deposits that the depositor has a legal right to withdrawal on demand," because it was believed that the objective of the Act could be achieved without applying it to certain institutions that did not take demand deposits (including, at that time, industrial banks).  This could be called an activities definition.  But the 1966 amendment was not thought to change the underlying purposes of the Act.

In 1970, the definition was narrowed again to avoid including additional financial institutions whose activities also were thought not to affect the achievement of the underlying purposes of the Act.  And so, in 1970, a commercial lending requirement was added to the 1966 demand deposit requirement, allegedly to exempt the Boston Company (parent of the Boston Safe Deposit and Trust Company) from the Act.  Once again there is no evidence that the added requirement was a result of changes in the underlying purposes of the Act.

The 1970 amendment permitted the creation of "nonbank" banks (institutions with national or state bank charters that engage in deposit taking, credit granting and credit exchange but do not make commercial loans or, perhaps, do make commercial loans but do not take demand deposits).  This is reminiscent of the late 1960s activity of creating bank holding companies that controlled only one bank.  Such one-bank holding companies were not then covered by the literal wording of the BHCA.  In 1966, Congress determined that the purposes of the BHCA could be fulfilled without bringing one-bank holding companies under the Act.  That determination was followed by a dramatic increase in the number and relative size of one-bank holding companies.  Congress then found that the increase in one-bank holding companies did threaten the underlying purposes of the Act and determined in the 1970 amendments to include those companies within the Act's coverage.  S. Rep. No. 1084, 91st Cong., 2d Sess. (1970), *reprinted in* 1970 U.S. Code Cong. & Ad. News 5619, 5522.

As a consequence of the 1970 amendments, numerous organizations sought to acquire banks but avoid being subject to the BHCA by creating a nonbank bank. Corporations typically avoided the definition by taking the acquired bank out of the commercial loan business. Furniture stores and other retailers acquired "banks" by agreeing not to engage in commercial lending activities. By not acquiring a "bank" they did not have to subject themselves to the regulation and activity limitations of the BHCA. Congress could have avoided the problem of nonbank bank acquisitions by commercial and industrial enterprises if it had maintained a chartering definition, and granted the Federal Reserve the power to grant exemptions consistent with the purposes of the BHCA.

The Federal Reserve tried to control the growth of nonbank banks by regulation, but lost the argument in *Board of Governors v. Dimension Financial Corp.*, 474 U.S. 361 (1986). The Federal Reserve had tried to establish a broad definition of both demand deposit and commercial loan, on the basis that the BHCA's plain purpose was to regulate institutions functionally equivalent to banks. The Fed believed that nonbank banks posed three dangers to the national banking system: (1) by being outside the reach of many banking regulations, nonbank banks had a significant competitive advantage; (2) the proliferation of nonbank banks threatened the structure established by Congress for limiting the affiliation of banking and commercial enterprises; and (3) the interstate acquisition of multiple nonbank banks undermined the statutory proscriptions on interstate banking absent specific state legislative authority. The Court held that the plain language of the BHCA did not support the Fed's regulations, and concluded that "[i]f the Bank Holding Company Act falls short of providing safeguards desirable or necessary to protect the public interest, that is a problem for Congress, and not the Board or the courts, to address."

The Competitive Equality Banking Act of 1987 redefined "bank" to include any FDIC-insured institution. However, the ownership of the nonbank banks by approximately 160 commercial enterprises was grandfathered, with a few restrictions on their activities. There are limitations on the cross-marketing of products and services with the parent of the limited service bank, and such banks are restricted to an annual growth rate of 7 percent of deposits. 12 U.S.C.A. § 1843(f). Finally, the new definition of bank contains exemptions for both trust companies and credit card banks, as well as permitting owners of limited service banks to acquire failing thrift institutions with assets of $500,000,000 and up.

## D.  Geographical Restrictions on BHCs

### 1.  Nonbank Subsidiaries

Federal banking law historically has shown substantial deference to state law in regulating the geographical expansion of banks, thus allowing the states to burden interstate commerce.  But federal law is silent as to the geographical expansion of nonbank subsidiaries and affiliates of banks, thus providing BHCs with the protection of the dormant Commerce Clause in limiting the power of the states to regulate their expansion.

The Supreme Court considered the application of the dormant Commerce Clause to nonbank subsidiaries under the BHCA in *Lewis v. BT Investment Managers, Inc.,* 447, U.S. 27 (1980). The case provides an interesting perspective on how BHCs have used nonbank subsidiaries to engage in bank-like activities across state lines prior to the 1994 legislation. The case also shows the rather extensive Federal Reserve approval process.

Bankers Trust (a BHC) decided to seek approval to have its Delaware incorporated investment management subsidiary operate in Florida. A Florida statute prohibited an out-of-state BHC from owing any investment adviser company operating in Florida. The Court invalidated the Florida statute, holding, first, that the statute violated the dormant Commerce Clause, and, second, that the BHCA did not save the statute through either section 1842(d), regulating interstate bank acquisitions, or section 1846, permitting state to regulate BHCs in a nondiscriminatory manner more restrictive than does the BHCA itself.

While under the Commerce Clause the states do retain authority to regulate matters of legitimate local concern, even if they affect interstate commerce, there is no police power justification for the level of discrimination caused by the Florida statute. Even if financial activities are of profound local concern, the statute went too far in protecting that interest, as the complete prohibition of foreign BHCs from competing in local markets was more than an incidental burden necessitated by legitimate local concerns. It was evident that section 1842(d) did not apply because the subsidiary involved was not a bank subsidiary. And section 1846 only preserves a state's authority to enact limitations on BHCs as a class, but does not authorize states to control the approval or disapproval of a particular BHC transaction.

After *Lewis*, out-of-state BHCs were free to establish any nonbank subsidiary, subject only to the regulatory powers of the state requiring registration and fees substantially similar to those for domestic corporations.  Such state requirements may include registration of a foreign corporation doing business in the state and registration for a particular type of activity, such as investment advising.  Thus, an out-of-state BHC nonbank subsidiary is subject to the same regulation as subsidiaries of BHCs located in the host state.  They would also be subject to the same level of taxation for activities within the state.

Finally, note that 12 U.S.C.A. § 1846(a) specifically preserves the states' authority to regulate both banks and BHCs.  But it only provides an exemption from the limits of the Commerce Clause to the extent the state enacts legislation applicable to all BHCs.

## 2. Bank Subsidiaries

At least until June 1, 1997, and perhaps permanently in those states which opt-out of the interstate branching provisions of the 1994 Riegle-Neal Act, states have substantial authority under § 36 to limit interstate branching by out-of-state national banks. But just because the bank form of corporate structure cannot be used for geographical expansion does not mean that the BHC form of corporate structure is similarly limited.

While banks historically have been greatly limited in their power to expand geographically, until the BHCA was passed in 1956 multi-bank holding companies were not so restricted, because they were not banks and so were subject only to general corporation laws. But multi-bank holding companies began to gain importance in individual states as a way around branching restrictions, and also began to operate across state lines by acquiring a different bank in each state. Section 1842(d) of the 1956 BHCA, commonly known as the Douglas Amendment, provided that bank subsidiaries of a BHC could not be located outside the state in which the BHC's principal bank subsidiary was located, unless specifically authorized by the law of the other state. For almost two decades this had the effect of completely barring further interstate bank acquisitions because no state had enacted the requisite authorizing statute. Beginning with Maine in 1975, 49 states (not Hawaii) enacted legislation permitting interstate banking to one extent or another; ultimately 37 states permitted unrestricted entry while others permitted entry only by banks located in the same region or only for limited purposes such as issuance of credit cards.

The watershed case for interstate banking under the Douglas Amendment was *Northeast Bancorp. Inc. v. Board of Governors*, 472 U.S. 159 (1985). The Court upheld as constitutional so-called interstate banking compacts, allowing interstate banking among selected states on a reciprocal basis but excluding banks located in other states, such as the money center banks headquartered in New York and California.

The Douglas Amendment was effectively repealed by the Interstate Banking and Branching Efficiency Act of 1994. As previously noted, the Act contains an important distinction between interstate banking and interstate branching. Interstate banking involves BHCs acquiring banks in multiple states. Effective September 29, 1995, BHCs have the power to make interstate acquisitions of banks located anywhere in the United States without regard to state laws that might purport to limit such acquisitions. The amended text of § 1842(d) preempts the law of the 13 states not previously authorizing unlimited interstate banking, but it also gives states a clearer basis for enforcement of some state laws without risking dormant Commerce Clause violations or claims of federal preemption.

The new statute authorizes the Federal Reserve to approve an application for an acquisition of a bank by a BHC that is adequately capitalized and adequately managed, subject to the 10% national and 30% state insured deposits concentration limits.

### 3.  Interstate Banking

While states do not have the power to "opt-out" of interstate banking and so prohibit acquisitions of banks located in their state by out-of-state bank holding companies, states still can impose some limitations on BHC acquisitions.  A state can require that a target bank be in existence for up to five years before it can be acquired by an out-of-state bank holding company.  In addition, states can maintain laws concerning community reinvestment, fair lending, intrastate branching, and consumer protection, as long as such laws do not discriminate against out-of-state institutions.  Finally, federal law provides the above mentioned approval criteria that the Federal Reserve Board must consider in any application to acquire a bank under the interstate banking provisions.  This includes both federal and state Community Reinvestment Act compliance as well as state and national deposit concentration limits.

Consider the following problem.

*Problem 4-7*

Wyoming National Bank controls 35% of the total of $10 billion of deposits of insured depository institutions in Wyoming.  Wyoming has passed no state concentration limit law.  Octopus Bank Holding Company, headquartered in New York with assets of $30 billion, wishes to acquire Wyoming National Bank under the 1994 Act.  Can Octopus do so under § 1842(d)?  Would federal antitrust law prohibit the acquisition?

Assume that Octopus is prohibited from acquiring Wyoming National Bank because it already has a $10 million asset bank subsidiary in Wyoming.  As a consequence, it acquires Cheyenne State Bank which has 25% of deposits in Wyoming.  Wyoming has unlimited intrastate branching.  The state legislature now becomes quite concerned about the presence of Octopus in Wyoming and passes a law prohibiting banks, or affiliated banks in a bank holding company system, from branching once the bank or bank holding company has reached the 30% of deposits limit.  Is this state law enforceable or is Octopus, through its bank subsidiary, free to continue to branch de novo in Wyoming?  Is this legislation discriminatory?  As an alternative, under the new law could Octopus either have one of its bank subsidiaries branch de novo into Wyoming or sponsor a new bank in Wyoming that it would own?

———————————

The 10% and 30% concentration limits are a supplement to existing antitrust criteria applicable to local banking markets.  But, as you may recall from Chapter 2, it is quite possible that transactions permissible under the 10% federal and 30% statewide concentration limits may still be prohibited from acquisitions under the general antitrust laws, and vice versa.

# Section 4. Restrictions on BHC and Bank Subsidiary Activities

## A. Introduction

The initial policy question is whether and to what extent we should permit either BHC nonbank subsidiaries or bank direct downstream subsidiaries to engage in activities prohibited to banks. A related policy question is, to the extent we permit expansion of activities of entities affiliated with banks, should we encourage the activities diversification at the BHC level (the United States model), or at the downstream subsidiary of the bank level (the European or universal bank model).

Prior to the 1930s many banks and trust companies were able to combine the functions of commercial banking, investment banking, insurance and other financial activities without a BHC organizational structure. They managed estates and cared for real property and other investments. These wide powers attracted customers and investors.

The legislation of the 1930s was a watershed in terms of the organizational structure and regulatory climate governing financial services institutions. Stability was the overriding objective, with much government control instituted. The Banking Act of 1933, among other matters, created federal deposit insurance and appeared to separate commercial banking from investment banking. The idea was that a bank's asset activities were governed by its responsibility to meet deposit liabilities on demand. A bank should not seek additional profits by taking undue credit risks or undue risks in other activities, financial or nonfinancial.

Today, competition from non-bank lenders, foreign banks with broader powers, and the generally open financial services market, stimulated by rapid growth of computer and telecommunications technology, has both broadened the scope of available banking services and facilitated the channeling of credit activities outside the banking system. This changing environment, it is argued, requires that financial institutions be authorized to broaden their range of services in order to be economic competitors in our society. Additional powers, most probably, would be granted to affiliates of the banking organization outside of the bank entity, and so outside of the depository system, the federal deposit insurance safety net, and the payments system.

The most common corporate structure for additional activities is the BHC form, which seeks to insulate a bank from the risks of the activities of its corporate affiliates through the legal doctrine of corporate separateness. The other possible corporate structure is the bank/subsidiary form. While little statutory change has occurred in recent decades concerning the powers of banks and BHCs, much has occurred through regulatory and judicial determinations, such as the substantial erosion of those sections of the Banking Act of 1933 which appear to separate commercial and investment banking. Most of the expansions of bank and BHC powers have involved activities of a financial nature, such as securities and insurance. But some proposed statutory changes would go beyond activities of a financial nature and also eliminate the separation of banking from commercial and industrial enterprise, established statutorily in the Bank Holding Company Act of 1956 for BHCs and in § 24(7) for national banks.

The largest banks have had a particularly difficult time.  The largest bank customers, such as General Motors, have found cheaper sources of credit and other financial services outside the banking industry, particularly in the commercial paper market.  More and more institutions, such as American Express, General Electric, and Merrill Lynch, have gradually extended their range of activities across the full spectrum of financial services, beyond those that can be provided by banks.  In response, banks have tried to become department stores of financial services much like they were before the 1930s legislation, in order to provide their customers with an attractive array of products, such as securities, insurance, real estate, data processing, and leasing.  The money center banks argue that if they are to survive, there must be some relaxation of restrictions on their activities.

Congressional legislation has historically preferred the BHC structure.  But this may be no more than a reflection of the historical development of corporate law, which allowed one corporation to own another beginning only in the 1890s, long after it had been determined that banks could engage only in the business of banking.  The 1890s state legislation gave entrepreneurs the ability to own both banks and non-banks through the holding company structure, while under banking law banks still could not own nonbanks.

Today, while most activities closely related to banking are carried out in BHC subsidiaries, the authorization of interstate branching under the 1994 Act may cause the bank/subsidiary model to become the preferred corporate structure.  Recognizing this possibility, one should also recognize the conceptually identical possibility of an insurance or securities firm parent with non-insurance or non-security subsidiaries, including a bank subsidiary.

In addition to this practical reality it can be debated as a matter of policy which is the better corporate structure.  With BHC subsidiaries, any losses suffered in non-banking activities will be borne by the shareholders and creditors of the holding company, and not by the creditors or depositors of the bank or by the FDIC.  Further, the non-banking activities, under a holding company structure, would necessarily be capitalized by the holding company and would not be capitalized by funds drawn from the financial resources and capital of the bank.  But in response, a holding company might be willing to cut loose a failing bank subsidiary, while a bank as parent corporation will always have to maintain the bank's financial soundness as paramount in order to survive.  And, all that would be required to protect the bank from the activities of its non-bank subsidiaries would be separate capitalization and application of the same conflict of interests and self-dealing restrictions that are applicable to BHC affiliates under 12 U.S.C.A. § 371c. See 12 U.S.C.A. § 371c(b)(2)(A).

A second argument is that the holding company structure enables regulators to focus solely on the bank as a bank and not be concerned with the non-banking activities, because such activities undertaken in the holding company cannot directly affect the depository institution.  Since holding company non-banking activities are entirely separate from the bank, the bank's relationship with these activities can be supervised and controlled, but the same is not true if the activities are a subsidiary of the bank. Additionally, it is argued that there would be wasteful duplication of regulatory effort if bank subsidiaries were used for permissible non-banking activities. This is because, in the bank/subsidiary structure, *if* the bank were to provide substantial capital for a subsidiary's activities, the banking regulators would necessarily be concerned with those activities, which are more naturally governed by the SEC, insurance regulators, and others involved in the regulation of non-banking activities. This overlap of regulatory concern would (somehow) not occur in the holding company subsidiary structure.

Finally, it is suggested that the holding company structure, while protecting banks from the financial difficulties of the other subsidiaries, can provide financial strength to the bank if the other subsidiaries are successful. On the other hand, if the bank's subsidiaries have financial difficulties, the bank will not be protected from such difficulties.

A different view of BHC subsidiaries and bank subsidiaries suggests that the two structures represent only insubstantial differences of degree. It is difficult to believe that either in the eyes of the public, in the activities of management, or in the supervision of regulators it is any easier (or more difficult) to separate the benefits and burdens of non-bank activities from the bank itself. To the extent that banks need to be provided with or surrounded by a sense of safety and soundness and economic neutrality, the form of corporate structure separating the activities should make little difference. Effective separation may, in either form of organization, more obviously depend on regulation of affiliate transactions, of affiliate cross-selling of services, of separate business names and of separate physical locations, (none of which is affected by corporate structure), as well as separate capitalization and separate boards of directors.

The obvious benefit of any such structure is legal corporate separation for purposes of contagion control, regulatory supervision, and perhaps public comprehension of the different activities. While such a structure suggests, and in fact would require, separate capital, it does not necessarily require totally separate management and resources. While legal separation can be achieved, and fire walls can be used to attempt to enhance the separation, experience has suggested that the parent is greatly inclined to go beyond its legal investment to support a distressed subsidiary, most obviously to protect its general reputation and customer base. What this does, necessarily, is extend the safety net available to the bank to the subsidiary or affiliate that is assisted.

*Problem 4-8*

You are junior counsel to the United States Senate Banking Committee, and are asked whether corporate structure would have any effect on the practical problems arising out of the following transaction.

Assume that banks, securities firms and insurance companies are allowed free affiliation as separate entities.  Ace Holding Company owns a national bank, an insurance company, and a securities firm.  Ace National Bank makes a lending limit loan to the English China Clay Corporation.  Ace Insurance Company provides an insurance performance (contract completion) bond guaranteeing the completion by English China Clay of its contract to build a porcelain factory in Indonesia.  Ace Securities Corporation underwrites a public offering of English China Clay Corporation's stock, and Ace Holding Company purchases in the secondary market 5% of the stock sold.  Recall the availability of 12 U.S.C.A. § 1843(c)(6).

---

Consider whether the policies forming the basis of the BHCA are substantially related to those of the National Bank Act.  Two of the principles underlying the definition of the business of banking, discussed in chapter 3, are safety and soundness, and economic neutrality in the allocation of credit in our society.  In § 1843(c)(8), which is the fundamental section determining what nonbank activities are appropriate for BHCs, the statute provides:  "In determining whether a particular activity is a proper incident to banking . . . the Board shall consider whether its performance by an affiliate of a holding company can reasonably be expected to produce benefits to the public, such as greater convenience, increased competition, or gains in efficiency, that outweigh possible adverse effects, such as undue concentration of resources, decreased or unfair competition, conflicts of interests, or unsound banking practices."  The concerns about unfair competition and conflicts of interests can be viewed as analogous to concerns for economic neutrality.  The concern for unsound banking practices (or for soundness of our national economy) is similar to the concern for safety and soundness.  An additional concern elaborated in the BHCA is the antitrust concern for undue concentration of resources that we discussed in Chapter 2.

Is it fair to say that, unless a substantial justification can be made on the basis of safety and soundness or some other public policy, it appears that banks should be free to choose the corporate structure model that they prefer?  Is it a different point to say that financial institutions should be allowed to create forms of broader affiliation so long as they limit the risk to the deposit insurance fund?

In 1994, the following companies owned an FDIC insured depository institution and also engaged in insurance, securities, mutual funds, commercial lending, mortgage banking, credit cards, and consumer loan activities:  General Electric, Prudential, John Hancock, American Express, The Travelers, and Merrill Lynch.  These and other non-bank firms controlled almost half of all domestic consumer and business loans in 1995.  Does this create any regulatory problems?  As the distinctions blur among financial services providers, the issue is whether more effective regulation could be provided if there were a merger of financial services regulators. Or, should the various activities be in separately capitalized subsidiaries and affiliates so they can be individually regulated by those with the necessary specialized expertise?

If bank affiliations are to be limited to financial services, so that the separation of banking and commerce is continued, it will become important to come up with a definition of financial services. One example of the problem is American Express. While it is perhaps best known for its travel and entertainment card, it engages not only in that and other financial services, but also is substantially engaged in the travel business and publishing. On the other hand, while the practical issue of existing affiliations may be difficult, the definition itself may not be so difficult, as it could be limited to the ability to engage in any activity historically associated with banking, insurance, and securities–financial asset related instruments.

## B. Nonbank Activities of BHCs – Defining "Closely Related to Banking"

Bank holding companies own "non-bank" subsidiaries that engage in activities other than banking. These non-bank activities, however, must be activities specified in 12 U.S.C.A. § 1843 or, under § 1843(c)(8), they must be activities "so closely related to banking . . . as to be a proper incident thereto." Underlying the quoted section is the concept of the separation of banking and commerce, although this is not explicitly stated in the BHCA.

From 1956 to 1970 the BHCA regulated only multi-bank holding companies. Many feared that the expansion of one-bank holding companies into nonbanking fields in the late 1960s threatened the stability of the banks they controlled. In addition, many people believed that the nonbanking subsidiaries of unregulated one-bank holding companies had unfair advantages over their competitors who were not so affiliated, because of easier access to credit and other banking services. Under the 1970 amendments to the BHCA, one-bank holding companies were made subject to the same general restrictions that multi-bank holding companies had been subject to since 1956. The boundaries of permissible BHC interests in nonbanking organizations, and involvement in nonbanking activities, are contained in § 1843, listing numerous exemptions from the restrictions. Here, we deal with the most important exemption, the exemption for activities "so closely related to banking . . . as to be a proper incident thereto." 12 U.S.C.A. § 1843(c)(8). Because of the ambiguity in the language, a wider array of BHC activities has been sanctioned under this section than under any other exemption.

The procedures for obtaining the approval of the Federal Reserve Board to engage in activities under 12 U.S.C.A.§ 1843(c)(8) are contained in 12 C.F.R. § 225.23-.27. The activity must pass two tests, the public benefits (proper incident) test, and the closely related to banking test. As to the first test, the question is whether performance of an activity proposed by the holding company can reasonably be expected to produce benefits to the public, such as greater convenience, increased competition, or gains in efficiency, that outweigh possible adverse effects, such as undue concentration of resources, decreased or unfair competition, conflict of interests, or unsound banking practices.

Although many cases discuss only the public benefits test in detail, both the public benefits test and the closely related test must be met. An application by a BHC for permission to operate an automobile dealership or a restaurant chain would easily be dealt with under the closely related test if any BHC were foolish enough to make such an application. The fact that public benefits might result from such an operation would not save the application. Conversely, an activity might be closely related to banking, but not meet the public benefits test.

In the following case, it appears that both tests are relevant. Note that, in the view of the Board, the fact that there were substantial public benefits in an area where the service was not otherwise available was sufficient to satisfy § 1843(c)(8). However, the application failed, in the court's view, to meet the closely related test in some aspect. Consequently, the case illustrates some factors that enter into the Board's, as well as the courts', analyses of closely related and public benefits, and discloses the possibility that an activity can meet one of the tests but not the other. The current regulation is at 12 C.F.R. § 225.28(b)(10).

## National Courier Association v. Board of Governors
### 516 F.2d 1229 (D.C. Cir. 1975)

McGOWAN, Circuit Judge:

The Bank Holding Company Act of 1956, which generally prohibits bank holding companies from owning shares in companies other than banks, allows such ownership where the activities of the non-bank affiliate have been found by the Federal Reserve Board to be "so closely related to banking or managing or controlling banks as to be a proper incident thereto." 12 U.S.C. § 1843(c)(8) (1970). In the regulation herein challenged on direct review, the Board has enlarged the activities heretofore found by it to be "closely related." The addition consists of certain courier or high speed transportation services for

(i) the internal operations of the holding company and its subsidiaries; (ii) checks, commercial papers, documents, and written instruments (excluding currency or bearer-type negotiable instruments) as are exchanged among banks and banking institutions; (iii) audit and accounting media of a banking or financial nature and other business records and documents used in processing such media.

12 C.F.R. § 225.4(a)(11) (1974).

A fourth category of service that may be provided by bank-affiliated couriers is contained in the following "interpretation," also added to Regulation Y by the contested order:

[T]he furnishing of courier services for non-financially-related material upon the specific, unsolicited request of a third party when courier services are not otherwise reasonably available may be regarded as an incidental activity of a bank-related courier.

*Id.* § 225.129. . . .

## I

We note at the outset the limited nature of the question we have been asked to decide. Section 4(c)(8) of the Bank Holding Company Act provides that the general ban on the ownership by a bank holding company of shares in any company other than a bank shall not apply to

> shares of any company the activities of which the Board after due notice and opportunity for hearing has determined (by order or regulation) to be so closely related to banking or managing or controlling banks as to be a proper incident thereto.

12 U.S.C. § 1843(c)(8) (1970). By an amendment of the same section in 1970 the Board has been further instructed as follows:

> In determining whether a particular activity is a proper incident to banking or managing or controlling banks the Board shall consider whether its performance by an affiliate of a holding company can reasonably be expected to produce benefits to the public such as greater convenience, increased competition, or gains in efficiency, that outweigh possible adverse effects, such as undue concentration of resources, decreased or unfair competition, conflicts of interest, or unsound banking practices.

*Id.*

The parties are agreed that there are two distinct issues raised by a bank holding company's seeking to hold shares in a company engaged in non-banking activities, and that they correspond to the statutory segments set out above. The first is whether those activities are "closely related to banking." This is a question that asks only whether the activities in question are generally of a kind that Congress, having concluded that "banking and commerce should remain separate," forbade bank holding companies to engage in, without regard to the merits of such engagement in a particular case.

The second or so-called "public benefits" issue, derived from the 1970 amendments to the Act, is one which normally must be resolved upon specific facts. It poses the question whether the performance of a non-banking activity by a bank holding company affiliate will achieve a favorable balance of the kinds of benefits and adverse effects enumerated in the statute. Naturally the conclusion that the non-banking activity of one bank holding company would be anticompetitive or threaten "unsound banking practices" may not hold for a different bank holding company under different circumstances.

Recognizing this distinction in the nature of the two issues, the Board has reserved the latter for case-by-case resolution at the time of individual bank holding company applications to engage in courier service. The parties are therefore agreed that no Board determination on the "public benefits" of such engagement is now before this court for review. What is before us is the final resolution of the former or "closely related" issue with respect to the activities that the Board has added to Regulation Y. The Board's determination that these are not activities necessarily forbidden to bank holding companies takes the form of a rule intended to be binding on all future parties to individual application proceedings. Board Brief at 44.

## II

Courier services were described in the statement accompanying the Board's order as the "transportation of any item with a critical time schedule, provided such items are small in bulk, light in weight, and require only ordinary security measures." J.A. at 813. The items which are carried by courier service in far the greatest volume are financial documents and records — particularly banking instruments — which require speedy transportation from one place of business to another. It thus appears that the nation's banks are by far the largest consumers of courier services, accounting for more than half of that industry's sales. The industry itself is about thirty years old, and has thus far remained largely independent of the banks, though it is dominated by a very few firms.

Of the three categories of courier services that the Board has found to be "closely related" to banking, the first, that of courier services "for the internal operations of the holding company and its subsidiaries," is not in issue. The provision of services by one bank affiliate is expressly allowed by Section 4(c)(1)(C) of the statute. 12 U.S.C. § 1843(c)(1)(C) (1970).

The second category is that of courier services "for checks, commercial papers, documents, and written instruments (excluding currency or bearer-type instruments) as are exchanged among banks and banking institutions." What is meant are the so-called "cash letters" in which one bank transmits all the checks, drafts, and money orders that must be cleared or otherwise processed at another bank. As the Hearing Examiner explained:

> The some 13,000 commercial banks of the country, with their 30-odd thousand banking offices, have check-drawing customers who generate perhaps 25 billion checks a year, drawn on those banking offices. These checks are sent to payees by the drawers, and the payees either cash them at a bank, the corner druggist or some similar establishment, or "deposit" them for collection with their own banks. More often than not (say, 80 percent of the time), a given check thus deposited will be drawn on another bank.

> As is well known, the checks drawn on other banks are presented either directly to that bank, or if presented indirectly, through one or more intermediate collecting banks, which may include Federal Reserve banks. They are sent in what is called a "cash letter," which may be an adding machine tape or its equivalent, wrapped around the items, all of which are in an envelope or other container, suitably addressed. When indirect presentment occurs, the collecting banks in the chain are usually concentration points for the processing of huge volumes of checks.

J.A. 700-701.

The third category of "closely related" courier services are those "for audit and accounting media of a banking or financial nature and other business records and documents used in processing such media." The term "media" appears simply to refer to the physical form (paper documents, magnetic tapes, etc.) in which the financial data to be processed are conveyed. To cite a concrete example, one used by the Hearing Examiner, a bank which accepts demand deposits may find it efficient, particularly if it is a small bank, to employ a data processor to keep and update the records of those accounts in effect to perform a book-keeping function for it. As was testified at the hearings:

> In such a service, the inbound movement from the customer bank to the data center requires a pickup after the close of business at the customer's location of the data reflecting the day's transactions, and

delivery to the computer center in sufficient time to permit overnight processing of the data and a return of the reports updating the bank's accounts prior to the opening of business the next morning. J.A. 703.

The "data center" need not, of course, be a bank. In this respect the Board's order must be read in connection with an earlier section of Regulation Y permitting bank affiliates to provide financially related data processing services such as " . . . payroll, accounts receivable and payable, or billing services." 12 C.F.R. § 225.4(a)(8) (1974). In effect subsection (iii) of the present rule authorizes bank-affiliated couriers to furnish transportation services which complement the activities of fellow affiliates engaged in data processing, just as subsection (ii) of the rule authorizes them to provide transportation services which complement the activities of fellow affiliates engaged in banking.

The fourth category of authorized courier services, that contained in the Board's separate "interpretation," is largely self-explanatory. Bank- affiliated couriers may carry non-financially related material if requests for such service are unsolicited and it is not otherwise reasonably available. Any doubt as to the lack of limitation on the kind of material that may be carried under this heading was erased by the press release accompanying the Board's order, which gave as examples "human blood, exposed and processed film, repair parts and cut flowers." J.A. at 800.

## III

No challenge is made to the procedure by which the amendments to Regulation Y were adopted, but merely to their substance. In this respect our task is to set aside the Board's findings of fact if they are "arbitrary, capricious, an abuse of discretion, or otherwise not in accordance with law," while deciding "all relevant questions of law" ourselves. 5 U.S.C. § 706 (1970).

Without slighting the difficulties of separating questions of law and fact, but also without rehearsing them at any length, we address what seems to us the single "question of law" in the case, and that is the proper definition of the statutory phrase "closely related." Is it an intentionally vague phrase by which Congress very largely left it up to the Board to decide what kinds and degrees of relationships are sufficiently close? Or is there some more specific connection that the Board must find exists between banking and the assertedly related activity?

Unfortunately, no clear answers emerge from the legislative history of the statute. Its original passage in 1956 was accompanied by numerous expressions of the view that, in order to guard against conflicts of interest, bank holding companies should be confined to banking and to activities "closely related to the business of banking," but the quoted phrase was never elucidated. The Board interpreted this language restrictively, judging that it prohibited affiliation with any company whose activities were not directly related to the banking operations that the particular holding company was already engaged in. It was for this reason that the Board in 1969 proposed amendments to the Act which would give the bank holding companies greater flexibility.

A comparison of the wording of Section 4(c)(8) before and after it was amended might suggest that the Board had limited success. What had read:

. . . activities . . . which the Board . . . has determined to be so closely related to the business of banking or of managing or controlling banks as to be a proper incident thereto . . . .

70 Stat. 135 (1956), was amended to read:

. . . activities . . . which the Board . . . has determined . . . to be so closely related to banking or managing or controlling banks as to be a proper incident thereto.

12 U.S.C. § 1843(c)(8) (1970).

The history of these seemingly slight changes tells a different story, however. Though the precise amount of the intended increase in the latitude to be given the bank holding companies is something of a puzzle, it is plain that Congress intended to expand that latitude in substantial degree. The House and Senate each passed versions of the amendments which replaced the term "closely related" with the term "functionally related," and which were expressly intended, at least by the respective reporting committees, to relax the earlier restrictions. The term "functionally related" disappeared in conference (just how much of a retreat this represented is unclear, but the relaxation of restrictions did not. It is embodied in the substitution of the word "banking" for the phrase "the business of banking," the latter having been the source of the Board's earlier restrictive approach.

A substantial relaxation of the required closeness of the relation of bank affiliate activities to banking is of course consistent with Congress's simultaneous addition in 1970 of the public benefits test. The latter requires the Board to judge whether particular activities are "properly incident to banking" by specific reference to most if not all of the evils which the Act as a whole aims at preventing. See 12 U.S.C. § 1843(c)(8) *supra*. Congress has thus introduced a new and more refined test for the presence of those evils. The "closely related" test no longer bears the full load, and may now be thought of as setting off as forbidden to banks those activities which are so clearly of a purely commercial nature that the predominantly adverse effects of a bank's engaging in them may be presumed.

Against this background, and reminding ourselves that the matter is one expressly committed by the statute to the Board, we think we owe considerable deference to the Board's judgment that a particular activity is " closely related to banking." Rather than define that term with any precision, therefore, we simply require that the Board go about making its "closely related" decision in a reasoned fashion consistent with the legislative intent.

The Board must, we think, articulate the ways in which banking activities and the proposed activities are assertedly connected, and must determine, not arbitrarily or capriciously, that the connections are close. As to what kinds of connections may qualify, at least the following seem to us within the statutory intent: 1. Banks generally have in fact provided the proposed services. 2. Banks generally provide services that are operationally or functionally so similar to the proposed services as to equip them particularly well to provide the proposed service. 3. Banks generally provide services that are so integrally related to the proposed services as to require their provision in a specialized form. We turn, then, to the question of whether the Board has rationally found such connections in this case.

A.  Banking Material.

The Board appears to have found all three of the foregoing kinds of connections between banking and courier service for banking material. It made clear, for example, that it did not regard courier service as the exclusive historical province of specialized carriers. It noted that "three bank holding companies, all of which became subject to the Bank Holding Company Act as a result of the 1970 Amendments, are engaged in providing 'for hire' courier service."

As to the second kind of connection, the Board pointed out that the internal operation of a bank often involves it in transportation activities of the kind involved in courier service. According to the Board, "a number of banks, particularly those which operate a significant number of branches, engage in the transportation of such items as checks, internal memoranda and data processing material between branches . . ." J.A. at 814. The business of banking, after all, does not consist solely of abstract interest computations and lending and borrowing decisions. It is in an equally important sense the management of the torrential stream of documents and records that are the medium of financial transactions. And if it would be impossible to say that the management of that stream within a bank is not "banking," it would also be hard to say that the management of that stream between banks is not "closely related" to banking.

The third kind of connection — the dependence of banks on a specialized form of the proposed services — has been the most emphasized in this case. The Board concluded that "courier services for cash letters play a vital role in the check clearing process," and that "the transportation of a cash letter has been so integrated into the process by which checks are collected as to be part of the present payments mechanism." J.A. at 813-815. Petitioners do not really dispute the point, but urge that, if the necessity of a service to banking activities may justify the establishment of a bank affiliate to provide the service itself, then the banks may expand into any number of industries whose goods and services they consume. Telephone service is given as an example. Apart from noting that this kind of connection to banking is not the only one present in the case, we can only respond by emphasizing that the service must be required by the bank in a specialized form, as is not true of telephone service or of many others that banks employ.

The Board has thus articulated several ways in which banking and courier services for banking materials may properly be considered related. Record evidence in support of each is ample, and we cannot say that in finding the relation a "close" one the Board was arbitrary or capricious.

B. Financially Related Data Processing Materials.

The Board's findings with respect to financially related data processing materials, though less explicit than its findings with respect to " cash letters," were to the same effect. It did not specify whether the banks which it found were already engaged in "for hire" courier services had been transporting data processing as well as other materials, but the record suggests that such was the case. The Board specifically named data processing materials as among the items that banks with numerous branches often transport for their own purposes between branches. Once again, the greatest stress was put on the need for a specialized form of transportation service. The Board noted that the Hearing Examiner had found that "courier service is essential to the performance of data processing activities." The Hearing Examiner had in turn cited, in support of his conclusion that the transportation of audit media was "time critical," the following testimony of a data processing executive: "In the data processing part of the business, we sell accuracy and timeliness. The timeliness of what we sell is a function in competitiveness. We can print 1000 lines a minute, and if we can't get it to the client it is meaningless." Hearing Officer's Recommended Decision, J.A. at 704. In short, the Board treated the transportation of data processing material as bearing the same relation to data processing itself as the transportation of cash letters bears to banking, and we cannot say that it was arbitrary or capricious in doing so.

The difficult question, of course, is whether the similarity of these two relations was enough.

The record suggests that in many cases check processing and financially related data processing are carried on at the same locations and by the use of the same equipment. It would seem anomalous to require that similar material, quite possibly generated by a single customer and destined for a single bank computer, be transported by two separate couriers.

We have not overlooked the fact that no restrictions are placed by the challenged regulation upon whom a bank-affiliated courier may serve. The carriage of banking materials authorized in the second part of the Board's order will presumably be between banks, but neither need be an affiliate of the bank-affiliated courier. The carriage of data processing materials under the third part of the Board's order may be between two places of business neither of which is a bank, a bank affiliate, or a customer of either. A bank-affiliated courier may thus carry the financially related records of a firm with which it has no dealings (let us say a department store that does its banking elsewhere,) to the independent data processor of that firm's choice. It is at this point that the Board has put its discretion to determine the closeness of relations to banking under the greatest strain.

We do not think it has exceeded that discretion, however. Authorization to provide courier services to banks and bank affiliates must carry with it the authorization to provide the same services generally. The reason is that otherwise the bank-affiliated courier services, which may be of superior quality, would be "tied" by law to the other services which banks and their affiliates provide. The anti-competitive effects of such a tie in respect of banking services would contravene the Act's most basic purposes. Recognizing this, the Board has in fact not only authorized but intends to require bank affiliated couriers to provide their services generally and without discrimination. See 12 C.F.R. § 225.129 (1974).

C.  General Courier Services Where Unsolicited and Not Otherwise Available.

The Board has apparently not taken the manifestly untenable position that the transportation of non-financially related material becomes "closely related" to banking simply because such service is provided without solicitation and is not otherwise available. Its position appears instead to be that in such circumstances concededly non-closely related services may be provided because they are purely "incidental." It suggests, in other words, that in requiring that the "activities" of bank affiliates be closely related to banking, Congress meant only their ordinary or principal activities, and left them free to engage in other activities certified by the Board to be "incidental."

The notion that bank affiliates may be permitted to engage not only in activities that are "closely related to banking," but also in "incidental" activities was not first introduced by the Board in the context of courier services. It apparently takes the same view with respect to all categories of "closely related" activities, having announced in the first sentence of its Regulation Y:

. . . (A)ny bank holding company may engage, or retain or acquire an interest in a company that engages solely in one or more of the (closely related) activities specified below, *including such incidental activities as are necessary to carry on the activities so specified.*

12 C.F.R. § 225.4(a) (1974) (emphasis supplied). The Board has in fact gone on to specify the activities that may be engaged in as "incidental" to one other "closely related" activity, that of

financially related data processing.  Nor is the permissibility of activities "incidental" to those that are expressly authorized a notion that originated with the Board.  That section of the National Bank Act which circumscribes the activities of nationally chartered banks entitles them "(t)o exercise . . . all such incidental powers as shall be necessary to carry on the business of banking." 12 U.S.C. § 24 (1970).[21]

The idea is thus fairly well established that Congress intended some reasonable latitude in the limitations it placed upon the activities of banks and their affiliates.  In enumerating the activities that could be carried on, it certainly could not have meant to forbid engagement in such other "incidental" activities as were reasonably necessary to carrying out those that were enumerated.

The justification for the "incidental" courier services at issue here is, however, quite different.  It is not, as far as we can tell, that the carriage of non-financially related material is in any way necessary to the successful operation of the courier service affiliates.  Rather, it is that the provision of such service would serve "the convenience of the public."  We have in effect been asked to approve a doctrine of "incidental" activities under which the Board may permit bank affiliates to engage in such activities because such engagement would be a generally beneficial thing.  The Board has made quite an appealing case in this respect.  If requests for non-financially related courier services must be unsolicited, it may seem unlikely that a bank's courier affiliate would ever get very deeply involved in providing them.  If such services must be otherwise unavailable, then those who employ it would appear to gain, while no competitor of the bank loses.  It might thus be argued that the provision of general courier services under the conditions the Board has imposed offends none of the policies against economic concentration and conflicts of interest which underlie the statutory separation of commerce and banking.

But Congress did not instruct the Board to allow or disallow bank involvement in non-financial activities as may be required by the policies which counsel a separation of commerce and banking.  Having heeded that counsel itself, it decreed the separation, and instructed the Board to enforce it.  Its decision hardly seems an unreasonable one, even in the context of this case, for it is not at all clear that the Board's non-solicitation and non-availability conditions would in fact prevent bank-affiliated couriers from becoming substantially involved in general courier service.  The problem, of course, is the inexactitude of such terms as "unsolicited" and "not otherwise reasonably available."

The result is that while there may be some warrant in the statute for the Board's permitting as "incidental" those activities that are necessary to the bank affiliate's closely related activities, we can find no such warrant for its determination that non-financially related courier services are "incidental" and therefore permissible if unsolicited and otherwise unavailable.  The Board's order, which we have sustained in other respects, we decline to do so in this one. . . .

---

[21]    Examples of "incidental" activities that national banks have been permitted to engage in are the provision of travel services to customers, the maintenance of postal substations on bank premises, the provision of messenger services, and the acquiring of equity interests in community development projects, though such an interest would "clearly not (be) a bankable asset by ordinary standards."  12 C.F.R. §§ 7.7475, 7.7480, 7.7482, 7.7490 (1974).

The petition for review is denied in all respects with the exception that the so-called "interpretation" added to Rule Y . . . is set aside.

## Comments and Questions

1.  Note that the closely related test is only a threshold inquiry.  It merely forbids those activities "which are so clearly of a purely commercial nature that the predominantly adverse effects of a bank's engaging in them may be presumed."  What are these "adverse effects"?

2.  The emphasis of the *Courier* test is on what *banks* have done.  That seems to suggest something akin to our earlier discussion of the business of banking.  It certainly can be argued that the legislative history and underlying principles of the BHCA suggest a different test.  Should the closely related test be broader than *Courier,* or is *Courier* just a poor articulation of that test?  Is the value of the *Courier* test limited because it is backward looking?  Why don't we return to the original 1956 definition and recast it to allow affiliations with activities that are "of a financial, fiduciary or insurance nature" or are simply "financial in nature?"

3.  Arguably, the major consideration under the public benefits analysis is the possibility of the adverse impact of a subsidiary's failure on the banking operations of its bank affiliates.  The concern is similar to safety and soundness under the business of banking analysis.  Consider whether the public benefits analysis, as least as the basis for objection by competitors, should be abandoned as serving no public purpose.  Existing applicable principles can meet any public concern.  These principles are safety and soundness, economic neutrality, and the antitrust laws in the case of an acquisition of a "closely related to banking" subsidiary that is a going concern, rather than a de novo business.  Eliminating the public benefits test would reduce the substantial procedural delays and expense incurred under the current system, roadblocks usually caused by prospective competitors.  It is fair to suggest that if the activity is not a benefit to the public, the public will not utilize, pay for, and so support the activity?  The only issue would be whether the activity was "closely related to banking."  It would be difficult for competitors to relitigate that issue on a case by case basis.

### Problem 4-9

You are a new associate in a large law firm.  Your boss has scrawled out the following sets of facts for you on a scrap of paper the size of a gum wrapper and has asked you to predict the outcome of the case.  Basic Bank Holding Company wishes to form a subsidiary to engage in armored car transportation services, which activities would be fully insured from loss through private insurance for theft and fraud.  The services include transportation of cash, negotiable instruments, securities, and valuables; collecting currency and checks from commercial customers in non-bank financial institutions and transporting and depositing these collections at depository institutions; and delivering cash, negotiable instruments, securities, and valuables to commercial customers and non-bank financial institutions.   The BHC's bank subsidiaries would terminate their contracts with independent armored car companies and contract with the new BHC subsidiary for such services.   Is this a permissible activity under the BHCA?  See 12 C.F.R. § 225.28(b)(10). You vaguely remember the *Plant City* case and wonder whether it has any relevance. Also consider 12 U.S.C.A. § 371c-1.

### 1. Real Estate Activities

Various real estate activities have always attracted substantial investment interest from those in the financial markets.  We previously have discussed the real estate activities of banks under 12 U.S.C.A. §§ 29, 371 and 371d (ownership through foreclosure; mortgage lending; and bank premises).

The real estate powers of BHCs are primarily found in 12 C.F.R. § 225.28(b)(2) and (3).  The real estate leasing provisions, 12 C.F.R. § 225.28(b)(3), permit a BHC or its subsidiary to engage in leasing of real or personal property if it complies with the provisions of the regulation.  Generally, the provisions for leasing of personal property are substantially similar for both banks and bank holding companies.  Leasing of real property generally is prohibited for banks.  Real property leasing is, however, permitted for BHC subsidiaries under provisions substantially similar to those applicable to personal property leasing.

Are any of the evils thought to exist in bank ownership of real property likely to result from the leasing arrangements permitted by 12 C.F.R. § 225.28(b)(3)?  The basic idea of the pre-1997 leasing regulations was that only leases that are full payout leases and therefore constitute a lending transaction were permissible.  The rationale is that the lender is then able to recapture the principal and interest value of the financing from rentals, tax benefits, and residual value.  In other words, in the eyes of the regulators it was critical that there is little risk to the financial institution from the fluctuation in value of the underlying property.  But a lease transaction is noticeably different from a loan if the residual value benefit remains with the bank-lessor at the termination of the lease.  If the residual value benefit does remain with the financial institution, it raises issues similar to those raised in our discussion of equity kickers.

Recall that in 1987 § 24 was amended to permit national banks to engage in personal property lease transactions beyond leases that are the functional equivalent of loans. Under that authority, the OCC and the Federal Reserve lifted the limitations on using residual values to recover the investment in leased personal property, allowing up to 100 percent of the lease compensation to be derived from the property's residual value. Investment in leases expecting recovery of more than 25 percent of the acquisition cost from the residual are limited to 10 percent of the depository institution's assets.  12 C.F.R. §§ 23.1, 23.8.

In 1997 the Federal Reserve extensively amended 12 C.F.R. Pt. 225 by redefining and expanding the list of permitted nonbanking activities, now set out in 12 C.F.R. § 225.28. One important example concerns the leasing of personal or real property.  The new regulation removes several former restrictions on leasing: (1) that the lease must serve as the functional equivalent of an extension of credit (permissible high residual value leasing may not be the functional equivalent of an extension of credit); (2) that the property must be acquired only for a specific leasing transaction; (3) that the leased property must be released or sold within two years of the end of each lease; (4) that the maximum lease term not exceed 40 years; and (5) that no leased property may be held for more than 50 years. A few restrictions remain, in order to distinguish bank leasing activities from general property rental and real estate development.

Banks take mortgages on commercial and industrial, as well as residential, real estate. Bank trust departments manage real estate as part of the management of trust assets under their supervision. Banks frequently provide financing for real estate developments and syndications. Consequently, banks have a fair amount of real estate experience to draw on, and see no reason not to profit from such expertise.

Consider the following decision of the Federal Reserve. Some background may be helpful. At one time mortgage banking was a rather straightforward mortgage loan granting or mortgage loan placement activity. Commercial or industrial real estate brokerage, the placement of ownership equity interests, was a distinct activity. Times changed, primarily due to inflation. Sophisticated investors, such as insurance companies, decided that they could realize greater overall returns on their assets through investment in equity interests rather than in pure debt, mortgage interests. Mortgage bankers were quick to respond by offering ownership equity interests as well as traditional mortgages. Mortgage bankers affiliated with BHCs were faced with the choice of competing, by offering the same new products, or giving up a substantial portion of their business.

So far, we have focused on the BHC dealing with the owner/user of real estate and providing lease financing. In this decision, we deal with the BHC acting as a real estate investment adviser, but not as a real estate broker. How do you distinguish between the two activities? See 12 C.F.R. § 225.28(b)(2) and (3).

## In re BankAmerica Corp.
### 68 Fed. Res. Bull. 647 (1982)

BankAmerica Corporation, San Francisco, California, a bank holding company within the meaning of the Bank Holding Company Act, has applied for the Board's approval, under section 4(c)(8) of the act (12 U.S.C. § 1843(c)(8)) and section 225.4(a) of the Board's Regulation Y (12 C.F.R. § 225.4(a)), to engage through its subsidiary, BA Mortgage and International Realty Company, San Francisco, California ("BAMIRCO"), in the activity of arranging equity financing for certain types of income-producing properties.

Notice of the application, affording interested persons an opportunity to submit comments and views on the relatedness of the proposed activity to banking and on the balance of public interest factors regarding the application has been duly published . . . . The time for filing comments and views has expired and the Board has considered the application and all comments received in light of the public interest factors set forth in section 4(c)(8) of the act.

Applicant is a bank holding company by virtue of its control of Bank of America NT & SA, San Francisco, California (domestic deposits of $51.2 billion), the largest banking organization in California.  Bank of America controls 36.1 percent of total deposits in commercial banks in that state.  Applicant also engages in certain nonbanking activities, including mortgage banking, commercial lending and leasing, credit related insurance activities, investment advisory activities, and management consulting to depository institutions.

Applicant, through BAMIRCO, currently engages in mortgage banking and servicing activities for which it received Board approval under section 4(c)(8) of the act and sections 225.4(a)(1) and (3) of Regulation Y.  BAMIRCO also is authorized to provide investment advisory services under section 225.4(a)(5) of Regulation Y, including advice with respect to commercial or industrial real estate.

BAMIRCO currently provides to persons seeking financing for commercial or industrial income producing property a variety of financing services, including the provision or arrangement of traditional mortgage loans.  In this application, BAMIRCO seeks authority to provide these persons equity financing as an alternative to an extension of credit made or arranged by BAMIRCO.  The equity financing activity will be performed only by BAMIRCO, Applicant's mortgage banking subsidiary, and will be offered only as an alternative to traditional financing arrangements.  BAMIRCO will not solicit for properties to be sold, list or advertise properties for sale, or hold itself out or advertise as a real estate broker or syndicator.

In order to approve an application submitted pursuant to section 4(c)(8) of the act to engage in a nonbank activity, the Board is required to find that the activity is closely related to banking or managing or controlling banks.  In determining whether an activity is closely related to banking under section 4(c)(8) of the act, the Board has used the following guidelines recognized by the courts:  (1) whether banks have generally provided the proposed service; (2) whether banks generally provide services that are operationally or functionally so similar to the proposed service as to equip them particularly well to provide the proposed service; or (3) whether banks generally provide services that are so integrally related to the proposed service as to require their provision in specialized form.  In addition, the Board may consider other factors in deciding what activities are closely related to banking. . . .

Equity financing, as proposed by BankAmerica, involves arranging for the financing of commercial or industrial income-producing real estate through the transfer of the title, control and risk of the project from the owner/developer to one or more investors.  BAMIRCO would represent the owner/developer and would be paid a fee by the owner/developer for this service.  Neither BAMIRCO nor any of its affiliates will provide financing to the investors in connection with an equity financing arrangement.  BAMIRCO will arrange equity financing only in the case of commercial or industrial income-producing real property, only where the financing arranged exceeds $1 million, and will place equity financing only with institutional or wealthy, professional individual investors.

The evidence of record shows that, in performing the equity financing activity for commercial or industrial income-producing real estate, BAMIRCO needs and will utilize the type of expertise and analysis developed by financial institutions in evaluating and arranging mortgage financing for such property.  For example, Applicant states that BAMIRCO would consult with the developer/owner to determine the nature, objectives and financing requirements of a project; would consider the project's concept, architectural design, building layout, suitability for purpose and prospects; would analyze traffic flow, competing projects, source of customers, the nature of the market; would calculate projected rentals and income flows; and would review the developer/owner's timetable for the project; and availability of construction financing and long term financing for the property. Based upon its review, BAMIRCO would prepare a written analysis of the project and, in view of this analysis and its knowledge of the current real estate financing market, BAMIRCO would formulate financing alternatives, which might include equity financing. According to Applicant, in presenting a project to an investor this analysis is the same, whether the ultimate financing is in the form of a mortgage or equity financing.

The Board finds that the particular expertise and analysis required to provide equity financing for large commercial or industrial income-producing properties is functionally and operationally similar to the analysis and expertise that is required when a bank provides traditional mortgage financing services for such properties. Banking organizations have historically provided financing for commercial and industrial properties and thus are particularly well equipped to provide the proposed service. The Board's judgment is that the functional and operational similarity between mortgage banking and equity financing is further supported by the fact that equity financing can be viewed as an economic substitute for long-term mortgage financing. Evidence in the record shows that investors have increasingly turned to equity participations in projects as a means of increasing their yields and protecting themselves against inflation and interest rate fluctuations.

Moreover, the Board's view is that equity financing as proposed by Applicant and as conditioned by this Order bears a functional relationship to investment advisory services traditionally and lawfully performed by commercial banks with respect to commercial and industrial real estate. Accordingly, on these bases and based upon the evidence of record and subject to the conditions and limitations set forth in this Order, the Board finds that equity financing by Applicant is closely related to banking.[5]

The Board has imposed the conditions in this Order to confine the activity proposed by Applicant to equity financing and to prevent Applicant from engaging in real estate development or syndication. In equity financing, BAMIRCO's function is limited to acting as intermediary between developers and investors to arrange financing. Neither BAMIRCO nor any affiliate may acquire an interest in the real estate project for which BAMIRCO arranges equity financing nor have any role in the development of the project. Neither BAMIRCO nor any of its affiliates shall participate in managing, developing or syndicating property for which BAMIRCO arranges

---

[5]     In a 1972 decision, the Board required an applicant to divest a general real estate brokerage subsidiary because the applicant had not demonstrated that the proposed activity was closely related to banking. "Boatmen's Bancshares, Inc," 58 Federal Reserve Bulletin 427 (1972). Some comments on BankAmerica's proposal suggested that equity financing should be regarded as real estate brokerage and impermissible under the Board's "Boatmen's" decision. However, equity financing for income-producing properties was not an activity considered in the "Boatmen's" case. Moreover, economic conditions have changed significantly since 1972 when that determination was made, and, as noted below, equity financing has become an economic substitute for long-term mortgage financing. Because the particular expertise and analysis required for equity financing are not involved in general real estate brokerage, the Board's conclusion with respect to BAMIRCO's proposed activities does not represent a departure from the Board's position concerning the impermissibility of general real estate brokerage.

equity financing, nor promote or sponsor the development or syndication of such property. The fee BAMIRCO receives for arranging equity financing for a project shall not be based on profits derived, or to be derived, from the property and should not be larger than the fee that would be charged by an unaffiliated intermediary. The Board finds that Applicant's proposed equity financing activity will not constitute either real estate development or real estate syndication, provided the above-mentioned conditions and limitations are observed by Applicant and BAMIRCO.

Before approving a bank holding company's application to engage in an activity that the Board determines is closely related to banking, the Board must also find that consummation of the proposal can reasonably be expected to produce benefits to the public that outweigh possible adverse effects. With respect to the proposed equity financing activity, it appears from the record that authorizing the activity for bank holding companies would enhance competition and provide greater convenience, increased efficiencies, and lower costs, without resulting in any adverse consequences. Greater convenience and increased competition would result by providing a broader range of long-term financing alternatives and by aiding the flow of funds between investors and developers. This should also tend to produce lower costs and increased efficiencies. Moreover, competition would be enhanced since mortgage company subsidiaries of bank holding companies could better compete with independent mortgage companies, which may engage in both traditional mortgage banking and equity financing. Some concern was expressed by commenters on the application that consummation of the proposal might result in unfair competition by allowing bank holding companies to engage in real estate brokerage and might result in conflicts of interests with respect to subsidiary banks. As noted, the Board has limited the proposed activity to exclude general real estate brokerage. Moreover, in view of the commitments and representations furnished by Applicant, including the prohibition against the financing by BAMIRCO's affiliates of investors in an equity financing arrangement, the Board believes that approval of the activity is not likely to result in any conflicts of interest. . . .

Based upon the foregoing and other considerations reflected in the record, the Board has determined that the balance of the public interest factors that the Board is required to consider under section 4(c)(8) of the act is favorable. This determination is conditioned upon Applicant strictly limiting its activities as described in information provided in connection with this application and as provided in this Order.

Accordingly, the application is hereby approved. . . .

## Comments and Questions

1. On first consideration, it appears that this decision represents only a minor expansion of the powers of BHCs. The subsidiary will not solicit for properties to be sold, list or advertise properties for sale, or hold itself out as a real estate syndicator. But, because the subsidiary's customers are professional investors, it is hard to believe they will not know about the subsidiary offering equity financing placements.

2. What distinguishes equity financing from general real estate brokerage? It can be argued that the activity proposed by BankAmerica is synonymous with real estate brokerage and syndication. BankAmerica will provide equity investors the opportunity to

acquire income-producing property, which is the very essence of real estate brokerage and syndication. Consider footnote 5 in the opinion. Could a more principled distinction be made similar to that made between private placements and public offerings in securities law? A line could be drawn between "private placement" of investment properties with sophisticated investors—which relates to offering only financial services and financial judgments—and other brokerage, particularly single family home retail brokerage—which additionally involves more intangible, nonfinancial considerations.

3. On the other hand, general real estate brokerage can generate substantial income and does not require substantial capital investment. Banks, especially the smaller banks, are in a particularly strong position to offer such a service because they have numerous and regular customer contacts. Many smaller banks, which especially need to diversify their services, have excellent retail customer relations. Many banks could do "general" real estate brokerage very efficiently because they already have computerized facilities capable of maintaining property listings and customer lists. Such brokerage has none of the risks of real estate equity investments, such as cyclical prices, high capital costs, and skill or experience intensiveness. So, where should we draw the line?

4. As you will learn when we discuss financial institutions' securities powers, financial institutions have the power to engage in securities brokerage. They have a lesser power to engage in securities underwriting, which exposes substantial amounts of capital to the risk of the worth of the securities. Since brokerage has a lower risk to the financial security of a financial institution, should banks also be allowed to engage in real estate brokerage? They are both agency, not principal, activities. Apply the *Courier* test to real estate brokerage. Do banks generally provide the service? Do banks generally provide services that are operationally and functionally similar to real estate brokerage? Do banks generally provide services that are so integrally related to the proposed service as to require their provision in a specialized form? Is real estate brokerage financial in nature?

### 2. Data Processing

Data processing activities are principally governed by 12 C.F.R. § 7.1019 for banks and by 12 C.F.R. § 225.28(b)(14) for BHCs.

Electronic data processing has enabled banks to increase the efficiency of their internal operations and, consequently, to improve customer service. Data processing may also present the opportunity for banks to provide additional financial services to customers. The most obvious possibilities are infinite kinds of financial records processing. You might consider such possibilities as billing services for professionals, such as doctors, dentists and engineers; rent collection and accounting records for owners of real estate; inventory and cost accounting for commercial customers; and income tax accounting for individuals.

Overall, it is obvious that information processing and transfer is becoming increasingly important to banks and BHCs which are facing substantial competition from other entities with technological capabilities on the "information superhighway." For example, AT&T entered the financial services business with the Universal telephone and credit card in 1990, and five years later ranked second in Mastercard cards and VISA cards issued. With its general communications capabilities, AT&T has shown substantial interest in home banking and other electronic commercial activities.

Of a similar and perhaps even more formidable nature are the activities of Microsoft Corporation, as the leading providers of computers' basic operating systems, and its growing interest in home banking and the provision of unified financial services. Obviously Microsoft and AT&T, which has a telecommunications relationship with the majority of households in the United States, are major players in financial services technologies which are not limited by the BHCA. Consider whether the limitations imposed in the following case will ultimately cause banks and BHCs to become noncompetitive players in the technology of financial services.

## Association of Data Processing Service Organizations v. Board of Governors
### 745 F.2d 677 (D.C Cir. 1984)

SCALIA, Circuit Judge:

. . . On February 23, 1979, Citicorp applied for authority to engage, through its subsidiary Citishare, in the processing and transmission of banking, financial, and economic related data through timesharing, electronic funds transfer, home banking and other techniques. It also sought permission to sell its excess computing capacity and some computer hardware. The Board published notice of Citicorp's application, which was protested by ADAPSO, and set it for formal hearing. 45 Fed. Reg. 41,533 (July 19, 1980). Before the hearing was held, Citicorp amended its application to add certain activities and to request amendment of Regulation Y to permit the activities it had specified. The Board published an Amended Order for Hearing and invited public comments and participation. 45 Fed. Reg. 76,515 (Nov. 19, 1980). A formal hearing was held before an Administrative Law Judge in which the merits of both the application and the proposed rule were considered. In addition, more than sixty companies and individuals submitted written comments on the proposed rule. On March 29, 1982, the ALJ decided that the activities proposed by Citicorp were closely related to banking and would produce benefits to the public which would outweigh their costs. *In re: Application of Citicorp to Engage in Data Processing and Transmission Activities*, ALJ Recommended Decision, J.A. B-68 to B-123 ("Recommended Decision"). The ALJ also recommended amendments to Regulation Y that would permit those activities contained in the Citicorp application. On July 9, 1982, the Board adopted the ALJ's recommendation to approve the Citicorp application, with certain restrictions. On August 23, 1982, the Board adopted the ALJ's recommended amendments to Regulation Y, again with certain restrictions. ADAPSO, and two of its members, participants in the actions below, filed these petitions for review. . . .

### II. CLOSELY RELATED TO BANKING

This appeal requires us, then, to decide whether the Board of Governors acted arbitrarily or capriciously–either because no substantial evidence existed to support its factual premises, or in any other respect–when it concluded, based on the record of the proceedings before it, that the new activities Citicorp proposed were closely related to banking. The test which the Board applied was that developed by this court in *National Courier* . . .

The "Data Test"

Petitioners do not contend that the *National Courier* criteria are in themselves erroneous (they have subsequently been approved by the Supreme Court . . . ), but they do contend, preliminarily, that the Board erroneously applied them to *the kinds of data involved in the proposed services,* rather than to the *services themselves.*

The depth of confusion that surrounds this argument is suggested by the fact that the Board's brief denies that a data test was applied . . . while the briefs of intervenors supporting the Board acknowledge that, at least as to the Regulation Y order, it was applied but assert that its application was lawful . . . . We must address the Board's contention first.

The Board is quite correct that the Citicorp order specifically examined each of the eight categories of data processing the applicant proposed to provide.  But some of those categories were only described with reference to (1) the data processing technology employed and (2) the nature of the data to be provided or processed, and the Board clearly held that the former "is not determinative of whether [the] activity is permissible," Citicorp Order, 68 Fed. Res. Bull. at 507. The conclusion is therefore inescapable that, even in the Citicorp order, a data test was employed. With regard to timesharing services, for example, the applicant proposed to provide "data processing and transmission services for financial and non-financial institutions wherein the data being processed and transmitted are financial, banking or economic related." J.A. C-54.  The Board approved this, with the one change (which will be discussed further in another portion of this opinion) that "economic related" was altered to "economic."  Citicorp Order, 68 Fed. Res. Bull. at 507 n.8.  It is true that the application further provided some examples of the specific data processing *uses* to which the requested authority would be put:

> Such packaged financial systems permit customers at various locations to obtain the benefit of Citicorp's financial information systems and financial analysis expertise with respect to such applications associated with banking as financial modeling, loan analysis, accounting and bookkeeping, budget and profitability analysis, portfolio record-keeping and analysis, foreign exchange exposure, general ledger, bond analysis, international trade settlement, and economic forecasting.

J.A. C-54 to C-55.  The Board's opinion discussed several of these examples,[7] concluding that they in fact represented services provided by banks or were so similar to such services that banking organizations are particularly well equipped to provide them.  But that can only be understood as an attempted *demonstration* that its data test is as successful in concrete application as it is in theory.

It is even clearer that the Regulation Y order employs a data test.  No more is needed to establish this than the text of the new regulation which the order adopted.  Permissible activities of bank holding companies now include:

---

[7]    There is no doubt that the Board understood them to be, as they were phrased, merely *examples* of the data processing uses that would be made available.  Where its opinion meant to limit the applicant to the specific uses that were recited as currently contemplated, it said so.  *See* the portion of the Citicorp order dealing with home banking services, 68 Fed. Res. Bull. at 509-10, the conclusion of which is reflected in the Regulation Y Order, 47 Fed. Reg. 37,370.

Providing to others data processing and data transmission services, facilities (including data processing and data transmission hardware, software, documentation or operating personnel), data bases, or access to such services, facilities, or data bases by any technological means, if: (i) The data to be processed or furnished are financial, banking, or economic, and the services are provided pursuant to a written agreement so describing and limiting the services; (ii) The facilities are designed, marketed, and operated for the processing and transmission of financial, banking, or economic data; and (iii) The hardware provided in connection therewith is offered only in conjunction with software designed and marketed for the processing and transmission of financial, banking, or economic data, and where the general purpose hardware does not constitute more than 30 percent of the cost of any packaged offering.

12 C.F.R. § 225.25(b)(7). The Regulation Y order states that the amendment it adopts "will make it permissible for bank holding companies to engage in the data processing and transmission services the Board has approved by order in the [Citicorp] case." Regulation Y Order, 47 Fed. Reg. 37,369. But as the footnote accompanying that statement shows, this is a reference to the eight broad technological categories of service (*e.g.*, timesharing) rather than to the particular uses within those categories (*e.g.*, budgeting, bookkeeping, accounting) which petitioners complain a data test avoids. And when the Regulation Y order incorporates by reference "[t]he Board's findings on the permissibility of the services involved . . . set forth in detail in the Board's [Citicorp] order," *id.*, that incorporation, like the original findings themselves, must be for the purpose of exemplifying that in concrete application the data test will produce services closely related to banking.

As the insignificant nature of the textual changes in the portion of Regulation Y dealing with the current issue indicates, the present amendment does not fundamentally alter the approach of that regulation to data processing services. With regard to the data test point it is significant, we think, that the Board's staff recommendation proposing what in substance became the 1971 Regulation Y described its approach as follows:

In our view, the real issue is what kind of data should banking organizations be permitted to process. The technology employed is not the subject of the Act. . . . Accordingly, we recommend that the Board shift the emphasis of its proposal from the method of processing data to the kind of data being processed. Under this recommendation, bank holding companies would be permitted to process banking, financial, or other economic data, regardless of the tool used in the processing.

Legal Division Memo to Board of Governors (June 7, 1971), Applicant's Exhibit M-2 at 6. While this is the staff's description rather than the Board's we think it an accurate representation of what the Board did in 1971 and perpetuated in the present orders. . . .

We must confront, therefore, the stark question whether the data test, as the determinant of whether data processing services are closely related to banking, is arbitrary or capricious. We think not. It would of course be preferable, from the point of view of accuracy alone, to make every "closely related" determination on a more narrow, specific, case-by-case basis–to ask, as petitioners would have the Board do, whether data processing for budget analysis, for bookkeeping, and for accounting each separately qualifies for the exemption. Indeed, it would be even *more* accurate to get even *more* specific, and to ask whether budget analysis for manufacturing entities, budget analysis for retail sales entities, and budget analysis for personal service entities each separately qualifies. But the whole point of rulemaking as opposed to adjudication (or of statutory law as opposed to case-by-case common law development) is to incur a small possibility of inaccuracy in exchange for a large increase in efficiency and predictability. What the present controversy comes down to is simply whether there is reasonable assurance that the activities embraced within the data test–not all of which have been individually examined or even yet foreseen–will be closely related to banking under one or more of the broad *National Courier* tests. We think that there is.

As a theoretical matter, to begin with, the test is appealing. The record of this proceeding amply demonstrates, if any demonstration is needed, that banks regularly develop and process for their customers large amounts of banking, financial and economic data, and that they do so (and will presumably continue to do so) through the most advanced technological means. Once that is acknowledged, it is difficult to envision how any provision of data processing services dealing with data of that particular type would not meet at least the second of the *National Courier* tests:

> Banks generally provide services that are operationally or functionally so similar to the proposed services as to equip them particularly well to provide the proposed service.

*National Courier, supra*, 516 F.2d at 1237. Perhaps it may not be in the public interest for them to provide one or another of such services, for anticompetitive or other reasons. But that relates to the "public benefits" determination, which is made case-by-case rather than in the amended Regulation Y, and whose resolution in the Citicorp order is not under challenge on this appeal.

In addition to its theoretical reasonableness, there is the fact that the Board, in the course of this proceeding, considered specific applications of the principle to various specific data processing uses proposed by Citicorp–finding all of them to be within one of the *National Courier* criteria, and many to be within the most rudimentary criterion that "[b]anks generally have in fact provided the proposed services," *id.* We find adequate support in the record for those conclusions. . . .

We think these considerations amply justify the approach the Board has taken, an approach to which the petitioners have suggested no feasible alternative.

### Economic Data

We turn next to an objection of petitioners that relates not to the data test as such, but to the types of data which the data test embraces.

The previous version of Regulation Y permitted bank holding companies to engage in "storing and processing other banking, financial, or *related economic* data, such as performing payroll, accounts receivable or payable or billing services." 12 C.F.R. § 225.4(a)(8)(ii) (1972) (emphasis added). In the combined adjudication-rulemaking here at issue, the ALJ's Recommended Decision accepted Citicorp's proposal that this be expanded to include the processing and transmission of "banking, financial and *economic related* data." Recommended Decision at 49, J.A. B-120 (emphasis added). The Board rejected that recommendation, agreeing with petitioners here that "economic related data" was "too broad a category and includes data that are not closely related to banking." Regulation Y Order, 47 Fed. Reg. 37,369; Citicorp Order, 68 Fed. Res. Bull. at 507 n.8. It adopted, however, an expansion of the previous language to "banking, financial and *economic* [as opposed to *economic-related*] data," and permitted Citicorp to engage in such activities. *Id.* This expansion of prior authority was based upon its conclusion that "the record in this proceeding supports a finding that banks process *economic* data." Regulation Y Order, 47 Fed. Reg. 37,369. *See also* Citicorp Order, 68 Fed. Res. Bull. at 507 n.8 ("[t]he record supports a finding that banks engage in the processing and transmission of economic data").

We agree. The testimony amply establishes the proposition that banks have long served their customers by developing and making available information regarding the national and international economy, including economic projections useful for investment decisions. The existing Regulation Y itself permitted the provision of "general economic information and advice, general economic statistical forecasting services and industry studies." 12 C.F.R. § 225.4(a)(5)(iv) (1982). The current amendment of Regulation Y, which merely enables banks to make such information available in a new and more useful fashion, thus clearly meets the second of the *National Courier* criteria, and perhaps the first as well. Petitioners complain that "[n]owhere in the record has there been any demonstration that banks have historically provided economic services even approaching the sophistication, scale and business mode approved by the Board in its Orders." Petitioners' Brief at 42. Perhaps so, but that is progress. It is not the purpose of the Bank Holding Company Act restrictions to confine banks to the same level, or crudeness, or technological simplicity of services previously provided–but merely to services of a closely related nature.

We also reject petitioners' complaint that the Board has not defined "economic data." Petitioners' Brief at 35-36. In the context of these orders the meaning of the term is clear enough. It includes, as petitioners fear, "agricultural matters, retail sales matters, housing matters, corporate profit matters and anything 'of value in banking and financial decisions.'" *Id.* at 36 (*quoting* Citicorp Reply Brief before the Board at 13 & n.17).

Timesharing Services

Until the 1970s, data processing was performed in the "batch" mode, that is, the application of a computer program was applied to data recorded (keypunched) on small cards, which were physically delivered to the computer. Batch processing requires expensive data pick-up and delivery, often involves lengthy overall turnaround time, and permits only one job to be performed at a time. Technological advances now enable data to be transmitted electronically, typically over a telephone line, to and from the central processing unit and the user's terminal. That capability plus other technological advances permit "timesharing"–the simultaneous use of a computer by many users, each of whom can interact with the computer, *i.e.*, ask yes-no questions and receive immediate responses. The ALJ found timesharing particularly well suited to economic, financial, and banking operations. Recommended Decision at 9, J.A. B-80.

Timesharing was approved in both the Citicorp and the Regulation Y Orders, 68 Fed. Res. Bull. at 507; 47 Fed. Reg. 37,369. Of course one of petitioners' objections to this action is that the approval of this new service on the basis of the data test was impermissible; we have addressed that in a more general context above. Petitioners also claim, however, that timesharing, particularly when combined with customer use (which the orders permit) of applications software for such functions as modeling, forecasting and statistical analysis residing on holding company computers (as opposed to requiring customer creation and use of their own applications software) enables customers to use bank computer systems for "open-ended and general, non-financial services," Petitioners' Brief at 28, such as "race track handicapping or employee evaluation," *id.* at 27.

This objection is unfounded. To begin with, the Act places a limitation upon the services that bank holding companies can *offer*, not upon the uses to which others choose to put them. If the services proposed here were so well adapted to such uses unrelated to banking as employee evaluation that it could reasonably be thought that the services were *offered* for that purpose it would be one thing; but these services are no more invalidated by the mere *possibility* of such use, "unknown even to the holding company itself," Petitioners' Brief at 29, than was the service which we approved in *National Courier* invalidated by the obvious possibility that a customer might include some nonfinancial material in the courier packages. And such a possibility (at most) is all that petitioners established. They brought forward not a single instance of actual use of such services for such purposes. Even their theoretical horrible was refuted by testimony asserting that it would be prohibitively expensive to use financial programs for such nonfinancial purposes. Nov. 17, 1981 Tr. at 1178-79, 1214-15.

Moreover, as undocumented and as unrealistic as the petitioners' fears on this score appear to be, the Board nonetheless included provisions in its orders to calm this concern. In the Citicorp order the Board required that "all proposed data processing services provided by Citicorp to others outside the holding company for banking, financial and economic data must be provided pursuant to a written agreement so describing and limiting the services." Citicorp Order, 68 Fed. Res. Bull. at 507. The approval conferred by the amended Regulation Y applies only when "the data to be processed or furnished are financial, banking, or economic, and the services are provided pursuant to a written agreement so describing and limiting the services." 12 C.F.R. § 225.25(b)(7)(i). These agreements will be subject to scrutiny in connection with the Board's case-by-case "public benefits" determination. In addition, the amended Regulation Y specifically requires that the offered facilities (by which the Board means "data processing and transmission hardware, systems software, documentation and operating personnel," Citicorp Order, 68 Fed. Res. Bull. at 507 n.12) be "designed, marketed, and operated for the processing and transmission of financial, banking, or economic data," 12 C.F.R. § 225.25(b)(7)(ii), and the Citicorp order makes it clear that this imposes the obligation to "take the technical steps necessary to ensure" this result. 68 Fed. Res. Bull. at 508. It is unthinkable that any more should be required.

### Hardware

In both the Citicorp order and the Regulation Y order, the Board approved bank holding company provision of data processing hardware to their customers. Hardware is the equipment used in data processing systems, such as the mainframe computer, terminals, printers, memory devices, and the like. Software is the coded instructions which control the way data is processed, for example, individual programs. See Recommended Decision at 6-7, J.A. B-77 to B-78. For present purposes, data processing hardware provided by bank holding companies can be divided into two types, which were approved subject to different conditions and must be discussed separately.

*Specialized hardware* is specifically designed "to provide a permissible data processing or transmission service[ ], and is not likely to be used, to any significant extent, for nonfinancial purposes." Citicorp Order, 68 Fed. Res. Bull. at 508 n.14. The prime example is the automated teller machine (ATM), which is designed to execute banking transactions and has special security features appropriate to that purpose. The Board found that such hardware, when "offered only in conjunction with software designed and marketed for the processing and transmission of financial, banking, or economic data," 12 C.F.R. § 225.25(b)(7)(iii), meets the third *National Courier* test. Citicorp Order, 68 Fed. Res. Bull. at 508 & n.14, 509; Regulation Y Order, 47 Fed. Reg. 37,370. As noted earlier, that test reads as follows:

> Banks generally provide services that are so integrally related to the proposed services as to require their provision in a specialized form.

516 F.2d at 1237. Petitioners make several attacks upon this finding, none of which seems to us well taken. . . .

But at this point it begins to become foolish to devote one's analytic energy to a parsing of the *National Courier* tests as though they were the statute itself, instead of referring to the underlying intent of the "closely related" requirement of which *National Courier* is, and only purports to be, a partial elaboration. That is to say, surely one of the most significant elements of the *National Courier* criterion is its prologue. After noting that the 1970 amendments to the Bank Holding Company Act (which slightly altered the text of the "closely related" provision and added the "public benefits" requirement) mean that the "closely related" test "no longer bears the full load, and may now be thought of as setting off as forbidden to banks those activities which are so clearly of a purely commercial nature that the predominantly adverse effects of a bank's engaging in them may be presumed," 516 F.2d at 1237, we continued:

> Against this background, and reminding ourselves that the matter is one expressly committed by the statute to the Board, we think we owe considerable deference to the Board's judgment that a particular activity is "closely related to banking." Rather than define that term with any precision, therefore, we simply require that the Board go about making its "closely related" decision in a reasoned fashion consistent with the legislative intent.

> The Board must, we think, articulate the ways in which banking activities and the proposed activities are assertedly connected, and must determine, not arbitrarily or capriciously, that the connections are close. As to what kinds of connections may qualify, *at least the following* seem to us within the statutory intent. . . .

*Id.* (emphasis added).

Whether or not the provision of specialized computer hardware comes within the third *National Courier* test, we think the Board came to its decision in a reasoned fashion consistent with the legislative intent, and that that decision is not arbitrary or capricious. The Board noted, with adequate record support, that customers do not buy software and hardware but data processing. Citicorp Order, 68 Fed. Res. Bull. at 508-09; Regulation Y Order, 47 Fed. Reg. 37,370. Moreover, the Recommended Decision which the Board adopted discussed the impact of large scale integrated (LSI) circuits upon data processing technology, which now permit simple software functions, and in the future will permit more complex software functions, to be built into the hardware; and enable some of the computing function to be removed from the central computer and located in a customized "micro-processor" or "minicomputer" located at the point of use. Recommended Decision at 7-8, J.A. B-78 to B-79. This is the way some data processing is conducted now, and much more will be conducted in the future. Finally, the Recommended Decision also noted, with adequate record support, that a software producer marketing a "package" of software plus hardware is able to get a manufacturer's discount on the hardware, and is thus able to provide the full service to the purchaser at a more competitive price. Recommended Decision at 8, J.A. B-79. On the basis of these factors the Board concluded that "the activity of providing software without the corresponding authority to provide related hardware is of questionable economic feasibility." Citicorp Order, 68 Fed. Res. Bull. at 508 (footnote omitted). It is not the economic infeasibility in itself that impresses us, but the underlying cause of that infeasibility, recognized by the Board — that in both market contemplation and technological reality the service in question is a unitary one. The issue boils down, as Citicorp suggests, Citicorp Brief at 58, to almost "a tautology." In effect, to authorize the provision of banking, financial and economic data processing is to authorize the provision of banking, financial and economic hardware and software. Whether it be considered "integrally related" to the authorized service or, perhaps more realistically, simply part of it, the provision of specialized hardware is reasonably included.

*General purpose hardware* is, as the name would suggest, hardware that is designed to perform data processing functions in addition to banking, financial and economic. The Board approved bank holding company provision of this hardware, subject to the same condition that it be offered only in conjunction with banking, financial or economic data software, and subject to the additional condition that it "not constitute more than 30 percent of the cost of any packaged offering." 12 C.F.R. § 225.25(b)(7)(iii). The Board acknowledged that the sale of general purpose hardware "is not itself an activity that is closely related to banking," but found that with the limitations the Board imposed it would be permissible as "incidental" to the provision of permissible data processing services, Citicorp Order, 68 Fed. Res. Bull. at 508; *see also* Regulation Y Order, 47 Fed. Reg. 37,370.

The notion of permissibility of "any incidental activities that are necessary to carry on" activities closely related to banking has been embodied in Regulation Y since 1971. 12 C.F.R. § 225.21(a)(2). We approved it in *National Courier*, noting that "[i]n enumerating the activities that could be carried on, [Congress] certainly could not have meant to forbid engagement in such other 'incidental' activities as were reasonably necessary to carrying out those that were enumerated." 516 F.2d at 1240. We disapproved its application to bank courier handling of nonfinancial materials for the following reason:

The justification for the 'incidental' courier services . . . is not, as far as we can tell, that the carriage of non-financially related material is in any way necessary to the successful operation of the courier service affiliates. Rather, it is that the provision of such service would serve 'the convenience of the public.'

*Id.* (footnote omitted). Here, by contrast, the Board's justification was *precisely* that the provision of banking, financial and economic data processing services could not be successful unless they were offered in conjunction with the necessary hardware. Even where the hardware itself was not required to be specialized or to contain any software–so that the hardware could not be regarded as in itself the provision of banking, financial or economic data processing–the nature of the data processing market was such, the Board found, that hardware and software were a single package. The provision of data processing software in isolation, even where no specialized or software-inclusive hardware was required, was "of questionable economic feasibility." Citicorp Order, 68 Fed. Res. Bull. at 508, referred to in Regulation Y Order, 47 Fed. Reg. 37,370. There was record evidence to support this conclusion, and, as the excerpt from *National Courier* above suggests, the conclusion is sufficient to support the Board's action. Indeed, the Fifth Circuit Court of Appeals has permitted an even lesser connection to sustain bank holding company provision of liability insurance as "incidental" to the closely-related-to- banking activity of providing property damage insurance for the collateral in bank loans. *Alabama Association of Insurance Agents, supra.* While that court found evidence to sustain the proposition that, "from the consumer's point of view, packaged property damage and liability policies are more desirable than the same policies separately sold," 533 F.2d at 245, it did not make the further finding that the sale of the one had been shown to be "of questionable economic feasibility" without the sale of the other. In that respect, *Alabama Association* goes further than we were prepared to go in *National Courier*, though there was, it must be acknowledged, the added factor that liability insurance in itself to some degree increased the security of the banks' loans. In any case, we think that the reasoning of both *National Courier* and *Alabama Association* supports the proposition that the economic necessity of offering a service that is not closely related to banking in order to sell another service that is, justifies the provision of the one as "incidental" to the other.

There is an obvious limitation upon this principle: At some point the tail begins to wag the dog. If it should be found, for example, that data processing services cannot be sold in an economically feasible manner without manufacturing data processing hardware; and if the banks' profits from the latter should exceed their profits from the former; surely the provision of data processing services would be incidental to hardware manufacture rather than vice-versa. But the Board has adequately taken that limitation into account, by specifying, as described above, that the cost of the hardware (including both specialized and general purpose hardware) cannot exceed 30 percent of the cost of the package. The Board derived this figure by noting from the record that hardware costs for the data processing industry as a whole represent about 25 percent of total costs, Citicorp Order, 68 Fed. Res. Bull. at 509,–so that a "package" in which hardware accounted for about that percentage of the cost could reasonably be considered primarily a sale of data processing rather than a sale of processing hardware. We think that a reasonable way to proceed, and we cannot say that an element of a permissible service which constitutes less than one-third the cost of that service is not "incidental." . . . .

Denied.

## Comments and Questions

1. It is evident that banks and BHCs, with the substantial investments they have in computer hardware and EDP employees, have the capability to develop data processing services in areas not related to any underlying banking service. Should this capability be limited? Or, should banks and BHCs be permitted to develop freely their data processing capabilities and make those capabilities available to the public as a public benefit? Should BHCs have easier entry into the data processing field than banks?

2. It was determined that a BHC's processing of "economic related" data is not closely related to banking, but processing "economic" data is closely related. What does this mean in terms of which activities are permissible and which activities are prohibited? It is evident that at some point data processing becomes less and less incidental to banks and BHCs and more integral. Yet, then-Judge Scalia commented that "at some point the tail begins to wag the dog." Is this statement only applicable to limiting the offering of

general purpose hardware, or does it also limit the offering of permissible data processing services?

3.  The Federal Communications Commission denied Citicorp a common carrier license for digital termination service frequencies to provide EFT services and data communications.  It appears the basis for the ruling was that a BHC is limited in the type of data it may transmit, and so was not permitted by the Federal Reserve to be a common carrier.

4.  We previously have discussed various approaches to determining what is closely related to banking.  Specifically considering the *Citicorp* decision, was the court correct in focusing on the kind of data rather than the technology of the services provided?

5.  It is obvious that someone is going to create information management systems that give both businesses and individuals the capability to inquire about, preview, and purchase a full range of financial services at their own convenience.  To put it differently, is the technological delivery system a more critical element in competing for financial business than is the financial product or service it delivers?  How much of the business of banking becomes the business of managing financial information and its delivery systems?  To what extent is this question the critical element in providing other services such as travel services and health care services — can these services also be classified as the management of financial information? In general, what should be the scope of permissible data?

6.  In 1997 the Federal Reserve removed two restrictions on permissible data processing activities: (1) that the services must be provided pursuant to a written agreement; and (2) that data processing facilities must be designed, marketed and operated for processing and transmitting financial, banking or economic data.  Further, the new regulation permits BHCs to derive up to 30 percent of their data processing revenues from processing and transmitting data that are not financial, banking or economic.  Are these revisions necessary to allow BHCs to complete with other software providers and to recruit the most talented employees?

### Problem 4-10

Bank Onit Holding Company wishes to become involved in the multi-trillion dollar health care industry.  It wishes to engage in the following activities and seeks your considered advice.

1.  One idea is that the BHC would supply HMO patients with plastic identification cards which, when put through the appropriate electronic terminal, would provide the doctor with insurance information on deductibles, co-payment requirements, and other aspects of medical coverage.  Subsequent to appropriate medical services, the physician could complete and transmit the claim form to the appropriate insurance company, which would then credit the doctor's account at Bank Onit.

2.  Your client would like to create information systems that draw together doctor and hospital records for patients, as well as diagnostic and treatment expert pathways, and

so offer a complete range of electronic medical information and the necessarily related fund transfer services that ultimately result.

3. If they are allowed to engage in the above activities, do bank and bank affiliates have an unfair advantage on their non-bank competitors because, ultimately, the customers are going to have to use a bank to move the funds?

---

Banking law contains several significant exceptions to the separation of banking from commerce. One is 12 U.S.C.A. § 1843(c)(6), which provides that a BHC may own up to 5 percent of the voting shares of any company. The statute appears to be clear on its face that "any company" means what it says–it permits ownership of 5 percent of General Motors or Microsoft.

*Problem 4-11*

1. Venturous Bank Holding Company has a wholly owned nonbank subsidiary, Venturous Venture Capital. It places the following ad in Business Month magazine: "Venturous Venture Capital (Venturous) is interested in sponsoring new and emerging companies that have substantial growth potential. We are interested in anything (that is legal). We will purchase up to 5 percent of the voting stock of your corporation and supply necessary additional capital by purchasing nonvoting stock. This nonvoting stock shall be convertible into voting stock at any time such conversion is permissible under applicable federal and state law." Ridgets Inc. responds to the ad. An agreement is reached, wherein Venturous acquires 5 percent of the voting stock and 100 percent of the nonvoting stock of Ridgets, comprising 90 percent of its total capitalization. The agreement also provides that Ridgets may not merge with anyone else, or enter into any new business activity, without the express agreement of Venturous. Is this permissible? 12 C.F.R. § 225.143 prohibits such an arrangement with respect to acquisition of stock in banks or BHCs. If this regulation relevant? See also 12 U.S.C.A. § 1841(d).

2. May Venturous own 5 percent of a parcel of real estate, or of any other asset? Would it matter whether the ownership was in the form of a general partnership or a limited liability corporation?

## Comments and Questions

While under § 1843(c)(8) BHCs must ask the Federal Reserve for approval of an acquisition, no such requirement applies to § 1843(c)(6) acquisitions. But, if there is a question of violation of the 5 percent ownership limit, the Federal Reserve has the power to rule on the issue. In addition, there is something called the "source-of-strength" doctrine which we will discuss in greater detail in the next section. Essentially, the source of strength doctrine requires a BHC to have enough capital to support its bank subsidiaries before it directs funds to the support of nonbank investments. In general, the Federal Reserve will allow holding companies to own up to 4.9 percent of voting stock in a nonfinancial company and up to an additional 20 percent of nonvoting stock.  If these restrictions create difficulties for a BHC, it often is possible to turn to the Small Business Administration and the use of an SBIC–a BHC investment authorized under § 1843(c)(5). The banking regulators historically have deferred to the SBA's interpretations of the SBA statute and regulations.  The SBA frequently has given very liberal interpretations of what constitutes a small business, and the SBA can also offer exemptions for investments in companies that are based in distressed areas.

## C.  Nonbanking Activities of Bank Subsidiaries

The outer limits of permissible activities of *bank* subsidiaries is a separate but obviously related question.  Historically, national bank subsidiaries have been permitted to engage only in those activities authorized to the bank itself.  Is there a policy basis for this historic limitation?  Why should a bank subsidiary be treated differently than a BHC non-bank subsidiary?

In order to improve their economies and create jobs, some states have begun to expand the activities permissible to state-chartered banks or their subsidiaries.  For example, South Dakota enacted a law permitting South Dakota chartered banks, directly or through subsidiaries, to engage in "all facets of the insurance business."  S.D. Codified Laws Ann. § 51A-4-4.  Should the federal government step in to prohibit or regulate such activity, or is this just another chapter in the history of the dual banking system?  (We will return to this South Dakota statute in Chapter Sixteen.)

Begin by considering the two most common, large financial transactions engaged in by consumers.  First, an individual wishes to purchase an automobile but does not have sufficient cash.  A loan or lease is necessary.  The individual will have to purchase automobile insurance at the same time.  Second, a customer purchasing a house will require both a mortgage and homeowner's insurance.  It is evident that the various products are complementary.  The truth of this can be seen in the activities of real estate brokers providing mortgage brokerage services, and of automobile dealers providing automobile loan services.  Why can the automobile dealer offer loans, but the bank cannot sell automobiles?  The answer is deposit insurance.  In at least one sense, banks are different because they have access to deposit insurance.  Expanded powers potentially expose the insurance fund, the government and the taxpayers to the ultimate expense of loss.

The basic purposes behind the federal deposit insurance system are to protect the grocery money ($100,000) of consumers and to protect the stability of the banking and payments system by maintaining public confidence in its safety.  The central purposes of commercial banks in our society are to provide financial transaction and financial intermediation services.  Transaction services, such as checking accounts, facilitate payment for goods, services, and financial investments.  Intermediation services involve using the funds of savers, such as deposits, to invest in loans to business, consumers, and government units.  This lending activity is particularly important in the financing of smaller business enterprises, which require special skill in evaluating and monitoring individual situations, and generally do not have access to the securities markets to raise capital. Are these activities sufficiently important that we want persons involved in them focused solely on them? Are these activities difficult enough, without banks attempting to become experts in related financial activities, such as securities and insurance, or commercial activities, such as manufacturing or selling automobiles? Are your answers to these questions different for bank and BHC subsidiaries?

A truly surprising development over the last decade or so has been that the expansion of permissible bank activities has frequently been greater than the expansion of permissible bank holding company activities. Congress could not have expected this result–that greater powers are available to banks under the National Bank Act (and state law) than are available to BHCs under the Bank Holding Company Act.

The culmination of this development is that, effective January 1, 1997, the Comptroller adopted regulations allowing national banks to expand the activities of operating subsidiaries, on a case by case basis, potentially including insurance and securities underwriting, all data processing, real estate sales and leasing, and other undefined activities, even if the activities are not permissible to national banks themselves. The regulations contain firewalls intended to separate the national bank from its subsidiaries, such as a 10 percent cap on the amount of bank capital that can be invested in the subsidiaries, separate facilities and names, and section 371c type limitations on bank-subsidiary credit transactions. See 12 C.F.R. Pt. 5, particularly § 5.34; see also 61 Fed. Reg. 60,363 (Nov. 27, 1996) (implementing release). Consider how attractive this corporate structure may be to a small national bank which wishes to diversify its activities, such as owning a small insurance agency, and what effect it may have on state chartered banks and their regulators. (The Federal Reserve has proposed, but not adopted, similar regulations expanding the permissible activities of BHC nonbank subsidiaries.)

Twelve U.S.C.A. § 1843(c)(8) generally provides that non-bank subsidiaries of a BHC may only engage in activities that are closely related to banking. State banking laws, however, frequently authorize banks to engage in a greater variety of activities. Does the BHCA preempt such state laws under the supremacy clause? In addition, recall that 12 U.S.C.A. § 1831a empowers the FDIC to limit the activities of state-chartered FDIC insured banks as principal. But, this prohibition generally does not extend to agency activities, and the FDIC has indicated little interest in the activities of subsidiaries that are not within the insurance safety net.

Nevertheless, the historic position of the Federal Reserve Board has been that the activities of subsidiaries of state-chartered banks that are members of a BHC are subject to the limitations of the BHCA. Consider the following case.

## Citicorp v. Board of Governors ("Family Guardian")
### 936 F.2d 66 (2d Cir. 1991), *cert. denied*, 502 U.S. 1031 (1992)

JON O. NEWMAN, Circuit Judge:

Once again we consider an aspect of the broad issue of the extent to which banks are authorized to engage in nonbanking activities. That issue was before us just two years ago in *Independent Insurance Agents of America, Inc. v. Board of Governors*, 890 F.2d 1275 (2d Cir. 1989) (*Merchants II* ), *cert. denied*, 111 S. Ct. 44 (1990). We there ruled, in agreement with the Federal Reserve Board ("the Board" or "the Fed"), that the Bank Holding Company Act ("BHCA" or "the Act") did not preclude bank subsidiaries of a bank holding company from selling insurance. The question now before us is the one left open in *Merchants II*–whether the BHCA extends the regulatory authority of the Fed to the subsidiary of a holding company's bank subsidiary.

The question arises on a petition for review filed by Citicorp challenging the Board's September 5, 1990, order. That order requires one of Citicorp's bank subsidiaries, Citibank Delaware, to terminate insurance activities that the bank subsidiary was conducting through its operating subsidiary, Family Guardian Life Insurance Co. ("Family Guardian"). Though mindful of the deference due an agency's construction of the statute it is administering, we conclude that, once the BHCA has been construed to leave the regulation of a holding company's subsidiary banks to their chartering authorities, the Act cannot sensibly be interpreted to reimpose the authority of the Fed on a generation-skipping basis to regulate the subsidiary's subsidiary. We therefore grant the petition for review and vacate the Board's order.

### Background

Before introducing the facts, it will be helpful to outline briefly the pertinent statutory provisions of the BHCA, the construction placed on those provisions at the Board's urging by this Court in *Merchants II*, the Board's regulation concerning operating subsidiaries, and the pertinent aspects of the Delaware regulatory framework.

*The Statutory Framework.*

. . . In relevant part, section 4(c)(8) states that the section 4(a) nonbanking prohibitions shall not apply to

shares of any company the activities of which the Board after due notice and opportunity for hearing has determined (by order or regulation) to be so closely related to banking or managing or controlling banks as to be a proper incident thereto, but for purposes of this subsection it is not closely related to banking or managing or controlling banks for a bank holding company to provide insurance as a principal, agent or broker. . . .

*Id.*

*The Decision in Merchants II.* In 1989 the Board approved an application by Merchants National Corporation, a bank holding company, to permit two of its Indiana bank subsidiaries to engage in insurance activities. *Merchants National Corp.*, 75 Fed. Res. Bull. 388 (1989). That ruling was vigorously challenged in this Court by insurance interests who contended that the BHCA was intended to accomplish a nearly complete separation of banking and nonbanking activities by precluding bank holding companies and all entities within their systems from engaging in nonbanking activities, other than the "closely related to banking" activities specifically identified in section 4(c)(8) of the Act. The Board took the position that Congress had not gone so far. In the Board's view, Congress had precluded nonbanking activities by bank holding companies themselves but had not wished to displace the traditional authority of state and national bank chartering bodies to determine what nonbanking activities could appropriately be engaged in by banks that are subject to their regulatory authority, even though such banks were owned by a bank holding company under the jurisdiction of the Fed.

The dispute between the Board and the banking interests, on the one hand, and the insurance interests, on the other hand, was a substantial one. Ultimately, we ruled in favor of the Board. *Merchants II*, 890 F.2d at 1284. We acknowledged that the statute was not entirely clear and that arguments supporting each of the contending positions could plausibly be based on some of the language of the Act, some aspects of the structure of the Act, and some passages from the legislative history. *Id.* at 1281-84. After canvassing the available evidence, we concluded that the construction urged by the Board was a "reasonable interpretation" of the Act, "one that confides decisions concerning the scope of insurance and other nonbank activities of bank subsidiaries to their national and state chartering authorities." *Id.* at 1284.

In *Merchants II* we noted the Board's additional position that, although the Act denied the Board authority to preclude bank subsidiaries of a bank holding company from engaging in nonbank activities, it nonetheless empowered the Board to preclude the subsidiaries of bank subsidiaries from engaging in nonbank activities. Though the insurance interests pressed upon us the "apparent awkwardness and perhaps illogic," *id.* at 1282, of the Board's generation-skipping approach, we confined our ruling to approval of the Board's construction of the Act to permit nonbank activities by bank subsidiaries (the first generation after the holding company), and left for another day the issue of whether the Act could simultaneously be construed to bar nonbank activities by a subsidiary's subsidiaries (the second generation). That day has now arrived.

*The Board's Operating Subsidiary Rule.* Long before the administrative and judicial rulings in *Merchants II*, the Board had issued Regulation Y, the so-called "operating subsidiary rule," which purports to govern the activities of subsidiaries of a bank holding company. *See* 12 C.F.R. Pt. 225 (1990) (current version). In general, such subsidiaries must limit their activities to those banking and "closely related to banking" activities permitted by section 4 of the Act. However, one provision of Regulation Y permits state-chartered banks, without the Board's prior approval, to acquire

all . . . of the securities of a company that engages solely in activities in which the parent bank may engage, at locations at which the bank may engage in the activity, and subject to the same limitations *as if the bank were engaging in the activity directly.*

*Id.* § 225.22(d)(2)(ii) (emphasis added). Thus, under Regulation Y and the Board's construction of section 4, as endorsed in *Merchants II*, a subsidiary of a state-chartered bank subsidiary of a holding company may engage in nonbank activities permitted to the bank under state law, provided that the activities are conducted under the same limitations that would apply if the bank were engaging in the activities "directly."[1]

*The Delaware Regulatory Framework.* In May 1990, Delaware enacted the Bank and Trust Company Insurance Powers Act of 1989, 67 Del. Laws, c. 223 (1990) ("the Delaware statute"). The Delaware statute permits Delaware banks, under certain conditions, to engage in insurance activities (other than title insurance). The statute affords the banks the option of conducting insurance activities through a "department" or "division" of the bank or through a subsidiary of the bank. Whichever option is chosen, the statute requires substantial structural barriers between the bank's insurance activities and its banking activities.

For example, the statute requires that the assets of the bank may be applied only to satisfy the non-insurance liabilities of the bank and not those of the bank's insurance "division," *id.* § 8, and the assets of the insurance "division" may be applied only to satisfy the liabilities of that "division" and not the other liabilities of the bank, *id.* § 22. The statute places a 25 percent limit on the amount of the bank's total capital, surplus, and undivided profits that may be allocated to its insurance "division," *id.* § 10, and the minimum capital that the bank is required to maintain under Delaware banking law may not be used to meet the separate capital requirements of the "division" imposed by state insurance law, *id.* § 3. The statute provides that for purposes of the Delaware Insurance Code an insurance "division" of a bank is treated as an insurance company "in the same manner and to the same extent as if it were a separately incorporated subsidiary . . . with separate capital accounts, assets and liabilities." *Id.* § 17.

In general, Delaware authorizes its bank commissioner to regulate the banking activities of state-chartered banks and authorizes its insurance commissioner to regulate the insurance activities of a bank's insurance "division." *Id.* §§ 5, 38. However, the statute permits the bank commissioner to supervise the insurance "division" whenever he determines that the "division's" activities are "likely to have a materially adverse effect on the safety and soundness of the bank." *Id.* § 5.

*Citicorp's Banking and Insurance Activities in Delaware.* Citicorp is a bank holding company with assets of more than $200 billion. In 1982, Citicorp obtained a charter from Delaware for Citibank Delaware, a commercial bank wholly owned by Citicorp. Citibank Delaware has assets of more than $2 billion and serves customers in 35 states.

In 1986, with the approval of the Fed, Citicorp established Family Guardian as a wholly owned subsidiary to underwrite and sell certain credit-related insurance expressly authorized for bank holding companies by section 4(c)(8)(A) of the BHCA, 12 U.S.C. § 1843(c)(8)(A). The day after the Delaware statute was enacted, Citicorp transferred all of the voting shares of Family Guardian to Citibank Delaware in order to permit Family Guardian to transact the broader range of insurance activities authorized under the Delaware statute for insurance "divisions" and subsidiaries of Delaware banks. Family Guardian then began to expand its operations to include insurance underwriting and other insurance activities within the scope of Delaware law, though

---

[1]     A comparable regulation applies to operating subsidiaries of national banks. 12 C.F.R. § 225.22(d)(1) (1990).

beyond the scope of the "closely related to banking" activities specified in section 4(c)(8) of the BHCA.

*The Pending Litigation.* Soon after the expansion of Family Guardian's insurance activities, various insurance industry trade associations filed a petition with the Board, contending that Family Guardian's activities were not permitted under the operating subsidiary rule of Regulation Y. The complainants argued that the barriers required by the Delaware statute between the banking and insurance activities of a Delaware-chartered bank were so substantial that a Delaware bank, such as Citicorp Delaware, could not engage in insurance activities "directly" within the meaning of Regulation Y. Since Citicorp Delaware could not engage in these insurance activities "directly," the argument continued, its subsidiary, Family Guardian, was not operating within the limitations of Regulation Y.

The Fed accepted the contentions of the complainants, ruled that the activities of Family Guardian were not authorized by Regulation Y, and concluded that these activities, if not exempted by Regulation Y, were impermissible under the BHCA for an entity owned by a subsidiary of a bank holding company. *Citicorp.* 76 Fed. Res. Bull. 977 (1990). The Board ordered Citicorp to cause Family Guardian to cease providing any insurance activities beyond those authorized and approved by the Board under section 4(c)(8)(A). Citicorp then brought this petition for review to challenge the Board's ruling.

## Discussion

Citicorp makes two arguments. First, it contends that the insurance activities of Family Guardian are permitted for the bank subsidiary of Citicorp by virtue of the Board's operating subsidiary rule. Second it contends that, if the operating subsidiary rule does not permit insurance activities by Family Guardian, the Board lacks statutory authority under the BHCA to proscribe the activities of a subsidiary of a holding company's bank subsidiary.

1. Citicorp's Claim under Regulation Y.

Regulation Y, as we have noted, permits state-chartered banks to own a subsidiary company "that engages solely in activities in which the parent bank may engage . . . and subject to the same limitations as if the bank were engaging in the activities directly." 12 C.F.R. § 225.22(d)(2)(ii). Citicorp contends that the Delaware statute permits a Delaware-chartered bank, like Citicorp Delaware, to sell insurance and leaves it up to the bank whether to operate its insurance activity in a "division" within the bank or in a wholly owned subsidiary of the bank. With that proposition the Fed is in agreement. The dispute concerns the meaning of "directly" in Regulation Y. The Fed takes the position that the extent of separation between a bank and its insurance "division" required by the Delaware statute has the effect of precluding the bank from "directly" engaging in the insurance activities of its "division." Since, in the Fed's view, the bank could not engage in insurance activities "directly" within the bank, Regulation Y does not permit it to do so through an operating subsidiary. Citicorp contends that the separateness of an insurance "division," required by Delaware law, does not prevent the bank from engaging in insurance activities "directly." . . .

It would be a straightforward interpretation of Regulation Y to read it to mean that a bank may own a non-banking subsidiary so long as the subsidiary is subject to the same limitations that would apply if the activities of the subsidiary were being conducted within the bank itself. Under this reading "directly" would simply mean "within the bank," as distinguished from "through a subsidiary." . . . The Fed's reading, however, gives "directly" substantive content, interpreting it to mean that the bank must engage in the activity not only "within the bank" but in the absence of the degree of separateness mandated by the Delaware statute for a bank's insurance "division."

We confess to considerable wonderment as to why the Fed would want to construe its regulation to mean that insurance activities conducted in a "division" of a bank are not conducted by a bank "directly" just because the "division" is surrounded by protections designed to maintain the soundness of both the banking and the insurance activities of the bank.  It is not readily apparent why the Fed would be *more* willing to permit Citibank Delaware to sell insurance if Delaware provided *less* protection for the bank's assets from the risks of the bank's insurance activities. . . .

A further cause for concern about the Fed's position is the response of its General Counsel to a specific inquiry from a member of the Delaware House of Representatives during consideration of the bill that became the Delaware statute.  The inquiry sought advice as to the significance, for federal regulatory purposes, of the extent of separation between an insurance "division" and the rest of a bank's activities.  The General Counsel replied that under the proposed statute, Delaware banks may conduct broadened insurance activities "*directly within the bank* or in a separate subsidiary of the bank" and noted that, under the Board's operating subsidiary rule, "if a holding company state bank is permitted to conduct an activity *directly*, the bank may establish a wholly-owned nonbank subsidiary to conduct the activity."  Letter of J. Virgil Mattingly, Jr., to the Honorable John F. Van Sant (May 17, 1989) (emphasis added). . . .

Despite our considerable unease at the way the Board is construing the word "directly" in its regulation, especially in light of the advice its General Counsel furnished to the Delaware legislature, we are willing to assume, for purposes of this appeal, that the separation mandated by the Delaware statute precludes a bank from operating its insurance "division" "directly."  So long as the Board is exercising its statutory authority, it has ample discretion to frame regulations and accord to its chosen words any technical meaning it wishes that does not purport to deny those words any semblance of their ordinary meaning. . . . In this instance, the Board's view that a separate insurance "division" is not being operated "directly" by a bank presses that rule to its limit, and possibly beyond, but we will assume that the Board has fairly interpreted its own regulation and proceed to consider the statutory issue.

2. Citicorp's Claim under the BHCA.

Citicorp contends that the BHCA does not permit the Fed to regulate the activities of the subsidiary of a bank subsidiary of a holding company.  Before the *Merchants II* litigation, that contention would have posed a substantial issue because a major controversy then existed as to whether the BHCA permitted non-banking activities (other than those specifically authorized by section 4(c)(8)) to be conducted anywhere in a system controlled by a bank holding company. The insurance interests in *Merchants II* contended that neither a holding company, nor a bank subsidiary, nor the subsidiary of a bank subsidiary could engage in nonbanking activities. However, the Fed disagreed with that interpretation of the Act and argued that the bank subsidiaries of a holding company were beyond the Board's regulatory authority.  In the Fed's view, Congress intended to leave unimpaired the primary regulatory authority of state and national bank chartering agencies to determine the activities of institutions under their jurisdiction. We agreed with that construction of the statute.

Thus, in the aftermath of *Merchants II*, we take the Act as if it said in terms, "The Board is without authority to limit the activities of a bank subsidiary of a bank holding company." Now the question is whether the Board may nonetheless regulate the activities of a bank subsidiary's subsidiary. The rationale of the position that the Board successfully urged upon us in *Merchants II* requires an answer consistent with the interpretation the Board there urged us to adopt. The Board urged, and we agreed, that Congress wanted bank chartering agencies to regulate the activities of banks within their jurisdiction. By virtue of their authority over the banks that they charter, those agencies have ample authority to determine the permissible activities of the subsidiaries owned by the banks. We have been given no reason to believe that Congress wanted the jurisdiction of bank chartering authorities to end at the corporate structure of the bank itself, rather than extend throughout the chain of companies owned by the bank. Surely a bank chartering agency, charged with the responsibility to maintain the soundness of a bank, is vitally interested in the assets owned by a bank, including shares of wholly owned subsidiaries. In the pending case, Delaware has demonstrated that its regulatory authority over Delaware-chartered banks is not confined to activities occurring within the bank, but extends to insurance activities whether conducted within the bank (albeit in a separate "division") or in a subsidiary of the bank.

Moreover, the Board has provided no basis for believing that Congress wished to create two classes of state-chartered banks–those owned and those not owned by bank holding companies. Before *Merchants II*, such an argument was plausible; Congress might have wanted those state-chartered banks owned by holding companies to be confined to banking activities, leaving banks not so owned to have broader activity. But once the Board persuaded us to read the statute to leave all state-chartered banks free to sell insurance, subject to state, not Board, regulation, there is no basis for believing that Congress simultaneously adopted a generation-skipping approach and authorized the Board to bar the subsidiaries of state-chartered banks from selling insurance whenever those banks were in turn the subsidiaries of a holding company. . . .

The Board responds to these contentions by assailing Citicorp for making the "assumption" that Family Guardian is an operating subsidiary of Citicorp Delaware. *See* Brief of Respondent at 30 n.13. The Board's point here is simply a reaffirmation of its interpretation of Regulation Y: since Citicorp Delaware may not operate Family Guardian "directly" within the bank, it may not operate it as a subsidiary. The argument is entirely unpersuasive on the statutory issue. Even if, as we have indulgently assumed, Regulation Y may plausibly be read to mean that Family Guardian is not the sort of operating subsidiary specifically authorized by that regulation, it cannot be maintained that Family Guardian is not in fact an operating subsidiary of Citibank Delaware. Obviously it is; it operates a business and it is wholly owned by Citicorp Delaware. The Board's strained interpretation of Regulation Y cannot answer the statutory issue of whether the BHCA permits the Board to regulate the activities of an entity that is demonstrably the operating subsidiary of a state-chartered bank.

The Fed reminds us that in *Merchants II* we contemplated the possibility that the Fed might be correct both in its view that the BHCA permitted a state-chartered bank subsidiary of a holding company to be immune from coverage of the BHCA and in its view that the Act nevertheless reached the subsidiary's subsidiary. We there observed that "*if* the Board is right [in both views], this would not be the first time that Congress has adjusted the competing positions of strong forces with a compromise of imperfect symmetry." 890 F.2d at 1282 (emphasis added) (citation omitted). But in *Merchants II*, we were required to decide only whether the Board was entitled to read the Act to leave the regulation of the nonbank activities of holding company banks to chartering authorities. We were not obliged to endorse the Board's additional (and "perplexing," *id.*) view that the Act reached the subsidiary's subsidiary. The fact that we peered into the abyss of conflicting statutory constructions that occur in federal law and noted that in some instances they reflect political realities does not mean that we accepted both aspects of the Fed's views. In *Merchants II* we had to decide whether the possibility of an asymmetrical construction of the BHCA precluded the view advanced by the Fed with respect to coverage of holding company banks, and we agreed with the Fed that it did not. Now we face the issue whether the Fed's view concerning BHCA coverage of the subsidiary's subsidiary is only a tolerable inconsistency or an entirely untenable construction, and we conclude it is the latter. . . .

We are still obliged to begin our task by according deference to the view of the agency directly responsible for administering the Act. But when that view clashes with the construction of the statute that the same agency has urged us to adopt, we need not elevate deference to blind obeisance, and we can notice the contrary view of significant banking regulators.

In *Merchants II*, it is likely that we would have upheld the Board had it chosen to interpret the BHCA to bar nonbanking activities throughout a bank holding company's system, even though we ultimately agreed with the Board's interpretation that the Act permitted bank subsidiaries of holding companies to engage in nonbanking activities. As we acknowledged in *Merchants II*, the BHCA is not clear as to whether it requires bank holding companies and all subsidiaries within their systems to observe a total separation from nonbanking activities. But however that issue is resolved, the Act must be interpreted as a whole and must retain some internal coherence. The Board ruled that whether bank subsidiaries may engage in nonbanking activities is a matter for the chartering authorities of those banks, and not for the Board. Once that decision was made, we cannot agree that the Act can sensibly be construed to permit the Board to displace bank-chartering authorities in determining what activities are permitted for the subsidiaries of bank subsidiaries.

The petition for review is granted, and the order of the Board is vacated.

## Comments and Questions

1. Because the Federal Reserve determined in a regulation that it does not have the power to regulate the activities of state-chartered banks controlled by a BHC, the court determined that the Federal Reserve also does not have the power to regulate the activities of subsidiaries of BHC controlled state-chartered banks. Therefore, various state laws which authorize state-chartered banks to engage in a range of real estate, insurance, securities, travel agency and "leeway investment" activities cannot be limited by the "closely related to banking" requirement of 12 U.S.C.A. § 1843(c)(8).

State-chartered banks in many states have broad real estate powers, specifically including the authority to be a real estate broker. See West's Ann. Cal. Fin. Code §§ 750,

751.3, and 751.7 (1989).  Using a state-chartered bank with such powers will enable a BHC to skirt the BHCA problem of whether the activities are impermissible real estate brokerage as compared to permissible real estate investment advisory services.  A state license is required for real estate brokerage, which raises a related issue.  If the activity were authorized by the OCC for a national bank, would the OCC ruling preempt a state regulators' attempted application of a state licensing or prohibition law?

2.  In data processing, as in other areas, it is possible for a state-chartered bank to have greater powers than a national bank or a BHC.  In California, "a corporation subject to the Banking Law . . . may engage in any business activity not prohibited by the respective statutes and regulations to which it is subject." West's Ann. Cal. Corp. Code § 206 (Supp. 1990).  Consequently, if there is not a specific statutory prohibition, a state bank or its subsidiary may perform the activity.  Also under California law, a state bank may "provide electronic data-processing services," defined as "the process that encompasses all computerized and auxiliary automated information handling, including systems analysis and design, conversion of data, computer programming, information storage and retrieval, data transmission, requisite system controls, simulation, and all the related operator-machine interaction." West's Ann. Cal. Fin. Code § 778 (1989).  Could a California state-chartered bank receive an FCC license as a common carrier?

3.  Are the subsidiaries of national banks that are members of a BHC equally free to engage in the activities allowed to state-chartered banks under state law?  In one sense the answer is no, but in another sense the answer is yes.  Traditionally, operating subsidiaries of national banks are not allowed to engage in activities beyond the scope of the business of banking.  Yet the Comptroller has allowed operating subsidiaries of national banks to engage in activities that would appear to be impermissible to a nonbank subsidiary of a BHC under the Federal Reserve Board's interpretation of 12 U.S.C.A. § 1843(c)(8).  In the past two years, the Comptroller has indicated a willingness to authorize national bank subsidiaries to engage in activities national banks themselves may not perform.  So, while it is evident Congress assumed that BHCs would be able to engage in activities beyond those permissible to their bank subsidiaries with respect to both state- and national-chartered banks, what has occurred is that banks and their subsidiaries, through state law and federal agency interpretations, often may engage in activities well beyond those allowed to parent holding companies and their nonbank subsidiaries.  How can this be?

4.  Another benefit of having nonbank affiliates structured as subsidiaries of the bank rather than as subsidiaries of the BHC, is that profits from the subsidiaries could flow up to boost bank capital, but regulatory prohibitions could bar capital from flowing down to subsidiaries should substantial trouble arise there.  Similar to Delaware, it may be that there are some activities the Comptroller would approve as being within the business of banking, but for regulatory purposes would require the activity to be in a separately incorporated and capitalized subsidiary.  Thus, the Comptroller could allow expanded powers within the rubric of the business of banking, but protect the federal safety net from the risks of the new activities.

5. Recall our prior discussion of 12 U.S.C.A. § 1831a. Does it matter to the FDIC whether the various activities permissible under state law to state-chartered banks are conducted in the bank or in a separately incorporated subsidiary of the bank?

*Problem 4-12*

You represent a BHC with both state and national bank subsidiaries. Management of the BHC wishes to engage in a wide range of data processing, software development, and management consulting services. The BHC has several young employees with exceptional talents and does not want to lose them. One valuable employee is a computer programmer who exhibits exceptional talent in writing computer games with graphical interfaces, and who is in the early stages of developing a three-dimensional digital casino and entertainment website in virtual reality. The site would offer casino-style gaming and entertainment through interactive games and tutorials, and fully interactive gambling. The employee would like the BHC to acquire and finance the development and implementation of the website. The proposed website name is "Las Vegas Living Room."

Another young employee has shown exceptional skill in providing management consulting services to small financial institutions. The employee wants to offer a full range of management consulting services in competition with the Big Six accounting firms and other full-service management consultants. As always, BHC management is in urgent need of your knowledge and judgment. Are such activities permissible for the BHC or its subsidiaries, and if so, how would you structure the corporate organization of such activities? Consider 12 C.F.R. §5.34 and 12 C.F.R. § 225.28(b)(9) and (14).

## D. Unitary Savings and Loan Holding Companies

Twelve U.S.C.A. § 1467a is a regulatory regime for savings and loan holding companies conceptually similar to the BHCA. The scope of permitted activities of affiliates is actually more limited than those permissible to BHCs, with the exception that S&L holding companies do have the power to conduct an insurance agency business. Otherwise, they generally are limited to activities approved by the Federal Reserve Board by regulation (and not by individual order) for BHCs.

But there is one critical difference from the BHCA. Under 12 U.S.C.A. § 1467a(c)(3) an S&L holding company which controls only one savings association is not subject to any limitation on the activities of its affiliates, provided that the savings association is a qualified thrift lender. The qualified thrift lender test is found in § 1467a(m). While complex, it generally provides that a savings and loan is a qualified thrift lender if its housing related assets equal at least 65 percent of its total portfolio assets for 9 out of every 12 months. As a consequence, all savings and loan associations can be owned by commercial and industrial firms. Recall, however, that savings and loan associations have a variety of additional limitations on the assets they may hold. For example, in addition to the qualified thrift lender test, they are limited to investing 20 percent of their assets in commercial loans, although there does not appear to be any limit on the amount of loans that they could participate to others or securitize.

The scope of permissible activities of a savings and loan holding company returns us to a question posed in the introduction to this section–the affiliation of depository institutions with commerce. Would affiliations of banking with commerce have a strong influence on the flow of credit and so on business innovation and competition? How important is it that lenders make objective credit judgments, and that we have a financial system that supports the manufacturing and service economy without the potential for bias?

While the proper scope of the separation of banking from other activities is a recurring issue, there is scant historical support for abolishing entirely the separation requirement. The absence of such a requirement could lead to the repetition of the early banking experience in the United States, in which bank investment in commercial activities caused significant losses of depositors' funds. Even a prohibition of a bank's participation in such equity investments, coupled with authorization for general commercial enterprises to control banks, could adversely affect the economic neutrality of banks' credit-granting decisions.

On the other hand, there are numerous historical examples of affiliation between banks and other *financial* activities. One of the primary reasons for the National Bank Act was to put banks *in* the securities business. Trust activities as a form of investment services have been closely affiliated with banking at least since shortly after the Civil War. Some banks started out as insurance companies. Savings banks in New York and a few other states continue to sell life insurance today, although the 1982 Act amended § 1843(c)(8) to restrict significantly the insurance activities of bank holding companies.

There are reasons for the historical relations between banks and other financial activities. These relations do not obviously undermine the principles of the BHCA. Certainly, with respect to the financial markets, there is a functional relationship among banking, insurance and securities activities. All take some form of deposit (broadly defined), either as general deposits, insurance premium "deposits," or special "deposits" for investment purposes. All have as their primary activities the provision of money-related services. All provide for a form of investment opportunity. All serve as financial intermediaries between our capital markets and other sectors of the economy, by, for example, making consumer and commercial loans, and by buying commercial paper and corporate debt instruments. Banking, insurance and securities activities are critical points of exchange for financing general commercial enterprises in our economy. They all accept individual and entity financial assets and allocate our capital resources to their most efficient economic use. All are regulated with some concern for safety, soundness and economic neutrality, and all are important to the soundness of the national economy.

Consequently, it can be argued that the circle of permissible affiliations for banks should be broadened to include all forms of financial institutions and financial market activities, including all institutions that are engaged in receiving general or special "deposits" of money, credit granting, or provision of investment opportunities. While banking, insurance and securities entities could not be merged into a single corporate entity, arguably the three types of financial endeavors could be affiliated if properly identified to their clients as separate types of depositories with different consequential risks. The question is whether adequate safeguards could be provided and recognized by the public, ensuring maintenance of the generic policies that underlie all their activities: economic neutrality and disclosure and limitation (safety and soundness) of the various investment risks involved.

### Problem 4-13

High above Wall Street you lean back, put your feet on your desk, smile and fondly remember when you used to represent small restaurant owners and down-on-their-luck politicians. Your reveries are interrupted when your associate shows into your office an individual you know to be one of the wealthiest persons in the United States. The individual says, "Four of my friends and I want to own a depository institution." Further discussion uncovers that, in addition to desiring to own a United States depository empire, the individual and friends own several other enterprises, including a chain of retail drug stores, and a regional securities brokerage and investment management firm. Their current business operations span New York, Florida, Texas and California. They would like the operation of their depository institution to be equally extensive, and have come to you because of your extensive knowledge of the matrix of regulation of depository institutions.

Considering both the opportunities and limitations of federal and state depository institutions law, what advice would you give to the individual and friends with respect to creating and structuring their business empire?

### Problem 4-14

You are a staff attorney at the Federal Reserve. They have asked you to consider the following theoretical problems which might arise should the limitations on the affiliation of banking and commercial activities be eliminated.

1. Should it be a concern that a large corporation controlling a large bank could use it for extending credit to those who can particularly benefit the entire organization? Would it be a problem if the large bank, as does any bank, attracted funds at low cost through insured deposits and then used those funds to provide credit to retailers, manufacturers, and others who further the distribution of the parent's products and services?

2. Would you have any concern that the bank might withhold credit from those who are viewed as actual or potential competitors of the parent corporation?

3. Should there be any concern that difficulties in the commercial activities of the parent corporation and its commercial and industrial affiliates might cause the bank to be vulnerable? Suppose that the parent corporation was a famous failure, such as the W. T. Grant retail chain or the Penn-Central railroad. Would such a failure by the parent cause

the bank to be vulnerable to huge withdrawals of deposits, notwithstanding fire walls between the bank and its parent?

4. Are there any compensating benefits from affiliating banking and commercial enterprises? Might there be benefits from the industrial management experience of the parent?

# Section 5.  Financial Obligations of Bank Holding Companies

If banks or BHCs are given expanded powers outside the bank, and deposit insurance and other safety nets for banks are statutorily limited to avoid government insurance of the non-core, risk-taking activities of non-bank affiliates, one unresolved issue is whether a bank can effectively be insulated from the activities of its non-bank affiliates. Both of the two basic corporate structures attempt to accomplish this. The BHC is formed as a non-bank parent company with its business activities located in both bank and non-bank subsidiaries. The alternative structure is the bank/subsidiary form, with the bank as the parent company and the non-bank activities located in direct, non-bank subsidiaries.

The concepts of corporate separateness and limited liability appear to be of significant value, but there are real problems. For example, while we saw in our discussion of § 371c that there are substantial limitations on bank loans to affiliates, there are other problems in insulating a bank from the activities of affiliates. One difficult question is the practical scope of the doctrine of corporate separateness. It may well be that effective advertising and cross-selling of services by a BHC, as well as any permitted use of a common name, would induce the public, and possibly the courts, to limit the doctrine of corporate separateness in difficult situations.

A second obvious problem is the natural tendency of management to centralize decisionmaking power and resource allocation in the parent bank or BHC. It is doubtful that management would leave the bank and non-bank subsidiaries free to make the important business decisions as to activities, reinvestment of profits, and new markets. It is more likely that there is and would be significant centralization of decisionmaking at the parent company level, with management deciding what products and markets will be focused upon and how profits will be reallocated. Thus, the critical lending activity of a bank and its general safety may be less important than the profitability of the parent holding company as a whole. It would also be difficult to separate the affairs of the affiliates in terms of conflicts of interests. It is doubtful that a bank which is an affiliate of an automobile company would be actively seeking to make loans to competing automobile companies or their suppliers.

Yet a third concern would be the tendency toward the emergence of larger organizations. Just as with banks, regulators would be much more concerned about the ramifications of a major affiliate's failure, and the great difficulties in finding a buyer for all or part of a large bank holding company with complex affiliates.

In addition to legal corporate separateness, regulators have used "fire walls" in an attempt to respond to the concern that financial problems in one affiliate will be transmitted to other affiliates in the financial organization, whatever the legal corporate structure. Fire walls essentially are operational barriers between affiliates. Common types of fire walls include the prohibition of banks making loans to securities affiliates, of guaranteeing stocks or bonds issued by securities affiliates, or of financing the purchase of any securities underwritten by securities affiliates. Similarly, a securities affiliate might be prohibited from offering deposits in the insured institution. Fire walls could further bar mutual funds from borrowing from affiliated banks and limit the ability of bank officers to serve as directors of an affiliated mutual fund. Common names could be barred so that mutual funds could not suggest that they are somehow related to a federally insured depository institution.

Taken together, these fire walls can easily create economic inefficiencies and may frustrate a desire to operate as a coherent whole. But history has shown that there usually is an irresistible incentive for management to bring the total resources of the financial conglomerate to bear to prevent a failure.

Another way to manage contagion risk, beyond corporate separateness and firewalls, is substantial reporting, public disclosure, and aggressive regulatory oversight. We will more directly consider the values and limitations of these regulatory tools in chapter 5.

*Problem 4-15*

You are counsel to a financial conglomerate, for which the parent company is Horizon National Bank. Horizon is the investment adviser to an affiliated mutual fund, Pacific Prime Government Fund. On the advice of its adviser, the mutual fund acquired variable- and floating-rate notes issued by U.S. government agencies. These are known as "structured notes" on which the interest rates are calculated through formulas based on various published indices. When the Federal Reserve dramatically raised interest rates beginning in February, 1994, the Fund began to experience losses. Institutional investors began to make withdrawals from the Fund. To pay redemptions, the Fund eventually was forced to sell the structured notes, which would result in a loss of approximately 30% of their face value if the notes were sold at market value. Horizon wishes to put money into the Fund to cover the potential losses and to protect the net asset value of the shares from further decline, by purchasing the structured notes at face rather than at market value. This will cost $70 million, and Horizon has sufficient capital to do so.

1. Is a mutual fund adviser under any legal obligation to infuse capital?

2. If not, why would Horizon wish to bail out the Fund?

3. Would the bailout be a violation of 12 U.S.C.A. § 24(7) which prohibits national banks from purchasing and selling for their own account investment securities, other than those specified?

4. Would bailing out the Fund be an unsafe or unsound practice in violation of 12 U.S.C.A. § 1818?

5. Would the bailout be a violation of §§ 371c or 371c-1?

———————

Unlike most other countries, we regulate capital adequacy at the BHC as well as at the bank level.  An initial approach to this end was the development of the "source of strength" doctrine by the Federal Reserve, effectively defining a new standard of safety and soundness for BHCs by requiring them to serve as a source of strength for their bank subsidiaries.  Failure to do so could result in regulatory penalties, more fully discussed in the next chapter.  The source of strength concept was upheld in *Board of Governors v. First Lincolnwood Corp.*, 439 U.S. 234 (1978), where the Court affirmed the Federal Reserve's denial of an application to become a BHC on the basis that "holding companies should be a source of strength to subsidiary financial institutions."  The most prominent application of the Board's source-of-strength doctrine occurred in an administrative proceeding initiated in 1988 against MCorp. While the precedential value of the subsequent Fifth Circuit opinion is limited because the Supreme Court reversed the decision on procedural grounds, it remains the most important opinion on the Federal Reserve's doctrine. *MCorp Financial Inc. v. Board of Governors*, 900 F.2d 852 (5th Cir. 1990), *reversed in part on other grounds*, 502 U.S. 32 (1991).

The source of strength doctrine has two components. One is that a BHC should have sufficient managerial and financial resources to assist its bank subsidiaries in case they get into trouble. The second is that a BHC should actually use such resources to assist any subsidiary banks that become troubled. After 20 of MCorp's 25 banks failed and were placed into receivership by the bank regulators, MCorp, the BHC, had $400 million of assets which the Federal Reserve wanted applied to the capital account deficiencies in the failed banks.   In most industries there is little need to worry about the safety or soundness of a holding company's subsidiaries because the failure of a subsidiary imposes no cost on the public. Only the creditors of the subsidiary are hurt by failure, and they are assumed to be capable of protecting their own interests. The problem with a bank subsidiary failure is that it imposes cost on the public by increasing FDIC losses and depleting the insurance fund. Since BHC management directs the bank management, the Federal Reserve believed that the BHC should be responsible for losses caused by the bank failure.

The essence of MCorp's legal challenge was its assertion that the regulatory requirements for capital were limited to affirmative requirements that BHCs themselves be well-capitalized and prudently managed. The resulting Fifth Circuit opinion is based on pre-FIRREA (1989) and pre-FDICIA (1991) law. To support the source-of-strength regulation the Federal Reserve cited *First Lincolnwood Corp* and *Dimensions Financial*. The court distinguished *First Lincolnwood* because that case involved the Federal Reserve's consideration of an application to form a BHC, not the day to day operations of a BHC. In considering *Dimensions Financial*, the court said that the Federal Reserve's regulatory authority over BHCs was only to restain the undue concentration of commercial banking resources and to prevent possible abuses related to the control of commercial credit. In a footnote, the court suggested that the Federal Reserve could regulate the financial obligations of BHCs to bank subsidiaries by entering into negotiated capital maintenance agreements with BHCs at the time of an application. Consequently, the court held that the Federal Reserve did not have the statutory authority to issue the source-of-strength regulation.

Both FIRREA in 1989 and FDICIA in 1991 expanded on the theme of BHC financial obligations to troubled subsidiary banks, as part of the continuing change of approach to the regulation of banks and BHCs from limitation of activities to expanded capital regulation.  FIRREA enacted some measure of horizontal consolidation among affiliated banks by including a cross-guarantee provision that allows the FDIC to make a direct assessment on BHC commonly controlled banks whenever the FDIC incurs losses as the result of the failure of another federally insured depository institution within the same BHC system.  See 12 U.S.C.A. § 1815(e).  Note that this provision does not reach BHC resources invested in nonbank affiliates or the BHC itself.

The issue of vertical consolidation of financial obligations was addressed by Congress in FDICIA.  See 12 U.S.C.A. § 1831o.  First, the legislation imposes a series of supervisory restrictions on any depository institution that fails to meet its capital requirements.  The institution is to submit a capital restoration plan, including a guarantee from its parent holding company that the capital restoration plan will be achieved.  But the guarantee is limited to the lesser of five percent of the undercapitalized subsidiary's total assets, or the amount necessary to bring its undercapitalized subsidiary back into compliance.  Equally significant, compliance is optional with the holding company, and so a BHC may choose to cut its losses, decline to make the guarantee, and allow the regulators to apply their other supervisory enforcement powers, such as closure of the institution.  See 12 U.S.C.A. § 1831o(e)(2).

The result in the Fifth Circuit opinion in *MCorp* and subsequent legislation suggest several possibilities. One is that BHCs will tend to focus their future diversification outside their bank subsidiaries and to transfer activities from bank to nonbank subsidiaries. Second, current law is an incentive to encourage transactions between affiliates that favor nonbank affiliates through slightly mispriced business transactions, such as the provision of data processing and management services. A third concern is how coordination should occur between the authority of the Federal Reserve to regulate the capital of a BHC and the authority of the Comptroller or the FDIC to regulate the capital of bank subsidiaries.

Availability of the source-of-strength doctrine would encourage different activity, such as product diversification to reduce the risk of bank failures, whether the product diversification is inside or outside the bank subsidiaries. It would also eliminate the incentive to transfer resources from banks to nonbank affiliates. Finally, it would discourage risky activity within the bank because the risk would reflect to the BHC. While it can be argued that source-of-strength arbitrarily subjects BHC shareholders to greater liability than ordinary shareholders, perhaps that has been exchanged for the benefit of federal deposit insurance.

We can see that there are alternative approaches to regulating depository institutions and their affiliates. It is evident that in recent years we have chosen enhanced holding company financial obligations as a preferred path to regulatory supervision, over re-regulation of activities of banks and BHCs. At least in terms of safety and soundness, there are certain advantages to this route. Certainly there is less need for government to micro-manage the affairs of the financial institutions. The cross-guarantee and vertical guarantee provisions will tend to pierce the corporate veil and so cause holding companies to bear more of the costs of losses incurred by their bank subsidiaries. This should, in turn, allow BHCs to make more individually tailored judgments about their particular activities, rather than being subject to industry-wide detailed rules on particular activities. On the other hand, we already have seen that the regulation of capital adequacy can also become exceedingly complex.

The question for you to consider is which, if any, of these approaches represent appropriate regulatory policy–BHC capital adequacy regulation, source-of-strength obligations, mandatory depository institution cross-guarantees, optional BHC vertical guarantees, and activity regulation, whether of the rifle shot (no junk bonds) or broad gauge (presumption that federally insured state banks are precluded from engaging as principals in any activity not expressly authorized for national banks) variety of prohibition.

Consider the following excerpt from an article by one of the casebook co-authors, advocating increased reliance on financial obligations of holding companies. Are you persudaded that holding company obligations are an effective mechanism of regulatory control?

### Howell E. Jackson, The Expanding Obligations of Financial Holding Companies
107 Harv. L. Rev. 507 (1994)

Over the past two and a half decades, financial holding companies have emerged as the dominant organizational structures in this country's financial services industry. . . .

As financial holding companies have gained prominence in the nation's economy, the U.S. regulatory system has altered its treatment of corporations that own controlling interests in financial institutions. Until twenty years ago, financial holding companies were subject to varying degrees of regulatory control and supervision, but they had relatively few affirmative obligations with respect to their regulated subsidiaries . . . Over the past two decades, however, financial holding companies have become increasingly embroiled in the regulatory supervision of subsidiary financial institutions. . . . Many of these initiatives have targeted holding companies in the bank and thrift industries, where the pace of regulatory reform has been particularly brisk. . . . .

Although these new or "enhanced" obligations of financial holding companies take a variety of forms and are designed to effect a number of regulatory policies, far and away the most important category consists of legal requirements that holding companies guarantee (in whole or in part) the solvency of their regulated subsidiaries. As a result of these regulatorily imposed guarantees, financial holding companies are increasingly called upon to recapitalize insolvent subsidiaries or to compensate government authorities for losses that failed subsidiaries impose on public claimants (such as depositors . . . ) or public insurance funds (such as the Federal Deposit Insurance Corporation (FDIC) . . . ). As a conceptual matter, these new rules can be understood as a departure from the traditional rule of limited liability -- under which parent corporations are not held responsible for the liabilities of their subsidiaries -- in favor of a regime of unlimited (or at least less limited) liability for the special case of holding companies that control subsidiaries in the financial services industry.

. . . [T]he main advantage of enhanced obligations is that they transfer front-line supervisory responsibility from governmental agencies to the financial holding companies. Unlike many traditional regulatory strategies, which depend on government officials to anticipate and prevent high-risk activities, enhanced obligations look, in the first instance, to financial holding companies to monitor and restrain risk-taking in their regulated subsidiaries. Not only are financial holding companies apt to be more proficient than government officials in evaluating institutional behavior, but holding companies also can monitor risks at a lower cost than government agencies, because holding companies already have substantial information about their regulated subsidiaries as a result of ordinary managerial activities. Another advantage of enhanced obligations, as compared with other regulatory alternatives, is that they are apt to be more finely calibrated. With many other forms of regulation, regulatory authorities must set general behavioral standards that may be either unduly harsh or excessively lenient in any given case. With enhanced obligations, on the other hand, because holding companies are accountable only for those losses that their own subsidiary institutions actually incur, penalties are at least theoretically calibrated at an appropriate level.

[Thus,] enhanced holding company obligations are an attractive supplement to more traditional forms of regulation. Particularly in the depository institution field, where illiquid assets and severe informational asymmetries complicate traditional forms of risk-regulation by government agencies, holding company guarantees are a promising innovation in regulatory structure. Although the enhanced obligation regimes that have been developed to date are inadequate in many respects, it would be a relatively small step -- but one with potentially large regulatory rewards -- to reform our existing regulatory structure to capture the full potential of this new regulatory strategy. . . .

## Comments and Questions

1.  If our regulatory regime were to make greater use of financial guarantees from holding companies, how should independent depository institutions be treated?  For example, if a bank or thrift had no holding company parent, should it be exempt from this requirements or should the institution be required to obtain an alternative guarantee from some other entity?  Which approach would be more fair?  Which would be more efficient?  See also Lissa L. Broome, *Redistributing Bank Insolvency Risks: Challenges to Limited Liability in The Bank Holding Company Act Structure*, 26 U.C. DAVIS L. REV. 9385 (1993).

2.  Think back to the *Winstar* case, reproduced in Chapter 3, Section 7: Would Congress be free to impose enhanced obligations on financial holding companies that acquired depository-institution subsidiaries at a time when no such obligations existed?  See Branch v. United States, 69 F.3d 1571 (1995), *cert. denied,* 117 S. Ct. 55 (1996).

# CHAPTER FIVE

# TROUBLED AND FAILED BANKS

## Section 1. Introduction

Two primary purposes for ensuring the safety and soundness of banks are (1) to maintain public confidence in the stability of the payments and financial system, and (2) to protect depositors' "grocery money." Concerns relating to maintaining public confidence and so preventing financial panics, however, may be quite distinct from concerns relating to depositor protection. If individual depositors can be protected when a bank fails, public policy needs to be concerned with the bank's failure only to the extent that it causes deposit runs on soundly managed banks, or undermines confidence in the system. Arguably, so long as individual depositors are protected, banks may fail without endangering the general monetary system. Nevertheless, many believe that our financial institutions are so vital to the proper functioning of our economy that few can be allowed to fail before public confidence is shaken.

We already have considered many aspects of the regulatory effort to maintain the safety and soundness of financial institutions. Federal and state laws control entry into the banking business. Other examples of efforts to maintain safety and soundness include the portfolio-shaping rules prohibiting banks from holding certain types of assets and from engaging in various nonbanking activities; and regulations requiring certain levels of bank capital. Notwithstanding all of this, some financial institutions continue to have solvency difficulties, whether caused by fraud, mismanagement, or unforeseen economic occurrences.

The FDIC, and the other regulators, must deal with these "troubled" banks. Short of insolvency and receivership, regulators can attempt to correct the problems of faltering banks by prohibiting certain practices and utilizing various regulatory powers, some of which we have already considered briefly, such as capital directives and prompt corrective action. The supervisory enforcement powers also include the cease and desist power, the civil money penalty power, and the power to suspend or remove individuals from their bank positions of authority. See 12 U.S.C.A. §§ 1818, 1831o, 3907.

There is a major connection between troubled banks and the Federal Deposit Insurance Corporation as receiver of failed banks. Once a bank goes beyond being a supervisory problem and becomes a failed bank, it typically becomes the sole responsibility of the FDIC. But the entire process often involves several regulators. For example, when a national bank gets into trouble, the supervisory enforcement powers are utilized by the Comptroller. When a national bank becomes insolvent it is the responsibility of the FDIC to deal with the problem. But that often requires the cooperation of both the Federal Reserve and the Comptroller. The Federal Reserve frequently is needed as a lender of last resort to keep the bank open while the FDIC works out the best possible deal to resolve the problems; and only the Comptroller generally has the power to declare a national bank insolvent and close it.  Disagreements can easily occur among the regulators as to the seriousness of the problem and how best to handle it.

As the reins on permissible banking activities loosen, the problems of supervisory and solvency regulation become more difficult.  Most of the laws creating regulatory agencies and granting them increased powers were enacted in response to either financial crises or notable abuses of deposited funds.  Often there are subsequent proposals to reduce the regulatory restrictions and there is always pressure to expand the scope of permissible bank or bank affiliate activities.  Deregulation proposals typically are based on the desire to have market forces play some part in the regulation of both the activity and deposit sides of depository institutions.  At the same time, the presence of federal deposit insurance has caused a societal perception that dealing with banks is virtually risk free.  But both public confidence concerns and risk to the pervasive deposit insurance system are counterweights to the unregulated market.

Public confidence and solvency regulation are closely tied to the deposit insurance system.  There is no doubt that the system of deposit insurance has produced dramatic benefits in achieving a major objective of bank solvency regulation—the prevention of banking panics.  There is little doubt that the presence of federal deposit insurance is a major aspect of the stability of our banking structure and has contributed greatly to monetary and economic stability.

The Federal Deposit Insurance Corporation was established in 1933 to help restore public confidence in banks.  All but an insignificant portion of depository institutions are covered by the FDIC.  Initially, maximum insurance coverage was $2,500 per account.  In 1934 the coverage was boosted to $5,000, then to $10,000 in 1950, $15,000 in 1966, $20,000 in 1969, $40,000 in 1974, and most recently to $100,000 in 1980.  Bank failures have diminished radically since the establishment of the FDIC in 1933, although some of this certainly should be attributed to an improved economy rather than the establishment of the FDIC.  From 1934 through 1942, an average of 54 banks failed each year.  From 1943 until 1974 average failures per year dropped to approximately five out of 14,000 banks.  This is quite a contrast to the average of 588 failures per year between 1920 and 1929 and an average of 2,277 annually from 1930 to 1933.  In 1975 the numbers began to rise.  During the 1970s, there were 79 bank failures.  Beginning with 1982, bank failures steadily increased in each successive year until 1989, when they peaked at 206.  Since then, the number of failures gradually declined, falling to 13 in 1994.  Overall, from 1982 through 1994 a total of 1,496 banks failed, which was more than 10% of all banks in the United States in 1982.  In addition, thousands of savings and loan associations failed, resulting in the bankruptcy of the Federal Savings and Loan Insurance Corporation (FSLIC) and its eventual dissolution and merger into the FDIC.  The number of banks designated as problem banks by the FDIC exceeded 1,000 for the last several years of the 1980s, but declined to several hundred by 1995.  In 1995 there were about 10,000 insured banks and about 2,000 insured savings and loan associations.  While there is debate about the extent to which shortcomings in the regulatory system were responsible for depository institution failures, it is fair to say that the presence of deposit insurance prevented deposit runs and loss of public confidence.

Major changes in the financial institutions regulatory structure, particularly for thrift institutions, began with the enactment of the Garn-St Germain Act of 1982, which substantially expanded the types of loans and investments that could be made with insured deposits. Because of $100,000 deposit insurance, money brokers entered the picture, collecting high-rate deposits from both large and small depositors, and selling $100,000 units to the insured institutions willing to pay the highest interest rates. At the same time, the increased thrift powers attracted new financial institution owners with new goals, willing to pay high interest rates. State legislation, particularly in Florida, California, and Texas, gave state chartered thrifts broader powers, including direct investment in real estate development activities. The combination of $100,000 deposit insurance and broad investment powers effectively provided financial institution owners the right to retain all profits from their new activities and to pass along all losses to the federal insurance funds, and ultimately to the taxpayers.

From 1934 through 1972 the FDIC's total losses were only $75 million. In 1988 alone the FDIC suffered losses of about $4 billion, reducing the bank insurance fund to a value of approximately $14 billion, or about 0.7% of insured deposits, which were in excess of $2 trillion. The savings and loan federal insurance system became completely bankrupt. Finally, Congress passed the Financial Institutions Reform, Recovery and Enforcement Act of 1989 ("FIRREA"). The fundamental purposes of the Act were to reform the regulatory structure for the thrift industry and to reestablish financial soundness for the federal deposit insurance funds. The legislation authorized $50 billion to meet the obligations of the Federal Savings and Loan Insurance Corporation. The ultimate losses from the savings and loan crisis have been estimated to be $300 billion over 30 years, probably the largest financial loss ever suffered by American taxpayers. (In contrast, there were about 6,000 bank robberies in 1985, which cost the banks an aggregate of $46 million.) While exceedingly complex, FIRREA essentially gave the Federal Deposit Insurance Corporation the regulatory authority to deal with both bank and savings and loan association failures.

There has been much discussion about the reasons for the recent massive failures of insured depository institutions. Many have argued that the losses were caused simply by severe economic reverses in the 1980s in certain areas of our economy, particularly oil and gas, agriculture, and real estate. But in early 1990, the chairman of the FDIC disagreed, stating that approximately 60% of failed savings and loan associations had been victimized by serious criminal activity. Much of the apparent fraud appears to have occurred in complex real estate transactions, often involving the swapping of over-valued property several times between borrowers and various savings and loan associations. The transactions created false values and appraisals on which loans could be made, and generated substantial fees to appraisers, brokers, developers, and other participants, including insiders of the financial institutions.

A third view is that the great majority of such transactions were not fraudulent, but were lawful, albeit risky, activities authorized under the expanded powers granted by federal and state laws and regulations beginning in the early 1980s.  And so, the blame for the depository institution failures can be shared by legislators, regulators, and management of failed institutions.

The congressional response was passage of the Federal Deposit Insurance Corporation Improvement Act (FDICIA) in 1991.  For our purposes, the most significant part of FDICIA was the creation of the prompt corrective action (PCA) requirements.  12 U.S.C.A. § 1831o.  Prompt corrective action requires the regulators to address capital deficiencies and supervisory problems of depository institutions, leaving less regulatory discretion than is typically found in depository institution regulatory statutes.  It remains to be seen whether FIRREA and FDICIA will play a significant role in a permanent solution.

Where do we go from here–how do we regulate both to provide substantial assurance that such a financial disaster never happens again and to give substantial range to market forces and individual decisions?  A few preliminary thoughts may help to focus your thinking.  One obvious possibility is to reduce the $100,000 deposit insurance limit, which is far beyond protecting "grocery money."  Alternatively, some argue that banks can be made safer by expanding their powers, particularly in securities, insurance and real estate.  The arguments are that these activities would both create more competition and strengthen banks and their holding companies by enabling them to diversify their income sources.  Some, however, have challenged this view on either a safety and soundness, or an economic neutrality, basis.  Other suggestions include requiring depository institutions to carry their assets at market value at all times, rather than at cost as has generally been permitted.  Utilizing market values would reduce the ability of an institution to appear to be solvent when in fact it is insolvent on a balance sheet basis, but it would be counter to the concept of banks as sources of long-term credit decisions in the local economy.

One final element for your consideration is a different way to impose increased capital requirements.  Beyond the discussion of capital adequacy in Chapter 3, some have suggested that an individualized and forceful incentive for safe and sound financial institutions would occur if directors and principal officers were required to have a substantial amount of their own capital at risk.  Not only does capital in general act as a buffer against unexpected losses, but there may be no more effective way to align the decisions of financial institution managers with concerns about public confidence and deposit insurance than by requiring them to have a significant personal stake in the enterprise.

Federal deposit insurance has had an obvious effect on capital ratios.  In 1840 the leverage capital ratio of U.S. banks was about 50%.  This ratio gradually declined until the late 1920s, when the average was about 12%.  The reason for these pre-deposit insurance capital ratios was that they were necessary to maintain depositors' confidence.  Since creation of the FDIC, the financial markets have been willing to allow bank capital ratios to decline because of the various protections such as deposit insurance, the Federal Reserve as lender of last resort, and other methods that have appeared to reduce the risk to depositors.

An additional policy concern that often appears to exist in practice, though it can be found to a much lesser extent in the statutes, is that large banks should not be allowed to fail. This is commonly referred to as the too-big-to-fail doctrine. While Congress attempted to limit the doctrine in FDICIA, the ability to rescue any bank at any cost continues to exist provided that, the regulators find systemic risk to the banking system. The FDIC can then utilize such techniques as reimbursement of *uninsured* depositors, typically through financially assisted bank mergers. On the other hand, FDICIA attempts to discourage such too-big-to-fail bailout techniques by requiring public approval from the Treasury Department, the Comptroller, and the FDIC before treating a large bank specially as too-big-to-fail.

In 1873 Walter Bagehot, the founder of *The Economist* magazine, wrote: "There is a cardinal difference between banking and other kinds of commerce; you can afford to run much less risk in banking than in commerce, and you must take much greater precautions. In common business, the trader can add to the cost price of the goods he sells a large mercantile profit, . . . but the banker has to be content with the interest of money. . . . The business of a banker therefore cannot bear so many bad debts as that of a merchant. . . . And besides, a banker dealing with the money of others, and money payable on demand, must always be, as it were, looking behind him and seeing that he has reserve enough in store if anything should be asked for, which a merchant dealing mostly with his own capital need not think of. Adventure is the life of commerce, but caution . . . is the life of banking. . . ." WALTER BAGEHOT, LOMBARD STREET (1873).

In this chapter, first we will consider the reporting and examination requirements imposed on banks. Second, we will examine the regulators' statutory supervisory powers. In the last section of this chapter we will consider the powers of bank regulators for dealing with an insolvent institution and institution-affiliated parties, including attorneys.

# Section 2.  Bank Reports and Examinations

## A.  Introduction

The regulatory agencies use two tools for the initial, general supervision of all banks: reports and examinations. Periodic reports enable regulators to review the condition of each bank without an on-site inspection. They also help regulators prepare for periodic on-site inspections, called examinations. The data provided in the reports can be analyzed by computers to attempt to identify problems requiring special attention. These reports include reports of condition (basically a bank's balance sheet); reports of income and dividends; trust department reports; reports of international operations and foreign exchange activities; reports on stock ownership in the reporting bank and on indebtedness of executive officers and principal shareholders to the reporting bank and its correspondent banks; past due loan reports; reports filed under the federal securities laws; and foreign country lending exposure reports. The most important and widely utilized report is the "Call Report"–a combination of the condition and income reports. Reports of condition and income are public records, as are certain parts of past due loan reports.

The quarterly reports of income and condition filed with the regulatory agencies are helpful, particularly in comparing each institution with statistical early warning models that have been used by the agencies since the mid-1970s.  The reports can be of some value in determining the priority or urgency for on-site examinations.

As for examinations, the primary concern of the regulators is to ascertain the financial condition of the bank, in order to ensure the safety and soundness of the nation's banking system.  This involves not only checking the existence of assets (e.g., loans) and adequate collateral, but more significantly includes a review of the adequacy of the bank's planning and control measures for unanticipated changes in external conditions, such as interest rate fluctuations.  It is possible to have separate examinations of various areas of a bank, such as the commercial loan department, electronic data processing systems, the trust department, and the bank holding company.

After reviewing the reports and examinations, regulators attempt to resolve any problems with a bank through informal meetings and discussions.  If these informal actions fail, the actors proceed to the more formal enforcement actions dealt with in the next section of this chapter.

The Federal Financial Institutions Examination Council was formed in 1979.  One of its primary purposes is to make the bank supervisory system more standardized on various matters, including examination procedures and the measure of bank performance in determining financial solvency and soundness.  A major development has been the adoption of a uniform financial institutions rating system.  This system (often referred to by the acronym CAMELS) causes all agencies to use the same general framework in their analysis of individual banks.  The acronym identifies the six major factors that are assessed in rating a bank.  They are:  (1) capital adequacy; (2) asset quality; (3) management ability and effectiveness; (4) earnings quantity and quality; (5) liquidity (which is the ability to meet demands for payment of obligations, particularly deposits); and (6) sensitivity to market risk, such as fluctuations in interest rates.

Each factor is rated on the following scale of one to five:  (1) strong, significantly better than average; (2) satisfactory; (3) below average; (4) marginal, well below average; and (5) unsatisfactory, critically deficient.  The scores on each of the five factors are then combined into a composite rating showing the overall condition of the bank. The composite rating system also is on a scale of one to five, with one being the most favorable.

Beginning in 1996 the regulators implemented a "supervision by risk" examination program.  It rates a bank's risk exposure and risk management as a significant part of evaluating management within the CAMELS rating system.  One weakness of the CAMELS system is thought to be that it is a snapshot of a bank on a single day, and fails to give consideration to the potential of future events, whether expected or unanticipated, having an adverse impact on the bank's capital or earnings.  There are nine categories of risk.  The first seven are called explicit risks:  credit, liquidity, interest rate, price, foreign exchange, transaction, and compliance.

Credit risk is the potential that obligors will fail to pay their obligations. Liquidity risk is the possibility that a bank will be unable to meet its obligations as they become due. Interest rate risk is the effect of interest rate movements on a bank's income and expenses. Price risk is the change in value of financial instruments held by a bank. Foreign exchange risk involves the risk from movement in foreign exchange rates. Transaction risk involves problems with the bank's services, such as its operating systems and controls. Compliance risk stems from non-conformance with laws and regulations.

The remaining two risks are implicit risks. Strategic risk arises from bad business decisions, such as dealing with technology changes or new competition. Reputation risk arises from negative public opinion and affects a bank's ability to establish new or maintain existing customer relations. Even if all of these risks are difficult to quantify, focusing attention on these risks may at least be beneficial to the primary mandate of examinations to ensure safety and soundness.

Provisions of FIRREA provide additional mechanisms to limit bank risk-taking. In a partial reversal of the 1982 legislation, FIRREA called for the implementation of minimum collateral requirements for real estate loans, the establishment of appropriate appraisal standards for real estate loans, the prohibition of brokered deposit utilization by troubled institutions, and the expansion of supervisory enforcement powers. One example of those powers under FIRREA is that the penalty for filing a late or inaccurate report of income or condition can be as high as $1 million per day, and an inadvertent error in a report can result in a penalty of up to $2,000 per day.

The 1991 enactment of FDICIA added several examination related regulatory requirements on depository institutions. The law requires the filing of an annual management report that is available to the public and covers financial statements, internal controls, and compliance with identified safety and soundness laws. Each institution with assets above $500 million must have an audit committee composed solely of independent directors and undergo an annual independent audit of its financial statements. In addition, the CPA must certify certain statements of management concerning internal controls and compliance with safety and soundness laws.

## B.  "Unsafe or Unsound"

An all-encompassing regulatory power of the "appropriate Federal banking agency" (12 U.S.C.A. § 1813(q)) is its ability to terminate any activity of a bank that it finds to be an "unsafe or unsound" practice. 12 U.S.C.A. § 1818(a) and (b). The reason for the power is to assist regulators in maintaining banks' solvency, thus achieving the twin goals of protecting individual depositors while keeping banks out of trouble. The concept of unsafe or unsound banking practices is a concept that touches the entire operation of a bank. As a result, it is impossible to formulate a rigid and all-inclusive definition of the activities that are included within the concept. Nevertheless, the words "unsafe" or "unsound" as a basis for supervisory action have appeared in both federal and state law for many decades. In *People v. Bank of San Luis Obispo*, 154 Cal. 194, 97 P. 306, 309 (1908), the court held that the term "unsafe" had a broad and expansive definition. "It is true that the phrase 'unsafe . . . to continue to transact business,' as used in the act, is broader than the term 'insolvent,' and that a finding that it is unsafe for a banking corporation to continue business does not necessarily mean that it is insolvent. But the converse of this is not true. The act clearly contemplates that it is unsafe for an insolvent banking corporation to continue business . . . ."

The term "unsafe or unsound" has been utilized in federal law since the Banking Act of 1933. Since then "unsafe or unsound practices" has been ground for removal of a director or officer of a member bank. It has been grounds since 1935 for the termination of FDIC insurance. 12 U.S.C.A. § 1818(a).

The following statement made by the chairman of the FDIC during Senate hearings is illustrative of the approach regulators have taken in their attempts to clarify the concept of unsafe or unsound banking practices.

[A] particular activity not necessarily unsafe or unsound in every instance may be so when considered in light of all relevant facts. Like many other generic terms widely used in the law, such as "fraud," "negligence," "probable cause" or "good faith," the term "unsafe or unsound practices" has a central meaning which can and must be applied to constantly changing factual circumstances. Generally speaking, *an unsafe or unsound practice embraces any action, or lack of action, which is contrary to generally accepted standards of prudent operation, the possible consequences of which, if continued, would be abnormal risk or loss or damage to an institution, its shareholders, or the insurance fund administered by the corporation.*

George LeMaistre, Chairman, FDIC, Testimony Before the Senate Committee on the Subject of Overdrafts and Correspondent Banking Practices, CIS, 5-241-25 (1977) (emphasis added). The substantial equivalent of the emphasized passage can be found in the testimony of virtually every chairman of every financial supervisory agency in the last 20 years.

The Comptroller's efforts in this area appear to be concentrated on conflict of interests, self-dealing, and insider abuses. In 1977-78 Senate hearings, the following categories were listed as areas in which most of the unsafe or unsound banking problems arise: 1) Bank stock loans; (2) Loans to favored customers; (3) Overdrafts; (4) Failure to comply with banking laws or regulations; (5) Insurance commissions; (6) Double use of collateral; (7) Insider overreaching. CIS, S-241-25 (1977).

If unsafe or unsound practices are found, the enforcement powers of the regulatory agencies (the cease and desist, civil money penalty and removal powers) come into play. It is virtually impossible to find any regulatory elaboration, beyond that quoted above, of just what is meant by the term "unsafe or unsound" practices. See 12 C.F.R. Pt. 337.

# In re Seidman
## 37 F.3d 911 (3d Cir. 1994)

HUTCHINSON, Circuit Judge.

In these consolidated cases, Lawrence Seidman ("Seidman") and John Bailey ("Bailey") petition for review of the order of the Director ("Director") of the Office of Thrift Supervision ("OTS") subjecting them to administrative sanctions for their part in a loan transaction Crestmont Federal Savings and Loan ("Crestmont") considered while Seidman was Chairman of Crestmont's Board of Directors ("Board") and Bailey was one of its officers.  Specifically, Bailey petitions for review of that portion of the Director's order publicly directing him to cease and desist from participating in unsafe and unsound lending practices.  Seidman's petition seeks review of that portion of the Director's order removing him from his office at Crestmont and banning him from further participation in the banking industry.

### I.  *Factual and Procedural History*

#### A.  *Seidman's Business Dealings*

Lawrence Seidman is an attorney in his mid-forties who has been engaged in the practice of banking and securities law for twenty years.  During the past decade he has specialized in real estate investments and begun to pursue a career in banking.  In 1989, he headed a group of investors who purchased stock in Crestmont, a thrift institution in Edison, New Jersey.[3]  Seidman became a director of Crestmont and, in November 1989, was named Chairman of its Board of Directors.

In 1986, before he became a Crestmont director, Seidman formed a partnership, Fulton Street Associates ("FSA"), with James Zorlas ("Zorlas") and Lawrence Rappaport ("Rappaport") to purchase and develop industrial condominiums on a piece of commercial property ("Boonton Project").  FSA's partners made substantial capital contributions to the Boonton Project and obtained additional financing from United Jersey Bank ("UJB"), secured in part by all the partners' personal guarantees.  Seidman listed his affiliation with FSA on conflict disclosure forms he filed with Crestmont when he became a director.

In mid-1990, Seidman decided to focus his business activities on Crestmont.  Recognizing that his outside business ventures could create conflicts that would prevent Crestmont from making otherwise desirable loans, Seidman advised the Board that he had begun to withdraw from his outside business ventures and started disposing of various business interests to his former partners.  Rappaport agreed to acquire Seidman's interest in FSA, promising to indemnify Seidman against any continuing obligation on FSA's loan from UJB without any further consideration flowing to Seidman.  On June 1, 1991, Seidman's transfer of his interest in FSA to Rappaport became the subject of a formal agreement.  Seidman testified that he lost all of the $320,000 he had invested in FSA but that he thought Crestmont offered even greater potential for profit.

---

[3]    At the time the parties argued and briefed these cases, Crestmont was not one of the failed thrifts that led to the "S & L bailout."  We have not been advised of any change in this respect.

Months before the June 1st agreement, however, UJB started to worry about its loan to FSA. On January 21, 1991, it sent FSA a notice of default. UJB gave FSA a chance to cure the default, but FSA denied it was in default, contending any default would have been cured if an interest reserve fund had been properly credited against its debt. Though UJB then sent FSA a demand for immediate payment, negotiations between them continued.

James Risko ("Risko"), a Poole & Co. commercial loan broker, handled negotiations to resolve the dispute between FSA and UJB.  Poole & Co. was the commercial loan company that had placed the FSA loan with UJB.  Roger Eberhardt ("Eberhardt"), chairman of UJB's real estate management committee, and Thomas Stackhouse ("Stackhouse"), the UJB commercial lending officer assigned to the FSA loan, were key participants in the negotiations.  Risko, Eberhardt and Stackhouse all testified that the participants, including Seidman, discussed end-user financing for FSA's Boonton condominiums.[4]  Crestmont was mentioned as a potential source of end-user loans, but no one testified that Seidman or Crestmont promised to make any loan.  On May 20, 1991, the parties agreed to restructure the UJB loan.  As part of the restructuring, the FSA partners, including Seidman, signed personal guarantees covering $4.45 million.  Seidman's successful efforts to be released from the guarantee figure prominently in these proceedings, but other ongoing events also play a significant role.

## B.  *The Levine Loan*

John Bailey is the Executive Vice President of Crestmont.  His responsibilities include underwriting commercial loans, managing a commercial loan portfolio, producing new lending business and supervising Crestmont's loan officers.  Bailey had authority to approve loans of less than $500,000 if they did not directly involve the interests of Crestmont's directors but had no authority to approve loans in excess of $500,000 or loans in which Crestmont's officers or directors had an interest.  Loans over $500,000 went before a "Senior Loan Committee" made up of Bailey, Seidman and Crestmont's President, S. Griffin McClellan ("McClellan"). Commercial loans in which an officer or director had an interest were prohibited at Crestmont.

In December of 1990, Steven Levine ("Levine") of S & N Realty approached Bailey about end-user financing for a $466,000 office condominium in FSA's Boonton project.  Levine, who had been referred to Crestmont and Bailey by Zorlas, sought $375,000. On December 18, 1990, Bailey contacted Zorlas, Rappaport and Seidman about Levine's loan request and asked them how things stood on Seidman's partnership interest in FSA. All three FSA partners individually represented to Bailey that Seidman was in the process of withdrawing from the partnership and that the withdrawal would be completed "shortly."  Bailey Appendix ("Bailey App.") at 319. Bailey memorialized this conversation and placed a memo about it in a file marked "Seidman Financial Associates." *Id*. Rappaport testified he told Bailey no loan could be made to Levine until Seidman was out of the partnership.

Assured Seidman would soon be out of FSA, Bailey decided to get a head start on the Levine loan and assigned James Little ("Little"), a Crestmont loan officer, the task of writing it

---

[4]    End-user financing permits a person who plans to occupy a unit in a development to buy the unit or rent it to others.  The institution that has financed the project has a strong interest in facilitating end-user financing because it usually receives a substantial part of the price the end-user pays, thus reducing its exposure on the loan to the developer.

up. Little interviewed Levine and told him the loan could be approved but no other action could be taken on it until Seidman left FSA. Little became involved with other things and gave the paperwork on the loan back to Bailey to complete. Still assured that Seidman would soon be out of FSA, Bailey did extensive work on it.

Bailey prepared a Credit Summary for the Levine loan on February 21, 1991.[5]    On March 19, 1991, Bailey and Little approved the loan and issued a commitment letter to Levine.[6] Levine did not sign the commitment letter until May 30, 1991, when Bailey was given a check for $2,000 in exchange for the commitment.[7]

### C. *Crestmont's Loan Policies*

Crestmont had a loan policy which Bailey had authored. It was based on OTS regulations and stated:

The policy of the bank is to carefully administer extensions of credit which are subject to special reporting requirements. These loans include the following: . . . .

— [L]oans to individuals or entities that conduct business or have conducted business with officers or directors of the bank.

These situations are clearly described in the bank's loan committee credit summary. They are presented to the bank's Senior Loan Committee regardless of their size.

*Id.* at 314. Crestmont had another policy, also based on OTS regulations, which forbade it from

---

[5]    In the Credit Summary form there is a space headed "Bank Officers and Directors Interest." Bailey says he thought this heading referred to the officers and directors of the Levine partnership, not FSA, the developer. Bailey also listed the applicant as "[a] N.J. General Partnership, the ownership of which is 100% Steven K. Levine and Ned Levine." Bailey App. at 321. Clarence Hartwick, a twenty-seven year veteran in banking and an executive at First Fidelity Bank in New Jersey, corroborated Bailey's understanding at a hearing before an OTS ALJ. He testified:

That line refers to the borrower. Is the borrower an officer or director of the bank, it's as simple as that.

*Id.* at 304. Bailey entered the word "none" on the line calling for disclosure of "Bank Officers and Directors Interest." *Id.* at 321. Other underwriting documents included with the Credit Summary clearly disclosed FSA's interest.

[6]    The commitment was later modified and reissued on May 10, 1991. Unknown to Bailey, Levine had already entered into a Contract of Sale with FSA on or about May 10, 1991. Seidman did not formally withdraw from FSA until June 1, 1991. Questioned about what would have happened if Seidman had failed to withdraw from a similar transaction, Crestmont's President, McClellan, testified, "We would not have closed the loan. It was clearly understood by all involved that that was a condition to closing." *Id.* at 191.

[7]    Crestmont negotiated that instrument but the date of negotiation is unclear. OTS contends that the check was negotiated before June 1, 1991, the date Seidman transferred his interest, but Bailey contends the check was cashed after Seidman relinquished his partnership. Levine's delivery of the check for $2,000 resulted in a binding contract two days before Seidman's formal withdrawal. *See generally Restatement (Second) of Contracts* § 17 (1981).

either directly or indirectly mak[ing] any loan to or purchase . . . any loan made to any third party on the security of real property purchased from any affiliated person of the association unless the property was a single-family dwelling owned and occupied by the affiliated person as a permanent residence.

OTS Appendix ("OTS App.") at 96-97 (citing 12 C.F.R. § 563.43(c)(1)).  Crestmont's policies also put on its directors

a fundamental duty to avoid placing themselves in any position which creates, leads to or could lead to a conflict of interest or even the appearance of such conflict of interest between the accomplishment of the purposes of the association and the personal financial interests of the directors, officers and other affiliated persons.

*Id.* at 98-99 (citing 12 C.F.R. § 571.7).  Specifically, Crestmont's directors were supposed to avoid any transaction in which

a third party purchaser seeks to obtain a loan from the association secured by real estate acquired from the affiliated partnership or as to which the affiliated partnership holds a security interest.

*Id.* at 100.  Bailey and Seidman were fully aware of these policies.

### D.  *The Garden Park Loan*

At the same time that Crestmont was negotiating the Levine loan, Seidman and OTS were engaged in a tense dialogue over property owned by Garden Park Associates ("Garden Park"), for which Seidman was attempting to arrange financing at Crestmont.  Seidman had an interest in Garden Park and had also personally guaranteed the development loans for Garden Park.  Seidman fully disclosed his interest in Garden Park to the Crestmont Board and Crestmont formally asked OTS to permit it to make the Garden Park loan.  On May 23, 1991, OTS denied Crestmont's request citing 12 C.F.R. § 563.43(c)(1) (1991) which forbade certain transactions with affiliated parties.[8]  Seidman contacted OTS's Chief Examiner in charge of Crestmont, Joseph Donohue ("Donohue"), for a further explanation of OTS's position.  Donohue told Seidman that OTS considered the Garden Park loan impermissible so long as Seidman remained a guarantor of Garden Park's obligation.  Seidman asked for reconsideration, but OTS still refused to allow the loan.

### E.  *Seidman's Release from the UJB Guarantee*

Until his May 23, 1991, conversation with Donohue, Seidman seems to have believed that his withdrawal from FSA would permit Crestmont to make the Levine loan.  After speaking with Donohue about Garden Park, Seidman had second thoughts about his personal guarantee of FSA's loan from UJB and began to wonder whether it would disqualify Crestmont from loaning

---

[8]    OTS amended this regulation subsequent to the ALJ's decision, but the Code of Federal Regulations no longer contains any independent OTS conflict of interest rules.  Instead, 12 C.F.R. § 563.43 incorporates the Federal Reserve Board regulations found at 12 C.F.R. § 215.1 *et seq.  See* 57 Fed. Reg. 45,977 (1992) (codified at 12 C.F.R. § 563.43).  There is no provision in the Federal Reserve Board regulations comparable to former 12 C.F.R. § 563.43(c)(1).  For the text of former section 563.43(c)(1), *see infra* typescript at 930.

money to Levine even after Seidman completed his withdrawal from FSA. Seidman turned to James Poole ("Poole") of Poole & Co., who advised Seidman to get a release from the UJB guarantee and to discuss this with Risko. Seidman did so and Risko approached Eberhardt. Risko told Eberhardt that the conflict between Seidman's obligation on the guarantee and his fiduciary duties to Crestmont created problems in Crestmont's providing end-user financing for the FSA project. Eberhardt told Risko to put a proposal for Seidman's release in writing and UJB would consider it.

Events now moved rapidly. On May 30, 1991, the day Levine signed the commitment letter, Risko contacted Seidman and told him UJB would consider releasing Seidman. Risko suggested Seidman draft a letter asking for the release and that he, Risko, would sign a letter giving UJB the reasons for granting Seidman's request. Risko testified Seidman and he agreed that Seidman would do an initial draft of both the request for release and Risko's supporting letter. Risko testified he was only to approve and sign the supporting letter and that Seidman faxed him the draft. Seidman testified that Risko dictated the draft to Seidman's secretary and she forwarded it to Risko for review.

While drafts were being faxed back and forth between Risko and Seidman, OTS examiner Thomas Angstadt ("Angstadt") was at Crestmont on other business. While using a Crestmont fax machine, Angstadt saw a copy of the draft of Risko's letter lying on a desk. Angstadt secretly read and copied the draft.

The final version of Risko's letter was identical with the draft except for one sentence that Risko added.[9] Seidman had no objection to Risko's addition.

On June 7, 1991, UJB notified Seidman that it would release him from his guarantee of FSA's loan. Eberhardt later testified UJB understood that the release did not obligate Crestmont to provide such financing, but he prepared a handwritten memo that indicated availability of end-user financing from Crestmont was a consideration in UJB's decision to release Seidman.

In the meantime, on June 3, 1991, OTS prohibited the Garden Park loan, and Seidman again asked Donohue for an explanation. Donohue now told Seidman that OTS believed conflict of interest prevented a thrift from making a loan to an entity in which an officer or director of the thrift had had an interest, including liability on a guarantee, at any time within two years before

---

[9]    Risko's supporting letter reads as follows, with the sentence Risko added emphasized in bold face type:

As you are aware, Mr. Seidman is the Chairman of the Board of Crestmont Federal Savings and Loan Association and Crestmont is entertaining financing certain condo purchasers who are purchasing units from Fulton Street. His position as Chairman may make this financing impossible if he is also a partner in Fulton Street. The inability to finance the end users, in our opinion, does not serve either United Jersey Bank's position or that of the developer. At the present time, Crestmont is entertaining $700,000 in financing for two users and a third potential buyer has indicated the need for approximately $1 million in financing. **Crestmont would be willing to consider future financing of condo units in the Boonton area, assuming qualified buyers.**

OTS App. at 2 (emphasis added).

the loan was made. Seidman protested that such a policy had no support in OTS regulations, but Donohue was not moved.

Frustrated, Seidman ordered Bailey to stop considering commercial loans on projects in which Seidman had an interest either as a partner or guarantor. On June 4, 1991, Bailey sent both the Levine and the Garden Park loans to the Savings Bank of Rockland.[10] On June 5, 1991, OTS issued a supervisory directive forbidding Crestmont from making any commercial loans and launched the investigation for "conflict of interest" that gave rise to the cases now before us. It is undisputed that Crestmont never made the loans OTS questioned. . . .

### G. The Director's Decision

. . . . The Director independently held that Seidman's attempt to destroy evidence and cover-up his activities during the investigation violated section 1818(e)(1). He found the attempted cover-up, which involved giving misleading testimony, destroying the original record of the fax of the early draft of Risko's letter from Seidman to Risko and requesting that Risko forget about the letter, *inter alia*, constituted an unsafe or unsound practice. The Director concluded that these acts established personal dishonesty within the meaning of section 1818(e)(1)(C)(i) and conferred a personal benefit on Seidman within the meaning of section 1818(e)(1)(B)(iii).

The Director also held Bailey had engaged in an unsafe and unsound banking practice. He found Bailey knew of Seidman's interest in FSA, failed to disclose it to the Board of Directors or the Senior Loan Committee and issued a commitment letter for the Levine loan before Seidman withdrew from FSA. The Director concluded this created an "abnormal risk of loss" to Crestmont and that a cease and desist order was appropriate under section 1818(b). . . . .

### III. *Standard of Review*

The Administrative Procedure Act ("APA"), 5 U.S.C.A. § 706(2) (West 1977), defines the scope of judicial review over the Director's findings and conclusions of law. We must uphold the Director's order against Bailey and Seidman unless we determine that the Director has made an error of law or that his findings are not supported by substantial evidence on the whole record. *See Hoffman v. FDIC*, 912 F.2d 1172, 1173-74 (9th Cir.1990). Substantial evidence is "such relevant evidence as a reasonable mind might accept as adequate to support a conclusion." *Consolidated Edison Co. v. NLRB*, 305 U.S. 197, 229 (1938). Issues of law are subject to plenary review. *Dill v. INS*, 773 F.2d 25, 28 (3d Cir.1985). In deciding legal issues, we must defer to an agency's consistent interpretation of the statute it administers unless it is "arbitrary and capricious," *Chevron, U.S.A., Inc. v. Natural Resources Defense Council, Inc.*, 467 U.S. 837, 844 (1984). Nevertheless, when "bizarre" interpretations of a statute are made out of "regulatory zeal," deference is not appropriate. *See Wachtel v. OTS*, 982 F.2d 581, 585 (D.C.Cir.1993). Similarly, interpretations contrary to the plain meaning of the statute are unacceptable. *Elliot Coal Mining Co., Inc. v. Director, OWCP*, 17 F.3d 616, 629 (3d Cir.1994). . . .

---

[10]     Seidman is also a member of the Board of Directors at Rockland, but that lending institution is regulated by FDIC, not OTS.

## V. *The Charges Against Bailey*

Section 1818(b)(1) prohibits unsafe and unsound practices. OTS argues that Bailey's commitment to the Levine loan conflicts with Crestmont's policy of prohibiting purchase money loans on the security of real property in which a Crestmont officer or director had an interest. An officer's violation of a banking institution's policy, however, is not enough to justify a cease and desist order under section 1818(b)(1). While the statute gives the Director considerable discretion, it nevertheless requires substantial evidence showing that the violation of policy amounted to an unsafe and unsound practice. . . . .

Because the statute itself does not define an unsafe or unsound practice, courts have sought help in the legislative history. *See, e.g., Northwest Nat'l Bank v. United States*, 917 F.2d 1111, 1115 (8th Cir. 1990); *Gulf Federal Sav. & Loan Ass'n v. Federal Home Loan Bank Bd.*, 651 F.2d 259, 264 (5th Cir. 1981), *cert. denied*, 458 U.S. 1121 (1982). . . . . [The] courts have generally interpreted the phrase "unsafe or unsound practice" as a flexible concept which gives the administering agency the ability to adapt to changing business problems and practices in the regulation of the banking industry. . . .

Among the specific acts that may constitute an unsafe and unsound practice are "paying excessive dividends, disregarding a borrower's ability to repay, careless control of expenses, excessive advertising, and inadequate liquidity." *Gulf Federal Sav. & Loan Ass'n*, 651 F.2d at 264. In *Gulf Federal*, the court had to decide whether a bank's breach of contract was an unsafe or unsound practice that justified an FHLBB order to cease and desist. *Id.* at 262. The FHLBB concluded that the bank's potential liability for breach and possible "loss of public confidence in the institution" meant the breach was an unsafe and unsound practice that authorized the agency to order the bank to perform its contract. *Id.* at 264. The court disagreed and held that a breach of contract is not an unsafe or unsound practice that threatens a bank's financial soundness. *Id.* The court expressly rejected FHLBB's conclusion that liability for breach and consequent loss of public confidence in the bank's willingness to honor its commitments give rise to an unsafe or unsound practice that authorized a cease and desist order. *Id.* It stated:

> Such potential "risks" bear only the most remote relationship to [the bank's] financial integrity and the government's insurance risk. . . . We fail to see how the [FHLBB] can safeguard [the bank's] finances by making definite and immediate an injury which is, at worst, contingent and remote.

> Approving intervention under the [FHLBB's] "loss of public confidence" rationale would result in open-ended supervision. . . . The [FHLBB's] rationale would permit it to decide, not that the public has lost confidence in [the bank's] financial soundness, but that the public may lose confidence in the fairness of the association's contracts with its customers. If the [FHLBB] can act to enforce the public's standard of fairness in interpreting contracts, the [FHLBB] becomes the monitor of every activity of the association in its role of proctor for public opinion. This departs entirely from the congressional concept of acting to preserve the financial integrity of its members.

*Id.* at 264-65 (footnote omitted).

In *Northwest National Bank* the court upheld the Comptroller of the Currency's ("Comptroller's") conclusion that evidence showing failure to maintain an adequate loan to loss reserve and inadequate capital, together with deficient loan administration, established unsafe or unsound banking practices. *Northwest Nat'l Bank*, 917 F.2d at 1113-14. The court agreed with FHLBB that the bank's failure to maintain adequate reserves and capital was an unsafe or unsound practice. *Id.* at 1115. The court defined the phrase "unsafe and unsound banking practices" in general terms similar to those that appear in the legislative history: "Unsafe and unsound banking practices are . . . 'conduct deemed contrary to accepted standards of banking operations which might result in abnormal risk of loss to a banking institution or shareholder.'" *Id.* . . .

In *MCorp Financial, Inc. v. Board of Governors*, 900 F.2d 852 (5th Cir. 1990), *aff'd in part, rev'd in part on other grounds*, 112 S. Ct. 459 (1991), the Board of Governors of the Federal Reserve concluded that MCorp's failure to provide capital to its subsidiary banks was an unsafe or unsound practice and entered a cease and desist order directing MCorp to transfer assets to its banking subsidiaries. *MCorp Fin., Inc.*, 900 F.2d at 862. On review, the court of appeals concluded that Congress had failed to provide a clear definition of "unsafe or unsound practice." *Id.* at 862. *Limited by Chevron, U.S.A., Inc. v. Natural Resources Defense Council, Inc.*, 467 U.S. 837 (1984), but relying on *Gulf Federal Savings & Loan Association*, the court concluded that the Board of Governors' order directing MCorp to transfer assets to its troubled subsidiaries was itself contrary to "'generally accepted standard [ ] of prudent operation.'" *Id.* at 863 (quoting *Gulf Federal Sav.*, 651 F.2d at 254). "Such a transfer of funds would require MCorp to disregard its own corporation's separate status; it would amount to a wasting of the holding company's assets in violation of its duty to its shareholders." *Id.*

We think at least one common element of an unsafe or unsound banking practice relating to the health of the institution can be deduced from these cases and the legislative history. The imprudent act must pose an abnormal risk to the financial stability of the banking institution. This is the standard that the case law and legislative history indicates we should apply in judging whether an unsafe or unsound practice has occurred.

With this in mind, we turn to the specific imprudent acts OTS charges against Bailey. They are:

(a) failing to disclose Seidman's interest in Fulton Street Associates to the Senior Loan Committee . . ., (b) approving the Levine Loan without presenting the loan for review to Crestmont's Senior Loan Committee . . ., and (c) approving the Levine Loan even though Bailey knew that Seidman had an interest in Fulton Street Associates.

Bailey App. at 20. Only one of them has any potential for causing Crestmont loss–Bailey's premature issuance of the commitment letter.[21]

---

[21]    The first two grounds relied upon by the Director — a failure to disclose Seidman's interest in FSA to the Senior Loan Committee and Bailey's approval of the loan without submitting it to the Senior Loan Committee — were not material to Bailey's act of approving the loan and issuing a commitment letter. The record establishes that all the members of the Senior Loan Committee were fully aware of Seidman's interest and had agreed that the Levine loan was not to be approved until Seidman fully disassociated himself from FSA. Moreover, reliance on the omission of Seidman's interest on the Credit Summary form is misplaced. Undisputed testimony supported Bailey's claim that the entry on the form referred to an affiliated party's interest in the borrower. See *supra* note 5.

When Bailey issued the commitment letter, he made Crestmont responsible for the Levine loan. He did this despite the fact that Seidman had not extricated himself from the FSA partnership or from the UJB guarantee. When Levine accepted the commitment, Crestmont remained ineligible to make the loan. Thus, Crestmont became responsible for the loan despite the potential illegal conflict. We think this act was imprudent. Although all parties testified that their understanding was that the loan would not go through absent Seidman's complete withdrawal, Bailey had nevertheless obligated Crestmont to a loan it might not be able to make. Obligating one's institution to transactions that might be illegal is not in accord with "generally accepted standards of prudent operation." See *MCorp Fin., Inc.*, 900 F.2d at 862. After Levine accepted the commitment letter, Crestmont either had to make the loan, breach the agreement to make it or place the loan with another institution regardless of Seidman's position. Although, as it turned out, Crestmont was able to place the loan without incident or loss, we recognize that a risk was present when Bailey issued the commitment. Obliging an institution to choose between covering fluctuations in the interest rate, engaging in an illegal transaction or breaching a binding agreement is not prudent.

Imprudence standing alone, however, is insufficient to constitute an unsafe or unsound practice. A cease and desist order is designed to prevent actions that if repeated would carry a potential for serious loss. Although issuance of even this single commitment exposed Crestmont to some potential risk of loss, that potential risk did not begin to approach the abnormal risk involved in *Northwest National Bank*, where the bank was exposed to a serious threat to financial stability by its general failure to monitor its loans adequately and to maintain adequate reserves and capital. The potential loss to which Bailey subjected Crestmont is rather like that present in *Gulf Federal*. Contingent, remote harms that could ultimately result in "minor financial loss[es]" to the institution are insufficient to pose the danger that warrants cease and desist proceedings. *Gulf Fed. Sav. & Loan Ass'n*, 651 F.2d at 264. Though it is not particularly onerous to require a loan officer to satisfy himself that the institution may legally make a loan before the commitment is issued, we cannot conclude that the commitment Bailey authorized posed such an abnormal risk that Crestmont's financial stability was threatened.

We hold that Bailey's approval of the Levine loan and the commitment he issued on behalf of Crestmont in violation of its policies, while imprudent, did not pose an abnormal risk to Crestmont's financial stability and therefore was not an unsafe or unsound practice within the meaning of section 1818(b). Accordingly, we will grant Bailey's petition for review and vacate the part of the Director's order pertaining to Bailey.

VI. *The Charges Against Seidman*

2. *Did Seidman Engage in an Unsafe or Unsound Practice by Seeking the Release?*

Because Seidman did not act in violation of a law or regulation as required by section 1818(e)(1)(A)(i)(I) when he sought the release, we next consider whether by doing so he engaged in an unsafe or unsound practice under section 1818(e)(1)(A)(ii). The Director summarily concluded that Seidman's conduct in seeking a release from the UJB guarantee without informing the Board or the Senior Loan Committee of his interest in FSA, the second charge against him, constituted an unsafe or unsound practice. OTS urges us to affirm this holding.

As stated previously,

> an "unsafe or unsound practice" embraces any action, or lack of action, which is contrary to generally accepted standards of prudent operation, the possible consequences of which, if continued, would be abnormal risk of loss or damage to an institution, its shareholders, or the agencies administering the insurance funds.

*MCorp Fin., Inc.*, 900 F.2d at 862 (quotation omitted).  An unsafe or unsound practice has two components:  (1) an imprudent act (2) that places an abnormal risk of financial loss or damage on a banking institution.  See *supra* Part V.  OTS contends that Seidman's conduct in seeking a release from his UJB guarantee and failing to inform the Board or the Senior Loan Committee of his interest meets these requirements.

OTS and the Director equate the imprudence component of an unsafe or unsound practice with a breach of the fiduciary duty of due care, once called the "prudent man rule" and now more often described as the "business judgment" rule.  See Revised Model Business Corporation Act ("RMBCA") § 8.30 comment (1992).  In its brief, OTS asserts "[t]he prudent operation of Crestmont certainly requires that its directors and officers comply with OTS regulations concerning conflicts of interest as well as Crestmont's own policy governing conflicts." . . . .

While the same act may be both an unsafe or unsound practice under section 1818(e)(1)(A)(ii) and a breach of a fiduciary duty under section 1818(e)(1)(A)(iii), we hesitate to make one a proxy for the other.  If OTS seeks to prove a violation of section 1818(e)(1)(A)(ii), it must satisfy the definition of an unsafe or unsound practice.  Conversely, if OTS wishes to prove a violation of section 1818(e)(1)(A)(iii), it must do so under the standards that define a fiduciary's duty.  Our present inquiry is only whether the first charge against Seidman concerning his successful efforts to obtain a release from his guarantee of FSA's obligations to UJB was an unsafe and unsound practice.  So considered, we conclude Seidman's attempt to secure a release was not an unsafe and unsound banking practice with respect to Crestmont.  OTS not only placed Seidman in the position of selecting between his business life and his banking life but also compelled him to deprive Crestmont of potentially desirable loans.  OTS told Seidman he had to relinquish his outside interests and disengage himself from the obligations he had incurred while a partner in FSA and then, when he did so, charged him with an unsafe and unsound practice.  Seidman's successful effort to secure a release from his guarantee was potentially beneficial to Crestmont by giving it an added source of desirable loans.  The record does not support a conclusion that Seidman's attempts to extricate himself from the UJB guarantee were contrary to accepted banking practices for persons acting on behalf of Crestmont.

Even if we were to conclude that Seidman behaved imprudently in seeking the release, OTS would still have to show that his actions created an abnormal risk of financial loss for Crestmont. *See supra* Part V.  Unable to identify any specific harm to Crestmont, OTS argues, "if directors are free to make choices for the institutions they control based on the personal benefit that would result from their choice there would be an inherent risk that the interests of the depositors and the institution would take a back seat to the personal interest of the director." Appellee App. at 31. OTS again fails to recognize any distinction between the separate requirements of section 1818(e).  Its argument conflates the act of engaging in an unsafe practice with the prohibited effect of personal gain.  Compare 12 U.S.C.A. § 1818(e)(1)(A)(ii) with *id.* § 1818(e)(1)(B)(iii). This record does not show that Seidman's attempt to obtain relief from his guarantee and free

Crestmont from OTS's prohibition against end-user financing on FSA's Boonton development created an abnormal risk of loss or damage to Crestmont. We therefore turn to section 1818(e)(1)(A)(iii).

### 3. *Did Seidman Violate Any Fiduciary Duty In Seeking the Release?*

In a final attempt to demonstrate that Seidman's release from the UJB guarantee was an "act" under section 1818(e)(1)(A) and therefore one of the three elements needed to justify a removal and prohibition order, OTS argues that the Director correctly concluded that Seidman's efforts to secure his release constituted self-dealing and violated his fiduciary duty of loyalty to Crestmont under section 1818(e)(1)(A)(iii). As a member of the board and an officer of Crestmont, Seidman did owe a duty of loyalty to Crestmont. Section 8.42 of the RMBCA states:

(a) An officer with discretionary authority shall discharge his duties under that authority: (1) in good faith; (2) with the care an ordinarily prudent person in a like position would exercise under similar circumstances; and (3) in a manner he reasonably believes to be in the best interests of the corporation.

RMBCA § 8.42 (1992). Common law also imposes on a director a duty of loyalty to the corporation served. See *Fleishhacker v. Blum*, 109 F.2d 543, 547 (9th Cir.), *cert. denied*, 311 U.S. 665 (1940). The duty of loyalty includes a duty to avoid conflicts of interest. See *Pepper v. Litton*, 308 U.S. 295, 306, 310-11 (1939).

In *In re Bush*, OTS AP 91-16, 1991 WL 540753, 1991 OTS DD LEXIS 2 (April 18, 1991), the Director discussed both a director's duty of loyalty and the initial inquiry of whether a director has a conflicting interest in a transaction:

A fundamental component of the fiduciary duties of directors in every jurisdiction, however, is that directors owe a duty of loyalty to the institution they serve. This duty prohibits directors from engaging in transactions that involve conflicts of interest with the institution. . . .

The threshold inquiry in assessing whether a director violated his duty of loyalty is whether the director has a conflicting interest in the transaction. Directors are considered to be "interested" if they either "appear on both sides of a transaction [ ]or expect to derive any personal financial benefit from it in the sense of self-dealing, as opposed to a benefit which devolves upon the corporation or all stockholders generally."

*In re Bush*, OTS AP 91-16 at 11, 15-16, 1991 WL 540753 at 5, 6, 1991 OTS DD LEXIS at *18, *21 (footnote and citations omitted). The RMBCA defines a director's conflicting interest transaction as "a transaction effected or proposed to be effected by the corporation . . . respecting which a director of the corporation has a conflicting interest." RMBCA § 8.60(2) (1992). Perhaps because this definition tautologically defines the defined in terms of itself, the Commissioners, in commentary, observed that "[t]o constitute a director's conflicting interest transaction, *there must first be a transaction by the corporation, its subsidiary, or controlled entity in which the director has a financial interest.*" RMBCA § 8.6 comment 2(1) (emphasis added).

As Seidman points out, Crestmont never granted any loan secured by property whose sale could reduce Seidman's obligation on his guarantee or UJB's exposure on its loan to FSA, nor did Seidman ever promise anyone that Crestmont would make such loans in exchange for his release. OTS clearly suspected that Seidman promised UJB Crestmont's favorable consideration for end-user loans on FSA properties in return for UJB's release. Suspicion is not enough, however, and OTS's suspicion that Seidman had promised he would use his position at Crestmont to insure end-user financing on the FSA project is not supported by substantial evidence. Risko's letter does not show any such *quid pro quo* in either of its versions. Indeed, if we accept the Director's finding that Seidman prepared the original draft, the version of the evidence most favorable to OTS, it appears that Risko took pains to make it clear to UJB that no *quid pro quo* was promised in the version Risko finally sent to UJB without any objection from Seidman. The evidence on this record is just as consistent with a finding that UJB released Seidman because Crestmont was a good prospect for the end-user financing it needed to reduce its own exposure on a worrisome project as it is with the conclusion that UJB granted the release in exchange for Seidman's unlawful promise to use his influence to obtain Crestmont's approval of loans that would reduce its exposure on FSA's Boonton project and to favor end-user loans on the Levine property or any other property in the Boonton project.[32]

OTS's position puts Seidman in a "Catch-22." If he remained liable on his guarantee to UJB, Crestmont would be unable to consider potentially profitable end-user loans on the Boonton project; but when Seidman acted to secure a release from the guarantee, he subjected himself to removal from Crestmont's Board. The only way Seidman could avoid the conflict of interest that OTS saw in his relation to FSA was to extricate himself from the FSA partnership and all the entanglements it entailed, including the guarantee. This record shows that this is what he did. Moreover, when we consider the whole record, as we must, we see substantial evidence that Seidman did not act as he did to benefit himself at Crestmont's expense, but rather because he wished to eliminate outside interests that could have a potential for conflict with Crestmont's interests. Corporate law imposes a duty of loyalty not because the conflict appears improper to a third party but to "'prevent[ ] a conflict of opposing interest *in the minds of fiduciaries*, whose duty it is to act solely for the benefit of their beneficiaries.'" *FSLIC v. Molinaro*, 889 F.2d 899, 904 (9th Cir. 1989) (quoting *Restatement of Restitution* § 197 comment c (1937)) (emphasis added). This record shows Seidman acted to avoid that conflict, not because of it.

We do not think every appearance of wrongdoing justifies the sanction of removal and prohibition. Rather, we believe such a drastic sanction should require some evidence of actual misconduct or evidence from which a reasonable person acquainted with the facts could conclude there was misconduct. Here, Crestmont never made any loan to an end-user on the FSA project, and Seidman told Bailey to stop considering any loans in which Seidman had an interest before OTS began its investigation. Seidman did so as soon as he realized he could not persuade OTS that his guarantee did not matter. Seidman's earlier attempts to persuade OTS to the contrary were not improper. Viewed as a whole, we think this record contains substantial evidence that Seidman acted to further the interests of Crestmont, not just his own, when he attempted to obtain

---

[32]     Additional evidence which supports a conclusion that UJB's recognition that Crestmont could not lawfully supply end-user loans on the Boonton project unless UJB released Seidman's guarantee motivated its approval of the release. It shows that the release was good business for UJB, Seidman and Crestmont because it increased the pool of potential lenders in a tight market and gave Crestmont an opportunity to acquire good loans on their merits.

a release from his guarantee, and therefore his actions did not constitute a breach of the fiduciary duty of loyalty contained in section 1818(e)(1)(A)(iii).

In summary, we hold Seidman's conduct in seeking a release from the UJB guarantee did not violate any "law or regulation" under section 1818(e)(1)(A)(i)(I) or constitute an "unsafe or unsound" practice under section 1818(e)(1)(A)(ii) or a breach of fiduciary duty under section 1818(e)(1)(A)(iii). To the extent the Director relied on Seidman's conduct of seeking a release from his guarantee of FSA's indebtedness to UJB to support the order of removal and prohibition, the Director erred. . . .

### C. *Seidman's Attempt to Hinder the OTS Investigation*

Finally, we must consider whether Seidman's actions during the pendency of the OTS investigation support removal and prohibition. The Director found Seidman lied in his deposition of September 13, 1991, destroyed material evidence and encouraged Risko to testify falsely about events surrounding the draft of Risko's letter to UJB. The Director stated:

The OTS has a right to accurate and reliable information in the course of its examinations and investigations. Seidman's lack of integrity, evidenced by his misleading testimony, his attempts to destroy evidence and his attempts to solicit false and misleading testimony, poses as a natural consequence an abnormal risk of loss or damage to the institution, the very essence of an unsafe or unsound practice. The Director concludes that Seidman committed an unsafe and unsound practice by these attempts to obstruct the OTS investigation. . . .

Seidman benefitted from his efforts by depriving the OTS of reliable and material evidence, thwarting the OTS enforcement action and hampering the prompt resolution of the self-dealing charges. Seidman demonstrated personal dishonesty by giving misleading testimony and omitting material facts during an OTS investigation and examination; destroying evidence; and soliciting another witness to give false testimony and destroy material evidence.

Seidman App. at 119-20. While the Director did not directly relate his conclusions to the statutory requirements, it is clear he concluded that Seidman's conduct during the investigation constituted an unsafe or unsound practice under section 1818(e)(1)(A)(ii) and that Seidman satisfied the effect component of section 1818(e)(1)(B)(iii) by receiving a personal benefit.

We agree with the Director that hindering an OTS investigation is an unsafe or unsound practice as that term has come to be used in the banking industry. Section 1818(e)(1)(A) can be satisfied by evidence showing the conduct with which an affiliated person like Seidman is charged falls within section 1818(e)(1)(A)(ii)'s proscription of unsafe or unsound practices because it "is contrary to generally accepted standards of prudent operation" and "the possible consequences of [the act], if continued, would be abnormal risk or loss or damage to . . . the agenc[y] administering the insurance fund [ ]." *Gulf Federal Sav. & Loan Ass'n*, 651 F.2d at 264 (quotation omitted); *see also supra* Part V. We believe an attempt to obstruct an OTS investigation is such an act. OTS is statutorily charged with preserving the financial integrity of the thrift system. See 12 U.S.C.A. 1462a (West Supp. 1994); *id.* § 1463(a). To meet that responsibility, OTS has the power to investigate. See 12 C.F.R. § 509.16 (1993). Where a party attempts to induce another to withhold material information from the agency, the agency becomes unable to fulfill its regulatory function. Such behavior, if continued, strikes at the heart of the regulatory function. Seidman's attempt to obstruct the investigation, if continued, would pose an abnormal risk of damage to OTS. Accordingly, we hold that an attempt to hinder an OTS investigation constitutes an "unsafe or unsound practice," thus satisfying the act requirement of section 1818(e)(1)(A). . . .

## IX. *Conclusion*

For these reasons, we will grant Bailey's petition for review and reverse that part of the Director's order commanding him to cease and desist. We will also grant Seidman's petition for review of that portion of the Director's order removing him from his position as director and chairman of the board of Crestmont, reverse it and remand Seidman's case to the Director for further proceedings consistent with this opinion. Finally, we will vacate that part of the Director's order temporarily suspending Seidman from his office at Crestmont and from participating in Crestmont's business activities.

## Comments and Questions

1. It appears that the definition of unsafe or unsound banking practice suggested by the court includes two elements. The first requirement is that there be some violation of accepted standards of banking operations. The second element is an abnormal risk of loss or damage to the institution. Do you agree with the definition? The circuits are split on the proper definition of unsafe or unsound banking practice. For example, *Seidman* was expressly rejected in *Greene County Bank v. Federal Deposit Insurance Corp.*, 92 F.3d 633 (8th Cir. 1996), where the court stated that "It is well-settled in this Circuit, however, that an 'unsafe or unsound practice' exists where the conduct is 'deemed contrary to accepted standards of banking operations which might result in abnormal risk or loss to a banking institution or shareholder'", thus rejecting the requirement the practice have a reasonably direct effect on the bank's financial soundness.

2. Notice how a finding of an unsafe or unsound banking practice can serve as the basis for applying all of the supervisory enforcement powers—cease and desist, officer removal and prohibition, and civil money penalty. Also notice that the lack of a detailed definition of unsafe or unsound enables the regulatory agencies to challenge a broad range of claimed misconduct.

3. Is the range of conduct potentially encompassed by the term "unsafe or unsound banking practices" so broad as to be unfair, or is there a principled basis? Note the court's discussion concerning directors' fiduciary duties, particularly the duty of care and the business judgment rule. Are both the unsafe or unsound banking practices concept and the business judgment rule concept statements of a general duty of care of officers and directors? What are the possible similarities and differences between the two concepts of duty?

4. Do you agree with the holding of the case? Consider two factors; first, the standard of review and second, the question of risk of loss to the depository institution. For the court to hold as it did, it had to find that the determination of unsafe or unsound,

in the context of risk of loss, was not based in any substantial evidence. Note that the court did not disagree with the factual determination that Seidman had engaged in undisclosed negotiations with UJB to secure release of a $4.5 million personal obligation by intimating to UJB that Cresmont was willing to make end-user loans to financially qualified purchasers from a UJB debtor. How does this fact relate to the requirement of "abnormal risk of loss or damage?" Is that element not met here because the specific conduct engaged in in this particular case did not result in a loss? Is this the correct way to analyze the risk element, or should the risk element be found if loss ultimately is likely to occur if similar conduct were continued? While Seidman did not make a legally binding commitment to UJB on behalf of Cresmont, might his actions have a significant potential for affecting decisions at both UJB and Cresmont?

5. Why is the misleading testimony of Seidman an unsafe or unsound practice? Is it because the testimony constitutes perjury? Is it enough if the testimony is misleading?

6. How about Mr. Bailey? Bailey, probably influenced by Seidman, made a decision to commit the bank to Levine when Seidman had a conflicting interest that could influence Bailey's decision. In addition, it is obvious that Bailey had no plan to submit Levine's loan application to the senior loan committee before the financing was issued. In other words, Bailey agreed to enter into a substantial loan at a time when Seidman's personal fortunes were very much still tied to those of his real estate investment partnership.

7. FDICIA added 12 U.S.C.A. § 1831p-1, requiring the bank regulatory agencies to issue guidelines or regulations establishing standards for safety and soundness governing (1) internal controls, information systems, and internal audit systems; (2) loan documentation; (3) credit underwriting; (4) interest rate exposure; (5) asset growth; (6) compensation, fees and benefits; and (7) asset quality, earnings, and stock valuation. If a bank fails to meet the standards, it must develop a plan specifying how the deficiencies will be corrected, and the agencies may levy supervisory enforcement sanctions, without a formal hearing, for failure to do so. The stated purpose of the guidelines is to identify and address problems before capital becomes impaired. Regulatory guidelines became effective in 1995, providing vague standards such as that loans should be "prudent," and should consider concentrations of credit risk and the character, creditworthiness, and collateral offered by borrowers. What new benefit is gained by such regulation of safety and soundness? Does it expand safety and soundness beyond capital and solvency concerns? Does it alter the procedure for enforcement of perceived safety and soundness violations, much like the capital directive process we saw in *Choushatta*?

*Problem 5-1*

You are on the legal staff of the FDIC.  Bank examiners have brought the following matters to your attention and wish to know whether you consider them unsafe or unsound practices.  The FDIC wants to consider taking further action, as bank management in each case has shown itself unwilling to alter the situation voluntarily.  *Also see* 12 U.S.C.A. § 1821(e).

1.  Bank A has transferred $500,000 of its assets to Bank B to hold in escrow.  The money is to be used to make payments to several of Bank A's officers pursuant to employment agreements between those officers and the bank.  Among the events that would trigger the payments is the receivership of Bank A.  The position of the bank is that the agreements are legitimate means for Bank A to avoid losing key officials and management personnel.  The bank had a composite CAMELS rating of three for the past year.

2.  Bank C has permitted the securities discount brokerage subsidiary of its parent bank holding company to place offices in several of its bank lobbies.  Bank C is not charging any rent to the discount brokerage subsidiary.  The bank has a composite CAMELS rating of one.

3.  Under 12 U.S.C.A. § 84, a loan commitment ordinarily is not an extension of credit subject to that section's lending limits.  Bank D has entered into a large number of loan commitment agreements in order to generate immediate fee income.  Many holders of commitments are in difficult financial circumstances and will need to rely on these previously contracted arrangements in order to continue in business.  The bank has a composite CAMELS rating of four.

# Section 3.  Supervisory Enforcement Powers

## A.  Introduction

A reading of 12 U.S.C.A. §§ 1818, 1831o, and 3907 shows that the supervisory enforcement powers of the banking regulators go well beyond the basis of unsafe or unsound practices.  Perhaps because of the magnitude of the statutory supervisory enforcement powers of the bank regulators, there also exists an array of informal regulatory mechanisms to deal with the problems of troubled banks.

A regulator will identify problems based on either the filing of required reports or, more likely, a critical examination.  Typically the board of directors of the bank is asked to meet with the regulators.  A troubled bank may be faced with the choice of acquiescing with the terms of an informal supervisory action, or becoming enmeshed in a contested administrative enforcement proceeding.  However, the bank may persuade the examiners that the proposed action is not justified because, for example, the criticized matter has already been corrected, or there is some misunderstanding by the examiner.  In other words the first goal may well be to change the regulator's perception of the problem.

Second, there is often room for negotiation, as regulators also have limited resources to engage in extensive administrative proceedings.

The regulators utilize various phrasings to describe their informal supervisory actions. The terminology includes a board of directors' resolution, a commitment letter, and a memorandum of understanding. Although informal actions are not legally enforceable, a failure to honor informal actions often is viewed as strong evidence of the need for formal action.

The first level of informal action is a board of directors resolution, which is used to address minor deficiencies in well-run institutions. The board of directors of the institution passes a resolution which contains provisions tailored to respond to the deficiencies noted by the agency. The content of the resolution is suggested by the agency with the request that the board pass the resolution and notify the agency of that action. The second level of informal action is a commitment letter, which is used for institutions that are in good overall condition with minor problems in isolated areas of activity. The commitment letter is prepared by the agency and sent to the board of directors of the depository institution. The board is asked to execute the letter in which they agree to undertake certain commitments to correct the identified deficiencies.

A written memorandum of understanding is essentially a consensus between the regulator and the bank's board of directors as to what action should be taken. This informal action usually occurs where there are new problems that have developed recently. A memorandum of understanding is usually prepared by the agency. It is written in a style similar to that of a cease and desist order and contains provisions which require the depository institution to establish a business plan to correct the problems identified by the regulatory agency.

One provision of FIRREA requires that the banking agencies make public all final administrative orders and modifications or terminations of such orders. 12 U.S.C.A. § 1818(u). An institution desiring to avoid public attention thus may be encouraged to agree to informal supervisory action. When substantial compliance with an informal enforcement arrangement is achieved, the depository institution can request that termination of the arrangement be granted by the agency.

Until 1966, the primary formal statutory supervisory power of bank regulators was the authority to revoke the charter or to terminate the insurance of a bank. The severity of this penalty was so great that its use as a remedial supervisory instrument was impractical. The power simply could not be used for any but the most egregious transgressions of sound banking principles. Also, such an administrative proceeding frequently took years before an effective remedy against the institution was available. However, FIRREA amended § 1818(a) so that the termination of deposit insurance may become a more effective regulatory tool. Section 1818(a)(8) now provides for temporary suspension of insurance, which results in suspension of FDIC coverage on all deposits received after the order. Suspension of insurance requires that the institution notify all depositors.

The lowest level of formal administrative action is a formal written agreement. A formal written agreement is a document signed by a bank's board of directors and the regulator in which specific corrective and remedial measures are enumerated as necessary to return the bank to a safe and sound condition. While a bank cannot be forced to enter into such an agreement, the alternative may well be adversarial supervisory proceedings, such as a cease and desist proceeding. To the extent that formal written agreements are used, they usually are found in serious situations, but still situations where the regulator is confident that management will correct the problem. It is standard for such agreements to provide that the agreement is enforceable as a final cease and desist order, so that the agreement can later be enforced in a court of law without an administrative hearing.

Most cease and desist proceedings are settled by consent through a stipulation signed by the bank and the regulator. Such stipulations often contain language to the effect that, by stipulating, the parties do not concede the validity of the allegations contained in the notice of charges. This avoids collateral estoppel should the same claim be raised by private litigants.

In 1966 banking regulators were given the authority to issue cease and desist orders if an institution had engaged in an unsafe or unsound practice or had violated any other stated ground for issuance of an order. See 12 U.S.C.A. § 1818(b). An order may be issued after a trial-type administrative hearing. A second power authorized was the temporary cease and desist order, effective upon service. See 12 U.S.C.A. § 1818(c). A third power was the power to remove or suspend officers and directors, generally if such persons were found to be dishonest individuals. The particular value of this added power is that it enabled regulators to go directly against the individuals who caused the problem rather than against the institution.

In 1978 a further significant device was added, the civil money penalty, which can be assessed against any institution or person violating the terms of a cease and desist order that has become final. 12 U.S.C.A. § 1818(i). This power was thought to give the regulators greater flexibility in the imposition of sanctions, particularly against individuals. The sanction can be graded and utilized in instances where removal may be too harsh a penalty.

The passage of FIRREA in 1989 resulted in substantial changes to all supervisory enforcement powers. It broadened the group of individuals subject to supervisory enforcement powers to include "institution-affiliated parties": any person required to file a change in bank control notice; all shareholders, consultants, officers, directors, and others who participate in the conduct of an institution's affairs; and independent contractors (expressly including attorneys, appraisers and accountants) who knowingly or recklessly participate in violations of law that are likely to cause a significant adverse effect upon the institution. The Act broadened the remedies that the regulators can enforce in cease and desist proceedings to include payment of damages for losses caused to the bank, rather than having initially to seek such relief in court. Also, regulators may seek to remove an institution–affiliated party when the institution has been harmed or prejudiced, without requiring that the harm be substantial or the prejudice serious. Finally, the civil money penalty authority was dramatically expanded. FIRREA established a three-tier system of money penalties beginning with a maximum penalty of $5,000 per day for minor violations and escalating to a maximum penalty of $1 million per day for the most serious violations. The full range of these regulatory powers can only be discerned by a careful and complete reading of the statutes involved, particularly § 1818.

The bank regulators were given new authority under FDICIA in 1991 to take certain "prompt corrective action" (PCA) to resolve a bank's problems. Actions taken depend on a bank's capital level. For example, if a bank becomes undercapitalized it is required to submit a capital restoration plan. Depending on the severity of a bank's problems, a PCA directive can also be issued. During 1994, ten banks were required to submit a capital restoration plan, and two PCA directives were issued. The purpose of the legislation was to resolve a bank's problems at the least possible long-term cost to the deposit insurance fund. As we will see in section four, least cost disposition of failed banks has become a dominant policy concern.

Finally, while we will not further discuss the criminal aspects of banking law, it is worth knowing that the maximum criminal fine for certain financial institution offenses was raised from $5,000 to $1 million, the maximum jail term raised from 5 years to 20 years, and the statute of limitations increased from 5 years to 10 years. Also, the federal forfeiture statute, 18 U.S.C.A. § 981, was amended to expand the ability of the United States Justice Department to seize gains attributable to bank fraud offenses. The Act further provides that violations of 18 U.S.C.A. § 1344, the general bank fraud statute, constitute predicate acts under RICO. RICO also contains substantial forfeiture provisions.

## B. Cease and Desist Power

The agencies did not begin to use their supervisory enforcement powers until the mid-1970s. The first major case reviewing bank regulatory cease and desist orders was *First National Bank of Eden v. Department of the Treasury*, 568 F.2d 610 (8th Cir. 1977). Today, regulators may issue both permanent and temporary cease and desist orders. Such orders typically are based on one of two generic situations. The first is engaging in an unsafe or unsound banking practice. The second is a violation of applicable law or regulations pertaining to the depository institution. The remedies can involve a prohibitory injunction and affirmative corrective action—payment of restitution or reimbursement, or providing indemnification and guarantee against potential loss. See 12 U.S.C.A. § 1818(b)(6) and (7). Finally, the cease and desist orders and the remedies can be effective against both institutions and institution-affiliated parties.

### Problem 5-2

You represent Hibernia Bank and Trust, whose balance sheet and other financial statements are set out below. The bank president is worried because he has just received a Notice of Charges and of Hearing from the FDIC, which is proposing to issue a cease and desist order. The FDIC is primarily concerned that the bank has taken on a number of risky loans in an effort to improve earnings. The average of total loans to assets of banks in the state in 1996 was 58%. The relevant sections of the Notice are as follows:

(1) The Bank, its directors, officers and agents have engaged and are continuing to engage in unsafe and unsound practices in conducting the business of the Bank by following hazardous lending and collection practices and policies in that as of December 31, 1996, the Bank's adversely classified loans aggregated 9.4% of the total dollar volume of $109,840,334.

| | |
|---|---|
| Substandard | $ 6,774,750 |
| Doubtful | 2,603,210 |
| Loss | 935,594 |
| | $10,313,554 |

(2) ". . . in that that as of December 31, 1996 the Bank has allowed the total volume of loans and mortgages to exceed 76% of total deposits and to exceed 68% of total assets.

(3) ". . . in that the Bank has failed to diversify its securities portfolio. As of December 31, 1996 the Bank had investments in municipal bonds aggregating $30,704,761, or 214.4% of total book capital and reserves of $14.3 million. The municipal bonds have an average maturity of twenty-two years."

The board of directors has asked your judgment on two matters: (1) The Bank has not violated any specific law or regulation in its lending and securities activities. Does the FDIC have any right in these circumstances to take any action? What are the parameters which determine whether the FDIC has such a right? (2) If the FDIC should institute cease and desist proceedings, do you think you could successfully prevail in those proceedings based on the data given?

Counsel from the FDIC contacts you with the following proposal. The bank could avoid the embarrassment of a hearing and the possibility of a publicly disclosed order if it would stipulate to certain facts and consent to a cease and desist order. The FDIC would require the following:

1. The Bank would have to charge off 100% of the loans classified as "Loss" and 50% of the loans classified as "Doubtful". Substandard loans must be reduced. "Reduce" would mean to collect, to charge off, or to improve the quality of the loan (i.e., demand more security).

2. The Bank would have to agree not to extend credit to any borrower whose loan is now classified as "doubtful" or "loss."

3. The Bank would have to reduce its holdings of municipal bonds by $12 million per year until the total volume of municipal bonds equal $6 million or not more than 50% of bank capital and reserves.

4. Within thirty days the Bank would adopt and thereafter strictly follow written loan policies acceptable to the FDIC. The written loan policies would govern, but not be limited to, the following areas:

(a) The general fields of lending in which the Bank will engage and the kinds or types of loans within each general field;

(b) The lending authority of each loan officer;

(c) The lending authority of an executive or loan committee, if any;

(d) The responsibility of the board of directors in reviewing, ratifying, or approving loans;

(e) The guidelines under which unsecured loans will be granted;

(f) The guidelines for rates of interest and the terms of repayment for (i) unsecured loans and (ii) the documentation required by the Bank for each type of secured loan;

(g) The maintenance and review of complete and current credit files on each borrower;

(h) Appropriate and adequate collection procedures, including, but not limited to, the actions to be taken against borrowers who fail to make timely payments;

(i) Appropriate limitations on the extension of credit through overdrafts; and

(j) A description of the Bank's normal trade area and the circumstances under which the Bank may extend credit outside of such area.

5.  With regard to internal routine and controls, the Bank would adopt a corrective program which would require the Bank to do at least the following:

(a) Establish and maintain satisfactory liability ledger records;

(b) Maintain negotiable collateral under dual control;

(c) Rearrange the duties of employees so as to preclude one person from performing additional functions which give the person sole control over particular transactions or accounts;

(d) Provide for periodic review or audit of accrued or deferred accounts including unearned discount and similar accounts;

(e) Provide for an audit program by:

(i) Employment of a full-time internal auditor, or

(ii) Periodic employment of an independent auditor, or

(iii) Designation of an audit supervisor and an established program of internal audit by the Bank's own staff.

(f) Place the working supply of travelers' checks under the sole control of the person responsible for them; and

(g) Maintain charged-off assets under dual control.

At the meeting of the board of directors, the Bank president gave the following statement against acceptance of the FDIC proposal.

Hibernia Bank and Trust is one of the most profitable and community oriented banks in our community.  Each year's earnings have been greater than the last; in 1996 the bank earned $15.94 per share which is the highest rate in the bank's history and more than twice the 1995 rate of $6.39 per share. This earning level is the result of hard work on the part of an active and innovative management.

The FDIC proposes to cut by 80% the bank's investments in long-term municipal bonds which have enhanced the earning potential of Hibernia. Generally, the interest rate on long-term municipal bonds is much higher than other short-term investments. The municipal bonds held by Hibernia pay a return of 7% while shorter-term municipal bonds would earn 4-5%.

The long-term bonds also provide an important public service. Through its Municipal Finance Division, Hibernia serves about twenty-five municipalities. The municipalities are responsible for some $5 million in time deposits, the largest aggregate amount in the community. Hibernia has also become one of the few banks that bid on investments of all school districts in the community. In addition the bank has begun a follow-up service to maintain continual relationships with each client district.

The FDIC also proposes to dictate Hibernia's loan procedures and has complained that some of our loans are "risky." Hibernia has begun a policy of granting loans which do have a greater element of risk as defined by the bank examiners, but which also carry a higher interest rate. By our bank's standards, these loans are made to creditworthy individuals and businesses. The bank management is convinced that the bank's investments are now earning the highest rate of return and are also providing an important community service.

Hibernia has granted mortgage loans to several industrial concerns equal to 95% of the fair market value of the plants that are mortgaged. In 1996, loans were made totaling $10 million to manufacturers to expand, modernize or streamline operations in order to increase production. Ten loans, totaling $500,000 and including three "special consideration" loans, were made in 1996 to minority-owned businesses such as restaurants, a computer school, garages, grocery store, liquor store and ice cream store franchises. With almost $110 million loans outstanding Hibernia serves twice as many customers who are based in this community than any other bank. These customers include hospitals, schools, doctors, dentists and a variety of commercial enterprises. More money channeled into community investments means more jobs and more money ultimately being banked in the community.

Overall, the FDIC proposals will limit Hibernia's more profitable and community oriented activities. If the FDIC successfully forces Hibernia to conform with the conservative practices of other banks, the current rapid growth of bank earnings will be stifled and ultimately the community will suffer.

What do you as counsel for the bank recommend? How do you respond to the president's arguments?

## STATEMENT OF CONDITION

| As of December 31, | 1996 | 1995 |
|---|---|---|
| ASSETS | | |
| Cash and Due from Banks | $ 5,883,503 | $ 19,863,088 |
| Investment Securities–at Amortized Cost | | |
|     U.S. Treasury Securities | 7,524,244 | 17,873,007 |
|     Project Notes and Public Housing Authority | | |
|       Bonds (U.S. Gov't guaranteed) | 4,029,865 | 10,497,222 |
|     Securities of other U.S. Gov't Agencies | 1,827,910 | 7,612,951 |
|     Obligations of States and Political | | |
|       Subdivisions | 30,704,761 | 23,190,130 |
|     Other Securities | 733,577 | 2,307,958 |
| Total Investment Securities | $ 44,820,357 | $ 61,481,268 |
| Federal Funds Sold | -0- | -0- |
| Loans | | |
|     Loans and Discounts | $ 73,410,251 | $ 38,131,202 |
|     Real Estate Mortgages | 36,430,083 | 36,396,393 |
| Total Loans | $109,840,334 | $ 74,527,595 |
| Bank Premises and Equipment | 1,058,775 | 2,904,900 |
| Other Assets | 330,850 | 1,303,512 |
|     TOTAL ASSETS | $161,933,819 | $160,080,363 |
| LIABILITIES | | |
| Deposits | | |
|     Demand Deposits | $ 59,426,613 | $ 57,158,676 |
|     Time Deposits | 85,422,766 | 87,152,312 |
| Total Deposits | $144,849,379 | $140,310,988 |
| Unearned Income | 2,175,347 | 2,028,018 |
| Other Liabilities | 585,327 | 566,965 |
| Total Liabilities | $147,610,053 | $146,905,971 |
| Reserve for Losses on Loans | $ 1,355,066 | $ 1,262,501 |
| CAPITAL ACCOUNTS | | |
| Capital Notes (Rate 5% Due serially to | | |
|   October  15, 2009) | $ 700,000 | $ 800,000 |
| Stockholders' Equity: | | |
|     Common Stock, $10 Par Value | 2,727,130 | 2,159,040 |
|     Number shares outstanding 1996– | | |
|       272,713; 1995–215,904. | | |
| Surplus | 6,168,362 | 6,062,826 |
| Retained Earnings | 3,373,208 | 2,890,025 |
|     Total Stockholders' Equity | $ 12,268,700 | $ 11,111,891 |
|     Total Capital Accounts | $ 12,968,700 | $ 11,911,891 |
|     TOTAL LIABILITIES, RESERVE AND | | |
|       CAPITAL ACCOUNTS | $161,933,819 | $160,080,363 |

## COMPARATIVE STATEMENT OF EARNINGS

| As of December 31, | 1996 | 1995 |
|---|---|---|
| OPERATING INCOME | | |
| Interest and Fees on Loans | $ 8,219,981 | $ 5,180,432 |
| Interest on Federal Funds Sold | 383,416 | 101,396 |
| Interest and Dividends on Investments | | |
| U.S. Treasury Securities | 1,006,733 | 1,162,285 |
| Securities of other U.S. Gov't Agencies and Corporations | 327,978 | 473,290 |
| Obligations of States and Political Subdivisions | 2,382,754 | 1,318,547 |
| Other Securities | 120,765 | 132,273 |
| Trust Department Income | 414,116 | 318,953 |
| Service Charges on Deposit Accounts | 399,500 | 370,741 |
| Other Service Charges, Collection and Exchange Charges, Commissions and Fees | 190,008 | 149,873 |
| Other Operating Income | 36,808 | 33,562 |
| Total Operating Income | $ 13,482,059 | $ 9,241,352 |
| OPERATING EXPENSES | | |
| Salaries and Wages | $ 2,036,938 | $ 1,874,804 |
| Pensions and Other Employee Benefits | 559,370 | 516,742 |
| Interest on Deposits | 3,998,998 | 3,560,294 |
| Interest on Federal Funds Purchased | -0- | 12,156 |
| Interest on Borrowed Money | 9,397 | 4,764 |
| Interest on Capital Notes | 39,167 | 44,167 |
| Occupancy Expense of Bank Premises, Net | 472,555 | 449,063 |
| Furniture and Equipment Depreciation, Rental Costs, Servicing, Etc. | 284,019 | 251,069 |
| Provision for Loan Losses | 124,727 | 100,039 |
| Other | 1,233,369 | 1,022,974 |
| Total Operating Expenses | $ 8,758,540 | $ 7,836,072 |
| Income before Income Taxes and Security Gains or Losses | $ 4,723,519 | $ 1,405,280 |
| Applicable Income Taxes | 361,682 | 36,976 |
| Income before Security Gains or Losses | $ 4,361,837 | $ 1,368,304 |
| Net Securities Gains (Losses) after Income Tax Credit of $17,633 in 1996 and Income Tax of $10,433 in 1995 | (15,609) | 10,284 |
| NET INCOME | $ 4,346,228 | $ 1,378,588 |

# Rapaport v. Office of Thrift Supervision
## 59 F.3d 212 (D.C. Cir. 1995), *cert. denied*, 116 S. Ct. 775 (1996)

GINSBURG, Circuit Judge:

Robert D. Rapaport was the majority shareholder of a savings and loan association that failed. Thereafter the Office of Thrift Supervision, as successor to the Federal Savings and Loan Insurance Corporation, ordered him to pay approximately $1.5 million pursuant to his agreement personally to maintain the capital in the institution at no less than the minimum required by regulation. We hold that because the OTS has not shown that Rapaport was "unjustly enriched," it may not enforce the agreement against him in an administrative (as opposed to judicial) proceeding. Accordingly, we grant Rapaport's petition for review and set aside the agency's order.

## I. Background

Great Life Savings Association of Sunrise, Florida, a state-chartered institution, applied to the FSLIC for deposit insurance in April 1984. While Great Life's application was pending, the Federal Home Loan Bank Board–the governing body of the FSLIC–promulgated a regulation requiring that any individual who owned 25% or more of the stock of a newly insured savings association "personally guarantee the maintenance of the association's net worth at the regulatorily required level." See 49 Fed. Reg. 41237, 41244 (Oct. 22, 1984), codified at 12 C.F.R. § 571.6(c)(4)(i) (1985). Accordingly, when the FHLBB approved Great Life's application, it did so upon the condition that Rapaport, who planned to purchase 74% of the Great Life's shares, enter into a Net Worth Maintenance Agreement with the FSLIC.

Rapaport ultimately purchased 69.9% of Great Life's stock. In March 1985 he entered into a five-year Agreement that provided:

> [I]n consideration of the FSLIC granting insurance of accounts to the Association, the Acquiror agrees . . . pursuant to the requirements of 12 C.F.R. § 571.6(4), or any successor regulation thereto, to maintain the Association's net worth in compliance with the Net Worth Requirement applicable to the Association, computed in accordance with 12 C.F.R. § 563.13, or any successor regulation then in effect.

The FHLBB approved Great Life's insurance application and the thrift opened for business in May 1985.

Owing primarily to the number of non-performing commercial real estate loans on its books, Great Life, like many thrift institutions in the late 1980s, began to experience capital deficiencies. In November 1989 the OTS notified Rapaport that Great Life's capital was deficient by $152,000 and asked him to contribute $106,248 (69.9% of the total) pursuant to the Agreement. Rapaport responded that he was expending "great effort"–but not by actually contributing any capital–to improve Great Life's financial health. After further investigation, the OTS determined that Great Life's capital deficiency amounted to some $3.5 million as of December 31, 1989. In June 1990 the Resolution Trust Corporation was appointed receiver of Great Life, which has since been liquidated.

The OTS began an administrative proceeding against Rapaport in July 1990.  In April 1993 an Administrative Law Judge found that:  (1) Rapaport's role in the activities of Great Life "was limited solely to that of a stockholder"; (2) Rapaport was "unjustly enriched within the meaning of [12 U.S.C. § 1818(b)(6)(A)(i) ]" because he received the benefit of Great Life's having deposit insurance while retaining the capital he was supposed to contribute under the Agreement; and (3) under the Agreement Rapaport was obliged to contribute $1,946,000 to help cover Great Life's capital deficiency.

The Acting Director of the OTS affirmed the ALJ's decision, though he corrected it insofar as the ALJ had suggested that the benefit of insurance received by Great Life, rather than Rapaport's retention of what the Agreement allegedly required him to pay, was the basis for holding that Rapaport had been "unjustly enriched." (He also reduced Rapaport's liability to $1,536,675 based upon a revised valuation of one of Great Life's loans.)  Like the ALJ, the Acting Director based his decision that Rapaport was liable for his unjust enrichment upon Rapaport's personal responsibility, as a stockholder, for Great Life's capital shortfall; he did not rely upon any role that Rapaport might have played in the management of Great Life.

. . . Rapaport claims that the OTS failed to show that he was "unjustly enriched," as required by this court's decision in *Wachtel v. OTS*, 982 F.2d 581 (D.C. Cir. 1993). . . .

## II.  Analysis

Though we conclude that the OTS does have the authority administratively to enforce an agreement to which the FSLIC was a party, we also hold that the OTS failed in this case to make the required showing that Rapaport was "unjustly enriched."  We therefore set aside the agency's decision without addressing Rapaport's last two arguments. . . .

### B.  Unjust enrichment

In order for the OTS to order a party to undertake any "affirmative action to correct conditions resulting from violations or practices," it must show either that the party has been "unjustly enriched" or that his conduct "involved a reckless disregard for the law or any applicable regulations or prior order of [a] Federal banking agency."  12 U.S.C. § 1818(b)(6)(A); see *Wachtel v. OTS*, 982 F.2d 581, 586 (D.C. Cir. 1993).  The OTS's only theory throughout this case has been that Rapaport was "unjustly enriched," and therefore it must show as much before it can require him to pay a pro rata share of Great Life's capital deficiency.

The Acting Director's sole basis for concluding that Rapaport had, in fact, been unjustly enriched was simply that Rapaport "retain[ed] funds . . . belong [ing] to [Great Life]"–i.e., the contested capital contribution–"while [Great Life] received the benefits of deposit insurance." Rapaport claims that this is insufficient to make out a case of unjust enrichment within the meaning of § 1818(b)(6)(A), and we agree.

As a preliminary matter, the OTS argues that we should defer to its construction of § 1818 under *Chevron, U.S.A., Inc. v. Natural Resources Defense Council*, 467 U.S. 837 (1984).  We have already held in *Wachtel* that we owe no such deference to the OTS's interpretation of § 1818 because that agency shares responsibility for the administration of the statute with at least three other agencies. 982 F.2d at 585.  The alternative would lay the groundwork for a regulatory regime in which either the same statute is interpreted differently by the several agencies or the one agency that happens to reach the courthouse first is allowed to fix the meaning of the text for all.

Neither outcome is unthinkable, of course, but neither has the OTS suggested any reason to believe that the congressional delegation of administrative authority contemplates such peculiar corollaries. *Cf. Bowen v. American Hospital Association*, 476 U.S. 610, 642 n.30 (1986) (refusing to defer to agency's construction of Rehabilitation Act because "not the same basis for deference predicated on expertise" as in *Chevron*); *see also CF Industries, Inc. v. FERC*, 925 F.2d 476, 478 & n.1 (D.C. Cir. 1991) (dictum implying deference may be due when all agencies concerned "agree as to the which of them has exclusive jurisdiction"). Hence, we proceed de novo.

"Unjust enrichment" is a term of art at common law and we must presume that the Congress used it as such, *mutatis mutandis*, when it imported the term into the field of bank regulation. Turning to a commentary upon the common law, we learn that the fundamental characteristic of unjust enrichment is "that the defendant has been unjustly enriched by receiving something . . . that properly belongs to the plaintiff[, thereby] forcing restoration to the plaintiff." Dobbs, *Law of Remedies* § 4.1(2). The law of Florida is typical: The elements of a cause of action based upon unjust enrichment are that: (1) the plaintiff conferred a benefit upon the defendant; (2) the defendant accepted and retained the benefit; and (3) it would be unjust for the defendant not to pay the plaintiff the value of the benefit. *See, e.g., Hillman Construction Corp. v. Wainer*, 636 So. 2d 576, 577 (Fla. App. 1994).

The agency's argument that Rapaport was "unjustly enriched" by his failure to pay the amount he allegedly owed under the Agreement is deeply flawed, for it fails to satisfy even the first element of a claim for unjust enrichment. If Rapaport "benefitted" from his failure to contribute capital to Great Life–and that is at best an odd way to describe what happened–it was not because the OTS or its predecessor conferred something upon him. Nor did Rapaport profit from Great Life's continued operation because of anything that the agency did to shore up the institution. Rapaport just failed to pay up as allegedly required by his contract. A breach of contract might give rise to liability for damages measured by the loss to the plaintiff, but unjust enrichment simply does not lie when the plaintiff has not bestowed some sort of benefit upon the defendant.

At best, the FSLIC conferred an indirect benefit upon Rapaport in that it allowed him to own more than 25% of the shares in a federally insured institution (the direct beneficiary of the Agreement being Great Life). In other words, Rapaport got the opportunity to invest more than otherwise would have been allowed. (Ultimately, of course, his investment was worth nothing, but Rapaport's opportunity to invest was presumably of some value ex ante.) Nothing in either the ALJ's or the Acting Director's decision indicates that Rapaport received any other benefit from the FSLIC or from Great Life (at which he held no office).

There are two problems with the opportunity-to-invest-more concept of "benefit," however. First, it was not advanced in the decision of the OTS. Second, we doubt whether it would be sufficient in any event to establish that Rapaport was unjustly enriched.

Though the decisions of the ALJ and the Acting Director are somewhat opaque on the nature of the benefit, we know that they did not consider Rapaport's opportunity to invest more the benefit that he received because the OTS has maintained throughout this proceeding that the amount of the benefit to Rapaport is the amount that he would have had to contribute to Great Life had he complied with the Agreement to the agency's satisfaction. That amount, however, bears no relation whatever to the value to Rapaport of the FSLIC insuring Great Life's deposits, either at the outset or at the time of his alleged default.  The $1.5 million Rapaport was allegedly required to contribute may arguably approximate the amount of the agency's loss attributable to Rapaport's alleged breach, but no principle in the law of restitution is more clear than this: "Restitution is measured by the defendant's unjust enrichment, not by the plaintiff's loss." Dobbs, *Restitution* at § 4.5(1).  The Acting Director actually paid lip service to this principle, but he ignored it in fact when he concluded that Rapaport was "unjustly enriched" by retaining the money he allegedly should have paid in under the Agreement.  That is the equivalent of saying that the defendant must cover the plaintiff's loss, lest the defendant's failure to do so enrich him. The argument is circular, hardly more than a play upon words.

What makes this case even harder to square with any recognizable notion of unjust enrichment is that Rapaport's alleged obligation to contribute more funds did not even arise until the value of Rapaport's right to hold stock in excess of 25 percent had become, for reasons not attributable to Rapaport himself, little more than the right to lose that much more money. Whatever the value of the opportunity that Rapaport received from the OTS in 1985, he had neither realized any benefit from nor even retained it as of late 1989, when the OTS came calling for more funds; there was by then simply no benefit that he could be required to disgorge.  See *Restatement of Restitution* § 142, Comment a (1937) ("When events are such that a loss must be suffered by one of the parties . . . justice does not require that the recipient should bear this loss where he is guilty of no greater fault than that of the claimant").

In short, the OTS has failed to demonstrate either that Rapaport was enriched or, if he was, why that enrichment was unjust.  With only the Acting Director's *ipse dixit* to support the agency's claim, we see no reason to conclude that Rapaport was "unjustly enriched" by his failure to contribute capital to Great Life.

Even if we were to read the term "unjustly enriched" in § 1818(b)(6)(A) as having something other than its ordinary meaning at common law, our analysis in *Wachtel* of the history of the statute and of the related case law would lead us to the same conclusion. . . .

Here Rapaport allegedly failed to abide by his Agreement to contribute capital; this might have contributed to (or at least accelerated) Great Life's insolvency, but it certainly did not enrich Rapaport.

In essence, the OTS would have us approve the administrative assessment of personal liability in every case where a party agrees, but ultimately fails, to maintain the required level of capital, regardless whether he gains personally from the operation of the institution. The Congress clearly contemplated something more than failing to uphold one's end of a contract when it required that a party have been "unjustly enriched" before he can be held personally liable in an administrative proceeding.

*Akin v. OTS*, 950 F.2d 1180 (5th Cir. 1992), is not necessarily to the contrary. Akin, like Rapaport, had agreed to maintain the required level of capital at a thrift institution that ultimately failed. *Id.* at 1182. Unlike Rapaport, however, Akin had been the sole shareholder, President, Chief Executive Officer, and Chairman of the Board of the failed institution. *Id.* at 1181. Had Rapaport received the benefits of office as Akin did, he may well have been "unjustly enriched," at least to that extent, and that distinction may be enough to reconcile the two cases. *See* 12 U.S.C. § 1818(b)(6)(A) (party may be ordered to "make restitution or provide reimbursement, indemnification, or guarantee against loss" if unjustly enriched). We express no view on the Fifth Circuit's implicit conclusion that once a party has been unjustly enriched, he may be held liable for the institution's loss, i.e., for an amount in excess of his own enrichment.

To the extent that Akin's enrichment does not serve to reconcile these two cases, we respectfully disagree with the Fifth Circuit. Responding to Akin's claim that he had not been unjustly enriched, that court acknowledged that the OTS's position did not "dovetail[ ] neatly into a pattern of transfer of a benefit and restitution of that benefit from a party wrongfully retaining it," but it refused to require "a precision fit" between the OTS's position and "black letter contract law." *Id.* at 1184. Rather, the court thought that the terms of the particular provision should be read broadly because the statute "[r]ead in its entirety . . . manifests a purpose of granting broad authority to financial institution regulators." *Id.* Sometimes that follows, sometimes not. *Cf. Stomper v. Amalgamated Transit Union, Local 241*, 27 F.3d 316, 320 (7th Cir. 1994) (Easterbrook, J.: "A court must determine not only the direction in which a law points but also how far to go in that direction"). In this context, a "broad" reading of § 1818(b)(6)(A) is in effect an unlimited reading of a statute upon which the Congress intended to place a limit. Having read out of the law the limitation that the Congress had put into it, the Akin court was remitted to relying upon the mere hope that the OTS would limit itself; hence the precatory dictum that "restitution orders should [not] become a remedy of choice for OTS." 950 F.2d at 1184 n.5. Yet it is hard to see why that would not inevitably be the result of the Fifth Circuit's decision.

We are mindful that Rapaport made an agreement with the FSLIC that (unless his third argument is well-founded) he appears to have breached. Federal bank regulators are not without means to force a contract party to live up to his obligations, however. The Congress has simply made their "remedy of choice," to use the Fifth Circuit's phrase, a suit in district court under 12 U.S.C. § 93, where the safeguards and standards appurtenant to Article III courts apply. Only if Rapaport had been unjustly enriched—only if he had received and retained some personal benefit either from a federal regulator or from Great Life that he should in justice be required to disgorge—could the OTS force him onto the agency's own turf in order to exact restitution.

### III. Conclusion

The OTS has the authority under the FIRREA to enforce a capital maintenance or other agreement in an administrative proceeding only against a party who has either been unjustly enriched or has acted with reckless disregard for some aspect of federal regulation. Rapaport's alleged failure to contribute as agreed in order to maintain Great Life's required level of capital does not amount to such unjust enrichment. Accordingly, we grant his petition for review and set aside the agency's final order. . . .

### Comments and Questions

1. Have you previously considered the concept of unjust enrichment in either a contracts or a remedies course? If so, isn't it obvious that the court is correct in its common law definition of unjust enrichment? Should the statutory use of the term be limited to its common law meaning? The argument of OTS was one of economic advantage. It argued that Rapaport was richer than he would have been had he performed

the contract.  This led OTS to argue that Rapaport had been "enriched" and, it was "unjust" for Rapaport to keep such enrichment.

2.  Did the Court err in refusing to give deference to the agency's construction of the statute under *Chevron*?  Might the problem with the legal definition of unjust enrichment have had some effect on the court's lack of deference to the OTS interpretation of the statute?  Could Rapaport have prevailed if the *Chevron* standard of review had been applied?

3.  Notwithstanding the substantial deference given to statutory interpretations of regulatory agencies under *Chevron*, the regulators lost in both *Seidman* and *Rapaport*.  Is this some evidence of an attempt by the courts to rein in the regulators' dramatically expanded supervisory enforcement powers after FIRREA and FDICIA?  Might it be that the courts, however indirectly, are questioning the very validity of *Chevron*, and are suggesting that it is the proper role of the courts to determine questions of law, to determine that the regulators have not misconstrued the law?  As you read the remaining cases in this chapter, you may detect that the courts appear to be torn as to the proper resolution of the judicial reivew relationship between administrative agencies and courts.

4.  The 1989 and 1991 legislation generally expanded regulatory powers.  But both the case developments and the detailed elaboration of § 1818(b)(6) and (7) by Congress may have limited the definition of unsafe or unsound practice to financial problems.  On the other hand, the regulators do have a great deal of power if the basis for a cease and desist proceeding is a violation of law, regulation, or order, rather than the general catch-all of unsafe or unsound practice.  And now we also have 12 U.S.C.A. § 1831p-1, standards for safety and soundness.

5.  Compare the regulatory procedural steps required in a cease and desist proceeding based on a claim of unsafe or unsound practice, with those for a violation of a formal written agreement which may be enforced as if it were a final cease and desist order.  In the first case, the regulatory agency must go through a notice and administrative hearing process.  In the second case, the violation is much easier to prove and the agreement can be enforced in an Article III court without the administrative hearing process.

6.  Another important aspect of the supervisory enforcement powers is the range of possible remedies.  For example, in *Central National Bank of Mattoon v. Department of the Treasury*, 912 F.2d 897 (7th Cir. 1990), an examination by the OCC uncovered numerous violations of trust law and regulations, as well as imprudent trust investment practices.  The OCC gave notice of intent to revoke the bank's trust powers.  After an administrative hearing, the administrative law judge recommended only a cease and desist order.  The Comptroller instead ordered revocation of trust powers, and the Seventh Circuit upheld the decision.  The violations were largely admitted by the bank.  The court noted that the standard of review for the appropriateness of the remedy is similar to the standard of review for the underlying substantive claim, arbitrary or capricious.  Since a reasonable person could find the appropriate remedy to be termination of trust powers, rather than a cease and desist order, the remedy imposed was not arbitrary or capricious and the decision of the Comptroller stood.

7.   The temporary cease and desist power available in § 1818(c) is another exceptionally powerful regulatory provision.  Such orders were initially designed to address critical threats to an institution and allow an exception from normal adjudicatory procedures.  But FIRREA in 1989 significantly reduced the elements required for issuance of a temporary cease and desist order.

### Problem 5-3

Jane Lewis and Joe Fame are officers and directors of Corbin Bank.  They admit their responsibility for making loans within the bank's lending limit to Powers Furniture Store.  Powers fell on hard times and the bank incurred substantial losses on the loans.  Might Lewis and Fame be personally liable for the losses suffered by the bank, under § 1818(b)(6)?

Would your answer be different if at the time the loan was made to Powers, Lewis and Fame knew or should have known that Powers was not creditworthy, and so their conduct breached their fiduciary duty of care?  Would your answer yet again be different if the loan to Powers was made for a small amount, did not create any risk to the bank's financial integrity, was an isolated error of judgment, and was not part of any pattern of conduct?

### Problem 5-4

Prosser Bank fails and is placed into receivership.  The FDIC issues a notice of charges against all of the directors of the failed bank, including Fess Barker, alleging that the directors had violated laws, breached their fiduciary duties and otherwise engaged in unsafe or unsound banking practices that, in the opinion of the FDIC, had caused the bank and its depositors to suffer losses.  At the same time the FDIC also issues a temporary cease and desist order, ordering Barker to pay restitution in the amount of $13 million and preventing him from disposing of his personal assets except to pay for household expenses of not more than $5,000 per month.  Barker comes to you for advice, incredulous at the idea that the FDIC could engage in such activity under 12 U.S.C.A. § 1818(c).  Barker states that, while he and others may have engaged in poor business judgment, he certainly did not gain any financial benefit.  Can Barker appeal the temporary cease and desist order, and, if so, what is his likelihood of success?

## C.  Suspension, Removal, and Prohibition Power

Section 1818(e) provides the bank regulators with extensive powers concerning suspension or removal of officers and directors from depository institutions, as well as the power to prohibit such individuals from ever again working for a depository institution anywhere in the United States.  This sanction is potentially much more serious than a cease and desist order.

We previously caught a glimpse of this power in *In re Seidman,* in our consideration of unsafe or unsound practices. The OTS sought Seidman's removal from office and his permanent prohibition from participation in the thrift industry. Note the three part conjunctive test provided by § 1818(e)(1). The agency must show by substantial evidence that: 1) the individual has committed an unlawful act; 2) the act has either an adverse effect on the regulated institution or its depositors or confers a benefit on the individual; and 3) the act is accompanied by a culpable state of mind. The section deserves a careful reading. In *In re Seidman,* the Third Circuit found that Seidman's attempts to obstruct the OTS investigation constituted an unsafe or unsound banking practice, meeting the first element. This also constituted personal dishonesty, satisfying the third element. However, they found that the obstruction of the OTS investigation did not satisfy the second element. The more difficult burden of proof in removal actions is also evidenced by the following case.

## Kim v. Office of Thrift Supervision
### 40 F.3d 1050 (9th Cir. 1994)

LEAVY, Circuit Judge:

A former bank officer petitions for review of an order issued by an administrative agency that forever bans him from working in the American banking industry. For the reasons which follow we grant the petition and vacate the order.

### FACTS AND PRIOR PROCEEDINGS

Delta Savings Bank ("Delta") was a minority-owned, state-licensed savings and loan institution catering to the immigrant Asian community (i.e., principally Korean and Vietnamese families) in Southern California. Prior to September 1989, Delta had been an unprofitable bank: It had regularly reported losses of approximately $100,000 per month, and had failed to meet its minimum regulatory capital requirements since at least March 31, 1988.

On September 15, 1989, a group of local businessmen invested some $2.6 million of new capital in Delta and, two weeks later, took over the bank when their application for change of control was approved by the federal government. One of these investors, Young Il Kim ("Kim"), who initially put up $500,000 of his own money to acquire some of Delta's stock, became the bank's President and Chief Executive Officer. Yun Suk Seo ("Seo"), another investor, was elected Delta's Chairman of the Board. All of the investors, including Dr. Minh Ngoc Dang ("Dang") and Michael Kim (no relation to Kim), joined Delta's board of directors.

Delta began to prosper almost immediately after the new owners and managers took over. It started showing regular monthly gains within three months of the change of control; three months after that, the Office of Thrift Supervision ("OTS"), the regulatory and supervisory successor to the Federal Savings and Loan Insurance Corporation, awarded Delta a composite MACRO[1] rating of 3, an improvement over the previous year's rating of 4. Four months later

---

[1]     MACRO is an acronym standing for *M*anagement, *A*sset quality, *C*apital adequacy, *R*isk management and *O*perating results. It is a five-tiered system, with 1 being the highest and best rating.

(July 1990), the OTS rescinded its year-old Supervisory Agreement[2] in recognition of Delta's substantially improved position. By the end of 1990, Delta reported a $500,000 profit, 60% of which the Board voluntarily allocated to its loan loss reserves. Less than a year later, Delta's financial position had improved to the point where it had tangible capital of $3.5 million and a capital ratio of 5.4%, *i.e.*, nearly a 30% improvement over the previous year's ratio of 4.2%. (The tangible capital requirement at the time was 1.5%.)

On November 8, 1991, things dramatically changed: The OTS filed a Notice of Charges ("Notice") against Kim, Seo, Dang, and Michael Kim, alleging that the four had violated banking laws and regulations, engaged in unsafe and unsound financial practices, and breached their fiduciary duties to the bank. Simultaneously with the filing of the Notice, the OTS issued an order temporarily removing Kim from office and seizing the assets of the institution. The OTS then placed Delta in a conservatorship under the Resolution Trust Corporation ("RTC"). Six months later (May 8, 1992), Delta went into RTC receivership.

Kim and Michael Kim contested the Notice, leading to six days of hearings before an administrative law judge ("ALJ") in April and May 1992. On September 18, 1992, the ALJ issued a lengthy and detailed Recommended Decision and Order, including extensive findings of fact and conclusions of law. The ALJ determined that, while Delta's board of directors had engaged in some unsafe and unsound practices as evidenced by, *inter alia*, four questionable loans and the waiving of fees for one director's (Dang's) returned checks, no sanctions were recommended against either Kim or Michael Kim and no restitution was warranted.[4]

The OTS filed exceptions to the Recommended Decision, to which Kim and Michael Kim replied, and the matter was referred to the Acting Director ("AD") of the OTS. On April 15, 1993, the AD issued an Order and Decision that adopted the ALJ's findings of fact and accepted his recommendation that neither Kim nor Michael Kim should be required to make any restitution. However, the AD's Order and Decision rejected that part of the ALJ's recommendation that no sanctions were warranted and issued a Prohibition Order, i.e., an industry-wide ban against both former directors, forever prohibiting them from working in the American banking business. Kim has timely petitioned for review of that order; Michael Kim has not.

---

[2]    The OTS apparently uses Supervisory Agreements to restrict the operations of troubled financial institutions. The OTS had imposed the Supervisory Agreement in question on Delta's former owners and managers on June 5, 1989.

[4]    The ALJ found that at least one loan constituted both a statutory and a regulatory violation by exceeding the $500,000 limit for individual borrowers; that a $200,000 unsecured loan to Michael Kim constituted a commercial loan rather than a consumer loan and ran afoul of 12 C.F.R. § 563.43(b)(5); that Delta's failure to document certain director loans as having been made on the same terms and/or conditions generally available to the public constituted regulatory violations; that the waiving of late fees on one director loan, and the waiving of NSF charges for that same director's returned checks, involved unsafe and unsound banking practices (and, with respect to the former, constituted a regulatory violation as well); and that each of these transactions either did, or at least could have, cost Delta money.

## ANALYSIS

Kim attacks the AD's imposition of an industry-wide Prohibition Order on two grounds: First, the Order and Decision was based on factual findings not supported by substantial evidence; and second, the Prohibition Order was arbitrary and capricious. With respect to the former contention, we note that Kim asserted no direct administrative challenge to the ALJ's findings of fact, which were adopted *in toto* by the AD. Accordingly, the essence of Kim's argument for purposes of this appeal must be that, even taking those facts as given, the penalty imposed was arbitrary and capricious. . . .

In light of the above, Kim obviously does not attempt to dispute the AD's *authority* to impose an industry-wide Prohibition Order against him; rather, Kim argues that the *decision* to do so on these facts was arbitrary and capricious because Kim did nothing illegal, he did not profit from any of the actions complained of (indeed, he apparently lost his entire investment of $650,000), and Kim acted in reliance on the advice of legal counsel and the guidance of a former OTS official who joined Delta in 1990 as its Chief Operating Officer.[6]

While it is true, as Kim argues, that he was charged with no criminal wrongdoing and that he did not personally profit from any of the above, the OTS was not required to prove such blatant misconduct in order for the AD to impose the blanket Prohibition Order authorized by 12 U.S.C. § 1818(e)(1). All that the OTS had to show was that Kim, as an "institution-affiliated party" (§ 1818(e)(1)(A)), at least "indirectly violated" (§ 1818(e)(1)(A)(i)) one or more banking "law[s] or regulation[s]" (§ 1818(e)(1)(A)(i)(I)), or "participated in . . . unsafe or unsound practice[s]" (§ 1818(e)(1)(A)(ii)), any one of which could have caused Delta to "suffer financial loss or other damage" (§ 1818(e)(1)(B)(i)), and that this conduct involved "willful or continuing disregard . . . for the safety or soundness" of Delta (§ 1818(e)(1)(C)(ii)).

Put somewhat differently, 12 U.S.C. § 1818(e)(1) requires the OTS to prove three things before it may lawfully impose a permanent Prohibition Order against a banker: (1) "misconduct" under § 1818(e)(1)(A); (2) "effect" under § 1818(e)(1)(B); and (3) "culpability" under § 1818(e)(1)(C). Because we find substantial evidence supports the OTS's showing of the misconduct and effect prongs of this test, the only question before us is whether or not the OTS also proved culpability; i.e., did Kim's conduct rise (or, perhaps more accurately, descend) to the level of a "willful or continuing disregard" for Delta's financial security? Although this Circuit has not yet discussed this question in any published decision, other Circuits have.

In *Seidman v. Office of Thrift Supervision*, 37 F.3d 911 (3d Cir. 1994), the Court of Appeals for the Third Circuit held that, before the OTS could impose the "ultimate administrative sanction" of a permanent Prohibition Order against a banker, it had to prove by substantial

---

[6]    Several months after the bank had already approved a $200,000 unsecured loan to Michael Kim, Delta sought the advice of legal counsel for the ostensible purpose of clarifying the OTS's regulatory distinction between commercial and consumer loans as applied to a bank's own officers and directors. Adrienne Miller, a former OTS examiner, joined Delta as its Chief Operating Officer in May 1990. Twelve days after being hired, Miller presented her draft of a "Conflict of Interest and Corporate Conduct" policy and procedures manual ("Miller Policy") stating, in relevant part, that Delta could make secured loans to its directors up to $500,000, and unsecured loans up to $300,000 (aggregate). Delta's Board of Directors, including Kim, unanimously approved the Miller Policy.

evidence that "(1) the banker has committed an unlawful act; (2) the act has either an adverse effect on the regulated institution or its depositors or confers a benefit on the actor and (3) the act is accompanied by a culpable state of mind." *Id.* at 929-30 (footnote omitted).

Simiarly, in *Doolittle v. National Credit Union Admin.*, 992 F.2d 1531 (11th Cir. 1993), the Court of Appeals for the Eleventh Circuit held that "willful or continuing disregard" under section 1818(e)(1)(C)(ii) "must have the same magnitude as personal dishonesty." 992 F.2d at 1539 (citing decisions from the Fifth, Eighth, and D.C. Circuits). *Accord Oberstar v. Federal Deposit Ins. Corp.*, 987 F.2d 494, 502 (8th Cir. 1993) ("The more severe sanction of a Prohibition Order may only be imposed if the misconduct was more than inadvertent or technical," *i.e.*, "the FDIC . . . must prove 'some scienter' to establish culpability."). *Cf. Grubb v. Federal Deposit Ins. Corp.*, 34 F.3d 956, 961 (10th Cir. 1994) (under the FDIC's interpretation of its own regulations, "continuing disregard" requires a showing of at least "heedless indifference to the prospective consequences").

These decisions all hark back to the Eighth Circuit's seminal opinion in *Brickner v. Federal Deposit Ins. Corp.*, 747 F.2d 1198 (8th Cir. 1984). In that case the court held that "willful disregard" and "continuing disregard" were to be viewed in the disjunctive as separate tests because of Congress's use of "or" between the two. 747 F.2d at 1202-1203. While acknowledging that "willful disregard" required a showing of a higher degree of culpability than "continuing disregard," the court noted that "some sort of scienter" was nevertheless required for the latter, *i.e.*, "a mental state . . . akin to 'recklessness.'" *Id.* at 1203 & n.6.

In light of the above, we conclude with our sister Circuits that, before the OTS may impose the ultimate sanction of a Prohibition Order against a banker that forever bans him or her from working in the American banking industry, the OTS must show a degree of culpability well beyond mere negligence, *i.e.*, there must be a showing of scienter.

Despite the OTS's vehement use of such colorful words as "egregious" to describe Kim's conduct, the materials provided show only that Kim was one of several officers and directors who approved a few questionable loans–from none of which he personally profited–out of literally hundreds of good loans, and that a few relatively minor and technical violations of certain banking regulations occurred while Kim was at Delta's helm. While the facts may very well have justified OTS's decision to place Delta in a conservatorship, and may have warranted the issuance of a temporary prohibition against Kim from continuing to manage Delta's affairs after November 8, 1991, Kim's conduct in no way involved anything approaching the level of culpability required by 12 U.S.C. § 1818(e)(1)(C), and certainly does not justify the imposition of such a draconian measure as a permanent Prohibition Order.

Because the facts do not support a showing of culpability on the third prong of the test laid out by 12 U.S.C. § 1818(e)(1), the AD's decision to impose a Prohibition Order against Kim cannot stand. Accordingly, the Petition is GRANTED and the Prohibition Order is VACATED.

## Comments and Questions

1. Suppose the four loans (among hundreds of good loans) that turned out to be bad were all lawful (within the bank's lending limit) but imprudent loans, and in fact were the direct cause of the bank's ultimate failure. Would the prohibition order then be justified? If a person has had an active hand in destroying one bank, causing losses both to depositors and to the insurance fund, why should that person not be barred from again exposing the insurance fund to subsequent liability? Why does the court classify the loans as "questionable" rather than "negligent?"

2. Does scienter mean knowledge, or does it mean something less, *i.e.,* that a person should have reason to know that the loans could cause substantial financial harm to the institution?

3. Can the *Kim* case be of benefit to officers and directors from whom the banking regulators seek multi-million dollar damage awards under the affirmative action provisions of the cease and desist power? Does there have to be some degree of proportionality between the level of misconduct and the remedy sought, even if the directors admit that their few "questionable" loans caused multi-million dollars of damages to the institution? Is there a requirement of personal dishonesty in damage awards? Might it be that OTS's decision not to seek damages from Mr. Kim swayed the court's decision on the prohibition order, on the theory that the OTS implicitly admitted that the depository institution was not financially harmed by any of Mr. Kim's actions? Or, might it be that Mr. Kim did not have any assets?

4. Section 1818(e) does, in fact, place a burden of proof on the regulator greater than that found in § 1818(b). But is it possible to remove a person from office through what is known as a "back door removal" under § 1818(b), by placing limitations on the activities of the particular individual for the putative purpose of correcting unsafe or unsound practices or other violations? See § 1818(b)(6)(E) and (7). Is it also possible to have a backdoor removal as part of a temporary cease and desist order, as § 1818(c) has reference to § 1818(b)(6)? In general, how should § 1818(b) and (e) be reconciled?

5. The prompt corrective action provisions of FDICIA provide additional statutory authority, if an institution is undercapitalized, for bank regulators to dismiss officers and directors without any specific requirement for either a pre-dismissal evidentiary hearing or explicit post-dismissal judicial review. The statute does, however, provide for an informal post-dismissal hearing. But to gain reinstatement the dismissed officer or director has the burden of proving that his or her continued employment by the undercapitalized institution is vital to that institution's restoration and success. Any subsequent judicial review would seem to be based on the substantial evidence or arbitrary and capricious standard. The power does not appear to involve an industry-wide prohibition. On the other hand, there is no requirement of personal culpability. See 12 U.S.C.A. § 1831o(f)(2). Can bank regulators use this procedure to sidestep the more cumbersome procedural protections of § 1818(e)?

## D.  Civil Money Penalty Power

The federal banking agencies have the power to impose civil money penalties against both depository institutions and institution-affiliated parties.  The basis for imposing civil money penalties is set out in a three-tier structure elaborated in 12 U.S.C.A. § 1818(i).  First-tier violations require only a violation of a law, order, written agreement or condition.  Good faith is not a defense to a violation, but may be considered in determining the amount of the penalty, which can be up to $5,000 per day for each day the violation continues.  A second-tier violation can be based on the ground set out for a first-tier violation, but also includes engaging in an unsafe or unsound practice or breach of fiduciary duty.  In addition, the agency must establish that the conduct is part of a pattern, is likely to cause more than minimal loss, or has resulted in gain to the actor.  In essence, a second-tier violation requires proof of scienter and allows for a civil money penalty up to $25,000 per day for so long as the violation, practice, or breach continues.

A third-tier violation requires knowingly committing a first-tier or second-tier violation as well as knowingly or recklessly causing a substantial loss or receiving a substantial pecuniary gain.  The penalty generally can range up to $1 million per day.

Note that civil money penalties can be assessed whether or not damages have resulted, unlike the basis for ordering affirmative action under a cease and desist order.  Consider the following case.  (Section 1817(j), cited in the case, is identical to § 1818(i), discussed above.)

# Rapp v. Office of Thrift Supervision
## 52 F.3d 1510 (10th Cir. 1995)

VRATIL, District Judge.

Petitioners Tom Rapp, Harry Rapp, Mark Rapp, Lori Rapp, Patricia Rapp, Mary Rapp, Michael Rapp, and Debra Rapp Wallace ("the Rapps") petition for review of an order of the Director of the Office of Thrift Supervision ("OTS") dated December 4, 1992.  In that order, the Director found that the Rapps in concert had willfully acquired and/or retained control of a federally-insured thrift without filing prior notice, in violation of the Change in Bank Control Act of 1978 ("the Control Act"), 12 U.S.C. § 1817(j), and the Savings and Loan Holding Company Act ("the Holding Company Act"), 12 U.S.C. § 1467a.  Pursuant to that finding, the Director assessed various civil money penalties, in the aggregate amount of $1,415,243, against the individual Rapps. . . .

### A.  FACTUAL BACKGROUND

The Rapps are related family members.  Tom and Harry are brothers.  Harry is married to Patricia.  Tom is married to Mary and they have four children:  Mark, Lori, Michael, and Debra.

In 1984, Charles Bartlett recruited Tom to help organize First Northern Savings ("FNS"), a new local savings and loan association in Greeley, Colorado.  Tom believed that he had a conflict of interest due to his involvement with a local bank, so he suggested that his daughter Lori participate.  As a result, Lori became an organizer of FNS and served on its Board of

Directors from its inception in 1984 until August 21, 1990.  Although Tom was not formally an organizer of FNS, he was extremely active in marketing and selling FNS shares, and he vastly influenced the Rapp family's acquisition of FNS stock.  In addition, Tom served as director of FNS from July 15, 1985, through October 31, 1989, holding positions as chairman of the board and vice president.

Between October, 1984, and July, 1985, the Rapps and two Rapp-owned partnerships, RAPCO and TRASCO, collectively acquired at least 87,000 shares–43 percent–of outstanding FNS stock.  The Rapps acquired the stock as a short-term investment, expecting to sell a control block at two to three times its book value within several years.

In late August or early September of 1985, Tom divined through a newspaper article that the Rapp family might need government approval to own 43 percent of FNS stock.  As a result, he and FNS president Charles Bartlett solicited legal advice on behalf of FNS.  By letter dated September 17, 1985, counsel advised that the Rapp stock ownership constituted a control violation and that one of two things must occur:  either (1) the Rapps should give notice of their control ownership to the Federal Savings and Loan Insurance Corporation ("FSLIC") pursuant to 12 C.F.R. § 563.18-2 (1985), or (2) as a group, the Rapps should immediately divest sufficient shares to bring their combined ownership to less than 25 percent of total outstanding shares.  The Rapps elected not to file notice with FSLIC, but within one week they transferred 38,750 shares (approximately 45 percent of their holdings) to other individuals.

Specifically, on September 17, 1985, Harry and Patricia transferred 16,500 shares of FNS stock to Judy Nelson, who worked as a secretary at Harry's company.  On September 18, 1985, Tom and Mary transferred 12,250 shares to Ivan Shupe, a long-time family friend.  And on September 23, 1985, Mark transferred 10,000 shares to his business partner, Bruce Copp.  The Director found that these stock transfers were sham transactions, structured to reserve the attributes of ownership and control to the Rapp family while formally registering the stock in the names of third parties.[3]

After the stock transfers, the Rapps continued to search for potential buyers for the stock which they had already–at least nominally–sold to Nelson, Shupe and Copp.  Indeed, on March 17, 1986, Mark sold to Harold Winograd the stock which he had nominally transferred to Copp.

On August 20, 1987, Nelson asked Harry to take the FNS shares out of her name and cancel and return the promissory note and agreement.  On September 9, 1987, Harry cancelled and returned the agreement and promissory note, but he did not transfer the stock out of Nelson's name.  Shortly thereafter, Nelson informed FNS that she had assigned the stock back to Harry

---

[3]    Each transfer was structured as a "sale" in which the buyer executed a non-recourse, interest-bearing demand note for the full purchase price of the stock.  The Rapps retained the stock certificates, endorsed in blank by the buyers, as security.  The buyers executed hypothecation agreements which permitted the Rapps to pledge the stock as collateral.  These transactions were free of risk to the buyers.  The buyers were not responsible for interest or principal on the notes unless and until third parties purchased the stock.  In that event, depending upon the resale price, Nelson, Shupe or Copp could pay off the notes and retain the profit, or default on the notes and walk away from the transaction with no personal liability whatsoever.

and Patricia and on October 30, 1987, FNS notified the Federal Home Loan Bank Board ("FHLBB") that the Rapp family might be in violation of the Control Act.

On December 29, 1987, Harry transferred the "Nelson" shares to Harry Asmus, Tom's neighbor and long-time acquaintance, and Kathryn Landrum, Harry's sister-in-law. Through TRASCO, Harry's wife and sons provided full financing for the transactions and took back non-recourse demand notes secured by the stock. Asmus and Landrum endorsed the stock certificates and Harry retained possession of them. Asmus and Landrum paid no interest or principal on the notes. On December 9, 1988, Harry informed Landrum that he had overstated the financial condition of FNS and would discount her note to reflect year-end book value. Landrum replied that she had no alternative but to return the stock and that she expected Harry to cancel the note and waive interest to date. Harry subsequently sold the stock to an unrelated third party for half what Landrum had purportedly paid him.

After the Rapps learned of their control violation in September, 1985, and even after they had executed the nominal transfers to Nelson, Shupe and Copp, the Rapps acquired additional shares of FNS stock. On April 11, 1986, Tom purchased 500 FNS shares. On the same date Tom's sister, Katherine Rapp Miller, purchased 1,000 shares. On December 31, 1987, Lori exercised stock warrants for an additional 2,500 shares.

Throughout the time that the Rapp family was in violation of the control statutes, Tom was actively involved in efforts to sell a control block of FNS stock at a premium price. He placed numerous advertisements in national publications, claiming that he and his family and friends owned over 50 percent of FNS stock and offering to coordinate a sale of that stock for a personal fee.

On January 10, 1990, the OTS issued Enforcement Review Committee Resolution No. ERC 90-7, along with a Notice of Assessment of a Civil Money Penalty ("Notice of Assessment"), charging that since July, 1985, the Rapps had continually owned and had the power to vote more than 25 percent of the outstanding voting stock of First Northern Savings, in willful violation of Section 1817(j)(16) of the Control Act. The notice assessed a $1,000,000 penalty against Tom Rapp, with an additional $10,000 penalty for each day the violation continued. The notice also assessed penalties of $50,000, plus $1,000 for every day of continuing violation, against each of the seven remaining petitioners.[7]

On February 2, 1990, the Rapps answered the Notice of Assessment and requested an administrative hearing. The Administrative Law Judge ("ALJ") recommended summary judgment against the Rapps on, *inter alia*, the Rapps' affirmative defenses of estoppel and breach of contract. The ALJ held an administrative hearing from November 13 through 14, 1990, and April 16 through 19, 1991. On August 22, 1991, the ALJ issued his recommended decision, finding that the Rapps had engaged in a pattern of misconduct in willful violation of the Control Act. He recommended civil penalties in the amount of $100,000 against Tom Rapp and $20,000

---

[7]    The Notice of Assessment also imposed penalties against Stan Rapp, a brother of Tom and Harry. The Director found that penalties were not warranted as to Stan, because of his minimal involvement in the scheme. The Rapps do not challenge this finding and Stan is not a party to this appeal.

against each of the remaining Rapps.  Both the Rapps and the OTS filed exceptions to the ALJ's recommended decision.

On December 4, 1992, the OTS Director issued his *Decision and Order on Assessment of Civil Money Penalties ("Final Decision")*, which found that from June 26, 1985 through November 13, 1990, over consecutive time periods, the Rapps in concert had violated both the Holding Company Act and the Control Act.  More specifically, the Director found that from June 26, 1985, through December 31, 1989, the Rapps had violated the Holding Company Act, while from January 1, 1990, through November 13, 1990, the Rapps had violated the Control Act.  As a consequence of these findings, the Director imposed statutory penalties in the following amounts: $971,600 against Tom Rapp; $186,900 against Harry Rapp; $186,900 against Mark Rapp; $29,370 against Lori Rapp; $16,020 against Patricia Rapp; $13,585 against Mary Rapp; $5,434 against Michael Rapp; and $5,434 against Debra Rapp Wallace.

The Rapps challenge the penalties on three separate grounds. . . . Second, the Rapps assert that the record does not justify second-tier penalties against individual family members.  Finally, the Rapps claim that the OTS violated their constitutional due process rights.

## B.  STANDARD OF REVIEW

Judicial review of OTS action is governed by the Administrative Procedure Act ("APA"), 5 U.S.C. § 701 *et seq.*  Under the APA we must "hold unlawful and set aside agency [adjudicatory] action, findings, and conclusions found to be (A) arbitrary, capricious, an abuse of discretion, or otherwise not in accordance with law; [or] . . . (E) unsupported by substantial evidence. . . ." . . .

## C.  DISCUSSION

. . . . .

### 2.  Penalty Assessment

The Rapps challenge the Director's assessment of second-tier penalties–as opposed to lesser, first-tier penalties–under the Control Act.  The Control Act imposes second-tier penalties in the maximum amount of $25,000 per day for any violation which

(I) is part of a pattern of misconduct; (II) causes or is likely to cause more than a minimal loss to such institution; or (III) results in pecuniary gain or other benefit to such person.

12 U.S.C. § 1817(j)(16)(B)(ii).  A Control Act violation under Section 1817(j) which does not meet these criteria qualifies for first-tier penalties in the maximum amount of $5,000 per day. 12 U.S.C. § 1817(j)(16)(A).

The Director held that second-tier penalties were appropriate because the individual petitioners had engaged in a "pattern of misconduct" and had received "other benefit" under Sections 1817(j)(16)(B)(ii)(I) and (III), respectively.  Petitioners argue that the Director's statutory interpretation is unreasonable and that his factual findings are arbitrary, capricious and unsupported by the evidence.

### a. *Sham Transactions*

In finding a "pattern of misconduct," the Director concluded that the stock transfers to Nelson, Shupe and Copp were sham transactions. Petitioners challenge this conclusion, arguing that it is unsupported by the record. We disagree. On this record, the Director could easily find that the stock transfers to Nelson, Shupe and Copp were transfers in name only, designed to conceal the Rapps' control violation and buy time for them to find *bona fide* purchasers who would buy the stock at a premium price.

The Rapps assert that the transactions were legitimate because Nelson, Shupe and Copp received genuine investment opportunities, in that they could pay off the notes and retain any profit. The record reflects that Nelson, Shupe and Copp had no intent of paying off the notes, however, and that they acquired their stock at prices which substantially exceeded the "going prices" of FNS shares. The likelihood that they would ever realize any profit was apparently slim or none. On this record, we readily affirm the Director's conclusion that the stock transfers were sham transactions.

### b. *Pattern of Misconduct*

The Rapps challenge the Director's further finding that the control violations by individual Rapps were part of a "pattern of misconduct" under Section 1817(j)(16)(B)(ii)(I). Specifically, petitioners assert that a "pattern of misconduct" under subsection (I) requires two or more Control Act violations and that misconduct surrounding a single violation cannot give rise to a "pattern of misconduct" under the statute. The Rapps also complain that factually, the record does not support a finding that each individual engaged in a "pattern of misconduct."

The Control Act does not define a "pattern of misconduct" and the legislative history is seemingly silent on this point. Congress has not specifically addressed the issue and in fact has entrusted the OTS with responsibility for administering the statute. We therefore give considerable deference to the Director's interpretation and limit our review to a determination whether his construction of the statute is reasonable. . . .

Under the statute, any person who commits a control violation, "which violation . . . is part of a pattern of misconduct," is liable for second-tier penalties. 12 U.S.C. § 1817(j)(16)(B)(ii)(I). The statutory language does not limit second-tier penalties to patterns of Control Act violations, nor does it stipulate that in order to incur liability for second-tier penalties each member of an offending control group must independently demonstrate a separate "pattern of misconduct." The plain language of the statute authorizes second-tier penalties if the control violation is part of a pattern of misconduct. In our view, the Director acted reasonably in so construing it.

In this case, citing the Rapps' repeated efforts to conceal their control violations and their continuing refusal to comply with control regulations, the Director found a "pattern of misconduct" which authorized imposition of second-tier penalties. In support of his conclusion, the Director cited the Rapps' ongoing acquisition of FNS stock, the sham stock transfers, Tom's misrepresentations to state regulators and FNS directors concerning the propriety of the sham transactions, Harry's attempt to mislead state investigators with respect to Nelson's stock ownership, and subsequent stock purchases by Tom and Lori after they had clearly learned of the control violation. . . . .

These findings were supported by substantial evidence, and the Director did not exceed his authority in finding that each petitioner's violation was part of a "pattern of misconduct" under Section 1817(j)(16)(B)(ii)(I).

c. *Other Benefit*

In part, the Director based the imposition of second-tier penalties on his finding that although petitioners had not received pecuniary profit from their control violation, they had received "other benefit" under Section 1817(j)(16)(B)(ii)(III).  The Rapps contend that the Director erred in concluding that their control of FNS, without more, constituted "other benefit."

As a preliminary matter, contrary to petitioners' argument, the Director did not find that control ownership alone constituted "other benefit" sufficient to justify imposition of second-tier penalties in this case.  The Director did state that petitioners' control was a benefit, but he found that the benefit was more than *de minimis*.  Indeed, the Director outlined various benefits which the Rapps had secured as a result of their control violation:  they demanded and received seats on the FNS board of directors, with Tom serving as of chairman of the board, and through Tom, the Rapps advertised the institution for sale, demanding a premium price for the family's control block of stock and negotiating a personal fee to bring the transaction to completion.[12] . . . .

More importantly, on this record, the Director's conclusion that petitioners benefitted from their control violation is not arbitrary, capricious, or unsupported by the record.[13] . . . .

d. *Mitigating Factors*

The Rapps complain that the Director failed to properly consider mitigating factors, especially the fact that FNS did not suffer financial loss as a result of the Rapps' misconduct. In determining the penalty to be assessed against each individual Rapp, however, the Director reduced the tentative penalty by 80 percent because petitioners' conduct did not cause a loss or risk of loss to FNS, and because the Rapps had no prior control violations.  On this record, we find that the Director sufficiently considered mitigating factors and did not abuse his discretion in imposing the penalties.  *See, e.g., Morgan v. Secretary of Hous. and Urban Dev.*, 985 F.2d 1451, 1458 (10th Cir. 1993) (we will not disturb amount of penalty imposed unless it is abuse of discretion or otherwise arbitrary or capricious). . . .

For the foregoing reasons, we AFFIRM the Director's order.

## Comments and Questions

1.  Suppose that a regulator issues a cease and desist (or prompt corrective action) order requiring that the bank raise additional capital.  The officers and directors are unable

---

[12]    That the Rapps considered their control a "benefit" is demonstrated by their refusal to relinquish it–even when confronted with knowledge that it was illegal.

[13]    Because the Director specifically found that the Rapps derived non-pecuniary benefit from their control violation, we do not address petitioners' argument that control in itself is not a benefit under 12 U.S.C. § 1817(j)(16)(B)(ii)(III).  *But cf. Oberstar v. FDIC*, 987 F.2d 494, 502 (8th Cir. 1993) (obtaining effective control of financial institution is no doubt "other benefit" under § 1818(e)(1)(B)(iii)).

to do so. Does the regulator have the power to assess a civil money penalty for violation of the cease and desist order? Would it be a defense if a good faith effort had been made to raise capital?

2. Are the civil money penalty powers of the bank regulators part of a civil, or criminal, statute? In *United States v. Hudson*, 14 F.3d 536 (10th Cir. 1994), defendants filed motions to dismiss criminal indictments against them arising out of their alleged illegal operations of several banks. The court held that the defendants had possible double jeopardy defenses depending on whether the Comptroller's civil money penalties were solely remedial, or were in fact "punishment" that would preclude subsequent criminal prosecution. In *United States v. Barnette*, 10 F.3d 1553 (11th Cir. 1994), cert. denied, 513 U.S. 816 (1994), the court held that a 3 to 1 ratio of civil money penalties to the actual loss caused to the government was not so high as to constitute punishment which would result in a violation of the double jeopardy clause. This was so, notwithstanding that the government had already obtained restitution for the actual loss.

### Problem 5-5

The directors of a bank approve a loan relying on information, opinions, reports, and statements of bank employees who are their lending experts. It turns out that the key lending officer-expert, Dazzio, had clearly committed a fraud on the bank by hiding his financial relationship with a particular borrower, so that no reasonable officer or director could learn that the loan was in violation of 12 U.S.C.A. § 375a. The FDIC seeks to assess a civil money penalty against the directors who approved the loan. Would the above stated facts negate the basis for a civil money penalty assessment or would they merely be relevant to the amount of the assessment?

## E. Capital Directives and Prompt Corrective Action

We have previously considered capital directives (§ 3907) and prompt corrective action (§ 1831o) as part of our discussion of capital adequacy in Chapter 3, including consideration of *Bank of Coushatta*. The prompt corrective action (PCA) provisions are patterned after the capital directive procedure, and do not provide the statutory due process provisions that are otherwise available in general supervisory enforcement actions. Due process generally involves two concepts, a right to adequate procedures and a right to an adequate explanation of how the conclusions were reached by the regulator. These could be restated as a right to fairness and a right to accuracy. In *Bank of Coushatta*, the court said that all of this had occurred. And so it appears that PCA directives also will withstand constitutional objections.

Once the PCA provisions are triggered by their capital adequacy requirements, they greatly expand the powers of bank regulators. With few procedural limitations, regulators can impose restrictions much more easily through PCA than through traditional cease and desist orders, and, also with few procedural limitations, regulators have additional tools under PCA for removal of officers and directors. It is reasonable to expect that in the next round of depository institution failures the PCA powers will be used much more extensively than the traditional § 1818 provisions.

The various capital levels created by FDICIA act as the principal trigger for prompt corrective action, activating the regulatory power to address both capital deficiencies and supervisory problems.  Again, the five capital categories into which depository institutions are placed are:  1) well capitalized; 2) adequately capitalized; 3) undercapitalized; 4) significantly undercapitalized; and 5) critically undercapitalized.  An institution's capital category determines which measures the regulator either may or must take in response to the institution's capital deficiency.  The statute provides for three types of agency proceedings:  1) issuance of a PCA directive requiring an institution to take or refrain from certain actions; 2) reclassification of an institution from one PCA category to a lower category; and 3) dismissal of directors and senior executive officers of the institution.  PCA directives are similar to final cease and desist orders, in that they are enforceable in the United States district courts.  Further, violations of PCA directives are subject to the same levels of civil money penalties as violations of final cease and desist orders.  A reclassification action is likely to occur as the first step in the issuance of a PCA directive, and the dismissal of directors (as previously discussed) appears to be an unfettered route for removal proceedings.

The authority of the regulators under the PCA provisions reaches every important aspect of a depository institution's activities and operations.  Institutions can be required to sell additional capital, to restrict their transactions with affiliates, to limit their interest rates on deposits, to limit their asset growth or reduce their asset size, and to terminate any activity that the regulator determines poses excessive risks to the institution.  See § 1831o(f).

Note that, based upon supervisory information other than the capital of the institution, the regulators have the power to reclassify a well capitalized institution as adequately capitalized.  The adequately capitalized institution may then be required to comply with supervisory orders as if it were in the yet next lower capital category.  See § 1831o(g).  The regulators may reclassify an institution if they determine, after notice and the opportunity for an informal hearing, that the institution is in an unsafe or unsound condition or is engaging in an unsafe or unsound practice.  Further, an institution is deemed to be engaged in an unsafe or unsound practice if it has received a rating of 3 or worse in any one of the CAMELS categories of assets, management, earnings, or liquidity.

One deficiency of PCA, as with any regulatory system dependent on capital adequacy to determine safety and soundness, is that capital is a lagging indicator of institutional weakness.  PCA is triggered only after capital has or is about to decline due to asset or liability problems, such as defaulting loans.  Can you think of any more appropriate triggers that might better provide regulators with sufficient lead time for successful intervention at troubled banks?

*Problem 5-6*

1. John Hughes has been an outspoken critic of various bank regulators for years. He also happens to be the CEO of Centennial Bank and Trust Company. While neither Hughes nor Centennial has violated any specific banking laws or regulations, the bank is an agricultural lender that has suffered some loan losses, resulting in the bank being classified as undercapitalized. The regulator, for whatever reason, would like to remove Hughes from office, and asks you whether it can do so either under a § 1818(e) proceeding or a PCA dismissal order. Please advise.

2. The regulators define "significantly" undercapitalized as a 20% variance from the minimum leverage capital ratio, which is 3%. An institution therefore becomes significantly undercapitalized with a 2.4% leverage ratio. While Friends Bank has a 2.4% leverage ratio, it meets the risk-based capital requirement and is able to fund itself without reliance on either brokered deposits or government support. Can the bank be forced to sell additional stock through either a formal enforcement proceeding or a PCA directive?

3. Gateway National Bank has several loans outstanding to semiconductor manufacturers, none of which is in default. Because of volatile earnings in the semiconductor industry, OCC examiners decide that these loans should be considered "doubtful" and therefore written down by 50%. The write-down results in the capital of Gateway being lowered for purposes of determining PCA capital categories from adequately capitalized to undercapitalized. What sanctions is Gateway exposed to due to the examiner's judgment of the future expectations of payments on the loans to semiconductor manufacturers?

# Section 4.  The Failed Bank

## A.  Introduction

In the 1920s alone, over 5,000 banks failed in the United States. While recent times again brought a substantial numbers of failures, the response of the public was significantly different. In the late 1920s and early 1930s, a panic quickly cut short the boom economy. This resulted in the 1930s legislation which created the financial system we have today, banks that are mostly run-resistant because of the federal deposit insurance guarantee. The lack of an economic panic in the face of so many recent financial institution failures is notable. The difference is that now much of the loss is indirectly distributed to all depositors through insurance premiums or all taxpayers through federal appropriations.

Since the 1930s, the FDIC usually becomes the receiver when a bank fails. The "receiver" role is independent of the role as insurer of deposits and administrator of the deposit insurance system, which is the FDIC as "corporation." The FDIC as corporation in the failed bank situation is obligated to pay off, or in some form provide for, the insured deposits. The FDIC as receiver must engage in traditional receivership activities, i.e., collecting assets and paying creditors. The two roles are often performed simultaneously and can often be difficult to distinguish. Nevertheless, the distinction is important.

While we typically will discuss the activities of the FDIC as a receiver, the FDIC may also be appointed as a conservator.  A receiver typically is appointed for the purpose of liquidation, while a conservator typically is appointed to conserve assets and put the institution back on its feet.  Under 12 U.S.C.A. § 1821(c)(2)(A) the appropriate supervisory authority may appoint the FDIC as conservator of any insured federal depository institution, and the FDIC may accept the appointment.  While appointment and acceptance of a conservatorship is discretionary, the appointment and acceptance of the FDIC as receiver typically is mandatory.

The Federal Deposit Insurance Act was significantly amended by FIRREA in 1989 and FDICIA in 1991.  Here we will merely summarize many of the more important statutory changes.  Later we will consider several of them in more detail.  The statutory section that provides for most of the FDIC powers in acting either as a conservator or as a receiver of a failed bank is 12 U.S.C.A. § 1821.  Other powers, however, are found in additional, scattered sections. *See, e.g.,* §§ 1815, 1819, 1820, 1822 and 1823.  Overall, the amendments codify much of the common law that has developed in the bank failure area over the past sixty years.

FIRREA enlarged the Board of Directors of the FDIC from three to five members.  One is the Comptroller of the Currency, one is the Director of the Office of Thrift Supervision, and three are appointed by the President subject to approval by the Senate.  12 U.S.C.A. § 1812(a).

Several important definitions are found in 12 U.S.C.A. § 1813.  You should consider, particularly, the definitions of "appropriate federal banking agency," "institution-affiliated parties," and "default."

The FDIC is always appointed as receiver of a national bank through the power of the Comptroller of the Currency.  FIRREA significantly changed the appointment of a receiver for a state chartered insured institution, by empowering the FDIC to appoint itself as conservator or receiver under certain circumstances.  12 U.S.C.A. § 1821(c)(4), (5), (9) and (10).  If the FDIC takes this route, the receivership is treated as if the failed institution was federally chartered.  As a consequence, problems with particular state receivership laws can be avoided.  However, it is still typical that the FDIC accepts appointment as receiver by state authority.  12 U.S.C.A. § 1821(c)(3).  A change from prior law is that the FDIC no longer is required to accept the offer of receivership from the state regulator.

The prompt corrective action provisions of FDICIA provide that, if an institution is critically undercapitalized (leverage capital ratio below 2%) for 90 days, the appropriate federal banking agency must either appoint a receiver or conservator or take other action, with the concurrence of the FDIC, that they believe would better achieve the purposes of the prompt corrective action provisions.  If the institution remains critically undercapitalized for approximately one year the agency must appoint a receiver, unless it is concluded that the institution is viable and not expected to fail.  See 12 U.S.C.A. § 1831o(h).  Note that the provisions in § 1821(c)(5)(K) and (L) establish under capitalized, rather than critically undercapitalized, as the basis for appointment of a receiver.

As receiver, the FDIC has a variety of powers. For example, virtually any action to which the FDIC is a party is deemed to arise under federal law. 12 U.S.C.A. § 1819(b)(2)(A). Similarly, the FDIC may remove a case from state to federal court in virtually all circumstances. 12 U.S.C.A. § 1819(b)(2)(B).

FIRREA added important provisions dealing both with claims against and claims by the FDIC. Claims against the FDIC as receiver must initially be filed with the FDIC. If the claim is disallowed, the claimant, often a depositor, has a choice of either filing in a federal district court or going through an FDIC administrative claims procedure. 12 U.S.C.A. § 1821(d)(6) and (7). If the FDIC is the claimant, FIRREA provides a rather generous statute of limitations–six years for contract claims and three years for tort claims, from the later of the date that the institution fails, or the applicable state's statute of limitations commences. 12 U.S.C.A. § 1821(d)(14).

You may be aware that under federal bankruptcy law the trustee in bankruptcy is provided with an automatic stay against pending litigation. Under FIRREA, however, the FDIC may only request a stay of specifically identified pending litigation for a period of up to 90 days. The wording of the statute suggests that the court must grant the stay. 12 U.S.C.A. § 1821(d)(12). Also similar to the trustee in bankruptcy, the FDIC as receiver has the power to repudiate contracts. See 12 U.S.C.A. § 1821(e)(1). And the FDIC has the power to enforce contracts, notwithstanding provisions in a contract for termination upon receivership. 12 U.S.C.A. § 1821(e)(12).

When deposit insurance was first created, the deposit insurance limit was $2,500 per account. The general assumption was that the FDIC would act simply as liquidator of a bank when appointed as receiver. Gradually, however, through the use of assisted merger transactions and purchase and assumption agreements (where an existing bank agrees to purchase the assets and assume all the deposit liabilities of the failed bank) to resolve bank failures, until the 1980s the FDIC commonly arranged what amounted to complete deposit insurance, or complete payoff of all depositors, both insured and uninsured. But today any type of assistance is supposed to be given only if it is the course of action that will result in the "least cost" to the FDIC insurance fund. 12 U.S.C.A. § 1823(c)(4)(A)-(E). The underlying reasoning is that the purpose of the FDIC is not to eliminate the effects of bank failures by franchise sales, but to dispose of failed banks by the least costly methodology.

Either methodology (purchase and assumption, or liquidation) typically begins with the institution being placed in receivership. Then there is either a straight liquidation (deposit payoff) or a sale of the closed bank as a going business (purchase and assumption). In either case the old institution is terminated and the loss to the FDIC should be immediately realized. The historic exception to the least cost test was the "essential to the community" standard, later expanded to add "essential to the financial system." Today the only exception to least cost resolution is the systemic risk exception, 12 U.S.C.A. § 1823(c)(4)(G).

Actual FDIC failing bank transactions, however, are more complex. Whether through open bank assistance (§ 1823(c)(1)) or purchase and assumption transactions involving a closed bank, the FDIC has been regularly engaged in a variety of transactions that attempt to resurrect the failed bank so that the FDIC can recover the going concern or franchise value of the bank.  The "premium" paid for this asset is roughly measured as a percentage of retail deposits, such as 1-3 percent.  The most valuable asset of a closed bank is its deposits, which are its balance sheet liabilities.  The deposit liabilities are the real assets of the bank because they are a cheap source of funds to be used in the business of banking.  Further, the balance sheet assets, such as real estate, agricultural and other loans, are often viewed as liabilities, the part of the bank that someone else will least care to purchase.  The FDIC often tries to keep the going concern value of the institution by engaging in a purchase and assumption transaction and, by one manner or another, guaranteeing the acquiring institution against loss on the nonperforming assets that come with the bank.  Such a transaction is often called a total asset purchase agreement.  It casts the FDIC in the role of savior, rather than liquidator, of the institution.  But the FDIC's exposure to later losses on nonperforming assets raises difficult questions about the indeterminate nature of the "least cost" analysis, because the cost of the purchase and assumption transaction cannot be immediately determined.  Some believe that the taxpayers' interests would be better served by outright sales of assets that would immediately transfer the investment risk.  This can be done by entering into a yield maintenance agreement, with the FDIC guaranteeing a certain return on the investment that phases out over time.  Such a method of asset transfer immediately fixes the cost of the failure to the FDIC.

## B.  Open Bank Assistance and Least-Cost Resolution

While § 1823(c)(1) appears to allow the FDIC to provide various forms of assistance to an open but failing bank in order to keep it in existence, a variety of factors severely limit such assistance.  Section 1823(c)(8) allows the FDIC to consider providing financial assistance to an open bank only if (1) grounds for appointment of a conservator or receiver exist or likely will exist in the immediate future and it is unlikely that the bank will meet capital standards without assistance; and (2) the bank's management has been competent.  In addition, the PCA provisions of FDICIA require the banking agencies to pursue early resolution strategies.  Finally, the Resolution Trust Corporation Completion Act of 1993 added a separate provisions prohibiting the use of FDIC insurance funds in any manner that would benefit the shareholders of any failing bank.

The limitations on open bank assistance are logically related to two other concerns: (1) the power of the Federal Reserve to be the lender-of-last-resort and (2) the concept of "too-big-to-fail."  The general fear of regulators is that the failure of a large bank can create unforseen, systemic problems in the banking system and tax the resources of the FDIC to deal effectively with all the complications of such a failure.

In response to these concerns, FDICIA added the detailed least-cost resolution procedures in § 1823(c)(4) requiring the regulators always to utilize the least-cost methodology of dealing with a bank that is threatened with failure.  FDICIA also limited excessive use of discount window advances.  The congressional fear was that regulators could use Federal Reserve discount window loans to avoid the prompt corrective action provisions and ultimately increase failure costs to the federal deposit insurance funds. Under FDICIA the Federal Reserve banks may now advance funds to undercapitalized institutions for not more than 60 days in any 120-day period. See 12 U.S.C.A. § 347b(b). FDICIA also attempted to repeal the practical existence of the too-big-to-fail doctrine by generally prohibiting the FDIC from using funds to pay uninsured depositors or other creditors more than they would recover in a liquidation (§§ 1821(i)(2) and 1823(c)(4)(E)).

As a consequence, open bank assistance now appears to be available under § 1823(c)(4) only through the systemic risk exception of § 1823(c)(4)(G). The systemic risk exception must be initiated by either two-thirds of the FDIC's board of directors or two-thirds of the Federal Reserve Board. In addition, each body must approve the request of the other body and the Secretary of the Treasury must determine that the systemic risk exception is justified. Finally, the FDIC must recover any losses it suffers from using the systemic risk exception by a special assessment of all members of the insurance fund.

## Comments and Questions

1. The pre-FDICIA open bank assistance activities of the FDIC bring to mind the activities of the Reconstruction Finance Corporation, which was created by Congress in 1932 to restore capital strength in weak banks that had failed prior to the creation of the FDIC. The Reconstruction Finance Corporation typically not only provided loans but also took equity positions in the form of preferred stock. Those powers appear to be quite similar to the rather open-ended open assistance powers provided to the FDIC before 1991.

2. The FDIC has taken equity positions, through warrants or preferred stock, in closed bank transactions, where the institution is purchased from the FDIC as receiver and continued in business. See 12 U.S.C.A. § 1823(c)(5). Is it appropriate for the FDIC to hold equity interests in banks, acquired through the funding of bank rescues? How does that affect competition and regulation?

3. In such transactions the FDIC has also commonly provided an open-ended type of loan protection by guaranteeing against losses above a certain amount on loans purchased by the acquiring bank. Unless the transaction is done on a fixed price basis, how can the FDIC ever make an intelligent least-cost determination at the time of the rescue? In a fixed cost transaction, the acquirer of the failed bank makes up any shortfall in value in the asset portfolio which unexpectedly exceeds the amount of federal assistance. In an open-end transaction, the FDIC bears some or all of the risk of unexpected losses in the acquired institution's asset portfolio, even if the losses surface after the transaction with the FDIC is closed. While the FDIC can always say that it has minimized the loss of franchise value by not liquidating the institution, that would appear to be only one factor in performing the least-cost analysis. In other words, is there a concern not only for equity transactions by the FDIC, but also long-term, open-end extensions of government credit to purchasers? Is it possible that these transactions primarily avoid having the FDIC appear to be a liquidator while maintaining institutions and jobs at an unknown cost to the federal government? If existing owners show such disinterest in the franchise of a bank

that they are unwilling to recapitalize the operation, why should FDIC funds ever be expended?

4.  Do you see the critical difference between a liquidity problem and a solvency problem with respect to the Federal Reserve's power as lender of last resort?  If a bank is solvent, in the sense that its assets are worth more than its liabilities, the bank should experience little difficulty in obtaining sufficient liquidity through either asset sales or borrowings from other banks to meet deposit outflows.  This suggests that a solvent bank should rarely, if ever, need to utilize the Federal Reserve discount window.  The only way that a liquidity crisis could become an insolvency crisis would be if there were a flight from the deposits in banks not to deposits in other banks (thus keeping the money in the banking system), but to currency (thus taking money out of the banking system and forcing asset sales to meet deposit withdrawals).  This could cause a decrease in the value of assets generally, including collateral for bank loans.  This, in fact, is what occurred in the 1930s and is the systemic concern that the regulators have the discretion to deal with under FDICIA.  In such a case the Federal Reserve does have the power to meet the needs of all banks simultaneously to deal with deposit outflows and the avoidance of fire-sale losses of assets and collateral in the likelihood of multiple banks' liquidity problems expanding into solvency problems.

## C.  Determining Insolvency

As previously discussed, § 1821(c) provides an array of bases on which the regulatory authorities can determine that a conservator or receiver should be appointed for a depository institution.  The most common basis for appointment is that the institution is insolvent.  The discretion of the regulators in making insolvency determinations has always been quite broad.

There are many justifications for the regulators' broad discretion.  It is thought to be necessary for the regulators to be able to act quickly in order to protect the financial interests of depositors and creditors, as well as the welfare of the general public.  Bank insolvencies also present difficult questions of evaluation and appraisal of assets and liabilities which may be more quickly determined by a regulator than by a court.  To the extent that court review is available, it is based on the arbitrary, capricious, or abuse of discretion standard of the Administrative Procedure Act.  *Golden Pacific Bancorp. v. Clarke*, 837 F.2d 509 (D.C. Cir.), *cert. denied*, 488 U.S. 890 (1988).

There are two standard tests of insolvency, the balance sheet test and the equity test.  In the former, one is regarded as insolvent if liabilities exceed assets.  In the latter, one is regarded as insolvent if unable to meet debts as they become due.  A moment's thought will lead one to recognize that a bank or a business will often be insolvent under one test but not under the other.  For example, many students are insolvent under the balance sheet test, but are perfectly solvent according to the equity test and are capable of and do meet their debts as they become due.  Conversely, a bank or another business that has a valuable but nonliquid asset may be enormously well off according to its balance sheet but may, as they say in the trade, have "cash flow" problems and thus be insolvent according to the equity test.  In hard times the balance sheet test may be more generous to a debtor because it is incapable of liquidating a valuable asset. Conversely, in boom times a business that may appear to be insolvent on its balance sheet may be earning a great deal of money and may thus not be insolvent according to the equity test. Thus, neither is inherently more generous than the other to the debtor.

Surely any bank that meets the equity test of insolvency must be declared insolvent. The creditors of a bank are significantly different from the creditors of a typical industrial organization. The principal creditors of a bank are the depositors. Bank deposits represent the most liquid, and one of the most important, assets that most depositors hold. Thus, if the bank-debtor defaults by its inability to meet a depositor's demand for withdrawal, the depositor is immediately, if not seriously, injured. It is small consolation to the depositor that the bank may be solvent in the balance sheet sense and may in one, two or five years pay off its obligation. Conversely, the typical creditor of a nonbank business does not suffer such immediate harm by the debtor's failure to pay and can more comfortably await subsequent payment as the illiquid assets are sold. Thus, it seems that no one would seriously argue that a bank which meets the equity test of insolvency and is in fact defaulting on its credit obligations could or should remain in business without the intervention of the regulators.

One should appreciate the difficulties inherent in applying the balance sheet test to a bank. Some of the bank's assets will have no readily ascertainable fair market value; others will have a fair market value but it will be uncertain whether that is the proper value to use in arriving at the balance sheet totals. Assume, for example, that the bank in question has $100 million of loans outstanding. Commonly the bank's loans will be its principal asset, but how does one value such loans? Some, of course, must be discounted because the debtors who owe the loans to the bank may not be able to make repayment. But should loans also be discounted because they are long term and carry a low rate of interest, thus having a current fair market value of less than par (face value)? One may ask the same question concerning municipal bonds, another widely held bank asset. If the bank holds the bonds to maturity, they will pay 100% of principal at maturity and they will pay the stated interest in the interim. However, bonds issued at a time when the going municipal interest rate is 4% will have a fair market value of much less than par at a time when the going rate for municipal bonds of similar credit worthiness is 8%. Are all of these fluctuations to be taken into account in determining the value of the bank's assets?

If that is so, can a bank's liabilities be marked down for similar reasons? Assume, for example, that a bank has issued debentures which because of the low interest rate and the difficulties that the bank faces are traded at 50 cents on the dollar. May the bank write down its liability to that amount or, because it will eventually have to pay 100% (unless it buys on the open market) must it carry the liability at the full value? Overall, recall from Chapter 3 that banks prefer to use historic cost accounting, rather than market value, allowing for a potentially inaccurate depiction of a bank's current financial health.

If a bank that is healthy may carry its municipal bonds and loans at par, but a bank in danger of liquidation must carry them at fair market value, there is a kind of Catch 22 to the balance sheet determination of insolvency, for a "sound" bank continues along as entirely solvent with its assets valued at par, but once some determination has been made that it is "troubled," the assets are now down-valued to their fair market value and overnight the bank becomes insolvent.

## Comments and Questions

1. Suppose that many institutions are insolvent under the balance sheet test, but all continue to operate.  Do the regulators have the authority to close some of these institutions but not others that are arguably similarly situated?

2. Suppose an institution is insolvent under the balance sheet test according to the Comptroller but is in an attractive banking market.  Because of the banking market the shareholders could prove that the institution's goodwill–the amount of premium that a solvent institution would be willing to pay for the deposit accounts–was a substantial amount, which would cause the institution to be solvent on a balance sheet test if the goodwill asset were added.  Further, suppose that the institution has favorable long-term, assignable leases for its branch locations.  Could it avoid a regulatory determination of insolvency?

3. You will recall that 12 U.S.C.A. § 371c, the statutory provision regulating inter-affiliate transactions, permits BHCs to treat their bank subsidiaries as a branch system.  In fact, BHCs frequently engage in common name, cross-marketing and cross-advertising activities, as well as other sharing of services among the bank subsidiaries.  Also recall that § 1815(e), as added by FIRREA in 1989, establishes a "cross-guarantee" provision under which the FDIC may require a healthy bank subsidiary in a multibank holding company system to reimburse the FDIC for losses caused by the failure of another bank subsidiary in the same BHC system.

4. And FDICIA added 12 U.S.C.A. § 1831o(e)(2)(C)(ii) and (E), creating a bank holding company cross-guarantee capital obligation, but in a highly conditional way.  The section generally requires an undercapitalized bank to submit a capital restoration plan, and requires a controlling company to guarantee that the depository institution will comply with the plan.  But the guarantee is limited in amount to a maximum of 5% of the depository institution's assets, and the controlling company can refuse to execute the guarantee.  Consider the following problem.

## Problem 5-7

You are an attorney with the FDIC.  Its general counsel has asked for your advice concerning Pennsylvania Bank Holding Company, an organization with seventeen bank subsidiaries and several nonbank subsidiaries.  The holding company's flagship bank, Titanic Bank, a state-chartered institution, is in financial difficulty.  Titanic Bank has approximately $1 billion in assets and has been forced by circumstances to borrow $100 million from the Federal Reserve for the past 30 days.  The other sixteen bank subsidiaries are in good shape financially and appear to have reasonable net worth.  The FDIC's general counsel wants your evaluation of the power of the FDIC to engage in the following actions.

1. Can the FDIC place Titanic Bank in receivership? If it is possible, how should the FDIC proceed? See § 1821(c).

2. The general counsel would like to send a "bill" to the other sixteen banks and the BHC for the anticipated losses to be incurred by the FDIC upon the insolvency of Titanic Bank. Can it do this? How should the bill be allocated among the sixteen other banks and the BHC? If a billed bank or BHC becomes insolvent, what would be the priority of the FDIC's bill against other creditors of the billed entity, such as holders of subordinated bank debt, uninsured depositors, and beneficiaries of letters of credit? See §§ 1815(e) and 1831o(e)(2).

3. Pennsylvania BHC has a nonbank data processing subsidiary which has provided data processing services to all bank and nonbank subsidiaries of the holding company. The data processing subsidiary has been highly profitable, and has been charging fees to the affiliated banks at least as high, if not higher, than those charged by independent data processing companies. Is it possible for the FDIC to "bill" the data processing subsidiary for losses suffered in the receivership of Titanic Bank, or otherwise recover funds from the data processing subsidiary? See § 1831g.

---

The FDIC has various expenses both in its corporate and its receivership capacity. In its corporate capacity, it will incur administrative expenses in paying deposit claims. A careful reading of the statutes suggests that the FDIC does not have a preference for such a claim but shares pro rata with all other creditors with proved claims in the distribution of the failed bank's assets. However, all other FDIC expenses incurred in the liquidation of assets of a failed bank are charged to the receivership estate and are recovered first as administrative expenses from the receiver's collections. See § 1821(d)(11).

Similarly, balancing rights between the FDIC and depositors can have many tricky aspects. Consider the relationship between a customer and the failed bank where the customer is both a depositor and a borrower. Carefully read the first sentence of § 1813(m). The section does not appear to provide a clear rule for setting off loans against deposits. For example, if a loan is not yet due and payable, it would appear that the FDIC as receiver would not have the power to set off the loan against its deposit insurance obligation without the consent of the depositor. On the other hand, the depositor might wish to accelerate its loan under equitable set off principles in order to reduce its amount of uninsured deposits. In the next problem, consider how that might affect the obligation of the FDIC and the assets ultimately available for uninsured depositors and other general, unsecured creditors.

### Problem 5-8

Assume that a hypothetical bank in liquidation has eight depositors, five with accounts of $100,000 each and three with accounts of $200,000 each. One of these last three depositors also has a loan outstanding to the bank of $100,000. The FDIC as corporation pays out $800,000 to cover insured deposits and so satisfies all five of the $100,000 depositors, as well as $100,000 of the claims of the other three. The eighth depositor seeks to set off her $100,000 loan against $100,000 of her deposits, resulting in a net deposit of $100,000. Ultimately, the FDIC as receiver recovers $400,000 and in the process of this recovery expends $30,000 in salary and expenses. It proposes to absorb the entire $400,000 as payment for expenses and as subrogee of the claims of the depositors it has paid off. One of the $200,000 depositors without any loan outstanding asks your opinion on whether he has a claim to some part of the $400,000 and whether the FDIC improperly allowed the loan set off for the other $200,000 depositor. In dollars and cents, what possible recovery do the excess depositors have? See 12 U.S.C.A. §§ 1813(m), 1821(d)(11), 1821(g), and 1822. How would an unpaid supplier of janitorial services to the bank fare?

Would the result change if the loan set off was unsecured and had been participated (sold) to a third party assignee bank? If the power of set off was still effective, would this significantly change the status of the participating bank from having an unsecured claim against the borrower to having an unsecured claim against the receiver of the failed bank.

---

A reverse twist on protecting the insurance fund is that FIRREA provided to participants in complex financial arrangements the functional equivalent of insurance above $100,000, even in a bank liquidation. Recall from Chapter 3 that under 12 U.S.C.A. § 1821(e)(8)-(10) holders of "qualified financial contracts" have the power to terminate or liquidate the contracts, specifically including the power conferred under any security agreement to foreclose on bank assets held as collateral, thus rendering these contracts exempt from bank receivership powers. The right to liquidate collateral effectively removes potential receivership assets from the liquidation. Recall also that a general depositor in a bank cannot be granted a security interest in bank assets. 12 U.S.C.A. § 90. Do you see how § 1821(e)(8)-(10) has the potential to nullify the depositor preference of § 1821(d)(11)(A)(ii) provided to both uninsured depositors and the FDIC corporation as subrogee of insured depositors? This is most likely to occur in large bank failures, involving billions of dollars.

## D.  Resolution Costs of Bank Failures

When the FDIC is appointed receiver, it has the choice of engaging in a deposit payoff under 12 U.S.C.A. § 1821(f) or engaging in a purchase and assumption transaction under § 1823(c), subject to the requirement that the FDIC use the least costly resolution methodology. 12 U.S.C.A. § 1823(c)(4)(E). In a deposit payoff the bank is liquidated. Assets are collected and liabilities are paid. A purchase and assumption transaction is a merger or acquisition of the failed bank by a successful bank, with the successful bank paying a certain amount for the goodwill value of the failed bank, largely measured by the core deposits of the institution. A third method is a deposit transfer, using the general purchase and assumption methodology, but using deposit payoff values as the basis for paying creditors.  See 12 U.S.C.A. § 1821(i).

FIRREA codified much of the common law that had developed in the bank liquidation field.  In addition, section 1821(d)(1) gives the FDIC the power to prescribe regulations it determines to be appropriate for the conduct of receiverships.  Subsection (d)(2) of § 1821 provides a variety of general powers for the receiver, specifically including succession to all the rights of the institution and authorization to conduct all its business, including merging the institution and transferring assets and liabilities of the institution, without any approval in most cases.

As a troubled bank's condition deteriorates, the FDIC will commonly work closely with the Comptroller or with the state banking authorities, depending upon whether the bank has a national or state charter.  Neither the Federal Reserve nor the Comptroller has explicit authority to deal with a failing bank in the way the FDIC does.  The Federal Reserve, of course, can lend money to any bank in need, and nothing would prevent it from encouraging such a bank to merge with another, but nothing gives the Federal Reserve explicit authority to lend money or purchase assets to facilitate such a merger, nor does it have the authority to make long term loans to sustain a failing bank.

Most deposit payoff resolutions occurred in the early years of the FDIC.  Since then, the FDIC has entered into purchase and assumption transactions far more frequently than deposit payoffs, perhaps in an attempt to maintain public confidence in the system.  A purchase and assumption option has been used whenever possible with the larger bank failures, which tend to get broader coverage by the press.  By using the purchase and assumption methodology, the FDIC usually has been able to arrange complete or almost complete payoffs of all depositors, both insured and uninsured, as well as unsecured creditors.

But since FDICIA was enacted the FDIC's ability to use the purchase and assumption arrangement is dependent upon the least cost test.  And after depositor preference was added to § 1821(d)(11) in 1993, it is even harder to conclude that a traditional purchase and assumption transaction is the least costly resolution.  This has lead to an increase in the use of deposit payoffs, and particularly in the use of deposit transfers under § 1821(i).  (There also is a fourth resolution methodology, though we will not directly consider it.  The FDIC has the authority to own and operate a newly chartered national bank until a more permanent solution can be arranged for a failed bank.  This is known as a bridge bank, which provides a means of preserving the going-concern value of an institution until an acquirer can be found in due course of time.)

Uninsured depositors now can be protected through a purchase and assumption transfer to a successful bank only if the acquirer is willing to pay an additional, incremental premium for the franchise value of the failed bank that is greater than the uninsured depositors' portion of the insolvent institution's loss.  Also, the depositor preference provisions of § 1821(d)(11) require that the FDIC not payoff any general unsecured creditors of a failed bank until both the FDIC's insurance fund costs have been fully recovered (as the FDIC is subrogated to, and stands in the shoes of, the insured depositors) and all uninsured depositors are fully paid.  Consequently, while in the past purchase and assumption deals commonly protected general uninsured creditors, as well as uninsured depositors, it now will be much more difficult to arrange a purchase and assumption deal in which all of a bank's liabilities are transferred to a new owner.

Overall, to determine the least-cost method of resolution, the FDIC must compare its loss in a deposit payoff and liquidation transaction to its estimated loss under each bid received for purchase of the franchise of the failed bank.  As the statute indicates, other policy considerations are largely secondary to the least-cost test.  But these other policy considerations might be taken into account in particular circumstances.  For example, a determination of systemic risk to public confidence and stability in the banking system allows the regulators to avoid the least-cost test.

In a deposit payoff, the FDIC as corporation pays the full claim amount to all insured depositors and liquidates the assets of the failed bank.  The separate classes of uninsured depositors and other general creditors of the bank receive less than full reimbursement in the form of receivership certificates, which entitle them to a proportionate share of collections on the failed bank assets.  The uninsured depositors and the FDIC as subrogee to the insured depositors share pro rata to the full extent of their claims before unsecured creditors receive any reimbursement.

In an insured-deposit transfer transaction under § 1821(i), uninsured depositors and unsecured creditors are not fully protected.  Only the insured deposits and the secured liabilities are transferred to the acquiring bank.  Uninsured deposits and unsecured creditors remain with the receivership.  The FDIC corporation makes a cash payment to the acquiring institution.  This payment equals the amount of the insured deposits and secured and preferred liabilities less the assets transferred and any franchise premium paid.

A purchase and assumption transaction works as follows.  The FDIC, as receiver, holds all the assets of the failed bank.  The deposit liabilities and certain assets of the failed bank are transferred to a profitable bank.  If necessary, the FDIC corporation pays the assuming bank funds equal to the amount of deposit liabilities assumed less the value of the assets transferred and the premium paid for the perceived value of the franchise, similar to the computation in an insured deposit transfer.  Section 1821(d) gives the FDIC the authority to deal with itself in its two separate capacities, as receiver of the failed bank and as corporate insurer of deposits.  Under an agreement between the FDIC as receiver and FDIC in its corporate capacity, the FDIC-corporation assumes all of the liabilities not assumed by the purchasing bank and also takes title to all the assets not transferred to the purchasing bank.  FDIC-corporate then liquidates the assets that it has taken over.  FDIC-corporate next repays itself, from the funds realized through liquidation, whatever advance it has made to the assuming bank plus its expenses for liquidation and interest.  Any remaining funds and liabilities are returned to the FDIC-receiver in order to pay off other claims against the bank in receivership.

In determining the costs of alternative transactions, the FDIC is required to compute the cost of a deposit payoff and liquidation as of the date the receiver is appointed, but must determine the cost of any other transaction as of the date on which the FDIC provides assistance. See 12 U.S.C.A. § 1823(c)(4)(C). Therefore, the cost of liquidation to the FDIC can be computed as the total of the insured deposits less the present value of the assets of the institution, which must be shared pro rata with the uninsured depositors, but not with unsecured creditors. In effect, then, it is easy to create a balance sheet that shows only assets and liabilities of the failed institution, the assets being all of the assets from which values can be realized and the liabilities being the FDIC insured deposits and the uninsured deposits. The liabilities typically will exceed the assets, and the FDIC cost can be determined by computing the difference between the cost of the payout on the insured deposits and the FDIC's pro rata share of the assets. Unsecured creditors often get nothing.

In a purchase and assumption transaction, the place to start the computation of the transaction's cost to the FDIC is with the acquiring institution, as the assets and liabilities assumed by the acquiring institution must be equal. The asset side is generally evidenced by the failed bank assets acquired, the value of the premium that the acquiring bank is willing to pay, and the value of any necessary FDIC monetary assistance. The counterbalancing liabilities are typically made up of deposits and any other liabilities that are assumed. Some of these liabilities assumed might be secured creditors, but the FDIC may also wish to provide full protection of certain unsecured, nondeposit liabilities. Failure to protect certain unsecured creditors may adversely impact the going concern value of an institution. Such creditors often are providing some essential service, such as data processing or accounting services. 12 U.S.C.A. § 1821(i)(3) specifically authorizes such differential treatment of selected unsecured creditors.

For example, in the failure of U.S. National Bank the purchasing bank, Crocker Anglo, received $130 million in cash plus all of the bank's "clean" assets, worth $850 million. In exchange Crocker assumed $1,070 million of U.S. National Bank's liabilities, mostly deposits, for which it "paid" a $90 million premium. From Crocker's point of view, the transaction balanced. The FDIC also paid off U.S. National Bank's $30 million Federal Reserve loan. In addition, the FDIC, not Crocker, shared the remaining assets with those who ultimately procured judgments against the U.S. National Bank. The FDIC also indemnified Crocker against liabilities not specifically assumed by Crocker and not arising out of Crocker's own actions.

Try your hand at the deposit payoff, deposit transfer, or purchase and assumption alternatives in the following problem.

*Problem 5-9*

As counsel for the FDIC, you have obtained the following financial statements of Wappinger National Bank and the report of an FDIC examiner who recently examined the bank. The examiner's report states that:

(a) Ten percent of all loans should be classified as loss or uncollectible and completely charged-off against capital; 20% should be classified as doubtful of which one-half should be considered uncollectible and charged-off; and 23% are substandard, for which better or more security should be obtained.

(b) Eighty percent of the bank's deposits are covered by FDIC insurance.

Wappinger has been a troubled bank in the past and the FDIC has questioned their loan practices, but has not taken official action.  The capital accounts on the balance sheet show a little under $5 million from which more than $14.3 million must be subtracted as a result of the loan losses.

With such large amounts to be deducted from the capital accounts, the balance sheet now shows the bank to be insolvent.  No bank is willing to extend a large loan to Wappinger to help it out of its troubled condition.  With seven branch offices in Union (population 365,000) and Fishkill (population 461,000) counties, Wappinger National Bank is the third largest bank in the area.  Both counties, located near a large metropolitan area, have undergone rapid growth.  The household median income is usually above the state average, but the area has recently suffered from industry layoffs and shutdowns.  The unemployment of the area is at an all-time high of 10%.  There are five other banks in the two county area.

To facilitate a sale of the franchise to a bank in the area, the FDIC has offered to loan the highest bidder $20 million to repay Wappinger's secured loan from the Federal Reserve.  The purchasing bank would repay the loan in ten years at 6% interest. Since the interest rate is considerably lower than the prime rate, the FDIC-corporation estimates that it will lose $3 million in future earnings on the loan.  The FDIC-corporation will purchase Wappinger's uncollectible loans at their full book value and suffer the resulting loss.  The examiner estimates that the FDIC-receiver could liquidate the investment securities, and the bank premises and equipment, for seventy-five percent of their book value.

1.  Palatka National Bank, the largest bank in the Union-Fishkill area with twenty-two branch offices, has offered the only bids:  $10 million to assume all deposits and purchase the assets of Wappinger; or $9 million if only insured deposits are assumed.  Would either be financially more advantageous to the FDIC than a deposit payoff?  Should the FDIC demand a higher premium?

2.  If the FDIC must reject the Palatka offers because of antitrust problems, it may accept the offer of Fishkill Savings Bank, the smallest, bank in the Union-Fishkill area. Fishkill has offered to purchase the deposits and liabilities of Wappinger, but it can only pay a $2 million premium for all deposits.  According to the bank examiner, it would be less expensive to liquidate the bank's assets and pay off the depositors and creditors.

Hrothgar, president of Wappinger, urges you to accept the Fishkill proposal.  He argues that the FDIC's loss may not be limited to Wappinger since its failure could weaken public confidence in the solvent banks in the community and cause a run on these banks which could force many to fail.  He urges the FDIC to interpret section 1823(c) to include losses from the potential failure of other banks in the community.  Should the FDIC accept Fishkill's offer, liquidate Wappinger, or follow Hrothgar's advice?

## WAPPINGER NATIONAL BANK STATEMENT OF CONDITION

| As of December 31, | 1996 | 1995 |
|---|---|---|
| ASSETS | | |
| Cash and due from banks | $ 6,317,088 | 7,957,278 |
| Investment securities: | | |
| U.S. Treasury obligations | 776,607 | 7,878,122 |
| U.S. Government Agencies | 1,766,524 | 4,213,171 |
| State and municipal | 1,174,219 | 5,437,721 |
| Other | 898,696 | 731,814 |
| Total investment securities | $ 4,616,046 | $18,260,828 |
| Federal funds sold | --- | 2,500,000 |
| Loans | 71,601,979 | 41,083,467 |
| Bank premises and equipment, net | 2,862,804 | 2,802,048 |
| Interest receivable and other assets | 880,324 | 712,303 |
| TOTAL ASSETS | $86,278,241 | $73,315,924 |
| | | |
| LIABILITIES AND CAPITAL FUNDS | | |
| Demand deposits | $22,184,048 | $25,309,425 |
| Savings deposits | 17,142,679 | 19,826,981 |
| Other time deposits | 22,150,345 | 21,810,412 |
| Total deposits | 61,248,825 | 66,946,818 |
| Federal Reserve Loan Payable | 20,000,000 | 3,299,195 |
| Total Liabilities | 81,248,825 | 69,647,623 |
| Reserve for possible Loan Losses | 554,286 | 536,326 |
| Capital funds- | | |
| Subordinated capital notes | $ 1,000,000 | $ --- |
| | | |
| LIABILITIES AND CAPITAL FUNDS | | |
| Common stock, $7.50 par value, 238,518 shares authorized and outstanding | $ 1,788,885 | $ 1,490,742 |
| Surplus | 1,200,000 | 1,143,185 |
| Undivided profits | 486,245 | 498,048 |
| Shareholders' equity | $ 3,475,130 | $ 3,131,975 |
| Total capital funds | $ 4,475,130 | $ 3,131,975 |
| TOTAL LIABILITIES AND CAPITAL FUNDS | $86,278,241 | $73,315,924 |

## STATEMENT OF INCOME

| For the years ended December 31, | 1996 | 1995 |
|---|---|---|
| OPERATING INCOME: | | |
| Interest and fees on loans | $ 4,403,046 | $ 2,979,172 |
| Interest on Federal funds sold | --- | 221,096 |
| Income on investments | | |
| U.S. Treasury and | | |
| Agency securities | 45,819 | 503,090 |
| State and municipal obligations | 102,282 | 243,932 |
| Other securities | 60,530 | 31,333 |
| Service charges on | | |
| deposit accounts | 302,221 | 273,121 |
| Other income | 238,970 | 179,306 |
| TOTAL OPERATING INCOME | $ 5,152,868 | $ 4,431,050 |
| | | |
| OPERATING EXPENSES: | | |
| Salaries and employee benefits | $ 1,256,918 | 1,078,287 |
| Interest on deposits | 2,242,492 | 1,845,843 |
| Interest on capital notes | 73,135 | 7,289 |
| Net occupancy expense | 264,508 | 274,412 |
| Provision for possible | | |
| loan losses | 60,000 | 55,000 |
| General and administrative | | |
| expenses | 826,195 | 715,929 |
| TOTAL OPERATING EXPENSES | $ 4,723,248 | $ 3,976,760 |
| INCOME BEFORE INCOME TAXES | | |
| AND SECURITIES TRANSACTIONS | $ 429,620 | $ 454,290 |
| PROVISION FOR INCOME TAXES | 75,000 | 100,971 |
| INCOME BEFORE SECURITIES | | |
| TRANSACTIONS | $ 354,620 | $ 353,319 |
| SECURITIES GAINS (LOSSES), net of | | |
| related income tax effects of $300 | | |
| in 1996 and $1,200 in 1995 | (195) | 1,138 |
| NET INCOME | $ 354,425 | $ 354,457 |
| | | |
| EARNINGS PER SHARE, restated to | | |
| reflect a 20% stock dividend in 1996 | | |
| Income before securities | | |
| transactions | $1.48 | $1.48 |
| Securities transactions | --- | .01 |
| Net Income | $1.48 | $1.49 |

Numerous controversies can result from these failed bank resolution transactions between a solvent bank, the FDIC as receiver, and the FDIC in its corporate capacity. Typically, these controversies arise between the FDIC and shareholders of the failed bank, between the FDIC and the creditors of the failed bank, between the FDIC and debtors of the failed bank, and between the FDIC and other parties, particularly directors and officers of the failed bank. Several of these controversies will be discussed in more detail below. But first we will take a brief look at the failure of a BHC.

## E.  The Bankruptcy Code-Bank Receivership Interface

Despite substantial bankruptcy and bank receivership legislation, the interplay between the two areas of law remains quite uncertain when a bank holding company becomes insolvent. On March 27, 1989, MCorp stated its intention to file for protection from its creditors under Chapter 11 of the Bankruptcy Code. Two days later the bank regulators put into receivership twenty of MCorp's twenty-five bank subsidiaries. At the same time, the Federal Reserve initiated administrative cease and desist proceedings against MCorp. The following litigation ensued.

## Board of Governors v. Mcorp Financial, Inc.
### 502 U.S. 32 (1991)

Justice STEVENS delivered the opinion of the Court.

MCorp, a bank holding company, filed voluntary bankruptcy petitions in March 1989. It then initiated an adversary proceeding against the Board of Governors of the Federal Reserve System (Board) seeking to enjoin the prosecution of two administrative proceedings, one charging MCorp with a violation of the Board's "source of strength" regulation[1] and the other alleging a violation of § 23A of the Federal Reserve Act, as added, 48 Stat. 183, and amended.[2] The District Court enjoined both proceedings, and the Board appealed. The Court of Appeals held that the District Court had no jurisdiction to enjoin the § 23A proceeding, but that, under the doctrine set forth in *Leedom v. Kyne*, 358 U.S. 184 (1958), the District Court had jurisdiction to review the validity of the "source of strength" regulation. The Court of Appeals then ruled that the Board had exceeded its statutory authority in promulgating that regulation. 900 F.2d 852 (CA5 1990). We granted certiorari, 499 U.S. 904 (1991), to review the entire action but, because we conclude that the District Court lacked jurisdiction to enjoin either regulatory proceeding, we do not reach the merits of MCorp's challenge to the regulation.

---

[1]    The "source of strength" regulation provides in relevant part: "A bank holding company shall serve as a source of financial and managerial strength to its subsidiary banks and shall not con[d]uct its operations in an unsafe or unsound manner." 12 CFR § 225.4(a)(1) (1991).

[2]    Section 23A sets forth restrictions on bank holding companies' corporate practices, including restrictions on transactions between subsidiary banks and nonbank affiliates. See 12 U.S.C. § 371c.

I

In 1984, the Board promulgated a regulation requiring every bank holding company to "serve as a source of financial and managerial strength to its subsidiary banks."[3]  In October 1988, the Board commenced an administrative proceeding against MCorp,[4] alleging that MCorp violated the source of strength regulation and engaged in unsafe and unsound banking practices that jeopardized the financial condition of its subsidiary banks.  The Board also issued three temporary cease-and-desist orders.[5]  The first forbids MCorp to declare or pay any dividends without the prior approval of the Board.  App. 65-67.  The second forbids MCorp to dissipate any of its nonbank assets without the prior approval of the Board.  *Id.* at 68-70.  The third directs MCorp to use "all of its assets to provide capital support to its Subsidiary Banks in need of additional capital."  *Id.* at 85.  By agreement, enforcement of the third order was suspended while MCorp sought financial assistance from the Federal Deposit Insurance Corporation (FDIC).[6]

In March 1989, the FDIC denied MCorp's request for assistance.  Thereafter, creditors filed an involuntary bankruptcy petition against MCorp in the Southern District of New York, and the Comptroller of the Currency determined that 20 of MCorp's subsidiary banks were insolvent and, accordingly, appointed the FDIC as receiver of those banks.  MCorp then filed voluntary bankruptcy petitions in the Southern District of Texas and all bankruptcy proceedings were later consolidated in that forum.

At the end of March, the Board commenced a second administrative proceeding against MCorp alleging that it had violated § 23A of the Federal Reserve Act by causing two of its subsidiary banks to extend unsecured credit of approximately $63.7 million to an affiliate.  For convenience, we shall refer to that proceeding as the "§ 23A proceeding" and to the earlier proceeding as the "source of strength proceeding."

In May 1989, MCorp initiated this litigation by filing a complaint in the Bankruptcy Court against the Board seeking a declaration that both administrative proceedings had been automatically stayed pursuant to the Bankruptcy Code; in the alternative, MCorp prayed for an injunction against the further prosecution of those proceedings without the prior approval of the Bankruptcy Court.  On the Board's motion, the District Court transferred that adversary proceeding to its own docket.

---

[3]    See n.1, *supra*.  In 1987, the Board clarified its policy and stated that a "bank holding company's failure to assist a troubled or failing subsidiary bank. . . . would generally be viewed as an unsafe and unsound banking practice or a violation of [12 CFR § 225.4(a)(1) ] or both."  52 Fed. Reg. 15707-15708.

[4]    The term "MCorp" refers to the corporation and to two of its wholly owned subsidiaries, MCorp Financial, Inc., and MCorp Management.

[5]    MCorp timely challenged these orders in the District Court for the Northern District of Texas, pursuant to 12 U.S.C. § 1818(c)(2).  The District Court stayed MCorp's challenge pending resolution of this proceeding.  Brief for MCorp et al.

[6]    The current status of this order is unclear.  See Tr. of Oral Arg. 22-25, 41-42.  We address only MCorp's effort to enjoin the Board's administrative proceedings and express no opinion on the continuing vitality or validity of any of the temporary cease-and-desist orders.

In June 1989, the District Court ruled that it had jurisdiction to enjoin the Board from prosecuting both administrative proceedings against MCorp and entered a preliminary injunction halting those proceedings. The injunction restrained the Board from exercising "its authority over bank holding companies . . . to attempt to effect, directly or indirectly, a reorganization of the MCorp group [of companies] except through participation in the bankruptcy proceedings." *In re MCorp*, 101 B.R. 483, 491. The Board appealed.

Although the District Court did not differentiate between the two Board proceedings, the Court of Appeals held that the § 23A proceeding could go forward but that the source of strength proceeding should be enjoined. The court reasoned that the plain language of the judicial review provisions of the Financial Institutions Supervisory Act of 1966 (FISA), 80 Stat. 1046, as amended, 12 U.S.C. § 1818 *et seq.* (1988 ed. and Supp. II), particularly § 1818(i)(1), deprived the District Court of jurisdiction to enjoin either proceeding, but that our decision in *Leedom v. Kyne*, 358 U.S. 184 (1958), nevertheless authorized an injunction against an administrative proceeding conducted without statutory authorization. The Court of Appeals ruled that the Board's promulgation and enforcement of its source of strength regulation exceeded its statutory authority. Accordingly, the court vacated the District Court injunction barring the § 23A proceeding, but remanded the case with instructions to enjoin the Board from enforcing its source of strength regulation. Both parties petitioned for certiorari.

The Board's petition challenges the Court of Appeals' interpretation of *Leedom v. Kyne*, as well as its invalidation of the source of strength regulation. MCorp's petition challenges the Court of Appeals' interpretation of the relationship between the provisions governing judicial review of Board proceedings and those governing bankruptcy proceedings. We first address the latter challenge.

## II

A series of federal statutes gives the Board substantial regulatory power over bank holding companies and establishes a comprehensive scheme of judicial review of Board actions. See FISA; the Bank Holding Company Act of 1956 (BHCA), 12 U.S.C. § 1841 *et seq.* (1988 ed. and Supp. II); and the International Lending Supervision Act of 1983, 12 U.S.C. § 3901 *et seq.* In this litigation, the most relevant of these is FISA.[7]

FISA authorizes the Board to institute administrative proceedings culminating in cease-and-desist orders, 12 U.S.C. §§ 1818(a)-(b) (1988 ed., Supp. II), and to issue temporary cease-and-desist orders that are effective upon service on a bank holding company. § 1818(c). In addition, FISA establishes a tripartite regime of judicial review. First, § 1818(c)(2) provides that, within 10 days after service of a temporary order, a bank holding company may seek an injunction in district court restraining enforcement of the order pending completion of the related administrative proceeding. Second, § 1818(h) authorizes court of appeals review of final Board orders on the application of an aggrieved party. Finally, § 1818(i)(1) provides that the Board may apply to district court for enforcement of any effective and outstanding notice or order.

---

[7] Although the several "Notices of Charges and of Hearing" issued by the Board against MCorp relied on FISA *and* the BHCA, e.g., App. 57, 72, the parties have focused only on the former. We note, however, that the BHCA includes a preclusion provision that is similar to § 1818(i)(1) in FISA. See 12 U.S.C. § 1844(e)(2).

None of these provisions controls this litigation:  The action before us is not a challenge to a temporary Board order, nor a petition for review of a final Board order, nor an enforcement action initiated by the Board.  Instead, FISA's preclusion provision appears to speak directly to the jurisdictional question at issue in this litigation:  "[E]xcept as otherwise provided in this section no court shall have jurisdiction to affect by injunction or otherwise the issuance or enforcement of any notice or order under this section, or to review, modify, suspend, terminate, or set aside any such notice or order."  *Ibid.*  Notwithstanding this plain, preclusive language, MCorp argues that the District Court's injunction against the prosecution of the Board proceedings was authorized either by the automatic stay provision in the Bankruptcy Code, 11 U.S.C. § 362, or by the provision of the Judicial Code authorizing district courts in bankruptcy proceedings to exercise concurrent jurisdiction over certain civil proceedings, 28 U.S.C. § 1334(b).  We find no merit in either argument.

The filing of a bankruptcy petition operates as an automatic stay of several categories of judicial and administrative proceedings.[9]  The Board's planned actions against MCorp constitute the "continuation . . . [of] administrative . . . proceeding[s]" and would appear to be stayed by 11 U.S.C. § 362(a)(1).  However, the Board's actions also fall squarely within § 362(b)(4), which expressly provides that the automatic stay will not reach proceedings to enforce a "governmental unit's police or regulatory power."[10]

MCorp contends that in order for § 362(b)(4) to obtain, a court must first determine whether the proposed exercise of police or regulatory power is legitimate and that, therefore, in this litigation the lower courts did have the authority to examine the legitimacy of the Board's

---

[9]    The automatic stay provision provides in relevant part:

(a) Except as provided in subsection (b) of this section, a petition filed under section 301, 302, or 303 of this title, or an application filed under section 5(a)(3) of the Securities Investor Protection Act of 1970 (15 U.S.C. 78eee(a)(3)), operates as a stay, applicable to all entities, of

(1) the commencement or continuation, including the issuance or employment of process, of a judicial, administrative, or other action or proceeding against the debtor that was or could have been commenced before the commencement of the case under this title, or to recover a claim against the debtor that arose before the commencement of the case under this title; . . . .

(3) any act to obtain possession of property of the estate or of property from the estate or to exercise control over property of the estate; . . .

(6) any act to collect, assess, or recover a claim against the debtor that arose before the commencement of the case under this title. . . .

11 U.S.C. § 362(a).

[10]    Title 11 U.S.C. § 362(b)(4) provides:

(b) The filing of a petition under section 301, 302, or 303 of this title, or of an application under section 5(a)(3) of the Securities Investor Protection Act of 1970 (15 U.S.C. 78eee(a)(3)), does not operate as a stay − . . .

(4) under subsection (a)(1) of this section, of the commencement or continuation of an action or proceeding by a governmental unit to enforce such governmental unit's police or regulatory power. . . .

actions and to enjoin those actions.  We disagree.  MCorp's broad reading of the stay provisions would require bankruptcy courts to scrutinize the validity of every administrative or enforcement action brought against a bankrupt entity.  Such a reading is problematic, both because it conflicts with the broad discretion Congress has expressly granted many administrative entities and because it is inconsistent with the limited authority Congress has vested in bankruptcy courts. We therefore reject MCorp's reading of § 362(b)(4).

MCorp also argues that it is protected by §§ 362(a)(3) and 362(a)(6) of the Bankruptcy Code.  Those provisions stay "any act" to obtain possession of, or to exercise control over, property of the estate, or to recover claims against the debtor that arose prior to the filing of the bankruptcy petition.  MCorp contends that the ultimate objective of the source of strength proceeding is to exercise control of corporate assets and that the § 23A proceeding seeks enforcement of a prepetition claim.

We reject these characterizations of the ongoing administrative proceedings.  At this point, the Board has only issued "Notices of Charges and of Hearing" and has expressed its intent to determine whether MCorp has violated specified statutory and regulatory provisions.  It is possible, of course, that the Board proceedings, like many other enforcement actions, may conclude with the entry of an order that will affect the Bankruptcy Court's control over the property of the estate, but that *possibility* cannot be sufficient to justify the operation of the stay against an enforcement proceeding that is expressly exempted by § 362(b)(4).  To adopt such a characterization of enforcement proceedings would be to render subsection (b)(4)'s exception almost meaningless.  If and when the Board's proceedings culminate in a final order, and if and when judicial proceedings are commenced to enforce such an order, then it may well be proper for the Bankruptcy Court to exercise its concurrent jurisdiction under 28 U.S.C. § 1334(b).  We are not persuaded, however, that the automatic stay provisions of the Bankruptcy Code have any application to ongoing, nonfinal administrative proceedings.

MCorp's final argument rests on 28 U.S.C. § 1334(b).  That section authorizes a district court to exercise concurrent jurisdiction over certain bankruptcy-related civil proceedings that would otherwise be subject to the exclusive jurisdiction of another court[12]  MCorp's reliance is misplaced.  Section 1334(b) concerns the allocation of jurisdiction between bankruptcy courts and other "*courts*," and, of course, an administrative agency such as the Board is not a "court." Moreover, contrary to MCorp's contention, the prosecution of the Board proceedings, prior to the entry of a final order and prior to the commencement of any enforcement action, seems unlikely to impair the Bankruptcy Court's exclusive jurisdiction over the property of the estate protected by 28 U.S.C. § 1334(d).  In sum, we agree with the Court of Appeals that the specific preclusive language in 12 U.S.C. § 1818(i)(1) (1988 ed., Supp. II) is not qualified or superseded by the general provisions governing bankruptcy proceedings on which MCorp relies.

---

[12]    Title 28 U.S.C. § 1334(b) provides: "(b) Notwithstanding any Act of Congress that confers exclusive jurisdiction on a court or courts other than the district courts, the district court shall have original but not exclusive jurisdiction of all civil proceedings arising under title 11, or arising in or related to cases under title 11."

## III

Although the Court of Appeals found that § 1818(i)(1) precluded judicial review of many Board actions, it exercised jurisdiction in this litigation based on its reading of *Leedom v. Kyne*, 358 U.S. 184 (1958). *Kyne* involved an action in District Court challenging a determination by the National Labor Relations Board (NLRB) that a unit including both professional and nonprofessional employees was appropriate for collective-bargaining purposes–a determination in direct conflict with a provision of the National Labor Relations Act.  The Act, however, did not expressly authorize any judicial review of such a determination.  Relying on *Switchmen v. National Mediation Bd.*, 320 U.S. 297 (1943), the NLRB argued that the statutory provisions establishing review of final Board orders in the courts of appeals indicated a congressional intent to bar review of any NLRB action in the District Court.[15]  The Court rejected that argument, emphasizing the presumption that Congress normally intends the federal courts to enforce and protect the rights that Congress has created.  Concluding that the Act did not bar the District Court's jurisdiction, we stated:  "This Court cannot lightly infer that Congress does not intend judicial protection of rights it confers against agency action taken in excess of delegated powers." 358 U.S. at 190.

In this litigation, the Court of Appeals interpreted our opinion in *Kyne* as authorizing judicial review of any agency action that is alleged to have exceeded the agency's statutory authority.  *Kyne*, however, differs from this litigation in two critical ways.  First, central to our decision in *Kyne* was the fact that the Board's interpretation of the Act would wholly deprive the union of a meaningful and adequate means of vindicating its statutory rights.  "Here, differently from the *Switchmen*'s case, 'absence of jurisdiction of the federal courts' would mean 'a sacrifice or obliteration of a right which Congress' has given professional employees, for there is no other means, within their control. . . to protect and enforce that right." *Ibid.*  The cases before us today are entirely different from *Kyne* because FISA expressly provides MCorp with a meaningful and adequate opportunity for judicial review of the validity of the source of strength regulation.  If and when the Board finds that MCorp has violated that regulation, MCorp will have, in the Court of Appeals, an unquestioned right to review of both the regulation and its application.

The second, and related, factor distinguishing this litigation from *Kyne* is the clarity of the congressional preclusion of review in FISA.  In *Kyne*, the NLRB contended that a statutory provision that provided for judicial review implied, by its silence, a preclusion of review of the contested determination.  By contrast, in FISA Congress has spoken clearly and directly: *"[N]o court shall have jurisdiction to affect by injunction or otherwise the issuance or enforcement of any [Board] notice or order under this section."*  12 U.S.C. § 1818(i)(1) (1988 ed., Supp. II) (emphasis added).  In this way as well, this litigation differs from *Kyne*.

---

[15]    In *Switchmen v. National Mediation Bd.*, 320 U.S. at 306, the Court had reasoned:

When Congress in § 3 and in § 9 provided for judicial review of two types of orders or awards and in § 2 of the same Act omitted any such provision as respects a third type, it drew a plain line of distinction.  And the inference is strong from the history of the Act that that distinction was not inadvertent.  The language of the Act read in light of that history supports the view that Congress gave administrative action under § 2, Ninth a finality which it denied administrative action under the other sections of the Act.

Viewed in this way, *Kyne* stands for the familiar proposition that "only upon a showing of 'clear and convincing evidence' of a contrary legislative intent should the courts restrict access to judicial review." *Abbott Laboratories v. Gardner*, 387 U.S. 136, 141 (1967). As we have explained, however, in this case the statute provides us with clear and convincing evidence that Congress intended to deny the District Court jurisdiction to review and enjoin the Board's ongoing administrative proceedings.

## IV

The Court of Appeals therefore erred when it held that it had jurisdiction to consider the merits of MCorp's challenge to the source of strength regulation. In No. 90-913, the judgment of the Court of Appeals remanding the case with instructions to enjoin the source of strength proceedings is therefore reversed. In No. 90-914, the judgment of the Court of Appeals vacating the District Court's injunction against prosecution of the § 23A proceeding is affirmed.

## Comments and Questions

1. Do you see the conflicting policy objectives of the bank receivership statutes and the Bankruptcy Code? The bank receivership statute is largely focused on minimizing the loss to the deposit insurance fund by maximizing the receiver's claims to assets and minimizing claims against the receiver. In contrast, the Bankruptcy Code is designed to achieve a fair distribution of the debtor's assets among creditors. And if the debtor's estate is under Chapter 11 bankruptcy reorganization, an additional objective is to rehabilitate the debtor's business, continuing a valuable economic activity and maintaining jobs.

2. It is clear that the bankruptcy court does not have any jurisdiction over the assets of a bank in receivership. See 12 U.S.C.A. §§ 1821(d)(13)(C) and (D), 1821(j). If the bankruptcy court cannot reach the banks themselves, how is it possible for the bankruptcy court to develop a successful reorganization?

3. Does the case suggest that it may be prudent for a BHC to transfer as many of its activities as possible from its bank to its nonbank subsidiaries? For example, would it be prudent to place in nonbank subsidiaries such activities as data processing, discount brokerage, credit card operations, and to the extent possible the activities of the trust department? Note that the passage of FIRREA has strengthened the authority of the FDIC to reach the assets of all banks in a BHC system under the cross-guarantee provision. 12 U.S.C.A. § 1815(e). But the section does not reach the parent holding company or the nonbank subsidiaries, and the reach of 12 U.S.C.A. § 1831o(e)(2)(C)(ii) and (E) is highly conditional.

4. If the FDIC wished to recover various assets that it claims were improperly diverted from the failed banks, would the FDIC as receiver be forced to file a proof of claim in MCorp's bankruptcy? What effect would this have on the ability of bank regulators to deal with the nonbank subsidiaries in a bank rescue scenario? In the case, the Federal Reserve made a similar claim in its § 371c proceeding. If the Federal Reserve determines that § 371c was violated, how is that determination to be judicially reviewed —

by the bankruptcy court or by a circuit court?  How could the agency recover the assets, and with what priority?  Note that in *MCorp* the Court indicated the bankruptcy court has jurisdiction over the property of the bankrupt.  The Court appeared to leave open the question whether a bankruptcy court could stay enforcement of a banking agency final order that attempted to take property of the estate.  But in *Carleton v. First Corp.*, 967 F.2d 942 (4th Cir. 1992) the court allowed enforcement of an agency temporary cease and desist order that required a turnover of a subsidiary's stock (a savings and loan association) by the Chapter 11 debtor.  The significance of the case may be limited, however, because the holding company in Chapter 11 had entered into a capital maintenance agreement with the bank regulator which included an agreement to obtain bank regulatory approval before acquiring or disposing of savings and loan association subsidiaries.

5.  Does *MCorp* affect the ability of the FDIC receiver to deal with subsidiaries of the bank, as contrasted with subsidiaries of the bank holding company?  It appears that the answer is no.  In *In re Landmark Land Co. of Oklahoma, Inc.*, 973 F.2d 283 (4th Cir. 1992), the court determined that the bank receiver's powers over a failed depository institution extend to its non-bank subsidiaries that were in Chapter 11.  But difficult questions remain.  For example, it would seem that creditors of the bank's non-bank subsidiary that is in Chapter 11 would have a clear priority claim over the FDIC as receiver, which holds claims only as a shareholder, absent a claim of fraudulent conveyance or the like by the FDIC.

6.  Another difficult question is a bank in receivership holding as an asset a loan to a borrower that is in bankruptcy with claims against the failed bank.  Each party, through a separate insolvency regime, has a claim against the other.  In *In re Parker North American Corp.*, 24 F.3d 1145 (9th Cir. 1994), the court held that the jurisdictional bar of 12 U.S.C.A. § 1821(d)(13)(D) applied only to claims "by creditors" and therefore bankruptcy courts retain jurisdiction over claims "by debtors" against the bank in receivership.  But another circuit, in dictum, disagreed.  See *Freeman v. FDIC*, 56 F.3d 1394, 1401 (D.C. Cir. 1995).

7.  Does the *MCorp* decision determine whether bank regulations affecting affiliates are covered by the automatic stay of the bankruptcy court against all litigation, thus limiting attempts to deal with questionable transactions within a BHC system?  In other words, does *MCorp* effectively stop the regulatory process, rather than just execution on money judgments?  The Bankruptcy Code provides that the filing of a petition does not operate as a stay "of the enforcement of a judgment, other than a money judgment, obtained in an action or proceeding by a governmental unit to enforce such governmental unit's police or regulatory power."  11 U.S.C.A. § 362(b)(5).

## F.  Creditors and Priorities

### 1. In General

Those familiar with Article 9 of the Uniform Commercial Code and with the Bankruptcy Code appreciate the kind of legislation both the states and Congress have enacted to govern the rights of creditors and debtors in circumstances like those considered in this chapter.  When a bank becomes insolvent, however, it is clear that the lawyer cannot simply bring over Article 9 and the Bankruptcy Code and apply them to a bank.  First, banking corporations are specifically exempted from the federal Bankruptcy Code, 11 U.S.C.A. § 109(b)(2).  Thus, any bankruptcy law could only be applied to a bank's insolvency by analogy.  Second, the National Bank Act and the Federal Deposit Insurance Act are not as comprehensive as the Bankruptcy Code or Article 9, but they do have certain sections that determine creditors' rights and priorities and provide, for example, for the setting aside of preferences.  The presence of these sections makes it clear that Congress did not intend the state law of creditor's rights to apply in toto to national banks.  The question is whether Congress intended state law to apply at all.  Cases such as *Clearfield Trust Co. v. United States*, 318 U.S. 363 (1943), as well as cases dealing explicitly with the National Bank Act, form a basis for an argument that the claims of creditors against the national bank are to be resolved according to federal law – certain sections in the FDI and National Bank Acts, some sort of federal common law, and other applicable federal statutes.  However, we will see that recent cases have suggested that where there is an extensive federal statutory structure there is no supplementary federal common law.  And 12 U.S.C.A. § 1821(e)(11) provides that at least the state law according to perfection of security interests applies to the creditors of a national bank.

The federal statutory law has a series of sections that deal explicitly with some of the creditors' rights.  First is the provision in 12 U.S.C.A. § 1821(a) that provides for the FDIC's payment to "depositors" of up to $100,000 each.  Whether one calls this a priority, a preference or simply a federal guarantee, it is an obvious intentional preferring of one class of creditors.  Second, § 1821(e)(11) generally protects perfected security interests, and appears to treat security interests more favorably than does the Bankruptcy Code, disallowing security interests only if taken in contemplation of insolvency, rather than the 90 day improvement in position disallowance in bankruptcy.  Third, § 1821(d)(11) provides a simplified priority hierarchy for distribution from a failed depository institution.  The order of priority is:  (1) administrative expenses; (2) deposits; (3) general unsecured creditors; (4) subordinated unsecured creditors; and (5) shareholders.  Fourth, also different from bankruptcy, § 1821(i) allows the receiver to treat creditors of the same class differently, in two ways.  First, it limits the receiver's liability for a creditor's claim to the value it would have had if the depository institution had been liquidated.  This means that any franchise sale value from the sale of the failed bank goes to the FDIC, rather than to claims left behind, such as uninsured depositors and unsecured creditors.  Second, the section authorizes the FDIC to make nonratable distributions to some creditors by making "supplemental payments."  The result of these two provisions is that the FDIC has the power to pay unassumed creditors less for their claims than the FDIC pays creditors whose obligations are assumed in a purchase and assumption or deposit transfer transaction. The section is a substantial qualification of 12 U.S.C.A. § 194, which expresses the bankruptcy-like intent that creditors of the same class be treated equally. Rather, it emphasizes the FDIC's interest in "least-cost" payments from insurance funds, and the desire to minimize costs to the FDIC. In effect, then, § 1821(i) gives the FDIC as corporation a priority claim over other general creditors because the FDIC receives the going concern value of a franchise sale.

Although there is no statutory provision which allows the payment of interest on creditors' claims before any money is paid to the shareholders, all creditors, including the FDIC, receive interest on the amount of their claims from the date of insolvency to the date of payment. *FDIC v. Wilhoit*, 297 Ky. 339, 180 S.W.2d 72 (Ct. App. 1943). Otherwise, the creditors' funds would become a source of shareholders' income if the receiver were to refuse to pay interest to the FDIC and other creditors while it was winding up the affairs of the bank. *FDIC v. Citizens State Bank of Niangua*, 130 F.2d 102 (8th Cir. 1942).

Both §§ 91 and 1821(e)(11) invalidate all transfers of the bank's assets in contemplation of insolvency or after an act of insolvency that were made with the intent of preferring one creditor over another. To one familiar with the Bankruptcy Code, this has overtones of preference and fraudulent conveyance. Of course, these provisions are much less extensive than the comparable bankruptcy sections, and they have not been polished with a judicial gloss in the way the Bankruptcy Code has. Thus, it is not entirely clear how the sections would apply in many of the circumstances that a bankruptcy lawyer could pose.

Matters were somewhat clarified in 1989 by the passage of FIRREA. Topics that received Congressional consideration included the claims resolution procedure, the power to disaffirm or repudiate contracts, the power to stay litigation, the relevant statutes of limitations, and the power to enforce contracts of the failed bank.

Overall, the differences between bank insolvency law and the Bankruptcy Code are broad ranging. We have previously considered the interface between bank insolvency and the Bankruptcy Code primarily as a clash between the powers of the bank receiver and the trustee in bankruptcy, one example being that the automatic stay of the Bankruptcy Code does not apply to administrative proceedings of the banking agencies nor to the assets under the control of the bank receiver.

Here, the focus is on the differences in how creditors and debtors of an insolvent organization are dealt with under bank insolvency law and the Bankruptcy Code. As to debtors of the receivership, we have already considered the cross-guarantee provision in § 1815(e) which, unlike the Bankruptcy Code, empowers the bank receiver to assess the loss caused by the failure of one depository institution to be charged against an affiliated depository institution. The Bankruptcy Code has no provision allowing creditors to so reach the assets of affiliates. Similarly, in subsection G, we will examine briefly the power of the receiver to bar many claims and defenses of debtors that would have been valid against the depository institution when solvent, and generally would have been available had the Bankruptcy Code, rather than bank insolvency law, applied. This power is based in 12 U.S.C.A. § 1823(e).

Federal bank insolvency law also contains special provisions, different from those in the Bankruptcy Code, concerning repudiation of contracts, fraudulent conveyances, asset freezes, priorities among creditor claims, and agency enforcement powers, among others. Much of the new law is found in 12 U.S.C.A. § 1821(d) and (e). For a fuller discussion of these special bank insolvency rules, see Peter P. Swire, *Bank Insolvency Law Now That it Matters Again*, 42 DUKE L.J. 469 (1992).

## 2. Claims Against a Failed Financial Institution

Until the 1990s, most creditors (including depositors) of a failed financial institution were made whole through the mechanism of a purchase and assumption transaction. But under the least-cost test, the regulators now often leave uninsured depositors and unsecured liabilities with the receiver. With the existence of tens of thousands of lawsuits involving both creditors and debtors of failed institutions, it is obvious that the FDIC as receiver is involved in a massive business of liquidating billions of dollars of assets and distributing the proceeds to thousands of creditors.

FIRREA created an extensive claims administration process which, while outlining a logical claims administration structure, has also caused extensive litigation. There are several preliminary matters to consider before looking at the claims administration process itself. First is § 1821(j), which broadly deprives any court of the power to take any action that has the effect of restraining the FDIC, acting in its capacity as receiver, from exercising its powers. This includes the inability to restrain such activities as the FDIC conducting a nonjudicial foreclosure sale of assets acquired from a failed bank, even if the creditor disputes the validity of the foreclosure. The creditor's sole remedy is recovery of monetary damages through utilization of the claims administration process of § 1821(d) and subsequent court review. This is a rather drastic limitation on courts' power to grant equitable relief.

Frequently, difficult questions arise as to whether an aggrieved party is a creditor of the failed institution. This issue often arises where the party is also a debtor of the institution, or there is a dispute about which party materially breached a contract between the failed bank and the aggrieved party. In general, the courts have been broadly inclusive in determining who is a creditor, subjecting numerous persons to the elaborate claims process of 12 U.S.C.A. § 1821(d)(3)-(13). You should read the section carefully. Note the jurisdictional bar of § 1821(d)(5) and (13), which requires creditors to make timely use of the administrative claims process until exhaustion or be barred from any recovery.

Additional problems arise in other circumstances. One is that the claims process appears to encompass creditors beyond those to whom notice must be given, as § 1821(d)(13)(D) provides that "any claim relating to an act or omission of the institution or the Corporation as receiver" is subject to the administrative claims process exhaustion requirement. Another problem is where the FDIC fails to give notice. Consider this rather simple case.

# Simon v. Federal Deposit Insurance Corporation
## 48 F.3d 53 (1st Cir. 1995)

CYR, Circuit Judge.

Plaintiffs-appellants Franklin W. Simon ("Simon"), Webb Place Condominiums, Inc. ("Webb Place") and Greystone Condominiums, Inc. ("Greystone") initiated this action in Massachusetts state court against the Federal Deposit Insurance Corporation ("FDIC"), receiver of 1st American Bank for Savings ("Bank"), seeking declaratory and equitable relief relating to two real estate loan agreements between plaintiffs-appellants and the Bank. Following removal, the United States District Court for the District of Massachusetts dismissed the action on jurisdictional grounds pursuant to the Financial Institutions Reform, Recovery, and Enforcement Act ("FIRREA"), 12 U.S.C. § 1821(d)(13)(D) (1994). . . .

## I
## BACKGROUND

In January 1988, Simon, president and sole stockholder of Greystone and Webb Place (collectively: "Borrowers"), entered into two mortgage loan agreements with the Bank, whereby Greystone borrowed $2,500,000 and Webb Place borrowed a total of $3,150,000 with which to finance condominium development projects. The loans were secured by mortgages on the properties to be developed and by Simon's personal guaranty.

When the loans matured on January 31, 1990, the Borrowers sought extensions and further advances to enable completion of the projects. On August 14, 1990, with the outstanding loan balances at $2,500,000 on the Greystone loan and $2,295,490 on the Webb Place loan, the Borrowers entered into two separate Loan Modification Agreements ("Modification Agreements"), whereby the Bank waived all accrued and future interest on the original January 1988 loans and extended their maturity dates to May 31, 1992. The Bank further agreed to lend an additional $816,000 to Greystone and $520,942 to Webb Place, to be disbursed upon the Borrowers' request, for completion of the projects. Finally, the Bank agreed to provide end-loan financing to individual buyers of the completed condominium units.

The Borrowers in turn agreed to complete construction of the mortgaged properties under the supervision of an independent engineer, to devise a marketing plan acceptable to the Bank, and to pay the Bank 100% of the net proceeds from the sale of any unit in the mortgaged properties in return for a partial release of the Bank's mortgage lien. Simon secured his loan guaranties with two certificates of deposit and with mortgages on two real estate properties owned by him. In return, the Bank agreed to limit Simon's total liability on the personal guaranty to $900,000.

All construction loan requisitions by the Borrowers were honored in due course by the Bank until October 18, 1990, when a requisition for $204,657 was dishonored. The following day, the Bank closed and FDIC was appointed receiver.

On October 24, FDIC published notice of its appointment as receiver, alerting creditors that all claims against the Bank were to be submitted to FDIC by January 23, 1991 ("bar date"). On October 25, FDIC mailed notice to all known Bank creditors and, on October 31, notice of FDIC's appointment as liquidating agent of the Bank was mailed to plaintiffs-appellants.

Although plaintiffs-appellants did not receive FDIC's notice, they were aware prior to the bar date that FDIC had been appointed receiver of the Bank.

On October 31, plaintiffs-appellants requested that FDIC advise as to its position respecting further loan disbursements under the Modification Agreements.  FDIC did not reply.  On November 27, plaintiffs-appellants informed FDIC that the Bank was in default under the Modification Agreements for refusing their October 18 requisition.  Their letter demanded that the Borrowers' requisitions be met and that the collateral securing Simon's personal guaranty be released due to the Bank's default.  FDIC did not reply.

The present action was commenced on April 21, 1992, in state court.  Simon sued to recover all collateral pledged to secure his personal guaranty and for a judicial declaration that his personal obligations under the guaranty had been extinguished as a result of the Bank's and FDIC's defaults under the Modification Agreements.  The Borrowers sought a judicial declaration entitling them to a "priority position" among Bank creditors on all obligations incurred by the Borrowers to third parties after FDIC took possession of the Bank's assets.

After removal, the federal district court granted the FDIC motion for summary judgment.  It found that neither Simon nor the Borrowers had filed proofs of claim with FDIC despite having received actual notice of FDIC's appointment.  Plaintiffs-appellants thus having failed to exhaust their administrative remedies, the district court ruled that their claims were barred under 12 U.S.C. § 1821(d)(13)(D)(i).

## II

## DISCUSSION

### A. *The Simon Guaranty*

Simon contends that FDIC surrendered all claims to the collateral pledged to secure his personal guaranty because the Bank's (and FDIC's subsequent) breach of the Modification Agreements discharged Simon from all liability.

Section 1821(d)(13)(D)(i) bars all claims against the assets of a failed financial institution which have not been presented under the administrative claims review process ("ACRP"), *see* 12 U.S.C. § 1821(d)(3)-(10), governing the filing, determination, and payment of claims against the assets of failed financial institutions following FDIC's appointment as receiver. *Heno v. FDIC*, 20 F.3d 1204, 1206-07 (1st Cir. 1994).  Upon its appointment as receiver, FDIC is required to publish notice that the failed institution's creditors must file claims with FDIC by a specified date not less than ninety days after the date of publication.  12 U.S.C. § 1821(d)(3)(B).  FDIC is also required to mail notice to all known creditors of the failed institution.  *Id.* § 1821(d)(3)(C).  It has 180 days from the date of filing to allow or disallow claims.  *Id.* § 1821(d)(5)(A)(i).  Claimants have sixty days from the date of disallowance, or from the expiration of the 180-day administrative decision deadline, within which to seek judicial review in an appropriate United States district court.  *Id.* § 1821(d)(6)(A).  Failure to comply with the ACRP deprives the courts of subject matter jurisdiction over any claim to assets of the failed financial institution.  See *id.* § 1821(d)(13)(D)(I). . . .

Simon's position is and always has been that the Bank's *pre*-receivership refusal to honor the Borrowers' October 18 loan requisition constituted a material breach of the Modification Agreements, entitling him to recover his collateral.  It is clear, therefore, that the claim to the collateral securing the personal guaranty is barred as a "claim or action for payment from . . . the assets" of a failed financial institution for which FDIC has been appointed receiver.  See 12 U.S.C. § 1821(d)(13)(D)(i).

Simon concedes that the two real estate mortgages securing his personal guaranty are bank "assets."  Claims for the recovery of bank assets are barred absent compliance with the ACRP. *Id.*  Simon was aware of FDIC's appointment as receiver on October 19, 1990, well before the ACRP bar date.  Furthermore, Simon concededly knew, before the bar date, that he had a claim against FDIC for the return of the collateral.  In these circumstances, the failure to comply with the ACRP deprived the district court of jurisdiction over Simon's claim for recovery of the collateral securing his personal guaranty.

B.  *The Borrowers' Claims*

The Borrowers seek compensatory damages for FDIC's alleged post-bar-date repudiation of their pre-receivership Modification Agreements with the Bank.  *See id.* § 1821(e)(3)(i).  The Borrowers assert that all obligations they incurred to third parties *after* FDIC was appointed receiver are entitled to priority status against Bank assets, on the theory that the Modification Agreements remained executory at the time FDIC was appointed receiver.  Consequently, the Borrowers argue, the executory Modification Agreements remained open to affirmance or repudiation by FDIC within a reasonable period following its appointment.  See *id.* § 1821(e)(1)-(2).  Since FDIC has yet to affirm the Modification Agreements, the Borrowers conclude that the agreements have been repudiated.

Their claim is premature, for failure to exhaust administrative remedies.  See *Heno v. FDIC*, 20 F.3d at 1212-13 (publishing FDIC internal manual procedures for filing claims arising from FDIC's post-bar-date repudiation of executory prereceivership contracts with failed institution).  In *Heno*, we deferred to FDIC's construction of its enabling statute as according the agency first opportunity to evaluate alleged post-bar-date claims, including those arising after the ninety-day period following notice of FDIC's appointment as receiver, *id.* at 1209.  As the Borrowers have yet to exhaust their administrative remedies pursuant to the internal agency procedures published in *Heno*, we affirm the district court judgment, without prejudice to Borrowers' subsequent submission of an administrative claim to FDIC.

## Comments and Questions

1.  What happens if an aggrieved party never receives the required § 1821(d)(3)(C) notice?  The only statutorily specified exemption from the strict requirements of the process is provided if "the claimant did not receive notice of the appointment of the receiver in time to file such claim."  Section 1821(d)(5)(C).  And even in that case the only consequence is that the FDIC "may" consider a late filed claim.  In effect, then, § 1821(d)(3)(C) requiring notice to creditors imposes no consequence on the FDIC for failure to do so.  In *Elmco Properties, Inc. v. Second National Federal Savings Association*, 94 F.3d 914 (4th Cir. 1996), however, the court held that the creditor's constitutional due process rights were violated by the RTC denying the borrower's claim as untimely, where the borrower had neither actual nor inquiry notice of the claims process, and the RTC had not

sent notice. Constructive notice by publication also was constitutionally insufficient, and so the RTC was required to process the claim.

2. Several courts have held that if the receiver fails to rule on an administrative claim within the 180 day determination period, and the aggrieved party fails to seek judicial review within the subsequent 60 days, the claim is deemed to be disallowed and judicial review is foreclosed. *See, e.g., Astrup v. Resolution Trust Corporation*, 23 F.3d 1419 (8th Cir. 1994). If a claim is not filed under the administrative claims process, it appears that the claim still can be used as an affirmative defense or in recoupment should the FDIC bring a suit as plaintiff against the aggrieved party.

3. Another aspect of what constitutes a claim involves actions that occur after the date of receivership. As receiver in possession of a failed bank's assets, the FDIC might determine to take actions that result in an alleged breach of contract with respect to the assets taken over, such as the operation of a foreclosed shopping center. The courts appear to be split on whether such disputes are subject to the administrative claims process or are free of the jurisdictional bar. *See, e.g., Homeland Stores, Inc. v. Resolution Trust Corporation*, 17 F.3d 1269 (10th Cir.), cert. denied, 513 U.S. 928 (1994).

4. Read § 1821(d)(7). Must the FDIC grant a request for administrative review of a receiver's disallowance determination? Might the FDIC deny such a request for two reasons: a) it will tend to cause those with small claims to give up due to the cost of litigation in a federal court, and b) the requirement for a hearing on the record is so time consuming that it is not a cost-effective process for the FDIC to go back over ground that the receiver has already covered?

5. Under § 1821(d)(13)(A) the FDIC must abide by any "unappealable" judgment, but § 1821(d)(13)(C) provides that no attachment or execution may be issued by any court against assets held by a receiver. How is the claimant holding an unappealable judgment to collect on that judgment? Should such a party be viewed as an unsecured general creditor with a claim that has been allowed? Under § 1821(d)(13) and (i) may such a judgment creditor be left behind in a purchase and assumption or deposit transfer transaction?

6. Section 1821(d)(12) provides the FDIC, upon request, with a mandatory 90-day stay against any judicial action or proceeding. Subsection (d)(8) requires the FDIC to establish an expedited relief procedure, but only for a claimant with a perfected security interest who claims irreparable injury if forced to follow the routine claims procedure. This procedure appears to provide no protection for some, such as a borrower facing imminent foreclosure who has asked a court for a temporary restraining order to block the foreclosure of the real estate by the receiver. Under § 1821(d)(6) a claimant can only elect to go to court after the receiver's determination, which may be six months or more after the receivership commences.

7. As a comparison, the trustee in bankruptcy generally has an automatic stay of litigation of indefinite duration. Yet in bank receivership (a) the stay is not automatic—rather the receiver has to identify each piece of litigation it wishes to have stayed, and (b) the stay is for a limited duration and cannot be renewed. Why? If the

FDIC as receiver wishes to stay several pieces of litigation scattered among various federal and state courts, may it do so through a single application to one federal court?

### 3.  Repudiation of Contracts

One important new power of the FDIC as receiver relates to contracts entered into before its appointment as receiver.  12 U.S.C.A. § 1821(e).  The receiver may repudiate any contract or lease of the failed institution which is burdensome and the repudiation of which will promote the orderly administration of the receivership.  Repudiation must occur within a reasonable time.  The statute goes on to provide that any damages for repudiation are limited to actual direct compensatory damages.  Consider the following case.

## Modzelewski v. Resolution Trust Corporation
### 14 F.3d 1374 (9th Cir. 1994)

KOZINSKI, Circuit Judge:

Starting in the 1970s, MeraBank Savings and Loan offered high level employees "salary continuation agreements," presumably to secure the most talented managers.  Nonetheless, it went the way of many S & Ls this past decade. The Resolution Trust Corporation, as receiver, now refuses to honor the agreements, claiming that the right to payments terminated automatically pursuant to 12 C.F.R. § 563.39(b)(5) when the RTC took over.

### I.  Facts

Gene Rice devoted 35 years of service to MeraBank; Ernest Modzelewski gave 28.  As executives, they signed agreements providing for 120 monthly installments after certain triggering events:  retirement, death or termination without cause.

MeraBank was declared insolvent in January 1990; the RTC took over as receiver and promptly terminated both Rice and Modzelewski.  Adding injury to insult, it refused to pay them anything under their salary continuation agreements.  Rice and Modzelewski brought suit claiming they were entitled to compensatory damages under 12 U.S.C. § 1821(e)(3) because the RTC had repudiated its obligation under the contract.

The district court granted summary judgment to the RTC and Rice and Modzelewski appeal.  785 F. Supp. 1385.  Both sides claim attorney's fees.

### II.  The Merits

The parties agree that the RTC was entitled to repudiate Rice and Modzelewski's salary continuation agreements once it took over MeraBank.  The far-more-than-$64,000 question is whether it could do so without paying them compensation.  The RTC argues it was entitled to walk away from the salary continuation agreements because they were merely employment contracts which don't survive receivership, except insofar as rights thereunder are "vested," 12 C.F.R. § 563.39(b)(5).  Rice and Modzelewski argue that the salary continuation agreements are not employment contracts, but pension plans which arguably survive receivership pursuant to 12 C.F.R. § 563.47.  In any event, they argue their rights to receive benefits were vested.

### A.  The Nature of the Agreements

"Employment contract" is not defined in the applicable regulations.   Black's Law Dictionary 525 (6th ed. 1990) says it's an agreement setting forth "terms and conditions" of employment.   The regulations do define "pension plan" by reference to ERISA.   12 C.F.R. § 563.47(a).  ERISA, in turn, points us to the terms of the plan itself to see whether it provides for "retirement income" or "deferral of income . . . for a period extending to the termination of covered employment or beyond. . . ."

The parties draw different inferences from the terms of the salary continuation agreements. Rice and Modzelewski argue the agreements fit the definition of pension plan because they provide pay upon Rice's "termination" after age 57 and upon Modzelewski's "retirement" after age 65.   The agreements also calculate benefits according to age and length of service–another hallmark of pension plans.

The RTC, for its part, points out that the agreements also contain terms and conditions of employment.  In the "general agreement" under paragraph 1, the employee agrees to maintain no other employment without the employer's consent and to devote all his working time and ability to MeraBank; another paragraph establishes a covenant not to compete after retirement or termination as a condition of receiving benefits; a third authorizes MeraBank to discharge for cause and voids all benefits if that occurs.  Based on these provisions, the RTC asserts this is not a retirement plan but an employment contract.

Both sides are right to some extent.   Certain aspects of the salary continuation agreements plainly fall within ERISA's highly functional definition of a pension plan–a plan containing some provision for retirement or deferred income.  29 U.S.C. § 1002(2)(A).  We have interpreted this language broadly, holding that a pension plan is established if a reasonable person could "'ascertain the intended benefits, beneficiaries, source of financing, and procedures for receiving benefits'. . . .  That is clearly a sufficient allegation of the establishment of a plan." *Scott v. Gulf Oil Corp.*, 754 F.2d 1499, 1504 (9th Cir. 1985) (quoting *Donovan v. Dillingham*, 688 F.2d 1367, 1373 (11th Cir. 1982)); *see also Williams v. Wright*, 927 F.2d 1540, 1543-49 (11th Cir. 1991) (letter promising "continuation . . . of cash" after retirement to be paid from general assets of company in return for consultant services and continued loyalty constituted pension plan under ERISA definition).   The relevant paragraphs of the salary continuation agreement here–calculating payments based on age and length of service, identifying the beneficiaries and setting out a schedule for payments–satisfy our *Scott* requirements.

Nothing in ERISA's definition or the regulations, moreover, says that if pension plans also contain other terms–such as terms governing employment–they somehow cease to be pension plans.   In fact, ERISA makes specific provision for certain terms of employment like non-competition clauses in pension plans.  See 29 U.S.C. § 1053(a)(3); *Clark v. Lauren Young Tire Center Profit Sharing Trust*, 816 F.2d 480 (9th Cir. 1987).

At the same time, the agreements in question clearly contain terms related directly to employment, and hence are also employment contracts.  Indeed, the salary continuation aspect of the agreements is merely one bundle of rights and obligations within a broader employment relationship.  This is not at all unusual.  Because ERISA's definition of a pension plan is so broad, virtually any contract that provides for some type of deferred compensation will also establish a de facto pension plan, whether or not the parties intended to do so.

Since the agreements in question are both employment contracts and pension plans, we must consider whether, and to what extent, the RTC may abrogate them when it takes over the institution.  Rice and Modzelewski argue that, insofar as what's at issue here is their right to a pension, the applicable regulation is 12 C.F.R. § 563.47, which governs the administration of pension plans.  This regulation, Rice and Modzelewski point out, has no provision giving the RTC a right to abrogate, meaning that the RTC is powerless to cut off an employee's rights in a pension plan, even where that pension plan is part of an employment contract.  The RTC, for its part, sees section 563.47 as inapposite.  That section, the RTC argues, merely establishes housekeeping rules for the administration of pension plans set up by S & Ls; it has no bearing on whether an individual employee's right to collect under a particular plan is cut off pursuant to section 563.39(b)(4) or (b)(5).

The RTC has the better of the argument.  An individual employee's right to participate in a pension plan is a term of his employment contract.  Pensions and other deferred compensation arrangements are benefits of employment–not all that different from salaries and other fringe benefits.  As such, they are subject to termination when the RTC takes over, except to the extent the right to receive them has become vested.  12 C.F.R. § 563.39(b)(5); *see also Fentron Indus. v. National Shopmen Pension Fund*, 674 F.2d 1300, 1306 (9th Cir. 1982) (under ERISA, nonvested pension rights are subject to alteration or abolition at any time).  It's to the issue of vesting that we now turn.

### B.  Vested Rights

### i.  Rice

Under Rice's agreement, if he retired or died after age 57, he would be entitled to payment under the salary continuation agreement.  Rice was 59 when the RTC took over.  At that point–indeed, any time after he had turned 57–Rice could have claimed his full benefits by taking retirement; had he died, his estate would have been entitled to the payments.  There was nothing more he was required to do in order to earn the right to receive payments under the plan.

Nonetheless, Rice chose to keep working.  This means he could have been terminated for cause.  And, had he been so terminated, he would have lost all benefits under the agreement.  Thus, the RTC argues, Rice's right to collect under the agreements had not yet become unconditional at the time he was terminated and, therefore, was not vested.

The nub of the controversy, then, is whether the presence of this somewhat remote contingency kept Rice's rights from becoming vested as that term is used in section 563.39.  Since vesting isn't defined in the regulation, we look to analogous federal law.  Rice points us toward an IRS regulation which provides that property rights are "substantially vested" for tax purposes when they're "not subject to a substantial risk of forfeiture."  26 C.F.R. § 1.83-3.  This regulation specifies that termination for cause does not amount to a "substantial risk."  *Id.*

The RTC, for its part, relies on ERISA's definition of "nonforfeitable" which requires the right to be "unconditional."  *See* 29 U.S.C. § 1002(19).  Unfortunately for the RTC, neither it nor the few district court cases on which it relies took account of the conditions that follow this "unconditional" language.  *See id.* (citing 29 U.S.C. § 1053(a)(3)); *Hummell v. S.E. Rykoff & Co.*, 634 F.2d 446, 449 (9th Cir. 1980).  Thus, even under the ERISA definition, nonforfeitable does not mean that the payments must be absolutely unconditional.  The Supreme Court also has noted that vested pension rights may still be subject to certain conditions subsequent. *See, e.g.,* *Nachman Corp. v. Pension Benefit Guaranty Corp.*, 446 U.S. 359, 376-77 n.25, 378 (1980).

We conclude that, in order to be vested as that term is used in 12 C.F.R. § 563.39(b), rights need not be free of every contingency or possibility of divestiture. Rather, a right is vested when the employee holding the right is entitled to claim immediate payment. It's not material that the employee fails to make such a demand–exposing himself to the risk of divestiture–so long as the decision not to claim payment lies entirely within his control. Pursuant to this standard, Rice's rights under paragraph 2 of his agreement had vested because he had an unconditional right to retire and collect benefits under the salary continuation agreement when he reached age 57, two years before the RTC took over. Rice is therefore entitled to actual compensatory damages stemming from the RTC's repudiation of its obligation. 12 U.S.C. § 1821(e)(3)(A).

### ii. Modzelewski

The terms of Modzelewski's agreement are substantially the same as Rice's, but there is one significant difference: Modzelewski hadn't yet earned the right to claim benefits. He was entitled to benefits when he attained the age of 65; when the RTC took over, Modzelewski was only 53. His right to claim benefits was still subject to any number of substantial contingencies. For example, right before the RTC took over, Modzelewski would have forfeited all of his benefits had he quit MeraBank; had he died, his beneficiary would only have received 50% of his benefits; had MeraBank terminated him without cause, Modzelewski would have been entitled to only 10% of his benefits. The day before the RTC took over, Modzelewski simply could not have forced payment under the salary continuation agreement; he would have had to work at MeraBank for 12 more years before earning the right to receive benefits on demand. Modzelewski's rights therefore had not vested before the RTC took over MeraBank, and his salary continuation agreement terminated by operation of law before his rights could vest.

Modzelewski argues in the alternative that his rights vested at the moment the RTC took over. Another provision of his contract states that, upon a change in control of management, Modzelewski is entitled to full benefits as if he had reached retirement age. Thus, Modzelewski asserts that the RTC's takeover constituted such a change in control–vesting his rights even as they were voided. By the terms of the regulation, however, all the rights terminated upon the RTC's appointment except for "[a]ny rights . . . that have *already vested.*" 12 C.F.R. § 563.39(b)(5) (emphasis added). For Modzelewski's argument to work, his right would have had to vest before the RTC took over. As we hold above, they had not. . . .

*AFFIRMED as to Modzelewski (No. 92-15670), REVERSED as to Rice (No. 92-15865).*

## Comments and Questions

1. There has been substantial litigation over various employee compensation claims. In *Office and Professional Employees International Union v. FDIC*, 27 F.3d 598 (D.C. Cir. 1994), the court held that a collective bargaining agreement could be repudiated but that there was a valid legal claim for severance pay, even though the repudiation occurred after the FDIC's appointment, because severance pay constituted recoverable "actual direct compensatory damages." Would the answer be different if the claimant for severance pay were the bank's president?

2.  While the major issue in repudiation cases is typically damages, note that the contract repudiated must be burdensome and that the repudiation must occur within a reasonable time after the receivership commences.  These elements usually are easy to ascertain.

3.  If the FDIC does repudiate a contract, what is the measure of damages, the contract expectation interest or something less?  Are the contract reliance and restitution interests relevant to any attempt to define "actual direct compensatory damages?"  What is the measure of damages for breach of a qualified financial contract?  See 12 U.S.C.A. § 1821(e)(3).

4.  A converse provision, section 1821(e)(12), provides that a receiver may enforce any contract of the failed institution notwithstanding any contract provision providing for termination and the like.  There is a specific exception with respect to officers and directors liability insurance.  See *FDIC v. Aetna Casualty and Surety Co.*, 903 F.2d 1073 (6th Cir. 1990).

### Problem 5-10

The Comptroller declared the Falmouth National Bank of Falmouth, Tennessee, insolvent and appointed the FDIC as receiver.  The FDIC arranged a deposit transfer with Lamar State Savings Bank.  Lamar agreed to take $104,882,000 in deposits (leaving behind $2 million in uninsured deposits) and $94,882,000 in assets; thus Lamar would pay a $10 million premium to acquire the assets and liabilities of Falmouth.  The Federal Reserve held some of these assets as security for a $50 million loan made six months ago when the bank began its liquidity crisis.  The Federal Reserve Bank took possession of $40 million in securities and bonds six months ago and, the day before insolvency was declared, filed a financing statement for the security interest it has in $20 million worth of "accounts" or loans owed to Falmouth by various customer-debtors.  To facilitate the transfer, the FDIC corporation agreed to pay off the loan over a two-year period if the Federal Reserve would release its security interest in the assets transferred to Lamar.  In consideration of the FDIC's (as a corporation) repaying the Federal Reserve, the FDIC (as receiver) agreed to transfer to the Corporation the remaining assets received from the Federal Reserve which would still be subject to its security interest.

After the deposit transfer arrangement the FDIC as receiver held $10 million from liquidated assets to be distributed among the creditors.  It is unlikely that the receiver will obtain any of the proceeds from the liquidation of the assets held by the Federal Reserve.  The receiver has estimated the cost of liquidation and distribution of the assets to be approximately $500,000.

The following creditors of the bank were omitted from the deposit transfer arrangement and have presented the following claims.  The General Counsel of the FDIC has considered the claims and their legal basis and has written a rough outline of a proposed response to each claim.  She has been called out of town and wants you to finish the memorandum, comment on her suggestions, and determine how much money each creditor will receive.

1. Slippery Rock Savings Bank demanded payment of a $5 million loan it made to Falmouth Bancorp, which was Falmouth's holding company, and a $5 million loan to Falmouth National Bank. Falmouth Bancorp is now in bankruptcy and holds only the stock of Falmouth as an asset. Slippery Rock argued that the receiver should honor its BHC claim because the bank is the alter ego of the holding company and because the loan was actually made for the benefit of the bank. As for the bank loan, Slippery Rock argues that it should be treated like other creditors whose obligations were assumed by Lamar. See § 1821(i).

Response: Slippery Rock Savings Bank has no claim on the assets of the Falmouth Bank. The first loan was made to Falmouth Bancorp, which is a separate entity holding interests in several banks, a securities broker-dealer and a data processing company. The loan was made for the benefit of the holding company as a whole rather than any company affiliated with the Bancorp. Slippery Rock's only remedy is to present a claim in the bankruptcy proceedings of Bancorp. As to the loan to the bank, they should at least be subordinated to wage claims.

2. Several large stockholders claimed a secured interest in $2 million worth of assets for a loan made to the bank six months before insolvency. The stockholders correctly perfected their interest under state law one week before the bank was closed. See §§ 91 and 1821(e)(11).

Response: The security interest granted to the stockholders is a preference as a transfer made in contemplation of insolvency. The shareholders were influential in the affairs of the bank and, from their discussions with the bank examiners, were aware of the approaching insolvency of the bank at the time of perfection. The perfection of the security interest allows them to receive a greater share of the assets than they would have received under the "pro rata" rule of § 194. The shareholders must return any assets of the bank held as collateral for the loan and they cannot claim the collateral for their loans held by the receiver. They do have the right to receive their pro rata share as general creditors.

3. Holders of capital notes worth $2 million presented their claims. These note holders had agreed to be subordinated to all other creditors. See § 1821(d)(11).

Response: The capital note holders are creditors of the bank and have a valid claim, but any payment to them must await complete payment of all other creditors. The noteholders cannot argue that the subordination agreement which they had signed earlier is a violation of the "pro rata" rule for creditors of the same class under §§ 1821(d)(11) and 1821(i). The statute does not upset the valid contractual arrangements between the bank and its creditors and between one creditor and another after the bank has become insolvent.

4. The State of Tennessee deposited $1.5 million from state sales taxes in Falmouth and took possession of securities now worth $1.2 million.  The state presented a claim for $1.5 million.  See § 90.

Response:  The State of Tennessee has taken a valid pledge of assets for the deposit of public funds.  The state will receive a pro rate payment based on the entire amount of their debt up to $300,000.

5. Murray Computer Services, Inc. presented a claim for $500,000 from a judgment it received three days before the bank failed and a claim for $200,000 for post-receivership services.  Can Murray be treated differently than the Slippery Rock loan to the bank in claim #1?

Response:  Murray Computer Services has a valid claim as a lien holder.  Since Murray had received a judgment before the bank failed, the $500,000 claim cannot be attacked and Murray will receive the entire amount of its claim.  The claim for reimbursement for recent services is controlled by section 1821(d)(11) and Murray will receive its pro rata share.

6. There are also pre-bankruptcy claims of $55,000 for janitorial services, $25,000 for wages and salaries of bank employees, and $15,000 for utilities.

Response:  Any employee whose wages and salaries were not assumed by the purchasing bank as part of Falmouth's liabilities is entitled only to his or her pro rata share of the bank's assets remaining in the hands of the receiver.  The employees of a national bank are not entitled to the preference given by state law to employees in the distribution of the estate of their insolvent employer because the application of state law will disrupt the ratable distribution of the bank's assets.  The janitorial and utility companies will also receive their pro rata share.

7. The Oxnard Savings Bank presented a claim for $1 million which it had lent Falmouth on the federal funds market two days before the date of insolvency.  Oxnard was aware of Falmouth's difficulties and required security for the loan.  Falmouth gave Oxnard security in the same "accounts" in which the Federal Reserve held a security interest.  Oxnard filed a financing statement with the state authorities on the day the loan was made.  See § 1821(e)(8)-(10).

8. Of Falmouth's $105 million of deposits, $10 million are high-rate certificates of deposit that have two or more years to maturity.  Lamar asks that the FDIC as receiver repudiate those certificates of deposit and make them passbook savings accounts which the depositors can either keep on deposit with Lamar at savings account interest rates or immediately withdraw.  See § 1821(e).

Response:  I did not have time to consider the last two issues.  But you do.

## G.  Debtors of the Failed Bank

When the FDIC becomes the receiver of a failed bank, under the basic contract law of assignments it steps into the shoes of the bank.  The receiver both succeeds to the contract rights of the bank and becomes subject to most defenses that debtors have against the bank.  Of course, if the bank in its own right is a holder in due course, then the FDIC succeeds to that status and thus is protected against virtually all claims and defenses of debtors.  However, in most cases where the bank is the original payee of commercial paper evidencing a loan, the FDIC cannot become a holder in due course for a variety of reasons.  For example, often the obligations are already in default and so under the Uniform Commercial Code there cannot be a holder in due course upon transfer with notice that the note is overdue.  U.C.C. §§ 3-302(1) (c) and 3-304(3).  Also, the FDIC is a purchaser in bulk, not a purchaser in the regular course of the transferor's business.  U.C.C. § 3-302(3)(c).  Consequently, under state law it is subject to all defenses that the debtor has against the failed bank with whom it has dealt.  U.C.C. § 3-305(2).

Nevertheless, under both *D'Oench, Duhme and Co. v. FDIC,* discussed in the following case, and the subsequent enactment of 12 U.S.C.A. § 1823(e), the FDIC has appeared to achieve the status of holder in due course, and then some, through federal law.  Thus, most defenses and claims that bank debtors would expect to have available to them in litigation with the bank may be ineffective against the FDIC in either its corporation or receivership capacity.

FIRREA added § 1821(d)(9)(A), which provides that affirmative claims against a receiver are also subject to the requirements of § 1823(e).  Thus, an additional question is whether, and the extent to which, the requirements of § 1823(e) apply to situations where a bank now in receivership has breached an agreement.

## Murphy v. Federal Deposit Insurance Corporation
### 61 F.3d 34 (D.C. Cir. 1995)

GINSBURG, Circuit Judge:

Bruce Murphy, an investor in an unsuccessful real estate venture, seeks damages from the FDIC on the theory that the failed bank that financed the venture, of which the FDIC is the receiver, was responsible for his loss.  The district court granted summary judgment in favor of the FDIC upon the ground that the appellant's claims are barred both by federal common law, *see D'Oench, Duhme & Co., Inc. v. FDIC*, 315 U.S. 447 (1942), and by 12 U.S.C. § 1823(e).
. . .

### I.  BACKGROUND

In his complaint Murphy tells the following story (which we take as true for the purpose of this appeal).  In 1989 he paid approximately $515,000 for one "partnership unit" in the Orchid Island Associates Limited Partnership, which was then in the process of developing the Orchid Island Golf and Beach Club near Vero Beach, Florida.  The investment contract guaranteed that he would receive a "6.1 multiple return on investment" but to date he has received nothing.

Southeast Bank, N.A. was the lead lender for the Orchid Island project. In the late 1980's and early 1990's the bank made several loans to the partnership, in a total amount approximating $50 million. Southeast was also involved in a plan whereby Orchid would engage in a public bond offering to raise additional funds in order to complete the project. Pursuant to that plan, Orchid would take a "bridge loan" from Southeast to cover expenses until the bonds were sold, and the proceeds from the bond offering would be used both to repay the bridge loan and to reduce the amounts outstanding on Southeast's earlier loans. When Southeast informed Orchid's other lenders that the proposed bond financing would result in a lien on the project superior to theirs, however, they rejected the proposal and the deal fell through. Orchid subsequently defaulted on its loan obligations, and Southeast foreclosed upon the property. Shortly thereafter Southeast was itself declared insolvent, the FDIC was appointed receiver of the bank, and Murphy filed this lawsuit.

Although somewhat vague, the gravamen of Murphy's claim is that the bank effectively controlled Orchid and thus assumed the role, and the corresponding legal duties, of a joint venturer or partner. Murphy contends that the bank is therefore responsible for various misdeeds allegedly committed by Orchid officials, including: "failure to register securities" (count 3); "unlawful offer and sale of securities" (count 4); "breach of fiduciary duties" (count 5); "breach of contract" (count 6); and "accounting" improprieties (count 7). Murphy further contends that, in its role as promoter of the aborted bond offering, the bank itself engaged in "fraud" (count 8) and made "negligent misrepresentation[s]" (count 9). . . . Murphy seeks money damages (in counts 3-6 and 8-9), and an order requiring the FDIC to give him certain accounting statements (count 7) . . . .

Each of the loan agreements between Orchid and the bank contains a provision to the following effect: "The Lender is a lender only and shall not be considered a shareholder, joint venturer or partner of the Borrower." Relying upon those written provisions, Murphy's inability to point to any written agreement that supports his joint-venture theory of liability, the federal common law *D'Oench* doctrine, and 12 U.S.C. § 1823(e), the district court granted summary judgment in favor of the FDIC on counts 3 through 9. . . .

## II. ANALYSIS

Murphy raises distinct substantive and procedural points before this court. First, he argues that 12 U.S.C. § 1823(e) does not apply to his substantive claims and that the recent Supreme Court decision in *O'Melveny & Myers v. FDIC*[, 512 U.S. 79 (1994),] makes clear that the federal common law *D'Oench* doctrine has been displaced by a federal statute. Second, he renews his claim that the FDIC is required to establish an ADR procedure and to apply it to his claim.

### A. *12 U.S.C. § 1823(e)*

In 1950, eight years after the Supreme Court decided *D'Oench*, the Congress enacted the Federal Deposit Insurance Act, 12 U.S.C. § 1811 *et seq.*, which "bars anyone from asserting against the FDIC any agreement not properly recorded in the records of the bank that would diminish the value of an asset held by the FDIC." *E.I. du Pont de Nemours & Co. v. FDIC*, 32 F.3d 592, 596 (D.C. Cir. 1994). That provision, as modified in 1989 by the Financial Institutions Reform, Recovery, and Enforcement Act, Pub. L. No. 101-73, 103 Stat. 183 (better known as the FIRREA), currently provides that:

No agreement which tends to diminish or defeat the interest of the [FDIC] in any asset acquired by it under this section or section 1821 of this title, either as security for a loan or by purchase or as receiver of any insured depository institution, shall be valid against the [FDIC] unless such agreement–(A) is in writing, (B) was executed by the depository institution and any person claiming an adverse interest thereunder, including the obligor, contemporaneously with the acquisition of the asset by the depository institution, (C) was approved by the board of directors of the depository institution or its loan committee, which approval shall be reflected in the minutes of said board or committee, and (D) has been, continuously, from the time of its execution, an official record of the depository institution.

12 U.S.C. § 1823(e)(1). The Congress further provided in the FIRREA that "any agreement which does not meet the requirements set forth in section 1823(e) of this title shall not form the basis of, or substantially comprise, a claim against the [FDIC]." 12 U.S.C. § 1821(d)(9)(A).

By their terms, these statutory provisions bar any claim that (1) is based upon an agreement that is *either* (a) unwritten *or* (b) if in writing, does not meet the stringent requirements of §§ 1823(e)(1)(B)-(D), *and* (2) would diminish or defeat the interest of the FDIC in an asset acquired by it in its capacity as receiver of a failed depository institution. Murphy concedes that his claims (save one) are (1) premised upon the existence of an unwritten joint-venture agreement between the bank and Orchid, but argues that § 1823(e) does not bar his claims because (2) the FDIC has failed to demonstrate that its interest in any specific asset assigned from Southeast would be diminished were he to prevail. He points out that he is not a borrower (or "obligor" per the statute) attempting to avoid payment of a loan owed to Southeast Bank but is rather an investor in a failed business venture in which, he claims, the failed bank was a culpable participant. To be sure, Murphy's claims, if successful, would diminish the value of the bank in the hands of the FDIC but that, according to Murphy, is not sufficient to meet the "asset" requirement of § 1823(e). We agree.

We recently held that § 1823(e)(1) is "applicable only to cases involving a specific asset, usually a loan, which in the ordinary course of business would be recorded and approved by the bank's loan committee or board of directors" and that "the requirements of § 1823(e) effectively limit that provision to conventional loan transactions." *du Pont*, 32 F.3d at 597. That interpretation gains support from subsection (C) of § 1823(e)(1), which specifically requires that, if a suit is to go forward, the agreement upon which it is based must have been approved by "the board of directors of [the bank] or its loan committee." See *In re NBW Commercial Paper Litigation*, 826 F. Supp. 1448, 1463-64 (D.D.C. 1992) (§ 1823(e) applies primarily to loan transactions). An agreement that does not involve an extension of credit would not ordinarily be submitted to the board or to a loan committee for approval. Moreover, while any agreement to make a significant loan will ordinarily meet the exacting requirements of § 1823(e), see *Langley v. FDIC*, 484 U.S. 86, 92 (1987) (requirements of § 1823(e) "ensure mature consideration of unusual loan transactions by senior bank officials"), those requirements will almost never be met by an agreement between the bank and an investor, a trade creditor, or most clearly, a tort claimant (such as Murphy is, at bottom). Without so much as a "hint in any of Congress' pronouncements that such individuals should be disfavored," *du Pont*, 32 F.3d at 597 (quoting *NBW*, 826 F. Supp. at 1463), it would be positively wanton for a court to construe the asset requirement so broadly as to destroy their otherwise valid claims.

Even if we assume for the sake of argument that the asset requirement of § 1823(e) is so undemanding that § 1823(e) is a defense to any claim that would diminish the FDIC's interest in any asset that it has acquired from a failed bank, including an asset other than a loan, Murphy's claims would still survive.  The FDIC does not point to an interest in any specific asset of any type that would be diminished by Murphy's claims.  Indeed, the FDIC does not even respond directly to Murphy's assertion that its interest in no specific asset would be diminished, preferring instead to argue only that other courts have applied the federal common law *D'Oench* doctrine to bar claims that would not diminish its interest in a specific asset.  That response not only fails to speak to the proper interpretation of the asset requirement of § 1823(e), it amounts to a near concession that the statute does not bar Murphy's claims and that if the FDIC is to find any refuge it must be in federal common law.

In a footnote to its brief the FDIC does observe that its "recovery from the loan transactions would clearly be diminished by any liabilities arising out of the same transactions."  That statement could charitably be read implicitly to argue that the loans that Southeast made to Orchid are the specific assets in which the FDIC's interest would be diminished by Murphy's claims.  If that is the FDIC's argument, however, then we find it singularly unconvincing.  The value of the loans themselves would be diminished not at all by Murphy's claims.  The FDIC may collect those loans or execute upon the property securing them to the same extent regardless whether Murphy prevails upon his damage claims.  Only the overall value of the bankrupt's estate, not the receiver's interest in any specific asset, would be diminished if Murphy were to prevail.

Because the FDIC has failed to demonstrate that any specific asset–let alone a specific asset "which in the ordinary course of business would be recorded and approved by the bank's loan committee or board of directors," *du Pont*, 32 F.3d at 597–would be diminished were Murphy to succeed, we reverse the judgment of the district court (which did not discuss the specific asset requirement in holding that § 1823(e) bars Murphy's claims).  Although the FDIC does not rely separately upon § 1821(d)(9)(A), the statutory cousin of § 1823(e), we note also that that section simply "incorporates by reference the requirements of § 1823(e)," including the asset requirement, *du Pont*, 32 F.3d at 597, and therefore can not provide an independent ground for judgment in favor of the FDIC.

B.  *Federal common law:  herein of D'Oench, Duhme & Co.*

The *D'Oench* case involved a securities dealer who had sold certain bonds to a bank insured by the FDIC.  The issuer later defaulted on the bonds.  In order to allow the bank to avoid carrying past due bonds on its books, the securities dealer executed unconditional notes in the amount of the bonds, pursuant (the dealer alleged) to a secret side agreement that the bank would not call the notes for payment.  When the bank failed, however, the FDIC was appointed receiver and it demanded payment of the notes.  The Supreme Court held that to allow the securities dealer to rely upon the secret agreement as a defense to payment of its note would violate the policy behind the Federal Reserve Act, viz. "to protect [the FDIC], and the public funds which it administers, against misrepresentations as to the securities or other assets in the portfolios of the banks which [the FDIC] insures."  315 U.S. at 457.

Thus was born the federal common law doctrine that courts have since expanded "beyond the paradigm in which a debtor seeks to assert a defense to liability on a note held by the FDIC" to bar a variety of both claims made and affirmative defenses raised against the FDIC as receiver. *See du Pont*, 32 F.3d at 597-99 (and cases cited therein). Indeed, in the instant case the district court held that the *D'Oench* doctrine extends to (and therefore bars) Murphy's substantive claim that the bank by its actions assumed the liabilities of a joint-venturer because that theory of liability contradicts the written agreements between the bank and Orchid in the records of the bank.

Although various circuits, including this one, have had occasion to apply the common law *D'Oench* doctrine since the passage of the FIRREA in 1989, Murphy argues that the Supreme Court's recent decision in *O'Melveny & Myers* now makes clear that the common law doctrine was preempted by that statute. To be sure, in *O'Melveny & Myers* the Supreme Court does not flatly state that *D'Oench* has been preempted by the FIRREA, but it does set forth some more general propositions that, we think, lead ineluctably to that conclusion.

In *O'Melveny & Myers* the FDIC, as receiver of a California savings bank, sued a law firm that had performed services for the bank; it claimed that the firm had been negligent and had breached its fiduciary duty by failing to uncover the wrongdoing of certain officers of the bank. 512 U.S. at 82. The district court entered summary judgment in favor of the law firm, apparently upon the ground that under California law knowledge of the employees' misconduct is imputed to the employer–and thence to the FDIC as receiver in the employer's stead. *Id.* The FDIC argued that the question whether to impute knowledge of a bank employee's conduct to the FDIC is governed not by California law but by federal common law. *Id.* The Supreme Court unanimously rejected that contention, holding that the FIRREA preempted the creation of federal common law on this issue and that the rule of decision is therefore to be found either in the federal statute itself or in state law. *Id.* at 86-87.

The Court began its discussion of preemption with the proposition that it "would [not] adopt a court-made rule to supplement federal statutory regulation that is comprehensive and detailed; matters left unaddressed in such a scheme are presumably left subject to the disposition provided by state law." *Id.* The Court then turned to 12 U.S.C. § 1821(d)(2)(A)(i), which, as amended by the FIRREA, provides that the FDIC "shall . . . by operation of law, succeed to all rights, titles, powers, and privileges of the insured depository institution," and explained that this provision "appears to indicate that the FDIC as receiver steps into the shoes of the failed S & L [so that] any defense good against the original party is good against the receiver." *Id.*

The Court went on to hold that the above-quoted provision is an exclusive grant of rights to the FDIC as receiver, which can be neither "supplemented [nor] modified by federal common law." *Id.* Here the Court cited four provisions of the FIRREA–including § 1821(d)(9), which it described parenthetically as "excluding certain state-law claims against FDIC based on oral agreements by the S & L"–that "specifically create special federal rules of decision regarding claims by, and defenses against, the FDIC as receiver. . . . *Inclusio unius, exclusio alterius.*" *Id.* The Court concluded this aspect of the opinion with the broad observation:

> It is hard to avoid the conclusion that § 1821(d)(2)(A)(i) places the FDIC in the shoes of the insolvent S & L, to work out its claims under state law, except where some provision in the extensive framework of FIRREA provides otherwise. To create additional "federal common-law" exceptions is not to "supplement" this scheme, but to alter it.

*Id.*

Although the Court's reasoning appears to leave no room for a federal common law *D'Oench* doctrine, the FDIC here emphasizes that the continuing vitality of *D'Oench* was not directly before the Supreme Court and that the Court did not specifically mention *D'Oench* in its opinion. That is hardly compelling, however, when one considers that "[i]n cases of doubt, the institutional role of the Supreme Court weighs in favor of considering its rulings to be general rather than limited to the particular facts." *Cowin v. Bresler*, 741 F.2d 410, 425 (D.C. Cir. 1984). That point has particular force in this instance, for while the vitality of *D'Oench* was not directly at issue in *O'Melveny & Myers* the Court was specifically advised by both sides on brief and at oral argument that resolution of the issue before it could also affect the *D'Oench* doctrine. Moreover, although the opinion for the Court does not specifically mention *D'Oench*, it does expressly include one of the *D'Oench*-like statutory provisions (§ 1821(d)(9)) in the list of special federal statutory rules of decision from which it infers that "*[i ]nclusio unius, exclusio alterius.*" *O'Melveny & Myers*, 512 U.S. at 86. In so doing the Supreme Court, we think, necessarily decided the *D'Oench* question. To translate: the inclusion of § 1821(d)(9) in the FIRREA implies the exclusion of overlapping federal common law defenses not specifically mentioned in the statute–of which the *D'Oench* doctrine is one.

The FDIC next contends that this interpretation is inconsistent with both the Supreme Court's earlier decision in *Langley v. FDIC*, 484 U.S. 86 (1987), and the decisions of several lower courts (including this one) holding that *D'Oench* survives the enactment of the FIRREA. The FDIC suggests that in *Langley* the Court signalled the continuing validity of the *D'Oench* doctrine because it relied upon the *D'Oench* case itself to inform its interpretation of the term "agreement" in § 1823(e). Even if we accepted that interpretation of *Langley*, however, it would surely not dispose of the present issue because the Court decided *Langley* before the Congress enacted the FIRREA. In any event, in *Langley* itself the Court suggested, if anything, that *D'Oench* was even then a dead letter:

That "agreement" in § 1823(e) covers more than promises to perform acts in the future is confirmed by examination of the leading case in the area prior to the enactment of § 1823(e) in 1950 . . . *D'Oench, Duhme & Co. v. FDIC*, 315 U.S. 447 (1942). . . .

*Id.* at 92. Referring to *D'Oench* as the leading case "prior to the enactment of § 1823(e) in 1950" implies that *D'Oench* had lost its vitality as federal common law with the enactment of the FDIA in 1950. At most the Court in *Langley* left that question open.

As for the post-FIRREA decisions of the lower courts, the FDIC is undeniably correct in its assertion that many courts, including we, have either explicitly stated or implicitly assumed that the federal common law remains alive and well alongside its statutory cousin. *See, e.g., du Pont*, 32 F.3d at 596-97; *NBW*, 826 F. Supp. at 1457-61 (and cases cited therein). Most courts, however, have done so "without even considering the preemption question." *NBW*, 826 F. Supp. at 1458. More specifically, not one court has discussed the impact of last year's decision in *O'Melveny & Myers* upon the continuing vitality of *D'Oench*. . . .

By stating that "§ 1821(d)(2)(A)(i) places the FDIC in the shoes of the insolvent S & L, to work out its claims under state law, except where some provision in the extensive framework of FIRREA provides otherwise," *O'Melveny & Myers*, 512 U.S. at 87, the Supreme Court appears to have concluded that the Congress in the FIRREA did indeed address the question previously governed by *D'Oench*. It follows that the need for a body of federal common law under the rubric of *D'Oench* has now "disappeared" and that the district court erred in holding that Murphy's claims are barred under *D'Oench*. . . .

For the foregoing reasons, we affirm the district court's grant of summary judgment in favor of the FDIC on counts 1 and 2 and reverse the district court's grant of summary judgment on counts 3 through 9. . . .

## Comments and Questions

1. Would the result in the case be different if Murphy had stated the same causes of action but had borrowed the $515,000 he invested in Orchid Island from Southeast Bank rather than using funds he already had? In either case the Murphy's causes of action would be independent of the terms of any loan to him. Is the FDIC now generally subject to fraud claims against failed banks?

2. What is a receivership asset for purposes of § 1823(e)?

3. If the transaction does involve an agreement, note the requirement that the agreement must be maintained continuously as a record of the institution. Failed banks frequently have poor records. What can an innocent party to an apparently ordinary commercial loan transaction do to assure itself that the institution has satisfied this requirement, such as properly recording loan payments?

4. An interesting and complex case is *Astrup v. Midwest Federal Savings Bank*, 886 F.2d 1057 (8th Cir. 1989). A condominium developer sued its joint venture partner, a wholly owned subsidiary of a federal savings and loan association which subsequently went into receivership. The court held that § 1823(e) did not protect against a tort claim by the developer for breach of fiduciary duty, which each party to a joint venture owes to the others. The court analogized to the liability of an institution in receivership for a personal injury claim by a motorist who was in a collision with a vehicle owned and operated by a bank employee, a claim clearly not subject to § 1823(e). Do you think the analogy is apt?

5. Section 1823(e) literally provides that the FDIC can defeat an interest in an asset of a failed institution unless the agreement was executed "contemporaneously" with the institution's acquisition of the asset. In many common bank financial transactions this element may be difficult to meet. Suppose that a bank sells assets to a trust and agrees with the trustee to repurchase the sold assets under certain circumstances. Such a repurchase obligation often is collateralized by granting the trustee a security interest in other, preexisting assets of the bank. Thus, the agreement has not been executed "contemporaneously" with the acquisition of the asset by the bank. May the FDIC defeat such a security interest, or is this outside the "purpose" of the statute? Can the term "asset" in the statute be interpreted to mean the repurchase contract, so that the contemporaneous requirement is met? Consider the various statutory interpretation methodologies that you have encountered.

*Problem 5-11*

Rose McFarland executed a continuing guarantee agreement for $500,000 to guarantee all obligations of her son, Rory.  Over the years Rory had several loans from the Bank of Commerce.  In 1994 Rory restructured his loans, provided additional security, and secured the release of his mother's guarantee agreement.  The terms of this restructuring were set out in a letter dated April 2, 1995, delineating the terms of the restructuring and stating the bank's agreement to release Mrs. McFarland's guarantee agreement.  Rory McFarland signed and returned the letter agreement to the bank, but it cannot be found, even though the bank loan officer would testify that he remembers receiving the letter.  However, Mrs. McFarland's guarantee agreement remained in the bank's files.  In August, 1996, the bank was closed and the FDIC appointed receiver.  Rory defaulted on his loan, and the FDIC brought a suit against Rose on her guarantee, claiming that the bank's alleged release of Rose was not valid against the FDIC under § 1823(e).  What result?

## H.  Officer, Director, and Institution-Affiliated Party Liability

We previously have seen various aspects of officer and director liability.  In the case of *del Junco v. Conover*, 682 F.2d 1338 (9th Cir. 1982), *cert. denied*, 459 U.S. 1146 (1983), the Ninth Circuit upheld a cease and desist order of the Comptroller of the Currency that required directors to indemnify their bank for lost principal and interest on loans made in violation of § 84, for the bank's attorneys fees, and for the bank's efforts to collect the loans.

Our primary focus here, however, is on the liability of officers, directors, and professional advisers with respect to the failure of a bank.  Their duties and responsibilities are substantial.  Directors' duties include the duty of obedience, the duty of care, the duty of loyalty, and specific statutory duties related to the general duties.  The same can be said for officers and professional advisers.  In almost every bank failure case, suits are brought by the FDIC against such persons.

## Atherton v. Federal Deposit Insurance Corp.
### 117 S. Ct. 656 (1997)

BREYER, J., delivered the opinion of the Court.

The Resolution Trust Corporation (RTC) sued several officers and directors of City Federal Savings Bank, claiming that they had violated the legal standard of care they owed that federally chartered, federally insured institution.  The case here focuses upon the legal standard for determining whether or not their behavior was improper.  It asks where courts should look to find the standard of care to measure the legal propriety of the defendants' conduct--to state law, to federal common law, or to a special federal statute (103 Stat. 243, 12 U.S.C. § 1821(k)) that speaks of "gross negligence"?

## I

In 1989, City Federal Savings Bank (City Federal), a federal savings association, went into receivership. The RTC, as receiver, brought this action in the bank's name against officers and directors. (Throughout this opinion, we use the more colloquial term "bank" to refer to a variety of institutions such as "federal savings associations.") The complaint said that the defendants had acted (or failed to act) in ways that led City Federal to make various bad development, construction, and business acquisition loans. It claimed that these actions (or omissions) were unlawful because they amounted to gross negligence, simple negligence, and breaches of fiduciary duty.

The defendants moved to dismiss. They pointed to a federal statute,  12 U.S.C. § 1821(k), that says in part that a "director or officer" of a federally insured bank "may be held personally liable for monetary damages" in an RTC-initiated "civil action ... for gross negligence " or "similar conduct ... that demonstrates a greater disregard of a duty of care (than gross negligence)...." (Emphasis added.) They argued that, by authorizing actions for gross negligence or more seriously culpable conduct, the statute intended to forbid actions based upon less seriously culpable conduct, such as conduct that rose only to the level of simple negligence. The District Court agreed and dismissed all but the gross negligence claims.

The Third Circuit, providing an interlocutory appeal, 28 U.S.C. § 1292(b), reversed. It interpreted the federal statute as simply offering a safeguard against state legislation that had watered down applicable state standards of care--below a gross negligence benchmark. As so interpreted, the statute did not prohibit actions resting upon stricter standard of care rules-- whether those stricter standard of care rules originated in state law (which the Circuit found applicable in the case of state-chartered banks) or in federal common law (which the Circuit found applicable in the case of federally chartered banks). Resolution Trust Corp. v. Cityfed Financial Corp., 57 F.3d 1231, 1243-1244, 1245-1249 (1995). Noting that City Federal is a federally chartered savings institution, the Circuit concluded that the RTC was free "to pursue any claims for negligence or of breach of fiduciary duty available as a matter of federal common law." Id., at 1249.

The defendants, pointing to variations in the Circuits' interpretations of the "gross negligence" statute, sought certiorari. Compare Resolution Trust Corp. v. Frates, 52 F.3d 295 (C.A.10 1995) (§ 1821(k) prohibits federal common-law actions for simple negligence) with Cityfed, supra, at 1246-1249 (§ 1821(k) does not prohibit federal common-law actions for simple negligence). And we granted review.

## II

We begin by temporarily setting the federal "gross negligence" statute to the side, and by asking whether, were there no such statute, federal common law would provide the applicable legal standard. We recognize, as did the Third Circuit, that this Court did once articulate federal common-law corporate governance standards, applicable to federally chartered banks. Briggs v. Spaulding, 141 U.S. 132 (1891). But the Court found its rules of decision in federal common law long before it held, in Erie R. Co. v. Tompkins, 304 U.S. 64 (1938), that "[t]here is no federal general common law." Id., at 78. The Third Circuit, while considering itself bound by Briggs, asked whether relevant federal common-law standards could have survived Erie.

This Court has recently discussed what one might call "federal common law" in the strictest sense, i.e., a rule of decision that amounts, not simply to an interpretation of a federal statute or a properly promulgated administrative rule, but, rather, to the judicial "creation" of a special federal rule of decision.  See Texas Industries, Inc. v. Radcliff Materials, Inc., 451 U.S. 630, 640-643 (1981).  The Court has said that "cases in which judicial creation of a special federal rule would be justified ... are ... 'few and restricted.' "  O'Melveny & Myers v. FDIC, 512 U.S. 79, 87 (1994) (quoting Wheeldin v. Wheeler, 373 U.S. 647, 651 (1963)).  "Whether latent federal power should be exercised to displace state law is primarily a decision for Congress," not the federal courts.  Wallis v. Pan American Petroleum Corp., 384 U.S. 63, 68 (1966).  Nor does the existence of related federal statutes automatically show that Congress intended courts to create federal common-law rules, for " 'Congress acts ... against the background of the total corpus juris of the states....' "  Id., at 68 (quoting H. Hart & H. Wechsler, The Federal Courts and the Federal System 435 (1953)).  Thus, normally, when courts decide to fashion rules of federal common law, "the guiding principle is that a significant conflict between some federal policy or interest and the use of state law ... must first be specifically shown."  Ibid.  Indeed, such a "conflict" is normally a "precondition."  O'Melveny, supra, at 87.

No one doubts the power of Congress to legislate rules for deciding cases like the one before us.  Indeed, Congress has enacted related legislation.  Certain federal statutes specify, for example, how to form "national banks" (i.e., a federally chartered bank), how to amend the articles of association, how shareholders are to vote, directors' qualifications, the form of a bank's "organization certificate," minimum capital requirements, and a list of corporate powers.  See 12 U.S.C. § 21 et seq.  Other federal statutes regulate the activities of federally chartered savings associations in various ways.  E.g., 12 U.S.C. § 1464(b) (various regulations on savings associations, such as interest rate on loans).  No one argues, however, that either these statutes, or federal regulations validly promulgated pursuant to statute, set forth general corporate governance standards of the sort at issue applicable to a federally chartered savings association such as City Federal.  Cf. 12 C.F.R. § 7.2000 (1996) (discussed infra, at 673) (describing governance procedures applicable to federally chartered national banks, but not federal savings associations).  Consequently, we must decide whether the application of state-law standards of care to such banks would conflict with, and thereby significantly threaten, a federal policy or interest.

We have examined each of the basic arguments that the respondent implicitly or explicitly raises.  In our view, they do not point to a conflict or threat that is significant, and we shall explain why.  (The respondent, by the way, is now the Federal Deposit Insurance Corporation-- the FDIC--which has replaced the Resolution Trust Corporation pursuant to a new federal statute.  12 U.S.C. § 1441a(b)(4)(A).)

First, the FDIC invokes the need for "uniformity."  Federal common law, it says, will provide uniformity, but "[s]uperimposing state standards of fiduciary responsibility over standards developed by a federal chartering authority would ... 'upset the balance' that the federal chartering authority 'may strike....' "  Brief for Respondent 23.  To invoke the concept of "uniformity," however, is not to prove its need.

For one thing, the number of federally insured banks is about equally divided between federally chartered and state-chartered banks, Federal Deposit Insurance Corporation, 1 Statistics on Banking: A Statistical History of the United States Banking Industry, Table SI-9, p. B-9 (Aug.1995) (showing that, in 1989, there were 1,595 federally chartered institutions and 1,492 state- chartered ones); and a federal standard that increases uniformity among the former would increase disparity with the latter.

For another, our Nation's banking system has thrived despite disparities in matters of corporate governance. Consider, for example, the divergent state law governance standards applicable to banks chartered in different States, e. g., Ind.Code Ann. § 23-1-35-1(e)(2) (1994) (directors not liable unless conduct constitutes at least "willful misconduct or recklessness"); Iowa Code § 524.605 (1995) (providing ordinary negligence standard), as well as the different ways in which lower courts since 1891 have interpreted Briggs ' "federal common law" standard. Compare Federal Deposit Insurance Corporation v. Mason, 115 F.2d 548, 551-552 (C.A.3 1940) (applying standard similar to simple negligence) with Washington Bancorporation v. Said, 812 F.Supp. 1256, 1266 (D.D.C.1993) (Briggs did not apply "simple negligence" standard of care). See R. Stevens & B. Nielson, The Standard of Care for Directors and Officers of Federally Chartered Depository Institutions: It's Gross Negligence Regardless of Whether Section 1821(k) Preempts Federal Common Law, 13 Ann. Review Banking L. 169, 172 (1994) (in part because of "widely varying results, the federal common law standard of care is neither fully developed, nor well settled"). See also infra, at 672 (citing cases in which state governance law has been applied to national banks). Indeed, the Comptroller of the Currency, acting through regulation, permits considerable disparity in the standard of care applicable to federally chartered banks other than savings banks (which are under the jurisdiction of the Office of Thrift Supervision, 12 U.S.C. §§ 1462a, 1463(a)). See 12 C.F.R. § 7.2000 (1996) (permitting banks, within broad limits, "to follow the corporate governance procedures of the law of the state in which the main office of the bank is located ... [or] the Delaware General Corporation Law ... or the Model Business Corporation Act").

Second, the FDIC at times suggests that courts must apply a federal common-law standard of care simply because the banks in question are federally chartered. This argument, with little more, might have seemed a strong one during most of the first century of our Nation's history, for then state- chartered banks were the norm and federally chartered banks an exception--and federal banks often encountered hostility and deleterious state laws. See B. Klebaner, American Commercial Banking: A History 4-11 (1990) (tracing the origin of the dual banking system to the 1780 Philadelphia Bank and discussing proposals of a then-young Alexander Hamilton); B. Hammond, Banks and Politics in America: From the Revolution to the Civil War 41-66 (1957) (describing the controversial, but successful, Federalist proposals for the first and second federally chartered Bank of the United States).

After President Madison helped to create the second Bank of the United States, for example, many States enacted laws that taxed the federal bank in an effort to weaken it. This Court held those taxes unconstitutional. McCulloch v. Maryland, 4 Wheat. 316, 431, 4 L.Ed. 579 (1819) ("[T]he power to tax involves the power to destroy"). . . .

During and after the Civil War a federal banking system reemerged. Moved in part by war-related financing needs, Treasury Secretary (later Chief Justice) Salmon P. Chase proposed, and Congress enacted, laws providing for federally chartered banks, Act of Feb. 20, 1863, ch.

43, 12 Stat. 655, and encouraging state banks to obtain federal charters.  Act of June 3, 1864, ch. 106, 13 Stat. 99 (only federally chartered banks can issue national currency). . . .

This latter history is relevant because in 1870 and thereafter this Court held that federally chartered banks are subject to state law.  See National Bank v. Commonwealth, 9 Wall. 353, 361, 19 L.Ed. 701 (1869).  In National Bank the Court distinguished McCulloch by recalling that Maryland's taxes were "used ... to destroy," and it added that federal banks

"are subject to the laws of the State, and are governed in their daily course of business far more by the laws of the State than of the nation.  All their contracts are governed and construed by State laws.  Their acquisition and transfer of property, their right to collect their debts, and their liability to be sued for debts, are all based on State law.  It is only when the State law incapacitates the banks from discharging their duties to the government that it becomes unconstitutional."  9 Wall., at 362.

The Court subsequently found numerous state laws applicable to federally chartered banks.  See, e.g., Davis v. Elmira Savings Bank, 161 U.S. 275, 290 (1896) ("Nothing, of course, in this opinion is intended to deny the operation of general and undiscriminating state laws on the contracts of national banks, so long as such laws do not conflict with the letter or the general objects and purposes of Congressional legislation");  First Nat. Bank in St. Louis v. Missouri, 263 U.S. 640, 656 (1924) (national banks "are subject to the laws of a State in respect of their affairs unless such laws interfere with the purposes of their creation, tend to impair or destroy their efficiency as federal agencies or conflict with the paramount law of the United States");  Wichita Royalty Co. v. City Nat. Bank of Wichita Falls, 306 U.S. 103 (1939) (applying state law to tort claim by depositor against directors of a national bank);  Anderson Nat. Bank v. Luckett, 321 U.S. 233, 248 (1944) ("National banks are subject to state laws, unless those laws infringe the national banking laws or impose an undue burden on the performance of the banks' functions");  California Fed. Sav. & Loan Assn. v. Guerra, 479 U.S. 272 (1987) (applying state employment discrimination law to federally chartered savings and loan association).

For present purposes, the consequence is the following:  To point to a federal charter by itself shows no conflict, threat, or need for "federal common law."  It does not answer the critical question.

Third, the FDIC refers to a conflict of laws principle called the "internal affairs doctrine"--a doctrine that this Court has described as

"a conflict of laws principle which recognizes that only one State should have the authority to regulate a corporation's internal affairs--matters peculiar to the relationships among or between the corporation and its current officers, directors, and shareholders--because otherwise a corporation could be faced with conflicting demands."  Edgar v. MITE Corp., 457 U.S. 624, 645 (1982).

States normally look to the State of a business' incorporation for the law that provides the relevant corporate governance general standard of care.  Restatement (Second) Conflict of Laws § 309 (1971).  And by analogy, it has been argued, courts should look to federal law to find the standard of care governing officers and directors of federally chartered banks.  See Resolution Trust Corporation v. Chapman, 29 F.3d 1120, 1123-1124 (C.A.7 1994).

To find a justification for federal common law in this argument, however, is to substitute analogy or formal symmetry for the controlling legal requirement, namely, the existence of a need to create federal common law arising out of a significant conflict or threat to a federal interest. O'Melveny, 512 U.S., at 85, 87. The internal affairs doctrine shows no such need, for it seeks only to avoid conflict by requiring that there be a single point of legal reference. Nothing in that doctrine suggests that the single source of law must be federal. See Chapman, supra, at 1126-1127 (Posner, C.J., dissenting). In the absence of a governing federal common law, courts applying the internal affairs doctrine could find (we do not say that they will find) that the State closest analogically to the State of incorporation of an ordinary business is the State in which the federally chartered bank has its main office or maintains its principal place of business. Cf. 12 C.F.R. § 7.2000 (1996) (federally chartered commercial banks may "follow the corporate governance procedures of the law of the state in which the main office of the bank is located"). So to apply state law, as we have said, would tend to avoid disparity between federally chartered and state-chartered banks (that might be next door to each other). And, of course, if this approach proved problematic, Congress and federal agencies acting pursuant to congressionally delegated authority remain free to provide to the contrary.

Fourth, the FDIC points to statutes that provide the Office of Thrift Supervision, a federal regulatory agency, with authority to fine, or to remove from office, savings bank officers and directors for certain breaches of fiduciary duty. The FDIC adds that in "the course of such proceedings, the OTS, applying the ordinary-care standard [of Briggs ] ... has spoken authoritatively respecting the duty of care owed by directors and officers to federal savings associations." Brief for Respondent 23-25. The FDIC does not claim, however, that these OTS statements, interpreting a pre-existing judge-made federal common-law standard (i.e., that of Briggs ) themselves amounted to an agency effort to promulgate a binding regulation pursuant to delegated congressional authority. Nor have we found, in our examination of the relevant OTS opinions, any convincing evidence of a relevant, significant conflict or threat to a federal interest.

Finally, we note that here, as in O'Melveny, the FDIC is acting only as a receiver of a failed institution; it is not pursuing the interest of the Federal Government as a bank insurer--an interest likely present whether the insured institution is state, or federally, chartered.

In sum, we can find no significant conflict with, or threat to, a federal interest. The federal need is far weaker than was present in what the Court has called the "few and restricted instances," Milwaukee v. Illinois, 451 U.S. 304, 313 (1981), in which this Court has created a federal common law. . . . Indeed, the interests in many of the cases where this Court has declined to recognize federal common law appear at least as strong as, if not stronger than, those present here. . . .

We conclude that the federal common-law standards enunciated in cases such as Briggs did not survive this Court's later decision in Erie R. Co. v. Tompkins. There is no federal common law that would create a general standard of care applicable to this case.

### III

We now turn to a further question: Does federal statutory law (namely, the federal "gross negligence" statute), supplant any state-law standard of care? The relevant parts of that statute read as follows:

"*A director or officer* of an insured depository institution *may be held personally liable for* monetary damages in any civil action by, on behalf of, or at the request or direction of the Corporation ... acting as conservator or receiver ... for *gross negligence, including* any similar conduct or conduct that demonstrates *a greater disregard of a duty of care* (than gross negligence) including intentional tortious conduct, as such terms are defined and determined under applicable State law. *Nothing in this paragraph shall impair or affect any right of the Corporation under other applicable law.*" 12 U.S.C. § 1821(k) (emphasis added).

Lower courts have taken different positions about whether this statute, in stating that directors and officers "may be held personally liable" for conduct that amounts to "gross negligence" or worse, immunizes them from liability for conduct that is less culpable than gross negligence such as simple negligence.  Federal Deposit Insurance Corporation v. McSweeney, 976 F.2d 532, 537, n. 5 (C.A.9 1992), cert. denied, 508 U.S. 950 (1993);  Federal Deposit Insurance Corporation v. Canfield, 967 F.2d 443, 446, n. 3 (C.A.10) (en banc), cert. dism'd, 506 U.S. 993 (1992);  Federal Deposit Insurance Corporation v. Swager, 773 F.Supp. 1244 (D.Minn.1991).

In our view, the statute's "gross negligence" standard provides only a floor--a guarantee that officers and directors must meet at least a gross negligence standard.  It does not stand in the way of a stricter standard that the laws of some States provide.

For one thing, the language of the statute contains a savings clause that, read literally, preserves the applicability of stricter state standards.  It says "[n]othing in this paragraph shall impair or affect any right of the Corporation under other applicable law." 12 U.S.C. § 1821(k) (emphasis added).  The petitioner, in contending that the statute displaces federal common law, says that "any right" means only a right created elsewhere in the same Act of Congress, for example, by various regulatory enforcement provisions.  E.g., § 1818(b) (cease-and-desist provision).  But that is not what the Act says nor does its language compel so restrictive a reading.  That language, read naturally, suggests an interpretation broad enough to save rights provided by other state, or federal, law.

For another thing, Congress enacted the statute against a background of failing savings associations, see 135 Cong. Rec. 121 (1989) (statement of Rep. Roth);  135 Cong. Rec. 1760 (1989) (statement of Sen. Graham), large federal payments to insured bank depositors, and recent changes in state law designed to limit preexisting officer and director negligence liability.  See, e.g., Fla. Stat. § 607.0831 (1993) ("recklessness or an act or omission ... committed in bad faith or with malicious purpose");  Ohio Rev.Code Ann. § 1701.59(D) (1994) ("deliberate intent to cause injury to the corporation or undertaken with reckless disregard for the best interests of the corporation").  The state-law changes would have made it more difficult for the Federal Government to recover, from negligent officers and directors, federal funds spent to rescue failing savings banks and their depositors.  And the background as a whole supports a reading of the statute as an effort to preserve the Federal Government's ability to recover funds by creating a standard of care floor.

The legislative history, insofar as it is relevant, supports this conclusion.  Members of Congress repeatedly referred to the harm that liability-relaxing changes in state law had caused the Federal Government, hence the taxpayer, as federal banking agencies tried to recover, from negligent officers and directors, some of the money that federal insurers had to pay to depositors in their failed banks. E.g., 135 Cong. Rec. 7150-7151 (1989) (statement of Sen. Riegle) ("[T]he establishment of a Federal standard of care is based on the overriding Federal interest in protecting the soundness of the Federal Deposit Insurance Corporation fund and is very limited in scope.  It is not a wholesale preemption of longstanding principles of corporate governance ...").  To have pre-empted state law with a uniform federal "gross negligence" standard would have cured the problem in some instances (where state law was weaker) but would have aggravated it in others (where state law was stronger).

In fact, the legislative history says more.  The relevant Senate Report addresses the point specifically.  It says:

"This subsection does not prevent the FDIC from pursuing claims under State law or under other applicable Federal law, if such law permits the officers or directors of a financial institution to be sued (1) for violating a lower standard of care, such as simple negligence."  S.Rep. No. 101-19, p. 318 (1989).

This Report was not published until two weeks after Congress enacted the law.  But, as petitioner elsewhere concedes, the Report was circulated within Congress several weeks before Congress voted. . . .

The petitioner, in the courts below and as an alternative ground in this Court, made a final complicated argument to explain why § 1821(k) displaces federal common law.  He points to the universally conceded fact that the "gross negligence" statute applies to federal, as well as to state, banks.  He then assumes, for sake of the argument, that in the absence of the statute, federal common law would determine liability for federal banks.  He then asks why Congress would have applied the "gross negligence" statute to federal banks unless it wanted that statute to set an absolute standard, not a floor.  After all, on the assumption that, without the statute, federal common law would hold federal directors and officers to a standard as strict, or stricter, there would have been no need for the statute unless (as applied to federal banks) it intended to set a universal standard, freeing officers and directors from the potentially less strict standard of the common law, and not what, given the assumptions, would be a totally unnecessary floor.  This argument, taken to its logical conclusion, would also suggest that state standards of simple negligence would be displaced by the federal gross negligence statute.

One obvious short answer to this ingenious argument lies in the fact that our conclusion in Part II runs contrary to the argument's critical assumption, namely that federal common law sets the standard of liability applicable to federal banks.  State law applies.  Without that assumption, the need for a "gross negligence" floor in the case of federally chartered banks, is identical to the need in the case of state-chartered banks.  In both instances, the floor is needed to limit state efforts to weaken liability standards;  in both instances a floor serves that purpose; and the reasons for believing the statute only sets such a floor are equally strong.

A more thorough answer lies in the fact that Congress nowhere separated its consideration of federally chartered, from that of state-chartered, banks.  Congress did not ask whether one looked to federal common law or to state law to find the liability standard applicable to federally chartered banks.  Nor did it try to determine the content of federal common law.  One can reconcile congressional silence on the matter with a "gross negligence" statute, the language of which brings all banks (federal and state-chartered) within its scope, simply by assuming that Congress, when enacting the statute, wanted to leave other law, including the law applicable to federally chartered banks, exactly where Congress found it.  That, after all, is what the statute says. And the savings clause language taken at face value permits Congress to achieve its basic objective (providing a "gross negligence" floor) without having to unravel the arcane intricacies of federal common law.  In our view, this understanding of congressional intent better explains the statute's language and history than the petitioner's interpretation, imputing to Congress an intent to apply a uniform "gross negligence" standard to federally chartered, but not state-chartered, institutions.

For these reasons, the judgment of the Court of Appeals is vacated, and the case is remanded for proceedings consistent with this opinion.

Justice O'CONNOR, with whom Justice SCALIA and Justice THOMAS join, concurring in part and concurring in the judgment.

I join all of the Court's opinion, except to the extent that it relies on the notably unhelpful legislative history to 12 U.S.C. § 1821(k). As the Court correctly points out, the most natural reading of the savings clause in § 1821(k) covers both state and federal rights.  With such plain statutory language in hand, there is no reason to rely on legislative history that is, as the majority recognizes, "not all on one side."

## Comments and Questions

1.  Many states have enacted statutes that attempt to limit the liability of directors and officers for breaches of duty involving  gross negligence.  The principal reason Congress enacted § 1821(k) was to preempt these limitations.  After *Atherton*, not only will the standard of care applicable to officers and directors of a state chartered institution depend on the state common law and any subsequent statutory enactments, as limited by § 1821(k), but state laws also will determine the standard of care applicable to federally chartered depository institutions. Query: If a state adopted a liability rule making state bank directors responsible for simple negligence, would § 1821(k) preempt that standard as inconsistent with § 1821(k)?  Would directors of national banks located in the jurisdiction be held to that standard?

2.  A possible defense for officers and directors is the business judgment rule. Under the business judgment rule, a director is absolved from liability if he or she acts in good faith with the care an ordinarily prudent person would utilize under similar circumstances.  Officers and directors often comply with the business judgment rule by utilizing such mechanisms as audit committees, compliance officers, and good faith reliance on bank executive officers and expert consultants.  Will the scope of protection the business judgment rule vary by state for officers and directors of federally chartered depository institutions?

3.  Will *Atherton* affect the scope of agency discretion in administrative enforcement proceedings to sanction insider misconduct administratively through cease and desist orders (including restitution), suspension and removal orders, and civil money penalties?  Or is there no conflict?  Can the regulators effectively sanction negligent misconduct through their supervisory enforcement powers, with limited judicial review under *Chevron*?

4. The second major issue that has been litigated in connection with director and officer liability is whether the statute of limitations on the claim had run prior to the FDIC being appointed receiver. Read § 1821(d)(14). Subsection (A) provides a tort statute of limitations of either three years from the date the claim accrues or, if longer, the applicable state law statute of limitations. Subsection (B) states that the statute of limitations begins to run on the later of either the date of FDIC's appointment or the date on which the cause of action accrues. But case law requires that the claim must not be barred under state law at the time the FDIC is appointed receiver. The only way for the FDIC to avoid the running of the state statute of limitations prior to their appointment is to utilize the doctrine of adverse domination, which tolls the statute of limitations. Adverse domination exists where a bank is so dominated by those against whom it has a claim (i.e., officers and directors), that it is unable to pursue the claim. In general, courts have held that the adverse domination standard for tolling a statute of limitation is a question of state law.

---

The role of professional advisers, such as accountants and attorneys, to failed depository institutions has become a subject of congressional and regulatory attention. The most notorious controversy arose out of the widely-publicized insolvency of Charles Keating's Lincoln Savings and Loan Association of Irvine, California. Set out below is a chronology of the proceedings excerpted from a law review symposium on the case.

What is the legal basis for the proceeding against the law firm of Kaye, Scholer? From where does the OTS derive jurisdiction over the law firm? What is the applicable standard of conduct? Is it the legal profession's Rules of Professional Conduct or some other source of law? Recall that we have seen numerous references to institution-affiliated parties, a term defined by 12 U.S.C.A. § 1813(u) and explicitly made subject to the supervisory enforcement powers of the FDIC in § 1818.

The term "institutional-affiliated party" includes attorneys, accountants and appraisers, as well as any other independent contractor to a depository institution, if such person has (1) "knowingly or recklessly" participated in (2) any violation of law or regulation, any breach of fiduciary duty, or any unsafe or unsound practice, (3) "which caused or is likely to cause more than a minimal financial loss to, or a significant adverse effect on, the insured depository institution. "Under this definition, might incorrect legal or accounting advice, given in good faith, be a basis for supervisory enforcement action? Note that once the definition is met, all of the supervisory enforcement powers of § 1818 are available, such as the three-tiered civil money penalty power. If the conduct of the person also involves either personal dishonesty or a willful disregard for the safety and soundness of the institution, the regulators have the power to bar the person from representing any depository institution. See 12 U.S.C.A. § 1818(e). And, as we will see, §§ §§ 1818(b) and (c) allow the regulators to effectuate a freeze of the assets of an institution-affiliated party.

## James O. Johnston & Daniel S. Schecter, Kaye, Scholer and the OTS – Did Anyone Go Too Far?
### 66 S. Cal. L. Rev. 977, 979-83 (1993).

The issues raised by these articles are best understood by referencing the sequence of events that culminated in Kaye, Scholer's stunning settlement with the OTS.

Kaye, Scholer began representing Charles Keating's American Continental Corporation in 1977.  In February 1984, ACC acquired Lincoln and hired Kaye, Scholer to represent the thrift on various matters.  In early 1986, Lincoln retained the law firm of Jones, Day, Reavis & Pogue to represent it before the Federal Home Loan Bank Board in its semiannual examination of operations and financial condition ("1986 Examination").  Lincoln; however, became dissatisfied with Jones Day's cooperative, nonconfrontational dealings with the FHLBB's examiners and soon replaced the firm with Kaye, Scholer.

Kaye, Scholer partner Peter M. Fishbein immediately composed a caustic five-page letter to the FHLBB, denouncing the "abusive and costly" practices of the examiners and demanding that all further requests for information be given to specified Kaye, Scholer attorneys.  This demand baffled the FHLBB, the rules of which gave it the right to inspect thrift records at any time.  The request "reflects a fundamental misunderstanding of the examination process," wrote B.J. Davis, the FHLBB's regulator in charge of the 1986 Examination, in response to Fishbein's letter.  "Unfettered access, including the ability to appear at [a regulated institution] without advance notice, is essential to fulfillment of [the FHLBB's] function."  Nevertheless, the FHLBB complied, and for the remainder of the 1986 Examination the ten Kaye, Scholer lawyers working with Lincoln took a consistently hard-line approach to FHLBB requests.  "This was not a dialogue," noted one examiner.  "This was a stiff-arm day in and day out."

In April 1987, the FHLBB issued a very negative report of examination ("1986 ROE") for Lincoln and received a confidential recommendation from the examiners to appoint a receiver for the thrift, which had invested heavily in high-risk takeover stocks, junk bonds, and speculative real estate.  Kaye, Scholer responded to the 1986 ROE with a 768-page rebuttal, supplemented by more than 10,000 pages of exhibits, that portrayed Lincoln as a soundly managed, solvent institution.  The FHLBB, faced with Kaye, Scholer's threats of litigation and pressure from several U.S. Senators,[9] ultimately declined to pursue the matter.

In July 1988, the FHLBB once again began an examination of Lincoln, which continued to retain Kaye, Scholer.  The regulators' subsequent report of examination ("1988 ROE"), issued in December of that year, was similarly negative, concluding that Lincoln was managed in "an aggressive risk prone manner that has resulted in a level of problem assets that severely strains capital and places the continued viability of the association in jeopardy."  Also in December, the Securities and Exchange Commission issued a report stating that Lincoln had failed to meet its minimum capital requirements, prompting the resignation of Lincoln's accountant, Arthur Young & Company.  Kaye, Scholer nevertheless responded to the 1988 ROE, in January 1989, by asserting that "Lincoln's managerial skill its sound diversification of investments and its prudent underwriting are all demonstrated by the unqualified success of its investment program."

---

[9]     This intervening group of Senators later became known as "the Keating Five."

Just three months later, however, the FDIC (the predecessor to the OTS) seized Lincoln and found the thrift to be insolvent by more than $2.6 billion. Lincoln's subsequent challenge to the government takeover in federal court proved unsuccessful, as Judge Sporkin declared it to be "abundantly clear that Lincoln was in an unsafe and unsound condition to transact business and that [Lincoln] did in fact engage in numerous unsafe and unsound banking practices."[12] Judge Sporkin then proceeded to issue a blistering condemnation of Lincoln's professional advisers:

The questions that must be asked are:

Where were these professionals . . . when these clearly improper transactions were being consummated?

Why didn't any of them speak up or disassociate themselves from these transactions?

Where also were the outside accountants and attorneys when these transactions were effectuated?

What is difficult to understand is that with all the professional talent involved (both accounting and legal), why at least one professional would not have blown the whistle to stop the overreaching that took place in this case.

. . . Here it is clear that the private sector was not willing to cooperate with the public oversight regulators. Indeed, the private sector at times impeded the regulatory authorities from discharging their duties. All too often [Charles] Keating and those individuals working with him adopted strategies to thwart and frustrate the regulatory process.

Judge Sporkin's "Where were the professionals?" became a rallying cry at the OTS, which began to build a case against Kaye, Scholer. The seizure of Lincoln gave the OTS access to internal documents and the ability to waive the attorney-client privilege in order to use those documents against Kaye, Scholer, which it promptly did. More than a year and a half later, after a painstaking compilation of correspondence and depositions, the OTS filed a notice of ten claims against the firm. In brief, the OTS alleged the following:

1) Kaye, Scholer knew that Lincoln's directors had misleadingly backdated documents in order to take advantage of a rule permitting grandfathering of direct investments when "definitive plans" had been made for those investments.

2) Kaye, Scholer knowingly misrepresented the status of those direct investments to the FHLBB.

3) Kaye, Scholer knowingly failed to disclose that Arthur Andersen & Company, Lincoln's accountant in 1986, had resigned from service because of concerns about Lincoln's operations and asset management.

4) Kaye, Scholer knowingly omitted material facts in submissions to the FHLBB and engaged in obstructionist and improper conduct in its appearances before the agency.

5) Kaye, Scholer knowingly failed to disclose the existence of numerous "linked" transactions that improperly inflated Lincoln's income and net worth.

6) Kaye, Scholer knowingly failed to disclose that Lincoln had removed adverse documents and created favorable documents in preparation for the 1986 Examination.

7) Kaye, Scholer knowingly failed to disclose facts indicating that Lincoln had participated in limited partnership investments in order to finance personal tax shelters for ACC's control persons.

---

[12]    *Lincoln Sav. & Loan Ass'n v. Wall*, 743 F. Supp. 901, 905-06 (D.D.C. 1990).

8) Kaye, Scholer urged the FHLBB to rely on the opinions of Lincoln's auditors regarding certain joint venture transactions when it knew that those opinions had been prepared without adequate investigation.

9) Kaye, Scholer engaged in improper and unethical conduct by representing both ACC and Lincoln, thus creating a conflict of interest.

10) Kaye, Scholer obtained an illegal loan from Lincoln for one of its partners on favorable terms and in violation of the thrift's internal procedures.

Declaring that these charges constituted a prima facie showing that Kaye, Scholer had a "proclivity to violate laws and regulations, breach their fiduciary duties of loyalty and care and engage in unsafe an unsound practices," the OTS concurrently issued the temporary cease and desist order under 12 U.S.C. § 1818(c).

On the same day, Kaye, Scholer released a memorandum deeming the charges to be a "completely groundless . . . attempt by the OTS to create and apply new standard's for attorney conduct that are different from, and inconsistent with, generally accepted professional standards and ethical obligations for lawyers representing a client." In the release, the firm indicated an intent to "contest these charges vigorously and ultimately to prevail on the merits." Kaye, Scholer also released a nine-page summary of the opinion of Professor Geoffrey C. Hazard, Jr., a specialist in legal ethics. This document, which was prepared by Kaye, Scholer but signed by Professor Hazard, concluded, after nearly six pages of factual assumptions, with a ringing endorsement of the firm's conduct:

Kaye, Scholer did not violate existing standards of ethical conduct and professional responsibility, and Kaye, Scholer acted in accord with its duties under the law. The disclosures and representations that the OTS alleges should have been made to the [FHLBB] by Kaye, Scholer in fact would have violated the standards of ethical conduct and professional responsibility generally recognized in its role as litigation counsel.[27]

Despite Kaye, Scholer's protestations of innocence, however, the firm rapidly capitulated, settling with the OTS six days later. Kaye, Scholer's insurance covered only about half of the $41 million, leaving the firm's 110 partners to pay the rest. Because Kaye, Scholer did not give a reason for its rapid decision to accept this bitter pill, speculation has abounded. Some argue that the temporary cease-and-desist order gave the firm no other choice. "What the government wanted was to bludgeon [Kaye, Scholer] so they wouldn't have to prove the allegations," said Professor Dennis Aronowitz. "The most insidious part of the case was that aspect: the government throwing its weight around." Others, however, argue that the firm would have settled quickly even in the absence of the order. "It was a realization that the freeze was irrelevant!" Susan Beck and Michael Orey have claimed. "[N]othing else the firm could have done would have saved it from having to fight the OTS's $275 million claim . . . . The firm would likely have lost a long, public fight at the OTS."

---

[27]  *Summary of the Expert Opinion of Geoffrey C. Hazard, Jr.* 8 (Feb. 25, 1992), *reprinted in* KAYE, SCHOLER CASE, *supra* note 6, at 112. For a critique of Professor Hazard's opinion, see Susan Beck & Michael Orey, *Hazard Opinion: Read with Caution*, AM. LAW., May 1992, at 75.

## Comments and Questions

1. Who was Kaye, Scholer's client? Was it Charles Keating, or Lincoln Savings and Loan Association and its creditors, including depositors, who ultimately suffered a $2.6 billion loss? What do you think of the claim by Kaye, Scholer that it was merely performing its duties as litigation counsel, even though the OTS was involved in an examination of a federally insured depository institution, which under federal law gave it access to all of the depository institution's records?

2. On the other hand, are the claims of the OTS nothing more than an argument that lawyers have a duty to "rat" on their clients, in violation of the Rules of Professional Conduct? Is there a difference between shielding a client through aggressive legal arguments based on facts, rather than a misstatement or concealment of facts?

3. Consider the auditors for a bank as an institution-affiliated party. Is it reasonable for them to expect that the FDIC might rely on the auditor's report, at least as a point of inquiry, when performing bank examinations? Might the auditor be liable for a negligent audit of the bank, such as failing to identify and disclose significant amounts of loss or substandard loans?

4. Was it a conflict of interests for Kaye, Scholer to represent American Continental Corp., Lincoln's holding company, as well as Lincoln?

5. Does the attorney have a duty to advise the depository institution how to comply with its legal obligations? Can this be the basis for a malpractice claim against depository institution lawyers, should the institution fail and the FDIC as receiver acquire all the rights of the failed institution?

6. The government brought an administrative enforcement action rather than a civil law suit against Mr. Fishbein and Kaye, Scholer. The reason is that this gave the defendants fewer procedural means of defense. Particularly, the OTS imposed a freeze on certain assets belonging to Fishbein and Kaye, Scholer. The FDIC has the power to issue a temporary cease and desist order against institution-affiliated parties, including lawyers who "knowingly or recklessly participated" in a violation or in an "unsafe or unsound" banking practice. If the banking agency determines that the violation or unsafe or unsound practice is likely to cause insolvency or dissipation of earnings, the agency may issue a temporary order to cease and desist and also to take affirmative action to prevent or remedy the insolvency, dissipation or condition. See §§ 1813(u) and 1818(c)(1). Under § 1818(b)(6) the affirmative action that the agency may order includes restitution, a freeze on assets, and other powers, all without any requirement for a prior hearing. These powers appear to be available not only with respect to institutions close to insolvency but also with respect to failed institutions. Section 1818(c)(2) authorizes the party served with a temporary cease and desist order to apply within ten days to the district court for review. However, § 1818(d) may limit the court's discretion. Any violation of the temporary order can result in civil money penalties. And it is common for administrative hearings to drag on for months. Is all of this an excess of regulatory power, with insufficient checks and balances?

Kaye, Scholer was one of many law firms that found themselves subject to litigation arising out of the savings and loan crisis of the 1980s.  The following case involves one of the largest law firms in Los Angeles.  How does this litigation compare to the OTS's enforcement proceeding in Kaye, Scholer?  What is the legal basis for the government's claim?  What is the proper source of law governing attorneys who represent federal insured financial intermediaries?  To what extent does the nature of the client institution affect professional standards of conduct?  And what forum should define those standards?

Start by considering § 1821(d)(2)(A), which allows the FDIC to bring civil lawsuits against institution-affiliated parties as receiver of a failed institution, rather than administrative proceedings as regulator of the institution.  By standing in the shoes of the failed institution in court, the regulator does not have to meet the "knowingly or recklessly" requirement of § 1818(u), and so can bring any claim, such as a malpractice claim, based on any duty that a professional may have to its depository institution client.

## O'Melveny & Myers v. Federal Deposit Insurance Corporation
### 512 U.S. 79 (1994)

Justice SCALIA delivered the opinion of the Court.

The issue in this case is whether, in a suit by the Federal Deposit Insurance Corporation as receiver of a federally insured bank, it is a federal-law or rather a state-law rule of decision that governs the tort liability of attorneys who provided services to the bank.

I

American Diversified Savings Bank (ADSB or S& L) is a California-chartered and federally insured savings and loan.  The following facts have been stipulated to, or are uncontroverted, by the parties to the case, and we assume them to be true for purposes of our decision.  ADSB was acquired in 1983 by Ranbir Sahni and Lester Day, who respectively obtained 96% and 4% of its stock, and who respectively served as its chairman/CEO and president.  Under their leadership, ADSB engaged in many risky real estate transactions, principally through limited partnerships sponsored by ADSB and its subsidiaries.  Together, Sahni and Day also fraudulently overvalued ADSB's assets, engaged in sham sales of assets to create inflated "profits," and generally "cooked the books" to disguise the S & L's dwindling (and eventually negative) net worth.

In September 1985, petitioner O'Melveny & Myers, a Los Angeles-based law firm, represented ADSB in connection with two real estate syndications.  At that time, ADSB was under investigation by state and federal regulators, but that fact had not been made public.  In completing its work for the S & L, petitioner did not contact the accounting firms that had previously done work for ADSB, nor state and federal regulatory authorities, to inquire about ADSB's financial status.  The two real estate offerings on which petitioner worked closed on December 31, 1985.  On February 14, 1986, federal regulators concluded that ADSB was insolvent and that it had incurred substantial losses because of violations of law and unsound business practices. Respondent stepped in as receiver for ADSB, and on February 19, 1986, filed suit against Messrs. Sahni and Day in Federal District Court, alleging breach of fiduciary duty and, as to Sahni, RICO violations. Soon after taking over as receiver, respondent began receiving demands for refunds from investors who claimed that they had been deceived in connection with the two real estate syndications. Respondent caused ADSB to rescind the syndications and to return all of the investors' money plus interest.

On May 12, 1989, respondent sued petitioner in the United States District Court for the Central District of California, alleging professional negligence and breach of fiduciary duty. The parties stipulated to certain facts and petitioner moved for summary judgment, arguing that (1) it owed no duty to ADSB or its affiliates to uncover the S & L's own fraud; (2) that knowledge of the conduct of ADSB's controlling officers must be imputed to the S & L, and hence to respondent, which, as receiver, stood in the shoes of the S & L; and (3) that respondent was estopped from pursuing its tort claims against petitioner because of the imputed knowledge. On May 15, 1990, the District Court granted summary judgment, explaining only that petitioner was "entitled to judgment in its favor . . . as a matter of law." The Court of Appeals for the Ninth Circuit reversed, on grounds that we shall discuss below. 969 F.2d 744 (1992). Petitioner filed a petition for writ of certiorari, which we granted. 510 U.S. 989 (1993).

## II

It is common ground that the FDIC was asserting in this case causes of action created by California law. Respondent contends that in the adjudication of those causes of action (1) a federal common-law rule and not California law determines whether the knowledge of corporate officers acting against the corporation's interest will be imputed to the corporation; and (2) even if California law determines the former question, federal common law determines the more narrow question whether knowledge by officers so acting will be imputed to the FDIC when it sues as receiver of the corporation.[2]

The first of these contentions need not detain us long, as it is so plainly wrong. "There is no federal general common law," *Erie R. Co. v. Tompkins*, 304 U.S. 64, 78 (1938), and (to anticipate somewhat a point we will elaborate more fully in connection with respondent's second contention) the remote possibility that corporations may go into federal receivership is no conceivable basis for adopting a special federal common-law rule divesting States of authority over the entire law of imputation. See *Bank of America Nat. Trust & Savings Assn. v. Parnell*, 352 U.S. 29, 33-34 (1956). The Ninth Circuit believed that its conclusion on this point was in harmony with *Schacht v. Brown*, 711 F.2d 1343 (CA7 1983), *Cenco Inc. v. Seidman & Seidman*, 686 F.2d 449 (CA7 1982), and *In re Investors Funding Corp. of N.Y. Securities Litigation*, 523 F. Supp. 533 (S.D.N.Y. 1980), 969 F.2d, at 750, but even a cursory examination of those cases shows the contrary. In *Cenco*, where the cause of action similarly arose under state common law,

---

[2]    The Court of Appeals appears to have agreed with the first of these contentions. Instead of the second, however, it embraced the proposition that federal common law prevents the attributed knowledge of corporate officers acting against the corporation's interest from being used as the basis for an estoppel defense against the FDIC as receiver. Since there is nothing but a formalistic distinction between this argument and the second one described in text, we do not treat it separately.

the Seventh Circuit's analysis of the "circumstances under which the knowledge of fraud on the part of the plaintiff's directors [would] be imputed to the plaintiff corporation [was] merely an attempt to divine how Illinois courts would decide that issue." *Schacht*, 711 F.2d, at 1347 (citing *Cenco*, 686 F.2d, at 455).  Likewise, in *Investors Funding*, the District Court analyzed the potential affirmative defenses to the state-law claims by applying "[t]he controlling legal principles [of] New York law."  523 F. Supp. at 540.  In *Schacht*, the Seventh Circuit expressly noted that "the cause of action [at issue] arises under RICO, a federal statute; we therefore write on a clean slate and may bring to bear federal policies in deciding the estoppel question."  711 F.2d at 1347.

In seeking to defend the Ninth Circuit's holding, respondent contends (to quote the caption of its argument) that "The Wrongdoing Of ADSB's Insiders Would Not Be Imputed To ADSB Under Generally Accepted Common Law Principles," Brief for Respondent 12–in support of which it attempts to show that nonattribution to the corporation of dishonest officers' knowledge is the rule applied in the vast bulk of decisions from 43 jurisdictions, ranging from Rhode Island to Wyoming.  *See, e.g., id.* at 21-22 n.9 (distinguishing, *inter alia*, *Cook v. American Tubing & Webbing Co.*, 28 R.I. 41, 65 A. 641 (1905), and *American Nat. Bank of Powell v. Foodbasket*, 497 P.2d 546 (Wyo. 1972)).  The supposed relevance of this is set forth in a footnote: "It is our position that federal common law does govern this issue, but that the content of the federal common law rule corresponds to the rule that would independently be adopted by most jurisdictions."  Brief for Respondent 15 n.3.  If there were a federal common law on such a generalized issue (which there is not), we see no reason why it would necessarily conform to that "independently . . . adopted by most jurisdictions."  But the short of the matter is that California law, not federal law, governs the imputation of knowledge to corporate victims of alleged negligence, and that is so whether or not California chooses to follow "the majority rule."

We turn, then, to the more substantial basis for the decision below, which asserts federal pre-emption not over the law of imputation generally, but only over its application to the FDIC suing as receiver.  Respondent begins its defense of this principle by quoting *United States v. Kimbell Foods, Inc.*, 440 U.S. 715, 726 (1979), to the effect that "federal law governs questions involving the rights of the United States arising under nationwide federal programs."  But the FDIC is not the United States, and even if it were we would be begging the question to assume that it was asserting its own rights rather than, as receiver, the rights of ADSB.  In any event, knowing whether "federal law governs" in the *Kimbell Foods* sense–a sense which includes federal adoption of state-law rules, see *id.* at 727-729 – does not much advance the ball.  The issue in the present case is whether the California rule of decision *is* to be applied to the issue of imputation or displaced, and if it is applied it is of only theoretical interest whether the basis for that application is California's own sovereign power or federal adoption of California's disposition. . . . .

In answering the central question of displacement of California law, we of course would not contradict an explicit federal statutory provision.  Nor would we adopt a court-made rule to supplement federal statutory regulation that is comprehensive and detailed; matters left unaddressed in such a scheme are presumably left subject to the disposition provided by state law. . . . Petitioner asserts that both these principles apply in the present case, by reason of 12 U.S.C. § 1821(d)(2)(A)(i) (1988 ed., Supp. IV), and the comprehensive legislation of which it is a part, the Financial Institutions Reform, Recovery, and Enforcement Act of 1989 (FIRREA), Pub. L. 101-73, 103 Stat. 183.

Section 1821(d)(2)(A)(i), which is part of a Title captioned "Powers and duties of [the FDIC] as . . . receiver," states that "the [FDIC] shall . . . by operation of law, succeed to–all rights, titles, powers, and privileges of the insured depository institution. . . ." 12 U.S.C. § 1821(d)(2)(A)(i) (1988 ed., Supp. IV). This language appears to indicate that the FDIC as receiver "steps into the shoes" of the failed S & L, *cf. Coit Independence Joint Venture v. FSLIC*, 489 U.S. 561, 585 (1989), obtaining the rights "*of* the insured depository institution" that existed prior to receivership. Thereafter, in litigation by the FDIC asserting the claims *of* the S & L–in this case California tort claims potentially defeasible by a showing that the S & L's officers had knowledge–"'any defense good against the original party is good against the receiver.'" 969 F.2d at 751 (quoting *Allen v. Ramsay*, 179 Cal. App. 2d 843, 854, 4 Cal. Rptr. 575, 583 (1960)).

Respondent argues that § 1821(d)(2)(A)(i) should be read as a *nonexclusive* grant of rights to the FDIC receiver, which can be supplemented or modified by federal common law; and that FIRREA as a whole, by demonstrating the high federal interest in this area, confirms the courts' authority to promulgate such common law. This argument is demolished by those provisions of FIRREA which specifically create special federal rules of decision regarding claims by, and defenses against, the FDIC as receiver. See 12 U.S.C. § 1821(d)(14) (1988 ed., Supp. IV) (extending statute of limitations beyond period that might exist under state law); §§ 1821(e)(1), (3) (precluding state-law claims against the FDIC under certain contracts it is authorized to repudiate); § 1821(k) (permitting claims against directors and officers for gross negligence, regardless of whether state law would require greater culpability); § 1821(d)(9) (excluding certain state-law claims against FDIC based on oral agreements by the S & L). *Inclusio unius, exclusio alterius*. It is hard to avoid the conclusion that § 1821(d)(2)(A)(i) places the FDIC in the shoes of the insolvent S & L, to work out its claims under state law, except where some provision in the extensive framework of FIRREA provides otherwise. To create additional "federal common-law" exceptions is not to "supplement" this scheme, but to alter it.

We have thought it necessary to resolve the effect of FIRREA because respondent argued that the statute not only did not prevent but positively authorized federal common law. We are reluctant to rest our judgment on FIRREA alone, however, since that statute was enacted into law in 1989, while respondent took over as receiver for ADSB in 1986. The FDIC is willing to "assume . . . that FIRREA would have taken effect in time to be relevant to this case," Brief for Respondent 35 n.21, but it is not self-evident that that assumption is correct. See *Landgraf v. USI Film Products*, 511 U.S. 244, 268-70, 274 (1994); *cf. id.* at 290-91 (SCALIA, J., concurring in judgment). It seems to us imprudent to resolve the retroactivity question without briefing, and inefficient to pretermit the retroactivity issue on the basis of the FDIC's concession, since that would make our decision of limited value in other cases. As we proceed to explain, even assuming the inapplicability of FIRREA this is not one of those cases in which judicial creation of a special federal rule would be justified.

Such cases are, as we have said in the past, "few and restricted," *Wheeldin v. Wheeler*, 373 U.S. 647, 651 (1963), limited to situations where there is a "significant conflict between some federal policy or interest and the use of state law." *Wallis v. Pan American Petroleum Corp.*, 384 U.S. 63, 68 (1966). Our cases uniformly require the existence of such a conflict as a precondition for recognition of a federal rule of decision. . . . Not only the permissibility but also the scope of judicial displacement of state rules turns upon such a conflict. . . . What is fatal to respondent's position in the present case is that it has identified *no* significant conflict with an identifiable federal policy or interest. There is not even at stake that most generic (and lightly invoked) of alleged federal interests, the interest in uniformity. The rules of decision at issue here do not govern the primary conduct of the United States or any of its agents or contractors, but affect only the FDIC's rights and liabilities, as receiver, with respect to primary conduct on the part of private actors that has already occurred. Uniformity of law might facilitate the FDIC's nationwide litigation of these suits, eliminating state-by-state research and reducing uncertainty–but if the avoidance of those ordinary consequences qualified as an identifiable federal interest, we would be awash in "federal common-law" rules. . . .

The closest respondent comes to identifying a specific, concrete federal policy or interest that is compromised by California law is its contention that state rules regarding the imputation of knowledge might "deplet[e] the deposit insurance fund," Brief for Respondent 32. But neither FIRREA nor the prior law sets forth any anticipated level for the fund, so what respondent must mean by "depletion" is simply the forgoing of *any* money which, under any *conceivable* legal rules, might accrue to the fund. That is a broad principle indeed, which would support not just elimination of the defense at issue here, but judicial creation of new, "federal-common-law" causes of action to enrich the fund. Of course we have no authority to do that, because there is no federal policy that the fund should always win. Our cases have previously rejected "more money" arguments remarkably similar to the one made here. . . .

Even less persuasive — indeed, positively probative of the dangers of respondent's facile approach to federal-common-law-making — is respondent's contention that it would "disserve the federal program" to permit California to insulate "the attorney's or accountant's malpractice," thereby imposing costs "on the nation's taxpayers, rather than on the negligent wrongdoer." Brief for Respondent 32. By presuming to judge what constitutes malpractice, this argument demonstrates the runaway tendencies of "federal common law" untethered to a genuinely identifiable (as opposed to judicially constructed) federal policy. What sort of tort liability to impose on lawyers and accountants in general, and on lawyers and accountants who provide services to federally insured financial institutions in particular, "'involves a host of considerations that must be weighed and appraised,'" *Northwest Airlines, Inc.*, 451 U.S. at 98 n.41 (quoting *United States v. Gilman*, 347 U.S. 507, 512-513 (1954))–including, for example, the creation of incentives for careful work, provision of fair treatment to third parties, assurance of adequate recovery by the federal deposit insurance fund, and enablement of reasonably priced services. Within the federal system, at least, we have decided that that function of weighing and appraising "'is more appropriately for those who write the laws, rather than for those who interpret them.'" *Northwest Airlines*, 451 U.S. at 98 n.41 (quoting *Gilman*, 347 U.S. at 513).

We conclude that this is not one of those extraordinary cases in which the judicial creation of a federal rule of decision is warranted. As noted earlier, the parties are in agreement that if state law governs it is the law of California; but they vigorously disagree as to what that law provides. We leave it to the Ninth Circuit to resolve that point. The judgment is reversed and the case remanded for proceedings consistent with this opinion.

Justice STEVENS, with whom Justice BLACKMUN, Justice O'CONNOR and Justice SOUTER join, concurring.

While I join the Court's opinion, I add this comment to emphasize an important difference between federal courts and state courts. It would be entirely proper for a state court of general jurisdiction to fashion a rule of agency law that would protect creditors of an insolvent corporation from the consequences of wrongdoing by corporate officers even if the corporation itself, or its shareholders, would be bound by the acts of its agents. Indeed, a state court might well attach special significance to the fact that the interests of taxpayers as well as ordinary creditors will be affected by the rule at issue in this case. Federal courts, however, "unlike their state counterparts, are courts of limited jurisdiction that have not been vested with open-ended lawmaking powers." *Northwest Airlines, Inc. v. Transport Workers*, 451 U.S. 77, 95 (1981). Because state law provides the basis for respondent's claim, that law also governs both the elements of the cause of action and its defenses. Unless Congress has otherwise directed, the federal court's task is merely to interpret and apply the relevant rules of state law.

Cases like this one, however, present a special problem. They raise issues, such as the imputation question here, that may not have been definitively settled in the state jurisdiction in which the case is brought, but that nevertheless must be resolved by federal courts. The task of the federal judges who confront such issues would surely be simplified if Congress had provided them with a uniform federal rule to apply. As matters stand, however, federal judges must do their best to estimate how the relevant state courts would perform their lawmaking task, and then emulate that sometimes purely hypothetical model. The Court correctly avoids any suggestion about how the merits of the imputation issue should be resolved on remand or in similar cases that may arise elsewhere. "The federal judges who deal regularly with questions of state law in their respective districts and circuits are in a better position than we to determine how local courts would dispose of comparable issues." *Butner v. United States*, 440 U.S. 48, 58 (1979).

## Comments and Questions

1. On remand, 61 F.3d 17 (9th Cir. 1995), the court reinstated the claim under California state law rather than federal common law, and so reached the same holding it had originally.

2. Note that, as compared to Kaye, Scholer, *O'Melveny* represents the other way that attorneys can get in trouble—malpractice claims brought by the government as receiver.

3. You certainly are aware of the attorney-client privilege. Notice that the FDIC, as receiver, became the client and so was able to waive the attorney-client privilege.

---

The O'Melveny case and the Kaye, Scholer enforcement proceeding were among many actions brought against attorneys and other professionals following the savings and loan crisis of the 1980's. The following excerpt from, Howell E. Jackson, *Reflections on Kaye, Scholer: Enlisting Lawyers to Improve the Regulation of Financial Institutions*, 66 S. CAL. L. REV. 1019 (1993), summaries the legal theories underlying these cases.

Among the government's most effective legal weapons against outside counsel are claims that arise after a bank or thrift fails and a government agency — either the Federal Deposit Insurance Corporation or the Resolution Trust Corporation — becomes receiver or conservator for the institution, but that relate to legal services rendered while the institution was still in private hands. The government qua receiver succeeds to whatever malpractice or contract claims the defunct institution may have had as a result of defective legal services rendered to the institution before its demise. . . .

At the risk of oversimplification, differences between the government and defenders of past practices of the private bar can be grouped into three major categories. The first concerns the obligations of lawyers to inquire into the factual underpinnings of the advice they give to regulated entities-facts represented in filings with a government agency as well as facts relevant to legal advice given outside the regulatory process. On this point the relevant legal norms are accepted by both sides: An attorney should not "knowingly perpetuate a fraud upon a tribunal," nor should the attorney "assist [a] client in conduct that the lawyer knows to be illegal or fraudulent." Differences of interpretation arise in specifying the degree of knowledge the stricture contemplates. To what extent can lawyers plead ignorance of or at least uncertainty about underlying facts, and to what extent and under what circumstances do attorneys have an affirmative duty to unearth and confirm facts that bear on the legal advice they offer? The gist of the government's position is to push outside counsel toward a kind of due diligence obligation for factual predicates. The thrust of the private bar's defense is that no such obligation currently exists, save in a few specialized areas involving relatively formal opinions of counsel.

A second, related area of disagreement concerns the range of legal sources that attorneys are obliged to consider before rendering legal advice to a regulated thrift or bank. Critics of the government stress that it is the prerogative of the client to define an attorney's scope of engagement, and they argue that it is perfectly appropriate-indeed, desirable-for counsel to offer advice on comparatively narrow legal issues. Government attorneys, in contrast, emphasize how important it is for counsel to regulated entities to practice the "whole law," a formulation that former OTS Chief Counsel Harris Weinstein tirelessly championed. In the context of regulated depositories, the whole law includes not just technical requirements of statutes and regulations, but also more open-ended legal rules, such as the obligation of depository institutions to avoid "unsafe and unsound" practices. The government envisions a broad duty on the part of regulatory counsel to explore legal issues; the defenders of the private bar contemplate a narrower one.

The final general area of disagreement between the government and defenders of such firms as Kaye, Scholer might loosely be termed the duty to elevate. According to the government, this duty arises when an attorney becomes aware that a financial institution client has become enmeshed in illegal conduct, including conduct that might violate more open-ended legal norms, such as fiduciary duties or the prohibition against unsafe and unsound practices. At that point, the government claims, an attorney is precluded from furthering the unlawful activity and is obliged to elevate the issue to higher authority, including, if necessary, the institution's board of directors. If the higher authority fails to intercede, "[a] lawyer who neither withdraws or disaffirms continues at his peril," in the government's view. The objections to this duty to elevate proceed at several levels. . . . [T]he most important objections concern the level of awareness of wrongdoing that counsel must possess before this duty arises and the nexus that must exist between counsel's services and the illegal conduct in question. The defenders of the private bar take a relatively narrow view, focusing on when counsel is aware of illegal conduct and when counsel's actions further that conduct so substantially as to trigger a duty to elevate. The government argues for broader duties. . . . .

An alternative source of legal obligations for counsel to regulated firms is derivative liability for the misconduct of a client or employees and agents of a client. Many of the OTS counts against Kaye, Scholer included theories of derivative liability, particularly aiding-and-abetting claims under which the firm was alleged to have assisted Lincoln Savings in primary violations of law. . . .

The essence of an aiding-and-abetting claim is that when a professional adviser becomes sufficiently wound up in the wrongdoing of a client, the adviser becomes secondarily liable for the wrongdoing. . . . [T]he precise scope of aiding-and-abetting liability (and related forms of derivative liability) is difficult to articulate. At least as far as the securities laws are concerned, the federal circuit courts of appeals have adopted a variety of formulations of the degree of awareness and participation necessary to establish aiding-and-abetting liability. As was true of the theories of primary liability discussed earlier, the elements of aiding-and-abetting liability leave ample room for interpretation and expansion. As in its interpretation of the primary obligations of counsel, the government has argued for imposing liability on outside counsel with relatively low levels of knowledge and participation; defenders of Kaye, Scholer insist that such claims require higher levels.

Claims based on theories of agency are another variant of derivative liability that figured prominently in the Kaye, Scholer enforcement action. While the firm insisted that it was simply serving as "litigation counsel" for Lincoln Savings, OTS charged that partners at the firm allowed themselves to become agents for (and indeed the alter ego of) the client institution. As it turned out, no factual record on the issue was ever developed, and it is virtually impossible to untangle the parties' disagreements from the skeletal pleadings and statements available to the public, let alone to define precisely the legal standard for determining when an attorney or other outside adviser becomes susceptible to this form of derivative liability. But the dispute does establish that attorneys who insert themselves too deeply into relations between regulators and a regulated entity run the risk of being held to be agents of their client and thus primarily responsible for their client's violations of law.

A separate and increasingly important source of derivative liability for attorneys of federally insured thrifts and banks is the recently amended Financial Institutions Supervisory Act (FISA). That Act defines the jurisdiction of federal banking agencies, allowing them to bring enforcement actions against a group of individuals known as institution-affiliated parties. For attorneys and other professional advisers to banks and thrifts, the definition of institution-affiliated party [12 U.S.C. § 1813(u)] creates a statutory analog to the two common law forms of derivative liability described earlier. The analog to common law aiding-and-abetting liability is found in subsection (4) of the definition, which adds to the list of institution-affiliated parties "any independent contractor (including any attorney, appraiser, or accountant) who knowingly or recklessly participates in [certain illegal conduct] which caused or is likely to cause more than a minimal financial loss to, or a significant adverse effect on, the insured depository institution." The analog to agency liability is subsection (3), which adds to the definition any "consultant ... and any other person ... who participates in the conduct of the affairs of an insured depository institution."

Attorneys and other professional advisers who fall within the definition of institution-affiliated parties are susceptible to a variety of administrative enforcement actions. Some of these administrative actions can result in monetary assessments.  For example, civil money penalties on institution-affiliated parties can range from $5000 to $1 million a day per violation. Further monetary sanctions are possible in cease-and-desist orders, under which banking agencies can require restitution or indemnification from an institution-affiliated party who is found either to have been unjustly enriched by a violation or practice or to have acted in reckless disregard of applicable laws and regulations. This latter source of monetary sanctions was the one that the government deployed against the respondents in the Kaye, Scholer enforcement action.

FISA also allows for a wide range of nonmonetary sanctions.  The most common nonmonetary sanction is a cease-and-desist order, which . . . [can] be employed to require various affirmative actions, such as correcting conditions caused by past practices or violations.   Cease-and-desist orders can even be used to impose ongoing limitations on the activities of institution-affiliated parties. Another, more extreme form of nonmonetary penalty for such parties is a removal action, which can be enforced on an industrywide as well as a firm-specific basis. Finally, to round out the list of nonmonetary sanctions, FISA includes criminal referrals, which may result in incarceration as well as fines, and, of course, ex parte temporary injunctions of the sort that the OTS used to restrict Kaye, Scholer's bank accounts while the proceeding was pending.

As suggested earlier, the substantive predicates for FISA enforcement actions against attorneys and other advisers of regulated institutions are reminiscent of the substantive elements of their antecedents at common law- aiding-and-abetting liability and agency liability. . . .  The most important distinctions between common law derivative liability and FISA's statutory remedies appear to be not substantive but procedural. While common law remedies are defined in the first instance by judicial interpretation, the federal banking agencies have primary jurisdiction over the remedial provisions of FISA. . . . This deference allows banking agencies . . . considerable latitude in formulating standards of intention and nexus.  In a similar vein, FISA bestows upon federal banking agencies a much broader arsenal of monetary and nonmonetary sanctions than the government could traditionally have obtained in judicial enforcement proceedings. . . .

## Comments and Questions

The Jackson excerpt summarizes the range of legal theories now available to federal banking agencies seeking to bring actions against failed depository institutions.  To what extent should the government invoke these cases to bring actions against attorneys? Should they use such actions to compensate the government for losses caused by bank failures?  Should the government be dissuaded from bringing such cases if state bar associations have not censured the attorneys involved?  Is the aggressive use of enforcement actions against attorneys likely to prevent another savings and loan crisis from occurring?  Are there better ways to prevent the failure of financial institutions?

# CHAPTER SIX

# INTRODUCTION TO INSURANCE REGULATION

As we saw in earlier sections of this book, an essential function of depository institutions is to raise funds from the general public through the sale or issuance of debt instruments. These instruments range from demand deposits to long-term instruments, such as certificates of deposits and other forms of borrowing. While the rate of interest paid on bank deposits may vary, the distinguishing feature of these liabilities is that they represent fixed commitments on the part of the depository institutions to repay determinable sums at some point in the future. In this critical respect, insurance companies are fundamentally different than depository institutions. The economic function of insurance companies is to pool risks among many parties. Not all those risks come to pass. And so with respect to individual creditors of insurance companies (that is, policyholders), an insurance company's liabilities are contingent. Insurance companies promise to make payments upon the occurrence of certain events — most commonly, a death, a fire, an accident, an illness, or a lawsuit. Underwriting insurance, which involves developing and administering contracts to make these contingent payments, is a complex and subtle business, underlying many of the problems of insurance regulation that we will consider in this part of the book.

Our discussion of insurance regulation begins with a historical review of the industry in the United States from the colonial times until the present. We next consider the principal justifications underlying insurance regulation. As you work your way through these materials, consider how the history of insurance regulation and the policies underlying this regulatory structure compare to those we considered in our discussion of depository institutions.

## Section 1. History of Insurance Regulation

Insurance corporations are the only financial institutions in the United States that are regulated almost entirely at the state level. Accordingly, the content of insurance regulation varies somewhat from state to state. This reliance on state regulation is often difficult to reconcile with the current structure of the industry. The United States insurance industry is vast. As of 1996, the industry included some 1,136 life insurance companies and 2,418 property-casualty carriers; together these firms held over three trillion dollars in assets, and were supported by a nationwide network of more than 700,000 agents. Insurance companies often conduct their business on a national scale; many operate globally. To a large degree, the current structure of insurance regulation in this country reflects the historical circumstances under which the industry evolved.

## A. Colonial Times

Marine insurance was the predominant line of insurance during the colonial period.  The New England merchants' desire to insure their ships and cargo created the demand for this type of insurance.  Not a single building in the colonies was insured until 1752.  The colonists' insurance policies were often bought from British insurance companies.  This was due, in part, to the Act of Parliament of 1719 which made the organization of stock insurance companies illegal in the British colonies.  This prohibition was explicitly extended to the American colonies in 1741, though individuals and certain other unincorporated entities were still free to underwrite policies.

The development of a domestic insurance industry in the United States proceeded relatively slowly.  The earliest known advertisement for an opening of an insurance office occurred in 1721 in Philadelphia.  Another insurance office was established in Massachusetts in 1728.  The first known domestic insurance company was the Corporation for the Relief of Poor and Distressed Presbyterian Ministers and of the Poor and Distressed Widows and Children of Presbyterian Ministers headquartered in Philadelphia.  It issued its first policy on May 22, 1761.  By 1770, there were three insurance institutions in Philadelphia.

## B. Early Republic Through the Civil War: 1776-1865

The emergence of the corporate form was a key factor in the development of the insurance industry.  Individual underwriting, which constituted the bulk of colonial domestic insurance activity, was necessarily limited in scope.  The issuance of insurance policies by corporations opened up new possibilities.  The corporate form enabled the insurer to raise enough capital to issue a large number of insurance policies so as to allow for the diversification of risk.  Additionally, the indefinite life of a corporation allows the insurer to credibly enter into the long-term contractual obligations that insurance policies often require.

The use of the corporate form also offered the opportunity to the states to impose restrictions on the insurance corporation.  Incorporation at the time was usually granted by special enactment by the state legislature.  State legislatures would often condition the grant of incorporation on compliance with various restrictions.  Accordingly, the early insurance industry was regulated by a diverse collection of restrictions rather than by the modern practice of statutes that are generally applicable to the insurance industry.  The first domestic stock corporation was the Insurance Company of North America in 1794.  The statute granting incorporation placed restrictions on the type of investments the company could make and required a reserve for possible losses.  The granting of incorporation by special act of the legislature was a common practice until roughly the panic of 1837.  After the panic, general incorporation laws became the norm, at approximately the same time that free banking laws were popularized for depository institutions.  Michigan in 1837 adopted a general incorporation statute, and New York followed suit in 1849.

Although insurance companies have existed since the beginning of the United States, the industry did not experience its first period of rapid growth until roughly the 1830s.  Before this period, insurance was of marginal importance in the national economy.  In 1830 the amount of insurance in force was only $600,000.  By 1840 this figure had increased by more than sevenfold to $4.69 million, and then ballooned to $96 million by the end of the decade.  The number of insurance companies also increased dramatically, from nine in 1830, to fifteen in 1840, and it had increased to forty-three in 1860.  A large portion of the growth in the 1840s was in life insurance.  While economic growth no doubt contributed to the rise of the insurance industry in the mid-19th Century, some experts also attribute a portion of the industry's expansion to the introduction of the mutual form — an incorporated entity owned and controlled by policyholders, not shareholders.  Nearly all the special charters granted in New York City in the 1840s were for mutuals, such as Mutual Life in 1843.

During the pre-Civil War period, the predominant regulatory tool for the insurance industry was the use of public and periodical reports.  As early as 1807 Massachusetts required that the president and directors of domestic insurance companies provide a statement describing the financial status of the company to the legislature.  In 1818 Massachusetts required domestic companies to publish in a newspaper various financial data.  In 1827, Massachusetts required out-of-state agents to file and publish in a newspaper a copy of their company's charter, their power of attorney and annual financial statements.  Another popular regulatory feature was requiring the filing of a financial statement in a local public office where citizens could inspect it.

New York developed a regulatory structure similar to that of Massachusetts.  In 1824, New York imposed on foreign companies certain filing requirements.  In 1827-28, it enacted a statute requiring domestic corporations to file annually a form specifying certain financial information (for instance, debts owed by the corporation) that had to be submitted to the comptroller of the state.  If the comptroller believed something was amiss then a report was supposed to be filed with legislature.  This was keeping in line with the approach of other states at this early stage.  States usually delegated only limited powers to the officials in charge of insurance regulation.  Some combination of public reports and filings with state officials of financial data constituted a very common early regulatory structure.

In addition, some states enacted more substantive regulatory requirements.  Massachusetts at the early date of 1817 limited the risks of fire companies to 1/10 of their capital and forbade insurance companies from engaging in other types of businesses.  New York in 1851 required a $100,000 deposit for corporations, whether foreign or domestic, requesting to underwrite insurance in the state.  This concern with ensuring the financial health of insurance companies in time became a major focus of regulatory attention.

There were several motivations in enacting insurance regulation at this early date. One of the most important was the desire for revenue. Much of the early insurance legislation is contained in the taxing statutes. The earliest officials in charge of insurance regulation were fiscal officials. Massachusetts and Pennsylvania in 1827 named the state treasurer as the official in charge of the insurance filings. New York named the state comptroller. Imposing a requirement of filing financial information with state officials aided in the collection of revenue. Many states collected revenue from licensing fees. New York was the first state to adopt a tax on premiums in 1824. New Jersey followed in 1826 with its own premium tax. Taxes were also placed on insurance agents early on by Illinois and Maryland. Some of the motivation was protectionist or retaliatory in nature. Massachusetts required agents of foreign companies to post bonds. Pennsylvania in 1829 imposed a 20% tax on all premiums collected by agents of foreign companies.

In the 1850s independent administrative agencies emerged whose sole responsibility was to oversee the regulation of the insurance industry. The first board was established in 1851 by New Hampshire. Massachusetts established a board in 1852. The Massachusetts board's duties included examining the annual reports of the insurance companies and ensuring that the insurance laws were enforced. In 1854 and again in 1855 the power of the board was expanded. Massachusetts provided an annual salary to the members of the board. Soon other states followed Massachusetts' lead. In 1859 New York established a single superintendent of insurance with fairly extensive powers. The establishment of an independent administrative agency responsible for insurance regulation made possible more extensive regulation than was possible when the responsible official had other duties. The independent administrative board also allowed for specialization in insurance regulation; a necessary perquisite to administrating statutes more complex than the ones that had existed up to that point.

## C.  Post Civil-War Developments: 1865-1944

*The Insurance Industry's Attempt to Avoid State Regulation:* After the passage of the National Bank Act of 1864 the insurance industry sought relief from state regulation by attempting to convince Congress to pass a federal insurance law similar in scope. One of the focuses of the second meeting of the National Board of Fire Underwriters held in 1868 was the passage of a general federal insurance law. Although bills were introduced in Congress, these efforts never succeeded. The insurance industry turned towards the courts for relief. The landmark case of Paul v. Virginia, 75 U.S. (8 Wall.) 168 (1869), was the result.

Decided in 1869, Paul v. Virginia had a major impact on the course of insurance regulation. The dispute involved two related Virginia state statutes which subjected foreign insurance companies and their local agents to a licensing requirement. Paul applied for a Virginia license to represent unadmitted New York insurance companies as an agent. Paul refused to comply with the requirement that certain securities be deposited as a precondition to the granting of a license. The litigation was financed by the National Board of Fire Underwriters which hoped that the state statute would be declared unconstitutional. The insurance industry hoped to use a favorable outcome in the *Paul* case to strike similar restrictions in other state statutes and also to prompt congressional enactment of a national insurance statute, modeled on the National Bank Act.

The industry's strategy was thwarted, however, when the Court held that the Virginia statute did not violate the Commerce Clause. Justice Field explained that "[t]hey are not subjects of trade and barter offered in the market as something having an existence and value independent of the parties to them. They are not commodities to be shipped or forwarded from one State to another, and then put up for sale." Justice Field then added, "[s]uch contracts are not interstate transactions, though the parties may be domiciled in different states."

In subsequent cases, the Supreme Court repeatedly endorsed and expanded the "Paul doctrine". One of the most important cases in this line was New York Life Insurance Co. v. Deer Lodge County, 231 U.S. 495, 509 (1913). At issue was a Montana statute that imposed a higher tax on out-of-state insurance companies than it imposed on domestic firms. The insurance company argued that it was an unconstitutional burden on interstate commerce. The Supreme Court refused to distinguish the *Paul* case on the grounds that it dealt with fire insurance while the present dispute involved life insurance. The Court flatly stated that "The business of insurance is not commerce." After the *Deer Lodge* case it appeared that state authorities would have essentially unbridled authority to develop insurance regulations and taxes.

*Post Civil-War Regulatory Developments:* After the Civil War the country experienced rapid growth and increasing financial and economic concentration. The insurance industry participated in this growth. In 1860, there were $205 million of life insurance in force. By 1900 the figure was over $7.6 billion. Many lines of insurance developed for the first time in this period. Casualty insurance experienced growth of 318% in assets and 275.5% in income between 1894 and 1904. Before this period the size of the casualty insurance industry was insignificant. Personal accident insurance, introduced only in 1863, also experienced significant growth. Rapid growth in the health insurance industry, whose formation can be located in the 1890s, occurred at the turn of the century. For much of this period insurers grew faster than banks. This might be due in part to the comparatively late start of insurance and that insurance firms faced lighter regulation than their banking counterparts.

With the expansion of the insurance industry and the amount of insurance regulation by the states during the period following the Civil War the need for regulatory uniformity increased. In 1871, a group of state insurance commissioners began to hold meetings in New York to discuss issues such as establishing standardized annual forms and uniform methods of valuing the assets of insurance corporations. Over time, these meetings evolved into an organization known as the National Association of Insurance Commissioners (NAIC), which has played an important role over the years in coordinating insurance regulation across state lines and facilitating periodic reform efforts.

During the ante-bellum period, regulation of the insurance industry underwent several important extensions and reforms during this period:

(a) *Geographic Limitations on Investment.*     Throughout this period there was a widespread belief that the investments of insurance companies should be geographically limited so that they might serve local interests.     Fritz McCaster, an Insurance Commissioner of South Carolina, echoed the sentiments of many when he wrote that

> The natural channel for the investment of the savings of the people of South Carolina is in South Carolina securities... How will these investments find their natural channels if they are controlled by men in Boston, Mass., New York City or Newark, New Jersey or other points 1,000 miles away from South Carolina and by men who know little of and care less for the particular interests of such distant states?

One of the first laws that attempted to force local investment was passed by Wisconsin in 1865.  It was repealed in less than a year.  In 1907, Texas passed the "Robertson Law" which required that 75% of the Texas reserves be invested in Texas securities if one wished to receive a license to sell insurance there.  Many life insurance companies initially withdrew from Texas after the passage of this law, but they eventually returned.

(b) *Rate regulation:*    Throughout the latter half of the 19th Century, a recurrent problem in the fire insurance industry was the cyclical nature of fire insurance losses. When losses are low and profits high this attracts new insurers.  Entry into the insurance industry has historically required little capital.  The capital fund required by statutes were usually small.  In order to attract business, insurers, whether new or old, had an incentive to charge rates that were too low to sustain long-term profitability. Even if an insurer desired to charge appropriate rates it faced considerable uncertainty as to what that rate should be.  This problem was particularly acute during the nineteenth century because of the primitive state of actuarial science.  When a major fire occurred many of the insurers who had engaged in over-confident predictions of future losses became insolvent.  With the failure of concerted action by the insurers to prevent this destructive competition, the cycle repeated itself over and over again.  Of course, there were other important sources of insolvency; including mismanagement, fraud and a weak economy.   Responding to this cycle of "booms and busts," the president of the Fire Underwriter's Association of the Northwest in 1877 estimated that about 4000 insurance companies had come into existence at one point or another, and that only 1000 remained.  An industry committee in 1850 estimated that the fire insurance suffered a net loss from 1791 to 1850.

Destructive rate cutting was especially difficult to stop in this period. Not only did the insurers themselves have an incentive to cut rates but their agents did as well.  Even if an insurer was able to resist the temptation to cut rates it was difficult, sometimes impossible, for an insurer to prevent his agents from selling the insurance at below cost.  The agent had a powerful incentive to sell as much insurance at possible since the more insurance he sold the larger his commissions.  The downside, the liability of potential future losses, was borne by the insurer and not the agent.  This problem was exacerbated during this period because insurers were anxious not to upset their agents for fear of the agents switching, along with their business, to another company. Companies often tried to convince agents of another company to join their sale force. For example, one morning New York Life received notice that "their entire Manhattan office consisting of a general agent and over two hundred agents had gone over to Equitable."  In this highly competitive situation it was difficult to establish rates collectively.

The first systematic attempt to prevent destructive rate cutting was the establishment of local associations or boards that attempted to maintain minimum rates.  One of the first boards, the Salamander Society, was established in 1819. Informal agreements between companies existed as early as 1806.  The boards were usually dominated by local agents.  The boards generally proved to be ineffective.  The incentive to cheat during profitable times proved too powerful.  The rates established by the boards were often inadequate as well.

In 1864 and 1865, the industry suffered from heavy losses and rate cutting.  In response, the National Board of Fire Underwriters was established in 1866.  The first two planks in the National Board platform stated the goal of establishing a uniform system of rates and a uniform rate of compensation to agents.  The National Board relied on local boards of agents to establish rates.  Despite some initial success, in the years following the establishment of the National Board, as after previous attempts at concerted action, the incentive for insurers to rate cut undermined its effectiveness.  In 1871, two devastating fires occurred: the Chicago fire and a fire that destroyed the small city of Peshtigo, Wisconsin.  The Chicago fire alone caused approximately $200 million in property damage.  Approximately half of the losses were insured.  As a result, one third of the companies that incurred liability as a result of the fire went out of business. The following year fires ravaged Boston.  These fires, and the resulting insolvencies, revealed the pressing need for some system of rate maintenance.

A system more decentralized than had previously existed emerged.  The National Board focused its attention on fire prevention and insurance statistics.  Numerous regional organizations were established in an attempt to maintain adequate rates.  The Western Union was founded in 1879, the Southeastern Tariff Association in 1882 and the Pacific Insurance Union in 1884 among others.  These associations were usually dominated by the insurance companies, not the agents.  The associations used the technique of the compact and the stamping office to maintain discipline.  One of the first was the St. Louis Compact in 1879.  Under this arrangement, a compact manager would usually have the authority to establish rates and maintain discipline according to the terms of the compact.  With the stamping office, agents would have to send in information concerning the policies they had sold.  This information would be reviewed in order to ensure that the proper rates were charged.  Despite the elaborate methods used, the regional associations were not much more successful than previous attempts. There existed the perennial incentive to cheat. Furthermore, some companies simply refused to join the association or compact.

The attempt to maintain rate adequacy was given a further blow when many states in the late 1800s passed anti-compact legislation. During this period there was strong public feeling against monopolies and price fixing. This antitrust feeling manifested itself on the federal level with the passage of the Sherman Antitrust Act of 1890. On the state level one of its manifestations was laws forbidding price fixing among insurers. The first anti-compact legislation was enacted by Ohio and New Hampshire in 1885. By 1913 twenty-three states had enacted anti-compact legislation. Insurers vigorously opposed this legislation. The sentiments of the *American Underwriter* were typical. When discussing the anti-compact legislation it wrote that "vote-hunting politicians have perhaps more than counteracted any advances that have been made in scientific fire-rating." States varied the scope of the anti-price fixing prohibition. Some states, like Ohio and Wisconsin, prohibited only price fixing between companies while other states, like Kansas, prohibited agreements among agents. New Hampshire applied its legislation only to foreign corporations. However, most anti-compact legislation prohibited all agreements, whether between companies or agents.

There were various attempts to circumvent the anti-compact legislation Some companies attempted to avoid the prohibition by subscribing to "private" rating services which would publish "advisory" rates. In Missouri agents formed an 'Underwriter's Social Club' which attempted to maintain rates. Despite the failure to curb many of these avoidance techniques, rate cutting, as in the past, still occurred on a wide scale. The San Francisco fires of 1906, like the Chicago fire of 1871, highlighted the need for rate maintenance. The anti-compact laws, in many states, were gradually replaced by laws that regulated rates themselves.

The first rate regulatory laws banned differential pricing for insuring the same risk. These anti-discrimination laws were generally ineffective because of the inability to classify risks. In 1909, Kansas required insurers to file their rates with the commissioner. Once filed, insurers could not charge different rates. Most importantly, the commissioner had the authority to change the rates if the commissioner found them to be either too high or too low. This legislation was held to be constitutional by the Supreme Court in German Alliance Insurance Co. v. Lewis, 233 U.S. 389 (1914). Other states, sometimes as a result of their own investigations into insurance rates, followed Kansas's lead in permitting cooperative rate fixing with state supervision. The Joint Legislative Committee of New York, commonly known as the Merritt Committee, investigated fire insurance rates after the San Francisco fire of 1906. It recommended that some form of cooperative rate making supervised by the state be allowed. On the other hand, it did not endorse fixing rates at which companies would be forced to sell without their agreement. The Merritt Committee investigation resulted in legislation that made rate filings with the superintendent mandatory and cooperative price fixing legal. The superintendent had the authority to adjust rates so as to remove any discrimination. In the 1920s legislation was enacted that permitted insurers, with the superintendent's approval, to deviate from bureau rates. More importantly, the superintendent, like the Kansas commissioner, was given power to change any rates he found to be either too high or too low.  This regulatory structure remained intact in New York until 1969.  The NAIC in 1914 drafted model bills that allowed for cooperative price fixing.  Several states adopted the NAIC model bills when formulating their own insurance laws governing rate regulation.  Interestingly, as a general rule, states did not enact similar rate regulatory legislation in the casualty field during this entire period.

(c) *The Armstrong Reforms:*  Public distrust of the insurance industry was present from almost the start of the post-Civil War period.  During the last third of the nineteenth century there were many who believed that there were widespread abuses and corruption within the insurance industry.  This perception was part of a larger public distrust of the new industrial conglomerations and their perceived influence.  While some of the distrust directed at the insurance industry was based on imaginary abuses, others were real enough.

It was not uncommon for agents to promise future payments that were inflated.  Given the clout of agents during this period, insurance corporations generally did not have the means to effectively discipline their agents even if they so desired.  Some of the more serious abuses occurred with smaller "assessment," and "co-operative" companies which were largely unregulated and often had insufficient capital.   This distrust was exasperated when many insurance companies failed during the depression in the 1870s.  The extent of this distrust in some quarters can vividly be seen in the annual report of the Insurance Bureau of Kentucky:

> The nefarious system of speculative insurance, which has grown up so rapidly in some of our neighboring States and spread its baleful influence over the whole Union, has lately met with more than one severe check, notably in Pennsylvania, the home and birth-place of the most infamous of the foul brood. . . . The Commissioner trusts to do something, ... toward hunting down and driving out of our borders these unprincipled and shameless violators of the law.

At the turn of the century, the insurance industry was subjected to several state investigations which uncovered abuses within the industry.  The most famous and influential was the New York Legislative Insurance Investigation Committee of 1905, commonly referred to as the "Armstrong Investigation.  As a result of this investigation, and the abuses it uncovered, a number of laws were passed by the New York legislature; laws that acted as a model and a catalyst for other states.  The results of the Armstrong investigation were especially important because at the time more than half of the insurance industry's assets were held by New York insurance companies.

One of the Armstrong Committee's lines of investigation concerned the ties between the industrial interests and the life insurance industries: ties that powerful railroad firms, for example, had purportedly used to force the life insurance industry to purchase excessive quantities of railroad securities.  While modern scholars have come to question the validity of the Armstrong Committee's analysis, the turn-of-the-Century perception of untoward relations between insurance companies and industrial concerns prompted the Armstrong Committee to recommend, and the New York legislature to enact, a statute prohibiting life insurance companies from purchasing stock unless secured by collateral in which the company could have directly invested.  Other jurisdictions quickly emulated New York's restrictions on insurance investments in equity securities, and while these restrictions have been liberalized over time, they remain an important element of insurance regulation.

The Armstrong Committee made a number of other influential recommendations.  They included encouragement of the formation of mutual companies, standard policies for all companies, prohibition on the incorporation of assessment or cooperative insurance companies, annual distribution of dividends, and limitations on agents' commissions.  Many changes in the law were made by the New York legislature in response to the hearings and the report.  Companies had to advance loans to their policyholders in sums not exceeding the legal reserve required on the policy upon the security of the policy.  All policies by New York companies had to include provisions providing for annual distribution of dividends.  Standard policy forms were provided for by law.

Among the more significant reforms was legislation governing mutualization.  New laws enacted legislation that made it possible to organize mutual companies in New York, something that had been impossible during the previous fifty years.  The Armstrong Commission concluded that "while both stock and mutual corporations have exhibited the abuses incident to management without a becoming sense of responsibility, the later are more amenable to the demands of public sentiment."  In 1922, New York extended this policy of favoring mutual companies by prohibiting demutualization -- the conversion of mutual companies into stock form.  The NAIC followed New York by proposing a model law prohibiting demutualization in 1923.

## D.  Modern Insurance Regulation: 1944 to the Present

*The* SEUA *Case and the McCarran Act*:  Due to the *Paul v. Virginia* case and its progeny, insurance regulation remained the province of states.  Though the industry had initially resisted state supervisory authority when the *Paul* case was litigated, by the mid-20th Century, it had grown accustomed to local oversight and particularly the operation of state-sponsored rate bureaus. The 1940s, however, threatened the stability of this arrangement.

In response to complaints about price fixing among fire insurance companies, the Department of Justice initiated an investigation of the South-Eastern Underwriters Association (SEUA) which resulted in criminal indictments in 1944 of the Association, 198 member companies and 27 of its officers for violations of the federal anti-trust laws  The Association and its member companies were charged with organizing an illegal boycott of agents that dealt with insurance companies that were not members of the association. Invoking the Paul doctrine, the defendants persuaded the district court to dismiss the indictment on the grounds that the business of insurance was not commerce, and, therefore, the federal antitrust laws did not apply.

In United States v. South-Eastern Underwriters Association (SEUA), 322 U.S. 533 (1944), the Supreme Court reversed. The Court held that fire insurance transactions across state lines constituted interstate commerce. The Court explained:

> No commercial enterprise of any kind which conducts its activities across state lines has been held to be wholly beyond the regulatory power of Congress under the Commerce Clause. We cannot make an exception of the business of insurance.

Though the court attempted to distinguish *Paul v. Viriginia*, the *SEUA* decision clearly marked a dramatic change in the Court's approach to whether the business of insurance was interstate commerce. Both the industry and the state regulatory structure immediately perceived the *SEUA* decision as a serious threat. Application of the federal antitrust laws could hamper the operation of many industry rate-setting mechanisms, and the Court's reinterpretation of the federal Commerce Clause threatened to invalidate many aspects of state insurance regulations and taxes that differentiated between domestic and out-of-state insurance companies.

Reaction to the *SEUA* decision was strong and prompt. Even while the case was pending, there were efforts to pass federal legislation, which would exempt the insurance industry from the federal antitrust laws. The stock fire and casualty companies in particular wished for a return to the pre-*SEUA* regime. While the bill passed the House, it died in the Senate. Its defeat was due in part to the possible negative public reaction to exempting the insurance industry from antitrust legislation that applied to every other business and a feared presidential veto. The NAIC, along with representatives of the insurance industry, drafted an alternative bill which provided for only partial exemption from federal law. Under the NAIC bill, the insurance industry, after a phase-in period, would be subject to the federal antitrust law, with an exemption for state-approved cooperative rates, forms and underwriting plans. On December 18, 1944 Senators Pat McCarran and Homer Ferguson introduced legislation that essentially adopted the recommendations of the NAIC. The bill was signed by the President on March 9, 1945.

The McCarran-Ferguson Act, although a very short statute, has had a major impact on the structure of insurance regulation in the United States. It states that the silence of Congress is not to be construed as a barrier to the enactment of state laws governing the business of insurance. The statute affirmatively provides that the business of insurance "shall be subject to the laws of the several states which relate to the regulation or taxation of such business." Besides the antitrust laws, no federal law should be construed to invalidate, impair or supersede any state law regulating the "business of insurance" or imposing a tax on such business unless the law specifically relates to the business of insurance. The business of insurance is subjected to the Sherman Antitrust Act, Clayton Act, and the Federal Trade Commission Act to the extent to which it is not regulated by state law. This provision was a compromise between a group that wanted complete exemption from the federal antitrust laws and those desiring more federal involvement. The Sherman Antitrust Act exemption is inapplicable to "any agreement to boycott, coerce, or intimidate, or act of boycott, coercion or intimidation."

*Developments since passage of the McCarran-Ferguson Act:* As a result of the passage of the McCarran-Ferguson Act, it became important for states wishing to avoid application of the federal antitrust statutes to pass laws regulating rates. Model bills governing rate making, labeled the 'All-Industry' bills, were drafted by the NAIC and insurance representatives. These model bills were widely adopted. By March 1951, every state had adopted a fire and casualty insurance rating law. Most states eventually also passed an Unfair Trade Practices Acts to block application of the Federal Trade Commission Act. The effectiveness of these laws varied as a result of a number of factors; varying from differences in the abilities of commissioners to the size of the insurance departments' budgets.

The approach of fixing rates came under increasing criticism and pressure during the 1950s and 1960s. Consumers were dissatisfied with the rising cost of automobile insurance. In 1964 the NAIC undertook a comprehensive study of state rate regulation. In December of 1968, the NAIC released its findings. The report concluded:

The All-Industry laws were devised for an insurance market that was basically non-competitive. Since the enactment of that legislation in the late 1940's, marked changes have occurred in the fire and casualty business. In particular, the competitive setting has changed, bringing with its changes in the availability of insurance. . . . It is the sense of the Subcommittee, therefore, that, where appropriate, reliance be placed upon fair and open competition to produce and maintain reasonable and competitive prices...

Several states in the late 1960s and 1970s adopted laws which allowed for a greater role for competitive forces in setting rates. Naturally, these states varied in the extent to which rates were deregulated and how this deregulation was structured. Later developments added another dimension. During the 1980s several states began to subject the business of insurance to their antitrust laws to a greater extent than they had before, thereby making it more difficult for insurance corporations to restrain competition through collective action.

The McCarran-Ferguson Act, and the policy of leaving the states primarily responsible for insurance regulation, has recently come under attack. During the 1980s, liability insurance costs skyrocketed and several large insurance companies failed. Some commentators blamed these problems on inadequate state regulation. Repeal of the McCarran-Ferguson Act and the establishment of federal oversight were proposed as remedies. In addition, several powerful lobbying groups, including the commercial banking industry, favored repeal of the McCarran-Ferguson Act. The insurance industry has historically opposed its repeal. To date, efforts to repeal the Act have failed.

# Section 2.  Overview of Insurance Regulation

The following excerpt, from Spencer L. Kimball & Werner Pfennigstorf, The Regulation of Insurance Companies in the United States and the European Communities 23-42 (1981), gives a quick overview of the substance of insurance regulation in the United States.  The excerpt is updated with italicized amendments from Robert W. Klein, Structural Change and Regulatory Response in the Insurance Industry (1995).  As you read through this description, consider how the regulatory structure compares to the regimes applicable to depository institutions in the United States.  To what extent do the differences in regulatory approaches reflect distinctions in regulatory policy and to what extent are the differences simply the product of historical accident?

### 1. Regulation By Classes

Almost all state insurance codes contain extensive lists of the classes of insurance.  The lists serve to define the different classes and they provide the basis for differentiated capital requirements and for restrictions concerning the combination of several classes of business in the same carrier or in the same contract.  The existing lists show all the variety and lack of coherence that come with a long evolution.  While many state codes can be grouped into families, by virtue of having been copied from one another or having been drafted by the same consultant, the lists are difficult to compare with one another because they use different approaches to a taxonomy of the business.  In practice, the different classification systems do not seem to cause many problems.  Even where -- as in New York -- they continue the long-abandoned contrast between fire insurance and casualty insurance, it has not been necessary to revise them; all that was needed was an additional provision permitting the different classes to be combined.

Much more important for the practices of the insurance business and for supervising it is the classification used for reporting premiums, losses, and expenses as part of the annual statement.  Fortunately, this classification is uniform throughout the U.S. as part of the uniform annual statement blanks prepared by the National Association of Insurance Commissioners (NAIC).  The "lines" of the annual statements in fact provide the only basis for obtaining comparative data concerning the experience of individual companies as well as the industry as a whole.  There are now four major blanks:  one each for life and accident and health insurers, fire and casualty insurers, fraternal benefit societies, and nonprofit service plans.  Some states also have special blanks for town or county mutual fire insurance companies, title insurers, reciprocals, and other special carriers.

Most state insurance codes exempt certain organizations or transactions from all or part of the regulatory rules.  Typical cases are government insurance funds, charitable organizations, employee pension and welfare plans (for which federal law has displaced state regulation), and certain small mutual aid societies. . . .

### 2. Authorization to do business

All jurisdictions of the U.S. prohibit the transaction of an insurance business on their territories by anyone who has not obtained formal authorization to do so, which is granted upon satisfaction of certain conditions specified by law:

(a)    Restrictions on forms of enterprise -- The standard forms of organization for insurers are the stock company and the mutual insurance company. . . .    The ingenuity of promoters and the leniency of legislatures and regulators have however produced and permitted some unorthodox forms of organization.  Most are variations of the basic mutual model, and in practice function like any other insurer. . . .

(b)    Restrictions on ownership -- Over half the states (28) have provisions precluding the authorization of any insurer, or of any foreign or alien insurer, that is owned or controlled by a foreign government, or by any government. . . .

(c)    Restrictions on other business -- American insurance codes generally prohibit insurance companies from engaging in any other business not reasonably related to its insurance business.  Nonlife insurers, however, have long been permitted to hold controlling interests in unrelated businesses as part of their investments, and modern holding company laws permit them to have affiliates for a generously defined range of related activities; some states expressly permit affiliates for any lawful purpose.  Straight subsidiaries are no longer the only way to diversify--one modern sophisticated strategy is to have an upstream holding company that in turn can become the parent of all kinds of related and unrelated affiliates.

(d)    Separation and combination of lines -- Almost universally, with exceptions only for some very old companies, American insurance codes require legally separate carriers for the transaction of life and nonlife insurance, respectively; accident and health insurance may be transacted either by life or by nonlife insurers.

The nonlife business was for many years further divided into two major segments--fire and marine insurance, and casualty/surety insurance.  This division was abandoned in favor of multiple-line underwriting around 1950 but its vestiges are still much in evidence in the organization of the industry and the insurance codes. . . .

(e)    Required financial resources -- All states require newly formed domestic insurance companies to have a certain minimum amount of paid-in capital or, in the case of a mutual, of surplus, which must be maintained at the prescribed level at all times. . . . . *[Traditional fixed minimum capital and surplus standards, which typically range in the area of $500,000 - $6 million for a multi-line insurer, have been more appropriate for start-up operations than for established companies with significant premium volume and risk exposure. Insurers range widely in size and the types of risks they assume which makes fixed minimum capital standards inadequate for many companies. In practice, regulators can and do take action against troubled insurers before they fall below the minimum standard, but such actions are subject to legal challenges and regulators must convince a court that an insurer is in unsafe condition. The NAIC adopted model minimum risk based capital (RBC) requirements for life insurers in 1992 and for property/casualty insurers in 1993 which are intended to partially correct the deficiencies of fixed standards.]*

(f)    Special rules for foreign insurers -- Foreign insurers, that is, those domiciled in another state of the U.S., are treated like domestic insurers in most respects.  As a rule, they must show that they are lawfully organized and licensed in their home jurisdiction and that they have capital and surplus at least in the amount required of like domestic companies.  Only a few states require foreign companies to have a higher amount of capital or surplus.

More often foreign companies are required to make deposits but a deposit made in one state is recognized by all other states provided it has been made for the benefit of policyholders or creditors throughout the U.S.  Some states impose on foreign insurers deposit requirements that do not apply to domestic companies; in a few other states the amounts of required deposits are higher for foreign insurers.  In addition to the general deposits designed to protect policyholders and creditors everywhere in the U.S., some states require insurers in certain classes (especially the title and surety businesses) to establish special deposits for the benefit of the citizens of that particular state; these provisions, too, often specify a higher amount for out-of-state insurers than for domestic insurers.  Notwithstanding these numerous variations equal treatment of domestic and foreign insurers is more common.

(g)  Special rules for alien insurers -- Alien insurers, that is, insurers domiciled in a foreign country, are also to a remarkable extent treated like domestic insurers.  Like foreign insurers, they must furnish proof that they are lawfully organized and licensed in their home jurisdiction, and like foreign insurers, they are in a number of states admitted only if they have operated successfully elsewhere for a certain number of years.  In order to assure the insurers' ability to satisfy their obligations, great weight is placed on deposits, which are often larger than those required of domestic or foreign insurers and must be especially secured by trust agreements.  Several states require trust accounts equal to the capital and surplus required of domestic companies; others require them to correspond to the insurer's liabilities.  All but four jurisdictions also still formally require all alien insurers to comply with the capital and surplus standards set for domestic insurers.  The two requirements have separate purposes, though neither has been adequately thought out.  The capital and surplus requirements relate to the overall solidity of the company; the deposit requirements seek to make assets readily available if things go bad--to satisfy the claims of residents of the states requiring the deposit.  The amounts are often grossly inadequate for that purpose. . . .

(h)  Discretion and review -- Most state insurance codes do not distinguish among domestic, foreign, and alien insurers in providing legal remedies against denials of authorization and other adverse administrative actions. . . .

(i)  Reciprocity and retaliation -- In general, the states of the U.S. rely on each other to a large extent in regulating the insurance business.  Of course, the reliance placed on some states (notably New York) is greater than that placed on others.  In certain fields, mutual reliance and assistance are expressly conditioned on reciprocity; this is the case, for instance, under the uniform insurer rehabilitation and liquidation act.

On the other hand, almost all states have retaliatory provisions, which generally subject foreign and alien insurers, in addition to the regular conditions and requirements to be met by everyone, to any additional requirements, charges, fees or taxes that their home jurisdictions impose on insurers from the jurisdiction whose authorization is sought. . . .

3.  Supervision of the going concern

(a)  Financial requirements -- There is a general agreement among insurance companies and regulators that the need of an insurance operation for financial resources increases as its volume of business increases and that there should always be a reasonable ratio of surplus to premium volume.  A set of rough rules of thumb, known as the "Kenney rules", was once widely accepted as a general indicator of sound financial condition. *[Since the early 1970s, the NAIC has utilized IRIS [Insurance Regulatory Information System] to monitor insurers' financial condition at a national level and identify those insurers requiring further regulatory attention. Companies' financial data are first processed through a statistical phase consisting of a series of 11 financial ratios (12 for life/health insurers) as well as a series of additional screening criteria. Companies showing unusual results are analyzed further by a select team of state financial examiners and financial analysts who recommend further investigation by the companies' domiciliary regulators, if necessary. Companies deemed to be "high priority" are followed up by the NAIC's Examination Oversight Task Force which takes action if the domiciliary state fails to do so. . . .*

*Most states require insurers' investments to be diversified and many have placed limits on the amount of lower quality bonds and other high risk assets that insurers can invest in. Holding company laws control transactions between affiliated companies, including the payment of dividends from a subsidiary to a parent. Insurers are prohibited from improper delegation of authority to managing general agents in the areas of pricing, underwriting and paying claims. In general, insurance company managements are required to act prudently in protecting policyholders' interests and regulators are authorized to seize control if management actions threaten a company's solvency*

*. . . The NAIC, in 1991, established a working group to draft a comprehensive model law covering all insurer investments. . . . Several provisions of the draft model act have received considerable criticism from the insurance industry and investment community. Foreign investments would be limited to 3 percent (5 percent for property/casualty insurers) of admitted assets per country for countries in non-investment grade categories. Commercial mortgage loans would be limited to 30 percent (10 percent for property/casualty insurers) of admitted assets. Property/casualty insurers would be required to maintain an amount of liquid investments (cash, high and medium grade investments, common stocks and reinsurance recoverables on paid and unpaid losses) equal to their loss, loss adjustment expenses and unearned premium reserves, discounted to present value. Equity interest would be limited to 10 percent (25 percent for property/casualty and accident/health insurers) of admitted assets. Derivative investments would be restricted to hedging and limited income generation transactions. An insurer's board of directors also would be required to adopt a written investment plan that would govern the insurer's investment activity. Notwithstanding the provisions of the act, the insurance commissioner would be authorized to order an insurer to limit, dispose of, withdraw from, or discontinue an investment or investment practice, subject to due process requirements under administrative law. The model act also contains a "basket provision" which allows insurers to hold additional investments that exceed limitations contained in other provisions, subject to certain specified caps based on capitalization levels.]*

(b) Contract forms -- A large variety of provisions and practices aim at control of the terms of insurance contracts, trying to achieve such objectives as clarity and comparability of policies, fairness of terms, or politically motivated expansion of benefits. Provisions requiring policy forms to be submitted for approval before use are most common for life and accident and health insurance; some states prescribe approval for all policies. The approval process concentrates on compliance with statutory provisions concerning required clauses or prohibited clauses, although some states give the commissioner considerable latitude in evaluating the forms. In administrative practice there are even wider differences than in the laws.

(c) Premium rates -- The control of premium rates, especially for fire and casualty insurance, has for a long time been one of the most demanding, most controversial and most frustrating responsibilities of American insurance departments. The issue is closely related to the special statutes of the insurance industry in relation to the federal antitrust laws. For much of the first part of this century, the prevailing view in the industry and among regulators was that unrestrained price competition would lead to ruinous rate wars and massive failures. Premium cartels were therefore regarded as justified and indeed indispensable, and government control of rates was to provide the necessary safeguards.

Since about 1950, the premium cartels have all but disappeared and competition is increasingly relied on as the preferable regulator. The change is not yet complete, however, and is even less fully recognized by regulators than it should be. Consequently there exist in the states a variety of different approaches, ranging from uniform government-set rates, through various forms of approval or subsequent disapproval provisions, to complete freedom in ratemaking. Different rules apply to different classes of business, notably automobile insurance, fire and casualty insurance in general, and workers' compensation.

In life and accident and health insurance, there is no direct rate regulation but state-standard accident and health policy laws normally give the commissioner the power to disapprove policy forms if in his judgment the promised benefits are not reasonable in relation to the premiums charged.

(d) Other area of continuing supervision -- The scope of insurance regulation has had a tendency to expand in response to popular demands of more protection and politicians' desire to satisfy those needs. *[The NAIC and the individual states have strengthened consumer protections in a number of areas to respond to specific market abuses that arose or intensified during the 1980s. Regulation has been tightened in areas such policy terminations, assumption reinsurance, health insurance rating and underwriting, claims settlement practices, and credit insurance. Another issue that has received renewed attention recently is insurance availability and affordability in urban areas. The NAIC established a special task force to look at this issue after the 1992 Los Angeles riots renewed allegations that insurers are redlining against inner-city and minority communities. Concerns about fair access to insurance are confronting established industry business practices in underwriting selection and pricing. Urban activists advocate restricting geographic rate differentials, prohibiting use of underwriting criteria such as age and minimum value restrictions for homeowners insurance, and forcing insurers to appoint agents and offer replacement cost homeowners coverage in inner-city neighborhoods. The NAIC and a number of states have compiled ZIP code level data and are conducting an extensive study of conditions in urban insurance markets. Preliminary analysis of these data tends to support concerns about high prices and diminished availability of homeowners insurance in poor, minority neighborhood.]*

Advertising and solicitation by insurers and observation of the principles of fair trade have long been subject to surveillance both by state insurance departments and to a lesser extent by the Federal Trade Commission.

### 4. Administrative monitoring and enforcement

(a)    Sources of information -- The principal traditional source of information for insurance commissioners with respect to the control of the financial soundness of insurers has been the annual financial statement. The forms (blanks) for preparing the statements are uniform throughout the U.S., thanks to the efforts of the NAIC.

*[Insurance companies are required to maintain records and file annual and quarterly financial statements with regulators in accordance with statutory accounting principles (SAP) which differ somewhat from Generally Accepted Accounting Principles (GAAP). Statutory accounting seeks to determine an insurer's ability to satisfy its obligations at all times, whereas GAAP measures the earnings of a company on a going-concern basis from period to period. Under SAP, most assets are valued conservatively and certain non-liquid assets, e.g., furniture and fixtures, are not admitted in the calculation of an insurer's surplus. Statutory rules also govern such areas as how insurers should establish reserves for invested assets (life insurers only) and claims and the conditions under which they can claim credit for reinsurance ceded.*

*. . . Insurers are required to file annual financial statements for the previous calendar year by March 1 with their domiciliary state, every state in which they are licensed to do business, and the NAIC. Statements for the 1st, 2nd and 3rd quarters must be filed 45 days after the close of the quarter. Insurance departments typically subject statements to a "bench" or "desk" audit by an in-house financial analyst or examiner who assesses the accuracy and reasonableness of the information that is filed and determines whether the insurer requires further investigation before its next regularly scheduled on-site examination. The NAIC also scrutinizes insurers' financial statements and disseminates its analysis to insurance departments.*

*States generally prioritize the review of their domiciliary companies and any other companies which require expedited scrutiny. Most departments utilize some system of financial ratios or other tools to screen and prioritize insurers for analysis. Regulators also use NAIC financial information systems including the Insurance Regulatory Information System (IRIS), which includes the Financial Analysis and Surveillance Tracking (FAST) system, and other reports. Various additional sources of information are often tapped, including: Securities and Exchange Commission (SEC) filings; claims-paying ability ratings; complaint ratios; market conduct reports; correspondence from competitors and agents; news articles; and other sources of anecdotal information.]*

Insurance company examinations are conducted at the insurer's head office, most often by examiners who are on the permanent staff of the insurance departments, but sometimes by independent accountants who are retained by the insurance department for that purpose. In the case of large companies operating in all or many states, examinations are coordinated by the NAIC in such a manner that the insurance departments interested in examining the insurer are represented by examiners selected by geographical regions (Zone Examinations). *[The*

*NAIC's Financial Condition Subcommittee also may encourage non-domiciliary states to call a special association examination if an examination conducted by a company's domiciliary is inadequate or if the domiciliary state fails to conduct an examination when financial ratio results or other information indicate the need. There were 2,919 financial examinations in process in 1993 which means that roughly one in every three insurers was under examination sometime during the year. The frequency of examinations rose over the period 1986-1993 in response to increased concerns about insurer solvency.*]

(b)  Enforcement -- American insurance commissioners have a large assortment of enforcement powers, whose simple existence and deterrent effect make it possible for the commissioner in most cases to secure compliance with his suggestions without having to resort to enforcement measures.  The enforcement measures that are used most often include civil penalties or forfeitures, and suspension or revocation of license.  The state insurance codes also provide for a variety of criminal penalties for violations of the law.  Actual prosecutions are rare, however.

*[The size of insurance departments varies significantly depending on the size of their markets and other factors, such as the number of domicilary companies and whether they provide ancillary services. In 1993, the number of state insurance department personnel ranged from 24 in Wyoming to 1,098 in California. Total full-time equivalent staff for all departments combined amounted to 9,678, in addition to 2,134 contract staff. For fiscal year 1995, state department budgets ranged from $1.2 million in Wyoming to $97 million in California, with a total combined budget for all departments of approximately $647.9 million. Insurance department staff include actuaries, financial examiners and analysts, rates and forms analysts, market conduct examiners, attorneys, fraud investigators, and systems analysts. The availability of qualified actuaries to state insurance departments has been a special issue because of the actuarial questions involved in rate review and financial analysis. According to NAIC statistics, 36 departments had at least one staff actuary and an additional 11 departments had contract actuaries in 1993.]*

(c)  Rehabilitation and liquidation -- The insurance business is exempted from the federal bankruptcy law.  Instead, provisions concerning the rehabilitation and liquidation of insurers form a standard part of state insurance codes.  Coordination of liquidation proceedings against insolvent insurers with claims and assets in many jurisdictions has been attempted but has not fully succeeded.  There is no guaranty, therefore, that all the assets of an insolvent insurer will be pooled and distributed equitably among its insureds and other creditors regardless of where they live.  There are even considerable differences among the laws of the various states with respect to the rank order of preferred creditors.

(d)  Insolvency guaranty funds -- In response to public concern and adverse publicity and threats of federal takeover of insurance regulation following a series of failures in the 1960s, especially of automobile insurers, most states have introduced insurer insolvency guaranty funds, which pay the insurance claims of insolvent insurers; eventual deficits are borne by all other licensed insurers, either in the form of ad hoc assessments or in the form of advance contributions to a fund.  Most states have separate funds for life and nonlife insurance; there are also special insolvency funds in some states for workers' compensation insurance and for automobile insurance.

*[Most states limit coverage of property/casualty claims and death benefits to $300,000. Health insurance claims and cash values on life insurance policies and annuities are typically limited to $100,000. There are no limits on workers' compensation claims. All licensed insurance companies are required to be members of the state guaranty association. Guaranty funds are financed by assessments on member insurers' premiums written in covered lines of business in a state subject to an annual cap (usually one or two percent of premiums). With the exception of New York's property/casualty guaranty fund, assessments are made after an insolvency occurs to cover the claims of the insolvent insurer. New York has a pre-insolvency assessment property/casualty guaranty fund. Assessments also are made to cover the administrative expenses of guaranty funds. The burden of guaranty fund assessments are ultimately shared by: 1) all policyholders through higher insurance rates; 2) taxpayers because of state premium tax offsets (in some states) and deductions for federal income taxes; and 3) owners of insurers.]*

### 5. Special rules for reinsurers

The control of reinsurers by the states within the U.S. is limited. Since the transaction is one between the direct insurer -- which may itself be a foreign insurer -- and the reinsurer, and often takes place outside the state where the directly insured risk is located, the state is concerned less immediately than it is in the case of a direct insurance transaction. On the other hand, the existence and terms of reinsurance and the financial condition of the reinsurer are relevant to the financial condition of the direct insurer and its ability to perform on its promises. Since the state government cannot assert regulatory control directly over a foreign or alien reinsurer that has no local representative and deals with direct insurers in far-away places, whatever control is to be exercised over reinsurance is exercised indirectly using the direct insurer as an intermediary.

The lever applied against direct insurers to establish some minimum control over reinsurers is either an outright prohibition against dealing with reinsurers that have not been recognized by the state or that do not satisfy the state's financial resources requirements or a refusal to give credit to reinsurance coverages in valuing reserves. *[In 1989, the NAIC adopted a model law which tightened requirements for insurers to receive financial credit for ceded reinsurance. In order for the ceding insurer to receive credit, the reinsurer must be "authorized" or post security to cover its obligations, should it fail. To be authorized, a reinsurer must be licensed in at least one state and have capital and surplus of at least $20 million as well as meet other requirements. The credit that a ceding insurer receives also is reduced for uncollectible and overdue reinsurance payments. . . . In 1992, the NAIC proposed federal legislation that would establish the NAIC as a vetting office for alien insurers and reinsurers. Congress has not shown much interest in this legislation and the NAIC has explored how it might undertake certain elements of the proposal without federal action.]*

### 6. Nonadmitted insurance

It is an inherent requirement that any system of insurance regulation be closed to unlicensed insurers . . . . One compromise that has been found necessary is known as surplus lines or excess lines business. It is a compromise between the need to protect the public of a state so far as possible and the need to give the same public, or at least the commercial community, access to a broad and competitive insurance market outside the state for its coverage needs, if the domestic market does not satisfy those needs.

Most of those who look for coverage in the surplus lines market are thought to need less protection than the rest of the population. It is still considered necessary, however, to protect domestic and licensed foreign and alien insurers against unfair competition by unlicensed insurers and also to protect the state's premium tax revenue. In most states these problems have been solved by surplus lines laws that permit business to be written in the state by unlicensed insurers if the contracts are made by specially licensed brokers who affirm that the coverage could not be obtained in the regular market, who assume the responsibility for paying the applicable premium tax, and who are expected to satisfy themselves that the insurers selected are financially sound. Some states go further and permit surplus lines business only if placed with insurers that have been expressly declared eligible by the insurance commissioner. Most states, however, rely on the evaluation performed by the NAIC's Non-Admitted Insurers Information Office. That office compiles financial information on alien insurers doing business in the U.S. and annually publishers a list of those insurers that it considers sound on the basis of general financial standing, existence of an adequate trust account in the U.S., and reputation. In effect, therefore, the nonadmitted or surplus lines market is not unregulated but is regulated on different standards and with different methods than the regular licensed insurers. Moreover, the regulation of nonadmitted insurers is likely to become stricter.

There may be occasions, too, when a certain coverage is not available in either the regular licensed market or from eligible surplus lines insurers but is offered by an insurer that is not on the eligible list. Some laws do indeed permit such third-class business under those circumstances. . . .

### 7. Agents, brokers and other intermediaries

In all states of the U.S., agents and brokers have traditionally been required to obtain licenses from the insurance department, which usually requires successful completion of an examination designed to test technical competence. Licenses are usually renewable annually subject to payment of fees. There are wide variations in details and even wider variations in the enforcement practices of various state insurance departments.

There are no uniform criteria for distinguishing between agents and brokers, for instance, and some states do not distinguish at all. Several states also regulate other intermediaries, such as insurance consultants, and providers of ancillary services, such as adjusters.

### Comments and Questions

1. How does the regulatory structure described in this excerpt differ from the regime applicable to depository institutions? To what extent do these differences reflect the historical evolution of the insurance industry in the United States and to what extent do they respond to different regulatory challenges that the insurance function presents?

2.  In Spencer L. Kimball, *The Purpose of Insurance Regulation: A Preliminary Inquiry into the Theory of Insurance Law*, 45 Minn. L. Rev. 472 (1961), Professor Kimball developed what has become the classic exposition of the function of insurance regulation in the United States.  Of particular interest in this work is Professor Kimball's exploration of goals other than solvency (or solidity) regulation.  Are the considerations discussed in the following passage applicable to other areas of financial-institutions regulation?

### THE PRINCIPLE OF AEQUUM ET BONUM

Although it is hard to deny the propriety of utilizing legal controls to ensure the solidity of insurance companies, there is more disposition to question interference by the law on behalf of a congeries of objectives perhaps best expressed by the term *aequum et bonum*.  This term is chosen precisely because it lacks precision, thereby reflecting the vague character of the objectives and at the same time adequately expressing their general thrust.  The objective of *aequum et bonum* is present in some degree in most systems of insurance law and regulation.  It has many facets:  It is equity.  It is morality.  It is fairness, equality, reasonableness.  It may even by efficiency, economy, parsimony.

1.  *Reasonableness Between Company and Policyholders*

Two reciprocal aspects of this objective appear.  On the one side, social policy requires that the premium charges should be reasonable so that insurance buyers pay only what the coverage is worth.  On the other side, a complementary thrust of the objective would require the company to define its coverage in a way that is unambiguous and not unreasonably strict.  This may be regarded as ensuring that the insured gets what he pays for, or -- going somewhat further -- as requiring the company to give the insured what he must have assumed he was paying for.  The narrower interpretation would permit any constriction of coverage the company wished, provided only that the premium charges were appropriately reduced.  The broader meaning would focus on the dangers of ambiguity, and might even place lower limits on the definition of coverage -- quite irrespective  of ambiguity or of correlative reduction in premiums -- on the ground that such a limitation of coverage would be misleading.  In this extended sense the goal of reasonableness might, in the short run, come into conflict with the principle of solidity.  In the long run, premiums could be raised, in theory at least, to take account of any refusal of the courts, or of the insurance commissioner, to honor limitation in the policies.

Premium rate limitations do not exhaust the possibilities of the principle of reasonableness, even with respect to monetary concerns.  Thus, any statutory provisions which require non-forfeiture benefits on lapse and which set maximum surrender charges also constrain the companies to reasonable conduct in relation to policyholders as a group. It is possible, however, that when a company declines to give any benefits on lapse or when it charges excessive surrender fees, it is being reasonable with the whole body of policyholders but inequitable as among groups.  Thus non-forfeiture provisions have their most direct thrust in the preservation of equitable treatment among groups of policyholders.

Another aspect of reasonableness receives a great deal of attention, especially in the United States.  I refer here to the control of policy terms.  We have uniform fire policies, and standard provisions in accident and health insurance. Control over terms ensures both that coverage will be more precisely defined and that restrictive clauses will not unfairly prejudice the policyholder, whether by making his bargain a bad one or by misleading him.

This strong drive toward uniformity of policies has shifted the area of competition from coverage -- and especially from "gimmicks" -- to price and service, concepts which the individual policyholder can better understand.

### 2. *Equity Among Policyholders*

The aspect of *aequum et bonum* that I have called "equity" is a notion that policyholders should be treated without unfair discrimination. It is best illustrated in American law by the explicit requirement of the All-Industry laws that insurance premium rates shall not be "unfairly discriminatory." The requirement demands fair classification of policyholders for premium computation in order that each person need carry only the cost of his own insurance, so far as that can be worked out. No other objective of insurance regulation is so difficult to apply. In some sense every risk unit is unique and could be separately classified and rated. To carry refined classification to this extreme would be impossible for most lines, however. In the first place, an over-refinement of risk classification would increase administrative cost. In the second place, there is, in general, no way to measure risk directly; one can only measure risk indirectly through loss statistics which reflect experience with similar risks. Such statistics are valid only if they are "credible," a condition which exists when the collection of statistics is sufficiently large and dispersed that the effects of chance are eliminated. To give the quality of credibility to statistical data requires the combination in a single classification of a large number of risk units, categorized on some *a priori* basis. Thus it becomes apparent that a reasonable compromise must be sought between refined classification and the need for credibility in order to measure risk.

### 3. *Fairness to Policyholders*

Whereas the objective of reasonableness prohibits the mistreatment of the whole body of policyholders, and that of equity the mistreatment of policyholders in groups, the remaining objective of fairness prohibits mistreatment of policyholders as individuals. One of the most common examples of unfairness is in the handling of claims. Some companies make a practice of being unduly strict in claims payments or repeatedly insist on unmeritorious but available technical defenses. Likewise, some agents make misrepresentations to individual policyholders or induce them to replace existing policies. Individualized misconduct presents difficult problems of control, especially by a restructuring of the system of operation. Instead one has to rely, in general, on unwieldy administrative systems of enforcement akin to those developed for enforcement of the criminal law.

There seems to be no inherent conflict between the objective of fairness and the other objectives we have discussed so far. In practice, however, there may be conflict with the objective of solidity whenever a legal agency such as a court loses sight of the objective of solidity in seeking to implement the objective of fairness. Thus the construction of the insurance policy *contra proferentem* can lead in an individual case to an extreme decision in favor of the policyholder that creates real difficulties for the security of the insurance fund. For example, if an agent has made misrepresentations to a policyholder under circumstances that induce the court to hold the company responsible for the misrepresentation, the consequence may be to make the company pay a large sum outside the boundary of the coverage upon which its premiums are based. Of course it is not abstract fairness that produces this conflict, but its misapplication. Likewise, a decision reversing a line of previous decisions may bring a whole class of occurrences within the policy coverage and create difficulties for the fund. But if the company is making proper use of reinsurance and has the resilience resulting from appropriate contingency reserves and surpluses, then the conflict is less with solidity than with equity, for subsequent rate increases will redress the balance between the company and the whole body of policyholders . . . .

*Problem 6-1*

As a prelude to our discussion of insurance regulation, put yourself in the position of an insurance executive considering the sale of bicycle insurance in Cambridge, Massachusetts, an urban center with many bicycle riders. According to police reports for the Boston metropolitan market — where Cambridge is located — one in four bicycles are stolen each year. What annual premium should an insurance company charge for a $100 bicycle owned by a Cambridge resident? Do you think the insurance will be an attractive product for bicycle owners in Cambridge?

How much would you charge for fire insurance on a $100,000 property, if your actuaries told you that there was one chance in 300 that the property would be destroyed by fire in any particular year? Would that insurance be attractive to home owners?

# CHAPTER SEVEN

# ISSUES IN INSURANCE REGULATION

---

In this chapter, we explore a selection of problems that arise in the regulation of the insurance industry. In contrast to our discussion of the regulation of depository institutions, no effort will be made to offer comprehensive coverage of the field. Rather, our attention will be limit to selected topics. Many of the topics (including rate regulation and prohibitions against discriminatory rates) illustrate problems peculiar to the insurance industry. Other topics (such as solvency regulation and rules regarding the demutualization of insurance companies) present issues relevant to a variety of financial intermediaries.

## Section 1. The Definition of Insurance

We begin our analysis of insurance regulation by considering what kinds of financial transactions are subject to insurance regulations and which are treated as mere commercial contracts. The jurisdictional bounds of insurance regulation are often the subject of disputes, as is explored in the following three cases. As you review these cases, consider the policies underlying each of the decisions. What is it about the underlying transactions that warrants a special regulatory regime? What is special about insurance?

### State ex rel. Duffy v. Western Auto Supply Co.
### 134 Ohio St. 163 (Ohio 1938)

[In this case, the attorney general of Ohio brought an action in quo warranto against a corporation that had been offering certain "guarantees" as part of its retail business in automobile equipment and supplies. The attorney general, as relator, sought "a judgment of ouster" to prevent the respondent company from "enjoying the franchise and privilege of engaging in the business of insurance."]

The respondent operates retail stores in several cities in this state where, along with certain other articles of merchandise, it sells pneumatic rubber tires for automobiles, which tires bear various trade names and are of standard quality of material and workmanship. Two printed forms of so-called "guarantee" were employed by the company. Both of them served to guarantee the tire sold for a specified period which varied with the grade of tire which was indicated by the trade name, and also depended upon whether the tire was to be used on a passenger or commercial car. One form was a specific guarantee for the period stated therein "against blowouts, cuts, bruises, rim-cuts, under-inflation, wheels out of alignment, faulty brakes or other road hazards that may render the tire unfit for further service (except fire and theft)." It then provided that "In the event that the tire becomes unserviceable from the above conditions, we will (at our option) repair it free of charge, or replace it with a new tire of the same make at any of our stores, charging . . . th[e average] of our current price for each month which has elapsed since the date of purchase. The new tire will be fully covered by our regular guarantee in effect at time of adjustment. Furthermore: every tire is guaranteed against defects in material or workmanship without limit as to time, mileage or service." In the blank spaces were inserted the trade name of the tire, the period covered by the guarantee and the fractional part thereof represented by a single month's wear.

The other form constituted a guarantee "to wear" for not less than the period therein specified, and then provided as follows: "Should the tire fail within the replacement period, return it to the nearest Western Auto Store and we will either repair it free or replace it with a new tire, charging you a proportionate part of the current price for each month you have had the tire."

In some instances these statements of guarantee were supplemented by written statements in a catalogue or otherwise and by oral statements made to purchasers, but all in purpose and effect were substantially the same. It was further stipulated as follows: "All pneumatic tires, regardless of the quality of material and workmanship, are subject to failure in varying degrees by cuts, bruises, breaks, blow-outs, rimcuts, under-inflation, wheels out of alignment, faulty brakes and collision, as well as other road hazards not herein specifically enumerated."

The sole question presented by the record is whether these oral or written agreements or statements or either of them as employed by the respondent in connection with its sale of automobile tires constitutes insurance. It is contended by the relator that in the respect complained of the respondent is engaged in the business of insurance in violation of Section 665, General Code. Its provisions are as follows:

"No company, corporation, or association, whether organized in this state or elsewhere, shall engage either directly or indirectly in this state in the business of insurance, or enter into any contracts substantially amounting to insurance, or in any manner aid therein, or engage in the business of guaranteeing against liability, loss or damage, unless it is expressly authorized by the laws of this state, and the laws regulating it and applicable thereto, have been complied with. . . . ."

The relator concedes that any agreement in the sale of any product which is a warranty against defects in material or workmanship is not insurance, but contends that any agreement which goes further than to guarantee the material and workmanship is violative of the insurance laws of the state, and particularly of the section above quoted. Relator contends that the guarantee agreement is more than a warranty of material and workmanship because of the stipulation that tires are subject to injury and their failure may result from cuts, bruises, blow-outs and other road hazards. Relator further contends that the special guarantee of material and workmanship, unlimited as to time, shows that the general guarantee is for another and different purpose and relates to injuries sustained from exterior causes, and also that the clause, "should the tire fail within the replacement period," with no limitation as to cause, shifts from the buyer to the seller the risk of accidental damage or loss which is independent of and entirely unrelated to quality of material or workmanship.

The contention of the respondent is that the agreement of warranty in either of the forms it uses in the sale of its tires is intended only as a guarantee of material and workmanship and provides a method of carrying out and performing its contract of guarantee which, from its experience, has proved most satisfactory to its customers and the trade generally. It argues that in the absence of some such pre-determined method of adjustment, upon the failure of a tire to render the service expected of it if free from defects of workmanship and material, disputes between the manufacturer or dealer and the customer as to the cause of such failure are constant and annoying, and that it was by reason of the difficulties of reaching satisfactory adjustments and for the purpose of eliminating these disputes and disagreements between dealer and customer and to preserve and promote good will of the users of a product which is subject to failure from various causes often difficult of ascertainment that the type of unconditional or road hazard guarantee was adopted as the fairest, most practical and satisfactory method available.

It argues also that these agreements of guaranty have to do only with the product sold by the respondent and are a part of the sale transaction between itself and its customer, and that the undertaking is limited to a guarantee that the tire will render service for a stipulated period and that in neither of the forms employed is there any promise of financial return to the purchaser in any event, but only to repair the damaged tire without charge or to replace it upon the payment of the specified proportion of the current price covering the remainder of the stipulated period of service guaranteed.

Are such agreements of guarantee permissible as incidental to the sale of automobile tires; or do they constitute "the business of insurance" or "the business of guaranteeing against liability, loss or damage" or are these agreements of guarantee "contracts substantially amounting to insurance" within the purview of Section 665, General Code, and therefore inhibited?

What is insurance? "Broadly defined, insurance is a contract by which one party, for a compensation called the premium, assumes particular risks of the other party and promises to pay to him or his nominee a certain or ascertainable sum of money on a specified contingency. As regards property and liability insurance, it is a contract by which one party promises on a consideration to compensate or reimburse the other if he shall suffer loss from a specified cause, or to guarantee or indemnify or secure him against loss from that cause." It is a contract "to indemnify the insured against loss or damage to a certain property named in the policy by reason of certain perils to which it is exposed."

It seems well settled that to constitute insurance the promise need not be one for the payment of money, but may be its equivalent or some act of value to the insured upon the injury or destruction of the specified property. It is well settled, also, that the business of insurance is impressed with a public use and consequently its regulation, supervision and control are authorized and required to protect the general public and safeguard the interests of all concerned. We are in accord with the suggestion that business and enterprise should not be unduly restricted or interfered with but should be permitted as great freedom in the conduct and management of their affairs as is consistent with the public interest and welfare. However, our conclusion of the issue presented in this case must be determined from the provisions of our own statutes and our especial inquiry is whether the guarantees in question constitute insurance or are contracts substantially amounting to insurance.

Numerous decisions have been cited which deal with conditions and transactions so at variance with those involved in this case that they are of little assistance in reaching a conclusion of the legal question before us. It is essential that the distinction between warranty and insurance be clearly stated. Section 8392, General Code, defines an express warranty as follows: "Any affirmation of fact or any promise by the seller relating to the goods is an express warranty if the natural tendency of such affirmation or promise is to induce the buyer to purchase the goods, and if the buyer purchases the goods relying thereon." A warranty promises indemnity against defects in the article sold, while insurance indemnifies against loss or damage resulting from perils outside of and unrelated to defects in the article itself.

The respondent, in one of its forms of contract, specifically guarantees "against defects in material and workmanship without limit as to time, mileage or service"; but it goes further and undertakes to indemnify the owner of such tires against all road hazards (except fire and theft) which may render his tire unfit for service. The terms employed in the guarantee are sufficiently broad to include not only damage from blow-outs, cuts and bruises, whether resulting from under-inflation, faulty brakes or misalignment, but any and every hazard, including collisions, whether resulting from negligence of the owner or another. It clearly embraces insurance upon the property of the owner, such as is authorized by the provisions of Section 9556, General Code, to be written by companies required to comply with the insurance laws of the state.

The ultimate force and effect of the contract of indemnity embraced in this guarantee may be appreciated if extended to cover not only the automobile tire but the automobile itself. Surely no one would contend that an undertaking by an automobile manufacturer to replace an automobile damaged or destroyed (excepting only by fire and theft) within a specified period after its purchase is not a contract to reimburse one if he suffers loss from a specified cause, or to indemnify him against such loss.

The fact that such contract of indemnity is made only with the purchaser of the indemnitor's product does not relieve the transaction of its insurance character. When the sale is complete, title passes and the property which is the subject of insurance or indemnity belongs to the purchaser. If the contracts of indemnity involved here are not violative of the insurance laws, then every company may, in consideration of the purchase price paid therefor, furnish its product and also undertake to insure it against all hazards for a specified period. Even if such contract is an incident in the sale of merchandise and its use therein does not constitute the business of insurance, it in effect is a contract "substantially amounting to insurance" within the restrictive provisions of Section 665, General Code.

We are unable to discern any essential difference in the character or effect of the various forms of agreement of indemnity made by the respondent and advertised in its catalogue. Each constitutes an undertaking to indemnify against failure from any cause except fire or theft and therefore covers loss or damage resulting from any and every hazard of travel, not excepting negligence of the automobile driver or another. It is substantially an unconditional promise of indemnity, and that is insurance.

It follows that a judgment of ouster should issue in all respects as prayed for.

## Comments and Questions

How does the court distinguish between permissible guarantees and unauthorized insurance contracts? Is this a sensible distinction? Will this legal rule have a desirable effect on the way goods and services are produced? What is the public's interest in policing arrangements of this sort?

## Prepaid Dental Services, Inc. v. Day
### 615 P.2d 1271 (Utah 1980)

Plaintiff proposes to market a prepaid dental services plan which, it alleges, is not an insurance plan and not subject to regulation under the Insurance Code. The Utah State Insurance Commissioner (Commissioner), however, determined both that the plan is within the definition of insurance in § 31-1- 7 of Utah Code Ann., 1953, as amended, and is a Health Maintenance Organization (HMO), subject to regulation under § 31-42-1, et seq. The Commissioner also found that plaintiff did not propose to offer sufficient basic health services, required of HMOs under § 31- 42-3(6) and denied plaintiff a Certificate of Authority, forbidding it to conduct business.

Plaintiff brought action in the District Court of Salt Lake County praying for declaratory judgment that the plan it proposed is not subject to regulation by the Insurance Commissioner. Both parties moved for summary judgment upon stipulated facts. The District Court granted defendant's motion, sustained the findings of the Commissioner, and denied plaintiff's petition. Plaintiff appeals.

Plaintiff's plan consists of the following:

1. Plaintiff would contract with employers to arrange for specific dental services to be provided to the employer's employees, as needed. The employers would pay to plaintiff a specific monthly charge, determined by the number of employees and their families who agreed to be participants.

2. Plaintiff would also contract with licensed dentists to provide these specific dental services. Plaintiff would pay the dentists a monthly payment whether they performed any services or not, the payments also being determined by the number of participants enrolled.

3. A participant would be required to have the dental services provided by the dentists with whom plaintiff had contracted, rather than choosing a dentist of his own, and for certain services would make scheduled co-payments to the dentists.

4. Plaintiff would require a performance bond from the dentists to ensure that the promised services continued to be available to participants during a contract year.

5. Plaintiff's plan would not provide emergency care, in-patient hospital and physician care, out-of-area coverage or out-patient medical services.[2]

By § 31-1-7, the Utah Legislature has defined insurance:

Insurance is a contract whereby one undertakes to indemnify another or pay or allow a specified or ascertainable amount or benefit upon determinable risk contingencies.

Plaintiff asserts that its plan is not an insurance plan as the benefits it promises to participants do not involve determinable risk contingencies, and that plaintiff, by its various contracts, does not undertake to indemnify or assume any risk.

This Court has observed that insurance contracts involve "risk on the part of the insurer to pay on the happening of the contingency and the spreading of the risk over the group who pay the

---

[2]    HMO's are required to offer such services under § 31-42-6(2)(c).

premiums." . . . . To be sure, there is a certain risk, in this matter, that participants will need dental care, and that risk under plaintiff's plan would be spread over the group of participants. Nevertheless, that risk is not assumed by plaintiff under its plan. Plaintiff would obligate itself to pay to the dentists no more (and no less) if the participants need dental care than if they do not need such care. It was just such a lack of assumption of any risk that led this Court to determine that the contracts [prior cases] were not insurance contracts.

In Jordan v. Group Health Ass'n, 107 F.2d 239 (D.C.Cir.1939) the Court determined that a health plan, operated by a non-profit corporation which paid its enrolled doctors a monthly payment was not insurance, saying:

> Whether the contract is one of insurance or of indemnity there must be a risk of loss to which one party may be subjected by contingent or future events and an assumption of it by legally binding arrangement by another. Even the most loosely stated conceptions of insurance and indemnity require these elements. Hazard is essential and equally so a shifting of its incidence. If there is no risk, or there being one it is not shifted to another or others, there can be neither insurance nor indemnity. Insurance also, by the better view, involves distribution of the risk, but distribution without assumption hardly can be held to be insurance. These are elemental conceptions and controlling ones.

Most courts which have considered this question have determined that such contracts do not constitute insurance where the professional is paid a "retainer" as distinguished from a fee for the service provided. . . . .

The District Court distinguished [prior cases] on the ground that, here, plaintiff not only would agree to use its best efforts to obtain dental services for participants, but would require a performance bond of the dental group to assure the delivery of those services. The District Court held that the requirement of the performance bond indicated that plaintiff had assumed some risk. We do not agree. A performance bond might indicate that the indemnitor, or bondsman, had assumed a risk, but plaintiff, does not, under its plan, undertake to pay any benefit upon the happening of any contingency. Insurers are required under our code to maintain large deposits and reserves of assets in order to assure the public that the insurer will be able to meet its obligations to pay benefits upon the happening of a contingency, when it has assumed that risk. There is no reason to require such deposits and reserves of plaintiff as it would not obligate itself to pay anything in addition to the regular monthly payments to dentists pursuant to its contract with the dental group regardless of the happening of any contingency. Thus, plaintiff is not an insurer, as it would assume no risk.

Retainer plans, such as the one proposed by plaintiff have long been recognized as providing a beneficial and economical alternative to the dominant "fee for service" in delivery of health care. . . . In 1973, the Utah Legislature provided for limited regulation by the Commissioner of organizations offering comprehensive health care plans, operated on a per capita, or retainer basis under the Health Maintenance Organization Act § 31-42-1, et seq.[3] The legislative purpose of this act is stated in § 31-42-2:

---

[3]     Both the Commissioner and the District Court assumed that the Legislature intended HMOs to be deemed insurance companies merely because it placed the regulation of such organizations with the Insurance Commissioner. Yet the Legislature prohibited HMOs from using words descriptive of insurance in their titles or promotional materials (§ 31-42- 22), and specifically provided that HMOs should not be subject to regulation as insurers (§ 31-42-31).

As a guide to the interpretation and application of this act, the public policy of this state is declared to be as follows: The legislature wishes to eliminate legal barriers to the establishment of health maintenance organizations which provide readily available, accessible and quality *comprehensive health care* to their members and to encourage their development as an alternative method of health care delivery. The state of Utah must have reasonable assurance that health maintenance organizations offering health plans within this state are financially and administratively sound and that such organizations are in fact able to deliver the benefits which they offer. (Emphasis added.)

The Commissioner found that plaintiff's plan is within the definition of an HMO in § 31-42-3(4), which provides:

(4) "Health maintenance organization" means any person:

(a) Who furnishes, either directly or through arrangements with others, health care to an enrolled member in return for periodic payments; the amounts of said payments are agreed upon prior to the time during which the health care may be furnished; and

(b) Who is obligated to the member to arrange for or to directly provide available and accessible health care.

An individual is not a health maintenance organization when he contracts to render professional or personal services which he performs himself.

But the Commissioner also found that plaintiff is prohibited from transacting business as it does not provide basic health services, as defined in § 31-42- 3(6).

(6) "Basic health care services" means as a minimum, emergency care,

inpatient hospital and physician care, out-patient medical services, and out- of-area coverage.

Thus, plaintiff is, under the Commissioners's reasoning, prohibited from transacting business because it does not offer "comprehensive health care," though the Legislature has stated that its purpose is to regulate those organizations which do. Nowhere in the HMO Act do we find a provision that an HMO must provide dental services. It seems anomalous then that an organization which provides dental services must also offer medical and hospital services in order to operate.

It is our opinion that the Legislature did not intend that profit organizations offering only dental services on a prepaid, or retainer, basis should be regulated under the HMO Act, nor that by such Act, it intended to prohibit such organizations from transacting business. In so holding we express no opinion as to whether regulation of plaintiff's business is required under provisions of the Code other than those relating to insurers and HMOs.

## Comments and Questions

1. Note the emphasis the court places on the performance bond guaranteeing the Prepaid Dental Plan's obligations. Does the presence of this bond eliminate the need for any additional regulatory oversight in this context? In the prior case, would Western Auto have been permitted to offer its tire guarantees if it had obtained a similar performance bond? What if a more traditional health maintenance organization obtained such a bond?

2. Had the court concluded that the Prepaid Dental Plan was an insurance company, what effect would the decision have had on the plan's operations? Under what conditions

could the plan have had to operate?  Who would have borne the costs of those conditions?

---

In the next case, the definition of insurance question arises in a different context. Here, a state insurance commissioner sought to enjoin a national bank from engaging in an activity that the commission concluded was insurance underwriting.  Before reading this case, students may find it helpful to review our discussion of the business of banking in section 2 of Chapter Three.  Students should also consider that national banks have only limited express authority to engage in insurance activities.  See 12 U.S.C.A. § 92 (West 1996).  Traditionally, this limited authority was understood to establish an outer bound on the permissible insurance activities of national banks.  See, e.g., Saxon v. Georgia Association of Independent Insurance Agents, 399 F.2d 1010 (5th Cir. 1968).  More recently, however, the courts have allowed national banks make greater inroads into the insurance business, provided the Comptroller of the Currency ratifies the incursions in reasoned interpretation of statutory authority.  See, e.g., NationsBank, N.A. v. VALIC, 513 U.S. 251 (1995).

## First National Bank of Eastern Arkansas v. Taylor
### 907 F.2d 775 (8th Cir.), *cert. denied*, 498 U.S. 972 (1990)

In July, 1987, First National Bank of Eastern Arkansas (FNB) began offering debt cancellation contracts as additional-cost options to customers borrowing $10,000 or less. These contracts obligated FNB to cancel the unpaid loan balance remaining at the borrower's death, regardless of the cause of death. FNB offered the debt cancellation contracts at rates that did not vary with a borrower's age or medical condition. A regulation promulgated by the United States Comptroller of Currency (Comptroller) authorizes national banks to enter into debt cancellation contracts. See 12 C.F.R. 7.7495 (1990).[1]

I

In September, 1987, the Arkansas Insurance Department notified FNB that debt cancellation contracts were the equivalent of credit life insurance policies, and thus subject to state insurance laws. The Department requested that FNB stop offering the contracts.[2] FNB

---

[1]     12 C.F.R. § 7.7495 provides:

A national bank may provide for losses arising from cancellation of outstanding loans upon the death of borrowers. The imposition of an additional charge and the establishment of necessary reserves in order to enable the bank to enter into such debt cancellation contracts are a lawful exercise of the powers of a national bank and necessary to the business of banking.

[2]     The Department indicated in its letter to FNB that the bank's failure to stop offering debt cancellation contracts would result in enforcement action by the Commissioner. Under Ark. Code of 1987 Ann. § 23-65-105 (Supp. 1989), the Commissioner has authority to issue a cease and desist order against any person who engages in the business of insurance without a license.

complied, but then brought a suit in federal district court seeking a declaration that the Department's action was preempted by the National Bank Act . . . .

Our inquiry in this case is limited to the question whether the Arkansas Insurance Commissioner may prohibit FNB from entering into debt cancellation contracts.[6] The Commissioner initially urges that such a prohibition does not conflict with federal law because the National Bank Act does not grant national banks the power to offer debt cancellation contracts. The Commissioner argues that in authorizing the contracts, the Comptroller has exceeded his authority. We disagree.

In addition to enumerating specific powers, including the lending of money, the National Bank Act grants national banks the power to exercise "all such incidental powers as shall be necessary to carry on the business of banking." 12 U.S.C. § 24 (Seventh). The Comptroller, through 12 C.F.R. § 7.7495, has interpreted "incidental powers" to include the offering of debt cancellation contracts . . . .

The "incidental powers" of national banks are not limited to activities that are deemed essential to the exercise of express powers. Rather, courts have analyzed the issue by asking whether the activity is closely related to an express power and is useful in carrying out the business of banking. For example, the Supreme Court, in Colorado Nat'l Bank v. Bedford, 310 U.S. 41 (1939), held that a national bank was authorized to operate a safe-deposit business, reasoning that this activity was incidental to the bank's express power to accept special deposits. Id. at 49-50. . . .

As the district court found, the debt cancellation contracts at issue in this case are directly related to FNB's expressly-authorized lending power. The contracts are sold only in connection with loans made by FNB, and involve only FNB and its borrowing customers. The contracts provide borrowers with a convenient method of extinguishing debt in case of death, and enable FNB to avoid the time, expense, and risk associated with attempting to collect the balance of the loan from a borrower's estate. Because we agree with the district court that the debt cancellation contracts are directly connected to FNB's lending activities, we deem the Comptroller's authorization of this activity as reasonable and within the incidental powers granted by the National Bank Act.

---

[6]    Because the Commissioner's request that FNB stop offering debt cancellation contracts was grounded on FNB's failure to obtain a state license, the parties dispute whether this case should be regarded as one of prohibition or regulation. However, Arkansas law requires licensees to submit to extensive state regulation, including maintenance of specific capital and surplus levels, payment of licensing fees, financial information disclosure, and inspection by the Commissioner. Compliance with these requirements would pervert FNB's status as a federal instrumentality. Moreover, 12 U.S.C. § 484 (1988) prohibits states from exercising "visitorial powers" over national banks. For these reasons, we regard the Commissioner's request as a prohibition on FNB's issuance of debt cancellation contracts.

The Comptroller, in an amicus curiae brief, concedes that there may be particular state insurance regulations (e.g., those limiting premium rates) which apply to debt cancellation contracts and which do not conflict with national banking powers. We agree with the Comptroller's argument that these issues are more properly addressed on a case-by-case basis.

## II

Having found that the National Bank Act authorizes national banks to offer debt cancellation contracts as "incidental" to the business of banking, we find in favor of FNB under the principle of federal preemption. Because national banks are considered federal instrumentalities . . . , states may neither prohibit nor unduly restrict their activities. . . . Thus, the National Bank Act preempts the Commissioner's authority to prohibit FNB from offering debt cancellation contracts.

The Commissioner argues, however, that section 2 of the McCarran-Ferguson Act limits the preemptive power of the National Bank Act in this case because it forbids courts to construe the National Bank Act in a manner that impairs a state's authority to regulate the "business of insurance." 15 U.S.C. § 1012(b). The Commissioner urges that because debt cancellation contracts have the same effect as credit life insurance contracts, they are subject to the exclusive regulatory authority of the state under the McCarran-Ferguson Act. We reject this argument. We hold that because the debt cancellation contracts offered by FNB fall within the incidental powers granted by the National Bank Act, they do not constitute the "business of insurance" under the McCarran-Ferguson Act.

We reach this holding for two reasons. The primary reason is that the McCarran-Ferguson Act was not directed at the activities of national banks. The McCarran-Ferguson Act was passed by Congress in response to the Supreme court's decision in United States v. South-Eastern Underwriters Ass'n, 322 U.S. 533 (1944), which held that the insurance industry was subject to regulation by Congress under the Commerce Clause, and that insurance company activities were subject to federal antitrust laws. Id. at 553. The McCarran-Ferguson Act was designed to preserve traditional state regulation and taxation of insurance companies, and to provide insurance companies with a partial exemption from federal antitrust laws. Group Life & Health Ins. Co. v. Royal Drug Co., 440 U.S. 205, 217-18 (1979); Union Labor Life Ins. Co. v. Pireno, 458 U.S. 119, 129 (1982). In holding that certain pharmacy contracts involving health-care organizations were not the "business of insurance," the Court in Group Life expressed doubt as to whether the McCarran-Ferguson Act applied to entities commonly thought to be outside the insurance industry:

There is not the slightest suggestion in the legislative history that Congress in any way contemplated that arrangements such as the Pharmacy Agreements in this case, which involve the mass purchase of goods and services from entities outside the insurance industry, are the "business of insurance."
. . .

At the time of the enactment of the McCarran-Ferguson Act, corporations organized for the purpose of providing their members with medical services and hospitalization were not considered to be engaged in the insurance business at all, and thus were not subject to state insurance laws. . . . Since the legislative history makes clear that Congress certainly did not intend the definition of the "business of insurance" to be *broader* than its commonly understood meaning, the contemporary perception that health-care organizations were not engaged in providing insurance is highly significant in ascertaining congressional intent.

440 U.S. at 224-27 (emphasis in original). . . .

The McCarran-Ferguson Act was not intended to give states power to regulate beyond that which they had been thought to possess prior to the South-Eastern Underwriters decision. As the Court in SEC v. National Sec.. Inc., 393 U.S. 453 (1969) said,

The McCarran-Ferguson Act was an attempt to turn back the clock, to assure that the activities of insurance companies in dealing with their policyholders would remain subject to state regulation. As the House Report makes clear, "it [was] not the intention of Congress in the enactment of this legislation to clothe the States with any power to regulate or tax the business of insurance beyond that which they had been held to possess prior to the decision of the United States Supreme Court in the Southeastern Underwriters Association case." . . . .

Id. at 459. . . . Yet, well before the South-Eastern Underwriters decision, regulation of national banks was within the exclusive domain of the federal government. E.g., First Nat'l Bank v. California, 262 U.S. 366, 369 (1923). This strongly indicates that Congress did not intend the "business of insurance" to encompass lawful activities of national banks.

Our second reason for holding that the debt cancellation contracts offered by FNB are not the "business of insurance" is that debt cancellation contracts issued by banks in connection with loans differ significantly from traditional insurance contracts. Although debt cancellation contracts may, as the Commissioner argues, transfer some risk from the borrower to the bank,[8] the contracts do not require the bank to take an investment risk or to make payment to the borrower's estate. The debt is simply extinguished when the borrower dies. Thus, the primary and traditional concern behind state insurance regulation -- the prevention of insolvency -- is not of concern to a borrower who opts for a debt cancellation contract. As Justice Brennan said in his concurring opinion in S.E.C. v. Variable Annuity Life, 359 U.S. at 90-91, "The prevention of insolvency and the maintenance of 'sound' financial condition in terms of fixed-dollar obligations is precisely what traditional state regulation [of insurance] is aimed at." The fact that debt cancellation contracts issued by national banks in connection with loans do not implicate this central concern of insurance regulation, at least as it relates to the ability of the banks to fulfill their obligations under the contracts, adds further support to our holding that debt cancellation contracts should not be considered the "business of insurance."[9]

## Comments and Questions

1.   The *Taylor* decision relies, in part, on an interpretation of the McCarran-Ferguson Act and a series of Supreme Court cases holding that the Act's "business of insurance" exemption from federal anti-trust laws does not extend to all insurance company activities.   The *Taylor* court interprets this line of authority to preclude state

---

[8]   We acknowledge that in addition to the Commissioner a few state appellate courts have found debt cancellation contracts to fall within their states' definitions of "insurance." . . . . However, state law defining insurance is not controlling on the issue of whether an activity falls within the "business of insurance" as that term is used in the McCarran-Ferguson Act. . . . .

[9]   The responsibility of ensuring the financial condition of the national banking system has long been committed to the Comptroller. In the case of debt cancellation contracts, the Comptroller has indicated that banks must use prudent banking judgment, which may include the establishment of reserves to cover losses resulting from early debt cancellation. See 12 C.F.R. § 7.7495; Letter from J. Michael Shepherd, Senior Deputy Comptroller for Corporate and Economic Programs, to W.D. Glover, FNB Chairman and President, (Jan. 7, 1988). . . . . If a national bank is engaging in "unsafe or unsound" banking practices, the Comptroller, under 12 U.S.C. § 1818(b), may issue a cease and desist order.

insurance regulation from extending to duly authorizes activities of federally chartered banks.  In a subsequent cases, the Supreme Court has been more reluctant to preempt state insurance regulation.  See Barnett Bank  v. Nelson, 116 S. Ct. 1103 (1996).

2.     Later on, in our discussion of inter-sector competition (see Chapter 16), we will consider the jurisdictional line between banking and insurance in some detail.  For the time being, however, consider the approach taken by the *Taylor* court.  If national banks can offer debt cancellation contracts without complying with state insurance regulation, what regulatory structures govern these transactions.  Are these structures sufficient to safeguard purchasers  of  these  contracts?  To protect our banking system?  Recall that in our discussion of bank subsidiaries in section 4 of Chapter Four, we considered a case in which Delaware  had  authorized  its  state-chartered  banks  to  underwrite  insurance.  What regulatory structure did Delaware apply to those activities?  Why?

3.     In our discussion of bank powers, one of the issues we considered with the authority of national banks to issue standby letters of credit and bankers' acceptances, but not straightforward guarantees.  See section 4C of Chapter Three.   One reason this distinction is problematic is that all of these arrangements are the functional equivalent of financial default insurance underwritten by banks.  In recent years, it has become fashionable in financial economic circles to point out that any commercial loan can also be disaggregated into a risk-free loan plus default insurance on the borrower.  This perspective suggests that underwriting default insurance is inherent to the banking industry, and the Comptroller has adopted similar reasoning to authorize national bank underwriting of municipal bond insurance.  See Securities Industry Association v. Clarke, 885 F.2d 1034 (2d Cir. 1989), *cert. denied,* 493 U.S. 1070 (1990).  The *Taylor* case extends this analysis because the risk underwritten here also includes mortality risk, something banks have not traditionally underwritten. Have the *Taylor* court and the Comptroller of the Currency gone too far?  For a full discussion of bank insurance powers, see Chapter Sixteen.

## Section 2.  The Interpretation of Insurance Contracts

Once a transaction is deemed to be insurance, the party issuing the contract — that is, the insurance underwriter — becomes subject to comprehensive regulatory oversight. A large part of that regulatory structure concerns the content and interpretation of insurance contracts themselves.  Most insurance law casebooks devote most of their attention to this aspect of insurance regulation.  See KENNETH S. ABRAHAM, INSURANCE LAW AND REGULATION (2d ed. 1995); ALAN J. WIDISS, INSURANCE (1989).  Though the field offers many fascinating issues, we devote only a few pages to the subject, providing just two short cases to give a flavor of the subject.  As you review these cases, consider why we regulate insurance contracts so thoroughly but leave the content of bank loans and even deposit relationships largely to the province of private negotiation.  Should we be more concerned about the lending transactions and depository instruments?

# State Farm Mutual Automobile Insurance Co. v. Moore
## 544 A.2d 1017 (Pa. Super. Ct. 1988), *appeal denied*, 557 A.2d 725 (Pa. 1989)

The accident underlying this action occurred in 1980, while Brian Stuck was driving a 1961 Pontiac owned by Charles Royer and insured by Ohio Casualty [Insurance Company]. Although owned by Charles Royer the Pontiac was paid for and primarily used by his daughter Leigh Ann Royer. On the night of the accident Leigh Ann, Brian Stuck and some friends visited several bars. Initially, Leigh Ann drove the Pontiac. Later in the evening, when she wished to ride in her friends' car she gave Brian Stuck the keys to the Pontiac so that he could drive her car to the agreed upon destination. Brian Stuck did not have a driver's license. On the way to the destination an accident occurred.

Personal injury actions were brought naming Brian Stuck as defendant. Ohio Casualty denied coverage claiming, in part, that because Stuck was not licensed to drive he was excluded from coverage under the policy. At the time of the accident Stuck resided with his parents who had a no-fault insurance policy with State Farm Mutual Automobile Insurance Company. State Farm undertook the defense of claims asserted against Stuck. State Farm maintains that its policy provides only excess coverage. State Farm commenced the instant declaratory judgment action seeking a determination that primary liability coverage should be furnished by Ohio Casualty.

Following trial the jury returned a verdict specifically finding that Brian Stuck had a reasonable belief that he was entitled to use the vehicle in question. Accordingly, the trial court found Ohio Casualty's exclusion was avoided and that Brian Stuck was entitled to liability coverage under the Ohio Casualty policy. . . . .

Ohio Casualty contends that the trial court misconstrued the policy provision in question. This clause, contained in Ohio Casualty's policy, stated:

We do not provide Liability Coverage: . . . .

11. For any person using a vehicle without a reasonable belief that the person is entitled to do so.

Ohio Casualty argues that "entitled" encompasses not only permission of the owner but also possession of a driver's license.

The trial court instructed the jury that they were to decide the narrow issue of whether or not Mr. Stuck had a reasonable belief that he was entitled to operate the vehicle. In charging on the meaning of "entitled" the court stated:

Now, the other word which we have trouble with here is entitled. What does entitled mean? And if we go to Websters Dictionary, New Collegiate Dictionary, it was copyrighted in 1975, we find that "entitled" is stated as "to give a title to, designate". That's the definition one. "To furnish with proper ground for seeking or claiming something." As in "this ticket entitles bearer to free admission."

In this case, however, entitled, as I said, to give title to, designate. So, in this case here you must decide was Brian Stuck reasonable in his belief that he was entitled to drive the motor vehicle in question on that night? And in considering that, as I said, you should consider all the testimony including the question I asked Brian, "did you ever drive before?"

N.T., Judge's Charge to Jury, 6/26/86 at 26-27.  Additionally the court charged that:

> The term "entitled" as used in the Ohio Casualty policy means "permitted by the owner or person in lawful possession of the vehicle" . . . .

Id. at 28.  Ohio Casualty argues that this additional charge was erroneous.  It argues that the term "entitled" is not ambiguous and that it includes not only permission but also possession of a license.

The question of the meaning of "entitled" in the Ohio Casualty policy is a question of interpretation.  The often-quoted principles applicable to interpretation of insurance contracts provide that:

> The task of interpreting a contract is generally performed by a court rather than by a jury.  The goal of that task is, of course, to ascertain the intent of the parties as manifested by the language of the written instrument.  Where a provision of a policy is ambiguous, the policy provision is to be construed in favor of the insured and against the insurer, the drafter of the agreement.  Where, however, the language of the contract is clear and unambiguous, a court is required to give effect to that language.

Standard Venetian Blind Co. v. American Empire Insurance Co., 503 Pa. 300, 304-05, 469 A.2d 563, 566 (1983) (citations omitted).  As applied to the case at hand what is essential is the determination of whether the policy provision is ambiguous.  In determining this we have stated that:

> A provision of a contract of insurance is ambiguous if reasonably intelligent persons, considering it in the context of the whole policy, would differ regarding its meaning.

Musisko v. Equitable Life Assurance Society, 344 Pa.Super. 101, 106, 496 A.2d 28, 31 (1985) (citations omitted).

Considering the clause in the context of the whole policy, we believe reasonably intelligent persons would differ regarding its meaning.  Certainly one interpretation is that advanced by Ohio Casualty.  That is, for a person to reasonably believe that he is entitled to use a car a person must have the owner's permission and a valid driver's license.  However, the clause could also be interpreted to mean that a person can reasonably believe he is entitled to use a car once he has obtained the owner's permission.  The mere use of the word "entitled" in the policy language does not require that one interpretation be accepted to the exclusion of the other.  If Ohio Casualty had wanted to specifically exclude from coverage unlicensed drivers it could have defined the word "entitled" in its policy.  We note that it has a section entitled "Definitions" in its policy and "entitled" is not one of the words it chose to define.  Ohio Casualty could also have listed persons without a driver's license as an additional exclusion.  The clause we are now interpreting is number 11 of 12 separate exclusions.  Unlicensed drivers could have been specifically set forth as exclusion number 13.  This was not done.

Accordingly we find that "entitled" as it is used in the clause at issue is ambiguous.  As such, the provision is to be construed against the insurer, who was the drafter of the agreement. Standard Venetian Blind Co., supra.  As applied to these facts we then agree with the trial court that it is "sufficient to avoid Ohio Casualty's exclusion that Brian Stuck have had a reasonable belief that he had the permission of the owner or a person in lawful possession of the Royer vehicle."   The trial court's charge was not in error.   We find no merit to appellant's first argument.

. . . Ohio Casualty [also] directs this Court's attention to the summation of counsel for State Farm wherein counsel remarked that the insurance coverage would benefit not only Stuck but also those people injured as a result of the accident.   Ohio Casualty contends that this remark . . . prejudiced Ohio Casualty and resulted in a verdict based upon sympathy and prejudice.

We have carefully reviewed the remarks and . . . the summation of State Farm and the judge's charge in their entirety.   With respect to the remarks made during closing argument, counsel for Ohio Casualty asked the trial court to give correcting instructions.   The court gave such instructions and cautioned the jury to limit its deliberations to the facts at issue.   The court explained to the jury that they were not to be concerned with the accident that occurred, with the injured parties or with the fact that there may be more insurance money available.   The trial court is in a better position than we to observe the atmosphere at trial and determine whether a statement made by counsel had a prejudicial effect on the jury. . . . . [W]e find that the court's charge was proper and adequately dissipated any prejudicial effect appellees' counsel's remarks may have had on the jury. . .

MONTEMURO, Judge, concurring and dissenting:

. . . [T]his contract of automobile insurance does not contemplate coverage for the deliberate perpetration of an illegality, as is clear from the reasonableness requirement.   Had appellant's policy merely referred to the insurability of permissive users . . . , there would be no difficulty in finding coverage for Stuck. . . . . However, the clause here under examination speaks of reasonable belief, a phrase which implies the exercise of sound judgment.   Insofar as the test for such a belief is concerned, it "takes into account a variety of circumstances, including the borrower's age, personality, and social milieu, and the effect of such attendant influences on his judgment and mind as may be credibly discerned from the proofs."   Miller v. U.S.F. & G. Co., 28 D. & C.3d 389 (1983).

At the time of the accident Brian Stuck was 23 years old and a high school graduate.   He admitted, both in deposition and at trial, to knowledge that it was illegal to operate a motor vehicle without a license, and that his prior driving experience had been limited.   Although, given all these factors, it is remotely possible that Stuck thought himself "entitled," that is, empowered by permission of the owner to operate the car simply by virtue of having been handed the keys, that conclusion involves more wishful thinking than reasonableness.   Such judgment as it demonstrates is neither sound nor rational since it endows the (putative) teenage owner of an automobile with the authority to permit an activity, driving without a license, which the state clearly and specifically forbids.

The majority also finds that there is ambiguity in the concept of entitlement sufficient to require an express exclusion of unlicensed drivers from coverage.   From the dictionary definitions and usage of the word in the policy, I would find no lack of clarity.   Moreover, within the context of this case, the specifics of entitlement matter less than Stuck's knowledge that he was prohibited by law from operating any automobile.   We therefore arrive where we began, with the question of reasonableness.

## Comments and Questions

1. Note that this case involved a contest between State Farm, which had a policy issued to the parents of the unlicensed driver who caused the accident, and Ohio Casualty, which had a policy covering the vehicle itself. State Farm contended that Ohio Casualty's primary coverage should cover the accident, whereas Ohio Casualty attempted (unsuccessfully) to invoke an exclusion in its policy and thereby push liability onto excess coverage of State Farm's policy. Determining which insurance company is liable, when two or more policies arguably cover an accident, is a common subject of insurance litigation.

2. Both the opinions in this case focus on the reasonableness of the driver's understanding that he had permission to drive the vehicle. Which opinion do you find more persuasive? If, as the facts suggest, it was demonstrated that the driver was intoxicated when he got behind the wheel, would that be dispositive? Should the fact that automobile insurance is mandatory in most jurisdictions affect a court's interpretation of such clauses? For an analysis of conflicting authority interpreting this exclusion, see Note, *The Entitlement Exclusion in the Personal Auto Policy*, 84 KY. L.J. 349 (1995).

3. Interpreting policy exclusions presents difficulties in many areas of insurance. Particularly contentious in recent years has been the scope of exclusions for environmental damage in commercial liability policies as well as exclusions for experimental medical procedures in health insurance policies. For an introduction to these lines of authority, see Melody A. Hamel, *The 1970 Pollution Exclusion in Comprehensive General Liability Policies: Reasons for Interpretations in Favor of Coverage in 1996 and Beyond*, 34 DUQ. L. REV. 1083 (1996), and Note, *Insurers' and Courts' Response to High Dose Chemotherapy with Autologous Bone Marrow Transplants in the Treatment of Breast Cancer*, 43 DRAKE L. REV. 863 (1995). For an interesting overview of doctrines governing the interpretation of insurance contracts, see Kenneth S. Abraham, *A Theory of Insurance Policy Interpretation*, 95 MICH. L. REV. 531 (1996).

4. One distinctive feature of the insurance contracts is the prevalence of standardized forms used, with minor variations, by a large number of insurance companies or in some cases an entire sector of the industry. Many pragmatic considerations explain this prevalence of standardized contracts. First, in many contexts, state insurance authorities must approve the form of insurance contracts. Standardized contracts simplify this approval process. Standardized contracts also facilitate the development of a body of judicial authority with considerable precedential value. Furthermore, standardized contracts allow industry trade groups to develop loss data for standardized policies, which many members of the industry can then use for pricing decision. We will consider some potential drawbacks of standardized contracts in Chapter 8, Section 2. What might they be?

---

The next case explores a separate regulatory constraint on insurance contract: the requirement that the beneficiary of insurance policies have an "insurable interest" in the subject matter of the policy.   This principle, which evolved at common law and has statutory antecedents tracing back several hundred years, is recognized in one form or another in all U.S. jurisdictions.

## Johnson v. Allstate Insurance Co.
### 870 P.2d 792 (Okla App. Ct. 1993)

Appellant, Sherry A. Murdock Johnson (Sherry) sued Allstate Insurance Company (Allstate), Union National Bank of Arkansas (Bank), and Jack D. Murdock (Jack).   The purpose of the action was to collect the proceeds of an insurance policy covering her former home in Tulsa, Oklahoma, after it had been destroyed by fire.   The trial court overruled Sherry's motion for summary judgment. . . .   Sherry appeals.

Jack and Sherry were divorced on May 8, 1991.   The Divorce Decree, in its division of property, vested title to the home of the parties in Jack, subject to the balance due on a note, secured by a mortgage on the home in favor of Bank, which he was ordered to pay.   Jack was also ordered to pay various other debts of the parties, and to hold Sherry harmless as to them.   She was ordered to execute and deliver to Jack a quit claim deed to the home, and she did so.   The deed contained a recital that it was executed pursuant to the order in the Divorce Decree.   She was not given any lien or claim against the home as security in the event Jack failed to pay the debts of the parties, as ordered by the Court.   The quit claim deed did not reserve any such security interest.

In October, 1991, Jack filed for Chapter 7 Bankruptcy.   In the Federal Court, by objections filed October 24, 1991, Sherry contested Jack's right to a discharge of his obligation to her to pay the debts assigned to him by the Divorce Decree, and to hold her harmless.   However, the Bankruptcy Court held Jack's obligations in that respect were subject to discharge.

Sherry applied for insurance on the home, apparently to protect herself from possible liability on the note and mortgage to Bank.   Allstate issued an insurance policy on the home to Sherry, in her name, on October 26, 1991.   The policy covered the usual hazards, including fire, and contained a standard loss payable clause, as its interest appears, to Bank as mortgagee.   The policy contained a provision limiting Allstate's liability to Sherry's insurable interest.   It is consistent with Oklahoma's statutes, and is as follows:

> . . . Allstate . . . , to an amount not exceeding the limit of liability specified, does insure the Insured named in the Declarations and legal representatives, to the extent of the actual cash value of the property at the time of loss, but not exceeding . . . , nor in any event for more than the interest of the Insured, . . . .

On December 1, 1991, the home was destroyed by fire.   Allstate furnished Proof of Loss forms to Sherry.   About January 20, 1992, she returned the Proof of Loss to Allstate.   She claimed a loss for the value of the structure, but not for its contents.   Allstate took her sworn examination and also the sworn examination of Jack.   For reasons not readily apparent in this appeal, Allstate thought the circumstances of the fire were suspicious and caused an investigation to be made.

On April 2, 1992, Allstate advised Sherry, through her attorney, that it would pay Bank in full for all principal and interest due on its note and mortgage, but would not pay Sherry any additional sum of money because . . . Sherry's insurable interest was limited to the amount required to pay the balance due on the note and mortgage to Bank, and the payment to Bank satisfied [Allstates'] liability in full. Sherry contended she had the right to collect the balance of the policy because Jack's discharge in bankruptcy and his failure to hold her harmless on various debts (as listed in the Divorce Decree) caused her to be required to expend several thousand dollars in paying debts that Jack had been ordered to pay.

Sherry contends the [trial court] erred in holding her insurable interest in the home was limited to the amount due Bank on its note and mortgage. In effect, she contends Jack's failure to pay various debts, as ordered by the divorce court, gave her a security interest in the home. Applicable authority to support this contention has not been cited. In making her argument in support of her contentions, the holding of the Bankruptcy Court that Jack's obligation to her was dischargeable is not considered. If Jack received a discharge in bankruptcy, he would have no obligation to Sherry to pay debts. At the time of the hearing, in this case, the automatic stay, under bankruptcy laws, was in effect.

Sherry contends she executed and delivered a quit claim deed to Jack, which put the title to the home in his name, with the oral understanding that he would sell the home and pay their joint debts. This contention ignores the provision in the Divorce Decree ordering her to execute and deliver the deed, the provision in the Decree that it would constitute such a conveyance if she failed to do so, and the provision in the decree restraining her from claiming any interest in the home. In addition, the deed does not contain any reservation of any security interest. In addition, this contention does not consider the effect of [ Oklahoma real estate law] which requires a deed, mortgage, or conveyance of real estate or any interest in real estate . . . to be in writing and subscribed by the grantors.

Sherry contends Allstate is estopped from denying her payment of the full proceeds of the insurance policy (less the amount paid to Bank). Before estoppel may apply, the insurance policy must constitute a lawful contract. Contracts of insurance are valid and enforceable insofar as authorized by statute. Such contracts, not authorized by statute, have generally been held illegal and not enforceable because of public policy considerations and laws prohibiting gambling. Oklahoma statutes, as a prerequisite to validity of an insurance contract, require the beneficiary to have an insurable interest.

As pointed out in Allstate's brief, [Oklahoma insurance law] provides:

A. No insurance contract on property or of any interest therein or arising therefrom shall be enforceable as to the insurance except for the benefit of persons having an insurable interest in the things insured.

B. "Insurable interest" as used in this section means any actual, lawful, and substantial economic interest in the safety or preservation of the subject of the insurance free from loss, destruction, or pecuniary damage or impairment.

C. The measure of an insurable interest in property is the extent to which the insured might be damnified by loss, injury, or impairment thereof.

In Snethen v. Oklahoma State Union of the Farmers Educational And Co- operative Union of America, 664 P.2d 377 (Okl.1983), the Court . . . discussed the requirement of an "insurable interest". The Court said:

It is well settled that both the validity and enforceability of an insurance contract depend upon the presence of insurable interest in the person who purchased the policy. Considerations underlying the insurable interest concept are generally articulated in terms of policy (1) against allowing wagering contracts under the guise of insurance, (2) against fostering temptation to destroy the insured property in an effort to profit from it and (3) favoring limitation upon the sweep of indemnity contracts. . . .

While American jurisdictions generally agree with the public policy considerations that underl[ie] the necessity for an insurable interest, they stand divided on what constitutes an insurable interest. Two basic theories were evolved for measuring the nexus which must be present between the property and its insured for an insurable interest to attach. The literature refers to one of these as the "legal interest" and to the other as the "factual expectation" theory.

Sherry had no title, ownership, insurable interest, or other [legal] interest in the real property (the home) involved here. She had no factual expectation of an actual, lawful, substantial economic interest in Jack's general assets from which she would ever be satisfied.

The trial court correctly held that Sherry's "insurable interest" in the home was limited to the amount due to Bank on its note and mortgage.

## Comments and Questions

1. Did the court let Allstate off too easily? Should an insurance company have a responsibility to determine whether a party has an appropriate insurable interest before accepting premiums for the full face amount of the insurance policy? Or was it reasonable to make Shelly bear the risk that she would not be found to possess fully insurable interest once the property was destroyed? How does the court's approach square with the *contra proferentem* principle invoked in the preceding *State Farm* decision?

2. The insurable interest doctrine was initially based on a moral judgment that individuals should not enter into insurance contacts for speculative purposes, as well as on pragmatic considerations that such contracts present an acute moral hazard in that an insured party may be tempted to destroy the insured property in order to recover on the party's policy. Are these considerations still valid today? After all, in our modern economy, investors are permitted to speculate in futures and options contracts without having any underlying economic interests in these insurance-like contracts. Indeed, economists generally regard this sort of speculation as a valuable source of liquidity. Should we therefore allow insurance companies to underwrite traditionally uninsurable interests in order to broaden insurance pools and expand business opportunities?

*Problem 7-1*

The Joneses live in an economically depressed region of Pennsylvania. In 1990, they bought their current home for $100,000 and have ever since been insuring the property for its fair market value. Over the past few years, the home prices in their neighborhood have declined substantially, and now the Joneses estimate that their home's market value is less than $70,000, whereas it would cost them at least $125,000 to rebuild the house if it were destroyed. Can the Joneses insure the property up to its replacement cost? Should they be able to? Does the amount of outstanding balance due on the Joneses' mortgage matter?

---

Another distinguishing feature of insurance contracts is the manner in which they are marketed to the general public. Some insurance companies sell their policies directly, through their employees or the employees of affiliated agents. Other companies make use of independent agents, who offer policies from a variety of underwriters. The existence of separate system of licensed insurance agents adds a degree of complexity to the field. For an overview of the subject, see ALAN L. WIDISS, INSURANCE § 2.5 (1989). Our treatment of the matter, for present purposes, will be limited to the following brief case. Note, however, that the distinction between insurance underwriters and insurance agents will be important when we consider, in Chapter 16, the authority of banks in the United States to engage in insurance activities.

# Murphy v. Kuhn
## 660 N.Y.S.2d 371 (N.Y. 1997)

BELLACOSA, Judge.

The question for this case is whether an insurance agent should be liable to a former customer for tortious misrepresentation and breach of implied contract. The alleged wrongdoing is a failure of the defendant insurance agent to advise plaintiff Thomas Murphy as to possible additional insurance coverage needs. The theory of the lawsuit and the asserted duty is a special relationship and special level of advisory responsibility.

The Appellate Division affirmed an order of Supreme Court, which granted defendants' motion for summary judgment and dismissed the complaint. Plaintiffs appeal . . . .

Plaintiffs Thomas Murphy and Webster Golf Course, Inc. sued defendants Donald C. Kuhn, Kuhn & Pedulla Agency, Inc., and its predecessor Roman A. Kuhn Agency, alleging professional negligence and breach of implied contract. This dispute originates in a 1991 automobile accident in Florida involving Murphy's son. One person died and several others suffered serious injuries as a result of the accident. At that time, the title to the son's car was in his father's name and the personal insurance was placed under the commercial automobile policy covering Murphy's business, Webster Golf Course, Inc. After exhausting the $500,000 policy limit to settle the car accident claims, Thomas Murphy assertedly paid an additional $194,429.50 plus $7,500 in attorneys' fees. Then, he sued these defendants to recover the additional sums he had to pay personally.

Defendants began providing the property, casualty and liability insurance to plaintiffs in 1973 in connection with their golf business. Beginning in 1977, defendant Donald Kuhn also handled all of Murphy's personal insurance needs, providing him with both homeowners insurance and personal automobile coverage. In 1979, plaintiff Thomas Murphy and his partner, Edward Rieflin, completed their purchase of the Happy Acres Golf Course and formed Webster Golf Course, Inc. Happy Acres had been a client of the Roman A. Kuhn Agency since 1957.

In 1990, Kuhn placed personal automobile coverage for Murphy with The Hartford, as insurer. Later that year, Hartford notified Murphy that his coverage was in danger of cancellation due to the poor driving records of his children. Murphy then transferred the insurance covering his son's car, which was registered and titled in Murphy's name, from Murphy's personal policy to Webster Golf Course's commercial automobile insurance policy. Murphy testified at his deposition that it was his standard arrangement to place title and register his children's cars in his name. From 1984 until the time of the accident, the liability limits on the commercial policy were $250,000 per person and $500,000 total per accident. Murphy never requested higher liability coverage for his personal and family automobile insurance needs, which were subsumed within the commercial automobile liability policy.

Supreme Court concluded that, absent a request by the customer, an insurance agent "owes no continuing duty to advise, guide or direct the customer to obtain additional coverage." Therefore, acknowledging that on this record plaintiffs never specifically requested defendants to increase the liability limits on the commercial automobile policy, the court held that defendants owed no special duty of affirmative advisement to plaintiffs. The court also declined to adopt plaintiffs' "special relationship" theory.

Plaintiffs propose that insurance agents can assume or acquire legal duties not existing at common law by entering into a special relationship of trust and confidence with their customers. Specifically, plaintiffs contend that a special relationship developed from a long, continuing course of business between plaintiffs and defendant insurance agent, generating special reliance and an affirmative duty to advise with regard to appropriate or additional coverage.

Generally, the law is reasonably settled on initial principles that insurance agents have a common-law duty to obtain requested coverage for their clients within a reasonable time or inform the client of the inability to do so; however, they have no continuing duty to advise, guide or direct a client to obtain additional coverage (see, Wied v. New York Cent. Mut. Fire Ins. Co., 208 A.D.2d 1132, 1133, 618 N.Y.S.2d 467 . . . . . Notably, no New York court has applied plaintiffs' proffered "special relationship" analysis to add such continuing duties to the agent-insured relationship . . .

Recently, however, this Court recognized a special relationship in a commercial controversy, involving no generally recognized professional relationship (see, Kimmell v. Schaefer, 89 N.Y.2d 257, 260, 652 N.Y.S.2d 715, 675 N.E.2d 450). We held that the relationship between the parties "under the circumstances [there] required defendant to speak with care.". . . . Kimmell cautions, however, that "liability for negligent misrepresentation has been imposed only on those persons who possess unique or specialized expertise, or who are in a special position of confidence and trust with the injured party such that reliance on the negligent misrepresentation is justified." For example, "[p]rofessionals, such as lawyers and engineers, by virtue of their training and expertise, may have special relationships of confidence and trust with their clients, and in certain situations we have imposed liability for negligent misrepresentation when they have failed to speak with care" . . . ).

The Court concluded that given "the absence of obligations arising from the speaker's professional status" in the commercial context, "there must be some identifiable source of a special duty of care" in order to impose tort liability (id., at 264, 652 N.Y.S.2d 715, 675 N.E.2d 450). "The existence of such a special relationship may give rise to an exceptional duty regarding commercial speech and justifiable reliance on such speech" (id.). We determined, to be sure, that "[w]hether the nature and caliber of the relationship between the parties is such that the injured party's reliance on a negligent misrepresentation is justified generally raises an issue of fact" (id.). It is important to note that Kimmell is significantly distinguishable from the instant case, which involves an insurance agent- insured relationship and an alleged failure to speak. We therefore allude to Kimmell for its general relevance and disclaim any implication of a direct, precedential applicability in the insurance relationships context.

Even assuming the general applicability of the "special relationship" theory in the customer-agent automobile insurance coverage setting, we conclude that the relationship between these parties was insufficiently established to warrant or justify this case surviving a defense summary judgment motion. As a matter of law, this record does not rise to the high level required to recognize the special relationship threshold that might superimpose on defendants the initiatory advisement duty, beyond the ordinary placement of requested insurance responsibilities. Rather, the record in the instant case presents only the standard consumer-agent insurance placement relationship, albeit over an extended period of time. Plaintiffs' plight does not warrant transforming his difficulty into a new, expanded tort opportunity for peripheral redress. The record does not support plaintiffs' effort in this manner to shift to defendant insurance agent the customer's personal responsibility for initiating, seeking and obtaining appropriate coverage, without something more than is presented here.

We note in this respect that Murphy never asked Kuhn to increase the liability limits on the Webster Golf Course commercial automobile policy. In fact, there is no indication that Murphy ever inquired or discussed with Kuhn any issues involving the liability limits of the automobile policy. Such lack of initiative or personal indifference cannot qualify as legally recognizable or justifiable reliance. Therefore, there was no evidence of reliance on the defendant agent's expertise, as sharply distinguished from Kimmell (contrast, Kimmell v. Schaefer, supra, 89 N.Y.2d, at 264, 652 N.Y.S.2d 715, 675 N.E.2d 450).

The absence of reliance is further reflected in Murphy's deposition testimony that it was his standard procedure to simply register his children's cars in his name. Additionally, Murphy's deposition description of his relationship with Kuhn concerning the golf course's general insurance matters shows that he had not met personally with Kuhn to discuss the insurance needs of Webster Golf Course, Inc. for approximately 12 years preceding the accident in question.

Rather, his partner Rieflin was the one actively and personally involved in handling the insurance needs of the golf course.

We also note that Murphy's contention that he mistakenly believed that the commercial policy had a $1,000,000 liability limit on all covered vehicles can be given no weight in resolving this dispute on this theory. The liability coverage had remained the same since 1984 and Murphy's deposition testimony failed to establish the basis for his plainly unfounded assumption. Therefore, plaintiffs are not entitled to advance beyond the summary judgment stage of this lawsuit because they failed to establish the existence of a legally cognizable special relationship with their insurance agent in this standard set of circumstances.

Plaintiffs-appellants urge this Court to avoid generally absolving insurance agents from legal principles which subject other individuals to duties beyond those rooted in the common law. They overstate the concern and effect of this decision and the principle that emanates from it. Our decision today does not break any new ground and does not immunize insurance brokers and agents from appropriately assigned duties and responsibilities. Exceptional and particularized situations may arise in which insurance agents, through their conduct or by express or implied contract with customers and clients, may assume or acquire duties in addition to those fixed at common law. As with Kimmell, the issue of whether such additional responsibilities should be recognized and given legal effect is governed by the particular relationship between the parties and is best determined on a case-by-case basis (see, Kimmell v. Schaefer, 89 N.Y.2d 257, 264, 652 N.Y.S.2d 715, 675 N.E.2d 450, supra ).

Notably, other jurisdictions have recognized such an additional duty of advisement in exceptional situations where, for example, (1) the agent receives compensation for consultation apart from payment of the premiums (see, Sandbulte v. Farm Bur. Mut. Ins. Co., 343 N.W.2d 457, 464 [Iowa]; Nowell v. Dawn-Leavitt Agency, 127 Ariz. 48, 51, 617 P.2d 1164, 1168), (2) there was some interaction regarding a question of coverage, with the insured relying on the expertise of the agent (see, Trupiano v. Cincinnati Ins. Co., 654 N.E.2d 886, 889[Ind] [applying Michigan law] ); or (3) there is a course of dealing over an extended period of time which would have put objectively reasonable insurance agents on notice that their advice was being sought and specially relied on (see, Trotter v. State Farm Mut. Auto. Ins. Co., 297 S.C. 465, 377 S.E.2d 343). In these circumstances, insureds bear the burden of proving the specific undertaking (id.). The relationship established in the instant case does not rise to the level of these exceptional situations and we refrain from determining when the special relationship analysis may apply in the insurance context.

We do, however, take note that the uniqueness of customary and ordinary insurance relationships and transactions is manifested by "the absence of obligations arising from the speaker's professional status" with regard to the procurement of additional coverage (Kimmell v. Schaefer, supra, 89 N.Y.2d, at 264, 652 N.Y.S.2d 715, 675 N.E.2d 450). As stated, it is well settled that agents have no continuing duty to advise, guide, or direct a client to obtain additional coverage (see, Wied v. New York Cent. Mut. Fire Ins. Co., 208 A.D.2d 1132, 1133, 618 N.Y.S.2d 467, supra ). No doubt, therefore, public policy considerations will have to be weighed on the question of whether to override this settled principle by recognizing additional advisement duties on insurance agents and brokers (see, Farmers Ins. Co. v. McCarthy, 871 S.W.2d 82, 85-86 [Mo] ). But we do not reach that question here.

Insurance agents or brokers are not personal financial counselors and risk managers, approaching guarantor status (see, id.). Insureds are in a better position to know their personal assets and abilities to protect themselves more so than general insurance agents or brokers, unless the latter are informed and asked to advise and act (id.). Furthermore, permitting insureds to add such parties to the liability chain might well open flood gates to even more complicated and undesirable litigation. Notably, in a different context, but with resonant relevance, it has been observed that "[u]nlike a recipient of the services of a doctor, attorney or architect * * * the recipient of the services of an insurance broker is not at a substantial disadvantage to question the actions of the provider of services" (Video Corp. of America v. Frederick Flatto Assocs., 85 A.D.2d 448, 456, 448 N.Y.S.2d 498, mod 58 N.Y.2d 1026, 462 N.Y.S.2d 439, 448 N.E.2d 1350).

Accordingly, the order of the Appellate Division should be affirmed, with costs.

## Comments and Questions

1. Who was the principal for the Kuhn & Pedulla Agency? Thomas Murphy or the Hartford? Or both?

2. The *Murphy* decision is characteristic of a long line of judicial decisions revealing a reluctance on the part of courts to impose on insurance agents general disclosure obligations regarding opportunities to obtain additional coverage. As we will see when we explore the obligation of securities brokers in analogous contexts, judges have been more willing to craft detailed disclosure obligations for securities firms. See Chapter Ten, Section 2. Is there a good reason why insurance agents should be held to a lower standard of care? Is insurance less important than securities investments? Is there some reason to think insurance agents are less prone to ignore the best interest of their customers?

### Problem 7-2

Anna Smith is an independent insurance agent. Several years ago, the Joneses stopped by Ms. Smith's office to inquire about home-owners insurance. At the time, Mr. Jones expressed interest in acquiring an "umbrella policy," which would provide liability coverage in excess of that provided in a basic home-owners policy. Ms. Smith was unable to find an umbrella policy of the sort Mr. Jones desired, and so the Joneses obtained only home-owners insurance. For the past few years, Ms. Smith has sent the Joneses annual renewal notices for their home-owners policy, and each year they have renewed the policy without comment, sending Ms. Smith a check for the annual premium, from which she has deducted her commission before sending the balance of the payment to the company that underwrites the Joneses' policy.

Ms. Smith is about the send out the Joneses' renewal notice for the coming year. She has, however, just learned about an umbrella policy of the sort Mr. Jones had wanted. The policy is offered by a different insurance company than the one that currently underwrites the Joneses' home-owners insurance, and if the Joneses were to obtain an umbrella policy from this new company, they would also have to switch over their home-owners policy as well. Does Ms. Smith have to inform the Joneses of this new coverage option? What if the commissions that Ms. Smith would earn on the new policies are less than what she earns on the Joneses' current home-owners insurance? What if she also has concerns about the claims processing ability of the new company? What, if anything, does she have to tell the Joneses?

# Section 3.  The Regulation Of Insurance Company Solvency

Perhaps the most striking characteristic of the insurance regulation in the United States is the fact that the states retain primary responsibility for regulating most facets of the industry. In the previous chapter, we explored the historical origins of this regulatory structure. Now, we consider the practical significance of the structure. Here we focus our attention on two areas where the primacy of local regulation presents special problems. The first involves the disposition of failed insurance companies that operate on a national basis. The second concerns the coordinating role of the National Association of Insurance Commissioners (NAIC). As you read through these materials, consider the merits of a decentralized regulatory system in these contexts. Clearly, the structure increases administrative costs, but are there offsetting benefits of regulatory federalism?

## A.  Executive Life Insurance Company: A Case Study

Twenty years ago, Executive Life Insurance Company (ELIC) was a small and little-noticed life insurance company domiciled in California. In the 1980s, however, new management, led by Fred Carr, transformed ELIC and its New York affiliate:

As chief executive officer, Mr. Carr used [ELIC] to construct one of the largest insurance organizations in America in just 10 years. The numbers are staggering: Reported assets of Executive Life in California sky-rocked 1,578 percent from 1980 to 1990, and the assets of Executive Life in New York leapt 1,273 percent during the same period. By 1990, First Executive had become the 15th largest life insurer in the United States with combined assets exceeding $19 billion.

Mr. Carr and his associates achieved their heady success by turning the Executive Life companies into high-risk investment funds which obtained capital from the public under the guise of insurance policies, annuities, and guaranteed investment contracts. Risky investments in junk bonds and speculative real estate yielded very substantial short-term profits that enabled the Executive Life insurers to beat their competition in the insurance industry. They attracted hordes of policyholders who were delighted to earn generous rates of return equivalent to the investment markets, while maintaining their funds in the secure hands of State-regulated insurance companies. The obvious defect in this happy scenario was that the generous earnings propelling the First Executive empire were produced by businesses with inflated values that would easily falter.

During its heyday, First Executive amassed more than 60 percent of its insurance assets in the volatile and exceedingly risky junk bonds peddled by Michael Milken through the Drexel Burnham Lambert investment firm.  These bonds paid very high interest because they were issued and backed by marginal corporations, which could not qualify for the lower interest capital offered by traditional securities and bank loans.  When the junk bond market began to collapse precipitously in late 1989, gigantic write-downs in the investment portfolios at Executive Life in California triggered a policy redemption rush by worried customers.  The rush exposed the underlying financial vulnerabilities of First Executive, and sank the Executive Life insurance companies in 1991.

Wishful Thinking: A World View of Insurance Solvency Regulation, A Report by the Subcommittee on Oversight and Investigations of the House Committee on Energy and Commerce 19  (Oct. 1994).

ELIC's principal operating unit, the one domiciled in California, was placed into conservatorship on April 11, 1991.  The California Insurance Commissioner, who had statutory responsibility for overseeing rehabilitation of the firm, faced an immediate and daunting task.  The unit's accounts showed some $9.0 billion of policy and contract claims.  Of these liabilities, $1.8 billion were in the form of an innovative product known as municipal guaranteed investment contracts (or Muni-GIC's), and the balance were more traditional insurance products, including standard guarantee investment contracts (GICs) held by pension plans and individuals.  (We will examine litigation involving both of these liabilities shortly).  One of the Commissioner's primary problems was that the ELIC's remaining assets were worth much less than $9.0 billion when the firm failed.  Although many of the company's assets were hard to value -- particularly the junk bonds which were highly volatile at the time -- it appeared in the spring of 1991, that all of the firm's assets would be in the range of $5.0 to $6.0 billion.

By the fall of 1991, the Insurance Commissioner had developed a plan for resolving the ELIC conservatorship.  He explained the plan in the following correspondence:

September 6, 1991

To:     POLICYHOLDERS, ANNUITANTS, CONTRACT HOLDERS, OTHER CREDITORS AND INTERESTED PERSONS OF EXECUTIVE LIFE INSURANCE COMPANY, OF LOS ANGELES, CALIFORNIA

I wanted to let you know the status of our efforts to rehabilitate Executive Life Insurance Company (ELIC) . . . .

After a long series of negotiations, the first official bid from the company came from a group of French investors on August 8, 1991.  They agreed to purchase most of ELIC's assets and assume most of the policyholder and contract obligations which will provide approximately 81% of the ELIC contract value. . . . .

In an historic agreement of cooperation, the National Organization of Life and Health Insurance Guaranty Associations (NOLHGA) decided on August 27, 1991, that state guaranty associations would fund the remaining 19% to most contract values.  This means over 95% of the ELIC policyholders and contract holders will receive 100% of their original contract values. . . .

This agreement must be ratified by the individual guarantee associations. The California Life Guaranty Association has become the first to approve the agreement. This agreement would restore covered, allocated policyholders and contract holders (other than the Municipal-GICs) benefits to 100% of the ELIC contract account values for contracts up to the first $100,000. Contracts in excess of $100,0000 would also receive enhanced participations, including payments from a liquidating trust which will be created to carry out certain activities, including litigation designed to increase benefits to policyholders and contract holders. . . . . 　　　　　　　　　　　　　　　　　Sincerely,

　　　　　　　　　　　　　　John Garamendi
　　　　　　　　　　　　　　California Insurance Commissioner
　　　　　　　　　　　　　　Conservator of ELIC

　　　　　　　　　　　* * * * * * * * *

　　　　　　　　　　　January 29, 1992

To: Policyholders, Annuitants, Contract Holders, Other Creditors and Interested Persons of Executive Life Insurance Company, of Los Angeles, California

I am very happy to report that since my last communication with you we have made tremendous progress towards completing the sale of Executive Life. Last month, the Superior Court in Los Angeles approved my recommendation of [the French consortium] Altus/MAAF as the winning bidder in a vigorous competitive bidding process that saw eight different investor groups vying for the insurance company. . . . .As part of the sale Altus will pay $3.25 billion for the junk bond portfolio and other investors will contribute an additional $300 million to the new company, bringing the total infusion of capital to $3.55 billion. . . . .

The enclosed Rehabilitation/Liquidation Plan (the "Rehabilitation Plan") is the legal mechanism to accomplish the transition of Executive Life contracts to the new company established by Altus/MAAF, Aurora Natonal Life Assurance Corporation ("Aurora"). . . .

An important provision in the Rehabilitation Plan details how holders of Municipal Guaranteed Investment Contracts (Muni-GICs) should be paid. In our original proposal, we considered Muni-GICs to be Class 6 contracts, the same as general creditors under Insurance Code Section 1033. A higher priority, Class 5, was given to all other Executive Life policies and contracts. The Muni-GICs filed suit to challenge the position. The Superior Court held on November 15, 1991 that the bondholders [who benefit from the Muni-GICs] should receive the same treatment as other policyholders. We immediately appealed the decision and are awaiting a hearing date.

In the Rehabilitation Plan, we have recommended the if Muni-GICs are classified the same as insurance products, the account values of the Muni-GICs should be based on the purchase price of the bonds rather than their face value, which totals almost $2 billion. In order to provide equity and to avoid windfall profits, the account value of the Muni-Gics will reflect the price paid for the bonds purchased before the April 11, 1991 conservation proceedings, and the market price of the bonds on April 11, 1991 for bonds purchased after that date. It is our strong belief that bondholders should not receive a greater percentage of their actual investments than the insurance policyholders and annuitants.

If the Court of Appeal reverses the lower court and determines that Muni-GICs should be considered Class 6, insurance policyholder payments will rise from approximately 72 cents on the dollar to about 89 cents. This will primarily affect those policyholders and contract holders with account values over $100,000. . . . .

I realize this has been a difficult nine months for you, and I appreciate your patience and cooperation as we bring this complex process to a successful conclusion.

> Sincerely,
> John Garamendi
> California Insurance Commissioner
> Conservator of ELIC

---

Litigation over the Muni-GICs mentioned in the Commissioner's second letter lasted for several years. We will examine one opinion from the litigation shortly, but first some background on these instruments. ELIC designed the Muni-GICs for municipalities raising funds for public works projects of various sorts. After raising tax exempt funds through the sale of municipal bonds, the municipalities would place the funds with a trustee that would, in accordance with the provisions of a trust indenture, invest the funds in one of ELIC's customized Muni-GICs. The Muni-GICs typically paid a relatively high rate of interest, and allowed the indenture trustee to withdraw funds to make payments on the indenture's bonds and to cover drawdowns on the projects associated with the bonds. Since bonds financed in this manner were typically not general obligation bonds — that is, they were not guaranteed by the sponsoring municipality — losses on Muni-GICs were borne by holders of the municipal bonds. Thus bond holders were directly affected by the treatment of the Muni-GICs in ELIC's rehabilitation Plan.

The bondholders' most financially significant disagreement with the Commissioner was over the treatment of the Muni-GICs in ELIC's rehabilitation plan. For example, the bondholders claimed the Muni-GICs were entitled to Class 5 priority status, which would put them on a par with ELIC's more traditional insurance obligations. The Commissioner argued for Class 6 status, which would make the Muni-GICs subordinate to ELIC's insurance obligations and therefore unlikely to receive any payments from the conservatorship. In Texas Commerce Bank v. Garamendi, 11 Cal. App. 4th 460, 14 Cal. Rptr. 2d 854 (1992), the California Court of Appeal ruled that the Muni-GICs were entitled to Class 5 status because the instruments fell within the California insurance statute's definition of annuity. The Court rejected the Commissioner's attempts to distinguish Muni-GICs from traditional annuities on the grounds that the instruments were simply fixed-rate funding instruments unconnected to a human life. (Traditional annuity make payments to an individual, typically from retirement until death.)  Resolving the priority of Muni-GICs did not, however, end the litigation:

# Commercial National Bank v. Superior Court
## 14 Cal.App.4th 393,17 Cal.Rptr.2d 884  (1993)

EPSTEIN, Judge.

Immediately upon his appointment by the court as conservator of the [Executive Life Insurance Company ("ELIC")] estate on April 11, 1991, the [California Insurance] Commissioner proceeded to sequester and conserve the assets of the insolvent company. . . . Early in the insolvency proceedings, a dispute arose over the priority claim status of the eight [Municipal Bond Guarantee Contracts ("Muni-GIC's")] which had been purchased for a total sum of $1.8 billion.  In Texas Commerce Bank v. Garamendi, [11 Cal.App.4th 460, 14 Cal.Rptr.2d 854 (Nov. 30, 1992)], we held these instruments to be annuities and their holders to be entitled to class-5-priority status.

The Muni-GIC's were issued to banks that acted as indenture trustees for eight municipal entities.  Through these annuities, ELIC promised to make guaranteed, periodic accumulated interest payments to the trustee banks.  The indenture agreements with the municipal entities required the banks to purchase Muni-GIC's from ELIC with the proceeds of funds raised by the entities through the sale of municipal bonds.  The banks were required to transmit a part of the periodic annuity payments and special withdrawals from the Muni-GICs to the municipal entities, and, on their behalf, to pay all debts on a pro rata basis.

The result was that ELIC was the issuer and the trustee banks the policyholders of the Muni-GIC's.  The municipal entities were the sole intended third-party beneficiaries of these instruments, and the municipal bond purchasers were creditors of the municipal entities.

During the pendency of the Muni-GIC claim priority dispute, the Commissioner entertained bids for assumption of portions of ELIC's assets and liabilities through a rehabilitation plan.  This included sale of substantial portions of ELIC's "junk bond" portfolio, and a negotiated rehabilitation plan.  The successful bidder was New California Life Holdings, Inc. (Newco), a California insurance company.

The rehabilitation plan provides for transfer of essentially all liabilities and assets of insolvent ELIC to Aurora National Life Insurance Company (Aurora), a subsidiary that Newco acquired and recapitalized to effect the plan.  The present value of ELIC assets to be transferred is estimated at $7.2 billion or more, but no adjudication of the precise value has been made.  In addition to the transferred assets of ELIC, Aurora will have access to an additional $300 million capital infusion now held in trust by another Newco subsidiary, Altus.

The plan also incorporates benefits under an Enhancement Agreement negotiated through the National Organization of Life and Health Insurance Guaranty Associations.  Under that agreement, the guarantee associations of 43 states will supplement the rehabilitation plan with substantial assets for the benefit of insurance contracts which these associations are otherwise obligated to cover under the laws of their respective states.  The plan deems this contribution as fulfilling the statutory obligations of the associations to their respective covered policyholders.

Aurora will assume liability for all ELIC insurance contracts and will issue restructured insurance contracts to owners of ELIC contracts who agree to participate in the plan. Aurora will make lump-sum "liquidation" cash payments to contract holders who elect not to accept a restructured contract. The plan provides all policyholders the right to opt out, but it is designed to discourage that election. . . .

The value of each restructured contract for purposes of fixing its alternative liquidation cash-out payment is obtained by multiplying the account value by the "liquidation percentage." That percentage, in turn, is fixed by dividing the value of ELIC's distributable assets as of the April 11, 1991 insolvency date by the total account values of all contracts. The trial court has adjudicated the value of the distributable assets on April 11, 1991 to be $5,044 million. Based on that, the liquidation value of a restructured contract will be about 72 percent of its value for purposes of benefits as a continuing Aurora restructured contract.

While there was extensive expert opinion testimony about the valuation methods used in the plan, and about alternative methods, there were few significant disputes as to the material facts. The principal dispute is over a legal issue: whether the valuation methods used are arbitrary and improperly discriminatory . . . .

### The Two-Tier System

The central issue in this litigation is how policyholder accounts are to be valued for purposes of calculating the terms of restructured policies and the amount of lump-sum payments to be made to those who choose not to accept those policies.

In the case of Muni-GIC's, and for them alone, the plan sets up a valuation system that disregards the actual policyholders and the amounts they paid to purchase their annuities. This is the "two-tier" system, and it is the basis of the first challenge to the plan that we discuss.

The assumption of the two-tier system is that the trustee banks that purchased and that hold the Muni-GIC's, and to which they were issued, are not policyholders. Instead, the system looks through the banks and the municipalities that furnished the funds to buy the policies, to the current owners of the municipal bonds issued to raise funds used to purchase the annuities.[6] The valuation is not based on the amount raised from the sale of municipal bonds for purchase of the annuities or on what ELIC received for the annuities, but on what each bondholder of record actually paid for bonds on the primary or secondary market, if the acquisition was on or before the April 11, 1991 insolvency date. For purchases after that, the plan uses the market value of the bonds on April 11, 1991.

Stated in another way, the system disregards the $1.8 billion actually paid to ELIC for the Muni-GIC annuities, and looks instead to the out-of-pocket amounts paid by persons who were bondholders of record on April 11, 1991, and to the market price on that date for bondholders who purchased bonds thereafter.

---

[6]    For that reason, this aspect of the plan is alternatively called the "look through" system. The plan uses the term "Nominated Account Value" to describe the aggregate account value established by the system, apparently on the theory that the amount paid for the municipal bonds, originally or on the secondary market, "nominates" (i.e., fixes) the amount to be used in the valuation formula.

The effect of disregarding the premiums actually realized by ELIC is significant. It is undisputed that a large number of the municipal bond owners purchased their positions on the secondary market at prices below, and in some cases substantially below, the par-value issuance price. Devaluing the Muni-GIC's reduces the amount to be paid or credited to their owners, either in benefits or in opt-out payments. The money realized by this devaluation increases the value of other policies relative to the Muni-GIC's.

The Commissioner argues that rehabilitation proceedings are equitable in nature and that the plan is fair because it prevents profit-taking by those who purchased bonds for less than a par consideration. He also asserts that statutory requirements for recognition of consideration and ratable distribution are satisfied by focusing on the out-of-pocket amounts paid by the bondholders.

We cannot accept the two-tier approach as valid. It is based on an unjustified fiction, and it is not supported by law or reason.

Its most obvious infirmity is that it treats the municipal bondholders as "claimants" and "policyholders." They are neither. It also refers to the out- of-pocket payments for the bonds (or the market price on April 11, 1991 for bonds purchased after that date) as the "consideration" for the Muni-GIC's. They are not.

Section 1023 controls what must be shown for a creditor or policyholder claim to be allowed against the estate of the insolvent insurer. The statute requires that a claim based on a contractual obligation declare that the amount claimed is "justly owing from such person [the insolvent insurer] to the claimant" and state "the particulars thereof, and the consideration paid therefor." It is evident that section 1023 means consideration paid by or on behalf of the insured for the insurance contract, not consideration paid in some other transaction by parties not in privity with the insurer.

There can be no serious dispute that the record owners of the municipal bonds issued in 1985 and 1986 to fund the 1986 ELIC Muni-GIC's have no privity of contract with the insolvent insurer and did not pay section 1023 "consideration" to ELIC for the Muni-GIC's.

In Texas Commerce Bank v. Garamendi, supra, 11 Cal.App.4th 460, 14 Cal.Rptr.2d 854, we explained in substantial detail what constitutes an insurance annuity under section 101. We concluded that the 1986 ELIC Muni-GIC's are entitled to class 5 "policyholder" claim status against the ELIC estate because they qualify as insurance annuities under section 101. In arriving at this conclusion we examined the relationship between the Muni-GIC's and the underlying "indenture agreements" between the respective trustee banks and municipal entities.

Under the provisions of the Muni-GIC's, ELIC's only contractual obligations were to the trustee banks, as owners, and to the underlying municipal entities, which were designated in the GICs as the only intended third-party beneficiaries. The very terms of the Muni-GIC's state that the indenture trustees are the legal owners of those annuities. The Muni-GIC's expressly disclaim any intent to create any other third-party beneficiary or contractual obligation on the part of ELIC. While the underlying bonds were offered to the public with the representation that the municipal entities' obligations would be backed by the security of Muni-GIC's, this did not create a policyholder status in the bondholders or a contractual relationship between bond purchasers and ELIC.

The circumstance that the indenture agreements between the municipal entities and the bank indenture trustees require the banks to pay a portion of the Muni-GIC periodic payments to bondholders for accruing interest on the bonds, and generally subject the agreements to insolvency and bankruptcy laws, does not abrogate the legal status of ELIC as insurer, the trustee banks as the sole Muni-GIC policyholders, or the municipal entities as the only third-party beneficiaries under the indentures.

The requirements of section 1023 also are inconsistent with provisions in the plan that municipal bondholders are entitled to share ratably with class 5 priority claimants. Even if bondholders somehow could qualify as claimants on the theory that ELIC owed a debt to the municipal entities that the bondholders could reach, they would be, at best, class 6 general creditors, not entitled to share ratably or at all with the class 5 claimants.[7]

Besides its inconsistency with section 1023, the legal fiction that bondholders are policyholders also is inconsistent with the rationale of equitable distribution required by the controlling statutes and by the Carpenter rationale.

Sections 1025, 1033 and 1057, read together, manifest the principle that the insolvency trustee has a fiduciary duty to effect a pro rata distribution to all allowed policyholder claimants. Section 1025 controls the allowance of unliquidated claims, but requires that such claims, once proved and allowed, "... shall share ratably with other claims of the same class in all subsequent distributions." Section 1033 controls liquidation preferences of allowed claims. Its subdivision (a)(5) gives the same claim priority to "all claims of policyholders of an insolvent insurer that are not covered claims." Section 1057 provides that in insurance insolvency proceedings the Commissioner is deemed to be the trustee for the benefit of all creditors and other persons interested in the estate.

The principle embodied in sections 1023, 1033 and 1057 precludes the Commissioner from disregarding insurance contracts or the policyholders who filed claims based on those contracts. It also precludes him from reducing the value of those contracts in order to achieve objectives extraneous to the entitlements of the policy owners.

In fact and in law, the Muni-GIC's, not the municipal bonds, are the policies; the trustee banks, not the bondholders, are the claimants; and the $1.8 billion paid to ELIC by the banks, not the prices paid by bondholders for their bonds, is the "consideration paid" within the meaning of section 1023.

The discrimination against Muni-GIC policyholders by the two-tier system is manifest. They are the only group as to whom the actual purchase price paid for an insurance product is

---

[7]    We note, also, that the Commissioner's position that bondholders are policyholders is inconsistent with the position taken by the Commissioner in Texas Commerce Bank v. Garamendi, supra, 11 Cal.App.4th at p. 482, 14 Cal.Rptr.2d 854. In that litigation, which was pending during the briefing in this case, the Commissioner put forward the rationale that Muni-GIC's did not qualify as annuities under section 101 because they were sold to banks and had no human annuitants. That position is inconsistent with the argument he now makes that the banks and the municipalities should be "looked through" to find the true annuitants--the bondholders--many of whom the Commissioner acknowledges to be individual persons.

disregarded. We have pointed out that the use of this system seriously disadvantages Muni-GIC policyholders relative to other policyholders.

What is left is the claim that the authority to impose a "two-tier" system may be implied from the equitable nature of insurance insolvency proceedings.

It is not disputed that insurance insolvency proceedings are special proceedings controlled by statutory provisions requiring fairness with respect to allowed claims within the same claim priority class. But no authority has been cited and none has been found conferring discretion to the superior court to approve a valuation scheme that disregards the very insurance policies upon which claims were filed and approved, and disregards the legal owners of the policies who actually paid consideration for their contracts to the insolvent insurer and filed timely claims against the insolvent insurer. . . .

The "equity" argument is based in large part, if not entirely, on the notion that speculators who purchased municipal bonds at prices less than their par issuance value should not be allowed to profit. There is no showing or even an argument that any of the bond transactions are voidable or illegal in any way. The usual rule is that the buyer of a bond or similar instrument of debt is at least entitled to exercise the right of the seller, into whose shoes the buyer has stepped. There is nothing to suggest that this rule does not apply to bondholders who purchased bonds on the secondary market. Indeed, if it did not, there would scarcely be a secondary market.

The two-tier system vitiates the legal ownership rights of the trustee banks and diminishes by millions of dollars the account values of the Muni-GIC's. This indirectly diminishes the amount of ELIC funds that might ultimately be distributed to the legal owners of the Muni-GIC's and transmitted by them to the issuing municipal entities and their creditors, the current bondholders (including those who bought at par-value issuance prices or higher). Moreover, it does nothing to reimburse an original bond purchaser who sold at a distressed price.

We find nothing equitable in a system that disregards the very insurance policies upon which claims were filed and approved, disregards the legal owners of the policies who paid for them, and simply redirects a part of their entitlement for reasons unrelated to effectuation of the rehabilitation plan. . . . . .

### The Liquidation Valuation Date

The final issue we determine is whether the date ELIC conservatorship proceedings were commenced (April 11, 1991) is an appropriate date for setting the value of the distributable assets of the insolvent insurer that opting-out policyholders will share.

The selection of the April 11, 1991 conservatorship date, rather than a date closer to the effective date of the rehabilitation plan, relegates opting-out policyholders to share a fund acknowledged by all parties to be billions of dollars less than the value of the ELIC assets when the rehabilitation plan was approved, on July 31, 1992. The value of ELIC's assets as of April 11, 1991 was adjudicated by respondent to be $5,044 million. The parties dispute the value of the assets at present, but it is agreed that the estate has substantially appreciated (partly due to cessation of payments to most general creditors and reduced interim benefit payments to policyholders) and may amount to $7.6 billion.

The liquidation valuation date is important because it determines the amount of ELIC assets available for pro rata distribution among opting-out policyholders. Consequently, it also determines the amount of ELIC assets available to Aurora for purposes of carrying on the business of ELIC through the restructured policies of the opting-in policyholders. A calculation based on the liquidation value of the insolvent estate as of the date of implementation of the rehabilitation plan would increase the portion of ELIC assets available to opt-out policyholders and decrease the portion transferred to Aurora.

The Commissioner and Aurora contend that the April 11, 1991 date set by the plan is authorized by section 1019 and supported by equitable considerations. They also contend that setting the valuation date is a matter within the broad discretion conferred upon the Commissioner, acting as rehabilitator, and upon the superior court by section 1043 and the police power of the state.

We conclude that the valuation date selected cannot be supported.

Section 1019 provides: "Upon the issuance of an order of liquidation under section 1016, the *rights and liabilities* of any such person [the insurer in liquidation] and of creditors, policyholders, shareholders and members, and all other persons interested in its assets ... shall, *unless otherwise directed by the court*, be fixed as of the date of the entry of the order...." (Emphasis added.)

The Commissioner and Aurora read the section 1019 reference to "rights and liabilities" as including the determination of the total value of the distributable assets of the insolvent insurer for purposes of liquidation distribution. They urge that the statute's reference to a court order ("unless otherwise directed by court") confers discretion on the court to select either the date of the liquidation or any other date for the valuation. They conclude that section 1019 authorizes a rehabilitator under section 1043 to select any liquidation valuation date for purposes of determining how much is available for distribution to policyholders opting-out of the rehabilitation. . . . .

Use of the insolvency date provides an unrealistic result because, in most situations, significant time will pass from the date of the conservation order to the actual liquidation or rehabilitation distribution. If the estate appreciates after the conservation order and straight liquidation is ultimately necessary (when a rehabilitation plan fails or when rehabilitation is not a viable alternative), valuing the estate as of the conservation date will not yield the total net value of the estate available for distribution to claimants. Conversely, if the estate value decreases after entry of the conservation order, valuation of the estate assets as of the date of the conservation order yields a value in excess of that actually available to claimants upon liquidation or rehabilitation distribution. In either case, a second valuation as of the distribution date would be required.

Calculation of the "liquidation" value of assets as of the distribution date of a rehabilitation plan is more functional. It pragmatically fixes total distributable asset value as of the very date the liquidation distribution is actually to occur. No second calculation is required to account for interim fluctuation in the value of the distributable assets. . . . .

The Commissioner and Aurora also contend that April 11, 1991, is the appropriate "liquidation" valuation date for the insolvent insurer's assets because, since that date, the efforts of the Commissioner have been directed toward effecting a rehabilitation plan providing continuation of policy benefits to ELIC policyholders and greater recovery than could have been realized in a straight liquidation pursuant to section 1016.

From this they argue that policyholders who elect not to participate in the section 1043 rehabilitation plan, which was formulated by the Commissioner and approved by respondent approximately 14 months after commencement of the conservation proceedings, are not entitled to share in the accumulated value of the insolvency estate during that period. Instead, the plan would treat policyholders who elect not to accept restructured insurance contracts as if no rehabilitation plan were ever effected. They are not permitted to share in either the benefits or the burdens of the rehabilitation.

In contrast, it is argued, policyholders who agree to accept restructured policies under the plan deserve to have their restructured policy benefits calculated on the basis of the total value of the estate as of the effective date of the rehabilitation plan (estimated to be approximately $2 to $3 billion greater than the April 11, 1991, value).

The problem with this rationale is that it assumes that policyholders had a choice at the time the assets of ELIC were taken over on April 11, 1991. The fact is that, with very limited exceptions, all ELIC policyholders were compelled to wait over 14 months while the rehabilitation plan was being formulated and offered for court approval. They are still waiting. It is only when the plan is known that policyholders can intelligently determine whether to opt in or opt out. In the meantime, all policyholders were subjected to the same risk that the ELIC estate would depreciate in value by the time a plan was formulated and approved. There is no rational basis to penalize policyholders who are dissatisfied with the eventual plan on the theory that they are ungrateful dissidents who bore no risk of depreciation of the estate and deserve no share of the accumulations.

## Comments and Questions

1. The Commissioner's proposed valuation technique was intended to prevent holders of municipal bond from receiving windfall profits on their investments. Was this a legitimate concern? Would you recommend the California insurance statutes be amended to incorporate the Commissioner's position? What effect would such an amendment have on future insolvencies? The second issue considered in this case — the valuation date of ELIC's assets — also had implications for bondholders, as well as any other claimant of the conservatorship that was not fully protected by state guarantee funds. As a matter of public policy, should these claimants participate in the performance of conservatorship assets after the receivership has been declared? Or should the state agencies charged with supervising the receivership bear the risks from any increase or decrease in asset values? How is this issue resolved in the disposition of failed banks?

2. In certain respects, the rehabilitation proceedings of insolvent insurance companies such as ELIC resemble those we studied for depository institutions. Once again, the provisions of the federal bankruptcy code do not apply; rather specialized government agencies are responsible for the rehabilitation or liquidation of the entity. In addition,

government guaranty funds, analogous to the FDIC, protect eligible claimants from loss. (In ELIC's case, these guarantees typically did not extend to Muni-GICs.) Moreover, as the ELIC case illustrates, the preferred disposition technique for failed insurance companies is to transfer the failed entity's assets and liabilities to an existing or newly created firm to ensure continuity of operations. (This is similar to the purchase and assumption transaction in the failed bank context.)

Where insurance company resolution procedures differ from the depository institution practices is in the number of organizations involved. For banks and thrifts, the FDIC serves as both receiver and guaranty fund. In the insurance context, these functions are divided. In ELIC's case, for example, the California Insurance Commissioner served as conservator of the failed entity, but a collection of state guaranty funds indemnified eligible claimants for their coverage shortfalls. The California insurance fund would typically cover policyholders resident in that state, but out-of-state policyholders would ordinarily have seek indemnification from their own jurisdiction's guaranty fund. This network of guarantees considerably complicates insurance company insolvencies. As the ELIC case illustrates, all affected guaranty funds typically must sign off on final rehabilitation plans. Often there is uncertainty as to which state's guarantee fund covers a particular policy. (For example, which state covers a life insurance for a person who was a Minnesota resident when the policy was purchased ten years ago, but for the last five years has been living in Florida?) There is also considerable variation in the amount of guarantees offered in different states. For example, whereas California covers life insurance contracts up to $100,000, Pennsylvania guarantees comparable policies up to $300,000. See Unisys Corp. v. Pennsylvania Life & Health Insurance Guaranty Ass'n, 667 A.2d 1199 (Pa. Commonw. Ct. 1995). States even take different positions with respect to what kind of policies are covered, as the following case illustrates.

# Arizona Life & Disability Insurance Guaranty Fund v. Honeywell, Inc.
927 P.2d 806 (Ariz. Ct. App. Div. 1996), *rev'd*, 945 P.2d 805 (Ariz. 1997)

The Arizona Life and Disability Insurance Guaranty Fund ("the Fund") filed an action for declaratory relief in superior court seeking a declaration that it was not obligated to cover losses suffered by an employee retirement plan operated by Honeywell, Inc. . . . The issue presented is whether the Fund must assure payments by an insurer which had entered into Guaranteed Investment Contracts ("GIC's")[1] with the plan trustee.

---

[1]    The definition of a GIC varies. Recent Arizona legislation defined the term "Guaranteed Investment Contract" as

an investment contract, funding agreement or guaranteed interest contract in which an insurance company agrees to guarantee a fixed or variable rate of interest or a future payment that is based on an index or any other similar criteria and that is payable at a predetermined date on monies that are deposited with the insurance company without regard to the continuance of human life.

## I.

Honeywell is a Delaware corporation with its principal place of business in Minnesota. It operates manufacturing and research facilities in various locations in Arizona. Honeywell sponsors employee retirement plans for its employees. The assets of Honeywell's employee retirement plan are held in trust and are managed by the trustee.

Honeywell's employees voluntarily participated in the retirement plan. Employees elected to deduct a designated percentage from their pay to be invested on their behalf. Employees could select from among several different investment programs.

More than 7,000 of Honeywell's Arizona employees selected what was designated the "fixed income" or "protected interest" option. For those employees who selected this option, the trustee invested approximately 21 million dollars with the Executive Life Insurance Company ("ELIC"). ELIC was a California insurance corporation authorized to do business in Arizona.

The trustee purchased four GIC's from ELIC in January and April of 1988. The four contracts were substantially similar. Each named the trustee as the owner of the contract. As owner, the trustee was entitled to "exercise every contract right and enjoy every contract provision without the consent of any [Honeywell employee retirement plan] participant."

The trustee deposited a specified amount, either in a lump sum or in installments, with ELIC. Each GIC issued by ELIC provided a guaranteed interest rate on the deposit. Each GIC had a set maturity date at which time ELIC was obligated to pay the full "fund value." "Fund value" was defined in the contracts as "the sum of all deposits, less any withdrawals and scheduled payments, plus interest earned at the guaranteed rate...." Each GIC provided for annual payments of accrued interest to the trustee. Each GIC also provided that the full fund value was to be paid not in one installment but in a specified number of yearly installments.

Deductions from the fund value of the GIC's were allowed without penalty under specified conditions. Each GIC contained what we will refer to as "payout provisions":

> The Owner may direct [ELIC] to purchase an individual annuity contract for a participant before the retirement date. [ELIC] will withdraw the cost of annuity benefits for the participant on the date it withdraws the amount. The owner may also withdraw all or part of the fund value to provide for plan benefits, in accordance with the [Honeywell employee retirement plan's] provisions.[5]

If funds were withdrawn before the contract maturity date, interest payments on the amounts withdrawn ceased. Although the trustee could have withdrawn funds from the ELIC GIC's to purchase annuities on behalf of Honeywell's employees, it is undisputed that it made no such withdrawals.

Upon retirement, a plan participant could select three types of annuities: a life annuity, an annuity covering the participant for life with the remainder to a beneficiary, or a joint and

---

A.R.S. § 20-208 (Supp. 1995).

[5]   Honeywell's retirement plan allowed for distribution of retirement benefits upon retirement, disability, death or termination of employment.

survivor annuity.[6] When the trustee purchased annuities for retiring employees, it purchased the annuities from other insurance companies.[7] However, if a retiring employee did not wish to select an annuity, Honeywell's retirement plan allowed several other options, including a lump-sum distribution, a deferred lump-sum distribution, and payment over a term of years.

When an employee died, Honeywell's retirement plan provided three options for the surviving beneficiary. The survivor could request full payment of the dollar value of the deceased employee's accrued benefits in a lump sum, payment over a term of years, or payment in the form of an annuity to provide retirement income for the life of the beneficiary.

## II.

Because the issue in this case depends on whether Arizona's guaranty fund statute covers guaranteed investment contracts, we begin with an analysis of the relevant statutory provisions.

In 1977, the Arizona Legislature established the Life and Disability Guaranty Fund. The legislation was patterned after a model act developed by the National Association of Insurance Commissioners.

Although no statement of intent was adopted by the Arizona Legislature, the drafters of the model act wrote that the purpose of such a guaranty fund is "to protect policy-owners, insureds, beneficiaries, annuitants, payees and assignees against losses . . . which might otherwise occur due to an impairment or insolvency of an insurer."

Under the Arizona statutes, all member insurers are required to be members of the Fund as a condition of their authority to transact insurance in Arizona. A.R.S. § 20-683(A) (1990). All costs, expenses and liabilities of the Fund are paid from assessments levied against the member insurers. A.R.S. § 20-683(C) (1990).

When a non-Arizona insurer becomes impaired, the Fund is obligated to

1.     Guarantee, assume or reinsure . . . the covered policies of residents.

2.     Assure payment of the contractual obligations of the impaired insurer to residents [and]

3.     Provide such monies, pledges, notes, guarantees or other means as are reasonably necessary to discharge such duties . . . .

A.R.S. § 20-685(D) (Supp.1995).

However, the Fund's obligations are limited to certain kinds of insurance, namely:

to direct life insurance policies, disability insurance policies, annuity contracts and contracts supplemental to life and disability insurance policies and annuity contracts issued to residents of this state by persons authorized to transact insurance in this state. . . .

---

[6]     The GIC's contracts provided that, once the trustee applied for "an individual retirement annuity contract ... [t]he contract will be owned by the [employee retirement plan] participant, and will specify the dates and amounts of payments...."

[7]     If the retiring employee selected the annuity option, the retirement plan provided that the trustee would select the insurance company from which the annuity would be purchased.

A.R.S. § 20-682(A) (Supp.1995). The question of the Fund's obligation to cover the losses suffered by Honeywell's employee retirement plan after ELIC's liquidation depends on whether the GIC's are included in section 20-682 as "annuity contracts ... issued to residents of this state. . . ."

The first question is whether the GIC's were "issued to residents of this state." The Fund argues that they were issued to the non-resident trustee. While the trustee was legal owner of the GIC's, the equitable owners were the beneficiaries of the retirement plan trust. Many of the beneficiaries were Arizona employees of Honeywell. The contracts were "issued to" Arizona residents even though the trustee held legal title. See Unisys Corp. v. Pennsylvania Life and Health Ins. Guar. Ass'n, 667 A.2d 1199, 1204 (Pa.Commw.Ct.1995) (resident employees protected under Pennsylvania's Guaranty Fund even if owner of GIC's was the trustee of the employee benefit plan). But see Bennet v. Virginia Life, Accident and Sickness Ins. Guar. Ass'n, 251Va. 382, 468 S.E.2d 910, 913 (1996) (GIC's were issued to plan trustee, not plan participants, and were owned by trustee).

We agree with Honeywell that the Fund's interpretation of the phrase "issued to residents" leads to anomalous results. It would be possible under the Fund's construction for employees who are residents of other states to invoke the protection of Arizona's fund merely because an Arizona resident was trustee of their retirement plan. That would expose the Fund to coverage of benefits owed to unknown numbers of non-Arizonans, based merely on the selection of an Arizonan as trustee. On the other hand, the Fund's interpretation would deny coverage to Arizona employees merely because their trustee was not a resident of this State. That result would disserve the legislative purpose, which is to protect the interests of resident policyholders and insureds from the consequences of insurers' impairment.

[The next question is whether the ELIC GIC's are "annuity contracts."] The Fund statutes do not define the term, but elsewhere the term "Annuities" is defined. That term

> encompasses all agreements to make periodic payments ... where the making or continuance of all or some of a series of such payments, or the amount of such payment, is dependent upon the continuance of human life.

A.R.S. § 20-254.01 (1990).

Honeywell contends that the GIC's were annuities for two reasons. First, it argues that the GIC's themselves are annuities because they provided that ELIC would make life-contingent periodic payments. Second, Honeywell argues that the payout provisions requiring ELIC to issue an annuity to a Honeywell employee on the trustee's request satisfies the definition of annuity. We disagree with both contentions.

The GIC's themselves are not annuities because payments under the GIC's are not life-contingent. Under the terms of the GIC's, the trustee deposited specified sums with ELIC. ELIC then agreed to pay the fund value -- accrued interest and principal -- in yearly installments. Honeywell argues that these yearly installments constituted "periodic payments" as contemplated by A.R.S. section 20-254.01. Honeywell also contends that these payments were "dependent upon the continuance of human life" because the GIC's provided that amounts could be withdrawn from the fund value if a Honeywell employee died.

Honeywell's claim that the GIC's were life-contingent rests on a part of the retirement plan. The plan allowed for distribution of benefits upon the death of the employee. The GIC's in turn accommodated the plan provision by allowing the trustee to withdraw all or part of the fund value to provide for plan benefits, including the distribution upon death. Honeywell argues that the periodic payments of the fund value to the trustee were life contingent because -- if an employee died -- the trustee could make withdrawals to pay plan benefits. If this occurred, then some of ELIC's payments to the trustee would depend on the continuance of a human life.

The death benefit payout provision does not make the GIC's themselves annuities. Arizona's definition of annuities requires that some or all of the payments from the financial institution to the annuitant "*is* dependent upon the continuance of human life." A.R.S. § 20-254.01 (1990) (emphasis added). Honeywell's interpretation of the statute would require us to hold that a contract is an annuity if the making or amount of the payments "may" depend on the continuance of human life, or if the payments "potentially" depend upon the continuance of human life. ELIC's payments were not affected by the death of an employee alone, but were affected only if the trustee also elected to pay the employee's benefits by a withdrawal from the GIC. This further condition means that payments under the GIC's did not depend on the continuance of human life.

Because the GIC's themselves were not life-contingent, they resembled bank certificates of deposit more than annuities. Indeed, Honeywell's description of the GIC's to its employees represented that the GIC's were similar to bank investments at a guaranteed interest rate. In explaining the fixed income fund, Honeywell wrote that "[t]he Fixed Income Fund invests in insurance company investment contracts, bank investment contracts, and money market investments." It also noted:

> The Fund assets are invested primarily in insurance company investment contracts, which are issued by insurance companies and are usually for substantial amounts of money.... The Plan agrees to invest money with the insurance company for a fixed time, usually one to five years. In return, *the insurance company agrees to pay a fixed rate of interest and return the principal upon maturity of the contract.*
>
> *Bank investment contracts are similar to insurance company investment contracts except they are offered by banks rather than insurance companies.*

(Emphasis added). Although Honeywell's characterization of the trustee's investments in GIC's is not dispositive, it does suggest that GIC's are analogous to bank certificates of deposit, not to annuities.

Honeywell cites Board of Trustees of the Maryland Teachers & State Employees Supplemental Retirement Plans v. Life & Health Ins. Guar. Corp., 335 Md. 176, 642 A.2d 856 (1994) for its argument. The issue in Board of Trustees was whether GIC's sold by ELIC to the trustee of the state employee retirement plan were covered policies under Maryland's guaranty fund provisions.

Under Maryland law, the provisions of the guaranty fund law were applicable to "direct life insurance policies, health insurance policies, annuity contracts, and contracts supplemental to ... annuity contracts issued by persons authorized to transact insurance in this State." 642 A.2d at 858 (quoting Md.Code. Ann. Ins. § 522(1) (1957)). The Maryland Fund's obligations when a foreign insurer became impaired were the same as the obligations of the Arizona Fund when a foreign insurer is impaired. See A.R.S. § 20- 685(D) (Supp.1995). Maryland law further defined annuity as

> all agreements to make periodical payments where the making or continuance of all or some of a series of such payments, or the amount of any such payment, is dependent upon the continuance of human life.

Board of Trustees, 642 A.2d at 859 (quoting Md.Code Ann. Ins. § 65 (1957)).

The court in Board of Trustees addressed the Guaranty Fund's argument that the payout provisions in the GIC's were not life-contingent. In rejecting this argument, the court wrote:

> ELIC could be called upon, whenever a participant died, to pay its pro rata share of that participant's account in the Plan. This amount would be the initial value of the share together with interest at the guaranteed rate, compounded daily. The actual return which ELIC might have realized on its investment of the premium deposits . . . as of the times of demands for payments generated by death or illness of participants, could have been below the amount which ELIC had promised to pay the Board. Thus, ELIC's assumption of the economic risk was life-contingent. Indeed, ELIC's contractual assumption also included the risk, however remote, that a catastrophe or epidemic would result in the deaths of large numbers of participants in a relatively brief span of time.

Board of Trustees, 642 A.2d at 861.

We disagree with the conclusion in Board of Trustees that the death benefit payout provision makes the GIC's themselves life-contingent. The court in Board of Trustees noted that ELIC could be called upon to pay sums out of the fund value of the GIC's if an employee died. The very rationale in that case was that it was sufficient that ELIC's payments were potentially life- contingent. We do not agree that the definition of annuity under Arizona law can be read to include an arrangement that makes the life-contingent nature of the periodic payments speculative.

The court in Board of Trustees also relied heavily on considerations not present in this case. First, the court relied on administrative treatment of GIC's as covered annuities.[12] Maryland's Insurance Commissioner had approved GIC policy forms, evidencing an administrative interpretation in favor of coverage. Id. at 863. Also, administrative regulations adopted pursuant to Maryland's guaranty fund law defined group annuities as contracts "*purporting* to provide annuity benefits to more than one person." Id. at 865 (emphasis in original). Second, the court cited evidence of legislative acquiescence to the administrative decision to include GIC's in Maryland's guaranty fund law. Maryland law provided a specific method for evaluating GIC's, and the court concluded from this fact that the Legislature knew that GIC's were being written by life insurance companies in Maryland at a time when the Insurance Commissioner had determined that GIC's were covered under the guaranty fund law. Id. at 864. The court also noted that the Maryland legislature had rejected four bills that would have excluded GIC's from coverage under the guaranty fund. Id. at 865-66. The court held that the failed amendments to the guaranty fund laws evidenced legislative acquiescence to the administrative practice of treating GIC's as covered annuities. Id. at 866.

---

[12] The same is true of the decisions in Unisys Corp. v. Pennsylvania Life and Health Ins. Guar. Ass'n, 667 A.2d 1199 (Pa.Commw.Ct.1995) and Minnesota Life & Health Ins. Guar. Ass'n v. Dep't of Commerce, 400 N.W.2d 769 (Minn.App.1987). . . .

We are not under any similar compulsion to follow an administrative practice to include GIC's as covered annuities. No administrative body in Arizona has determined that GIC's are covered under Arizona's guaranty fund provisions.[13] We interpret the statutes without any prior administrative practice of accepting these contracts for coverage or of making fund assessments based on these contracts.[14] Because we are not constrained by administrative interpretations in favor of coverage, we can interpret the definition of annuity according to its plain meaning: payments which depend in whole or in part on the continuance of human life rather than payments which might be contingent on the continuance of human life.

Honeywell's second argument is that the GIC's are annuities because the payout provisions provide for the purchase of an annuity from the fund value of the GIC's upon the retirement of a Honeywell employee. We also reject this argument. The possibility that an annuity would be purchased is even more speculative than the possibility of a withdrawal to pay the benefits upon death.

The provision allowing the purchase of an annuity is not itself an annuity. Rather, it is a clause accommodating a provision of the pension plan for purchase of an annuity. ELIC's contract accommodated this plan provision by allowing withdrawals to pay for the annuity.[15] The annuity entitled the employee to payments of retirement income for his or her life. After the employee exercised this option, the employee was designated as the owner of the annuity.

Whether an annuity would be purchased was entirely speculative. First, an employee who invested in the fixed income fund must have retired. Second, the employee would had to have selected the annuity option from the number of options available under Honeywell's retirement plan. Third, the trustee must have elected to direct ELIC to purchase the annuity by withdrawing money from the fund value of the GIC's, as opposed to purchasing an annuity from other funding sources. Given the contingencies that stood in the way of a purchase of an annuity under ELIC's

---

[13]    Honeywell claims that an opinion of the Arizona Attorney General favors a finding of coverage. In an opinion written in 1983, the Attorney General wrote that the guaranty fund "covers individual lives insured under a group policy." Op. Ariz. Att'y Gen. I83-053 (R83-036) (May 11, 1983). This opinion is not helpful because it lacks any factual context. At best, the opinion demonstrates that coverage will not be denied to "a master plan encompassing many individual lives." Id. Even if group insurance policies or annuities are covered, this does not answer the question of what constitutes an annuity.

[14]    The Fund argues that the insurance department has by inaction determined that GIC's are not covered under the guaranty fund law. It notes that the insurance department has never applied the "form filing" requirements to GIC's and that ELIC was never required to pay premium taxes on the GIC's. . . . . The parties have not briefed the applicability of the form filing requirements or of the premium tax to annuity contracts. Assuming that an annuity contract is subject to these two requirements, we do not agree with the Fund that administrative inaction is evidence of an administrative interpretation to the effect that GIC's are not covered annuities.

[15]    It was only when an employee retired that the trustee could direct ELIC to withdraw money from the fund value of the GIC's to purchase an annuity. When an employee was otherwise entitled to benefits--upon death, disability and termination--the contract with ELIC provided that the trustee could withdraw funds to pay the employee's benefits. In the latter situation, there was no requirement that ELIC purchase an annuity for the employee.

contracts with the trustee, we cannot hold that the payout provisions mean that the GIC's are "annuity contracts."

## Comments and Questions

1.  On appeal, the Supreme Court of Arizona held that "[t]he ELIC GICs are annuity contracts as defined under [Arizona statute] and therefore eligible for Fund coverage" and "vacate[d] that part of the court of appeals opinion holding that the ELIC GICs are not annuity contracts." 945 P.2d 805, 817 (Ariz. 1997) The majority opinion explained: "GICs in and of themselves are not life-contingent, . . . [but] the GICs are part of [Investment Plus Plan] . . . [and] therefore . . . incorporat[e] the Plan, subject to all the Plan's provisions." *Id.* at 812. The dissented countered that "[i]n deciding whether GICs are annuities, [he] would look at the GICs alone without reference to the employer's Plan." *Id.* at 817.

2.  As the divergent decisions in the Arizona courts reveal, there has been considerable variation in the way state guarantee funds have treated ELIC GICs issued to pension plans.  Since the decisions typically involve interpretations of state law, the U.S. Supreme Court will not likely resolve these conflicts.  Is the result is a healthy illustration of the states' serving as laboratories for regulatory experimentation?  Or is it is simply inefficient and inequitable?  Could you design a system that did a better job of dealing with insurance company insolvencies without moving to a national system comparable to what exists in the depository institution field?

3.  Both the Arizona decisions and the preceding case arose from ELIC's insolvency: the earlier decision dealt with the conservatorship in California and this one involves guaranty fund coverage in Arizona.  How would you compare the two decisions?  Do they approach ELIC's failure in a consistent manner?  Note in particular the ways in which these decisions treat the beneficiaries of ELIC's contracts: municipal bondholders in the first decision and Honeywell's employees in this case.  Are the respective decisions consistent in their willingness to look beyond the nominal contract holders?

4.  Another distinctive feature of our insurance insolvency procedures is the use of industry assessments to cover costs the guaranty funds incur when a company fails.  Typically, these costs are assessed on insurance companies in the same line of business in that state.  Assessments are also typically pro-rated based on amount of premiums written, and most states have an annual cap on the level of assessments each year (typically two percent of total premium income).  In almost all U.S. jurisdictions, assessments are made only after an insolvency takes place.  In many jurisdictions, insurance companies are permitted to deduct all or a portion of these assessments from state taxes.

4.  This post-funded assessment system has been criticized in recent years.  Some have questioned whether the system has the capacity to handle the simultaneous failure of one or more large insurance firms.  See U.S. General Accounting Office, Insurer Failures: Life/Health Insurer Insolvencies and Limitations of State Guarantee Funds (1992) (GAO-GGD-92-44).  Statutory limits on the amount of annual assets, in particular, restricts the ability of insurance regulators to raise funds quickly, and one of the lessons of the thrift

crisis of the 1980's is that undercapitalized guarantee funds can make costly mistakes by postponing closures in order to preserve resources. An alternative approach would be for insurance regulators to move towards the FDIC's deposit insurance system which entails pre-funding on a national basis. Would you favor such a change? Why or why not?

## B. The NAIC and Its Accreditation Project

The failure of ELIC and several other large insurance companies in the late 1980s and early 1990s prompted congressional leaders and other experts to question the efficacy of our state-based system of regulating an industry that often operates on a national basis. Of particular concern was the perceived inability on the part of state insurance commissions to coordinate their efforts. Rogue companies domiciled in one jurisdiction posed a threat to the entire system. In the case of ELIC, for example, subsequent congressional investigation reached the following conclusions:

- The regulators in other States relied entirely upon California and New York to supervise the Executive Life companies, rather than having many separate checks by different commissions on the company's excesses. Nobody else took any action until the insurers' collapse was imminent.

- There was minimal communication and cooperation among State agencies. Dating back to 1980, New York had found . . . serious management wrongdoing. In February 1987, the department finally ordered a $250,000 fine and a $151 million capital infusion, and also banished the California company and the offending officers from New York. The California commission did not discover these regulatory actions until 3 months later, after the $151 million was paid without notice in violation of California law. . . . [T]he new California commissioner said the First Executive holding company basically "raided Executive Life of California to protect the New York Company." . . . .

- State regulators did not share important information. The Minnesota commission became deeply concerned about the condition of Executive life in early 1990, and sought to obtain current information from California. The California commission would not provide such data or agree to an immediate examination. . . .

- The NAIC's Securities Valuation Office, which is supposed to catch improper investments, allowed First Executive to create the illusion of investment grade securities by transferring $789 million of junk bonds to affiliated companies in exchange for new securities that were collateralized by the junk bonds . . . .

- Although State regulatory agencies have existing general powers to order an insurer to halt any practice which might result in a hazardous financial condition, no agency used these powers against the Executive Life companies. . . .

Wishful Thinking: A World View of Insurance Solvency Regulation, A Report by the Subcommittee on Oversight and Investigations of the House Committee on Energy and Commerce 21-22 (Oct. 1994). At the time, parallels to the still unfolding thrift crisis were common:

The need to adapt to the increasingly competitive environment has presented problems for many types of financial institutions--commercial banks, savings and loans, securities firms, and insurers. We see these stresses in the insurance industry in increasing insolvencies among both the property/casualty and life/health insurers. For property/casualty insurers, the average number of liquidations from 1970 to 1983 was about six per year. However, from 1984 to 1989, the average number of property/casualty liquidations increased to 24 per year, with a high of 36 in 1989. For life/health insurers, the average number of liquidations from 1975 to 1983 was about five per year. However, from 1984 to 1990, the average number of life /health liquidations was about 19 per year, with a high of 43 in 1989.

Insurance Regulation: Assessment of the NAIC, Statement of Richard L. Fogel, Assistant Comptroller General of the General Accounting Office Before the Subcommittee on Oversight and Investigations of the House Committee on Energy and Commerce (May 22, 1991).

Increasingly, Representative John Dingell (D-Mich.) and other influential congressional leaders were calling for a federal role in the regulation of the insurance industry. In response to these developments, the NAIC instituted an accreditation program which is the subject of the following testimony from an official of the U.S. General Accounting Office. As you review this testimony, consider the extent to which the NAIC's program offers a viable response to the problems of the prior regime.

## Statement of Richard L. Fogel
## Assistant Comptroller General of the General Accounting Office
### Before the Subcommittee on Oversight and Investigations
### House Committee on Energy and Commerce
### (June 9, 1993)

NAIC's financial regulation standards were adopted in June 1989 and fall into three categories:

- First, there are twenty-seven Part A standards covering laws and regulations, seven of which were added by NAIC in March 1993. State insurance departments have until January 1, 1996 to comply with these new standards. According to NAIC, the Part A standards address whether the state insurance department has the needed authority to regulate an insurer's corporate and financial affairs. These standards cover such things as regulatory authority to examine firms, minimum required capital levels, prescribed accounting practices, and appropriate corrective actions for troubled companies.

- Second, there are twelve Part B standards covering regulatory practices and procedures. According to NAIC, these standards address whether the state insurance department has the necessary resources and capabilities to conduct financial analysis and examinations of firms operating within the state.

- The third part of the program consists of six Part C standards covering organizational and personnel practices. According to NAIC, these standards address whether a state insurance department has professional development and minimum educational requirements for its staff that will promote effective regulatory practices.

In June 1990, NAIC adopted its accreditation program to encourage states to implement the standards. In a full accreditation review, an independent on-site team of about five individuals assesses the state insurance department's compliance with these standards. The on-site visits generally last about 5 days. Subsequent on-site re-accreditation reviews are to be scheduled every 5 years with annual off-site evaluations by NAIC in the interim. To attain accreditation, a state insurance department must

- have authorities through laws, regulations, or administrative practices that substantially comply with Part A standards;

- have sufficient resources and appropriate procedures and practices to comply with each of the part B and part C standards, as measured by a rating of at least "acceptable" on a rating scale of "excellent," "good," "acceptable," and "unacceptable"; and

- receive an average score of "good" or better for the Part B standards taken together and for the Part C standards taken together.

To date, there is no penalty, other than peer pressure, for being an unaccredited state. However, beginning in January 1994 accredited states, except under certain circumstances, will not accept examination reports prepared by nonaccredited states on those states' domiciled insurance companies. This could require companies domiciled in nonaccredited states to get a second examination performed by an accredited state insurance department. This still does not penalize the unaccredited state directly. NAIC expects this sanction to lead insurers to lobby their home states to become accredited in order to avoid the expense of multiple examinations under differing state rules.

We continue to support NAIC's objective of improving the quality and consistency of solvency regulation and believe its accreditation program has helped to improve the overall quality of state regulation. We also recognize that a new program will inevitably experience unanticipated problems and that a learning curve can be expected as changes are adopted to improve the program.

While NAIC's standards have been a catalyst in some states to make improvements in insurance regulation, our concern with the process is the speed with which NAIC is moving and its willingness to develop clear standards and apply them rigorously. NAIC's accreditation program still does not convincingly demonstrate that accredited states can effectively regulate. . ...

## STANDARDS ARE NOT SPECIFIC, ALLOWING PERMISSIVE INTERPRETATION

For the accreditation program to be credible, it must establish consistent minimum standards that apply to each accredited state. NAIC and its review teams, however, continue to interpret the Financial Regulation Standards permissively. Therefore, states with weak regulatory authorities and practices are being accredited.

For example, most of the standards on laws and regulations require the state insurance department to have a particular NAIC model or authorities that are "substantially similar." In most instances, NAIC has not specified criteria for determining whether state variations from NAIC models actually provide the minimum level of solvency regulation intended by the standard. NAIC has said that these determinations are left primarily to the judgment of the review teams and ultimately the Financial Regulation Standards and Accreditation Committee. NAIC's President has said that this creates a problem for the review teams as well as for the committee. We are concerned that liberal interpretation of what is "substantially similar" to the NAIC models specified in the standards allows inconsistent or inadequate regulation.

Our review of the accreditation documentation revealed that all of the accredited states had variations from the NAIC models. Sometimes the states lacked model provisions, and sometimes the language of provisions was simply different from that of the NAIC models. In other cases, states had provisions not found in NAIC models; sometimes these provisions were stricter than the models but other times appeared to negate the intent of the models. Without specific criteria defining "substantially similar," we could not assess whether the teams' or the committee's determinations were appropriate or consistent. In light of the many variations cited by the review teams, we question whether the accreditation program will result in uniform, or even consistent, solvency regulation as NAIC envisions.

NAIC is trying to make several of the accreditation standards more specific. These include the standard for minimum capital requirements and the standard requiring that a state have a guaranty fund. We do not know when or if these changes will be adopted. However, in our view, NAIC failed in its much publicized attempt to clarify one of the financial regulation standards. In October 1991, NAIC ruled that, to become accredited, states had to have a particular provision of the Model Insurance Holding Company System Regulatory Act precisely as it was stated in the model. This particular language, setting regulatory approval, was added to the model law in 1986. This provision was added following the failure of Baldwin-United where, according to regulators, the parent holding company milked the insurance subsidiaries to service its own debt. By the time that NAIC made its decision to require the specific model language, several states with weaker thresholds than the model had already been accredited. Subsequently, NAIC reversed its ruling requiring the stricter threshold and approved a number of alternative provisions that it will accept as "substantially similar." According to NAIC, this action was taken because it believed that requiring only the model provision was "too rigid". However, some industry analysts have characterized NAIC's acceptance of the alternatives as weakening the standard.

We are concerned that liberal interpretation of what is accepted in the accreditation program as "substantially similar" may allow significant variation among states and potentially weak regulatory performance rather than a consistent and definable floor in state systems . . . .

## GROWING RESISTANCE TO DEMANDS OF ACCREDITATION PROGRAM
## MAY LIMIT ITS SUSTAINABILITY

According to NAIC, the accreditation program is dynamic, and standards will be added or amended to keep pace with changing industry practices. The evolutionary nature of NAIC's accreditation program will require states to periodically adopt new authorities or amend their regulatory programs to maintain their accredited status. For example, states have until January 1, 1996, to comply with seven new standards recently adopted by NAIC. Given the nature of the state-based insurance regulatory system, changes in the accreditation program require each state to revisit issues already addressed and considered resolved by its state legislature. We continue to question whether NAIC can sustain its program over time because it lacks authority to require states to adopt and use its standards.

Many state insurance departments are still working to adopt the original standards and may not be able to keep pace with NAIC's ever evolving standards. In March of this year, New York--

one of the first states to be accredited--had its accreditation suspended by NAIC for failing to adopt several model laws or regulations added to the original standards. Recently, a number of regulators, industry representatives and state legislators have expressed resistance to NAIC's efforts to clarify vague standards and add new ones. Opposition from these participants in the regulatory process raises further doubts about the long-term viability of the program.

## LACK OF FOCUS ON PERFORMANCE ALLOWS STATES WITH WEAK EXAMINATION QUALITY TO BE ACCREDITED

Insurance regulators have two tools that they routinely use to monitor insurers' financial condition and identify solvency problems. These are on-site examinations and off-site analyses of insurer-reported financial information. The accreditation documentation we reviewed revealed a disturbing pattern of weaknesses in the way states do insurance company examinations--a fundamental regulatory function. We found that NAIC's review teams consistently identified deficiencies in states' examination systems. This is troubling because examinations, which are generally required only every 3 to 5 years, are the principal means that state regulators have to verify insurer-reported data and to detect financial problems.

In our review of states accredited in 1991, we found numerous instances in which the review teams' workpapers appeared to indicate clear noncompliance with the regulatory practices and procedures standards on examinations. For example, some state insurance departments did not examine insurers in a timely fashion, and some did not have the necessary and required specialists available to assist examiners. Several states also did not comply with the accreditation requirement that they follow the policies and procedures of NAIC's Examiners Handbook. Nevertheless, the review teams certified departmental compliance with NAIC's standards as acceptable for accreditation, despite these noted deficiencies.

Again this year, the review teams' documentation suggested that minimum capabilities and procedures necessary for effective examination processes were not truly in place in all accredited states. In 7 of the 10 states accredited during 1992, the documentation indicated that examinations did not generally follow the Examiners Handbook in areas crucial for solvency monitoring. While the extent of the problems varied among the states, the accreditation review teams found inadequate testing of policy and loss reserves, lack of comprehensive internal control assessments, and reliance on unverified insurer-produced data and on the work of insurers' external auditors without assessing the quality and reliability of the auditors' work.

With these documented weaknesses in insurance company examinations, we question the state regulators' abilities to effectively detect solvency problems. Without proper assessment of insurance reserves, examiners have no reliable basis to understand an insurer's primary business operation. Without comprehensive assessments of internal controls, regulators have little assurance that examinations will detect all major control weaknesses. As a result, regulators could fail to find problems before they seriously erode an insurer's financial condition. Using unverified data and the work of external auditors without reviewing the scope and quality of that work also increases the risk that examiners will not detect potential problems.

# Summary of States' Adoption of NAIC Models Related to Accreditation
## (NAIC Data as of May 12, 1993)

| NAIC Model | Date Model Adopted by NAIC | ---- Number of States With ---- Changes to Legislation or Regulation Pending | Initial Legislation or Regulation Pending |
|---|---|---|---|
| Examination Authority | 1991 | 2 | 6 |
| Regulation to Define Standards and Commissioner's Authority for Companies in Hazardous Financial Condition | | 0 | 3 |
| Holding Company Act | 1985 | 13 | 0 |
| Holding Company Regulation | 1969 | 4 | 1 |
| Credit for Reinsurance Act | 1971 | 3 | 2 |
| Credit for Reinsurance Regulation (1) | 1984 | 0 | 4 |
| Regulation for Life and Health Reinsurance Agreements (2) | 1991 | | |
| Standard Valuation Law (1) | 1986 | 1 | 3 |
| Actuarial Opinion and Memorandum Regulation (1) | 1943 | 4 | 0 |
| CPA Audit Regulation (1) | | | |
| Rehabilitation and Liquidation Model Act | 1991 | 0 | 4 |
| IRIS Model Act | 1980 | 2 | 0 |
| Risk Retention Act | 1978 | 1 | 2 |
| Business Transacted w/Producer Controlled P/C Insurer Act (3) | 1985 | 1 | 3 |
| Managing General Agent Act | 1983 | 4 | 2 |
| Reinsurance Intermediaries Act | 1991 | 2 | 7 |
| Life and Health Insurance Guaranty Association Act | 1989 | 2 | 5 |
| Post-Assessment Property and Liability Insurance Guaranty Association Act | 1990 | 2 | 9 |
| | 1971 | 7 | 0 |
| | 1970 | 3 | 0 |

Legend:

(1) States have until January 1996 to adopt.

(2) California is the only state to enact a more comprehensive version of this model adopted by NAIC in 1992.  States have until January 1996 to adopt the new version.

(3) States have until June 1993 to adopt.

These procedural weaknesses are exacerbated by a lack of quality controls over the consistency and reliability of examiners' work. The review teams often found inadequate documentation of what examination work was performed. They also found little explanation about why certain work was not performed. Both findings indicated to the teams that supervisory review was lacking or inadequate. Without proper documentation and supervisory review of work performed, there is a high likelihood that errors in examiner judgment could go unchallenged and that incorrect conclusions could result.

In testimony before this Subcommittee last year, NAIC said that it does not accredit states on a conditional basis. But, in reality, it had already done so. In 1991, Iowa was accredited on the condition that it was to demonstrate compliance with the regulatory practices and procedures standards during the year following its accreditation. In 1992, 3 of the 10 newly accredited states — Texas, North Dakota, and Minnesota — received accreditation contingent once again upon a full on-site reevaluation of their compliance with the regulatory practices and procedures standards in 1 year.

Texas was recommended for accreditation by the review team, and the committee accredited the state on the condition that Texas improve how it did financial analysis and financial examinations. Specifically, Texas was told to conduct its financial analysis on a more timely basis and implement more comprehensive examination procedures. North Dakota received accreditation but the review team believed it was only "minimally acceptable" with respect to its use of specialists and its compliance with the Examiners handbook. The review team in Minnesota recommended accreditation but also characterized the state's compliance with the examiners Handbook and supervisory review standards as "minimally acceptable." The review team further recommended that Minnesota's accreditation be withdrawn in 1 year unless it could demonstrate "significant improvement" in its compliance with those standards.

Under NAIC's scoring system, the need for significant improvement to comply with a standard is the definition of a failing score. Furthermore, according to the accreditation procedures, a state can become accredited only if it successfully meets or exceeds all minimum accreditation standards. A state failing to meet any minimum accreditation standard cannot be accredited.

If these three states met the requirements for accreditation, why were they accredited for only 1 year? If they did not meet the requirements, why were they accredited at all? Given the review teams' documentation, the stated criteria of the accreditation program, and NAIC's own recognition that these states did not comply fully with the requirements for accreditation, we question the NAIC's decision to accredit these states.

Last year, we suggested that NAIC consider recognizing publicly a qualified or conditional accreditation status for states which are found not to be in full compliance on all standards and, thus, are not prepared for full accreditation. NAIC's current policy is to publicly announce full accreditation for each state, but NAIC did not publicly disclose that four states' accreditations were contingent on passing another full on-site review in 1 year after their accreditations. The difference between these two alternatives may appear to some to be merely semantic. However, if NAIC is to hold up its program as a basis for assuring the public that the states are doing a good job of regulating the industry, it should be willing to share publicly the results of its assessments of state efforts. Public sharing of this information also could be a catalyst for making improvements.

## CRITERIA ARE INADEQUATE FOR ASSESSING THE QUALITY
## OF FINANCIAL ANALYSIS

Insurance departments also assess an insurance company's financial condition through analysis of insurer-provided financial information. Like examinations, financial analysis is a component of NAIC's standards and the accreditation review process. However, whereas NAIC's Examiners Handbook contains specific work procedures and guidelines for planning, supervising, and conducting examinations, similar procedures or guidelines that could be used as criteria in assessing how well a state insurance department analyzes insurer financial statements do not exist. As a result, we are unable to determine what constitutes an acceptable level of performance for the financial analysis process.

Because the scoring for each of the regulatory practices and procedures standards is not independent, the limited criteria for financial analysis is a significant concern. That is, although the program specifies that a state must receive a passing score on each standard, NAIC told us that weaknesses in one area can be offset by perceived strengths in other areas. In fact, as we reported last year, NAIC said that examination weaknesses in one accredited state were not a problem because the state had a good financial analysis system.

## CONCLUSIONS

We support state efforts to improve the quality and effectiveness of insurance regulation through adoption of the Financial Regulation Standards set forth in NAIC's accreditation program. We believe that NAIC's standards have been a catalyst encouraging state insurance departments to regulate better.

So far, however, the program still does not credibly distinguish effective from ineffective solvency regulation. The standards are applied permissively. Thus, accreditation does not establish a meaningful minimum level of performance. Nevertheless, NAIC's accreditation review teams' efforts reveal a troubling pattern--poor quality of examinations in accredited states. These examinations are critical for effective solvency regulation. As long as the standards for accreditation of state insurance departments are vague and liberally interpreted, NAIC will not achieve uniformity, or even consistency, in state-by-state regulation. Moreover, we continue to question NAIC's ability to successfully sustain the program over the long term without the inherent authority to enforce its standards.

### Comments and Questions

1. Since Mr. Fogel presented this testimony, the NAIC accreditation program has continued to evolve. By June 1995, 46 states and the District of Columbia had been accredited. In addition, the NAIC adopted several new mandatory statutes, including a Risk-Based Capital for Insurers Model Act that accredited states are supposed to have adopted by January 1, 1997. Does the continued accreditation of states suggest that Mr. Fogel was unduly skeptical of the NAIC's efforts with this initiative?

2.  One of the GAO's concerns about the NAIC's accreditation program has been the ability of the organization to force states to comply with the standards. And, indeed, there has been some resistance at the state level to the NAIC's intiatives. In particular, the National Conference of Insurance Legislators ("NCOIL"), a voluntary organization representing 33 jurisdictions, has been a vocal critic of the NAIC's efforts. NCOIL's principal objections have concerned the large number of bills that state legislators are required to adopt even when the bills address problems that do not exist in all jurisdictions and the fact that the NAIC often insists that the model statutes be adopted verbatim, without amendment or modification to reflect local circumstances. Are these legimate complaints? The NOILC and other critics of NAIC accreditation have proposed that the system be amended to make mandatory only those model statutes that have already been adopted by a certain number of jurisdictions, perhaps a majority. Would you favor such an amendment?

3.  As originally envisioned, the NAIC accreditation program was supposed to be self-enforcing. After January 1, 1994, accredited states were supposed to refuse to accept examinations from unaccredited states, thereby forcing insurance companies from unaccredited states to submit to additional examinations. This mechanism, however, has proven ineffective. For one thing, unaccredited states, such as New York, adopted retaliatory legislation threatening to reject regulatory examinations of insurance companies domiciled in states that rejected examinations from the legislating state. Threats of this sort dissuaded most jurisdictions from enforcing the accreditation sanctions. In addition, insurance companies from unaccredited states discovered a loophole in the original sanctioning mechanism. By submitting themselves to "zone" examinations, in which regulatory authorities from several states participated, a company domiciled in an unaccredited jurisdiction could claim that it was examined by an accredited jurisdiction if at least one accredited jurisdiction participated in the examination. Should the NAIC have amended its accreditation program to close this loophole?

4.  The problem of multi-jurisdictional regulation reasserts itself in almost all areas of regulation in the international context. Many large financial institutions operate on a global basis. How are the problems of multi-jurisdictional operations solved in this context? Should there be a multi-national analog to the NAIC to coordinate regulation of the financial services industry around the world? What powers should it (or could it) have over sovereign nations?

## Section 4.  Insurance Rates and Risk Classifications

One of the most distinctive features of insurance regulation is its close attention to the terms and pricing of insurance companies' dominant liability: the insurance contract. Special rules governing the interpretation of insurance contract, explored briefly in section 2 of this chapter, are one illustration of this phenomenon. We now turn to two more prominent examples: the regulation of insurance rates and risk classification systems. In contrast to our discussion of insurance solvency regulations, where many parallels could be drawn to the regulation of depository institutions, these regulatory structures have few analogs in other sectors of the financial services industry.   What is it about insurance transactions that warrants such extensive governmental oversight of pricing and marketing decisions?

## A. Rate Regulation

One of the most publicized aspects of insurance regulation is the government's role in approving or, in some circumstances, setting the prices that insurance companies charge their consumers.  The regulation of insurance rates, which is typically confined to the property/casualty side of the industry, is a relatively modern development.  Until the 1940s, insurance companies in most jurisdictions had considerable freedom to establish whatever rates they choose, and often collaborated with each other through the use of rate bureaus to pool loss data and establish uniform prices.  With the Supreme Court's decision in United States v. South-Eastern Underwriters Association, 322 U.S. 533 (1944), however, these practices became vulnerable  to challenge under the federal anti-trust laws.   In 1945, the McCarran-Ferguson Act granted the industry a limited exemption to federal anti-trust law, but only to the extent that the industry was subject to state regulation.  The NAIC promptly developed model laws for rate regulation, which all of the states eventually adopted with various modifications.  The following excerpt introduces the rate regulation process as it has evolved over the past fifty years.

## Kenneth S. Abraham, Insurance Law and Regulation 106-12 (2d ed. 1995)

In contrast to regulation for solvency, where *financial data* regarding an insurer's assets and liabilities is used to assess the economic health of the company, in ratemaking *statistical data* on claims and losses takes center stage.  Insurance premiums, like prices for most products in imperfectly competitive markets, tend to be set with one eye on cost and profitability, and the other on market share.  Unlike most products, however, the lion's share of an insurer's costs are unknown at the time it must set a price for coverage.  Admittedly, this difference between insurance and other products is sometimes exaggerated.  Companies in other lines of business also must make decisions in the face of uncertainty about the future.  For example, General Motors must decide whether to build a new plant, open a new assembly line, hire more employees, or design a new model vehicle before it knows what all of its costs will be and how future economic forces will affect demand for its product.  But insurers probably know with certainty a smaller proportion of the costs they will ultimately incur when they set their prices than most businesses that operate in other sectors of the economy.

### Operating Profit: Underwriting Results and Investment Income

Both the process of insurance ratemaking and the regulation of that process are somewhat uncertain undertakings.  If an insurer is to earn an *operating profit*, then the sum of its *underwriting* and *investment* profit and loss must be positive.  The underwriting side of the insurance business is the sale of insurance and the payment of claims.  Generally, underwriting profit and loss are expressed as the ratio of claim payouts and expenses to premiums earned.  If this *combined ratio* is below 100 (or 1.00, depending on the scale used) then the insurer has earned an underwriting profit. If the combined ratio exceeds 100, the insurer has incurred an underwriting loss. For example, an insurer might find that its payouts ("losses") for a given year in a particular line were $.88 for every dollar of premium earned, and that its expenses (for marketing, administration, claim processing, etc.) per dollar of premium were $.22. Its combined ratio would then be 110. Notice that the combined ratio is the result of a comparison (like any ratio) of two numbers: losses-plus-expenses as compared to premiums. Consequently, this ratio will rise either when losses-plus-expenses increase, or when premiums decline similarly, the combined ratio will fall either when losses-plus-expenses fall or when premiums rise.

The underwriting experience measured by the combined ratio, however, is only half the story. Because the insurer holds premiums for a period of time before it must pay claims against its policies, it can earn income on those premiums by investing them prior to payout. Positive investment income at least partially offsets underwriting losses, and sometimes more than offsets these losses. The longer the insurer holds premiums, the greater the income it can earn by investing them. In a *long-tail* line (one in which the claims against a single year's policies are issued) such as medical malpractice or products liability, investment income may be able to offset sizeable underwriting losses. As a consequence, premiums should be lower than they would be for coverage of the same aggregate expected loss with a shorter tail. In contrast, in *short-tail* lines such as automobile collision or fire insurance, most claims are made and paid shortly after the expiration of the policy period, and investment income constitutes a smaller percentage of profit or loss. Thus, in a world where insurance companies compete for business, premiums are inevitably set with potential investment income taken into account. Similarly, once all the results are in, a complete picture of an insurer's profitability cannot be obtained without taking its investment income into account.[1]

### Ratemaking

Unfortunately, it is a fact of insurance life that at the time an insurer sets rates--and at the time a regulator scrutinizes them--neither can know for certain whether the level at which rates are set will produce profit or loss. In the absence of certainty about the future, past underwriting results are some evidence of what the future may bring. For two reasons, however, even past underwriting results must be adjusted to take account of the future. First, some differences between past and future results may already be known. Comparative negligence may have been adopted, or a statute requiring the installation of sprinkler systems in all public buildings may have been enacted. Second, unless the past underwriting results used as a ratemaking building block are complete, they may be an inaccurate predictor of the future; and to the extent that these results are complete, they may be older than would be ideal for use as predictors. For example, suppose that in 1995 an insurer wanted to set a rate for products liability insurance in 1996. If it looked at data regarding losses paid under 1995 policies, there would be very little data,

---

[1]    Of course, the fact that insurers earn income on invested premiums does not necessarily mean that they have an incentive to delay settling claims. Even a coldly calculating insurance executive who had no concern for public relations would need to predict whether the inflation in claim value (because of economic or legal factors) that resulted from any delay in payment of claims exceeded the investment yield on the sum for which the claim could be settled without delay, plus the legal and other expenses incurred in delaying the claim.

because claims would only just be coming in.  Data on losses paid under 1989 policies would be much more complete; but that data would also be less relevant, because of changes in the social, economic, and legal environments in the interim.

Consequently, when insurers project the future based on underwriting experience in recent years, the validity of their projections depends heavily on the completeness of the data used. When that data is incomplete, insurers follow accounting conventions for projecting the ultimate magnitude of claims and payouts against a particular year's policies, and then draw conclusions regarding the profitability of that year based on these projections.  As a result, conclusions about the profitability of long-tail lines of coverage sold in a recent year are partly historic statements, but these conclusions also are partly predictions.

For example, in 1995 an insurer may attempt to determine how profitable its 1994 products liability insurance was, or (what amounts to almost the same thing) how profitable it ultimately will be.  The insurer may know that it has paid $500,000 in claims against 1994 policies, and that claims likely to result in payouts of an additional $1,000,000 have already been reported.  It will therefore *reserve* $1,000,000 for these reported claims.  Then, on the basis of past experience, the insurer may also project that claims payouts in the first year after a given year's products liability policies have been issued plus sums reserved for claims already-reported-but-not-yet-paid usually have turned out to constitute only 20 percent of ultimate payouts against that year's policies.  The insurer will therefore estimate, based on this past pattern of *loss development*, that it will ultimately incur an additional $6,000,000 in losses against 1995 policies for claims *incurred but not reported* (IBNR).  It may also note, however, that each year for the past several years its loss development estimates of this sort have turned out to be low; an additional *loss development factor* may therefore be added.  In addition, the insurer will employ a *trend factor* to revise this figure upward, based on the pattern of increases in loss rates that it has observed over the past years.

Notice that this entire exercise involves prediction of the future by projecting past results. On top of these projections of past experience, the insurer may also include a factor to take account of the economic and legal inflation that it predicts for the period during which these 1995 policies still will be exposed to claims.  In the aggregate, these estimates of the total losses that ultimately will be paid by 1995 policies produce a projection of ultimate underwriting experience that may be used as part of the bases for setting 1996 rates.  As long as everyone involved understands what is going on, statements about the underwriting profitability of recent policy years for particular insurance lines can be understood for what they are: the best estimates that may be available, but estimates nonetheless.

If there were no regulation of insurance rates, all this would merely be a description of some of the factors insurers take into account in setting rates.  Any insurer that overestimated its future losses--deliberately or in error--might fool its shareholders for a short time, but ultimately other insurers would make more accurate projections and increase their market shares by underpricing the first insurer.  To a great extent that kind of competition can and does occur in the existing insurance markets. . . . [H]owever, in at least some lines of property/casualty insurance a somewhat more collective process of ratemaking is the norm, arguably because of the inability of even the largest companies to make rates based on the limited loss data available to them individually.

Partly for this reason, and partly out of independent concern that certain segments of the insurance market are not completely competitive, insurance rates are subject to regulatory scrutiny. Ostensibly, such regulation has been motivated by the tripartite concern that rates not be "excessive, inadequate, or unfairly discriminatory," to quote the standard provision in almost every state's regulatory legislation. In practice, however, most regulatory scrutiny of rates is not focused on whether they are inadequate (a solvency concern) or unfairly discriminatory, though the latter is receiving increasing emphasis. Rather, the typical Insurance Commissioner in a rate hearing, or in deciding whether to have a hearing, is concerned to assure that rates are not excessive.

At an administrative hearing considering the proposed rate increase, both parties (and/or others, depending on the nature of the proceeding and those granted standing) would present evidence in support of their contentions. . . . Normally this testimony will be from experts who have examined the insurer's claims experience, and who have made projections based in part on this experience (or the total claims experience of the companies represented by a rate service bureau such as ISO) and in part on judgments about future trends that are not subject to objective proof. The Commissioner would then rule depending on the nature of his authority under the state's insurance code or statutes.

### Forms of Rate Regulation

The method by which Insurance Commissioners exercise their authority varies from state to state, and the lines of insurance subject to different regulatory requirements are likely to vary within each state. Property/casualty insurance rates tend to be more carefully scrutinized than life and health insurance rates. With these caveats, the received understanding is that these methods fall into four general categories, although there are of course hybrids of the four and slight variations in actual use:

*State prescription of rates.* This is a relatively rare approach [though it is the one used in Massachusetts, as the following case illustrates]. In practice, the difference between this and the prior approval method is likely to turn on the burden of going forward with evidence in support of or against a rate increase, since insurers supply data on which state-prepared rates are based, and the rates set by a Commissioner may be challenged in court.

*Prior approval.* Insurers file proposed rates with the Insurance Commissioner, who must approve them before they may be used. In many states, unless the Commissioner disapproves a rate filing within a statutory period (usually 90 days or less) the filed rate goes automatically into effect, or is "deemed" to be approved.

*File and use.* Under this approach rates become effective immediately upon filing with the Commissioner, but may be disapproved within a specified period. A hybrid of this and the prior approval approach is *flex-rating,* under which rate changes within a specified band may flex through file and use, but changes beyond the band (usually more than 15 or 25 percent) require prior approval.

*Open Competition.* Insurers need not even file rates in lines where it has been determined that competition can effectively regulate rates, although the Commissioner has residual regulatory authority.

Whatever the form of regulation, a Commissioner's scrutiny of a rate involves consideration of roughly the same issues.  Few really informed observers believe that all segments of the insurance market are always fully competitive, and few believe that there is always widespread parallel action by insurers, let alone outright conspiracy.  The basic philosophical difference between proponents of regulation and proponents of open competition, therefore, turns on their level of confidence (or lack of it) in the capacity of insurance regulators to make the kinds of pricing decisions that would otherwise be made by market forces.

Private automobile insurance is one area in which state insurance regulators have been particularly active in policing rates. A variety of factors explain the more extensive regulation of automobile insurance.  To begin with, private automobile insurance is a significant expenditure for many individuals.  In 1993, for example, consumers spent more than $93.4 billion on automobile insurance (or more than $500 for every licensed driver).    While some of this expenditure is voluntary,  much is not.  Almost all U.S. jurisdictions have some form of mandatory automobile insurance law requiring automobiles to be covered by certain minimum amounts of insurance, typically to provide coverage for personal injuries and property damage caused to third parties.

### J. W. Wilson & Associates
### A HYPOTHETICAL RATE CASE
**(dollars in thousands)**

|  | As Seen By: | |
| --- | --- | --- |
|  | **Insurer** | **Consumer** |
| Earned Premium (Current Rates | $1,597,265 | $1,597,26 |
| Incurred Losses (Current Year) | $1,287,416 | $1,287,41 |
| Trend Factor | 1.100 | 1.060 |
| Loss Development Factor | 1.150 | -- |
| Composite Factor (3 x 4) | 1.265 | 1.060 |
| Ultimate Losses (2 x 5) | $1,628,581 | $1,364,661 |
| Loss Adjustment Expense Factor | 1.120 | 1.110 |
| Ultimate Losses & LAE (6 x 7) | $1,824,010 | $1,514,774 |
| Current Loss & LAE Ratio (8/1) | 1.142 | 0.948 |
| . Commission & Expense Factor | 1.250 | 1.10 + $159,72 |
| . Profit & Contigency Factor | 1.050 | 0.90 |
| . Indicated Rate Change Factor (9 x 10 x 11) | 1.499 | .939 + $143,754 |
| . Required Rate Increase | $797,035 | $46,321 |
| . Percentage Increase (13/1) | + 49.9% | + 2.9% |

**Notes**

1. Both parties agree on total premiums earned last year.

2. Both accept the insurer's stated "losses"--which includes those paid and those incurred but not paid.

3.-5.    The consumer advocate wants to combine development and trend factors into a single number; more importantly, the consumer's projection of development plus trend is .205 lower than the insurer's. In effect, the consumer advocate argues that the insurer's prediction of future increases in loss payouts is excessive.

6. The result is a substantial difference in future projected costs.

7.-8.    Differences between the parties as to the projected increase in loss adjustment expenses (in liability insurance, mainly counsel fees) further separates their estimates.

9. Summarizes this difference in the form of a projected combined ratio for this year.

10. The parties also differ about how to project other expense increases--the consumer advocate uses actual expenses plus a factor for future increases, while the insurer simply uses an increase factor.

11. Because the insurer projects an underwriting loss, see item 9 above, it counts on its investment income to offset it, while the consumer advocate projects an underwriting profit, and wants 10 percent of the insurer's investment income used to reduce premiums.

12.-13.    This difference between the parties results in different total rate change factors, and a different dollar increase in rates requested.

14. Because of the differences noted, the percentage increase in rates suggested by the parties are radically different.

---

Because the state requires such large personal expenditures on private automobile insurance, regulatory authorities often feel an obligation to insure that the product is available to all drivers at a fair price. As of 1993, twenty one states subjected automobile insurance to prior approval procedures, and twenty three other states had "file and use" or some variant thereon. Massachusetts maintains the most elaborate rate regulation structure, an administratively developed pricing system applicable to all insurance companies selling automobile insurance in the jurisdiction. Each year, the Massachusetts Commissioner of Insurance establishes a fee structure for all private automobile insurance sold in the Commonwealth. In many years, the insurance industry challenges the Commissioner's ruling, as it did in the following case. As you review this case, consider the factors the Commissioner must take into account in this rate setting process. How likely is it that the Commissioner will evaluate these factors accurately? Would a private insurance company likely do better? How would the process differ if Massachusetts used a prior approval system?

---

## Automobile Insurers Bureau v. Commissioner of Insurance
### 650 N.E.2d 1234 (Mass. 1995)

The decision of the Commissioner of Insurance (commissioner) establishing private passenger motor vehicle insurance rates for 1995 resulted in an over-all rate reduction of 6.1%. The Automobile Insurers Bureau of Massachusetts[3] (AIB) and ten of its member companies filed a complaint for judicial review.

1. The proceedings. The commissioner determined that competition was insufficient to assure that private passenger automobile insurance rates would not be excessive. See G.L. c. 175E, § 5 (1992 Ed.). The commissioner therefore invoked the procedures of G.L. c. 175, § 113B, to fix and establish automobile insurance rates for calendar year 1995. Interested parties were invited to participate in the proceedings. Four parties formally intervened: the AIB; the State Rating Bureau, pursuant to G.L. c. 26, § 8E (1992 Ed.); the Attorney General, pursuant to G.L. c. 12, § 11F (1992 Ed.); and the Professional Independent Insurance Agents of Massachusetts (PIIAM), a trade association.

On December 15, 1994, the commissioner issued a decision resolving . . . the effect of recent law changes, particularly the 1994 mandatory seat belt law, on loss pure premiums. . . . The commissioner concluded that the seat belt law would produce savings to the industry and therefore reduced the bodily injury portion of rates by 4.9%, which represents an over-all rate decrease of approximately 2.2%. The commissioner concluded that other legal and regulatory changes did not warrant any rate adjustment.

2. Seat belt law adjustment. The commissioner reduced loss pure premiums[8] for bodily injury coverage to reflect anticipated savings from the 1994 seat belt law, St.1993, c. 387, which mandated the use of seat belts as of February 1, 1994.[9] The plaintiffs argue that this reduction was not authorized, that the model used to establish the amount of the reduction was faulty, and that the inputs used in applying this model were improper.

a. Authority to reduce rates. The seat belt law provides that "[t]he commissioner of insurance shall mandate a minimum five percent reduction in bodily injury premiums if the observed seat belt use rate among all occupants equals or exceeds fifty percent one year after this law has been in effect." St.1993, c. 387, § 7.[10] The seat belt law had not been in effect for one

---

[3]    "The Automobile Insurers Bureau of Massachusetts is an unincorporated voluntary association of insurance companies licensed to write automobile insurance in Massachusetts." Automobile Insurers Bureau of Mass. v. Commissioner of Ins., 415 Mass. 455, 456 n. 1, 614 N.E.2d 639 (1993).

[8]    "Loss pure premiums" are the portion of premiums allocated to losses or claims. . . .

[9]    This statute inserted a new section, § 13A, in G.L. c. 90, which requires operators and passengers of most motor vehicles to wear seat belts, subject to a fine of twenty-five dollars for noncompliance. St.1993, c. 387, § 1. The section is to be enforced "only when an operator of a motor vehicle has been stopped for a violation of the motor vehicle laws or some other offense." Id.

[10]    This statute also provides that, "[i]f at any time the safety belt use rate in the commonwealth exceeds the national average, additional reductions in bodily injury premiums shall take effect."

year at the time the commissioner made the rate reduction. It thus was impossible to observe seat belt use one year after the law took effect. The plaintiffs assert that the commissioner erred because she was not authorized to reduce insurance rates to reflect the effect of the law. We do not agree.

The commissioner had the authority to effect the rate reduction under her broad rate setting powers. The commissioner has the statutory authority, and duty, under G.L. c. 175, § 113B, to establish insurance rates that are adequate, just, reasonable, and nondiscriminatory. In so doing, she can, and indeed must, consider all changes in conditions which affect rates, including changes in the law. See, e.g., Massachusetts Auto. Rating & Accident Prevention Bureau v. Commissioner of Ins., 389 Mass. 824, 842-844, 453 N.E.2d 381 (1983) (adjustment for increased sanctions for driving under the influence); Massachusetts Auto. Rating & Accident Prevention Bureau v. Commissioner of Ins., 384 Mass. 333, 338-339, 424 N.E.2d 1127 (1981) (adjustment for merit rating); Massachusetts Auto. Rating & Accident Prevention Bureau v. Commissioner of Ins., 381 Mass. 592, 599-600, 411 N.E.2d 762 (1980) (adjustment for raised drinking age).

The rate-reduction language in the 1994 seat belt law does not limit the commissioner's ability to consider seat belt use in setting rates under her powers pursuant to G.L. c. 175, § 113B. It simply sets a minimum reduction (i.e., five per cent) in the event of a certain occurrence (i.e., "the observed safety belt use rate among all occupants equals or exceeds fifty percent one year after" the law takes effect). St.1993, c. 387, § 7. "Specific authority to act in a particular respect does not bar other action that is consistent under general statutory authority." Massachusetts Elec. Co. v. Department of Pub. Utils., 419 Mass. 239, 246, 643 N.E.2d 1029 (1994). See Grocery Mfrs. of Am., Inc. v. Department of Pub. Health, 379 Mass. 70, 76, 393 N.E.2d 881 (1979). The reduction for 1995 is consistent with a further reduction for 1996 if observed seat belt use equals or exceeds fifty per cent after February 1, 1995.[11]

b. The model. The plaintiffs also contest the model by which the commissioner determined the amount of the rate reduction. The model used by the commissioner in determining the rate reduction was previously used to take account of the effects of the 1986 seat belt law[12] in determining insurance rates for 1986, 1987, and 1988. The model seeks to establish the effect of changes of seat belt usage, as a result of the law, on the loss experience for bodily injuries, and, in turn, on insurance costs. It compares prelaw and postlaw seat belt usage, multiplied by the efficacy of seat belts in reducing four major classes of injury (fatal, severe, moderate and

---

St.1993, c. 387, § 7. The commissioner did not base the rate reduction on this provision.

[11]    The commissioner's rate reduction furthers the seat belt law's intent of reducing rates to reflect seat belt usage. Not only does the law provide for the aforementioned minimum rate reduction, but it also provides that "[a]nnual safety belt survey results shall be a criterion in all future regulatory actions regarding bodily injury premiums." St.1993, c. 387, § 7. In reducing the rates, the commissioner considered safety belt survey results. Disallowing the reduction, as suggested by the plaintiffs, would conflict with both the purpose of this law and the purpose of G.L. c. 175, § 113B, to set rates that are "just" in light of known factors. See Hadley v. Amherst, 372 Mass. 46, 51, 360 N.E.2d 623 (1977) ("a statute is to be interpreted in harmony with prior enactments to give rise to a consistent body of law").

[12]    This law was in effect for only ten months as it was repealed by voter referendum.

minor). These amounts are then multiplied by the distribution of injury costs for vehicle occupants for each category of injury. The resulting amounts are applied to reduce loss pure premiums.

In reviewing the commissioner's decision, under G.L. c. 175, § 113B, "our inquiry is limited to 'whether the rates have reasonable support in evidence.' " Aetna Casualty & Sur. Co. v. Commissioner of Ins., 408 Mass. 363, 378, 558 N.E.2d 941 (1990), quoting Massachusetts Auto. Rating & Accident Prevention Bureau, 384 Mass. at 337, 424 N.E.2d 1127. "[T]his standard is indistinguishable from the substantial evidence standard." Automobile Insurers Bureau of Mass. v. Commissioner of Ins., 415 Mass. 455, 457, 614 N.E.2d 639 (1993), quoting Aetna Casualty & Sur. Co., supra at 378 n. 14, 558 N.E.2d 941. . . .

There was substantial evidence supporting the commissioner's decision. It was reasonable for the commissioner to conclude that the clearly evidenced increase in seat belt use would reduce losses. See Attorney Gen. v. Commissioner of Ins., 370 Mass. 791, 819, 820-821, 353 N.E.2d 745 (1976). To determine the amount by which to reduce rates, the commissioner used an existing, accepted model. The plaintiffs did not meet their burden of showing that the commissioner's choice of methodology was erroneous. See Massachusetts Bonding & Ins. Co. v. Commissioner of Ins., 329 Mass. 265, 280, 107 N.E.2d 807 (1952) (party challenging methodology has burden of establishing that commissioner's order is erroneous); Aetna Casualty & Sur. Co., supra at 373, 558 N.E.2d 941 (can continue to use previously used methodologies where party does not provide adequate reason not to).

The plaintiffs argue that the model should have been rejected because it proved to be erroneous in its prior application. They argue that, contrary to the model's prediction, the 1986 seat belt law did not reduce insurance costs and that, if it did, the model overstated the effect of the law. The commissioner found these arguments unpersuasive. Instead, she accepted the evidence of a relative deceleration in loss pure premiums in 1986 and evidence that the seat belt law was a cause of this drop.

The plaintiffs argue that there is no information on which to draw a direct correlation between the loss pure premium drops and the use of seat belts. The existing data reflected the result of all factors that influence loss pure premiums in either direction. Although the effect of increased seat belt use could not be isolated, there was evidence that after the 1986 law took effect, the number of motor vehicle occupant injuries declined by 20% while seat belt use increased from 20% to 35%-37% of motor vehicle occupants. After the 1986 law was repealed, seat belt use declined to 24% and the number of motor vehicle occupant injuries increased 11%.

It was reasonable for the commissioner to conclude that, because bodily injury loss pure premiums ultimately derive from injuries, the correlation between increased seat belt use and reduced loss pure premiums was shown. The commissioner should not decline to consider this correlation simply because it is difficult to quantify. See Massachusetts Auto. Rating & Accident Prevention Bureau v. Commissioner of Ins., 401 Mass. 282, 301, 516 N.E.2d 1132 (1987) ("The industry argues that there was not sufficient basis for an exact quantification of the excess, so the commissioner should not have made the reduction. Apparently, the industry believes that when an area of excess is difficult to quantify, the presumption should be that the excess will be born by the policyholders until it can be precisely measured. We cannot agree"). While the data were insufficient to prove that the degree of reduced loss pure premiums was accurately predicted by the model, the commissioner's decision was justified by the logic of the model, the available data, and the absence of evidence to the contrary. See Aetna Casualty & Sur. Co., supra at 375, 558 N.E.2d 941 ("It lies within the discretion of the commissioner to determine the weight to be given to certain evidence supporting or detracting from reliance on particular methodologies or data").

c. The inputs. The plaintiffs next dispute the use of three pieces of data by the commissioner in applying the model. The commissioner's use of these data is supported by substantial evidence.

First, the plaintiffs dispute the level of prelaw seat belt use applied by the commissioner. The commissioner used the 1993 seat belt use rate of 34.5%. The plaintiffs suggested a use rate of 39%, based on an alleged trend of increasing seat belt use over the five years prior to the law. The commissioner's use of the 1993 level, as determined by a survey by Boston University, was supported by substantial evidence. In deciding on this rate, the commissioner looked at the rates of seat belt use in 1993 and 1994. See id. at 379, 558 N.E.2d 941 (evidence supported commissioner's use of two years of historical data, rather than the six recommended by the AIB). Contrary to the plaintiffs' assertions, the data do not show a steady increase in seat belt use during the years prior to the law's effect, but rather, shows a fluctuation, with the level dropping slightly and then remaining essentially steady during the three years immediately preceding the law.[15]

Second, the plaintiffs dispute the accuracy of the commissioner's estimates of the effectiveness of seat belts in reducing loss costs. The commissioner used the same estimates used in testing the effect of the 1986 law. The plaintiffs argue that the estimates were erroneous because they do not account for improvements in vehicle safety which may lower the significance of seat belt use. The commissioner correctly rejected this argument because it was not supported by any quantitative evidence and because the AIB did not provide alternative estimates of effectiveness. Further, the limited data available supported the continued use of the old estimates.[16]

Third, the plaintiffs argue that the model's distribution of injury types is outdated as a result of the trend to less severe injuries that are less affected by seat belt use.[17] The AIB did not, however, quantify the effect of this trend or provide an alternative distribution of injury types. Further, the commissioner had before her evidence that changing the distribution weightings did not materially affect the over-all outcome of the model. Thus, the commissioner's decision was warranted.[18]

_____

[15]    The survey showed that seat belt use was 27% in December, 1986, dropped to 26% in December, 1987, increased gradually to 36% in May, 1991, dropped to 34% by June, 1992, and remained at that level until June, 1993.

[16]    The Boston University survey showed a 20% reduction in fatalities as a result of increased seat belt use. This is the same as the estimate used by the model. We note, however, that the survey recognized that other factors may have contributed to the reduction.

[17]    The trend to less severe injuries may be the result of increased seat belt use.

[18]    The plaintiffs point out that many insurance claims are fraudulent or inflated, see Automobile Insurers Bureau of Mass. v. Commissioner of Ins., 415 Mass. 455, 461, 614 N.E.2d 639 (1993), and therefore unaffected by the use of seat belts. They do not, however, show that such claims have become

3. *Other law changes.* The plaintiffs argue that the commissioner should have increased premiums to account for two law changes: a revision in regulations governing the referral shop system and the deregulation of the towing industry. They argue that, in deciding that these changes did not warrant rate adjustments, the commissioner impermissibly placed a higher burden of proof on the AIB to show that a rate increase would be proper than it required for a decrease due to the seat belt law. See Medical Malpractice Joint Underwriting Ass'n of Mass. v. Commissioner of Ins., 395 Mass. 43, 47, 478 N.E.2d 936 (1985). The commissioner's determination that these changes did not warrant a rate increase was warranted.

First, regulations governing the referral shop system were changed. Under this system, insurers enter into agreements with repair shops to act as referral shops. If an insured has a vehicle repaired at a referral shop, the insurer guarantees the cost and quality of the repairs. The insured need not go to a referral shop, but, if the insured has his vehicle repaired elsewhere, the insurer does not guarantee price or quality. Prior to the change, insurers were required to provide insureds with a list of at least five referral shops in a geographically convenient area. They also had to disclose that insureds could have their vehicles repaired at a nonreferral shop, but in that case, the insurer would not guarantee the quality of the repair and the insured could incur additional expense.

On May 1, 1994, a regulatory change was made, codified at 211 Code Mass.Regs. § 123.00, requiring insurers to provide insureds with a list of all registered body shops in the county where the insured resides or, on request, another county. Insurers can highlight or underline referral shops but must give the same disclosure about using nonreferral shops. The plaintiffs argue that this change will increase insurance costs because it will reduce the use of referral shops and therefore reduce the ability of insurers to negotiate reduced prices with such shops.

The commissioner properly concluded that an increase in rates was not warranted by this regulatory change. There was no evidence of a decrease or expected decrease in the use of referral shops or number of referral shops. The incentive for insureds to use referral shops remains unchanged. While the AIB did present evidence of an increase in supplemental payments[19] since May, 1994, it did not show the magnitude of such payments or the reason for them. There was no evidence linking the increase in such payments to the regulatory change. In short, there was no evidence supporting AIB's contention. The commissioner's decision was therefore not erroneous.

Second, police-ordered towing charges were deregulated.[20] As of January 1, 1995, the Federal government has preempted the ability of the States to regulate rates for towing motor

---

more prevalent, thus making the earlier model outdated. Again, they provide no quantitative evidence or alternative.

[19] "A supplemental payment [occurs] after a claimant disputes the initial appraisal as underestimating the actual cost of repairs.... This may occur when, for instance, damage is discovered during the repair process which was not visible at the time of the initial appraisal." Massachusetts Auto Body Ass'n v. Commissioner of Ins., 409 Mass. 770, 776, 570 N.E.2d 147 (1991).

[20] "Police-ordered towing charges," in this context, refers to the costs of towing following collisions.

vehicles.    49 U.S.C. § 11501(h).    Prior to this time, the Department of Public Utilities (department) had established a maximum charge for all police-ordered towing.  See G.L. c. 159B, § 6B (1992 Ed.);  220 Code Mass.Regs. § 272.00 (1993).  The plaintiffs argue that the costs of police-ordered towing will rise and insurers will therefore incur higher claim costs.  In support of this, they point to a petition to the department by the State Towing Association (STA) stating that the regulated tow rate produced a revenue deficiency of $34.61 per tow.  The commissioner determined that the AIB's unqualified adoption of these unsupported data did not provide sufficient support for an adjustment to premiums.  Because the actual effect of the deregulation was speculative, the commissioner deferred consideration.

There was no error.  The AIB produced no evidence other than testimony about the contents of the STA's petition.  It admitted that it would not have supported the petition before the department absent evidence that the proposed figures were correct and that the towers needed more revenue.  Where a party admits that it does not know the basis for its evidence, the commissioner's rejection of that evidence as speculative is amply supported. See Massachusetts Auto. Rating & Accident Prevention Bureau, 389 Mass. at 845, 453 N.E.2d 381.

## Comments and Questions

1. Almost every year, the Massachusetts high court hears a case challenging the Insurance Commissioner's automobile rate regulation.  In other decisions the court has resolved challenges to a host of rate setting practices:

- The basis of the Commissioner's calculation of the federal income tax rate applied to insurance company earnings on investment and other income.  Compare Massachusetts Auto. Rating & Accident Prevention Bureau v. Commissioner of Insurance, 516 N.E.2d 1132 (Mass. 1987), with  Massachusetts Auto. Rating & Accident Prevention Bureau v. Commissioner of Insurance, 453  N.E.2d 381 (Mass 1983) .

- The effect of projected medical savings from recently enacted hospital cost containment statute. See  Massachusetts Auto. Rating & Accident Prevention Bureau v. Commissioner of Insurance, 453  N.E.2d 381 (Mass 1983).

- The use of a "Competition Adjustment Factor," as a result of which the Commissioner reduced projected industry expenses by a certain amount (for example, 15 percent) on the grounds that there was considerable variation in the expense level of individual insurance companies and that variation, without more, indicated that industry-wide cost savings were possible.  See Massachusetts Auto. Rating & Accident Prevention Bureau v. Commissioner of Insurance, 411 N.E.2d 762 (Mass. 1980).

2. Rate regulation of the sort employed in the Massachusetts has been the subject of intense criticism in the insurance industry.  See e.g., Orin Kramer, *Rate Suppression and its Consequences*, 10 J. INS. REG. 523 (1992).  Industry representatives assert that states such as Massachusetts deny insurance companies sufficient returns to ensure long-term solvency and argue that the industry should be allowed to charge higher rate that would prevail in a competitive market.  Industry critics, on the other hand, reject the claim that state-

controlled insurance rates are inadequate and warn that a return to unregulated markets will facilitate collusive behavior and artificially inflated prices. See J. Robert Hunter, *'Rate Suppression And Its Consequences:' A Critique*, 11 J. INS. REG. 333 (1993). How should the Massachusetts Insurance Commissioner resolve theoretical disputes of this sort? What sort of evidence would be probative? Is it, for example, relevant that Massachusetts is typically among the five most expensive states in which to purchase automobile insurance, and premiums in the Commonwealth are usually 30 to 40 percent over the national average?

4. Since the early 1980's when Congress eliminated most federal restrictions on interest paid of federally insured deposits, there has not be a direct analog to rate regulation for depository institutions. What explains this difference? Do banks and thrifts face indirect analogs to rate regulation?

---

Whereas Massachusetts has traditionally heavily regulated automobile insurance rates, California has historically been a low-regulation jurisdiction, relying primarily on competitive forces to control costs. In the 1980s, however, rising insurance rates, particularly in automobile lines, pushed insurance issues to the forefront of California products. Initially, reform efforts focused on the legal liability system as the industry supported various efforts to move away from traditional tort liability rules, with their relatively high administrative costs and potentially excessive jury awards, to a presumably less costly no-fault liability system. (For an empirical analysis of the relative costs of no-fault and traditional tort liability, see Jeffrey O'Connell et al., *The Comparative Costs of Allowing Consumer Choice for Auto Insurance in All Fifty States*, 55 MD. L. REV. 160 (1996).) When these efforts failed to restrain rising insurance costs, consumer advocate invoked the state's referendum procedures to deal address the problem more directly.

## Calfarm Insurance Co. v. Deukmejian
### 771 P.2d 1247 (Cal. 1989) (en banc)

In this case we consider various challenges to Proposition 103, an initiative measure enacted November 8, 1988, making numerous fundamental changes in the regulation of automobile and other types of insurance.[1] . . . .

The initiative begins with a statement of findings and purpose, asserting that "[e]normous increases in the cost of insurance have made it both unaffordable and unavailable to millions of

---

[1]   Proposition 103 applies to "all insurance on risks or on operations in this state, except those listed in Section 1851." Insurance Code section 1851 lists reinsurance, life insurance, title insurance, certain types of marine insurance, disability insurance, workers' compensation insurance, mortgage insurance, and insurance transacted by county mutual fire insurers.

Californians," and that "the existing laws inadequately protect consumers and allow insurance companies to charge excessive, unjustified and arbitrary rates." The initiative's stated purpose is to ensure that "insurance is fair, available, and affordable for all Californians."

Insurance rates are to be immediately reduced to "at least 20 percent less" than those in effect on November 8, 1987 (approximately the date when the initiative was proposed, and one year prior to its enactment). (§ 1861.01, subd. (a); all statutory references are to the Insurance Code, unless otherwise stated.)[3] All rate increases require the approval of the Insurance Commissioner, who may not approve rates which are "excessive, inadequate, unfairly discriminatory or otherwise in violation of [the initiative]." (§ 1861.05.) Prior to November 8, 1989, however, rates may be increased only if the commissioner finds "that an insurer is substantially threatened with insolvency." (§ 1861.01, subd. (b).) Certain procedures are specified for hearing applications for rate approvals. (§§ 1861.04-1861.10.)

The initiative prohibits an insurer from declining to renew a policy except for nonpayment of premium, fraud, or significant increase in the hazard insured against. (§ 1861.03, subd. (c).) Insurers are required to mail notices to policy holders informing them they may join a nonprofit corporation to be formed to represent their interests by persons appointed for this purpose by the Insurance Commissioner. (§ 1861.10.) The Board of Equalization is directed to adjust the tax rate on insurance premiums to avoid any loss of tax revenues as a result of decreases in the rates charged by insurers. (Rev. & Tax.Code, § 12202.1.) Finally, the initiative contains a severance provision stating that the invalidity of any portion of the initiative "shall not affect other provisions or applications of the act which can be given effect without the invalid portion...."[4]

**1. Provisions relating to the reduction and subsequent adjustment of insurance rates.**

The constitutional test for the validity of state price controls was established in Nebbia v. New York (1934) 291 U.S. 502, 539: "Price control, like any other form of regulation, is unconstitutional only if arbitrary, discriminatory, or demonstrably irrelevant to the policy the legislature is free to adopt, and hence an unnecessary and unwarranted interference with individual liberty." The United States Supreme Court reaffirmed this test in Pennell v. City of San Jose (1988) 485 U.S. 1. We followed it in Birkenfeld v. City of Berkeley (1976) 17 Cal.3d 129, 130 Cal.Rptr. 465, 550 P.2d 1001, a rent control case, and went on to explain that "[t]he

---

[3]    Section 1861.01 further provides: "(d) For those who apply for an automobile insurance policy for the first time on or after November 8, 1988, the rate shall be 20% less than the rate which was in effect on November 8, 1987, for similarly situated risks. [¶] (e) Any separate affiliate of an insurer, established on or after November 8, 1987, shall be subject to the provisions of this section and shall reduce its charges to levels which are at least 20% less than the insurer's charges in effect on that date." Our discussion of the initiative's rate rollback and reduction provisions applies to subdivisions (d) and (e) as well as to subdivision (a) of section 1861.01.

[4]    Other provisions of the initiative, not challenged here, require that automobile insurance rates, beginning in November 1989, be based on driving record, number of miles driven, years of driving experience, and other factors approved by the commissioner, that good drivers receive a 20 percent discount on automobile insurance rates, that the insurance industry be subject to the Unruh Civil Rights Act (Civ.Code, §§ 51-53), antitrust laws and unfair business practice laws, and that the Insurance Commissioner be an elective office beginning with the 1990 election.

provisions are within the police power if they are reasonably calculated to eliminate excessive rents and at the same time provide landlords with a just and reasonable return on their property." (P. 165, 130 Cal.Rptr. 465, 550 P.2d 1001.)

The state and federal Constitutions are concerned not so much with the way in which the initial rates are set as with whether the rates as finally set are confiscatory.[5] "[I]t is the result reached not the method employed which is controlling." (Power Comm'n v. Hope Gas Co. (1944) 320 U.S. 591, 602; see Duquesne Light Co. v. Barasch (1989) 109 S.Ct. 609, 617.) In Fisher v. City of Berkeley (1984) 37 Cal.3d 644, 683, 209 Cal.Rptr. 682, 693 P.2d 261, we reaffirmed the rule that "whether a regulation produces a return that is confiscatory or fair depends ultimately on the result, and ... we will invalidate an ordinance on its face only if its terms preclude avoidance of confiscatory results." Petitioners must show that the law is "so restrictive as to facially preclude any possibility of a just and reasonable return" (Hutton, supra, 350 A.2d 1, 16); that "its terms will not permit those who administer it to avoid confiscatory results" (Birkenfeld v. City of Berkeley, supra, 17 Cal.3d 129, 165, 130 Cal.Rptr. 465, 550 P.2d 1001).

Consequently, we focus less on the rate specified in the statute than on the ability of the seller to obtain relief if that rate proves confiscatory. The face of a statute rarely reveals whether the rates it specifies are confiscatory or arbitrary, but necessarily discloses its provisions, if any, for rate adjustment. Recognizing that virtually any law which sets prices may prove confiscatory in practice, courts have carefully scrutinized such provisions to ensure that the sellers will have an adequate remedy for relief from confiscatory rates. . . .

We therefore begin our discussion by considering the provisions in Proposition 103 which would permit an insurer to seek relief from any rate it considers confiscatory. Section 1861.05 provides that "[e]very insurer which desires to change any rate shall file a complete rate application with the commissioner." Subdivision (a) states that the commissioner may not approve or permit any rate "which is excessive, inadequate, unfairly discriminatory or otherwise in violation of this chapter"--language which makes it clear that the commissioner can grant relief from confiscatory rates. Section 1861.01, subdivision (b), however, qualifies section 1861.05 by limiting rate adjustments prior to November 1989 to insurers substantially threatened with insolvency. Petitioners attack the constitutionality of this limitation.

Section 1861.01, subdivision (b), provides that "[b]etween November 8, 1988, and November 8, 1989, rates and premiums reduced pursuant to subdivision (a) may be only increased if the commissioner finds, after a hearing, that an insurer is substantially threatened with insolvency." "Insolvency" has various meanings, but none will allow us to construe subdivision (b) to conform to the constitutional standard of a fair and reasonable return. A company may be insolvent because it has more liabilities than assets, or because it is unable to pay its obligations as they fall due. . . .

---

[5]    The terms "fair and reasonable" and "confiscatory" are antonyms, not separate tests. (See FPC v. Texaco, Inc. (1974) 417 U.S. 380, 392; Board of Comm'rs v. N.Y. Tel. Co. (1926) 271 U.S. 23, 31; Hutton Park Gardens v. Town Council (1975) 68 N.J. 543, 350 A.2d 1, 15 [hereafter Hutton ].)

The insolvency standard of subdivision (b) refers to the financial position of the company as a whole, not merely to the regulated lines of insurance.[10]    Many insurers do substantial business outside of California, or in lines of insurance within this state which are not regulated by Proposition 103.  If an insurer had substantial net worth, or significant income from sources unregulated by Proposition 103, it might be able to sustain substantial and continuing losses on regulated insurance without danger of insolvency.  In such a case the continued solvency of the insurer could not suffice to demonstrate that the regulated rate constitutes a fair return.

The effect of section 1861.01, subdivision (b), is thus to bar safely solvent insurers from obtaining relief from "inadequate" rates until November 1989. Temporary rates which might be below a fair and reasonable level might compel insurers to return to their customers surpluses exacted through allegedly excessive past rates.  But the concept that rates may be set at less than a fair rate of return in order to compel the return of past surpluses is not one supported by precedent.  "The just compensation safeguarded to the utility by the Fourteenth Amendment is a reasonable return on the value of the property used at the time that it is being used for the public service....  [T]he law does not require the company to give up for the benefit of future subscribers any part of its accumulations from past operations.  Profits of the past cannot be used to sustain confiscatory rates for the future."  (Board of Comm'rs v. N.Y. Tel. Co., supra, 271 U.S. 23, 31-32; accord, American Toll Bridge Co. v. Railroad Com. (1938) 12 Cal.2d 184, 203, 83 P.2d 1.) Hutton, supra, said that if past rents were excessive an ordinance could refuse to give landlords credit for current cost increases if the diminished rate of return was still just and reasonable.  (350 A.2d at p. 16.)  But no case supports an unreasonably low rate of return on the ground that past profits were excessive.

Proponents urge that the insolvency standard can be sustained as a temporary or emergency measure.  They point out that temporary freezes while administrative machinery is set up are commonly approved, even if they lack any method whereby a seller can get relief.  (See, e.g., Trans Alaska Pipeline Rate Cases (1978) 436 U.S. 631;  United States v. SCRAP (1973) 412 U.S. 669;  Western States Meat Packers Assn., Inc. v. Dunlop (T.E.C.A.1973) 482 F.2d 1401.)  Most freezes are for periods of much less than one year, but courts have sustained freezes of a year or longer.  (See, e.g., Mass. Med. Society v. Comm'r of Ins. (1988) 402 Mass. 44, 520 N.E.2d 1288 [two-year freeze on medical malpractice insurance rates].)  The cases, however, proceed on the assumption that the frozen prices were those set by a seller in a competitive market, and thus were fair rates, so that the only concern is increased costs during the freeze. (See discussion in Birkenfeld v. City of Berkeley, supra, 17 Cal.3d 129, 166, 130 Cal.Rptr. 465, 550 P.2d 1001.)  Here we have a law which mandates not maintenance of a rate set by the seller, but a reduction to at least 20 percent less than former rates.  The risk that the rate set by the statute is confiscatory as to some insurers from its inception is high enough to require an adequate method for obtaining individualized relief.

---

[10]    Proponents point out that rates are generally regulated by considering each line of insurance separately, and suggest that "substantially threatened with insolvency" could be analyzed in a like manner.  But subdivision (b) refers to the solvency of an "insurer," not a line of insurance.  One can speak of a line of insurance as unprofitable, or causing losses, but it would be strained usage to speak of it as threatened with insolvency.

Proponents further argue that the insolvency standard in Proposition 103 was inserted to combat an emergency created by unavailable and unaffordable insurance. They assert that between 1983 and 1986 automobile insurance rates doubled, while commercial rates increased over 200 percent. They observe also that in 1984 the Legislature enacted the Robins-McAlister Financial Responsibility Act (Stats.1984, ch. 1322), requiring all motorists to purchase liability insurance and carry proof of financial responsibility.

We recognize that emergency situations may require emergency measures. As the court explained in Hutton, a rent control case, "[t]he term 'confiscatory' must be understood in light of the surrounding circumstances. There are undoubtedly times of great public exigency during which landlords may temporarily be required to rent their property at rates which do not permit them to obtain what would ordinarily be considered a fair return." (350 A.2d at p. 13.) Numerous cases confirm that measures enacted to combat an emergency of limited duration may be valid even though they do not guarantee a fair rate of return. . . .

To justify a measure which deprives persons of a fair return, however, "an emergency would have to be a temporary situation of such enormity that all individuals might reasonably be required to make sacrifices for the common weal." (Hutton, 350 A.2d 1, 14.) We do not believe that the circumstances which inspired Proposition 103 meet this requirement. Our concern is not with the magnitude of the problem, but with its character. The asserted rise in insurance rates, rendering insurance unavailable or unaffordable to many, is not a temporary problem; it is a long term, chronic situation which will not be solved by compelling insurers to sell at less than a fair return for a year. Over the long term the state must permit insurers a fair return; we do not perceive any short term conditions that would require depriving them of a fair return. We therefore conclude that subdivision (b) cannot be sustained as a emergency measure fashioned to meet a temporary exigency.

Having determined that section 1861.01, subdivision (b), precludes adjustments necessary to achieve the constitutional standard of fair and reasonable rates, and that the subdivision cannot be sustained as a temporary or emergency measure, we hold it invalid under the due process clauses of the state and federal Constitutions . . . .

The invalidation of this subdivision leaves untouched the general standard for rate adjustment set out in section 1861.05, subdivision (a). That provision states that "[n]o rate shall be approved or remain in effect which is excessive, inadequate, unfairly discriminatory, or otherwise in violation of this chapter. In considering whether a rate is excessive, inadequate or unfairly discriminatory no consideration shall be given to the degree of competition and the commissioner shall consider whether the rate mathematically reflects the insurance company's investment income."

Petitioners raise no question of the constitutionality of rates set pursuant to that section. Its prohibition on excessive or inadequate rates echoes similar language in the laws of most states, as well as former section 1852 which it replaces. Since a confiscatory rate is necessarily an "inadequate" rate under the statutory language, section 1861.05 requires rates within that range which can be described as fair and reasonable and prohibits approval or maintenance of confiscatory rates. . . . .

Petitioners argue, however, that even if section 1861.05 provides a constitutionally valid standard for rate adjustment, insurers will be compelled to charge confiscatory rates pending administrative relief.  They compare the procedures established by Proposition 103 with those in Birkenfeld v. City of Berkeley, supra, 17 Cal.3d 129, 130 Cal.Rptr. 465, 550 P.2d 1001, where we invalidated a rent control ordinance because "the inexcusably cumbersome rent adjustment procedure" was "not reasonably related to [its] stated purpose of preventing excessive rents." (P. 173, 130 Cal.Rptr. 465, 550 P.2d 1001.)

The city ordinance at issue in Birkenfeld governed rents for about 22,000 units.  (17 Cal.3d at p. 169, 130 Cal.Rptr. 465, 550 P.2d 1001.)  No landlord could apply for a rent increase for any unit until he had obtained a certificate of compliance from the city building inspector.  (P. 170, 130 Cal.Rptr. 465, 550 P.2d 1001.)  Every application required a hearing, regardless of the size of the increase, the reason for the request, or the consent of the tenant.  (P. 171, 130 Cal.Rptr. 465, 550 P.2d 1001.)  The rent control board was required to hear each application personally;  it could not consolidate applications or delegate the task to a hearing officer.  (Ibid.) "In short, [the board was] denied the means of reducing its job to manageable proportions through the formulation and application of general rules, the appropriate delegation of responsibility, and the focusing of the adjudicative process upon issues which cannot fairly be resolved in any other way." (Ibid.)

We find no similar barriers to efficient decision making in Proposition 103.  It does not establish a detailed method of processing and deciding rate applications.  It contains a few provisions relating to public notice and participation (i.e., §§ 1861.05, subd. (c), 1861.06, 1861.07 & 1861.10), but hearings are generally held in accordance with provisions of the Administrative Procedure Act.  (See § 1861.08, which provides generally that "[h]earings shall be conducted pursuant to Sections 11500 through 11528 of the Government Code.")  Much is necessarily left to the Insurance Commissioner, who has broad discretion to adopt rules and regulations as necessary to promote the public welfare. (Credit Ins. Gen. Agents Assn. v. Payne (1976) 16 Cal.3d 651, 656, 128 Cal.Rptr. 881, 547 P.2d 993; see Garris v. Carpenter (1939) 33 Cal.App.2d 649, 653, 92 P.2d 688.)  Unlike Birkenfeld, supra, 17 Cal.3d 129, 130 Cal.Rptr. 465, 550 P.2d 1001, there are no prerequisites to the filing of an application for an increase. Increases of no more than 7 percent for personal lines, or 15 percent for commercial lines, are automatically granted without a hearing unless one is requested.  The commissioner is expressly authorized to delegate hearings to administrative law judges. (§ 1861.08.)  No provision bars the commissioner from consolidating cases or issuing regulations of general applicability.  Thus there is nothing here which prevents the commissioner from taking whatever steps are necessary to reduce the job to manageable size.  It "is to be presumed that the [administrative agency] will exercise its power in conformity with the requirements of the Constitution; and if it does act unfairly, the fault lies with the [agency] and not the statute." (Fisher v. City of Berkeley, supra, 37 Cal.3d 644, 684, 209 Cal.Rptr. 682, 693 P.2d 261, quoting Butterworth v. Boyd (1938) 12 Cal.2d 140, 149, 82 P.2d 434.)

Moreover, the commissioner has the power to grant interim relief from plainly invalid rates. Her powers are not limited to those expressly conferred by statute;  "rather, '[i]t is well settled in this state that [administrative] officials may exercise such additional powers as are necessary for the due and efficient administration of powers expressly granted by statute, or as *may fairly be implied* from the statute granting the powers.' " (Rich Vision Centers, Inc. v. Board of Medical Examiners (1983) 144 Cal.App.3d 110, 114, 192 Cal.Rptr. 455, quoting Dickey v. Raisin Proration Zone No. 1 (1944) 24 Cal.2d 796, 810, 151 P.2d 505.)  The power to grant interim relief is necessary for the due and efficient administration of Proposition 103, and may fairly be implied from its command that "[n]o rate shall ... *remain in effect* which is excessive, inadequate, unfairly discriminatory or otherwise in violation of this chapter." (§ 1861.05, subd. (a).) (Italics added.)

In short, any insurer who believes the rates set by section 1861.01, subdivision (a), are confiscatory may file an application with the Insurance Commissioner for approval of a higher rate. If that application is filed before November 8, 1989, the insurer may immediately begin charging that higher rate[17] pending approval from the commissioner. After that date insurance rates subject to Proposition 103 must be approved by the commissioner prior to their use, but, as we have explained, the commissioner can approve an interim rate pending her final decision. If the commissioner finds the initiative's rate, or some other rate less than the insurer charged, is fair and reasonable, the insurer must refund excess premiums collected with interest. No insurer, however, will be compelled to charge the rates set by the initiative unless it either acquiesces in that rate or is unable to prove that a higher rate is constitutionally required.[18] In view of these safeguards we conclude that the initiative provision requiring a reduction in rate to at least 20 percent below 1987 rates does not, on its face, violate the due process rights of insurers.

In summary, we have concluded (a) that section 1861.01, subdivision (b), limiting first-year-rate adjustments to insurers substantially threatened with insolvency, is facially invalid . . . ; (b) that the procedures for adjustment of insurance rates--including application to the commissioner, the opportunity to seek interim relief, a hearing in accordance with the Administrative Procedure Act, and judicial review--meet constitutional standards; and (c) that in view of the safeguards described in this opinion, the rate rollback and reduction of Proposition 103 is not invalid on its face, but the rates thereby established are necessarily subject to the right of an insurer to demonstrate that a particular rate is, as applied to it, a confiscatory rate.

### 2. Restrictions upon the insurers' right to refuse to renew policies.

Proposition 103, in section 1861.03, subdivision (c) [hereafter nonrenewal provision], provides: "Notwithstanding any other provision of law, a notice of cancellation or non-renewal of a policy for automobile insurance shall be effective only if it is based on one or more of the following reasons: (1) nonpayment of premiums; (2) fraud or material misrepresentation affected the policy or insured; (3) a substantial increase in the hazard insured against." Before enactment

---

[17]   Proposition 103 provides that "insurance rates subject to this chapter must be approved by the commissioner prior to their use" (§ 1861.01, subd. (c)), but this provision takes effect November 8, 1989. Although the insolvency standard (§ 1861.01, subd. (b)) contemplated that during the first year of the initiative an insurer could not raise rates without a prior hearing, we have held this provision invalid. With its deletion, there remains no provision requiring prior approval of rate increases before November 8, 1989.

[18]   Proposition 103 contemplates that any rate set by the commissioner will be subject to judicial review. (See § 1861.09.) At the time of any such review, the court will have before it an administrative record that will undoubtedly contain vital ratemaking information and the commissioner's evaluation of the impact of that rate on the insurer and the insureds. That record will make possible a more informed analysis of any claim that the rate set by Proposition 103 is confiscatory as to a particular insurer and line of insurance.

of Proposition 103 insurers had an unfettered right to refuse to renew policies (see Greene v. Safeco Ins. Co. (1983) 140 Cal.App.3d 535, 538, 189 Cal.Rptr. 616).[19]

Respondent Attorney General and proponents contend that the nonrenewal provision applies to policies issued before enactment of Proposition 103. Petitioners agree that the provision was intended to apply to policies in force when Proposition 103 was enacted but maintain that the application of this provision to such policies would in effect alter their terms, and thereby violate the constitutional prohibition against a "law impairing the obligation of contracts." (U.S. Const., art. I, § 10; see Cal.Const., art. I, § 9.) . . . .

Three relatively recent United States Supreme Court decisions have considered the impairment-of-contract clause. In Allied Structural Steel Co. v. Spannaus (1978) 438 U.S. 234, the court struck down a Minnesota statute which required a company terminating operations in Minnesota to transfer to the state a sum sufficient to fund pension obligations to local workers. (Under prior law the company had the right to terminate the pension by refunding the trust amounts.) The court emphasized the narrow focus of the legislation--it was apparently aimed at only a few companies--and the fact that it concerned a subject not previously regulated.

Energy Reserves Group v. Kansas Power & Light, supra, 459 U.S. 400, upheld a Kansas law which established rates for natural gas sales and prohibited rate increases based on certain escalator clauses in existing contracts between gas sellers and public utilities. The court distinguished Allied Structural Steel, supra, 438 U.S. 234, primarily on the ground that the parties were operating in a heavily regulated industry.

The most recent decision, Exxon Corp. v. Eagerton (1983) 462 U.S. 176, upheld an Alabama law which imposed a severance tax on oil and gas and prohibited price increases which would pass on the burden of the tax even though some sellers had contracts which expressly authorized such price increases. The decision explained that "[a]lthough the language of the Contract Clause is facially absolute, its prohibition must be accommodated to the inherent police power of the State 'to safeguard the vital interests of its people.' . . . ." (462 U.S. at pp. 190-192.)

None of the United States Supreme Court cases has considered the contract clause in connection with insurance regulation, but a number of lower court decisions have discussed this matter. Hinckley v. Bechtel Corp. (1974) 41 Cal.App.3d 206, 116 Cal.Rptr. 33 involved a law which limited the period during which a retiring employee could exercise his right to convert a group life insurance policy to an individual policy without proof of insurability. Holding that the law could be applied to existing policies, the Court of Appeal stated: "The cases are legion which hold that the police power of the state to regulate insurance business cannot be contracted away, and the economic interest of the state may justify the exercise of its continuing protective power notwithstanding interference with existing contracts." (P. 215, 116 Cal.Rptr. 33.)

Decisions of other states also offer an analogy. Smith v. Department of Insurance, 507 So.2d 1080 [(Fla.1987)], offers something for both sides. Florida passed a law which limited

---

[19]    "Cancellation," as opposed to "non-renewal," refers to termination of a policy before its expiration date. Insurers' power to cancel policies was severely restricted by section 661 before enactment of Proposition 103. The only effect of Proposition 103 upon this section was to eliminate the 60-day grace period following issuance of a policy during which section 661 placed no limits on cancellation.

noneconomic tort damages, froze insurance rates, required a partial rebate of premiums on existing policies, and prohibited insurers from cancelling or refusing to renew existing policies in order to avoid the rate freeze or rebate.  The court held the rebate provision unconstitutional, applying a Florida rule that "virtually no degree of contract impairment is tolerable in this state." (Pomponio v. Claridge of Pomponio Condominium, Inc. (Fla.1979) 378 So.2d 774, 780, cited in Smith, supra, 507 So.2d at p. 1094.)  But it upheld without discussion all other provisions relating to insurance policies, including the section limiting the insurers' right to refuse to renew policies.

The State of Massachusetts, after regulating insurance rates for many years, discontinued rate regulation as of January 1, 1977.  When insurance rates rose rapidly, the state legislature reimposed regulation retroactive to January 1, directed that all policies written since January 1 be rewritten at reduced rates, and excess premiums rebated.  In American Mfrs. Mut. Ins. Co. v. Comm'r of Ins., 372 N.E.2d 520 (Mass. 1978), the Supreme Judicial Court of Massachusetts upheld the statute.  The court relied on the urgent need for immediate correction of insurance rates, and reasoned that insurers, as part of an intensely regulated industry, "were on notice that the premiums received were not firm against legislative adjustment." (372 N.E.2d at p. 528.)

When New York enacted no-fault insurance in 1973, it required insurers to offer that coverage to existing policyholders, and imposed a three-year restriction on nonrenewal of policies. In Country-Wide Ins. Co. v. Harnett (S.D.N.Y.1977) 426 F.Supp. 1030, 1035, a three-judge federal court upheld a law extending the restriction for an additional three years, stating that "[t]he law accomplishes a legitimate public goal and any contract rights must yield to it."[25]

We now apply these principles and precedents to the renewal provision of Proposition 103. We begin by assessing the severity of the impairment, since that assessment "measures the height of the hurdle the state legislation must clear" (Allied Structural Steel v. Spannaus, supra, 438 U.S. 234, 245), then examine the public interest advanced to justify the impairment.

In the present case the impairment, while not so low as to escape constitutional scrutiny, is relatively moderate and restrained, and the hurdle correspondingly low.  The insurer may still refuse to renew policies for nonpayment of premium, fraud or misrepresentation, or substantial increase in the hazard insured against.  And when it renews pursuant to Proposition 103 it is guaranteed fair and reasonable rates.

Insurance, moreover, is a highly regulated industry, and one in which further regulation can reasonably be anticipated.  As we said in Carpenter v. Pacific Mut. Life Ins. Co. (1937) 10 Cal.2d 307, 74 P.2d 761: "It is no longer open to question that the business of insurance is affected with a public interest.... Neither the company nor a policyholder has the inviolate rights that characterize private contracts.  The contract of the policyholder is subject to the reasonable

---

[25]    One decision has reached a contrary result.  In Health Ins. Ass'n of America v. Harnett (1978) 44 N.Y.2d 302, 405 N.Y.S.2d 634, 376 N.E.2d 1280 the court held that a law requiring health insurers to offer maternity coverage could not constitutionally be applied to existing health insurance policies. The decision rests on a view of state power far more limited than appears in the California cases, that "[o]nly on rare occasions and in extreme circumstances do rights fixed by the terms of a contract willingly entered into give way to a greater public need." (405 N.Y.S.2d 634, 641, 376 N.E.2d 1280, 1287.)

exercise of the state's police power." (P. 329, 74 P.2d 761; see People v. United National Life Ins. Co. (1967) 66 Cal.2d 577, 595, 58 Cal.Rptr. 599, 427 P.2d 199 and cases there cited.) Indeed it is clear that during the year prior to November 8, 1988--a year during which almost all automobile insurance policies in effect on that date were issued or renewed--insurers were well aware of the possibility that initiatives or ordinary legislation might be enacted that would affect existing policies.

Finally, Proposition 103 does not prevent an insurer from discontinuing its California business.  Sections 1070 through 1076 spell out the procedure by which an insurer may withdraw from California by surrendering its certificate of authority.  The initiative did not repeal those sections, and indeed recognizes the possibility that insurers may withdraw from some insurance markets by authorizing the commissioner to establish a joint underwriting authority to serve such markets.[21]

We turn now to examine the public interest to determine whether it justifies the impairment.  As we noted earlier, the drafters and the voters were evidently concerned that the enactment of Proposition 103 might cause some insurers not to renew some or all of their existing policies, an action which would undermine Proposition 103's goal of making insurance "available" for all Californians.  Indeed if many insurers refused to renew the state could face a crisis in which many of its residents would be unable to obtain insurance and thus could not legally drive, and others would be forced to accept inadequate protection.  We conclude that the public interest in averting this danger, when measured against the relatively low degree of impairment of contract rights involved, is sufficient to justify Proposition 103's nonrenewal provision, and accordingly that this provision can be applied to existing policies without violating the state or federal Constitutions.

### 3. Notice of formation of a consumer-advocacy corporation.

Section 1861.10, subdivision (c), provides for the creation of a consumer-advocacy corporation, and notice to all California policyholders of their opportunity to become members of the corporation.  It reads in full as follows:  "(1) The commissioner shall require every insurer to enclose notices in every policy or renewal premium bill informing policyholders of the opportunity to join an independent, non-profit corporation which shall advocate the interests of insurance consumers in any forum.  This organization shall be established by an interim board of public members designated by the commissioner and operated by individuals who are democratically elected from its membership.  The corporation shall proportionately reimburse insurers for any additional costs incurred by insertion of the enclosure, except no postage shall be charged for any enclosure weighing less than 1/3 of an ounce.  (2) The commissioner shall by regulation determine the content of the enclosures and other procedures necessary for implementation of this provision.  The legislature shall make no appropriation for this subdivision."

---

21    [S]ection 1861.11 . . . provides:  "In the event that the commissioner finds that (a) insurers have substantially withdrawn from any insurance market covered by this article, including insurance described by section 660 [automobile insurance], and (b) a market assistance plan would not be sufficient to make insurance available, the commissioner shall establish a joint underwriting authority in the manner set forth by Section 11891, without the prior creation of a market assistance plan."

Petitioners contend that the foregoing provision violates article II, section 12 of the California Constitution, which states: "No amendment to the Constitution, and no statute proposed to the electors by the Legislature or by initiative, that names an individual to hold any office, or names or identifies any private corporation to perform any function or to have any power or duty, may be submitted to the electors or have any effect." Petitioners further argue that since the constitutional provision says that no statute which violates it "may ... have any effect," the invalid language is nonseverable and invalidates the whole of Proposition 103. We hold that the consumer-advocacy provision of Proposition 103 does violate article II, section 12, but is severable and does not affect the balance of the initiative. . . . .

## Comments and Questions

1. The heart of Proposition 103 was its 20 percent roll-back provision. A number of factors contributed to popular support for this aspect of the initiative. To begin with, in the five years preceding passage of the initiative, the cost of private automobile insurance in California had been growing at an annual rate of between 12 and 22 percent. According to survey data, sixty-five percent of respondents believed that the industry was overcharging for premiums, and a similar percentage either agreed or strongly agreed with the proposition that California property-insurance companies "ma[d]e a killing but pretend[ed] they are not making money." Dwight W. Jaffee & Thomas Russell, The Causes and Consequences of Rate Regulation in the Auto Insurance Industry (Sept. 1995) (NBER Working Paper 5245). The perceived inequity of rising rates was particularly intense in urban areas:

For example, in Los Angeles county, in the 5 year period 1983-1988, the frequency of claims for bodily injury liability was 2.4 times the statewide average for these claims. Yet, in this 5 year period, the actual total of incurred claims in L.A. was 71,890 on an "installed base" of 1,464,079 autos. Thus 95% of all insured automobiles in Los Angeles County had no claims in 5 years. Nevertheless, these Los Angeles county drivers faced insurance premiums about 2.4 times as high as the state average.

Id. at 13. Subsequent analysis of voting patterns has revealed that high-premium counties such as Los Angeles were among the most ardent supporters of Proposition 103. Some analysts have suggested that this data implies that Proposition 103 was simply a self-interested transfer of wealth from low-premium counties to high-premium jurisdictions. Are there other, more public-spirited justifications for the initiative?

2. Under the *Calfarm* decision, insurance companies were entitled to contest the roll-back provision as confiscatory. A number of companies sought such relief, and the California Insurance Department eventually held a number of hearings on this issue, and developed a methodology designed to ensure firms an 11.2 percent return on invested equity. See 20th Century Insurance Co. v. Garamendi, 878 P.2d 566 (Cal. 1994). Does this approach satisfy the standards articulated in the *Calfarm* decision? How does it compare to the approach employed in Hypothetical Rate Case discussed earlier?

3. Proposition 103 also dealt with permissible classification systems for future premiums. The relevant provisions, summarized above in footnote four of the case,

authorized three permissible factors: prior safety record, miles driven annually, and years of driving experience.  Notably absent from the list was geographic location of the vehicles — a principal rate-setting factor in the industry.  Proposition 103 did, however, authorize the Insurance Commissioner to consider other factors "that have a substantial relationship to the risk of loss."  Under intense pressure from the industry, the commissioner has invoked this residual authority, at least initially, to allow premiums to reflect geographic considerations.  The results of this accommodation is described in the following excerpt:

[A] study of the state's 14 largest insurers, which together control 82 percent of California's market, demonstrates that insurers use a driver's address as a critical element in setting premiums. That, despite the passage seven years ago of Proposition 103, the voter-approved initiative that ordered the practice halted but which was blunted in the courts by challenges from insurers and resulted in a continuously renewed series of emergency regulations.

Under those emergency regulations modifying Prop. 103, insurers have continued to use zip codes, age, marital status and other factors in determining coverage. . . . For example, a good driver in Los Angeles County pays an average of $1,009 annually for coverage; in Northern California counties the same driver pays $407, according to the survey.

After Los Angeles, the costliest counties were Orange, at $729; San Bernardino-Riverside counties at $555; the San Francisco Bay area at $547; and San Diego-Imperial counties at $473.

Overall, the state wide average premium for a 30-year-old good driver was $566 during 1994, a slight increase over the year before. . . .

But the average costs do not reflect the extremes of premium rates. A good driver in Los Angeles' South Central district, for example, pays an average of $2,315 a year for coverage, while the equivalent driver in Palos Verdes pays as little as $359 for the same policy, depending on the carrier. . . .

The most dramatic costs were reported in family coverage. A husband and wife, with one speeding ticket each and driving a 1994 Ford Explorer and a 1992 Toyota Camry, and with a 17-year-old son licensed for one year and covered as an occasional operator, can pay more than $500 a month - $6,500 annually - in Los Angeles County, and $3,253 in northern California counties.

The cost of family coverage also varied dramatically according to the carrier. The survey found that a couple with a teenage son and two automobiles would be charged $3,422 from one carrier, while another insurer would charge a whopping $10,393 for the same coverage.

*California Drivers Pay Wide Range of Premiums*, Nat'l Underwriter Property & Casualty Risk Management, Oct. 16, 1995, at 30.  Query: What do you make of the fact, noted in the last paragraph of this excerpt, that there is a near three-fold difference in the price companies charge for the same insurance?  How can the market allow for this variation in prices?

In response to public outcry over continuing rate disparities, Insurance Commissioner Chuck Quackenbush subsequently proposed new rules eliminating geographic factors but authorizing fifteen other optional factors — "type of vehicle, type of use, the number of vehicles in a household, the academic standing of the driver, the sex of the driver, the marital status of the driver, whether the driver smokes and whether the driver has completed a driver training course." "Automobile Insurance Rates to Change in California," San Francisco Examiner, July 9, 1996, at A5.   Do you approve of the Commissioner's rules?

---

Intense regulation of premiums, of the sort practiced in both Massachusetts and California, often gives rise to disputes over the terms under which insurance companies are permitted to withdraw from doing business in the jurisdictions.   See Travelers Indemnity Co. v. Gillespie, 785 P.2d 500 (Cal. 1990) (exploring the relationship between Proposition 103's mandatory renewal provisions and the rights of insurance companies to cease doing business in the state); Aetna Casualty & Surety Co. v. Gailey, 753 F. Supp. 46 (D. Mass. 1990) (dismissing for want of ripeness a challenge to Massachusetts restrictions on withdrawal).  Similar issues are at play in the following decision.

## In re Twin City Fire Insurance Co.
### 609 A.2d 1248 (N.J. 1992), *cert. denied*, 506 U.S. 1086 (1993)

Twin City Fire Insurance Company (Twin City) challenges the constitutionality of the order issued by the Commissioner of Insurance (Commissioner) conditioning the termination of its authority to write insurance in New Jersey.

I.

Twin City is a property-casualty insurer licensed for more than twenty years to transact business in each of the fifty states and the District of Columbia. It has no plan to surrender its license in any jurisdiction other than New Jersey.   Twin City primarily writes private-passenger and commercial automobile insurance in New Jersey.  Its 1989 private-passenger insurance premiums aggregated $16.3 million, or 1.032% of that market; its aggregate 1989 commercial-insurance premiums were $49.6 million, representing 13% of the market.   Twin City is a wholly-owned subsidiary of Hartford Fire Insurance Company (Hartford Fire), as are the other six Twin City affiliated companies affected by the Commissioner's order, as modified. . . . Hartford Fire and the other six Twin City affiliates generated approximately $120 million in aggregate premiums from New Jersey insurance business in 1989, of which approximately $9 million was attributable to private-passenger automobile premiums and the balance to multiple lines of property and casualty insurance.

On March 7, 1990, Twin City tendered its Certificate of Authority for surrender to the Acting Commissioner of Insurance, accompanied by a letter forecasting that the impending adoption of [Fair Automobile Insurance Reform Act of 1990, L.1990, c. 8 (the Reform Act or the Act) (requiring automobile insurers to participate equitably in the shifting of residual-market insureds to the voluntary market)] would cause Twin City to incur "devastating losses in future years." The Reform Act was signed by Governor Florio on March 12, 1990.  Section 72 of the Act, which applied retroactively to requests by insurers for surrender of Certificates of Authority submitted on or after January 25, 1990, provides:

An insurance company of another state or foreign country authorized under chapter 32 of Title 17 of the Revised Statutes to transact insurance business in this State may surrender to the commissioner its certificate of authority and thereafter cease to transact insurance in this State, or discontinue the writing or renewal of one or more kinds of insurance specified in the certificate of authority, only after the submission of a plan which provides for an orderly withdrawal from the market and a minimization of the impact of the surrender or discontinuance on the public generally and on the company's policyholders in this State. The plan shall be approved by the commissioner before the withdrawal or discontinuance takes effect. In reviewing a plan for withdrawal under this section, the commissioner shall consider, and may require as a condition of approval, whether some or all other certificates of authority issued pursuant to chapter 17 or 32 of Title 17 of the Revised Statutes held by the company or by other companies in the same holding company as the company submitting the plan should be surrendered. The certificate of authority of the company shall be deemed to continue in effect until the provisions of the approved plan have been carried out. The provisions of this section shall apply to any request for withdrawal, surrender or discontinuance filed on or after January 25, 1990.

[O]n April 30, 1990, Twin City submitted a plan for orderly withdrawal, effective the following day, in which it proposed to withdraw from private-passenger automobile-insurance business in New Jersey by non-renewing its policies and withdrawing its rating system, retaining the authority to write other forms of insurance in the state. Twin City's rationale for its proposed withdrawal from the private-passenger automobile-insurance market . . . relied on financial projections prepared by Twin City in anticipation of adoption of the Reform Act. Those projections, prepared on the basis of estimated rate increases of 6.4% in 1990 and 8% in 1991 and 1992, calculated that Twin City would sustain underwriting losses in those three years of $ 3.8 million, $19 million, and $23.5 million, respectively, if it continued its present private-passenger automobile-insurance business.

In his Administrative Decision and Order of August 14, 1990 (No. A90-151), the Commissioner approved Twin City's plan subject to fourteen conditions. In challenging the Commissioner's Order and the constitutionality of Section 72 of the Reform Act in the Appellate Division, Twin City objected specifically to four of the conditions:

A. The "Five Year Condition"

Twin City must attempt to place its private-passenger automobile business with other insurers. If unsuccessful after five years, Twin City may then issue notices of non-renewal. Twin City cannot withdraw from the market until all of its policies have been placed with other carriers or have expired.

B. The "Other Business Condition"

Twin City shall be required to seek replacement carriers for its other lines of business for a period of five years. After five years Twin City must non-renew any remaining policies in force as they expire.

C. The "Forfeiture Condition"

Twin City's ITT Hartford affiliates must submit orderly plans of withdrawal from their respective markets providing for the termination of their transaction of insurance business within five years.

D. The "New-Business Condition"

During its withdrawal from the private-passenger automobile-insurance business over a five-year period, Twin City must comply with all provisions of the Reform Act including the requirement that it participate proportionately in the shifting of "assigned risk" or residual market insureds to the voluntary market.

II.

A. History and Overview of the Reform Act

A basic familiarity with the events and circumstances that prompted passage of the Reform Act, as well as an appreciation of the Act's anticipated impact on the private-passenger automobile-insurance market, are essential prerequisites to an informed evaluation of the validity of the Commissioner's order. The Act's background and objectives are described comprehensively in State Farm Mutual Automobile Insurance Co. v. State, 124 N.J. 32, 590 A.2d 191 (1991), in which this Court sustained the constitutionality of the Reform Act against a facial challenge.

For years, New Jersey's system of automobile insurance regulation, like those of many other states, has faced an intractable problem of providing coverage for high-risk drivers. Prior to 1983, drivers who could not obtain coverage directly from insurers in the voluntary market were insured through an Assigned Risk Plan (N.J.S.A. 17:29D-1), under which the Commissioner of Insurance apportioned high-risk drivers among all auto insurers doing business in New Jersey. In 1983, the Automobile Full Insurance Availability Act, N.J.S.A. 17:30E-1 through -24, replaced the assigned-risk system with the New Jersey Automobile Full Insurance Underwriting Association, commonly known as the Joint Underwriting Association or JUA. All insurers licensed to write automobile insurance in New Jersey were required to be members of the JUA. The objective of the new scheme was to create a more extensive system of allocating high-risk drivers to carriers, and through the JUA, to provide such drivers with coverage at rates equivalent to those charged in the voluntary market....

The JUA, a good deal more complex than the prior Assigned Risk Plan, worked as follows. Insurers (and subsequently certain qualified non-insurer entities) could apply to become "servicing carriers," which would bear administrative responsibility for collecting premiums, arranging coverage, and the like, and which would receive fees for such services from the JUA. However, the statute, the Plan of Operation, and the agreements between the JUA and servicing carriers all provided that claims and liabilities of the JUA would be borne by it independently; servicing carriers were to be insulated from such claims and liabilities.

Because the JUA insured high-risk drivers but also required that their rates be the same as voluntary-market rates (see N.J.S.A. 17:30E-13), it was anticipated that premium revenues would not cover costs of claims against JUA policies. Therefore, in addition to normal premium income, the JUA was also given income from Department of Motor Vehicle surcharges for moving violations and drunken driving convictions, policy "flat charges," and "residual market equalization charges," or RMECs, to be added to policy rates for voluntary-market insureds. N.J.S.A. 17:30E-8. Thus, the JUA was a system in which the insurance costs of high-risk drivers were subsidized by the imposition of fees on segments [on] the general population of motorists. The JUA was supposed to be operated on a no-profit, no-loss basis, with RMECs increased or decreased as needed to accomplish that result.

However one may view the objectives of the JUA, the system did not achieve its goals. More and more drivers became unable to procure voluntary-market coverage, until by 1988 over 50% of New Jersey drivers had to be insured through the JUA. Claims against JUA insureds were sizeable and greatly exceeded the JUA's available income. Despite the imposition of substantial RMECs from

1988 through 1990, the JUA nonetheless accumulated a deficit of over $3.3 billion in unpaid claims and other losses.

Automobile insurance reform, including the reduction of the cost of insurance, and particularly some plan for eliminating the unwieldy JUA, repaying its debt, and replacing it with a more workable distribution of the automobile insurance market, became a priority for the Legislature and the executive branch in 1990. By March of that year the Reform Act had been adopted.

The principal goals of the Act were to reduce insurance costs for most New Jersey drivers, to depopulate the JUA by switching insureds to the voluntary market, and to create a funding mechanism to pay off the JUA debt. To these ends, the Act provided that the JUA would cease writing or renewing policies as of October 1, 1990. The "depopulation" of the JUA would be accomplished by classifying insured drivers into three categories: (1) high-risk drivers in the (revived) Assigned Risk Plan (10% of the market); (2) "non-standard" risk drivers, who would be insured by private insurers directly, but who could be charged rates up to 135% of those of standard risks (15% of the market); and (3) standard-risk, voluntary-market insureds covered at prevailing rates (the remaining 75% of the market). Presumably, the higher rates now to be charged high-risk and "non-standard" risk drivers should bring the premium income on such coverage in line with actual costs, and this coverage would no longer be subsidized.

There remains, however, the problem of how to pay off the JUA's prior accumulated debt of over $ 3.3 billion; this, too, is addressed by the Reform Act. The Act creates the New Jersey Automobile Insurance Guaranty Fund (Auto Fund), a separate fund within the State Treasury, to collect and disburse the various payments designed to pay off the JUA debt. Reform Act, Section 23; N.J.S.A. 17:33B-5. The Act assigns to the Auto Fund certain sources of income that under the prior scheme went to the JUA, e.g., surcharges for driving violations and drunken driving convictions. It also creates new sources of revenue for the Auto Fund, e.g., fees on lawyers, doctors, and auto body repair businesses, higher automobile registration fees, and, most significant in the context of this litigation, the imposition of additional assessments and surtaxes on insurers.

The assessments imposed on insurance carriers are collected through the Property Liability Insurance Guaranty Association (PLIGA). Reform Act, Section 74, N.J.S.A. 17:30A-8a(9). PLIGA was created in 1974 to impose assessments on New Jersey property-casualty insurers to pay claims against carriers that had become insolvent. (L. 1974, c. 17; N.J.S.A. 17:30A-1 through 17:30A-20). The Reform Act requires PLIGA to make additional assessments to be applied exclusively to the JUA debt. These assessments, denominated by the Act as "loans," are paid into the Auto Fund. N.J.S.A. 17:30A-8a(10). They are to be set at rates designed to net $ 160 million per year for eight years (1990 through 1997); for 1990, the assessments represented 2.7% of net premiums of the property-casualty insurers.

Section 75 of the Reform Act, N.J.S.A. 17:30A-16, addresses recoupment from policyholders of PLIGA assessments both for insolvencies and for the JUA bailout. Insurers have always been permitted to pass through the insolvency assessments to policyholders. The insolvency passthrough originally was accomplished by rate increases, but in 1979 the method was changed to direct surcharges on policy premiums. The surcharges for insolvency assessments continue to be authorized under the Reform Act. N.J.S.A. 17:30A-16a. However, the Act expressly prohibits such surcharges to recover the new assessments for the JUA bailout. Section 75b states:

> No member insurer shall impose a surcharge on the premiums of any policy to recoup assessments paid pursuant to [the provision requiring assessments to be loaned to the Auto Fund]. [N.J.S.A. 17:30A-16b.]

In addition to the new assessments, the Reform Act, Section 76, imposes a special surtax on insurers to go toward the JUA bailout. N.J.S.A. 17:33B-49. This surtax is a greater amount, 5% of net premiums, but is imposed for a shorter period (only three years, 1990, 1991 and 1992), than the assessments. The additional surtax is designed to net a total of $300,000,000 over the three-year period into the Auto Fund. Reform Act, Section 77, N.J.S.A. 17:33B-50. Because the objective is to secure $ 300 million in net proceeds, the 5% surtax rate can be adjusted, depending upon the amount of insurers' net premiums. The 5% rate cannot be exceeded, and it is theoretically possible that the Director of Taxation could lower the rate; but such a lowering could occur only if automobile insurance net premiums increased significantly, a highly unlikely event given both the supposed premium-reducing effects of the Act and current market conditions. The Reform Act, Section 78, addresses the question of whether the additional surtaxes can be charged to consumers: The Commissioner of Insurance shall take such action as is necessary to ensure that private passenger automobile insurance policyholders shall not pay for the surtax imposed pursuant to section 76.

[N.J.S.A. 17:33B-51.] [124 N.J. at 40-45, 590 A.2d 191 (citations omitted).]

In State Farm, the insurers had argued that those provisions of the Reform Act that prohibited the passthrough to policyholders of the assessments and surcharges imposed by the Act to pay off the JUA's $ 3.3 billion indebtedness would necessarily cause the insurers to operate at a loss and thus be deprived of a constitutionally-adequate rate of return. We noted, however, that Section 2g of the Act, N.J.S.A. 17:33B-2g, which had been added by an amendment introduced when the Reform Act was before the Assembly Appropriations Committee, specifically provided that "insurers 'are entitled to earn an adequate rate of return'" through the ratemaking process. 124 N.J. at 57-58, 590 A.2d 191. We also observed that "emergency regulations" adopted by the Commissioner while the State Farm litigation was pending established a new procedure to afford rate relief to insurers that could demonstrate that payment of the surtaxes and assessments had denied them a fair rate of return. Id. at 59-61, 590 A.2d 191. Hence, we rejected the facial challenge to the constitutionality of the Reform Act because we were satisfied that the regulatory provisions for rate relief and the legislative assurance of a fair rate of return demonstrated that the passthrough prohibitions of Sections 75 and 78 of the Act "do not necessarily preclude all insurers from earning a fair rate of return." Id. at 61-62, 590 A.2d 191. . . .

III.

Before us, Twin City and amicus curiae, American Insurance Association, have focused their challenge to the Commissioner's order on two of the fourteen conditions, the "forfeiture condition," requiring Twin City's affiliates to terminate business in New Jersey within five years, and the "new-business condition," which requires Twin City during its withdrawal from New Jersey to comply with the Reform Act and participate equitably in the shift of residual-market insureds to the voluntary market. . . .

A. Substantive Due Process

Although Twin City limits its due-process argument to the new-business condition, apparently conceding the validity under due-process principles of the forfeiture condition, our analysis is sufficiently broad to embrace both conditions. Our decisions have established, as have those of the United States Supreme Court, that "a state statute does not violate substantive due process if the statute reasonably relates to a legitimate legislative purpose and is not arbitrary or discriminatory. * * * [I]f a statute is supported by a conceivable rational basis, it will withstand a substantive due process attack." Greenberg v. Kimmelman, 99 N.J. 552, 563, 494 A.2d 294 (1985) (citations omitted). We described the proper function of the courts in this area in Hutton Park Gardens v. Town Council, 68 N.J. 543, 350 A.2d 1 (1975):

"So far as the requirement of due process is concerned, and in the absence of other constitutional restriction, a state is free to adopt whatever economic policy may reasonably be deemed to promote public welfare, and to enforce that policy by legislation adapted to its purpose. The courts are without authority either to declare such policy, or, when it is declared by the legislature, to override it." . . .

In assessing the constitutionality of Section 72 of the Reform Act and of the conditions imposed by the Commissioner pursuant to its authorization, we observe at the outset that insurance is "a business to which the government has long had a 'special relation.'" California State Auto. Ass'n v. Maloney, 341 U.S. 105, 109 (1951). The principle that "the insurance business is strongly affected with a public interest and therefore properly subject to comprehensive regulation in protecting the public welfare" is long settled and well-established. Sheeran v. Nationwide Mut. Ins. Co., 80 N.J. 548, 559, 404 A.2d 625 (1979).

In the context of the broad and comprehensive regulatory authority of the state over the business of insurance and the tolerant standard by which due-process challenges to such regulation must be addressed, we find no merit in Twin City's contention that the new-business condition violates its due-process rights. Viewed against the backdrop of New Jersey's chronic difficulties in assuring coverage for substandard private-passenger automobile insureds, the justification for imposing that condition on Twin City's right to withdraw is not merely rational, it is compelling. To the extent Twin City's contention addresses the obligation to renew existing policies during its five-year withdrawal process, that obligation is hardly an onerous one. As it withdraws over a five-year period, Twin City must either place its existing policies with other carriers or renew them in order that its insureds not be disadvantaged by its withdrawal. We sustained an analogous requirement in Sheeran, supra, 80 N.J. at 561, 404 A.2d 625, and entertain no doubt about its reasonableness or its validity.

We are also convinced that due process is not offended by the Commissioner's requiring Twin City to comply, during its withdrawal period, with the Reform Act's mandate that the shift of insureds from the residual to the voluntary market be shared equitably by all insurers. As long ago as 1951 the United States Supreme Court upheld against a due-process challenge a California statute authorizing that state's insurance commissioner to approve "a reasonable plan for the equitable apportionment" among insurers of substandard risk drivers. California State Auto. Ass'n, supra, 341 U.S. at 107, 110-11. New Jersey's extraordinary difficulties with assigned-risk drivers, resulting in the JUA's staggering deficit, provoked the Reform Act's mandatory residual-market depopulation provisions. State Farm, supra, 124 N.J. at 41-42, 590 A.2d 191. Because the Act requires all insurers to participate equitably in the shift from the residual to the voluntary market, see N.J.S.A. 17:30E-14, the Commissioner's imposition of that statutory obligation as a condition of Twin City's withdrawal is not only rational and fair but virtually required by the Act. That an insurer who enjoyed profitable operations during the pre-Reform Act period could abandon entirely the remedial burdens imposed by the Act on all private-passenger insurers would be inequitable. Twin City's obligation to participate in depopulation of the residual market is limited to five years or such shorter period within which it places its policies with other carriers. The new-business condition does not violate due process.

We are equally convinced that, although not asserted as a due-process violation, the forfeiture condition does not violate the due-process rights of Twin City and its affiliates in ITT Hartford. In its challenge to the forfeiture condition as an unconstitutional taking of property without just compensation, see infra at 412-419, 609 A.2d at 1260-1264, Twin City protests that the Commissioner had no regulatory basis for ignoring the separate corporate status of its affiliates by requiring the termination of their New Jersey business as a condition of Twin City's withdrawal. Although the United States Supreme Court has acknowledged that the "rationality" standard determinative of substantive-due-process challenges to State regulation is less stringent than the "takings" standard, which requires that the taking "substantially advance" the State interest to be achieved, Nollan v. California Coastal Comm'n, 483 U.S. 825, 834 n.3 (1987), both tests focus on the strength of the connection between the government's objective and its regulatory action. By either standard, Twin City's interrelationship with its affiliates is indisputably sufficient to justify a regulatory approach that treats them pragmatically as a single entity.

Twin City's own Plan of Withdrawal establishes that ITT Hartford owns and controls Hartford Fire and, in turn, owns and controls Twin City and its other affiliates. The companies market their products under common names, use the same insurance agents designated for them by ITT Hartford, process their claims collectively through employees of Hartford Fire, and participate in reinsurance-pooling agreements with other ITT Hartford companies. At oral argument, counsel acknowledged that ultimately the decision whether Twin City and the affiliates would remain or withdraw from New Jersey would be made by ITT Hartford's management. Whether Twin City and its affiliates operate as divisions of a single corporation or as subsidiary corporations of an integrated insurance holding company, a responsible regulator could hardly ignore their common ownership and operational interdependence.

Although the Reform Act unquestionably renders more burdensome and less profitable the private-passenger automobile-insurance business in New Jersey, our decision in State Farm determined that the Act contemplates that insurers will earn a fair return, and it thus cannot facially be construed to deny insurers a fair rate of return. 124 N.J. at 62, 590 A.2d 191. Twin City's decision to withdraw apparently reflects the unwillingness of ITT Hartford to subject Twin City to what may be a difficult and burdensome regulatory process. The option of Twin City's withdrawal, however, would be unavailable to ITT Hartford if the affiliates were divisions under common ownership rather than subsidiaries under common control.

As the Commissioner's order observed, the withdrawal of any private-passenger insurers in the current difficult regulatory climate increases the burdens on those insurers who remain, burdens attributable to the more favorable regulatory conditions enjoyed by Twin City before the passage of the Reform Act. Other private-passenger insurers have also sought withdrawal, following Twin City's example. In such a period of regulatory turmoil and uncertainty, nothing short of severe regulatory measures imposed on private-passenger insurers threatening to withdraw -- in other words, strong medicine -- would be effective. If the forfeiture condition discourages withdrawal, a substantial State interest -- retention of private-passenger insurers -- will have been advanced. If it fails to discourage Twin City's withdrawal, the availability for acquisition of its affiliates' insurance business may operate as an inducement to other multi-line carriers to remain in New Jersey, thereby advancing an analogous and equally substantial State interest.

Twin City's reluctance to assert a substantive due-process challenge to the forfeiture condition rather persuasively demonstrates the strength of the regulatory interest advanced by that condition. We hold that that regulatory interest is more than adequate to sustain the forfeiture condition against a substantive-due-process challenge. That the forfeiture condition also "'substantially advance[s]' the 'legitimate state interest' sought to be achieved," Nollan, supra, 483 U.S. at 834 n. 3 (quoting Agins v. Tiburon, 447 U.S. 255, 260 (1980)) -- the Nollan Court's governmental-interest test for takings -- is also self-evident from our analysis.  See infra at 419, 609 A.2d at 1264.

## [B]. The Takings Issue

Twin City's principal contention before us is that the forfeiture condition, requiring its affiliates to forfeit their licenses and transfer their New Jersey insurance business to competitors, constitutes an unconstitutional "taking" of its property for public use without just compensation. U.S. Const. amend. V; N.J. Const. art. I, para. 20.  It argues that the Appellate Division, in addressing the "takings" issue, improperly focused on the losses Twin City would incur if it remained in New Jersey rather than on its affiliates' forced surrender of approximately $ 120 million in aggregate annual-premium income in the event Twin City elects to surrender its license.

As the United States Supreme Court has recently observed, "takings" cases can generally be divided into two distinct categories: cases in which the government takes title to or physically occupies property, generally requiring that compensation be paid; and cases in which the government regulates the permitted uses of property, which require fact-specific determinations on whether  compensation is mandated.  Yee v. City of Escondido, 112 S.Ct. 1522, 1525 (1992). "A 'taking' may more readily be found when the interference with property can be characterized as a physical invasion by government * * * than when interference arises from some public program adjusting the benefits and burdens of economic life to promote the common good." Penn Central Transp. Co. v. New York City, 438 U.S. 104, 124 (1978). Concerning the second class of cases, the Court observed: But where the government merely regulates the use of property, compensation is required only if considerations such as the purpose of the regulation or the extent to which it deprives the owner of the economic use of the property suggest that the regulation has unfairly singled out the property owner to bear a burden that should be borne by the public as a whole.  See, e.g., Penn Central Transp. Co. v. New York City, 438 US 104, 123-125 (1978).  The first category of cases requires courts to apply a clear rule; the second necessarily entails complex factual assessments of the purposes and economic effects of government actions.  [City of Escondido, supra, 112 S.Ct. at 1526.]

As a general proposition, the Supreme Court has recognized that the "Fifth Amendment's guarantee * * * [is] designed to bar Government from forcing some people alone to bear public burdens which, in all fairness and justice, should be borne by the public as a whole." Armstrong v. United States, 364 U.S. 40, 49 (1960).  Nevertheless, the Court consistently has refrained from proposing or adopting rigid or precise principles for determining when a compensable taking has occurred, favoring instead a "highly nonformal, open ended, multi-factor balancing method." Frank Michelman, Takings, 1987, 88 Colum.L.Rev. 1600, 1621 (1988). As Justice Brennan acknowledged in Penn Central, supra, 438 U.S. 104, the Court has simply been unable to develop any "set formula" for determining when "justice and fairness" require that economic injuries caused by public action be compensated by the government, rather than remain disproportionately concentrated on a few persons.  See Goldblatt v. Hempstead, 369 US 590, 594 (1962).  Indeed, we have frequently observed that whether a particular restriction will be rendered invalid by the government's failure to pay for any losses proximately caused by it depends largely "upon the particular circumstances [in that] case." [Id., at 124 (quoting United States v. Central Eureka Mining Co., 357 U.S. 155, 168 (1958)).]

Nevertheless, as a guide to the ad hoc inquiry implicated by regulatory "takings" claims, the Court has identified three factors as having particular significance: the character of the governmental action, the economic impact of the regulation, and whether the regulation interfered with reasonable investment-backed expectations. See Kaiser Aetna v. United States, 444 U.S. 164, 175 (1979); accord Connolly v. Pension Benefit Guar. Corp., 475 U.S. 211, 224-25 (1986); Penn Central, supra, 438 U.S. at 124.

Before evaluating those critical factors in the context of the forfeiture condition, we observe preliminarily that Twin City's "takings" claim is somewhat incongruent with the Supreme Court's application of its regulatory "takings" doctrine. That application heretofore has been concentrated almost exclusively on governmental regulations restricting use of tangible property, usually some form of real estate, as opposed to regulations that interfere with or diminish only the profits of a business enterprise. . .

In a handful of cases involving regulatory "takings" of commercial property interests other than land, the Court generally has been reluctant to conclude that compensation was required. .

Against that context of decisional law, we consider the specific factors generally emphasized in regulatory "takings" cases. We emphasize that application of those factors necessarily involves a balancing of the private interests affected by the regulation against the public interests that are advanced. We have already elaborated on the character of the governmental action, noting that the forfeiture condition was a forceful but relevant regulatory measure imposed to advance the substantial State interest in discouraging Twin City's withdrawal from the private-passenger automobile market, as well as the State's interest in encouraging other multi-line carriers to continue in that market. The regulatory crisis in New Jersey's private-passenger automobile-insurance market supports and enhances the reasonableness of and necessity for strong regulatory measures to promote market stability while the planned depopulation of the residual market is implemented.

The second factor, the economic impact of the regulation, emphasizes the potential significance of the financial loss that the Twin City affiliates may sustain if Twin City ceases to operate in New Jersey. We note preliminarily that because the property affected by the regulation is the value of the Twin City affiliates' New Jersey insurance business, we have no occasion to consider application of those decisions involving real property that categorically find a compensable taking when a regulation "denies all economically beneficial or productive use of land." See, e.g., Lucas, supra, 112 S.Ct. at 2893. The record indicates that the affiliates' businesses generate aggregate annual premiums of $ 120 million and that those businesses are generally profitable, although no estimate of lost profits has been presented. The record does not indicate whether the affiliates could sell or otherwise receive compensation from other insurers interested in succeeding to lines of business written by one or more of Twin City's affiliates. We take for granted, however, that the surrender by Twin City's affiliates of their respective licenses would not necessarily result in the elimination of all commercial value inherent in the affiliates' New Jersey business operations, some aspects of which undoubtedly could be applied to business in other states. Nevertheless, we cannot speculate on whether, conceding the significant economic loss that the affiliates would sustain if forced to surrender their New Jersey markets, ITT Hartford would be able to recoup that loss by expanding its marketing efforts in other states with a less-restrictive regulatory climate. At least one commentator has noted that competition among state governments tends to prevent overregulation, offering companies choices in determining those States' regulatory systems to which it will subject its business operations. See Vicki Bean, "Exit" as a Constraint on Land Use Exactions: Rethinking the Unconstitutional Conditions Doctrine, 91 Colum.L.Rev. 473, 508-09 (1991).

The third factor, whether the regulation interfered with reasonable investment-backed expectations, lends itself to either side of the argument. On the one hand, Twin City would undoubtedly acknowledge the strong, well-recognized governmental interest in regulating the business of insurance.. Moreover, the Appellate Division observed that Twin City and its investors had fair warning that the Legislature would link appellants' licenses to write other lines of insurance with their continuing to write private passenger automobile policies. In his 1987 veto message of Senate Committee Substitute for Senate Bill No. 2318 and Assembly Bill No. 2404, Governor Kean specifically called for legislation similar to Section 72:

> We need to say to insurance companies that before they quit doing business in New Jersey in one line of insurance, they must be able to show that they are doing so for a good reason. If not, the Insurance Commissioner must have the power to require surrender of the company's licenses for all lines . . . . The language that I am recommending to be added includes reasonable limits on the authority of the Insurance Commissioner to require the surrender of other licenses in the holding company system of the company wishing to withdraw from our State. . . .

On balance, we are fully satisfied, considering the specific factors ordinarily emphasized in regulatory "takings" analysis in the context of existing and developing "takings" jurisprudence, and weighing the compelling public interest against the private interests adversely affected, that no compensable taking of property under either the Federal or State Constitutions is implicated by the forfeiture condition. We consider that condition to be more in the nature of a regulatory limitation on Twin City's right to abandon its responsibilities in the private-passenger automobile market than a "taking" of its affiliates' property for public use. As in Connolly, supra, 475 U.S. at 224, the State has taken none of the affiliates' businesses for its own use; rather, it has terminated the affiliates' authority to do business as a condition of Twin City's withdrawal. That Twin City's affiliates will lose profits because of the restriction imposed by the Commissioner does not give rise to a compensable taking of property, in view of our conclusion that the underlying regulation is valid. Moreover, we have already determined that the objective of the forfeiture condition is sufficiently related to the State's regulatory power to supervise Twin City's withdrawal from the market as to satisfy the enhanced standard set forth in Nollan, supra, 483 U.S. at 834 n.3, that the "taking" substantially advance the State interest to be achieved. We also have carefully considered the public interest served by the forfeiture condition in the context of the economic impact of that condition on Twin City's affiliates and the extent to which it interferes with their investment-backed expectations. Although the economic impact is potentially quite severe, we are thoroughly persuaded that the public interest advanced by the regulation substantially outweighs its adverse effect on ITT Hartford. Accordingly, we find no merit in Twin City's contention that the forfeiture condition imposes a compensable taking of its affiliates' property.

## Comments and Questions

1. How does the *Twin City* case compare with the California Supreme Court's decision in *Calfarm*? Are the two opinions consistent? Does the Twin City decision deny multi-line carriers such as Hartford Fire a fair return on its investments in New Jersey? Does it matter that the New Jersey statute makes it more costly for a larger insurance conglomerate to withdraw from New Jersey than it does for a small, single line operation? For a critical analysis of the New Jersey statute, see Note, *Withdrawal Restrictions in the Automobile Insurance Market*, 102 Yale L.J. 1431 (1993).

2. The fiscal shortfall underlying the Twin City case derives from underwriting losses from automobile policies that the "voluntary" markets would not cover. As the decision illustrates, New Jersey has over the two decades experimented with several devices for handing such policies. Before 1983, the state maintained an assigned risk program in which each insurance company in the market was required to underwrite a pro rata share of the unwanted drivers. The JUA replaced this system with a public residual pool, administered but not underwritten by private companies. The Reform Act of 1990 put in place a hybrid system including a publicly underwritten pool for 10 percent of the market, and a privately underwritten (and rate regulated) allocation system for another 15 percent. What are the relative strengths and weaknesses of these approaches? How are losses allocated in each system? What are the justifications for providing subsidized automobile insurance to drivers the private market does not underwrite voluntarily?

3. In the *Twin City* case, New Jersey regulated Twin City and all of its affiliates on a consolidated basis, at least with respect to the penalty imposed for withdrawal from private automobile insurance markets in the jurisdiction. How does this approach compare with the approach the United States takes with respect of banking organizations that we considered in some detail Chapter Four? When is it appropriate to hold organizations accountable for the activities of affiliated, but legally distinct entities?

## B. Risk Classifications

The classification of risks is one of the most important and potentially controversial aspects of insurance regulation. In the following article, a leading academic expert sketches out the basic trade-off between efficiency and fairness that characterizes this area of the law.

## Kenneth S. Abraham, *Efficiency and Fairness in Insurance Risk Classification*
71 Va. L. Rev. 403, 404-08, 421-24, 428-29 (1985)

Insurance operates best in the face of a very special sort of uncertainty. The tension between risk assessment and risk distribution is so characteristic of the operation of insurance that risksharing schemes from which the tension is missing seem only to resemble what we think of as insurance. For example, if we knew precisely how many losses of a certain sort would occur, but nothing about who would suffer them, then insurance against such losses would be feasible. It would be insurance embodying only the distribution of risk among those insured, however, with no assessment of the extent of each individual's risk: each insured would pay the same premium. Similarly, if we knew who was at risk of suffering a loss if it occurred, but nothing about how many of those at risk would suffer losses, insurance would also be feasible: insureds would be charged retroactively for their proportionate share of whatever losses ultimately occurred. Again, this arrangement would embody risk distribution, but no individualized risk assessment. Although both of these schemes involve risk sharing, each is simpler than the standard insurance arrangement because neither involves any individual risk assessment.

Typically, however, insurers know something about individual risks. Because in such instances it is usually possible both to assess and to distribute risk, the tension between assessment and distribution is inevitable. Risk assessment through classification of insureds into groups posing similar risks necessarily limits the amount of risk distribution achieved by an insurance arrangement, because it uses knowledge about risk expectancies to set different prices for members of different groups. No risk classification system, however, can classify and price individual risks with anything near complete accuracy; the future is too uncertain for that. Nevertheless, when reasonably accurate risk assessment is feasible, insurance classification can promote economically efficient behavior by encouraging insureds to compare the cost of insurance with the cost of investment in loss prevention that would reduce the sum of these two costs. In contrast, when risk assessment is inaccurate but insurance is still available, inefficient behavior is a likely result. This is the 'moral hazard' of insurance.

Often a classification scheme can be made more efficient. [H]owever, promoting efficiency through risk classification sometimes requires sacrificing other values. The burdens of inaccuracy may be unevenly distributed; risk classes may be based on variables not within the control of insureds; and certain variables may have unacceptable social or moral connotations. . . . Although these concerns are similar in that each sometimes demands inefficient forms of risk classification, risk-distributional fairness itself is not a monolithic notion. Without attention to the differences among these concerns, proposed remedies will be overbroad, undereffective, or both.

A variety of legal tools is available for addressing these issues and regulating the combination of efficiency and risk distribution reflected in the insurance market's classification practices. Legislatures can exercise control through statutes governing insurance classification or through general prohibitions against various forms of discrimination. Legislation in almost every state also delegates considerable authority to insurance commissioners to regulate risk classification and premium rates. Often these commissioners are required to assure that premium rates are not 'excessive, inadequate, or unfairly discriminatory.' This mandate affords commissioners broad discretion to fashion compromises between the twin goals of efficiency and risk-distributional fairness. Finally, the courts also play a role through judicial enforcement of statutory standards and through oversight of administrative action. In short, the inevitable tensions between risk assessment and risk distribution create the context in which the institutions that make law governing risk classification operate.

## THE NATURE OF INSURANCE CLASSIFICATION AND PRICING

The starting point for any analysis of insurance classification is an obvious but fundamental fact: insurance is only one of a number of ways of satisfying the demand for protection against risk. With few exceptions, insurance need not be purchased; people can forgo it if insurance is too expensive. Indeed, as the price of coverage rises, the amount purchased and the number of people purchasing will decline. Instead of buying insurance, people will self-insure by accumulating savings to serve as a cushion in the event of loss, self-protect by spending more on loss prevention, or simply use the money not spent on insurance to purchase other goods and services. An insurer must compete against these alternatives, even in the absence of competition from other insurers.

One method of competing for protection dollars is to classify potential purchasers into groups according to their probability of loss and the potential magnitude of losses if they occur. Different risk classes may then be charged different premiums, depending on this expected loss. Were it not for the need to compete for protection dollars, an insurer could simply charge each individual a premium based on the average expected loss of all its insureds (plus a margin for profit and expenses), without incurring classification costs.

An insurer can capture protection dollars by classifying because, through classification, it can offer low-risk individuals lower prices. Classification, however, involves two costs. First, the process of classification is costly. Insurers must gather data and perform statistical operations on it; marketing may also be more costly when prices are not uniform. Second, classification necessarily raises premiums for poor risks, who purchase less coverage as a result. In the aggregate, classification is thus worthwhile to an insurer only when the gains produced from extra sales and fewer pay-outs outweigh classification costs plus the costs of lost sales. Even in the absence of competition from other insurers, an insurer who engages in at least some classification is likely to capture more protection dollars than it loses.

When there is not only competition for available protection dollars, but competition among insurers for premium dollars, the value of risk classification to insurers becomes even clearer. The more refined (and accurate) an insurer's risk classifications, the more capable it is of 'skimming' good risks away from insurers whose classifications are less refined. If other insurers do not respond, either by refining their own classifications or by raising prices and catering mainly to high risks, their 'book' of risks will contain a higher mixture of poor risks who are still being charged premiums calculated for average risks. These insurers will attract additional poor risks, and this resulting adverse selection will further disadvantage their competitive positions.

## RISK ASSESSMENT AND ECONOMIC EFFICIENCY

Other things equal, insurers strive to charge insureds in accord with expected costs, which equal their expected losses plus a portion of the other costs of providing coverage. To the extent that risk classes and prices conform to this standard, a number of results follow. The first effect is that individual insureds pay premiums based on expected losses and thereby share the risk of random losses. The members of each class are charged in accord with their expected costs, so that total premiums cover the aggregate losses of the class. No subsidies run from one risk class to another. The only subsidy under this ideal flows from the lucky members of the class to the unlucky.

Even efficiently classified insurance coverage, therefore, has elements of both risk assessment and risk distribution, but the scope of each is distinct. Individual insureds are assessed the risk of suffering expected losses and are charged on that basis. The risk of suffering random losses is distributed among all insureds.

The second effect of an efficient classification system is that it does not discourage insureds from allocating an optimal amount of resources to loss prevention. Because insurance is priced in accord with expected cost, insureds have the incentive to compare the cost of protecting against risk through insurance with the cost of reducing risk through loss prevention. Efficient classification discourages insureds from purchasing insurance when they can more cheaply protect against risk by investing in loss prevention. In contrast, inefficient classification may produce suboptimal loss prevention incentives. When coverage is priced below expected cost, for example, insureds may not take safety precautions that would otherwise be worthwhile. In this situation, they can obtain equivalent protection against risk by purchasing insurance at a lesser cost than the precautions.

Finally--and this is a vital point--an efficient classification system does not strive to make its prices equal expected cost when improvement in accuracy is not worth the cost of achieving it. Information about expected cost is accumulated and risk classes are thereby refined only so long as the competitive benefits of refinement are worth their cost. Consequently, efficient classification does not recognize all individual differences. When an insurer can no longer attract or make enough profit from additional low-risk insureds to justify discovering and classifying them, an equilibrium is reached and no further refinement occurs. Some groups may then seem to 'subsidize' or be 'subsidized' by others.

For example, suppose that people raised on farms are especially poor drivers or that obstetricians born in Ohio are unusually immune to malpractice suits. Because classification systems are unlikely to have the information necessary to make these variables the basis of risk classes, neither farm-born drivers nor Ohio-born obstetricians will be charged exactly in accord with their true expected costs. Thus, the former may seem to be subsidized by other drivers, and the latter may seem to subsidize other insured physicians. It is a bit misleading, however, to say that a situation involves a subsidy even when it would be inefficient to make the investment necessary to discover and eliminate the 'subsidy.'

This example makes it plain that there is nothing special or preordained about the classifications that turn out to be efficient. Had insurers begun decades ago to maintain data about farm-born drivers or the birth places of obstetricians, it might now be efficient to use these variables for classification. In many cases, however, a new approach cannot be taken without sacrificing real economies. Even if restructuring a classification system would otherwise be efficient, probably no individual insurer would have an incentive to restructure. Competitors would take advantage of the classifications introduced by the innovating insurer and compete on an equal basis for the newly-discovered low-risk insureds, but without having made the investment required of the innovator. Some form of collective action would therefore be required for the innovation to occur.

To sum up the implications of the discussion thus far, insurance relies on group rather than individual estimates of expected loss. With few exceptions (such as large enterprises with detailed loss histories and frequent current losses), estimating expected loss 'individually' is impossible. Most individual loss experience is not statistically credible enough to warrant individual rating, though a few insurers occasionally gamble on unique risks--the well- being of [a top ranked tennis player]'s left arm, for example. Group probabilities provide the credibility necessary to the predictions that are at the heart of the insurance system. Until an individual insured is treated as a member of a group, it is impossible to known his expected loss, because for practical purposes that concept is a statistical one based on group probabilities. Without relying on such probabilities, it would be impossible to set a price for insurance coverage at all. In this sense there is risk sharing even within the risk assessment component of insurance classification. For practical purposes, no individual can have a 'true' expected loss. Rather, insureds share the risk that characteristics of those in their risk class, not considered in the classification, render the class's expected loss higher than it would be were those characteristics considered in setting premium rates.

## RISK-DISTRIBUTIONAL FAIRNESS

In addition to asking how well a classification system assesses risk to produce efficient results, we may also raise a series of different questions regarding how insurance classification and pricing systems distribute risk. Because these questions are not always clearly formulated, they need both explication and evaluation. Moreover, because the questions are not all of the same order, it is important to consider the different solutions that are available for the different kinds of unfairness that these questions highlight. Certain solutions may appropriately be fashioned within the insurance system, but for other risk-distributional problems, noninsurance approaches are more suitable. This part begins the analysis of such solutions by examining the distributional objections to the drive for efficiency in classification.

Criticisms of risk classification schemes seem to fall into three general categories. The first cluster of criticisms is composed of accuracy-equity concerns: demands that classification and pricing closely reflect expected cost, so that low-risk insureds are not forced to subsidize high-risk insureds and so that the burdens of inaccuracy are equitably distributed. Accuracy concerns obviously have much in common with the efficiency notions discussed in the preceding section. Efficiency, however is a characteristic of an entire system; risk-distributional fairness is a notion that also pertains to the treatment of individuals within that system and touches on more than economic considerations alone. The second category of criticisms is composed of control-causality concerns. These involve the contention that risk classes should be based on variables that are within the control of or at least caused by the insured. The third set of criticisms is directed at the use of suspect variables. These criticisms are occasioned by the use of variables that are 'suspect,' even apart from accuracy-equity or control-causality issues. A fourth consideration, different from these criticisms, is one in favor of redistributional policies. This consideration does not necessarily raise fairness questions in the same way as the first three; rather, it involves separate objectives of public policy.

---

The following case offers a concrete illustration of these issues

# Department of Insurance v. Insurance Services Office
434 So.2d 908 (Fla. Dist. Ct. App. 1983), *pet. denied*, 444 So.2d 416 (Fla. 1984)

The [Florida Insurance] Department appeals the final order of a hearing officer of the Division of Administrative Hearings, in a rule challenge proceeding, declaring its Rule 4- 43.03 to be an invalid exercise of delegated legislative authority.[1]

In January, 1978, Dade County petitioned the Department to adopt two rules, one prohibiting the continued use of age,[2] sex, marital status, and scholastic achievement as automobile insurance rating factors and the other prohibiting the use of arbitrary territorial boundaries as a factor.

The insurance companies (whose premium rates are formulated using sex, marital status or scholastic achievement, or some combination thereof) challenged the validity of the rule on the ground[ that] the rule extends, modifies, conflicts with or enlarges upon the requirements of the Florida Insurance Code and thus exceeds the Department's rule-making authority . . . .

At the heart of this controversy is section 626.9541(15)(h), Florida Statutes (1979), one of the laws being implemented by Rule 4-43.03, which provides as follows:

> (h) No insurer shall, with respect to premiums charged for automobile insurance, unfairly discriminate solely on the basis of age, sex, marital status, or scholastic achievement.

In enacting this statute the legislature obviously intended to permit discrimination based on sex, marital status, and scholastic achievement so long as this discrimination is not unfair or based solely on these factors. Yet the Department, by promulgating Rule 4-43.03, imposed a total prohibition against the use of sex, marital status or scholastic achievement in the formulation of premiums or rate classifications. The legislative history of Section 626.9541(15)(h) irrefutably shows that the legislature expressly considered, but rejected, provisions which would prohibit the

---

[1]    Rule 4-43.03 Unfair Discrimination in Private Passenger Motor Vehicle Insurance Rates-- Based on Sex, Marital Status and Scholastic Achievement.

(1) No insurer authorized to engage in the business of insurance in the State of Florida shall establish classifications or premium rates for any policy, contract or certificate of private passenger motor vehicle insurance based upon the sex, marital status or scholastic achievement of the person or persons insured.

(2) This rule shall become effective on March 1, 1980.

[2]    Noticeably, the use of age as a rating factor was not prohibited in Rule 4-43.03, as the Department found a strong correlation between age classifications and loss experience resulting from vehicle accidents. Further, no workable alternative to age as a primary risk assessment factor was suggested, and without that, it was concluded that elimination of age as a rating variable would lead only to greater inequities. Interestingly, the Department has also not come forth with verified alternatives to sex, marital status and scholastic achievement, although these have proven reliability as rating factors. Yet use of these factors seems to have been forbidden in large part because they are "socially unacceptable." Florida's Automobile Insurance Rate Classification System:  Report To The Insurance Commissioner And The Commissioner's Orders and Findings.

use of these factors as unfairly discriminatory.[5] This provides strong evidence that the legislature did not intend, by enactment of Section 626.9541(15)(h), to completely prohibit the use of these factors. This history provides strong support for the hearing officer's determination that the Department's contrary construction of the statute in Rule 4-43.03 is unauthorized. . . . .

Nevertheless, the Department urges that the rule does not conflict with the statute because the use of sex, marital status, and scholastic achievement in the formulation of premium rates necessarily unfairly discriminates solely on the basis of those criteria. Hence, the Department contends that in promulgating Rule 4-43.03, it implemented Section 627.031(1)(a), Florida Statutes (1979), which provides that it is the purpose of the Insurance Code to "... promote the public welfare by regulating insurance rates ... to the end that they shall not be ... unfairly discriminatory...." The Department also maintains that it implemented Section 627.062(1), Florida Statutes (1979), which provides: "The rates for all classes of insurance to which the provisions of this part are applicable shall not be ... unfairly discriminatory."

"Unfairly discriminatory" is not defined in the Code. However, Section 627.0651, Florida Statutes (1979) (also implemented, according to the Department, in its promulgation of Rule 4-43.03), provides several standards to be applied by the Department in making a determination as to whether a rate is unfairly discriminatory. In particular, Section 627.0651(6) provides:

> (6) One rate shall be deemed unfairly discriminatory in relation to another in the same class if it clearly fails to reflect *equitably* the difference in expected losses and expenses. (emphasis supplied)

It is the Department's contention that "unfairly discriminatory" and "equitably" are not technical terms of art and should be given their common ordinary meaning. Giving these words their common ordinary meaning, the Department urges, a rating factor will be deemed unfairly discriminatory and inequitable unless it has a causal connection to expected losses. Thus the Department reasons that since sex, marital status and scholastic achievement have no direct or indirect causal connection to a person's driving habits they are necessarily unfairly discriminatory and inequitable rating factors. The Department further reasons that these rating factors are always unfairly discriminatory because their use results in the misclassification of a large number of individuals who share the distinguishing feature of the group (e.g. male sex) but do not share the "average" driving characteristics of the group.

On the other hand, the insurance companies contend that "unfairly discriminatory" and "equitable" are technical words, with a particular meaning in the insurance industry, and that Section 626.9541(15)(h) must be construed with this meaning in mind. United States v. Cuomo, 525 F.2d 1285, 1291 (5th Cir.1976). Reading Section 627.0651(6) in pari materia with the other standards contained in Section 627.0651(3) through (8), the insurance companies urge that the word "equitably" (used in Section 627.0651(6)), means "accurately" in the actuarial sense. The hearing officer agreed, finding that the most equitable classification factors are those that are the

---

[5]    Senate Bill 1181, which amended Section 626.9541(15) by adding paragraph (h) was passed by voice vote of the Senate on May 18, 1977, 1977 Senate Journal 438. A previously proposed amendment read: "Rates for any class based solely on age, sex, school grades, education or lack of driver education shall be deemed unfairly discriminatory." This was considered but rejected in the Senate Commerce Committee on May 10, 1977.

most actuarially sound. In making this finding, the hearing officer relied upon the testimony of the Department's own Chief Actuary and Director of the Division of Rating. The hearing officer further found that the classification factors of sex, marital status and scholastic achievement, in light of the present state of the art in the industry, enhanced the actuarial soundness of a rate classification for automobile insurance.[8] Thus, as the hearing officer concluded, the Department has not established that the use of the criteria prohibited by Rule 4-43.03 necessarily results in unfair discrimination.

We find it highly significant that in presenting its argument on this point the Department has changed its own interpretation of the word "equitably," as used in Section 627.0651(6), as well as its interpretation of the phrase "unfairly discriminatory," relevant to this proceeding. Historically, the Department has measured the equitableness of a rating factor by its predictive accuracy. Further, until the enactment of the challenged rule, the Department interpreted the insurance code and Section 626.9541(15)(h) as permitting rate classification plans using sex, marital status and scholastic achievement criteria in their formulation.

We also attach great significance to the finding of the hearing officer that the Department did not offer evidence or testimony sufficient to establish that factual changes of any nature have occurred, or that the Department has become aware of new factual information, which would support a deviation from their historic interpretation of the Florida Insurance Code. . . . .

Turning again to the statutes, we note that when the legislature enacted Section 626.9541(15)(h), it also reenacted Section 627.0651(3) through (8), which correspond with the Department's settled interpretation that rates "reflect equitably the difference in expected losses" if the rates reflect those differences as accurately as possible. Thus, by implication, the legislature approved the interpretation that rates based upon sex, marital status or scholastic achievement are unfair only if those rating factors are found to be actuarially unsound. As previously stated, the evidence below overwhelmingly shows these factors are actuarially sound. We conclude, therefore, that even under the alternate theory advanced by the Department, the statutes do not authorize a blanket prohibition against use of these factors.

---

[8]    The Department does not dispute this finding and has in fact admitted that within some groups (all policyholders 25 years of age and under, in a similar usage category) the subgroup consisting of all females has a lower actual or expected loss experience than the subgroup consisting of all males, and that a subgroup consisting of all married policyholders also has a lower actual or expected loss experience than the subgroup consisting of all unmarried policyholders. Further, there was testimony that there are differences in expected loss experience between those who qualify for scholastic achievement discount and those who do not.

## Comments and Questions

1. In the order overturned by the court in this case, the Florida Insurance Department offered the following justification:

> Charging more or less to policyholders on the basis of race, religion, or economic status would be socially unacceptable regardless of any statistical justification a company might offer. Several witnesses at the hearings argued that it is socially unacceptable to continue the use of sex and marital status to justify lower premiums to women and married couples. . . . . [However], it was apparent from the hearings that the insurance industry does not have such reservations with respect to any existing rate classifications. . . . . [T]here were indications from the testimony that fears of being placed at a competitive disadvantage might in part be responsible for a lack of industry introspection as to the social acceptability of current rating factors.

> Therefore, it is clear that the power and responsibility to make public policy in this area must rest with the regulator. The private sector has neither the incentive nor the will to make such judgments. To leave the determination of social acceptability to the private sector would serve only to further retard the already slow movement in the direction of ending discrimination based on certain classifications which the Supreme Court has found to be invidious.

434 So.2d at 935 (appendix to dissenting opinion). Is the Department correct in suspecting that the private sector is incapable of assuming responsibility in this area?

2. The use of gender as a classification factor in automobile insurance was a deeply contested issue in the 1980s. A number of jurisdictions prohibited the practice. See, e.g., Hartford Accident & Indemnity Co. v. Insurance Commissioner, 482 A.2d 542 (Pa. 1984) (affirming Pennsylvania Insurance Commissioner's decision to ban gender-based automobile rates). A number of states of adopted similar restrictions, and one state — Montana — has banned to use of gender in all insurance classifications (including life insurance.) The equitable case against gender-based or similar classifications is summarized in a 1978 Report of Rates and Rating Procedures of the NAIC Task Force of the Automobile Insurance Subcommittee:

> In terms of simplicity and consistency (i.e., stability and ease of verification), age, sex and marital status receive high marks as rating factors. This is not the case from the viewpoint of causality. Causality refers to the actual or implied behavioral relationship between a particular rating factor and loss potential. The longer a vehicle is on the road, for example, the more likely it is that the vehicle may be involved in a random traffic accident; thus, daily or annual total mileage may be viewed as a causal rating factor. To the extent that sex and marital status classifications may be defended on causal grounds, the implied behavioral relationships rely largely on questionable social stereotypes. . . . Given the significant changes in traditional sex roles and social attitudes which have occurred in recent years, justifications for rating plans on the grounds of such implied assumptions are unacceptable.

How strong a causal link should we require before accepting a risk classifications? Are there costs, in terms of economic efficiency or some other values, in requiring causality as opposed to mere correlation with loss experience?

3. Another risk classification practice that has attracted controversy concerns the use of credit histories. As one industry executed admitted in a recent press account:

> [My] insurance company uses credit reports . . . "to help us identify where not to renew business" . . . . Poor credit histories "seem to correlate directly to greater exposure to arson cases or situations where jewelry and other valuables items 'disappear.' When people need money because of credit problems, it just seems that those types of claims are more likely to occur."

*Credit Reports Aid Underwriters*, Best's Review— Life-Health Edition, July 1, 1995, at 36. Do you think this is an appropriate classification system? Would your views changed if it turned out that minorities were substantially more likely to have poor credit histories than other members of the population? See *Auto Insurance Study Shows Gaps in Minority Areas*, L.A. Times, Mar. 2, 1995, at 1 (reporting that 9 of 10 motorists in inner-city Los Angles neighborhoods lacked insurance). Should insurance regulators develop regulations similar to those imposed on depository institutions under the Community Reinvestment Act?

---

The following problem explores an emerging issue in life and health insurance classifications. (For further reading on the subject, see Jill Gaulding, *Race, Sex, and Genetic Discrimination in Insurance: What's Fair?*, 80 CORNELL L. REV. 1646 (1995).)

### Problem 7-3

Scientists from the National Institutes of Health have just announced the development of a new and inexpensive genetic test that predicts, with a fair degree of accruacy, the probability than an otherwise healthy individual will contract various types of cancer and heart disease. Several insurance companies have expressed interest in using this new test to set premiums for individual life insurance and health insurance policies. Industry sources have indicated that use of the test could dramatically reduce insurance premiums with favorable test results, but consumer groups have protest that the tests would discriminate unfairly against individuals with unfavorable test results, many of whom may never contract cancer or heart disease.

The genetic test has become a major issue in the upcoming election for Insurance Commissioner of your home state. The candidate's staff has tentatively recommended a ban on using any form of genetic testing to set insurance premiums, but the details of the ban have not yet been worked out. Several of the candidates' advisers are concerned about the effect of such a ban on insurance markets in the state. The candidate has turned to you for advice on the following issues. Should the state ban the use of genetic classifications in the pricing of insurance? Are there any practical impediments to imposing such a ban? Would it matter if other states in the region did not impose a similar sort of ban?

# Section 5. The Mutual Form

We now turn our attention from the primary focus of insurance regulation -- the relationship between insurer and insured -- to issues of organizational form. One peculiarity of the insurance industry is that many major firms are organized as "mutuals" -- that is legal entities that lack traditional equity shareholders.  For example, in the life insurance industry as of 1994, mutual insurance companies held forty-one percent of industry assets.  Moreover, six of the ten largest life insurance companies were organized in mutual form.   On the property-casualty side, mutuals are somewhat less significant (holding more than a quarter of sector assets), but still constituted a substantial segment of the industry.

The focus of attention in this section of the casebook is the "demutualization process," which consists of the legal arrangements whereby mutuals change their corporate form, either through liquidation or conversion into more traditional stock corporations. Demutualization is not unique to insurance companies, and has applications to other types of financial intermediaries, most notably savings and loan associations and savings banks, which also often organize themselves in mutual form. While this section is primarily concerned with the demutualization of insurance companies, we also consider briefly a parallel development in the savings bank industry.

## A. Demutualization of Insurance Companies

To understand the demutualization process, one must first have a general appreciation of the legal relationship between mutual insurance companies and their policyholders.  That relationship is explored in the following excerpt:

## J.A.C. Hetherington, *Fact v. Fiction: Who Owns Mutual Insurance Companies* 1969 Wis. L. Rev. 1068, 1970-84

### THE MUTUAL POLICYHOLDER AS AN OWNER

The formal legal status of the mutual insurance policyholder is somewhat analogous to that of the stockholder in a stock company.  Like the shareholder, he is said to be the owner of the corporation.  The black letter "rule" has often been repeated by courts and text writers.  In part, the mutual policyholder is thought to be an owner because superficially he looks like one. He has the right to elect the management of the company, a function traditionally reserved to the owners of a business enterprise.  He is also owner by a process of elimination:  in the case of a mutual organization, the only available candidates are the members, and in a mutual insurer this means the policyholders.  However, the meaning of "ownership" is neither specific nor obvious; it varies with the context and the subject matter to which it is applied.  In our law of business associations, the owner is generally identified and characterized by his exposure to the risk of personal liability in the event of insolvency, or at least the risk of loss of his investment; his right to the profits; and finally, his right and, usually his ability to control the management.  An examination of the relationship between the mutual policyholder and the insurer clearly revels that he substantially lacks all three of these attributes.

## A. *Risk*

Generally, mutual insurance policyholders are not exposed to personal liability as a result of the insolvency of the mutual insurance carrier. An exception exists in the case of assessable policies which may be issued by mutual insurers, but in practice are issued only during the formative stages of the enterprise. Assessable policies are not issued by the large established commercial mutual, and in Wisconsin may not be issued by life insurers. As a practical matter, therefore, mutual policyholders, like shareholders, are not exposed to personal liability for the debts of the corporation on insolvency. Again, like shareholders, the risk to which they are exposed in the event of insolvency, is the loss of whatever ownership interest they may have in the company. The extent of this exposure depends on the amount of the investment, which varies greatly from one type of insurance to another, and from one policyholder to another.

At the outset, it will be helpful to consider the premium paid by the mutual nonlife policyholder as consisting of two elements: first, the portion which covers the cost of the protection he is buying, including the operating costs of the company. The determination of the amount of this part of the premium is based on the losses anticipated by the company on the basis of past experience and other factors, including its expenses of operation. The second portion of the premium consists of any excess over the first amount. Any such excess is a direct contribution to the surplus of the company.

Policyholders generally pay premiums for their insurance in advance of the period of coverage. The period of the payment may be annually, quarterly, monthly, or even weekly in life, health and accident, and automobile insurance; in homeowners' property-liability insurance the premiums may be paid every three years. With respect to the portion of the premium which covers the cost of the insurance coverage purchased, the policyholder is like any other buyer who pays in advance for a product or service. As a buyer who paid in advance the policyholder is a "financing buyer," a creditor of the insurer. He resembles, for example, the purchaser of a magazine subscription who has not yet received all the issues for which he has paid. As the period of subscription or policy progresses, the buyer receives in installments the product for which he has paid. The amount of unearned premium at any given time is an investment by the policyholder in the company in the same way that a magazine subscription is an investment in the publishing company by the subscriber. Both are purchasers of a product who, like any financing buyer who has not received the product or service he has paid for, is a creditor of the seller. If the contract is terminated (and the buyer is not liable for breach), prima facie he is entitled to recover from the seller the amount of the prepayment. And like any creditor, he is exposed to a risk of loss if his debtor becomes insolvent and is unable to return the prepayment or provide the product or service contracted for. The risk of loss of his unearned premium resulting from insolvency is the same from the standpoint of the policyholder, as the loss he sustains if the insurer is unable to pay a claim arising under his policy, except that it is likely to be less serious. Protection against this customer risk is the *raison d'etre* of insurance regulation. This risk is distinguishable from the characteristic risk of an owner of an enterprise that his property (or his investment in the case of limited liability) is chargeable with the debts owed by the enterprise to others. Policyholders of stock insurance companies are subject to the same nonproprietary risk.

The risk of the insolvency of the supplier is always on the buyer who prepays. In one respect, this is a particularly important risk for the insurance buyer, as compared with other purchasers of goods and services. The insured buys a continuing future and contingent performance which the supplier can provide only if it remains solvent. For this reason, the financial "solidity" of the insurer is of the greatest importance to him. . . .

In one respect, however, the mutual policyholder is more than a customer. This is because he has a pro rata interest in the company's surplus. This surplus is derived from two sources: first, the amount of premium paid in by policyholders which exceeds the costs, including administrative expenses of the insurer's performance under its outstanding policies. The second source of surplus is investment earnings.

As is demonstrated in the following section this investment is inaccessible to the policyholder, except in unusual circumstances over which he has no control. It is therefore questionable whether this interest in surplus should properly be regarded as an investment which the policyholder may "lose" if the insurer becomes insolvent. The importance of such a loss, should it occur, would be minimal to the insured, since it is an investment over which he has no control and from which he derives no benefit. The loss of this investment is not a subject of any importance in insurance insolvency proceedings which are exclusively concerned about the inability of the company to pay claims under its outstanding policies and the loss of protection suffered by all policyholders. These again are losses and risks which the policyholders suffer as customers, not as investors.

## B. *Profits*

The fight to share in profits after all creditors of the enterprise have been paid is the essence of ownership of a business. The mutual policyholder shares in the "profits" of the enterprise principally through dividends paid on his policy. Dividends are usually not paid in cash, but are applied on the next premium. In some companies, they are "deducted from premiums in advance" so that the policyholder sees nothing that looks like a dividend. In either case, for income tax purposes, mutual dividends are considered a return of previously paid premium and are not income to the policyholder. Dividends are that portion of the previously paid premium which exceeds the cost of the protection under the policyholder's contract. However, the entire excess is generally not returned, because surpluses are accumulated by the insurer for purposes of expansion.

As "owners" of the company, and through it of its assets, mutual policyholders should have a legally or equitably recognizable claim to share in the accumulations of assets made by the company during their time as policyholders. They have none. In property-liability companies, the full extent of their claim to the company's surplus, is their right to receive whatever dividend the board of directors may declare.

Life companies are often required to pay some portion of the surplus back to policyholders. Surplus is determined after "such contingency reserve as may be deemed necessary" is first deducted. The courts have uniformly held that life policyholders have no claim against the insurer beyond their rights under the terms of their insurance contracts. . . . [T]hey have neither control of, nor legally enforceable claim to, the portion of surplus, which the company may lawfully accumulate.

Furthermore, in the absence of a statute or a controlling policy provision, the management may terminate the policyholder's membership by canceling or refusing to renew his policy, and may exercise this right for any or no reason. This power of expulsion from the membership group is antithetical to any conception of the policyholder as an owner, especially since the departing member takes nothing with him and has nothing to sell. Traditionally, the owner of a business enterprise has the right, subject to limitations imposed by law, to terminate the association of employees, suppliers and customers with the enterprise. The fact that policyholders in a mutual insurance company, like policyholders in any insurance organization, may be "fired" by the management who are theoretically their employees, is strongly indicative of the non-proprietary character of their relationship to the company. . . .

## C. *Control*

With minor exceptions, the business and affairs of mutual insurance companies are by statute required to be managed by a board of directors elected by the policyholders. For a variety of reasons, policyholder participation is minimal, and the procedure has far less actual or even potential significance than it does in a widely held stock corporation. . . . .

The practice in both property-casualty and life companies plainly reflects the almost total nonparticipation of policyholders in the selection of management. In the great mutual life companies in Wisconsin and elsewhere, the management is routinely returned to office, without difficulty or interruption, by the votes of a few dozen policyholders. The same is true of property-liability company management. Sometimes in property-liability companies permanent proxies are used, which enable management to vote without consulting the policyholders.

Voting practices in the mutual insurance industry contrast sharply with the practices in publicly held stock companies. Under either organization, management is reelected without opposition in the vast majority of cases, but in a stock company, at least fifty percent of the shares must be voted. An elaborate and expensive effort to inform the electorate is combined with the annual solicitation of proxies. Though shareholder opposition is exceptional, a regular reading of the *Wall Street Journal* during the annual meeting season clearly shows it is not rare. Among commercial mutual insurance companies, on the other hand, there are no exceptions. The conclusion is inescapable that mutual policyholders not only do not select the management, they exert no influence on management through the election process.

---

The autonomy enjoyed by management of mutual insurance companies has led to more than one creative plan of reorganization. Consider the transaction before the court in the following case:

## Allyn v. Hull
## 99 A.2d 128 (Conn. 1953)

The plaintiff as insurance commissioner of the state of Connecticut instituted this action against five individuals who formerly had been directors of the Madison Mutual Fire Insurance Company. His main purpose was to obtain a declaratory judgment concerning the disposition of the company's assets. The court sustained a demurrer addressed to the complaint. From the judgment subsequently rendered for the defendants upon the refusal of the plaintiff to plead over, the latter has appealed.

The complaint alleges the following facts: The Madison Mutual Fire Insurance Company, hereinafter called the company, was organized under a special charter in 1855. Over the succeeding years, policies insuring against loss by fire and other casualties were issued to various persons, many of whom abandoned their interest in the company upon the expiration or other termination of their policies. In February, 1946, the defendant Steele, as attorney for the company, wrote to the insurance commissioner, inquiring about the mechanics of liquidation. The commissioner replied that '[t]here appears to be no provision in the Connecticut Insurance Law which would vest this Department with jurisdiction over a liquidation of this nature. While there are provisions under which the Commissioner has authority in the liquidation of an insolvent domestic insurance company, the Madison appears to be solvent with a surplus of approximately $20,000.00 according to its 1945 annual statement. Our conclusion, therefore, is that the Directors should proceed in this matter under the general law governing corporate liquidations.'

On May 15, 1946, the five defendants and one other were directors of the company. On that date they voted to write no new business and to renew no existing policy after May 31, 1946. They also voted to accept a proposal of the New London County Mutual Fire Insurance Company to reinsure, for the single premium of $2500, all risks outstanding on June 1, 1946. The risks were then represented by policies in the total face amount of $301,850, held by 198 persons. Of the 198, six were the company's directors, to each of whom had been issued, on May 31, 1946, a new five-year policy for $1000. These six policies were excepted from the contract of reinsurance with the New London company. As the policies held by the other 192 persons expired, after June 1, 1946, they were not renewed but each policyholder received from the company a cash dividend equal to the amount of the premium he had paid. At the expiration of all policies except those held by the directors, the company still had undistributed assets approximating $17,000.

In 1949, the company again wrote to the insurance commissioner concerning the further disposition of its assets. The commissioner replied that 'this is purely a legal matter over which we have no jurisdiction.' On May 31, 1951, five policies, being renewals of those written on the same date in 1946, were issued to the five defendants, who still remained directors of the company. The sixth of the original directors' policies had been previously canceled.

Thereafter, the five directors entered into negotiations with the Glover Insurance Agency of South Norwalk for the sale of the charter. On February 5, 1952, the directors met in special meeting and, purporting to act as the sole policyholders, voted to distribute to themselves the company's remaining assets, less such an amount as would meet any unpaid bills. On February

7, 1952, the company wrote five new policies in the names of persons designated by the Glover agency. At the annual meeting of the company held on the same day, those five persons and the defendants elected themselves directors, and at a subsequent directors' meeting, those representing the Glover interests were elected to the various offices. The defendants then resigned as directors. Purporting to act under the vote of February 5, 1952, the defendants distributed to themselves the company's assets of $19,240, which included $2000 paid for the charter. The several grounds of demurrer, addressed to the complaint, revolve around the one question determinative of this appeal. That question, as the parties concede, is whether the plaintiff has the legal right or power to institute this action.

The plaintiff is a state official whose office was created by the General Assembly. General Statutes § 6025. Like other comparable public officials, he has only such power and authority as are clearly conferred or necessarily implied. State v. Hartford Accident & Indemnity Co., 138 Conn. 334, 339, 84 A.2d 579; Mechem, Public Officers, § 511; 43 Am.Jur. 68, § 249. Section 6029 prescribes his powers and duties. It requires him, among other things, to 'see that all laws respecting insurance companies are faithfully executed.' Undoubtedly, this vests him with a wide range of discretion. American Casualty Ins. & Security Co. v. Fyler, 60 Conn. 448, 460, 22 A. 494. That discretion, however, cannot be exercised on everything bearing directly or indirectly upon the subject of insurance. See Noyes v. Byxbee, 45 Conn. 382, 385. The legislative mandate which we have quoted does not endow him with limitless authority to do whatever he thinks he ought to do. The statute does not speak of laws relating to insurance. It refers to laws respecting 'insurance companies.' The authority granted by it to the plaintiff, therefore, is circumscribed. The statute permits him to supervise the activities of insurance companies only so far as to see that they fulfil the obligations imposed upon them by law. It gives him no power over the directors of insurance companies in their individual capacities.

The complaint does not purport to state a cause of action against the company. Indeed, the company is not even a party defendant. Nor has the action been brought against the defendants as directors. In short, the plaintiff seeks to compel neither the company nor its directors to execute any legal duty. The gist of the complaint is that the defendants, as individuals, should respond because of some act of alleged misconduct. Justification for the maintenance of the present action cannot be found in § 6029.

The plaintiff maintains that, on the face of the admitted facts, a grievous wrong, intentional or otherwise, has been done to 192 policyholders. Whether this is so, or what rights, if any, they may have under a different alignment of parties, we do not determine on this appeal. We go no further than to hold that this plaintiff is without power to bring the instant action. However commendable may be his purpose, the plaintiff lacks the necessary authority to sue as he has done.

## Questions

Do you agree with the Connecticut court's decision in this case. Was the transaction abusive? Who should have been entitled to receive the remaining surplus in Madison Mutual? Why didn't the former policyholders challenge the transaction instead of the Attorney General?

————————

As the Hetherington excerpt and *Allyn* case indicate, traditional legal structures offer limited control over the management of mutual organizations. Over the years, economic studies of the performance of mutual insurance companies have generally confirmed that these firms operate less efficiently than their stock counterparts. In additional, mutual firms are disadvantaged in their ability to raise funds in the capital markets and to diversify through holding company affiliates. Given the drawbacks of the mutual ownership form, the continuing importance of the mutual form in the insurance industry is something of an anomaly, particularly inasmuch as stock corporations and partnerships dominate most other fields of business activity.

Some analysts attribute the presence of mutual insurance firms to historical accident. During the 19th Century, when the insurance industry grew to maturity in the United States regulatory supervision was relatively lax. At the time, the general public favored mutual life insurance companies because they were perceived to be less prone to risk-taking than stock corporations. This tendency was particularly important in the life insurance field where firms made relatively long-term commitments and policyholders needed assurances that firms would not change investment policies before those commitments were honored. On the property-casualty side, mutual firms were also thought less prone to opportunistic pricing and perhaps more adept at appropriately classifying policyholder risks. Legislative reforms at the turn of the century, most prominently the Armstrong Commission of 1905, encouraged many stock life insurance companies to convert into mutual form.

Over the past few decades, as the regulation of insurance companies has become more effective, the desirability of retaining such a large portion of the industry in mutual form has increasingly become a subject of debate. Policy analysts have questioned whether the form is simply a remnant of historical accident, and managements of mutual firms have increasingly chafed at the organization limits of this business form. In response to these pressures, a number of state legislatures, most notably New York where many of the larger mutuals are domiciled, have elected to eliminate old prohibitions on demutualizations and adopted new statutes to facilitate the process. See *Going Public: The Critical Choice*, Best's Review -- Life-Health Insurance Edition (Jan. 1985). Although the pace of insurance company demutualizations is still relatively slow, a trend in that direction has begun.

The following excerpt is from an administrative order approving a recent demutualization in the Commonwealth of Massachusetts. As you review this order, consider how the Massachusetts demutualization statute deals with the issues presented in the *Allyn* case. Is this a fair resolution of the problems associated with demutualization? (In reviewing the order, you may find it useful to consult the pro forma financial statement reproduced at the end of the excerpt. Who is getting the value that State Mutual has accumulated since it was initially chartered?)

## In re State Mutual Life Assurance Co. of America
### Executive Office of Consumer Affairs, Massachusetts Division of Insurance
### Docket No. F-95-1 (Aug. 2. 1995)

### INTRODUCTION

1.    On February 28, 1995, the Board of Directors of State Mutual Life Assurance Company of America ("State Mutual" or "the Company") adopted a Plan of Reorganization (the "Plan") whereby State Mutual proposes to convert from a mutual life insurance company to a stock life insurance company and become a wholly owned subsidiary of Allmerica Financial Corporation ("AFC"). On that same date, State Mutual filed the Plan with the Commissioner of Insurance (the "Commissioner") seeking approval of the conversion, pursuant to Section 19E of chapter 175 of the Massachusetts General Laws ("M.G.L.") ("Section 19E" or the "demutualization statute"). . .

### BACKGROUND

#### A. The Demutualization Statute

2.    In 1991, the Massachusetts Legislature passed Section 19E which authorizes the conversion of domestic mutual life insurance companies to domestic stock life insurance companies, a process known as "demutualization. " The demutualization statute requires that a converting insurer meet certain mandates and prescribes generally the manner in which a conversion shall be accomplished. It places upon the Commissioner the responsibility of protecting the policyholders of the insurer and the insuring public by, among other things, requiring a finding that the plan of conversion filed with the Division of Insurance (the "Division") is not prejudicial to them. Section 19E also mandates that no demutualization can occur without the affirmative vote of two-thirds of the votes of the voting policyholders. M.G.L. c. 175, § 19E.

3. State Mutual is the first Massachusetts insurance company to file a reorganization plan under Section 19E, making this an important case of first impression for Massachusetts insurance regulators and the policyholders of Massachusetts mutual life insurance companies. The Division has allocated unprecedented resources to its review of State Mutual's submissions. . .

### THE REORGANIZATION

A.    Structure of the Reorganization

21.    Section 19E permits the conversion of a mutual life insurance company to a stock life insurance company "as part of a plan of reorganization in which a majority or all of the common shares of the domestic stock life insurance company is acquired by a parent corporation or

another corporation which may be, but need not be, a corporation organized for such purposes and may be a subsidiary or other affiliate of such domestic mutual life insurance company prior to such acquisition...." M.G.L. c. 175, § 19E (introductory paragraph). Under the Plan, State Mutual will change its name to First Allmerica Financial Life Insurance Company and become a wholly owned subsidiary of AFC, a Delaware Corporation formed for the purpose of becoming the publicly owned Holding Company of State Mutual after the demutualization.

22.   State Mutual represents that, after the reorganization, it will continue to honor all of its contractual commitments to its policyholders. All policies will remain continuously in force and policy values, premiums and guarantees will not be changed in any way by the demutualization. In addition, dividend paying policies will continue to pay policy dividends as declared.

B.   Purpose of the Reorganization

23.   The stated purposes of the Plan are "to demutualize State Mutual so that it can improve its access to capital markets and raise capital to permit [it] to grow its existing business and develop new business opportunities in the insurance and financial services industries." State Mutual management believes this will be beneficial to policyholders because the reorganized State Mutual will be stronger financially, more efficiently operated, and therefore, better able to meet its contractual commitments to policyholders.

24.   The flexibility to raise capital as a stock company may have distinct advantages in enabling a company to react to the exigencies of the insurance business, such as downgrades by major ratings agencies. In March 1995, financial ratings agency Standard & Poor's ("S&P") lowered its rating of State Mutual's claims-paying ability to A+ ("Good") and placed it on credit watch subject to the consequences of both the timing of the demutualization and the success of the related capital raising efforts contained in State Mutual's Plan. S&P reported that the Plan would be beneficial to State Mutual, and if related capital raising efforts are successful, the ratings could be upgraded. However, S&P also reported that if the reorganization is significantly delayed or not completed, the ratings could be negatively affected.

25.   On June 19, 1995, Moody's Investors Service ("Moody's") downgraded the insurance financial strength ratings of State Mutual and its subsidiary, SMA Life Assurance Company, from "Aa3" Like S&P, Moody's also stated that the proposed demutualization and the related initial public offering ("IPO") will improve State Mutual's access to the public capital markets and its ability to allocate capital across its lines of business.

26.   According to a submission by the three named policyholders [who intervened to challenge aspects of the transaction], A.M. Best recently affirmed State Mutual's current "A" (Excellent) rating and stated that it would view favorably the increased flexibility available to a publicly traded (demutualized) company.

27.   Implementation of the Plan, therefore, is expected to at least maintain, and possibly improve, State Mutual's claims paying ratings, enabling State Mutual to compete more successfully in the insurance industry and enhancing State Mutual's ability to satisfy its obligations to its policyholders. I find that these benefits are in the interest of State Mutual's policyholders and the insuring public, and that State Mutual has demonstrated the importance of expedited access to public capital markets.

C. The Closed Block, Plan

*Purpose of the Closed Block*

28.    The reorganization requires the creation of a special arrangement, known as a "Closed Block," to protect the policy dividend expectations of certain policyholders with respect to policies defined in the Plan as the Closed Block Business. The Company must set aside assets in the Closed Block in an amount that is expected to produce cash flows sufficient to support Closed Block Business, including the payment of policy benefits and certain taxes and to provide for the continuation of 1994 policy dividend scales. These assets may not be reallocated, transferred, or otherwise removed from the Closed Block without the Commissioner's prior approval.

29.    By means of this segregation of assets and policies, the Closed Block is designed to protect the policy dividend expectations of the Closed Block policies from the vagaries of the market forces that could affect other parts of the newly capitalized public company. In this way, the Plan assures individual policyholders that post-demutualization dividend scales will be determined on a basis consistent with the way they were determined prior to demutualization. . . .

40.    Based on the foregoing, I find that the composition, operation, and funding of the Closed Block, is fair, reasonable, and not prejudicial to the policyholders or to the insuring public.

D. The Initial Public Offering

41.    The effective date of the Plan is the date of the closing of an IPO in which new shares of the Holding Company's common stock will be issued and offered for sale to the general public. This IPO, together with certain debt offerings set forth in the Plan, will result in the raising of capital. This capital will then be used to purchase assets for the Closed Block, pay cash up to an amount to be approved by the Commissioner to certain policyholders electing to receive cash and those required to receive it, fund policy credits, pay the expenses of the demutualization, and contribute cash to the capital of the reorganized State Mutual.

42.    State Mutual presently intends to conduct capital raising transactions under the Plan consisting of an IPO of $207 million (the Plan requires an IPO of at least $100 million) and a public note offering of $200 million.

43.    The infusion of new capital will strengthen the Company to the benefit of its policyholders, who will receive as consideration stock, cash and policy credits representing the entire pre-IPO value of State Mutual. The new capital will increase the value of the Company, shares of which initially will be owned by both policyholders and, to a lesser extent, by IPO purchasers.

44.    I find that the capital-raising transactions are reasonably structured to allow the Company to (1) raise capital sufficient to make the required contributions to State Mutual under the Plan (including approximately $124 million for additional Closed Block funding, $4.5 million for mandatory cash payments and policy credits, $24 million for cash elections and $25 million for demutualization expenses) and (2) raise capital in additional amounts to contribute to the capital of State Mutual to support its life, health and retirement operations.

45.    The IPO will also establish a public market for shares of AFC enabling policyholders who receive stock to sell it. The Plan requires the Holding Company to arrange to list its common

stock on a national securities exchange, and to use its best efforts to maintain that listing for as long as the common stock is publicly traded. AFC has already taken the first step towards meeting that requirement by filing an application to list the stock on the New York Stock Exchange. The policyholders will thus have the opportunity after the demutualization to sell their stock in the secondary market at the potentially higher price paid by an informed and active market. By retaining their shares, policyholders also have the opportunity to realize the full value of any possible increase in the price of the stock over time.

46. The IPO will also set the price per share of the common stock, which will determine the value of the individual policyholder consideration. As a means of determining the price per share of the common stock, I find that the IPO is a fair and reasonable basis on which to calculate the policyholder consideration and policy credits under the Plan. The price per share reflects the value that investors are willing to pay for the stock following informational and marketing efforts by management and underwriters, a review of the offering prospectus and other materials, consultation with industry experts and research analysts, and a comparison of the Company to comparable companies and alternative investment opportunities as well as taking into account other relevant financial considerations.

### Continuing Regulatory Review of IPO Process

47. State Mutual and the Holding Company have signed a letter undertaking that the Division's financial advisors, Alex. Brown, will be permitted to monitor the IPO process. As part of that undertaking, State Mutual and AFC have also committed to the Division that the IPO process will be conducted in a manner consistent with customary practices for reasonably comparable IPOs. The final pricing decision on the IPO will be made by a special committee or committees of the Holding Company and State Mutual's Boards, which will have a majority of outside, independent directors.

48. State Mutual and the Holding Company shall provide at least 24 hours and not more than 48 hours notice to the Division and Alex. Brown of the time and place of execution of the underwriting agreement and of its expected terms and conditions, including documents.

49. State Mutual and AFC also commit that they will not enter into any underwriting agreement if they receive notification that the Division has not received confirmation from Alex. Brown that they have complied with the terms of the undertaking letter.

### The Pricing Committee

50. The three named policyholders raised an issue as to whether members of the Board of Directors of the Company who have affiliations with financial institutions that may purchase shares of the Holding Company in the IPO should be precluded from serving on the Pricing Committees based upon possible conflicts of interest. However, there are a number of safeguards to prevent even the appearance of a conflict from becoming a conflict in fact. Members of State Mutual's Board have a fiduciary obligation to act in the best interest of the Company and its policyholders. In addition, there are monitoring procedures established by the Division's financial Consultants, including their attendance at the final pricing meetings of the Pricing Committees of the Boards of Directors. Moreover, under the federal securities laws, any purchase by any such affiliate would be required to be on the same terms and conditions as all other purchasers in the IPO and on the same available information concerning State Mutual and AFC. Nevertheless, the Pricing Committees of the State Mutual and Holding Company Boards of

Directors have been reconfigured so that their members (Directors Nichols, Varnum and Harrison) are not affiliated with financial institutions that might purchase shares in the IPO.

### Value Received By Policyholders

51.    Certain policyholders have asserted that the current structure of the IPO will result in the policyholders receiving less than the full fair market pre-conversion value of the Company. They also claim that the investors who participate in the IPO will experience a windfall due to the rebound effect to the price per share sometimes caused by the alleged discount built into such offerings. These policyholders claim that, consequently, they will forego profits due to the anticipated appreciation of the publicly issued stock. There is more than adequate testimony in the Record that the policyholders will receive the full pre-IPO value of the Company for their aggregate membership interests in the distribution of consideration under the Plan. Likewise, although there is often a discount to the market value of a company in the pricing of an IPO, there is no guarantee that the initial price of the stock will increase in the six month to one year period following the offering.

52.    The policyholders will therefore receive the full pre IPO value of State Mutual when they receive the consideration called for in the Plan, and the IPO will not result in a "windfall" to IPO investors, as there are no guarantees that the stock price will rise after the IPO. If a rise does occur, those policyholders receiving stock will realize the appreciation to the same extent as outside investors.

53    I find that the IPO is a fair and reasonable method of determining the value of the policyholder consideration, both individually and in the aggregate, and the participation of the Division's financial Consultants will ensure that the pricing process will be conducted in an open manner, consistent with industry practice. . . .

### ELEMENTS OF SECTION 19E AND THE PLAN

55.    Among other things, the Commissioner must find compliance with each of the elements of Section 19E. . . .

### D. Policyholder Consideration

*Appropriate consideration must be given to eligible policyholders under the Plan in exchange for their membership interests in the company, and must be "determinable under a fair and reasonable formula approved by the commissioner, and shall be based on the insurer's entire surplus as shown by the insurer's financial statement most recently filed with the commissioner [prior to adoption of the plan] . . . including all voluntary reserves but excluding contingently repayable and outstanding guaranty capital shares at the redemption value thereof, and without taking into account the value of nonadmitted assets or insurance business in force." Section 19E(3).*

### Aggregate Consideration

76.    Under the Plan the aggregate consideration is the total pre-IPO value of the Company, which is to be distributed to eligible policyholders. The amount of the aggregate consideration will be set by the market in the IPO, which will result in the issuance of shares of stock in AFC, State Mutual's new parent holding company. The IPO is an appropriate method to determine the value of the consideration to be given to eligible policyholders, as market forces will determine the share price in an objective, and fair and reasonable manner.

77.  The Company's outside financial advisor, Merrill Lynch, has opined that the aggregate consideration to be received under the Plan by eligible policyholders is fair from a financial perspective. Moreover, the Division's outside financial advisor, Alex. Brown, has also determined that the aggregate consideration received by policyholders is fair. No credible evidence to the contrary was submitted to the Record. Therefore, I find that the consideration received by policyholders under the Plan is appropriate, determinable under a fair and reasonable formula, in conformity with the requirements of Section 19E(3).

### Allocation of Policyholder Consideration

78.  In determining the allocation of consideration among eligible policyholders, the Company has employed a method consisting of a fixed component and a variable component. The fixed component represents approximately ten percent of the total consideration given to eligible policyholders.

79.  The fixed component consists of an allocation of twenty-eight shares per policy of common stock of AFC. The fixed component is paid on a per policy basis and is not tied to the number of votes which are represented by a particular policy.[30] Use of a fixed component (while not mandatory) insures that all eligible policyholders receive a minimum amount of consideration, irrespective of their contribution to surplus, and also provides compensation for their membership interests other than their right to the company's divisible surplus. The amount of the fixed component under the Plan is consistent with, and falls within the upper range of, fixed components of consideration given to policyholders in other, prior, demutualizations. I find that

---

[30]  The three named policyholders have alleged that the determination of the fixed component "eviscerates" the voting power of the policyholders and benefits institutional group policies, because it fails to take into account the number of votes an individual policyholder may have held.

Under the Plan, each eligible policy, whether assigned one or twenty votes, receives the same number of shares for the cancellation of the holder's membership interests other than the right to participate in the divisible surplus of the Company, which right is compensated by receipt of the variable component of consideration. Section 19E is silent as to the calculation of consideration for the cancellation of the right to vote and there is no statutory requirement that the number of votes allocated to each policy be taken into account when determining consideration. Section 19E requires only that consideration be based on a fair and reasonable formula.

The number of votes allocated to each policy is determined with reference to applicable statutes. Individual policies are granted anywhere from one to twenty votes, depending on the size of the policy, up to a maximum of twenty votes (for $100,000 or more in coverage). Policies with coverage over that amount receive no more than the twenty allocated votes, although an individual could have more than twenty votes if he had more than one policy. Group policies, on the other hand, have but one vote held by the "holder" or the "employer," regardless of the amount of the policy.

Varying the amount of the fixed component based on the number of votes would not be fair to those holders of single large policies as against holders of several small policies. The small policyholder would likely have considerably more votes than the large policyholder, yet have no greater interest in or effect on the company's condition or future.

Thus, the basis allocation of a minimum and *non-varying* number of shares to each eligible policy is fair and reasonable and is not prejudicial to the policyholders or the insuring public.

this formula is fair and reasonable and constitutes an appropriate method for determining and allocating the fixed component.

80.    The variable component, which is intended to compensate policyholders for their rights to the divisible surplus, is determined under the Plan pursuant to a formula that takes into account both past and anticipated future contributions of participating policies to the Company's surplus. This method, known as the historic plus prospective method of allocation, employs the Company's reported surplus as of December 31, 1993.

81.    The three named policyholders claim that Section 19E(3) mandates the use of the historic-only method. Contrary to this claim, Section 19E is flexible and does not expressly require, or preclude, the use of any one method. It requires simply that policyholder consideration be "appropriate," that it be determinable under a "fair and reasonable formula" and that it be "based upon" the insurer's entire surplus. . . .

84.    The only suggestion to the contrary is the testimony of Tierney, unsupported by any evidence, presented on behalf of the three named policyholders, that Section 19E requires use of the historic only method of policyholder allocation. Tierney asserts that the method of allocation under the Plan favors group policyholders to the detriment of individual policyholders. Tierney testified that, if read as an actuarial communication, Section 19E would compel the use of the historic only method. (Id.) Section 19E is not an actuarial communication, however, and I do not find persuasive, in light of all the evidence, the unsupported contention that Section 19E requires the use of the historic only method. In fact, Section 19E does not dictate that only one method be used. The evidence here supports a flexible reading of Section 19E and a conclusion that the historic plus prospective method of allocation is fair and reasonable in this case.[31] . . .

85.    In addition, the use of the historic plus prospective method of allocating policyholder consideration is supported by the Report of the Task Force of the Society of Actuaries on Mutual Life Insurance Company Conversion ("SOA Report"), published in July 1987, which states that the allocation of policyholder consideration should be "based primarily on the relative contributions of policyholders to the surplus of the company" and that such contributions should include both past and anticipated future contributions to surplus.

---

[31]    Tierney was presented as an expert witness at the Hearing and testified concerning his views on actuarial and financial issues relating to the Plan and how provisions of a conversion plan could be selected or voted on by policyholders. Tierney has a Master of Science in Actuarial Science from Northeastern University and is a Fellow by examination in the Society of Actuaries. He has no degree in business or finance, however, and testified that he has never served as a financial consultant in connection with an IPO. He worked in various capacities at John Hancock Mutual Life Insurance Company from 1965 to 1977, although while there he performed no work on demutualizations. He noted that he is a pension actuary and testified that most recently approximately ten to fifteen percent of his work involves life or health insurance companies. While Tierney is an actuary, and might be qualified to testify as an expert on pension matters, he is not sufficiently qualified in the specific fields of demutualizations and IPOs to render expert actuarial or financial opinions on those matters. Nor does he possess any legal expertise to provide any meaningful interpretation of Section 19E. Accordingly, his testimony will be treated as that of an informed lay person with a background in actuarial science, and will be accorded only the weight that such a non-expert qualification would allow.

## E. Preemptive Rights

*The Plan must "give each eligible policyholder a preemptive right to acquire his proportionate part of all of the proposed capital stock of the insurer . . within a designated reasonable period, and to apply upon the purchase thereof the amount of his consideration, . . . provided . . . in the instance of a plan of reorganization in which the appropriate consideration received by eligible policyholders . . . is stock of a corporation in a transaction authorized under this section, or other consideration as approved by the commissioner or, without limiting the generality of the foregoing . . . the plan shall provide either (i) that no policyholder shall have any preemptive right to acquire any of the proposed capital stock of the insurer or of the proposed parent or other corporation or (ii) for preemptive rights on such other terms as approved by the commissioner. . . ." Section 19E(4)*

88.  As stated, the consideration to be given to each of the eligible policyholders in exchange for their membership interests includes shares of common stock of AFC. Since the Plan explicitly states that no policyholder or other person will have any preemptive right to acquire shares of stock of AFC or State Mutual, I find that the Plan conforms to the requirements of Section 14E(4). . . .

## G. Share Price to Policyholders

*Under the Plan, "shares are to be offered to policyholders at a price not greater than to be thereafter offered under the plan to others." Section 19E(6).*

90.  In exchange for their membership interest, policyholders will receive either common stock in AFC ("Common Stock"), cash, or policy credits. The value of the cash and policy credits will be based upon an allocation to the policyholder of a specific number of shares of Common Stock, which are then converted into cash or policy credits, the amount depending on the price per share in the IPO.  At the same time, the Holding Company will be offering shares of the same Common Stock to the public in the IPO, at a price to be fixed by special Pricing Committees of AFC and State Mutual, in consultation with the lead underwriter of the IPO, Merrill Lynch & Co. Moreover, as stated, there will be no preemptive rights offering. Accordingly, it is clear that the per share price of the Common Stock that will be received by the policyholders in exchange for their membership interests, either directly or as a measurement of the cash or policy credits they are to receive, will be the same as that offered for sale in the IPO, as the stock price will be set by the IPO. Therefore, I find that the Plan conforms to Section 19E(6) which prohibits the offering of shares at a price greater than to be thereafter offered under a conversion plan to others. . . .

## M. Costs related to Commissioner's review of Plan

*All reasonable costs related to the review of the Plan "including those costs attributable to the use of staff personnel" by the Commissioner, must "be borne by the insurer making the filing." Section 19E(9).*

107. The expenses of the conversion of State Mutual are estimated to total approximately $25.8 million. Approximately half of that total cost relates to the costs of Consultants retained by the Division and the NYSID. State Mutual has followed the reimbursement and payment policy in the Plan, which expressly provides that such costs shall be borne by State Mutual. Therefore, I find that all reasonable costs related to the review of the Plan, including those costs

attributable to the use of staff personnel and outside consultants by the Commissioner have been borne by State Mutual in compliance with Section 19E(9).

## LEGAL CONCLUSIONS

108. The State Mutual Plan of Reorganization conforms to each of the requirements of Section 19E. . . .

---

Presented below is a pro forma balance sheet, reflecting the State Mutual balance sheet before and after the demutualization. The post-demutualization balance sheet also reflects the public offering of 11 million shares of common stock at an initial offering price of $15 per share. Of the $231 million raised in this offering, $15 million were to be allocated to underwriting discounts and related offering expenses. The post-demutualization balance sheets also reflect proceeds from a $200 million issuance of senior debentures (that is, long term debt), of which $2.3 million were to be allocated to underwriting discounts and related offering expenses.

The total net proceeds of the stock offering and subordinated debenture issuance was to be $413.7 million. Of this amount, $28.3 million were to be transferred to Eligible Policyholders as cash payments or policy credits. Another $8.2 million were to be expended for non-recurring reorganizational expenses. As a result of these and other minor adjustments for expenses, the pro-forma balance sheets show an increase in retained earnings of $179 million after the demutualization.

After completion of the demutualization, it was anticipated that the company would have 48.5 million shares of common stock outstanding, 11 million sold in the public offering and the balance of the shares issued to Eligible Policyholders under terms of the reorganization. As mentioned above, certain Eligible Policyholders were to receive cash or policy credits in lieu of or in addition to common stock.

### Comments and Questions

1.    Demutualization statutes of the sort underlying this transaction balance many competing interests: current policyholders versus future shareholders, individual policies versus policies issued through group accounts, and policyholders assigned to the Closed Account and other policyholders. How does the Massachusetts statute resolve those conflicts? Does the resolution seem sensible to you?

# Pro Forma Balance Sheet

## (June 30, 1995)

| | Pre-Demutalization (in $millions) | Post-Demutualization (in $millions) |
|---|---|---|
| **Assets** | | |
| Investments | $9,942 | $9,305 |
| Cash and cash equivalents | $319 | $564 |
| Reinsurance receivables | $923 | $922 |
| Premiums, accounts and notes receivable | $524 | $523 |
| Other assets | $1,432 | $1,392 |
| Separate account assets | $3,659 | $3,659 |
| Closed Block assets | $0 | $815 |
| **Total Assets** | **$16,799** | **$17,179** |
| | | |
| **Liabilities** | | |
| Policy liabilities and accruals | $10,410 | $9,517 |
| Short-term debt | $28 | $28 |
| Other liabilities | $1,482 | $1,474 |
| Senior debentures payable | $0 | $200 |
| Separate account assets | $3,659 | $3,659 |
| Closed Block liabilities | $0 | $902 |
| **Total Liabilities** | **$15,569** | **$15,770** |
| | | |
| **Equity** | | |
| Common stock | $0 | $1 |
| Capital in excess of par | $0 | $1,313 |
| Retained earnings | $1,135 | $0 |
| Net unrealized appreciation on investments | $96 | $96 |
| Total Equity | $1,230 | $1,409 |
| | | |
| **Total Liabilities and Equity** | **$16,799** | **$17,179** |

2.    In addition to the factors outlined in the edited version of the order, the Massachusetts Demutualization statute required the Division of Insurance to ensure that upon completion of the transaction, no person acquires more than a ten percent beneficiary interest in the resulting entity and that State Mutual's officers and directors receive no additional compensation as a result of this transaction. What purpose do these additional restrictions serve? Are they likely to be effective?

## B.  Conversion of Savings Banks

The State Mutual transactions notwithstanding, relatively few mutual life insurance company have actually implemented demutualization plans. Demutualization of savings and loan associations and mutual savings banks has, in contrast, been highly popular over the past two decades. Hundreds of savings associations and savings banks have completed demutualization transactions (also known as conversions), and mutual thrifts now constitute a minority of an industry they once dominated. In the early 1990s, roughly 100 mutuals converted each year. At this rate of conversion, mutual thrifts could become extinct early in the 21$^{st}$ Century. A series of recent savings demutualizations are described in the following article. As you read through this piece -- and the following materials on savings bank conversions -- consider how these mechanisms for conversion compare with the rules that governed the State Mutual transaction. Which legal regime is better?

## Getting In on Savings Bank Conversion
### N.Y. Times, Feb. 5, 1994, § 1, at 34

When the Green Point Savings Bank converted to stock ownership a week ago, its stock soared 27 percent on the first day of trading. Depositors who bought shares of the Flushing, Queens, institution in advance booked a tidy paper profit.

Similar deals remain plausible. Although bank regulators and Congressmen are concerned about windfalls going to bank officials and have put such conversions on hold, their efforts may merely delay the inevitable. About 1,200 mutual savings institutions remain, and 75 have more than $500 million in assets.

"Any bank over $500 million is a good prospect for demutualization, " said Paul A. Bauer, president of Bauer Financial Reports, a bnk research firm in Coral Gables, Fla. "The only way for them to grow is to generate some capital." So even if you missed out on the deal for Green Point, a small deposit at another mutual savings bank may be worth more than its face value some day. Depositors in conversions have generally been allowed to acquire a certain amount of stock before outsiders, although additional restrictions are possible.

The initial stock offering can be as low as half the book value. "As a short-term investment, the price usually rises 30 to 40 percent over the offering," Mr. Bauer said. "And if the thrift then takes the money and uses it properly, it should get up to one and a half times book." Market professionals have opened savings accounts at large mutual savings banks for this potential profit. In response, many banks restrict new accounts to state residents.

In response to transactions such as the Green Point Savings Bank conversion, the FDIC initiated a rule-making process in 1994, culminating in this final rule:

## FDIC Rule on Mutual-to-Stock Conversions of Savings Banks
### 59 Fed. Reg. 61,233 (Nov. 30, 1994)

In June 1994 the FDIC issued a proposed rule to add specific substantive requirements to its mutual-to-stock conversion regulations (Proposed Rule) (59 FR 30316 (June 13, 1994)). . . .

The Proposed Rule would have:

- required the submission of a full appraisal report, including a complete and detailed description of the elements that make up an appraisal report, justification for the methodology employed and sufficient support for the conclusions reached therein;

- required a depositor vote on all mutual-to-stock conversions of State Savings Banks and prohibited management's use of previously executed (or "running") proxies to satisfy depositor voting requirements;

- for one year following the date of the conversion, among other things, required that any management recognition plans (MRPs) or stock option plans be implemented only after shareholder approval is received, required that stock options (if any) be granted at no lower than the market price at which the stock is trading at the time of grant and prohibited MRPs funded by conversion proceeds;

- required that the record date for determining depositors eligible to receive rights to participate in the subscription offering of the conversion stock not be less than one year prior to the date of adoption of the plan of conversions by the converting bank's board of trustees; required that the subscription offering provide a preference to eligible depositors and others in the bank's "local community" (as defined in the proposed rule) or within 100 miles of the bank's home office or branch(es);

- required that employee stock ownership plans (ESOPs) not have a priority over subscription rights of "eligible depositors" (as defined in the proposed rule);

- required the submission of a business plan, including, among other things, a detailed discussion of how management intends to deploy the capital raised through the sale of stock in the conversion; [and]

- prohibited stock repurchases within one year following the conversion.

### Summary of Comments and Discussion of Issues

#### 1. The FDIC's Oversight Role

In general, the comments acknowledged that there had been notable examples of insider abuse in mutual-to-stock conversions of State Savings Banks in the recent past and suggested how future potential abuses could be avoided. Many of those who commented recommended that the FDIC continue to play an oversight role in the mutual-to-stock conversions of State Savings Banks, noting that federal oversight will continue to safeguard the integrity of the process. One noted that "present abuses in several recent and proposed conversions have demonstrated the need for the FDIC to maintain oversight of the conversion process, to ensure that issues of both safety and soundness and of fiduciary care are identified and adequately addressed". A trade group commented that "with recent publicity over some apparent abuses in the [conversion] process and resulting Congressional concerns, . . . it is most appropriate and important for the FDIC to assert regulatory jurisdiction over conversions by state nonmember banks". One state regulator noted that the Interim Final Rule was an "excellent set of rules" with a "very conservative, realistic approach to a situation which could have gotten out of hand if left to go unchecked". One savings bank said simply that "past abuses [in mutual-to-stock conversions] support the need for FDIC oversight". . . . . Some commenters contended that state regulation was sufficient in the area of mutual-to-stock conversions and that the requirements in the [Proposed Rule] are not necessary. One mutual savings bank asserted that the "averments made by the FDIC in support of the [Rule] that it is needed for safety and soundness reasons and to protect the interest of depositors are without merit and are being offered only to support continued federal intrusion into issues which are primarily the concern of state law and regulation." One state mutual savings bank stated that the "proposed policy statement is overkill" and that "state regulation can handle insider abuse issues." One state banking and thrift regulator asserted that state regulators are not to blame for insider abuses in conversions and that "states' rights should not be tramped on". The regulator suggested that a committee of state and federal regulators work together to address issues and concerns. . . .    The Board has determined that each of the requirements in the final rule is necessary to satisfy specific FDIC concerns about safety and soundness, breaches of fiduciary duty and other violations of law in connection with mutual-to-stock conversions. At the same time, the FDIC believes that it is essential to consider the existence of state regulation and supervision in determining the proper role in the conversion process for the FDIC as the primary federal regulator of State Savings Banks. As discussed above, many of the comments that the FDIC received on the Proposed Policy Statement, the [Proposed Rule] expressed agreement with the FDIC's federal oversight role in mutual-to-stock conversions of State Savings Banks, but several also suggested the FDIC have a limited role in conversions of State Savings Banks and that deference be paid to states' rights on issues outside the FDIC's areas of concern.

    With the issuance of the final rule, the Board is attempting to strike the proper balance in this regard. In particular, the final rule includes a provision stating that, in the event that a State Savings Bank proposing to convert determines that compliance with any provision of the final rule would be inconsistent or in conflict with applicable state law, the bank may file with the FDIC a written request for waiver of compliance with the provision. The request must demonstrate that the requested waiver would not be detrimental to the safety and soundness of the bank, entail a breach of fiduciary duty by the bank's management, or otherwise be detrimental or inequitable to the bank, its depositors, any other insured depository institution(s), the federal deposit insurance funds or the public interest. In this connection, the Board does not believe that state-wide exemptions from the requirements of the final rule are appropriate or practical. Establishing exemption criteria and applying those criteria equitably and consistently would prove very difficult, if not unrealistic. The Board prefers the case-by-case approach contained in the final rule.

    As indicated in the Proposed Rule, many of the requirements of the final rule are prompted by the Board's concerns about bank management's proper exercise of its fiduciary duties. As discussed in the preambles to the [Proposed Rule], the duties and obligations of directors/trustees and officers of mutual savings banks are identical to the responsibilities the FDIC has historically enunciated and enforced concerning directors and officers of commercial banks.  The two principal duties of care and loyalty that directors and officers of commercial banks must exercise on behalf of the institution and its constituencies (i.e., depositors, creditors and shareholders) also apply to directors/trustees of mutual savings banks.  Both duties have long antecedents in the common law of corporations and financial institutions.

Directors/trustees (as well as officers) of mutual savings institutions are held to the same standard of care and loyalty as directors and officers of stock banks.  Thus, the directors/trustees and officers of mutual State Savings Banks must fulfill their duty of loyalty to the institution by administering its affairs with the utmost candor, personal honesty and integrity.  They are prohibited from advancing their own personal or business interests or those of others at the expense of the bank.  This general fiduciary duty has been frequently interpreted to include an element of fairness and good faith which, in the context of mutual-to-stock conversions, affords protection to the various stakeholders (particularly depositors) of mutual savings banks. The FDIC, through the final rule, also requires the directors/trustees and officers of mutual savings banks to adhere to the same standards of loyalty and care that are required of directors and officers of stock institutions in order to prevent insider abuse. As indicated throughout, the requirements in the final rule are rooted in concerns about safety and soundness, breaches of fiduciary duty and/or other violations of law.

### 2. Appraisals

The Proposed Rule included a requirement that State Savings Banks intending to convert to stock ownership submit to the FDIC, along with the other required materials, a full appraisal report on the value of the converting bank and the pricing of the conversion stock.  As discussed in the Proposed Rule, many states require that a converting mutual savings bank sell its capital stock at a total price equal to its estimated pro forma market value, based on an independent valuation.  Despite this requirement, many converted institutions have exhibited significant increases in the immediate post-conversion trading market price for the stock.

As explained in detail in the Proposed Rule, the FDIC is concerned that the history of increases in market prices resulted from appraisal reports (submitted in connection with these conversions) that significantly undervalued the stock--the effect of which has several ramifications. If an appraisal is too low and the shares of stock are underpriced, the institution receives less of an increase in capital than it should from the sale of conversion stock and the deposit insurance fund is provided with less of a capital cushion than would have resulted if the stock sales price was based on a proper and adequate appraisal.  Also, an underpriced appraisal enriches the insiders who purchase or are granted a significant interest in the converting institution by enticing them to undertake a conversion (in order to acquire shares below their fair value) that may not be in the best interest of the institution. Sophisticated investors also are able to benefit, undeservedly, from the sale of underpriced conversion stock.. . . .

The FDIC received several comments on the proposed appraisal requirements.  Most who commented on this issue favored the required submission of a full appraisal report.  Some expressed concern, however, that an over-emphasis on immediate post-conversion share price increases might force appraisers to overvalue the stock of converting institutions, resulting in a detriment to the institution and its stockholders. They also suggested that there must be some expectation of an early increase in stock price to entice investors to purchase stock of a converting mutual. A few of those commenting said the FDIC should publish the standards it will use in judging appraisals. One suggested that the OTS and the FDIC should issue joint appraisal standards. . . .

Based on the comments received and the FDIC's view that the proper valuation of a converting mutual savings bank is a crucial factor in assuring an equitable mutual-to-stock conversion, the Board has decided to adopt the appraisal requirements in the Proposed Rule. Thus, the FDIC will continue to review appraisal reports to ensure that converting institutions are properly valued and will continue to object to proposed conversions supported by unacceptable appraisal reports. . . . .

### 3. Voting Requirement/Prohibition Against Running Proxies

The Proposed Rule included a requirement that depositors and other stakeholders of a State Savings Bank vote in favor of a mutual-to-stock conversion in order for the FDIC not to object to the proposed conversion. It also proposed a prohibition on the use of running proxies in mutual-to-stock conversions of State Savings banks.

As discussed in detail in the Proposed Rule, the Board believes that, in order for a board of directors or trustees of a mutual savings bank to properly exercise its fiduciary responsibilities to the bank and its depositors, the board should obtain a vote of depositors in favor of the proposed conversion before the proposed conversion is completed. Most states, but not all, require a depositor vote for mutual-to-stock conversions. The OTS also requires both federal and state savings associations to obtain a majority vote of association members as one of the pre-conditions to converting. Some states, however, require only that the board of directors or trustees (or similar group) approve the plan of conversion and do not require a vote of members.

As also discussed in the Proposed Rule, in the same vein, the Board also believes that a proxy specifically designed for the proposed conversion should be used to obtain a depositor vote on the conversion. In some states the management of converting banks and savings associations, subject to certain conditions, may use so-called "running proxies" (proxies obtained when a depositor opened his or her account with the institution) to vote in favor of the proposed conversion.

The FDIC received numerous comments on these related issues. Several of the comments voiced opposition to "voting rights" for depositors in states that do not provide such rights. One state bank asserted that "voting rights should be left to state law. To impose some sort of depositor approval requirement in a state that does not have depositor voting could lead to expanded ownership claims by depositors that could operate to the detriment of mutuals". One state regulator asserted that "any FDIC requirement of a depositor vote in a mutual-to-stock conversion . . . [would be] wholly unsupported by any expressly preemptive federal statute". Many banks in Massachusetts commented that any depositor voting right requirements imposed by the FDIC would put undue pressure on mutuals in that state to convert to stock ownership. . . .

In response to these comments, the Board continues to believe that it is necessary and appropriate for the FDIC to require a depositor vote on proposed conversions. Such a requirement will not necessarily contradict state laws (that do not require a depositor vote), but will supplement the state law by requiring the member vote. The FDIC's concern is with the board of directors'/

trustees' proper exercise of its fiduciary duties of loyalty and care to the bank and its depositors. The Board believes that the proper exercise of such duties requires that depositors, as stakeholders of the bank, have the opportunity to approve or disapprove the proposed conversion. This requirement is, in part, rooted in the concern that bank insiders often benefit personally from bank conversions. This almost inherent conflict of interest (between self interest and the interests of the bank) may be mitigated by the existence of a depositor vote on the proposed conversion. The Board also believes that any additional expense caused by the voting requirement and prohibition against running proxies is outweighed by the need to ensure the proper participation of depositors and other stakeholders in the proposed conversion. The final rule, therefore, adopts the requirement in the Proposed Rule for a depositor vote in favor of the proposed conversion of a State Savings Bank to stock form.. . . .

5. Eligibility Record Date, Priority to Depositors Residing in the Bank's Local Community (Local Depositor Preference), Priority of ESOPs

A. Eligibility Record Date

The Proposed Rule included a requirement that the eligibility record date for determining the stock subscription purchase priority for depositors of a State Savings Bank be set at no less than one year prior to the date of the board of directors'/trustees' adoption of the plan of conversion (from mutual to stock form). As indicated in the Proposed Rule, the Board believes that, in order for a board of directors/trustees of a State Savings Bank to carry out its fiduciary responsibilities to the bank and its depositors, the board must assure an equitable and lawful conversion process. From the numerous comments received and from a review of proposed and completed conversions, it is apparent that so-called "professional depositors", who place funds in mutual banks and savings associations in order to gain a purchase priority if the institution converts to stock form, have reaped substantial profits on conversions of mutual institutions. A proper exercise of fiduciary responsibilities toward the bank and its longer-term depositors dictates that "professional depositors" not be allowed to experience windfall gains in conversions. Requiring that the eligibility record date be no less than one year prior to the board's adoption of the plan of conversion will help assure that longer-term depositors are more likely than professional depositors to benefit from the stock purchase priority.

Many of those who commented on this issue expressed support for it. A state banking commissioner and a consumer group each commented that a one-year eligibility record date would help curb insider abuses. One person said the FDIC should not set an eligibility record date. Another person expressed support for the one-year eligibility requirement but suggested that it might not weed out professional depositors because many of them have deposits with savings banks for over a year. A state regulator said a 90-day eligibility requirement might be sufficient. . . .

Based on the comments received on this issue, the Board has determined that the one-year period is sufficient and that, given the factual nature of the requirement, attempting to establish a starting period based on when a bank's board of directors/trustees first considered whether to convert to stock ownership would be very difficult to implement and regulate. Thus, the Board has decided to adopt the eligibility record date requirement of the Proposed Rule because, as stated in the comments, it properly protects the legitimate interests of core depositors and provides sufficient assurance that long-term supporters of an institution are given priority. Also, as stated in the Proposed Rule, the one-year period is a minimum time period. Converting State Savings Banks are encouraged to designate longer time periods if appropriate to encompass longer-term depositors in the local communities served by the bank.

### B. Local Depositor Preference

The Proposed Rule also included a required stock purchase preference for eligible depositors in the bank's "local community" or within 100 miles of a home or branch office of the converting bank. The FDIC proposed the Local Depositor Preference requirement to promote local community participation by long-term depositors in the conversion process and to ensure that the opportunity for local depositors to fully participate in the subscription offering in a mutual-to-stock conversion is not diminished by large purchases made by "professional depositors".

The FDIC received numerous comments on this proposed requirement. Thirteen expressed support for the rule, contending that the preference would rightfully promote local control of the bank and limit the participation of "professional depositors" in conversions. They also noted that the Local Depositor Preference would give depositors in the local community a more meaningful opportunity to participate in the conversion and reduce the problem of outside investors tending to put undue pressure on management to achieve a higher stock value more rapidly than may be feasible through safe and sound operations.

Eight of those who commented on the proposed requirement opposed it, asserting that the rule constituted an unlawful geographic discrimination. They contended that all depositors have ownership, voting and liquidation rights and, thus, a subscription purchase priority should not be related to where a depositor lives. Several of those who commented said that the rule should at least be modified to provide for long-term depositors who moved away from the bank; they and others criticized the 100-mile rule as unworkable.

After a review of the comments and an internal review of the issue, the Board has decided to defer to the judgment of the converting bank's board or directors or trustees and the applicable state law on whether a stock purchase priority is provided to local depositors. The FDIC continues to believe, generally, that local depositors, collectively, should be granted a preference because they typically have made significant long-term contributions to the financial success of the converting State Savings Bank, in contrast to certain non-local depositors who have made deposits solely in anticipation of a conversion. The FDIC also believes, however, any potential abuse by professional depositors can and should be handled on a case-by-case basis by the converting bank's management, under the applicable state law. Thus, the final rule does not require the local depositor preference contained in the Proposed Rule. The FDIC will consider, on a case-by-case basis, the reasonableness of any local depositor preference included in a proposed conversion. In that connection, the Board notes that it will not object to a local depositor preference based on the definition of "local community" contained in the OTS Revisions.

### C. Priority for ESOPs

The proposed rule included a provision requiring that ESOPs not be accorded a higher subscription right priority than "eligible depositors". As noted above, the term "eligible depositors" was defined as depositors holding qualifying deposits at the bank as of a date designated in the bank's plan of conversion that is not less than one year prior to the date of adoption of the plan of conversion by the converting bank's board of directors/trustees. This proposed requirement was prompted by the Board's belief that ESOPs (tax- qualified or otherwise) should not be accorded higher purchase priority rights than long-term depositors. This is in keeping with the principle of fiduciary duty requiring that the board of directors/trustees of a State Savings Bank put the interest of long-term depositors ahead of the interests of management and employees.

The FDIC received several comments on this proposed requirement. In essence, they were evenly divided between those for and against the proposal. Those in favor of the requirement argued that eligible depositors of a converting State Savings Bank should be accorded the first priority in purchasing stock in the conversion. Those opposed asserted that the employees make the bank successful and, thus, should be accorded the first subscription priority. One group commented that ESOP participants and eligible depositors should share priority on a pro rata basis.

The Board does not disagree that ESOPs promote greater employee productivity and motivation and that the employees of a State Savings Bank should be permitted to benefit, through the purchase of subscription stock by an ESOP, in the bank's mutual-to-stock conversion. The Board continues to believe, however, that, under general principles of fiduciary duty, ESOPs should not be accorded higher purchase priority rights than long-term depositors. Thus, the Board has decided to include in the final rule the requirement that "eligible depositors" be accorded a higher subscription priority than ESOPs. . . .

7. Stock Repurchases

The Proposed Rule included a provision to prohibit State Savings Banks from repurchasing stock for one year following the bank's conversion to stock form. After that period the FDIC would consider such proposed repurchases on a case-by-case basis under section 18(i)(1) of the FDI Act (12 U.S.C. 1828 (i)(1)) (Section 18(i)). Section 18(i) prohibits state nonmember banks from reducing or retiring capital without the prior consent of the FDIC.

The FDIC received several comments on this issue, the majority of which opposed stock repurchase restrictions. Those against it asserted that the inability to repurchase stock for one year would constitute an unnecessary and inappropriate restriction on the ability of officers and trustees to carry out their duty to maximize the value of the shares of the bank. Those for the restriction stated that it would help prevent insider abuse. One state regulator said any such restriction should be determined by the bank's primary regulator.

As indicated in the Proposed Rule, the Board is concerned that a substantial stock buyback program begun immediately after the bank's conversion to stock form may not have a legitimate business purpose and would raise issues about whether the conversion stock was appropriately valued. The Board is also concerned that a recently converted institution have a capital base adequate to safeguard against possible unexpected losses that may occur under the new organizational structure. Thus, upon consideration of the comments, the Board has decided to implement the one-year restriction. To allow for some flexibility in this respect, however, the final rule modifies the restriction to allow limited stock repurchases up to 5 percent during the first year where compelling and valid business reasons are established. This would give the FDIC the explicit ability to permit repurchases during the first year after the conversion where it is in the best interests of the bank and its shareholders. All proposed stock repurchases by State Savings Banks are considered by the FDIC on a case-by-case basis under section 18(i).

8. Merger/Conversions

In some cases mutual institutions convert to stock ownership simultaneously with a merger or acquisition transaction with another depository institution or holding company. This is generally known as a merger/conversion. In merger/conversions depositors of the converting institutions obtain the right to purchase stock in the acquiring institution and not the converting savings bank. In exercising its fiduciary responsibilities the board of directors/trustees of a mutual State Savings Bank must assure that: (1) The value of the converting institution is fairly determined; and (2) That value is distributed to the proper constituents of the bank.

[B]ased on the proposed conversions the FDIC has reviewed in the recent past and other merger conversions it has studied, the Board has observed that, in virtually every merger conversion, the acquiring institution has captured a large portion of the value of the converting institution. It has not been uncommon in merger/conversions for the management of the converting mutual institution to receive extremely generous compensation and benefit packages. Thus, an apparent conflict of interest exists: whether the management of a mutual institution is opting for a merger/conversion, instead of a standard conversion or no conversion at all, based on the best interests of the institution and its depositors or in response to the level of benefits offered to management by the acquiring entity. [T]here have been numerous complaints by depositors and others that permitting healthy mutual savings banks to be acquired by means of a merger/conversion has resulted in some savings bank insiders putting their interests ahead of the interests of the converting bank and its constituents.

In the Proposed Rule, the FDIC requested specific comment on this topic and specifically whether a moratorium should be placed on merger/conversions involving sufficiently capitalized State Savings Banks. Most of those who commented on the issue said the FDIC should not prohibit merger/conversions and that the FDIC should review such proposed transactions on a case-by-case basis. A bank holding company commented that merger/conversions are desirable because they increase competition in the industry and support safety and soundness. It noted that state law is the "proper authority" to regulate management compensation issues in merger/conversions. A state banking and thrift regulator suggested that the FDIC and OTS collaborate in a joint determination on whether merger/conversions will be approved in the future and, if so, adopt specific requirements to provide parity among savings associations and savings banks. A state banking and thrift industry trade group recommended that merger/conversions be permitted only in the case of undercapitalized institutions or at the discretion of the regulators .
. . .

Others expressed general opposition to merger/conversions. A national consumer group said merger/conversions should be prohibited. An individual commented that merger/conversions should not be allowed because they "only serve management's interests and not the depositors". He suggested that any merger take place only after an initial "free-standing" standard conversion. A national banking and thrift industry trade group said it would not oppose a "regulatory pause by the FDIC to evaluate its rules governing merger/conversions".

Upon consideration of the comments and based on the factors discussed above, the Board continues to believe that merger/conversions should, in most cases, be permitted only in situations where a State Savings Bank is "undercapitalized" "significantly undercapitalized" or "critically undercapitalized", as defined in the FDIC's capital maintenance regulations. The Board still believes, however, that it is unnecessary at this time to impose a blanket prohibition on non-supervisory merger/conversions. Such merger/conversions may be considered in situations where the value of a State Savings Bank is determined in a fair manner and that value is delivered to the rightful recipients, as determined by the directors/trustees of the bank in the proper exercise of their fiduciary responsibilities under the applicable state law. In no instance will an acquiring institution be considered a rightful recipient.

In response to comments requesting that the FDIC specify, in its mutual-to-stock conversion regulations, the terms and conditions of a merger/conversion that would be acceptable to the FDIC, the FDIC notes only the general criteria that: (1) The value of the converting institution be fairly determined, and (2) the value be proposed to be distributed to the proper constituents of the bank. Industry innovation is encouraged in this regard. State law factors also are an important consideration. As noted above, because historically merger/conversions have been a source of considerable insider abuse, the FDIC will continue to closely scrutinize such proposed transactions, particularly for potential breaches of fiduciary duty.

Owing to the same historical concerns in this area, the OTS Revisions continue to prohibit non-supervisory merger/conversions. In response to the comment that the FDIC and the OTS adopt similar regulations on merger/conversions, the FDIC notes that, in its conversion regulations, the OTS retains its general waiver authority to permit a merger/conversion under the appropriate circumstances. Thus, the OTS approach (that it would not prohibit a non- supervisory merger/conversion in certain circumstances) is consistent with the FDIC's approach of considering merger/conversions on a case-by-case basis.

9. Convenience and Needs

[O]ne of the factors the FDIC currently considers in reviewing proposed conversions of State Savings Banks is "the extent of any existing and planned contributions to or investments in the community" . . . .

The FDIC received eight comments on this issue. . . . Some argued that a convenience-and-needs requirement should not be imposed because a conversion involves only a financial recapitalization and not a change in services. Others said they favored such a requirement. Two comments that opposed the proposal questioned the FDIC's legal authority to impose such a requirement. They also noted that the FDIC has ample opportunity to review a savings bank's CRA performance in the context of a post-conversion CRA evaluation. One commenter suggested that it was a legislative, not a regulatory, matter.

Based on the comments received and an internal review of this issue, the Board has decided to consider, as part of its review of proposed mutual-to- stock conversions of State Savings Banks, how the bank intends to serve, or continue to serve, the convenience and needs of its community. This provision adds a convenience-and-needs component to the factors the FDIC considers in reviewing proposed conversions of State Savings Banks, but does not impose a convenience-and-needs or CRA requirement upon banks proposing to convert.

## Comments & Questions

1.    How do the FDIC conversion regulations differ from the Massachusetts demutualization statute applied in the State Mutual Order?  Which regime is preferable.

2.    A key and recurring question in the regulation of conversions (or demutualizations) is how to allocate  the accumulated value that often exists in mutual institutions.  The following article proposes another approach.   Would you support it?

## Robyn Meredith, *CBO Wants U.S. to Share in Thrift Executive Bonanzas*
### Am. Banker, Mar. 1, 1994

The Congressional Budget Office on Monday added its voice to those calling for the government to share in the windfalls that occur when mutual thrifts sell stock for the first time. While the CBO did not say thrift executives should be denied all benefits from such deals, the agency debunked the argument that managers deserve a share of the equity because they helped build the thrift and were paid less than their counterparts at publicly held institutions.

"Management has already been paid for performing those functions," the CBO said. "Compensation relative to the assets or to the number of employees at thrifts is slightly higher at mutual savings and loans than at stock-owned savings and loans," the congressional agency said. The nation's 1,240 mutual thrifts, which have more than $230 billion in assets, have been converting to stock ownership in large numbers lately, particularly in states with laws that permit management to capture a large share of the equity. . . .

Under current regulations, "since no one actually owns the equity in the institution, the existing value is captured as a windfall gain by the initial stockholders," the CBO said. "The federal government has a reasonable claim to a portion of these gains by virtue of the role deposit insurance has played in helping thrifts accumulate their net worth."  The CBO said that had the government granted itself an option to buy 15% of the thrift conversion stock issued in the first three quarters of 1993 and exercised those options, it "would have made the government about $60 million richer." . . . .

[One industry spokesman] said that if all management perks are stripped from stock conversions, "at least half of those would decide that it would be safer for them" to stay mutual. "I think it is bad anytime you discourage capital from coming into the industry. . . . Some of those that have excess capital now who might be conversion candidates and who probably would need the capital as (interest rate) spreads narrow and as rates increase might not have the same incentives to go forward."

Does the government have a legitimate claim on the retained earnings of mutual savings ːs?  How does government's interest here compare with what California accomplished with ɔosition 103 or New Jersey did in the *Twin City* case?

# CHAPTER EIGHT

# FEDERAL-STATE RELATIONS IN INSURANCE REGULATION

---

As explored earlier in our discussion of the history of insurance regulation in the United States, one of the distinguishing characteristics of this field is the preeminence of state regulation. The federal authority does, however, lurk in the background. This chapter examines three areas where this residual federal presence is most important: constitutional limitations on state insurance regulation, reservations of federal authority under the McCarran-Ferguson Act, and the special rules governing employee benefit plans under the Employee Retirement Income Securities Act of 1974, as amended ("ERISA").

## Section 1. Constitutional Limitations

In many areas of financial regulation, the U.S. Constitution limits the authority of the states to impose legal regimes that burden interstate commerce or subvert the operations of federal instrumentalities or regulatory regimes. In the depository institution field, we saw these limitations at work in several areas. In the landmark decision of *McCulloch v. Maryland*, the Supreme Court struck down a Maryland taxation scheme that threatened the Second Bank of the United States. Many lesser cases and administrative interpretations deal with the authority of states to impose legal rules governing national banks (modern descendants of the Second Bank). The dormant Commerce Clause is also often an issue in the depository institution filed. For example, in *Lewis v. BT Investment Managers, Inc.* (discussed in Chapter Four) the Court set aside a Florida statute that unfairly burdened out-of-state bank holding companies.

In the insurance field, constitutional limitations are also at work, although in a slightly different way. In our discussion of rate regulation, we read several decisions that tested the validity of state regulations under the Takings, Due Process, and Contract Clauses of the U.S. Constitution. In this section, we will consider further constitutional limitations on state insurance rules. Federal preemption (the doctrine underlying the *McCulloch* decision) is not as important in the insurance field because very little federal legislation deals directly with the regulation of the insurance industry (aside from ERISA's extensive regulation of employment-based benefits plans) and the federal government has not historically chartered general purpose insurance companies. Nor is the dormant Commerce Clause (relevant in the *Lewis* case) generally applicable, as the McCarran-Ferguson Act alters that provision's operation in this context. (See Section 2 below.) As the following case illustrates, however, analogous restraints are imposed under another provision of the U.S. Constitution.

In reading through the decision, consider the substance of the state statute at issue. Why did Alabama adopt this kind of legislation? Constitutional limitations aside, is this the kind of local initiative that should be encouraged in a federal system? Are there analogs to this kind of statute in the depository institution field?

## Metropolitan Life Insurance Co. v. Ward
### 470 U.S. 869 (1985)

Justice POWEL delivered the opinion of the Court.

This case presents the question whether Alabama's domestic preference tax statute, Ala.Code §§ 27-4-4 and 27-4-5 (1975), that taxes out-of-state insurance companies at a higher rate than domestic insurance companies, violates the Equal Protection Clause.

I

Since 1955,[1] the State of Alabama has granted a preference to its domestic insurance companies by imposing a substantially lower gross premiums tax rate on them than on out-of-state (foreign) companies.[2] Under the current statutory provisions, foreign life insurance companies pay a tax on their gross premiums received from business conducted in Alabama at a rate of three percent, and foreign companies selling other types of insurance pay at a rate of four percent. Ala.Code § 27-4-4(a) (1975). All domestic insurance companies, in contrast, pay at a rate of only one percent on all types of insurance premiums. § 27-4-5(a). As a result, a foreign insurance company doing the same type and volume of business in Alabama as a domestic company generally will pay three to four times as much in gross premiums taxes as its domestic competitor.

Alabama's domestic preference tax statute does provide that foreign companies may reduce the differential in gross premiums taxes by investing prescribed percentages of their worldwide assets in specified Alabama assets and securities. § 27-4-4(b). By investing 10 percent or more of its total assets in Alabama investments, for example, a foreign life insurer may reduce its gross premiums tax rate from 3 to 2 percent. Similarly, a foreign property and casualty insurer may reduce its tax rate from four to three percent. Smaller tax reductions are available based on

---

[1]    The origins of Alabama's domestic preference tax statute date back to 1849, when the first tax on premiums earned by insurance companies doing business in the State was limited to companies not chartered by the State. Act No. 1, 1849 Ala.Acts 5. A domestic preference tax was imposed on and off throughout the years until 1945, when the State restored equality in taxation of insurance companies in response to this Court's decision in United States v. South-Eastern Underwriters Assn., 322 U.S. 533, (1944). Act No. 156, 1945 Ala.Acts 196-197. In 1955, the tax was reinstated, Act No. 77, 1955 Ala.Acts 193 (2d Spec.Sess.), and with minor amendments, has remained in effect until the present.

[2]    For domestic preference tax purposes, Alabama defines a domestic insurer as a company that both is incorporated in Alabama and has its principal office and chief place of business within the State. Ala.Code § 27-4-1(3) (1975). A corporation that does not meet both of these criteria is characterized as a foreign insurer. § 27-4-1(2).

investment of smaller percentages of a company's assets. Ibid. Regardless of how much of its total assets a foreign company places in Alabama investments, it can never reduce its gross premiums tax rate to the same level paid by comparable domestic companies. These are entitled to the one-percent tax rate even if they have no investments in the State. Thus, the investment provision permits foreign insurance companies to reduce, but never to eliminate, the discrimination inherent in the domestic preference tax statute.

## II

Appellants, a group of insurance companies incorporated outside of the State of Alabama, filed claims with the Alabama Department of Insurance in 1981, contending that the domestic preference tax statute, as applied to them, violated the Equal Protection Clause. They sought refunds of taxes paid for the tax years 1977 through 1980. The Commissioner of Insurance denied all of their claims on July 8, 1981.

Appellants appealed to the Circuit Court for Montgomery County, seeking a judgment declaring the statute to be unconstitutional and requiring the Commissioner to make the appropriate refunds. . . . On cross-motions for summary judgment, the court ruled . . . that the Alabama statute did not violate the Equal Protection Clause because it served "at least two purposes, in addition to raising revenue: (1) encouraging the formation of new insurance companies in Alabama, and (2) encouraging capital investment by foreign insurance companies in the Alabama assets and governmental securities set forth in the statute." The court also found that the distinction the statute created between foreign and domestic companies was rationally related to those two purposes and that the Alabama Legislature reasonably could have believed that the classification would have promoted those purposes.

[A]ppellants appealed to the Court of Civil Appeals. It affirmed the Circuit Court's rulings as to the existence of the two legitimate state purposes, but remanded for an evidentiary hearing on the issue of rational relationship, concluding that summary judgment was inappropriate on that question because the evidence was in conflict.. Appellants then waived their right to an evidentiary hearing on the issue whether the statute's classification bore a rational relationship to the two purposes found by the Circuit Court to be legitimate, and they requested a final determination of the legal issues with respect to their equal protection challenge to the statute. The [Alabama] Supreme Court denied certiorari on all claims. . . .

## III

Prior to our decision in Western & Southern Life Ins. Co. v. State Board of Equalization of California, 451 U.S. 648 (1981), the jurisprudence of the applicability of the Equal Protection Clause to discriminatory tax statutes had a somewhat checkered history. Lincoln National Life Ins. Co. v. Read, 325 U.S. 673 (1945), held that so-called "privilege" taxes, required to be paid by a foreign corporation before it would be permitted to do business within a State, were immune from equal protection challenge. That case stood in stark contrast, however, to the Court's prior decisions in Southern R. Co. v. Greene, 216 U.S. 400 (1910), and Hanover Fire Ins. Co. v. Harding, 272 U.S. 494 (1926), as well as to later decisions, in which the Court had recognized that the Equal Protection Clause placed limits on other forms of discriminatory taxation imposed on out-of-state corporations solely because of their residence.

In Western & Southern, supra, we reviewed all of these cases for the purpose of deciding whether to permit an equal protection challenge to a California statute imposing a retaliatory tax on foreign insurance companies doing business within the State, when the home States of those companies imposed a similar tax on California insurers entering their borders. We concluded that Lincoln was no more than "a surprising throwback" to the days before enactment of the Fourteenth Amendment and in which incorporation of a domestic corporation or entry of a foreign one had been granted only as a matter of privilege by the State in its unfettered discretion. 451 U.S. at 665. We therefore rejected the longstanding but "anachronis[tic]" rule of Lincoln and explicitly held that the Equal Protection Clause imposes limits upon a State's power to condition the right of a foreign corporation to do business within its borders. 451 U.S. at 667. We held that "[w]e consider it now established that, whatever the extent of a State's authority to exclude foreign corporations from doing business within its boundaries, that authority does not justify imposition of more onerous taxes or other burdens on foreign corporations than those imposed on domestic corporations, unless the discrimination between foreign and domestic corporations bears a rational relation to a legitimate state purpose." Id., at 667-668.

Because appellants waived their right to an evidentiary hearing on the issue whether the classification in the Alabama domestic preference tax statute bears a rational relation to the two purposes upheld by the Circuit Court, the only question before us is whether those purposes are legitimate.[5]

## A(1)

The first of the purposes found by the trial court to be a legitimate reason for the statute's classification between foreign and domestic corporations is that it encourages the formation of new domestic insurance companies in Alabama. The State contends that this Court has long held that the promotion of domestic industry, in and of itself, is a legitimate state purpose that will survive equal protection scrutiny. In so contending, it relies on a series of cases, including Western & Southern, that are said to have upheld discriminatory taxes.

In Western & Southern, the case principally relied upon, we did not hold as a general rule that promotion of domestic industry is a legitimate state purpose under equal protection analysis. Rather, we held that California's purpose in enacting the retaliatory tax--to promote the interstate business of domestic insurers by deterring other States from enacting discriminatory or excessive taxes--was a legitimate one. 451 U.S., at 668. In contrast, Alabama asks us to approve its purpose of promoting the business of its domestic insurers in Alabama by penalizing foreign insurers who also want to do business in the State. Alabama has made no attempt, as California did, to influence the policies of other States in order to enhance its domestic companies' ability to operate interstate; rather, it has erected barriers to foreign companies who wish to do interstate business in order to improve its domestic insurers' ability to compete at home.

---

[5]    The State and the intervenors advanced some 15 additional purposes in support of the Alabama statute. As neither the Circuit Court nor the Court of Civil Appeals ruled on the legitimacy of those purposes, that question is not before us, and we express no view as to it. On remand, the State will be free to advance again its arguments relating to the legitimacy of those purposes. . . .

The crucial distinction between the two cases lies in the fact that Alabama's aim to promote domestic industry is purely and completely discriminatory, designed only to favor domestic industry within the State, no matter what the cost to foreign corporations also seeking to do business there.  Alabama's purpose, contrary to California's, constitutes the very sort of parochial discrimination that the Equal Protection Clause was intended to prevent.

(2)

The State argues nonetheless that it is impermissible to view a discriminatory tax such as the one at issue here as violative of the Equal Protection Clause.  This approach, it contends, amounts to no more than "Commerce Clause rhetoric in equal protection clothing."  Brief for Appellee Ward 22.  The State maintains that because Congress, in enacting the McCarran-Ferguson Act, 15 U.S.C. ss 1011-1015, intended to authorize States to impose taxes that burden interstate commerce in the insurance field, the tax at issue here must stand.  Our concerns are much more fundamental than as characterized by the State.  Although the McCarran-Ferguson Act exempts the insurance industry from Commerce Clause restrictions, it does not purport to limit in any way the applicability of the Equal Protection Clause.  As noted above, our opinion in Western & Southern expressly reaffirmed the viability of equal protection restraints on discriminatory taxes in the insurance context.[8]

Moreover, the State's view ignores the differences between Commerce Clause and equal protection analysis and the consequent different purposes those two constitutional provisions serve.  Under Commerce Clause analysis, the State's interest, if legitimate, is weighed against the burden the state law would impose on interstate commerce.  In the equal protection context, however, if the State's purpose is found to be legitimate, the state law stands as long as the burden it imposes is found to be rationally related to that purpose, a relationship that is not difficult to establish.  See Western & Southern, 451 U.S. at 674, (if purpose is legitimate, equal protection challenge may not prevail so long as the question of rational relationship is " 'at least debatable' " (quoting United States  v. Carolene Products Co., 304 U.S. 144, 154 (1938)).

The two constitutional provisions perform different functions in the analysis of the permissible scope of a State's power--one protects interstate commerce, and the other protects persons from unconstitutional discrimination by the States.  See Bethlehem Motors Corp. v. Flynt, 256 U.S. 421, 423-424 (1921).  The effect of the statute at issue here is to place a discriminatory tax burden on foreign insurers who desire to do business within the State, thereby also incidentally placing a burden on interstate commerce.  Equal protection restraints are applicable even though the effect of the discrimination in this case is similar to the type of burden with which the Commerce Clause also would be concerned.  We reaffirmed the importance of the Equal Protection Clause in the insurance context in Western & Southern and see no reason now for reassessing that view.

---

[8]    In fact, as we noted in Western & Southern, the legislative history of the McCarran-Ferguson Act reveals that the Act was Congress' response only to United States v. South-Eastern Underwriters Assn., 322 U.S. 533 (1944), and that Congress did not intend thereby to give the States any power to tax or regulate the insurance industry other than what they had previously possessed.  Thus Congress expressly left undisturbed this Court's decisions holding that the Equal Protection Clause places limits on a State's ability to tax out-of-state corporations.  See 451 U.S., at 655, n. 6.

## B

The second purpose found by the courts below to be legitimate was the encouragement of capital investment in the Alabama assets and governmental securities specified in the statute. We do not agree that this is a legitimate state purpose when furthered by discrimination. Domestic insurers remain entitled to the more favorable rate of tax regardless of whether they invest in Alabama assets. Moreover, the investment incentive provision of the Alabama statute does not enable foreign insurance companies to eliminate the discriminatory effect of the statute. No matter how much of their assets they invest in Alabama, foreign insurance companies are still required to pay a higher gross premiums tax than domestic companies. The State's investment incentive provision therefore does not cure, but reaffirms, the statute's impermissible classification based solely on residence. We hold that encouraging investment in Alabama assets and securities in this plainly discriminatory manner serves no legitimate state purpose.

## IV

We conclude that neither of the two purposes furthered by the Alabama domestic preference tax statute and addressed by the Circuit Court for Montgomery County . . . is legitimate under the Equal Protection Clause to justify the imposition of the discriminatory tax at issue here. The judgment of the Alabama Supreme Court accordingly is reversed, and the case is remanded for further proceedings not inconsistent with this opinion. It is so ordered.

Justice O'CONNOR, with whom Justice BRENNAN, Justice MARSHALL, and Justice REHNQUIST join, dissenting.

This case presents a simple question: Is it legitimate for a State to use its taxing power to promote a domestic insurance industry and to encourage capital investment within its borders? In a holding that can only be characterized as astonishing, the Court determines that these purposes are illegitimate. This holding is unsupported by precedent and subtly distorts the constitutional balance, threatening the freedom of both state and federal legislative bodies to fashion appropriate classifications in economic legislation. Because I disagree with both the Court's method of analysis and its conclusion, I respectfully dissent. . . .

The policy of favoring local concerns in state regulation and taxation of insurance, which the majority condemns as illegitimate, is not merely a recent invention of the States. The States initiated regulation of the business of insurance as early as 1851. In 1944, however, this Court overruled a long line of cases holding that the business of insurance was an intrastate activity beyond the scope of the Commerce Clause. United States v. South-Eastern Underwriters Assn., 322 U.S. 533. "The decision provoked widespread concern that the States would no longer be able to engage in taxation and effective regulation of the insurance industry. Congress moved quickly, enacting the McCarran-Ferguson Act within a year of the decision in South-Eastern Underwriters." St. Paul Fire & Marine Insurance Co. v. Barry, 438 U.S. 531, 539 (1978).

The drafters of the Act were sensitive to the same concerns Alabama now vainly seeks to bring to this Court's attention: the greater responsiveness of local insurance companies to local conditions, the different insurance needs of rural and industrial States, the special advantages and constraints of state-by-state regulation, and the importance of insurance license fees and taxes as a major source of state revenues. See, e.g., Hearings on S. 1362 before the Senate Subcommittee on the Judiciary, 78th Cong., 1st Sess., 3, 10, 16-17 (1943) (letter of Gov. Sharpe of South

Dakota stressing role of domestic insurers that provide "poor man" and rural policies adapted to farming concerns); 90 Cong.Rec. 6564 (1944) (remarks of Rep. Vorhis). "As this Court observed shortly afterward, '[o]bviously Congress' purpose was broadly to give support to the existing and future state systems for regulating and taxing the business of insurance.' Prudential Insurance Co. v. Benjamin, 328 U.S. 408, 429 (1946)." St. Paul Fire & Marine Insurance Co. v. Barry, supra, 438 U.S., at 539. . . .

The contemporary realities of insurance regulation and taxation continue to justify a uniquely local perspective. Insurance regulation and taxation must serve local social policies including assuring the solvency and reliability of companies doing business in the State and providing special protection for those who might be denied insurance in a free market, such as the urban poor, small businesses, and family farms. . . . Currently at least 28 of the 50 States employ a combination of investment incentives and differential premium taxes favoring domestic insurers to encourage local investment of policyholders' premiums and to partially shelter smaller domestic insurers from competition with the large multistate companies.

State insurance commissions vary widely in manpower and expertise. In practice, the State of incorporation exercises primary oversight of the solvency of its insurers. . . . Even the State of incorporation's efforts to regulate a multistate insurer may be seriously hampered by the difficulty of gaining access to records and assets in 49 other States. Thus the security of Alabama's citizens who purchase insurance from out-of-state companies may depend in part on the diligence of another State's insurance commissioner, over whom Alabama has no authority and limited influence. In the event of financial failure of a foreign insurer the State may have difficulty levying on out-of-state assets. Since each State maintains its own insurance guarantee fund, the domestic insurers of the States where a multistate insurer is admitted to do business may ultimately be forced to absorb local policyholders' losses.

. . . . This Court cannot ignore the exigencies of contemporary insurance regulation outlined above simply because it might prefer uniform federal regulation. Given the distinctions in ease of regulation and services rendered by foreign and domestic insurers, we cannot dismiss as illegitimate the State's goal of promoting a healthy local insurance industry sensitive to regional differences and composed of companies that agree to subordinate themselves to the Alabama Commissioner's control and to maintain a principal place of business within Alabama's borders. Though economists might dispute the efficacy of Alabama's tax, "[p]arties challenging legislation under the Equal Protection Clause cannot prevail so long as 'it is evident from all the considerations presented to [the legislature], and those of which we may take judicial notice, that the question is at least debatable.' " Western & Southern Life Ins. Co. v. State Board of Equalization of California, 451 U.S., at 674, quoting United States v. Carolene Products Co., 304 U.S., at 154.

## Comments and Questions

1. Does the *Ward* decision amount to "Commerce Clause rhetoric in equal protection clothing," as the state contended? Or is the constitutional test applied in this case somehow different than traditional Commerce Clause analysis? In the years following the *Ward* decision, state insurance regulators were called upon to defend a variety of

premium taxation schemes from equal protection challenges.  After *Ward,* how might you defend a tax that charged lower premiums for companies organized and doing business substantially all their business with the state's boundaries?  See William T. Barker & Robert E. Wagner, *State Insurance Tax Differentials and Regulatory Objectives,* 8 J. INS. REG. 128 (1990) (offering a defense of the Illinois state premium tax system).  What happened to *Ward* on remand?

2.   It is interesting to compare the *Ward* decision with the Court's decision in the *Northeast Bancorp* case, which was decided the same Term.  (The *Northeast Bancorp* case ruled that the Douglas Amendment to the federal Bank Holding Company Act permits states to establish regional compacts, and was discussed in Chapter IV materials reviewing the history of geographic expansion by banks.) Plaintiffs in the *Northeast Bancorp* case also challenged the compacts on equal protection grounds.

# Northeast Bancorp Inc. v. Board of Governors
## 472 U.S. 159 (1985)

Justice REHNQUIST delivered the opinion of the Court.

[In previous sections of the opinion, the Court ruled that the Northeastern regional compact (which permitted, among other things, Massachusetts and Connecticut bank holding companies to make acquisitions into each others' home jurisdictions) did not violate the Commerce Clause of the U.S. Constitution on the grounds that the Douglas Amendment to the Bank Holding Company Act implicitly authorized such compacts.  The Court then considered a separate constitutional challenge to regional compacts.]

Petitioners [also] argued before the [Federal Reserve] Board and the Court of Appeals that the Massachusetts and Connecticut statutes violated the Equal Protection Clause,  U.S. Const., Amdt. 14, § 2, by excluding bank holding companies from some States while admitting those from others.  This claim was abandoned in their petition for  certiorari and their briefs on the merits, but after our decision in Metropolitan Life Insurance Co. v. Ward, 470 U.S. 869 (1985), petitioners filed a supplemental brief urging us to consider the equal protection issue.  Because the issue was fully reviewed by the Board and the Court of Appeals and because it would undoubtedly cloud other pending applications for acquisitions by bank holding companies, we elect to decide it.

In Metropolitan Life we held that encouraging the formation of new domestic insurance companies within a State and encouraging capital investment in the State's assets and governmental securities were not, standing alone, legitimate state purposes which could permissibly be furthered by discriminating against out-of-state corporations in favor of local corporations.  There we said:

"This case does not involve or question, as the dissent suggests, post, at 900-901, the broad authority of a State to promote and regulate its own economy. We hold only that such regulation may not be accomplished  by imposing discriminatorily higher taxes on nonresident corporations solely because they are nonresidents." Id., at 882, n. 10.

Here the States in question -- Massachusetts and Connecticut -- are not favoring local corporations at the expense of out-of-state corporations.  They are favoring out-of-state corporations domiciled within the New England region over out-of-state corporations from other parts of the country, and to this extent their laws may be said to "discriminate" against the latter.  But with respect to the business of banking, we do not write on a clean slate; recently in Lewis v. BT Investment Managers, Inc., 447 U.S., at 38, we said that "banking and related financial activities are of profound local concern." This statement is a recognition of the historical fact that our country traditionally has favored widely dispersed control of banking.  While many other western nations are dominated by a handful of centralized banks, we have some 15,000 commercial banks attached to a greater or lesser degree to the communities in which they are located.  The Connecticut legislative Commission that recommended adoption of the Connecticut statute in question considered interstate banking on a regional basis to combine the beneficial effect of increasing the number of banking competitors with the need to preserve a close relationship between those in the community who need credit and those who provide credit.  4 App. in No. 84-4047 (CA2), pp. 1239-1241.  The debates in the Connecticut Legislature preceding the enactment of the Connecticut law evince concern that immediate acquisition of Connecticut banks by holding companies headquartered outside the New England region would threaten the independence of local banking institutions.  See, e. g., App. to Pet. for Cert. A157-A160.  No doubt similar concerns motivated the Massachusetts Legislature.

We think that the concerns which spurred Massachusetts and Connecticut to enact the statutes here challenged, different as they are from those which motivated the enactment of the Alabama statute in Metropolitan, meet the traditional rational basis for judging equal protection claims under the Fourteenth Amendment.  Barry v. Barchi, 443 U.S. 55, 67 (1979); Vance v. Bradley, 440 U.S. 93, 97 (1979).

Justice O'CONNOR, concurring.

I agree that the state banking statutes at issue here do not violate the Commerce Clause, the Compact Clause, or the Equal Protection Clause.  I write separately to note that I see no meaningful distinction for Equal Protection Clause purposes between the Massachusetts and Connecticut statutes we uphold today and the Alabama statute at issue in Metropolitan Life Insurance Co. v. Ward, 470 U.S. 869 (1985).

The Court distinguishes this case from Metropolitan Life on the ground that Massachusetts and Connecticut favor neighboring out-of-state banks over all other out-of-state banks.  It is not clear to me why completely barring the banks of 44 States from doing business is less discriminatory than Alabama's scheme of taxing the insurance companies from 49 States at a slightly higher rate.  Nor is it clear why the Equal Protection Clause should tolerate a regional "home team" when it condemns a state "home team." See id., at 878.

The Court emphasizes that here we do not write on a clean slate as the business of banking is "of profound local concern." Ante, at 177.  The business of insurance is also of uniquely local concern.  Prudential Insurance Co. v. Benjamin, 328 U.S. 408, 415-417 (1946).  Both industries historically have been regulated by the States in recognition of the critical part they play in securing the financial well-being of local citizens and businesses. Metropolitan Life Insurance Co. v. Ward, supra, at 888-893 (dissenting opinion).  States have regulated insurance since 1851.

Like the local nature of banking, the local nature of insurance is firmly ensconced in federal law. 470 U.S., at 888-889. The McCarran-Ferguson Act, enacted in 1945, states:

"Congress hereby declares that the continued regulation and taxation by the several States of the business of insurance is in the public interest, and that silence on the part of the Congress shall not be construed to impose any barrier to the regulation or taxation of such business by the several States." 59 Stat. 33, 15 U. S. C. § 1011.

The Court distinguishes the Connecticut and Massachusetts banking laws as having a valid purpose: "to preserve a close relationship between those in the community who need credit and those who provide credit." Ante, at 178. This interest in preserving local institutions responsive to local concerns was a cornerstone in Alabama's defense of its insurance tax. It survives as one of the "15 additional purposes" the Court remanded for reconsideration. Metropolitan Life Insurance Co. v. Ward, supra, at 875-876, n. 5.

Especially where Congress has sanctioned the barriers to commerce that fostering of local industries might engender, this Court has no authority under the Equal Protection Clause to invalidate classifications designed to encourage local businesses because of their special contributions. Today's opinion is consistent with the longstanding doctrine that the Equal Protection Clause permits economic regulation that distinguishes between groups that are legitimately different -- as local institutions so often are -- in ways relevant to the proper goals of the State.

### Comments and Questions

1. Does the Court satisfactorily distinguish *Ward* from *Northeast Bancorp*?

2. Suppose a state adopts an ad valorem tax on intangibles, including bank deposits, at a rate of 25 cents per 100 dollars of value, but also adopts an exclusion which reduces to 12.5 cents the tax for deposits in any bank organized under the laws of the state or any national bank located in the state. The legislative history of the tax justifies the differential on the grounds that it is more costly for the state to collect taxes from out-of-state institutions and, in practice, the tax is never collected on some out-of-state deposits. Cf. St. Ledger v. Commonwealth of Kentucky, 912 S.W.2d 34 (Ky. 1995) (presenting analogous situation).

## Section 2.  The McCarran-Ferguson Act

As was outlined in section 2.D of Chapter Six, Congress enacted the McCarran-Ferguson Act at the behest of the insurance industry in the wake of the Supreme Court's 1944 decision in *United States v. South-Eastern Underwriters Association (SEAU)*. The Act allocates supervisory power authority over the insurance industry between federal and state authorities. While federal intrusion into the field remains a constant and perhaps increasingly serious threat (as we saw in our discussion of solvency regulation), the balance of power in this area currently tilts strongly in favor of the states. The text of the McCarran-Ferguson Act , 15 U.S.C.A. §§ 1011-1015 (West 1995), reads as follows:

### Section One. Declaration of Policy

The Congress hereby declares that the continued regulation and taxation by the several States of the business of insurance is in the public interest, and that silence on the part of the Congress shall not be construed to impose any barrier to the regulation or taxation of such business by the several States.

### Section Two. Regulation by State law and Certain Federal Laws

(a) State regulation. The business of insurance, and every person engaged therein, shall be subject to the laws of the several States which relate to the regulation or taxation of such business.

(b) Federal regulation. No Act of Congress shall be construed to invalidate, impair, or supersede any law enacted by any State for the purpose of regulating the business of insurance, or which imposes a fee or tax upon such business, unless such Act specifically relates to the business of insurance: Provided, That after June 30, 1948, the [Sherman Act, the Clayton Act, and the Federal Trade Commission Act] shall be applicable to the business of insurance to the extent that such business is not regulated by State law.

### Section Three. Suspension of certain Federal laws

(a) Until June 30, 1948, the [Sherman Act and certain other federal antitrust laws] shall not apply to the business of insurance or to acts in the conduct thereof.

(b) Nothing contained in this Act shall render the said Sherman Act inapplicable to any agreement to boycott, coerce, or intimidate, or act of boycott, coercion, or intimidation.

### Section Four. Applicability of National Labor Relations Act, etc.

Nothing contained in this Act shall be construed to affect in any manner the application to the business of insurance of the [NLRA and certain other federal labor laws].

### Section 5. Definition of "State"

As used in this Act, the term "State" includes the several States, Alaska, Hawaii, Puerto Rico, Guam, and the District of Columbia.

The McCarran-Ferguson Act presents many fascinating issues of statutory interpretation. Some have labeled the legislation quasi-constitutional, because it allocates regulatory authority between the states and the federal government. To what extent should the Act be understood to influence the courts' interpretation of legislation adopted by subsequent Congresses? Should the Act be relevant to statutes adopted before the 1940's?

Under the McCarran-Ferguson Act, one of the most significant enclaves of residual federal power in the regulation of the insurance industry concerns antitrust enforcement. Section 2 of the Act grants the "business of insurance" general exemption from federal laws (including anti-trust laws) unless the federal law "specifically relates" to the business of insurance. The Act goes on to reimpose anti-trust laws on the "business of insurance" in two separate ways. First, section 2 reinstates federal anti-trust rules "to the extent that such business is not regulated by State law". Second, section 3(b), makes the federal antitrust laws applicable to "any agreement to boycott, coerce, or intimidate, or act of boycott, coercion, or intimidation."

In this section and in later sections of the book, we will consider several important interpretative issues under the McCarran-Ferguson  What is the "business of insurance"? Under what circumstances will that business be considered "not regulated by state law." What is the scope of section 3(b)? But before turning to these issues, consider the effect of the Act on the Supreme Court's decision in *SEUA*.  Did the Act restore the *status quo ante*?  Or did it change the balance between federal and state authority over the insurance industry?

## A.  The Business of Insurance

A concept central to the McCarran-Ferguson Act is the "business of insurance."  The U.S. Supreme Court has on numerous occasions decided cased interpreting these words. Many of the most important of these decisions have involved private suits challenging insurance industry practices alleged to fall outside the bounds of the "business of insurance" and therefore subject to liability under federal anti-trust laws.  In Union Labor Life Insurance Co. v. Pireno, 458 U.S. 119 (1982), the Court articulated a three-part test designed to clarify the concept.  The *Pireno* test, which has been applied in numerous subsequent cases, is discussed in the following decision, which involves the application to a federal priority statute to an insolvency proceeding administered by a state insurance commissioner.

## U.S. Department of Treasury v. Fabe
### 508 U.S. 491 (1993)

Justice BLACKMUN delivered the opinion of the Court.

The Ohio priority statute was enacted as part of a complex and specialized administrative structure for the regulation of insurance companies from inception to dissolution.  The statute proclaims, as its purpose, "the protection of the interests of insureds, claimants, creditors, and the public generally."  Ohio Rev. Code Ann. § 3903.02(D).  Chapter 3903 broadly empowers the State's Superintendent of Insurance to place a financially impaired insurance company under his supervision, or into rehabilitation, or into liquidation.  The last is authorized when the Superintendent finds that the insurer is insolvent, that placement in supervision or rehabilitation would be futile, and that "further transaction of business would be hazardous, financially or otherwise, to [the insurer's] policyholders, its creditors, or the public."  § 3903.17(C).  As liquidator, the Superintendent is entitled to take title to all assets, § 3903.18(A);  to collect and invest moneys due the insurer, § 3903.21(A)(6);  to continue to prosecute and commence in the name of the insurer any and all suits and other legal proceedings, § 3903.21(A)(12);  to collect reinsurance and unearned premiums due the insurer, §§ 3903.32 and 3903.33;  to evaluate all claims against the estate, § 3903.43;  and to make payments to claimants to the extent possible, § 3903.44.  It seems fair to say that the effect of all this is to empower the liquidator to continue to operate the insurance company in all ways but one--the issuance of new policies.

Pursuant to this statutory framework, the Court of Common Pleas for Franklin County, Ohio, on April 30, 1986, declared American Druggists' Insurance Company insolvent. The court directed that the company be liquidated, and it appointed respondent, Ohio's Superintendent of Insurance, to serve as liquidator. The United States, as obligee on various immigration, appearance, performance, and payment bonds issued by the company as surety, filed claims in excess of $10.7 million in the state liquidation proceedings. The United States asserted that its claims were entitled to first priority under the federal statute, 31 U.S.C. § 3713(a)(1)(A)(iii), which provides: "A claim of the United States Government shall be paid first when ... a person indebted to the Government is insolvent and ... an act of bankruptcy is committed."

Respondent Superintendent brought a declaratory judgment action in the United States District Court for the Southern District of Ohio seeking to establish that the federal priority statute does not pre-empt the Ohio law designating the priority of creditors' claims in insurance-liquidation proceedings. Under the Ohio statute, as noted above, claims of federal, state, and local governments are entitled only to fifth priority, ranking behind (1) administrative expenses, (2) specified wage claims, (3) policyholders' claims, and (4) claims of general creditors. § 3903.42. Respondent argued that the Ohio priority scheme, rather than the federal priority statute, governs the priority of claims of the United States because it falls within the anti-pre-emption provisions of the McCarran- Ferguson Act, 15 U.S.C. § 1012.

The District Court granted summary judgment for the United States. Relying upon the tripartite standard for divining what constitutes the "business of insurance," as articulated in Union Labor Life Ins. Co. v. Pireno, 458 U.S. 119 (1982), the court considered three factors:

> " 'first, whether the practice has the effect of transferring or spreading a policyholder's risk; second, whether the practice is an integral part of the policy relationship between the insurer and the insured; and third, whether the practice is limited to entities within the insurance industry.' " App. to Pet. for Cert. 36a (quoting Pireno, 458 U.S., at 129).

Reasoning that the liquidation of an insolvent insurer possesses none of these attributes, the court concluded that the Ohio priority statute does not involve the "business of insurance." App. to Pet. for Cert. 45a.

A divided Court of Appeals reversed. 939 F.2d 341 (CA6 1991). The court held that the Ohio priority scheme regulates the "business of insurance" because it protects the interests of the insured. Id., at 350-351. Applying Pireno, the court determined that the Ohio statute (1) transfers and spreads the risk of insurer insolvency; (2) involves an integral part of the policy relationship because it is designed to maintain the reliability of the insurance contract; and (3) focuses upon the protection of policyholders by diverting the scarce resources of the liquidating entity away from other creditors. Id., 939 F.2d, at 351-352. . . .

"[T]he starting point in a case involving construction of the McCarran- Ferguson Act, like the starting point in any case involving the meaning of a statute, is the language of the statute itself." Group Life & Health Ins. Co. v. Royal Drug Co., 440 U.S. 205, 210 (1979). Section 2(b) of the McCarran-Ferguson Act provides: "No Act of Congress shall be construed to invalidate, impair, or supersede any law enacted by any State for the purpose of regulating the business of insurance ... unless such Act specifically relates to the business of insurance." 15 U.S.C. § 1012(b). The parties agree that application of the federal priority statute would "invalidate, impair, or supersede" the Ohio priority scheme and that the federal priority statute does not "specifically relat[e] to the business of insurance." All that is left for us to determine, therefore, is whether the Ohio priority statute is a law enacted "for the purpose of regulating the business of insurance."

This Court has had occasion to construe this phrase only once. On that occasion, it observed: "Statutes aimed at protecting or regulating this relationship [between insurer and insured], directly or indirectly, are laws regulating the 'business of insurance,' " within the meaning of the phrase. SEC v. National Securities, Inc., 393 U.S. 453, 460 (1969). The opinion emphasized that the focus of McCarran-Ferguson is upon the relationship between the insurance company and its policyholders:

> "The relationship between insurer and insured, the type of policy which could be issued, its reliability, interpretation, and enforcement--these were the core of the 'business of insurance.' Undoubtedly, other activities of insurance companies relate so closely to their status as reliable insurers that they too must be placed in the same class. But whatever the exact scope of the statutory term, it is clear where the focus was--it was on the relationship between the insurance company and the policyholder." Ibid.

In that case, two Arizona insurance companies merged and received approval from the Arizona Director of Insurance, as required by state law. The Securities and Exchange Commission sued to rescind the merger, alleging that the merger-solicitation papers contained material misstatements, in violation of federal law. This Court held that, insofar as the Arizona law was an attempt to protect the interests of an insurance company's shareholders, it did not fall within the scope of the McCarran-Ferguson Act. Ibid. The Arizona statute, however, also required the Director, before granting approval, to make sure that the proposed merger "would not 'substantially reduce the security of and service to be rendered to policyholders.' " Id., at 462, The Court observed that this section of the statute "clearly relates to the 'business of insurance.' " Ibid. But because the "paramount federal interest in protecting shareholders [was] perfectly compatible with the paramount state interest in protecting policyholders," id., at 463, the Arizona statute did not preclude application of the federal securities laws.

In the present case, on the other hand, there is a direct conflict between the federal priority statute and Ohio law. Under the terms of the McCarran-Ferguson Act, 15 U.S.C. § 1012(b), therefore, federal law must yield to the extent the Ohio statute furthers the interests of policyholders.

Minimizing the analysis of National Securities, petitioner invokes Royal Drug and Pireno in support of its argument that the liquidation of an insolvent insurance company is not part of the "business of insurance" exempt from pre-emption under the McCarran-Ferguson Act. Those cases identified the three criteria, noted above, that are relevant in determining what activities constitute the "business of insurance." See Pireno, 458 U.S., at 129. Petitioner argues that the Ohio priority statute satisfies none of these criteria. According to petitioner, the Ohio statute merely determines the order in which creditors' claims will be paid, and has nothing to do with the transfer of risk from insured to insurer. Petitioner also contends that the Ohio statute is not an integral part of the policy relationship between insurer and insured and is not limited to entities within the insurance industry because it addresses only the relationship between policyholders and other creditors of the defunct corporation.

To be sure, the Ohio statute does not directly regulate the "business of insurance" by prescribing the terms of the insurance contract or by setting the rate charged by the insurance company. But we do not read Pireno to suggest that the business of insurance is confined entirely to the writing of insurance contracts, as opposed to their performance. Pireno and Royal Drug held only that "ancillary activities" that do not affect performance of the insurance contract or enforcement of contractual obligations do not enjoy the antitrust exemption for laws regulating the "business of insurance." Pireno, 458 U.S., at 134, n. 8. In Pireno, we held that use of a peer review committee to advise the insurer as to whether charges for chiropractic services were reasonable and necessary was not part of the business of insurance. The peer review practice at issue in that case had nothing to do with whether the insurance contract was performed; it dealt only with calculating what fell within the scope of the contract's coverage. Id., at 130. We found the peer review process to be "a matter of indifference to the policyholder, whose only concern is whether his claim is paid, not why it is paid" (emphases in original). Id., at 132. Similarly, in Royal Drug, we held that an insurer's agreements with participating pharmacies to provide benefits to policyholders was not part of the business of insurance. "The benefit promised to Blue Shield policyholders is that their premiums will cover the cost of prescription drugs except for a $2 charge for each prescription. So long as that promise is kept, policyholders are basically unconcerned with arrangements made between Blue Shield and participating pharmacies." Id., at 213-214 (footnote omitted).

There can be no doubt that the actual performance of an insurance contract falls within the "business of insurance," as we understood that phrase in Pireno and Royal Drug. To hold otherwise would be mere formalism. The Court's statement in Pireno that the "transfer of risk from insured to insurer is effected by means of the contract between the parties ... and ... is complete at the time that the contract is entered," 458 U.S., at 130, presumes that the insurance contract in fact will be enforced. Without performance of the terms of the insurance policy, there is no risk transfer at all. Moreover, performance of an insurance contract also satisfies the remaining prongs of the Pireno test: it is central to the policy relationship between insurer and insured and is confined entirely to entities within the insurance industry. The Ohio priority statute is designed to carry out the enforcement of insurance contracts by ensuring the payment of policyholders' claims despite the insurance company's intervening bankruptcy. Because it is integrally related to the performance of insurance contracts after bankruptcy, Ohio's law is one "enacted by the State for the purpose of regulating the business of insurance." 15 U.S.C. § 1012(b).

Both Royal Drug and Pireno, moreover, involved the scope of the antitrust immunity located in the second clause of § 2(b). We deal here with the first clause, which is not so narrowly circumscribed. The language of § 2(b) is unambiguous: the first clause commits laws "enacted ... for the purpose of regulating the business of insurance" to the States, while the second clause exempts only "the business of insurance" itself from the antitrust laws. To equate laws "enacted ... for the purpose of regulating the business of insurance" with the "business of insurance" itself, as petitioner urges us to do, would be to read words out of the statute. This we refuse to do.

The broad category of laws enacted "for the purpose of regulating the business of insurance" consists of laws that possess the "end, intention, or aim" of adjusting, managing, or controlling the business of insurance. Black's Law Dictionary 1236, 1286 (6th ed. 1990). This category necessarily encompasses more than just the "business of insurance." For the reasons expressed above, we believe that the actual performance of an insurance contract is an essential part of the "business of insurance." Because the Ohio statute is "aimed at protecting or regulating" the performance of an insurance contract, National Securities, 393 U.S., at 460, it follows that it is a law "enacted for the purpose of regulating the business of insurance," within the meaning of the first clause of § 2(b).

Our plain reading of the McCarran-Ferguson Act also comports with the statute's purpose. As was stated in Royal Drug, the first clause of § 2(b) was intended to further Congress' primary objective of granting the States broad regulatory authority over the business of insurance. The second clause accomplishes Congress' secondary goal, which was to carve out only a narrow exemption for "the business of insurance" from the federal antitrust laws. 440 U.S., at 218, n. 18.

Petitioner, however, also contends that the Ohio statute is not an insurance law but a bankruptcy law because it comes into play only when the insurance company has become insolvent and is in liquidation, at which point the insurance company no longer exists. We disagree. The primary purpose of a statute that distributes the insolvent insurer's assets to policyholders in preference to other creditors is identical to the primary purpose of the insurance company itself: the payment of claims made against policies. And "mere matters of form need not detain us." National Securities, 393 U.S., at 460. The Ohio statute is enacted " for the purpose of regulating the business of insurance" to the extent that it serves to ensure that, if possible, policyholders ultimately will receive payment on their claims. That the policyholder has become a creditor and the insurer a debtor is not relevant. . . .

Finding little support in the plain language of the statute, petitioner resorts to its legislative history. Petitioner relies principally upon a single statement in a House Report:

> "It is not the intention of Congress in the enactment of this legislation to clothe the States with any power to regulate or tax the business of insurance beyond that which they had been held to possess prior to the decision of the United States Supreme Court in the South-Eastern Underwriters Association case." H.R.Rep. No. 143, 79th Cong., 1st Sess., 3 (1945).

From this statement, petitioner argues that the McCarran-Ferguson Act was an attempt to "turn back the clock" to the time prior to South-Eastern Underwriters. At that time, petitioner maintains, the federal priority statute would have superseded any inconsistent state law.

Even if we accept petitioner's premise, the state of the law prior to South-Eastern Underwriters is far from clear. Petitioner bases its argument upon United States v. Knott, 298 U.S. 544 (1936), which involved the use and disposition of funds placed with the Florida Treasurer as a condition of an insurer's conducting business in the State. According to petitioner, Knott stands for the proposition that the federal priority statute pre-empted inconsistent state laws even before South-Eastern Underwriters. But this proffered analogy to Knott unravels upon closer inspection. In that case, the Court applied the federal priority statute only when the State had not specifically legislated the priority of claims. Id., at 549-550 ("But it is settled that an inchoate lien is not enough to defeat the [Federal Government's] priority.... Unless the law of Florida effected ... either a transfer of title from the company, or a specific perfected lien in favor of the Florida creditors, the United States is entitled to priority"). Moreover, other cases issued at the same time reached a different result. See, e.g., Conway v. Imperial Life Ins. Co., 207 La.

285, 21 So.2d 151 (1945) (Louisiana statute specifically providing that deposited securities are held by state treasurer in trust for benefit and protection of policyholders supersedes federal priority statute).

More importantly, petitioner's interpretation of the statute is at odds with its plain language. The McCarran-Ferguson Act did not simply overrule South-Eastern Underwriters and restore the status quo. To the contrary, it transformed the legal landscape by overturning the normal rules of pre- emption. Ordinarily, a federal law supersedes any inconsistent state law. The first clause of § 2(b) reverses this by imposing what is, in effect, a clear- statement rule, a rule that state laws enacted "for the purpose of regulating the business of insurance" do not yield to conflicting federal statutes unless a federal statute specifically requires otherwise. That Congress understood the effect of its language becomes apparent when we examine other parts of the legislative history.[7]   The second clause of § 2(b) also broke new ground: it "embod[ied] a legislative rejection of the concept that the insurance industry is outside the scope of the antitrust laws--a concept that had prevailed before the South-Eastern Underwriters decision." Royal Drug, 440 U.S., at 220.

Petitioner's argument appears to find its origin in the Court's statement in  National Securities that "[t]he McCarran-Ferguson Act was an attempt to turn back the clock, to assure that the activities of insurance companies in dealing with their policyholders would remain subject to state regulation." 393 U.S., at 459. The Court was referring to the primary purpose underlying the Act, namely, to restore to the States broad authority to tax and regulate the insurance industry. Petitioner would extrapolate from this general statement an invitation to engage in a detailed point-by-point comparison between the regime created by McCarran-Ferguson and the one that existed before. But it is impossible to compare our present world to the one that existed at a time when the business of insurance was believed to be beyond the reach of Congress' power under the Commerce Clause. . . .

We hold that the Ohio priority statute, to the extent that it regulates policyholders, is a law enacted for the purpose of regulating the business of insurance. To the extent that it is designed to further the interests of other creditors, however, it is not a law enacted for the purpose of regulating the business of insurance. Of course, every preference accorded to the creditors of an insolvent insurer ultimately may redound to the benefit of policyholders by enhancing the reliability of the insurance company. This argument, however, goes too far:  "But in that sense, every business decision made by an insurance company has some impact on its reliability ... and its status as a reliable insurer." Royal Drug, 440 U.S., at 216-217. Royal Drug rejected the

---

[7]    Elaborating upon the purpose animating the first clause of § 2(b) of the McCarran-Ferguson Act, Senator Ferguson observed:

"What we have in mind is that the insurance business, being interstate commerce, if we merely enact a law relating to interstate commerce, or if there is a law now on the statute books relating in some way to interstate commerce, it would not apply to insurance. We wanted to be sure that the Congress, in its wisdom, would act specifically with reference to insurance in enacting the law." 91 Cong.Rec. 1487 (1945).

This passage later confirms that "no existing law and no future law should, by mere implication, be applied to the business of insurance" (statement of Mr. Mahoney). Ibid.

notion that such indirect effects are sufficient for a state law to avoid pre-emption under the McCarran-Ferguson Act. Id., at 217.

We also hold that the preference accorded by Ohio to the expenses of administering the insolvency proceeding is reasonably necessary to further the goal of protecting policyholders. Without payment of administrative costs, liquidation could not even commence. The preferences conferred upon employees and other general creditors, however, do not escape pre-emption because their connection to the ultimate aim of insurance is too tenuous.

The judgment of the Court of Appeals is affirmed in part and reversed in part, and the case is remanded to that court for further proceedings consistent with this opinion.

Justice KENNEDY, with whom Justice SCALIA, Justice SOUTER and Justice THOMAS join, dissenting.

The function of the Ohio statute before us is to regulate the priority of competing creditor claims in proceedings to liquidate an insolvent insurance company. On its face, the statute's exclusive concentration is not policyholder protection, but creditor priority. The Ohio statute states that its comprehensive purpose is "the protection of the interests of insureds, claimants, creditors, and the public generally, with minimum interference with the normal prerogatives of the owners and managers of insurers." Ohio Rev.Code Ann. § 3903.02(D) (1989). It can be said that Ohio's insolvency scheme furthers the interests of policyholders to the extent the statute gives policyholder claims priority over the claims of the defunct insurer's other creditors. But until today that result alone would not have qualified Ohio's liquidation statute as a law enacted for the purpose of regulating the business of insurance. The Ohio law does not regulate or implicate the "true underwriting of risks, the one earmark of insurance." S.E.C. v. Variable Annuity Life Ins. Co. of America, 359 U.S. 65, 73 (1959) (footnote omitted). To be sure, the Ohio priority statute increases the probability that an insured's claim will be paid in the event of insurer insolvency. But such laws, while they may "furthe[r] the interests of policyholders," ante, at 2208, have little to do with the relationship between an insurer and its insured, National Securities, 393 U.S., at 460, and as such are not laws regulating the business of insurance under the McCarran-Ferguson Act. The State's priority statute does not speak to the transfer of risk embodied in the contract of insurance between the parties. Granting policyholders priority of payment over other creditors does not involve the transfer of risk from insured to insurer, the type of risk spreading that is the essence of the contract of insurance.

## Comments and Questions

1. The *Fabe* majority distinguished between the first and second clause of section 2(b) of the McCarran-Ferguson Act. What is the textual basis of this distinction? Is it compelling? For a substantive defense of the *Fabe* decision, see Jonathan R. Macey & Geoffrey P. Miller, The *McCarran-Ferguson Act of 1945: Reconceiving the Federal Role of Insurance Regulation*, 68 N.Y.U. L. REV. 13 (1993).

2. Suppose the staff of the Federal Trade Commission concluded that an insurance company was televising misleading advertisements about certain insurance products. Could the Commission institute an enforcement proceeding against the companies? Would it make a difference if the practice took place in a state that had a statute

prohibiting insurance companies from making false and deceptive statements? See FTC v. National Casualty Co., 357 U.S. 560 (1958) (per curiam).

3. Recall that in our discussion of depository institutions, we considered in several context the "business of banking." How do the standards developed in those areas compare with the Supreme Court's interpretations of the "business of insurance" under the McCarran-Ferguson Act? Are different approaches justified?

## B.  Boycotts Under McCarran-Ferguson

A separate strain of McCarran-Ferguson Act cases concern section 3(b)'s reinstatement of federal anti-trust law for boycotts, coercion, and intimidation involving insurance companies. Over the past fifteen years, this provision has been the subject of frequent litigation. Many of the reported cases arise out of what is often loosely referred to as the liability crisis in the insurance industry. Before turning to those cases, we include a brief overview of the scope of this crisis, as experienced in the mid-1980s, and a summary of principal academic theories of the cause of the crisis.

## George L. Priest, The Current Insurance Crisis and Modern Tort Law
### 96 Yale L.J. 1521, 1521-25 (1987)

[T]he crisis in insurance . . . has recently disrupted product and service markets in the United States. From press accounts, the crisis seemed to peak in the early months of 1986, when reports became common of extraordinary changes in commercial casualty insurance markets. Insurers had increased premiums drastically for an unusual set of products, such as vaccines, general aircraft, and sports equipment, and for an equally diverse set of services, such as obstetrics, ski lifts, and commercial trucking. In still other cases -- intrauterine devices, wine tasting, and day care -- insurers had refused to offer coverage at any premium, forcing these products and services to be withdrawn from the market. . . . .

Over time, product manufacturers and service providers adjusted to these insurance difficulties. Recently, some commentators have interpreted the decline in the volume of complaints as evidence that the insurance crisis has subsided. But this is an incomplete and unrealistic view of the problem. Although there has allegedly been some increase in insurance availability, the huge premium increases of early 1986 are largely intact, necessitating sustained price increases and reducing demand for affected products and services. Moreover, many of the effects of the crisis have become permanent. A recent Conference Board study of liability problems of the country's largest corporations--those whose size and self-insurance capability make them least vulnerable to changes in commercial insurance markets--reports that twenty-five percent had removed products or withdrawn services from the market. The effect on national income of increased prices and the withdrawal of products and services is obvious. . . .

Three sets of theories have been put forth to explain the insurance crisis and to propose its cure. The first set views the crisis as collusively engineered by insurance companies, either by explicit price-fixing or by financial manipulation of insurance reserve accounts. A second set of theories explains the crisis with reference to the cyclical effect of changes in interest rates on investment returns and, thus, on insurance premiums. According to this theory, the crisis is the direct result of recent declines in interest rates which have forced insurance premiums to increase. In a slightly different version, the crisis is attributed to an earlier period of high interest rates during which insurers, shortsightedly, underpriced risks to gain premiums for investment, risks which must be recalculated at higher premiums today. The collusion and the insurance cycle theories both imply that these insurance problems will disappear in time, either through the breakdown of the cartel (or by antitrust enforcement or regulation), through the cyclical return of higher interest rates, or through the more accurate evaluation of risks by chastened insurers.

A third theory, most prominently espoused by the Justice Department, attributes the crisis to modern tort law's expansion of corporate liability exposure, which has necessitated insurance premium increases. According to the Justice Department, only wide-ranging tort law reform can cure the crisis. Within the past eighteen months, on the basis of the Department's and other attributions of the crisis to tort law, forty-two states have enacted tort reform or insurance legislation. Although there are differences among the states, the general similarity in approach and the sudden spontaneity of the response represent the most extraordinary state law development having national impact since the states' unanimous adoption of the Uniform Commercial Code. Indeed, the Justice Department now claims that this legislation--though in effect only for scant months--has largely cured the insurance problem.

None of these three theories, however, fully or adequately explains the phenomena of the recent insurance crisis. Virtually all commentators, in characterizing the crisis, have focused solely on the sudden increases in insurance premiums and the occasional withdrawal of insurance coverage during early 1986. The crisis, however, has been attended by a much broader group of related phenomena, which must be addressed by any comprehensive explanation. For example, long before 1986, there began to occur increasing shifts toward corporate self-insurance for expected tort liability. In addition, in recent months, while simultaneously increasing premiums, insurers have fundamentally redrafted the basic commercial insurance policy--raising deductibles, lowering levels of aggregate coverage, and revising specific policy exclusions. A comprehensive theory of the crisis must account for all of these phenomena, and must explain their peculiar concentration within commercial casualty lines only, rather than across the broad range of insurance offerings. None of the three existing theories of the insurance crisis can do so.

[My own] theory of the crisis . . . attributes these changes in insurance coverage to modern tort law, but by a mechanism much different from that suggested by the Justice Department. In my view, it is simplistic to no more than assert a connection between expanding tort liability and the disruption of insurance coverage. The relationship between legal liability and the insurance function obviously is more complicated: The demand for commercial insurance coverage derives from tort liability. The expansion of tort liability might well create opportunity, rather than crisis, for the insurance industry. [I] argue . . . that the characteristic of contemporary tort law most crucial to understanding the current crisis is the judicial compulsion of greater and greater levels of provider third-party insurance for victims. The progressive shift to third-party corporate insurance coverage, since its beginnings in the mid-1960's, has systematically undermined insurance markets. The decline in interest rates within the past two years has led the most fragile of these markets--those for which third-party coverage is least supportable--to collapse. The collapse is signalled by the accelerating conversion to self-insurance. This conversion, in turn, forces insurers to exact drastic premium increases, as well as to restructure the terms of the basic insurance policy, in order to salvage a market among remaining insureds. Where these salvage efforts have proven unsuccessful, insurers have refused to offer coverage altogether.

This explanation of the crisis uncovers what I believe to be a tragic paradox of our modern civil liability regime. The expansion of liability since the mid- 1960's has been chiefly motivated by the concern of our courts to provide insurance to victims who have suffered personal injury. The most fundamental of the conceptual foundations of our modern law is that the expansion of tort liability will lead to the provision of insurance along with the sale of the product or service itself, with a portion of the insurance premium passed along in the product or service price. Expanded tort liability, thus, is a method of providing insurance to individuals, especially the poor, who have not purchased or cannot purchase insurance themselves. This insurance rationale suffuses our modern civil law, and must be acknowledged as one of the great humanitarian expressions of our time.

The paradox exposed by my theory is that the expansion of tort liability has had exactly the opposite effect. The insurance crisis demonstrates graphicly that continued expansion of tort liability on insurance grounds leads to a reduction in total insurance coverage available to the society, rather than to an increase. The theory also shows that the parties most drastically affected by expanded liability and by the current insurance crisis are the low-income and poor, exactly the parties that courts had hoped most to aid.

## Comments and Questions

1. As this excerpt suggests the prevalence of boom-bust cycles in the insurance industry presents something of a puzzle. Is there something about the nature of the insurance business that makes underwriters prone to wide swings in profitability? To what extent do our legal rules — insurance regulation as well as ancillary fields of tort law and nuisance — exacerbate the problem? Beyond the crisis of the past few decades, what lessons can be drawn from the history of the insurance industry in the United States? What other legal developments over the past few years can also be understood as a response to the insurance industry crisis?

2. The literature on the boom-bust cycle of insurance markets is voluminous and fascinating. For a rebuttal to Professor Priest's emphasis on judicially-imposed third-party coverage, see Steven P. Croley & Jon D. Hanson, *What Liability Crisis? An Alternative Explanation for Recent Events in Products Liability*, 8 YALE. J. REG. 1 (1991). For another perspective of the issue, see Ralph A. Winter, *The Liability Crisis and the Dynamics of Competitive Insurance Markets*, 5 YALE J. REG. 455 (1988).

————

The insurance industry has responded to the liability crisis in many different ways, but one of the industry's most important efforts has been to change the content of insurance contracts to narrow the scope of policies. For example, in Rhode Island in the 1970s, St. Paul Fire & Marine Insurance Company announced that it would no longer underwrite medical malpractice insurance on an "occurrence basis," but would only provide "claims made" policies. With an occurrence policy, the insured doctor is covered for any claims arising of injuries that occurred while the policy was in effect; "claims made" policies cover only claims made while the policy is in effect. From an insurance company's perspective, "claims made" policies are advantageous because they allow companies to reprice policies from year to year as claims experience develops. So, if medical malpractice claims continued to rise in the future, a claims made policy would allow St. Paul to increase its insurance premiums, rather than being locked into premiums set when injuries occurred but before actual claims rates were known.

This change in St. Paul's policies, accompanied as it was by a collective refusal on the part of all Rhode Island malpractice underwriters to offer alternative policies to St. Paul's existing customers, led a group of Rhode Island doctors to challenge the practice under federal anti-trust laws. In St. Paul Fire & Marine Insurance Co. v. Barry, 438 U.S. 531 (1978), the Supreme Court agreed that practice was actionable under federal law because it constituted a "boycott" for purposes of section 3(b) of the McCarran-Ferguson Act. In reaching this conclusion, the Court stressed that the alleged collusion between St. Paul and its competitors was curtailing the availability of coverage previously offered to Rhode Island doctors and was thereby coercing the physicians to accept what they considered a less attractive product.

The *St. Paul* decision raised a number of interpretive questions about the application of section 3(b)'s boycott provision, several of which the Supreme Court considered in the following decision. The underlying suit, brought by a number of state attorneys general, also grew out of the liability crisis of the 1980s. According to the states' theory of the case, members of the U.S. insurance industry conspired together with foreign and domestic reinsurers to limit the availability of certain types of insurance policies. Whether this alleged conspiracy was susceptible to prosecution under the federal anti-trust laws was the issue before the Court. As you read through the following opinions, consider how you would describe the scope section 3(b)'s boycott exemption today.

# Hartford Fire Insurance Co. v. California
## 509 U.S. 764 (1993)

Justice SOUTER announced the judgment of the Court and delivered the opinion of the Court with respect [to section 2(b) of the McCarran-Ferguson Act].

The Sherman Act makes every contract, combination, or conspiracy in unreasonable restraint of interstate or foreign commerce illegal. 26 Stat. 209, as amended, 15 U.S.C. § 1. These consolidated cases present questions about the application of that Act to the insurance industry, both here and abroad. The plaintiffs (respondents here) allege that both domestic and foreign defendants (petitioners here) violated the Sherman Act by engaging in various conspiracies to affect the American insurance market. A group of domestic defendants argues that the McCarran-Ferguson Act precludes application of the Sherman Act to the conduct alleged; a group of foreign defendants argues that the principle of international comity requires the District

Court to refrain from exercising jurisdiction over certain claims against it. We hold that most of the domestic defendants' alleged conduct is not immunized from antitrust liability by the McCarran-Ferguson Act . . . .

## I

The two petitions before us stem from consolidated litigation comprising the complaints of 19 States and many private plaintiffs alleging that the defendants, members of the insurance industry, conspired in violation of § 1 of the Sherman Act to restrict the terms of coverage of commercial general liability (CGL)[1] insurance available in the United States. Because the cases come to us on motions to dismiss, we take the allegations of the complaints as true.

## A

According to the complaints, the object of the conspiracies was to force certain primary insurers (insurers who sell insurance directly to consumers) to change the terms of their standard CGL insurance policies to conform with the policies the defendant insurers wanted to sell. The defendants wanted four changes.

First, CGL insurance has traditionally been sold in the United States on an "occurrence" basis, through a policy obligating the insurer "to pay or defend claims, whenever made, resulting from an accident or 'injurious exposure to conditions' that occurred during the [specific time] period the policy was in effect." App. 22 (Cal. Complaint P 52). In place of this traditional "occurrence" trigger of coverage, the defendants wanted a "claims-made" trigger, obligating the insurer to pay or defend only those claims made during the policy period. Such a policy has the distinct advantage for the insurer that when the policy period ends without a claim having been made, the insurer can be certain that the policy will not expose it to any further liability. Second, the defendants wanted the "claims-made" policy to have a "retroactive date" provision, which would further restrict coverage to claims based on incidents that occurred after a certain date. Such a provision eliminates the risk that an insurer, by issuing a claims-made policy, would assume liability arising from incidents that occurred before the policy's effective date, but remained undiscovered or caused no immediate harm. Third, CGL insurance has traditionally covered "sudden and accidental" pollution; the defendants wanted to eliminate that coverage. Finally, CGL insurance has traditionally provided that the insurer would bear the legal costs of defending covered claims against the insured without regard to the policy's stated limits of coverage; the defendants wanted legal defense costs to be counted against the stated limits (providing a "legal defense cost cap").

To understand how the defendants are alleged to have pressured the targeted primary insurers to make these changes, one must be aware of two important features of the insurance industry. First, most primary insurers rely on certain outside support services for the type of insurance coverage they wish to sell. Defendant Insurance Services Office, Inc. (ISO), an association of approximately 1,400 domestic property and casualty insurers (including the primary insurer defendants, Hartford Fire Insurance Company, Allstate Insurance Company, CIGNA Corporation, and Aetna Casualty and Surety Company), is the almost exclusive source of support services in this country for CGL insurance. ISO develops standard policy forms and

---

[1]    CGL insurance provides "coverage for third party casualty damage claims against a purchaser of insurance (the 'insured')."

files or lodges them with each State's insurance regulators; most CGL insurance written in the United States is written on these forms. All of the "traditional" features of CGL insurance relevant to this case were embodied in the ISO standard CGL insurance form that had been in use since 1973 (1973 ISO CGL form). For each of its standard policy forms, ISO also supplies actuarial and rating information: it collects, aggregates, interprets, and distributes data on the premiums charged, claims filed and paid, and defense costs expended with respect to each form, and on the basis of this data it predicts future loss trends and calculates advisory premium rates. Most ISO members cannot afford to continue to use a form if ISO withdraws these support services.

Second, primary insurers themselves usually purchase insurance to cover a portion of the risk they assume from the consumer. This so-called "reinsurance" may serve at least two purposes, protecting the primary insurer from catastrophic loss, and allowing the primary insurer to sell more insurance than its own financial capacity might otherwise permit. Thus, "the availability of reinsurance affects the ability and willingness of primary insurers to provide insurance to their customers." Insurers who sell reinsurance themselves often purchase insurance to cover part of the risk they assume from the primary insurer; such "retrocessional reinsurance" does for reinsurers what reinsurance does for primary insurers. Many of the defendants here are reinsurers or reinsurance brokers, or play some other specialized role in the reinsurance business; defendant Reinsurance Association of America (RAA) is a trade association of domestic reinsurers.

### B

The prehistory of events claimed to give rise to liability starts in 1977, when ISO began the process of revising its 1973 CGL form.. For the first time, it proposed two CGL forms (1984 ISO CGL forms), one the traditional "occurrence" type, the other "with a new 'claims-made' trigger." The "claims-made" form did not have a retroactive date provision, however, and both 1984 forms covered "'sudden and accidental' pollution" damage and provided for unlimited coverage of legal defense costs by the insurer. Within the ISO, defendant Hartford Fire Insurance Company objected to the proposed 1984 forms; it desired elimination of the "occurrence" form, a retroactive date provision on the "claims-made" form, elimination of sudden and accidental pollution coverage, and a legal defense cost cap. Defendant Allstate Insurance Company also expressed its desire for a retroactive date provision on the "claims-made" form. Majorities in the relevant ISO committees, however, supported the proposed 1984 CGL forms and rejected the changes proposed by Hartford and Allstate. In December 1983, the ISO Board of Directors approved the proposed 1984 forms, and ISO filed or lodged the forms with state regulators in March 1984.

Dissatisfied with this state of affairs, the defendants began to take other steps to force a change in the terms of coverage of CGL insurance generally available, steps that, the plaintiffs allege, implemented a series of conspiracies in violation of § 1 of the Sherman Act. The plaintiffs recount these steps as a number of separate episodes corresponding to different Claims for Relief in their complaints; because it will become important to distinguish among these counts and the acts and defendants associated with them, we will note these correspondences.

The [complaints] charge the four domestic primary insurer defendants and varying groups of domestic and foreign reinsurers, brokers, and associations with conspiracies to manipulate the ISO CGL forms. In March 1984, primary insurer Hartford persuaded General Reinsurance Corporation (General Re), the largest American reinsurer, to take steps either to procure desired changes in the ISO CGL forms, or "failing that, [to] 'derail' the entire ISO CGL forms program." General Re took up the matter with its trade association, RAA, which created a special committee that met and agreed to "boycott" the 1984 ISO CGL forms unless a retroactive-date provision was added to the claims-made form, and a pollution exclusion and defense cost cap were added to both forms. RAA then sent a letter to ISO "announcing that its members would not provide reinsurance for coverages written on the 1984 CGL forms," and Hartford and General Re enlisted a domestic reinsurance broker to give a speech to the ISO Board of Directors, in which he stated that no reinsurers would "break ranks" to reinsure the 1984 ISO CGL forms.

The four primary insurer defendants (Hartford, Aetna, CIGNA, and Allstate) also encouraged key actors in the London reinsurance market, an important provider of reinsurance for North American risks, to withhold reinsurance for coverages written on the 1984 ISO CGL forms. As a consequence, many London-based underwriters, syndicates, brokers, and reinsurance companies informed ISO of their intention to withhold reinsurance on the 1984 forms, and at least some of them told ISO that they would withhold reinsurance until ISO incorporated all four desired changes into the ISO CGL forms.

For the first time ever, ISO invited representatives of the domestic and foreign reinsurance markets to speak at an ISO Executive Committee meeting. At that meeting, the reinsurers "presented their agreed upon positions that there would be changes in the CGL forms or no reinsurance." The ISO Executive Committee then voted to include a retroactive-date provision in the claims-made form, and to exclude all pollution coverage from both new forms. (But it neither eliminated the occurrence form, nor added a legal defense cost cap.) The 1984 ISO CGL forms were then withdrawn from the marketplace, and replaced with forms (1986 ISO CGL forms) containing the new provisions. After ISO got regulatory approval of the 1986 forms in most States where approval was needed, it eliminated its support services for the 1973 CGL form, thus rendering it impossible for most ISO members to continue to use the form.

The [complaints also] charge a conspiracy among a group of London reinsurers and brokers to coerce primary insurers in the United States to offer CGL coverage only on a claims-made basis. The reinsurers collectively refused to write new reinsurance contracts for, or to renew long-standing contracts with, "primary . . . insurers unless they were prepared to switch from the occurrence to the claims-made form"; they also amended their reinsurance contracts to cover only claims made before a "'sunset date,'" thus eliminating reinsurance for claims made on occurrence policies after that date.

[The complaints further] charge another conspiracy among a somewhat different group of London reinsurers to withhold reinsurance for pollution coverage. The London reinsurers met and agreed that all reinsurance contracts covering North American casualty risks, including CGL risks, would be written with a complete exclusion for pollution liability coverage. In accordance with this agreement, the parties have in fact excluded pollution liability coverage from CGL reinsurance contracts since at least late 1985.

[The complaints also] charge a group of domestic primary insurers, foreign reinsurers, and the ISO with conspiring to restrain trade in the markets for "excess" and "umbrella" insurance by drafting model forms and policy language for these types of insurance, which are not normally offered on a regulated basis. The ISO Executive Committee eventually released standard language for both "occurrence" and "claims-made" umbrella and excess policies; that language included a retroactive date in the claims-made version, and an absolute pollution exclusion and a legal defense cost cap in both versions.

[Finally, the complaints] charge a group of London and domestic retrocessional reinsurers with conspiring to withhold retrocessional reinsurance for North American seepage, pollution, and property contamination risks. Those retrocessional reinsurers signed, and have implemented, an agreement to use their "'best endeavors'" to ensure that they would provide such reinsurance for North American risks "'only . . . where the original business includes a seepage and pollution exclusion wherever legal and applicable.'"

## C

Nineteen States and a number of private plaintiffs filed 36 complaints against the insurers involved in this course of events, charging that the conspiracies described above violated § 1 of the Sherman Act. After the actions had been consolidated for litigation in the Northern District of California, the defendants moved to dismiss for failure to state a cause of action, or, in the alternative, for summary judgment. The District Court granted the motions to dismiss. In re Insurance Antitrust Litigation. It held that the conduct alleged fell within the grant of antitrust immunity contained in § 2(b) of the McCarran-Ferguson Act, because it amounted to "the business of insurance" and was "regulated by State law" within the meaning of that section; none of the conduct, in the District Court's view, amounted to a "boycott" within the meaning of the § 3(b) exception to that grant of immunity.. . . .

The Court of Appeals reversed. Although it held the conduct involved to be "the business of insurance" within the meaning of § 2(b), it concluded that the defendants could not claim McCarran-Ferguson Act antitrust immunity for two independent reasons. First, it held, the foreign reinsurers were beyond the regulatory jurisdiction of the States; because their activities could not be "regulated by State law" within the meaning of § 2(b), they did not fall within that section's grant of immunity. Although the domestic insurers were "regulated by State law," the court held, they forfeited their § 2(b) exemption when they conspired with the nonexempt foreign reinsurers. Second, the Court of Appeals held that, even if the conduct alleged fell within the scope of § 2(b), it also fell within the § 3(b) exception for "acts of boycott, coercion, or intimidation." . . . .

## II

Petitioners are all of the domestic defendants in the consolidated cases: the four domestic primary insurers, the domestic reinsurers, the trade associations ISO and RAA, and the domestic reinsurance broker Thomas A. Greene & Company, Inc. They argue that the Court of Appeals erred in holding, first, that their conduct, otherwise immune from antitrust liability under § 2(b) of the McCarran-Ferguson Act, lost its immunity when they conspired with the foreign defendants, and, second, that their conduct amounted to "acts of boycott" falling within the exception to antitrust immunity set out in § 3(b).

## A

By its terms, the antitrust exemption of § 2(b) of the McCarran-Ferguson Act applies to "the business of insurance" to the extent that such business is regulated by state law. While "business" may mean "[a] commercial or industrial establishment or enterprise," Webster's New International Dictionary 362 (2d ed. 1942), the definite article before "business" in § 2(b) shows that the word is not used in that sense, the phrase "the business of insurance" obviously not being meant to refer to a single entity. Rather, "business" as used in § 2(b) is most naturally read to refer to "mercantile transactions; buying and selling; [and] traffic." Ibid.

The cases confirm that "the business of insurance" should be read to single out one activity from others, not to distinguish one entity from another. In Group Life & Health Ins. Co. v. Royal Drug Co., 440 U.S. 205 (1979), for example, we held that § 2(b) did not exempt an insurance company from antitrust liability for making an agreement fixing the price of prescription drugs to be sold to Blue Shield policyholders. Such activity, we said, "would be exempt from the antitrust laws if Congress had extended the coverage of the McCarran-Ferguson Act to the 'business of insurance companies.' But that is precisely what Congress did not do." Id., at 233 (footnote omitted). And in Union Labor Life Ins. Co v. Pireno, 458 U.S. 119 (1982), we explicitly framed the  question as whether "a particular *practice* is part of the 'business of insurance' exempted from the antitrust laws by § 2(b)," id., at 129 (emphasis added), and each of the three criteria we identified concerned a quality of the practice in question: "*first*, whether the practice has the effect of transferring or spreading a policyholder's risk; *second*, whether the practice is an integral part of the policy relationship between the insurer and the insured; and *third*, whether the practice is limited to entities within the insurance industry." Ibid. (emphasis in original).

The Court of Appeals did not hold that, under these criteria, the domestic defendants' conduct fell outside "the business of insurance"; to the contrary, it held that that condition was met.  Nor did it hold the domestic defendants' conduct to be "unregulated by State law." Rather, it constructed an altogether different chain of reasoning, the middle link of which comes from a sentence in our opinion in Royal Drug Co. "Regulation . . . of foreign reinsurers," the Court of Appeals explained, "is beyond the jurisdiction of the states," and hence § 2(b) does not exempt foreign reinsurers from antitrust liability, because their activities are not "regulated by State law." Under Royal Drug Co., "an exempt entity forfeits antitrust exemption by acting in concert with nonexempt parties." 440 U.S., at 231. Therefore, the domestic insurers, by acting in concert with the nonexempt foreign insurers, lost their McCarran-Ferguson Act antitrust immunity. This reasoning fails, however, because even if we were to agree that foreign reinsurers were not subject to state regulation (a point on which we express no opinion), the quoted language from Royal Drug Co., read in context, does not state a proposition applicable to this case.

The full sentence from Royal Drug Co. places the quoted fragment in a different light. "In analogous contexts," we stated, "the Court has held that an exempt entity forfeits antitrust exemption by acting in concert with nonexempt parties." 440 U.S., at 231. We then cited two cases dealing with the Capper-Volstead Act, which immunizes from liability under § 1 of the Sherman Act particular activities of certain persons "engaged in the production of agricultural products."  § 1 of the Capper-Volstead Act. Because these cases relied on statutory language referring to certain "persons," whereas we specifically acknowledged in Royal Drug Co. that the McCarran-Ferguson Act immunizes activities rather than entities, the analogy we were drawing was of course a loose one. The agreements that insurance companies made with "parties wholly outside the insurance industry," we noted, such as the retail pharmacists involved in Royal Drug Co. itself, or "automobile body repair shops or landlords," are unlikely to be about anything that could be called "the business of insurance," as distinct from the broader "'business of insurance companies.'" The alleged agreements at issue in the instant case, of course, are entirely different; the foreign reinsurers are hardly "wholly outside the insurance industry," and respondents do not contest the Court of Appeals's holding that the agreements concern "the business of insurance."

These facts neither support even the rough analogy we drew in Royal Drug Co., nor fall within the rule about acting in concert with nonexempt parties, which derived from a statute inapplicable here. Thus, we think it was error for the Court of Appeals to hold the domestic insurers bereft of their McCarran-Ferguson Act exemption simply because they agreed or acted with foreign reinsurers that, we assume for the sake of argument, were "not regulated by State law."[12]

Justice SCALIA delivered the opinion of the Court [with respect to section 3(b) of the McCarran-Ferguson Act].

Determining proper application of § 3(b) of the McCarran-Ferguson Act to the present case requires precise definition of the word "boycott." It is a relatively new word, little more than a century old. It was first used in 1880, to describe the collective action taken against Captain Charles Boycott, an English agent managing various estates in Ireland. The Land League, an Irish organization formed the previous year, had demanded that landlords reduce their rents and had urged tenants to avoid dealing with those who failed to do so. Boycott did not bend to the demand and instead ordered evictions. In retaliation, the tenants "sent Captain Boycott to Coventry in a very thorough manner." J. McCarthy, England Under Gladstone 108 (1886). "The population of the region for miles round resolved not to have anything to do with him, and, as far as they could prevent it, not to allow any one else to have anything to do with him. . . . The awful sentence of excommunication could hardly have rendered him more helplessly alone for a time. No one would work for him; no one would supply him with food." Id., at 108-109; see also H. Laidler, Boycotts and the Labor Struggle 23-27 (1968). Thus, the verb made from the unfortunate Captain's name has had from the outset the meaning it continues to carry today. To "boycott" means "to combine in refusing to hold relations of any kind, social or commercial, public or private, with (a neighbour), on account of political or other differences, so as to punish him for the position he has taken up, or coerce him into abandoning it." 2 The Oxford English Dictionary 468 (2d ed. 1989).

Petitioners have suggested that a boycott ordinarily requires "an absolute refusal to deal on any terms," which was concededly not the case here. We think not. As the definition just recited provides, the refusal may be imposed "to punish [the target] for the position he has taken up, or coerce him into abandoning it." The refusal to deal may, in other words, be conditional, offering its target the incentive of renewed dealing if and when he mends his ways. This is often the case -- and indeed seems to have been the case with the original Boycott boycott. Cf. McCarthy, supra, at 109 (noting that the Captain later lived "at peace" with his neighbors). Furthermore, other dictionary definitions extend the term to include a partial boycott -- a refusal to engage in some, but not all, transactions with the target. See Webster's New International Dictionary 321 (2d ed. 1950) (defining "boycott" as "to withhold, wholly or in part, social or business intercourse from, as an expression of disapproval or means of coercion").

It is, however, important -- and crucial in the present case -- to distinguish between a conditional boycott and a concerted agreement to seek particular terms in particular transactions. A concerted agreement to terms (a "cartelization") is "a way of obtaining and exercising market

---

[12]    The Court of Appeals's assumption that "the American reinsurers . . . are subject to regulation by the states and therefore prima facie immune," appears to rest on the entity-based analysis we have rejected. As with the foreign reinsurers, we express no opinion whether the activities of the domestic reinsurers were "regulated by State law" and leave that question to the Court of Appeals on remand.

power by concertedly exacting terms like those which a monopolist might exact." L. Sullivan, Law of Antitrust 257 (1977). The parties to such an agreement (the members of a cartel) are not engaging in a boycott, because: "They are not coercing anyone, at least in the usual sense of that word; they are merely (though concertedly) saying 'we will deal with you only on the following trade terms.'    ". . . Indeed, if a concerted agreement, say, to include a security deposit in all contracts is a 'boycott' because it excludes all buyers who won't agree to it, then by parity of reasoning every price fixing agreement would be a boycott also. The use of the single concept, boycott, to cover agreements so varied in nature can only add to confusion." Ibid.

Thus, if Captain Boycott's tenants had agreed among themselves that they would refuse to renew their leases unless he reduced his rents, that would have been a concerted agreement on the terms of the leases, but not a boycott. The tenants, of course, did more than that; they refused to engage in other, unrelated transactions with Boycott -- e. g., selling him food -- unless he agreed to their terms on rents. It is this expansion of the refusal to deal beyond the targeted transaction that gives great coercive force to a commercial boycott: unrelated transactions are used as leverage to achieve the terms desired.

The proper definition of "boycott" is evident from the Court's opinion in Eastern States Retail Lumber Dealers' Assn. v. United States, 234 U.S. 600 (1914). The associations of retail lumber dealers in that case refused to buy lumber from wholesale lumber dealers who sold directly to consumers. The boycott attempted "to impose as a condition . . . on [the wholesale dealers'] trade that they shall not sell in such manner that a local retailer may regard such sale as an infringement of his exclusive right to trade." We held that to be an "artificial condition," since "the trade of the wholesaler with strangers was directly affected, not because of any supposed wrong which he had done to them, but because of a grievance of a member of one of the associations." In other words, the associations' activities were a boycott because they sought an objective -- the wholesale dealers' forbearance from retail trade -- that was collateral to their transactions with the wholesalers.

Of course as far as the Sherman Act (outside the exempted insurance field) is concerned, concerted agreements on contract terms are as unlawful as boycotts. For example, in Paramount Famous Lasky Corp. v. United States, 282 U.S. 30 (1930), and United States v. First National Pictures, Inc., 282 U.S. 44 (1930), we held unreasonable an agreement among competing motion picture distributors under which they refused to license films to exhibitors except on standardized terms. We also found unreasonable the restraint of trade in Anderson v. Shipowners Assn. of Pacific Coast, 272 U.S. 359 (1926), which involved an attempt by an association of employers to establish industry-wide terms of employment. These sorts of concerted actions, similar to what is alleged to have occurred here, are not properly characterized as "boycotts," and the word does not appear in the opinions.[3] In fact, in the 65 years between the coining of the word and

---

[3]    Justice SOUTER points out that the Court in St. Paul Fire & Marine Ins. Co. v. Barry, 438 U.S. 531, 57 L. Ed. 2d 932, 98 S. Ct. 2923 (1978), found the term boycott "does not refer to ' "a unitary phenomenon,"'" ante, at 20 (quoting Barry, supra, at 543 (quoting P. Areeda, Antitrust Analysis 381 (2d ed. 1974))), and asserts that our position contradicts this. Ante, at 26-27. But to be not a "unitary phenomenon" is different from being an all-encompassing one. "Boycott" is a multifaceted "phenomenon" that includes conditional boycotts, punitive boycotts, coercive boycotts, partial boycotts, labor boycotts, political boycotts, social boycotts, etc. It merely does not include refusals to deal because of objections to proposed terms.

enactment of the McCarran-Ferguson Act in 1945, "boycott" appears in only seven opinions of this Court involving commercial (nonlabor) antitrust matters, and not once is it used to describe a concerted refusal to engage in particular transactions until the terms of those transactions are agreeable. . . .

The one case in which we have found an activity to constitute a "boycott" within the meaning of the McCarran-Ferguson Act is St. Paul Fire & Marine Ins. Co. v. Barry, 438 U.S. 531 (1978). There the plaintiffs were licensed physicians and their patients, and the defendant (St. Paul) was a malpractice insurer that had refused to renew the physicians' policies on an "occurrence" basis, but insisted upon a "claims made" basis. The allegation was that, at the instance of St. Paul, the three other malpractice insurers in the State had collectively refused to write insurance for St. Paul customers, thus forcing them to accept St. Paul's renewal terms. Unsurprisingly, we held the allegation sufficient to state a cause of action. The insisted-upon condition of the boycott (not being a former St. Paul policyholder) was "artificial": it bore no relationship (or an "artificial" relationship) to the proposed contracts of insurance that the physicians wished to conclude with St. Paul's competitors.

Under the standard described, it is obviously not a "boycott" for the reinsurers to "refuse to reinsure coverages written on the ISO CGL forms until the desired changes were made," ante, at 21, because the terms of the primary coverages are central elements of the reinsurance contract -- they are what is reinsured. See App. 16-17 (Cal. Complaint P P 26-27). The "primary policies are . . . the basis of the losses that are shared in the reinsurance agreements." 1 B. Webb, H. Anderson, J. Cookman, & P. Kensicki, Principles of Reinsurance 87 (1990); see also id., at 55; Gurley, Regulation of Reinsurance in the United States, 19 Forum 72, 73 (1983). Indeed, reinsurance is so closely tied to the terms of the primary insurance contract that one of the two categories of reinsurance (assumption reinsurance) substitutes the reinsurer for the primary or "ceding" insurer and places the reinsurer into contractual privity with the primary insurer's policyholders. See id., at 73-74; Colonial American Life Ins. Co. v. Commissioner, 491 U.S. 244, 247 (1989); T. Newman & B. Ostrager, Insurance Coverage Disputes 15-16 (1990). And in the other category of reinsurance (indemnity reinsurance), either the terms of the underlying insurance policy are incorporated by reference (if the reinsurance is written under a facultative agreement), see J. Butler & R. Merkin, Reinsurance Law B.1.1-04 (1992); R. Carter, Reinsurance 235 (1979), or (if the reinsurance is conducted on a treaty basis) the reinsurer will require full disclosure of the terms of the underlying insurance policies and usually require that the primary insurer not vary those terms without prior approval, see id., at 256, 297.

Justice Souter simply disregards this integral relationship between the terms of the primary insurance form and the contract of reinsurance. He describes the reinsurers as "individuals and entities who were not members of ISO, and who would not ordinarily be parties to an agreement setting the terms of primary insurance, not being in the business of selling it." Ante, at 21. While this factual assumption is crucial to Justice SOUTER's reasoning (because otherwise he would not be able to distinguish permissible agreements among primary insurers), he offers no support for the statement. But even if it happens to be true, he does not explain why it must be true -- that is, why the law must exclude reinsurers from full membership and participation. The realities of the industry may make explanation difficult:

"Reinsurers also benefit from the services by ISO and other rating or service organizations. The underlying rates and policy forms are the basis for many reinsurance contracts. Reinsurers may also subscribe to various services. For example, a facultative reinsurer may subscribe to the rating service, so that they have the rating manuals available, or purchase optional services, such as a sprinkler report for a specific property location." 2 R. Reinarz, J. Schloss, G. Patrik, & P. Kensicki, Reinsurance Practices 18 (1990). . . .

Under the test set forth above, there are sufficient allegations of a "boycott" to sustain the relevant counts of complaint against a motion to dismiss. For example, the complaints allege that some of the defendant reinsurers threatened to "withdraw entirely from the business of reinsuring primary U.S. insurers who wrote on the occurrence form." Construed most favorably to the respondents, that allegation claims that primary insurers who wrote insurance on disfavored forms would be refused all reinsurance, even as to risks written on other forms. If that were the case, the reinsurers might have been engaging in a boycott -- they would, that is, unless the primary insurers' other business were relevant to the proposed reinsurance contract (for example, if the reinsurer bears greater risk where the primary insurer engages in riskier businesses). Cf. Gonye, Underwriting the Reinsured, in Reinsurance 439, 463-466 (R. Strain ed. 1980); 2 R. Reinarz, J. Schloss, G. Patrik, & P. Kensicki, Reinsurance Practices 21-23 (1990) (same). Other allegations in the complaints  could be similarly construed. For example, the complaints also allege that the reinsurers "threatened a boycott of North American CGL risks," not just CGL risks containing dissatisfactory terms; that "the foreign and domestic reinsurer representatives presented their agreed upon positions that there would be changes in the CGL forms or no reinsurance;" that some of the defendant insurers and reinsurers told "groups of insurance brokers and agents . . . that a reinsurance boycott, and thus loss of income to the agents and brokers who would be unable to find available markets for their customers, would ensue if the [revised] ISO forms were not approved."

Many other allegations in the complaints describe conduct that may amount to a boycott if the plaintiffs can prove certain additional facts. For example, General Re, the largest American reinsurer, is alleged to have "agreed to either coerce ISO to adopt [the defendants'] demands or, failing that, 'derail' the entire CGL forms program." If this means that General Re intended to withhold all reinsurance on all CGL forms -- even forms having no objectionable terms -- that might amount to a "boycott." Also, General Re and several other domestic reinsurers are alleged to have "agreed to boycott the 1984 ISO forms unless a retroactive date was added to the claims-made form, and a pollution exclusion and a defense cost cap were added to both [the occurrence and claims made] forms." Liberally construed, this allegation may mean that the defendants had linked their demands so that they would continue to refuse to do business on either form until both were changed to their liking. Again, that might amount to a boycott.

## Comments and Questions

1. A year after the Supreme Court's decision in *Hartford Fire*, the parties settled the litigation.  The industry defendants agreed to contribute $36 million dollars to a newly created public entity founded to make educational and technical services available to entities that purchase general liability insurance.  In addition, the ISO agreed to change the composition of its board to include more directors who are not affiliated with insurance companies. Which side prevailed in the *Hartford Fire* case?  What sort of boycotts are now actionable under section 3(b)?

2. Within the industry, one of the most closely followed aspects of the *Hartford Fire* litigation was the Ninth Circuit's ruling that domestic defendants lost their McCarran-Ferguson exemption from anti-trust liability because they contract with foreign reinsurers that were not adequately regulated by state law. The Supreme Court reversed this aspect of the appellate court's decision. But this element of the case raises an interesting question of the role of foreign reinsurers in the U.S. markets. The function of reinsurance is to allow primary insurance companies to reduce their exposure to certain risks. With reinsurance, a primary insurance company cedes a portion of its underwriting risk (say for home-owners insurance in coastal Florida) to a reinsurer. Foreign reinsurers, such as Lloyd's of London and the foreign defendants in the *Hartford Fire* case, are major suppliers of reinsurance to the U.S. market. As the *Hartford Fire* decision indicates, state regulators exercise some degree of control over foreign reinsurers, but the extent of that control is not as extensive or thorough as the supervision of domestic companies. Some analysts have expressed concern that the failure of one or more major foreign reinsurers could jeopardize the solvency of domestic insurers, particularly if the failure occurred in the aftermath of a major natural disaster (such as substantial hurricane or earthquake) which could force a large number of domestic insurers to recover on their reinsurance policies. For an introduction to this area of insurance regulation, see Insurance Regulation: State Reinsurance Oversight Increased, but Problems Remain (May 1990) (GAO/GGD-90-82).

3.   Problems presented by foreign reinsurers also figure into the perennial debate over whether the federal government should play a more active role in the insurance industry. Consider the legislative proposal described in the following press account.

### Dingell Unveils Insurance Industry Bill
Wall St. J., Apr. 10, 1992, at A6

Rep. John Dingell, chairman of the Energy and Commerce Committee, introduced his long-awaited bill to impose federal regulation for the first time on the insurance industry.

The 234-page bill, the product of years of investigation into the insurance industry, is unlikely to pass this late in the congressional session. But the clout of the Michigan Democrat makes the bill of acute importance to insurers because it increases the likelihood of some form of federal regulation in the industry. The insurers largely oppose federal regulation in favor of the current state-by-state system.

Under the bill, a Federal Insurance Solvency Commission, modeled after the Securities and Exchange Commission, would be the sole financial regulator for companies that meet certain minimum standards for capital and other safety measures. The commission would have the authority to suspend or revoke certificates for financially weak companies or for those that fail to comply with standards. It also would certify reinsurance companies, as well as foreign insurers operating in the U.S.

These federally certified insurers would be required to join a National Insurance Protection Corp., which would cover the claims of policyholders at failed companies. Those claims would be paid by other solvent companies; the U.S. government wouldn't guarantee the federal program. . . .

States would continue to monitor the safety of insurance companies that chose not to join the federal system, or didn't meet federal standards. States, moreover, also would continue to regulate rates and marketing rules.

But such a dual system is what the industry fears most. "If there is any lesson of the S&Ls and banks, it's that there are serious problems with a dual system," said William McCartney, president of the National Association of Insurance Commissioners and insurance commissioner for Nebraska. "You wind up with no one in charge."

Do you agree that it would be impractical to impose a federal system of solvency regulation for large insurance companies and general oversight of reinsurance companies? How burdensome would it be to retain rate and other regulatory functions at the state level? The NAIC's accreditation program (discussed in Chapter Seven, Section 3.B) was originally envisioned as an alterative to the nationalization of insurance regulation. Which is better?

4. Another less intrusive way for the federal government to increase its role in insurance regulation would be to amend the McCarran-Ferguson Act to allow federal anti-trust laws to govern a broader range of insurance industry activities. For example, in 1991, House Judiciary Committee Chairman Jack Brooks introduced the Insurance Competitive Pricing Act, which would have prohibited insurance companies from engaging in "price-fixing" and certain other anti-competitive practices. Should federal authority be extended in this way?

# Section 3. Employee Benefit Plans Under ERISA

The McCarran-Ferguson Act is not the only piece of federal legislation that affects the allocation of federal and state regulation in the insurance field. The Employee Retirement Income Security Act of 1974, as amended ("ERISA"), also has an important impact on how many American obtain certain kinds of insurance. Though principally concerned with retirement benefits, ERISA also extends to employer-sponsored plans providing "medical, surgical, or hospital care or benefits, or benefits in the event of sickness, accident, disability, death or unemployment, or vacation benefits, apprenticeship or other training services, or day care centers, scholarship funds, or prepaid legal services." Section 3(1)(A) of ERISA. In other words, whenever a private employer offers a fringe benefit that insures employees against risks, ERISA's regulatory requirements potentially come into play. In many instances, those requirements supersede otherwise applicable state insurance laws.

ERISA's substantive requirements are extraordinarily complex and generally beyond the scope of this casebook. (For an excellent introduction to the subject, see JOHN H. LANGBEIN & BRUCE A. WOLK, PENSION AND EMPLOYEE BENEFIT LAW (2d ed. 1995).) The basic structure of these requirements will, however, be familiar to studentsacquainted with other forms of financial-institution regulation. For example, ERISA plans must file periodic financial reports with the federal agencies charged with enforcing the statute (the

Department of Labor, the Internal Revenue Service, and for some plans the Pension Benefit Guaranty Corporation (PBGC)). Plan participants must also receive summary plan descriptions on a regular basis. Financial resources committed to ERISA plans must generally be held in trust, and federal fiduciary standards govern the management of these assets, requiring among other things that the resources be prudently invested and used for the exclusive benefit of plan participants and beneficiaries. In addition, ERISA imposes strict prohibited transaction rules designed to prevent plan fiduciaries and sponsors from doing business with affiliated ERISA plans.

For pension plans governed by ERISA, an additional layer of rules applies. To begin with, ERISA imposes funding requirements -- similar to capital requirements for the depository institution or reserve requirements in the insurance field -- to insure that pension plans have sufficient resources to meet their obligations to plan participants and beneficiaries. Participants in ERISA pension plans are also protected by mandatory vesting and accrual rules, designed to prevent employers from revoking pension promises or otherwise frustrating the expectations of beneficiaries and participants. Some ERISA-regulated pension plans are further protected by PBGC insurance, similar to FDIC coverage for bank and thrift deposits or state guaranty fund coverage for many insurance policies. Finally, ERISA imposes an elaborate system of "anti-discrimination" rules on pension plans intended to ensure that employers provide lower-paid workers pension benefits comparable to those offered higher-paid workers. The anti-discrimination rules and many other ERISA provisions are largely enforced through the Internal Revenue Code which conditions favorable tax treatment on a plan's meeting a host of ERISA requirements. See I.R.C. § 401(a). Among other things, these Internal Revenue Code rules puts a cap on the amount of contributions employers are permitted to make to their pension plans each year and also limits the terms on which participants can make withdrawals from pensions or assign interests in plan assets.

From this very summary description of ERISA's requirements, how would you say the regime compares to others that you have already studied? Consider the following discussion of ERISA and its relationship to earlier legal regimes.

## Robert C. Clark, The Four Stages of Capitalism
### 94 Harv. L. Rev. 561, 562-73 (1981)

The history of capitalist enterprise in the United States over the last two hundred years can be meaningfully organized into four distinct stages. The progression between stages displays a dual theme that suggests that some important basic processes are continually at work in our economy. [E]ach stage is characterized by a distinctive set of problems to which the legal system has tried to respond by employing regulatory strategies appropriate for that stage. . . .

### A. The Four Stages

The four stages are like generations. They overlap with one another -- indeed, none are dead, and all may continue indefinitely -- but each in turn has had its own time of rapid growth. Each stage has its characteristic business entity . . . . The first stage is the age of the entrepreneur, the fabled promoter-investor-manager who launched large-scale business organizations in corporate form for the first time in history. (Depending on one's perspective, he might also be called the "bourgeois capitalist" or the "robber baron.") He was primarily a nineteenth century phenomenon. The objective correlate of his activity was the rise of the corporation as a form of business organization. Its legal correlates were the increased enactment of general incorporation statutes and "enabling" laws.

The second stage, which reached adulthood in the first few decades of the twentieth century, is the age of the professional business manager. He appeared when the entrepreneurial function was split into ownership and control. . . . The characteristic institution of the age was the modern publicly held corporation. The second stage required the legal system to develop stable relationships between professional managers and public investors, ostensibly aimed at keeping the former accountable to the latter, but also at placing full control of business decisions in the managers' hands. A major legal correlate was the enactment of the federal securities laws during the Depression. . . .

The third stage of capitalism has been growing since the beginning of this century, and probably reached young adulthood in the 1960's. It is the age of the portfolio manager, and its characteristic institution is the institutional investor, or financial intermediary. As the second stage split entrepreneurship into ownership and control, and professionalized the latter, so the third stage split ownership into capital supplying and investment, and professionalized the investment function. . . .

The increasing separation of the decision about how to invest from the decision to supply capital for investment is one of the most striking institutional developments in our century. Since 1900, the proportion of savings channeled through financial intermediaries has grown steadily, and about eighty cents of every dollar saved now finds its way to some intermediary. Concomitantly, the role of financial intermediaries in the major financial markets has increased. Consider all financial claims (stocks, bonds, and other debt instruments) against ultimate users of capital funds (governments, corporations, and home buyers). Since World War II, the proportion of such claims held directly by individual investors or "households" has significantly decreased, and the proportion held by financial intermediaries (banks, thrift institutions, insurance companies, pension plans, and investment companies) has increased. The relative volume of trading in financial claims by individuals and institutions shows a similar, even strong, trend. The institutionalization of the major American stock exchanges is only part of the phenomenon; equally important is the large role played by institutional investors in the other major kinds of capital markets -- those for corporate bonds, governmental securities of various types, and home mortgages -- and the growth of financial intermediation in the rest of the capitalist world.

Can the fourth stage be predicted? It can, for it is already discernible in its infancy. One fumbles for an apt label, but perhaps it could be called the age of the savings planner. Just as the third stage split the capital ownership function into the decision to supply capital funds and active investment management, and professionalized the latter, so the fourth stage seems intent upon splitting capital supplying into the possession of beneficial claims and the decision to save, and professionalizing the savings-decision function. Today, decisions about whether and how much to save are increasingly being made by group representatives on behalf of a large number of group members, rather than by each individual whose present consumption is being deferred in favor of future consumption. The objective signs of this change are the steadily increasing predominance of group over individual health and life insurance policies, and the rapid growth since World War II of employee pension plans, especially as compared to the relative stagnancy of the individual annuities business. Today, the decision to save is only indirectly controlled by many of the workers who are to benefit from these plans (which can no longer accurately be described as "fringe" benefits), just as the decision to invest in particular financial claims is only rarely controlled by public suppliers of capital to financial intermediaries. And those new professional savings planners -- for example, the sponsors and administrators of large corporate pension plans -- rarely perform the active investment function. Most pension plan sponsors and administrators contract with outside bank trust departments, insurance companies, and investment advisory firms for investment management services. . . .

### B. The Succession of Regulatory Strategies

In stage one, large-scale corporate enterprises were perceived by many persons as problematic or dangerous. They might grow too fast, do too much, accumulate excessive power, or corrupt markets and legislatures. Among the methods used in the fitful attempts to protect society from them were individual chartering by legislatures, sharp limits on the powers and "personality" of the corporate entity, and the antitrust laws. By the turn of the century, the first two strategies had been abandoned. The legal system also aimed at protecting the entrepreneurs from one another. A large part of traditional, nonfederal "corporate" law, much of which retains force and utility in the context of closely held corporations, arose to establish rules of fair play among the members of the relatively small entrepreneurial groups involved with stage one corporations. These participant were typically viewed as inhabiting the same peer group. Although inequalities of power would certainly exist in particular enterprises, the participants often shared reasonably good access to information and a realistic ability to enter individualized consensual arrangements with one another.

The basic problem presented to the legal system by the second stage was concentrating and legitimating power over business decisions in the hands of professional managers, while nevertheless providing controls of some sort over their use of that power. The controls were designed to keep the professionals working in the interest of the public security holders, so that the confidence of the latter would not be lost, and their investable funds wasted. It came to be recognized that they were not in the same peer group as their managers. Their access to information was systematically poorer, and the transaction costs of entering into individualized consensual arrangements with managers were often forbidding. The basic strategies were not those of limiting corporate powers and attributes and mandating fair interactions, but those of facilitating the growth of efficient securities markets and making managers responsible for breach of externally imposed -- and frequently nonnegotiable -- fiduciary duties, many of which concerned transactions in publicly traded corporate securities. Market facilitation was important because managers are strongly, though often impersonally disciplined by effectively functioning capital markets. Their failure to maximize profits produces difficulty in raising new capital, and thus increases the threat of takeover and ouster. Congress attempted to facilitate the growth and functioning of capital markets by such techniques as affirmative disclosure requirements, antifraud rules, and government control over immediate market participants such as broker-dealer firms -- in brief, by enacting the federal securities laws. By contrast, much of the task of developing operational meanings for the open-ended fiduciary duties of managers was left to the state courts, which also deployed a clever and potent enforcement mechanism, the stockholders' derivative action.

But disclosure and conflict-of-interest rules assume less significance in the third stage. Stage two capitalists were still *investment* decisionmakers, and so could be protected by adequate and accurate information relevant to such decisionmaking, and assurance that business managers did not cheat them by violating the explicit or implicit conditions of their grant of power.  Stage three capitalists are very little involved, however, in the process of choosing investments.  Indeed, a major efficiency advantage of financial intermediation is *precisely* that it frees capital suppliers from having to know about portfolio management and the relative merits of specific issuers of securities.  Their only investment decision is whether to relinquish funds to a particular intermediary.  It would make little sense, obviously, to hold capital suppliers at their own peril to assess and assume whatever risks were presented by the intermediaries, since that would force them to duplicate the portfolio managers' efforts and thus defeat the scheme.  Moreover, many individual capital suppliers could be quite distressed by adverse fluctuations in their share of capital income.  The basic regulatory approach to this situation can be summed up in the concept of soundness.  By a variety of methods, public suppliers of capital are insulated from the consequences of financial failure of intermediaries.  This general aim has clearly and consistently been the generative, unifying force behind a staggering multiplicity of laws and regulations affecting banks, insurance companies, and the like.

In the fourth stage, the broad general orientation of regulatory efforts must shift yet again. Legislators and courts are moving beyond power limits and fair play, beyond disclosure and fiduciary duties, and beyond soundness regulation, to what might be called consumer protection. Of course, beneficiaries of employee benefit plans depend on the soundness of the plans, and their portfolio managers depend on the issuing companies to disclose adequate information.  But the beneficiaries must also be concerned about the terms upon which they are brought into or excluded from a collectivity of savers, and the ways in which their interests in a benefit plan are conditioned and limited.  Consequently, it was virtually inevitable that pension fund legislation such as the Employee Retirement Income Security Act of 1974 (ERISA) would include major provisions concerning acceptable participation, vesting, benefit-accrual, and break-in-service rules.  Moreover, the most important *disclosure* provisions of employee benefit law are not those that require disclosure about a plan's investment assets, but rather are those that tell the employee about his terms of participation and his particular expected benefits.  Only with such information can the employee rationally exercise whatever discretion he retains to trade off work against leisure, and present against future consumption. . . .

In significant measure, the regulatory techniques most characteristic of the earlier stages are not completely abandoned in the regulatory system governing the institutions typical of the later stages. ERISA, for example, imposes funding requirements and plan termination insurance -- that is, soundness regulation -- on many pension plans.  Indeed, in some respects older regulatory techniques may be intensified:  conflict-of-interest regulation is stricter for banks and insurance companies than for ordinary business corporations, for example, and under ERISA employee benefit plans are subject to the most stringent conflict-of-interest regulation.  But the main point is that with each new stage a fundamentally new *kind* of regulation is added. . . .

## Comments and Questions

1. Dean Clark's provocative essay traces the evolution of legal institutions from corporate law, through the regulation of securities and investment managers, down to the law of savings planners, as exemplified by ERISA. Where would you place depository institutions and traditional insurance companies into his framework?

2. More than a decade and a half has passed since this essay was published. Has the era of the savings planner continued to unfold? Within the world of pension law, one of the most striking developments of the past decade has been the expansion of self-directed 401(k) plans in which individual employees decide both how much of their income to set aside for retirement savings and how that savings should be invested. (Recall our analysis of various 401(k) investments in Executive Life GICs in Chapter Seven, section 3.) Is this development representative of a society in the fourth stage of capitalism? Should ERISA be amended to prohibit this kind of individual participation in retirement savings?

## A. Preemption of State Law

In terms of the structure of financial regulation in the United States, one of the most interesting aspects of ERISA is its relationship to state insurance law. That relationship is defined by section 514 of ERISA which states in relevant part:

(a) Except as provided in subsection (b) of this section, the provisions of [ERISA] supersede any and all State laws insofar as they may now or hereafter relate to any employee benefit plan . . . .

(b) . . . .(2)

(A) Except as provided in subparagraph (B), nothing in this subchapter shall be construed to exempt or relieve any person from any law of any State which regulates insurance, banking, or securities.

(B) Neither an employee benefit plan . . . nor any trust established under such a plan, shall be deemed to be an insurance company or other insurer, bank, trust company, or investment company or to be engaged in the business of insurance or banking for purposes of any law of any State purporting to regulate insurance companies, insurance contracts, banks, trust companies, or investment companies.

ERISA's preemption provision is essentially the inverse of the McCarran-Ferguson Act. Rather than establishing a presumption of state authority, ERISA's expressly trumps local law. The scope of the preemption is also unusually broad — displacing not just conflicting state rules, but all state laws that "relate to" employee benefit plans. The preemption provision does, however, have limits. Subsection 514(b)(2)(A), known as the "savings clause," carves out an exception for state insurance, banking, and securities regulation. However, the savings clause is itself limited by subsection (b)(2)(B), the "deemer clause," which stipulates that ERISA plans shall not be "deemed" to be financial institutions for purposes of local regulation.  The tension between the savings clause and the deemer clause is discussed below.

A combination of reasons explain ERISA's strong bias for federal law in the field of employee benefit plans.  In part, the Congress that enacted ERISA was concerned that large national corporations could be burdened by conflicting and opportunistic local regulations if the state were retained concurrent jurisdiction over ERISA plans.  In part too, the premise of ERISA was that the statute would establish a regulatory framework in which employers and employees would have considerable freedom to bargain over appropriate fringe benefit packages.  So, while ERISA sets various parameters on fringe benefits, much is left to private negotiation.  The mandatory nature of state insurance and other local rules, it was thought, might conflict with this contractual model (*see* Daniel M. Fox & Daniel Schaffer, *Semi-Preemption in ERISA*, 7 AM. J. TAX POLICY 47 (1988)), and so a strong preemption provision was added to the final version of the statute.  In addition, the political climate at the time of ERISA's enactment — the summer of 1974 — was a high-water mark for national and congressional power in the United States.  In this environment it seemed entirely reasonable to make federal authority exclusive.

Whatever policies underlay its enactment, the ERISA preemption provision has been one of the most litigated sections of the United State Code.  Since 1974, the Supreme Court has decided more than a dozen cases interpreting this provision.  Even after all this judicial attention, the provision remains a constant source of dispute and litigation.  As you read through the following three illustrative cases, consider why it is that the courts have had such difficulty interpreting section 514 of ERISA.  Is there a better way to divide jurisdiction between federal and state authorities in this field?

# Metropolitan Life Insurance Co. v. Massachusetts
## 471 U.S. 724 (1985)

Justice BLACKMUN delivered the opinion of the Court.

A Massachusetts statute requires that specified minimum mental-health-care benefits be provided a Massachusetts resident who is insured under a general insurance policy, an accident or sickness insurance policy, or an employee health-care plan that covers hospital and surgical expenses.  The question before us  is whether the state statute, as applied to insurance policies purchased by employee health-care plans regulated by the federal Employee Retirement Income Security Act of 1974, is pre-empted by that Act.

### I

### A

General health insurance typically is sold as group insurance to an employer or other group. Group insurance presently is subject to extensive state regulation, including regulation of the carrier, regulation of the sale and advertising of the insurance, and regulation of the content of the contracts. Mandated-benefit laws, that require an insurer to provide a certain kind of benefit to cover a specified illness or procedure whenever someone purchases a certain kind of insurance, are a subclass of such content regulation.

While mandated-benefit statutes are a relatively recent phenomenon, statutes regulating the substantive terms of insurance contracts have become commonplace in all 50 States over the last 30 years. . . . The substantive terms of group-health insurance contracts, in particular, also have been extensively regulated by the States. For example, the majority of States currently require that coverage for dependents continue beyond any contractually imposed age limitation when the dependent is incapable of self-sustaining employment because of mental or physical handicap; such statutes date back to the early 1960's. And over the last 15 years all 50 States have required that coverage of infants begin at birth, rather than at some time shortly after birth, as had been the prior practice in the unregulated market. Many state statutes require that insurers offer on an optional basis particular kinds of coverage to purchasers. Others require insurers either to offer or mandate that insurance policies include coverage for services rendered by a particular type of health-care provider.

Mandated-benefit statutes, then, are only one variety of a matrix of state laws that regulate the substantive content of health-insurance policies to further state health policy. Massachusetts Gen.Laws Ann., ch. 175, § 47B (West Supp.1985), is typical of mandated-benefit laws currently in place in the majority of States. With respect to a Massachusetts resident, it requires any general health-insurance policy that provides hospital and surgical coverage, or any benefit plan that has such coverage, to provide as well a certain minimum of mental-health protection. In particular, § 47B requires that a health-insurance policy provide 60 days of coverage for confinement in a mental hospital, coverage for confinement in a general hospital equal to that provided by the policy for nonmental illness, and certain minimum outpatient benefits.

Section 47B was designed to address problems encountered in treating mental illness in Massachusetts. The Commonwealth determined that its working people needed to be protected against the high cost of treatment for such illness. It also believed that, without insurance, mentally ill workers were often institutionalized in large state mental hospitals, and that mandatory insurance would lead to a higher incidence of more effective treatment in private community mental-health centers. . . .

In addition, the Commonwealth concluded that the voluntary insurance market was not adequately providing mental-health coverage, because of "adverse selection" in mental-health insurance: good insurance risks were not purchasing coverage, and this drove up the price of coverage for those who otherwise might purchase mental-health insurance. The legislature believed that the public interest required that it correct the insurance market in the Commonwealth by mandating minimum-coverage levels, effectively forcing the good-risk individuals to become part of the risk pool, and enabling insurers to price the insurance at an average market rather than a market retracted due to adverse selection. Section 47B, then, was intended to help safeguard the public against the high costs of comprehensive inpatient and outpatient mental-health care, reduce nonpsychiatric medical-care expenditures for mentally related illness, shift the delivery of treatment from inpatient to outpatient services, and relieve the Commonwealth of some of the financial burden it otherwise would encounter with respect to mental-health problems.

It is our task in these cases to decide whether such insurance regulation violates or is inconsistent with federal law.

## B

The federal Employee Retirement Income Security Act of 1974 (ERISA) comprehensively regulates employee pension and welfare plans. An employee welfare-benefit plan or welfare plan is defined as one which provides to employees "medical, surgical, or hospital care or benefits, or benefits in the event of sickness, accident, disability [or] death," whether these benefits are provided "through the purchase of insurance or otherwise." § 3(1). Plans may self-insure or they may purchase insurance for their participants. Plans that purchase insurance--so-called "insured plans"--are directly affected by state laws that regulate the insurance industry.

ERISA imposes upon pension plans a variety of substantive requirements relating to participation, funding, and vesting. §§ 201-306. It also establishes various uniform procedural standards concerning reporting, disclosure, and fiduciary responsibility for both pension and welfare plans. §§ 101-111, 401-414. It does not regulate the substantive content of welfare-benefit plans. See Shaw v. Delta Air Lines, Inc., 463 U.S. 85, 91 (1983).

ERISA thus contains almost no federal regulation of the terms of benefit plans. It does, however, contain a broad pre-emption provision declaring that the statute shall "supersede any and all State laws insofar as they may now or hereafter relate to any employee benefit plan." § 514(a). Appellant Metropolitan argues that ERISA preempts Massachusetts' mandated-benefit law insofar as § 47B restricts the kinds of insurance policies that benefit plans may purchase.

While § 514(a) of ERISA broadly pre-empts state laws that relate to an employee-benefit plan, that pre-emption is substantially qualified by an "insurance saving clause," § 514(b)(2)(A),, which broadly states that, with one exception, nothing in ERISA "shall be construed to exempt or relieve any person from any law of any State which regulates insurance, banking, or securities." The specified exception to the saving clause is found in § 514(b)(2)(B), the so-called "deemer clause," which states that no employee-benefit plan, with certain exceptions not relevant here, "shall be deemed to be an insurance company or other insurer, bank, trust company, or investment company or to be engaged in the business of insurance or banking for purposes of any law of any State purporting to regulate insurance companies, insurance contracts, banks, trust companies, or investment companies." Massachusetts argues that its mandated-benefit law, as applied to insurance companies that sell insurance to benefit plans, is a "law which regulates insurance," and therefore is saved from the effect of the general pre-emption clause of ERISA.

## II

Appellants are Metropolitan Life Insurance Company and Travelers Insurance Company (insurers) who are located in New York and Connecticut respectively and who issue group-health policies providing hospital and surgical coverage to plans, or to employers or unions that employ or represent employees residing in Massachusetts. Under the terms of § 47B, both appellants are required to provide minimal mental-health benefits in policies issued to cover Commonwealth residents.

In 1979, the Attorney General of Massachusetts brought suit in Massachusetts Superior Court for declaratory and injunctive relief to enforce § 47B. The Commonwealth asserted that since January 1, 1976, the effective date of § 47B, the insurers had issued policies to group policyholders situated outside Massachusetts that provided for hospital and surgical coverage for certain residents of the Commonwealth. It further asserted that those policies failed to provide Massachusetts-resident beneficiaries the mental- health coverage mandated by § 47B, and that the insurers intended to issue more such policies, believing themselves not bound by § 47B for policies issued outside the Commonwealth. In their answer, the insurers admitted these allegations.

## III

. . . . The narrow statutory ERISA question presented is whether Mass.Gen.Laws Ann., ch. 175, § 47B (West Supp.1985), is a law "which regulates insurance" within the meaning of § 514(b)(2)(A), and so would not be pre-empted by § 514(a).

### A

Section 47B clearly "relate[s] to" welfare plans governed by ERISA so as to fall within the reach of ERISA's pre-emption provision, § 514(a). The broad scope of the pre-emption clause was noted recently in Shaw v. Delta Air Lines, Inc., supra, where we held that the New York Human Rights Law and that State's Disability Benefits Law "relate[d] to" welfare plans governed by ERISA. The phrase "relate to" was given its broad common-sense meaning, such that a state law "relate[s] to" a benefit plan "in the normal sense of the phrase, if it has a connection with or reference to such a plan." 463 U.S., at 97. The pre-emption provision was intended to displace all state laws that fall within its sphere, even including state laws that are consistent with ERISA's substantive requirements. Id., at 98-99. "[E]ven indirect state action bearing on private pensions may encroach upon the area of exclusive federal concern." Alessi v. Raybestos- Manhattan, Inc., 451 U.S. 504, 525 (1981).

Though § 47B is not denominated a benefit-plan law, it bears indirectly but substantially on all insured benefit plans, for it requires them to purchase the mental-health benefits specified in the statute when they purchase a certain kind of common insurance policy. The Commonwealth does not argue that § 47B as applied to policies purchased by benefit plans does not relate to those plans, and we agree with the Supreme Judicial Court that the mandated-benefit law as applied relates to ERISA plans and thus is covered by ERISA's broad pre-emption provision set forth in § 514(a).

### B

Nonetheless, the sphere in which § 514(a) operates was explicitly limited by § 514(b)(2). The insurance saving clause preserves any state law "which regulates insurance, banking, or securities." The two pre-emption sections, while clear enough on their faces, perhaps are not a model of legislative drafting, for while the general pre-emption clause broadly pre-empts state law, the saving clause appears broadly to preserve the States' lawmaking power over much of the same regulation. While Congress occasionally decides to return to the States what it has previously taken away, it does not normally do both at the same time. . . .

To state the obvious, § 47B regulates the terms of certain insurance contracts, and so seems to be saved from pre-emption by the saving clause as a law "which regulates insurance." This common-sense view of the matter, moreover, is reinforced by the language of the subsequent subsection of ERISA, the "deemer clause," which states that an employee-benefit plan shall not be deemed to be an insurance company "for purposes of any law of any State purporting to regulate insurance companies, insurance contracts, banks, trust companies, or investment companies." § 514(b)(2)(B). By exempting from the saving clause laws regulating insurance contracts that apply directly to benefit plans, the deemer clause makes explicit Congress' intention to include laws that regulate insurance contracts within the scope of the insurance laws preserved by the saving clause. Unless Congress intended to include laws regulating insurance contracts within the scope of the insurance saving clause, it would have been unnecessary for the deemer clause explicitly to exempt such laws from the saving clause when they are applied directly to benefit plans.

The insurers nonetheless argue that § 47B is in reality a health law that merely operates on insurance contracts to accomplish its end, and that it is not the kind of traditional insurance law intended to be saved by § 514(b)(2)(A). We find this argument unpersuasive.

Initially, nothing in § 514(b)(2)(A), or in the "deemer clause" which modifies it, purports to distinguish between traditional and innovative insurance laws. The presumption is against pre-emption, and we are not inclined to read limitations into federal statutes in order to enlarge their pre-emptive scope. Further, there is no indication in the legislative history that Congress had such a distinction in mind.

Appellants assert that state laws that directly regulate the insurer, and laws that regulate such matters as the way in which insurance may be sold, are traditional laws subject to the clause, while laws that regulate the substantive terms of insurance contracts are recent innovations more properly seen as health laws rather than as insurance laws, which § 514(b)(2)(A) does not save. This distinction reads the saving clause out of ERISA entirely, because laws that regulate only the insurer, or the way in which it may sell insurance, do not "relate to" benefit plans in the first instance. Because they would not be pre-empted by § 514(a), they do not need to be "saved" by § 514(b)(2)(A). There is no indication that Congress could have intended the saving clause to operate only to guard against too expansive readings of the general pre-emption clause that might have included laws wholly unrelated to plans. Appellants' construction, in our view, violates the plain meaning of the statutory language and renders redundant both the saving clause it is construing, as well as the deemer clause which it precedes, and accordingly has little to recommend it.

Moreover, it is both historically and conceptually inaccurate to assert that mandated-benefit laws are not traditional insurance laws. As we have indicated, state laws regulating the substantive terms of insurance contracts were commonplace well before the mid-70's, when Congress considered ERISA. The case law concerning the meaning of the phrase "business of insurance" in the McCarran-Ferguson Act, also strongly supports the conclusion that regulation regarding the substantive terms of insurance contracts falls squarely within the saving clause as laws "which regulate insurance."

Cases interpreting the scope of the McCarran-Ferguson Act have identified three criteria relevant to determining whether a particular practice falls within that Act's reference to the "business of insurance": "*first*, whether the practice has the effect of transferring or spreading a policyholder's risk; *second*, whether the practice is an integral part of the policy relationship between the insurer and the insured; and *third*, whether the practice is limited to entities within the insurance industry." Union Labor Life Ins. Co. v. Pireno, 458 U.S. 119, 129 (1982) (emphasis in original). . . . Application of these principles suggests that mandated-benefit laws are state regulation of the "business of insurance."

Section 47B obviously regulates the spreading of risk: as we have indicated, it was intended to effectuate the legislative judgment that the risk of mental- health care should be shared. It is also evident that mandated-benefit laws directly regulate an integral part of the relationship between the insurer and the policyholder by limiting the type of insurance that an insurer may sell to the policyholder. Finally, the third criterion is present here, for mandated-benefit statutes impose requirements only on insurers, with the intent of affecting the relationship between the insurer and the policyholder.

Nor is there any contrary case authority suggesting that laws regulating the terms of insurance contracts should not be understood as laws that regulate insurance. In short, the plain language of the saving clause, its relationship to the other ERISA pre-emption provisions, and the traditional understanding of insurance regulation, all lead us to the conclusion that mandated-benefit laws such as § 47B are saved from pre-emption by the operation of the saving clause.[21]

Nothing in the legislative history of ERISA suggests a different result. There is no discussion in that history of the relationship between the general pre-emption clause and the saving clause, and indeed very little discussion of the saving clause at all. In the early versions of ERISA, the general pre-emption clause pre-empted only those state laws dealing with subjects regulated by ERISA. The clause was significantly broadened at the last minute, well after the saving clause was in its present form, to include all state laws that relate to benefit plans. The change was made with little explanation by the Conference Committee, and there is no indication in the legislative history that Congress was aware of the new prominence given the saving clause in light of the rewritten pre-emption clause, or was aware that the saving clause was in conflict with the general pre-emption provision. There is a complete absence of evidence that Congress intended the narrow reading of the saving clause suggested by appellants here. Appellants do call to our attention a few passing references in the record of the floor debate to the "narrow" exceptions to the pre-emption clause, but these are far too frail a support on which to rest appellants' rather unnatural reading of the clause.

We therefore decline to impose any limitation on the saving clause beyond those Congress imposed in the clause itself and in the "deemer clause" which modifies it. If a state law "regulates insurance," as mandated- benefit laws do, it is not pre-empted. Nothing in the language, structure, or legislative history of the Act supports a more narrow reading of the clause, whether it be the Supreme Judicial Court's attempt to save only state regulations unrelated to the

---

[21]    That mandated-benefit laws fall within the terms of the definition of insurance in the McCarran-Ferguson Act is directly relevant in another sense as well. Congress' "primary concern" in enacting McCarran-Ferguson was to "ensure that the States would continue to have the ability to tax and regulate the business of insurance." Group Life & Health Ins. Co. v. Royal Drug Co., 440 U.S. 205, 217-218 (1979). That Act provides: "The business of insurance, and every person engaged therein, shall be subject to the laws of the several States which relate to the regulation or taxation of such business." 59 Stat. 34, 15 U.S.C. § 1012(a). The ERISA saving clause, with its similarly worded protection of "any law of any State which regulates insurance," appears to have been designed to preserve the McCarran-Ferguson Act's reservation of the business of insurance to the States. The saving clause and the McCarran-Ferguson Act serve the same federal policy and utilize similar language to define what is left to the States. Moreover, § 514(d) of ERISA, 29 U.S.C. § 1144(d), explicitly states in part: "Nothing in [ERISA] shall be construed to alter, amend, modify, invalidate, impair, or supersede any law of the United States." Thus application of the McCarran- Ferguson Act lends further support to our ruling that Congress did not intend mandated-benefit laws to be pre-empted by ERISA.

substantive provisions of ERISA, or the insurers' more speculative attempt to read the saving clause out of the statute.

We are aware that our decision results in a distinction between insured and uninsured plans, leaving the former open to indirect regulation while the latter are not.  By so doing we merely give life to a distinction created by Congress in the "deemer clause," a distinction Congress is aware of and one it has chosen not to alter.[25]  We also are aware that appellants' construction of the statute would eliminate some of the disuniformities currently facing national plans that enter into local markets to purchase insurance.  Such disuniformities, however, are the inevitable result of the congressional decision to "save" local insurance regulation.  Arguments as to the wisdom of these policy choices must be directed at Congress.

## Comments and Questions

1. Mandatory benefits of the sort required by the Commonwealth of Massachusets in Section 47B are analogous to some of the provisions of the Utah statute we considered in connection with the *Pre-paid Dental Plan* case back in Chapter Seven, section 1.  From the perspective of public policy, should it matter that employers made the purchasing decision in this case, and not individual policy holders?

2.  In its interpretation of ERISA's savings clause, section 514(b)(2)(A), the *Metropolitan Life* decision incorporates the McCarran-Ferguson Act's "business of insurance" test.  Does the language of ERISA justify this interpretive convention?  Are there sound policy justifications for using the same test in the McCarran-Ferguson context and here?

3. In its final paragraphs, the *Metropolitan Life* decision distinguishes between group health plans purchased from a traditional insurance company and self-insured plans under which the employer itself bears the cost of medical expenses.  What is the significance of this distinction?  How would you expect employers to respond to this distinction?

---

[25]   A 1977 Activity Report of the House Committee on Education and Labor recognized the difference in treatment between insured and noninsured plans:  "To the extent that [certain programs selling insurance policies] fail to meet the definition of an 'employee benefit plan' [subject to the "deemer clause"], state regulation of them is not preempted by section 514, even though such state action is barred with respect to the plans which purchase these 'products.' "  H.R.Rep. No. 94-1785, p. 48.  A bill to amend the saving clause to specify that mandated-benefit laws are preempted by ERISA was reported to the Senate in 1981 but was not acted upon.

# FMC Corp. v. Holliday
## 498 U.S. 52 (1990)

Justice O'CONNOR delivered the opinion of the Court.

This case calls upon the Court to decide whether the Employee Retirement Income Security Act of 1974 (ERISA) pre-empts a Pennsylvania law precluding employee welfare benefit plans from exercising subrogation rights on a claimant's tort recovery.

I

Petitioner, FMC Corporation (FMC), operates the FMC Salaried Health Care Plan (Plan), an employee welfare benefit plan within the meaning of ERISA, § 3(1), that provides health benefits to FMC employees and their dependents. The Plan is self-funded; it does not purchase an insurance policy from any insurance company in order to satisfy its obligations to its participants. Among its provisions is a subrogation clause under which a Plan member agrees to reimburse the Plan for benefits paid if the member recovers on a claim in a liability action against a third party.

Respondent, Cynthia Ann Holliday, is the daughter of FMC employee and Plan member Gerald Holliday. In 1987, she was seriously injured in an automobile accident. The Plan paid a portion of her medical expenses. Gerald Holliday brought a negligence action on behalf of his daughter in Pennsylvania state court against the driver of the automobile in which she was injured. The parties settled the claim. While the action was pending, FMC notified the Hollidays that it would seek reimbursement for the amounts it had paid for respondent's medical expenses. The Hollidays replied that they would not reimburse the Plan, asserting that § 1720 of Pennsylvania's Motor Vehicle Financial Responsibility Law, 75 Pa.Cons.Stat. § 1720 (1987), precludes subrogation by FMC. Section 1720 states that "[i]n actions arising out of the maintenance or use of a motor vehicle, there shall be no right of subrogation or reimbursement from a claimant's tort recovery with respect to ... benefits ... payable under section 1719."[1] Section 1719 refers to benefit payments by "[a]ny program, group contract or other arrangement."

II

We indicated in Metropolitan Life Ins. Co. v. Massachusetts, 471 U.S. 724 (1985), that the[ ERISA preemption] provisions "are not a model of legislative drafting." Id., at 739. Their operation is nevertheless discernible. The pre-emption clause is conspicuous for its breadth. It establishes as an area of exclusive federal concern the subject of every state law that "relate[s]

---

[1]    Section 1720 of Pennsylvania's Motor Vehicle Financial Responsibility Law is entitled "[s]ubrogation" and provides:

"In actions arising out of the maintenance or use of a motor vehicle, there shall be no right of subrogation or reimbursement from a claimant's tort recovery with respect to workers' compensation benefits, benefits available under section 1711 (relating to required benefits), 1712 (relating to availability of benefits) or 1715 (relating to availability of adequate limits) or benefits in lieu thereof paid or payable under section 1719 (relating to coordination of benefits)."

to" an employee benefit plan governed by ERISA. The saving clause returns to the States the power to enforce those state laws that "regulat[e] insurance," except as provided in the deemer clause. Under the deemer clause, an employee benefit plan governed by ERISA shall not be "deemed" an insurance company, an insurer, or engaged in the business of insurance for purposes of state laws "purporting to regulate" insurance companies or insurance contracts.

### III

Pennsylvania's antisubrogation law "relate[s] to" an employee benefit plan. We made clear in Shaw v. Delta Air Lines, [463 U.S. 85, 95 (1983)] that a law relates to an employee welfare plan if it has "a connection with or reference to such a plan." Id., 463 U.S., at 96-97 (footnote omitted). We based our reading in part on the plain language of the statute. Congress used the words " 'relate to' in § 514(a) [the pre-emption clause] in their broad sense." Id., at 98. It did not mean to pre-empt only state laws specifically designed to affect employee benefit plans. That interpretation would have made it unnecessary for Congress to enact ERISA § 514(b)(4), which exempts from pre- emption "generally" applicable criminal laws of a State. We also emphasized that to interpret the pre-emption clause to apply only to state laws dealing with the subject matters covered by ERISA, such as reporting, disclosure, and fiduciary duties, would be incompatible with the provision's legislative history because the House and Senate versions of the bill that became ERISA contained limited pre-emption clauses, applicable only to state laws relating to specific subjects covered by ERISA. These were rejected in favor of the present language in the Act, "indicat[ing] that the section's pre-emptive scope was as broad as its language." Shaw v. Delta Air Lines, 463 U.S., at 98.

Pennsylvania's antisubrogation law has a "reference" to benefit plans governed by ERISA. The statute states that "[i]n actions arising out of the maintenance or use of a motor vehicle, there shall be no right of subrogation or reimbursement from a claimant's tort recovery with respect to ... benefits ... paid or payable under section 1719." 75 Pa.Cons.Stat. § 1720 (1987). Section 1719 refers to "[a]ny program, group contract or other arrangement for payment of benefits." These terms "includ[e], but [are] not limited to, benefits payable by a hospital plan corporation or a professional health service corporation." § 1719.

The Pennsylvania statute also has a "connection" to ERISA benefit plans. In the past, we have not hesitated to apply ERISA's pre-emption clause to state laws that risk subjecting plan administrators to conflicting state regulations. See, e.g., Shaw v. Delta Air Lines, supra, at 95-100 (state laws making unlawful plan provisions that discriminate on the basis of pregnancy and requiring plans to provide specific benefits "relate to" benefit plans); Alessi v. Raybestos-Manhattan, Inc., 451 U.S. 504, 523-526 (1981) (state law prohibiting plans from reducing benefits by amount of workers' compensation awards "relate[s] to" employee benefit plan). To require plan providers to design their programs in an environment of differing state regulations would complicate the administration of nationwide plans, producing inefficiencies that employers might offset with decreased benefits. See Fort Halifax Packing Co. v. Coyne, 482 U.S. 1, 10 (1987). Thus, where a "patchwork scheme of regulation would introduce considerable inefficiencies in benefit program operation," we have applied the pre-emption clause to ensure that benefit plans will be governed by only a single set of regulations. Id., at 11.

Pennsylvania's antisubrogation law prohibits plans from being structured in a manner requiring reimbursement in the event of recovery from a third party. It requires plan providers to calculate benefit levels in Pennsylvania based on expected liability conditions that differ from those in States that have not enacted similar antisubrogation legislation. Application of differing state subrogation laws to plans would therefore frustrate plan administrators' continuing obligation to calculate uniform benefit levels nationwide. Accord, Alessi v. Raybestos-Manhattan, Inc., supra (state statute prohibiting offsetting worker compensation payments against pension benefits pre-empted since statute would force employer either to structure all benefit payments in accordance with state statute or adopt different payment formulae for employers inside and outside State). As we stated in Fort Halifax Packing Co. v. Coyne, supra, at 9, "[t]he most efficient way to meet these [administrative] responsibilities is to establish a uniform administrative scheme, which provides a set of standard procedures to guide processing of claims and disbursement of benefits."

There is no dispute that the Pennsylvania law falls within ERISA's insurance saving clause, which provides, "[e]xcept as provided in [the deemer clause], nothing in this subchapter shall be construed to exempt or relieve any person from any law of any State which regulates insurance," § 514(b)(2)(A). Section 1720 directly controls the terms of insurance contracts by invalidating any subrogation provisions that they contain. See Metropolitan Life Ins. Co. v. Massachusetts, 471 U.S., at 740-741. It does not merely have an impact on the insurance industry; it is aimed at it. See Pilot Life Ins. Co. v. Dedeaux, 481 U.S. 41, 50 (1987). This returns the matter of subrogation to state law. Unless the statute is excluded from the reach of the saving clause by virtue of the deemer clause, therefore, it is not pre-empted.

We read the deemer clause to exempt self-funded ERISA plans from state laws that "regulat[e] insurance" within the meaning of the saving clause. By forbidding States to deem employee benefit plans "to be an insurance company or other insurer ... or to be engaged in the business of insurance," the deemer clause relieves plans from state laws "purporting to regulate insurance." As a result, self-funded ERISA plans are exempt from state regulation insofar as that regulation "relate[s] to" the plans. State laws directed toward the plans are pre-empted because they relate to an employee benefit plan but are not "saved" because they do not regulate insurance. State laws that directly regulate insurance are "saved" but do not reach self-funded employee benefit plans because the plans may not be deemed to be insurance companies, other insurers, or engaged in the business of insurance for purposes of such state laws. On the other hand, employee benefit plans that are insured are subject to indirect state insurance regulation. An insurance company that insures a plan remains an insurer for purposes of state laws "purporting to regulate insurance" after application of the deemer clause. The insurance company is therefore not relieved from state insurance regulation. The ERISA plan is consequently bound by state insurance regulations insofar as they apply to the plan's insurer.

Our reading of the deemer clause is consistent with Metropolitan Life Ins. Co. v. Massachusetts, supra. That case involved a Massachusetts statute requiring certain self-funded benefit plans and insurers issuing group health policies to plans to provide minimum mental health benefits. Id., 471 U.S., at 734. In pointing out that Massachusetts had never tried to enforce the portion of the statute pertaining directly to benefit plans, we stated, "[i]n light of ERISA's 'deemer clause,' which states that a benefit plan shall not 'be deemed an insurance company' for purposes of the insurance saving clause, Massachusetts has never tried to enforce [the statute] as applied to benefit plans directly, effectively conceding that such an application of [the statute] would be pre-empted by ERISA's pre-emption clause." Id., at 735, n. 14 (citations omitted). We concluded that the statute, as applied to insurers of plans, was not pre-empted because it regulated insurance and was therefore saved. Our decision, we acknowledged, "results in a distinction between insured and uninsured plans, leaving the former open to indirect regulation while the latter are not." Id., at 747. "By so doing, we merely give life to a distinction created by Congress in the 'deemer clause,' a distinction Congress is aware of and one it has chosen not to alter." Ibid.

Our construction of the deemer clause is also respectful of the presumption that Congress does not intend to pre-empt areas of traditional state regulation. See Jones v. Rath Packing Co., 430 U.S., at 525. In the McCarran-Ferguson Act, 59 Stat. 33, as amended, 15 U.S.C. § 1011 et seq., Congress provided that the "business of insurance, and every person engaged therein, shall be subject to the laws of the several States which relate to the regulation or taxation of such business." 15 U.S.C. § 1012(a). We have identified laws governing the "business of insurance" in the Act to include not only direct regulation of the insurer but also regulation of the substantive terms of insurance contracts. Metropolitan Life Ins. Co. v. Massachusetts, supra, 471 U.S., at 742-744. By recognizing a distinction between insurers of plans and the contracts of those insurers, which are subject to direct state regulation, and self-insured employee benefit plans governed by ERISA, which are not, we observe Congress' presumed desire to reserve to the States the regulation of the "business of insurance."

Respondent resists our reading of the deemer clause and would attach to it narrower significance. According to the deemer clause, "[n]either an employee benefit plan ... nor any trust established under such a plan, shall be deemed to be an insurance company or other insurer, bank, trust company, or investment company or to be engaged in the business of insurance or banking for purposes of any law of any State purporting to regulate insurance companies [or] insurance contracts." § 514(b)(2)(B). Like the Court of Appeals, respondent would interpret the deemer clause to except from the saving clause only state insurance regulations that are pretexts for impinging upon core ERISA concerns. The National Conference of State Legislatures et al. as amici curiae in support of respondent offer an alternative interpretation of the deemer clause. In their view, the deemer clause precludes States from deeming plans to be insurers only for purposes of state laws that apply to insurance as a business, such as laws relating to licensing and capitalization requirements.

These views are unsupported by ERISA's language. Laws that purportedly regulate insurance companies or insurance contracts are laws having the "appearance of" regulating or "intending" to regulate insurance companies or contracts. Black's Law Dictionary 1236 (6th ed.1990). Congress' use of the word does not indicate that it directed the deemer clause solely at deceit that it feared state legislatures would practice. Indeed, the Conference Report, in describing the deemer clause, omits the word "purporting," stating, "an employee benefit plan is not to be considered as an insurance company, bank, trust company, or investment company (and is not to be considered as engaged in the business of insurance or banking) for purposes of any State law that regulates insurance companies, insurance contracts, banks, trust companies, or investment companies." H.R.Conf.Rep. No. 93-1280, p. 383 (1974), U.S.Code Cong. & Admin.News 1974, pp. 4639, 5162.

Nor, in our view, is the deemer clause directed solely at laws governing the business of insurance. It is plainly directed at "any law of any State purporting to regulate insurance companies, insurance contracts, banks, trust companies, or investment companies." § 514(b)(2)(B). Moreover, it is difficult to understand why Congress would have included insurance contracts in the pre-emption clause if it meant only to pre-empt state laws relating to the operation of insurance as a business. To be sure, the saving and deemer clauses employ differing language to achieve their ends--the former saving, except as provided in the deemer clause, "any law of any State which regulates insurance" and the latter referring to "any law of any State purporting to regulate insurance companies [or] insurance contracts." We view the language of the deemer clause, however, to be either coextensive with or broader, not narrower, than that of the saving clause. Our rejection of a restricted reading of the deemer clause does not lead to the deemer clause's engulfing the saving clause. As we have pointed out, the saving clause retains the independent effect of protecting state insurance regulation of insurance contracts purchased by employee benefit plans.

Congress intended by ERISA to "establish pension plan regulation as exclusively a federal concern." Alessi v. Raybestos-Manhattan, Inc., 451 U.S., at 523 (footnote omitted). Our interpretation of the deemer clause makes clear that if a plan is insured, a State may regulate it indirectly through regulation of its insurer and its insurer's insurance contracts; if the plan is uninsured, the State may not regulate it. As a result, employers will not face " 'conflicting or inconsistent State and local regulation of employee benefit plans.' " Shaw v. Delta Air Lines, Inc., 463 U.S., at 99 (quoting remarks of Sen. Williams). A construction of the deemer clause that exempts employee benefit plans from only those state regulations that encroach upon core ERISA concerns or that apply to insurance as a business would be fraught with administrative difficulties, necessitating definition of core ERISA concerns and of what constitutes business activity. It would therefore undermine Congress' desire to avoid "endless litigation over the validity of State action," see 120 Cong.Rec. 29942 (1974) (remarks of Sen. Javits), and instead lead to employee benefit plans' expenditure of funds in such litigation.

In view of Congress' clear intent to exempt from direct state insurance regulation ERISA employee benefit plans, we hold that ERISA pre-empts the application of § 1720 of Pennsylvania's Motor Vehicle Financial Responsibility Law to the FMC Salaried Health Care Plan. We therefore vacate the judgment of the United States Court of Appeals for the Third Circuit and remand the case for further proceedings consistent with this opinion.

Justice STEVENS, dissenting.

The Court's construction of the statute draws a broad and illogical distinction between benefit plans that are funded by the employer (self-insured plans) and those that are insured by regulated insurance companies (insured plans). Had Congress intended this result, it could have stated simply that "all State laws are pre-empted insofar as they relate to any self-insured employee plan." There would then have been no need for the "saving clause" to exempt state insurance laws from the pre-emption clause, or the "deemer clause," which the Court today reads as merely reinjecting into the scope of ERISA's pre-emption clause those same exempted state laws insofar as they relate to self-insured plans.

From the standpoint of the beneficiaries of ERISA plans--who after all are the primary beneficiaries of the entire statutory program--there is no apparent reason for treating self-insured plans differently from insured plans. Why should a self-insured plan have a right to enforce a subrogation clause against an injured employee while an insured plan may not? The notion that this disparate treatment of similarly situated beneficiaries is somehow supported by an interest in uniformity is singularly unpersuasive. If Congress had intended such an irrational result, surely it would have expressed it in straightforward English. At least one would expect that the reasons for drawing such an apparently irrational distinction would be discernible in the legislative history or in the literature discussing the legislation.

The Court's anomalous result would be avoided by a correct and narrower reading of either the basic pre-emption clause or the deemer clause.

## Comments and Questions

1. Opinions such as the *FMC* decision confirmed the advantages of self-insured plans for employers, and over the past few years, self-insured plans have become increasingly prevalent in the United States. So, while only six million Americans were covered through self-insured plans when ERISA was enacted in 1974, some 55 million people and 40 percent of all group coverage was through self-insured plans by the late 1980s. See Gail A. Jensen & Kevin D. Cotter, *State Insurance Regulation and the Decision to Self-Insure*, 62 J. RISK & INS. 185 (1995). To qualify as self-insured for purposes of ERISA's preemption provision, a plan need not sever all ties with the insurance industry. Most self-insured plans contract with insurance companies to process claims and provide other administrative services for self-insured plans. Suppose an employer was concerned about incurring unexpectedly large medical claims from its self-insured plan. Suppose further that the employer purchased stop-loss coverage from an insurance company to recover losses incurred if its medical plan experienced more than $1 million in claims in any calendar year. How would ERISA's preemption provision apply to this arrangement? See Thompson v. Talquin Building Products Co., 928 F.2d 649 (4th Cir. 1991).

2. During the health care debates of the past few years, ERISA's preemption provision has been a source of controversy. Proponents of an increased federal presence in the field have argued that the provision has retarded state efforts to reform health care at the local level. Litigation culminating in the following decision was often cited as symptomatic of the kinds of barriers the preemption provision poses to state reforms. To what extent has the Supreme Court resolved these difficulties?

## New York State Conference v. Travelers Insurance Co.
### 514 U.S. 645 (1995)

Justice SOUTER delivered the opinion of the Court.

A New York statute requires hospitals to collect surcharges from patients covered by a commercial insurer but not from patients insured by a Blue Cross/Blue Shield plan, and it subjects certain health maintenance organizations (HMOs) to surcharges that vary with the number of Medicaid recipients each enrolls. N. Y. Pub. Health Law § 2807-c (McKinney 1993). This case calls for us to decide whether the Employee Retirement Income Security Act of 1974 (ERISA) pre-empts the state provisions for surcharges on bills of patients whose commercial insurance coverage is purchased by employee health-care plans governed by ERISA, and for surcharges on HMOs insofar as their membership fees are paid by an ERISA plan. We hold that the provisions for surcharges do not "relate to" employee benefit plans within the meaning of ERISA's pre-emption provision, § 514(a) and accordingly suffer no pre-emption.

## I

New York's Prospective Hospital Reimbursement Methodology (NYPHRM) regulates hospital rates for all in-patient care, except for services provided to Medicare beneficiaries.[1] N. Y. Pub. Health Law § 2807-c (McKinney 1993). The scheme calls for patients to be charged not for the cost of their individual treatment, but for the average cost of treating the patient's medical problem, as classified under one or another of 794 Diagnostic Related Groups (DRGs). The charges allowable in accordance with DRG classifications are adjusted for a specific hospital to reflect its particular operating costs, capital investments, bad debts, costs of charity care and the like.

Patients with Blue Cross/Blue Shield coverage, Medicaid patients, and HMO participants are billed at a hospital's DRG rate. N. Y. Pub. Health Law § 2807-c(1)(a); see also Brief for Petitioners Pataki et al.4. Others, however, are not. Patients served by commercial insurers providing in-patient hospital coverage on an expense-incurred basis, by self-insured funds directly reimbursing hospitals, and by certain workers' compensation, volunteer firefighters' benefit, ambulance workers' benefit, and no-fault motor vehicle insurance funds, must be billed at the DRG rate plus a 13% surcharge to be retained by the hospital. N. Y. Pub. Health Law § 2807-c(1)(b). For the year ending March 31, 1993, moreover, hospitals were required to bill commercially insured patients for a further 11% surcharge to be turned over to the State, with the result that these patients were charged 24% more than the DRG rate. § 2807-c(11)(i).

New York law also imposes a surcharge on HMOs, which varies depending on the number of eligible Medicaid recipients an HMO has enrolled, but which may run as high as 9% of the aggregate monthly charges paid by an HMO for its members' in-patient hospital care. § 2807-c(2-a)(a) - (2-a)(e). This assessment is not an increase in the rates to be paid by an HMO to hospitals, but a direct payment by the HMO to the State's general fund. . . .

On the claimed authority of ERISA's general pre-emption provision, several commercial insurers, acting as fiduciaries of ERISA plans they administer, joined with their trade associations to bring actions against state officials in United States District Court seeking to invalidate the 13%, 11%, and 9% surcharge statutes.. . .

## II

Since pre-emption claims turn on Congress's intent, . . . we begin as we do in any exercise of statutory construction with the text of the provision in question, and move on, as need be, to the structure and purpose of the Act in which it occurs. . . . The governing text of ERISA is clearly expansive. Section 514(a) marks for pre-emption "all state laws insofar as they . . . relate to any employee  benefit plan" covered by ERISA, and one might be excused for wondering, at first blush, whether the words of limitation ("insofar as they . . . relate") do much limiting. If "relate to" were taken to extend to the furthest stretch of its indeterminacy, then for all practical purposes pre-emption would never run its course, for "really, universally, relations stop nowhere," H. James, Roderick Hudson xli (New York ed., World's Classics 1980). But that, of course, would be to read Congress's words of limitation as mere sham, and to read the presumption against pre-emption out of the law whenever Congress speaks to the matter with

---

[1]    Medicare rates are set by the Federal Government unless States obtain an express authorization from the United States Department of Health and Human Services.

generality. That said, we have to recognize that our prior attempt to construe the phrase "relate to" does not give us much help drawing the line here.

In Shaw, [463 U.S. 85  (1983),] we explained that "[a] law 'relates to' an employee benefit plan, in the normal sense of the phrase, if it has a connection with or reference to such a plan." 463 U.S., at 97. The latter alternative, at least, can be ruled out. The surcharges are imposed upon patients and HMOs, regardless of whether the commercial coverage or membership, respectively, is ultimately secured by an ERISA plan, private purchase, or otherwise, with the consequence that the surcharge statutes cannot be said to make "reference to" ERISA plans in any manner. Cf. Greater Wash. Bd. of Trade, 506 U.S.[___ (1992)] (striking down District of Columbia law that "specifically refers to welfare benefit plans regulated by ERISA and on that basis alone is pre-empted"). But this still leaves us to question whether the surcharge laws have a "connection with" the ERISA plans, and here an uncritical literalism is no more help than in trying to construe "relate to." For the same reasons that infinite relations cannot be the measure of pre-emption, neither can infinite connections. We simply must go beyond the unhelpful text and the frustrating difficulty of defining its key term, and look instead to the objectives of the ERISA statute as a guide to the scope of the state law that Congress understood would survive.

## A

As we have said before, § 514 indicates Congress's intent to establish the regulation of employee welfare benefit plans "as exclusively a federal concern." Alessi v. Raybestos-Manhattan, Inc., 451 U.S. 504, 523 (1981). We have found that in passing § 514(a), Congress intended

> "to ensure that plans and plan sponsors would be subject to a uniform body of benefits law; the goal was to minimize the administrative and financial burden of complying with conflicting directives among States or between States and the Federal Government . . ., [and to prevent] the potential for conflict in substantive law . . . requiring the tailoring of plans and employer conduct to the peculiarities of the law of each jurisdiction." Ingersoll-Rand, 498 U.S., at 142.

This objective was described in the House of Representatives by a sponsor of the Act, Representative Dent, as being to "eliminate the threat of conflicting and inconsistent State and local regulation." 120 Cong. Rec. 29197 (1974). Senator Williams made the same point, that "with the narrow exceptions specified in the bill, the substantive and enforcement provisions . . . are intended to preempt the field for Federal regulations, thus eliminating the threat of conflicting or inconsistent State and local regulation of employee benefit plans." Id., at 29933. The basic thrust of the pre-emption  clause, then, was to avoid a multiplicity of regulation in order to permit the nationally uniform administration of employee benefit plans.

Accordingly in Shaw, for example, we had no trouble finding that New York's "Human Rights Law, which prohibited employers from structuring their employee benefit plans in a manner that discriminated on the basis of pregnancy, and [New York's] Disability Benefits Law, which required employers to pay employees specific benefits, clearly 'related to' benefit plans." 463 U.S., at 97. These mandates affecting coverage could have been honored only by varying the subjects of a plan's benefits whenever New York law might have applied, or by requiring every plan to provide all beneficiaries with a benefit demanded by New York law if New York law could have been said to require it for any one beneficiary. Similarly, Pennsylvania's law that prohibited "plans from . . . requiring reimbursement [from the beneficiary] in the event of recovery from a third party" related to employee benefit plans within the meaning of § 514(a). FMC Corp. v. Holliday, 498 U.S. 52, 60 (1990). The law "prohibited plans from being structured in a manner requiring reimbursement in the event of recovery from a third party" and "required plan providers to calculate benefit levels in Pennsylvania based on expected liability conditions that differ from those in States that have not enacted similar antisubrogation legislation," thereby "frustrating plan administrators' continuing obligation to calculate uniform benefit levels nationwide." Ibid. Pennsylvania employees who recovered in negligence actions against tortfeasors would, by virtue of the state law, in effect have been entitled to benefits in excess of what plan administrators intended to provide, and in excess of what the plan provided to employees in other States. Along the same lines, New Jersey could not prohibit plans from setting workers' compensation payments off against employees' retirement benefits or pensions, because doing so would prevent plans from using a method of calculating benefits permitted by federal law. Alessi, supra, at 524. In each of these cases, ERISA pre-empted state laws that mandated employee benefit structures or their administration. Elsewhere, we have held that state laws providing alternate enforcement mechanisms also relate to ERISA plans, triggering pre-emption. See Ingersoll-Rand, supra.

B

Both the purpose and the effects of the New York surcharge statutes distinguish them from the examples just given. The charge differentials have been justified on the ground that the Blues pay the hospitals promptly and efficiently and, more importantly, provide coverage for many subscribers whom the commercial insurers would reject as unacceptable risks. The Blues' practice, called open enrollment, has consistently been cited as the principal reason for charge differentials, whether the differentials resulted from voluntary negotiation between hospitals and payers as was the case prior to the NYPHRM system, or were created by the surcharges as is the case now. . . . Since the surcharges are presumably passed on at least in part to those who purchase commercial insurance or HMO membership, their effects follow from their purpose. Although there is no evidence that the surcharges will drive every health insurance consumer to the Blues, they do make the Blues more attractive (or less unattractive) as insurance alternatives and thus have an indirect economic effect on choices made by insurance buyers, including ERISA plans.

An indirect economic influence, however, does not bind plan administrators to any particular choice and thus function as a regulation of an ERISA plan itself; commercial insurers and HMOs may still offer more attractive packages than the Blues. Nor does the indirect influence of the surcharges preclude uniform administrative practice or the provision of a uniform interstate benefit package if a plan wishes to provide one. It simply bears on the costs of benefits and the relative costs of competing insurance to provide them. It is an influence that can affect a plan's shopping decisions, but it does not affect the fact that any plan will shop for the best deal it can get, surcharges or no surcharges.

There is, indeed, nothing remarkable about surcharges on hospital bills, or their effects on overall cost to the plans and the relative attractiveness of certain insurers. Rate variations among hospital providers are accepted examples of cost variation, since hospitals have traditionally "attempted to compensate for their financial shortfalls by adjusting their price . . . schedules for patients with commercial health insurance." Thorpe, [Does All-Payer Rate Setting Work? The Case of the New York Prospective Hospital Reimbursement Methodology, 12 J.

Health Politics, Policy, & Law 391, 394 (1987).] Charge differentials for commercial insurers, even prior to state regulation, "varied dramatically across regions, ranging from 13 to 36 percent," presumably reflecting the geographically disparate burdens of providing for the uninsured. Id., at 400 . . . .

If the common character of rate differentials even in the absence of state action renders it unlikely that ERISA pre-emption was meant to bar such indirect economic influences under state law, the existence of other common state action with indirect economic effects on a plan's costs leaves the intent to pre-empt even less likely. Quality standards, for example, set by the State in one subject area of hospital services but not another would affect the relative cost of providing those services over others and, so, of providing different packages of health insurance benefits. Even basic regulation of employment conditions will invariably affect the cost and price of services.

Quality control and workplace regulation, to be sure, are presumably less likely to affect premium differentials among competing insurers, but that does not change the fact that such state regulation will indirectly affect what an ERISA or other plan can afford or get for its money. Thus, in the absence of a more exact guide to intended pre-emption than § 514, it is fair to conclude that mandates for rate differentials would not be pre-empted unless other regulation with indirect effects on plan costs would be superseded as well. The bigger the package of regulation with indirect effects that would fall on the respondent's reading of § 514, the less likely it is that federal regulation of benefit plans was intended to eliminate state regulation of health care costs.

Indeed, to read the pre-emption provision as displacing all state laws affecting costs and charges on the theory that they indirectly relate to ERISA plans that purchase insurance policies or HMO memberships that would cover such services, would effectively read the limiting language in § 514(a) out of the statute, a conclusion that would violate basic principles of statutory interpretation and could not be squared with our prior pronouncement that "preemption does not occur . . . if the state law has only a tenuous, remote, or peripheral connection with covered plans, as is the case with many laws of general applicability." District of Columbia v. Greater Washington Board of Trade, 506 U.S. 125, 130 n. 1 (1992) (internal quotation marks and citations omitted). While Congress's extension of pre-emption to all "state laws relating to benefit plans" was meant to sweep more broadly than "state laws dealing with the subject matters covered by ERISA[,] reporting, disclosure, fiduciary responsibility, and the like," Shaw, 463 U.S., at 98, and n. 19, nothing in the language of the Act or the context of its passage indicates that Congress chose to displace general health care regulation, which historically has been a matter of local concern, see Hillsborough County v. Automated Medical Laboratories, Inc., 471 U.S. 707, 719 (1985); 1 B. Furrow, T. Greaney, S. Johnson, T. Jost, & R. Schwartz, Health Law §§ 1-6, 1-23 (1995).

In sum, cost-uniformity was almost certainly not an object of pre-emption, just as laws with only an indirect economic effect on the relative costs of various health insurance packages in a given State are a far cry from those "conflicting directives" from which Congress meant to insulate ERISA plans. See 498 U.S., at 142. Such state laws leave plan administrators right where they would be in any case, with the responsibility to choose the best overall coverage for the money. We therefore conclude that such state laws do not bear the requisite "connection with" ERISA plans to trigger pre-emption.

C.

This conclusion is confirmed by our decision in Mackey v. Lanier Collection Agency & Service, Inc., 486 U.S. 825 (1988), which held that ERISA pre-emption falls short of barring application of a general state garnishment statute to participants' benefits in the hands of an ERISA welfare benefit plan. We took no issue with the argument of the Mackey plan's trustees that garnishment would impose administrative costs and burdens upon benefit plans, id., at 831, but concluded from the text and structure of ERISA's pre-emption and enforcement provisions that "Congress did not intend to forbid the use of state-law mechanisms of executing judgments against ERISA welfare benefit plans, even when those mechanisms prevent plan participants from receiving their benefits." Id., at 831-832. If a law authorizing an indirect source of administrative cost is not pre-empted, it should follow that a law operating as an indirect source of merely economic influence on administrative decisions, as here, should not suffice to trigger pre-emption either.

The commercial challengers counter by invoking the earlier case of Metropolitan Life Insurance Co. v. Massachusetts, 471 U.S. 724 (1985), which considered whether a State could mandate coverage of specified minimum mental-health-care benefits by policies insuring against hospital and surgical expenses. Because the regulated policies included those bought by employee welfare benefit plans, we recognized that the law "directly affected" such plans. Id., at 732. Although we went on to hold that the law was ultimately saved from pre-emption by the insurance savings clause, § 514(b)(2)(A), respondents proffer the first steps in our decision as support for their argument that all laws affecting ERISA plans through their impact on insurance policies "relate to" such plans and are pre-empted unless expressly saved by the statute. The challengers take Metropolitan Life too far, however.

The Massachusetts statute applied not only to " 'any blanket or general policy of insurance . . . or any policy of accident and sickness insurance' " but also to " 'any employees' health and welfare fund which provided hospital expense and surgical expense benefits.' " 471 U.S., at 730, n. 11. In fact, the State did not even try to defend its law as unrelated to employee benefit plans for the purpose of § 514(a). Id., at 739. As a result, there was no reason to distinguish with any precision between the effects on insurers that are sufficiently connected with employee benefit plans to "relate to" the plans and those effects that are not. It was enough to address the distinction bluntly, saying on the one hand that laws like the one in Metropolitan Life relate to plans since they "bear indirectly but substantially on all insured benefit plans, . . . requiring them to purchase the mental-health benefits specified in the statute when they purchase a certain kind of common insurance policy," id., at 739, but saying on the other that "laws that regulate only the insurer, or the way in which it may sell insurance, do not 'relate to' benefit plans," id., at 741. Even this basic distinction recognizes that not all regulations that would influence the cost of insurance would relate to employee benefit plans within the meaning of § 514(a). If, for example, a State were to regulate sales of insurance by commercial insurers more stringently than sales by insurers not-for-profit, the relative cost of commercial insurance would rise; we would nonetheless say, following Metropolitan Life, that such laws "do not 'relate to' benefit plans in the first instance." Ibid. . And on the same authority we would say the same about the basic tax exemption enjoyed by non-profit insurers like the Blues since the days long before ERISA, see Marmor, New York's Blue Cross and Blue Shield, 1934-1990: The Complicated Politics of Nonprofit Regulation, 16 J. Health Politics, Policy, & Law 761, 769

(1991) (tracing New York Blue Cross's special tax treatment as a prepayment organization back to 1934); 1934 N. Y. Laws, ch. 595; and yet on respondent's theory the exemption would necessarily be pre-empted as affecting insurance prices and plan costs.

In any event, Metropolitan Life can not carry the weight the commercial insurers would place on it. The New York surcharges do not impose the kind of substantive coverage requirement binding plan administrators that was at issue in Metropolitan Life. Although even in the absence of mandated coverage there might be a point at which an exorbitant tax leaving consumers with a Hobson's choice would be treated as imposing a substantive mandate, no showing has been made here that the surcharges are so prohibitive as to force all health insurance consumers to contract with the Blues. As they currently stand, the surcharges do not require plans to deal with only one insurer, or to insure against an entire category of illnesses they might otherwise choose to leave without coverage.

### D

It remains only to speak further on a point already raised, that any conclusion other than the one we draw would bar any state regulation of hospital costs. The basic DRG system (even without any surcharge), like any other interference with the hospital services market, would fall on a theory that all laws with indirect economic effects on ERISA plans are pre-empted under § 514(a). This would be an unsettling result and all the more startling because several States, including New York, regulated hospital charges to one degree or another at the time ERISA was passed. . . . And yet there is not so much as a hint in ERISA's legislative history or anywhere else that Congress intended to squelch these state efforts.

### III

That said, we do not hold today that ERISA pre-empts only direct regulation of ERISA plans, nor could we do that with fidelity to the views expressed in our prior opinions on the matter. See, e.g., Ingersoll-Rand, 498 U.S., at 139; Pilot Life Ins. Co. v. Dedeaux, 481 U.S. 41, 47-48 (1987); Shaw, 463 U.S., at 98. We acknowledge that a state law might produce such acute, albeit indirect, economic effects, by intent or otherwise, as to force an ERISA plan to adopt a certain scheme of substantive coverage or effectively restrict its choice of insurers, and that such a state law might indeed be pre-empted under § 514. But as we have shown, New York's surcharges do not fall into either category; they affect only indirectly the relative prices of insurance policies, a result no different from myriad state laws in areas traditionally subject to local regulation, which Congress could not possibly have intended to eliminate.

### Comments and Questions

1. Did the *Travelers Insurance* decision adequately distinguish the Court's earlier rule in *Metropolitan Life*? Which state law put a more substantial burden on ERISA plans, New York surcharges or Massachusetts' mandatory mental-health provision? For a thorough analysis of the *Travelers Insurance* decision and an  assessment of its likely effect on subsequent interpretations of ERISA's preemption provision, see Karen A. Jordan, *Travelers Insurance: New Support for the Argument to Restrain ERISA Pre-emption*, 13 YALE J. REG. 255 (1996).

2. Suppose, in response to lobbying from various trade unions, a state adopts a rule requiring all contractors on state construction projects to post a surety bond guaranteeing

payment of all labor costs associated with work done on state projects. Would employees be permitted to recover on such a bond if a contractor failed to fund a health insurance plan promised its workers? What if state law expressly required the bond to cover all employee health benefits? What if the law provided that the surety would cover all labor costs except for benefit plans covered by ERISA? See Williams v. Ashland Engineering Co., 45 F.3d 588 (1ˢᵗ Cir.), *cert. denied,* 116 S. Ct. 51 (1995).

## B.  Private Enforcement of ERISA Requirements

As described in passing in some of the decisions we have already considered, ERISA has its own civil and administrative enforcement provisions. These rules are the subject of the following two decisions. How do they compare to the enforcement mechanisms available in traditional insurance regulation under state law? What is the justification for imposing different enforcement mechanisms in this context?

## Firestone Tire & Rubber Co. v. Bruch
### 489 U.S. 101 (1989)

Justice O'CONNOR delivered the opinion of the Court.

### I

Late in 1980, petitioner Firestone Tire and Rubber Company (Firestone) sold, as going concerns, the five plants composing its Plastics Division to Occidental Petroleum Company (Occidental). Most of the approximately 500 salaried employees at the five plants were rehired by Occidental and continued in their same positions without interruption and at the same rates of pay. At the time of the sale, Firestone maintained three pension and welfare benefit plans for its employees: a termination pay plan, a retirement plan, and a stock purchase plan. Firestone was the sole source of funding for the plans and had not established separate trust funds out of which to pay the benefits from the plans. All three of the plans were either "employee welfare benefit plans" or "employee pension benefit plans" governed (albeit in different ways) by ERISA. By operation of law, Firestone itself was the administrator, ERISA § 3(16)(A)(ii), and fiduciary, ERISA § 3(21)(A), of each of these "unfunded" plans. At the time of the sale of its Plastics Division, Firestone was not aware that the termination pay plan was governed by ERISA, and therefore had not set up a claims procedure, § 503, nor complied with ERISA's reporting and disclosure obligations, §§ 101-111, with respect to that plan.

Respondents, six Firestone employees who were rehired by Occidental, sought severance benefits from Firestone under the termination pay plan. In relevant part, that plan provides as follows:

"If your service is discontinued prior to the time you are eligible for pension benefits, you will be given termination pay if released because of a reduction in work force or if you become physically or mentally unable to perform your job.

"The amount of termination pay you will receive will depend on your period of credited company service."

Several of the respondents also sought information from Firestone regarding their benefits under all three of the plans pursuant to certain ERISA disclosure provisions. See §§ 104(b)(4), 105(a). Firestone denied respondents severance benefits on the ground that the sale of the Plastics Division to Occidental did not constitute a "reduction in work force" within the meaning of the termination pay plan. . . .

Respondents then filed a class action on behalf of "former, salaried, non-union employees who worked in the five plants that comprised the Plastics Division of Firestone." The action was based on § 502(a)(1), which provides that a "civil action may be brought ... by a participant or beneficiary [of a covered plan] ... (A) for the relief provided for in [§ 502(c) ], [and] (B) to recover benefits due to him under the terms of his plan." In Count I of their complaint, respondents alleged that they were entitled to severance benefits because Firestone's sale of the Plastics Division to Occidental constituted a "reduction in work force" within the meaning of the termination pay plan. . . .

The District Court granted Firestone's motion for summary judgment. 640 F.Supp. 519 (ED Pa.1986). With respect to Count I, the District Court held that Firestone had satisfied its fiduciary duty under ERISA because its decision not to pay severance benefits to respondents under the termination pay plan was not arbitrary or capricious. Id., at 521- 526. . . .

The Court of Appeals reversed. . . . 828 F.2d 134 (CA3 1987). With respect to Count I, the Court of Appeals acknowledged that most federal courts have reviewed the denial of benefits by ERISA fiduciaries and administrators under the arbitrary and capricious standard. Id., at 138 (citing cases). It noted, however, that the arbitrary and capricious standard had been softened in cases where fiduciaries and administrators had some bias or adverse interest. Id., at 138-140. See, e.g., Jung v. FMC Corp., 755 F.2d 708, 711-712 (CA9 1985) (where "the employer's denial of benefits to a class avoids a very considerable outlay [by the employer], the reviewing court should consider that fact in applying the arbitrary and capricious standard of review," and "[l]ess deference should be given to the trustee's decision"). The Court of Appeals held that where an employer is itself the fiduciary and administrator of an unfunded benefit plan, its decision to deny benefits should be subject to de novo judicial review. It reasoned that in such situations deference is unwarranted given the lack of assurance of impartiality on the part of the employer. 828 F.2d, at 137-145. . . .

II

ERISA provides "a panoply of remedial devices" for participants and beneficiaries of benefit plans. Massachusetts Mutual Life Ins. Co. v. Russell, 473 U.S. 134, 146 (1985). Respondents' action asserting that they were entitled to benefits because the sale of Firestone's Plastics Division constituted a "reduction in work force" within the meaning of the termination pay plan was based on the authority of § 502(a)(1)(B). That provision allows a suit to recover benefits due under the plan, to enforce rights under the terms of the plan, and to obtain a declaratory judgment of future entitlement to benefits under the provisions of the plan contract. The discussion which follows is limited to the appropriate standard of review in § 502(a)(1)(B) actions challenging denials of benefits based on plan interpretations. We express no view as to the appropriate standard of review for actions under other remedial provisions of ERISA.

## A

Although it is a "comprehensive and reticulated statute," Nachman Corp. v. Pension Benefit Guaranty Corp., 446 U.S. 359, 361 (1980), ERISA does not set out the appropriate standard of review for actions under § 502(a)(1)(B) challenging benefit eligibility determinations. To fill this gap, federal courts have adopted the arbitrary and capricious standard developed under  a provision of the Labor Management Relations Act, 1947 (LMRA). . . .In light of Congress' general intent to incorporate much of LMRA fiduciary law into ERISA, see NLRB v. Amax Coal Co., 453 U.S. 322, 332 (1981), and because ERISA, like the LMRA, imposes a duty of loyalty on fiduciaries and plan administrators, Firestone argues that the LMRA arbitrary and capricious standard should apply to ERISA actions.  See Brief for Petitioners 13-14.  A comparison of the LMRA and ERISA, however, shows that the wholesale importation of the arbitrary and capricious standard into ERISA is unwarranted.

In relevant part, [the LMRA]  authorizes unions and employers to set up pension plans jointly and provides that contributions to such plans be made "for the sole and exclusive benefit of the employees ... and their families and dependents."  The LMRA does not provide for judicial review of the decisions of LMRA trustees.  Federal courts adopted the arbitrary and capricious standard both as a standard of review and, more importantly, as a means of asserting jurisdiction over suits . . . by beneficiaries of LMRA plans who were denied benefits by trustees. . . . Unlike the LMRA, ERISA explicitly authorizes suits against fiduciaries and plan administrators to remedy statutory violations, including breaches of fiduciary duty and lack of compliance with benefit plans.  See ERISA §§ 502(a), 5022(f).  See generally Pilot Life Ins. Co. v. Dedeaux, 481 U.S. 41, 52-57 (1987) (describing scope of § 502(a)).  Thus, the raison d'etre for the LMRA arbitrary and capricious standard--the need for a jurisdictional basis in suits against trustees--is not present in ERISA.  See Note, Judicial Review of Fiduciary Claim Denials Under ERISA:  An Alternative to the Arbitrary and Capricious Test, 71 Cornell L.Rev. 986, 994, n. 40 (1986). Without this jurisdictional analogy, LMRA principles offer no support for the adoption of the arbitrary and capricious standard insofar as § 502(a)(1)(B) is concerned.

## B

ERISA abounds with the language and terminology of trust law.  See, e.g., ERISA § 3(7) ("participant"), 1002(8) ("beneficiary"), 3(21)(A) ("fiduciary"), 403(a) ("trustee"), 404 ("fiduciary duties"). ERISA's legislative history confirms that the Act's fiduciary responsibility provisions, ERISA §§ 401-414, "codif[y] and mak[e] applicable to [ERISA] fiduciaries certain principles developed in the evolution of the law of trusts." H.R.Rep. No. 93-533, p. 11 (1973), U.S.Code Cong. & Admin.News 1974, pp. 4639, 4649.  Given this language and history, we have held that courts are to develop a "federal common law of rights and obligations under ERISA- regulated plans."  Pilot Life Ins. Co. v. Dedeaux, supra, at 56.  See also Franchise Tax Board v. Construction Laborers Vacation Trust, 463 U.S. 1, 24, n. 26  (1983) (" '[A] body of Federal substantive law will be developed by the courts to deal with issues involving rights and obligations under private welfare and pension plans' ") (quoting 129 Cong.Rec. 29942 (1974) (remarks of Sen. Javits)).  In determining the appropriate standard of review for actions under § 502(a)(1)(B), we are guided by principles of trust law. Central States, Southeast and Southwest Areas Pension Fund v. Central Transport, Inc., 472 U.S. 559, 570  (1985).

Trust principles make a deferential standard of review appropriate when a trustee exercises discretionary powers. See Restatement (Second) of Trusts § 187 (1959) ("[w]here discretion is conferred upon the trustee with respect to the exercise of a power, its exercise is not subject to control by the court except to prevent an abuse by the trustee of his discretion"). See also G. Bogert & G. Bogert, Law of Trusts and Trustees § 560, pp. 193-208 (2d rev. ed. 1980). A trustee may be given power to construe disputed or doubtful terms, and in such circumstances the trustee's interpretation will not be disturbed if reasonable. Id., § 559, at 169-171. Whether "the exercise of a power is permissive or mandatory depends upon the terms of the trust." 3 W. Fratcher, Scott on Trusts § 187, p. 14 (4th ed. 1988). Hence, over a century ago we remarked that "[w]hen trustees are in existence, and capable of acting, a court of equity will not interfere to control them in the exercise of a *discretion vested in them by the instrument* under which they act." Nichols v. Eaton, 91 U.S. 716, 724-725, 23 L.Ed. 254 (1875) (emphasis added). See also Central States, Southeast and Southwest Areas Pension Fund v. Central Transport, Inc., supra, 472 U.S., at 568 ("The trustees' determination that the trust documents authorize their access to records here in dispute has significant weight, for the trust agreement explicitly provides that 'any construction [of the agreement's provisions] adopted by the Trustees in good faith shall be binding upon the Union, Employees, and Employers' "). Firestone can seek no shelter in these principles of trust law, however, for there is no evidence that under Firestone's termination pay plan the administrator has the power to construe uncertain terms or that eligibility determinations are to be given deference. See Brief for Respondents 24-25; Reply Brief for Petitioners 7, n. 2; Brief for United States as Amicus Curiae 14-15, n. 11.

Finding no support in the language of its termination pay plan for the arbitrary and capricious standard, Firestone argues that as a matter of trust law the interpretation of the terms of a plan is an inherently discretionary function. But other settled principles of trust law, which point to de novo review of benefit eligibility determinations based on plan interpretations, belie this contention. As they do with contractual provisions, courts construe terms in trust agreements without deferring to either party's interpretation. "The extent of the duties and powers of a trustee is determined by the rules of law that are applicable to the situation, and not the rules that the trustee or his attorney believes to be applicable, and by the terms of the trust *as the court may interpret them*, and not as they may be interpreted by the trustee himself or by his attorney." 3 W. Fratcher, Scott on Trusts § 201, at 221 (emphasis added). A trustee who is in doubt as to the interpretation of the instrument can protect himself by obtaining instructions from the court. Bogert & Bogert, supra, § 559, at 162-168; Restatement (Second) of Trusts § 201, Comment b (1959). See also United States v. Mason, 412 U.S. 391, 399 (1973). The terms of trusts created by written instruments are "determined by the provisions of the instrument as interpreted in light of all the circumstances and such other evidence of the intention of the settlor with respect to the trust as is not inadmissible." Restatement (Second) of Trusts § 4, Comment d (1959).

The trust law de novo standard of review is consistent with the judicial interpretation of employee benefit plans prior to the enactment of ERISA. Actions challenging an employer's denial of benefits before the enactment of ERISA were governed by principles of contract law. If the plan did not give the employer or administrator discretionary or final authority to construe uncertain terms, the court reviewed the employee's claim as it would have any other contract claim--by looking to the terms of the plan and other manifestations of the parties' intent. See, e.g., Conner v. Phoenix Steel Corp., 249 A.2d 866 (Del.1969); Atlantic Steel Co. v. Kitchens, 228

Ga. 708, 187 S.E.2d 824 (1972); Sigman v. Rudolph Wurlitzer Co., 57 Ohio App. 4, 11 N.E.2d 878 (1937).

Despite these principles of trust law pointing to a de novo standard of review for claims like respondents', Firestone would have us read ERISA to require the application of the arbitrary and capricious standard to such claims. ERISA defines a fiduciary as one who "exercises any discretionary authority or discretionary control respecting management of [a] plan or exercises any authority or control respecting management or disposition of its assets." ERISA § 3(21)(A)(i). A fiduciary has "authority to control and manage the operation and administration of the plan," § 402(a)(1), and must provide a "full and fair review" of claim denials, § 503(2). From these provisions, Firestone concludes that an ERISA plan administrator, fiduciary, or trustee is empowered to exercise all his authority in a discretionary manner subject only to review for arbitrariness and capriciousness. But the provisions relied upon so heavily by Firestone do not characterize a fiduciary as one who exercises entirely discretionary authority or control. Rather, one is a fiduciary to the extent he exercises any discretionary authority or control. Cf. United Mine Workers of America Health and Retirement Funds v. Robinson, 455 U.S. 562, 573-574 (1982) (common law of trusts did not alter nondiscretionary obligation of trustees to enforce eligibility requirements as required by LMRA trust agreement).

ERISA was enacted "to promote the interests of employees and their beneficiaries in employee benefit plans," Shaw v. Delta Airlines, Inc., 463 U.S. 85, 90 (1983), and "to protect contractually defined benefits," Massachusetts Mutual Life Ins. Co. v. Russell, 473 U.S., at 148 . . . . Adopting Firestone's reading of ERISA would require us to impose a standard of review that would afford less protection to employees and their beneficiaries than they enjoyed before ERISA was enacted. Nevertheless, Firestone maintains that congressional action after the passage of ERISA indicates that Congress intended ERISA claims to be reviewed under the arbitrary and capricious standard. At a time when most federal courts had adopted the arbitrary and capricious standard of review, a bill was introduced in Congress to amend § 1132 by providing de novo review of decisions denying benefits. See H.R. 6226, 97th Cong., 2d Sess. (1982), reprinted in Pension Legislation: Hearings on H.R. 1614 et al. before the Sub-committee on Labor-Management Relations of the House Committee on Education and Labor, 97th Cong., 2d Sess., 60 (1983). Because the bill was never enacted, Firestone asserts that we should conclude that Congress was satisfied with the arbitrary and capricious standard. See Brief for Petitioners 19-20. We do not think that this bit of legislative inaction carries the day for Firestone. Though "instructive," failure to act on the proposed bill is not conclusive of Congress' views on the appropriate standard of review. Bowsher v. Merck & Co., 460 U.S. 824, 837, n. 12 (1983). The bill's demise may have been the result of events that had nothing to do with Congress' view on the propriety of de novo review. Without more, we cannot ascribe to Congress any acquiescence in the arbitrary and capricious standard. "[T]he views of a subsequent Congress form a hazardous basis for inferring the intent of an earlier one." United States v. Price, 361 U.S. 304, 313 (1960).

Firestone and its amici also assert that a de novo standard would contravene the spirit of ERISA because it would impose much higher administrative and litigation costs and therefore discourage employers from creating benefit plans. See, e.g., Brief for American Council of Life Insurance et al. as Amici Curiae 10-11. Because even under the arbitrary and capricious standard an employer's denial of benefits could be subject to judicial review, the assumption seems to be that a de novo standard would encourage more litigation by employees, participants, and beneficiaries who wish to assert their right to benefits. Neither general principles of trust law nor a concern for impartial decisionmaking, however, forecloses parties from agreeing upon a narrower standard of review. Moreover, as to both funded and unfunded plans, the threat of increased litigation is not sufficient to outweigh the reasons for a de novo standard that we have already explained.

As this case aptly demonstrates, the validity of a claim to benefits under an ERISA plan is likely to turn on the interpretation of terms in the plan at issue. Consistent with established principles of trust law, we hold that a denial of benefits challenged under § 502(a)(1)(B) is to be reviewed under a de novo standard unless the benefit plan gives the administrator or fiduciary discretionary authority to determine eligibility for benefits or to construe the terms of the plan. Because we do not rest our decision on the concern for impartiality that guided the Court of Appeals, see 828 F.2d, at 143-146, we need not distinguish between types of plans or focus on the motivations of plan administrators and fiduciaries. Thus, for purposes of actions under § 502(a)(1)(B), the de novo standard of review applies regardless of whether the plan at issue is funded or unfunded and regardless of whether the administrator or fiduciary is operating under a possible or actual conflict of interest. Of course, if a benefit plan gives discretion to an administrator or fiduciary who is operating under a conflict of interest, that conflict must be weighed as a "facto[r] in determining whether there is an abuse of discretion." Restatement (Second) of Trusts § 187, Comment d (1959). . . .

## Comments and Questions

1. What is the significance of the Bruch decision? How would you expect employers to respond to the decision? Suppose, for example, employers amended their plans to grant a plan administrator discretion to deny benefits. To what sort of judicial review would such a provision be subject? See John H. Langbein, *The Supreme Court Flunks Trusts*, 1990 SUP. CT. REV. 207.

2. How does traditional insurance regulation deal with problems of this sort? Which approach is preferable? Why?

## Mertens v. Hewitt Associates
### 508 U.S. 248 (1993)

Justice SCALIA delivered the opinion of the Court.

The question presented is whether a nonfiduciary who knowingly participates in the breach of a fiduciary duty imposed by the Employee Retirement Income Security Act of 1974 (ERISA), as amended, is liable for losses that an employee benefit plan suffers as a result of the breach.

I

According to the complaint, the allegations of which we take as true, petitioners represent a class of former employees of the Kaiser Steel Corporation (Kaiser) who participated in the Kaiser Steel Retirement Plan, a qualified pension plan under ERISA. Respondent was the plan's actuary in 1980, when Kaiser began to phase out its steelmaking operations, prompting early retirement by a large number of plan participants. Respondent did not, however, change the plan's actuarial assumptions to reflect the additional costs imposed by the retirements. As a result, Kaiser did not adequately fund the plan, and eventually the plan's assets became insufficient to satisfy its benefit obligations, causing the Pension Benefit Guaranty Corporation (PBGC) to terminate the plan. Petitioners now receive only the benefits guaranteed by ERISA, which are in general substantially lower than the fully vested pensions due them under the plan.

Petitioners sued the fiduciaries of the failed plan, alleging breach of fiduciary duties. See Mertens v. Black, 948 F.2d 1105 (CA9 1991) (per curiam ) (affirming denial of summary judgment). They also commenced this action against respondent, alleging that it had caused the losses by allowing Kaiser to select the plan's actuarial assumptions, by failing to disclose that Kaiser was one of its clients, and by failing to disclose the plan's funding shortfall. Petitioners claimed that these acts and omissions violated ERISA by effecting a breach of respondent's "professional duties" to the plan, for which they sought, inter alia, monetary relief. In opposing respondent's motion to dismiss, petitioners fleshed out this claim, asserting that respondent was liable (1) as an ERISA fiduciary that committed a breach of its own fiduciary duties, (2) as a nonfiduciary that knowingly participated in the plan fiduciaries' breach of their fiduciary duties, and (3) as a nonfiduciary that committed a breach of nonfiduciary duties imposed on actuaries by ERISA. . . .

II

ERISA is, we have observed, a "comprehensive and reticulated statute," the product of a decade of congressional study of the Nation's private employee benefit system. Nachman Corp. v. PBGC, 446 U.S. 359, 361 (1980). The statute provides that not only the persons named as fiduciaries by a benefit plan, but also anyone else who exercises discretionary control or authority over the plan's management, administration, or assets, is an ERISA "fiduciary." Fiduciaries are assigned a number of detailed duties and responsibilities, which include "the proper management, administration, and investment of [plan] assets, the maintenance of proper records, the disclosure of specified information, and the avoidance of conflicts of interest." Massachusetts Mut. Life Ins. Co. v. Russell, 473 U.S. 134, 142- 143 (1985); see 29 U.S.C. § 1104(a). Section 409(a), 29 U.S.C. § 1109(a), makes fiduciaries liable for breach of these duties, and specifies the remedies available against them: the fiduciary is personally liable for damages ("to make good to [the] plan any losses to the plan resulting from each such breach"), for restitution ("to restore to [the] plan any profits of such fiduciary which have been made through use of assets of the plan by the fiduciary"), and for "such other equitable or remedial relief as the court may deem appropriate," including removal of the fiduciary. Section 502(a)(2) -- the second of ERISA's "six carefully integrated civil enforcement provisions," Russell, supra, at 146 -- allows the Secretary of Labor or any plan beneficiary, participant, or fiduciary to bring a civil action "for appropriate relief under section [409]."

The above described provisions are, however, limited by their terms to fiduciaries. The Court of Appeals decided that respondent was not a fiduciary, see 948 F.2d, at 610, and petitioners do not contest that holding. Lacking equivalent provisions specifying non fiduciaries as potential defendants, or damages as a remedy available against them, petitioners have turned to § 502(a)(3), which authorizes a plan beneficiary, participant, or fiduciary to bring a civil action:

> "(A) to enjoin any act or practice which violates any provision of [ERISA] or the terms of the plan, or (B) to obtain other appropriate equitable relief (i) to redress such violations or (ii) to enforce any provisions of [ERISA] or the terms of the plan...."

See also § 502(a)(5) (providing, in similar language, for civil suits by the Secretary based upon violation of ERISA provisions). Petitioners contend that requiring respondent to make the Kaiser plan whole for the losses resulting from its alleged knowing participation in the breach of fiduciary duty by the Kaiser plan's fiduciaries would constitute "other appropriate equitable relief" within the meaning of § 502(a)(3).

We note at the outset that it is far from clear that, even if this provision does make money damages available, it makes them available for the actions at issue here. It does not, after all, authorize "appropriate equitable relief" at large, but only "appropriate equitable relief" for the purpose of "redress[ing any] violations or ... enforc[ing] any provisions" of ERISA or an ERISA plan. No one suggests that any term of the Kaiser plan has been violated, nor would any be enforced by the requested judgment. And while ERISA contains various provisions that can be read as imposing obligations upon nonfiduciaries, including actuaries,[4] no provision explicitly requires them to avoid participation (knowing or unknowing) in a fiduciary's breach of fiduciary duty. It is unlikely, moreover, that this was an oversight, since ERISA does explicitly impose "knowing participation" liability on cofiduciaries. See § 405(a). That limitation appears all the more deliberate in light of the fact that "knowing participation" liability on the part of both cotrustees and third persons was well established under the common law of trusts. See 3 A. Scott & W. Fratcher, Law of Trusts § 224.1, p. 404 (4th ed. 1988) (hereinafter Scott & Fratcher) (cotrustees); 4 Scott & Fratcher § 326, p. 291 (third persons). In Russell we emphasized our unwillingness to infer causes of action in the ERISA context, since that statute's carefully crafted and detailed enforcement scheme provides "strong evidence that Congress did not intend to authorize other remedies that it simply forgot to incorporate expressly." 473 U.S., at 146-147. All of this notwithstanding, petitioners and their amicus the United States seem to assume that respondent's alleged action (or inaction) violated ERISA, and address their arguments almost exclusively to what forms of relief are available. And respondent, despite considerable prompting by its amici, expressly disclaims reliance on this preliminary point. Thus, although we acknowledge the oddity of resolving a dispute over remedies where it is unclear that a remediable wrong has been alleged, we decide this case on the narrow battlefield the parties have chosen, and reserve decision of that antecedent question.[5]

Petitioners maintain that the object of their suit is "appropriate equitable relief" under § 502(a)(3). They do not, however, seek a remedy traditionally viewed as "equitable," such as injunction or restitution. (The Court of Appeals held that restitution was unavailable, see 948

---

[4]    For example, a person who provides services to a plan is a "party in interest," and may not offer his services or engage in certain other transactions with the plan for more than reasonable compensation.

[5]    The dissent expresses its certitude that "the statute clearly does not bar such a suit." Post, at 2073, n. 1. That, of course, is not the issue. The issue is whether the statute affirmatively authorizes such a suit. To meet that requirement, it is not enough to observe that "trust beneficiaries clearly had such a remedy [against nonfiduciaries who actively assist in the fiduciary's breach] at common law." Ibid. They had such a remedy because nonfiduciaries had a duty to the beneficiaries not to assist in the fiduciary's breach. A similar duty is set forth in ERISA; but as we have noted, only some common-law "nonfiduciaries" are made subject to it, namely, those who fall within ERISA's artificial definition of "fiduciary."

F.2d, at 612, and petitioners have not challenged that.)  Although they often dance around the word, what petitioners in fact seek is nothing other than compensatory damages -- monetary relief for all losses their plan sustained as a result of the alleged breach of fiduciary duties.  Money damages are, of course, the classic form of legal relief.  Curtis v. Loether, 415 U.S. 189, 196 (1974);  Teamsters v. Terry, 494 U.S. 558, 570-571 (1990);  D. Dobbs, Remedies § 1.1, p. 3 (1973).  And though we have never interpreted the precise phrase "other appropriate equitable relief," we have construed the similar language of Title VII of the Civil Rights Act of 1964 (before its 1991 amendments)--"any other equitable relief as the court deems appropriate,")--to preclude "awards for compensatory or punitive damages."

Petitioners assert, however, that this reading of "equitable relief" fails to acknowledge ERISA's roots in the common law of trusts, see Firestone Tire & Rubber Co. v. Bruch, 489 U.S. 101, 110-111 (1989).  "[A]lthough a beneficiary's action to recover losses resulting from a breach of duty superficially resembles an action at law for damages," the Solicitor General suggests, "such relief traditionally has been obtained in courts of equity" and therefore "is, by definition, 'equitable relief.' "  It is true that, at common law, the courts of equity had exclusive jurisdiction over virtually all actions by beneficiaries for breach of trust.  See Lessee of Smith v. McCann, 24 How. 398, 407, 16 L.Ed. 714 (1861);  3 Scott & Fratcher § 197, p. 188.  It is also true that money damages were available in those courts against the trustee, see United States v. Mitchell, 463 U.S. 206, 226 (1983);  G. Bogert & G. Bogert, Law of Trusts and Trustees § 701, p. 198 (rev. 2d ed. 1982) (hereinafter Bogert & Bogert), and against third persons who knowingly participated in the trustee's breach, see Seminole Nation v. United States, 316 U.S. 286, 296-297 (1942);  Scott, Participation in a Breach of Trust, 34 Harv.L.Rev. 454 (1921).

At common law, however, there were many situations--not limited to those involving enforcement of a trust--in which an equity court could "establish purely legal rights and grant legal remedies which would otherwise be beyond the scope of its authority."  1 J. Pomeroy, Equity Jurisprudence § 181, p. 257 (5th ed. 1941).  The term "equitable relief" can assuredly mean, as petitioners and the Solicitor General would have it, whatever relief a court of equity is empowered to provide in the particular case at issue.  But as indicated by the foregoing quotation--which speaks of "legal remedies" granted by an equity court--"equitable relief" can also refer to those categories of relief that were typically available in equity (such as injunction, mandamus, and restitution, but not compensatory damages).  As memories of the divided bench, and familiarity with its technical refinements, recede further into the past, the former meaning becomes, perhaps, increasingly unlikely;  but it remains a question of interpretation in each case which is intended.

In the context of the present statute, we think there can be no doubt.  Since all relief available for breach of trust could be obtained from a court of equity, limiting the sort of relief obtainable under § 502(a)(3) to "equitable relief" in the sense of "whatever relief a common-law court of equity could provide in such a case" would limit the relief not at all. We will not read the statute to render the modifier superfluous.  Regarding "equitable" relief in § 502(a)(3) to mean "all relief available for breach of trust at common law" would also require us either to give the term a different meaning there than it bears elsewhere in ERISA, or to deprive of all meaning the distinction Congress drew between "equitable" and "remedial" relief in § 409(a) and between "equitable" and "legal" relief in the very same section of ERISA . . . .  Neither option is acceptable.  The authority of courts to develop a "federal common law" under ERISA, see Firestone, supra, 489 U.S. at 110, is not the authority to revise the text of the statute.

Petitioners point to ERISA § 502(*l*), which was added to the statute in 1989. . . and provides as follows:

"(1) In the case of -- (A) any breach of fiduciary responsibility under (or other violation of) part 4 by a fiduciary, or (B) any knowing participation in such a breach or violation by any other person, the Secretary shall assess a civil penalty against such fiduciary or other person in an amount equal to 20 percent of the applicable recovery amount."

The Secretary may waive or reduce this penalty if he believes that " the fiduciary or other person will [otherwise] not be able to restore all losses to the plan without severe financial hardship." " Applicable recovery amount" is defined (in § 502(*l*)(2)(B)) as "any amount ... ordered by a court to be paid by such fiduciary or other person to a plan or its participants or beneficiaries in a judicial proceeding instituted by the Secretary under [§ 502](a)(2) or (a)(5)." It will be recalled that the latter subsection, § 502(a)(5), authorizes relief in actions by the Secretary on the same terms ("appropriate equitable relief") as in the private-party actions authorized by § 502(a)(3). Petitioners argue that § 502(l ) confirms that § 502(a)(5)--and hence, since it uses the same language, § 502(a)(3)--allows actions for damages, since otherwise there could be no "applicable recovery amount" against some "other person" than the fiduciary, and the Secretary would have no occasion to worry about whether any such "other person" would be able to "restore all losses to the plan" without financial hardship.

We certainly agree with petitioners that language used in one portion of a statute (§ 502(a)(3)) should be deemed to have the same meaning as the same language used elsewhere in the statute (§ 502(a)(5)). Indeed, we are even more zealous advocates of that principle than petitioners, who stop short of applying it directly to the term "equitable relief." We cannot agree, however, that § 502(l ) establishes the existence of a damages remedy under § 502(a)(5)--i.e., that it is otherwise so inexplicable that we must give the term "equitable relief" the expansive meaning "all relief available for breach of trust." For even in its more limited sense, the "equitable relief" awardable under § 502(a)(5) includes restitution of ill-gotten plan assets or profits, providing an "applicable recovery amount" to use to calculate the penalty, which the Secretary may waive or reduce if paying it would prevent the restoration of those gains to the plan; and even assuming nonfiduciaries are not liable at all for knowing participation in a fiduciary's breach of duty, cofiduciaries expressly are, see § 405(a), so there are some "other person[s]" than fiduciaries-in-breach liable under § 502 (l )(1)(B). These applications of § 502(l ) give it meaning and scope without resort to the strange interpretation of "equitable relief" in § 502(a)(3) that petitioners propose. The Secretary's initial interpretation of § 502(l ) accords with our view. The prologue of the proposed regulation implementing § 502(l ), to be codified at 29 CFR § 2560.502l-1, states that when a court awards "equitable relief"--as opposed to "monetary damages"--a § 502(l ) penalty will be assessed only if the award involves the transfer to the plan of money or property. 55 Fed.Reg. 25288, 25289, and n. 9 (1990).

In the last analysis, petitioners and the United States ask us to give a strained interpretation to § 502(a)(3) in order to achieve the "purpose of ERISA to protect plan participants and beneficiaries." Brief for Petitioners 31. They note, as we have, that before ERISA nonfiduciaries were generally liable under state trust law for damages resulting from knowing participation in a trustees's breach of duty, and they assert that such actions are now pre- empted by ERISA's broad pre-emption clause, § 514(a). Thus, they contend, our construction of § 502(a)(3) leaves beneficiaries like petitioners with less protection than existed before ERISA, contradicting

ERISA's basic goal of "promot[ing] the interests of employees and their beneficiaries in employee benefit plans."

Even assuming (without deciding) that petitioners are correct about the pre-emption of previously available state-court actions, vague notions of a statute's "basic purpose" are nonetheless inadequate to overcome the words of its text regarding the specific issue under consideration. This is especially true with legislation such as ERISA, an enormously complex and detailed statute that resolved innumerable disputes between powerful competing interests--not all in favor of potential plaintiffs. The text that we have described is certainly not nonsensical; it allocates liability for plan-related misdeeds in reasonable proportion to respective actors' power to control and prevent the misdeeds. Under traditional trust law, although a beneficiary could obtain damages from third persons for knowing participation in a trustee's breach of fiduciary duties, only the trustee had fiduciary duties. ERISA, however, defines " fiduciary" not in terms of formal trusteeship, but in functional terms of control and authority over the plan, thus expanding the universe of persons subject to fiduciary duties--and to damages-- under § 409(a). Professional service providers such as actuaries become liable for damages when they cross the line from advisor to fiduciary; must disgorge assets and profits obtained through participation as parties-in- interest in transactions prohibited by § 406, and pay related civil penalties, see § 502(i); and (assuming nonfiduciaries can be sued under § 502(a)(3)) may be enjoined from participating in a fiduciary's breaches, compelled to make restitution, and subjected to other equitable decrees. All that ERISA has eliminated, on these assumptions, is the common law's joint and several liability, for all direct and consequential damages suffered by the plan, on the part of persons who had no real power to control what the plan did. Exposure to that sort of liability would impose high insurance costs upon persons who regularly deal with and offer advice to ERISA plans, and hence upon ERISA plans themselves. There is, in other words, a " tension between the primary [ERISA] goal of benefitting employees and the subsidiary goal of containing pension costs." . . . .We will not attempt to adjust the balance between those competing goals that the text adopted by Congress has struck.

Justice WHITE, with whom THE CHIEF JUSTICE, Justice STEVENS and Justice O'CONNOR join, dissenting.

The majority candidly acknowledges that it is plausible to interpret the phrase "appropriate equitable relief" as used in § 502(a)(3) at least standing alone, as meaning that relief which was available in the courts of equity for a breach of trust. . The majority also acknowledges that the relief petitioners seek here--a compensatory monetary award--was available in the equity courts under the common law of trusts, not only against trustees for breach of duty but also against nonfiduciaries knowingly participating in a breach of trust  Finally, there can be no dispute that ERISA was grounded in this common-law experience and that "we are [to be] guided by principles of trust law" in construing the terms of the statute. Firestone Tire & Rubber Co. v. Bruch, 489 U.S. 101, 111 (1989). Nevertheless, the majority today holds that in enacting ERISA Congress stripped ERISA trust beneficiaries of a remedy against trustees and third parties that they enjoyed in the equity courts under common law. Although it is assumed that a cause of action against a third party such as respondent is provided by ERISA, the remedies available are limited to the "traditional" equitable remedies, such as injunction and restitution, and do not include compensatory damages--"the classic form of legal relief." Because I do not believe that the statutory language requires this result and because we have elsewhere recognized the anomaly of construing ERISA in a way that "would afford less protection to employees and their beneficiaries than they enjoyed before ERISA was enacted," Firestone, supra, at 114, I must dissent.

## Comments and Questions

1. One of the puzzles for courts interpreting ERISA is the relationship between decisions such as *Mertens* and the Act's preemption provision.  For example, under ERISA § 502(a) the remedies available to private litigants are generally limited to accrued benefits, declaratory judgments and injunctions. Suppose an ERISA health care plan was negligent in its denial of medical services to a participating employee and the employee suffered serious and permanent injuries as a result.  What recovery could the employee seek from the plan under ERISA?  Could the employee bring a malpractice claim against the plan?  Suppose the treatment decision were made by a Health Maintenance Organization applying utilization protocols established under the HMO's contract with the plan.  Could the employee recover on a malpractice claim against the HMO or the doctors on its staff?  See Corcoran v. United HealthCare, 965 F.2d 1321 (5th Cir.), *cert. denied,* 506 U.S. 1033 (1992).

2. Is there a better way to integrate the regulation of employee benefits plans and traditional insurance and health care regulation?

---

The following recent cases pulls together a number of the themes we have been exploring in this section of the casebook.

## Andrews-Clarke v. Travelers Insurance Co.
### 984 F. Supp. 49 (D. Mass. 1997)

YOUNG, District Judge.

Richard J. Clarke and his wife, Diane Andrews-Clarke, lived in Haverhill, Massachusetts, with their four young children, Deanna, Lacey, Carly, and Justin.  Diane Andrews-Clarke, an employee of AT & T, maintained a family health insurance policy with Travelers Insurance Co. through her AT & T employee benefit plan.  Her husband and children were named beneficiaries of that policy.

Richard Clarke drank to excess.  On April 22, 1994, Dr. Smita Patel admitted Richard Clarke to St. Joseph Hospital in Nashua, New Hampshire, for alcohol detoxification and medical evaluation.  St. Joseph Hospital contacted Greenspring, the utilization review provider that must pre-approve treatment under the terms of Clarke's health plan, regarding Clarke's admission.  Greenspring authorized only a five day hospital stay for detoxification.  Despite the fact that the Travelers' insurance policy held by Andrews-Clarke specifically stated that each insured beneficiary is entitled to at least one thirty day inpatient rehabilitation program per year, Greenspring refused to approve Clarke's enrollment in a thirty day inpatient alcohol rehabilitation program.

After this five day hospital stay, Clarke was discharged from St. Joseph Hospital with a diagnosis of alcohol dependence, alcohol withdrawal symptoms, elevated liver function, and low hemoglobin.  He remained alcohol-free for twenty-five days, but then resumed drinking.  On September 12, 1994, he voluntarily admitted himself to Baldpate Hospital in Georgetown, Massachusetts, seeking help to stop drinking.  Although aware both of Clarke's medical condition and the clear terms of the Travelers' insurance policy, Greenspring refused to authorize more than eight days of inpatient treatment.  Baldpate discharged Clarke on September 20, 1994.

Less than twenty-four hours later, Clarke drank a substantial amount of alcohol, ingested cocaine, swallowed a handful of prescription drugs, and attempted to commit suicide by locking himself in the garage with the car engine running.  His wife saved his life, breaking through the garage door to find him slumped on the floor.  She shut off the car engine and dialed 911.  Although Clarke had no detectable pulse or respiration when the ambulance arrived, the paramedics were able to revive him.  Clarke was then flown to Henrietta Goodall Hospital in Sanford, Maine, where he was placed in a hyperbaric chamber and successfully treated for carbon monoxide poisoning.

By now, it was tragically apparent to everyone but Travelers and its agent, Greenspring, that Clarke was a danger to himself and perhaps others.  After conducting a commitment hearing, the Haverhill District Court so found, and ordered Clark committed to a thirty-day detoxification and rehabilitation program.  The court referred the issue of Clarke's placement to the Court Clinic, which in turn sought Greenspring's approval for an insured admission to a private hospital.  When Greenspring--despite the fact that enrollment in a thirty-day inpatient detoxification program is a defined benefit of the Travelers insurance policy--incredibly refused to authorize such a private admission, the court ordered Clarke committed to the Southeastern Correctional Center at Bridgewater for his detoxification and rehabilitation.[11]

Clarke's life now spiralled inexorably down and out of control.  While a patient at Bridgewater, he was forcibly raped and sodomized by another inmate in his unit.  He received little in the way of therapy or treatment.  After his release from Bridgewater on October 25, 1994, he made his way back to Haverhill where his wife and four minor children still lived.  Diane Andrews-Clarke told Clarke that he could return to the marital home only if he remained sober.  Unable to do so without hospitalization, Clarke began a three-week drinking binge.

After an episode of heavy drinking on November 10, 1994, Clarke was placed in protective custody by the Pelham, New Hampshire, police.  Later that day, he was admitted to the Southern New Hampshire Medical Center in full respiratory arrest, with a blood alcohol level of .380 and a head injury.  Southern New Hampshire Medical Center made no effort to treat Clarke's alcoholism and did not seek to obtain a detoxification admission at any other facility.  Clarke spent the night sleeping on a stretcher because it was too cold to discharge him and there were no beds available in area shelters.  He was released the next morning.

---

[11]    By breaking its contract with the Clarkes and thus containing its own costs, Travelers shifted these costs to the citizens of the Commonwealth in the form of increased taxes.  As will become apparent, the Congress of the United States has, as a functional matter, authorized Travelers to impose these taxes on the citizens of the Commonwealth.

Upon leaving Southern New Hampshire Medical Center, Clarke purchased a six- pack of Meisterbrau beer, which he immediately began to consume. At 3:06 a.m. on November 12, 1994, the Pelham, New Hampshire, police discovered Clarke's body in a parked car, with a garden hose extending from the tailpipe to the passenger compartment. Clarke, age forty-one, sat lifeless in the front seat, clasping a sixteen ounce beer can in his right hand. He was pronounced dead at the scene.

Subsequent to Clarke's death, Diane Andrews-Clarke commenced this action against Travelers and Greenspring in the Superior Court of the Commonwealth of Massachusetts sitting in and for the County of Essex, individually and as administratrix of Clarke's estate and as next friend of their four minor children. Andrews-Clarke asserts that her husband's death was the direct and foreseeable result of the improper refusal of Travelers and its agent Greenspring to authorize appropriate medical and psychiatric treatment during Clarke's repeated hospitalizations for alcoholism in 1994. She brought claims against them for breach of contract, medical malpractice, wrongful death, loss of parental and spousal consortium, intentional and negligent infliction of emotional distress, and specific violations of the Massachusetts consumer protection laws.[13]

Travelers and Greenspring promptly removed her case to this Court and then, just as promptly, asked this Court to throw her out without hearing the merits of her claim.

This, of course, is ridiculous. The tragic events set forth in Diane Andrews-Clarke's Complaint cry out for relief. Clarke was the named beneficiary of a health insurance policy offered through an employee benefit plan. That policy expressly provided coverage for certain medical and psychiatric treatments, including enrollment in a thirty-day inpatient alcohol detoxification and rehabilitation program. Doctors at several hospitals, and even the courts of the Commonwealth of Massachusetts, determined that Clarke was in need of such treatment, but the insurer and its agent, the utilization review provider repeatedly and arbitrarily refused to authorize it. As a consequence of their failure to pre-approve--whether willful, or the result of negligent medical decisions made during the course of utilization review--Clarke never received the treatment he so desperately required, suffered horribly and ultimately died needlessly at age forty-one.

Under traditional notions of justice, the harms alleged--if true--should entitle Diane Andrews-Clarke to some legal remedy on behalf of herself and her children against Travelers and Greenspring. Consider just one of her claims-- breach of contract. This cause of action--that contractual promises can be enforced in the courts--pre-dates Magna Carta. It is the very bedrock of our notion of individual autonomy and property rights. It was among the first precepts of the

---

[13]   Diane Andrews-Clarke invokes Massachusetts General Laws ch. 93A, ch. 176D, § 3, and ch. 175 § 47B. Mass. Gen. L. ch. 93A is a Consumer Protection Act that prohibits unfair or deceptive acts or practices by persons engaged in the conduct of "trade or commerce." Mass. Gen. L. ch. 93A, § 2.

Mass. Gen. L. ch. 176D, § 3 defines unfair methods of competition and unfair or deceptive acts or practices in the business of insurance.

Mass. Gen. L. ch. 175, § 47B requires any insurance policy that furnishes coverage for hospital and surgical expenses to also provide certain minimum mental health care benefits.

common law to be recognized in the courts of the Commonwealth and has been zealously guarded by the state judiciary from that day to this. Our entire capitalist structure depends on it.

Nevertheless, this Court had no choice but to pluck Diane Andrews-Clarke's case out of the state court in which she sought redress (and where relief to other litigants is available) and then, at the behest of Travelers and Greenspring, to slam the courthouse doors in her face and leave her without any remedy.

This case, thus, becomes yet another illustration of the glaring need for Congress to amend ERISA to account for the changing realities of the modern health care system. Enacted to safeguard the interests of employees and their beneficiaries, ERISA has evolved into a shield of immunity that protects health insurers, utilization review providers, and other managed care entities from potential liability for the consequences of their wrongful denial of health benefits.

All of Diane Andrews-Clarke's cognizable state law causes of action arise out of the alleged improper processing of Clarke's claims for benefits under an ERISA employee benefit plan, and are therefore preempted. At the same time, however, it is undisputed that ERISA's civil enforcement provision does not authorize recovery for wrongful death, personal injury, or other consequential damages caused by the improper refusal of an insurer or utilization review provider to authorize treatment. Thus, the practical impact of ERISA in this case is to immunize Travelers and Greenspring from any potential liability for the consequences of their denial of benefits.[27]

. . . .

## THE LARGER ISSUES

Perhaps even more disturbing than the perverse outcome generated by ERISA in this particular case is the fact that, in the current health care system, the misconduct alleged by Diane Andrews-Clarke may not be atypical. [Seventy-five percent] of insured Americans now receive their health care through some type of "managed care" plan. Although the advent of managed care has eliminated many of the excesses that plagued the traditional fee-for-service system and

---

[27]    Several recent cases have held that when the doctors who actually treated the plan beneficiary are actual or ostensible agents of the plan (as is often the case in a staff-model HMO) a malpractice claim against the plan based upon a theory of vicarious liability is not preempted by ERISA. . . .

In the case, at bar, however, the malpractice claims against Travelers and Greenspring are premised upon a theory of direct rather than vicarious liability. Diane Andrews-Clarke does not allege that the doctors who treated Clarke at St. Joseph Hospital, Southern New Hampshire Medical Center, or Baldpate Hospital were actual or ostensible agents of Travelers or Greenspring, or that Travelers or Greenspring directed Clarke to seek treatment at these hospitals, but rather wishes to recover for negligent medical decisions made during the utilization review process.

As a general matter, this Court further notes that the vicarious liability crack in the shield of ERISA preemption is one of narrow applicability. Unlike fully integrated staff-model HMOs, which hire physicians as employees, the majority of managed care plans contract with independent groups or networks of physicians. . . . A beneficiary cannot assert a malpractice claim against such a plan premised upon a theory of vicarious liability unless she can demonstrate that the plan held out the treating physician as its employee. . . . This showing will become increasingly difficult as managed care plans begin to realize that a clear communication to its enrollees that the plan does not directly furnish medical treatment is all that is necessary to avoid liability.

has, at least temporarily, stabilized the growth of health care costs, it has also spawned a whole new set of potential abuses. In contrast to the old system, in which doctors had incentives to provide too much care, under managed care, the incentives are to provide as little treatment as possible. Indeed, there is a growing body of anecdotal evidence that managed care plans often deny necessary, and even life-saving medical treatment in the name of cutting costs.

Congress, the states, and even the health care industry have recognized the need for reform. In 1997 alone, state legislatures across the country have introduced approximately 1,000 bills regulating managed care, 182 of which have already been enacted into law. At both the federal and state levels, considerable emphasis has been placed on legislating quality standards for individual treatments and procedures. In response to public outcry concerning "drive-through deliveries," Congress enacted the Newborns' and Mothers' Health Care Protection Act of 1996 which requires all health plans to provide coverage for a minimum hospital stay of 48 hours after childbirth. In addition, Congress is presently considering bills that would force health plans to provide coverage for 1) certain emergency medical services, 2) minimum hospital stays for mastectomies and lumpectomies, 3) reconstructive breast surgery, 4) annual mammography screenings for women over the age of 40;  and 5) gynecological services. Numerous states have already passed or are considering legislation similar to some or all of these proposals.

As matter of public policy, such piecemeal reforms are inadequate because they target the symptoms while ignoring the underlying pathology--the incentives for undercare which now pervade America's health care system. Persons who suffer from medical conditions that affect only a small or historically underrepresented portion of the population are left unprotected. Furthermore, although certain procedures such as mastectomy and child birth seem to lend themselves to uniform regulation, innumerable other medical conditions require more idiosyncratic treatment protocols. Attempts to draw bright-line rules regarding what levels of treatment are "medically necessary" for such conditions will ultimately "impede even proper denials" of treatment, and thus needlessly drive up health care costs.

Rather than seeking directly to regulate managed care procedure-by-procedure, the more efficient approach is to allow insurers and utilization review providers to make benefit determinations on a case-by-case basis, but hold them legally accountable for the consequences of their decisions. By ensuring that bad medical judgments made during the utilization review process do not "end up being cost-free to the plans that rely on [utilization review] to contain medical costs," plan administrators will have more incentive to "seek out those [utilization review providers] that can deliver both high quality services and reasonable prices."

Some have argued that exposing managed care plans to the threat of direct liability will result in over-deterrence, and therefore undermine legitimate cost containment efforts. Congress, certainly sensitive to these concerns, of course has the power to cap the amount of damages that beneficiaries can recover against insurers and utilization providers, or to take other steps to limit industry liability. Under any criterion, however, the shield of near absolute immunity now provided by ERISA simply cannot be justified.

This Court takes judicial notice that Congress is now considering two bills which would remove the shield of de facto immunity that ERISA provides for managed care insurers and utilization review providers. The Managed Care Plan Accountability Act of 1997 would amend ERISA's civil enforcement provision, Section 502(c), to provide a federal remedy to any ERISA plan participant or beneficiary who is wrongfully denied benefits under a managed care plan pursuant to a "clinically or medically inappropriate decision or determination resulting from the application of any cost containment technique ... [or] any utilization review directed at cost containment." The Patient Access to Responsible Care Act of 1997, in contrast, would make ERISA's preemption provision, section 514(a), inapplicable to "any State cause of action to recover damages for personal injury or wrongful death against any person that provides insurance or administrative services to or for an employee welfare benefit plan maintained to provide health care benefits." Although both of these bills are still in the early stages of the legislative process, Congress is at least aware of the current gap in remedies.

The very reason that most "people seek health insurance is to have some medical security in a crisis." For the more than 50% of American workers who receive their health insurance through an ERISA-governed plan, however, such security is sorely lacking because of the de facto immunity that the law now confers upon insurers and utilization review providers associated with such plans. Unfortunately, to date, "ERISA [has proven] an excellent example of the classic observation that it is a great deal more difficult for Congress to correct flawed statutes than it is to enact them in the first place ....because interests coalesce around the advantageous aspects of the status quo." Although the alleged conduct of Travelers and Greenspring in this case is extraordinarily troubling, even more disturbing to this Court is the failure of Congress to amend a statute that, due to the changing realities of the modern health care system, has gone conspicuously awry from its original intent.

Does anyone care?

Do you?

## Comments and Questions

1. Judge Young's opinion in the *Andrews-Clarke* decision has helped focus national attention on the problem of inadequate remedies for denial of medical benefits provided under employer-sponsored health plans. As of the summer of 1998, Congress was considering various solutions to the problem. One approach, associated with the Republican Party, would mandate expert review boards, created to ensure that employees could obtain prompt and impartial resolution of disputed benefit requests. A second approach, associated with the Democratic Party, would favor the restoration of traditional common law remedies — that is, punitive and consequential damages — for breaches of contract involving employee benefits. Which approach would you favor?

2. The premise of Judge Young's decision is that something has gone serious wrong in this area of the law. With ERISA, Congress preempted traditional state law remedies for materials related to employee benefit plans (that's the preemption line of cases), and then created a limited and inadequate set of federal remedies in the field (that is the *Bruch/Mertens* line). Is it clear that Judge Young is right? The tragedy of the *Andrews-Clarke* decision is clear, but might it simply be an exceptional case? Can't we rely on market forces to develop appropriate employee benefit plans and police their administration? Is this is an appropriate area for creating a one-size-fits-all system of mandatory remedies?

# CHAPTER NINE

# INTRODUCTION TO THE SECURITIES INDUSTRY

With this chapter, we begin our study of the securities industry. As with the regulation of depository institutions and insurance companies, the supervision of securities firms has evolved in a distinctive manner that has left its mark on our modern regulatory structure. Securities firms generally are of two types: broker-dealers and investment advisers. We will focus principally on broker-dealers. In the first few decades of this century, when the industry first became the subject of serious regulatory attention, the states were the exclusive regulators of broker-dealers. Only with the passage of the Securities Exchange Act of 1934 did the federal government begin to regulate broker-dealers. Today, all significant broker-dealers are regulated at both the state and federal level. Thus, like depository institutions, broker-dealers operate under a dual system of regulation. In the broker-dealer field, however, federal regulation is preeminent, and the states serve to supplement federal authority, rather than to compete with it.

Another distinguishing characteristic of U.S. broker-dealer regulation is the prominence of private organizations that perform quasi-governmental functions. The National Association of Securities Dealers, Inc. ("NASD"), the stock exchanges, and a variety of lesser organizations play important roles in supervising broker-dealers. As you read through these chapters, pay attention to the role of private organizations in this field and consider whether similar systems of statute-based self-regulation should be encouraged in other financial fields.

Finally and most significantly, the regulation of securities firms is not based on the sort of mandatory rules -- such as restrictions on activities and formal rate-making procedures -- that characterize the depository institution and insurance fields. Rather, disclosure obligations and fiduciary norms form the core of broker-dealer regulation in this country. How does this mixture of regulatory controls compare with regulatory structures we have already studied? Is there something about the activities of broker-dealers that make it necessary to employ a different regulatory strategy in this field? Or, would it be preferable to move towards greater uniformity in regulation? If you think uniformity is desirable, in which direction would you propose we move?

This chapter offers an introduction to the regulation of broker-dealers. The first section reviews the history of the securities industry in the United States and charts the growth of regulatory structures. The second section provides a brief overview of the business of broker-dealers. The final section outlines the current structure of broker dealer regulation.

# Section 1.  History of Broker-Dealers and their Regulation

In the second half of the nineteenth century, when the basic forms of depository institutions and insurance companies were already well-established, a separate class of institutions specializing in the underwriting of corporate securities emerged as a new and significant economic force.   These precursors of today's securities industry included J.P. Morgan & Co., Kidder, Peabody, and Brown Brothers.  The firms tended to be located in the eastern financial centers of New York, Boston, and  Philadelphia, and many of the larger firms were affiliated with correspondent firms in Europe.  As a group, these early American investment banks played a major role in the industrialization of the American economy, helping railroads and industrial firms like U.S. Steel raise large amounts of capital.   Until the end of the century, securities underwritten through American private banks were primarily debt instruments, which were largely placed with (that is, sold to) institutional holders or wealthy clients.   With the turn of the century, however, the securities business underwent several profound changes, transforming the industry and our regulatory structure:

A number of factors coalesced to create active public securities markets during [the last years of the nineteenth century].The growth of large industries such as railroads and heavy manufacturing stimulated unprecedented demands for capital. At the same time, increases in wealth among the middle classes created a new source of capital that could be tapped effectively by means of public securities issuance. Developments in transportation and communication technology made widespread promotion and distribution of securities practicable. Realizing the potential purchasing power of the rising middle class, bond issuers began to offer securities in denominations of $100 instead of the traditional denominations of $1,000 or even $10,000. A surge of new investment followed.

Most securities sold to investors during this period were reputable and safe -- the classic examples being railroad and municipal bonds. Interest rates on these securities were low, however.  For the investor with a taste for risk, plenty of speculative issues were available in the market. . . . [T]he speculative securities in the early 1900s were typically equity securities issued by mining and petroleum companies, land development schemes (such as irrigation and tract housing projects), and patent development promotions.

Speculative securities were distributed outside the usual channels for blue chip issues. The elite investment banks would not touch them, and they were not listed on the New York or Curb Exchanges, although in the case of mining and oil securities, they often would be listed for trading on the San Francisco, Spokane, or Los Angeles Stock Exchanges. Lacking traditional distribution channels, these securities were marketed by face-to-face solicitation, newspaper advertisements, and mass mailings. . . .

Sales of speculative securities surged in the period from 1910 to 1911. The relatively high inflation prevailing during this period spurred investors to seek high-yielding investments such as bonds of smaller railroads, public utilities, and industrial firms. These investments, while still relatively safe, paid as much as 6 percent as compared with blue chip bonds at 4 to 4 1/2 percent. Equity securities offered even greater potential yields -- albeit coupled with greater risk -- while hedging against inflation. Meanwhile a strong agricultural economy from

1910 to 1912 placed disposable income in the hands of the American farmer, who sometimes invested in securities that were as alluring as they were ultimately unwise.

Johnathan R. Macey & Geoffrey P. Miller, *Origins of the Blue Sky Laws*, 70 TEX. L. REV. 347, 352-56 (1991).

The First World War, and more particularly the government's efforts to finance the war through the sale of Liberty Bonds to the general public, accelerated the expansion of the securities industry:

> The sale of government bonds to finance the war on a massive scale, unduplicated since the days of Jay Cooke's Civil War campaigns, caused a revolution in the ownership pattern of securities and in their methods of distribution. Financial institutions were expected to assist the government in widely distributing the large war loans. They were encouraged to lend investors the purchase price of government bonds on liberal repayment terms. By the end of the war, every large urban bank throughout the country was involved in the creation of an atmosphere favorable to securities investment that ultimately reach over 14 million Americans.
>
> . . . After 1919, corporations of all types, not just railroads and heavy industries, discovered an American public, now committed to the investing habit, very receptive to new security issues of an unprecedented frequency and dollar volume. As a consequence of this new access to the supply of long-term capital, many companies found they were far less reliant on banks to provide short-term, seasonal financing. In addition, high profits gave many corporations such a large cash flow that outside borrowing was unnecessary. This decline in loan demand threatened the earning power of commercial banks and encouraged them to seek other opportunities for profit. An expansion of investment banking functions to offset the reduction in loan revenues was a course chosen by more and more large urban banks.

Edwin J. Perkins, *The Divorce of Commercial and Investment Banking: A History*, 88 BANKING L.J. 483, 491-93 (1970).

The forays of commercial banks into investment banking in the 1920s were arrested in 1933 with the passage of the Glass-Steagall Act, a statute we will consider in Chapter 15. For now, however, we focus on the problems that the expanding securities industry created in the first few decades of the twentieth century, and the ways in which first the states and then the federal government responded to those problems.

## A. Early Regulation and State Blue Sky Laws

Perhaps not surprisingly in light of their primacy in other forms of financial regulation at the time, the states were the first to develop a supervisory structure for the emerging securities industry. Kansas's adoption of legislation in 1911 is generally considered to be the first state securities regulation statute, and forty-six other jurisdictions followed suit before any action was taken at the federal level. The following excerpt provides a brief overview of these early state regulatory initiatives and the problems they faced:

> State securities statutes were known as 'blue sky' laws, because some lawmakers believed that 'if securities legislation was not passed, financial pirates would sell citizens everything in [the] state but the blue sky.' Legislators were reacting to both genuine and spurious complaints received from investors regarding fraudulent securities deals. . . .

Blue sky laws varied from state to state but can be classified into two broad categories: antifraud laws and licensing laws. Antifraud laws did not take effect until evidence appeared that fraud had been or was about to be committed in the sale of securities. State authorities were empowered by statute to investigate suspected fraud and could enjoin such fraudulent activities and in some cases undertake criminal proceedings. Licensing laws gave state officials control over traffic in securities by prohibiting sales until an application was filed and permission granted by the state. Officials of the state agency, charged with enforcement of this type of blue sky law, usually reviewed detailed information supplied by the issuer regarding the issuer's financial history and present status and passed judgment on the soundness of the securities offering. If the securities appeared to meet the statutory requirements, the issuer was permitted to sell the securities within the state. In some instances, securities with no record of earnings could be sold by issuers only with the express label: 'This is a speculative security.'

Many states boasted of great success with their blue sky legislation, but there was little documented proof as to their effectiveness. In reality, the laws proved quite ineffective for several reasons. First, responsibility for the enforcement of these laws was delegated to 'unspecialized attorneys working for state officials as disparate as the railroad commission or the state auditor. When political administrations changed, responsibility for blue sky law enforcement frequently also was reassigned.' In addition to the lack of expertise among the enforcers, state funding was generally inadequate to support the fulltime manpower needed to investigate the securities and to take remedial or prosecutional action. Also, many states were deliberately lax in the regulation of securities traffic in order to attract outside industry and to prevent the exodus of industry to more lenient states.

The victims of securities fraud were another factor in the inadequate enforcement of state security laws. Typically, promoters and dealers, facing prosecutorial investigation, would offer refunds to prosecution witnesses. Often a witness would accept a refund and the case would fail for lack of sufficient evidence. Insurance funds set up by fraudulent dealers would be used for 'placating the more dangerous of the defrauded investors.' While this practice interfered with effective enforcement of the laws, the objectives of the blue sky laws were met in an indirect way by forcing dealers to return money to some investors.

In 1917, the Supreme Court clearly established the constitutionality of the blue sky laws. [See Hall v. Geiger-Jones Co., 242 U.S. 539 (1917).] By that time the laws had already been analyzed by the securities industry, in particular, the Investment Banker's Association (IBA), an organization interested in resisting regulation. In 1915, the IBA informed its members that the blue sky laws could be evaded easily by operating across state lines. Promoters could sell their securities through the mails in other states, as long as the sale was finalized through an acceptance from the seller's office by mail or telegram. Since a sale consists of an offer and acceptance, until the buyer accepts an offer there is no sale. Under the law of contracts, the sale is legally made at the place where the acceptance is given. Sellers took great care to avoid the jurisdiction of states that had effective statutes. Even with offers that were strictly intrastate, effective lobbying, principally by the IBA, riddled the statutes with exemptions.

Securities listed on the New York Stock Exchange were exempted from regulation under most of the state laws, since the listing requirements of the exchange were more stringent than most states' requirements. Legislatures began to provide exemptions for securities listed on other exchanges which had not developed listing requirements adequate to protect investors. These exemptions provided a way for issuers with less than 'sound' financial histories to escape the scrutiny of state examiners. Once these issuers were listed with one of the exempt minor exchanges, they could offer securities within the state, unaffected by the state regulation.

The blue sky laws were not much of an obstacle for the fraudulent promoter. According to contemporary reports, promoters used the devices noted above to continue their dealings. They selected ventures, such as mining, oil, or real estate, and set up companies with no legitimate prospects, in order to sell stock. In 1922, a movement was begun to draft uniform blue sky legislation directed at eliminating some of the inherent problems that permitted evasion of the laws. At the time of the enactment of the federal securities laws, no state had adopted the uniform act that had been drafted between 1922 and 1930 by the National Conference of Commissioners on Uniform State Laws. Without universal adoption of the uniform laws, the purposes of such legislation could still have been subverted.

Elisabeth Keller & Gergory A. Gehlmann, *A Historical Introduction to the Securities Act of 1933 and the Securities Exchange Act of 1934*, 49 OHIO ST. L.J. 329, 331-33 (1988).

## B. Federal Securities Regulation and the New Deal

Though federal legislation was not adopted until the 1930s, a number of congressional investigations presaged that development. For example, following the lead of the Armstrong Commission's study of corruption in the New York life insurance industry, a congressional investigation popularly known as the Pujo Committee instituted in 1912 its own investigation of J.P. Morgan and other members of the so-called Money Trust. Many of the committee's findings, which concerned excessive compensation and favoritism of investment bankers, found their way into Louis Brandeis's celebrated *Other People's Money* (1914), which propounded mandatory disclosure as the appropriate response to the excesses of Wall Street: "Publicity is justly commended as a remedy for social and industrial diseases. Sunlight is said to be the best of disinfectants; electric light the most efficient policeman."

Despite the early support for federal intervention and the increasingly obvious deficiencies of state blue sky laws, no significant federal legislation was adopted in the 1920s. The Republican administrations of the post-World War I era were reluctant to interfere with the business world, and the not-yet overturned *Paul v. Virginia* decision cast doubt on the constitutionality of federal regulation over securities transactions. (These concerns were not entirely resolved until the Supreme Court implicitly endorsed the constitutionality of the federal securities laws in Jones v. SEC, 298 U.S. 1 (1936).) The Republicans' laissez-faire attitude came to an end with the Crash of 1929:

Between September 1, 1929, and July 1, 1932, the value of all stocks listed on the New York Stock Exchange shrank from a total of nearly $90 billion to just under $16 billion — a loss of 83 percent. In a comparable period, bonds listed on the New York Stock Exchange declined from a value of $49 billion to $31 billion. . . . Nor did these figures, staggering as they were, fully gauge the extent of the 1929-1932 stock market crash. During the post-

World War I decade, approximately $50 billion of new securities were sold in the United States.  Approximately half or $25 billion would prove near or totally valueless.  Leading "blue chip" securities, including General Electric, Sears, Roebuck, and U.S. Steel common stock, would lose over 90 percent of their value between selected dates in 1929 and 1932.

JOEL SELIGMAN, THE TRANSFORMATION OF WALL STREET: A HISTORY OF THE SECURITIES AND EXCHANGE COMMISSION AND MODERN CORPORATE FINANCE 1 (2d ed. 1995).

The Crash and the depression that followed transformed American finance.  In the presidential elections of 1932, New York Governor Franklin Roosevelt defeated Herbert Hoover, and brought to Washington a new team of economic advisers intent on imposing vigorous federal authority to oversee the country's financial markets.  Their offensive began with a congressional investigation into stock exchange practices. Under the leadership of Ferdinand Pecora, counsel of the Senate Banking Committee and former New York prosecutor, the hearings explored a number of charges of corruption and shady practices:

*Disclosure problems:* According to many witnesses, underwriters had marketed securities to the general public without revealing critical information about the purpose of the offering or the prospects of the issuer.  For example, a securities firm affiliated with a large New York bank sold a number of Latin American bond issues without revealing that issuing countries were on the brink of insolvency and that the bonds would largely be used to repay loans from an affiliated bank.

*Manipulation:* Another set of allegations had to do with market manipulation by securities firms.  In a typical scheme, called a bear raid, securities firms would collude to depress the price of a particular stock (either through short sales or even illusory wash sales) with the intention of prompting other investors to sell their shares in a panic and then buying the securities back at a lower price.

*Conflicts of interest:* Witnesses also repeatedly charged securities firms with favoritism in their treatment of customers.  Hearings uncovered many instances in which either officers of the securities firms or else colleagues and acquaintances were given investment opportunities that were not shared with the general public.  These charges were reminiscent of the Pujo Committee's earlier suspicions that the leading securities firms constituted the lynchpin in an elaborate and self-serving money trust.

By bringing these charges and other evidence of corruption in the securities industry to light, the Pecora hearings awakened the public to the need for federal regulation.

Precisely what form this federal regulation should take remained a subject of considerable debate for the first few years of the first Roosevelt Administration.  Some of the more diehard New Dealers argued that the government had to take an active role in reviewing the quality and appropriateness of publicly-traded securities, a role the government had in fact played to a limited degree during the First World War.  (A number of state blue sky laws in place at the time operated in this way )  The alternative view opposed such intrusive government involvement and advanced a Brandeisian vision of a disclosure-based regulation.

## 1. The Securities Act of 1933 — Oversight of Public Offerings

The first of the New Deal securities statutes, the Securities Act of 1933 (the 1933 Act), established a federal system for the registration of new issues of securities. Thus the direct subjects of the 1933 Act's regulation were corporations making public offerings. From the perspective of the securities industry, the primary importance of this legislation was its imposition of federal authority over the underwriting process. (Under the federal securities laws, "underwriting" is a term of art, see section 2(11) of the 1933 Act, which entails the distribution of securities to the general public.) Among other things, the 1933 Act established elaborate procedural and disclosure requirements for public offerings of securities. The 1933 Act required the registration statement to contain specified information about the security, the issuer, and the underwriters. The 1933 Act also established a stringent system of civil, administrative, and criminal sanctions designed to ensure compliance with the Act's procedural and disclosure requirements.

While it had a profound effect on capital formation, the 1933 Act was recognized from the start as simply the first phase of federal regulation over the securities industry. The 1933 Act, for example, had little impact on the secondary securities market — that is, the trading markets where many of the abuses uncovered in the Pecora hearings had occurred — nor did the Act directly regulate securities firms themselves. Indeed, as far as the securities industry was concerned, the 1933 Act was arguably not even the most important piece of federal legislation passed that year. From a structural perspective, the Banking Act of 1933, which included the Glass-Steagall provisions mandating the separation of commercial and investment banking, was more important because it caused a large portion of the industry to be separated from commercial banking affiliates.

## 2. The Securities Exchange Act of 1934 — Regulation of Exchanges

The Securities Exchange Act of 1934 (the 1934 Act) addressed the more complex problem of establishing federal oversight in the country's trading market. Because the 1934 Act is a multi-faceted statute, it is more difficult to summarize than the 1933 Act. As a preliminary matter it is important to recognize that the political climate had changed to a considerable degree between 1933 and 1934. Worsening economic conditions had caused some in Congress and many in the business world to question the wisdom of the stringent new requirements of the 1933 Act. (And indeed, a portion of the 1934 Act constituted amendments to the earlier legislation, weakening its liability rules somewhat.) Accordingly, the Roosevelt Administration was more inclined to seek compromises in 1934, and the legislation enacted that year reflects that attitude.

The central compromise of the 1934 Act was its acceptance of the continued importance of the major stock exchanges, most notably the New York Stock Exchange (NYSE), which was then as it is now our largest and more prominent trading market. Rather than imposing direct federal control over the trading markets, the 1934 Act made the exchanges themselves instruments of federal regulation. This transformation from private enterprise to quasi-public self-regulatory organization (or SRO) was effected in two ways. First, all stock exchanges were required to register with the federal government and become, along with their member firms, subject to indirect federal oversight. Second, all companies with securities listed on registered exchanges were required to comply with periodic disclosure requirements similar to the 1933 Act's requirements for public offerings.

The 1934 Act also created a new federal agency, the Securities and Exchange Commission (SEC), and charged it with overseeing the exchanges and also administering the requirements of the 1933 Act, which had previously been under the jurisdiction of the Federal Trade Commission. The initial staffing of the Commission reflected the pragmatism of the time. While a number of prominent New Dealers were appointed as members of the Commission, President Roosevelt picked former market manipulator Joseph P. Kennedy to be the SEC's first chair. According to one witness to the decision: "The President has great confidence in him because he has made his pile . . . and know all the tricks of the trade. Apparently he is going on the assumption that Kennedy would now like to make a name for himself for the sake of his family." While Kennedy stayed on as SEC chair only a year, he played a major role in launching the agency by attracting an expert staff and developing a reputation for effective and pragmatic oversight.

The 1934 Act also gave the Commission a number of tools to improve the integrity of the nation's markets. For example, the Act included several substantive rules designed to curb manipulation of trading in the secondary markets. These rules addressed specific practices like "bear raids" and manipulative short selling that the Pecora hearings had uncovered. The 1934 Act also granted the SEC open-ended rulemaking authority with which to address other manipulation and fraudulent activities. The most prominent example of this power is section 10(b), under which the Commission promulgated the now familiar Rule 10b-5 in 1942. (Recall our brief discussion of rule 10b-5 in section 9 of Chapter Three (Bank Trust Activities).) Section 15(c) of the Act includes a similarly broad mandate for the SEC to develop specialized anti-fraud rules for the broker-dealer industry. In an effort to restrain speculation, the 1934 Act also authorized the Federal Reserve Board to regulate credit used to finance stock purchases.

### 3. The 1938 Amendments and the Creation of the NASD

Perhaps not surprisingly in light of the many compromises written into the 1934 Act, the years immediately following the Act's enactment were characterized by low-level warfare between the existing exchanges (primarily the NYSE) and the Commission over dominance in the securities industry. Politically, the exchange — and its President Richard Whitney — were well connected and maintained close ties with both the Roosevelt Administration and Congress. Although the federal securities laws were a centerpiece of the New Deal, experts remained divided over how much the Commission should be allowed to impose upon the NYSE in its dealings with its members. Defenders of the NYSE argued that the new federal securities laws were contributing to the continuing economic problems of the Great Depression and asserted that further regulation would only worsen the situation.

In 1938, the tide moved against the exchanges. There was internal division within the NYSE's membership as the old guard (the elite private banking houses represented by Whitney) increasingly opposed governmental intrusions into their enclave, while rank and file members, who had extensive retail networks and depended on consumer confidence for their livelihood, favored reform efforts to improve their situation. The final blow fell when Whitney was discovered to have been embezzling client funds and was convicted of grand larceny.   In the wake of the Whitney scandal, the NYSE revised its internal operations to ensure a more rigorous review of members.  In addition, the position of the retail-broker members of the exchange was generally enhanced at the expense of the old guard.

When William O. Douglas became chair of the SEC in 1937, one of his primary goals was to bring the over-the-counter (OTC) markets under commission control.  As Douglas recognized, the 1934 Act had left an asymmetry of regulation between exchanges and over-the-counter markets: securities listed on the exchanges were subject to a more extensive system of regulation than those traded on the OTC markets, and securities firms that were members of exchanges came under indirect SEC oversight whereas broker-dealers that limited themselves to OTC markets were, effectively, free from federal regulation, aside from several general and inadequately enforced anti-fraud rules.  The OTC markets were, moreover, a difficult environment to supervise.  Unlike the exchanges, these markets had no physical location; rather they typically consisted of a loose network of dealers connected through telegraph lines or the circulation of quotation sheets.  In addition, unlike the exchanges, the OTC markets had no formal organizational structure onto which federal supervision could be superimposed.  Under the original 1934 Act, the only way for the Commission to reach the over-the-counter markets was through direct federal oversight, and the size and complexity of the market made that approach a daunting prospect.

Douglas found the solution to this dilemma on another plank of New Deal platform.  At roughly the same time the federal securities law were enacted, Congress had adopted the National Industrial Recovery Act, under which industries were encouraged to form themselves into trade associations and adopt binding codes of fair trade practices to alleviate perceived problems of excessive competition.  In Schechter Poultry Corp. v. United States, 295 U.S. 495 (1935), the Supreme Court had struck down the legislation as an unconstitutional delegation of power, but before the Act's demise, the Investment Banker's Association had begun to fashion a Code Committee to oversee OTC market activities.

In December 1937, Douglas invited leaders of the investment banking community to discuss means of better coordinating enforcement activities.  At the meeting several bankers agreed with an SEC proposal to amend the Securities Exchange Act to give voluntary associations like the Investment Bankers Conference an official status similar to that of the organized exchanges "in order to enable the associations to undertake effective programs of enforcement." Douglas soon emphasized to a congressional committee that if effective self-regulation of the securities exchanges were to succeed, the SEC could not compromise its enforcement role, but should play a residual role: "Government would keep the shotgun, so to speak, behind the door, loaded, well oiled, cleaned, ready for use but with the hope it would never have to be used."

JOEL SELIGMAN, *supra*, at 185.

With the passage of the Maloney Act of 1938, Congress accepted Douglas's recommendation and created a self-regulatory system for the OTC market based on the principle of "cooperative regulation". Modeled after the original Act's treatment of exchanges, the 1938 amendments provided for the formation of "national securities associations" that would, under the supervision of the Commission, have the power to promulgate rules governing voluntary membership of non-exchange broker-dealers. The National Association of Securities Dealers, Inc. (NASD) is the only such association ever to form, and survives as lineal descendent of the National Industrial Recovery Act.

### 4. Further Refinements of the Modern Era

In the years following the Maloney Act, the Commission's authority over the broker-dealer industry and the trading market gradually expanded and solidified. Between 1945 and 1962, the number of salespersons registered with the NASD increased from 25,000 to 95,000 and the number of broker-dealer branch offices from 790 to 4,713. However, the professionalism of many of the new entrants was uneven, and a number of registered representatives were inadequately trained and poorly supervised. In response to these and other concerns, the Commission undertook a Special Study of the securities industry, which resulted in the Securities Act Amendments of 1964. These amendments expanded the substantive authority of the Commission over broker-dealer affairs and mandated additional standards regarding broker-dealer competence and capital. In addition, prior to 1964 the Commission could only suspend or revoke a firm's registration; the amendments extended this power to include the authority to censure and placed limitations on the activities, functions, or operations of a broker-dealer. The 1964 Amendments also closed the last major loophole in OTC regulation: the disclosure obligations of issuers of securities trading in that market. As mentioned earlier, the original 1934 Act had imposed mandatory disclosure obligations only on issuers with securities listed on registered exchanges. Not until the 1964 amendments did Congress expand the 1934 Act to establish similar periodic disclosure requirements for public companies with securities traded in OTC markets.

The next important amendment to the federal securities laws came in 1970, when Congress enacted a series of changes designed, among other things, to respond to the "back office" crisis of the 1960s during which a number of broker-dealers fell into insolvency and many customer securities were lost or misapplied, leaving customers unable to recover their assets from a bankruptcy trustee or receivership. In addition to tightening financial standards for the industry, the 1970 amendments created the Securities Investor Protection Corporation ("SIPC") to guarantee the safekeeping of customer securities and cash balances held by registered broker-dealers and to oversee broker-dealer liquidations. SIPC provides coverage for up to $500,000 in losses for an individual account, not more than $100,000 of which may be in cash balances. SIPC coverage does not extend to losses on securities from market fluctuations or to losses from fraudulent or manipulative activities by broker-dealers. Analogous to the FDIC, SIPC is financed by an annual assessment of members, supported by a residual and as-yet-unused billion-dollar line of credit from U.S. Treasury.

In 1975, Congress again adopted major amendments to the 1934 Act. Most of the 1975 amendments were designed to increase competition in trading markets and to develop a more unified national market system. (Chapter Eleven discusses these aspects of the amendments in some detail.)  The 1975 reforms also expanded the scope of SEC authority over pockets of the securities industry that previously had been exempted from federal oversight.  Most significantly, the 1975 Amendments expanded SEC authority over municipal securities broker-dealers, and established a new SRO — the Municipal Securities Rulemaking Board (MSRB) — to develop uniform guidelines for this segment of the industry.  Eleven years later, in 1986, Congress made a comparable extension of broker-dealer coverage when it enacted yet another registration requirement for broker-dealers that limited their business to U.S. government securities.

The past fifteen years have seen numerous additional refinements of SEC authority over the broker-dealer industry.  For example, in 1984 and 1988, Congress enacted a series of technical amendments aimed at reducing insider trading and imposing new supervisory obligations on the broker-dealer industry.  In 1990, Congress further amended the 1934 Act to expand the array of the SEC's supervisory powers, making them roughly comparable to the enhanced powers granted federal bank and thrift regulators in the post-thrift crisis reforms of 1989.  The 1990 reforms also included a new statutory directive for the regulation of penny stock fraud, which we will discuss in Chapter Ten, and enhanced SEC powers to dealing with sudden market drops, such as the market break of October 1987.

### 5.  Realignment of Federal-State Authority over Broker-Dealers

The enactment of the National Securities Market Improvements Act of 1996 marks the most recent amendment to the 1934 Act and signals a realignment of supervisory authority over the securities industry.  The original federal securities statutes enacted in the 1930s were intended to supplement, not supersede, existing state blue sky laws.  Both the 1933 Act and the 1934 Act had savings clauses that expressly preserved state law, unless in direct conflict with federal requirements.  See section 16 of the 1933 Act; Section 28(a) of the 1934 Act.  Out of concern that overlapping state and federal regimes impose unnecessary costs, the National Securities Market Improvements Act of 1996 partially repealed the traditional joint federal-state oversight.  In particular, the Act added section 15(h) to the 1934 Act, which invalidates all state or local laws that "establish capital, custody, margin, financial responsibility, [record-keeping], bonding, or financial or operational reporting requirements for brokers, dealers, municipal securities dealers, government securities brokers, or government securities dealers that differ from, or are in addition to the requirements" of the 1934 Act.  Apparently left unaffected by this new provision are state anti-fraud rules and other common law rights and remedies.  For a review of the impact of the 1996 legislation, see Howard M. Friedman, *The Impact of NSMIA on State Regulation of Broker-Dealers and Investment Advisers*, 53 BUS. LAW. 511 (1998).

### Comments and Questions

The federal regulation of the securities industry followed a several-decade-long experiment with regulation of securities markets solely through the state blue-sky laws.  The cataclysm of the Great Depression triggered a change in jurisdictional authority.  In the insurance industry, in contrast, state regulators were given a much longer period of time to develop effective regulatory mechanisms and remain the primary source of insurance regulation in the United States.  Could the states also have developed effective tools for policing the securities industry?  Or are there fundamental differences between insurance and securities products that necessitate national regulation in this field?  In our increasingly global economy, must securities regulation now move to some supra-national level of oversight?

# Section 2: The Business of Securities Firms

The following reading, which is excerpted from a leading treatise on broker-dealer regulation authored by Professor Poser of Brooklyn Law School, introduces the current business environment of the securities industry.

## Norman S. Poser, The Economics and Structure of the Securities Industry
### Broker-Dealer Law and Regulation 5-19 (2d ed. 1998)

The securities industry is part of the larger financial services industry, whose overall role is to act as an intermediary between providers and users of capital. . . .     Nevertheless,because of the central role played by brokers and dealers in raising capital, directing the savings of millions of individual investors, facilitating mergers and acquisitions, and making secondary markets in securities, the relative amount of financial assets that they hold gives an inadequate picture of the importance of these firms in the economy. . . .

The securities industry includes a large number of firms and individuals.  In 1995, approximately 7,700 broker-dealers were registered with the SEC.  More than one-half of these firms were organized as corporations, about one-fourth as sole proprietorships, and the remainder as partnerships.  They employed a total of approximately 550,000 persons, about one-quarter of whom worked in New York City, the financial center of the United States.

In terms of the amount of business done, by far the most important segment of the securities industry consists of the 487 member firms of the NYSE, including 309 firms that do business directly with the public.  Although this latter group of firms comprises only 6 percent of all broker-dealers, it accounts for 68 percent of all revenues and 76 percent of all assets of the securities industry.  In 1995, NYSE member firms doing business with the public employed about 120,000 salespersons (called "registered representatives" by the NYSE), who worked in a total of approximately 9,400 sales offices located throughout the country and in foreign countries (about 4,000 registered representatives in 282 foreign sales offices).  Approximately  200 NYSE member firms, which do not do business with the public, act as brokers, traders, and specialists (that is, market makers) on the floor of the NYSE.

The Securities Industry Association, the securities industry's trade and research group, divides the industry into five principal categories: (1) national full-line firms; (2) large investment banks; (3) New York City-based  firms; (4) regional firms; and (5) discount brokerage firms.  While the data discussed below cover aggregate industry revenues and expenses, it should be remembered that economic and business conditions affect each category of firms differently.  For example, a decline in the volume of trading will have the greatest impact on discount brokerage firms, which depend most heavily on commission income, whereas a decline in merger-and-acquisition activity is likely to have a disproportionate effect on the large investment banks, for which this activity is an important part of their total mix of business.

### Industry Concentration

Despite its broad membership base, the securities industry is highly concentrated.  In 1996, the ten largest firms in terms of their capital accounted for 51 percent of the revenues and 58 percent of the capital of all such firms, and the largest 25 firms accounted for 75 percent of all revenues and 77 percent of capital.  Over the years, the number of broker-dealer firms has steadily shrunk.  Even in the banner year of 1993, when industry revenues and profits reached record highs, the number of firms continued to drop, from 7,793 in the previous year to 7,441.  In fact, during the four years following the 1987 market crash, 20 percent of all NASD member firms disappeared.

Industry concentration is the result of a number of developments that have given a substantial advantage to large, well-capitalized firms.  The Securities Act Amendments of 1975 forced the stock exchanges to abandon their traditional practice of fixing the commission rates that brokers charged their customers.  The immediate effect of unfixing commissions was to introduce pricing competition into the brokerage business and to reduce drastically the level of commissions paid to brokerage firms by institutional investors.

The unfixing of rates caused many firms to reassess the mix of their business in search of other sources of profits to make up for their reduced commission revenues.  It contributed to the tendency of broker-dealers to engage in principal transactions involving risk, including proprietary trading, risk arbitrage, making "bridge loans" in connection with mergers and acquisitions, and "merchant banking" (that is, investing the firms' own money in leveraged buyouts and other types of deals that they manage).  Principal transactions created a greater need for capital than did the industry's traditional agency business, thus favoring large, well-capitalized firms.

Another regulatory change that gave an advantage to the largest firms was the SEC's adoption in 1982 of Rule 415, the so-called shelf registration rule.  Rule 415 allows an issuer of securities to register an offering of securities for future distribution at an opportune time.  The issuer can then put the offering up for competitive bids by underwriters, giving an opportunity to a single well-capitalized investment banker to handle the entire offering, instead of syndicating the offering among a large group of underwriters and dealers.  The impact of Rule 415 is evident from the fact that 87 percent of all corporate bonds underwritten in 1989 were done without syndication, as compared to only 2 percent in 1981.  Although Rule 415 reduced the control that investment bankers had traditionally exercised over their "captive" corporate clients, it also had the effect of excluding smaller and regional firms from participation in underwritings and thus gave a competitive edge to large firms.

Mergers and acquisitions also increased industry concentration.  Several of the largest securities firms were acquired by -- and therefore have gained access to the capital of -- corporate giants whose main business lay outside the securities business.  Thus, Bache was acquired by Prudential Insurance; Shearson and Smith Barney were acquired by Travelers Group; Dean Witter was acquired by Sears (but in 1994 was spun off to become an independent company again); and Kidder Peabody was acquired by General Electric (but was sold to Paine Webber in 1994).  Three other firms -- Drexel Burnham Lambert, E. F. Hutton, and Thomson McKinnon -- went out of business or were absorbed by other brokerage firms.  Of the top ten retail firms in 1980, only three -- Dean Witter, Merrill Lynch, and Paine Webber -- were independent firms at the end of 1994. Even these latter two firms have to some extent become conglomerates, having diversified their activities from their traditional businesses of brokerage and underwriting into asset management, real estate, and so on.

Firms specializing in investment banking have experienced a similar shake-out. By the early 1990s, only a dozen or so American investment banking firms of any importance remained in business, and only half that number -- CS First Boston, Goldman Sachs, Lehman Brothers, Merrill Lynch (a leading retail firm and a leading investment bank), Morgan Stanley, and Salomon Brothers -- were large enough to compete in the worldwide arena with such foreign securities firms and banks as Nomura, Deutsche Bank, and the Union Bank of Switzerland. According to Professor Samuel Hayes, the six leading U.S. investment banks "are now global in their perspective, have outposts all over the world, and have been prolific in the way they have build their size and their scope." It is hardly surprising that the capital available to these major financial institutions has grown enormously. For example, Morgan Stanley's capital increased from $10 million in the early 1970s to $9.81 billion in 1993. . . .

### Industry Diversification and the Increase in Broker-Dealers' Proprietary Trading

Broker-dealers today engage in many kinds of activities, ranging far beyond their traditional role of acting as agents for customers in the purchase and sale of securities. Many of these activities are performed through separate affiliates or subsidiaries established for the purpose. A 1992 report by the U.S. General Accounting Office describes the broad scope of broker-dealer functions:

> The broker-dealer entity, around which most . . . securities firms were built, remains as their principal operating unit in the United States. Broker-dealers buy and sell securities products, such as stocks, options, bonds, and debt instruments. They may trade these products as "agents," on behalf of investors or as "principals," for the firm's own trading and investment accounts. Broker-dealers also underwrite, or bring to the marketplace, new issues of securities products.

> In addition to these activities, broker-dealers provide research and investment advice to customers, lend securities to other broker-dealers, and often maintain custody of the securities their customers purchase. Some securities firms offer investment advice and asset management services through their broker-dealer or through a separate subsidiary. . . . In exchange for such services, broker-dealers receive sales commissions and fees, which provide revenue for the firm.

> Many securities firms are also active participants in futures markets. . . . Large securities firms trade, and may underwrite, U.S. government securities, mortgage-backed government securities, and debt obligations of other federal agencies. . . .

> Other prominent lines of business for large securities firms include corporate finance, merchant banking, and related activities. These firms receive substantial fees for negotiating, advising, and financing corporate mergers, acquisitions, and leveraged buyouts. The financing for these transactions may involve underwriting corporate debt securities or providing bridge loans. . . .

> [S]ecurities firms . . . have established . . . subsidiaries that engage in a variety of financial and non-financial activities. Some of these subsidiaries include insurance companies, energy-related partnerships, commodities dealers, mortgage companies, clearing corporations, and companies that specialize in real estate advice, investment, development or management. Other subsidiaries, such as those that issue and trade commercial paper, exist primarily to raise funds for the rest of the firm.

Securities firms also engage in special financial activities, such as repurchase agreements, foreign currency trading, and interest rate or foreign currency swaps.[1]

During the 1980s, the focus of broker-dealer activity shifted significantly. Brokerage commissions and other revenues resulting from the role of securities firms as agents for their customers declined in relative importance. Instead, the major preoccupation of securities firms became the management of their own capital. As Senator Christopher Dodd stated in 1990: "Over the last eight or ten years the industry appears to have taken a different course. It's fee driven, transaction oriented, becoming the player rather than the agent." As profitability of member firms (and the markets) soared during the mid-1990s, this trend has reversed to some extent. In 1996, $20.1 billion, or 17 percent of the $120.2 billion of total revenues of NYSE member firms, consisted of net gains from the firms' own trading and investment accounts. At several firms, trading profits comprise well over 25 percent of total revenues.

There are several reasons proprietary trading has become a major source of profit, which has been described as "the engine powering Wall Street." Competitive pressures have forced down the level of brokerage commissions paid by institutional customers since the abolition of fixed commission rates in 1975; volume declined on the stock exchanges during the late 1980s; the highly lucrative business of advising corporate customers on mergers and acquisitions dried up after the 1987 market break; and greater volatility in interest rates created profitable opportunities for trading in bonds. A growing portion of the firms' trading profits have been derived from esoteric new "derivative products" such as currency options, financial futures, and interest-rate swaps. According to the SIA:

> The trend towards proprietary trading has been one of the most fundamental changes in the securities business since the introduction of negotiated rates. As the profitability of the agency business declined, securities firms turned to other business activities to bolster their profitability. One of the most natural was taking principal positions in securities. Other trading activities, such as arbitrage and other niche trading specialties, have also come into their own during the last few years. In total, trading gains have grown to a $12 billion business and account for about one-fifth to one-quarter of industry revenues.

The largest source of revenue for the securities industry in 1996 was what the SIA labels "other revenue related to the securities business" and amounted to $47.1 billion. These revenues consist chiefly of interest income from reverse repurchase agreements and fees from handling and giving advice on private placements, mergers, and acquisitions.

Although NYSE member firms' revenues from commission rose rapidly between 1991 and 1996 (from$10.6 billion to $18.4 billion), this long-term trend has been for commissions to decline as a percentage of total revenues. In 1996, securities commissions accounted for $18.4 billion, or 15 percent of total industry revenues. This represented a substantial decline, in percentage terms, from 1965, when securities commissions represented 61 percent of industry revenues. As recently as 1980, the figure was still 35 percent, or more than twice its present level.

---

[1]    U.S. General Accounting Office, Securities Firms: Assessing the Need to Regulate Additional Financial Activities 35-37 (1992).

Other sources of 1996 broker-dealer revenues included underwriting revenue, which accounted for $11.2 billion, or 9 percent of the total; margin interest ($7.1 billion, or 6 percent); revenues from the sale of mutual fund shares ($4.5 billion, or 4 percent); asset management fees ($5.3 billion, or 4 percent), and revenues from commodities (1.1 billion, or 1 percent).

Thus, the traditional type of revenues of brokers and dealers -- commissions received from customers -- has declined dramatically in the past decade, while the industry's revenues from proprietary trading have remained constant (as a percentage of total revenues), although it should be kept in mind that some firms, including at least one national full-line firm and several regional brokerages, have remained profitable by continuing to concentrate on their agency business.

The relative decline in overall commission income is to a large extent the result of individual investors withdrawing from direct participation in the market in favor of investing indirectly through mutual funds and other types of institutions.  In an attempt to stem the erosion of commission business, brokerage firms have tried to attract and motivate salespersons who are big "producers" by increasing the percentage of commissions that they receive as compensation. Between 1982 and 1989, salespersons' average compensation increased from 33 percent to 43 percent of the gross.  In late 1990, several large firms  -- in apparent defiance of the laws of economics -- attempted to compensate for their loss of commission revenues by actually increasing their commission rates by about 5 percent, thus asking their remaining customers to supply the commission income they had lost by the departure of other customers.  In addition, several large firms have imposed a variety of charges on their customers in addition to commissions, including fees for inactive accounts, annual fees to pay for the privilege of being a customer, and fees for the confirmations they are required to send customers after each transaction.  It is unclear whether these increases in transaction costs, imposed principally on small investors, will increase overall revenues or will simply induce more customers to withdraw from direct participation in the markets in favor of investing indirectly, through mutual funds or other financial institutions.

The decline of commissions as a source of revenues for the securities industry and the increased importance of proprietary trading have undoubtedly influenced the way in which the managers of broker-dealer firms view their fiduciary duties to their customers.  A firm that depends on trading for its own account in order to remain profitable is unlikely to give its customers the same degree of loyalty as one whose customers represent its chief source of income.  Awareness of this danger appears to have been one reason Shearson Lehman separated its retail brokerage business from its investment banking business in 1990, although cost control was also an important factor.  The competing demands of profitmaking by trading and loyalty to customers raise conflicts-of-interest issues that are difficult or even impossible to resolve. . . .

**Expenses and Profitability**

Following the market crash of October 1987, the securities industry suffered from a severe profit squeeze.  In 1990, the industry as a whole suffered a pre-tax loss of $162 million. However, beginning in 1991 there was a dramatic turnaround, with pre-tax net income reaching a record high of $11.3 billion in 1996.  The renewed profitability of the industry was due to several factors, including (1) a rising stock market; (2) low short-term interest rates, which resulted in high stock and bond prices and permitted broker-dealer firms to borrow money at low rates and invest it in higher-yielding assets; (3) a boom in securities underwritings; (4) renewed interest among individual and institutional investors in the securities markets; and (5) a revival of merger-and-acquisition activity, which had been relatively dormant during the years immediately following the crash.

To a certain extent, however, the profitability of the securities industry during the early 1990s was due to cost cutting during the previous years.  Approximately 35,000 jobs in the securities industry disappeared during the two years directly following the market crash, and as business improved the industry added back only one employee for every two that it had let go in the two years following the 1987 market break.  Thus, the industry as a whole employed about the same number of employees in 1996 as it had in 1987  (264,000, compared with 260,000).  Furthermore,  20 percent of the firms that had existed at the time of the 1987 crash were no longer in existence in 1996, so there were fewer firms around to share in the industry's increased business.

The largest single expense in 1996 was for interest, which amounted to $49.2 billion or 45 percent of total expenses.  Compensation of managers and employees amounted to $36.8 billion or 34 percent of the total.  Other categories of expense include communications costs, leases and equipment, promotional costs, and regulatory fees. . . .

Although the securities industry suffered from overcapacity and declining profitability after the 1987 market crash, it continued to pay extraordinarily high salaries and bonuses to its managers. One explanation is that the genuine talents of many of these managers merit their high pay.  Another explanation, equally plausible, is that, because of the lack of formal training programs at most brokerage firms, it is usually easier and less costly to poach people from other firms by offers of high compensation than to recruit entry-level people and train them." . . . .

## Section 3.  Current Regulatory Structure

The following memorandum offers a summary of both broker-dealer registration and on-going regulation in the United States.  In the next two chapters we will consider certain aspects of this structure in greater detail, but as an introductory matter, we consider the structure as a whole.

### U.S. Broker-Dealer Registration and Regulation
Coudert Brothers, http://www.coudert.com/usbroker.htm (Oct. 10, 1996)

This memorandum describes briefly some of the principal considerations under the United States securities laws concerning broker-dealer registration and some of the principal consequences of registration.  Part I describes the major elements of the federal registration process and application for membership with the National Association of Securities Dealers, Inc. ("NASD").  Part II discusses some of the major regulatory consequences of registration.  The final section, Part III, notes the existence of state securities laws, which impose separate registration and regulatory requirements similar to the federal requirements described in the preceding sections.

## I. The Registration Process

A.    *SEC Registration:* Form BD. The basic document for registration with the Securities and Exchange Commission ("SEC") is Form BD. This form solicits detailed information concerning the broker-dealer applicant, its principals and controlling persons.

Since Form BD serves not only as an initial application form but also as one of the sources of current information concerning registered broker-dealers maintained by the SEC, it must be updated or amended whenever there is any material change in the information included in the form.

B.    *NASD Membership.* The system of broker-dealer regulation under the Exchange Act provides for a rather large degree of industry self-regulation, subject to SEC oversight, by industry organizations as well as by direct SEC regulation. Each securities exchange (e.g., New York Stock Exchange) is responsible for setting standards of qualification and business conduct, and for exercising supervisory responsibilities over its exchange members. The NASD is the professional association that exercises this function with respect to broker-dealers in the over-the-counter securities market.

Every registered broker-dealer, except for certain stock exchange members who carry no customer accounts and who conduct all of their business on the exchange, must become a member of the NASD and accordingly must satisfy the NASD's membership requirements and observe its rules. Effectively, a broker-dealer may not conduct business until its NASD membership has been approved. Prior to January, 1993, broker-dealer registrants were required to file separate applications for SEC registration and NASD membership. As a result of certain rule amendments adopted by the staff of the SEC, all broker-dealer registrants are now directed to file one application for registration on Form BD with the NASD. The NASD, in turn, passes the application information on to the SEC for review. . . .

In addition to the Form BD, the NASD requires a number of additional materials before it will grant membership approval. These include, among others:

1. a statement of financial condition (including trial balances, balance sheet, supporting schedules and computation of net capital);

2. a copy of written supervisory procedures for the conduct of the applicant's business and supervision of its personnel;

3. evidence of fidelity bonding;

4. fingerprint cards and Form U-4 registration applications for individuals conducting business on behalf of the applicant (discussed below);

5. an NASD initial membership fee of between $1,500 and $5,000; and

6. a clearing agreement with a clearing broker-dealer, if applicable.

The NASD will also conduct a pre-membership interview of one of the applicant's registered principals in order to review the applicability of various securities regulations to the applicant's proposed operations and in order to determine the applicant's ability and qualifications to engage in such operations. The pre-membership interview will not be scheduled until after the application has been completed and at least one principal has passed the examination for principals described in the next section.

The NASD does not permit applicants to have names that are confusingly similar to the names of existing members or other applicants. Prospective members should have their choice of names approved by the NASD in advance of submitting their membership application.

C.    *Registration and Examination of "Principals" and "Representatives".* NASD membership requires that certain key "persons associated with a member" be qualified to engage in the securities business. Such persons must pass an examination administered by the NASD and must be individually registered with the NASD prior to engaging in business activities on behalf of a member. The term "person associated with a member" is defined as follows:

> every sole proprietor, partner, officer, director or branch manager of any member, or any natural person occupying a similar status or performing similar functions, or any natural person engaged in the investment banking or securities business who is directly or indirectly controlling or controlled by such member. . . .

For purposes of the NASD's qualification and registration requirements, there are two relevant categories of persons associated with a member: "principals" and "representatives". Any person who is actively engaged in the management or supervision of the member's business must qualify and register as a principal. Any employee (other than a principal) who is engaged in the member's investment banking or securities business must qualify and register as a representative. Persons who perform merely clerical or ministerial functions, and persons whose functions relate solely to the need for nominal corporate officers (e.g., an attorney who serves as a corporate officer) or the need for financial capital (e.g., limited partners), are exempt from the qualification and registration requirements. Each of the President and Chief Executive Officer of a broker-dealer must register as a principal, whether or not he is involved in the applicant's securities business.

All persons associated with a member must pass the appropriate written examination, either for principals or representatives, covering various professional and legal aspects of the securities business. The NASD publishes various guides that, in conjunction with certain recommended texts and study courses, are designed to prepare applicants for the examinations. For categories of principal registration (including general securities principal), in addition to passing a principal examination, an applicant must previously have been qualified as a representative.

A Form U-4 must be submitted to the NASD for each candidate who intends to apply for registration as a principal or representative. The Form U-4 requires individual applicants to provide detailed biographical information, including information regarding work experience and involvement in any securities industry related disciplinary proceeding or adjudication. In addition, all principals and representatives must be fingerprinted. Pursuant to Section 17(f) of the Securities Exchange Act of 1934 (the "Exchange Act"), these fingerprints are forwarded to the U.S. Attorney General.

The obligation of associated persons to file amendments to Form U-4 and to satisfy the qualification requirements for principals or representatives is a continuing obligation that must be observed so long as a broker-dealer remains a member of the NASD.

Except under special circumstances, every firm applying for NASD membership must have at least two officers or partners who are qualified as principals. In addition, one principal must register and pass an additional examination as the applicant's Chief Financial and Operations Principal, unless an exemption is granted by the NASD. An exemption will ordinarily be granted to a broker-dealer that does not carry customer accounts and otherwise qualifies for the $5,000 minimum net capital requirement discussed below.

D.    *Fidelity Bond.* All NASD members must carry a blanket fidelity bond, in form and amount satisfactory to the NASD, covering the loss, theft, forgery, alteration and misplacement of securities by its personnel. In general, the bond must be 120% of the minimum net capital requirement applicable to the applicant, subject to a minimum bond of $25,000.

E.    *SIPC Membership.* Under the Securities Investor Protection Act of 1970, all registered broker-dealers are required to become members of the Securities Investor Protection Corporation ("SIPC"). SIPC is a quasi-governmental corporation that administers an insurance fund providing customers of financially distressed broker-dealers with insurance coverage of up to $100,000 for cash owed to each customer and $500,000 for securities owed to each customer. All SIPC members are required to pay annual assessments into the SIPC insurance fund in amounts that depend upon the member's gross income.

F.    *Other.* Registered broker-dealers must, in general, register as direct or indirect inquirers in the Securities Information Center's Lost and Stolen Securities Program.

## II. Consequences of Registration: Procedural Rules

Registered broker-dealers are subject to a wide variety of specific duties and restrictions affecting the conduct of their business. The principal sources of these rules are the Exchange Act and the SEC regulations thereunder and the by-laws and rules of the NASD. These rules may be broadly divided into substantive rules of business conduct affecting securities transactions and dealings with customers, and procedural rules regarding the creation and preservation of records, the maintenance of adequate capitalization, the filing of periodic reports, and other general operating procedures. The following are among the major requirements of a procedural nature:

A.    Recordkeeping. Section 17(a) of the Exchange Act, and SEC Rules 17a-3 and 17a-4 thereunder, require the creation and preservation (for a specified number of years) of numerous records, including the following:

a. daily blotters itemizing all purchases and sales of securities, all receipts and deliveries of securities (including certificate numbers), all cash receipts and disbursements and all other debits and credits;

b. a general ledger reflecting all assets and liabilities, income and expenses, and capital accounts;

c. ledgers separately itemizing all securities transactions and all debits and credits in each account;

d. position books reflecting all long and short positions in each security as of each clearance date;

e. memoranda of each brokerage order or instruction, indicating the account, the time of entry, the terms of the order and the details of the execution;

f. copies of all confirmations of securities transactions and all debit and credit advices;

g. records containing the name, address and signatures of all persons for whom accounts are carried;

h. detailed information concerning the identity, background and qualifications of all employees; and

    i.  monthly trial balances and other information in connection with the "net capital" computations described below.

The foregoing summarizes only the basic record-creation and maintenance requirements. In addition to these requirements, there are rules regarding the preservation of other items, such as all written agreements entered into by the broker-dealer, originals of all communications received and copies of all communications sent (including interoffice memoranda), checkbooks, canceled checks, working papers and so forth.  From time to time, the SEC and the NASD may conduct inspections to monitor compliance with these recordkeeping provisions and other internal operating procedures.  Section 15(b)(2)(C) of the Exchange Act requires that the SEC or NASD conduct at least one such inspection within the first six months following registration of a broker-dealer.

    B.  *The "Net Capital Rule"*.  Section 15(c)(3) of the Exchange Act requires the SEC to establish minimum financial responsibility standards for all broker-dealers, whether registered or unregistered.  SEC Rule 15c3-1 -- the "Net Capital Rule" -- specifies these requirements. . . . .

    C.  *Periodic Financial Reporting*.  All broker-dealers are required to file with the SEC annual financial statements, prepared in accordance with United States "generally accepted accounting principles" and certified by an independent accountant, containing the information specified in SEC Rule 17a-5.  Copies of these statements must also be furnished to the NASD and generally to customers as well.  Unaudited financial reports, which must include net capital computations and other financial information specified in SEC Rule 17a-5, must be filed with the SEC or the NASD on a monthly basis by broker-dealers that carry customer accounts or that clear securities transactions, and on a quarterly basis (in a somewhat simplified format) by broker-dealers that do not carry accounts or clear transactions.  These periodic financial and operational reports are referred to as FOCUS Reports.

    Under Rule 17h-1T and 17h-2T, certain broker-dealers that maintain capital in excess of $250,000 are required to maintain extensive records concerning "associated persons", including records detailing the relationship between the broker and associated person, the financial integrity of the associated person and related information.  Brokers subject to these provisions are also required to file quarterly reports with the SEC using the data required to be maintained concerning associated persons. . . .

    D.  *Continuing Education Program Requirements*.  In 1995, the NASD and SEC introduced Continuing Education Program requirements, consisting of a "Regulatory Element" and a "Firm Element".  The Regulatory Element requires individual registered persons to complete NASD administered continuing education sessions within 120 days of the anniversary of their second, fifth and tenth years of registration.  Individual registrants who are past their tenth anniversary and who have no disciplinary histories within that time frame would be exempt from the requirement.  Individual registrants who fail to complete the required sessions are not permitted to function in any capacity requiring registration (e.g. trading securities, offering or selling privately placed securities etc.)

    The Firm Element requires NASD member broker-dealers to implement, maintain and administer their own internal continuing training programs for all "covered registered persons". A "covered registered person" is defined to include any registered person who either (A) has direct contact with customers in the conduct of the member's securities sales, trading and investment banking activities or (B) is the immediate supervisor of any such person. . . .

Each member firm *at least annually* must (A) evaluate and prioritize its own particular training needs and (B) develop a written training plan. The training program must address at least the following matters concerning securities products and services offered by the member: general investment features and associated risk factors; suitability and sales practice considerations; and applicable regulatory requirements. Firms are required to maintain records (i) documenting the contents of its training program and (ii) evidencing the completion of the firm training programs by all covered registered persons. . . .

A detailed review of the many substantive regulations governing the day to-day operation of registered broker-dealers is beyond the scope of this memorandum. Applicants for broker-dealer registration should be aware, however, that the SEC, NASD and each national securities exchange have detailed regulations on how a broker-dealer may conduct its business. The NASD's Rules of Fair Practice (supplemented by frequent NASD interpretation), for example, sets out detailed regulations on the conduct of business. Many of the substantive rules of the SEC, NASD and the exchanges are directed at fraudulent practices such as churning customer accounts (i.e. excessive trading to generate commissions), misusing inside information, mishandling customer funds (e.g. recommending unsuitable investments for a particular customer), failing to properly supervise employees, charging excessive commissions or dealer mark-ups on securities, failing to make bona fide public offerings of "hot issues" (i.e. free-riding and withholding). In addition to anti-fraud rules, the NASD and national securities exchanges have detailed rules covering such important operational matters as production and distribution of customer confirmation of transactions, trading procedures and market-making activities. The lending activities of broker-dealers are regulated by both national securities exchanges and by the Federal Reserve Board's margin regulations . . . .

### III. State "Blue Sky" Laws

Practically every state has its own securities laws requiring, among other things, the registration of broker-dealers and the registration of securities being offered to the public. These "blue sky" laws must be complied with in any state in which a broker-dealer conducts business. Although the significance of these blue sky laws should not be minimized, it is generally the case that state broker-dealer requirements are no more onerous than the federal and NASD requirements. Indeed, in most states, the same registration forms that are required for SEC and NASD purposes can be used to comply with the state registration requirements. [Moreover, the National Securities Markets Improvement Act of 1996 barred states from imposing capital requirements or other portfolio shaping rules on broker-dealers. See section 15(h) of the 1934 Act.] Associated persons . . . , however, may have to take the Uniform Securities Agent State Law Examination (the Series 63 examination), also administered by the NASD, in order to qualify in certain states. . . . .

### Comments and Questions

How does this regulatory structure compare with the ones we have considered in connection with depository institutions and insurance companies? Where are there differences? What seems familiar? Is there something about the securities business that necessitates a different approach to regulation? Or it is an accident of economic history?

# CHAPTER TEN

# THE REGULATION OF BROKER-DEALERS

Our discussion of the substance of broker-dealer regulation is intended to be suggestive rather than comprehensive. The chapter is divided into four parts. The first concerns the definition of broker-dealer for purposes of federal securities laws. The second section turns to the obligations of broker-dealers in doing business with the general public. The third section explores recent trends towards arbitration of disputes in the securities industry. And finally, we consider the SEC's net capital rules for registered broker-dealers as well as other related standards of financial responsibility.

## Section 1. The Definition of Broker-Dealer

As in other fields of financial regulation, a critical threshold issue is the definition that brings business firms within the regulatory structure. Under section 3(a)(4) of the Securities Exchange Act of 1934, as amended (the "1934 Act"), a broker is defined to be "any person engaged in the business of effecting transactions in securities for the account of others, but does not include a bank." Section 3(b)(5) offers a similar definition for dealer as "any person engaged in the business of buying and selling securities for his own account, through a broker or otherwise, but does not include a bank, or any person insofar as he buys or sells securities for his own account, either individually or in some fiduciary capacity, but not as a part of a regular business." Implicit in both definitions is a threshold requirement of being "engaged" in certain kinds of business.

A basic question that arises in this context is how much activity must be undertaken before this threshold is crossed. Through a series of rulings over the years, the SEC has defined a number of attributes that together determine when a person or entity is sufficiently immersed in the securities business to warrant regulation under the statute. See David A. Lipton, *A Primer on Broker-Dealer Registration*, 36 CATH. U.L. REV. 899 (1987). In general, the standard contemplates a certain regularity or continuity of participation, and not simply an association with a few isolated transactions. Thus, the definition has been understood to include a de minimus exception for episodic participation in securities transactions.

One area of recurring difficulty concerns individuals who help sell shares on behalf of a corporate employer that is itself engaged in the sale of securities. If employees assists in such an underwriting, must these individuals register under the 1934 Act? The following correspondence deals with that issue:

# Old Stone Corp.
## SEC No-Action Letter, 1985 WL 51933 (Nov. 20, 1984)

Colleen C. Harvey, Esq.
Deputy Chief Counsel
Division of Market Regulation
Securities and Exchange Commission
450 Fifth Street, N.W., Room 5027
Washington, D.C. 20549

Re: Old Stone Corporation— Sections 3(a)(4), 15(a), 15(b), 15(c)
     and Rule 15c3-1 of the Securities Exchange Act of 1934

Dear Ms. Harvey:

Our firm represents Old Stone Corporation ("Old Stone"), a general business corporation incorporated under the laws of the State of Rhode Island for the primary purpose of operating as a financial institution holding company, which proposes to offer and sell notes ("Old Stone Notes") through three of its wholly owned subsidiaries, Old Stone Bank, a Federal Savings Bank (the "Federal Savings Bank"), the deposits of which are insured by the Federal Savings and Loan Insurance Corporation ("FSLIC"), Perpetual Savings and Loan Association, Inc. ("Perpetual"), the deposits of which are insured by the Financial Institutions Assurance Corporation, and Guild Loan & Investment Co. ("Guild"), the deposits of which are insured by the Rhode Island Share and Deposit Indemnity Corporation. The purpose of this letter is to request the Division to recommend that the Commission take no action if the Federal Savings Bank, Perpetual and Guild and their officers and other employees participate in the sale of the Old Stone Notes without registration as brokers pursuant to Sections 15(a) and 15(b) of the Securities Exchange Act of 1934 (the "1934 Act") and without meeting the net capital requirements of Section 15(c) of the 1934 Act and Rule 15c3-1 of the General Rules and Regulations under the 1934 Act ("Rule 15c3-1").

Background

Old Stone was formed in 1969; its principal offices are located in Providence, Rhode Island. On October 19, 1984, Old Stone consummated a reorganization (the "Reorganization") of certain of its subsidiaries in conjunction with Old Stone's acquisition of Rhode Island Federal Savings and Loan Association ("Rhode Island Federal"). In connection with the Reorganization, among other things, (i) Rhode Island Federal converted from a federal mutual savings and loan association to a federal stock savings bank named "Old Stone Bank, a Federal Savings Bank", all of the outstanding stock of which was issued to and is held by Old Stone, and (ii) all of the outstanding stock of Old Stone Bank, the Rhode Island chartered commercial bank which, immediately prior to the Reorganization, was the principal operating subsidiary of Old Stone (the "State Bank"), was transferred from Old Stone to a newly- formed, wholly-owned subsidiary of the Federal Savings Bank, and all of the assets and liabilities of the State Bank, other than its charter, its assets relating to its trust activities, and the minimum capital required under Rhode Island law to operate a bank, were transferred by the State Bank to the Federal Savings Bank.

The operations of the Federal Savings Bank, which is now Old Stone's principal operating subsidiary, consist of the former businesses and operations of the State Bank (other than its trust operations) and of Rhode Island Federal. The State Bank has changed its name to "Old Stone Trust Company" and amended its charter to operate as a limited purpose trust company. Certain activities of the State Bank's money market division as conducted prior to the Reorganization will be transferred to Old Stone Securities Company ("OSSC"), a newly-formed, wholly-owned subsidiary of Old Stone. OSSC's business will be limited to broker-dealer activities in municipal and United States government securities for its customers, and its own account and its operations will not be conducted in any of the branch offices of the Federal Savings Bank or Perpetual. OSSC has applications pending for broker-dealer registration with the Commission and the State of Rhode Island and has applied for membership in the National Association of Securities Dealers . . . .

Prior to the Reorganization, the State Bank was regulated by the Federal Deposit Insurance Corporation ("FDIC"). The FDIC in connection with its approval of the transfer of assets and liabilities from the State Bank to the Federal Savings Bank imposed a condition that the Federal Savings Bank achieve by December 31, 1985, a tangible capital to assets ratio in accordance with the FDIC's proposed capital guidelines. As one means of satisfying this requirement, Old Stone proposes to offer and sell up to $30 million aggregate principal amount of Old Stone Notes to the general public through the Federal Savings Bank's 33 offices in the State of Rhode Island, Perpetual's seven offices in the State of North Carolina and Guild's two offices in Rhode Island. As much as $20 million of the net proceeds from the sale of the Old Stone Notes may be transferred from Old Stone to the Federal Savings Bank.

By avoiding an underwriting commission, Old Stone believes that it can maximize the net proceeds from the sale of the Old Stone Notes. The Old Stone Notes will be registered with the Commission under the Securities Act of 1933 and will be sold under a trust indenture qualified under the Trust Indenture Act of 1939. Officers and other employees of the Federal Savings Bank who participate in the offer and sale of the Old Stone Notes will comply with a number of regulatory and other restrictions including guidelines issued by the staff of the Federal Home Loan Bank Board ("FHLBB"), as operating head of the FSLIC, which provide that securities issued by a thrift institution holding company may be sold at the offices of its FSLIC-insured thrift institution subsidiary only if:

1. No commissions are paid to any employee or other person;

2. No offers or sales are made by tellers or at the teller counter;

3. Offers and sales are made only by regular, full-time employees;

4. No unsolicited telephone calls or visits are made by the FSLIC-insured institution to any person in connection with any offers or sales; and

5. The FSLIC-insured institution's net worth at the commencement of and during the offering meets its regulatory net worth requirement calculated under generally accepted accounting principles
. . . .

Old Stone, the Federal Savings Bank, Perpetual and Guild will also take appropriate steps to ensure that the following conditions are also satisfied:

1. No officer, other employee or director of OSSC who is engaged in the selling activities of OSSC will participate in the offer and sale of the Old Stone Notes in any manner;

2. Common officers, other employees and directors of OSSC and Old Stone, the Federal Savings Bank, Perpetual or Guild will be involved in the distribution of the Old Stone Notes only to the extent that their status as officers, employees and directors of Old Stone, the Federal Savings Bank, Perpetual and Guild obligate them to take part in the decision to conduct the public offering and/or to perform administrative duties associated with such offering. Their activities during the public offering will not involve engaging in the solicitation of prospective purchasers or effecting transactions in the Old Stone Notes; and

3. The requirements of paragraphs (a)(1), (a)(2), and (a)(4)(ii) of proposed 1934 Act Rule 3a4-1 will be satisfied.[*]

Discussion

It is our view that, under the circumstances outlined above, officers and other employees of the Federal Savings Bank, Perpetual and Guild should not be considered to be acting as brokers if they participate in the offer and sale of the Old Stone Notes and that the Federal Savings Bank, Perpetual and Guild should not be required to register as brokers or satisfy 1934 Act net capital requirements. As noted by the Commission in 1934 Act Release No. 20943 (May 9, 1984), which reproposed the so-called "safe harbor" from broker registration under 1934 Act Rule 3a4-1, the safe harbor should not be available, for example, to agents retained by an issuer specifically for selling securities on a commission basis. Nor should the safe harbor be available to promoters who are regularly marketing securities. Neither is the case in the proposed offer and sale of the Old Stone Notes.

The transaction is unique in that: (1) it will be conducted in response to the higher capital to assets ratio imposed by the FDIC; (2) management of Old Stone, the Federal Savings Bank, Perpetual and Guild do not anticipate that future offers and sales of Old Stone Notes or other securities issued by Old Stone, the Federal Savings Bank, Perpetual or Guild will again be made in the manner presently contemplated; (3) persons associated with OSSC will not participate in the Old Stone Note offering; and (4) the officers and other employees of the Federal Savings Bank, Perpetual and Guild who will participate in the offering will be regular, full-time employees not compensated on a commission basis, or any other basis that varies with or depends solely upon their efforts to sell the Old Stone Notes.

It should also be indicated that the proposed offering appears to satisfy all of the relevant conditions of the Rule 3a4-1 safe harbor except possibly a technical noncompliance with paragraph (a)(3), which provides that the proposed Rule's safe harbor is not available to persons who are "associated persons of a broker or dealer." Although OSSC might technically qualify as such an "associated person," as a practical matter, however, the proposed arrangements outlined in this letter should not create the concerns set forth in 1934 Act Release No. 20943.

---

\*    [These regulatory requirements mean that officers and employees participating in the sale of notes have not been subject to disciplinary actions, will not receive commissions from the sales, and are primarily engaged in activities not involving securities transactions. Eds.]

As stated in that Release, "associated persons of a broker or dealer" have been excluded from the scope of Rule 3a4-1 for two reasons: (1) possible integration of their brokerage activities and sales of the issuer's securities; and (2) the potential for abusive tactics or confusion of investors. In view of the fact that: (1) OSSC has been organized for a limited purpose which does not include authority to underwrite securities such as the Old Stone Notes; (2) customers of OSSC will primarily be institutions, whereas Old Stone Note purchasers will primarily be individuals; (3) OSSC's operations are physically separated from the branch operations of the Federal Savings Bank, Perpetual and Guild; and (4) persons associated with OSSC will not be allowed to participate in the Old Stone Note offering, the concerns expressed in 1934 Act Release No. 20943 should not arise in the offer and sale of the Old Stone Notes.

Conclusion

For all the reasons stated above and in view of the possible technical noncompliance with Rule 3a4-1 as presently proposed, we respectfully request the Staff to recommend that the Commission take no enforcement action if the Federal Savings Bank, Perpetual and Guild and their officers or other employees participate in the offering of Old Stone Notes proposed above and do not register with the Commission as brokers pursuant to Section 15(a) and 15(b) of the 1934 Act or do not meet the net capital requirements of Section 15(c) of the 1934 Act and Rule 15c3-1.

If you have any questions regarding this matter, please do not hesitate to call the undersigned. We are available to meet with you, if a meeting will facilitate your consideration of our request.


Very truly yours,
McKENNA, CONNER & CUNEO
By Edward B. Crosland, Jr.

---

Edward Crosland, Jr., Esq.
McKenna, Conner & Cuneo
1575 Eye Street, N.W.
Washington, D.C. 20005

Dear Mr. Crosland:

This is in response to your letter of November 20, 1984, in which you requested the staff's advice regarding the applicability of the broker-dealer registration requirement of Section 15(a) of the Securities Exchange Act of 1934 (the "Act") to a proposed arrangement under which your client, Old Stone Corporation ("Old Stone"), will offer and sell notes ("Old Stone Notes") through its officers, directors and employees and through three of its wholly owned subsidiaries, Old Stone Bank, a Federal Savings Bank (the "Federal Savings Bank"), Perpetual Savings and Loan Association, Inc. ("Perpetual"), and Guild Loan & Investment Co. ("Guild"), and their officers, directors and employees. . . .

Based on the facts and representations presented, this Division will not recommend any enforcement action to the Commission if the Federal Savings Bank, Perpetual and Guild and their officers, directors and other employees participate in the proposed offering of Old Stone Notes without registering with the Commission as broker-dealers under Section 15(b) of the Act. You should understand that the foregoing is a staff position regarding enforcement action only and should not be understood to express any legal conclusions regarding the applicability of statutory or regulatory provisions of the federal securities laws. This position is based solely on the representations you have made in your letter and during our telephone conversations; any different facts or conditions of a material nature might require a different response.

Sincerely,

Amy C. Natterson
Office of Chief Counsel
Securities and Exchange Commission

## Comments and Questions

1. Note the context of these letters: an SEC "no-action letter" interpreting a "safe-harbor" regulation. The correspondence thus illustrate two ways in which the SEC communicates its interpretations of various statutory provisions to the general public. Safe-harbor rules are of more general application, and provide private parties protection from not only SEC enforcement actions but also most civil litigation. See section 23(a)(1) of the 1934 Act. No-action letters, in contrast, only represent a commitment on the part of the SEC staff not to recommend enforcement proceedings for an individual transaction involving a single correspondent. In practice, however, no-action letters offer unofficial guidance to a wider range of parties, and are occasionally even cited as authority in judicial decisions. See X LOUIS LOSS & JOEL SELIGMAN, SECURITIES REGULATION 4542-45 (3d ed. 1990). What are the relative advantages and weakness of these two approaches?

2. What policies underlie the particular safe-harbor at issue in this correspondence: Rule 3a4-1? Is it appropriate to allow unlicenced individuals to sell securities for their employer? Does the absence of commissions offer an adequate safeguard? Does it help in this context that the issuer was a regulated institution, albeit not a registered broker-dealer? Consider the following press account:

Charles Keating Jr., former chief executive officer of Lincoln Savings and Loan, was found guilty of securities fraud by a Los Angeles jury (California v. Keating, CalifSuperCt, No. BA-025326, 12/4/91).

The jury found Keating guilty on 17 of 18 counts of securities fraud relating to the sale of junk bonds by the thrift, according to Los Angeles deputy district attorney John Hodgman. . . . Keating is facing a maximum prison term of 10 years and a possible fine of $250,000 per count, or $4.25 million. . . .

The infractions, he said, came in connection with sales of American Continental Corp. bonds through Lincoln branches. ACC, Lincoln's holding company, had been ordered by the state department of savings and loans not to sell the bonds through Lincoln branches. ACC then proceeded to open sales offices in proximity to the thrift's retail outlets. . . .

The real illegality, he explained, came in the form of omissions and misrepresentations made to bonds purchasers as to ACC's financial condition. The truth, Hodgman said, was that ACC "was sliding down the tubes financially," although bond purchasers were never informed of this fact. ACC declared bankruptcy in April 1989.

*Charles Keating Convicted Of Fraud In Sale Of Junk Bonds*, BNA Securities Regulation & Law Report (Dec. 10, 1991).

# Section 2.  The Obligations of Broker-Dealers

In addition to registering with the SEC and state securities commissions, broker-dealers (and their employees) are required to abide by a number of substantive provisions of the federal securities laws as well as the codes of conduct of the various self-regulatory organizations.  These restrictions greatly influence the manner in which broker-dealers participate in the distribution of new security issues and in the trading of outstanding securities in the U.S. secondary markets.

The following materials suggest the tenor and complexity of these regulations, as well as the role that the NASD and other self-regulatory organizations play in the supervision of broker-dealers.  A distinctive feature of broker-dealer regulation is its focus on individual accountability.  Whereas individually imposed penalties were, until recently, unusual in the insurance industry and depository institution fields, such penalties have been the norm in securities enforcement for many years.  Individual suspensions and fines are also common punishments for errant broker-dealers.  Why do the enforcement mechanisms in this field focus on individuals as well as institutions?  Should a similar system of individual based penalties be imposed in other areas of financial-institution regulation?

Another distinguishing characteristic of broker-dealer regulation is its emphasis on protection through disclosure. Often times, broker-dealers are subject to sanctions not because of the substance of transactions they have engaged in, but rather because of their failure to make adequate disclosures to their customers.  Is this a model of regulation that could be adopted in other fields?  Under what conditions are disclosure-based regulations sufficient? Under what conditions are substantive requirements preferable?  Does it matter that not all individuals will be able to understand and act upon disclosures?

## A. Early Cases

We begin with two cases handed down in the 1940s when the federal securities laws were still new statutes and our modern regulatory structure had yet to develop.  The principles developed in these cases have been of enduring importance and are reflected in many subsequent judicial decisions and regulatory enactments. As you read through these cases and the materials that follow, consider the extent to which the law in this area draws upon traditional fiduciary principles.  To what extent has the jurisprudence in this field expanded upon its equitable foundations? Should we continue to rely upon open-ended legal principles enforced through case-by-case adjudication to police the securities industry? Or should we move towards more detailed regulations tailored to address special legal problems?

# Charles Hughes & Co. v. Securities and Exchange Commission
## 139 F.2d 434 (2d Cir.), *cert. denied*, 321 U.S. 786 (1943)

This is a petition, pursuant to § 25(a) of the Securities Exchange Act of 1934, to review an order of the Securities and Exchange Commission, entered July 19, 1943, under § 15(b) of that Act, in which petitioner's registration as a broker and dealer was revoked. The order developed from a proceeding which was instituted by the Commission to determine whether or not petitioner had willfully violated § 17(a) of the Securities Act of 1933, and § 15(c)(1) of the Securities Exchange Act of 1934.

Petitioner was incorporated on April 9, 1940, under the laws of New York, and maintains its principal office and place of business in New York City. It is engaged in over-the-counter trading in securities as a broker and dealer, being registered as such with the Commission under the 1934 statute cited above. The dealings which resulted in the revocation were continued sales of securities to customers at prices very substantially over those prevailing in the over-the-counter market, without disclosure of the mark-up to the customers. The Commission concluded that such practices constituted fraud and deceit upon the customers in violation of § 17(a) of the Securities Act, § 15(c)(1) of the Securities Exchange Act, and its own Rule 15c1-2.

Petitioner's dealings which are here in question were carried out by various of its customers' men. The customers were almost entirely single women or widows who knew little or nothing about securities or the devices of Wall Street. An outline of the sales plan used with Mrs. Stella Furbeck gives a representative picture of how petitioner worked. Stillman, a Hughes & Co. agent, having her name as a prospect, called Mrs. Furbeck on the telephone and told her of a "wonderful" stock that she should buy. She replied that she was not interested. The next day he called again, and he persisted in his calls until she finally relented and made a purchase. From that time on, he and a co-employee of his, one Armstrong, worked their way so completely into her confidence that she virtually placed complete control of her securities portfolio in their hands. Every few days one or the other would have another "marvelous" buy - one that was definitely "beyond the usual" - and she would add it to her collection, selling a more reputable security in order to finance the transaction.

The prices which Mrs. Furbeck and other customers paid for the securities purchased in this manner ranged from 16.1 to 40.9 percent over market value. In addition, most of the transactions involved little or no risk for petitioner, because an order was usually confirmed before it bought the securities that it was selling. There is conflict in the record as to whether Stillman and Armstrong made any direct representations to Mrs. Furbeck of the relation of the price paid to market value. She claims that every time she made a purchase it was directly induced by the statement that the price would be under that current in the over-the-counter market, while they deny such statements completely. It is unchallenged, however, that at no time did either Stillman or Armstrong reveal the true market price of any security to Mrs. Furbeck or the fact that petitioner's profits averaged around 25 percent. Similar evidence as to other customers all amply furnished the "substantial evidence" required by the statute to make conclusive the Commission's finding of a course of business by petitioner to sell at excessive mark-up prices without disclosure of market values to its customers . . . .

There is evidence in the record to show a threefold violation of § 17(a) of the Securities Act, viz., the obtaining of money "by means of any untrue statement of a material fact"; the "omission to state a material fact" necessary to make statements actually made not misleading; and the engaging in a course of business which operates "as a fraud or deceit upon the purchaser." It is true that the only specific evidence of false statements of a material fact is that of Mrs. Furbeck that the sales price was under the market price, and, as we have noted, these statements were denied by the salesmen. Although the Commission has neglected to make any finding of fact on this point, we need not remand for a specific finding resolving this conflict, for we feel that petitioner's mark-up policy operated as a fraud and deceit upon the purchasers, as well as constituting an omission to state a material fact.

An over-the-counter firm which actively solicits customers and then sells them securities at prices as far above the market as were those which petitioner charged here must be deemed to commit a fraud.[1] It holds itself out as competent to advise in the premises, and it should disclose the market price if sales are to be made substantially above that level. Even considering petitioner as a principal in a simple vendor purchaser transaction (and there is doubt whether, in several instances at least, petitioner was actually not acting as broker-agent for the purchasers, in which case all undisclosed profits would be forfeited), it was still under a special duty, in view of its expert knowledge and proffered advice, not to take advantage of its customers' ignorance of market conditions. The key to the success of all of petitioner's dealings was the confidence in itself which it managed to instill in the customers. Once that confidence was established, the failure to reveal the mark-up pocketed by the firm was both an omission to state a material fact and a fraudulent device. When nothing was said about market price, the natural implication in the untutored minds of the purchasers was that the price asked was close to the market. The law of fraud knows no difference between express representation on the one hand and implied misrepresentation or concealment on the other.

We need not stop to decide, however, how far common-law fraud was shown. For the business of selling investment securities has been considered one peculiarly in need of regulation for the protection of the investor. "The business of trading in securities is one in which opportunities for dishonesty are of constant recurrence and ever present. It engages acute, active minds, trained to quick apprehension, decision and action." Archer v. Securities and Exchange

---

[1]    The Commission points out that the National Association of Securities Dealers, Inc., an organization registered under § 15(a) of the Securities Exchange Act, of which petitioner was a member at the time of the transaction in question, has a rule limiting mark-up prices in over-counter securities to those which are fair, and calls attention to a decision of the Association's District Business Conduct Committee reported in the NASD News for October, 1943, imposing a fine of $500 and censure upon a member found to have violated rules of the Association by a practice of charging mark-ups of approximately 10 percent on transactions in listed and unlisted securities. . . . .

Commission , 133 F. 2d 795, 803 (8th Cir., cert. denied, 319 U.S. 767 (1943). The well-known "blue sky laws" of 43 states have in fact proved inadequate, so that in 1933 Congress after the most extensive investigations started on a program of regulation, of which this is one of the fruits. In its interpretation of § 17(a) of the Securities Act, the Commission has consistently held that a dealer cannot charge prices not reasonably related to the prevailing market price without disclosing that fact. Had we been in doubt on the matter we should have given weight to these rulings as a consistent and contemporaneous construction of a statute by an administrative body. As we have hitherto said of "the peculiar function" of the Commission: "One of the principal reasons for the creation of such a bureau is to secure the benefit of special knowledge acquired through continuous experience in a difficult and complicated field. Its interpretation of the act should control unless plainly erroneous. But we are not content to rest on so colorless an interpretation of this important legislation.

The essential objective of securities legislation is to protect those who do not know market conditions from the overreachings of those who do. Such protection will mean little if it stops short of the point of ultimate consequence, namely, the price charged for the securities. Indeed, it is the purpose of all legislation for the prevention of fraud in the sale of securities to preclude the sale of "securities which are in fact worthless, or worth substantially less than the asking price." If after several years of experience under this highly publicized legislation we should find that the public cannot rely upon a commission-licensed broker not to charge unsuspecting investors 25 percent more than a market price easily ascertainable by insiders, we should leave such legislation little more than a snare and delusion. We think the Commission has correctly interpreted its responsibilities to stop such abusive practices in the sale of securities.

Petitioner's final contention is that the actual market price of the securities was never satisfactorily proved. We agree, however, with the Commission that the evidence of the quotations published in the National Daily Quotation Sheets, a recognized service giving "daily market indications," as petitioner stipulated, and the prices paid concurrently by petitioner itself sufficiently indicated prevailing market price in the absence of evidence to the contrary.

## Comments and Questions

1. What was the relationship between the securities firm and its customers in this case? Was the firm simply an agent/broker? Or was it a principal/dealer? Do merchants selling other products and services operate under similar obligations? Should they? Within the securities bar, the theory articulated in this decision (sometimes called "*Hughes I*" to distinguish the following decision) has come to be known as the "shingle theory," and derives from a notion that when a securities firm hangs out its shingle to do business it implicitly represents that it will deal fairly with the general public. For a discussion of how this theory and the underlying concept of fair dealing has evolved over the years, see Roberta S. Karmel, *Is the Shingle Theory Dead?*, 52 WASH. & LEE L. REV. 1271 (1995).

2. How do the obligations imposed in this decision compare to the responsibilities of depository institutions or insurance firms? What obligations do we impose on depository institutions and insurance companies to ensure that they charge a fair price to

their customers?  Should standards of fair dealing as imposed on broker-dealers be expanded to other areas of financial regulation?  Why or why not?

## Hughes v. Securities and Exchange Commission
### 174 F.2d 969 (D.C. Cir. 1949)

The case is before this court on petition of Arleen W. Hughes, doing business as E.W. Hughes & Company, to review and set aside an order of respondent Securities and Exchange Commission revoking her registration as a broker and dealer.

Petitioner, referred to below as the registrant, has been engaged in the securities business as a broker and dealer since 1928.  She is now the sole proprietor of the above-named business.  In 1940, petitioner was registered as a broker and dealer under Section 15 of the Securities Exchange Act of 1934, as amended.  In 1942, she was registered as an investment adviser under Section 203 of the Investment Advisers Act of 1940.  Petitioner does business with about 175 clients residing in at least nine different states of the United States.  The petitioner's place of business is Colorado Springs, Colorado.  Following her registration as an investment adviser petitioner entered into a "Memorandum of Agreement" with each of her clients in which it was provided that the "Company, when acting as investment adviser, shall act as Principal in every such transaction, except as otherwise agreed." This agreement also contained a schedule of rates and charges to be paid by the client to the petitioner.  The advice which petitioner sells to her clients is based upon information she gathers and analyzes.  The cost to the client for this advice or "service" is slightly higher per transaction than is the ordinary dealer profit where a dealer sells a security to a customer.  Mrs. Hughes testified that her clients follow her investment advice "in almost every instance.". . . . Petitioner fills a client's order for the purchase of a security either by supplying it from her own inventory or by purchasing the security for her (petitioner's) own account and then selling it as principal to the client.

In the years 1944, 1945, and 1946, various members of respondent's staff, including individuals in the Commission's regional office in Denver, conducted an investigation of petitioner's business in an effort to determine whether her methods of conducting her business violated any of the anti-fraud provisions of any of the federal statutes administered by the respondent.  That investigation was primarily directed toward the adequacy of the disclosure which petitioner, acting as a fiduciary, made to her clients.  The investigation was accomplished through numerous oral and written discussions and communications between petitioner and respondent's agents.

. . . . After [an administrative hearing], the Commission issued an opinion dated February 18, 1948, in which the Commission found that petitioner was a fiduciary, that as such she was under a duty to make full disclosure of her adverse interest, that no such complete disclosure was made, and that her clients had not given their "informed consent" to her taking a position adverse to their interests.  The Commission also found that the proceedings were properly based in part upon alleged violations of the Securities Act and the Securities Exchange Act, and that the violations were willful.  Accordingly, and we think properly, the Commission concluded that the "revocation of the registrant's broker-dealer registration is compelled in the public interest."

[On petition for judicial review, t]here was filed in this court, prior to oral argument of the case and pursuant to order of this court, a brief on behalf of 120 of petitioner's 175 clients, who call themselves amici curiae. That brief purports to speak for a majority of the clients themselves. It argues that the clients have at all times had full knowledge and understanding of the Memorandum of Agreement and the capacity in which petitioner dealt with her clients and that the action of the Commission deprives the clients "of the right to continue to do business with Petitioner under a contractual relationship which they fully understand, and which has afforded them a high degree of investment protection, financial gain and security and financial peace of mind, * * *" Therefore, amici urge reversal of the order of revocation. Assuming arguendo the truth of the unverified statements in the amici brief, many of which are based on matters outside the record in the instant case, such statements do not constitute grounds for overturning the decision of the Commission in this case. If the Commission's decision that petitioner had wilfully violated specified anti-fraud sections of pertinent statutes and regulations is legally correct and supported by substantial evidence of record, it is immaterial whether or not a majority, or even all, of petitioner's clients understood completely the nature of their dealings with petitioner and were satisfied with, and had profited by, petitioner's method of doing business with them. Therefore, we will give no further consideration to the claims of amici for it is our understanding that the Commission is by statute empowered, and, in fact, is required to revoke a broker-dealer registration where there has been wilful violation of statute and where such revocation is in the public interest. This is true whether or not the clients of the broker-dealer happen to have knowledge of, completely understand, or condone and profit by the acts of the broker-dealer which constitute wilful violation of statute. Assuming the existence of both of the above-stated prerequisites for revocation, the revocation is proper even if one, or none, of the particular clients here involved has been misled or has suffered injury.

. . . In this case the Commission has expressly found that petitioner has wilfully violated the above-quoted anti-fraud sections of the two Acts. The Commission also expressly found that the revocation of petitioner's registration is in the public interest. If those two express findings have substantial evidentiary support in the record before us, we cannot set aside the order of revocation. Such support does exist in this record.

In the vast majority of transactions between this petitioner and her clients, petitioner concededly acted as a fiduciary. The record shows clearly that, except for a few isolated instances, petitioner acted simultaneously in the dual capacity of investment adviser and of broker and dealer. In such capacity, conflicting interests must necessarily arise. When they arise, the law has consistently stepped in to provide safeguards in the form of prescribed and stringent standards of conduct on the part of the fiduciary. More than 100 years ago the Supreme Court set forth this principle as follows:

> "In this conflict of interest, the law wisely interposes. It acts not on the possibility, that, in some cases, the sense of that duty may prevail over the motives of self-interest, but it provides against the probability in many cases, and the danger in all cases, that the dictates of self-interest will exercise a predominant influence, and supersede that of duty."[12]

---

[12]    Michoud et al. v. Girod et al., 1846, 4 How. 503, 554-555, 45 U.S. 503, 554-555, 11 L.Ed. 1076. Petitioner urges that the Michoud case is readily distinguishable and petitioner is correct.

But the Commission in this case did not, and we in turn do not, base the validity of the revocation order upon common law principles of fraud or deceit. Section 17(a) of the Securities Act of 1933, Sections 10(b) and 15(c)(1) of the Securities Exchange Act of 1934, and Commission-made rules thereunder, all quoted supra, in prohibitory language, set out the statutory prescription as to the conduct of the business of a broker and dealer in securities. If any one of these statutes or rules has been wilfully violated by petitioner and revocation is found to be in the public interest, the respondent, by virtue of Section 15(b), supra, has authority to revoke.

It cannot now be doubted that, as respondent points out, the securities field, by its nature, requires specialized and unique legal treatment. This is recognized by the very statutes and regulations here under consideration as well as by recent federal and state court decisions.

"The business of trading in securities is one in which opportunities for dishonesty are of constant recurrence and ever present. It engages acute, active minds, trained to quick apprehension, decision and action. The Congress has seen fit to regulate this business. Though such regulation must be done in strict subordination to constitutional and lawful safeguards of individual rights, it is to be enforced notwithstanding the frauds to be suppressed may take on more subtle and involved forms than those in which dishonesty manifests itself in cruder and less specialized activities."[13]

The acts of petitioner which constitute violations of the antifraud sections of statutes and of regulations thereunder are acts of omission in that petitioner failed to fully disclose the nature and extent of her adverse interest. The Commission found that petitioner failed to disclose to her clients (1) the best price at which the securities could be purchased for the clients in the open market in the exercise of due diligence and (2) the cost to petitioner of the securities sold by her to her clients. In no less than three places in the above-quoted statutes and regulations we find that, "any omission to state a material fact necessary in order to make the statements made, in the light of the circumstances under which they were made, not misleading," is expressly made unlawful. These quoted words as they appear in the statute can only mean that Congress forbid not only the telling of purposeful falsity but also the telling of half-truths and the failure to tell the "whole truth." These statutory words were obviously designed to protect the investing public as a whole whether the individual investors be suspicious or unsuspecting. The best price currently obtainable in the open market and the cost to registrant are both material facts within the meaning of the above-quoted language and they are both factors without which informed consent to a fiduciary's acting in a dual and conflicting role is impossible.

Petitioner strongly urges that she has fully and completely fulfilled any disclosure requirement by the insertion in the Memorandum of Agreement (entered into with each of her clients since 1943) of the clause that the "Company, when acting as investment adviser, shall act as Principal in every such transaction, except as otherwise agreed," and that, in any event, petitioner has always stood ready to provide any further information which her clients desired. The clause inserted in the Memorandum of Agreement does not even approach the minimum disclosure requirements. In the first place, it is certainly doubtful whether petitioner's clients

---

However, neither its age nor its distinguishability can detract from the force and vigor of the general doctrine set out therein.

[13]    Archer v. SEC, 133 F. 2d 795, 803 (8th Cir. 1943), *cert. denied*, 319 U.S. 767 (1943).

either knew of or understood the legal effect of this technical language inserted in fine print in the printed document which each client signed when he or she first became a client of petitioner. Secondly, even assuming, as urged by amici, that all of petitioner's clients are persons of more than average experience and intelligence with regard to the conceded intricacies of securities transactions, an assumption which is at best dubious in view of the present record,[14] their full knowledge that petitioner either sold them securities she then owned or bought securities in her own name and then resold them to the clients cannot be considered sufficient knowledge to enable the clients to give their informed consent.   When Mrs. Hughes took the witness stand in the proceedings below she categorically denied that she ever disclosed to her clients either the price she paid for a security, its market price, or any bid and ask prices for the security.   She thereafter stated: "If at any time one of my clients wants to ask anything, why, of course, I will answer them and they all know that." Based upon petitioner's own testimony then, the Commission's finding that her disclosure was inadequate was reasonable and correct and supported by substantial evidence of record.  It is not enough that one who acts as an admitted fiduciary proclaim that he or she stands ever ready to divulge material facts to the ones whose interests she is being paid to protect.  Some knowledge is prerequisite to intelligent questioning.  This is particularly true in the securities field.  Readiness and willingness to disclose are not equivalent to disclosure.  The statutes and rules discussed above make it unlawful to omit to state material facts irrespective of alleged (or proven) willingness or readiness to supply that which has been omitted.

## Comments and Questions

1.  How does the holding in this *Hughes-II* decision compare with the holding of *Hughes-I*, decided just a few years earlier.  Are the securities firms in both cases offering the same service?  Are their pricing strategies equivalent?

2.  An interesting and unusual aspect of the *Hughes-II* decision is the intervention of a large number of the petitioner's customers.  Were the Commission and court unduly dismissive of these customers' assertion that revocation of the petitioner's registration was unwarranted?  Is it really "immaterial whether . . . all . . of petitioner's clients understood completely the nature of their dealings with petitioner and were satisfied with . . . petitioner's method of doing business?"  Might the court have considered the customer's execution of the Memorandum of Agreement as a waiver of their rights to receive subsequent information about contemporaneous costs and alternative sources of supply. Would such a waiver be permissible under the federal securities laws?  See section 29(a) of the 1934 Act.

---

[14]    Two of the nine clients who testified below showed a completely inadequate understanding of the term "principal" in the clause in their agreement with petitioner.  None of the nine could recall that this term or that clause had ever been explained to them by petitioner.  Further, none of the nine could compute with accuracy the amount of petitioner's net profit by consulting the schedule of rates contained in the agreement.

## B. The Advisory Relationship

As *Hughes* I and *Hughes II* suggest, broker-dealers often provide not just access to the securities market but investment advice on which securities to buy and sell. In this section, we consider a number of ways in which the federal securities laws police the investment advice given by broker-dealers and other regulated entities.

### 1. The Appropriateness of Recommendations

A number of broker-dealer obligations are designed to ensure the appropriateness of investment advice. The following case is illustrative.

## Mihara v. Dean Witter & Co.
### 619 F.2d 814 (9th Cir. 1980)

On April 26, 1974, Samuel Mihara filed this action in United States District Court for the Central District of California. He alleged both federal statutory and California common law fiduciary duty claims arising from the handling of Mihara's securities accounts by defendants. Specifically, plaintiff alleges that the defendants, Dean Witter & Company and its account executive, George Gracis, engaged in excessive trading or "churning" in plaintiff's securities account, and purchased "unsuitable" securities which did not conform to Mihara's stated investment objectives. Plaintiff sought relief under Section 10(b) of the Securities Exchange Act of 1934 and Rule 10b-5 promulgated thereunder, as well as for breach of fiduciary duties. Plaintiff sought both compensatory and punitive damages, and demanded a jury trial.

On February 2, 1978, after a jury trial, a verdict was entered for Mihara and against the defendants on both the Rule 10b-5 claim and the State breach of fiduciary duty claim. Compensatory damages in the amount of $24,600 were awarded to Mihara, a punitive damages award of $66,666 was assessed against Dean Witter & Company, and a $2,000 punitive damage award was assessed against defendant Gracis. . . .

On January 6, 1971, plaintiff Mihara opened a joint securities account with the Santa Monica office of Dean Witter. At that time Mihara was employed by the McDonnell-Douglas Corporation as a supervisory engineer. He was 38 years old and possessed a Bachelor of Science and Master's Degree in Engineering. He and his wife were the parents of two daughters. Mihara's assets at the time consisted of approximately $30,000 in savings, an employee's savings account at McDonnell-Douglas of approximately $16,000, an equity in his home for approximately fifteen to seventeen thousand dollars. He also held shares of McDonnell-Douglas stock obtained through an employee payroll deduction plan.

Prior to opening his account with Dean Witter, Mihara had invested in securities for approximately ten years. He had dealt with several other firms during that period, but apparently felt that his account had not received adequate attention, and was looking for a new investment firm. Mihara opened his account with Dean Witter in January of 1971 by telephoning Stuart Cypherd, the office manager for Dean Witter's Santa Monica office, and asking to be assigned an account executive. Cypherd, in turn, instructed defendant Gracis to phone Mihara to set up an appointment.

The evidence as to the content of the initial meeting between Mihara and Gracis is conflicting. Mihara testified that as an engineer he lacked a finance and economics background and was looking for someone with expertise on which he could rely. He also stated that he was concerned about possible cutbacks at McDonnell-Douglas, noting that layoffs were common in that industry. He indicated that he was concerned about the education of his two daughters, and their financial security.

Gracis' testimony with regard to their initial meeting, and specifically relating to Mihara's investment objectives, differs substantially. Gracis testified that Mihara was not concerned about a possible layoff, that he was primarily interested in growth, and that he was knowledgeable about margin accounts and broker call rates.

Mihara invested $30,000 with Dean Witter. This money was to be invested according to Gracis' recommendations but subject to Mihara's approval.

The history of Mihara's investment account with Dean Witter & Company reflects speculative investments, numerous purchases and sales, and substantial reliance on the recommendations of Gracis. The initial recommendations of Gracis were that Mihara purchase shares of companies engaged in the double-knit fabric industry. These stocks included Venice Industries, Devon Apparel, Edmos, Fab Industries, D. H. J. Industries, Leslie Fay, Graniteville, Duplan, and United Piece and Dye. From 1971 to 1973, Mihara's account lost considerable sums of money. Since many of the purchases were on margin, Mihara would often have to come up with additional funds as the equity in his account declined. The final trading losses in the account totaled $46,464. This loss occurred during the period of January 1971 to May 1973.

Mihara first began to complain of the handling of his account when it showed a loss in April 1971. At that time he complained to Gracis because his account was losing money, then about $3,000. Throughout 1971, as Mihara's account lost money, he continued to complain to Gracis. In October of 1971, Mihara went to Mr. Cypherd, the office manager for the Santa Monica office of Dean Witter. Mihara complained to Cypherd about the handling of the account by Gracis. He did not, however, close out the account. As the value of Mihara's securities account continued to dwindle, he visited Cypherd on several occasions to complain further about Gracis. While Cypherd told Mihara he was "on top" of the account, the performance and handling of the account did not improve.

At about the same time that Mihara first contacted him, Cypherd was also made aware of substantial trading in the account by means of a Dean Witter Monthly Account Activity Analysis. This analysis was initiated by the Dean Witter computer whenever an account showed 15 or more trades in one month or commissions of $1,000 or more. Because Mihara's account reflected 16 trades for the month of April 1971, Cypherd was alerted to the problem at that time. In May of 1971, the Dean Witter computer generated another monthly account activity analysis as the result of 21 trades during that month in Mihara's account. Mihara's account in March of 1971 reflected 33 transactions, however, the computer did not generate an account analysis.

In November 1973, Mihara went to the San Francisco office of Dean Witter and complained to Paul Dubow, the National Compliance Director for Dean Witter, Inc. At that point Mihara's account had suffered considerable losses. Apparently not satisfied with the results of that meeting, Mihara filed this suit in April 1974.

The case experienced several delays in getting to trial. The trial was initially set for September 27, 1977. On May 2, 1977, plaintiff's counsel advised defense counsel that he intended to obtain another expert witness to testify at trial. On August 17, 1977, defendants moved for a continuance of the upcoming trial, or in the alternative, to exclude plaintiff's new expert, who at that time had not been designated. Immediately thereafter, plaintiff's counsel informed defendants that the additional expert witness was Mr. Robert McCuen, made him available for deposition, and the parties stipulated that the trial should be continued until November 15, 1977. Defense counsel was apparently unable to depose McCuen, and obtained a continuance of the trial until January 17, 1978. . . .

At trial plaintiff gave his recollection of the initial meeting with Gracis. He testified that Gracis recommended securities which did not appear to conform to those objectives. He also related the dismal record of the account, and how attempts to remedy the situation through meetings with Gracis' superiors proved fruitless. Plaintiff also introduced the Dean Witter Account Executive Manual (Plaintiff's Exhibit 1) which stated that Dean Witter account executives had a "sacred trust to protect" their customers, that Dean Witter customers have confidence in the firm, and "under no circumstances should we violate this confidence."

Mr. Paul Dubow, the National Compliance Director for Dean Witter from November 1971 through July 1974, testified as to his company's compliance duties, internal monitoring systems, and the responsibilities of supervisory personnel in monitoring clients' accounts. Mr. Dubow was also questioned by plaintiff's counsel regarding various New York Stock exchange (NYSE) and National Association of Security Dealers (NASD) rules and regulations. Both Mr. Dubow and Mr. Cypherd were specifically questioned regarding NYSE Rule 405 which requires that all account executives learn all essential facts about their clients (the "Know Your Customer Rule") and Article 3, Section 1 of the NASD Rule of Fair Practice which requires supervisory personnel to make sure that account executives are dealing fairly and within the objectives of their clients and to "know the client".

Plaintiff's expert, Mr. White, a former attorney with the Securities & Exchange Commission, testified at trial that the pattern of trading in the Mihara account reflected a pattern of churning. Plaintiff's Exhibit 20, Chart G, introduced at trial, indicated the following holding periods for Mihara's securities. In 1971, 50% of the securities were held for 15 days or less, 61% for 30 days or less, and approximately 76% were held for 60 days or less. Through June of 1973, 81.6% of the securities in the Mihara account were held for a period of 180 days or less. White also relied on the "turnover rate" in Mihara's account in reaching his conclusion. The turnover rate for a given period is arrived at by dividing the total dollar amount of stock purchases for a given period by the average monthly capital investment in the account. Plaintiff's Exhibit No. 20, Chart C, indicates that between January 1971 and July 1973, Mihara's average monthly investment of $36,653 was turned over approximately 14 times. On an annualized basis, Mihara's average capital monthly investment in 1971 of approximately $40,000 was turned over 9.3 times. His average capital investment in 1972 was $39,800 and that was turned over approximately 3.36 times. His average monthly capital investment for the first half of 1973 was $23,588 and that was turned over approximately .288 times. White testified that a substantial turnover in the early stages of the account followed by a significant decline in the turnover rate was typical of a churned account.

White also testified that the holding periods for securities in Mihara's account reflected a pattern of churning. He noted that churned accounts usually reflect significant turnover in the early stages, that is, a very short holding period for the securities purchased, followed by longer holding periods in the later stages of the account. Thus, the typical churned account is churned in the early stages of the account generating large commissions at the outset, followed by less trading and longer holding periods in the latter stages of the account, after significant commissions have been generated. Mihara's account reflects precisely that pattern. The cumulative total of commissions earned by Gracis was $12,672, the majority of which came in the early stages of the account.

In addition to the testimony of Mr. White that, in his expert opinion, Mihara's account had been "churned," plaintiff's expert witness McCuen also testified that in his opinion the securities purchased from Mihara's account were not suitable for Mihara's stated investment objectives. Mr. McCuen based his analysis in part on rankings found in reports in the "Value Line" investment service newsletter which rates those stocks poorly. Mr. McCuen noted that the securities in question were rated as high risk securities with below average financial strength.

At the close of plaintiff's presentation of evidence on the issue of liability, defense counsel moved for a directed verdict for failure to establish a prima facie case on both claims and on the grounds the plaintiff's testimony revealed existence of defenses as a matter of law. The Court denied the motion.

The defendant Gracis testified that Mihara was more interested in riskier growth potential investments. He stated he recommended such stocks, but also noted the drawbacks of such investments. Gracis testified that he also warned of the dangers of utilizing a margin account. Gracis also confirmed Mihara's testimony concerning complaints about losses . . . .

A stock broker at an investment firm Mihara had dealt with in the past testified that Mihara had been interested in growth stocks, had discussed margin accounts, though never initiated one, and had a "good knowledge" of the stock market.

Mr. William Bedford, an investment counselor, testified as defendant's expert witness regarding the suitability of the Mihara account. Bedford testified that given an aggressive growth investment objective, the securities in plaintiff's account were not unsuitable, nor the transactions excessive.

Finally, Mr. Cypherd testified regarding his supervisory function at Dean Witter, noting that he received various daily documents and reports relating to customer accounts and that he would regularly make inquiries of brokers regarding their customers' accounts. He testified that in October of 1971 he advised plaintiff that he was dealing in volatile securities, that he was paying considerable commissions and that perhaps his use of a margin account was excessive. Cypherd also verified that he had spoken with Gracis about the account on several occasions and that he would mention conversations between himself and Mihara to Gracis. . . .

When a securities broker engages in excessive trading in disregard of his customer's investment objectives for the purpose of generating commission business, the customer may hold the broker liable for churning in violation of Rule 10b-5. Hecht v. Harris Upham & Company, 430 F.2d 1202 (9th Cir. 1970). In order to establish a claim of churning, a plaintiff must show (1) that the trading in his account was excessive in light of his investment objectives; (2) that the broker in question exercised control over the trading in the account; and (3) that the broker acted with the intent to defraud or with the willful and reckless disregard for the interests of his client. Rolf v. Blyth, Eastman, Dillon & Company, Inc., 424 F.Supp. 1021, 1039-1040 (S.D.N.Y., 1977) aff'd at 570 F.2d 38 (1978), cert. denied 439 U.S. 1039 (1978).

Whether trading is excessive is a question which must be examined in light of the investment objectives of the customer. While there is no clear line of demarcation, courts and commentators have suggested that an annual turnover rate of six reflects excessive trading. See Rolf v. Blyth, Eastman, Dillon & Company, 424 F.Supp., at 1039. See also Churning by Securities Dealers, 80 Harv.L.Rev. 869 (1967). In Hecht v. Harris Upham & Company, 283 F.Supp. 417 (N.D.Cal., 1968), aff'd at 430 F.2d 1202, 1210 (9th Cir., 1970), this Court affirmed a finding of churning where an account had been turned over 8 to 11.5 times during a six-year ten-month period. In that case, 45% of the securities were held for less than six months, 67% were held for less than nine months, and 82% were held for less than a year. Under this Court's holding in Hecht, the evidence in the present case clearly supports a finding of excessive trading.

With regard to the second prerequisite, we believe that Gracis exercised sufficient control over Mihara's account in the present case to support a finding of churning. The account need not be a discretionary account whereby the broker executes each trade without the consent of the client. As the Hecht case indicates, the requisite degree of control is met when the client routinely follows the recommendations of the broker. The present case, as in Hecht, reflects a pattern of de facto control by the broker.

The third requisite element of a 10b-5 violation scienter has also been established. The manner in which Mihara's account was handled reflects, at best, a reckless disregard for the client's investment concerns, and, at worst, an outright scheme to defraud plaintiff. Perhaps in recognition of this, appellants have constructed a curious argument as to the scienter element. They suggest that plaintiff must establish an intent to defraud as to each trade executed by the broker. This assertion is entirely without merit. The churning of a client's account is, in itself, a scheme or artifice to defraud within the meaning of Rule 10b-5. With regard to the definition of scienter, this circuit has held that reckless conduct constitutes scienter within the meaning of Ernst & Ernst v. Hochfelder, 425 U.S. 185 (1976). . . .

Appellants' second contention is that plaintiff failed to establish a prima facie case of breach of fiduciary duty under California law. The central theme of this argument is that no fiduciary relationship was ever established between plaintiff and defendants, Dean Witter and Gracis, because defendants never accepted a fiduciary duty or position of trust with respect to plaintiff's account. Appellants' argument attempts to view the establishment of a fiduciary relationship in contractual terms of offer and acceptance. They contend that they never "accepted" a fiduciary responsibility toward plaintiff. This argument is without merit. The Dean Witter Account Executive Manual introduced at trial instructs securities brokers that "our client has a right to believe and trust you" and that Dean Witter has "a sacred trust to protect our customers." Even without these statements as to how Dean Witter viewed its relationship with its clients, the account executive has a duty not to place his interests over those of his client by generating commissions through excessive, unwarranted trading.

Appellants also argue that the defenses of estoppel, waiver, ratification, laches, and failure to mitigate damages were established as a matter of law. Appellants rely principally on Hecht v.

Harris Upham & Company, supra. In that case the District Court found that plaintiffs were barred from complaining about the specific purchases of stock by estoppel, laches, and waiver. As in the present case, the plaintiff in Hecht received confirmation slips stating exactly what had been purchased and indicating the amount paid. The Court in Hecht went on to find, however, that while the plaintiff was barred from complaining about specific purchases of stock, she was not estopped from maintaining a claim for excessive trading. The Court concluded that while confirmation slips were sufficient to inform plaintiff of the specific transactions made, they were "not sufficient to put her on notice that the trading of her account was excessive." Hecht v. Harris Upham, 430 F.2d, at 1210. Thus, the defenses raised by appellants apply only to plaintiff's claims regarding the suitability of the stocks purchased, and not to the claim of churning.

### Comments and Questions

1. The measure of damages in churning cases is often a contested issue. Traditionally, damages were limited to the amount of excess commissions. More recently, some courts have also allowed recovery for losses suffered on a churned portfolio. See, e.g., Miley v. Oppenheimer & Co., 637 F.2d 318 (5th Cir. 1981). Which is the more appropriate measure? Suppose a brokerage firm churned an account, but the account still earned substantial profits. Could the client still recover excessive commissions? See Nesbit v. McNeil, 896 F.2d 380 (9th Cir. 1990).

2. The *Mihara* decision refers to NYSE Rule 405 (the "Know Your Customer" Rule) as well as the NASD Rules of Conduct. These rules, developed through self-regulatory organizations ("SRO's") have played an important role in defining the obligations of broker-dealers. As we will see, these rules can form the basis of SRO enforcement proceedings. In addition, although courts have declined to infer private rights of action under SRO rules, these rules do create important background norms for cases such as the *Mihara* decision. In terms of protecting customers from inappropriate investment advice, one of the most significant SRO rules is the NASD's suitability rule, which provides in relevant part:

> In recommending to a customer the purchase, sale or exchange of any security, a member shall have reasonable grounds for believing that the recommendation is suitable for such customer upon the basis of facts, if any, disclosed by such customer as to his other security holdings and as to his financial situation and needs.

NASD Rules of Conduct, Rule 2310(a). In 1990, the NASD amended this rule to impose an additional affirmative obligation to become familiar with the financial needs of non-institutional customers before executing recommended transactions. *Id.* Rule 2310(b). See generally Stuart D. Root, *Suitability - the Sophisticated Investor - and Modern Portfolio Management*, 3 COLUM. BUS. L. REV. 287 (1991).

3. Several years before the Mihara case was decided, the U.S. Supreme Court handed down a series of cases cutting back on the scope of federal securities laws. For example, in Santa Fe Industries v. Green, 430 U.S. 462 (1977), the Court ruled that anti-fraud claims under rule 10b-5 must be based on deception (that is, the withholding of material information) rather than simple unfairness or breach of fiduciary duty. In a similar spirit,

Ernst & Ernst v. Hochfelder, 425 U.S. 185 (1976), held that violations of rule 10b-5 must entail intentional misconduct, not mere negligence. Many proceedings against broker-dealers, like the *Mihara* case itself, include claims arising under rule 10b-5. Should the restrictions of *Ernst & Ernst* and *Santa Fe* cases be read into these actions? Do the specialized anti-fraud provisions for broker-dealers authorize a broader scope of liability in this area. See section 15(c) of the 1934 Act; Rule 15c1-2. *Compare* Donald C. Langevoort, *Fraud and Deception by Securities Professionals*, 61 TEX. L. REV. 147 (1983) (arguing against a strict application of *Santa Fe*'s deception requirement in this context), *with* Roberta S. Karmel, *Is the Shingle Theory Dead?*, 52 WASH. & LEE. L. REV. 1271 (1995) (arguing that intervening Supreme Court decisions have vitiated the shingle theory).

*Problem 10-1*

John, 72, worked for many years as a high-school basketball coach, and recently retired with several hundred thousand dollars of savings, which he wants to use to support retirement income for himself and his wife Jane, 57, also retired. John's broker, Dibble & Sons, is keen on several start-up firms in the region which though speculative are potentially quite profitable. Can Dibble recommend investments in these firms to John? Should they recommend long-term U.S. government securities instead? Would it affect your answer if John had recently completed a college course in investment strategies?

### 2. Knowledge of Recommended Securities

Another obligation of broker-dealers is the duty to become educated about the securities being recommended to customers.

# Hanly v. Securities and Exchange Commission
## 415 F. 2d 589 (2d Cir. 1969)

Five securities salesmen petition to review an order of the Securities and Exchange Commission which barred them from further association with any broker or dealer. The Commission found that petitioners, in the offer and sale of the stock of U.S. Sonics Corporation (Sonics) between September 1962 and August 1963, willfully violated the antifraud provisions of Section 17(a) of the Securities Act of 1933, Sections 10(b) and 15(c)(1) of the Securities Exchange Act of 1934, and Rule 10b-5. Specifically, the Commission held that 'the fraud in this case consisted of the optimistic representations or the recommendations . . . without disclosure of known or reasonably ascertainable adverse information which rendered them materially misleading . . .. It is clear that a salesman must not merely avoid affirmative misstatements when he recommends the stock to a customer; he must also disclose material adverse facts of which he is or should be aware.' Petitioners individually argue that their violations of the federal securities laws were not willful but involved at most good faith optimistic predictions concerning a speculative security, and that the sanctions imposed by the Commission exceeded legally permissible limits. . . . . .

### Violations

Sonics was organized in 1958. It engaged in the production and sale of various electronic devices. From its inception the company operated at a deficit. During the period of the sales of its stock here involved, the company was insolvent.

By 1962 the company had developed a ceramic filter which was said to be far superior to conventional wire filters used in radio circuits. Sonics' inability to raise the capital necessary to produce these filters led it to negotiate with foreign and domestic companies to whom Sonics hoped to grant production licenses on a royalty basis. Licenses were granted to a Japanese and to a West German company, each of which made initial payments of $25,000, and to an Argentine company, which made an initial payment of $50,000. License negotiations with domestic companies continued into 1963 without success; negotiations terminated with General Instrument Corporation on March 20, 1963 and with Texas Instruments, Incorporated, on June 29, 1963. In addition, testing of the filter by prospective customers provided unsatisfactory results.

Merger negotiations with General Instrument and Texas Instruments likewise proved unsuccessful. Sonics' financial condition continued to deteriorate with the cancellation by the Navy of anticipated orders for hydrophones. On December 6, 1963 bankruptcy proceedings were instituted against Sonics, and on December 27, 1963 it was adjudicated a bankrupt.

During most of the relevant period petitioners were employed by Richard J. Buck & Co., a partnership registered as a broker-dealer. Gladstone and Fehr were co-managers of the firm's Forest Hills, N.Y., branch office. Hanly was the manager of its Hempstead, N.Y., office. Stutzmann and Paras were salesmen in the Hempstead office.

Gladstone (along with Paras) first heard of Sonics in September 1962 during a conversation with one Roach who had been a sales manager for his prior employer, Edwards and Hanly. Roach compared Sonics to Ilikon, whose stock he had previously recommended and which had been highly successful. Sonics was praised for its good management, large research and development expenses and, most important, its development of a ceramic filter. In January 1963 Roach told Gladstone of the possibility of a domestic license and furnished him with a copy of an allegedly confidential 14 page report which predicted a bright future for the company. In February Gladstone met with Eric Kolm, Sonics' president, who confirmed most of the statements in the report. During the spring of 1963 Gladstone learned of the licensing and merger negotiations mentioned above.

On the basis of this information and knowing that Sonics had never shown a year end profit since its inception, that it was still sustaining losses, and that the 14 page report was not identified as to source and did not contain financial statements, Gladstone told Hanly, Stutzmann and Paras about the company and made certain representations to his customers.

Evidence of affirmative misrepresentations by Gladstone to his customers regarding Sonics stock included the following: Sonics was a winner and would make money. It had a fabulous potential and would double or triple. It would make Xerox look like a standstill and would revolutionize the space age industry. Gladstone himself had purchased the stock for his own account and he would be able to retire and get rich on it. It had possibilities of skyrocketing and would probably double in price within six months to a year. Although it had not earned money in the past, prospects were good for earnings of $1 in a year. Sonics had signed a contract with General Instrument. The stock would go from 6 to 12 in two weeks and to 15 in the near future.  The 14 page report had been written by Value Line.  The company was not going bankrupt.  Its products were perfected and it was already earning $1 per share.  It was about to have a breakthrough on a new product that was fantastic and would revolutionize automobile and home radios.

In addition to these affirmative misrepresentations, the testimony disclosed that adverse information about Sonics' financial difficulties was not disclosed by Gladstone; that some customers had received confirmations for orders they had not placed; and that literature about the company was not provided.  Most of the customer-witnesses testified that they had purchased in reliance upon the recommendations of Gladstone.

Paras learned of Sonics during the same September 1962 conversation between Roach, Gladstone and Paras referred to above.

Evidence of affirmative misrepresentations by Paras to his customers regarding Sonics stock included the following: Sonics had a good growth possibility.  It should double after three or four weeks (to one customer); it could double, i.e. increase 8 to 10 points, within four to six months (to another customer); and it would rise 10 to 15 points (to still another customer).  Paras had bought the stock himself.  The company was about to enter into a favorable contract for its filters with Texas Instruments and Texas Instruments might acquire Sonics.

In addition to these affirmative misrepresentations, Paras never mentioned Sonics' adverse financial condition; he never provided any literature about the company; and in at least one instance he sent a confirmation to a customer who claims not to have ordered the stock.

When asked by the hearing examiner why he recommended a stock like Sonics when the commissions he would receive would be negligible, Paras replied that on the basis of his reliable information he hoped that Sonics would make money for his customers who would refer others to him.  'It would be a feather in my cap to buy a stock at $8 and sell it at $29 or $30.'

Stutzmann learned of Sonics, including its weak financial condition, through information given him by Gladstone and Paras and through examination of the anonymous 14 page report referred to above.

Evidence of affirmative misrepresentations by Stutzmann to his customers regarding Sonics stock included the following: Sonics had just acquired a big contract and should reach 15 in a year.  Sonics is similar to Ilikon.  Although its past earnings were not impressive, they would soon get bright because of licensing royalties.  The price would double in six months.  Since the price had dropped, this was a good time to buy.  It was a hot prospect.

As with Gladstone and Paras, customer-witnesses testified that Stutzmann did not provide any adverse financial information or any literature, and that he falsely claimed to have bought Sonics stock himself.

Fehr, with Gladstone, was a co-manager of the Forest Hills, N.Y., branch office of Buck & Co.  He first learned of Sonics at a meeting in February 1963 attended by Gladstone, Roach, Eric Kolm and Fehr.  It was Fehr, together with Gladstone, who conveyed to Hanly, Stutzmann and Paras information concerning Sonics, including its poor financial condition and its record of losses.

Despite Fehr's admission that he had received from Sonics' president, Kolm, the exact 1962 financial information regarding the company, he failed to disclose to Buck's customers interested in Sonics (including a customer to whom he made a direct sale of the stock) that the company had sustained operating losses for four consecutive years, that it had a large accumulated deficit, that it had no working capital and that it was insolvent.

Instead, in recommending the purchase of Sonics stock to a customer in March 1963, Fehr represented that the company was engaged in negotiations which, if successful, would lead to a price rise of 3 to 4 points; that the company was about to break through on a product he thought would be substantial; and that Sonics stock was an extremely good speculation. To another customer, who was concerned with the decline of the stock following his purchase upon representations by Gladstone, Fehr said between March and May 1963 that the stock was worth holding; that it was a good stock; that its decline was only temporary; and that he had purchased the stock for himself and a member of his family (which he had). On another occasion, Fehr told a group of people in the Buck office that there was nothing to worry about concerning Sonics.

Hanly, manager of the Hempstead, N.Y., office of Buck & Co., learned of Sonics and its weak financial condition from Gladstone and Fehr.

Although fully aware of Sonics' financial condition, Hanly did not disclose any financial information regarding the company to either of the two customers who purchased the stock on March 1, 1963 upon his recommendation.

Instead, Hanly told one of these customers that Sonics had a new invention that would rock the world; that it would merge with another company in the near future; and that its stock would rise from 8 to 12 or 15 in a short time. Although this customer instructed Hanly to hold any loss on her $3000 investment to $300, he failed to do so; when she demanded satisfaction, Hanly predated a sell order to minimize her loss.

## Law Applicable to Violations

In its opinion the Commission quoted from the record in attributing the representations discussed above respectively to each of the petitioners. It concluded that their optimistic representations or recommendations were materially false and misleading. Fraud was found both in affirmative falsehoods and in recommendations made without disclosure of known or reasonably ascertainable adverse information, such as Sonics' deteriorating financial condition, its inability to manufacture the filter, the lack of knowledge regarding the filter's commercial feasibility, and the negative results of pending negotiations.

The Commission found that the sophistication of the customers or prior relationships which many of them had enjoyed with the respective petitioners were irrelevant. It held that the absence of a boiler room did not justify affirmative misrepresentations or a failure to disclose adverse financial information. The relevance of a customer's nonloss of money or a salesman's speculation in the stock likewise was discounted.

The sensitivity of operations in the securities field and the availability of opportunities where those in a position of trust can manipulate others to their own advantage led Congress to pass the antifraud provisions of the statutes with which the instant proceedings are concerned. Congress committed to the Commission the responsibility of supervising the activity of broker-dealers and registered representatives.

When a securities salesman fraudulently violates the high standards with which he is charged, he subjects himself to a variety of punitive, compensatory and remedial sanctions. In the instant proceedings petitioners have not been criminally charged, nor have they been sued for damages by their customers arising from the alleged misrepresentations. Instead, in private proceedings initiated by the Commission, each petitioner's privilege of being employed in the securities industry has been revoked. It is in this context that the issues before the Court must be considered. More particularly, we are here concerned with the expertise of the Commission in its assessment of how the public interest best may be protected from various kinds of intentional fraud and reckless misconduct which often threaten securities transactions, especially, as here, in the over the counter market.

Brokers and salesmen are 'under a duty to investigate, and their violation of that duty brings them within the term 'willful' in the Exchange Act.' Thus, a salesman cannot deliberately ignore that which he has a duty to know and recklessly state facts about matters of which he is ignorant. He must analyze sales literature and must not blindly accept recommendations made therein. The fact that his customers may be sophisticated and knowledgeable does not warrant a less stringent standard. Even where the purchaser follows the market activity of the stock and does not rely upon the salesman's statements, remedial sanctions may be imposed since reliance is not an element of fraudulent misrepresentation in this context.

A securities dealer occupies a special relationship to a buyer of securities in that by his position he implicitly represents he has an adequate basis for the opinions he renders. While this implied warranty may not be as rigidly enforced in a civil action where an investor seeks damages for losses allegedly caused by reliance upon his unfounded representations, its applicability in the instant proceedings cannot be questioned.[14]

Sonics was an over the counter stock. Those who purchased through petitioners could not readily confirm the information given them. In Charles Hughes & Co., Inc. v. SEC, 139 F.2d 434 (2 Cir. 1943), cert. denied, 321 U.S. 786 (1944), this Court recognized the difficulties involved in over the counter stocks and the special duty imposed upon those who sell such stocks not to take advantage of customers in whom confidence has been instilled.

In summary, the standards by which the actions of each petitioner must be judged are strict. He cannot recommend a security unless there is an adequate and reasonable basis for such recommendation. He must disclose facts which he knows and those which are reasonably

---

[14] Petitioners argue that their activities are to be distinguished from those of a 'boiler room' and that, absent a finding of boiler room operations here, the Commission's strict standards should not be applied against petitioners. A boiler room usually is a temporary operation established to sell a specific speculative security. Solicitation is by telephone to new customers, the salesman conveying favorable earnings projections, predictions of price rises and other optimistic prospects without a factual basis. The prospective buyer is not informed of known or readily ascertainable adverse information; he is not cautioned about the risks inherent in purchasing a speculative security; and he is left with a deliberately created expectation of gain without risk. . . . Salesmen in a boiler room are held to a high duty of truthfulness which is not met by a claim of lack of knowledge. The Commission having previously refused to condone misrepresentation in the absence of a boiler room, we specifically reject petitioners' argument that absence of boiler room operations here is a defense to a charge of misrepresentation.

ascertainable.  By his recommendation he implies that a reasonable investigation has been made and that his recommendation rests on the conclusions based on such investigation. Where the salesman lacks essential information about a security, he should disclose this as well as the risks which arise from his lack of information.

A salesman may not rely blindly upon the issuer for information concerning a company, although the degree of independent investigation which must be made by a securities dealer will vary in each case.  Securities issued by smaller companies of recent origin obviously require more thorough investigation.

## Sanctions

The Commission is authorized by Section 15(b)(7) of the Securities Exchange Act, to bar any person from association with a broker or dealer 'if the Commission finds that such . . . barring . . . is in the public interest . . .,' and that such person has willfully violated the Securities Act or the Securities Exchange Act.

Acting pursuant to this statutory authority and upon a finding that it was in the public interest to do so, the Commission, having found that each petitioner had violated the antifraud provisions of the securities laws, ordered that each be barred from further association with any broker or dealer, except that Fehr was barred for only 60 days, after which he may return to the securities business in a non-supervisory capacity and upon an appropriate showing that he will be adequately supervised.[16]

The courts, including ours, uniformly have recognized the fundamental principle that imposition of sanctions necessarily must be entrusted to the expertise of a regulatory commission such as the SEC; and only upon a showing of abuse of discretion-- such as the imposition of a sanction unwarranted in law or without justification in fact-- will a reviewing court intervene in the matter of sanctions.

For the most part, petitioners' attacks upon the sanctions here imposed do not merit discussion.  Their arguments were fully considered by the Commission which, in accordance with its undoubted authority, gave different weight to such arguments than petitioners would like. . . . . [T]he obvious disparity in culpability between petitioners, reflected in our summary above of the evidence of violations by each, is not a proper basis for challenging the Commission's sanctions; nor is the fact that in the case of one or more petitioners only one investor witness testified against him.  And of course even the permanent bar order which the Commission in its discretion has imposed as to four of the petitioners is not necessarily an irrevocable sanction; upon application,  the Commission, if it finds that the public interest no longer requires the

---

[16]    In thus imposing sanctions, the Commission agreed with the hearing examiner's determination that Gladstone should be barred from association with any broker or dealer, but it found inadequate the sanctions imposed upon the other petitioners.  The examiner had ordered Fehr, Stutzmann and Paras suspended from association with any broker or dealer for five months, Hanly for four months; and the reinstatement of Stutzmann and Paras was conditioned upon a showing of adequate supervision in accordance with the Commission's usual practice.  The three sanctions authorized by the statute are censure, barring, or suspension.  Section 15(b)(7) of the 1934 Act.

applicant's exclusion from the securities business, may permit his return-- usually subject to appropriate safeguards.

There is one aspect of the sanction issue in the instant case which does merit brief mention: the Commission's imposition of greater sanctions upon four of the petitioners than ordered by the hearing examiner. This appears to be a matter of first impression, at least in this Court. The Commission clearly has the authority to modify, including the authority to increase, sanctions ordered by a hearing examiner in his initial decision, and we so hold.

## Comments and Questions

1. The *Hanly* decision extends the *Hughes I* and *Hughes II* line of cases in that it defines the responsibilities of broker-dealers when recommending securities to clients. A variety of SEC rules serve a similar purpose. For example, rule 15c2-11 specifies the financial information that a broker-dealer must possess before it can publish a quotation (that is, set a price) for a security. Under this rule, publishing a quotation without the requisite information is a fraudulent and manipulative act for purposes of section 15(c)(1) of the 1934 Act. Is it inherently fraudulent and manipulative to quote prices without information of the sort specified in rule 15c2-11? Would it be better to impose a more open-ended standard of reasonableness in this area?

2. An interesting and controversial aspect of *Hanly* decision is its suggestion that the implied warranty in this case "may not be as rigidly enforced in a civil action." In other words, the court is suggesting that while the Securities and Exchange Commission can bring an enforcement action in this case, one of the customers who suffered a loss as a result of the brokers' recommendations might not be able to recover. What is the statutory basis of this distinction? Is it sound policy?

3. A critical issue in cases such as the *Hanly* enforcement action is the sanction imposed on individual violators. In this case, several individuals were barred from the securities industry for life. Is this an appropriate penalty? In Steadman v. SEC, 450 U.S. 91 (1981), the Supreme Court ruled that administrative sanctions of this sort need only be supported by "the preponderance of the evidence." How does this compare to the safeguards built into comparable provisions applicable to depository institutions? (See Chapter Five, Section 3.C.)

4. Shortly after the *Hanly* decision was handed down, the SEC began an enforcement action against Merrill Lynch, one of the nation's largest brokerage firms. An investigation had revealed problems similar to those underlying the *Hanly* case: members of the Merrill sales force had allegedly made false and misleading statements about a company's securities and the firm's research department had failed to make an adequate investigation into the company's past performance and future prospects. The Commission eventually settled the matter on the following basis:

[A]fter consideration of the offer of settlement of Merrill Lynch wherein the firm offers: to accept the imposition of a censure; to pay a sum of up to $1,600,000 pursuant to the terms of its offer to compensate customers of Merrill Lynch who suffered losses resulting from transactions in Scientific; to undertake to review, and, where appropriate, adopt new or modified guidelines relating to its research and sales activities; and, to undertake to review and, where necessary, strengthen its Account Executive Training Programs, the Commission accepts Merrill Lynch's offer of settlement.

In deciding to accept this offer, the Commission has given weight to the fact that the violations occurring herein, although serious in nature, related to a small portion of Merrill Lynch's total business and a relatively small number of the firm's total employees. The Commission recognizes that since the occurrence of the violations found herein Merrill Lynch has improved the quality of its research capability by increasing the number of security analysts the firm employs in its research department and by reducing the number of securities each analyst is assigned to follow. The Commission also recognizes that the violations took place in a somewhat speculative climate of the late 1960s when high technology companies were in vogue. However, the Commission warns that a speculative climate, no matter how rampant, will not attenuate duties imposed by the security laws.

Twenty nine individual respondents have submitted offers of settlement wherein seven individuals offer to accept suspensions and twenty two individuals offer to accept censures. After consideration of these offers, the Commission has determined to accept them as being in the public interest. . . .

Merrill Lynch, Pierce, Fenner & Smith, Inc., SEA Rel. No. 14,149 (Nov. 9, 1977).

How does this penalty compare to the one imposed in the Hanly case? Is it appropriate for large firms to be treated differently?

### 3. The Investment Advisers Act of 1940

An important limitation of the 1934 Act's regulation of broker-dealers is the fact that the regulatory structure applies only to those in the businesses of "effecting transactions in securities" for others or of "buying or selling securities" for their own accounts. The mere rendering of advice about securities does not, without more, bring one within the scope of these definitions. A separate federal statute — the Investment Advisers Act of 1940 (the "Advisers Act") — does, however, extend to

[A]ny person who, for compensation, engages in the business of advising others, either directly or through publications or writings, as to the value of securities, or as to the advisability of investing in, purchasing, or selling securities, or who, for compensation and as part of a regular business, issues or promulgates analyses or reports concerning securities.

Section 202(a)(11) of the Advisers Act.

Those who fall within this definition and who do not qualify under a variety of institutional exemptions (including several for professionals, such as lawyers, accountants, and broker-dealers, whose advice is solely incidental to the conduct of regular business) must comply with separate federal and state registration systems that are substantially less onerous and protective than the ones applicable to registered broker-dealers. (As a result of the National Securities Markets Improvements Act of 1996, investment advisers that manage less than $25 million are principally regulated at the state level, whereas those with larger accounts are principally governed under the Advisers Act.)  The following case explores some of the substantive obligations imposed under the Advisers Act.

# Securities and Exchange Commission v. Capital Gains Research Bureau
## 375 U.S. 180 (1963)

Justice GOLDBERG delivered the opinion of the Court.

We are called upon in this case to decide whether under [section 206 of] the Investment Advisers Act of 1940 the Securities and Exchange Commission may obtain an injunction compelling a registered investment adviser to disclose to his clients a practice of purchasing shares of a security for his own account shortly before recommending that security for long-term investment and then immediately selling the shares at a profit upon the rise in the market price following the recommendation.  The answer to this question turns on whether the practice — known in the trade as "scalping" — "operates as a fraud or deceit upon any client or prospective client" within the meaning of the Act. . . .

Respondents publish two investment advisory services, one of which — "a Capital Gains Report" — is the subject of this proceeding.  The Report is mailed monthly to approximately 5,000 subscribers who pay an annual subscription price of $18.  It carries the following description:

An Investment Service devoted exclusively to (1) The protection of investment capital. (2) The realization of a steady and attractive income therefrom. (3) The accumulation of CAPITAL GAINS thru the timely purchase of corporate equities that are proved to be undervalued.

Between March 15, 1960, and November 7, 1960, respondents, on six different occasions, purchased shares of a particular security shortly before recommending it in the Report for long-term investment.  On each occasion, there was an increase in the market price and the volume of trading of the recommended security within a few days after the distribution of the Report.  Immediately thereafter, respondents sold their shares of these securities at a profit. They did not disclose any aspect of these transactions to their clients or prospective clients.

On the basis of the above facts, the Commission requested a preliminary injunction as necessary to effectuate the purposes of the Investment Advisers Act of 1940.  The injunction would have required respondents, in any future Report, to disclose the material facts concerning, inter alia, any purchase of recommended securities "within a very short period prior to the distribution of a recommendation * * *,' and "[t]he intent to sell and the sale of said securities * * * within a very short period after distribution of said recommendation * * *."

The decision in this case turns on whether Congress, in empowering the courts to enjoin any practice which operates "as a fraud or deceit upon any client or prospective client," intended to require the Commission to establish fraud and deceit "in their technical sense," including intent to injure and actual injury to clients, or whether Congress intended a broad remedial construction of the Act which would encompass nondisclosure of material facts. . .

The Investment Advisers Act of 1940 was the last in a series of Acts designed to eliminate certain abuses in the securities industry, abuses which were found to have contributed to the stock market crash of 1929 and the depression of the 1930s. It was preceded by the

Securities Act of 1933, the Securities Exchange Act of 1934, the Public Utility Holding Company Act of 1935, the Trust Indenture Act of 1939, and the Investment Company Act of 1940. A fundamental purpose, common to these statutes, was to substitute a philosophy of full disclosure for the philosophy of *caveat emptor* and thus to achieve a high standard of business ethics in the securities industry. As we recently said in a related context, "It requires but little appreciation * * * of what happened in this country during the 1920s and 1930s to realize how essential it is that the highest ethical standards prevail" in every facet of the securities industry. Silver v. New York Stock Exchange, 373 U.S. 341, 366.

The Public Utility Holding Company Act of 1935 "authorized and directed" the Securities and Exchange Commission "to make a study of the functions and activities of investment trusts and investment companies * * *." Pursuant to this mandate, the Commission made an exhaustive study and report which included consideration of investment counsel and investment advisory services. This aspect of the study and report culminated in the Investment Advisers Act of 1940.

The report reflects the attitude--shared by investment advisers and the Commission — that investment advisers could not "completely perform their basic function — furnishing to clients on a personal basis competent, unbiased, and continuous advice regarding the sound management of their investments — unless all conflicts of interest between the investment counsel and the client were removed." The report stressed that affiliations by investment advisers with investment bankers or corporations might be "an impediment to a disinterested, objective, or critical attitude toward an investment by clients * * *."

This concern was not limited to deliberate or conscious impediments to objectivity. Both the advisers and the Commission were well aware that whenever advice to a client might result in financial benefit to the adviser — other than the fee for his advice — "that advice to a client might in some way be tinged with that pecuniary interest [whether consciously or] subconsciously motivated * * *." The report quoted one leading investment adviser who said that he "would put the emphasis * * * on subconscious" motivation in such situations. It quoted a member of the Commission staff who suggested that a significant part of the problem was not the existence of a "deliberate intent" to obtain a financial advantage, but rather the existence "subconsciously [of] a prejudice" in favor of one's own financial interests. The report incorporated the Code of Ethics and Standards of Practice of one of the leading investment counsel associations, which contained the following canon:

> "(An investment adviser) should continuously occupy an impartial and disinterested position, as free as humanly possible from the *subtle* influence of prejudice, *conscious or unconscious*; he should scrupulously avoid any affiliation, or any act, which subjects his position to challenge in this respect." (Emphasis added.)

Other canons appended to the report announced the following guiding principles: that compensation for investment advice "should consist exclusively of direct charges to clients for services rendered"; that the adviser should devote his time "exclusively to the performance" of his advisory function; that he should not "share in profits" of his clients; and that he should not "directly or indirectly engage in any activity which may jeopardize [his] ability to render unbiased investment advice." These canons were adopted "to the end that the quality of services to be rendered by investment counselors may measure up to the high standards which the public has a right to expect and to demand."

Hearings were then held before Committees of both Houses of Congress. In describing their profession, leading investment advisers emphasized their relationship of "trust and confidence" with their clients and the importance of "strict limitation of [their right] to buy and sell securities in the normal way if there is any chance at all that to do so might seem to operate against the interests of clients and the public." The president of the Investment Counsel Association of America, the leading investment counsel association, testified that the

> "two fundamental principles upon which the pioneers in this new profession undertook to meet the growing need for unbiased investment information and guidance were, first, that they would limit their efforts and activities to the study of investment problems from the investor's standpoint, not engaging in any other activity, such as security selling or brokerage, which might directly or indirectly bias their investment judgment; and, second, that their remuneration for this work would consist solely of definite, professional fees fully disclosed in advance."

Although certain changes were made in the bill following the hearings, there is nothing to indicate an intent to alter the fundamental purposes of the legislation. The broad proscription against "any * * * practice * * * which operates * * * as a fraud or deceit upon any client or prospective client" remained in the bill from beginning to end. And the Committee Reports indicate a desire to preserve "the personalized character of the services of investment advisers," and to eliminate conflicts of interest between the investment adviser and the clients as safeguards both to "unsophisticated investors" and to "bona fide investment counsel." The Investment Advisers Act of 1940 thus reflects a congressional recognition "of the delicate fiduciary nature of an investment advisory relationship," as well as a congressional intent to eliminate, or at least to expose, all conflicts of interest which might incline an investment adviser — consciously or unconsciously — to render advice which was not disinterested. It would defeat the manifest purpose of the Investment Advisers Act of 1940 for us to hold, therefore, that Congress, in empowering the courts to enjoin any practice which operates "as a fraud or deceit," intended to require proof of intent to injure and actual injury to clients.

This conclusion moreover, is not in derogation of the common law of fraud, as the District Court and the majority of the Court of Appeals suggested. To the contrary, it finds support in the process by which the courts have adapted the common law of fraud to the commercial transactions of our society. It is true that at common law intent and injury have been deemed essential elements in a damage suit between parties to an arm's-length transaction. But this it not such an action. This is a suit for a preliminary injunction in which the relief sought is, as the dissenting judges below characterized it, the "mild prophylactic" of requiring a fiduciary to disclose to his clients, not all his security holdings, but only his dealings in recommended securities just before and after the issuance of his recommendations. . . .

We turn now to a consideration of whether the specific conduct here in issue was the type which Congress intended to reach in the Investment Advisers Act of 1940. It is arguable — indeed it was argued by "some investment counsel representatives" who testified before the Commission — that any "trading by investment counselors for their own account in securities in which their clients were interested * * *" creates a potential conflict of interest which must be eliminated. We need not go that far in this case, since here the Commission seeks only disclosure of a conflict of interests with significantly greater potential for abuse than in the situation described above. An adviser who, like respondents, secretly trades on the market effect of his own recommendation may be motivated--consciously or unconsciously--to recommend a given security not because of its potential for long-run price increase (which would profit the client), but because of its potential for short-run price increase in response to anticipated activity from the recommendation (which would profit the adviser). An investor seeking the advice of a registered investment adviser must, if the legislative purpose is to be served, be permitted to evaluate such overlapping motivations, through appropriate disclosure, in deciding whether an adviser is serving "two masters" or only one, "especially * * * if one of the masters happens to be economic self-interest." United States v. Mississippi Valley Generating Co., 364 U.S. 520.. Accordingly, we hold that the Investment Advisers Act of 1940 empowers the courts, upon a showing such as that made here, to require an adviser to make full and frank disclosure of his practice of trading on the effect of his recommendations.

Respondents . . . argue first that Congress could have made, but did not make, failure to disclose material facts unlawful in the Investment Advisers Act of 1940, as it did in the Securities Act of 1933, and that absent specific language, it should not be assumed that Congress intended to include failure to disclose in its general proscription of any practice which operates as a fraud or deceit. But considering the history and chronology of the statutes, this omission does not seem significant. The Securities Act of 1933 was the first experiment in federal regulation of the securities industry. It was understandable, therefore, for Congress, in declaring certain practices unlawful, to include both a general proscription against fraudulent and deceptive practices and, out of an abundance of caution, a specific proscription against nondisclosure. It soon became clear, however, that the courts, aware of the previously outlined developments in the common law of fraud, were merging the proscription against nondisclosure into the general proscription against fraud, treating the former, in effect, as one variety of the latter. For example, in Securities & Exchange Comm'n v. Torr, 15 F.Supp. 315 (D.C.S.D.N.Y.1936), rev'd on other grounds, 2 Cir., 87 F.2d 446, Judge Patterson held that suppression of information material to an evaluation of the disinterestedness of investment advice "operated as a deceit on purchasers," 15 F.Supp., at 317. Later cases also treated nondisclosure as one variety of fraud or deceit. In light of this, and in light of the evident purpose of the Investment Advisers Act of 1940 to substitute a philosophy of disclosure for the philosophy of caveat emptor, we cannot assume that the omission in the 1940 Act of a specific proscription against nondisclosure was intended to limit the application of the antifraud and antideceit provisions of the Act so as to render the Commission impotent to enjoin suppression of material facts. The more reasonable assumption, considering what had transpired between 1933 and 1940, is that Congress, in enacting the Investment Advisers Act of 1940 and proscribing any practice which operates "as a fraud or deceit," deemed a specific proscription against nondisclosure surplusage. . . .

Respondents argue, finally, that their advice was "honest" in the sense that they believed it was sound and did not offer it for the purpose of furthering personal pecuniary objectives. This, of course, is but another way of putting the rejected argument that the elements of technical common-law fraud — particularly intent — must be established before an injunction requiring disclosure may be ordered. It is the practice itself, however, with its potential for abuse, which "operates as a fraud or deceit" within the meaning of the Act when relevant information is suppressed. The Investment Advisers Act of 1940 was "directed not only at dishonor, but also at conduct that tempts dishonor." United States v. Mississippi Valley Generating Co., 364 U.S. 520, 549.  Failure to disclose material facts must be deemed fraud or deceit within its intended meaning, for, as the experience of the 1920s and 1930s amply reveals, the darkness and ignorance of commercial secrecy are the conditions upon which predatory practices best thrive.  To impose upon the Securities and Exchange Commission the burden of showing deliberate dishonesty as a condition precedent to protecting investors through the prophylaxis of disclosure would effectively nullify the protective purposes of the statute.  Reading the Act in light of its background we find no such requirement commanded. Neither the Commission nor the courts should be required "to separate the mental urges," Peterson v. Greenville, 373 U.S. 244, 248, of an investment adviser, for "[t]he motives of man are too complex * * * to separate * * *." Mosser v. Darrow, 341 U.S. 267, 271.  The statute, in recognition of the adviser's fiduciary relationship to his clients, requires that his advice be disinterested.  To insure this it empowers the courts to require disclosure of material facts.  It misconceives the purpose of the statute to confine its application to "dishonest" as opposed to "honest" motives.  As Dean Shulman said in discussing the nature of securities transactions, what is required is "a picture not simply of the show window, but of the entire store * * * not simply truth in the statements volunteered, but disclosure." The high standards of business morality exacted by our laws regulating the securities industry do not permit an investment adviser to trade on the market effect of his own recommendations without fully and fairly revealing his personal interests in these recommendations to his clients.

Experience has shown that disclosure in such situations, while not onerous to the adviser, is needed to preserve the climate of fair dealing which is so essential to maintain public confidence in the securities industry and to preserve the economic health of the country.

## Comments and Questions

1.  The *Capital Gains* decision is in certain respects analogous to the decisions in *Hughes I* and *Hughes II*. In all three cases, the courts found a breach of a disclosure obligation arising out of the status of the regulated entity. In *Capital Gains*, however, the material omission was in a published report distributed to a wide number of customers. How important is it to prohibit this sort of offense?  After all, if a newsletter consistently promotes stock with little intrinsic value, no one will pay for subscriptions.  On the other hand, if a publication's recommendations are sound, what difference does it make if the publisher also profits on the investment?  Should we be concerned that imposing liability on investment advisers might inhibit free speech protected under the First Amendment? See Lowe v. Securities & Exchange Commission, 472 U.S. 181 (1985).

2.  Although, as the *Hughes II* case reveals, some broker-dealers also register under the Advisers Act, the Act itself includes an exemption for broker-dealers whose performance of advisory services "is solely incidental to the conduct of [their business as broker-dealers] and who receive[] no special compensation therefor."   Section 202(a)(11)(C) of the Advisers Act.  Suppose a broker-dealer qualified for this exemption and then engaged in practices similar to those that gave rise to the *Capital Gains* case. Would the broker-dealer have breached an obligation under the 1934 Act?

3.  As mentioned above, regulation under the Advisers Act is generally less stringent than regulation of broker-dealers.  Among other things, SEC-regulated advisers

are not subject to the same qualification, test-taking, and on-going supervision applicable to registered broker-dealers. (Advisers subject to state regulation are, however, sometimes subject to licensing and qualification requirements analogous to those applicable to SEC-regulated broker-dealers.) In addition, there is no self-regulatory organization analogous to the NASD for investment advisers. Finally, the broad private rights of actions available under the 1934 Act are not replicated in the Advisers Act. See Transamerica Mortgage Advisers Inc. v. Lewis, 444 U.S. 11 (1979) (rescission as opposed to compensatory damages are the only private remedy available under the Advisers Act). For an overview of federal and state regulation in this area, see John A. Gray, *Reforms to Improve Client Protection and Compensation Against Personal Financial Planners' Unethical Business Practices*, 32 AM. BUS. L.J. 245 (1994). Given the significant substantive obligations arising out of advice given by broker-dealers, does it make sense for the regulatory constraints imposed on other financial planners to be so much more lenient?

4. One area in which the Adviser's Act is more rigorous than the 1934 Act is in its regulation of performance fees. Section 205(a)(1) of Advisers Act generally prohibits the use of performance based fees for most smaller investors. What are the advantages of such a restriction? Are there any disadvantages? Recall that in *Mihara* and other churning cases, brokers were tempted to increase the turnover of customer securities because their compensation depends on commissions, not the overall performance of a portfolio. Should we mandate performance base fees, rather than prohibit them?

### Problem 10-2

Charleston, Inc. (CI), is a full-service securities firm with offices in thirty-five cities around the country. CI would like to offer its customers a "financial account package (FAP)," under which the firm would offer customers special advisory services for brokerage accounts with portfolios worth more than $100,000. The advice would include recommendations with respect to specific investments — stocks, bonds, mutual funds, options and futures, variable annuities, etc. — and also assessments of larger market trends. In exchange for these services, CI proposes to charge an annual fee equal to one percent of the market value of the FAP portfolio plus a supplemental charge equal to five percent of the amount, if any, by which the account outperforms the return on the S&P 500 index each calendar year. Clients who effect fewer than twenty transactions per year would be entitled to a 10 percent reduction of the FAP account fee. Can the firm offer this package? Should it?

## C. Broker-Dealers as Market-Makers and Underwriters

We now turn our attention to the responsibilities of securities firms in contexts where they perform several different functions. Often times, these multiple functions present real or potential conflicts of interest. Back in the 1930s, some reformers were so concerned with these conflicts that they recommended the brokerage side of the securities business be completely segregated from the rest of the securities business. The idea behind this proposal was that the only effective way to protect consumers from market manipulation and overly aggressive underwriting was to prohibit those sectors of the industry from dealing with customers directly. (As we will discuss in Chapter Fifteen, similar considerations motivated the passage of the Glass-Steagall Act, which was intended to divorce commercial and investment banking.) Practical considerations and a sluggish economy ultimately persuaded New Deal legislators not to subdivide the securities industry in this way. Instead, the courts and the Commission have developed a complex system of rules and standards to ameliorate potential problems. As you read through the following materials, consider whether complete segregation would have been a better solution.

## Chasins v. Smith, Barney
### 438 F.2d 1167 (2d Cir. 1970)

This is an appeal by Smith, Barney & Co., Inc., a stock brokerage firm [hereinafter "Smith, Barney"] from a judgment for damages on a determination by Judge Dudley B. Bonsal in the United States District Court for the Southern District of New York that Smith, Barney had violated Rules 10b-5 and 15c1-4, in not disclosing to appellee (Chasins) that it was making a market in the securities it sold Chasins in the over-the-counter market. . . .

This action brought by Chasins in the district court under the Securities Act of 1933, and the Securities Exchange Act of 1934, for damages resulting from Smith, Barney's alleged violations of the Acts . . . in handling Chasins' securities brokerage account was tried to the court without a jury. At the time the four transactions in question in his appeal occurred,[3] Chasins was the musical director of radio station WQXR in New York City and was the commentator on a musical program sponsored by Smith, Barney. According to Chasins it was due to this relationship that he opened his brokerage account with Smith, Barney by orally retaining it to act as his stock broker. Smith, Barney acted in at least two capacities in these transactions, namely as Chasins' stockbroker and as principal, i.e., the owner of the security being sold to Chasins. In all four transactions Smith, Barney sold the securities to Chasins in the over-the-counter market, and although it revealed in the confirmation slips that it was acting as principal and for its own account in selling to Chasins, Smith, Barney did not reveal that it was "making a market" in the securities involved as was the fact. Nor did Smith, Barney disclose how much it had paid for the securities sold as principal to Chasins or that it had acted as an "underwriter" as defined by the Securities Act of 1933 in connection with the distribution of securities of Welch Scientific Company and Howard Johnson Company, two of the companies whose securities Smith, Barney sold to Chasins.

Preceding the four sales of July and August, 1961, Smith, Barney sent Chasins a written analysis of his then current security holdings and its recommendations in regard to his objective of aggressive growth of his holdings. The recommendations included strong purchase recommendations for securities of Welch Scientific, Tex-Star Oil and Gas Corp., and Howard Johnson Company. Chasins and Thomas N. Delaney, Jr., an authorized agent of Smith, Barney

---

[3]    . . . . Total cost of the securities to Chasins was $34,950; he subsequently sold these securities on June 28, 1962 for $16,333.36. . . . .

had various telephone conversations prior to the transactions in question. Delaney testified that at least at the times of the four transactions in question Smith, Barney was "making a market" in those securities, i.e., it was maintaining a position in the stocks on its own account by participating in over-the-counter trading in them; Smith, Barney's records indicated that at least from June 30, 1961, it had been trading in those stocks and had held positions in them during the times Chasins purchased the securities from it.[4] There was no testimony that Chasins had any knowledge or notice that Smith, Barney was "making a market" in the securities of the three companies.

The decision of the district court was based on conflicting evidence as to whether Chasins had a "discretionary account" with Smith, Barney and on the four transactions above. Although the court ruled that Smith, Barney had not violated any common law fiduciary duty to Chasins, Smith, Barney was found to have violated Rules 10b-5 and 15c1-4 (the latter in a supplemental opinion) in not disclosing its market making (or dealer) status in the securities that it recommended Chasins purchase, when Chasins followed that advice and purchased the securities and Smith, Barney was the other principal in the sales. Damages were awarded to Chasins in the amount of $18,616.64, with interest, which constituted the difference between the price at which Chasins purchased the securities from Smith, Barney and the price at which he later sold them (prior to discovering Smith, Barney's market making in the securities). . . .

Smith, Barney's major contention in attacking the district court's finding of a violation of Rules 10b-5 and 15c1-4 is that failure to disclose its "market making" role in the securities exchanged over the counter was not failure to disclose a material fact. Appellant contends that the district court's holding went farther than any other decision in this area and that no court had ever found failure to disclose a "market making" role by a stock brokerage firm to a client-purchaser to be a violation of Rule 10b-5. Smith, Barney also asserts that all brokerage firms had followed the same practice and had never thought such disclosure was required; moreover, the SEC had never prosecuted any firm for this violation. However, even where a defendant is successful in showing that it has followed a customary course in the industry, the first litigation of such a practice is a proper occasion for its outlawry if it is in fact in violation. See Opper v. Hancock Securities Corp., 250 F. Supp. 668, 676 (S.D.N.Y.1966), aff'd 367 F.2d 157 (2d Cir. 1966). In any event, it cannot fairly be said that no one in the trade had ever considered such nondisclosure to be significant. Appellant's own customers man (Delaney) testified that at the time (1961) he was disclosing to retail clients the firm's role as a market maker in a given security whenever he was aware of it.

Appellant also points to the fact that in over-the-counter trading, a market maker with an inventory in a stock is considered the best source of the security (the best available market); thus, the SEC has even punished a brokerage firm for not going directly to a firm with an inventory in a stock, i.e., interposing another firm between them. See e. g. In re Thomson &

---

[4]    Market maker has been defined by SEC Rule 17a-9(f) (1) as follows:

(1) The term "market-maker" shall mean a dealer who, with respect to a particular security, holds himself out (by entering indications of interest in purchasing and selling in an inter-dealer quotations system or otherwise) as being willing to buy and sell for his own account on a continuous basis otherwise than on a national securities exchange.

McKinnon, CCH Fed.Sec.L.Rep. para. 77,572, p. 83, 203 (1967-69 SEC Rulings). However, the fact that dealing with a market maker should be considered by some desirable for some purposes does not mean that the failure to disclose Smith, Barney's market-making role is not under the circumstances of this case a failure to disclose a material fact. The question here is not whether Smith, Barney sold to Chasins at a fair price but whether disclosure of Smith, Barney's being a market maker in the Welch Scientific, Tex-Star Oil and Gas and Howard Johnson securities might have influenced Chasins' decision to buy the stock. . . .The test of materiality "* * * is whether a reasonable man would attach importance * * * in determining his choice of action in the transaction in question. * * *". . . In applying that test in this case, the question of materiality becomes whether a reasonable man in Chasins' position might well have acted otherwise than to purchase if he had been informed of Smith, Barney's market making role in the three stocks in addition to the fact that Smith, Barney was the other principal in the transaction. The broker-dealer, Smith, Barney, had undertaken to make a written evaluation of Chasins' securities holdings and had strongly recommended sales of some of his holdings and purchases of these three stocks in which Smith, Barney was dealing as a principal.

Knowledge of the additional fact of market making by Smith, Barney in the three securities recommended could well influence the decision of a client in Chasins' position, depending on the broker-dealer's undertaking to analyze and advise, whether to follow its recommendation to buy the securities; disclosure of the fact would indicate the possibility of adverse interests which might be reflected in Smith, Barney's recommendations. Smith, Barney could well be caught in either a "short" position or a "long" position in a security, because of erroneous judgment of supply and demand at given levels. If over supplied, it may be to the interest of a market maker to attempt to unload the securities on his retail clients. Here, Smith, Barney's strong recommendations of the three securities Chasins purchased could have been motivated by its own market position rather than the intrinsic desirability of the securities for Chasins. An investor who is at least informed of the possibility of such adverse interests, due to his broker's market making in the securities recommended, can question the reasons for the recommendations. The investor, such as Chasins, must be permitted to evaluate overlapping motivations through appropriate disclosures, especially where one motivation is economic self-interest. See SEC v. Capital Gains Research Bureau, Inc., 375 U.S. 180 at 196 (1963).

In the case at bar, the broker-dealer had undertaken at its customer's request to make a written evaluation of his securities holdings and recommendations for further purchases and sales knowing that the customer, who was, as pointed out above, musical director of a radio station and commentator on a musical program sponsored by Smith, Barney, would rely on its report to him. In this situation failure to inform the customer fully of its possible conflict of interest, in that it was a market maker in the securities which it strongly recommended for purchase by him, was an omission of material fact in violation of Rule 10b-5.

The Securities and Exchange Commission is presently engaged in consideration of the advisability of rules on disclosure of the fact of market making, to delineate the extent and time of disclosure to be required, and whether distinction should be made as, for instance, between situations where the particular broker-dealer is the sole or dominant market maker and situations where it is one of a number of market makers and the price is competitive with quotes of other market makers. Such rules and similar rules of the self-regulatory agencies may well promote full and fair disclosure, while, in the words of the SEC "furthering customer protection." We do not attempt to address ourselves to the question of the best mechanics for disclosure. We here go so far only as to hold that under the particular circumstances proved in this case the court was correct in holding that the failure to disclose was the omission of a material fact.

To the extent that reliance is necessary for a finding of a 10b-5 violation in a non-disclosure case such as this, the test is properly one of tort "causation in fact." Chasins relied upon Smith, Barney's recommendations of purchase made without the disclosure of a material fact, purchased the securities recommended, and suffered a loss in their resale. Causation in fact or adequate reliance was sufficiently shown by Chasins.

FRIENDLY, J., dissenting from denial of rehearing en banc.

The transactions here in question were in securities traded on the "over-the-counter" market. Section 15(c) (1) of the Securities Exchange Act, which deals with this subject, provides:

> No broker or dealer shall make use of the mails or of any means or instrumentality of interstate commerce to effect any transaction in, or to induce the purchase or sale of, any security (other than commercial paper, bankers' acceptances, or commercial bills) otherwise than on a national securities exchange, by means of any manipulative, deceptive, or other fraudulent device or contrivance. The Commission shall, for the purposes of this subsection, by rules and regulations define such devices or contrivances as are manipulative, deceptive, or otherwise fraudulent.

Responsive to this Congressional direction, the SEC adopted Rule 15c1-4, which provides in pertinent part:

> The term "manipulative, deceptive, or other fraudulent device or contrivance," as used in section 15(c) (1) of the Act, is hereby defined to include any act of any broker or dealer designed to effect with or for the account of a customer any transaction in, or to induce the purchase or sale by such customer of, any security (other than United States Tax Savings Notes, United States Defense Savings Stamps, or United States Defense Savings Bonds, Series E, F and G) unless such broker or dealer, at or before the completion of each such transaction, gives or sends to such customer written notification disclosing (1) whether he is acting as a broker for such customer, as a dealer for his own account, as a broker for some other person, or as a broker for both such customer and some other person; * * *

The district court initially found that the confirmations here, which disclosed that Smith Barney was selling "as principal for our own account," were in full compliance with the rule. Although Rule 17a-9(f) defines "market-maker," this is in a reporting requirement; it is conceded that in 1961 no rule of the SEC (other than, allegedly, the inevitable Rule 10b-5), the NASD or the New York Stock Exchange required disclosure of that fact to a customer.

The complaint nowhere asserted that Smith Barney was under a duty to tell Mr. Chasins it was a "market-maker" in the three over-the-counter stocks that he bought. It alleged rather that defendant did not disclose the "best price" at which these and other securities could have been bought or sold in the open market, or the prices it had paid or received, and that plaintiff was deceived by Smith Barney's failure to disclose "the material fact of its adverse interest, the extent of which is today still unknown to and not determinable by plaintiff." The plaintiff, a noted musicologist, said nothing about market-making in his testimony. The closest he came to making the claim now sustained was that, despite his alleged inability to comprehend financial matters, he would have understood if told that the stock reflected by the confirmations was owned by the defendant, since "if you have a great picture, for example, and you know that the picture is going to be worth a lot more the next year or five years or ten, I don't think you would be anxious to dispose of it." Although this is hardly convincing, since great pictures are constantly being sold and bought under exactly such circumstances, Mr. Chasins had been plainly told of defendant's ownership by the confirmation slips. In addition, the Smith Barney research report he had received on Tex-Star contained the legend in common use at the time: "We point out that in the course of our regular business we may be long or short of any of the above securities at any time," and the prospectus he received of Welch Scientific Company disclosed that Smith Barney was one of the underwriters of that stock, which had only recently been placed on the market. All that the trial record contained about non-disclosure of market making was a statement by Delaney, a registered representative of Smith Barney, that he normally would bring this fact to the attention of clients if he knew it; that he did know Smith Barney was making a market in the three stocks; and that he couldn't recall whether or not he had brought this to Mr. Chasins' attention. . . .

The conclusions on the materiality of disclosure of market making by the district court and in this court's opinion are predicated on an essential misconception of the role of the market maker in over-the-counter transactions. When a reputable house like Smith Barney acts as one of several market makers, as was the case here, it serves a highly desirable purpose in reducing the spreads characteristic of over-the-counter trading. It has been widely recognized that the "best price" can be obtained by dealing directly with market makers, for one reason because a commission to an intermediary is avoided. . . . The district judge's fears concerning the ability of a market maker to set an arbitrary price are inapplicable when as here there were several market makers, as Smith Barney pointed out in its post-trial motion and the SEC now confirms in its letter to us as amicus curiae. Moreover Smith Barney offered to prove that in fact Mr. Chasins bought at the lowest available price. So far as concerns the fears of ulterior motives voiced by the district judge and now by the court, the market maker, who buys as well as sells, is less likely to be interested in palming off a stock than a dealer with only a long position. Yet the confirmation here would plainly have been adequate for such a dealer, and we held only recently, in a case curiously not cited, that a dealer need not make the additional disclosure that it had originally acquired the stock for investment and not with a view towards distribution, something considerably more material than being one of several market makers, S. E. C. v. R. A. Holman & Co., 366 F.2d 456, 457 (2 Cir., 1966). At the very least the materiality of market making to an investment decision was an issue on which Smith Barney was entitled to submit proofs. It never had a fair opportunity to do this, although we read the court's opinion as leaving this open to defendants in future cases.

## Comments and Questions

1. The *Chasin* case illustrates the problem of defining the scope of the broker-dealer's obligation to disclose material information to customers. As is true in many cases of this sort, the transaction took place in a highly regulated environment. The SEC had adopted fairly detailed rules regarding the kinds of information broker-dealers must include in the confirmation slips issued in connection with every securities transaction. (These requirements are currently codified in rule 10b-10 under the 1934 Act.) When the transactions at issues in the *Chasins* case were executed, SEC confirmation rules did not

require disclosure of Smith Barney's market-maker status. Should the absence of such government mandated disclosures have been a complete defense for the firm?

2. How do the obligations of broker-dealers in this area compare with those of insurance agents in analogous situations? Should the rules differ in these two contexts?

*Problem 10-3*

Hansen Ltd., a brokerage firm, wants to develop its reputation for expertise in small over-the-counter stocks. To align its sales force with this corporate objective, Hansen would like to establish a sales incentive program under which registered representatives receive additional compensation for transactions involving OTC securities as opposed to NYSE listed shares. Should the terms of the program be revealed to customers? (Note that the customers would pay the same commission regardless where the securities was traded.) See Shivangi v. Dean Witter, 825 F.2d 885 (5th Cir. 1987).

―――――――

The next case deals with markups on securities prices, an issue we have already considered in the *Hughes I* case. The following decision deals with the problem in the context of a full-service firm that serves as both market-maker and retail broker.

# In re Alstead, Dempsey & Co.
## Securities Exchange Act Rel. No. 20,825 (Apr. 5, 1984)

I.

Alstead, Dempsey & Company, Incorporated ("registrant"), a registered broker-dealer, appeals from the decision of an administrative law judge. The law judge found that registrant charged retail customers excessive markups in 84 sales of the securities of Flight Transportation Corporation ("FTC") and A.T. Bliss & Company, but dismissed allegations that registrant charged unfair markups in many additional transactions in those securities. He concluded that registrant's broker-dealer registration should be suspended for thirty days.

II.

This case raises questions concerning the proper pricing practices of an integrated dealer, a market maker who simultaneously makes a wholesale market in an over-the-counter security while selling the same security at retail. Before considering the particular facts at issue, we shall briefly review our policy in the markup area.

As early as 1939, this Commission held that a dealer violates antifraud provisions when he charges retail customers prices that are not reasonably related to the prevailing market price at the time the customers make their purchases. The key issue in cases involving allegations of unfair pricing has always been how to determine the prevailing market price, on the basis of which retail markups are computed. Once that price is determined, we have consistently held that, at the least, markups more than 10% above that level are fraudulent in the sale of equity securities.

The prevailing market price means the price at which dealers trade with one another, i.e., the current inter-dealer market. When a dealer is not simultaneously making a market in a security, we have consistently held that, in the absence of countervailing evidence, a dealer's contemporaneous cost is the best evidence of the current market. That standard, which has received judicial approval, reflects the fact that prices paid for a security by a dealer in actual transactions closely related in time to his retail sales are normally a highly reliable indication of prevailing market price. However, in the case of an integrated dealer, different considerations may be applicable.

In the recent case of Peter J. Kisch,[1] we noted that a market maker often purchases stock from other dealers at or around its bid and sells to other dealers at around its asked or offering price. Thus a rigid application of the "contemporaneous cost" rule (in effect using a dealer's bid as the basis for computing retail markups) may not be appropriate. We indicated that, where a market maker is involved, markups may be computed on the basis of the contemporaneous prices charged by the firm or other market makers in actual sales to other dealers or, if no such prices are available, on the basis of representative asked quotations. But in Kisch, as in other cases involving market makers, it is essential to examine the nature of the inter-dealer market in order to determine the extent to which it may legitimately serve as the basis for findings of prevailing market price.

Although the Kisch firm was the dominant market maker in the stock there at issue, Mini Computer Systems, Inc. ("MCS"), Kisch was only one of 14 firms making a market in that security. Moreover, the other 13 firms accounted for more than half the trading volume in that stock during the period in question. On the basis of the evidence, it was clear that Kisch did not control the inter-dealer market in MCS and, accordingly, that the prices paid Kisch for MCS stock by other dealers were an accurate reflection of the prevailing market price. We have consistently used such inter-dealer sales prices as the basis for computing markups in similar situations.

The use of quotations as the basis for computing markups is more problematic. By their very nature, quotations only propose a transaction; they do not reflect the actual result of a completed arms-length sale. Thus, as we have frequently pointed out, quotations for obscure securities with limited inter-dealer trading activity may have little value as evidence of the current market. They often show wide spreads between the bid and ask prices and are likely to be subject to negotiation.

However, there are situations involving a market maker, such as that presented in Kisch, where the use of representative asked quotations in the absence of actual inter-dealer sales is appropriate in determining prevailing market price. Where there is an active, independent market for a security, and the reliability of quoted offers can be tested by comparing them with actual inter-dealer transactions during the period in question, such quotations may provide a proper basis for computing markups. Thus, if inter-dealer sales occur with some frequency, and on the

---

[1]    Securities Exchange Act Release No. 19005 (August 24, 1982), 25 SEC Docket 1533.

days when they occur they are consistently effected at prices at or around the quoted offers, it may properly be inferred that on other days such offers provide an accurate indication of the prevailing market.

With that background, we now turn to a consideration of the particular facts at issue.

### III.A.

On November 30, 1979, FTC made the first public offering of its securities, 560,000 shares of its common stock at $3.25 per share. Registrant was underwriter of that offering on a "best efforts" basis, and sold 95.7% of the offering, or 537,150 shares, to its own customers. When the offering was completed on February 4, 1980, registrant decided to become a market maker in FTC. It accordingly placed quotations for the stock in the NASDAQ system, as did two other brokerage firms.

During the period at issue, the total trading volume in FTC stock was about 345,000 shares, and registrant's transactions with other dealers and customers amounted to more than 297,000 shares, or 86% of that volume. Since most FTC stock was held by registrant's customers, registrant effectively controlled the supply. And most of its trading volume resulted from principal transactions with its customers who purchased 133,840 shares and sold 130,200 shares during the period in question. The two other dealers who placed quotations in NASDAQ were the only other market makers in FTC, and their combined transactions with dealers other than registrant totaled only 7,750 shares, or 2.2% of the total trading volume.

Under these circumstances, it is clear that there was no independent competitive market in FTC stock. Registrant dominated the market to such a degree that it controlled wholesale prices. Thus the only reliable basis for determining the prevailing market price is the contemporaneous prices that registrant was willing to pay other dealers for the FTC stock it purchased from them. On the basis of the prices registrant paid such dealers on the day before or the same day as its sales to customers, we find that it charged customers excessive markups in 80 transactions. The markups in those sales ranged from 11.1% to 14.7% in 13 transactions, from 15.4% to 19.4% in 41 transactions, and over 20% in the remaining 26 transactions.

### B.

Although several market makers were listed with respect to Bliss in the nationally distributed "pink sheets" published by the National Quotation Bureau, Inc., numerical quotations appeared in those sheets only from July 28 through July 31. Registrant entered numerical quotations for Bliss in regional inter-dealer sheets published in Minneapolis. It argues that its published offers in those sheets should be accepted as the best evidence of prevailing market price. We cannot agree.

During the relevant period, registrant purchased a total of 116,500 shares of Bliss from other dealers and 28,650 shares from its own customers. It sold 138,650 shares to customers, but made only two inter-dealer sales totaling 2,500 shares. Those sales, on June 10 and June 16, 1980, were both made to the same firm. Except for one day during the period in question, registrant's offering price for Bliss was 4. But it never effected any sales at that figure. The two sales it made to another dealer were at prices of 3-7/16 and 3-1/2, and even its sales to retail customers were consistently below its published wholesale offering price. Moreover, on seven occasions when registrant was short and purchased Bliss stock from another dealer, a strong indication that registrant initiated the transactions and thus paid the other dealer's offering price, registrant paid prices ranging from about 2-3/4 to 3-3/8.

In view of the foregoing, it is clear that registrant's offering price was wholly illusory, and cannot be accepted as evidence of the prevailing market. Since there is no indication that registrant controlled the market for Bliss, the prices it charged the other dealer in two transactions may properly be used as a basis for computing markups. In all other instances during the period in question, the best evidence of the prevailing market is the price registrant paid for Bliss in contemporaneous transactions.

Accordingly, computing registrant's markups on the basis of the prices it charged in contemporaneous inter-dealer sales, and, in other instances, on the basis of its contemporaneous costs, we find that, in 207 retail sales of Bliss, registrant charged excessive markups ranging from 11.1% to 24% above the prevailing market price.

We conclude that, in connection with the retail sales of FTC and Bliss stock cited above, registrant willfully violated the antifraud provisions of Section 17(a)(1) of the Securities Act and Section 10(b) of the Securities Exchange Act and Rule 10b-5 thereunder. We also find that registrant willfully violated the antifraud provisions of Sections 17(a)(2) and 17(a)(3) of the Securities Act.

## Comments and Questions

As the *Alstead* ruling suggests, the rules governing markup has evolved considerably since the Hughes I case. In brief, under NASD Rules of Fair Practice, markups of five percent or less are considered presumptively reasonable; markups of more than ten percent are presumptively problematic; and between five and ten percent is something of a grey area. Of course, as the *Alstead* case reveals, determining the price from which this markup is to be measured can be complex. For an introduction to broker-dealer compensation, see David L. Ratner, *Regulation of the Compensation of Securities Dealers*, 55 CORNELL L. REV. 348 (1970). For a more recent survey of broker-dealer compensation, produced by a committee formed at the request of SEC Chairman Arthur Levitt, see Report on Broker-Dealer Compensation (Apr. 10, 1995) (executive summary available at http://www.sec.gov/news/studies/bkrcomp.txt).

———————

In the next case, we consider a broker-dealer acting as an underwriter for a public offering of securities. The underwriting process is the primary focus of the Securities Act of 1933, and securities firms that participate in underwriting are heavily regulated under that Act. However, the 1934 Act also has a series of anti-fraud and anti-manipulation rules that also bear on this process. Some are discussed in the following case:

# Pagel, Inc. v. Securities and Exchange Commission
## 803 F.2d 942 (9th Cir. 1986)

Pagel, Inc., a Minneapolis registered broker-dealer in securities, its president and sole stockholder, Jack W. Pagel, and its executive vice president, Duane A. Markus, petition for review of a final order of the Securities and Exchange Commission revoking the broker-dealer registration of Pagel, Inc., and barring Pagel and Markus from association with any broker or dealer.

Pagel, Inc., served as the principal underwriter for the first public offering of the securities of FilmTec Corporation in March 1979. Pursuant to the underwriting agreement, the firm was to underwrite the sale of 320,000 shares of FilmTec stock at $3.25 per share, with an option to purchase an additional 32,000 shares should customer allocations exceed the original number of shares. Retaining the balance for itself, the firm allotted only 34,800 shares of the issue to other dealers. On March 26, 1979, Pagel, Inc., began offering FilmTec at 3 1/4. The offering was ostensibly completed on March 29, 1979, when the firm exercised its over-allotment option, increasing its share of the offering to 317,200 shares, or over 90% of the total issue.

On March 30, 1979, aftermarket trading began, with the firm's opening prices for FilmTec stock set at 4 3/8 bid and 4 5/8 offered, increases of 35% and 42%, respectively, over the offering price of 3 1/4. At this time, Pagel, Inc., began to maintain a "long" position in Filmtec, or an excess of purchases from its customers over sales to them, which would continue until March 1980. The firm's Filmtec trading activities were all at the direction of Pagel and Markus. Within the first fifteen minutes of trading, the firm's customers sold 49,300 shares of FilmTec to the firm and purchased 39,205 shares, including 7,650 shares purchased by Markus through nominees, and the firm raised the price of FilmTec to 5 3/4 bid and 7 offered. By the day's closing, Pagel, Inc., had purchased a total of 70,455 shares from its customers and sold a total of 56,830 shares, charging as much as 7 3/4.

During the next seven trading days, April 2-10, 1979, the firm's customers sold 88,987 shares and purchased 66,680 shares, a 33% excess of sales over purchases. By April 10, 1979, the firm's long position had increased to 48,607 shares, but seven other dealers were short FilmTec stock in the amount of 4,750 shares. Pagel, Inc., and its customers cumulatively owned 329,875 shares, or 93.7% of the 352,000-share public offering. Despite the lack of customer demand, evidenced by the excess of customers' sales over purchases, Pagel, Inc., was offering FilmTec at a high of 10 1/2, an increase of more than 300% above the offering price of 3 1/4.

Between April 11, 1979, and the end of February 1980, Pagel, Inc., continued to dominate the FilmTec market, and the stock remained at a fairly constant price level. Throughout March 1980, however, the firm steadily lowered its prices for FilmTec, this despite the fact that customers' purchases exceeded customers' sales for the month. The firm's prices for FilmTec declined from 14 bid and 15 1/2 offered on March 3, to 7 bid and 8 1/2 offered on March 31, a 50% drop in price in one month. On March 21, 1980, with a bonus the firm gave to him, Pagel purchased 32,000 shares of FilmTec from the firm, apparently its entire inventory, at a price of 7 1/2. The sale enabled Pagel, Inc., to realize a $180,000 tax loss at the close of its fiscal year on March 31, offsetting the firm's trading profits. Furthermore, Pagel acquired stock with a potential for realizing long-term capital gains.

On June 9, 1982, the Commission ordered a public proceeding to determine whether petitioners had violated provisions of the securities laws and to determine what remedial action, if any, would be appropriate. An evidentiary hearing was held before an Administrative Law Judge (ALJ) on December 13-21, 1982. On August 29, 1983, the ALJ found that Pagel, Inc., Pagel, and Markus had violated the fraud, manipulation, and record keeping provisions of the securities laws by: (1) manipulating the price of FilmTec stock in the initial eight days of public trading; (2) manipulating the price of FilmTec stock in March 1980 to secure significant tax and investment benefits; (3) purchasing FilmTec stock within the period of distribution; and (4) failing to maintain records identifying the beneficial ownership of nominee accounts through which Pagel and Markus traded. The ALJ recommended the revocation of the firm's broker-dealer registration and the barring of Pagel and Markus from association with any broker or dealer.

Petitioners appealed the ALJ's decision to the Commission, which held that petitioners had violated the prohibitions of fraud and manipulation in securities dealings contained in section 17(a) of the Securities Act of 1933, and section 10(b) of the Securities Exchange Act of 1934, and Rule 10b-5 thereunder. The Commission also found that petitioners had violated the provisions of Rule 10b-6, prohibiting the purchase of securities by an underwriter participating in a distribution of the securities. Additionally, the Commission found that Pagel, Inc., had violated, and Pagel and Markus aided and abetted its violations of, the record keeping provisions of section 17(a) of the Securities Exchange Act of 1934, and Rule 17a-3(a)(9) thereunder.

Petitioners challenge the sufficiency of the evidence supporting the Commission's findings with respect to the violations of section 17(a) of the Securities Act, section 10(b) of the Securities Exchange Act, and Rule 10b-5. They also argue that the Commission erred in drawing an adverse inference from the individual petitioners' invocation of their fifth amendment privilege against self-incrimination and in approving the ALJ's exclusion of expert testimony. Petitioners argue further that the Commission imposed excessive sanctions.

First, petitioners argue that the evidence does not support the Commission's finding of manipulation of the market in FilmTec stock. They contend that "regardless of how much prominence [Pagel, Inc.] had in the making of the FilmTec market during the periods in question and the effect its trades had on price, there was no unlawful purpose, intent to induce others to act, artificial prices, or prices based on factors other than legitimate ones." . . . .

In connection with the securities markets, manipulation is a "term of art * * * connot[ing] intentional or willful conduct designed to deceive or defraud investors by controlling or artificially affecting the price of securities." Ernst & Ernst v. Hochfelder, 425 U.S. 185 (1976). As this case illustrates, there is room for considerable disagreement whether manipulation may be present on a given set of facts. The Commission, however, did not find petitioners liable solely because of their dominant position in the FilmTec market. Rather, it determined that petitioners had manipulated the market by abusing their position both during the first eight days of aftermarket trading and in March 1980. The Commission stated:

When individuals occupying a dominant market position engage in a scheme to distort the price of a security for their own benefit, they violate the securities laws by perpetrating a fraud on all public investors. In addition, their failure to disclose that market prices are being manipulated not only constitutes an element of a scheme to defraud, but is also a material omission of fact in the offer and sale of securities.

The Commission primarily relied on evidence of the price movements of FilmTec stock and the trading activities of petitioners during the periods at issue to conclude that manipulation had occurred. We agree that "rapidly rising prices in the absence of any demand are well-known symptoms of * * * unlawful market operations." Dlugash v. Securities & Exchange Commission, 373 F.2d 107, 109 (2d Cir.1967). Moreover, the Commission also considered other factors, such as the use of nominee accounts and the timing of the bulk sale to Pagel near the end of the Pagel, Inc., tax year, in reaching its conclusions. . . .

Petitioners argue further, however, that the Commission failed to establish the requisite element of intent, or "scienter." The Commission noted its finding of scienter in a footnote to its opinion. Scienter is the "mental state embracing intent to deceive, manipulate, or defraud." Ernst & Ernst, 425 U.S. at 193 n. 12. In Aaron v. Securities & Exchange Commission, 446 U.S. 680, 689-91 (1980), the Supreme Court held that the Commission must prove scienter in actions under sections 10(b) and 17(a)(1), but that it need only prove negligence in actions under sections 17(a)(2) or (3). Although the Commission could have been more explicit in its findings here, we cannot say that its conclusion on this issue is without substantial support in the evidence. Proof of scienter need not be direct but may be "a matter of inference from circumstantial evidence." Herman & MacLean v. Huddleston, 459 U.S. 375, 390 n. 30 (1983). We believe the Commission could reasonably have inferred from the evidence of price movement, trading activity, and other factors that the manipulation was undertaken for the purpose of securing financial and tax benefits for petitioners and thus was intentional.

Second, petitioners argue that the Commission impermissibly drew an adverse inference against Pagel and Markus based on their invocation of the fifth amendment privilege against self-incrimination. Although they concede that an adverse inference may be drawn against a party in a civil proceeding, they assert that in this case it was impermissible because there was insufficient evidence independent of their silence to support the Commission's findings.

In determining whether an inference may be drawn from invocation of the fifth amendment, a distinction is made between civil and criminal cases. Rosebud Sioux Tribe v. A & P Steel, Inc., 733 F.2d 509, 521 (8th Cir.), cert. denied, 469 U.S. 1072 (1984). In Baxter v. Palmigiano, 425 U.S. 308, 318-320 (1976), the Supreme Court held that the fifth amendment privilege against self- incrimination did not forbid drawing adverse inferences from an inmate's failure to testify at his own disciplinary proceedings. The Court noted that the fifth amendment " 'does not preclude the inference where the privilege is claimed by a party to a *civil cause*.' " Id. at 318 (quoting 8 J. Wigmore, Evidence 439 (McNaughton rev. 1961)) (emphasis in original). The Baxter Court also found, however, that silence alone would be insufficient to support an adverse decision against one who refuses to testify. Id. at 317. This principle was reiterated in Lefkowitz v. Cunningham, 431 U.S. 801, 809 n. 5(1977): "Respondent's silence in Baxter was only one of a number of factors to be considered by the finder of fact in assessing a penalty, and was given no more probative value than the facts of the case warranted * * *." It is clear that the Commission did not rely solely on Pagel's and Markus' refusal to testify but also, as we have stated above, on the evidence of FilmTec price movements, petitioners' trading activities, and other relevant facts. Furthermore, in earlier proceedings the ALJ chose not to draw an adverse inference against petitioners and still found violations. Consequently, the Commission's inference served only to support already established findings. . . . .

Finally, petitioners argue that the sanctions imposed are excessive. The Commission's choice of sanctions is not to be overturned unless we find them "unwarranted in law or without justification in fact." Brickner v. Federal Deposit Insurance Corp., 747 F.2d 1198, 1203 (8th Cir.1984). In imposing these sanctions, the Commission considered the overpayments customers made for purchases of FilmTec stock during the first eight days of trading and the lower prices they received on sales in March 1980. The Commission also considered the fact that petitioners previously had been sanctioned, pursuant to an offer of settlement, for violations of customer protection, credit extension, record keeping, and reporting provisions. The Commission could reasonably have concluded that protection of the public interest required the sanctions it imposed, see Berdahl v. Securities & Exchange Commission, 572 F.2d 643, 649 (8th Cir.1978). Accordingly, we find no abuse of discretion in the imposition of these sanctions.

## Comments and Questions

1. How did the petitioner's actions injure the investing public in this case? Didn't the petitioners run substantial risks pursuing the trading strategy outlined here?

2. A number of provisions of the 1934 Act are designed to prevent market manipulating schemes of the sort described in the *Pagel* decision. See, e.g., Section 9 of the 1934 Act (outlawing specific manipulative practices for securities traded on exchanges). In addition, the SEC has promulgated numerous rules implementing general prohibitions against manipulative practices. For example, rule 10b-6, which is one of the rules the *Pagel* petitioners were found to have violated, prohibits certain trading practices while an underwriting is in progress. Within the securities bar, there is an on-going debate over whether manipulative practices must entail an element of non-disclosure, or whether the prohibitions should also extend to activities that are either substantively unfair or otherwise disruptive of trading markets. For an introduction to this debate, see Daniel R. Fischel & David J. Ross, *Should The Law Prohibit 'Manipulation' in Financial Markets?*, 105 HARV. L. REV. 503 (1991). Would you characterize the *Pagel* decision as a case of non-disclosure? What would full disclosure accomplish in these situations?

3. As the *Pagel* decision suggests, targets of SEC enforcement actions may also face parallel criminal prosecutions. See section 32 of the 1934 Act (establishing criminal penalties for willful violations of the 1934 Act.) The coordination of civil and criminal proceedings presents numerous complex tactical and legal issues. Note, for example, the use the Commission made in this case of Pagel's invocation of the Fifth Amendment privilege against self-incrimination. For an overview of some of the problems associated with parallel civil and criminal proceedings, see THOMAS LEE HAZEN, THE LAW OF SECURITIES REGULATION § 9.5, at 438-39 (3rd ed. 1996).

---

The *Pagel* and *Alstead* cases illustrate a recurring problem in the broker-dealer industry. Firms obtain control over the market for shares of small, thinly traded companies, and then promote those shares to unsophisticated customers at prices that bear little relation to underlying values. Often times, these practices violated numerous legal standards, including suitability rules, markup regulations, and more general fiduciary standards. However, difficulties of proof and limitations in regulatory resources have made it difficult for the government to police these practices effectively. The Commission responded in 1989 with adoption of new Penny Stock regulations, now codified as Rule 15g-9 under the 1934 Act.

*Problem 10-4*

Assume you represent a group of clients interested in establishing a new brokerage house formed to specialize in small emerging companies. The firm's founders are recent business school graduates, and hope to market their services to former classmates and other young professionals who may be attracted to investment opportunities with significant upside potential. They would like to know what effect, if any, Rule 15g-9 would have on their operations. As you respond to this inquiry, consider whether the Rule is likely to prevent the kinds of abuses identified in the *Pagel* and *Alstead* cases. What other effects might the rule have?

## D. The Obligation to Supervise

Another distinguishing feature of broker-dealer regulation is its attention to supervisory responsibilities of managements. Under the federal securities laws, controlling persons are potentially liable for violations committed by their subordinates. See, e.g., Section 20(a) of the 1934 Act. And, special oversight responsibilities govern the liability of controlling persons for civil penalties imposed on insider trading. See Section 21A(b) of the 1934 Act. The following reading explores the contours of oversight responsibilities imposed on broker-dealer supervisors under Section 15(b)(4)(E) of the 1934 Act.

## In re John H. Gutfreund
### 52 S.E.C. Docket 2849 (Dec. 3, 1992)

[This proceeding arises out of a series of false bids that Paul Mozer, head of the Salomon Brothers, Inc. ("Salomon") Government Trading Desk, submitted in the first half of 1991 in an effort to corner the trading markets of certain issues of government securities. In late April of 1991, three members of the senior management of Salomon -- Chief Executive Officer John Gutfreund, President Thomas Strauss, and Vice Chairman John Meriwether— became aware of Moser's activities. They discussed the matter with Donald Feuerstein, the firm's chief legal officer, who informed them that Mozer's actions appeared to be criminal and recommended that the matter be reported to the government. Despite Feuerstein's advice, senior management failed to intervene effectively, and Mozer continued to submit false bids until the summer of 1991 when the practice became public and SEC investigation ensued.]

## 1. Legal Principles

Section 15(b)(4)(E) of the Exchange Act authorizes the Commission to impose sanctions against a broker-dealer if the firm has:

> failed reasonably to supervise, with a view to preventing violations [of federal securities laws], another person who commits such a violation, if such person is subject to his supervision.

Section 15(b)(6) of the Exchange Act incorporates Section 15(b)(4)(E) by reference and authorizes the Commission to impose sanctions for deficient supervision on individuals associated with broker-dealers.

The principles which govern this proceeding are well-established by the Commission's cases involving failure to supervise. The Commission has long emphasized that the responsibility of broker-dealers to supervise their employees is a critical component of the federal regulatory scheme. As the Commission stated in Wedbush Securities, Inc.:[15]

> In large organizations it is especially imperative that those in authority exercise particular vigilance when indications of irregularity reach their attention.

The supervisory obligations imposed by the federal securities laws require a vigorous response even to indications of wrongdoing. Many of the Commission's cases involving a failure to supervise arise from situations where supervisors were aware only of "red flags" or "suggestions" of irregularity, rather than situations where, as here, supervisors were explicitly informed of an illegal act.[16]

Even where the knowledge of supervisors is limited to "red flags" or "suggestions" of irregularity, they cannot discharge their supervisory obligations simply by relying on the unverified representations of employees.[17] Instead, as the Commission has repeatedly emphasized, "[t]here must be adequate follow-up and review when a firm's own procedures detect irregularities or unusual trading activity...."[18] Moreover, if more than one supervisor is involved in considering the actions to be taken in response to possible misconduct, there must be a clear definition of the efforts to be taken and a clear assignment of those responsibilities to specific individuals within the firm.[19]

---

[15]    48 S.E.C. 963, 967 (1988).

[16]    See, e.g., William L. Vieira, Exchange Act Release No. 26576 (February 26, 1989); Nicholas A. Bocella, Exchange Act Release No. 26574 (February 7, 1989); First Albany Corporation, Exchange Act Release No. 30515 (March 25, 1992).

[17]    See Shearson Lehman Hutton Inc., Exchange Act Release No. 26,766 (April 28, 1989); Prudential-Bache Securities, Inc., Exchange Act Release No. 22755 (January 2, 1986).

[18]    Prudential-Bache Securities, Inc., supra.

[19]    See, e.g., William E. Parodi, Sr., Exchange Act Release No. 27299 (September 27, 1989); Gary W. Chambers, Exchange Act Release No. 27963 (April 30, 1990). Supervisors who know of wrongdoing cannot escape liability for failure to supervise simply because they have failed to delegate or assign responsibility to take appropriate action

## 2. The Failure to Supervise

As described above, in late April of 1991 three supervisors of Paul Mozer-- John Meriwether, Thomas Strauss, and John Gutfreund--learned that Mozer had submitted a false bid in the amount of $3.15 billion in an auction of U.S. Treasury securities. Those supervisors learned that Mozer had said that the bid had been submitted to obtain additional securities for another trading area of the firm. They also learned that Mozer had contacted an employee of the customer whose name was used on the bid and falsely told that individual that the bid was an error. The supervisors also learned that the bid had been the subject of a letter from the Treasury Department to the customer and that Mozer had attempted to persuade the customer not to inform the Treasury Department that the bid had not been authorized. The supervisors were also informed by Salomon's chief legal officer that the submission of the false bid appeared to be a criminal act.

The information learned by the supervisors indicated that a high level employee of the firm with significant trading discretion had engaged in extremely serious misconduct. As the cases described above make clear, this information required, at a minimum, that the supervisors take action to investigate what had occurred and whether there had been other instances of unreported misconduct. While they could look to counsel for guidance, they had an affirmative obligation to undertake an appropriate inquiry. If they were unable to conduct the inquiry themselves or believed it was more appropriate that the inquiry be conducted by others, they were required to take prompt action to ensure that others in fact undertook those efforts. Such an inquiry could have been conducted by the legal or compliance departments of the firm, outside counsel, or others who had the ability to investigate the matter adequately. The supervisors were also required, pending the outcome of such an investigation, to increase supervision of Mozer and to place appropriate limitations on his activities.

The failure to recognize the need to take action to limit the activities of Mozer in light of his admitted misconduct is particularly troubling because Gutfreund and Strauss did place limitations on Mozer's conduct in connection with the June two-year U.S. Treasury note auction at a time when they thought the firm had not engaged in misconduct, but press reports had raised questions about the firm's activities. Although they had previously been informed that a serious violation had in fact been committed by Mozer, they failed for over three months to take any action to place limitations on his activities to deal with that misconduct.

The need to take prompt action was all the more critical in view of the fact that the potential unlawful conduct had taken place in the market for U.S. Treasury securities. The integrity of that market is of vital importance to the capital markets of the United States, as well as to capital markets worldwide, and Salomon occupied a privileged role as a government-designated primary dealer. The failure of the supervisors to take vigorous action to address known misconduct by the head of the firm's Government Trading Desk caused unnecessary risks to the integrity of this important market.

To discharge their obligations, the supervisors should at least have taken steps to ensure that someone within the firm questioned other employees on the Government Trading Desk, such as the desk's clerk or the other managing director on the Desk. Since the supervisors were informed that Mozer had said that he submitted the false bid to obtain additional securities for another trading desk of the firm, they should also have specifically investigated any involvement of that area of the firm in the matter. The supervisors should also have reviewed, or ensured that others reviewed, documentation concerning the February 21, 1991 auction. Such a review would have revealed, at a minimum, that a second false bid had been submitted in the auction and that false trade tickets and customer confirmations had been created in connection with both false bids. Those facts would have raised serious questions about the operations of the Government Trading Desk, and inquiries arising from those questions might well have led to discovery of the additional false bids described above. . . .

Each of the three supervisors apparently believed that someone else would take the supervisory action necessary to respond to Mozer's misconduct. There was no discussion, however, among any of the supervisors about what action should be taken or about who would be responsible for taking action. Instead, each of the supervisors assumed that another would act. In situations where supervisors are aware of wrongdoing, it is imperative that they take prompt and unequivocal action to define the responsibilities of those who are to respond to the wrongdoing. The supervisors here failed to do that. As a result, although there may be varying degrees of responsibility, each of the supervisors bears some measure of responsibility for the collective failure of the group to take action.

After the disclosure of one unauthorized bid to Meriwether, Mozer committed additional violations in connection with the submission of two subsequent unauthorized customer bids. Had limits been placed on his activities after the one unauthorized bid was disclosed, these violations might have been prevented. While Mozer was told by Meriwether that his conduct was career-threatening and that it would be reported to senior management and to the government, these efforts were not a sufficient supervisory response under the circumstances. The supervisors were required to take action reasonably designed to prevent a repetition of the misconduct that had been disclosed to them. They could, for instance, have temporarily limited Mozer's activities so that he was not involved in the submission of customer bids pending an adequate review of what had occurred in the February 21, 1991 auction, or they could have instituted procedures to require verification of customer bids.

Under the circumstances of this case, the failure of the supervisors to take action to discipline Mozer or to limit his activities constituted a serious breach of their supervisory obligations. Gutfreund, Strauss and Meriwether thus each failed reasonably to supervise Mozer with a view to preventing violations of the federal securities laws.[20] . . . .

Donald Feuerstein, Salomon's chief legal officer, was informed of the submission of the false bid by Paul Mozer in late April of 1991, at the same time other senior executives of Salomon learned of that act. Feuerstein was present at the meetings in late April at which the supervisors named as respondents in this proceeding discussed the matter. In his capacity as a legal adviser, Feuerstein did advise Strauss and Gutfreund that the submission of the bid was a criminal act and should be reported to the government, and he urged them on several occasions to proceed with disclosure when he learned that the report had not been made. However, Feuerstein did not direct that an inquiry be undertaken, and he did not recommend that appropriate procedures, reasonably designed to prevent and detect future misconduct, be

---

[20]   Salomon did not have established procedures, or a system for applying those procedures, which together reasonably could have been expected to detect and prevent the violations. The affirmative defense provisions of Section 15(b)(4)(E) thus do not apply in this case.

instituted, or that other limitations be placed on Mozer's activities. Feuerstein also did not inform the Compliance Department, for which he was responsible as Salomon's chief legal officer, of the false bid.[22]

Unlike Gutfreund, Strauss and Meriwether, however, Feuerstein was not a direct supervisor of Mozer at the time he first learned of the false bid. Because we believe this is an appropriate opportunity to amplify our views on the supervisory responsibilities of legal and compliance officers in Feuerstein's position, we have not named him as a respondent in this proceeding.[23] Instead, we are issuing this report of investigation concerning the responsibilities imposed by Section 15(b)(4)(E) of the Exchange Act under the circumstances of this case.

Employees of brokerage firms who have legal or compliance responsibilities do not become "supervisors" for purposes of Sections 15(b)(4)(E) and 15(b)(6) solely because they occupy those positions. Rather, determining if a particular person is a "supervisor" depends on whether, under the facts and circumstances of a particular case, that person has a requisite degree of responsibility, ability or authority to affect the conduct of the employee whose behavior is at issue.  Thus, persons occupying positions in the legal or compliance departments of broker-dealers have been found by the Commission to be "supervisors" for purposes of Sections 15(b)(4)(E) and 15(b)(6) under certain circumstances.

In this case, serious misconduct involving a senior official of a brokerage firm was brought to the attention of the firm's chief legal officer. That individual was informed of the misconduct by other members of senior management in order to obtain his advice and guidance, and to involve him as part of management's collective response to the problem. Moreover, in other instances of misconduct, that individual had directed the firm's response and had made recommendations concerning appropriate disciplinary action, and management had relied on him to perform those tasks.

Given the role and influence within the firm of a person in a position such as Feuerstein's and the factual circumstances of this case, such a person shares in the responsibility to take appropriate action to respond to the misconduct. Under those circumstances, we believe that such a person becomes a "supervisor" for purposes of Sections 15(b)(4)(E) and 15(b)(6). As a result, that person is responsible, along with the other supervisors, for taking reasonable and appropriate action. It is not sufficient for one in such a position to be a mere bystander to the events that occurred.

Once a person in Feuerstein's position becomes involved in formulating management's response to the problem, he or she is obligated to take affirmative steps to ensure that appropriate action is taken to address the misconduct. For example, such a person could direct or monitor an investigation of the conduct at issue, make appropriate recommendations for limiting the activities of the employee or for the institution of appropriate procedures, reasonably designed to prevent

---

[22]    In late May or early June, Feuerstein did speak with the head of the Compliance Department about the need to develop compliance procedures with respect to the firm's activities in government securities.

[23]    We note that Feuerstein has represented that he does not intend to be employed in the securities industry in the future.

and detect future misconduct, and verify that his or her recommendations, or acceptable alternatives, are implemented. If such a person takes appropriate steps but management fails to act and that person knows or has reason to know of that failure, he or she should consider what additional steps are appropriate to address the matter. These steps may include disclosure of the matter to the entity's board of directors, resignation from the firm, or disclosure to regulatory authorities.[26]

These responsibilities cannot be avoided simply because the person did not previously have direct supervisory responsibility for any of the activities of the employee. Once such a person has supervisory obligations by virtue of the circumstances of a particular situation, he must either discharge those responsibilities or know that others are taking appropriate action.

## ORDER

In view of the foregoing, the Commission deems it appropriate and in the public interest to impose the sanctions specified in the Offers of Settlement submitted by John H. Gutfreund, Thomas W. Strauss, and John W. Meriwether.

Accordingly, IT IS HEREBY ORDERED that:

A. John H. Gutfreund be, and he hereby is:

(i) ordered to comply with his undertaking not to associate in the future in the capacity of Chairman or Chief Executive Officer with any broker, dealer, municipal securities dealer, investment company or investment adviser regulated by the Commission; and

(ii) ordered to pay to the United States Treasury a civil penalty aggregating $100,000 pursuant to Section 21B(a)(4) of the Exchange Act;

B. Thomas W. Strauss be, and he hereby is:

(i) suspended from associating with any broker, dealer, municipal securities dealer, investment company or investment adviser for a period of six (6) months; and

(ii) ordered to pay to the United States Treasury a civil penalty aggregating $75,000 pursuant to Section 21B(a)(4) of the Exchange Act;

C. John W. Meriwether be, and he hereby is:

(i) suspended from associating with any broker, dealer, municipal securities dealer, investment company or investment adviser for a period of three (3) months; and

(ii) ordered to pay to the United States Treasury a civil penalty aggregating $50,000 pursuant to Section 21B(a)(4) of the Exchange Act.

---

[26] Of course, in the case of an attorney, the applicable Code of Professional Responsibility and the Canons of Ethics may bear upon what course of conduct that individual may properly pursue.  52 S.E.C. Docket 2849, 51 S.E.C. 93, Release No. 34-31554, 1992 WL 362753 (S.E.C.)

## Comments and Questions

1. Within the legal community, one of the most interesting aspects of the Gutfreund decision is its discussion of the responsibilities of Donald Feuerstein, who was the firm's legal officier but did not have direct supervisory authority over Mozer. The decision suggests that liability can attach to anyone with "a requisite degree of responsibility, ability or authority to affect the conduct of the employee." In the future, those in Feurestein's position may face sanctions if they fail to prevent violations of this sort. Is this an appropriate scope of responsibility? See Robert S. De Leon, *The SEC's Deputization of Non-Line Managers and Compliance Personnel*, 23 SEC. REG. L.J. 273 (1995). How does it compare to comparable rules applicable to depository institutions?

2. In the final footnote of the decision, the Commission acknowledges that attorneys may also be bound by rules of professional responsibility. For someone in Feuerstein's position, what effect would these rules have?

3. How do the legal obligations of compliance officers of SEC-registered broker-dealers compare to those applicable to legal counsel for federally-insured depository institutions. See Chapter 5, Section 4.H. Compare 12 U.S.C. § 1813(u) (definition of institution affiliated party) with section 15(b)(4) of the 1934 Act.

### Problem 10-5

Sonya Smith is the compliance officer for McNeil Smith, Inc., a full service brokerage house. Twelve months ago, one of the firm's branch managers noticed an unusual pattern of trading in 10 of the 500 accounts of a broker named Gypsum, and asked Smith to keep an eye on the broker. In response, Smith made several informal calls to a few of the Gypsum's customers, none of whom expressed concern over the transactions. Gysum had been subject to one serious disciplinary action five years ago, and at the time Smith had investigated the his activities as well as those of several other brokers in the same office, and subsequently monitored their activities on an active basis for several years. After her preliminary inquiries twelve months ago, Smith chose not to reinstitute active supervision of Gypsum or to take further action. Unfortunately, Gypsum had in fact begun to churn his customers accounts and was recently found to have expanded the misconduct to a wider circle of clients. Is Smith subject to SEC enforcement proceedings? Is it relevant that she supervised Gypsum closely in the past? That she uncovered misconduct by other brokers? Does it matter if Smith is legal counsel to McNeil-Smith?

# Section 3.  Arbitration of Disputes

We now turn our attention to a Supreme Court decision that has revolutionized the way in which customer disputes are resolved in the securities industry.

## Shearson/American Express Inc. v. McMahon
### 482 U.S. 220 (1987)

This case presents two questions regarding the enforceability of predispute arbitration agreements between brokerage firms and their customers.  The first is whether a claim brought under § 10(b) of the Securities Exchange Act of 1934 (Exchange Act), must be sent to arbitration in accordance with the terms of an arbitration agreement. . . .

I

Between 1980 and 1982, respondents Eugene and Julia McMahon, individually and as trustees for various pension and profit-sharing plans, were customers of petitioner Shearson/American Express Inc. (Shearson), a brokerage firm registered with the Securities and Exchange Commission (SEC or Commission). Two customer agreements signed by Julia McMahon provided for arbitration of any controversy relating to the accounts the McMahons maintained with Shearson. The arbitration provision provided in relevant part as follows:

> "Unless unenforceable due to federal or state law, any controversy arising out of or relating to my accounts, to transactions with you for me or to this agreement or the breach thereof, shall be settled by arbitration in accordance with the rules, then in effect, of the National Association of Securities Dealers, Inc. or the Boards of Directors of the New York Stock Exchange, Inc. and/or the American Stock Exchange, Inc. as I may elect." 618 F.Supp. 384, 385 (1985).

In October 1984, the McMahons filed an amended complaint against Shearson and petitioner Mary Ann McNulty, the registered representative who handled their accounts, in the United States District Court for the Southern District of New York.  The complaint alleged that McNulty, with Shearson's knowledge, had violated § 10(b) of the Exchange Act and Rule by engaging in fraudulent, excessive trading on respondents' accounts and by making false statements and omitting material facts from the advice given to respondents. . . .

II

The Federal Arbitration Act, 9 U.S.C. § 1 et seq., provides the starting point for answering the questions raised in this case.  The Act was intended to "revers[e] centuries of judicial hostility to arbitration agreements," Scherk v. Alberto-Culver Co., 417 U.S. 506, 510 (1974), by "plac[ing] arbitration agreements 'upon the same footing as other contracts.' " 417 U.S., at 511, quoting H.R.Rep. No. 96, 68th Cong., 1st Sess., 1, 2 (1924).  The Arbitration Act accomplishes this purpose by providing that arbitration agreements "shall be valid, irrevocable, and enforceable, save upon such grounds as exist at law or in equity for the revocation of any contract."  9 U.S.C. § 2.  The Act also provides that a court must stay its proceedings if it is satisfied that an issue before it is arbitrable under the agreement, § 3;  and it authorizes a federal district court to issue an order compelling arbitration if there has been a "failure, neglect, or refusal" to comply with the arbitration agreement, § 4.

The Arbitration Act thus establishes a "federal policy favoring arbitration," Moses H. Cone Memorial Hospital v. Mercury Construction Corp., 460 U.S. 1, 24 (1983), requiring that "we rigorously enforce agreements to arbitrate." Dean Witter Reynolds Inc. v. Byrd, 470 U.S. 213, 221 (1985). This duty to enforce arbitration agreements is not diminished when a party bound by an agreement raises a claim founded on statutory rights. As we observed in Mitsubishi Motors Corp. v. Soler Chrysler-Plymouth, Inc., "we are well past the time when judicial suspicion of the desirability of arbitration and of the competence of arbitral tribunals" should inhibit enforcement of the Act " 'in controversies based on statutes.' " 473 U.S. 614, 626-627 (1985), quoting Wilko v. Swan, 346 U.S. 427, 432(1953). Absent a well- founded claim that an arbitration agreement resulted from the sort of fraud or excessive economic power that "would provide grounds 'for the revocation of any contract,' " 473 U.S., at 627, the Arbitration Act "provides no basis for disfavoring agreements to arbitrate statutory claims by skewing the otherwise hospitable inquiry into arbitrability." Ibid.

The Arbitration Act, standing alone, therefore mandates enforcement of agreements to arbitrate statutory claims. Like any statutory directive, the Arbitration Act's mandate may be overridden by a contrary congressional command. The burden is on the party opposing arbitration, however, to show that Congress intended to preclude a waiver of judicial remedies for the statutory rights at issue. See id., at 628. If Congress did intend to limit or prohibit waiver of a judicial forum for a particular claim, such an intent "will be deducible from [the statute's] text or legislative history," ibid., or from an inherent conflict between arbitration and the statute's underlying purposes. See Id., at 632- 637; Dean Witter Reynolds Inc. v. Byrd, 470 U.S., at 217.

To defeat application of the Arbitration Act in this case, therefore, the McMahons must demonstrate that Congress intended to make an exception to the Arbitration Act for claims arising under . . . the Exchange Act, an intention discernible from the text, history, or purposes of the statute. . . .

III

When Congress enacted the Exchange Act in 1934, it did not specifically address the question of the arbitrability of § 10(b) claims. The McMahons contend, however, that congressional intent to require a judicial forum for the resolution of § 10(b) claims can be deduced from § 29(a) of the Exchange Act, which declares void "[a]ny condition, stipulation, or provision binding any person to waive compliance with any provision of [the Act]."

First, we reject the McMahons' argument that § 29(a) forbids waiver of § 27 of the Exchange Act. Section 27 provides in relevant part:

> "The district courts of the United States ... shall have exclusive jurisdiction of violations of this title or the rules and regulations thereunder, and of all suits in equity and actions at law brought to enforce any liability or duty created by this title or the rules and regulations thereunder."

The McMahons contend that an agreement to waive this jurisdictional provision is unenforceable because § 29(a) voids the waiver of "any provision" of the Exchange Act. The language of § 29(a), however, does not reach so far. What the antiwaiver provision of § 29(a) forbids is enforcement of agreements to waive "compliance" with the provisions of the statute. But § 27 itself does not impose any duty with which persons trading in securities must "comply." By its terms, § 29(a) only prohibits waiver of the substantive obligations imposed by the

Exchange Act. Because § 27 does not impose any statutory duties, its waiver does not constitute a waiver of "compliance with any provision" of the Exchange Act under § 29(a).

We do not read Wilko v. Swan, 346 U.S. 427 (1953), as compelling a different result. In Wilko, the Court held that a predispute agreement could not be enforced to compel arbitration of a claim arising under § 12(2) of the Securities Act. The basis for the ruling was § 14 of the Securities Act, which, like § 29(a) of the Exchange Act, declares void any stipulation "to waive compliance with any provision" of the statute. At the beginning of its analysis, the Wilko Court stated that the Securities Act's jurisdictional provision was "the kind of 'provision' that cannot be waived under § 14 of the Securities Act." 346 U.S., at 435. This statement, however, can only be understood in the context of the Court's ensuing discussion explaining why arbitration was inadequate as a means of enforcing "the provisions of the Securities Act, advantageous to the buyer." Ibid. The conclusion in Wilko was expressly based on the Court's belief that a judicial forum was needed to protect the substantive rights created by the Securities Act: "As the protective provisions of the Securities Act require the exercise of judicial direction to fairly assure their effectiveness, it seems to us that Congress must have intended § 14 ... to apply to waiver of judicial trial and review." Id., at 437. Wilko must be understood, therefore, as holding that the plaintiff's waiver of the "right to select the judicial forum," id., at 435, was unenforceable only because arbitration was judged inadequate to enforce the statutory rights created by § 12(2).

Indeed, any different reading of Wilko would be inconsistent with this Court's decision in Scherk v. Alberto-Culver Co., 417 U.S. 506 (1974). In Scherk, the Court upheld enforcement of a predispute agreement to arbitrate Exchange Act claims by parties to an international contract. The Scherk Court assumed for purposes of its opinion that Wilko applied to the Exchange Act, but it determined that an international contract "involve[d] considerations and policies significantly different from those found controlling in Wilko." 417 U.S., at 515, 94. The Court reasoned that arbitration reduced the uncertainty of international contracts and obviated the danger that a dispute might be submitted to a hostile or unfamiliar forum. At the same time, the Court noted that the advantages of judicial resolution were diminished by the possibility that the opposing party would make "speedy resort to a foreign court." Id., at 518. The decision in Scherk thus turned on the Court's judgment that under the circumstances of that case, arbitration was an adequate substitute for adjudication as a means of enforcing the parties' statutory rights. Scherk supports our understanding that Wilko must be read as barring waiver of a judicial forum only where arbitration is inadequate to protect the substantive rights at issue. At the same time, it confirms that where arbitration does provide an adequate means of enforcing the provisions of the Exchange Act, § 29(a) does not void a predispute waiver of § 27--Scherk upheld enforcement of just such a waiver.

The second argument offered by the McMahons is that the arbitration agreement effects an impermissible waiver of the substantive protections of the Exchange Act. Ordinarily, "[b]y agreeing to arbitrate a statutory claim, a party does not forgo the substantive rights afforded by the statute; it only submits to their resolution in an arbitral, rather than a judicial, forum." Mitsubishi Motors Corp. v. Soler Chrysler-Plymouth, Inc., 473 U.S., at 628. The McMahons argue, however, that § 29(a) compels a different conclusion. Initially, they contend that predispute agreements are void under § 29(a) because they tend to result from broker overreaching. They reason, as do some commentators, that Wilko is premised on the belief "that arbitration clauses in securities sales agreements generally are not freely negotiated." See, e.g.,

Sterk, Enforceability of Agreements to Arbitrate:  An Examination of the Public Policy Defense, 2 Cardozo L.Rev. 481, 519 (1981). According to this view, Wilko barred enforcement of predispute agreements because of this frequent inequality of bargaining power, reasoning that Congress intended for § 14 generally to ensure that sellers did not "maneuver buyers into a position that might weaken their ability to recover under the Securities Act." 346 U.S., at 432. The McMahons urge that we should interpret § 29(a) in the same fashion.

We decline to give Wilko a reading so far at odds with the plain language of § 14, or to adopt such an unlikely interpretation of § 29(a).  The concern that § 29(a) is directed against is evident from the statute's plain language: it is a concern with whether an agreement "waive[s] compliance with [a] provision" of the Exchange Act.  The voluntariness of the agreement is irrelevant to this inquiry:  if a stipulation waives compliance with a statutory duty, it is void under § 29(a), whether voluntary or not.  Thus, a customer cannot negotiate a reduction in commissions in exchange for a waiver of compliance with the requirements of the Exchange Act, even if the customer knowingly and voluntarily agreed to the bargain.  Section 29(a) is concerned, not with whether brokers "maneuver[ed customers] into" an agreement, but with whether the agreement "weaken[s] their ability to recover under the [Exchange] Act." 346 U.S., at 432.  The former is grounds for revoking the contract under ordinary principles of contract law; the latter is grounds for voiding the agreement under § 29(a).

The other reason advanced by the McMahons for finding a waiver of their § 10(b) rights is that arbitration does "weaken their ability to recover under the [Exchange] Act." Ibid.  That is the heart of the Court's decision in Wilko, and respondents urge that we should follow its reasoning.  Wilko listed several grounds why, in the Court's view, the "effectiveness [of the Act's provisions] in application is lessened in arbitration." 346 U.S., at 435.  First, the Wilko Court believed that arbitration proceedings were not suited to cases requiring "subjective findings on the purpose and knowledge of an alleged violator." Id., at 435-436.  Wilko also was concerned that arbitrators must make legal determinations "without judicial instruction on the law," and that an arbitration award "may be made without explanation of [the arbitrator's] reasons and without a complete record of their proceedings." Id., at 436.  Finally, Wilko noted that the "[p]ower to vacate an award is limited," and that "interpretations of the law by the arbitrators in contrast to manifest disregard are not subject, in the federal courts, to judicial review for error in interpretation." Id., at 436-437.  Wilko concluded that in view of these drawbacks to arbitration, § 12(2) claims "require[d] the exercise of judicial direction to fairly assure their effectiveness." Id., at 437.

As Justice Frankfurter noted in his dissent in Wilko, the Court's opinion did not rest on any evidence, either "in the record ... [or] in the facts of which [it could] take judicial notice," that "the arbitral system ... would not afford the plaintiff the rights to which he is entitled." Id., at 439.  Instead, the reasons given in Wilko reflect a general suspicion of the desirability of arbitration and the competence of arbitral tribunals--most apply with no greater force to the arbitration of securities disputes than to the arbitration of legal disputes generally.  It is difficult to reconcile Wilko's mistrust of the arbitral process with this Court's subsequent decisions involving the Arbitration Act. . . . .

Indeed, most of the reasons given in Wilko have been rejected subsequently by the Court as a basis for holding claims to be nonarbitrable.  In Mitsubishi, for example, we recognized that arbitral tribunals are readily capable of handling the factual and legal complexities of antitrust claims, notwithstanding the absence of judicial instruction and supervision. See 473 U.S., at 633-634. Likewise, we have concluded that the streamlined procedures of arbitration do not entail any consequential restriction on substantive rights. Id., at 628. Finally, we have indicated that there is no reason to assume at the outset that arbitrators will not follow the law; although judicial scrutiny of arbitration awards necessarily is limited, such review is sufficient to ensure that arbitrators comply with the requirements of the statute. See id., at 636- 637, and n. 19 (declining to assume that arbitration will not be resolved in accordance with statutory law, but reserving consideration of "effect of an arbitral tribunal's failure to take cognizance of the statutory cause of action on the claimant's capacity to reinstate suit in federal court").

The suitability of arbitration as a means of enforcing Exchange Act rights is evident from our decision in Scherk. Although the holding in that case was limited to international agreements, the competence of arbitral tribunals to resolve § 10(b) claims is the same in both settings. Courts likewise have routinely enforced agreements to arbitrate § 10(b) claims where both parties are members of a securities exchange or the National Association of Securities Dealers (NASD), suggesting that arbitral tribunals are fully capable of handling such matters. See, e.g., Axelrod & Co. v. Kordich, Victor & Neufeld, 320 F.Supp. 193 (SDNY 1970), aff'd, 451 F.2d 838 (CA2 1971); Brown v. Gilligan, Will & Co., 287 F.Supp. 766 (SDNY 1968). And courts uniformly have concluded that Wilko does not apply to the submission to arbitration of existing disputes, see, e.g., Gardner v. Shearson, Hammill & Co., 433 F.2d 367 (CA5 1970); Moran v. Paine, Webber, Jackson & Curtis, 389 F.2d 242 (CA3 1968), even though the inherent suitability of arbitration as a means of resolving § 10(b) claims remains unchanged. Cf. Mitsubishi, 473 U.S., at 633.

Thus, the mistrust of arbitration that formed the basis for the Wilko opinion in 1953 is difficult to square with the assessment of arbitration that has prevailed since that time. This is especially so in light of the intervening changes in the regulatory structure of the securities laws. Even if Wilko' s assumptions regarding arbitration were valid at the time Wilko was decided, most certainly they do not hold true today for arbitration procedures subject to the SEC's oversight authority.

In 1953, when Wilko was decided, the Commission had only limited authority over the rules governing self-regulatory organizations (SROs)--the national securities exchanges and registered securities associations--and this authority appears not to have included any authority at all over their arbitration rules. See Brief for Securities and Exchange Commission as Amicus Curiae 14- 15. Since the 1975 amendments to § 19 of the Exchange Act, however, the Commission has had expansive power to ensure the adequacy of the arbitration procedures employed by the SROs. No proposed rule change may take effect unless the SEC finds that the proposed rule is consistent with the requirements of the Exchange Act, section 19(b)(2) of the 1934 Act; and the Commission has the power, on its own initiative, to "abrogate, add to, and delete from" any SRO rule if it finds such changes necessary or appropriate to further the objectives of the Act, section 19(c) of the 1934 Act. In short, the Commission has broad authority to oversee and to regulate the rules adopted by the SROs relating to customer disputes, including the power to mandate the adoption of any rules it deems necessary to ensure that arbitration procedures adequately protect statutory rights.

In the exercise of its regulatory authority, the SEC has specifically approved the arbitration procedures of the New York Stock Exchange, the American Stock Exchange, and the NASD, the organizations mentioned in the arbitration agreement at issue in this case. We conclude that where, as in this case, the prescribed procedures are subject to the Commission's § 19 authority, an arbitration agreement does not effect a waiver of the protections of the Act. While stare decisis concerns may counsel against upsetting Wilko's contrary conclusion under the Securities Act, we refuse to extend Wilko's reasoning to the Exchange Act in light of these intervening regulatory developments. The McMahons' agreement to submit to arbitration therefore is not tantamount to an impermissible waiver of the McMahons' rights under § 10(b), and the agreement is not void on that basis under § 29(a). . . .

We conclude, therefore, that Congress did not intend for § 29(a) to bar enforcement of all predispute arbitration agreements. In this case, where the SEC has sufficient statutory authority to ensure that arbitration is adequate to vindicate Exchange Act rights, enforcement does not effect a waiver of "compliance with any provision" of the Exchange Act under § 29(a). Accordingly, we hold the McMahons' agreements to arbitrate Exchange Act claims "enforce[able] ... in accord with the explicit provisions of the Arbitration Act." Scherk v. Alberto-Culver Co., supra, at 520

### Comments and Questions

1. Two years after the *McMahon* decision, the Supreme Court extended its reasoning and ruled that predispute arbitration agreements would also govern claims arising under the Securities Act of 1933. See Rodriguez de Luijas v. Shearson/American Express, Inc., 490 U.S. 477 (1989). As a result of these decisions, individuals who have signed predispute arbitration agreements are generally unable to obtain judicial resolution of federal securities law claims arising out of brokerage transactions. The principal exceptions to this rule are class actions, which are generally not subject to arbitration, and situations in which the arbitration agreement was fraudulently induced. See Joel Seligman, *The Quiet Revolution: Securities Arbitration Confronts the Hard Questions*, 33 HOUSTON L. REV. 327, 338, 341-42 (1996).

2. After arbitration agreements were held enforceable, the question arose whether securities firms could make such agreements a mandatory condition of all customer accounts. Massachusetts attempted to prohibit the mandatory arbitration agreements, but its effort was ruled preempted by the Federal Arbitration Act. See Securities Industry Association v. Connolly, 883 F.2d 1114 (1st Cir. 1989), *cert. denied*, 495 U.S. 956 (1990). Are mandatory arbitration agreements consistent with the NASD standards of fair practice? Should the SEC intervene to ensure customers the option of resolving disputes in court?

3. Underlying much of the debate over securities arbitration is the question of whether arbitration procedures are fair to investors. In the *McMahon* decision, the Supreme Court accepted the industry's view that advances in SRO and SEC oversight elevated the quality of arbitration procedures. Members of the plaintiffs' bar have, however, remained skeptical about the fairness of arbitration proceedings, particularly when those proceedings are conducted under the rules of the industry's self-regulatory organizations (SRO's), such as the NASD and NYSE, as opposed to the more

independent American Arbitration Association. But see U.S. General Accounting Office, Securities Arbitration: How Investors Fare (May 1992) (GAO/GGD-92-74) (finding SRO arbitration results generally comparable to those of the AAA). In a response to these concerns, the NASD appointed a task force, chaired by former SEC Commissioner David Ruder, which recently made a series of recommendations to improve NASD arbitration proceedings. Among other things, the Ruder Task Force proposals concerned the training and selection of arbitrators, discovery rules for arbitration, and the scope of permissible remedies in arbitration (defining in particular the availability of punitive damage awards). See Arbitration Policy Task Force, NASD Securities Arbitration Reform (1996). Might the Ruder task force have gone too far?

4. Implicit in most of the opposition to arbitration is an assumption that plaintiffs do better in court than before an arbitration panel. Not everyone accepts this assumption:

[Consider] the suitability rule that requires the broker to make only recommendations that are appropriate for the customers and to disclose investment risks. . . . If a court hears a suitability dispute, the court will see the dispute as a disclosure issue under old familiar Rule 10b-5, and the court will look to see whether appropriate disclosures were made. . . . . As the law presently stands, if the requisite disclosures are in the documents, the court is required to dismiss the case. . . . . [I]n arbitration, the decisionmaker behaves quite differently. Inherently, arbitrators look at the reasonableness of the investment advice given by the broker-dealer. Even with disclosure of investment risks in the documents, the question is going to be, "how could you, Prudential, Merrill Lynch, or whoever, have let this person put half his or her portfolio in these risky securities? We do not care what the disclosure says."

Commentary of John C. Coffee, 33 HOUSTON L. REV. 376, 380 (1996). Does this ring true?

5. One of the principal advantages of arbitration is that it offers a cheaper forum for resolving disputes. Over the long run, this cost advantage might be thought to benefit both the industry and its customers. However, as more and more securities disputes are channeled through arbitration and other alternative dispute resolution mechanisms -- all of which characteristically do not generate written opinions — legal precedents in the field will become less common. Since the federal securities laws were enacted in the 1930s, the judiciary has played a major role in developing the law governing broker-dealers. Should we be concerned that the expansion of arbitration will lock us in to a future that will have to rely on primarily upon pre-*McMahon* precedents? See David A. Lipton, *Generating Precedent in Securities Industry Arbitration*, 19 SEC. REG. L.J. 26 (1991).

# Section 4: Financial Obligations of Broker-Dealers

As outlined in Chapter Nine, broker-dealers are subject to various financial obligations under section 15 of the 1934 Act. The most prominent of these are the SEC's net capital requirements, analogous to the capital requirements for depository institutions. The following enforcement action illustrates their application.

# Hinkle Northwest, Inc. v. Securities and Exchange Commission
### 641 F.2d 1304 (9th Cir. 1981)

Petitioners seek review of a suspension order of the Securities and Exchange Commission ("SEC") following a finding that they willfully violated recordkeeping, reporting, and financial-responsibility rules. We find that petitioners were correctly determined to be owners of the securities in issue, that the SEC was not collaterally estopped from so asserting, and that the sanctions imposed were justifiable. We therefore affirm.

### I.

In early 1975, Benjamin Franklin Savings and Loan Association ("Franklin") of Portland, Oregon opened an account with Hinkle Northwest, Inc. ("Northwest"), a registered broker-dealer and investment adviser. Jack Wied, at that time treasurer and a vice-president of Franklin, conducted his employer's business with Northwest. Wied engaged in municipal securities trading for Franklin's account.

Some months later, Wied entered into an arrangement with the officers of Northwest to use Franklin's credit to buy, in two transactions, over $125,000,000 in securities for Northwest's account through the mechanism of open reverse repurchase agreements ("reverse repos").[1] Although Franklin's credit was to be used for these purchases, Northwest was to be the owner of the securities and the transactions were to be concealed from Franklin. Northwest's officers approved the transactions, and Northwest ultimately reaped over $120,000 in profit without having pledged any of its own credit as collateral. Northwest paid over $15,000 in "gratuities" to Wied.

In 1977, Wied was convicted of misapplying Franklin's credit and making false entries. The SEC brought civil proceedings against Northwest and its officers/directors, Ernest F. Hinkle, Kenneth T. LaMear, and Dennis B. Reiter. The SEC, affirming the findings of an administrative law judge, found Northwest and its three directors in violation of recordkeeping and minimum net capital provisions. Specifically, the SEC found that Northwest, aided and abetted by Hinkle, LaMear, and Reiter, willfully violated the following provisions:

1. Section 17(a), Securities Exchange Act of 1934 and Rule 17a-3 thereunder, in that the two reverse repos were not properly recorded in Northwest's books;

---

[1]     By a reverse repurchase agreement, a seller in effect loans to a buyer the money with which to purchase a security from the seller. In practice, the seller sells a security to the buyer, who immediately sells it at the same price back to the seller, pays interest on the purchase price, and agrees to buy it back again at a later date. The original seller all the while retains a possessory security interest in the security pending repayment. The transaction is subsequently "unwound" when the security is sold on the open market. When, as here, the date of unwinding is not specified, the reverse repo is termed "open." The original buyer realizes a gain only if, at the time of unwinding, the market price of the security has so appreciated as to exceed the original purchase price (principal) plus accrued interest. Otherwise, the buyer is liable to the seller for the resulting deficiency.

2. Section 15(c)(3), Securities Exchange Act of 1934, and Rule 15c3-1 thereunder,, in that unrealized losses on the reverse repos caused Northwest to operate with impermissibly high net capital deficiencies on five occasions during April, 1975;

3. Section 17(a), Securities Exchange Act of 1934, and Rule 17a-11 thereunder, in that Northwest failed to give the required telegraphic notice of its net capital deficiencies and to file the required follow-up financial reports; and

4. Section 17(a), Securities Exchange Act of 1934, and Rule 17a-5 thereunder, in that Northwest's annual report of May 31, 1975 did not disclose the account balances relating to the reverse repos.[2]

The SEC order suspended Northwest from underwriting activities for 30 days, suspended Hinkle, LaMear, and Reiter from association with any broker or dealer for, respectively, 12 months, 12 months, and 3 months, and barred Hinkle, LaMear, and Reiter from collecting any money from Northwest or from participating in Northwest's activities in any manner during the periods of their suspension. Northwest and its directors petition this court for review of that order.

## II.

The SEC found petitioners in violation of the above regulatory provisions based upon various factual findings. We must accept those findings unless they are unsupported by substantial evidence. . . .

A. Northwest Owned the Securities

The central issue in this case revolves around whether Northwest owned the securities purchased by means of the reverse repos. Petitioners concede that if they owned the securities they were under an obligation, subject to their other defenses, to comply with the recordkeeping and net capital provisions. The SEC in turn acknowledges that if Northwest was not the securities' owner, Northwest and its directors would no more be in violation of the provisions than would any unrelated third party.

The SEC opinion determined that Wied was purchasing securities for registrant's (Northwest's) account, and that registrant would have all the attributes of ownership. It could dispose of the securities when it wished, and stood to gain any profit and suffer any loss. Petitioners concede that Wied purchased the securities for Northwest's account and that Northwest accepted the risk of loss or gain on the transaction. They quarrel, however, with the conclusion that Northwest owned the securities.

"Ownership" is "a collection of rights to use and enjoy property including the right to sell and transmit the same." Energy Oils, Inc. v. Montana Power Co., 626 F.2d 731, 736 (9th Cir. 1980) (citations omitted). See VI American Law of Property s 26.1 at 409 (A. Casner, ed. 1952).

---

[2]  At the same time, the SEC also found Hinkle and LaMear in violation of section 5(b)(1) of the 1933 Act for engaging in a "hard sell" under an improper prospectus and found Hinkle in violation of section 15(b)(4)(E) of the 1934 Act for inadequate supervision of an employee. Petitioners do not seek review of those findings.

Northwest enjoyed these powers as well as other indicia of ownership, including risk of profit or loss. The record contains ample support for the finding of ownership.[3]

### B. Sufficient Willfulness Was Demonstrated

Petitioners contend that the SEC failed to demonstrate that they violated the securities rules willfully. They claim that only acts of omission have been shown (e. g., failure to file reports, failure to meet net capital requirement), and that no inference of willfulness can be drawn from such.

In certain circumstances, "willfulness" does not carry a "connotation of evil intent; it means only that the act was a conscious, intentional action." Nees v. Securities and Exchange Com'n, 414 F.2d 211, 221 (9th Cir. 1969) (construing section 15 of Securities Exchange Act of 1934). In the instant case, petitioners were aware that Wied was purchasing securities for their account, and that they would have all the attributes of ownership, yet they failed to report the transactions on the company books or to file the appropriate forms with the SEC. Petitioners had substantial expertise in the securities field. The SEC found that they should have been, and almost certainly were, aware that purchases of securities had to be recorded on their books, adjusted to reflect market value. See Rule 15c3-1(c)(2)(i). Petitioners' intentional action, as experienced security brokers, in authorizing Wied to proceed on their behalf, together with their dereliction of regulation requirements, furnishes the requisite level of intent.

Petitioners answer that when the instant transactions were undertaken in 1975, the reverse repurchase agreement was a new mechanism. (The SEC adopted no accounting standards explicitly geared to reverse repos until 1976.) From this fact, they contend that the pre-existing securities rules, which the SEC alleged petitioners violated, were inapplicable to reverse repos. They conclude, accordingly, that they could not have willfully violated the regulations.

Petitioners' only evidence as to how reverse repos should have been treated under the existing rules was the testimony of David Asson, an accountant. Asson testified that proper accounting under the rules would have required no recordation of the reverse repos. He, however, based his opinion on the hypothetical assumption that the financial institution (Franklin) rather than the broker (Northwest) could determine if and when to sell the securities. Here, Northwest, not Franklin, had the power to sell. Thus, Asson's testimony did not address proper accounting procedure for the facts of this case. Accordingly, petitioners have not demonstrated that the absence of specific accounting standards for reverse repos excused their failure to comply with the requirements attendant upon all purchases of securities by registered broker-dealers. Moreover, Asson admitted on cross-examination that brokerage firms are required to compute their net capital based upon the market price of any security in their account, adjusting for any unrealized profit or loss.

---

[3]    Anglo-American law places little emphasis on the term ownership in a technical sense. J. Cribbet, Principles of the Law of Property 16 (2d ed. 1975). This may explain why, although it is of central importance to the case, neither side discusses the determinants of ownership.

## Comments and Questions

1. The *Hinkle Northwest* case is a fairly straightforward enforcement action. In contrast to prior cases, however, the underlying violation here concern the financial obligations of broker-dealer, and not fiduciary style duties to customers. In our discussion of depository institutions, we considered some analogous proceedings. What were they? How would you compare the disputes we've considered in these two areas?

2. We will shortly embark on a more detailed discussion of the net-capital rules described briefly in the *Hinkle Northwest* case. Readers should be aware, however, that the SEC has also promulgated extensive regulations governing segregation of customer securities and cash reserves, and the hypothecation (that is, pledging) of customer securities. In addition, broker-dealers must comply with elaborate Federal Reserve Board regulations governing the extension of credit to purchase securities. "Margin" loans of this sort pose special risks for investors. For an overview of these and related topics, see VII LOUIS LOSS & JOEL SELIGMAN, SECURITIES REGULATION 3107-328 (3d ed. 1991).

---

The following excerpts, which has been slightly reorganized from its original presentation, offers an overview of the broker-dealer net capital rules.

# Gary Haberman, **Capital Requirements of Commercial and Investment Banks**
Quarterly Rev. Fed. Res. Bank of New York, Autumn 1987, at 1, 3-7

### Securities and Exchange Commission Uniform Net Capital Rule for Brokers and Dealers

The SEC first adopted a capital rule in 1944 to establish a standard of financial responsibility for registered brokers and dealers. The most recent comprehensive update of the rule was implemented in 1982. Firms that provide retail brokerage services and that underwrite or deal in corporate or municipal securities must abide by the rule.

The capital rule is a liquidity test in the sense that it seeks to ensure that liquid assets, adjusted for trading risk, exceed senior liabilities by a required margin of safety. A broker-dealer should be able to liquidate quickly and to satisfy the claims of its customers without recourse to formal bankruptcy proceedings. The test is a two-step procedure: first, a determination of the amount of net capital available to meet a firm's capital requirement, and second, a determination of the capital requirement (that is, the margin of safety). Net capital is total capital reduced by various charges and by haircuts that measure trading risk. (See Figure 1.)

*Total capital:* Total capital equals net worth plus subordinated liabilities and is augmented by allowable credits. It is determined by generally accepted accounting principles on a mark-to-market basis. To be counted as capital, subordinated debt must have a minimum term of one year and may not be prepayable without the prior written approval of the broker-dealer's examining authority (New York Stock Exchange or NASD). Subordinated debt may be in the form of either borrowed cash or borrowed securities, the latter service as collateral for "secured demand notes." The rule also allows two forms of temporarily borrowed capital. Broker-dealers are permitted to obtain temporary subordinations not exceeding 45 days in maturity as often as three times a year to capitalize underwriting and extraordinary activities. A firm may also have a revolving subordinated loan agreement providing for prepayment within a year.

---

**Figure 1**
**SEC Net Capital Computation**

Total capital:  Equity, Allowable subordinated debt, and Allowable credits

[D]eductions:  (Illiquid assets), (Unsecured receivables), (Charges for aged credit exposure), and (Market risk haircuts) . . . .

Net Capital:  [Total Capital minus Deductions]

Requirement:  6 2/3 percent aggregated indebtedness, or
2 percent aggregate debit items

Excess Capital:  Net Capital [minus] Requirement

---

All of the above are treated as satisfactory subordination agreements by the rule and thereby qualify for total capital. However, the rule establishes more demanding specifications that, if met, would qualify subordinated borrowings from a partner or stockholder as what can best be called "near equity." Net worth plus this near equity must equal or exceed 30 percent of the total of net worth and subordinated debt.

Allowable credits to total capital include certain deferred income tax liabilities and accrued liabilities that are payable solely at the discretion of the firm, such as bonuses and profit sharing.

Broker-dealers are prohibited from distributing equity capital (for example, through dividends or unsecured loans to owners) if doing so would reduce the firm's net capital below warning levels. Supervisory authorities set warning levels somewhat higher than the minimum requirement; for example, one is 120 percent of the basic requirement.

*Capital charges*: Total capital is reduced by nonallowable assets and various special charges. An asset is considered nonallowable if it cannot be immediately or quickly converted into cash. This definition applies to fixed and intangible assets, investments [in] and unsecured receivables from affiliates and subsidiaries, most other unsecured receivables, and nonmarketable securities. Special charges include specified types of receivables from other broker-dealers not collected within 30 days and other specified receivables aged beyond 11 or 60 days. Credit exposure is also deducted for purchased securities not received within 30 days and for most sold securities not delivered within 5 days. There are also charges for giving excessive margin on repurchase transactions when a dealer borrows. (If excessive margin is taken when a dealer lends under a resale agreement, the requirement is increased.) Such charges encourage good business practices.

*Haircuts*: The rule recognizes that the prices of marketable assets and liabilities may move adversely during liquidation, thereby reducing net capital available to cover a firm's obligations. The deduction for price risk in the firm's proprietary positions, haircuts, are percentages of the market value of security and forward positions held by the broker-dealer. As a measure of price risk, haircut factors vary in accordance with the type and remaining maturity of securities held or sold short.

---

**Figure 2**
**Summary of Haircuts Applied to Unhedged Positions**

Government and agency  securities:
   0 to 6 percent in 12 maturity subcategories
   6 percent applied to 25 year bonds

Municipal securities:
   0 to 7 percent in 16 maturity categories
   7 percent applies to 20 year bonds

Commercial paper, bankers acceptances, and certificates of deposits:
   0 to 0.5 percent in 5 maturity categories
   0.5 percent applies to 9 month paper

Investment grade corporate debt:
   2 to 9 percent in 9 maturity categories
   9 percent applies to 25 year bonds

Preferred stock:
   10 percent

Common stock and "all other":
   30 percent under the basic method
   15 percent under the alternative method

---

For government and high-grade corporate debt, some forms of hedging serve to reduce haircuts. Moreover, within the several maturity subcategories into which government, high-grade corporate and municipal debt securities are grouped, short positions serve to offset long positions fully. Forward contracts receive the haircuts applicable to their underlying securities. Futures and options positions are also explicitly treated. The rule specifies additional haircut charges where the broker-dealer has an undue concentration in securities of a single issuer. For broker-dealers choosing the alternative method of calculating required capital, lower haircut percentages may be taken on certain securities positions, including undue concentration and underwriting commitments. Most important, the haircut on common stock and "all other" securities is 15 percent instead of 30 percent.

*Capital requirement*: Net capital must exceed a minimum absolute dollar level and one of two standards that relate to the size of a broker-dealer's business.

The basic method requires that net capital exceed 6 2/3 percent of aggregate indebtedness, which includes all liabilities less those specifically exempted. In essence, aggregate indebtedness is any liability not adequately collateralized, secured, or otherwise directly offset by an asset of the broker-dealer. It also includes contingent, off-balance sheet obligations. Few large investment houses choose to use the basic method because, as noted above, it requires a 30 percent haircut on common stock and "all other" securities. This method is usually chosen by smaller retail-oriented brokerage firms.

The alternative method requires that net capital exceed two percent of aggregate debit items computed in accordance with the Reserve Formula under the Customer Protection Rule. These debit items are the gross debit balances of particular asset accounts and generally represent good quality customer receivables. The rule uses these debit items as a proxy for the size of customer-related business. For small broker-dealers whose business is heavily retail-oriented, these aggregate debit items can represent a majority of a firm's assets. However, for most large broker-dealers who are not heavily retail-oriented, these debit items usually constitute less than 25 percent of total assets.

For major firms, the alternative method applies a lower percentage factor to a smaller base than does the basic method and permits a 15 percent haircut on "all other" securities rather than 30 percent. To qualify for this method, however, a firm must hold a greater reserve under the Customer Protection Rule calculation.

**Broker-dealer capital requirement: a liquidation measure**

The underlying logic of the SEC's capital rule is that a broker-dealer should be able to wind down its activities and protect its customers within one month. The Commission evaluates the risk-adjusted liquidity of the firm with a conservative view of those assets that can be sold or collected in order to meet senior obligations in the very near term. The SEC's rule starts with total capital, applies a series of deductions to derive "net capital," and compares this measure to a required safety margin. Broker-dealers must operate with capital in excess of the requirement. Because a firm must cease operating if it fails the standard, the required margin is quite small. The supervisory process, however, also employs several higher "warning level" tests. Firms operating with net capital at or below warning levels are subject to special restrictions and close supervisory scrutiny. They must scale down their activities in line with their capital.

The permitted components of total capital reflect the short time frame of the capital rule. Equity and subordinated debt with more than one year to maturity are the core elements, but other subordinated debt of quite temporary duration is also allowed as capital. For example, an unusually large underwriting may be capitalized with temporary subordinated debt repayable within 45 days. Owners may also provide debt capital by pledging marketable securities instead of investing cash in the firm. Moreover, accrued liabilities for discretionary bonuses and some tax deferrals are allowable additions to capital.

The SEC requires three types of deductions from total capital. The first set addresses liquidity and includes intangible, fixed, and other illiquid assets, securities that do not meet a stringent test of marketability, and "disallowed" assets such as most unsecured receivables. The deduction of unsecured receivables reflects both liquidity and credit risk concerns. The next set of deductions addresses other forms of credit risk and introduces into the rule several incentives for efficient market practices.[4]  Capital adjusted to this point in the calculation can be viewed as "liquid capital."

The third set of deductions from the total capital, called haircuts, gauges potential trading risk, that is, how much securities might decline in value prior to being sold.  Net capital, which remains after all deductions, is compared to a minimum requirement and higher warning levels.  The requirement is a small fraction of a proxy for the size of the firm.  Broker-dealers can choose either a proxy for the size of senior obligations (6.67 percent of aggregate indebtedness under the basic method) or a proxy for the size of "customer" business (2 percent of aggregate debit items under the alternative method).[5]

Liquid capital, as a measure, differs significantly from total capital.  Liquid capital is the excess of marketable and easily liquidated assets over senior liabilities.  Liquidity, thereby, is given primary importance, and unmarketable, unsecured assets are heavily penalized with a 100 percent capital requirement.  In this context, the SEC applies a definition of marketability which is quite stringent in most circumstances:  the security must be exchange traded, or bid and offer quotations must be readily available and settlement of sales at such prices must be possible within a relatively short time.  Marketable assets and liabilities must be valued at current prices and unrealized gains and losses reflected in net worth each day.  Marketable assets are assumed to be saleable, but this is not the point of the capital charge; liquidity is.  A security that does not pass the marketability test need not be deducted from total capital to the extent that a bank has already lent funds secured by the asset.

Most unsecured receivables and advances are also deducted in full, although a few routine receivables are only deducted when aged.  To secure a receivable under the rule, collateral must meet the same marketability tests as inventory.  This aspect of the rule helps insulate broker-dealers from their affiliates because it encourages firms to take marketable collateral to secure receivables.

The capital rule's focus on liquidity is designed to work in concert with the SEC's Customer Protection Rule.[6]  Put simply, the Customer Protection Rule seeks to compel a broker-dealer to (1) balance its liabilities to customers with receivables due from customers plus a segregated cash reserve, and (2) place all fully paid for customer securities in possession or control (a custodial obligation).[7]  Moreover, if a firm maintains a greater segregated cash reserve, it may choose the less burdensome alternative capital requirement.

Trading risk is explicitly treated to gauge how marketable assets might decrease in value, and marketable liabilities might increase in value, if a firm must be liquidated.  Risk factors (haircuts) for investment grade securities have been developed from statistical measures of price

---

[4]    For example, there is a capital charge for securities purchased but not yet received within 30 days, while the capital charge for securities sold but not yet delivered applies after only 5 days.

[5]    "Customers" are specifically defined within the SEC rules.  Not all counterparties are customers; principals of the firm and other broker-dealers are excluded.

[6]    Rule 15c3-3, the Customer Protection Rule, was established in the early 1970s in response to the back office problems suffered on Wall Street during the late 1960s.

[7]    That is, customer securities are those for which the broker has already received full payment and exclude securities purchased on margin.

volatility.[8] For example, three-month Treasury bills are haircut 0.5 percent and 30-year bonds are haircut 6 percent of market value. Haircuts are also applied to off-balance sheet market exposures such as futures, forwards, and options. Many forms of hedging and arbitrage are recognized as having less risk than uncovered positions. "All other" securities, such as common stock and low-rated bonds, require 15 percent capitalization.[9]

Credit risk is subsumed into this structure at several points. The credit risk on marketable debt securities is covered by the market risk haircuts. Broker-dealers usually sell such assets long before a default occurs.[10] Temporary credit exposures resulting from routine transactions are not treated consistently by the SEC because broker-dealers are presumed to avoid credit losses rather than to reserve for them. Capital charges for unsettled transactions, while based on credit risk, are designed to encourage efficient business practices. In contrast, most other unsecured receivables require 100 percent capital coverage, while secured receivables and the default risk on forward trades incur no capital charges. Finally, the 100 percent deduction for unmarketable assets to meet the liquidity intent of the rule more than sufficiently covers credit risk as well.

The structure of the SEC's rules, coupling the Net Capital Rule requirement for liquidity and the Customer Protection Rule requirement for coverage of customer payables, has practical application to the treatment of a failing firm. As a securities house weakens toward warning levels, it must constrain its business. It should not be able to double its bets and risk tripling its losses. Once a warning level is breached, the examining authority would seek further constraint. Thus, a firm's ability to compete, already weak, would be further undermined at a time when it still had positive liquid capital, that is, liquid assets in excess of senior liabilities. Facing an untenable position, management would then seek to sell or merge the company before the situation required a SIPC-managed failure. This approach has been used many times during the past two decades and, when it worked as intended, SIPC faced little or no loss. As a result, the insurance corporation operates with a low level of reserves, $393 million (as of August 1987), and a minimal $100 per firm annual premium. Of course, in cases of fraud neither this, nor most other structures work neatly.

*Observed capital levels*: Market pressures, rather than regulations, determine how much excess net capital securities firms need to compete successfully. Wall Street firms place great importance on the absolute amount of their excess net capital because it demonstrates their ability to serve large customers and handle large transactions. Most firms have increased their capitalization in recent years. At year end 1986 sixteen diversified firms reported average net capital 7.3 times larger than minimum requirements. In absolute terms, average excess capital was $408 million, while the average requirement was only $65 million. In comparison, total

---

[8]    The haircuts reflect price volatility measured over several years and cover relatively large price changes. The factors do not, however, cover the extraordinary price movements that occurred in October 1987.

[9]    Most major houses choose the alternative requirement and are subject to a 15 percent haircut on "all other" securities. Under the basic requirement, this haircut is 30 percent.

[10]    Defaulting debt securities usually trade at a small fraction of face value. The broker-dealer would, therefore, reflect losses day by day as the price dropped rather than wait until the asset was weak enough to warrant a write-off.

capital averaged $1.4 billion, with a range from under $300 million to over $3 billion. Equity constituted 61 percent of total capital in this sample.

The relationship between total, net and required capital is determined by the composition of a firm's business. Dealing, arbitrage and underwriting generate high haircuts that reduce net capital but change each day. Haircuts may not be particularly high on those days for which financial statements are prepared. Firms specializing in these activities tend to report more than 40 percent of their total capital as "excess." In contrast, retail brokerage causes other deductions and the final requirement to be larger. Several of the large retail houses report only 20 percent of their total capital as excess.

Although the minimum requirement is a proxy for size, it is not tied to assets. Among the sixteen firms, the minimum requirement ranged from 0.1 to 1 percent of total assets. The effective capital requirement of the SEC standard can be viewed as the difference between total and excess capital. This measure combines most aspects of the SEC rule to show how much of the firm's total capital is in use. The effective requirement reported by the sixteen firms averaged 5.1 percent of assets–a figure on par with banking standards of 5.5 percent. However, the effective requirements ranged from 1.6 to 16 percent.

*Holding company implications*:   Because regulations extend only to the licensed subsidiaries of investment houses, the firms frequently perform in unregulated affiliates activities that would be uneconomic if held to SEC requirements. This consequence of securities industry regulation has grown in importance with recent capital market innovations. As investment houses have broadened their activity to include new products that entail nonmarketable credit exposure, the portion of their business accomplished in unregulated affiliates has grown. Swaps, whole-mortgage loan trading, and bridge loans are among the innovations handled in affiliates. In consequence, the SEC, the CFTC and the Treasury have all written their capital rules to foster financial separation of affiliates. Transactions between regulated and unregulated affiliates are treated harshly; for example, unsecured loans require a 100 percent capital charge and have the effect of transferring liquid capital. Moreover, even secured transactions are closely reviewed by examining authorities. This structure, however, does not forbid advances to or investments in affiliates; it merely applies a strict capital evaluation. A firm willing to move liquid capital out of its regulated unit is not constrained by regulation so long as its net capital remains above warning levels. The investment houses usually publish consolidated holding company financial statements that display gross capital. The reports footnote the excess net capital within the firms' regulated broker-dealer subsidiaries. Competitive pressures to report impressive excess capital figures are a strong incentive to maximize the liquid capital within registered broker-dealer subsidiaries.

## Comments and Questions

1.  How do these rules described in this excerpt compare to those applicable to depository institutions? Do the differences between the business activities of broker-dealers and depository institutions justify such different systems of capital regulation? Would you support or oppose a unified capital system for broker-dealers and depository institutions? Should a unified system also cover insurance companies? If a unified system of capital regulation is impractical at the present time, should capital regulation of depository institutions and insurance companies at least be moving towards the kind of market-based system of accounting and capital requirements used for the securities industry?

2.   Several years after the foregoing excerpt was written, both Congress and the SEC revisited the issue of broker-dealer financial responsibility and adopted significant amendments described in the following release. As you read through this release, consider why the prior approach to broker-dealer net-capital regulation proved inadequate. Will the corrective measures described in this release solve those problems?

*Problem 10-6*

Refer back to the balance sheet of the bank described in Problem 3-4 of Chapter Three, Section 3.C. Would that bank meet the SEC's net capital requirements? What might the firm do to improve its compliance with these requirements?

# Proposed Temporary Risk Assessment Rules
## SEC Release No. 34-29635, 56 Fed. Reg. 44,014 (Sept. 6, 1991)

### Background

During the past decade, the securities markets have experienced expansion and evolution. The volume of trading on the securities exchanges and in the over-the-counter markets has grown tremendously.  The development of innovative financial products, such as stock index futures, has linked the securities and commodities futures markets through complex trading strategies implemented by major market participants.  Advances in communications and information technology have accelerated the pace at which information is disseminated through the markets, increasing the speed at which the markets react to information.  Trading has expanded beyond national borders; a global marketplace has unfolded.

Market participants have adapted and transformed along with the markets.  Where formerly participants in the U.S. securities markets were primarily individual investors, today's markets are often dominated by institutional investors.  The broker-dealer community has reacted to the changes in the financial landscape through expansion and diversification.  Many broker-dealers have begun to rely less on traditional revenue sources, such as agency transactions, and have become involved in activities such as proprietary trading and merchant banking, which require large capital bases.  To acquire the capital necessary to remain competitive in a rapidly expanding global marketplace, firms have turned to the public equity markets, have increased their leverage, or have merged or affiliated themselves with other entities.

As a consequence, many large investment banking firms are now owned by holding companies that have other subsidiaries engaging in financial and securities related activities throughout the globe.  In many instances, the holding companies or affiliates of the broker-dealer operate with little or no regulatory oversight.  These unregulated entities can attain a degree of leverage and assume credit risks which registered broker-dealers, subject to the Commission's net capital and customer protection rules, cannot. Specifically, many potentially risky activities, such as interest rate swaps, bridge loans, and foreign currency transactions are affected by unregulated holding companies and affiliates of the broker-dealer.[1]   In some cases, the registered

---

[1]    The Staff of the Commission, based on conversations with investment banking representatives and financial experts, has estimated that some of the affiliate entities of the major broker-dealers have outstanding, at any given point in time, $50 billion to $100 billion in interest rate swaps (based on the notional amount of those transactions) and $15 billion in foreign currency transactions. In addition, the

broker-dealer's parent or affiliates have significantly less capital than the broker-dealer. Where this occurs, creditors may rely on the credit standing of the broker-dealer and the ability of the holding company to obtain capital from the broker-dealer to support bridge financing or other extensions of credit.

### Existing Regulatory Framework

Existing Commission regulations deal with capital requirements designed to insulate broker-dealers and their customers from the business failure of the regulated broker-dealer. Specifically, the net capital rule requires that capital sufficient to meet reasonable anticipated business and trading losses remain in the broker-dealer at all times. Moreover, the customer protection rule ensures that customers' fully paid and excess margin securities are segregated and imposes strict controls on use of other customer funds and securities.

Rule 15c3-1 under the Exchange Act, the Commission's net capital rule, protects customers and creditors of registered broker-dealers from monetary losses and delays that can occur when the registered broker-dealer fails. In this way, the net capital rule acts to prevent systemic risk from the failure of a financial intermediary. The net capital rule requires registered broker-dealers to maintain sufficient liquid assets to enable firms that fall below the minimum capital requirements to liquidate in an orderly fashion without a formal proceeding. By concentrating on the financial condition of the broker-dealer, the net capital rule insulates the broker-dealer and its customers from financial failures or difficulties of affiliated entities.[2]

Rule 15c3-3 under the Exchange Act, the customer protection rule, complements the net capital rule by preventing the misallocation or misuse of customer funds or securities by broker-dealers. Among other things, the customer protection rule limits a broker-dealer's use of customer monies to finance the broker-dealer's businesses, except as necessary to finance customer transactions. Both the customer protection and the net capital rules focus specifically on the broker-dealer itself; the financial condition or the activities of holding companies, affiliates, or subsidiaries are not taken into account. Other recordkeeping and reporting rules enable the Commission to obtain records relating to the financial viability of the registered broker-dealer. Rule 17a-5 under the Exchange Act, requires registered broker-dealers to file with the Commission and the broker-dealer's designated examining authority various reports concerning the financial and operational condition of the broker-dealer.[3]

---

Staff estimates that the holding companies of the ten largest firms have outstanding approximately $2 billion in bridge loans.

[2]    However, the fate of a broker-dealer may be inextricably linked to that of its affiliates. Recently, the Commission adopted amendments to the net capital rule concerning the withdrawal of capital from a broker-dealer by a parent or an affiliate. See Securities Exchange Act Release No. 28927 (February 28, 1991); 56 FR 9124, (March 5, 1991). The amendments require broker-dealers to notify the Commission of large capital withdrawals made to benefit affiliates, subsidiaries and other persons related to the broker- dealer. The amendments also prohibit withdrawals of capital if the withdrawals would cause the broker-dealer's net capital to be less then 25 percent of the deductions required by the net capital rule as to the broker-dealer's readily marketable securities. Finally, the amendments give the Commission the authority to halt, by order, certain withdrawals of capital on a temporary basis in emergency situations. The amendments reflect the Commission's growing concern about the effect that related entities can have on the viability of a broker-dealer.

[3]    These reports are filed on the Financial and Operational Combined Uniform Single Report (commonly known as the FOCUS report). Rules 17a-3 and 17a-4 under the Exchange Act, provide for record maintenance and preservation. Rule 17a-3 specifies which records broker-dealers must preserve

Overall, the Commission's financial responsibility and reporting rules have successfully provided a regulatory framework for the protection of customers and creditors of registered broker-dealers. However, while these rules call for detailed financial and operational information of the registered broker-dealer, they do not require the broker-dealer to maintain and preserve records with respect to the activities of its holding company or affiliated parties. Although the rules provide a sound regulatory structure, they do not completely shelter the broker-dealer from the failures of affiliated entities. Broker-dealers are affected by the financial difficulties of affiliated entities both directly, by the withdrawal of capital to meet the obligations of affiliates, and indirectly, by the effect such difficulties can have on the broker-dealers' ability to obtain financing.

This impact on a broker-dealer can be exacerbated in times of market stress. Access to information concerning the activities of associated persons of broker-dealers is particularly pertinent during periods of steep market decline and volatility. For instance, the Commission was particularly concerned about the liquidity and funding of broker-dealers during both the October 1987 market break and the market turbulence of October 1989. Those incidents demonstrated that plunging stock prices may generate an environment of uncertainty that will impact the financial operation of broker-dealers. An abrupt decline in the market can increase the credit risk involved in lending to broker-dealers holding large inventories of equity relative to their capital; lenders may thus become reluctant to continue extending credit. In addition, some broker-dealers may experience temporary difficulties in marketing instruments the proceeds of which are needed to satisfy the financial obligations (e.g., bridge loans) of their clients. Events such as these could lead to a funding or liquidity problem for the holding company parent of a broker-dealer, which may be forced to look to the net capital of the broker-dealer as a means of funding the parent's business.

Likewise, regulatory concerns about the financial condition of broker-dealers can arise at times other than periods of market decline. For example, the activities carried out by the affiliates of a broker-dealer are, in the aggregate, generally more highly leveraged and riskier than permitted by the net capital rule. If a highly leveraged holding company or other affiliate encounters financial difficulties, its financial distress may extend to the registered firm. Financial problems at the holding company level or in a significant affiliate or subsidiary could impact the ability of the broker-dealer to obtain short-term financing to meet its operating and settlement obligations.

Short-term-financings, particularly through the commercial paper market and repurchase agreements, are common financing devices for broker-dealers. If the holding company complex faced a financial predicament, a creditor or contra party might force the broker-dealer to provide additional securities as margin for its repurchase agreements. Even a small increase in required margin levels could force the broker-dealer to liquidate its repurchase agreements and might drastically reduce the firm's short-term financing ability. Similarly, banks may withdraw lines of credit or restrict lending arrangements with broker-dealers because the fiscal health of a related entity has deteriorated. Accordingly, the ability of a broker-dealer to continue operations if a major affiliate ceased operations or met with financial difficulties could be severely impaired.

---

and maintain. Rule 17a-4 specifies, among other things, that the records and other information required to be kept pursuant to Rule 17a-3 must be maintained in a readily accessible place. Rule 17a-4 also specifies the time periods that broker-dealers must preserve the records required by it and by Rule 17a-3.

Furthermore, the abrupt liquidation of transactions by a large broker-dealer could seriously affect other market participants as well as disturb the markets themselves.

These concerns are illustrated by the bankruptcy of Drexel Burnham Lambert Group, Inc. ("Drexel"), the holding company parent of Drexel Burnham Lambert, Inc. ("DBL"), a registered broker-dealer.  In this case, Drexel had over $1 billion in commercial paper and other unsecured short-term borrowings outstanding.  As a result of significant losses and a downgrade in the rating of its commercial paper, Drexel found it increasingly difficult to renew its short-term borrowings.  Drexel was then forced to turn to the only liquid sources of capital in its assets--the excess net capital of DBL and that of an affiliated government securities dealer.

In a period of approximately three weeks, and without the knowledge of the Commission or the New York Stock Exchange, Inc. ("NYSE"), approximately $220 million of the excess capital was transferred from the broker-dealer to the holding company in the form of short-term loans.  When the Commission became aware of the situation, Drexel or its affiliates had more than $400 million in short-term liabilities maturing in two weeks and an additional $330 million maturing the next month.

Ultimately, the Commission and the NYSE intervened and prohibited further withdrawals of capital from the registered broker-dealer.  Nonetheless, after the bankruptcy filing by its parent Drexel, DBL was forced to declare bankruptcy and liquidate its assets.  This case clearly demonstrated that the viability and the ultimate survival of a broker-dealer can be linked to that of its associated persons.

### The Market Reform Act

Recently, Congress passed the Market Reform Act of 1990 (the "Reform Act") in response to these and other factors.[4]  The Reform Act is designed to strengthen the system of regulatory oversight over the securities markets and improve the Commission's regulatory supervision over broker-dealers.  Section 4 of the Reform Act entitled "Risk Assessment for Holding Company Systems" added section 17(h) of the Exchange Act.[5]

Section 17(h) requires broker-dealers to maintain and preserve such risk assessment information as the Commission by rule prescribes with respect to those associated persons of the broker-dealer whose "business activities are reasonably likely to have a material impact on the financial and operational condition" of the broker-dealer, including the broker-dealer's "net capital, its liquidity, or its ability to finance its operations".  The statute provides that the records should concern the broker-dealer's "policies, procedures, or systems for monitoring and controlling financial and operational risks to it resulting from the activities" of its material associated persons and should "describe, in the aggregate, each of the financial and securities activities conducted by, and the customary sources of capital and funding" of associated persons

---

[4]    Pub. L. No. 101-432, 104 Stat. 963 (1990).  The Reform Act also addresses other changes in the nation's securities markets.

[5]    Section 17(h) provides the Commission with specific authority to obtain information regarding certain activities of broker-dealer affiliates, but does not provide the Commission with any new authority to regulate the activities of those affiliates.  New Section 17(h) augments the Commission's broad authority with respect to matters relating to the financial responsibility of broker-dealers and builds on the Commission's statutory authority to adopt recordkeeping and reporting requirements for broker-dealers under section 17(a) of the Exchange Act.

whose business activities are reasonably likely to have a material impact on the broker-dealer". In addition, the Reform Act authorizes the Commission to require broker-dealers to file, no more frequently than quarterly, summary reports of the information and records maintained pursuant to the risk assessment rules.

The Reform Act does not contain a definition of the term "financial and securities activities"; however, the legislative history of the bill illustrates the types of activities that are intended to be included in this term.[10] The list encompasses activities generally understood to be engaged in by entities active in the financial markets. However, several activities, such as manufacturing, consumer lending and certain insurance activities are excluded and are beyond the scope of the risk assessment rules.

Section 17(h) of the Act also empowers the Commission to obtain more detailed reports (sometimes referred to as "call reports") during periods of market stress or when information contained in the quarterly reports or other information leads the Commission to conclude that supplemental information is necessary.

The risk assessment provisions provide the Commission with broad authority, either by rule or by order, to exempt persons or classes of persons from the recordkeeping or reporting requirements. The Commission may grant conditional, permanent or temporary exemptions. The statute directs the Commission to consider a number of factors in granting exemptions . . . .

The statute provides that, notwithstanding any other provision of law, the Commission may not be compelled to disclose any information required to be reported by a broker-dealer pursuant to the risk assessment rules or supplied to the Commission by any domestic or foreign regulatory agency. The statute expressly exempts risk assessment information from disclosure to the public under the Freedom of Information Act. However, the Commission is not authorized by the statute to withhold risk assessment information from Congress, or from complying with a request for information from any other Federal agency or department requesting the information for purposes within the scope of such agency or department's jurisdiction, or from complying with an order of a court of the United States in an action brought by the United States or the Commission.

### Comments and Questions

1. In 1992, the SEC promulgated Final Temporary Risk Assessment Rules, largely codifying the proposed temporary rule set forth above. See SEC Release No. 34-30929, 1992 WL 172803 (July 16, 1992) (codified at Rule 17h-1T and 17h-2T). How does this approach to broker-dealer affiliates compare to the treatment of affiliates in the depository institution field? Would it be feasible to relax the restrictions of the Bank Holding Company Act and adopt the approach reflected in the Market Reform Act of 1990 and these implementing regulations?

2. For a recent comparative analysis and critique of capital requirements for banks, securities firms, and insurance companies, see U.S. General Accounting Office, Risk-Based Capital: Regulatory and Industry Approaches to Capital and Risk (July 1998) (GGD-98-153).

---

[10]    See H.R. Rep. No. 3657, 101st Cong., 2d Sess., at 34 (1990) (hereinafter "H. Rep.").

# CHAPTER ELEVEN

# THE REGULATION OF TRADING MARKETS

We now turn our attention from the regulation of the relationship between securities firms and their customers — the focus of the preceding chapter — to the regulation of markets themselves. Here, once again, the role of self-regulatory organizations (SROs) is critical. The principal trading market in the United Sates, the New York Stock Exchange (NYSE), is itself an SRO. Under the 1934 Act, the NYSE is both a regulated entity and a regulator of its member firms and listed companies. Similarly, our second largest trading market — the National Association of Securities Dealers Automated Quotation System (NASDAQ) — is overseen by a self-regulatory organization, the NASD, which itself is responsible for supervising much of the over-the-counter market. The regulation of trading markets is complex and contested. As you read through this chapter, consider the extent to which the government has a role in overseeing trading markets. Is this an area in which we can rely on the SROs to compete among themselves in the development of efficient trading systems? Or is government intervention necessary to safeguard the public interest?

## Section 1. Introduction

This chapter is divided into two substantive sections. The first considers two prominent cases in which the SEC challenged SRO management of trading markets: the fixed-commission controversy of the 1970s and the debate over dual-class securities of the late 1980s. The second section explores the role of broker-dealers in trading markets, and considers two instances in which practices of securities firms were alleged to have undermined market integrity. Before turning to these substantive issues, we begin with a brief overview of the current structure of the U.S. trading markets, excerpted from Polly Nyquist, *Failure to Engage: The Regulation of Proprietary Trading Systems*, 13 YALE L. & POL'Y REV. 281 (1995).

### 1. The Primary Exchanges: NYSE and AMEX

The New York Stock Exchange is and always has been the dominant securities market in the U.S. [As of the end of 1996, there were 3,530 securities trading on the NYSE, representing 2907 listed companies. The average daily share volume on the NYSE in 1996 was roughly 410 million shares, and its total annual dollar volume of trading was over $ 4 trillion.] In 1993, the NYSE accounted for 82% of the consolidated tape trading volume in NYSE stocks and 70% of the reported consolidated tape trades. . . . In addition, the NYSE also represents the largest chunk of the total market capitalization in the U.S., $4.54 trillion [ in 1993], which outstrips all other markets combined.

The NYSE is an auction market; it has a physical exchange floor where customers' orders interact directly with one another through their brokers, or interact with the floor specialist who is making a market in the particular security. The specialist post acts as a meeting place for all brokers interested in a particular issue. The specialist manages the supply and demand flow in the issue. The specialist also keeps the limit order book where customers can enter and display their orders for holding until the buy/sell price is met.

In addition to the NYSE, the American Stock Exchange (AMEX) is also considered a "primary" exchange, although it does not have nearly the trading volume of the NYSE. AMEX does not provide a market for NYSE-listed companies, but instead lists companies independently.

### 2. The Other Exchanges: Regional Exchanges, NASDAQ, and the Third and Fourth Markets.

The NYSE competes with several other markets, including the regional markets, the third and fourth markets, and the Proprietary Trading Systems (PTSs) for volume in its own securities. There are five other exchanges, like the NYSE, which are auction markets with physical trading floors. These are generally referred to as the "regional" markets, and include the Boston Stock Exchange (BSE), the Philadelphia Stock Exchange (Phlx), the Cincinnati Stock Exchange (CSE), the Chicago Stock Exchange (CHX), and the Pacific Stock Exchange (PSE). These markets handle about 20% of the trading in NYSE securities; most of it, however, is at the best bid/offer on the Intermarket Trading System (ITS), thus limiting their role in price competition for the NYSE. Trading of NYSE-listed securities also takes place in the so-called "third market." Although the third market has not been consistently defined in the literature, the SEC has referred to over-the-counter (OTC) trading of exchange-listed securities as such a third market. This trading accounts for a fairly small portion of volume (7.4% of NYSE volume in 1993), and is primarily in small orders executed by discount brokers.

Finally, the "fourth market" refers to trading done without any intervention by a market professional, either directly between institutional investors or internal crossing between accounts within a single institution. The fourth market includes trading in any issues, including both NYSE and NASDAQ listings. Institutional investors engage in these transactions to avoid the market impact of exposure and the commissions paid to intermediaries. Because these trades are not run through an institution with reporting requirements, like a broker-dealer or an exchange, they are invisible to both the regulatory authorities and the market in general. Thus, they present possible problems for both the efficiency and accuracy of the public markets, and for regulatory authorities. Many of the concerns about fourth market trading have also been articulated with respect to PTSs. Although the size of this market cannot be measured accurately, the SEC estimates that it accounts for several million shares a day, and institutional money managers note that this process has been operating for years, despite its logistical difficulties.

The NYSE's major competitor for listings is NASDAQ, which, although it is the second largest market in the U.S., is not an "exchange" registered under section 6 of the Act, but rather is regulated as a "national securities association" under section 15A of the Act. [As of year end 1996, NASDAQ listed over 6300 securities of 5556 companies. NASDAQ's average daily share volume in 1996 was 543 million shares and its total dollar volume for the year was $3.3 trillion] All brokers and dealers must be members of a national securities association, and currently there is only one such organization, the National Association of Securities Dealers (NASD). The

NASD owns and operates NASDAQ, which is an automated interdealer quote system. It has no physical location or trading floor, and instead of offering continuous trading facilitated by a designated floor specialist, the NASDAQ market depends on dealers who act as "market makers" in a particular security. These market makers offer to buy or sell at "firm" prices entered on the NASDAQ system, which is sometimes referred to as a "dealer" market. These prices are then displayed on the screens of terminals located on the desks of other brokers and dealers. For the majority of trading, brokers or dealers wishing to execute a transaction with one of the market makers must pursue the execution through telephone communication. Unlike on the NYSE floor, where there is just one designated specialist making a market in a particular security, any dealer can make a market in a security on NASDAQ provided they follow NASD rules. Thus, for heavily traded issues, there may be more than one dealer making a market and competing for transactions. In contrast, more thinly traded issues may have only one market maker willing to buy or sell. Theoretically, this competition should make the spread smaller on NASDAQ issues, but as the recent NASD antitrust litigation indicates, there is some argument that spreads have not been reduced in proper amounts. Most NASDAQ stocks are subject to real time reporting to the Consolidated Tape (CT). NASDAQ is currently linked to the ITS for listed stocks that are not subject to off-board trading restrictions.

### 3. Proprietary Trading Systems

Proprietary trading systems, also known as "automated trading systems" or "broker dealer trading systems," are screen-based trading systems operated for profit by individual broker-dealers that offer automated execution in various forms and with various additional services. PTSs are used almost exclusively by institutional and other professional investors and are typically neither useful for, nor accessible to individual investors. Generally, PTSs offer customers direct access to contra trading [that is, trading against a party with an opposite interest] without the participation of intermediaries [such as specialists] found in the other organized exchanges.

### The Securities Act of 1933 and the Securities Exchange Act of 1934

The current regulatory framework for the U.S. securities markets is a product of the Securities Act of 1933 and the Securities Exchange Act of 1934 (or "the 1934 Act"). These legislative enactments established the basic regulatory structure and rules, most of which were designed primarily to protect the interests of individual investors. The 1934 Act was part of the congressional reaction to the Great Depression, the beginning of which was blamed on the 1929 stock market crash. The newly formed SEC was given regulatory responsibility for monitoring the various exchanges, which together constituted the "market." In a unique approach, the 1934 Act adopted a two-tiered regulatory structure. In addition to the general regulatory oversight of the SEC, the exchanges were to operate under the supervision of the SROs, which are responsible for the daily operation of the exchanges and promulgate the operating rules for each exchange. The SROs themselves are then subject to oversight by the SEC.

With this two-tiered structure, Congress intended to strike a balance between protection of the integrity of the markets . . . and the flexibility necessary to maintain an economically vigorous capital market. The structure was also intended to balance the need for the participation of the market professionals, achieved through SRO self- regulation, and the need for an independent watchdog, the SEC. To achieve these equilibria, Congress asked the SEC in its original mandate to wear two different hats. Under the first, known as the "sunlight" hat, the SEC was to encourage the disclosure of truthful and complete information by corporations so investors could more accurately assess the value of the security. The second was as a "market regulator," a hat which envisioned the SEC monitoring the structure and functioning of the markets themselves. . . .

The original structure also created a dual role for the SROs. . . . While the SEC asked the SROs to assume significant oversight responsibilities, their members rely on them to protect their turf in a competitive market environment. This latter role may require the SROs to ask for the removal of the very regulatory restraints they are also asked to enforce. The SROs' conflict of interest may encourage them to fashion their rules in a manner that is favorable to their own interests, rather than being responsive to the needs of the national securities markets.

———————

The relationship between SROs and the SEC is the focus of this chapter. As the preceding excerpt suggests, there are certain tensions built into the relationship. For example, how can the SEC ensure that these quasi-public entities serve the public interest and not the interest of their member firms? Analysis of such questions is further complicated by the fact that the theoretical justifications for regulating trading markets (as opposed to customer-broker relations) is not well understood. In a recent release, the SEC offered the following explanation of the regulation of trading markets:

———————

[I]nvestors are more likely to trade on a market when prices are current and reflect the value of securities, when they are confident that they will be able to buy and sell securities easily and inexpensively, and when they believe that they can trade on a market without being defrauded or without other investors having an unfair advantage. The competition for global investment capital among the world's exchanges and the many opportunities available to U.S. and foreign investors make it more important than ever for U.S. exchanges to protect these investor interests in order to attract order flow. Appropriate regulation is often necessary to protect these interests, by helping to ensure fair and orderly markets, to prevent fraud and manipulation, and to promote market coordination and competition for the benefit of all investors.[20]

In the United States, Congress decided that these goals should be achieved primarily through the regulation of exchanges and through authority it granted to the Commission in 1975 to adopt rules that promote (1) economically efficient execution of securities transactions, (2) fair competition, (3) transparency, (4) investor access to the best markets, and (5) the opportunity for investors' orders to be executed without the participation of a dealer. In promulgating the

———————

[20] Experience in both the United States and world markets has repeatedly shown that commercial incentives alone are insufficient to protect investors adequately and ensure fair markets. In adopting the Exchange Act, Congress noted that, however zealously exchange authorities may supervise the business conduct of their members, the interests with which they are connected frequently conflict with the public interest. . . .

Exchange Act, Congress gave the Commission means to achieve these and other goals of regulation,[23] by requiring every market that meets the definition of "exchange" under the Exchange Act to either register as a national securities exchange or be exempted from registration on the basis of limited transaction volume.[24] Congress also gave the exchanges authority to enforce their members' compliance with the goals of the securities laws and, in 1983, required every broker-dealer to become a member of an exchange[25] or securities association.

As SROs, every registered exchange and securities association is required to assist the Commission in assuring fair and honest markets, to have effective mechanisms for enforcing the goals of regulation, and to submit their rules for Commission review. This statutory structure has given the Commission ample authority to oversee securities markets and ensure compliance with the Exchange Act. Although regulation cannot prevent all manipulation, fraud, or collusion, it has proven effective in ridding markets of the most egregious of these practices and consequently in inspiring a high degree of investor confidence.

Concept Release on Regulation of Exchanges, 62 Fed. Reg. 30,485, 30,440 (June 4, 1997). As you read through the following materials consider how well the SEC achieves these regulatory goals in this field. Also consider the extent to which the justifications for the regulation of trading markets are well-founded.

## Section 2.  The Role of Self-Regulatory Organizations

We now go back more than two decades to a Supreme Court decision that chronicles one of the most important changes in the structure of U.S. securities markets in the second half of the Twentieth Century: the demise of fixed commissions. As you read this opinion, consider the roles that the NYSE, the SEC, and Congress played in this process.

---

[23]  Congress also directed the Commission in the 1975 . . . to advance  the concept of equal regulation so that persons enjoying  similar privileges, performing  similar functions, and having similar potential  to affect markets  would be  treated equally. The  Commission was  charged with ensuring  that no member or  class of members had an  unfair advantage  over other members  as a result of a disparity in  regulation not necessary or appropriate  to further  the objectives of  the Exchange Act.

[24]  There  are  currently  eight  registered national securities  exchanges  and one  exempted exchange. AZX (formerly known as Wunsch Auction Systems) was exempted  from  the  registration requirements  of Sections 5 and 6 of  the Exchange Act, based  on  the exchange's  expected limited volume  in  trading  of securities. . . .

[25]  Markets  operated  by  registered  securities associations serve  many of the same  functions as exchanges.  Registered securities associations are regulated under Section  15A of the Exchange  Act, and  are subject to  requirements that are virtually  identical to those applicable to registered exchanges under the Exchange Act.

# Gordon v. New York Stock Exchange
## 422 U.S. 659 (1975)

Mr. Justice BLACKMUN delivered the opinion of the Court.

This case presents the problem of reconciliation of the antitrust laws with a federal regulatory scheme in the particular context of the practice of the securities exchanges and their members of using fixed rates of commission.

In early 1971 petitioner Richard A. Gordon, individually and on behalf of an asserted class of small investors, filed this suit against the New York Stock Exchange, Inc. (NYSE), the American Stock Exchange, Inc. (Amex), and two member firms of the Exchanges. The complaint challenged a variety of exchange rules and practices and, in particular, claimed that the system of fixed commission rates, utilized by the Exchanges at that time for transactions less than $500,000, violated §§1 and 2 of the Sherman Act. Other challenges in the complaint focused on (1) the volume discount on trades of over 1,000 shares, and the presence of negotiated rather than fixed rates for transactions in excess of $500,000; (2) the rules limiting the number of exchange memberships; and (3) the rules denying discounted commission rates to nonmembers using exchange facilities.[3]

Commission rates for transactions on the stock exchanges have been set by agreement since the establishment of the first exchange in this country. The New York Stock Exchange was formed with the Buttonwood Tree Agreement of 1792, and from the beginning minimum fees were set and observed by the members. That Agreement itself stated: "We the Subscribers, Brokers for the Purchase and Sale of Public Stock, do hereby solemnly promise and pledge ourselves to each other, that we will not buy or sell from this day for any person whatsoever, any kind of Public Stock at a less rate than one-quarter per cent. Commission on the Specie value, and that we will give a preference to each other in our Negotiations." F. Eames, The New York Stock Exchange 14 (1968 ed). Successive constitutions of the NYSE have carried forward this basic provision. Similarly, when Amex emerged in 1908--1910, a pattern of fixed commission rates was adopted there.

These fixed rate policies were not unnoticed by responsible congressional bodies. For example, the House Committee on Banking and Currency, in a general review of the stock exchanges undertaken in 1913, reported that the fixed commission rate rules were 'rigidly enforced' in order 'to prevent competition amongst the members.' H.R.Rep. No. 1593, 62d Cong., 3d Sess., 39 (1913). The report, known as the Pujo Report, did not recommend any change in this policy, for the Committee believed

'The present rates to be reasonable, except as to stocks, say, of $25 or less in value, and that the exchange should be protected in this respect by the law under which it shall be incorporated against a kind of competition between members that would lower the service and threaten the

---

[3]     The relief requested included an injunction prohibiting the implementation of certain negotiated commission rates that were to be placed in effect on April 5, 1971, or, alternatively, requiring that negotiated rates be available for transactions of any size. Petitioner also requested treble damages amounting to $1.5 billion and an award of attorneys' fees of $10 million plus interest and costs.

responsibility of members. A very low or competitive commission rate would also promote speculation and destroy the value of membership.'

Id., at 115--116.

Despite the monopoly power of the few exchanges, exhibited not only in the area of commission rates but in a wide variety of other aspects, the exchanges remained essentially self-regulating and without significant supervision until the adoption of the Securities Exchange Act of 1934, as amended. At the lengthy hearings before adoption of that Act, some attention was given to the fixed commission rate practice and to its anticompetitive features.

Perhaps the most pertinent testimony in the hearings preparatory to enactment of the Exchange Act was proferred by Samuel Untermyer, formerly chief counsel to the committee that drafted the Pujo Report. In commenting on proposed [legislation], Mr. Untermyer noted that although the bill would provide the federal supervisory commission with 'The right to prescribe uniform rates of commission, it does not otherwise authorize the Commission to fix rates, which it seems to me it should do and would do by striking out the word 'uniform.' That would permit the Commission to fix rates. 'The volume of the business transacted on the exchange has increased manyfold. Great fortunes have been made by brokers through this monopoly. The public has no access to the exchange by way of membership except by buying a seat and paying a very large sum for it. Therefore it is a monopoly. Probably it has to be something of a monopoly. But after all it is essentially a public institution. It is the greatest financial agency in the world, and should be not only controlled by the public but it seems to me its membership and the commissions charged should either be fixed by some governmental authority or be supervised by such authority. As matters now stand, the exchange can charge all that the traffic will bear, and that is a burden upon commerce.' See Hearings on S.Res. 84 (72d Cong.) and S.Res. 56 and 97 (73d Cong.) before the Senate Committee on Banking and Currency, 73d Cong., 1st and 2d Sess., pts. 13, 15, and 16, pp. 6075, 6080, 6868, and 7705, 7705 (1934) (hereafter Senate Hearings).

As finally enacted, the Exchange Act apparently reflected the Untermyer suggestion, for it gave the SEC the power to fix and insure 'reasonable' rates. Section 19(b) provided:

The Commission is further authorized, if after making appropriate request in writing to a national securities exchange that such exchange effect on its own behalf specified changes in its rules and practices, and after appropriate notice and opportunity for hearing, the Commission determines that such exchange has not made the changes so requested, and that such changes are necessary or appropriate for the protection of investors or to insure fair dealing in securities traded in upon such exchange or to insure fair administration of such exchange, by rules or regulations or by order to alter or supplement the rules of such exchange (insofar as necessary or appropriate to effect such changes) in respect of such matters as . . . (9) the fixing of reasonable rates of commission, interest, listing, and other charges.

This provision conformed to the Act's general policy of self-regulation by the exchanges coupled with oversight by the SEC. . . .

With this legislative history in mind, we turn to the actual post-1934 experience of commission rates on the NYSE and Amex. After these two Exchanges had registered in 1934 under § 6 of the Exchange Act, both proceeded to prescribe minimum commission rates just as they had prior to the Act. These rates were changed periodically by the Exchanges, after their submission to the SEC pursuant to § 6(a)(4) and SEC Rule 17a--8. Although several rate changes appear to have been effectuated without comment by the SEC, in other instances the SEC thoroughly exercised its supervisory powers. Thus, for example, as early as 1958 a study of the NYSE commission rates to determine whether the rates were 'reasonable and in accordance with the standards contemplated by applicable provisions of the Securities Exchange Act of 1934,' was announced by the SEC. SEC Exchange Act Release No. 5678 (Apr. 14, 1958). This study resulted in an agreement by the NYSE to reduce commission rates in certain transactions, to engage in further study of the rate structure by the NYSE in collaboration with the SEC, and to provide the SEC with greater advance notice of proposed rate changes. SEC Exchange Act Release No. 5889 (Feb. 20, 1959). The SEC specifically stated that it had undertaken the study 'in view of the responsibilities and duties imposed upon the Commission by Section 19(b) . . . with respect to the rules of national securities exchanges, including rules relating to the fixing of commission rates.' Ibid.

Under subsection (d) of § 19 of the Act (which subsection was added in 1961), the SEC was directed to investigate the adequacy of exchange rules for the protection of investors. Accordingly, the SEC began a detailed study of exchange rules in that year. In 1963 it released its conclusions in a six-volume study. SEC Report of Special Study of Securities Markets, H.R.Doc. No. 95, 88th Cong., 1st Sess. The study, among other things, focused on problems of the structure of commission rates and procedures, and standards for setting and reviewing rate levels. Id., pt. 5, p. 102. The SEC found that the rigid commission rate structure based on value of the round lot was causing a variety of 'questionable consequences,' such as 'give-ups' and the providing of special services for certain large, usually institutional customers. These attempts indirectly to achieve rate alterations made more difficult the administration of the rate structure and clouded the cost data used as the basis for determination of rates. These effects were believed by the SEC to necessitate a complete study of the structure. Moreover, the SEC concluded that methods for determining the reasonableness of rates were in need of overhaul. Not only was there a need for more complete information about the economics of the securities business and commission rates in particular, but also for a determination and articulation of the criteria important in arriving at a reasonable rate structure. . . .

Meanwhile, the NYSE began an investigation of its own into the particular aspect of volume discounts from the fixed commission rates. This study determined that a volume discount and various other changes were needed, and so recommended to the SEC. The Commission responded in basic agreement. The NYSE study continued over the next few years and final conclusions were presented to the SEC in early 1968. . . .

In 1968, the SEC, while continuing the study started earlier in the decade, began to submit a series of specific proposals for change and to require their implementation by the exchanges. Through its Exchange Act Release No. 8324 (May 28, 1968), the SEC requested the NYSE to revise its commission rate schedule, including a reduction of rates for orders for round lots in excess of 400 shares or, alternatively, the elimination of minimum rate requirements for orders in excess of $50,000. These changes were viewed by the SEC as interim measures, pending further consideration 'in the context of the Commission's responsibilities to consider the national policies embodied both in the securities laws and in the antitrust laws.' In response to these communications, the NYSE (and Amex) eventually adopted a volume discount for orders exceeding 1,000 shares, as well as other alterations in rates, all approved by the SEC.

Members of the securities exchanges faced substantial declines in profits in the late 1960s and early 1970. These were attributed by the NYSE to be due, at least in part, to the fact that general commission rates had not been increased since 1958. The NYSE determined that a service charge of at least the lesser of $15 or 50% of the required minimum commission on orders of fewer than 1,000 shares should be imposed as an interim measure to restore financial health by bringing rates in line with costs. This proposal, submitted to the SEC pursuant to its Rule 17a--8, was permitted by the SEC to be placed into operation on a 90-day interim basis. Continuation of the interim measure was thereafter permitted pending further rate structure hearings undertaken by the SEC. The interim rates remained in effect until the rate structure change of March 1972.

In 1971 the SEC concluded its hearings begun in 1968. Finding that 'minimum commissions on institutional size orders are neither necessary nor appropriate,' the SEC announced that it would not object to competitive rates on portions of orders above a stated level. Although at first supporting a $100,000 order as the cutoff below which fixed rates would be allowed, the SEC later decided to permit use of $500,000 as the breakpoint. After a year's use of this figure, the SEC required the exchanges to reduce the cutoff point to $300,000 in April 1972. Statement of the SEC on the Future Structure of the Securities Markets (Feb. 2, 1972) (Policy Study).

Further reduction followed relatively quickly. By March 29, 1973, the SEC was considering requiring the reduction of the breakpoint on competitive rates to orders in excess of $100,000. In June, the SEC began hearings on the rate schedules, stimulated in part by a request by the NYSE to permit an increase of 15% of the current rate on all orders from $5,000 to $300,000, and to permit a minimum commission on small orders (below $5,000) as well. Three months later, after completion of the hearings, the SEC determined that it would allow the increases. The SEC also announced, however, that '(i)t will act promptly to terminate the fixing of commission rates by stock exchanges after April 30, 1975, if the stock exchanges do not adopt rule changes achieving that result.'

Elaboration of the SEC's rationale for this phasing out of fixed commission rates was soon forthcoming. In December 1973, SEC Chairman Garrett noted that the temporary increase in fixed rates (through April 1975) was permitted because of the inflation in the cost of operating the Exchanges, the decline in the volume of transactions on the exchanges, and the consequently severe financial losses for the members. SEC Exchange Act Release No. 10560 (Dec. 14, 1973). Indeed, without the rate increase, 'the continued deterioration in the capital positions of many member firms was foreseeable, with significant capital impairment and indirect, but consequential, harm to investors the likely result.' Id., at 36. The rate increase also would forestall the possibility that the industry would be impaired during transition to competitive rates and other requirements. . . . Although not purporting to elucidate fully its reasons for abolishing fixed rates, the SEC did suggest several considerations basic to its decision: the heterogeneous nature of the brokerage industry; the desirability of insuring trading on, rather than off, the Exchanges; doubt that small investors are subsidized by large institutional investors under the fixed rate system; and doubt that small firms would be forced out of business if competitive rates were required.

In response to a request by the NYSE, the SEC permitted amendment to allow competitive rates on nonmember orders below $2,000. SEC Exchange Act Release No. 10670 (Mar. 7, 1974). Hearings on intramember commission rates were announced in April 1974. SEC Exchange Act Release No. 10751 (Apr. 23, 1974). The SEC concluded that intramember rates should not be fixed beyond April 30, 1975. SEC Exchange Act Release No. 11019 (Sept. 19, 1974). At this time the SEC stated: '(I)t presently appears to the Commission that it is necessary and appropriate (1) for the protection of investors, (2) to insure fair dealing in securities traded in upon national securities exchanges, and (3) to insure the fair administration of such exchanges, that the rules and practices of such exchanges that require, or have the effect of requiring, exchange members to charge any person fixed minimum rates of commission, should be eliminated.' Id., at 63. The SEC formally requested the exchanges to make the appropriate changes in their rules. When negative responses were received from the NYSE and others, the SEC released for public comment proposed Securities Exchange Act Rules 19b--3 and 10b--22. Proposed Rule 19b--3, applicable to intramember and nonmember rates effective May 1, 1975, would prohibit the exchanges from using or compelling their members to use fixed rates of commission. It also would require the exchanges to provide explicitly in their rules that nothing therein require or permit arrangements or agreements to fix rates. Proposed Rule 10b--22 would prohibit agreements with respect to the fixing of commission rates by brokers, dealers, or members of the exchanges. See SEC Exchange Act Release No. 11073 (Oct. 24, 1974).

Upon the conclusion of hearings on the proposed rules, the SEC determined to adopt Rule 19b--3, but not Rule 10b--22. SEC Exchange Act Release No. 11203 (Jan. 23, 1975). Effective May 1, 1975, competitive rates were to be utilized by exchange members in transactions of all sizes for persons other than members of the exchanges. Effective May 1, 1976, competitive rates were to be mandatory in transactions for members as well, i.e., floor brokerage rates. Competition in floor brokerage rates was so deferred until 1976 in order to permit an orderly transition. The required transition to competitive rates was based on the SEC's conclusion that competition, rather than fixed rates, would be in the best interests of the securities industry and markets, as well as in the best interests of the investing public and the national economy. Ibid. This determination was not based on a simplistic notion in favor of competition, but rather on demonstrated deficiencies of the fixed commission rate structure. Specifically mentioned by the SEC were factors such as the rigidity and delay inherent in the fixed rate system, the potential for distortion, evasion, and conflicts of interest, and fragmentation of markets caused by the fixed rate system. Acknowledging that the fixed rate system perhaps was not all bad in all periods of its use, the SEC explicitly declined to commit itself to permanent abolition of fixed rates in all cases: in the future circumstances might arise that would indicate that reinstitution of fixed rates in certain areas would be appropriate.

The SEC dismissed the arguments against competitive rates that had been raised by various proponents of the status quo. First, the SEC deemed the possibility of destructive competition to be slim, because of the nature of the cost curve in the industry.[10] Second, there was substantial doubt whether maintenance of fixed rates, in fact, provided various subsidies that would be beneficial to the operation of the securities markets. For example, it was unlikely that small investors reaped a subsidy from higher rates charged larger investors, because of separation of the business between large and small investors. Nor did the SEC believe that regional brokers

---

[10]    In order for destructive competition to occur on a large scale, fixed costs must be a high percentage of total costs, and there must be economies of scale in a wide range of production. Neither of these factors was found to be present in the brokerage industry.

were substantially benefited by maintenance of fixed rates. Third, the possibility of an exodus from membership on the exchanges was unlikely, and should be dealt with only as it occurred. In any event, inasmuch as the SEC anticipated that there would be detailed studies of the operation of the competitive rates effectuated by its orders, any problems that arose could be effectively resolved upon further consideration.

During this period of concentrated study and action by the SEC, lasting more than a decade, various congressional committees undertook their own consideration of the matter of commission rates. Early in 1972, the Senate Subcommittee on Securities concluded that fixed commission rates must be eliminated on institution-size transactions, and that lower fees should be permitted for small transactions with 'unbundled' services than for those having the full range of brokerage services. Senate Committee on Banking, Housing and Urban Affairs, 92d Cong., 2d Sess., Securities Industry Study (For the Period Ended Feb. 4, 1972), 4 (1972) (containing a report of the Subcommittee on Securities). The Subcommittee objected particularly to the failure of the fixed rate system to produce 'fair and economic' rates, id., at 59, and to distortion in the rate structure in favor of the institutionally oriented firms.

The Subcommittee was perturbed at the SEC's actions regarding fixed commission rates for several reasons. . . . [T]he Subcommittee report stressed:

(I)t is essential that fixed commission rates be phased out in an orderly and systematic manner, and that a date certain be set promptly for elimination of fixed commissions on institutional-size transactions, which have resulted in the most serious distortions. Based on the SEC's conclusions and on testimony submitted to the SEC and to this Subcommittee, this could best be achieved by eliminating fixed rates on orders in excess of $100,000.

Securities Industry Study, supra, at 60.

The House Committee on Interstate and Foreign Commerce, in a report issued only six months after the Senate Report, supra, concluded that fixed rates of commission were not in the public interest and should be replaced by competitively determined rates for transactions of all sizes. Such action should occur 'without excessive delay.' H.R.Rep. No. 92--1519, pp. xiv, 141, 144--145, 146 (1972). Although prodding the SEC to take quick measures to introduce competitive rates for transactions of all sizes, the House Committee determined to defer enacting legislation so long as reasonable progress was being made. These conclusions resulted from a detailed study, by the Subcommittee, of asserted costs and benefits of competitive versus fixed rates, and reflected information gained through lengthy hearings. Id., at 131-- 146, and related Study of the Securities Industry, Hearings before the Subcommittee on Commerce and Finance of the House Committee on Interstate and Foreign Commerce, 92d Cong., 1st and 2d Sess., serials 92--37 to 92--37h (1971--1972). Similarly, after lengthy analysis, the Senate Subcommittee on Securities concluded both that competitive rates must be introduced at all transaction levels, and that legislation was not required at that time in view of the progress made by the SEC. Securities Industry Study Report of the Subcommittee on Securities of the Senate Committee on Banking, Housing and Urban Affairs, S.Doc. No. 93--13, pp. 5--7, 43--63 (1973), and Hearings on S. 3169 before the Subcommittee on Securities of the Senate Committee on Banking, Housing and Urban Affairs, 92d Cong., 2d Sess. (1972).

In 1975 both Houses of Congress did in fact enact legislation dealing directly with commission rates. . . .

The new legislation amends § 19(b) of the Securities Exchange Act to substitute for the heretofore existing provision a scheme for SEC review of proposed rules and rule changes of the various self-regulatory organizations. Reference to commission rates is now found in the newly amended § 6(e), generally providing that after the date of enactment 'no national securities exchange may impose any schedule or fix rates of commissions, allowances, discounts, or other fees to be charged by its members.' An exception is made for floor brokerage rates which may be fixed by the exchanges until May 1, 1976. Further exceptions from the ban against fixed commissions are provided if approved by the SEC after certain findings: prior to and including November 1, 1976, the Commission may allow the exchanges to fix commissions if it finds this to be 'in the public interest,' § 6(e)(1)(A); after November 1, 1976, the exchanges may be permitted by the SEC to fix rates of commission if the SEC finds (1) the rates are reasonable in relation to costs of service (to be determined pursuant to standards of reasonableness published by the SEC), and (2) if the rates 'do not impose any burden on competition not necessary or appropriate in furtherance of the purposes of this title, taking into consideration the competitive effects of permitting such schedule or fixed rates weighed against the competitive effects of other lawful actions which the Commission is authorized to take under this title.' § 6(e)(1) (B)(ii). The statute specifically provides that even if the SEC does permit the fixing of rates pursuant to one of these exceptions, the SEC by rule may abrogate such practice if it finds that the fixed rates 'are no longer reasonable, in the public interest, or necessary to accomplish the purposes of this title.' § 6(e)(2).

As of May 1, 1975, pursuant to order of the SEC, fixed commission rates were eliminated and competitive rates effectuated. Although it is still too soon to determine the total effect of this alteration, there have been no reports of disastrous effects for the public, investors, the industry, or the markets.

This lengthy history can be summarized briefly: In enacting the Securities Exchange Act of 1934, the Congress gave clear authority to the SEC to supervise exchange self-regulation with respect to the 'fixing of reasonable rates of commission.' Upon SEC determination that exchange rules or practices regarding commission rates required change in order to protect investors or to insure fair dealing, the SEC was authorized to require adoption of such changes as were deemed necessary or appropriate. . . . Since the Exchange Act's adoption, and primarily in the last 15 years, the SEC has been engaged in thorough review of exchange commission rate practices. The committees of the Congress, while recently expressing some dissatisfaction with the progress of the SEC in implementing competitive rates, have generally been content to allow the SEC to proceed without new legislation. As of May 1, 1975, the SEC, by order, has abolished fixed rates. And new legislation, enacted into law June 5, 1975, codifies this result, although still permitting the SEC some discretion to reimpose fixed rates if warranted. . . .

This Court has considered the issue of implied repeal of the antitrust laws in the context of a variety of regulatory schemes and procedures. Certain axioms of construction are now clearly established. Repeal of the antitrust laws by implication is not favored and not casually to be allowed. Only where there is a 'plain repugnancy between the antitrust and regulatory provisions' will repeal be implied. United States v. Philadelphia National Bank, 374 U.S. 321, 350-51 (1963).

The starting point for our consideration of the particular issue presented by this case, viz., whether the antitrust laws are impliedly repealed or replaced as a result of the statutory provisions and administrative and congressional experience concerning fixed commission rates, of course, is our decision in Silver v. New York Stock Exchange, 373 U.S. 341 (1963). There the Court considered the relationship between the antitrust laws and the Securities Exchange Act, and did so specifically with respect to the action of an exchange in ordering its members to remove private direct telephone connections with the offices of nonmembers. Such action, absent any immunity derived from the regulatory laws, would be a per se violation of s 1 of the Sherman Act. 373 U.S., at 347, 83 S.Ct. at 1251. Concluding that the proper approach to the problem was to reconcile the operation of the antitrust laws with a regulatory scheme, the Court established a 'guiding principle' for the achievement of this reconciliation. Under this principle, '(r)epeal is to be regarded as implied only if necessary to make the Securities Exchange Act work, and even then only to the minimum extent necessary.' Id., at 357, 83 S.Ct. at 1257.

In Silver, the Court concluded that there was no implied repeal of the antitrust laws in that factual context because the Exchange Act did not provide for SEC jurisdiction or review of particular applications of rules enacted by the exchanges. It noted: 'Although the Act gives to the Securities and Exchange Commission the power to request exchanges to make changes in their rules, § 19(b), and impliedly, therefore, to disapprove any rules adopted by an exchange, see also § 6(a)(4), it does not give the Commission jurisdiction to review particular instances of enforcement of exchange rules.' Ibid. At the time Silver was decided, both the rules and constitution of the NYSE provided that the Exchange could require discontinuance of wire service between the office of a member and a nonmember at any time. There was no provision for notice or statement of reasons. While these rules were permissible under the general power of the exchanges to adopt rules regulating relationships between members and nonmembers, and the SEC could disapprove the rules, the SEC could not forbid or regulate any particular application of the rules. Hence, the regulatory agency could not prevent application of the rules that would have undesirable anticompetitive effects; there was no governmental oversight of the exchange's self-regulatory action, and no method of insuring that some attention at least was given to the public interest in competition.

The Court, therefore, concluded that the absence in Silver of regulatory supervision over the application of the exchange rules prevented any conflict arising between the regulatory scheme and the antitrust laws. . . . The Court in Silver cautioned, however, that '(s)hould review of exchange self-regulation be provided through a vehicle other than the antitrust laws, a different case as to antitrust exemption would be presented.' 373 U.S., at 360, 83 S.Ct. at 1258. It amplified this statement in a footnote: 'Were there Commission jurisdiction and ensuing judicial review for scrutiny of a particular exchange ruling . . . a different case would arise concerning exemption from the operation of laws designed to prevent anticompetitive activity, an issue we do not decide today.' Id., at 358, n. 12, 83 S.Ct. at 1257.

It is patent that the case presently at bar is, indeed, that 'different case' to which the Court in Silver referred. In contrast to the circumstances of Silver, § 19(b) gave the SEC direct regulatory power over exchange rules and practices with respect to 'the fixing of reasonable rates of commission.' Not only was the SEC authorized to disapprove rules and practices concerning commission rates, but the agency also was permitted to require alteration or supplementation of the rules and practices when 'necessary or appropriate for the protection of investors or to insure fair dealings in securities traded in upon such exchange.' Since 1934 all rate changes have been brought to the attention of the SEC, and it has taken an active role in review of proposed rate changes during the last 15 years. Thus, rather than presenting a case of SEC impotence to affect application of exchange rules in particular circumstances, this case involves explicit statutory authorization for SEC review of all exchange rules and practices dealing with rates of commission and resultant SEC continuing activity.

Having determined that this case is, in fact, the 'different case,' we must then make inquiry as to the proper reconciliation of the regulatory and antitrust statutes involved here, keeping in mind the principle that repeal of the antitrust laws will be 'implied only if necessary to make the Securities Exchange Act work, and even then only to the minimum extent necessary.' 373 U.S., at 357, 83 S.Ct., at 1257. We hold that these requirements for implied repeal are clearly satisfied here. To permit operation of the antitrust laws with respect to commission rates, as urged by petitioner Gordon and the United States as amicus curiae, would unduly interfere, in our view, with the operation of the Securities Exchange Act. . . . .

[T]he statutory provision authorizing regulation, § 19(b)(9), the long regulatory practice, and the continued congressional approval illustrated by the new legislation, point to one, and only one, conclusion. The Securities Exchange Act was intended by the Congress to leave the supervision of the fixing of reasonable rates of commission to the SEC. Interposition of the antitrust laws, which would bar fixed commission rates as per se violations of the Sherman Act, in the face of positive SEC action, would preclude and prevent the operation of the Exchange Act as intended by Congress and as effecutated through SEC regulatory activity. Implied repeal of the antitrust laws is, in fact, necessary to make the Exchange Act work as it was intended; failure to imply repeal would render nugatory the legislative provision for regulatory agency supervision of exchange commission rates.

## Comments and Questions

1.  Who won the *Gordon* case?

2.  How does the application of anti-trust rules in this area compare with what we have seen elsewhere in the financial services industry?    In particular, how does it compare to the federal regulation of competitive practices in the insurance industry?

3.  Given our legal system's general aversion to price fixing conspiracies, why did it take so long for the era of NYSE fixed commissions to end?  A close reading of the *Gordon* case reveals several plausible justifications for restricting price competition among exchange members?  What were those justifications?  Are they plausible? Could such arguments ever offer a credible basis for restraining competition in capital markets? If so, under what circumstances?

———

As the *Gordon* case illustrates, 1975 marked the end of fixed commissions on the New York Stock Exchange.  Something of a revolution in the securities industry then ensued. A new breed of discount brokerage houses emerged, which, as we will discuss in Chapter 15, opened the door for depository institutions to enter the securities business.  The controversy over fixed commissions also increased public attention over the SEC's role as regulator of trading markets. The following excerpt, which is also from Polly Nyquist, *Failure to Engage: The Regulation of Proprietary Trading Systems*, 13 YALE L. & POL'Y REV. 281 (1995), explores some of the ways in which the 1975 Amendments changed the structure of our trading markets.

### The 1975 Amendments to the Securities Exchange Act

[Along with the controversy over fixed commissions on the NYSE, a] "back room" crisis in the 1960s, caused by the paper-driven market's inability to deal with an increasing trade volume, led to the enactment of the 1975 Amendments to the Securities Exchange Act, the first major structural reform effort since 1934. The primary focus of the 1975 Amendments was adoption of section 11A of the 1934 Act, which gave the SEC the mandate to establish a "National Market System" (NMS). This term was not defined, as Congress wanted to give the SEC and market forces the ability to create the best system. However, Congress outlined the goals it had for this system: (1) create a level playing field for competition among various market participants; (2) increase the dissemination of price quotes; (3) increase the efficiency of the market; and (4) ensure "best execution."

The debate over the meaning of the congressional mandate with respect to the development of the NMS illustrates the underlying theoretical tension in the regulation of the securities markets. As with the original drafting of the securities regulation laws, the current debate vacillates between the desire for centralized trading, which enhances price discovery, liquidity, and best execution, and the desire for competition among the markets that will improve the entire system through the "survival of the fittest." With the 1975 Amendments, Congress and the SEC, in its rule-making activities, seem to have sought both to encourage centralization through greater transparency and to encourage intermarket competition. The NMS legislation did not resolve this tension and thus leaves the SEC with an unclear mandate as to how to deal with an issue such as the regulation of PTSs which implicates both goals.

The SEC and the markets have undertaken several projects designed to implement the 1975 Amendments. The first, and perhaps the most successful to date, was the establishment of the Consolidated Tape for real-time reporting of trading in "eligible" securities, and the Consolidated Quotation System (CQS), which collects firm quotes from the various exchanges and OTC dealers. The second major project, the Intermarket Trading System (ITS), electronically links eight national exchanges and the NASD. The ITS provides brokers on the floor of any participating exchange with a means of executing a trade in any of the other markets, thus allowing the broker or specialist to execute their transaction at the best displayed price. The ITS also allows all participants to enter pre-opening interest in securities that will be executed when the market opens. The participants in the ITS have developed a set of uniform trading rules in order to enhance the effectiveness of the system in actually linking the markets.

### The Current System: Changes Since 1975

The U.S. securities markets have seen several dramatic changes since the enactment of the 1975 Amendments, which may question the continuing viability of these reforms. The purpose of the SEC's "Market 2000" study, announced in 1992 and released in January 1994, was to analyze these market changes and determine what, if any, regulatory response was needed.

### 1. Changes in Volume

The first important change is the increase in the total volume and dollar amount of equity securities traded in the United States. In 1975, the total market value of U.S. equities was $85 billion. By 1992, the total market value reached $5 trillion. More individuals participate in the markets today than ever before, either as individual investors or as members of the increasingly large and popular mutual funds and pension plans. More businesses are turning to the markets for their capital needs. Technological advances have allowed the markets and the market professionals to handle the increasing demand for access to the markets. Arguably, this huge growth means that the SEC, now more than ever, needs to take an active role to protect the increasing percentage of U.S. savings that are at risk in the markets.

### 2. Changes in Investors

One of the most important changes is the so-called "institutionalization" of the ownership of equity securities in the U.S. In 1975, institutional investors owned 30% of U.S. equity securities, but by 1992, they owned slightly over 50% of the market. Thus, individual investors now account for less than 50% of the market. A 1990 survey by the NYSE indicated that 51 million individuals in the U.S., or about 21% of the population, own corporate stock. This is compared to the approximately 25 million individuals that owned equity issues in 1975. Individuals do not trade directly on the markets or with each other. Rather, individual investors trade through a professional intermediary, such as a broker-dealer. . . .

Institutional investors are professional money managers or financial institutions who execute large numbers of transactions and manage large sums of money. The largest of these are the private pension plans, which in 1992 owned about 20% of U.S. equities, an increase from the less than 13% the pension funds owned in 1975. The second largest are the mutual funds, whose market share has more than doubled since 1975, jumping from 4% to 9.1% in 1992. Other types of institutional investors are hedge funds (typically involving less than 100 individual investors), insurance companies, and public pension funds. . . .

### 3. Changes in the Markets

The markets themselves have also been changing in response to the changing demands of the investors. The most striking changes are the shift in the distribution of volume between the various exchanges and the increased use of technology by both existing and emerging markets. Although the NYSE is and always has been the largest of the equity markets, it is currently losing market share to the regionals, NASDAQ, and other markets. This shift is due in part to the activities of the institutional investors who like to route their block trades through the regionals, where the specialists are less likely to interfere with the crosses or force them to be exposed to the limit order book. For the same reason, the PTSs often favor the regionals for execution of their trades, which are often matched within the system before transfer to the floor. The potential for increased market fragmentation that results has been met with concern by both academics and the regulators.

As the dominance of the NYSE has been challenged by other markets, the NYSE has moved to preserve itself in several ways. First, it has vigorously defended its remaining anti-competitive rules, such as restrictions on member off-board trading activity. Second, the NYSE has made several adaptations to match the services offered by its competitor markets. These efforts include development of the "upstairs" or "off-board" market where institutional investors can negotiate large block trades without exposing them to the market, and the addition of two after-hours crossing sessions to stem the flow of after-hours transactions to the international markets or PTSs.

Perhaps the NYSE's most fundamental change has been the partial automation of its functions through the addition of its Designated Order Turnaround (DOT) system that offers members the ability to execute or route orders to the specialist posts without the time-consuming process of using slips of paper carried by their floor brokers. The DOT experienced a significant operational failure during the 1987 Market Break, after which members were asked to curtail use of the system for program trading. Since that time, the NYSE has enhanced and strengthened it.

Like the NYSE, the regional markets have also modernized their services by developing automated routing and execution systems for smaller orders. One regional, the CSE, has eliminated its trading floor entirely and replaced it with an entirely computerized automated system, which makes it strikingly similar to the proprietary trading systems. NASDAQ has also tried to increase efficiency through the introduction of computerization with its SelectNet program. By using NASDAQ's SelectNet, users can avoid time consuming telephone conversations, and can enter buy or sell orders for execution directly into their computer terminals. SelectNet, however, is available only to dealers, a fact that annoys some institutional investors.

The rising popularity of PTSs is dramatic evidence of the invasion of computer technology. Although these systems currently account for a relatively small percentage of the total markets, 1.4% of NYSE and 13% of NASDAQ/NMS trading volume in 1993, their recent explosive growth, and their future potential, make them a real issue for both market users and regulators. In 1991, 2.9 billion shares traded though PTSs, but in only the first six months of 1993, that number had jumped to 4.7 billion shares. A vast majority of that trading, 87%, is in NASDAQ-listed issues where use of PTSs avoids paying dealer spreads and may allow users to take advantage of the interquote prices currently unavailable on NASDAQ. [Institutional i]nvestor participation in PTSs is particularly high, with TIAA-CREF, for example, recently reporting that it routes almost 75% of its orders through these systems. Institutional investors are drawn to these systems because they offer both anonymity and lower commission costs without the technical hassle of fourth market trading. They are particularly attractive to passive investors, such as funds managed by indexing, who do not need the continuous trading offered by the traditional exchanges. Investors trading in NASDAQ stocks may also be able to use the systems to avoid paying the dealer spreads. [In subsequent analysis, the SEC has estimated that alternative trading systems in 1997 accounted for roughly 20 percent of orders for NASDAQ securities and almost 4 percent of NYSE orders.]

## Comments and Questions

1. As this Nyquist excerpt indicates, one of the principal developments in our trading markets over the past twenty years has been the emergence of new trading systems. The NYSE is no longer the dominant force it once was, and the 1975 Amendments' goal of increasing competition across markets has been realized, at least in part. Questions remain, however, over whether the fragmentation of markets is necessarily a good thing. Some of the new markets — such as the proprietary trading systems — are only available to large institutional investors. Retail investors cannot currently gain access to these markets. Should the SEC be concerned with this trend? Is it consistent with the SEC's over-arching goal of protecting investors? Are there other costs associated with market fragmentation?

2. A related issue concerns the manner in which we regulate new trading markets. The SEC does not consider proprietary trading systems to be "exchanges" for purposes of the 1934 Act, and thus subjects them to a substantially less burdensome regulatory structure as compared to that imposed on the New York Stock Exchange and other traditional markets. Should all trading markets be regulated in the same way? Or, does the limited function of proprietary trading systems warrant more lenient supervision? For an introduction to these and related issues of market regulation, see Market 2000: U.S. Equity Market Structure, Exchange Act Release 30,920, 57 Fed. Reg. 32, 587 (July 22, 1992). See also Board of Trade v. SEC, 923 F.2d 1270 (7th Cir. 1991) (considering whether a system for trading options on government securities should be considered an exchange under the 1934 Act).

### Problem 11-1

The SEC recently issued a concept release exploring several policy implications of the rising of alternative trading systems. See Concept Release on Regulation of Exchanges, 62 Fed. Reg. 30485 (June 4, 1997). How should the securities industry respond to this initiative?

The questions raised by technological developments in the U.S. markets could be addressed in a variety of ways. As an initial matter, the Commission is soliciting comment on whether the current statutory and regulatory framework remains appropriate in light of the myriad new means of trading securities made possible by emerging and evolving technologies. The Commission is also soliciting comment on alternative ways of addressing these issues within the existing securities law framework. The release discusses two alternatives in particular that would integrate alternative trading systems more fully into mechanisms that promote market-wide transparency, investor protection, and fairness.

First, the Commission could continue to regulate alternative trading systems as broker-dealers and develop rules applicable to these systems, and their supervising SROs that would more actively integrate these systems into NMS mechanisms. The Commission could, for example, require alternative trading systems to provide additional audit trail information to SROs, to assist SROs in their surveillance functions, and to adopt standard procedures for ensuring adequate system capacity and the integrity of their system operations. The

Commission could then require SROs to integrate trading on alternative trading systems into their ongoing, real-time surveillance for market manipulation and fraud, and to develop surveillance and examination procedures specifically targeted to alternative trading systems they supervise.  In addition, the Commission could require alternative trading systems to make all orders in their systems available to their supervising SROs, and require such SROs to incorporate those orders into the public quotation system.  The Commission could also require that alternative trading systems provide the public with access to these orders on a substantially equivalent basis as provided to system participants.

Alternatively, the Commission could integrate alternative trading systems into the national market system as securities exchanges, by adopting a tiered approach to exchange regulation.  The first tier, under this type of approach, could consist of the majority of alternative trading systems, those that have limited volume or do not establish trading prices, which could be exempt from traditional exchange requirements.  For example, exempt exchanges could be required to file an application and system description with the Commission, report trades, maintain an audit trail, develop systems capacity and other operational standards, and cooperate with SROs that inspect their regulated participants.  Most alternative trading systems currently regulated as broker-dealers would be exempt exchanges.

The second tier of exchanges under this approach could consist of alternative trading systems that resemble traditional exchanges because of their significant volume of trading and active price discovery.  These systems could be regulated as national securities exchanges.  The Commission could then use its exemptive authority to eliminate barriers that would make it difficult for these non-traditional markets to register as exchanges, by exempting such systems from any exchange registration requirements that are not appropriate or necessary in light of their business structure or other characteristics.  For example, the Commission could exempt alternative trading systems that register as exchanges from requirements that exchanges have a traditional membership structure, and from requirements that limit exchange participation to registered broker-dealers.  The Commission could also use its exemptive authority to reduce or eliminate those exchange requirements that are incompatible with the operation of for-profit, non-membership alternative trading systems.

This approach could integrate these alternative trading systems more fully into NMS mechanisms and the plans governing those systems, potentially by requiring these systems to become members of those plans.  Because alternative trading systems differ in several key respects from currently registered exchanges, this could require revision of those plans in order to accommodate diverse and evolving trading systems.

Finally, a third tier of exchanges, consisting of traditional membership exchanges, could continue to be regulated as national securities exchanges.  The Commission could then use its exemptive authority to reduce overall exchange requirements.  In this regard, the Commission is considering ways to reduce unnecessary regulatory requirements that make it difficult for currently registered exchanges to remain competitive in a changing business environment.  The Commission, for example, could further accelerate rule filing and approval procedures for national securities exchanges and securities associations, and allow fully automated exchanges to meet their regulatory requirements in non-traditional ways.

One way for the Commission to implement this tiered approach would be to expand its interpretation of the definition of "exchange." For example, the Commission could reinterpret the term "exchange" to include any organization that both: (1) consolidates orders of multiple parties; and (2) provides a facility through which, or sets material conditions under which, participants entering such orders may agree to the terms of a trade.

---

In the mid-1990s, concern over anti-competitive practices in the securities industry arose again — this time in the over-the-counter markets — when a widely publicized academic study suggested that NASDAQ market makers might be colluding to maintain artificially wide spreads on NASDAQ stocks. See William G. Christie & Paul H. Schultz, *Why Do NASDAQ Market Makers Avoid Odd-Eight Quotes?*, 49 J. FIN. 1813 (1994). Investigations by the SEC and the Justice Department ensued, as did an internal study by the NASD. Two years later, the inquiries culminated in the following SEC release:

## In re National Association of Securities Dealers, Inc.
### Exchange Act Release No. 37,538 (Aug. 8, 1996)

The Securities and Exchange Commission ("Commission") deems it appropriate and in the public interest that public proceedings be instituted pursuant to Section 19(h) of the Securities Exchange Act of 1934 ("Exchange Act") against the National Association of Securities Dealers, Inc. ("the NASD"). In anticipation of this proceeding, the NASD has submitted an Offer of Settlement which the Commission has determined to accept. [T]he NASD, by its Offer of Settlement, without admitting or denying the Commission's findings, consents to the entry of this Order Instituting Public Proceedings, Making Findings and Imposing Remedial Sanctions.[1]

### A. RESPONDENT

The NASD is a Delaware nonstock corporation which is and at all relevant times was registered with the Commission as a national securities association pursuant to Section 15A(b) of the Exchange Act. At all relevant times, the NASD operated the Nasdaq Stock Market, Inc. ("the Nasdaq market"), an over-the-counter securities market featuring the electronic display of dealer price quotations. In January 1996, the NASD incorporated NASD Regulation, Inc. ("NASDR") as a wholly owned subsidiary to be delegated day-to-day responsibility for the self-regulatory operations of the NASD.

### B. MISCONDUCT IN THE NASDAQ STOCK MARKET

The Nasdaq market has not always operated in an open and freely competitive manner. Nasdaq market makers have engaged in conduct which has resulted in artificially inflexible

---

[1]    Simultaneously with the issuance of this Order the Commission released a Report Pursuant to Section 21(a) of the Securities Exchange Act of 1934 the NASD and the Nasdaq Market (the "Report"). The findings made herein are solely for the purpose of this proceeding and are not binding on any other person or entity named as a respondent or defendant in any other proceeding. . . .

spreads between dealer price quotations for many Nasdaq securities and unduly disadvantageous prices to investors trading in those securities. A number of Nasdaq market makers have also taken action to discourage competition. At the same time, various Nasdaq market makers have coordinated price quotations, transactions and transaction reports in order to protect or advance their proprietary interests, to the detriment of investors and other market participants. Many Nasdaq market makers have also failed to satisfy their basic obligations to transact at quoted prices and to report transactions in a timely and accurate manner. These activities involved potentially serious violations of NASD rules and the federal securities laws.

## C.  THE NASD'S PERFORMANCE AS A SELF-REGULATORY ORGANIZATION

The Exchange Act requires the NASD, as a self-regulatory organization, to comply with, and vigorously enforce, in an evenhanded and impartial manner, the provisions of the Exchange Act, the rules and regulations thereunder and its own rules, in carrying out its role as the entity responsible for the day-to-day oversight of its members and the Nasdaq market. The NASD has an affirmative obligation to be vigilant in surveilling for, evaluating, and effectively addressing issues that could involve violations of such provisions.

The NASD, during the period covered in the Report, did not comply with certain of its rules or satisfy its obligations under the Exchange Act to enforce its rules and the federal securities laws. It has inadequately enforced rules applicable to market makers while applying, in certain cases, ad hoc standards and criteria not embodied in NASD rules. This is attributable, in part, to the undue influence of Nasdaq market makers in the regulatory processes of the NASD. As a result of these regulatory failures, the NASD has violated [its Exchange Act] duties. . . .

### 1.  THE NASD'S INADEQUATE RESPONSE TO MISCONDUCT IN NASDAQ

By 1990, the NASD was aware of information suggesting that its members were engaged in misconduct which had potential anticompetitive implications and could be detrimental to the interests of investors. This information included: (a) facts and circumstances evidencing a convention among dealers that resulted in many stocks being quoted almost invariably in even-eighths; (b) evidence of spreads and dealer quotations being artificially inflexible with market makers having little incentive to narrow them; and (c) facts indicating that some market makers retaliated against other market makers who attempted to improve upon quotations otherwise prevailing in the market. The NASD failed to take appropriate action to thoroughly investigate these problems and take effective regulatory action. In particular, the NASD did not utilize the NASD's surveillance and enforcement resources to inquire into the conduct of market makers to ascertain whether violations of the NASD's rules or the federal securities laws had occurred and whether disciplinary action against market makers for such conduct was warranted.

### 2.  FAILURE TO ENFORCE FIRM QUOTE RULE

Market makers on Nasdaq have the obligation to trade at their quotations.[3] Many market makers, however, have repeatedly failed to honor their quotations even though no exception was available. The NASD is required to enforce the market makers' obligation to trade at their

---

[3]    The firm quote rule is Exchange Act Rule 11Ac1-1, and similar requirements are found in the NASD's rules. NASD Manual, Article III, Rules of Fair Practice, § 6, and NASD Bylaws, Schedule D, Part V, § 2(b) and Part VI, § 2. These rules require that market makers trade up to the amount of their quotations at whatever prices they have posted. Market makers are excepted from this duty only if (1) they change a quotation before receiving an order, or (2) they are in the process of executing a transaction when they receive an order, and send a new quotation to the Nasdaq immediately upon executing that transaction.

quotations, but has failed to adequately enforce compliance by market makers with this obligation.

### 3.  FAILURE TO ENFORCE TRADE REPORTING RULE

Market makers on Nasdaq have the obligation to report transactions on a timely and accurate basis.[4] Many market makers, however, have repeatedly failed to report transactions on a timely and accurate basis.  The NASD is required to enforce the market makers' obligation to report transactions on a timely and accurate basis, but has failed to adequately enforce compliance by market makers with this obligation.

### 4.  FAILURE TO COMPLY WITH RULES RELATING TO NASD MEMBERSHIP

The NASD processed the applications for membership of certain firms in a manner inconsistent with its rules.  It required such applicants to satisfy criteria not enumerated in the rules, failed to process their applications within a reasonable time, placed improper restrictions on their activities as a condition to membership and prevented such members, once admitted, from seeking modifications to their restriction agreements as permitted by the NASD rules.[5]

### D.  CONCLUSION

Based upon the foregoing, the Commission finds that during the relevant period the NASD has failed to comply with certain NASD rules and, without reasonable justification or excuse, failed to enforce compliance with the Exchange Act, the rules and regulations thereunder and its own rules, in violation of Section 19(g) of the Exchange Act.

The NASD has represented that in conjunction with the undertakings set forth below and other remedial measures it has taken and will take, the Board of Governors of the NASD and the Board of Directors of NASDR have authorized $25 million and have committed to expend an additional $75 million over the next five years, to enhance its systems for market surveillance, including the development and implementation of an enhanced audit trail, and to increase its staffing in the areas of examination, surveillance, enforcement, and internal audit.

In recognition of this commitment, the Commission has determined not to seek a monetary penalty from the NASD.

### ORDER

A.  The NASD be, and hereby is, censured.

---

[4]    Pursuant to Rules 11Aa3-1 and 11Aa3-2 under the Exchange Act of 1934, the NASD adopted a transaction reporting plan for National Market System securities in 1982.  Securities Exchange Act Release No. 18590 (March 31, 1982), 47 Fed. Reg. 13617.  As part of this plan, transactions in designated Nasdaq securities must be reported within 90 seconds after execution.  NASD Manual, Schedule D to the By-Laws, Part X, § 2(a), (1995).

[5]    The rules relating to membership applications are set forth in the NASD By-Laws.  NASD Manual, Schedule C to the By-Laws, Part I.  This Order makes no findings as to the NASD's processing or final determination of any specific membership application.

B. The NASD shall comply with the following undertakings within the next twelve months (or within such other time period as is otherwise noted below):

1. To implement and maintain at least fifty percent independent public and non-industry membership in its Board of Governors, the Board(s) of Governors or Directors of all of its subsidiaries and affiliates that exercise or have delegated self-regulatory functions, and the following: the National Nominating Committee, the Trading/Quality of Markets Committee, the Arbitration Committee, the Market Surveillance Committee, the National Business Conduct Committee, the Management Compensation Committee, and all successors thereto.

2. To provide that NASDR and any successor thereto has, consistent with the NASD's By-Laws and Plan of Delegation, as amended from time to time and as approved by the Commission, primary day-to-day responsibility for the regulation, surveillance, examination and disciplining of NASD member firms and registered persons, with respect to market activities as well as other self-regulatory matters, with full access to the records of the Nasdaq market.

3. To institute the participation of professional hearing officers (who shall be attorneys with appropriate experience and training) to preside over disciplinary proceedings.

4. To provide for the autonomy and independence of the regulatory staff of the NASD and its subsidiaries such that the staff, subject only to the supervision of the Board of Governors of the NASD and the Boards of Directors of NASDR and Nasdaq, and any successor thereto, (a) has sole discretion as to what matters to investigate and prosecute, (b) has sole discretion to handle regulatory matters such as approval of applications for membership and the conditions and limitations that may be placed thereon, (c) prepares rule proposals, rule interpretations and other policy matters with any consultations with interested NASD constituencies made in a fair and evenhanded manner, and (d) is generally insulated from the commercial interests of its members and the Nasdaq market. Among other things, the District Business Conduct Committees and the Market Surveillance Committee shall not have any involvement in deciding whether or not to institute disciplinary proceedings, nor shall the District Committees, or any subcommittee thereof, have any involvement in the review or approval of applications for membership in the NASD. Subject to the foregoing, the regulatory staff of the NASDR engaged in the disciplinary process may, solely on their own initiative, inform themselves on matters of market or other securities industry expertise by consulting with representatives of member firms or committees of the NASD or its subsidiaries.

5. To promulgate and apply on a consistent basis uniform standards for regulatory and other access issues, such as admission to the NASD as a member firm, and conditions to becoming a market maker; and institute safeguards to ensure fair and evenhanded access to all services and facilities of the NASD.

6. To ensure the existence of a substantial, independent internal audit staff which reviews all aspects of the NASD (including the regulatory function, the disciplinary process and the Nasdaq stock market and its systems) and reports directly to an audit committee of the NASD Board of Governors which includes a majority of public and non-industry Governors and is chaired by a public Governor.

7. To design and implement within the next twenty-four months (or as specified by further order of the Commission) an audit trail sufficient to enable the NASD to reconstruct markets

promptly, effectively surveil them and enforce its rules; which audit trail shall, subject to the Commission's approval, at a minimum, (a) provide an accurate time-sequenced record of orders and transactions, beginning with the receipt of an order at the first point of contact between the broker-dealer and the customer or counterparty and further documenting the life of the order through the process of execution (or partial or non-execution) of that order, and (b) provide for Nasdaq marketwide synchronization of clocks utilized in connection with the audit trail.

8. To improve substantially the surveillance and examination of order handling.

9. To improve substantially the reliability of the reporting through, among other things, enhancement of surveillance, examination, and enforcement.

10. To upgrade substantially the NASD's capability to enforce the firm quote rule, by (a) implementing a process for backing away complaints to be addressed as they are made during the trading day so that valid complaints may be satisfied with a contemporaneous trade execution; and (b) taking other appropriate actions.

11. To propose a rule or rule interpretation for Commission approval which expressly makes unlawful the coordination by or among market makers of their quotes, trades and trade reports, and which prohibits retribution or retaliatory conduct for competitive actions of another market maker or other market participant.

12. To enforce Article III, Section 1 of the NASD Rules of Fair Practice, with a view to enhancing market maker competitiveness by (a) Acting to eliminate anticompetitive or unlawfully enforced or maintained industry pricing conventions, and to discipline market makers who harass other market makers for narrowing the displayed quotations in the Nasdaq market, trading not more than the quantities of securities they are required to trade under the NASD's rules, or otherwise engaging in competitive conduct; (b) Acting to eliminate coordination between or among market makers of quotes, trades and trade reports; (c) Acting to eliminate concerted discrimination and concerted refusals to deal by market makers.

13. To redefine or repeal the excess spread rule so as to eliminate any disincentive to narrow the displayed quotations in the Nasdaq market.

14. To retain an independent consultant, acceptable to the Commission staff, to review and report to the Audit Committee of the NASD Board of Governors on the implementation of these undertakings. The Audit Committee shall report the findings of the independent consultant with respect to such implementation to the Chairman of the NASD Board of Governors and to the Commission's Divisions of Market Regulation and Enforcement beginning six (6) months after the date of this Order and thereafter annually for three years, beginning the first anniversary of this Order and concluding with the third anniversary of this Order; provided, however, that the appointment activities of the independent consultant shall no way limit the lawful authority of the Commission or its staff with respect to the NASD.

## Comments & Questions

1. As indicated in this release, the Commission also released a detailed report, pursuant to section 21(a) of the 1934 Act, summarizing the results of its investigation of the NASD and the NASDAQ trading market. A month before the release was issued, the Justice Department dropped its inquiry into alleged price fixing among NASDAQ dealers in exchange for agreement on the part of two dozen securities firms to tape-record random trader conversations on their over the counter desks and to undertake other supervisory actions. See *U.S. Settlement with NASDAQ Suggest Weak Collusion Case*, Wall St. J. , July 15, 1996, at A3. How do NASD practices in this area compare to the subject matter of the *Gordon* case? How do they compare to anti-competitive issues we have confronted elsewhere in the financial services industry?

2. In May of 1994, a private class action law suit was filed charging market-making firms with colluding to maintain artificially wide-spreads in 1,659 NASDAQ stocks over a five year period. Though representatives of the defendant firms denied that their market making practices were unlawful, most of the defendant had, by year end 1997, agreed to settlements totaling more than $1 billion dollars, reportedly the largest such recoveries in the history of federal or state anti-trust laws. See *Dealer Firms to Pay $910 Million To Settle Investors' Price-Fixing Charges*, BNA Securities Law Daily, Dec. 30, 1997.

---

We next consider the relationship between market regulation and corporate governance. One of the traditional functions of established trading markets, such as the New York Stock Exchange, has been to develop listing standards for the issuers of securities. By developing and enforcing listing requirements, it is believed, markets can make themselves more attractive to the investing public and lower capital costs for corporate issuers. The mandatory disclosure obligations of the federal securities laws — applicable to most publicly traded securities in the United States — supplement traditional listing requirements and serve a similar function. See John C. Coffee, *Market Failure and the Economic Case for a Mandatory Disclosure System*, 70 VA. L. REV. 717 (1984). The following case, which arises out of the take-over boom of the 1980s, involves an SEC initiative to augment traditional listing requirements in an unusual way. In reviewing the validity of the rule, the decision explores the line between SEC oversight and SRO autonomy.

# Business Roundtable v. Securities and Exchange Commission
## 905 F.2d 406 (D.C. Cir. 1990)

In 1984 General Motors announced a plan to issue a second class of common stock with one-half vote per share. The proposal collided with a longstanding rule of the New York Stock Exchange that required listed companies to provide one vote per share of common stock. The NYSE balked at enforcement, and after two years filed a proposal with the Securities and Exchange Commission to relax its own rule. The SEC did not approve the rule change but responded with one of its own. On July 7, 1988, it adopted Rule 19c-4, barring national securities exchanges and national securities associations, together known as self-regulatory organizations (SROs), from listing stock of a corporation that takes any corporate action "with the effect of nullifying, restricting or disparately reducing the per share voting rights of [existing common stockholders]." Voting Rights Listing Standards; Disenfranchisement Rule, 53 Fed.Reg. 26,376, 26,394 (1988) ("Final Rule"). The rule prohibits such "disenfranchisement" even where approved by a shareholder vote conducted on one share/one vote principles. . . .[1]

Two components of § 19 give the Commission authority over the rules of self-regulatory organizations. First, § 19(b) requires them to file with the Commission any proposed change in their rules. The Commission is to approve the change if it finds it "consistent with the requirements of [the Exchange Act] and the rules and regulations thereunder applicable" to the self-regulatory organization. § 19(b)(2). This provision is not directly at issue here, but, as we shall see, both the procedure and the terms guiding Commission approval are important in understanding the scope of the authority the Commission has sought to exercise. That is found in § 19(c), which allows the Commission on its own initiative to amend the rules of a self-regulatory organization as it deems necessary or appropriate [1] to insure the fair administration of the self-regulatory organization, [2] to conform its rules to requirements of [the Exchange Act] and the rules and regulations thereunder applicable to such organization, or [3] otherwise in furtherance of the purposes of [the Exchange Act]. § 19(c) (enumeration added). As no one suggests that either of the first two purposes justifies Rule 19c-4, the issue before us is the scope of the third, catch-all provision.

---

[1]    . . . [F]or academic commentary on the wisdom of the rule and of its federal adoption, see, e.g., Ronald J. Gilson, Evaluating Dual Class Common Stock: The Relevance of Substitutes, 73 Va.L.Rev. 807 (1987); Joel Seligman, Equal Protection in Shareholder Voting Rights: The One Common Share, One Vote Controversy, 54 Geo.Wash.L.Rev. 687 (1987) (arguing for a broad prohibition on all dual class capitalizations); George W. Dent, Jr., Dual Class Capitalization: A Reply to Professor Seligman, 54 Geo.Wash.L.Rev. 725, 754-55 (1986) (arguing the creation or sale of stock with disproportionate voting rights should be prohibited unless approved by a majority of disinterested shareholders); Louis Lowenstein, Shareholder Voting Rights: A Response to SEC Rule 19c-4 and to Professor Gilson, 89 Col.L.Rev. 979 (1989) (agreeing on the need to regulate dual class capitalizations but disagreeing with the methodology of the SEC's approach). For an exception to the general approval, see Daniel R. Fischel, Organized Exchanges and the Regulation of Dual Class Common Stock, 54 U.Chi.L.Rev. 119 (1987) (arguing that competition among securities markets will produce the most efficient rules). . . .

First it seems indisputable that the NYSE's proposed rule modifying its one share/one vote listing standard is a "rule" covered by § 19(b) and, correspondingly, that Rule 19c-4 does not fall outside of § 19(c)'s ambit for any want of being a "rule of a self-regulatory organization." As enacted in 1934, § 19 of the Exchange Act gave the Commission power to amend the rules of an exchange "in respect of" 12 explicitly enumerated "matters," including "the listing or striking from listing of any security," and "similar matters." Securities Exchange Act of 134, § 19(b). The 1975 amendments to the Exchange Act, far from narrowing that authority, removed the enumeration and replaced it with a general power under new §§ 19(b) & (c) both to review and to amend all self-regulatory organization rules.

The practice of the securities industry confirms the broad sweep of § 19(b)'s review mechanism. For the past fifteen years, the exchanges have routinely submitted changes in listing standards for approval and the Commission has reviewed them without any commenting party expressing doubt of its jurisdiction. Indeed, exchanges followed this practice with the proposals that led directly to the regulations challenged here. Many of the past proposals dealt with matters of internal corporate governance, but in no such case did the SEC seek to exercise its veto.[5] Accordingly, while the practice confirms that the "rules of a self-regulatory organization" required to be vetted by the Commission under s 19(b) are all-encompassing, it tells us nothing about the criteria of judgment the Commission may apply under subsection (b) or (c).

As mentioned above, the Commission does not suggest that it might support Rule 19c-4 by reference to the first two of the possible heads of jurisdiction in § 19(c)--assurance of fair administration of the self- regulatory organization itself and conformity to the requirements of the Exchange Act or rules thereunder applicable to the organization. Thus it is driven to the third--"otherwise in furtherance of the purposes" of the Exchange Act.

What then are the "purposes" of the Exchange Act? The Commission supports Rule 19c-4 as advancing the purposes of a variety of sections, see Final Rule, 53 Fed.Reg. at 26,390/1, but we first take its strongest--§ 14's grant of power to regulate the proxy process. The Commission finds a purpose "to ensure fair shareholder suffrage." See Final Rule, 53 Fed.Reg. at 26,391/2. Indeed, it points to the House Report's declarations that "[f]air corporate suffrage is an important right," H.R.Rep. No. 1383, 73d Cong., 2d Sess. 13 (1934) ("1934 House Report"), and that "use of the exchanges should involve a corresponding duty of according to shareholders fair suffrage," id. at 14. The formulation is true in the sense that Congress's decision can be located under that broad umbrella.

But unless the legislative purpose is defined by reference to the means Congress selected, it can be framed at any level of generality--to improve the operation of capital markets, for instance. In fact, although § 14(a) broadly bars use of the mails (and other means) "to solicit ... any proxy" in contravention of Commission rules and regulations, it is not seriously disputed that Congress's central concern was with disclosure. See J.I. Case Co. v. Borak, 377 U.S. 426, 431 (1964) ("The purpose of § 14(a) is to prevent management or others from obtaining authorization for corporate action by means of deceptive or inadequate disclosure in proxy solicitation."); see

---

[5]    The Commission has on occasion, however, given hints that eventuated in the exchanges' proposing a change, a practice viewed by one observer as "regulation by raised eyebrow." See Donald E. Schwartz, Federalism and Corporate Governance, 45 Ohio St.L.J. 545, 571 (1984).

also Santa Fe Industries, Inc. v. Green, 430 U.S. 462, 477-78 (1977) (emphasizing Exchange Act's philosophy of full disclosure and dismissing the fairness of the terms of the transaction as "at most a tangential concern of the statute" once full and fair disclosure has occurred).

While the House Report indeed speaks of fair corporate suffrage, it also plainly identifies Congress's target--the solicitation of proxies by well informed insiders "without fairly informing the stockholders of the purposes for which the proxies are to be used." 1934 House Report at 14. The Senate Report contains no vague language about "corporate suffrage," but rather explains the purpose of the proxy protections as ensuring that stockholders have "adequate knowledge" about the "financial condition of the corporation ... [and] the major questions of policy, which are decided at stockholders' meetings." S.Rep. No. 792, 73d Cong., 2d Sess. 12 (1934) ("1934 Senate Report"). Finally, both reports agree on the power that the proxy sections gave the Commission--"power to control the conditions under which proxies may be solicited." 1934 House Report at 14. See also 1934 Senate Report at 12 (similar language).

That proxy regulation bears almost exclusively on disclosure stems as a matter of necessity from the nature of proxies. Proxy solicitations are, after all, only communications with potential absentee voters. The goal of federal proxy regulation was to improve those communications and thereby to enable proxy voters to control the corporation as effectively as they might have by attending a shareholder meeting. Id. See also S.Rep. No. 1455, 73d Cong., 2d Sess. 74 (1934); Sheldon E. Bernstein and Henry G. Fischer, The Regulation of the Solicitation of Proxies: Some Reflections on Corporate Democracy, 7 U.Chi.L.Rev. 226, 227-28 (1940).

We do not mean to be taken as saying that disclosure is necessarily the sole subject of § 14. See Louis Loss, Fundamentals of Securities Regulation 452-53 (1988) (asserting that § 14 is not limited to ensuring disclosure), quoted in Final Rule, 53 Fed.Reg. at 26,391 n. 163. For example, the Commission's Rule 14a-4(b)(2) requires a proxy to provide some mechanism for a security holder to withhold authority to vote for each nominee individually. It thus bars a kind of electoral tying arrangement, and may be supportable as a control over management's power to set the voting agenda, or, slightly more broadly, voting procedures. . . . But while Rule 14a-4(b)(2) may lie in a murky area between substance and procedure, Rule 19c-4 much more directly interferes with the substance of what the shareholders may enact. It prohibits certain reallocations of voting power and certain capital structures, even if approved by a shareholder vote subject to full disclosure and the most exacting procedural rules.

The Commission noted in the preamble to the Proposed Rule its conviction that collective action problems could cause even a properly conducted shareholder vote (with ample disclosure and sound procedures) to bring about results injurious to the shareholders. See Proposed Rule, 52 Fed.Reg. at 23,672/1 (detailing collective action problem in the shareholder voting process and expressing "concern[ ]" over the "effect of that vote"). We do not question these findings. But we think the Commission's reliance on them is a clue to its stretch of the congressional purposes. As the Commission itself observed, "[s]ection 14(a) contains an implicit assumption that shareholders will be able to make use of the information provided in proxy solicitations in order to vote in corporate elections." Final Rule, 53 Fed.Reg. at 26,391/3. In 1934 Congress acted on the premise that shareholder voting could work, so long as investors secured enough information and, perhaps, the benefit of other procedural protections. It did not seek to regulate the stockholders' choices.  If the Commission believes that premise misguided, it must turn to Congress.

With its step beyond control of voting procedure and into the distribution of voting power, the Commission would assume an authority that the Exchange Act's proponents disclaimed any intent to grant.  Noting that opponents expressed alarm that the bill would give the Commission "power to interfere in the management of corporations," the Senate Committee on Banking and Currency said it had "no such intention" and that the bill "furnish[ed] no justification for such an interpretation."  1934 Senate Report at 10.  See also H.R. Conf. Rep. No. 1838, 73d Cong., 2d Sess. 35 (1934) (deleting as unnecessary section 13(d) of the bill, which made explicit that the Commission could not "interfere with the management of the affairs of an issuer").

There are, of course, shadings within the notion of "management."  With the present rule the Commission does not tell any corporation where to locate its next plant.  But neither does state corporate law;  it regulates the distribution of powers among the various players in the process of corporate governance, and the Commission's present leap beyond disclosure is just that sort of regulation.  The potpourri of listing standards previously submitted to the Commission under § 19(b) suggests the sweep of its current claim.  These govern requirements for independent directors, independent audit committees, shareholder quorums, shareholder approval for certain major corporate transactions, and other major issues traditionally governed by state law.  If Rule 19c-4 is closely enough related to the proxy regulation purpose of § 14, then all these issues appear equally subject to the Commission's discretionary control.

Surprisingly, the Commission does not concede a lack of jurisdiction over such issues.  When questioned at oral argument as to what state corporation rules are not related to "fair corporate suffrage," SEC counsel conceded only that further intrusions into state corporate governance "would present more difficult situations."  In fact the Commission's apparent perception of its § 19 powers has been immensely broad, unbounded even by any pretense of a connection to § 14.  In reviewing the previous SRO rule changes on issues of independent directors and independent audit committees, it grounded its review in a supposed mandate to "protect investors and the public interest." . . .  The Commission made no attempt to limit the concept by reference to the concrete purposes of any section.  Rather, it reasoned that the rule changes protected investors by "creat[ing] uniformity that helps to assure investors that all the companies traded in those markets have the fundamental safeguards they have come to expect of major companies."  If Rule 19c-4 were validated on such broad grounds, the Commission would be able to establish a federal corporate law by using access to national capital markets as its enforcement mechanism.  This would resolve a longstanding controversy over the wisdom of such a move in the face of disclaimers from Congress and with no substantive restraints on the power. It would, moreover, overturn or at least impinge severely on the tradition of state regulation of corporate law. As the Supreme Court has said, "[c]orporations are creatures of state law, and investors commit their funds to corporate directors on the understanding that, except where federal law expressly requires certain responsibilities of directors with respect to stockholders, state law will govern the internal affairs of the corporation."  Santa Fe Industries, 430 U.S. at 479, 97 S.Ct. at 1304, quoting Cort v. Ash, 422 U.S. 66, 84 (1975)).  At least one Commissioner shared this view, stating "[s]ection 19(c) does not provide the Commission carte blanche to adopt federal corporate governance standards through the back door by mandating uniform listing standards."  Final Rule, 53 Fed.Reg. at 26,395/1 (Grundfest, Comm'r, concurring). . . . We read the Act as reflecting a clear congressional determination not to make any such broad delegation of power to the Commission.

If the Commission's one share/one vote rule is to survive, then, some kind of firebreak is needed to separate it from corporate governance as a whole. But the Commission's sole suggestion of such a firebreak is a reference to "the unique historical background of the NYSE's one share, one vote rule." It is true that in the Senate hearings leading to enactment of the Exchange Act there were a few favorable references to that rule. . . . But these few references are culled from 9500 pages of testimony in the Senate hearings. No legislator directly discussed the NYSE's rule and no references were made to it in any of the Committee Reports. The most these references show is that legislators were aware of the rule and that it was an important part of the background. Even if we imputed the statements to a member of Congress, none comes near to saying, "The purposes of this act, although they generally will not involve the Commission in corporate governance, do include preservation of the one share/one vote principle." And even then we doubt that such a statement in the legislative history could support a special and anomalous exception to the Act's otherwise intelligible conceptual line excluding the Commission from corporate governance.

The Commission also rests on §§ 6(b)(5) and 15A(b)(6) for its broad vision of the Act's purposes. These sections, which contain identical language, allow the Commission in registering an exchange (§ 6(b)(5)) or an association of brokers and dealers (§ 15A(b)(6)) to consider whether its rules "in general, ... protect investors and the public interest." This open-ended standard, however, is part of a larger list of more specific standards concerning the administration and operation of the self-regulatory organizations themselves, not the fairness of the issuers' corporate structures. Under one maxim of interpretation (eiusdem generis ), the general standard at the end of this list should be construed to embrace only issues similar to the specific ones. But even if this canon is not applied, "public interest" is never an unbounded term. As the Supreme Court said in NAACP v. FPC, 425 U.S. 662 (1976), rejecting a claim that the Federal Power Commission was authorized to oversee its licensees' compliance with civil rights legislation, broad "public interest" mandates must be limited to "the purposes Congress had in mind when it enacted [the] legislation." Id. at 670, 96 S.Ct. at 1812. . . . Upholding the Commission's advance into an area not contemplated by Congress would circumvent the legislative process that is virtually the sole protection for state interests. . . . The Supreme Court's point in a slightly different context is relevant here: "Absent a clear indication of congressional intent, we are reluctant to federalize the substantial portion of the law of corporations that deals with transactions in securities, particularly where established state policies of corporate regulation would be overridden." Santa Fe Industries, Inc. v. Green, 430 U.S. 462, 479 (1977).

Perhaps realizing that a vague "public interest" standard cannot be interpreted without some confining principle, the Commission attempted to relate §§ 6(b)(5) and 15A(b)(6) to "the policies implicit in the Act," specifically those in § 14. See Final Rule, 53 Fed.Reg. at 26,392/2; Proposed Rule, 52 Fed.Reg. at 23,676 n. 115. As this approach simply piggybacks on the Commission's flawed view of § 14, it must also fail. . . .

Finally the Commission invokes § 11A, which Congress added as part of the 1975 amendments to give the Commission authority to "facilitate the establishment of a national market system for securities." § 11A(a)(2). In a preambular phrase, Congress found that it was "in the public interest ... to assure ... fair competition among brokers and dealers, among exchange markets, and between exchange markets and markets other than exchange markets."  § 11A(a)(1)(C)(ii).  The Commission here asserts that it is not "fair" for any self-regulatory organization "to compete for listings by lowering listing standards concerning shareholder voting rights" below a certain "minimum."  Final Rule, 53 Fed.Reg. at 26,392/3-26,393/1.  This reasoning -- essentially that exchanges might engage in a "race to the bottom" in their competition to secure corporate listings -- is again one that potentially engulfs all state corporate law.  Indeed, if coupled with § 11A's express interest in fostering a national market system, the theory can easily federalize corporate law for all companies wishing access to the national capital markets.  Yet nothing in the statute and legislative history suggests so broad a purpose.

The Commission points to a statement in the Conference Report supporting the view that § 11A gives authority "to remove unjustified disparities in regulation as may result in unfair competitive advantages."  H.R.Conf.Rep. No. 229, 94th Cong., 1st Sess. 94 (1975) ("1975 Conference Report"), U.S.Code Cong. & Admin.News 1975, 179, 321, 325.  The Committee was here discussing § 11A(c)(1)(F), which gives the Commission authority to "assure equal regulation of all markets for qualified securities and all exchange members, brokers, and dealers effecting transactions in such securities."  In a vacuum, this section and its description in the legislative history could be seen as allowing SEC imposition of uniform rules as needed to forestall a race to the bottom.  But the subtitle to the section of the Committee Report quoted is "Communication among and dissemination of information about securities markets," id. at 93, U.S.Code Cong. & Admin.News 1975, 324, and the section of which subsection 11A(c)(1)(F) is a part, § 11A(c)(1), concerns only the dissemination of "information with respect to quotations for or transactions in any security."  The Conference Report made clear that this section dealt with "communications systems ... [that] will form the heart of the national market system."[9]  Id.  The Senate Report gave a number of examples confirming its limited reach:

Examples of the types of subjects as to which the SEC would have the authority to promulgate rules under these provisions include:  the hours of operation of any type or quotation system, trading halts, what and how information is displayed and qualifications for the securities to be included on any tape or within any quotation system. 1975 Senate Report at 11, U.S.Code Cong. & Admin.News 1975, 189.  Even the final element in this list, which may sound similar to listing standards, seems to refer only to the qualifications relevant to inclusion within any particular information database (e.g., amount of trading activity, type of security, etc.).  See 1975 Conference Report at 92-93, U.S.Code Cong. & Admin.News 1975, 323-24 (both Houses intended that "all securities ... be eligible to be qualified for trading in the national market system," although the SEC may have to establish subsystems "tailored to the characteristics of the particular types of securities.").  Indeed Congress made clear that the power to regulate central information processing was not intended to give the SEC "either the responsibility or the

---

[9]    For example, elements of the national market system that have been realized include the Composite Quotation System (which reports bid and offer prices from several exchanges and the over-the-counter market), the Intermarket Trading System (a computer system linking terminals on trading floors in major exchanges), and the Consolidated Tape (which reports transactions on the New York, American and some regional exchanges).  See generally Donald L. Calvin, The National Market System:  A Successful Adventure in Industry Self-Improvement, 70 Va.L.Rev. 785, 800-01 (1984).

power to operate as an 'economic czar.' "  1975 Senate Report at 12, U.S.Code Cong. & Admin.News 1975, 190.  To argue that Congress's "equal regulation" mandate supports SEC control over corporate governance through national listing standards is to gamble that the court will accept a Commission spin on a statutory fragment without even a glance at its context. Wrong court, bad gamble.

The Commission's theory is, moreover, a rather odd reading of what was a cornerstone in Congress's 1975 desire to establish a national market system and "to break down the unnecessary regulatory restrictions ... which restrain competition among markets and market makers."  1975 Senate Report at 12-13, U.S.Code Cong. & Admin.News 1975, 191.  See also Jonathan R. Macey and David D. Haddock, Shirking at the SEC:  The Failure of the National Market System, 1985 U.Ill.L.Rev. 315, 315 (1975 amendments were essentially "deregulatory legislation");  1975 Conference Report at 94, U.S.Code Cong. & Admin.News 1975, 325 ("The Commission was directed to remove existing burdens on competition and to refrain from imposing, or permitting to be imposed, any new regulatory burden 'not necessary or appropriate in furtherance of the purposes' of the Exchange Act.").  To the extent these congressional views recognize a continuing need for regulation, the need is predicated upon purposes found elsewhere in the Exchange Act, and thus provides no independent purpose to sustain Rule 19c-4.

The Commission also invokes its power under § 11A(a)(2) to "designate the securities or classes of securities qualified for trading in the national market system."  See Final Rule, 53 Fed.Reg. at 26,392/2-3.  Even if we aggregated the individual exchanges into the "national market system" (which is doubtful, as they are only "components of the fragmented trading network that Congress wanted to reform," Dent, 54 Geo.Wash.L.Rev. at 732), the Commission's § 11A authority does not sustain its broad notion of the Exchange Act's purposes.  The power to designate securities as "qualified" for trading on the national market system is necessarily constrained by Congress's purposes in authorizing the Commission to foster that system.  See § 11A(a)(2) (requiring Commission to use its authority "in accordance with the findings and to carry out the objectives set forth in paragraph (1) of this subsection"); 1975 Conference Report at 92-95, U.S.Code Cong. & Admin.News 1975, 323-26.  Cf. Karmel, 36 Cath. U.L.Rev. at 829. Again, the Commission has failed to identify in § 11A or its history a purpose justifying regulation of corporate governance.

The petition for review is granted and Rule 19c-4 is vacated.

## Comments and Questions

1.  Was the court right in rejecting the SEC's final argument that Rule 19c-4 was necessary to facilitate the development of a national market system for securities?  Can we trust trading markets to compete among themselves to develop the most desirable trading environments, or is there a chance that the markets will engage in a destructive "race to the bottom."  If not the SEC, who can we depend upon to police trading markets? Broker-dealers? Issuers? Investors?   For an insightful discussion of inter-market competition, see Jonathan Macey & Hideki Kanda, *The Stock Exchange as Firm: The Emergence of Close Substitutes for the New York and Tokyo Stock Exchanges*, 75 CORNELL L. REV. 1007 (1990).

2. In the years since the Roundtable decision was decided, the debate over dual class stock has shifted back to the SROs, which have voluntarily adopted restrictions similar to those that Rule 19c-4 would have mandated. Does this development mean that SEC intervention was unnecessary? For further readings on these developments, see Stephen M. Bainbridge, *The Short Life and Resurrection of SEC Rule 19c-4*, 69 WASH. U.L.Q. 565 (1991); Douglas Ashton, *Revisiting Dual-Class Stock*, 68 ST.. JOHN'S L. REV. 863 (1994).

3. In a portion of the *Roundtable* decision not included here, the Court considered the puzzling relationship between section 19 of the 1934 Act and section 6(b)(5), which provides that the Commission should not register an exchange unless it determines that the exchanges' rules " are not designed . . . to regulate by virtue of any authority conferred by [the 1934 Act] matters not related to the purposes of [the 1934 Act] or the administration of the exchange." The puzzle here is how long-standing one-share/one-vote rules could be acceptable under section 6(b)(5) if the Commission lacked authority to impose them under section 19(b). The court resolved this dilemma by concluding that enforcement of listing requirements does not constitute regulation under the Act., thus distinguishing regulatory and non-regulatory functions of SROs. For an interesting discussion and criticism of this aspect of the court's opinion, see Douglas C. Michael, *Untenable Status of Corporate Governance Listing Standards Under the Securities Exchange Act*, 47 BUS. LAW. 1461 (1992) (suggesting that the 1934 Act should be understood to prohibit listing standards designed to enhance market regulation).

4. Given the quasi-government role of SROs, should we consider the exchanges and NASD as state actors for purposes of the Due Process Clause and other constitutional protections when, for example, they take enforcement actions against members or listed firms? What if the proceeding involves an SRO rule that the SEC itself would lack power to impose under the *Roundtable* decision? See generally, Richard L. Stone & Michael A. Perino, *Not Just a Private Club: Self Regulatory Organizations As State Actors When Enforcing Federal Law*, 2 COLUM. BUS. L. REV. 453 (1995).

*Problem 11-2*

The New York Stock Exchange has for many years restricted the ability of companies with securities listed on the NYSE to withdraw their securities from trading on the exchange. Under Exchange rules, a listed company may not withdraw a class of securities unless the withdrawal is approved by two-thirds of the holders of outstanding securities and no more than ten percent of the holders object to the withdrawal. Finding that this restriction is inhibiting some new companies from listing on the NYSE, the Exchange would like to change its listing requirements to allow withdrawal provided a simple majority of securities holders approve the decision. To what extent do the federal securities laws constrain the Exchange's ability to change this requirement? What role, if any, does the SEC have in reviewing such a change?

# Section 3: Broker-Dealers in Trading Markets

We now turn our attention to another mechanism for regulating trading markets: the supervision of broker-dealers. To some extent, these materials reprise doctrinal issues presented in Chapter Ten, where we were principally concerned with investor protections. Here, however, the integrity of trading markets also informs the structure of governmental intervention.

## A. Limit Orders

### In re E.F. Hutton & Co.
### 41 S.E.C. Docket 413, Release No. 34-25887 (July 6, 1988)

E.F. Hutton & Company Inc., now known as Shearson Lehman Hutton Inc. ("Hutton"), a member of the National Association of Securities Dealers ("NASD"), appeals from NASD disciplinary action.[1]

The pertinent facts, which are undisputed, may be summarized as follows. On January 11, 1984, William Manning placed an open limit order with Hutton's Rochester, New York branch office to sell 5,000 shares of Genex Corporation stock in his account at 17 1/8 .[2] Hutton accepted Manning's order and a ticket was prepared and sent to Hutton's over-the-counter ("OTC") trading department.

When Manning gave his order, Hutton was a registered NASDAQ market maker in Genex. The inside Genex quotation on NASDAQ was 17 bid, 17 1/8 asked,[3] and Hutton's quotation was 17 bid, 17 1/2 asked. While Hutton was holding Manning's order, it sold 4,755 shares of Genex from its own inventory at prices of 17 1/4 and 17 1/2 , higher than the 17 1/8 sought by

---

[1]    Unlike most NASD disciplinary actions, this proceeding was initiated and conducted by a public customer, William Manning. See Article IV, Section 2, of the NASD's Rules of Fair Practice (NASD Manual P 2202, p. 2203), and Article II, Sections 1 and 2 of the NASD's Code of Procedure (NASD Manual PP 3021-3022, p. 3041).

[2]    A limit order for the sale of stock allows the customer to set a specific price at or above which he will sell securities. An open limit order stays in effect until such time as it is executed or cancelled by the customer. The Hutton salesman who took Manning's order was to receive a "production credit" of 1/8 . Manning understood that his order would be executed only at 17 1/8 or higher.

[3]    The inside quotation is the highest bid and the lowest asked prices from the dealers entering quotations into the NASDAQ system. There were nine NASDAQ market makers in Genex at the time Hutton accepted Manning's order.

Manning.[4] Subsequently, the price of Genex declined substantially. Although Manning's order did not call for "all-or-none" execution, no part of the order was ever executed.

The NASD concluded that, by accepting Manning's limit order, Hutton had an obligation to give that order priority over its own proprietary position unless it had previously arrived at a different understanding with Manning. Since the NASD found that no such understanding had been reached, it concluded, among other things, that Hutton did not fulfill its fiduciary duty to Manning. The NASD accordingly found that Hutton had violated Article III, Section 1 of the NASD's Rules of Fair Practice.[5]

Hutton contends that it had no obligation to execute Manning's limit order. It points out that, as Manning knew, Hutton was making a market in Genex. It accordingly argues that, because the inside bid never reached the price set by Manning, it had no obligation to buy his stock. It also contends that it had no obligation to step aside and allow Manning's order to take preference in filling incoming buy orders that Hutton received as a market maker.

Both Hutton and the Securities Industry Association ("SIA") further assert that it is contrary to industry practice for OTC market makers to grant priority to customer limit orders over the market makers' proprietary trades. They maintain that, generally, such orders are executed only if a quotation reflecting "contra-side interest" (in this case a bid) reaches the limit order price. They argue that the concept of limit order priority (although applicable to exchanges where customer orders are centrally held, matched and given priority over specialists' proprietary trading) is fundamentally inconsistent with the dispersed nature of the OTC market and would, if adopted, entail serious adverse consequences.[8] Finally, they contend that the obligation imposed on Hutton by the NASD cannot reasonably or fairly be implied from existing law and that, if the NASD wishes to impose such an obligation, it must do so by adopting a rule.

At the outset, it should be emphasized that the NASD's decision does not impose a "limit order priority rule" on the OTC market. Market makers and other broker-dealers do not have to accept limit orders if they choose not to do so. Moreover, if they do accept such orders, they are free to specify the terms governing the orders' execution provided that those terms are fully and

---

[4] The bid and asked prices quoted by a market maker are the prices at which it is willing to buy stock from or sell it to other dealers. However, when a market maker is approached by a dealer that wishes to buy or sell stock, an acceptable transaction price may be negotiated; that price is normally around the market maker's bid or asked quotation. In the case of a retail sale from inventory, the market maker charges the customer a markup above the price being paid by dealers. The prices that Hutton obtained above the limit price for the 4,755 Genex shares do not include markups paid by retail customers.

[5] That provision requires NASD members to "observe high standards of commercial honor and just and equitable principles of trade." NASD Manual P 2151, p. 2014.

[8] Hutton claims that giving such a priority would encourage customers to usurp the dealer's spread by placing limit orders at a price between the dealer's bid and asked quotations. Thus, Hutton argues, some firms would stop accepting limit orders or stop making markets altogether which would diminish OTC liquidity. Hutton also states that customers would not benefit because firms would charge higher commissions on limit orders to offset the loss in profits normally received from the spread.

clearly disclosed to the customer, and the customer agrees to them, at the time that any such order is placed. The only questions presented by this appeal are: (1) whether under the NASD's rules a broker-dealer that accepts a customer's limit order may trade for its own proprietary account ahead of that order without having informed the customer that this is the practice it intends to follow, and (2) whether a determination that the type of conduct in which Hutton engaged was improper can be reached through adjudication or only through rulemaking.

When Manning entrusted his limit order to Hutton, and Hutton agreed to accept that order and act on Manning's behalf in obtaining execution, Hutton assumed certain fiduciary obligations. Those obligations were not extinguished even though Hutton could have acted in a principal capacity in executing Manning's order. A broker-dealer's determination to execute an order as principal or agent cannot be "a means by which the broker may elect whether or not the law will impose fiduciary standards upon him in the actual circumstances of any given relationship or transaction."[10]

Our aim is to give effect to the reasonable expectations of the parties to the relationship. Where there is no explicit agreement to the contrary and the relationship is a fiduciary one, the law governing fiduciary duties provides presumptive definition for such expectations. We need not consider whether in some circumstances an industry practice might be so universal and overt that investor expectations inconsistent with that practice are unreasonable, since we are not persuaded that such is the situation here. Thus Manning was entitled to expect that industry practice would comport with fiduciary principles and that conflicts of interest would be disclosed. It is hornbook law that, absent disclosure and a contrary agreement, a fiduciary cannot compete with his beneficiary with respect to the subject matter of their relationship.[12] Thus, far from being a "technical matter" that only involves the manner of executing a limit order, the practice at issue affects the fundamentals of the broker-dealer--customer relationship.

Hutton's willingness to sell Genex stock for its own account at prices equal to or higher than the price of Manning's limit order created a conflict between the interests of Hutton and Manning that affected the task Hutton had undertaken on Manning's behalf. Hutton was, in effect, competing with Manning with respect to the subject matter of their relationship--the execution of Manning's order. As the facts in this case illustrate, this can result in a broker-dealer seizing a customer's only opportunity for execution at his limit order price. Thus, as the NASD

---

[10]    Opper v. Hancock Securities Corp., 250 F.Supp. 668, 675 (S.D.N.Y.), aff'd, 367 F.2d 157 (2d Cir.1966).

[12]    See Restatement (Second) of Agency, Section 393, Comment b (1957). See also Wolfson, Phillips and Russo, Regulation of Brokers, Dealers and Securities Markets, P 2.03 at 2-15 (1977) ("the developing law--both in the Commission and the courts--supports the imposition of an affirmative duty of disclosure whenever a broker-dealer has a substantial interest in a transaction which may be adverse to his client"); Chasins v. Smith, Barney & Co., 438 F.2d 1167 (2d Cir.1970). For the disclosure obligations imposed on a fiduciary, see, generally, Securities Exchange Act Release No. 13662 (June 23, 1977), 12 SEC Docket 947, 966; United States v. Dial, 757 F.2d 163 (7th Cir.), cert. denied, 106 S.Ct. 116 (1985); Arleen W. Hughes, 27 SEC 629, 635-636, aff'd sub nom. Hughes v. SEC, 174 F.2d 969 (D.C.Cir.1949); L. Loss, Fundamentals of Securities Regulation at 965 (1983).

concluded, Hutton was required to disclose the priorities that would govern its handling of Manning's order unless it was willing to refrain from competing with him.[13]

If Manning had known that Hutton would execute its own transactions ahead of his, he would have had an opportunity to decide whether to leave his order with Hutton and have it executed on Hutton's terms, attempt to negotiate better terms with Hutton, or look for another broker willing to give his limit order priority in filling incoming buy orders.[14] However, Hutton deprived Manning of that opportunity.

Absent a conflict of interest, the only affirmative obligation Hutton assumed by accepting Manning's limit order was to execute the order when the inside bid reached the limit order price. Here, however, there was such a conflict. And Hutton traded for its own account ahead of Manning without having made any disclosure of that conflict. We think it clear that, by doing so, it violated "high standards of commercial honor and just and equitable principles of trade." We accordingly affirm the NASD's finding of violation.

Chairman RUDER, concurring:

I agree with the views expressed in the majority opinion, but write separately to emphasize the fundamental tenets of agency and fiduciary law that lie at the heart of that decision, tenets that are not recognized by the dissenting opinions.

A broker-dealer who undertakes to act as an agent for a customer for purposes of obtaining execution is a fiduciary for that purpose. The broker-dealer may not conceal interests adverse to

---

[13]    Hutton contends that the NASD's decision is unfair to integrated firms because it reduces the profits earned by market makers in connection with their marketmaking activities. Specifically, Hutton claims that, absent disclosure, the decision permits customers to usurp the market maker's spread, the difference between its bid and asked quotations, by placing limit orders at a price between those quotations. It is true that, if Hutton chooses to conceal its willingness to prefer its own interests and accepts a customer's limit order to sell securities, it must use the customer's limit order securities first in filling incoming buy orders at prices at or above the limit price. On such transactions, Hutton may forego all or part of its spread. However, it would still be compensated by charging both the retail seller and retail buyer of the limit order securities a commission (or commission equivalent) for the service it performs in executing their trades. On the other hand, by disclosing its potential conflict of interest and obtaining a customer's informed consent to the terms governing his order, Hutton can continue to obtain the spread by trading ahead of the customer. Thus no unfairness results.

[14]    Hutton argues that disclosure to Manning was unnecessary because Manning knew that his limit order would not be filled until the inside bid reached the limit order price. Manning acknowledges that he understood that trades by other firms might occur at prices above his limit price and that, on previous occasions when he complained to Hutton that a limit order had not been executed, Hutton informed him that it was because the inside bid never reached his price. He states, however, that he was never aware until the present situation arose that Hutton would prefer its own proprietary position to his. Hutton's branch manager conceded that neither he nor his salesmen told customers that Hutton would trade for its own account ahead of them. Thus the record amply supports the NASD's conclusion that "Manning never realized that [transactions at a price higher than his limit price] could occur for the account of the dealer with which he placed his order."

the customer that may affect the broker-dealer's ability to achieve the customer's purpose. Likewise, the broker-dealer may not place those undisclosed interests ahead of the customer's interest. As has been aptly stated: In other words, when one is engaged as agent to act on behalf of another, the law requires him to do just that. He must not bring his own interests into conflict with his client's. If he does, he must explain in detail what his own self-interest in the transaction is in order to give his client an opportunity to make up his own mind whether to employ an agent who is riding two horses.

The Commission did not invent these principles. They are "nothing more than good old-fashioned agency law."

It would be ironic indeed if the Commission, charged with the protection of investors, were to superimpose on the law of agency a requirement that there be further evidence of a relationship of trust and confidence between a securities customer and a broker-dealer before the customer is entitled to this basic protection. "[T]he law of agency does not and cannot make any exceptions in favor of the securities business." Quite the contrary, our capital markets depend upon holding securities professionals, who operate as the gateway to those markets, to higher legal standards than those which govern other facets of commerce.

To require a search for evidence of an additional expectation of trust and confidence as a precondition to imposing on an agent such as Hutton the fiduciary duty to disclose its policy of preferring itself over its customer with respect to the task entrusted to the agent--obtaining the execution of Manning's limit order--changes agency law. Inherent in all agency relationships is the beneficiary's right to expect and rely upon the agent's loyalty in carrying out the duties for which the agency was created. Here, where Hutton agreed to become Manning's agent for the purpose of obtaining execution of Manning's limit order, the trust and confidence that Commissioner[] Grundfest would require to be proved inheres, as a matter of law, in the agency relationship itself. The characteristics of the agency will determine the extent of the trust and confidence that inheres in the agency relationship. Here, Manning, in entrusting a limit order to Hutton for execution, was entitled to protection against the undisclosed self-preferencing by Hutton over Manning in executing that order, and Manning had no duty to prove that some special additional feature existed.

The degree of Manning's "sophistication" does not lead to a conclusion that Manning had an obligation to prove the existence of special features before Hutton's duty to refrain from undisclosed self-preferencing conduct arose. The limit order customer necessarily depends upon the broker-dealer, as agent, for access to the market and the customer relies upon the broker-dealer to monitor the market and obtain execution when the market reaches the limit order price. This is true regardless of whether the customer is sophisticated or inexperienced. Given the protections afforded under ordinary agency law and the overall objective of the securities statutes to promote investor confidence, neither the novice nor the experienced investor should be required to show the existence of special features of the agency relationship in order to protect against broker-dealer self-interest with respect to obtaining execution of a limit order.

It is possible that Hutton could have shown that it was relieved of its agent's duty to refrain from undisclosed self-preferencing conduct. It could have done so either by showing that Manning knew of its practices or by showing that Manning, as a sophisticated investor, must have known of a practice known to all sophisticated investors. Here the evidence showed, and the

NASD found, that Manning did not know of Hutton's practices. Likewise, Hutton did not prove the existence of a universal and overt practice known either to Manning or to sophisticated investors generally. To suggest, without such proof, that as a sophisticated investor Manning was not "reasonable" in failing to presume that its agent, Hutton, might prefer itself over Manning reverses the normal agent/principal obligations. . . . .

Commissioner GRUNDFEST, dissenting:

. . . . I write . . . to emphasize that: (1) a broker-dealer's obligation to a customer depends on the facts and circumstances of the relationship; (2) Mr. Manning was a sophisticated customer; (3) the record indicates that Hutton disclosed its "inside bid" policy to Manning; and (4) the NASD's own general counsel provided evidence that industry practice regarding limit orders is not uniform. . . .

Fiduciary Duties. When Hutton agreed to accept Mr. Manning's limit order, Hutton assumed certain fiduciary obligations. To call Hutton a fiduciary, however, "only begins the analysis."[2] Fiduciary duties are not all created equal, and "the nature of fiduciary duty owed will vary, depending on the relationship between the broker and the investor." Accordingly, the nature and extent of Hutton's disclosure obligations with respect to Mr. Manning's limit order "depends on all the circumstances, including the degree of sophistication and the course of conduct between them." In this regard, the obligations owed to an unsophisticated customer will not necessarily be the same as those owed to a customer who is knowledgeable about the securities market and can bargain effectively to protect his own interests.

Industry practice is also relevant in determining the nature and extent of Hutton's fiduciary obligation to Mr. Manning. In the absence of regulations governing the practice at issue, courts consider whether the conduct deviates from an industry norm. An indication that an industry engages in a widespread practice tends to negate an inference that clients expect to be treated differently. Of course, the fact that a practice is endemic within an industry does not, in and of itself, require that the practice be condoned.

Finally, we must keep in mind the rationale for the creation of fiduciary duties. In this case, where there are sophisticated parties on both sides of the transaction, a "fiduciary duty is a standby or off-the-rack guess about what parties would agree to if they dickered about the subject explicitly."[7] The law imposes fiduciary duties "on a case-by-case basis by fashioning obligations that approximate what the parties would have contracted ex ante had they anticipated the particular events,"[8] and requires a "careful analysis ... to determine what is the particular duty

---

[2]   SEC v. Chenery Corp., 318 U.S. 80, 85-86 (1943).

[7]   Jordan v. Duff & Phelps, Inc., 815 F.2d 429, 436 (7th Cir.1987), cert. dismissed, 108 S.Ct. 1067 (1988).

[8]   Pross v. Katz, 784 F.2d 455, 458 (2d Cir.1986).

of a fiduciary under specific circumstances."[9] As the majority puts it, the aim is to "give effect to the reasonable expectations of the parties to the relationship."

Sophistication and Course of Conduct. When it comes to the over-the-counter market, Mr. Manning is hardly a babe in the woods. Mr. Manning spent ten years with Merrill Lynch and became the leading producer in its Rochester office. For the past 15 years Mr. Manning has been president of Manning & Napier, a firm that manages more than $1.4 billion in assets and effects 40-50 securities transactions each business day. During 1983, the calendar year prior to the transaction at issue, Mr. Manning's account was the largest single account trading over-the-counter securities and generated more commission dollar volume than any other in Hutton's Rochester office. The vast majority of Mr. Manning's over-the-counter transactions consisted of limit orders. Mr. Manning also knew, as of the time of his trade, that Hutton was a market maker in Genex stock.

In the course of his dealings with Hutton, Mr. Manning had complained about a lack of execution on a number of occasions when he had observed prices of transactions in excess of his limit prices. The majority recognizes that Manning: "understood that trades by other firms might occur at prices above his limit price and that, on previous occasions when he complained to Hutton that a limit order had not been executed, Hutton informed him that it was because the inside bid never reached his price. [Manning] states, however, that he was never aware until the present situation arose that Hutton would prefer its own proprietary position to his. Hutton's branch manager conceded that neither he nor his salesmen told customers that Hutton would trade for its own account ahead of them."

Thus, properly phrased, the issue is not whether Hutton was under some general duty to explain the details of its limit order priority policy. Rather, the issue is whether, having explained to a sophisticated investor that limit orders are not executed until the inside bid reaches the limit price, Hutton had a further obligation to explain that it would give its own trading priority over Mr. Manning's limit order although the inside bid had not reached the limit price.

If Hutton's statement is interpreted literally, then Mr. Manning cannot complain of his treatment at Hutton's hands. After all, Hutton said it wouldn't trade until the inside bid reached the limit price and that is exactly what Hutton did. Only if there was a substantial basis for Mr. Manning's belief that there was or should have been an exception to the stated "inside bid" policy does the possibility even arise that Hutton violated "just and equitable principles of trade" in its transaction with Mr. Manning. Here, however, the only evidence is Mr. Manning's assertion as to his state of mind. . . . .

Industry Practice. Clearly, if the practice in the over-the-counter market is to provide limit order protection, then Mr. Manning might be justified in assuming an exception to Hutton's "inside bid" policy. The evidence on industry practice in executing limit orders in the over-the-counter market, however, tends to negate Mr. Manning's assertion that he was entitled to presume limit order priority. . . .

There is no suggestion in the NASD's own [correspondence with Manning] that the price at which a market maker will execute a customer's limit order is affected by whether the market

---

[9]    Epstein v. United States, 174 F.2d 754, 764. (6th Cir. 1949).

maker sells the same security from its own account. To the contrary, in his letter to Manning, the NASD General Counsel explains that market makers are not required always to sell customers' securities ahead of their own: "[U]nder the established custom and usage in the over-the-counter market, and the Association's rules, the members are not required to always sell customers' securities ahead of their own sales from market maker positions in which they may have substantial risks. The obligations of members in this regard depend on the express terms of the order which the customer is totally free to negotiate. As I understand the facts contained in your letter, it would appear that E.F. Hutton, absent any contrary directions from you, treated your sell order as an instruction to purchase the securities from you for its own inventory or sell the securities to another market maker when the inside NASDAQ bid reached 17 1/8 which it never did during the time period in question."

The NASD General Counsel's description of "established custom and usage" thus negates the suggestion that industry practice would lead Mr. Manning to believe that Hutton should have provided an exception to its "inside bid" policy. While the existence of a duty to disclose the lack of a limit order priority rule "depends on the facts involved," "established custom and usage" is one of those facts.

Reasonable Expectations and the Economics of the Over-the-Counter Market. The majority explains that its "aim is to give effect to the reasonable expectations of the parties to the relationship." Given Mr. Manning's expertise in the operation of the over-the-counter market, it is appropriate to consider the extent to which the economics of the over-the- counter market would lead a sophisticated investor to expect to receive limit order priority. Similarly, it is appropriate to consider the extent to which the economics of the market would fashion Hutton's expectations regarding the adequacy of its disclosure to Mr. Manning.

The spread between "bid" and "asked" prices is a source of compensation for market makers who bear the risk and capital cost of maintaining securities in inventory.[19] Mr. Manning asserts that it was reasonable for him to believe that Hutton would shut down its sell side marketmaking activities and effectively forego the opportunity to earn the spread on any sales from its inventory as long as Mr. Manning's limit order was alive on Hutton's books.

There is, however, no indication that Hutton charged Mr. Manning any more for his limit orders than for any market order that would have enabled Hutton to earn its customary spread. While it is possible that Hutton might be willing to provide a more expensive limit order priority service at the same price as it charges for a market order, it is not immediately apparent why Mr. Manning would assume that Hutton would do so, particularly in light of their past course of conduct.

Stated somewhat differently, Mr. Manning's expectation was that he, ahead of Hutton, would be able to sell at the "asked" price that was generally available only to dealers and not to customers. Had any dealer other than Hutton sold shares at prices better than Mr. Manning's 17 1/8 limit order, Mr. Manning would have no reason to complain because, as had already been explained to him, his order would not be executed until it equaled the inside bid. Indeed, had Mr. Manning entered a market sell order he would have obtained a price no better than 17. However,

---

[19]   See, e.g., Cohen, K.J., et al., The Microstructure of Securities Markets 93-129 (1986).

because Hutton happened to be the dealer who executed sales at "asked" prices above Mr. Manning's limit, Mr. Manning urges that he be allowed the inter-dealer benefit of the prices available to Hutton. Thus, it is relevant to consider the extent to which Mr. Manning was reasonable in presuming that, absent specific negotiations, the entry of a limit order would either keep Hutton out of the sell side of the inter-dealer market, or allow him to obtain better execution than any market order would ever have obtained. Put another way, given Mr. Manning's sophistication, how reasonable was it for him to presume that silence implied limit order priority under the facts and circumstances of this case?

The Concurring Opinion. Chairman Ruder's inquiry ends at the point when it should begin and therefore slides by the difficult issues presented in this case. Of course, a "broker-dealer may not conceal interests adverse to the customer that may affect the broker-dealer's ability to achieve the customer's purpose," and "may not place those undisclosed interests ahead of the customer's interest." Nothing in this dissent suggests otherwise. Nor would I "reduce the customer's protection below the common law agency standard." The concurring opinion, however, simply recites platitudes about the nature and scope of fiduciary duties and fails to confront the very difficult issues raised by the unusual facts of this case.

As the concurring opinion makes clear, the duty at issue in this case is based on the customer's expectation that his broker-dealer will "monitor the market and obtain execution when the market reaches the limit order price." But the market never reached the limit order price. Thus, by Chairman Ruder's own formulation, the customer's expectation was never frustrated.

## Comments and Questions

1. The majority and concurring opinions view this case as a simple extension of fiduciary principles to the context of limit orders. On what basis does the dissent disagree? Which opinion do you find more compelling?

2. The E.F. Hutton decision prompted a reexamination of the treatment of limit orders and related issues. After an extensive rulemaking procedure, the Commission adopted a rule requiring market-makers to display the price and size of customer limit orders when those orders represent buying and selling interest that is a better price than the market maker's public quote. See Final Rules on Order Execution Obligations, 61 Fed. Reg. 48,290 (Sept. 12, 1996) (adopting new Rule 11Ac1-4 and amending Rule 11Ac1-1). In the following excerpt from its statement accompanying the new rule, the Commission justified its action on the following grounds:

[T]he 1975 Amendments [to the Securities Exchange Act of 1934] contain an explicit statutory mandate for the establishment of a national market system. Congress considered mandating certain minimum components of the national market system, but instead created a statutory scheme granting the Commission broad authority to oversee the implementation, operation and regulation of the national market system. At the same time, Congress charged the Commission with the responsibility to assure that the national market system develop and operate in accordance with specific goals and objectives. The Commission believes that the adoption of a limit order display rule furthers these goals and objectives determined by Congress.

Specifically, the display of customer limit orders advances the national market system goal of the public availability of quotation information, as well as fair competition, market efficiency, best execution and disintermediation. The enhanced transparency of such orders increases the likelihood that limit orders will be executed because contra-side market participants will have a more accurate picture of trading interest in a given security. Further, this increased visibility will enable market participants to interact directly with limit orders, rather than rely on the participation of a dealer for execution.

Moreover, the display of limit orders that are priced better than current quotes addresses at least three regulatory concerns. First, displaying customer limit orders in the quotation can increase quote competition. If the quotes from a market or market maker represent only market maker buying and selling interest in a given security, the market or market maker faces less price competition than if customer buying and selling interest is made public. As a result, the price discovery process may be constrained. Second, the display of limit orders can narrow quotation spreads. Third, because many markets and market makers offer automatic executions of small orders at the best displayed quotes, the display of limit orders that improve the best displayed quotes can result in improved executions for these orders.

Limit orders currently are handled differently in the various auction and dealer markets. Generally, the rules of most exchanges require that a limit order be displayed in the quotation for a security when it improves the best bid or offer. NYSE specialists, for example, must reflect a customer limit order in their quotations at the limit price when requested to do so. In addition, the NYSE's order handling procedures assume that all limit orders routed to a specialist through SuperDOT contain a display request. Therefore, except in the unusual and infrequent circumstance where a specialist believes market conditions suggest the likelihood of imminent price improvement, a limit order received by a specialist through SuperDOT should be reflected in the specialist's quote as soon as practicable following receipt of the order. According to the NYSE, 93% of all SuperDOT limit orders that improve the best bid or offer displayed are reflected in the specialist's quote within two minutes of receipt, while 98% of such limit orders are reflected within five minutes of receipt. . . .

Currently in the OTC market, the quote for any security typically represents a dealer's own bid and offer. The rules of the NASD do not require market makers to display customer limit orders, whether or not they better the best bid or offer for the security. Generally, customer limit orders in OTC securities either will be routed to a broker-dealer's market making desk or to another market maker for execution if the customer's firm does not make a market in the security. In the past, market makers typically did not execute limit orders until the best bid (for sell orders) or offer (for buy orders) displayed on Nasdaq reached the limit price. This practice has changed, however, in recent years. In June 1994, the Commission approved a rule change filed by the NASD that prohibits broker-dealers from trading ahead of their customers' limit orders. This rule was expanded in May 1995, to prohibit broker-dealers from trading ahead of customer limit orders they accept from other brokers. . . . .

The Commission received numerous comments concerning whether the optimal degree of pre-trade disclosure of limit orders was being achieved within the U.S. equity markets. Some commentators alleged that specialists and third market dealers sometimes fail to display limit orders priced better than the displayed quotation. Questions also were raised about the lack of limit order exposure on Nasdaq. . . .

### a. Basis for Adoption of the Rule

After carefully considering all of the comments as well as economic research regarding the Display Rule, and based on the Commission's experience and knowledge of current market practices and conditions, the Commission believes that adoption of the Display Rule will promote transparency and enhance execution opportunities for customer orders, and encourage liquidity. . . .

The Commission believes that limit orders are a valuable component of price discovery. The uniform display of such orders will encourage tighter, deeper, and more efficient markets. Limit orders convey buying and selling interest at a given price. The display of limit orders can be expected to narrow the bid-ask spread when this buying and selling interest is priced better than publicly disclosed prices. Both large and small orders stand to benefit from the Display Rule's effect on price discovery. In fact, the importance of limit orders in the trading process was documented in recent studies.[51] The author quantified the impact of exposing limit orders on quoted spreads and effective transaction costs. Using NYSE data, he determined that the quote spreads resulting from participation of the limit order book were approximately 4 to 6 cents smaller than the spreads not set by the limit order book. Further, trading costs on the NYSE were approximately 3-4 cents less per share on a "round trip" transaction when both the purchase and the sale were executed against the limit order book.

The uniform display of limit orders also will lead to increased quote-based competition. Market makers will not only be competing amongst themselves, but also against customer limit orders represented in the quote. The Commission believes that this result will reduce the possibility of certain trading behavior on Nasdaq that was recently the subject of a Commission investigation. As reported in the 21(a) Report, Nasdaq market makers widely adhered to a "pricing convention," whereby Nasdaq market makers maintained artificially inflexible quotations and as a result often traded with the public at prices unduly favorable to such market makers. . . .

[T]he Commission believes the requirement to display customer limit orders in market maker quotes would inhibit market makers from engaging in the conduct described above. Moreover, the display of limit orders reduces the potential for certain other conduct described in the 21(a) Report, including market maker collaboration and coordination of trade and quote activities. Market makers will be less able to improperly coordinate such behavior due to the display of competing customer order flow and the resulting transparency of ultimate buying and selling interest. The Commission believes that the display requirement will both foster renewed quote-based competition among market makers and introduce new competition from customer limit orders.

---

[51]    See Jason T. Greene, The Impact of Limit Order Executions on Trading Costs in NYSE Stocks (An Empirical Examination), December 1995 ("Greene Study"); see also Jason T. Greene, Limit Order Executions and Trading Costs for NYSE Stocks, June 1996 ("Greene Study II").

The Commission also believes that overall market liquidity should be enhanced due to the increased trading volume that is expected to result from the display of limit orders. As noted previously, customer limit orders account for a significant percentage of total customer orders on the NYSE, where customer limit orders generally are required to be displayed when they represent a better price. Moreover, previous Commission initiatives designed to enhance transparency have resulted in increased competition and liquidity for the markets.

Customers also will be better able to monitor the quality of their executions. Currently, the failure to display limit orders often results in inferior or missed executions for these orders. The Commission has received frequent complaints from customers whose limit orders have not been filled while other executions are reported at prices inferior to their limit order prices. Requiring the display of customer limit orders in specialist and market maker quotes, although not guaranteeing that such limit orders will be executed, will help ensure that other orders are not executed at inferior prices until better priced limit orders are executed. Similarly, customers entering market orders will be able to determine whether their orders are receiving the best price available. Customers also will be in a better position to compare the execution quality provided by different broker-dealers.

The absence of a uniform limit order display requirement across all markets has contributed to the controversy among market participants regarding the availability of true price improvement opportunities. Many claim that "hidden" limit orders in exchange markets contribute to distorted price improvement figures for these markets. This potential distortion also hinders a customer's ability to monitor execution quality. Pursuant to the Display Rule, the vast majority of limit orders will be publicly disclosed, thus enabling a more accurate comparison of price improvement opportunities, and enabling customers and broker-dealers to make more informed order routing decisions. . . .

In sum, the Commission believes the adoption of the Display Rule is an important step in furthering the goals expressed by Congress in the 1975 Amendments. The Display Rule will provide enhanced opportunities for public orders to interact with other public orders, consistent with congressional goals. In addition, the display requirement will, among other things, narrow quotes, enhance market liquidity, and improve an investor's ability to monitor the quality of its executions. This will create a better environment for execution of both limit and market orders without the participation of a dealer. The increased order interaction will result in quicker and more frequent executions of customer limit orders. The Display Rule, therefore, will increase the likelihood that limit orders will be executed, a result that the Commission believes is consistent with the duty of best execution.

———————

How do these considerations compare to those underlying the *E.F. Hutton* decision? Why doesn't the Commission rely on market forces to deal with the problems of transparency and liquidity? Are there any risks in forcing the narrowing of spreads through rules of this sort? What would you expect the result of this regulatory initiative to be? To review an NASD summary of the initial results of the SEC Order Handling Rules, see Market Quality Monitoring: Overview of 1997 Market Changes, http://www.nasd.com/mr6z.html. (avail. Sept. 21, 1998).

## B.  Payment for Order Flow

Our final subject for this chapter concerns another controversial securities industry practice that combines both fiduciary obligations and issues of market structure: payments-for-order flow.  We begin with a brief overview of the practice and potential public policy concerns.  We then turn to a recent court decision challenging the practice.

## Note, The Perils of Payment for Order Flow
### 107 Harv. L. Rev. 1675 (1994)

A number of familiar problems in the securities broker-customer context have been adequately addressed by enforcement initiatives and by structural changes that properly align broker incentives.  In recent years, however, problems associated with the relatively new practice of "payment for order flow" (POF) have caused critics to call for regulation of that practice. More specifically, critics contend that "hidden kickbacks"--payment for orders--to brokers by market-makers and regional specialists distort broker incentives so that their choices diverge from what would best serve customers.  Critics also claim that these distortions do more than disserve individual investors--they damage the market structure itself.

Stock markets in the United States come in two basic types.  First are the centralized exchange markets, in which a restricted group of dealers trade listed securities.  The exchanges are agency-auction markets.  In this type of market, customers trade with one another through commission brokers, who search for other brokers whose clients want to buy or sell at the price that their own clients are seeking.  Second is the over-the-counter (OTC) market, in which customers trade directly with broker-dealers, who use a computerized network that allows them to trade in any stock. The OTC market is a dealer market, not an agency-auction market.  Unlike the exchanges, "the OTC market [does] not depend on centralizing order flow activity in one physical location." Customers buy and sell from an OTC dealer who maintains his own portfolio in certain stocks.

A "third market" straddles these two basic markets.  It consists of approximately fifty OTC market-makers who trade certain stocks listed on the New York Stock Exchange (NYSE) or the American Stock Exchange (AMEX). The existence of this additional market means that a broker can choose to execute a customer order for a stock listed on the NYSE or AMEX either on the primary exchanges or on the third market.  The stream of customer orders from a broker either to an exchange or to the third market is referred to as "order flow."

Market-makers profit from orders by capturing the "spread" on each trade--the dealer buys a security at the lower "bid" price, sells a stock at the higher "offer" price, and captures the difference with every trade.  Payment for Order Flow (POF) is the practice whereby OTC market-makers and regional specialists pay brokers one to two cents per share for sending them order flow.  This practice originated with similar payments made by wholesale firms to their regional correspondents.  Because retail brokers--particularly discount brokers-- are likely to engage in POF, the practice has its greatest impact on small investors.

POF has become particularly controversial in the past several years as regional specialists and OTC market-makers have extended their order flow payments beyond transactions in OTC stocks to transactions in exchange-listed stocks. According to the most recent SEC estimates, fifteen to twenty percent of order flow in listed stocks is directed pursuant to payment-for- order-flow arrangements--arrangements that divert trades from the exchanges to the OTC market.  This development is one of the major causes of the recent decrease in trading on the NYSE--a drop from 79% of the total number of trades of NYSE-listed stocks in 1982 to 65% in 1992.

## I. BENEFITS OF THE PRACTICE

Supporters of POF argue that the practice contributes to efficient competition among markets, which ultimately improves capital allocation and maximizes investor returns. On this view, the payors behind POF are market-makers who can execute customer orders more efficiently than other dealers.  The benefits of the competition that these payors provide, proponents maintain, will be "indirectly passed through to customers in the form of lower commission rates, more expeditious executions, and enhanced services." POF is thus said to lead to reduced per-trade execution costs. Moreover, payments compensate order-routing firms for efficient aggregation of orders. Loss of business by markets that do not efficiently compete for order flow through improved execution facilities, order-routing mechanisms, and technology is thus a "natural phenomenon of competition and not one to be interfered with lightly by regulation."

## II. DANGERS ASSOCIATED WITH PAYMENTS FOR ORDER FLOW

### A. Best Execution

Under SEC guidelines, "[b]roker-dealers are under a duty to seek to ensure that their customers obtain the 'best execution' of their orders." Despite the assertions of POF proponents that brokers who take part in payment-for-order-flow arrangements do fulfill their duty of best execution by obtaining for customers the benefit of the quick, price-guaranteed executions that characterize their market, structural incentives and the weight of the evidence both indicate otherwise.  Moreover, the problem of skewed incentives is exacerbated because customers are handicapped by information deficiencies.

POF causes brokers to conduct their business in ways that, were they known to the customers, might not meet with the customers' approval.  For example, customers may prefer to wait fifteen seconds or even half an hour and have the opportunity to price-improve on the primary exchange rather than execute quickly at the best posted price;  but customers are not given the opportunity to choose, because the broker--who benefits from the payment-- exercises virtually invisible and therefore unchecked discretion. Moreover, because the mechanics of order-flow-payment arrangements require execution in a predetermined market, the customer loses the benefit of trade- by-trade assessment of execution quality.  Also problematic is the fact that the customer does not get the premium paid by the dealer and so does not obtain the true best inside-market price.

For customers, however, the most significant disadvantage of POF is that diversion of order flow from the NYSE floor destroys the opportunity for customers to execute their orders in between the spread or, if the spread is only 1/8 , to obtain a price cheaper by one-eighth.  A "market order" routed to the NYSE floor is not necessarily executed immediately at the best displayed quote. Instead, the specialist exposes it to the market and allows other investors to interact with the order at a price superior to the posted bid or offer; the specialist cannot trade as long as there are other investors willing to better his price. By contrast, most OTC market-makers who pay for order flow tend to execute orders immediately at the "prevailing displayed best bid or offer."

Empirical studies bolster the best execution argument against POF. One study suggests that an investor in 1989 was approximately twice as likely to get an execution between the spread on the NYSE as on the OTC market. The same study found that investors' non-NYSE executions cost them 0.7 to 1.0 cents more per share than an NYSE execution. This resulted in a total cost to investors of thirteen to eighteen million dollars in 1988, and thirty-six to forty-seven million dollars in 1989. Although the costs of non-NYSE executions are increasing, the flow away from the NYSE also appears to be increasing. One conclusion that can be drawn is that the exodus from the NYSE is due to the incentive POF gives brokers to move away from the primary exchanges.

Some of the firms that pay for order flow argue that they have implemented price-improvement mechanisms that obtain performance superior to that of the exchanges. These mechanisms, they contend, have reduced the spread throughout a major portion of the primary market, thereby creating savings for all customers. There are several reasons to think that this price- improvement argument is tenuous, however. First, although some firms do price- improve, there is little evidence that many other market-makers that pay for order flow engage in any scheme of price improvement. Second, such price-improvement measures are optional. Third, when exposing orders for price improvement, the firms in question apparently only expose them for a short period of time, do not expose the whole order, and display orders only on the Cincinnati Exchange or on NASDAQ. Fourth, some of these firms apparently offer price improvement only if the spread is greater than 1/8 --a requirement that approximately 30% of the total number of their trades meet.

### B. Market Structure

In addition to endangering best execution for customers, POF threatens the structure of the equity-trading market. POF-related fragmentation may erode crucial aspects of a healthy capital market, such as liquidity, price discovery, pricing efficiency, public confidence, competitiveness, and price stability. Proponents of the practice concede that POF may result in some fragmentation, but they argue that this is the natural result of an unregulated market and claim that fragmentation actually improves market structure by multiplying the number of market-makers, thereby increasing liquidity. In addition, proponents contend that the OTC participants contribute to the creation of public goods such as price discovery.

Primary exchanges provide liquidity, which is a necessary element of a healthy capital market. Liquidity is available in a centralized exchange because the probability of linking customers increases with the flow that comes to the floor. Because POF diverts order flow away from the exchanges, it erodes the exchanges' ability to provide liquidity. The fragmentation that POF causes will lead buyers and sellers to arrive at the market at different times, and may result in "transaction induced volatility."

POF also impairs the price-discovery function of the centralized exchanges. In a centralized exchange, accurate price discovery is achievable because posted prices reflect valuation by many traders instead of only a few, and are therefore more likely to reflect the true value of a security. POF-related fragmentation may thus hide from the economy "significant messages concerning the most efficient allocation of resources." Failure to reveal the payments for order flow to the public further contributes to the distortion of pricing by hiding part of the trade price. The resulting inaccurate securities prices may also lead to "fundamental volatility."

Even as POF impairs price discovery by fragmenting the market, it also exacerbates the problem of "free riding" on the price information produced by the NYSE. The NYSE provides a forum for determining the price of a NYSE-listed security. This price is then used by other traders, like OTC market-makers, who do not contribute to the investment made to produce it. If payors for order flow continue to free-ride on the public goods of liquidity and price discovery, not only will they erode these elements of the market, but the exchanges may not generate enough revenue to stay profitable. Impairing the primary exchanges may endanger the supply of these public goods, and potentially endanger the trading markets themselves.

As a result of the diversion of profitable stocks and trades from the NYSE, POF may result in wider spreads. Many payors for order flow cherry-pick safer stocks, leaving NYSE specialists to trade riskier ones. The evidence also suggests that payors for order flow divert small retail orders from the floor--orders that do not threaten a specialist because they are unlikely to be based on information that the specialist does not have. This means that the specialist is left to trade the larger and riskier orders--the very ones that may be based on information that the specialist does not have. The combination of POF diversion of both profitable stocks and small orders ultimately forces a specialist to widen spreads in order to gain enough profits to subsidize his riskier role.

POF may also foster oligopolistic concentration within the broker-dealer market, because brokers will tend to direct their orders to "large dealers to assure for themselves the maximum and most efficient payment of rebates." By the same token, dealers have an incentive to give larger payments to large brokers, thereby securing the maximum order flow at the minimum operational expense. This increased concentration of both market-makers and brokers will ultimately hurt public investors by decreasing competitive pressures on price.

POF may harm the market in other ways as well. Because POF involves secret payments, it may diminish public confidence in the market and lead to decreased investment. Payments for order flow divert trading away from primary exchanges, and so hurt the public investors who are favored by the rigid regulation in these markets. Finally, because payors for order flow receive a guaranteed quantity of orders from brokers, they may have less incentive to attract customers by posting competitive quotes with a narrow spread.

---

# Guice v. Charles Schwab & Co.
## 89 N.Y.2d 31, 674 N.E.2d 282 (N.Y.1996)

The plaintiffs in these appeals are former retail customers of defendants Charles Schwab & Co., Inc. (Schwab) and Fidelity Brokerage Services, Inc. (Fidelity). Schwab and Fidelity are "discount" stock brokerage houses, operating nationwide, who charge reduced commissions for effecting securities transactions for their clientele and hold themselves out as offering quicker executions of orders on behalf of customers who have already decided upon what securities to buy or sell. . . . .

All of the plaintiffs' causes of action arise out of defendants' receipt of what is known in the securities industry as "order flow payments." The practice of order flow payment consists of remuneration in the form of monetary or other benefits given to retail securities broker-dealers for routing customers' orders for execution to wholesale dealers or other market makers in the subject securities. Paying for order flow originated many years ago in the over-the-counter (OTC) market, when regional broker-dealers were paid a fee by wholesale market makers in the OTC security bought or sold, for directing orders to them for execution.[2] With the advent of computer technological advances capable of providing an entirely automated market system independent of the floor of any stock exchange (such as the National Association of Securities Dealers Automated Quotation [NASDAQ] System), and automated trading systems permitting accelerated execution of orders by regional exchange specialists, OTC market makers and member firms of the regional stock exchanges could compete for orders in listed stocks with the national New York and American Stock Exchanges.[3] Thus, routing orders in listed stocks to OTC market makers and regional exchange specialists has more recently become a major source of order flow payments to retail broker-dealers.[4]

Plaintiffs' complaints allege that the defendants' acceptance of order flow payments breached the fiduciary relationship between them and their customers in the plaintiff member classes under common-law agency principles. Plaintiffs also allege that the acceptance of order flow payments itself is illegal and actionable because it violates a broker's duty to obtain the "best execution" (i.e., execute the transaction under the most favorable possible terms) of its customers' orders. . . .

Schwab and Fidelity moved to dismiss the complaints on grounds, inter alia, that enforcing plaintiffs' state common-law and statutory causes of action would violate the United

---

[2]    Payment For Order Flow, SEC Exchange Act Release No. 34-33026 (Oct. 6, 1993), reprinted in 58 Fed Reg 52934, 52935-52936; Facciolo and Stone, Avoiding the Inevitable: The Continuing Viability of State Law Claims in the Face of Primary Jurisdiction and Preemption Challenges Under the Securities Exchange Act of 1934, 1995 Colum Bus Law Rev 525, 640 (hereinafter cited as "Facciolo and Stone").

[3]    Securities and Exchange Commission Division of Market Regulation, Market 2000, An Examination of Current Equity Market Developments, at 8-9 (1994)

[4]    SEC Exchange Act Release No. 34-33026, supra, 58 Fed Reg, at 52936.

States Constitution's Commerce Clause (U.S. Const, art I, § 8) and Supremacy Clause (id., art VI, cl 2), and interfere with the primary jurisdiction of the Securities and Exchange Commission (SEC). In each case, the complaint was dismissed by Supreme Court [of New York] under the Supremacy Clause, on the ground that plaintiffs' causes of action were pre-empted by the Securities Exchange Act of 1934, as amended, and the SEC Regulations promulgated thereunder.

The Appellate Division . . . noted that plaintiff "as limited by his brief, does not seek to bar totally the practice of payments for order flow, 'except where, as here, "full and frank disclosure" has not been made' " The Court concluded that, upon that basis, plaintiff Guice's causes of action were not pre-empted by federal law and that the primary jurisdiction doctrine was not a bar. . . .

The Supremacy Clause of the United States Constitution, directing that federal laws "shall be the supreme Law of the Land * * * any Thing in the Constitution or Laws of any State to the Contrary notwithstanding" (U.S. Const, art VI, cl 2), thereby vests in Congress the power to supersede not only state statutory or regulatory law but common law as well (see, Freightliner Corp. v. Myrick, 115 S Ct 1483, 1487; International Paper Co. v. Ouellette, 479 U.S. 481, 496). The pre-emption question is ultimately one of congressional intent (see, Barnett Bank of Marion County v Nelson, 116 S Ct 1103, 1107; California Fed. Sav. & Loan Assn. v Guerra, 479 U.S. 272, 280). As recapitulated most recently in Barnett Bank (supra, 116 S Ct, at 1107-1108), congressional pre-emptive intent may be shown from express language in the federal statute; it may also be established implicitly because the federal legislation is so comprehensive in its scope that it is inferable that Congress wished fully to occupy the field of its subject matter ("field pre-emption"), or because state law conflicts with the federal law. Implied conflict pre-emption may be found when it is impossible for one to act in compliance with both the federal and state laws, or when "the state law * * * 'stan[ds] as an obstacle to the accomplishment and execution of the full purposes and objectives of Congress' " (id., at 1108, quoting Hines v. Davidowitz, 312 U.S. 55, 67; City of New York v. Job-Lot Pushcart, 88 N.Y.2d 163, 170).

Moreover, federal administrative agency regulations, promulgated pursuant to congressional delegation of discretionary quasi-legislative authority to effectuate congressional purposes, may also pre-empt state law (see, Capital Cities Cable, Inc. v Crisp, 467 U.S. 691, 699-700). "When the administrator promulgates regulations intended to pre-empt state law, the court's inquiry is * * * limited: 'If [h]is choice represents a reasonable accommodation of conflicting policies that were committed to the agency's care by the statute, we should not disturb it unless it appears from the statute or its legislative history that the accommodation is not one that Congress would have sanctioned' " (Fidelity Fed. Sav. & Loan Assn. v de la Cuesta, 458 U.S. 141, 154, quoting United States v. Shimer, 367 U.S. 374, 383 [brackets in the original] ).

The potential collision here of plaintiffs' state law causes of action with federal law arises out of the 1975 amendments to the Securities Exchange Act of 1934 and the implementing regulations of the SEC. The 1975 amendments were enacted in response to a congressional perception of "the securities industry's languor in the face of great change and great opportunity." Congress identified the causes of that languor to include "price fixing [of] commission rates; artificial * * * [and] unjustified barriers to access to markets and market makers; opposition to market integration from powerful vested interests; * * * [and] the absence of effective control of market developments and operations by the Securities and Exchange Commission"

Thus, Congress concluded that new legislation was necessary whereby "the SEC is granted broad and flexible authority to shape a new market system adequate to the needs of investors in this country and around the world" The bill was designed to give the SEC power to "eliminate all unnecessary or inappropriate burdens on competition," "pursue the goal to centralized trading of securities" and "provide leadership for the development of a more coherent and rational regulatory structure to correspond to and to police effectively the new national market system."

Accordingly, to the original Securities Exchange Act's enumerated reasons for requiring regulation of the securities industry, the 1975 amendments added the necessity "to remove impediments to and perfect the mechanisms of a national market system for securities and a national system for the clearance and settlement of securities transactions" (Section 2 of the 1934 Act). Congress made specific findings that it was in the public interest to assure "economically efficient execution of securities transactions; [and] fair competition among brokers and dealers, among exchange markets, and between exchange markets and markets other than exchange markets" (Section 11A[a][1][C] [i], [ii] of the 1934 Act ).

Under the 1975 amendments, the SEC was "directed, therefore, having due regard for the public interest, the protection of investors, and the maintenance of fair and orderly markets, to use its authority under this chapter to facilitate the establishment of a national market system for securities * * * and to carry out the objectives set forth in paragraph (1) of this subsection (Section 11A[a][2] of the 1934 Act).

Congress also authorized implementing regulations to "assure the prompt, accurate, reliable, and fair collection * * * [and] distribution * * * of information with respect to * * * transactions in such securities and the fairness and usefulness of the form and content of such information" (Section 11A[c][1][B] of the 1934 Act).

Acting under the foregoing legislative directions and delegation of authority, in 1977 the SEC adopted Rule 10b-10, regarding information to be disclosed on customers' confirmation statements upon the execution of customers' orders. The disclosure requirements of Rule 10b-10 were proposed by the SEC as "a uniform rule applicable to all who wish to effect transactions for or with investors" (Securities Confirmations Proposed Rule, SEC Exchange Act Release No. 12806 [Sept. 16, 1976], reprinted in 41 Fed Reg 41432, 41432). The SEC decided the nature and extent of such disclosure by "adjust[ing] regulatory requirements to eliminate those for which compliance costs appear to be disproportionate to the practical benefits of investor protection thereby obtained" (id.). Thus, as originally adopted, Rule 10b-10 contained a requirement that on a customer's confirmation statement the broker-dealer disclose "whether any other remuneration [other than the amount received from the customer and certain specified sources] has been or will be received and that the source and amount of such other remuneration will be furnished upon written request" (Securities Confirmations, SEC Exchange Act Release No. 34-13508 [May 5, 1977] [announcing adoption of Rule 10b-10], reprinted in 42 Fed Reg 25318, 25323, codified as amended at Rule 10b-10[a][7][iv] ).

### Federal Regulation of Order Flow Payments

The SEC has monitored and studied securities industry assessments of the practice of order flow payments for over a decade (SEC Exchange Act Release No. 34-33026, supra, 58 Fed Reg, at 52935). The agency conducted a round table discussion on the subject in 1989 (id.). The

SEC consistently applied the confirmation statement remuneration disclosure mandate of the original Rule 10b-10 to order flow payments (Release No. 34-33036, supra, 58 Fed Reg, at 59936-37 ["Thus, Rule 10b-10 currently requires a broker-dealer to indicate specifically if it is receiving payments for order flow in connection with a particular trade."] ). It is uncontested that Schwab and Fidelity complied with the applicable disclosure requirements of then Rule 10b-10 on the confirmation statements they sent to all of the putative plaintiff class members here.

In 1993, the SEC proposed to amend and add to its disclosure regulations in order to address with more particularity the practice of order flow payments (SEC Exchange Act Release No. 34-33026, supra). The SEC's decision-making process entailed the same interest balancing and cost/benefit analysis as was utilized in initially adopting Rule 10b-10. The SEC reviewed the potential detrimental effects of order flow payments, including potential conflicts of interest between customer and broker (Release No. 34-33036, supra, 58 Fed Reg, at 52936), possible breach of duty of best execution of orders under common-law agency principles and possible commission of commercial bribery under federal and state law (id., 58 Fed Reg, at 52937-52939, 52941). Thus, the agency recognized that there were critics who advocated drastic restrictions on order flow payments, if not outright elimination of the practice (id., 58 Fed Reg, at 52941).

Conversely, the SEC's 1993 proposed rulemaking on order flow payments recognized that the securities industry gained economic advantages from the practice, which ultimately benefitted the investor public (id., 58 Fed Reg, at 52939-52940).

The SEC rejected any extreme approach in favor of a proposed rule to expand disclosure of the receipt of order flow payments. The agency proposed to amend Rule 10b-10: (1) to include a broad definition of the practice itself, that would also cover various commonly employed forms of nonmonetary remuneration; and (2) to require confirmation statement disclosure of the receipt of order flow payments and the specific dollar "amount of any monetary payment, discount, rebate or reduction of fee" received (Release No. 34-33026, supra, 58 Fed Reg, at 52940). Additionally, the SEC proposed a new Rule 11 Ac1-3 to require disclosure on each new customer's account statement and annually thereafter as to the broker-dealer's policies concerning the receipt of order flow payments and annual disclosure of the aggregate dollar amount of such payments, rebates, etc. (id., 58 Fed Reg, at 52940). The agency invited comment on its proposal and upon more drastic alternative regulation of order flow payments, including outright elimination of the practice or requiring dealers to pass onto customers the order flow payment received (id., 58 Fed Reg, at 52941-42).

Approximately a year later, the SEC announced adoption of its final rule for regulation of order flow payments (Payment For Order Flow, SEC Exchange Act Release No. 34-34902 [Oct. 27, 1994], reprinted in 59 Fed Reg 55006).[6] It explained that it rejected elimination of order flow payments entirely because the practice did not necessarily violate a broker-dealer's best

---

[6]    In pertinent part the final rule added a new paragraph (9)(e) (defining payment for order flow), added a new subparagraph (a)(7)(iii) (governing disclosure of order flow payment at confirmation), and added a new Rule 11Ac1-3 (governing disclosure on customer account statements). These changes were codified respectively at Rule 10b-10(a)(9)(e), (a)(7)(iii), and Rule 11Ac1-3. Additionally, former subparagraph (a)(7)(iii) of Rule 10b-10--the original confirmation statement remuneration requirement--was redesignated subparagraph (a)(7)(iv).

execution obligation, and that the practice benefitted the securities industry in lowering execution costs, in facilitating technological advances in retail customer order handling practices and in enhancing competition among broker- dealers and the various exchange and nonexchange securities markets and, thus, also worked to the advantage of investors (id., 59 Fed Reg, at 55007- 55011). The SEC also noted the serious enforcement problems that elimination of the practice would entail and the drastic impact that an outright ban would have on the securities industry (id., 59 Fed Reg, at 55011).

The SEC's 1994 final rule regulating the practice of order flow payments largely followed the disclosure requirements it had proposed a year earlier. However, the agency--again employing cost/benefit analysis--eliminated the proposed disclosure requirements that confirmation statements and annual account statements show dollar amounts received for order routing. The SEC was apprehensive that mandatory disclosure of specific monetary receipts might be "unworkable" (id., Fed Reg 59, at 55010) and would, at the least, impose "an extreme burden" upon broker-dealers "to determine the amounts received from each order in time for a confirmation" and would entail expenses disproportionately high in relation to the potential benefits to customers (id., 59 Fed Reg, at 55010 n 39).

**Pre-Emption Analysis As Applied to Plaintiff's Common-Law Agency Causes of Action**

Pre-emption analysis must begin with a description of the nature of plaintiffs' causes of action and whether they represent colorable claims from which liability could be imposed. In this Court, as before the Appellate Division, plaintiffs have abandoned their statutory and common-law claims based on the per se illegality of defendants' receipt of order flow payments. Instead, plaintiffs rely exclusively on allegations in their identical complaints that Schwab and Fidelity violated their common-law agency relationships with customers comprising the putative plaintiff classes. Specifically, they allege that Schwab and Fidelity breached their common-law duties, owed to each member of the plaintiff classes, of undivided loyalty under which they were limited to acting in any stock transaction solely in the interest of each firm's principal.

Plaintiffs allege that the acceptance by defendants of order flow payments, which they characterize as "kickbacks," violated the agency relationship with each class member because customers' orders were accepted and routed "without full and frank disclosure" of each defendant's dual role in the transaction, which disclosure "to be effective must lay bare the truth, without ambiguity or reservation, in all its stark significance" (Complaints, ¶ 8). Plaintiffs aver that defendants' disclosures to the members of the class were inadequate (rendering their dual role and self-dealing actionable) in failing to inform the "class members prior to the execution of any transaction that [defendants] would be receiving a kickback, let alone the amount thereof" (Complaints, ¶ 9). They allege that the disclosure on the customers' confirmation statements (in compliance with then Rule 10b-10 [a][7][iii] ), that remuneration was received and would be further described upon request, "falls far short of the full and frank disclosure required by law" (id.).

Plaintiffs' allegations of the standard of disclosure which must be made by an agent, having a personal interest in the principal's transaction prior to the execution of the transaction, has support in New York agency law precedents. Indeed, plaintiffs plead verbatim this Court's articulation of an agent's obligation to make a full and complete disclosure of any conflict of interest in a transaction conducted for the principal:

Disclosure . . . indefinite and equivocal does not set the agent free to bargain for his own account or for the account of a corporation which acts through him alone. If dual interests are to be served, the disclosure to be effective must lay bare the truth, without ambiguity or reservation, in all its stark significance (Wendt v Fischer, 243 N.Y. 439, 443 [Cardozo, J.].

In such conflict of interest situations, the Restatement (Second) of Agency states that advance disclosure by the agent is required of "all facts which the agent knows or should know would reasonably affect the principal's judgment" whether to consent to the agent's dual role (Restatement [Second] of Agency, § 390 and comment a, at 208-209). Thus, facially, plaintiffs have pleaded actionable claims under New York common-law agency principles, and similar claims could have been brought in the courts of other States who subscribe to the views of the Restatement (Second) of Agency. And a jury could have found against Schwab or Fidelity under these principles because no specific pre-transaction disclosure of defendants' receipt of order flow payments was made, nor of the dollar amounts of such payments to be received in the transaction, which disclosure might have affected the judgment of the customers.

Upon the basis of the legislative history of the 1975 amendments to the Securities Exchange Act and the history of SEC's implementing regulations applicable to order flow payment disclosure, we are convinced that permitting the courts of each State to enforce the foregoing common-law agency standards of disclosure on the practice of order flow payments in civil damage actions would unavoidably result in serious interference with the "accomplishment and execution of the full purposes and objectives of Congress" (Hines v. Davidowitz, supra, 312 US, at 67), in enacting the 1975 amendments, and would directly conflict with SEC regulations limiting the disclosure requirements regarding receipt of order flow payments to less exacting, post- transaction information on customer confirmation statements and disclosure of general policies of the broker on initial and annual customers' account statements.

As we have shown, the 1975 amendments to the Securities Exchange Act were intended to give the SEC the power administratively to develop a "coherent and rational regulatory structure to correspond to and to police effectively the new national market system" Among the goals of Congress in that legislation was to spark the creation of such a national market system for security trading, which would assure more "economically efficient execution of securities transactions" and promote greater competition among all securities industry players, including competition "between exchange markets and markets other than exchange markets" (Section 11A[a][1][C] of the 1934 Act). The SEC was directed administratively to promote those goals. Congress also recognized that its objectives would require SEC regulation of disclosures regarding securities transactions, including "the fairness and usefulness of the form and content of such information" (Section 11A[c] [1][B] of the 1934 Act).

Acting pursuant to that delegated authority, the SEC fashioned customer disclosure requirements applicable to the receipt of order flow payments in 1977 under the original Rule 10b-10, and in 1994 by amendments to Rule 10b-10 and the adoption of new Rule 11Ac1-3. In each instance, the agency determined the nature and extent of the disclosure requirements, based on an interest-weighing, cost/benefit analysis. In applying the former Rule 10b-10 disclosure requirements to order flow payments and in specifically addressing the practice in its 1994 rulemaking on the subject, the SEC recognized that order flow payments further the purposes of Congress by enhancing more efficient and less costly execution of customers' orders and by promoting competition for order executions among all markets, with demonstrated beneficial results for individual investors.

Permitting the courts of each State to impose civil liability on national securities brokerage firms, such as Schwab and Fidelity, for failure to meet more stringent common-law agency standards of disclosure of receipt of order flow payments (rather than the federally-mandated uniform specific disclosure on post-transaction confirmation statements and general disclosure on new customer account statements and annual statements, under the SEC's amended Rule 10b-10 and Rule 11Ac1-3) would inevitably defeat the congressional purpose of enabling the SEC to develop and police that "coherent regulatory structure" for a national market system. Securities broker-dealers, confronted with the risk of nation-wide class action civil damage liability, including restitution of commissions and punitive damages--as plaintiffs seek here-- would be impelled to tailor their disclosures to each State's common-law agency jurisprudence, and the carefully-crafted SEC disclosure requirements would have little, if any, influence.[7] Surely, "[i]t is unlikely--to say the least--that Congress intended to establish such a chaotic regulatory structure" (International Paper Co. v. Ouellette, supra, 479 US, at 497).

When, thus, a State's regulation, through the imposition of common-law tort liability or otherwise, adversely affects the ability of a federal administrative agency to regulate comprehensively and with uniformity in accordance with the objectives of Congress, "then the state law may be pre- empted even though 'collision between the state and federal regulation may not be an inevitable consequence' " ( Schneidewind v. ANR Pipeline Co., 485 U.S. 293, 310, quoting Northern Natural Gas Co. v State Corp. Commn. of Kansas, 372 U.S. 84, 91-92).

State civil actions based upon common-law agency doctrine would thwart the objectives of Congress in a second respect. As already noted, the SEC determined that the practice of order flow payments brings about constructive results furthering the goals of Congress in the 1975 amendments to the Securities Exchange Act. It also found that stricter disclosure requirements than those ultimately adopted under its rules might be unworkable or costly out of all proportion to possible benefits to investors. Thus, the SEC rejected proposals for more exacting disclosure, anticipating that, at the least, the increased cost of such disclosure would be passed onto customers in higher commissions or to market makers in higher fees for order routing--outcomes clearly counterproductive to congressional objectives of economically-efficient execution of orders, lower execution costs and vigorous competition among OTC and exchange markets. At worst, onerous stricter disclosure costs plus the threat of lawsuits all around the country, based on breach of common-law agency relationships, would likely result in many brokerage firms abandoning acceptance of order flow payments altogether, an even more drastic undermining of congressional objectives. . . . [T]he SEC, acting reasonably within its rule-making authority, adopted a policy, incorporated in regulations, of permitting the practice of order flow payments and not unduly inhibiting the practice by oppressive disclosure requirements. These goals and policies of the SEC are "antithetical to threshold limitations placed" on order flow payment practices in the form of severely, if not prohibitively, burdensome additional disclosure

---

[7]    Securities industry representatives expressed to the SEC their apprehension of exposure to liability if common-law agency principles were allowed to prevail over SEC uniform disclosure requirements . . .

requirements imposed by application of each State's common-law of agency in civil damage actions.

We reject plaintiffs' contention that there is no pre-emption here because compliance with State common-law disclosure standards under agency doctrine would not prevent compliance with SEC regulatory disclosure requirements, and because greater disclosure promotes the same investor- protection purposes of the federal regulations. Even if the goals of federal and state law are the same, "[a] state law also is preempted if it interferes with the methods by which the federal statute was designed to reach this goal" (International Paper Co. v. Ouellette, 479 US, at 494, supra). The stricter standards of order flow payment disclosure which may be required under State common-law agency principles inevitably will supplant the disclosure rules of the SEC on the same subject and come to dominate the relationship between broker and customer, since the broker would not be able to avoid civil liability for acceptance of order flow payments merely by complying with federal regulations.

Unquestionably, however, state common-law standards for disclosure when an agent has a financial stake in a transaction effected on behalf of a principal are set generally, and would be applied to broker-dealer receipt of order flow payments, without engaging in the policy choices and balancing of the competing legitimate interests of investors, exchange and nonexchange markets and other participants in the securities industry, that the SEC was charged by Congress to perform and that are involved in regulation of order flow payments. Thus, although both state common-law actions and federal regulations may promote broker-dealers' disclosure to customers, state enforcement of agency law standards of disclosure cannot help but upset the policy-based delicate balance Congress directed the SEC to achieve in the regulatory regime envisaged under the 1975 amendments to the Securities Exchange Act. . . .

### The Effect of Securities Exchange Act § 28(a) on the Pre-emption Issue

Plaintiffs contend that any inference of pre-emptive intent by Congress under the 1975 amendments to the Securities Exchange Act is negated by the "savings" clauses incorporated in the statute by section 28(a) of the Act. That section provides that the Exchange Act's rights and remedies are "in addition to any and all other rights and remedies that may exist at law or in equity," and that the Act does not "affect the jurisdiction of [state securities regulatory bodies] over any security or any person *insofar as it does not conflict* with the provisions of this chapter or the rules and regulations thereunder" (emphasis supplied). We conclude that section 28(a) does not foreclose the implied conflict pre-emption we find here. First, the legislative history of section 28(a) indicates that its purpose was to "leave the States with as much leeway to regulate securities transactions as the Supremacy Clause would allow them in the absence of such a provision," and particularly, "to save state blue-sky laws from pre-emption" (Le Roy v. Great Western United Corp., 443 U.S. 173, 182 n 13 [describing the testimony of the principal draftsman of the Exchange Act in Senate hearings on the legislation]).

Substantially similar savings clauses have been interpreted as only negating implied field pre-emption, but not conflict pre-emption, leaving the courts to determine when any given state regulation is impliedly pre-empted because it prevents compliance with the federal law or the full achievement of congressional objectives (International Paper v. Ouellette, supra, 479 US, at 492-494).

Finally, the Supreme Court in Freightliner Corp. v. Myrick (115 S Ct 1483, supra), held that inclusion of an express provision in a federal statute dealing with the pre-emption issue may support an inference negating implied pre-emption, but this "does not mean that the express clause entirely forecloses any possibility of implied pre-emption" (115 S Ct, at 1488). Any inference negating implied pre-emption was completely overcome here because, as we have demonstrated, enforcement of state common-law duties of disclosure under its agency jurisprudence not only would have "the potential," but would inevitably "undermine [the finely-crafted and balanced federal] regulatory structure" (International Paper Co., supra, 479 US, at 497).

## Comments and Questions

1. In the final section of its decision, the *Guice* court discusses the impact of section 28(a) of the 1934 Act. How persuasive do you find this aspect of the decision? Should the court have given weight to the fact that in the National Securities Market Improvements Act of 1996, Congress expressly preempted a number of state registration and recordkeeping requirements for broker-dealers but elected not to disturb residual anti-fraud rules? Would the plaintiffs be precluded from recasting this case as a federal anti-fraud claim?

2. In the course of its decision, the court recounts the SEC's recent rulemaking efforts to deal with payments-for-order-flow. How would you characterize those efforts? How likely are they to address the policy concerns presented by the practice?

3. As a further effort to crack down on payment-for-order-flow and related practices, one SEC commissioner has called for the "decimalization" of trading markets whereby stock prices would be permitted to tick up or down in increments of five cents or less, rather than the normal one-eighth of a dollar (12.5 cent) movements currently used in most U.S. markets. See *SEC Member Wants Prices Quoted in Dollars and Cents*, Wall St. J., Sept. 26, 1996. What effect would such a proposal have? Would you recommend the Commission require decimalization?

### Problem 11-3

As law clerk to a federal district court judge, you have been asked to evaluate the following complaint. Does it state a cause of action under federal law?

Defendants in this case, Merrill Lynch Pierce Fenner & Smith, Inc. ("Merrill Lynch"), PaineWebber, Inc. ("PaineWebber") and Dean Witter Reynolds, Inc. ("Dean Witter"), are "integrated broker/dealer" brokerage companies that transact trades both as agents and as principals. Plaintiffs Bruce Zakheim IRA FBO Bruce Zakheim ("Zakheim"), a Merrill Lynch customer, Gloria Binder ("Binder"), a Painewebber customer, and Jeffrey Phillip Kravitz ("Kravitz"), a Dean Witter customer retained defendants to either conduct trades on their behalf or to trade with them directly in various over-the-counter ("OTC") securities.

The gravamen of plaintiffs' complaint is as follows:

1) As agents, defendants relied exclusively on the National Best Bid and Offer ("NBBO"), a price quotation representing the best bid and best offer of any OTC market maker in a particular security on the two-sided NASDAQ market, to fulfill their duty to execute their customers' market orders[1] at the best available price, despite the availability of better prices from a number of sources of liquidity. Those sources included SelectNet [NASDAQ's on-line trading system], Instinet [a proprietary on-line trading system], in-house limit orders, in-house market orders, and the SOES [Small Order Execution System] limit order file. Plaintiffs contend that by failing to take advantage of these other sources and by failing to disclose such neglect, defendants breached a fiduciary duty they owed to plaintiffs by dint of the broker/customer relationship that existed between them.

2) As principals, defendants not only failed to execute plaintiffs' market orders at the best available price but also employed a number of fraudulent devices to secretly accrue profits for themselves. Failure to disclose both the accrual of such profits and the practice of failing to execute at the best available price, according to plaintiffs, amounted to fraud. Moreover, defendants were unjust enriched by the accrual of secret profits.

The parties agree that all the transactions in question here were executed by defendants, either as agents or principals, at prices that were equivalent to the NBBO at the time of each transaction.

The fraudulent devices alleged by plaintiffs to have been employed by the defendants in their role as principals, are as follows:

1) Failure to reference sources other than the NBBO when setting prices, as principals, for transactions with retail customers: By setting the price of their transactions as principals with reference exclusively to the NBBO, defendants arbitrarily made parity with the NBBO the de facto standard for best execution. Because prices superior to the NBBO, from the standpoint of the retail customer, were in fact available from other sources of liquidity at the time of those transactions, defendants were able to establish market positions, both long and short, that were, in fact, better, from their standpoint, than those that represented the "best available price" at any given time. By establishing such superior positions, defendants were able to profit from the difference between the NBBO and the best available price.

2) Failure to cross in-house market orders: Plaintiffs contend that when defendants received contemporaneous market orders to buy and sell shares in the same stock they systematically failed to execute those orders at a price between the bid and ask, executing each instead at the NBBO quote, thereby appropriating the "spread" between the bid and asked prices on the two-sided NASDAQ market while incurring no risk to themselves.[2]

---

[1]    An instruction from a retail customer to buy or sell securities at the best available market price that is distinguished from a "limit order," an instruction to buy or sell at a particular price, specified by the customer.

[2]    Plaintiffs distinguish between situations in which balanced numbers of buy and sell orders are received, and situations in which unbalanced orders were received. The same failure to cross market orders is alleged in both cases. The difference is that in the unbalanced case, defendants are alleged to

3) Failure to cross customers' market orders with in-house limit orders: Plaintiffs contend that defendants executed customers' market orders at the NBBO despite having received corresponding "limit" orders in the same security from other customers. Defendants thereby appropriated the "spread" while incurring no risk to themselves.

4) Failure to cross customers' market orders with SOES limit orders: executing orders to either sell or buy shares of particular stocks at the NBBO despite the currency of "limit" orders on the SOES limit order file.

5) Re-trading at the inside price on the "same side" of the spread: executing market orders to either sell or buy shares of particular stocks at the NBBO quotes despite better prices being available, and then immediately retrading those same shares at those better prices for defendants' own profits, incurring no risk by trading on the same side of spread. Amended Complaint ¶ 37.

6) Selling order flow: Without knowledge or consent of the customers placing the orders and in exchange for payments ("payment for order flow"), defendants allegedly routed plaintiffs' market orders to other brokers who failed to execute them at the best available price and who used one or more of the above fraudulent devices to secretly accrue profits to themselves.

See In re Merrill Lynch et al., 911 F. Supp. 754 (D.N.J. 1995), *aff'd*, 115 F.3d 1127 (3d Cir. 1997), *reversed en banc*, 1998 WL 32535 (3d Cir. Jan. 30, 1998).

---

have taken advantage of another fraudulent device, using the NBBO rather than a better available price on SelectNet or Instinet, with respect to the remaining shares.

# CHAPTER TWELVE

# INTRODUCTION TO INVESTMENT COMPANIES

Investment companies are vehicles for the pooled investment of funds under the management of a third party. Thus, as a functional matter, investment companies are similar to bank collective trust funds and insurance company separate accounts, products that are discussed elsewhere in this book. Investment companies serve two important economic functions. First, they provide small investors, who otherwise would not be able to afford a private money manager nor have the expertise to make complicated investment decisions, with professional management advice. Second, investment companies offer investment diversification that individual investors would have difficulty achieving with direct investments in stocks and bonds.

Investment companies are fundamentally different from most business enterprises in both their structure and operation. Unlike a typical corporation in which management is internally organized, most investment companies are dominated by an outside entity — typically, an investment adviser. The investment company itself is generally a "legal shell" consisting only of a collection of assets. In the United States, investment companies do not typically have employees or any physical plant. Rather, the investment company contracts with the sponsor and other affiliated parties for all services necessary to manage the company's investments and distribute its shares to the public.

In this chapter and the next, we offer an introduction to the regulation of investment companies in the United States. Section One presents an overview of the history of the investment company industry and briefly summarizes the current structure of the U.S. investment company industry and its regulation. Section Two offers an overview of the many legal and business decisions relevant to the formation of an investment company.

Readers interested in a comprehensive treatment of the field should consult Tamar Frankel's excellent treatise, THE REGULATION OF MONEY MANAGERS: THE INVESTMENT COMPANY ACT AND THE INVESTMENT ADVISERS ACT (1978 & Supp.). For a looseleaf service with up-to-date information on the subject, see THOMAS P. LEMKE, ET AL., REGULATION OF INVESTMENT COMPANIES (1996 & Supp.). For the SEC's last substantial study of investment company regulation, see PROTECTING INVESTORS: A HALF-CENTURY OF INVESTMENT COMPANY REGULATION (May 29, 1992).

# Section 1. History of the Investment Companies

Unlike banks and insurance companies, investment companies are regulated almost exclusively at the federal level. Before the mid-1930s, investment companies had only to comply with state blue sky rules, corporation laws (if applicable) and a few state statutes. But, federal legislative initiatives soon came to dominate these laws. For many years, investment companies like broker-dealers had to comply with both federal and state laws. But in 1996, Congress largely preempted state blue-sky oversight of investment companies.

The first federal moves to regulate investment company practice were the Securities Act of 1933 and the Securities Exchange Act of 1934. These statutes provided an expansive set of issuer disclosure requirements triggered by the offer, sale, and trading of securities and anti-fraud rules which were to protect defrauded investors. However, they did not address the specific regulatory needs of investment companies.

Subsequently, in 1940, Congress adopted the Investment Company Act which established the first comprehensive federal regulatory framework for investment companies. Its purpose was to protect shareholders of investment companies from a broad array of abuses found in the industry before its enactment. It thus contains broad prohibitions on many activities, requires disclosure of particular information, and forces companies into a corporate governance style self-regulatory system.

A companion act, the Investment Advisers Act of 1940, placed regulations on those who give investment advice. It set up standards for advisers, established anti-fraud causes of action for defrauded clients and gave regulatory control over advisers to the SEC. Since then, the 1940 Acts have remained relatively unchanged, with only one series of amendments occurring in the 1970's. An appreciation of the abusive practices committed by investment companies before these two Acts is essential for a clear understanding of the Acts' particular rules and the regulatory structures they put into place.

## A. Origin and Development of the Investment Company

*English Roots*

The U.S. investment company structure traces its origins to Scotland and England in the mid-nineteenth century. Its development was occasioned by two primary social and economic conditions -- foreign nations needed capital and a more affluent British public had capital to spare. After the Napoleonic Wars, England became the leading creditor nation, financing foreign governments, colonies, and private industry. Because of the practical difficulties of investing capital abroad, joint investment structures were formed with professional advisers. In fact, many investment companies were set up to invest in the United States, mainly in railroad securities. Robert Fleming, largely considered to be the father of investment companies, formed the first Scottish association to invest in railway bonds in 1873.

Owing to the English industrial revolution, wealth spread over a larger populace and families and individuals accumulated excess savings available for investment. However, the combination of the difficulties related to foreign investment, the inexperience of investors in making investment decisions and the lack of financial resources that would be required to hire private investment managers left a gap to be filled by professional investment managers. Companies such as the Foreign and Colonial Government Trust were thus formed to "provide the investor of moderate means the same advantages as the large capitalist, in diminishing the risk of investing in Foreign and Colonial Government Stocks, by spreading the investment over a number of different stocks."

*Early Investment Companies in the United States*

The development of investment companies in the United States was influenced by the examples and experiences of British investment companies. The first wave of investment companies, also known as investment trusts, formed following World War I. Similar to English experience, at that time the United States had become a creditor nation, exporting capital to help rebuild European economies. In the United States, this was also a time of relatively widespread prosperity. The general public, awakened to the benefits of investments in the stock market in the 1920s, turned to professional managers. In response, a slew of investment companies were formed by bankers, brokers, investment counsel and industrialists who had experience in the capital markets, or wanted to (legally or illegally) gain from the investment company funds. They principally arose in the large East-coast cities, such as New York, Chicago, and Boston. In fact, one of the interesting features of the development of the investment company industry, and in particular the mutual fund industry, is the relative importance of Boston in the process.

As early as the mid-nineteenth century, Boston was known for its numerous private trustees managing individual and family wealth. The "Boston trustee" quickly became associated with the investment company business in the 1920s. In 1924, what is considered to be the first open-end or "mutual" fund, Massachusetts Investors Trust ("MIT"), was formed in Boston. MIT was unique in that it had a "share-liquidation" feature — that is, it allowed shareholders to redeem their shares with the trust upon demand. It later became the largest investment company for a quarter of a century. State Street Investment Corporation and Incorporated Investors, both also considered "open-end" funds because of their share-redemption features, opened their doors soon thereafter.

Before the 1920s, relatively few investment companies formed. By 1927 there were about 160 investment companies with total assets of around $1 billion. In 1928, the flood of new investment companies continued. One hundred forty new companies were formed; and in 1929, 186 new companies appeared. By the end of 1929, there were 675 investment companies with total assets close to $7 billion. Of these, 174 were closed-end funds with assets of $2.6 billion. Nineteen were open-end funds with $140 million in assets. In these early years, the corporate structure of investment companies varied greatly. However, most were corporations, of the closed-end variety; most had a complicated capital structure; and most were "pyramided" or owned or were owned by other investment companies.

Despite this rapid growth in investment companies, regulation of the industry was minimal at best. Governing their conduct and development were state blue sky laws, laws related to corporate governance, fraud, private contract and a few quasi-fiduciary obligations found in the common-law. Some states, including Ohio, Minnesota, Michigan, Alabama, Kentucky, and New Hampshire established substantial regulation governing the sale of investment trust securities within those states. Others, such as New York, passed and tried to enforce anti-fraud legislation.

*The Thirties*

After the stock market crash of 1929, the value of investment company assets declined and most closed-end companies' stocks began trading in the secondary markets at a discount to their net asset values. Some companies failed; others were swept up in a wave of consolidation that spread through the industry. Management services were up for sale, and many investment companies received new advisers. While from 1927 to 1936 about 1,100 new investment companies were formed, by 1936 after the consolidations, liquidations, and failures only about 560 remained.

Anxiety over the stock market crash affected the public desire to buy investment company securities, particularly shares of closed-end companies. New public offerings for closed-end companies virtually ceased. In fact, immediately after the crash, the public turned away from all management companies, investing primarily in "fixed trusts." Fixed trusts are companies that invest shareholder capital in a fixed set of stocks. This trend was short-lived and by the mid 1930s sales virtually ceased.

The hey-day of the open-end company or the "mutual-fund" was just beginning. The Thirties saw the first real increase in the organization of mutual funds. Historians believe that this expansion of open-end companies was driven by the redemption privilege (at net asset value) which protected shareholders from the risk of their shares trading below net asset value and the fact that they did not suffer the negative public reaction that befell the closed-end companies. By 1932 almost all newly organized investment companies adopted the mutual fund form.

The stock market crash precipitated new, strong federal regulation of securities and other markets. But the initial wave of New Deal securities legislation did not specifically address investment companies, and had little impact on the investment company industry. Possibly of more importance was the 1936 Revenue Act which allowed highly diversified investment companies to pass income to shareholders without an entity tax. In 1942, the qualifications for "diversified" status were reduced and remain similar today.

## B. Abuses Preceding the Reforms of 1940

Before 1940, federal and state regulation of investment companies was rudimentary at best and investors had little control over investment companies. Furthermore, there were many factors which offered managers and sponsors many opportunities to abuse their powers. First, because investment companies developed in order to aid unsophisticated investors, managers were in a position to take advantage of these investors' lack of knowledge. Second, the nature of the discretion given to the managers regarding portfolio investing gave them the freedom to change the nature of the their company's investment policies from conservative to speculative, to invest in affiliated companies, or to invest in the securities underwritten by affiliated investment banks. Third, the liquid nature of the investment company's assets facilitated manager embezzlement and looting.

*Disclosure*

One of the greatest abuses of investment company practice was the rapidity and irresponsibility with which some managements totally changed the nature of their business — in most cases, without the knowledge of the shareholders. Stockholders who had invested in self-styled "diversified" companies could be committed overnight to highly illiquid positions in any other business. Most spectacular was General Investment Company's sudden acquisition of a $70,000,000 subway in Buenos Aires which tied up practically all of its assets and was later sold for about 10% of its cost. Added to this was the power of managers to sell the investment company (or the advisory service) to other, sometimes unscrupulous, groups, and often without the knowledge or consent of the investors. At best, this meant different investment policies. At worst, the new management looted the fund.

In other cases, investors were given inadequate or deceptive reports about the performance of their investment company. Auditor reports of some companies showed misleading accounts of profits. For example, some accounting firms failed to distinguish between income and new capital and included fictitious profits arising out of inter-company transactions among affiliated firms.

*Self-dealing*

Other abusive practices involved management "self-dealing"-- investment companies often operated in the interest of their managers and affiliated companies rather than in the interests of the investors. There were examples of insiders and affiliates using investment companies to "unload" unmarketable securities, loans and other property in which they had an interest. One investment company sustained large losses as a consequence of buying the stock of its banking affiliate to support the affiliate's price in a falling market.

Other practices gave preferential treatment to insiders and affiliates who owned stock, at the expense of other shareholders. These management practices usually left non-insider/affiliate stock worth less per share (i.e., "shareholder dilution"). For example, insiders were frequently permitted to subscribe to newly issued stock at reduced prices and sometimes able to redeem their stock on a more favorable basis.

Open-end companies similarly engaged in abusive practices resulting in shareholder dilution.  For example, many insiders or affiliates were not required to pay "sales loads," or distribution fees paid upon buying shares of the company.  Additionally, some companies engaged in "backwards pricing," in which investors bought shares based on the price of the previous day.  According to an SEC report, "In a rising market, insiders and favored customers, who did not pay a sales load, could purchase shares based upon the previous day's lower price, turn around and redeem their shares the next day, and be assured of riskless profits, which resulted in dilution of the remaining shareholders' holdings."

*Capital Structure*

At that time, many commentators believed the complicated capital structures of investment companies with high debt loads and many classes of voting and non-voting shares served to harm public investors or at least create a strong potential of harm.  Leverage, or "trading on the equity," was thought to dangerously increase the risks of losses to shareholders. Many thought the mere existence of senior and junior securities to be dangerous.  Across the board, commentators attacked the voting structure of the companies in which insiders and affiliates normally owned all of the voting stock of the companies.  The public owned the senior securities - preferred stock and debentures.  After the crash, the common stock of many companies was worthless, and thus prompted these junior holders, who have voting control, to take larger risks.  Generally, as we have seen, this could mean a sale of the company or management services to other companies or management investing in more speculative ventures.

*Misappropriation of Funds*

Fraud, larceny and embezzlement by the management were not uncommon in the Twenties and, particularly, in the Thirties.  In some cases, individuals bought control of an investment company in order to "loot" the company, making off with its portfolio of investments.  In some cases, the looting was not limited to one investment company.  Instead, some of the assets of the company were used to buy control of other companies which were in turn looted.

One notorious example occurred in 1937 when a group composed mainly of lawyers discovered a way to gain control of investment companies without investing any money of their own. The  group carried on its operations through a personal holding company called the Fiscal Management Company.  The first victim was a small investment company with assets of $540,000.  They gained control of the company by paying the previous management a borrowed $110,000 for the Class A stock which had sole voting power.  As collateral for the $110,000 loan, the thieving group took securities having a market value of $152,000 from the portfolio of the victim company.  The $42,000 difference was retained by the Fiscal Management group as "commission" and "profit" on the deal.  Later, most of the remaining portfolio of marketable securities was liquidated.  The proceeds were used to buy securities of doubtful value from or make loans to the new management and their associates.  Finally, the investment company was taken over for liquidation by the Michigan State Securities Commission. Investors lost almost all they had paid for the securities of this concern.

But this was only the beginning. The next victim was a bank-sponsored investment company with $3 million in assets. Money was again borrowed to pay for 44% of the common stock. Portfolio securities were again sold, with "commissions" of $114,000 to insiders. Subsequently, the remaining portfolio of securities was liquidated to make personal loans and investments of dubious quality (including an investment in a South American utility project and loans to members of a brokerage firm, management, and other associates) and to purchase other investment companies. In fact, two other trusts were similarly acquired and grossly mismanaged by the same group. As a result of large losses, this investment company filed for reorganization in 1938. Ultimately, the individuals involved were indicted for fraud and larceny. One plead guilty and the others were acquitted. Later, three of those connected to the scams were convicted in federal court for using the mails to defraud the stockholders of the victimized companies.

## C. Passage of the Investment Company Act and the Investment Advisers Act

By the late 1920s and particularly in the 1930s, as the abuses in the organization and operation of investment companies became more apparent, calls for regulation of the industry increased. And, when Congress passed the Public Utility Holding Company Act of 1935, they authorized the Securities and Exchange Commission, which had itself been established only the previous year, to conduct a study of the investment company industry. That study, which was released in numerous volumes over the next seven years, reported substantial abuses and led directly to the Investment Company Act of 1940 and its companion Act, the Investment Advisers Act. These two Acts, as amended, provide the statutory basis for the regulation of investment companies today.

*Politics of the Act*

The original version of the Act, "a bill to provide for the registration and regulation of investment companies," was drafted by the SEC and introduced in Congress on March 14, 1940. A unique aspect of the enactment process and hearings was that there was virtually no disagreement between the investment company industry and the Commission on the question of the need for regulation. In fact, the final bill had the firm support of both the industry and the Commission. Yet, while the industry agreed that some regulation was necessary and wanted to restore investor confidence in the industry, there were divergent views as to the nature and extent of the regulations — particularly regarding the discretionary power given to the Commission in the original draft.

In the end, however, the final Act did give significant power to the SEC. In general, the Commission has the power to bring actions in federal district courts to enjoin practices constituting violations of the Act. Under some sections, the SEC has the discretion to adopt general rules and regulations. But the most controversial power given to the Commission by the Act is the power of exemption. See e.g. sections 6(c)("The

Commission . . . may conditionally or unconditionally exempt any person, security, or transaction . . . from any provision"). The SEC can exercise this power by *order* — that is, with reference to specific persons, securities, or transactions — as well as by general rules and regulations.

Although initially objecting, the industry ultimately accepted these discretionary powers as an alternative to strict statutory rules. The SEC's exemptive power at least offered greater flexibility to companies in particular cases. In the years after the Act was passed, we will see an extensive use of these powers, particularly the exemptive power.

*Structure of the Investment Company Act.*

The stated purpose of the Investment Company Act of 1940 ("1940 Act") is to remedy certain abuses listed in Section 1 of the Act. Though the method of regulation varies with different sections of the Act, in general the methods used are (1) company disclosure, to provide investors with more information; (2) shareholder voting and a "watchdog" board of directors, to equip the company with the self-regulatory features found in a corporate democracy; and (3) prohibitions on or heavy regulation of certain transactions and interrelationships that may lead to abuses.

A. *Registration:* All "investment companies" are required to register with the Commission. Thus, the scope of the legislation is determined by the definition of an "investment company" under the Act. With some exclusions, this definition includes all companies which "are or hold themselves out to be engaged primarily" in the investment business and those companies 40% of whose assets are in investment securities. Section 3(a).

Those found to be "investment companies" under the Act are further sub-classified for different treatment. Registered companies are divided into three categories: "Face-amount certificate companies" which sell unsecured debentures on an installment plan; "unit investment trusts" which sell shares in a fixed or semi-fixed bundle of securities deposited with a trustee; and "management companies" which are the focus of the Act and with which we will be most concerned. Management companies are further divided in two ways (a) open-end companies (mutual funds) and closed-end companies, and (b) diversified and non-diversified companies. The Act's requirements depend on and will vary based on the above classifications.

B. *Disclosure.* Some of the greatest abusive practices involved the rapid and often fraudulent changes in investment policies that were made without the knowledge or consent of the investors. In the banking and insurance sectors, we saw federal and state agencies' "solution" was to restrict the types of activities and investments permitted. This alternative was discussed in Congress as a possible cure for investment company problems. However, as with the regulation in the broker-dealer industry, the final Act turned to at least in the first instance to disclosure instead. For example, in Section 8, each company is required to disclose its investment policies and those activities it "reserves freedom of action to engage in." This includes any company plans to issue senior securities, to concentrate its portfolio in a certain industry, or to make loans to other persons.

Companies must adhere to these policies until a change is authorized by majority vote of the stockholders pursuant to Section 13.

Supplementing the specific disclosure requirements of the Investment Company Act are the more comprehensive disclosures rules in the Securities Act of 1933 and the Securities Exchange Act of 1934, both of which apply to registered investment companies. The 1933 Act mandates disclosure when securities are registered for a public offering and requires that written offers to sell investment company securities be accompanied or preceded by a prospectus meeting certain prescribed standards. The prospectus must reflect the policies and activities required by the registration statement under the 1940 Act. The 1934 Act provides for similar public disclosure (e.g., proxies, annual reports) of information by issuers whose securities are listed on the exchanges. Over the years, the SEC has developed special forms that tailor the disclosure requirements of the 1933 and 1934 Acts for different types of investment companies.

C. *Regulation of Activities and Operations.* Many provisions in the Investment Company Act were designed to attack the abusive activities found in the Commission's study, and go well beyond mere disclosure.

*Self-dealing.* To combat one of the most prolific sources of "self-dealing," the 1940 Act prohibited many direct transactions between "affiliated persons" and investment companies. Section 17 provides, with a few exceptions, strictly regulates transactions between an investment company (or its agents) and affiliates and other insiders of that investment company. The Commission has the power to exempt specific transactions that are fair and consistent with the company's policy and the purposes of the Act. Under Section 21, most loans to affiliated persons are prohibited. In addition, to prevent an underwriter from "dumping" unmarketable securities with an affiliated investment company, Section 10(f) prohibits an investment company from purchasing securities from an underwriting syndicate if a member of the syndicate is affiliated with the investment company in certain ways. Again, the Commission has the authority to exempt transactions by rule or order.

*Investments.* Other sections place limits on portfolio investments available to the company. Section 12(d) attacks the problem of "pyramiding" in which one investment company controls other investment companies by owning a large block of their shares. It forbids one investment company from acquiring more than 3% of a diversified company and 5% of a non-diversified investment company. Additionally, some risky investments are prohibited; for example, buying securities on margin and, with some exceptions, various investments in other firms in the financial services industry. Section 12.

*Capital Structure.* The original draft of the 1940 Act had permitted only common stock to be issued by investment companies in the future. However, the final draft allowed closed-end companies to issue bonds and preferred stock as long as certain asset coverage levels were met. Because of their continuous obligation to redeem their stock, the Act is more restrictive on open-end companies, forbidding them from issuing "senior securities" (Section 18(f)). In addition, all new issues of stock must have full voting rights, and bondholders and preferred stockholders in closed-end companies are given some rights to elect members of the Board.

The Act was also concerned with problems of shareholder dilution arising from self-dealing and complex capital structures.  To eliminate some of the most widely used methods of rewarding promoters and other insiders, no securities may be issued by a closed-end company to pay for services or property and repurchases may only occur on the open market.  "Private" share repurchases from selective persons is prohibited. See Section 23. Open-ended companies (or their principal distributors), which made money from the additional sales loads when shareholders exchanged shares for another fund, are prevented from making any offer involving an exchange of securities on any basis other than relative net asset values, unless approved by the Commission. Section 11. To protect shareholders from dilution when shares are sold to the public at different prices, Section 22(d) prevents any investment company, its principal underwriters and dealers from selling shares of the investment company except at a current public offering price described in its prospectus.

D.  *Shareholder Powers*. To combat the abuses of the Twenties and Thirties, the 1940 Act did more than prohibit certain transactions and relationships; it adopted the traditional corporate governance mechanisms to make sure advisers would be accountable for their actions.  Thus, it called for shareholder voting and, as discussed in the next section, forced investment companies to create independent boards of directors that could act as watchdogs over wayward managers.  As one method of increasing the authority of the shareholders over the affairs of their investment companies, Section 18 requires, with limited exceptions, that all shares of investment company stock "be voting stock and have equal voting rights with every other outstanding voting stock."  Certain voting powers are reserved for shareholders under the 1940 Act.  The most important example is the requirement that all changes in investment policy be approved by a shareholder vote. (Section 13).

The Act also calls for shareholder voting with regard to some investment company contracts. (Section 15).  All contracts with an investment adviser and underwriter must be in writing and must be approved by a majority of the voting securities or, in some cases, by the board of directors.  To prevent the transfer of an advisory contract without the vote of the shareholders, Section 15 provides for the "automatic termination" of these contracts in the event of an assignment.  Additionally, by a majority vote, shareholders can terminate either the advisory contract or accounting contract.  Contracts with accountants are also required to have the approval of a majority of the shareholders or board of directors.

E.  *Independent Directors*. Another strategy used by the 1940 Act was to force all investment companies to create shareholder-elected boards of directors (or board of trustees) to act as "watchdogs" over potential management conflicts of interest.  Initially, the Commission had supported very restrictive rules governing management/affiliate conflicts of interest, for example, prohibiting directors and managers of investment companies from holding similar positions in other investment companies, commercial banks, principal underwriters or principal brokers of the company. However, the final draft essentially relied on protection by independent directors, a percentage of which must be disinterested. (Section 10). Section 10 of the 1940 Act provides that no more than 60 percent of an investment company's board of directors shall be "interested persons." (See section 2(a)(19).) The board is required to supervise adviser conflicts of interest and approve some contracts. For example, in the absence of shareholder approval, the board must annually approve the company's underwriting and advisory contract.

*The Structure of the Investment Advisers Act.*

The Investment Advisers Act, a part of the legislative package in 1940, was also designed to deal with some of the abusive practices discovered by the Commission's study. The Act, however, focused on the regulation of investment *advisers*. Some of the important provisions include forced registration of all advisers with the SEC and, with some exceptions, prohibitions against performance-based compensation, such as compensation based on the capital gains in a client's account. Like the Investment Companies Act, this Act prohibits advisers from assigning their advisory contract to another party without the approval of the advises and prohibits fraudulent and deceitful transactions between the adviser and the client. The SEC is empowered to discipline violators of the statute and of its rules.

The Advisers Act has generally been considered a fairly weak statute, primarily because of its limited scope and relatively lax enforcement provisions. For example, the definition of an investment adviser include several exceptions, allowing many providers of investment advise to escape regulation under the Act. (Section 202(a)(11).) In addition, plaintiffs bringing private actions against violators of the Advisers Act are entitled to more limited damages than those bringing comparable enforcement actions under the 1934 Act. See Transamerica Mortgage Advisors Inc. v. Lewis, 444 U.S. 1 (1979).

## D. Evolution of Investment Companies Since 1940

*Growth of the Industry and Expanding Economic Role*

Investment companies grew cautiously at first, but by the 1970s the industry took off. In 1941, total assets invested in the companies registered with the Commission were $2 ½ billion. Mutual funds experienced much stronger growth after the Acts. By 1944, the aggregate assets of mutual funds exceeded those of closed-end companies, which had been the dominant type of fund throughout the Twenties. By 1970, the aggregate assets of mutual funds were $50 billion, or almost twelve times those of closed-end companies at $4 billion.

In the past twenty-fives years, investment company assets have skyrocketed, particularly in the mutual fund side of the industry. As of November 1997, there were reportedly over 6700 mutual funds on the market, with $4.43 trillion in assets under management. This represents a large increase even since 1990, when there were only 3105 mutual funds with $1.067 trillion in assets. This rapid rate of growth reflects the mutual fund industry's substantial inroads into retail markets. As of 1994, 38 million individuals, representing 31% of all US households, owned shares in mutual funds.

The current industry leader is Fidelity Investments. No other company comes close to matching Fidelity's $427 billion in assets under management (as of year end 1996) or 302 funds to choose from. The crown jewel of Fidelity has for many years been its Magellan Fund, which was managed by the highly successful and much publicized Peter Lynch during the 1980s. The Magellan Fund remains the country's largest mutual with $63 billion in assets as of the fourth quarter 1997, followed by the Vanguard Index Trust: 500 Portfolio with $48.2 billion in total assets.

One reason for the growth of the industry involves the stronger marketing of mutual fund shares and reduced or non-existent "sales loads." (In some cases, investment companies have replaced sales loads with "12b-1 fees," distribution costs paid directed by investment companies.) In 1940, most buyers of mutual fund shares also paid a "sales load" which went directly to the "sellers" — the underwriter, the dealers, and salespersons — to pay for their expenses and profits. In the 1960s the sales load was typically 8.5 percent of the offering price per share. "No-load" funds, whose shares are directly marketed to the public, were few. Today, no-load funds have dramatically increased, representing 35 percent of stock, bond, and income fund sales in 1990. One of the biggest promoters of "no load" trend is the Vanguard Company group of funds, which is the second largest mutual fund complex with roughly $245 billion in total mutual fund assets as of year end 1996.

*New Investment Company Structures.* Over the years, investment company structures have become more prominent since the Act. Today, most companies are arranged in "complexes." Under these arrangements, different funds cluster into groups that are managed by a common adviser, sold by a common distributor, and frequently have the same board of directors. (As of year end 1996, the top six complexes — each of which had more than $135 billion of mutual fund assets under management — accounted together for more than $1.1 trillion of mutual fund assets or just under a third of total mutual fund assets.) Some of the groups are comprised of "separate" investment companies; others are organized as one investment company which issues several series of stock, each series representing a different portfolio. Each "complex" might include a variety of "investment media" — mutual funds, closed-end funds, private advisory accounts, and variable annuities. We will see that these structures raise many conflict of interest issues — particularly because the adviser often has a greater self-interest in some funds than in others.

*New Products and Service Providers.* A host of new pooled securities products and new service providers have also emerged since the 1940 Act. Money market funds, or mutual funds which invest primarily in "safe" securities such as government-issued securities and high grade commercial paper, emerged in the late 1970s. By 1991, they held 41 percent of the investment company industry assets. Banks and insurance companies are beginning to move into the mutual fund field. Today, many banks offer money market funds as an alternative to savings accounts. An increasing number also offer other mutual funds.

*Legal Developments*

Since the 1940s, the Investment Company Act has remained relatively unchanged. Reforms occurred in the 1970s when several amendments were passed by Congress. Basically, the SEC's exemption power has been the alternative many companies have turned to when the Act is unclear or constrains them.

*The 1970 Amendments:* Concern over the quickly rising assets invested in investment company shares prompted three studies in the early to mid 1960s: The *Wharton School Report,* focusing on mutual funds (H.R. Rep. No. 2274, 87th Cong., 2d Sess. (1962)); the *Report of the Special Study of Securities Markets,* which dealt in passing with investment companies (H.R. Doc. No.95, pts.1 to 4, 88th Cong. 1st Sess. (1963)); and the *Report of the Securities and Exchange Commission on the Public Policy Implications of Investment Company Growth* (H.R. Rep. No.2337, 89th Cong., 2d Sess. (1966)). These reports highlighted a series of concerns about managerial compensation, sales loads, competition among retail sellers, brokerage commissions, the increasing size of some funds; and advertising.

Reforms of the 1970s purported to resolve at least one of these problems: management compensation. For the most part, the original 1940 Act did not impose restrictions on advisory fees but gave managers a large measure of discretion — discretion that was subject to shareholder and director review. In practice, adviser compensation was and still is normally based on a percentage of a fund's net asset value. By the 1960s with substantial increases in fund assets, the compensation for some advisers increased dramatically. Many argued that this fee was not justified because greater assets meant greater economies of scale — benefits that were not being realized by the investors. According to the Wharton Report's 1960 survey, of 20 of the largest funds, only 7 had scaled down advisory fee schedules to reflect the greater economies of size.

In the 1970 Amendments, Congress brought about two major changes. First, with an amended section 15(c), it demanded a stronger role for independent directors in the evaluation and approval of advisory contracts. Second, Congress adopted Section 36(b) which imposes a fiduciary duty upon investment advisers with regard to their compensation. Formerly, Section 36 only imposed on advisers a prohibition against gross abuse of trust or gross misconduct. The modified Section 36(b) gave shareholders a private right of action against their adviser with respect to the adviser's fee and a reduced standard of proof.

The 1970 Amendments also increased the importance of the Investment Advisers Act. These amendments amended the original act to expand its coverage and include many "advisers" previously exempted from the Act's registration requirements. In addition, it strengthened substantive provisions prohibiting performance fees for investment advisers. In the Securities Act Amendments of 1975, Congress expanded the information necessary for registration under the Advisers Act.

*SEC's Power of Exemption*

Under the 1940 Act, the SEC has the power to exempt any person, security, or transaction from any provision of the Act. As the financial markets have evolved and new products, structures and sponsors have emerged, investment companies and those wanting to set up or buy investment companies have increasingly turned to the SEC for relief. In 1991, the number of applications for exemption stood at 310.

Some examples of the SEC's use of this power include permitting Money Market Funds to use alternative valuation methods and allowing mutual funds to issue different classes or series of funds. In the past decade, Commission orders have also permitted new sales and distribution practices in the mutual fund industry. Some of these orders have later been codified as general rules. For example, rule 12b-1 allows those mutual funds to replace front-end loads (distributions fees paid by *buyers* of mutual fund shares) with "12b-1" fees, or distribution fees paid by the *owners* of mutual fund shares based on a percentage of the fund's daily average net assets.

### Reforms of 1996

In the National Securities Market Improvements Act of 1996, Congress reformed the regulation of investment companies by, among other things, preempting state registration, qualification, and disclosure requirements for most investment companies. The Act preserved state authority to bring enforcement actions involving fraud and other misconduct on the part of broker-dealers in connection with the sale of investment company shares. In addition, the states retained the right to impose filing and registration fees on investment companies. Collectively, the 1996 reforms greatly diminish the role of state regulators in supervising substantive aspects of investment company operations. This is the same piece of legislation that reallocated jurisdiction between investment advisers, establishing, in essence, a bifurcated regulatory in system under which state authorities supervise investment advisers with less than $25 million in assets under management, and the SEC oversees those with larger portfolios.

## Section 2. Organizing a Mutual Fund

Our next reading is from an article that reviews the many organizational issues a sponsor must consider in establishing a investment company today. To some extent, this excerpt overlaps with the preceding introduction. This perspective, however, is more practical in orientation and offer a more detailed (albeit still summary) view of applicable legal rules. As you read through this excerpt, consider how the regulation of investment companies differs from the rules we have studied for other financial intermediaries. What aspects of this structure are familiar? What are new to our study of financial institutions?

**Victoria E. Schonfeld & Thomas M.J. Kerwin, Organization of a Mutual Fund**
49 Bus. Law. 107 (Nov. 1993)

## WHY ORGANIZE A MUTUAL FUND

The sponsor of a new mutual fund typically is the fund's prospective investment adviser, administrator, or distributor. The sponsor functions like a movie producer -- bringing together all the elements necessary for launching the fund. The sponsor also typically provides personnel to manage and operate the fund, including officers and affiliated directors. In addition, the sponsor recruits unaffiliated persons to serve as independent directors and identifies affiliated or outside contractors to provide ancillary services to the fund . . . .

Depending on the size of the fund and other factors, organizing a mutual fund may involve start-up costs in the range of $250,000 to $400,000 or more -- including legal, accounting, and printing fees, and registration of the fund and its shares with the Securities and Exchange Commission (SEC) and various state securities regulatory authorities. Initial expenses generally are lower when an existing series fund offers a new series. The sponsor usually acts as the fund's initial shareholder, investing $100,000 or more in seed capital necessary to offer fund shares to the public. The sponsor often also provides on-going management, advisory or other services to the fund. The sponsor receives shares of the fund in exchange for its investment . . . .

## PRELIMINARY DECISIONMAKING PHASE

### INVESTMENT COMPANY STATUS

Under the Investment Company Act of 1940 (ICA), a mutual fund must register as a "registered investment company" . . . . Except for certain common trust funds and small business-related "business development companies," registration as an investment company also is a requirement for taxation as a "regulated investment company."[9] Regulated investment company tax status permits the fund to be treated as a pass-through vehicle, so that the fund's income flows through to shareholders without being taxed as the fund level.[10] . . .

---

[9]    I.R.C. § 851(a) (1992). Other requirements for "regulated investment company" tax status are that the fund (i) derive 90% of its income from dividends, interest, payments for securities loans, and gains from certain securities transactions, (ii) derive less than 30% of its income from certain securities held for less than three months (the so-called "short-short rule," occasionally targeted for repeal), and (iii) maintain at the close of each quarter (a) at least 50% of assets in cash, government securities, securities of other regulated investment companies, or other securities whose value, as to the securities of any one issuer, does not exceed 5% of the fund's total assets or 10% of the outstanding voting shares of the issuer, and (b) not more than 25% of assets, other than government bonds or shares of other investment companies, in shares of any one issuer, or shares of two or more issuers controlled by the fund and engaged in related businesses. *Id.* § 851(b).

[10]    *See id.* § 852. In addition to meeting the requirements of a "regulated investment company," if the fund is to operate on a substantially tax-free basis, it must distribute to shareholders currently as dividends at least 90% of its taxable income derived from ordinary income and exempt interest (excluding net capital gain, as to which no percentage requirement applies) on an annual basis, and must

## TYPES OF INVESTMENT COMPANIES

There are several types of registered investment companies. One primary classification, "management investment company," embraces most mutual funds and other investment companies such as closed-end funds. Non-management investment companies include unit investment trusts and face amount certificate companies. If on-going management of a portfolio is desired, management investment company status is necessary.

Management investment companies are subclassified into open-end or closed-end companies. Open-end companies (otherwise known as mutual funds) currently account for about eighty-five percent of investment company assets. An open-end fund issues securities that must be redeemable at all times, and typically also offers its securities on a continuous basis. The closed-end classification embraces all other management investment companies which do not redeem securities continuously, but typically sell a fixed number of shares in traditional underwritten offerings that later trade in secondary markets, through stock exchanges or over the counter. Once a new company designates its status as an open-end or closed-end company, any change in subclassification requires shareholder approval.

An open-end fund bears greater management and administrative burdens than a closed-end fund. The sales and redemption of shares on a continuous basis imposes substantial distribution burdens. Other open-end fund burdens include the need to adjust investment strategy to cope with unexpected cash inflows or outflows, restricting most investments to those meeting asset liquidity standards to facilitate shareholder redemptions, and calculating the fund's net asset value at least daily. Open-end funds also face tighter restrictions on borrowing, which generally prohibit the issuance of "senior securities" other than limited bank debt. By continuously offering shares, however, an open-end fund may increase its assets more readily than a closed-end company. In addition, investors may find open- end fund shares more attractive because shares can be redeemed at any time at net asset value less any sales charge or redemption fee. . . . .

Management investment companies are further subclassified into diversified and non-diversified companies. A mutual fund that calls itself "diversified" must allocate its assets among issuers of securities to a required extent, while a non-diversified company need not. The primary consequence of non-diversified as opposed to diversified status is that non-diversified funds must disclose the risk of narrower issuer selection. In some circumstances, a change from diversified to non-diversified status requires shareholder approval.

---

meet certain other conditions. *Id.* § 852(b)-(f). The fund then can take advantage of a regulated investment company's special deduction from taxable income for all dividends it pays currently. *Id.* § 852(b)(2)-(9). If less than all earnings and profits are distributed as dividends, but the distributions still meet the 90% minimum threshold, only undistributed ordinary income and undistributed net capital gain are taxed. *Id.* § 852(a)(1), (b)(2)(D), (b)(3)(A), (b)(5)(A), (c). However, a fund that schedules dividend distributions to defer taxation for a year -- such as by failing to pay its shareholders during each calendar year at least 98% of its calendar year ordinary income and at least 98% of its capital gain net income (determined using a twelve-month period ending October 31) -- may be subject to a 4% excise tax. *Id.* § 4982.

## FORM OF ORGANIZATION

A mutual fund may be organized as a corporation, association, jointstock fund, or business trust. A few investment companies, particularly business development companies, are organized as limited partnerships. Most mutual funds and other management investment companies are structured as business trusts (usually under Delaware law or Massachusetts law) or as corporations (usually under Maryland law).

A business trust is an unincorporated association governed by a board of trustees. Under state law, if permitted by the trust declaration, trustees can take most actions without ratification by shareholders, and can issue an unlimited number of shares of beneficial interest. In Delaware, the business trust form insulates its shareholders from liability in much the same way as a corporation. Trustees theoretically may have potential liability for obligations of the trust, but steps can be taken to protect them. Trusts also are permitted to limit trustees' liability for breaches of fiduciary duty other than the duty of loyalty, although the ICA imposes fiduciary duties of its own and limits the practical effectiveness of such disclaimers. Because business trusts dispense with traditional corporate formalities like annual shareholder meetings and shareholder approval of the issuance of additional shares, the trust form dovetails well with the ICA's limited role for shareholders and its flexibility concerning other governance issues. The trustees of a business trust have the same responsibilities under the ICA as those assigned to the directors of a corporation. . . . .

## SEPARATE ENTITIES VERSUS SERIES FUND

A fund sponsor faces a fundamental decision if it plans to offer more than one investment portfolio. On the one hand, the sponsor may create a family of different funds, with a separate legal entity for each. On the other hand, the sponsor may use a single legal entity to offer multiple portfolios or series of shares, each having different investment objectives, policies, and potential investors.

A family of funds, with a separate legal entity for each fund, has the advantage of clarity of purpose for each fund. Separate entities also may be desirable if different funds are to have differing distribution or administrative arrangements. Also, it may be easier to market a single portfolio as a separate legal entity than as one of a series. Multiple legal entities, however, inevitably require duplication and expense resulting from separate boards, agreements with service providers, prospectuses, periodic reports, and other regulatory filings.

In contrast, a single entity offering multiple series of shares, a "series fund," can eliminate some duplication. A single board of directors governs the series fund. Different investment advisers may manage each portfolio, but the same distributor, custodian, transfer agent, and other service-providers generally handle other operating responsibilities under one set of agreements. A single prospectus may suffice as well, although separate marketing of each series would require separate prospectuses.

Each series in a series fund represents a segregated portfolio of the fund's assets. Each series must vote separately on matters not affecting all series alike. For example, each series must vote to approve its investment advisory agreement (which generally will differ for each series), or to approve changes in fundamental investment policies. Other matters are excepted, however, from the requirement of voting by series. These include election of the fund's board of directors, approval of the fund's auditors, and ratification of underwriting agreements.

Series funds raise other potential issues. As to fund-wide votes, holders of similar numbers of shares in different series may have the same voting power, despite any disparity in the net asset values of their shares. To avoid this problem, some funds recently have arranged to have shareholder votes determined by the dollar value of shares rather than the number of shares. In addition, different series may be restricted as "affiliated persons" from engaging with each other in cross-acquisitions, joint distribution plans, and other joint enterprises — although similar restrictions apply to affiliated funds. Furthermore, recent judicial rulings giving the shareholder of one series standing to sue a sponsor on behalf of all series in a fund for allegedly excessive management fees lessen the desirability of series fund structure for some fund sponsors. The SEC proposed action to eliminate the former ability of a series fund to establish a new series by filing an automatically effective post-effective amendment to a previously filed registration statement.

## NAME OF THE FUND

The name of the fund may be an important marketing tool, and therefore merits careful consideration. The fund's name may reflect its investment objectives and any fund family or series affiliation. The name must not be deceptive or misleading. If the fund's name implies that it invests primarily in one type of securities, such as the securities of one foreign country, the fund must invest at least sixty-five percent of the value of its total assets in such securities. A "balanced fund" must invest at least twenty-five percent of the value of its assets in fixed-income senior securities. Funds whose names imply that they invest in federal-tax-exempt securities must invest at least eighty percent of their assets in such securities. To use the word *international* in its name, a fund must invest in at least three different countries outside the United States; *global*, *world*, or *atlas* funds must invest in at least three countries, one of which may be the United States. . . .

## INVESTMENT OBJECTIVES AND OTHER POLICIES

The fund prospectus must set forth the fund's investment objectives and policies. Certain objectives and policies are deemed "fundamental." Once those objectives and policies are identified in the registration statement, shareholders will have to approve any deviation from the fundamental objectives and policies, or any deviation from other policies declared in the registration statement to be changeable only by shareholder vote. Accordingly, a fund should identify carefully its fundamental policies and draft them broadly to avoid the need to later solicit shareholder votes to approve changes.

## ADMINISTRATION AND OPERATION

### Directors/Trustees

A mutual fund is governed by a board of directors or trustees, whose members supervise the fund's business operations. Independent directors play a critical role in the ICA's mandate to protect the shareholders' interests. Among other responsibilities, independent directors approve and review the fund's contracts and other arrangements and monitor fund performance and operations.

Under the ICA, independent directors must be disinterested — that is, not "interested persons" of the mutual fund. An "interested person" of the fund is defined broadly; it includes an "affiliated person" of the fund as well as an "interested person" of an investment adviser or principal underwriter. A person is not an "interested person," however, solely by reason of being a director or shareholder of the fund, or a relative of such a person.

Except in limited circumstances, a fixed portion of the fund's directors, normally at least forty percent, must qualify as independent. . . .

Whether or not required by law, mutual funds are well advised to retain a substantial majority of independent directors. Under the statutory standards explained *infra*, independent directors inadvertently may lose their "disinterested" status in a variety of ways, often unknowingly. The actions of an invalidly constituted board (fewer than forty percent of whose members are independent) may be void *ab initio*. Finding new independent directors on short notice may be difficult, and appointing them may require shareholder elections in some cases. Moreover, the deliberations and actions of independent directors are very important, and courts sometimes have commented favorably on the presence of a majority of independent directors in judicially endorsing board actions.

The most important duties of independent directors include approving the fund's investment advisory arrangements and monitoring the fund's relationships with the investment adviser and other insiders. In addition, tasks assigned to fund directors include monitoring the fund's investment performance, approving and reviewing agreements with other service providers, selecting the fund's independent auditors, approving the fund's fidelity bond coverage, reviewing the allocation of the fund's brokerage and affiliated brokerage transactions, supervising the administration of the fund's legal compliance program and code of ethics, valuing investments for which market prices are not readily available, setting the time of day for pricing an open-end fund's shares, and monitoring the quality and cost of other services being provided to the fund. An audit committee consisting solely of independent directors often performs the additional duty of meeting with the fund's independent auditors to review the fund's financial statements and discuss its internal procedures.

A new fund's sponsor may nominate both inside and independent directors, and the initial shareholder elects the original board. In the case of startup funds, the SEC staff no longer requires an undertaking to solicit a public shareholder vote to elect directors within sixteen months of effectiveness. Once the initial board is elected, it may fill vacancies occurring between shareholder meetings, if after the board action at least two- thirds of all directors were elected by shareholders (which may include the sole initial shareholder). If at any time less than half of all directors holding office were elected by shareholders, the board generally must hold shareholder elections to fill vacancies within sixty days. In practice, because most funds do not have annual shareholder meetings and fund boards are extremely static, the public shareholders rarely elect directors. . . .

Because one group of directors is permitted to serve on more than one fund, fund families or complexes may allocate director responsibilities in a variety of ways. For example, one family of funds may have one board of directors responsible for all of its equity funds and another board for all of its debt funds. Another fund complex may assign different inside directors to each fund, but assign responsibility for all funds to just one set of independent directors. Another complex may have three or four groups of directors, each of which serves on several funds and all of which meet concurrently on a quarterly basis. Other complexes may prefer one separately constituted board for each fund, particularly to supervise a fund with multiple series.

In addition to the requirement that the board include a percentage of independent directors, several other limitations affect the composition of the board, as well as any "advisory board" that the fund may wish to establish. A director may not be an "affiliated person" of an investment banker or of the fund's regular broker, or an "interested person" of the fund's principal underwriter, unless a majority of the fund's directors are not affiliated with the investment banker, broker, or principal underwriter, subject to narrow exceptions. Because many funds have at least one director affiliated with such an institution, in practice the majority of such a fund's directors must be unaffiliated with the institution. In addition, a majority of directors may not be affiliated with any one bank. . . . .

### Investment Adviser/Manager

The investment adviser manages the fund's assets, investing them in accordance with the fund's investment objectives and policies as stated in the registration statement. The adviser, in turn, may retain one or more subadvisers. The adviser also may have administrative duties and refer to itself as the fund's "manager." In addition, the adviser or an affiliate may act as distributor of the fund's shares. The adviser commonly is the fund's sponsor and its initial shareholder. The adviser (and any subadvisers) must be registered under the Investment Advisers Act of 1940, unless exempt from the registration requirement.

The adviser, in its various roles, will have incentives and opportunities to favor its own economic interests over those of the fund or its shareholders. To minimize the risk of self-dealing, and because of the crucial nature of the adviser's duties, the ICA places important oversight responsibilities on the fund's directors, particularly the independent directors. Among other duties, fund directors must assess carefully any proposed agreement between the fund and its adviser, approve the agreement, and monitor its performance. In conducting that assessment, the directors are required, among other responsibilities, to request and evaluate all information they deem reasonably necessary to evaluate the terms of the agreement. The adviser has a corresponding duty to provide such information.

A majority of independent directors must approve in person the initial execution and any renewal of the fund's investment advisory agreement -- as must a majority of all directors. The fund may continue the advisory agreement beyond a two-year initial period upon annual approval by the directors or the shareholders. For new funds, the SEC staff no longer requires an undertaking to solicit a public shareholder vote on an advisory agreement within sixteen months of effectiveness. Shareholder approval still is necessary, however, to amend an existing advisory agreement. . . .

### Affiliate Transactions

The investment adviser, other "affiliated persons" of the fund, and the distributor/principal underwriter, as well as their affiliates, are subject to a broad range of important prohibitions intended to protect the fund from conflicts of interest, unfair dealing, or overreaching in across-the- table, principal-agent, or joint dealings between affiliates and the fund. For across-the-table dealings, except in compliance with SEC rules, affiliated persons are prohibited from, among other things, selling securities to, purchasing securities from, or borrowing from the fund as principal. Exemptive relief may be available from the SEC if a proposed transaction is reasonable and fair, does not involve overreaching, and is consistent with the purposes of the ICA and the policies of the fund -- but obtaining exemptive relief is likely to be a difficult and time-consuming process.

With respect to principal-agent relationships, the ICA bars an affiliate, acting as agent for the fund, from receiving compensation from any source (other than regular salary from the fund) for the purchase or sale of property for or to the fund, except under a rule which authorizes certain payments to affiliated brokers. For joint dealings, certain common or parallel action between the fund and an adviser, other affiliated person, distributor/principal underwriter, or second-tier affiliate may implicate the broad provisions requiring SEC approval of transactions with the fund as a "joint" participant.

Investment advisory agreements and some distribution agreements are exempt from these prohibitions of section 17. Other arrangements between the fund and affiliated entities--such as a service contract between the fund and an affiliate of the investment adviser--may be permissible if fund directors review and approve such arrangements much as they do advisory agreements. The SEC staff indicated that fees for such ancillary service contracts may be in addition to advisory fees, and that such service contracts with affiliates are "within the plain language of" section 36(b) of the ICA and should be reviewed by directors.

*Manager/Administrator*

As noted supra, the investment adviser also may perform administrative functions as the mutual fund's manager or administrator. Administrative functions, like advisory responsibilities, may be divided among different service providers in a variety of ways. For example, the fund's manager may subcontract out both advisory and administrative responsibilities to other entities and merely oversee the activities of the subadviser and administrator. The manager also may perform advisory services itself, but subcontract out administrative responsibilities to a fund administrator, shareholder servicing administrator, or transfer agent. In the alternative, the fund may retain an administrator independent of the separate investment adviser. In these cases, the "subcontractors" are paid by the primary contractor from the fee it receives from the fund.

The manager typically assists the fund's officers in managing the fund, and prepares documents such as the fund's financial statements and, often, initial drafts of public filings. The manager also may oversee the performance of services by the investment adviser, custodian, and transfer agent, and provide required information to the directors. In addition, the manager may perform functions otherwise handled by the transfer agent, such as recordkeeping, accounting, and shareholder services. The manager's and/or administrator's fee, like that of the adviser, is typically an annual percentage of the fund's average net assets, which often is combined with the advisory fee into a unified management fee. If the manager is affiliated with the investment adviser, another affiliated person of the mutual fund, or the distributor/principal underwriter, it is subject to the broad prohibitions intended to protect the fund from self-dealing by affiliates.

*Distributor/Principal Underwriter*

The distributor or principal underwriter contracts with the mutual fund to purchase and resell the fund's shares to the public. In general, an open-end fund may effectively market its own shares through an affiliated investment adviser or distributor, or it may leave distribution to an affiliated or unaffiliated distributor aided by a sales force including brokers, financial planners, life insurance companies, or bank representatives. The underwriting of open-end funds as a separate function may not always be profitable. For that and other reasons, the distributor of an open-end fund often is affiliated with the investment adviser or other service-provider.

For open-end funds, the contract between a fund and its distributor must receive considerable director scrutiny. Majorities of both the independent directors and the board as a whole must approve in person the initial underwriting contract. Shareholder approval of an initial contract is not necessary, but the contract cannot continue for more than two years without annual approval by the directors or shareholders. The ICA limits the effectiveness of contract provisions attempting to shield underwriters from liability for willful misfeasance, bad faith, gross negligence, or reckless disregard of duty.

As in other fund arrangements, persons having records of criminal or other misconduct, or their affiliates, are ineligible to serve as principal underwriter for any open-end fund or certain other types of investment companies. In addition, if any fund director, officer, or employee is an interested person of the underwriter (even indirectly, such as through an affiliate relationship between underwriter and adviser), the fund ordinarily must have a majority of directors who are not interested persons of the underwriter.

Except in compliance with SEC exemptive rules, if any fund director, officer, employee, or adviser is an affiliated person of the fund's principal underwriter, the fund is restricted from purchasing other securities principally underwritten by that underwriter (or by any other underwriter or person affiliated with the fund, or by any person with whom fund directors, officers, employees, or the adviser are affiliated) during the pendency of the underwriting or selling syndicate. The SEC staff took an expansive view of this restriction, interpreting *underwriting* to include the private placement of tax-exempt securities with investment companies through an affiliated broker-dealer acting as agent for the issuers of the securities.

Like the investment adviser and other affiliated persons of the fund, the distributor/principal underwriter may be subject to broad affiliate transaction restrictions intended to protect the fund from self-dealing by affiliates. The principal underwriter of an open-end mutual fund also owes fiduciary duties imposed by the ICA to the fund and its shareholders.. . . .

### *Officers*

The adviser or other sponsor usually nominates the new fund's officers for consideration by the directors. Officers' duties may be limited, depending on the extent to which the adviser or manager delegates responsibilities to them. Officers often are affiliated with the adviser, which may pay their salaries. An officer may not be an "affiliated person" of an investment banker or of the fund's regular broker, or an "interested person" of the fund's principal underwriter, unless a majority of the fund's directors are not affiliated with the investment banker, broker, or principal underwriter. Persons with records of criminal or other misconduct are ineligible to serve as officers. Officers also may serve as directors, but an officer is an interested person of the fund by definition.

*DISTRIBUTION METHOD*

The mutual fund's distribution method is of great importance to its success, as it is the means by which the fund offers and sells its shares to the public. Because shares can be redeemed and usually purchased at any time, distribution is a vital on-going need. Many otherwise successful funds fail due to lack of an adequate distribution network. The costs and burdens of distribution are substantial, including printing prospectuses, complying with state and federal offering requirements, identifying potential investors and responding to inquiries, devising effective advertising or maintaining a sales force, executing purchase and redemption transactions, and providing other investor services. The primary decision for a new fund sponsor is whether the fund should assume some or all of these burdens for itself and its sponsor by direct marketing of its shares -- or instead should employ a broker-dealer sales force consisting of securities firms or brokers, financial planners, life insurance companies, or bank representatives.

### Direct Marketing: "No-load" Funds

To reduce costs, some funds and their sponsors prefer to handle distribution burdens themselves, without retaining and compensating a sales force. The ICA ostensibly bars a fund -- except for certain exempted no-load funds -- from acting as its own distributor other than through an underwriter, if in contravention of any rules established by the SEC. Nevertheless, direct marketing is possible in a number of ways.

For years, the SEC did not implement the statutory bar to self- distribution. Although most mutual funds distributed their shares through an underwriter and charged a front-end load to cover costs, some funds effectively distributed their own shares, usually without charging a sales load. While permitting this method, the SEC opposed the use of any current shareholders' funds, in the form of existing fund assets, to pay for distributing additional shares to new shareholders -- with certain exceptions. As a practical matter, the investment adviser or other sponsor generally absorbed a self-distributing fund's marketing expenses.

As the popularity of no-load funds increased, their sponsors requested the SEC to permit use of fund assets to pay for distribution expenses to compete with load funds. Load funds also desired greater flexibility in financing distribution costs. In 1980, after years of examining the issue, the SEC promulgated rule 12b-1.

Rule 12b-1 prohibits an open-end fund from distributing its own shares other than through an underwriter except as permitted by the rule or the statutory exemption for certain no-load fund shares. The rule permits a mutual fund to act as a distributor of its securities, provided that any payments made by the fund in connection with the distribution are made pursuant to a written plan describing all material aspects of the proposed financing, that all agreements relating to the plan are in writing, and that the plan contains certain procedural requirements.

Many no-load funds have adopted rule 12b-1 plans to assist their sponsors in covering costs such as sales commissions, printing of prospectuses and sales literature, advertising, and related distribution expenses -- subject to recently effective restrictions on use of the "no-load" label. Load funds also widely adopted rule 12b-1 plans, using them to supplement sales load revenues in compensating a broker sales force.

Despite the reaffirmation of the statutory bar to self-distribution in rule 12b-1, distribution of shares without an underwriter or a rule 12b-1 plan is permitted if distribution costs are not paid from fund assets. Under the rule, a fund acts as its own distributor if it "engages directly or indirectly in financing" any sales activity. Thus, a fund may distribute its own shares if it does not finance the activity itself. In practice, such an arrangement requires the fund's sponsor to expend its own resources, primarily through advertising.

Funds marketed under self- or affiliate-distribution arrangements generally are called no-load funds, although some direct-marketed funds do impose low sales loads. Any distributor must sell fund shares at the net asset value of the fund plus any applicable load, under guidelines described in the fund's prospectus. The shares of many no-load funds also may be purchased through unaffiliated brokers and banks, sometimes for a sales commission rather than a load, often supplemented by a service fee or other payment from the fund's distributor to the broker.

Investors who resist payment of loads and do not need a broker's advice may find no-load fund shares attractive. No-load funds gain some exposure to investors through publications such as Morningstar, Inc. that regularly review fund performance. Nevertheless, a no-load fund may find it difficult to attract or retain sufficient investors to achieve optimum profitability, or to realize desirable economies of scale. The burdens of distribution without a broker network or other sales force are considerable. The fund or its sponsor must develop effective advertising and public relations expertise to compensate for the absence of a sales force. Moreover, some investors may feel a need for a sales representative's on-going guidance about fund investments. Limited advice may be obtained by purchasing no-load funds through a broker, but load funds and recurring rule 12b-1 plan fees may encourage more on-going service by the broker.

### Use of Sales Force: Load Funds

To minimize distribution burdens, the new fund may decide to distribute its shares through a sales force, such as through brokers, life insurance companies, or depository institutions. That method normally requires a sales load to compensate the underwriter and the individual registered representatives -- although no-load funds also may be sold through a broker for a commission or service fee instead of a sales load. The underwriter and selling group members must charge uniform sales loads, or uniform scheduled variations, to each class of investors in a particular load fund.

Load funds commonly charge one of several types of sales loads, including a front-end load, a contingent deferred sales load, or a combination of both. These load arrangements may be supplemented by asset-based sales charges under a rule 12b-1 plan, or supplanted altogether by rule 12b-1 charges under a "level load" plan. Service fees, or "trailers" paid to broker-dealers for on- going shareholder services, also are permitted under NASD rules. Funds also may impose contingent or noncontingent redemption fees to discourage short-term trading; such redemption fees generally are not distribution-related, are paid to the fund rather than the distributor, and should be distinguished from deferred loads paid to the distributor.

A front-end load is a percentage commission paid to the distributor from invested assets at the time of the sale. The commission currently may range as high as 8.5%, although market pressures have reduced typical loads to 2% to 6%. High front-end loads are increasingly unattractive to investors, because of the wide availability of no-load or low-load funds, and deferred loads.

A contingent deferred sales load may be an appealing alternative to a front- end load. These fees typically are required to be paid only if the shareholder redeems fund shares within a specified number of years, usually five or six, from the date of initial purchase and are taken out of the proceeds of redemption. A typical fee would be five percent the first year, declining by one percent each succeeding year until it reaches zero.

A fund selling deferred load shares usually has a rule 12b-1 plan in effect as well. Under the typical rule 12b-1 plan, the fund agrees to pay the distributor a fixed annual percentage -- or up to a maximum percentage, depending on the plan -- of the fund's average net assets. The payment assists in covering distribution costs, and often funds an on-going trail commission or service fee for shareholder services. A new rule 12b-1 plan must be approved by independent directors and, for an existing fund, by shareholders; amendments to the plan that do not materially increase the amount expended under the plan may be approved by directors alone.

In a fund with a rule 12b-1 plan and a deferred load, after an investor purchases shares, the distributor gradually recoups its sales costs through rule 12b-1 plan charges (other than on-going service fees) against the investor's funds and other fund assets. If the investor redeems the shares before a fixed date, the investor may pay a contingent deferred sales load to cover distribution expenses not recouped under the plan. . . .

NASD rule[s] . . . affect the structure of distribution methods. . . . [and] appl[y] to contingent deferred sales loads, asset-based charges and service fees, and front-end loads. . . .

## ANCILLARY SERVICE PROVIDERS

Providers of ancillary services to the mutual fund and its management include the custodian, transfer agent, regular broker-dealers, counsel, and auditors.

### Custodian

The fund contracts with a custodian to retain custody of all fund cash and securities, receive and deliver fund assets pursuant to instructions from the fund and its adviser, maintain the fund's general ledger, and generally compute the net asset value of shares and the total asset value of the fund. The custodian must have fiduciary holding powers and data processing capability. It may be a bank with aggregate capital, surplus, and undivided profits of $500,000 or more, a securities firm that is a member of a national securities exchange, or, in limited circumstances, the fund itself. A clearing agency or other securities depository also may hold fund assets generally through arrangements with another intermediary custodian such as a bank. Custodial fees vary substantially depending on the size of the mutual fund and the type of assets . . . .

### Transfer Agent

The transfer agent, shareholder servicing agent, or dividend disbursement agent contracts with the mutual fund to provide services to shareholders. Specific functions may include recording share ownership, purchases and redemptions, responding to shareholder communications, processing shareholder transactions, paying dividends and distributions, and performing other shareholder accounting functions. The transfer agent may be affiliated with the fund's investment adviser, custodian, or another fund affiliate. Transfer agency fees vary substantially with the activity in the fund's shares and the size of customer accounts. . . .

### Broker-Dealers

A mutual fund may have a regular relationship with one or more broker- dealers. Such a broker-dealer also may be the sponsor of the fund, or may be affiliated with the fund's investment adviser or distributor. A fund director may not be affiliated with the fund's "regular broker" unless a majority of the fund's directors are not affiliated with the broker. Accordingly, if a fund director is affiliated with the fund's regular broker, more than one-half of the fund's directors must be independent of the broker.

Under rule 17e-1, a broker-dealer that is affiliated with the fund may receive commissions from the fund pursuant to procedures approved by the board of directors. Commissions charged by an affiliated broker-dealer must be "reasonable and fair," as compared to the usual and customary compensation received by other brokers in comparable arm's length transactions. The directors must review commission payments quarterly and annually. If a broker affiliated with a fund acts as a principal underwriter of newly-issued securities, the fund typically adopts procedures that will permit it to purchase such securities. . . . .

### Counsel, Auditors, and Other Service Providers

The mutual fund will need legal counsel to assist in organizing the fund, drafting the registration statement, and other procedures. The sponsor also may require counsel. Counsel for the distributor or the fund may handle matters such as preparing filings with state blue-sky authorities, and clearing advertisements with the National Association of Securities Dealers (NASD). Once the fund is fully operational, the fund's counsel will perform regular legal tasks such as preparing or reviewing public filings, preparing a memorandum for the board's annual meeting at which the fund's agreements and procedures are considered, and advising the board about its responsibilities. The independent directors may retain their own counsel, particularly when considering changes in advisory or distribution agreements or facing a specific conflict or other important issue requiring independent advice.

An employee of the administrator often performs the fund's internal accounting work, or the fund may retain an accounting firm experienced in mutual fund matters. The fund's independent auditors are selected by a majority of the independent directors. At present, shareholders must ratify the selection at the next annual meeting, if such a meeting occurs, although the SEC no longer requires new funds to hold a shareholders' meeting for that purpose. . . .

## DOCUMENT PREPARATION AND OTHER ACTIONS

### REGISTRATION UNDER THE ICA AND THE SECURITIES ACT OF 1933

Before mutual fund shares can be offered to the public, the fund must register as an investment company under the ICA, and its securities must be registered under the Securities Act of 1933 (Securities Act). The two registrations normally are combined in the same procedure. The process begins with the filing of a notification of registration (Form N-8A) stating basic identifying information about the fund, after which the fund is deemed registered under the ICA. Within three months thereafter (or three months after the end of the fund's fiscal year, if later), the fund must file the initial Securities Act registration statement.

The registration statement for most open-end investment companies is Form N-1A. The form comprises three parts, consisting of the prospectus, the statement of additional information, and other information filed with the SEC. The form and its accompanying guides set forth the required disclosures. It requires disclosure, among other things, of the structure and classification of the mutual fund, the fund's primary investment objectives and policies, information about each person and entity affiliated with the fund, and information about each fund officer and director.

The prospectus is not only a disclosure document, but also a sales document. While much of what is in the prospectus is required, the style should reflect the fund's marketing strategy. Care is essential in precisely describing how the fund will invest, as the document will govern the fund's day-to-day operations. The prospectus should reflect input from the fund's portfolio managers about the instruments to be purchased (such as options and commodity futures) and strategies to be used (such as leverage) as well as the "back office" as to such details as the procedures for purchasing and redeeming shares. The process of drafting the prospectus often reveals and resolves internal uncertainty about fund objectives.

An open-end fund provides supplemental sales literature as part of the registration statement. In addition, the fund is required to furnish copies of any periodic reports it may have filed, and all other information and documents that would be necessary to register the fund's securities under the Securities Act and to comply with the Exchange Act.

The item-by-item instructions for Form N-1A, and regulations relating to mutual fund filings under the Securities Act and the ICA, supply detailed information about the registration statement. The SEC guidelines for Form N-1A and the SEC staff's generic comment letters also should be reviewed carefully when drafting and preparing the registration statement, as they reflect the SEC staff's views on many disclosure issues.

Preparation of the registration statement may require three to six weeks or more, depending on the certainty of management about disclosure items and the complexity and novelty of issues addressed. After the fund files the initial registration statement, the SEC staff issues comments within thirty to forty-five days, although staff delays often require a longer period. The registration statement then is revised to reflect initial staff comments. For an open-end fund, once the SEC staff and the fund have agreed on language, the staff accelerates the effectiveness of the registration statement, and the fund thereafter can issue the final prospectus and issue shares.

The filing fee currently is $1000 for the ICA portion of the registration statement. The filing fee for the Securities Act registration statement depends on whether an indefinite number of shares are registered, as permitted for an open-end fund, and how many actually are issued. Ordinarily, a fund elects to register an indefinite number of shares and pays a $500 initial fee, making later payments as shares are issued.

Because an open-end fund normally is engaged in a continuous offering of its shares, it must maintain a current prospectus. The fund does this by filing regular post-effective amendments to the registration statement, including a revised prospectus, to provide updated financial statements, performance data, and other information such as the number of shares issued to date.

## ADVERTISEMENTS AND OTHER SUPPLEMENTAL SALES MATERIALS

A fund may advertise after filing a registration statement. Until a registration statement has been filed, no offer of the fund's shares may be made. During the period when a registration statement has been filed but is not yet effective, oral offers may be made but any written material that could be construed as an offer is severely restricted. After the registration statement becomes effective, sales literature may be disseminated so long as it is accompanied by the fund's prospectus. The fund must file sales literature with the SEC within ten days after using the literature in distributing shares.  Some sales information other than that submitted with the registration may be filed with the NASD in lieu of the SEC.

One sales tool that the new fund's sponsor may consider is presentation of information about the past performance of the investment adviser. This information, if intended for use in offering shares of a fund, can be advertised publicly only through an "omitting" prospectus under rule 482 of the Securities Act. Tombstone advertisements under the more liberal rule 134 presently cannot include performance data.  Under rule 482, an omitting prospectus advertisement currently can contain only information "the substance of which" is stated in the fund's full statutory prospectus issued under section 10(a) of the Securities Act.  Thus, if the sponsor wishes publicly to advertise performance data in sales literature or otherwise, much the same information also must appear in the fund's statutory prospectus. A performance data advertisement or omitting prospectus, like the statutory prospectus, is subject to section 12[a](2) of the Securities Act, which imposes liability for false or misleading statements of fact, and to related rule 156.

A public advertisement may be necessary for a direct-marketed fund, and helpful for a sales force-marketed fund intended primarily for individual investors. In any case, the use of prior performance data must be considered particularly by counsel. Performance data are reviewed carefully by the SEC staff, and their use may delay considerably the registration process. The data must disclose all material facts to avoid any false or misleading implications. The possible effect of specific investment company limitations on future performance also should be disclosed. Certain representations such as testimonials are prohibited, and restrictions apply to discussion of specific past recommendations of the adviser or model performance results.

The SEC proposed an amendment to rule 482 that would permit a new "off-the-page" advertising prospectus for mutual funds which is not limited to information contained in the statutory prospectus. The rule would not substantially alter existing restrictions on the disclosure of investment performance.

The NASD also adopted standards concerning investment company advertising. Those standards supplement applicable laws and regulations, and may in some cases be more restrictive.

# CHAPTER THIRTEEN

# THE REGULATION OF INVESTMENT COMPANIES

As we did in our discussion of insurance companies and securities firms, this chapter on the substantive regulation of investment companies focuses on a selection of regulatory issues that illuminate characteristic features of supervision in this field.

## Section 1.  The Definition of an Investment Company

Section 3 of the 1940 Act defines the term investment company.  Subsection (a) establishes the outer boundary of that definition, establishing a presumption that certain kinds of companies should be subject to regulation under the 1940 Act.  Subsections (b) and (c) create a number of exemptions from section 3's broad reach.  As you look over this statutory structure, consider the jurisdictional line it draws.  Business organizations that fall within the definition of investment company are subject to strict and intrusive regulatory requirements.  Other entities — including the vast majority of public corporations in the United States — are supervised far less stringently.  Are investment companies so different from other types of business organizations as to warrant such different regulation? Consider how the 1940 Act definitions were applied in the following case:

### SEC v. Fifth Avenue Coach Lines, Inc.
### 289 F. Supp. 3 (S.D.N.Y. 1968), *aff'd*, 435 F.2d 510 (2d Cir. 1970)

[Fifth Ave. Coach Lines (Fifth) was a New York corporation with almost 900,000 issued shares held by 2,300 stockholders.  Fifth had a wholly owned subsidiary called Surface Transit, Inc. (Surface), which in turn had a wholly owned subsidiary called Westchester Street Transportation Company, Inc. (Westchester).  Fifth and Surface operated bus lines in New York City; Westchester operated bus lines in Westchester County.  In 1962, the City of New York by condemnation acquired all the bus lines of Fifth and Surface, but did not take over Westchester.  After litigation, the City of New York in late 1966 and 1967 paid a total award of over $38 million to Fifth and Surface.  Once creditors were paid, $11.5 million of this award actually went to the managers of Fifth.  Fifth and its subsidiaries were run by Muscat, Cohn and Krock.  From late 1966 onwards, these three men led Fifth into a series of complicated transactions which became the basis of this lawsuit by the SEC.]

### Section 3(a)(1)

It has been said that Section 3(a)(1) describes the "orthodox investment company," i.e., a company that knows that it is an investment company and does not claim to be anything else, whereas Section 3(a)(3) "catches the inadvertent investment company," i.e., a company which does something else but suddenly comes up against the 40 per cent test.  See Kerr, The Inadvertent Investment Company, 12 Stan.L.Rev. 29, 32 (1959-60).

The court is not persuaded that this attempted distinction is wholly sound.  Section 3(a)(1) says that a company is an investment company if it is engaged primarily in the business of investing, reinvesting or trading in securities, or *holds itself* out as being engaged primarily in that business, or *proposes* to engage primarily in that business.  "Holding out" and "proposing" imply intent, but "is" does not necessarily imply it.  It would seem to be possible for a company to find itself at a given point in time to be actually engaged primarily in this business, even though it originally did not intend to be so engaged.  The key word is "primarily."  To determine whether a company is engaged primarily in the business of investing, its total activities of all sorts must be considered.

As has been pointed out earlier in this opinion, between March 1962 and October 1966, Fifth itself, as a practical matter, was not engaged in any business.  It was merely marking time until it received payment of the condemnation award.  Through Westchester, a subsidiary of a subsidiary, it was engaged in operating a bus line in Westchester County.  Since that was its only business, it must have been its "primary business" during that period, and although carried on indirectly, the company at that point would seem to have been specifically excluded from investment company status by Section 3(b)(1) of the Act.  In any event, no one claims that before October 1966 Fifth was an investment company.

Plaintiff says, however, that Fifth became one in October 1966, at the moment that it received the award.  The court does not agree.  The mere possession of $11,500,000 in cash does not make a company an investment company.  It is necessary to examine Fifth's activities thereafter to see what it did with the cash, in other words, to see in what business it became primarily engaged.

In fairness, it should be noted that plaintiff's contention that Fifth became an investment company immediately in October 1966 is based in part on the verbs "holding out" and "proposes," rather than the "is" in Section 3(a)(1). This has reference to the fact that in the President's Letter dated July 28, 1966, in Fifth's annual report for 1965, Muscat stated:

"As soon as the first monies are received from the City of New York the Surface mortgage bondholders will be paid in full, and the Company intends to make proper and advantageous investments for the benefit of the Company."

Furthermore, at the annual meeting of stockholders held on August 10, 1966. Cohn read a statement of Muscat which said:

"There are bargains available today in the form of investments in transportation, in related fields, and in brand new fields — bargains which others cannot take advantage of because they do not have the cash available.

We have been actively exploring several of these opportunities and we will be ready to move forward boldly when the funds are paid over to us.

We have waited more than four years. But we will be in a position to put the money to work profitably for you as soon as it is received."

These statements are predictions as to what Fifth plans to do in the future. They are too general in nature to justify a finding that they amounted to such a "holding out" or "proposing" that Fifth would engage *primarily* in the business of investing as to require the conclusion that Fifth became an investment company immediately when the funds were received.

When Fifth first received the $11,500,000, it deposited the cash in a number of different banks. Some of these deposits were time deposits, usually for ninety days, but in some instances longer. Fifth received interest on its time deposits. Plaintiff calls this "investing." The court does not believe that merely putting one's money in the bank, even though one thereby obtains some interest, in and of itself is "investing, reinvesting or trading in securities" within the meaning of Section 3(a)(1). Surely a company which has suddenly come into possession of a substantial amount of cash is entitled to a reasonable time to decide what to do with it without violating the Investment Company Act.

Within a month or so Fifth began buying stocks with some of this money. It bought 31,461 shares of the Defiance stock at a cost of $340,568.94. It also bought a small block of American Steel, 923 shares, for $13,125. Fifth has continued to hold these.

In November and December 1966, it bought small amounts of stock in Wilson Brothers, Standard Packaging, Horn & Hardart Company and Republic Corporation. It disposed of all these in late 1966 or early 1967.

In December 1966 Fifth made its first tender offer for Austin, Nichols stock, as we have seen. At the end of December 1966, as has been recounted, Fifth spent $717,200 for Gateway stock which, within a few weeks, it turned over to Gray Line.

At December 31, 1966 Fifth owned considerable stock. It still had on hand, however, a substantial amount of cash. It had immediately available cash of $3,147,594 plus certificates of deposit of $616,000 plus foreign time deposits of $750,000, a total of $4,513,594.

The court believes that up to that time Fifth was still in a period of transition. It still had not fully committed its liquid resources. It had not yet made investing its primary business. Under the 3(a)(1) test, it was not then an investment company.

Defendants say that they were looking around for opportunities for Fifth to buy control of other companies. There is evidence to support that contention. In the fall of 1966 Muscat, Krock and Cohn considered several different proposals for the acquisition of companies by Fifth. All of them fell through for one reason or another.

Fifth announced publicly in December 1966 that it sought to buy 51 per cent of Austin, Nichols. As events turned out, Fifth never came close to achieving that objective. By December 31, 1966, Fifth had not acquired control of any company, except the 60 per cent interest in Gateway which it almost immediately passed over to Gray Line.

In 1967 Fifth continued to buy stock. It was particularly active in buying bank stocks. In January it spent $3,609,884.35 to acquire 33,401 shares of Mercantile, a 26 per cent interest in the company. In February it bought 595 shares of University for $554,600 and lent its credit to American Steel to buy considerably more. It also purchased a comparatively small block of Guaranty, 2,087 shares, for $83,480.

The Austin, Nichols tenders were consummated in the winter and early spring of 1967. These took a sizable portion of Fifth's cash reserves. Fifth paid $2,312,582.54 for the 105,538 shares of Austin, Nichols common stock.

By June 30, 1967 Fifth owned substantially more securities and possessed substantially less cash than it had on December 31, 1966. As of June 30, its immediately available cash was $843,100 which, when added to time deposits of $775,000, made a total of $1,618,100 as compared to the $4,513,594 which it had had on December 31, 1966.

The time must eventually come when a corporation initially possessed of cash and no real business, by spending its cash becomes engaged in a business of some sort. That time had come by June 30, 1967.

What business was Fifth primarily engaged in on June 30? In the court's opinion, the only business that it can fairly be found to be primarily engaged in was the business of investing in securities. That was what it spent its money for. That is where its income came from. It had no other business which could reasonably be called "primary."

Westchester's buses and VIP's limousines were a negligible factor in Fifth's business. According to Fifth's own figures prepared by its new treasurer, Ellenbogen, the total income of Fifth and Surface on a consolidated basis for the first six months of 1967 was $266,158.60. Of this only $16,749.72 came from Westchester. VIP produced a loss of $175,957.22. And it cannot be said, merely because the securities owned by Fifth included stock constituting 26 per cent of Mercantile, that Fifth on June 30 was primarily engaged in the banking business.

Defendants argue that Fifth was not engaged primarily in the business of investing in securities on June 30, 1967 or at any other time because its policy was to buy stocks for the purpose of obtaining control of other companies. Although, as previously stated, the evidence indicates that at least at the outset this was Fifth's policy, Fifth has been markedly unsuccessful in carrying out that policy. The only company that it can be said to control is Mercantile.

But regardless of whether the policy was successful or not, the answer to defendants' argument, in the court's opinion, is that it finds no support in the language of the Act and indeed runs counter to the normal meaning of that language and to the fundamental purpose of the Act. The statute does not recognize an exception for the business that defendants claim Fifth is and was engaged in, i.e., the business of acquiring control of other companies. . . .

On all the evidence the court finds that on June 30, 1967 Fifth was an investment company within the meaning of Section 3(a)(1). There is no evidence to indicate that Fifth has changed its business since June 30, 1967. It follows that it is now an investment company.

### Section 3(a)(3)

There are two elements to the test set up by this section. In the first place, the company must engage or propose to engage in the business of investing, reinvesting, owning, holding or trading in securities. In the second place, it must meet a mechanical standard, i.e., the value of its 'investment securities' must exceed 40 per cent of the value of its total assets, as defined in the section.

Plaintiff claims, and defendants deny, that Fifth was an investment company under this test on December 31, 1966 and on June 30, 1967. Those specific dates have been selected for the valuation of Fifth's assets. For the reasons hereinafter set forth, the court finds that Fifth was not an investment company under the Section 3(a)(3) test on December 31, 1966 but that it was one on June 30, 1967.

*December 31, 1966*

The short answer to plaintiff's contention is that on that date Fifth was not yet engaged in the business of investing or holding securities. . . .

The court, however, does not rest its determination of Fifth's status on December 31, 1966 solely on this ground. It finds that on that date Fifth did not meet the second branch of the Section 3(a)(3) test either.

Application of the 40 per cent test involves two factors: (1) the value of a company's total assets, as defined in the section, (2) the value of its "investment securities." In this case, each side called an expert to testify on this subject. As might be expected, they disagreed on both factors.

*Fifth's Total Assets on December 31, 1966*

The problem as to assets involves the interpretation of the phrase "government securities and cash items" which the statute requires to be excluded from total assets for the purpose of this computation. This apparently simple language raises difficulties in the case which one would not normally expect to encounter. The court's conclusions on these matters will be briefly stated.

Plaintiff claims that Fifth's total assets for computation purposes on December 31, 1966 were $6,146,809. The court finds that they were $6,538,809. The difference arises in two ways: (1) plaintiff has included in assets amounts which the court finds should have been excluded as "cash items"; (2) plaintiff has excluded as cash items amounts which the court finds were not cash items and therefore should have been included.

The term is defined in Section 6-03.1 of Regulation S-X, a regulation which prescribes accounting rules for investment companies. It reads as follows:

"1. Cash and cash items.-- State separately (a) cash on hand, demand deposits, and time deposits; (b) call loans; and (c) funds subject to withdrawal restrictions. Funds subject to withdrawal restrictions and deposits in closed banks shall not be included under this caption unless they will become available within 1 year."

It will be observed that while this rule deals with "time deposits," it does not mention the term "certificate of deposit." A certificate of deposit is merely a piece of paper evidencing the existence of a time deposit. The court sees no valid distinction, as far as Section 3(a)(3) is concerned, between a time deposit which is not evidenced by a certificate and one that is. Except in special circumstances, a time deposit is defined to be a cash item. When it is evidenced by a certificate, it should still be regarded as a cash item. . . .

*Investment Securities on December 31, 1966*

Plaintiff contends that the total value of Fifth's investment securities on December 31, 1966 was $4,259,017. The court finds it to be $1,286,887.

The relevant statutory definitions have previously been set forth. To recapitulate briefly: Section 3(a)(3) says that "investment securities" means all securities except "government securities" and securities "issued by majority owned subsidiaries of the owner which are not investment companies." The long-winded definition of "security" in Section 2(a)(35) includes the phrase "evidence of indebtedness." Plaintiff says that an indebtedness may be "evidenced" orally. Thus, it treats this phrase as though it read "indebtedness," and consequently, regards every indebtedness which is not a government bond or the stock of a non-investment company subsidiary as an "investment security." This interpretation of the definitions leads in some instances to results which seem to the court to border upon the absurd.

Thus, plaintiff includes among Fifth's investment securities its claim against Krock for the return of the $175,000 duplicate payment which had not been returned by December 31, 1966. The court rejects this classification. The word "investment" in the section must have some significance. The court does not see how a claim for the return of a payment erroneously made can conceivably be called an investment.

Plaintiff also claims that the ninety day certificate of deposit totalling $616,000 and the Suizo time deposit of $250,000 are investment securities. As previously found, these items are cash and hence should not be in the computation at all. . . .

The court has found that the assets of Fifth, for computation purposes, on December 31, 1966 totalled $6,538,809. Forty per cent of that figure is $2,615,523. It is obvious, therefore, that investment securities aggregating only $1,286,887 do not meet the 40 per cent test. They constitute only approximately 20 per cent of the total assets. Hence, Fifth was not an investment company on December 31, 1966 under the Section 3(a)(3) test.

*June 30, 1967*

Here there is no difficulty with the first branch of the Section 3(a)(3) test. The court has already found that as of June 30, 1967, investing in securities was Fifth's primary business. As to the 40 per cent formula constituting the second branch of the test, the court finds that this was met as well on June 30, 1967. . . .

The most important question as of June 30, 1967, both as to assets and as to investment securities, is the proper treatment to be given to Fifth's claim against New York City for intangibles. By June 30, 1967, this claim had been reduced to judgment in the sum of $1,257,500, according to the opinion of Mr. Justice Hecht at Special Term. Matter of City of New York (Fifth Avenue Coach Lines, Inc.), N.Y.L.J., April 18, 1967, pp. 18, 19. . . .

Mr. Justice Hecht also awarded Surface $1,320,000 on its claim for intangibles. The award to Surface is not separately shown as such in the total of Fifth's assets because Section 3(a)(3) requires that the computation be made "on an unconsolidated basis." The award is taken into account, however, in the value attributed to Fifth's stock in Surface. The parties have stipulated that apart from the award, this stock had a value of minus $400,000.

At a meeting held on December 18, 1967, Fifth's board of directors determined that the fair value of Fifth's claim for intangibles was $13,490,000, and the fair value of Surface's claim was $16,520,000, a total of $30,010,000.  The board acted on the advice of independent counsel recently retained by Fifth who represented Fifth on the trial of this action. . . . .

The figure of $30,010,000 is substantially the same figure as Fifth and Surface claimed before Mr. Justice Hecht and in the Appellate Division and which they now claim in the New York Court of Appeals.  Mr. Justice Hecht's opinion characterized this claim as "grossly disproportionate to the allowances in the cases relied on in the majority opinion of the Court of Appeals." . . .

The court does not doubt the good faith of Fifth's present independent counsel in advising the board of what he believed to be its rights.  Moreover, the court assumes, without deciding, that in setting the value at the figure for which Fifth has consistently contended, Fifth's directors were acting in good faith, even though Mr. Justice Hecht found a very much lower figure.  But in the court's opinion, it was not open to Fifth's directors to value this asset . . . once the Supreme Court, New York County, had determined its value. . . .

The court has found that the assets of Fifth, for computation purposes, on June 30, 1967, were $15,266,033.  Investment securities of $8,389,463 is approximately 55 per cent of this total.  Therefore, on June 30, 1967, Fifth met the 40 per cent test and was an investment company under Section 3(a)(3). . . .

## Comments and Questions

1.  The *Fifth Avenue* case is an example of what practitioners refer to as an "inadvertent investment company" — a problem that arises when a commercial firm inadvertently restructures its assets in way that transforms the entity into an investment company for purposes of section 3.  The SEC has adopted a variety of regulations to alleviate this problem in a number of situations, but still the definitional provisions constitute a trap for the unwary.  See Section 3(b)(2) of the 1940 Act; see also Rule 3a-1 & 3a-2.  The interesting and difficult policy issues underlying these exceptions is the question of when a commercial firms becomes a vehicle for pooled investments such that the firm should be required to abide by the 1940 Act's restrictions.  Was, for example, the *Fifth Avenue* case correctly decided as a matter of regulatory policy?  Accepting the court's characterization in this case, what kind of investment company was involved in this case?  See sections 4 and 5 of the 1940 Act.

2. The structure of exemptions from the 1940 Act's basic definition of investment are complex, but several of the exemptions are instructive.  For example, read over subsection 3(c)(3).  Why is this exemption necessary?  Have we seen similar exemptions elsewhere? Note too subsection 3(c)(1), which exempts "private" investment companies — those with fewer than 100 beneficial owners.  The existence of this exemption has been critical for the development of certain segments of the financial services industry — most notably hedge funds.  Compare section 3(c)(1) with section 3(c)(7).  What is the difference between these two exemptions?  See also Section 2(a)(51) of the 1940 Act.  Are both exemptions necessary?

*Problem 13-1*

Victoria Lynn has been for many years a technical analyst for a large investment company complex, where she specializes in the tracking movements in foreign exchange markets. She is thinking of quitting her job to establish a small fund designed to make speculative and potentially extremely profitable investments in foreign exchange. She anticipates that she will be able to attract between 200 and 300 hundred investors to such a fund. Most of these investors would be wealthy individuals or corporations, but several dozen are acquaintances or relatives with more modest resources. Can she take on all these clients without registering under the 1940 Act? If her own net worth is less than a million dollars can she herself participate in the investments?

*Problem 13-2*

Warren Buffett has been one of the most successful investment managers of the past thirty years. His company, Berkshire Hathaway, holds substantial investments in a number of companies. Most of these investments are held through a Nebraska insurance company that is itself a wholly-owned subsidiary of Berkshire Hathaway. Berkshire Hathaway is a public company with numerous shareholders. Is Berkshire Hathaway subject to the 1940 Act?

---

In the preceding discussion, we have been considering situations in which the 1940 Act does not apply to entities excluded from the definition of investment company. As the following legal opinion illustrates, however, there are also situations in which companies regulated under the 1940 Act may find themselves also subject to other regulatory structures.

## Opinion of the Attorney General of the State of Oregon
### 42 Op. Atty Gen. Ore. 273 (Feb. 11, 1981)

QUESTION PRESENTED

Does the Cash Management Account (CMA) program operated by Merrill Lynch, Pierce, Fenner & Smith, Incorporated (Merrill Lynch) constitute "banking business" under ORS 706.005(4)?

DISCUSSION

The Cash Management Account (CMA) program operated by Merrill Lynch, as described in its July 1, 1981, program prospectuses, consists of three parts: a securities margin account, three related money market funds, and a VISA check/card account maintained by Bank One of Columbus, N.A. (Bank One).

The securities account is a conventional margin account which may be used to purchase and sell securities and options on margin or on a fully paid basis.  An interest charge is made for margin loans, with the maximum loan value of common stocks which may be sold on margin under the program now set at 50 percent of their current market value.  The securities account is maintained pursuant to the rules and regulations of the Securities and Exchange Commission (SEC), the Board of Governors of the Federal Reserve System, and the New York Stock Exchange.  Each investor with assets in the securities account has the benefit of up to $ 500,000 in protection through the Securities Investor Protection Corporation.

Two CMA programs are available.  These programs are identical, except that one offers only one money market fund while the other offers a choice of three money funds.  Free credit cash balances in the securities account are automatically invested, not less frequently than weekly, in shares of one of these funds at their current net asset value.  At any time, as with any securities account, free cash balances held in the securities account may be withdrawn by the investor by notifying Merrill Lynch.  Dividends are declared daily on money fund shares and are reinvested daily in additional shares.  The prospectuses state:

". . . Unlike the Securities Account, Money Fund shares are not subject to the protection of the Securities Investor Protection Act or to protection by the Federal Deposit Insurance Corporation or any other governmental insurance agency. . . ."

Money fund shares are redeemed at net asset value on the customer's request.  Shares are automatically redeemed as necessary to satisfy debit balances in the securities account, or amounts owed on the VISA account.

The third component of the CMA program is the VISA account.  Bank One issues a VISA card and checks to each customer (with certain minor exceptions).  The card may be used to make purchases of merchandise or services at participating VISA establishments, or to obtain cash advances from participating banks.  The checks may be used to draw upon the VISA account for any purpose, but neither the card nor the checks may be used to purchase securities in the securities account or money fund shares.  The amount available for VISA purchases, cash advances and checking is the sum of any uninvested free cash balance in the securities account, the net asset value of the money fund shares, and the available margin loan value of securities in the securities account.

Through use of computer interface, Bank One will notify Merrill Lynch daily of any charges made against the VISA account, and Merrill Lynch will pay Bank One on behalf of its customer from the CMA accounts on the same day.  Payments are made first from the free cash balances, if any, held in the securities account pending investment; second, from proceeds of redemption of money fund shares; and finally, from margin loans to the customer by Merrill Lynch from  the available margin loan value of securities in the securities account.

Participation in the CMA program requires a minimum investment of $ 20,000 in securities or cash.

The question presented is whether the CMA program, as described above, constitutes "banking business" under ORS 706.005(4), which provides:

"(4) Banking business means the business of soliciting, receiving or accepting money or its equivalent on deposit as a regular business whether the deposit is made subject to check or is evidenced by a certificate of deposit, a pass book or other writing, but does not include:

"(a) Depositing money or its equivalent in escrow or with an agent, pending investments in . . . securities for or on account of a principal. . . ." . . . .

In letter opinion OP-4340, issued May 30, 1978, to Mr. John B. Olin, Superintendent of Banks, we concluded, although acknowledging that it was a close question, that a program virtually identical to the CMA program described above did constitute "banking business" under this statute. That opinion was based on the conclusion that both the free credit balances in the securities account and the CMA money fund shares were "deposits of money or its equivalent," and that these deposits were not being held by an agent pending investments in securities. Our reexamination of this opinion leads us to conclude that it was in error. We do not believe that either the free credit balance in the securities account or the money fund shares represent "deposits" within the meaning of ORS 706.005(4), but even if they did constitute such deposits, they represent "money or its equivalent" deposited "pending investments in . . . securities" and thus are excepted from the definition of "banking business."

Funds deposited with a bank by its customer create a debtor-creditor relationship. See Dahl & Penne v. State Bank of Portland, 110 Or 68, 222 P 1090 (1924). The customer has a right to demand an equivalent amount of funds at some time in the future.

Free credit balances are subject to regulation by the SEC under the Securities Exchange Act of 1934. See Rule 15co-3 defines "free credit balance" as:

". . . [L]iabilities of a broker or dealer to customers which are subject to immediate cash payment to customers on demand, whether resulting from sales of securities, dividends, interest, deposits or otherwise, excluding, however, funds in commodity accounts which are segregated in accordance with the Commodity Exchange Act or in a similar manner."

In our opinion, the free credit balance does not constitute a "deposit" within the meaning of ORS 706.005(4), although it shares some of the characteristics of such a deposit. Free credit balances are subject to payment to the account holder on demand, but under the CMA program such funds are contractually committed to investment in shares of the money fund, i.e., to investment in a security. Funds in the free credit balance are transitory and in a constantly changing amount resulting from sales of securities, dividends, interest or, in some cases, cash additions to the securities account. The chief characteristic of the free credit balance, however, is that it represents a by-product of securities investment activity.

Free credit balances as described in the SEC rule, supra, are a common element of securities brokerage activity. We are aware of no case in which they have been declared to be "deposits" within the meaning of banking laws similar to ORS 706.005(4).

Our former opinion relied solely upon Western Investment Banking Co. v. Murray, 6 Ariz 215, 56 P 728 (1899), for its conclusion that free credit balances were deposits within the meaning of ORS 706.005(4). That case dealt with the question of whether a company was a banking institution, for purposes of a tax statute, if it received money from customers, invested the money in the customers' names by making loans and collecting rents and interests thereon, and made the interest and rents subject to check by the customer. The court impliedly held that the moneys received were deposits, but did not discuss this issue.  We do not find this case helpful in deciding the issues presented in this opinion.

Our former opinion also concluded that the CMA money fund shares were "deposits" under the banking statute, again relying on a single case for its conclusion.  That case, Security & Bond Deposit Co. v. State ex rel Seney, 105 Ohio 113, 136 NE 891 (1922), involved the following factual situation, as described by the court:

"It is disclosed by the record that the plan of operation of the business of the defendant company was to borrow securities, in the main Liberty Bonds, paying therefor a stipulated rate of interest, calculated on the par value thereof, in addition to the interest payable by the government under the terms of such bonds.  These securities thus borrowed would then be used as collateral by the company to secure loans of money to itself, denominated 'its cash working fund.'  As concisely stated by the president of the company, 'instead of selling stock to create our entire working fund we borrow securities and in turn borrow cash on the securities.'  The advertising matter of the defendant company informed the public that --

"To deposit your securities with the Security & Bond Deposit Company is similar to depositing your cash in a bank, as we pay from two per cent, to four per cent, annually on securities in addition to the amount of interest your securities are earning.  Therefore, you receive not only the amount of interest your securities are earning but also the additional interest we pay you for the use of your securities, which is the same as a bank paying for per cent for the use of your cash.'"

This case thus involved a company which was borrowing securities from the public and paying interest thereon.  The company and its depositors had a debtor-creditor relationship.  Security & Bond Deposit, supra, 136 NE at 894.

The money fund shares of the CMA represent a wholly different concept.  An investor in the money shares is an owner pro tanto of the fund.  An interest in the money fund is an equity interest providing capital gains and losses to investors.  The value of an interest in the share rises and falls with the value of the fund's portfolio of investments.  It thus differs from the debt represented by a bank deposit, the value of which is not subject to fluctuation.

For the reasons stated above, we do not believe that either the free credit balance or the money fund shares of the CMA program represent "deposits" under the banking law.  Even if they did represent such deposits, however, it is clear that these funds are deposited "pending investments in . . . securities" and are therefore within the exception to ORS 706.005(4).  The free credit balance and money funds are integrally related to the securities account, and simply provide a convenient "parking place" for investment funds pending investment in the securities account.

The CMA prospectuses have gone to great lengths to emphasize the distinctions between the CMA program and bank accounts.  The cover of the prospectuses dated July 31, 1981, states in part:

"Investors should be aware that the Cash Management Account service is not a bank account.  As with any investment in securities, the value of the shareholder's investment in the Funds will fluctuate."

On page ii this statement appears:

"... Unlike the Securities Account, Money Fund shares are not subject to the protection of the Securities Investor Protection Act or to protection by the Federal Deposit Insurance Corporation or any other governmental insurance agency."

On page v it is stated:

"Investors should be aware that the checking feature of the CMA program is intended to provide customers with easy access to the assets in their account and that the CMA account is not a bank account. As with any investment in securities, the value of a shareholder's investment in the Money Funds may fluctuate."

These explicit disclaimers make it highly unlikely that a person investing in the CMA program would believe that the investment represented a bank deposit or had the regulatory and insurance protections associated with such a deposit.

We also note that, since our earlier opinion was issued, a number of Attorneys General in other states have considered the question here presented. In no case has the CMA program been found to constitute banking business. ... We are informed that the CMA program is now offered in some 37 states without challenge.

This opinion is limited to the CMA program described herein and in the Merrill Lynch CMA prospectus dated July 1, 1981.

## Comments and Questions

1. The CMA program at issue in this case represented an important innovation in the financial services industry. The heart of the program was a money market mutual fund. The SEC has developed specialized rules governing the regulation of these entities, and we will discuss these rules in some detail later in this chapter. See Section 4.C infra. For the time being, consider the more general question that this order presents: should arrangements such as the CMA Program be regulated as banks or as investment companies? Which regulatory structure is more appropriate?

2. The growth of money market mutual funds such as the ones associated with Merrill Lynch's CMA program has been substantial. By year-end 1997, more than $1 trillion dollars of assets were invested in these funds, up from $498 billion at the end of 1990. Over the same period, deposits in commercial banks and savings associations grew much more solely. Why? Should we be concerned if money market mutual funds continue to grow at the expense of depository institutions?

# Section 2.  Fiduciary Duties and the Role of Directors

As outlined in the previous chapter, fiduciary duties and independent directors play an essential role in the regulation of investment companies.  To some extent, these legal requirements build upon the fiduciary obligations of broker-dealers.  However, the content of fiduciary obligations differ in this context.  Moreover, these fiduciary duties represent only part of the regulatory regime applicable to investment companies.  As your read through this section, consider whether such an elaborate system of fiduciary obligation is necessary in light of the other elements of investment company regulation — particularly, mandatory disclosure rules and various portfolio-shaping rules. Are additional fiduciary obligations cost-effective in this context?

## A.  Brokerage Allocation

We begin our discussion with what many consider to be the most influential line of cases in the investment company field.  These cases involve "brokerage allocation" practices of investment companies in the 1960s and early 1970s.  To understand this cases, you must recall that they took place during the era of fixed commissions on NYSE transactions.  (These commissions were the focus of the *Gordon* case, which we studied in Chapter Eleven.)  During this period, large institutional investors such as investment companies were required to pay excessively high brokerage commissions when trading securities in their portfolios ("portfolio securities").  The brokerage allocation practices at issue in the next two cases represented an effort on the part of some investment companies to recoup these commissions.  As you read through these cases, try to figure out how these transactions worked and also who, if anyone, was injured.  Also consider the legal duties these cases establish.  How likely is it that future compliance with these duties will solve the problems underlying these cases?

### Moses v. Burgin
### 445 F.2d 369 (1st Cir.), *cert. denied*, 404 U.S. 994 (1971)

ALDRICH, Chief Judge.

Plaintiff Moses, a shareholder of Fidelity Fund, Inc. (Fund), a Massachusetts-incorporated investment company, in December 1967 filed a complaint, and in November 1968 an amended complaint, in this derivative action.  Fund is an open-end mutual fund, registered under the Investment Company Act of 1940.  Defendants, in addition to Fund, are Fidelity Management and Research Company (Management), Fund's investment adviser; The Crosby Corporation (Crosby), a wholly owned subsidiary of Management and sometimes included within that term, an underwriter whose sole business is selling shares of Fund to independent broker-dealers; E. C. Johnson 2d, president and director of Fund, and president, director and principal voting stockholder of Management; E. C. Johnson 3d, director of Fund since April 1968, and director and substantial voting stockholder of Management; and C. R. Burgin, G. R. Harding, G. H. Hood, Jr., R. Jones, G. K. McKenzie and H. Schermerhorn, who are or were directors of Fund who claim not to be "affiliated" within the meaning of section 10(a) of the Act, hereinafter the unaffiliated directors. . . .

Fund's shareholders are numbered in five, and its assets in the upper nine, figures. The amount of its assets, apart from changes in the market value of its investments, depends upon the number of shares that it can sell as against the number it must redeem. Both activities are continual. The purchasers of individual participating interests, or shares, pay their net worth in terms of the current value of Fund's assets, plus a 1 1/2% Sales charge to Crosby and a brokerage commission of 6%. In response to advice by Management, Fund is constantly changing its portfolio. This is done through independent broker-dealers, and mostly involves trading by them on the New York and regional stock exchanges. . . .

The exchanges, at all relevant times, set required commission rates, with no quantity discounts. Because of the size of many mutual fund transactions brokers competing for business were willing to give up a portion of the commissions they received from the fund. "Anti-rebate" rules adopted by every exchange prevented any rebate or discount, direct or indirect, that would bring the net commission paid below the minimum level set by the exchange. As will be described, the total effect of these rules was in doubt, but they at least prevented direct cash refunds to the customer. On Fund's instructions, at Management's behest, the so-called customer-directed give-ups were paid over to brokers who sold shares of Fund acquired from Crosby to the public, in proportion to their success, in order to stimulate sales.[3] Customer-directed give-ups are to be distinguished from broker-directed give-ups, a long-recognized practice whereby two or more brokers who have shared in the work divide the commission between themselves. Give-ups which are customer- directed (which is what we shall mean by the term "give-up" hereafter) are inherently and necessarily, as the district court found, in the nature of a refund, or rebate to the customer.[4]

Plaintiff's complaint is double-barreled. First, she complains of Fund's give-up practices because they resulted in the loss of the value of brokerage commissions which could have been recaptured. She claims recapture was possible either by creation of a broker affiliate that could participate in Fund portfolio transactions, or by channeling present give-ups to an affiliate, with the result that in either case the sums involved would be credited to Fund. Second, she complains that the give-up practices, pursued to the exclusion of either course she suggests, benefitted Management and Crosby, since stimulating sales of Fund's shares increased Crosby's commissions, and increased Management's advisory fee, which was measured by the size of Fund's portfolio. Accordingly, plaintiff claims that Management and the two Johnsons, who together owned 90% of its voting stock, were using Fund's assets to their own private advantage. More pointedly, she claims in particular that Fund's board never considered these possibilities because relevant information regarding them was improperly withheld from the unaffiliated

---

[3]    To a lesser extent give-ups were also used to reward brokers who supplied statistical information to Management for use in making investment decisions.

[4]    "When an executing broker at the direction of his customer gives up part of the commission to another broker who has not participated in the transaction * * * the executing broker is giving the customer a rebate."

directors by the Management defendants.[5] Recovery is sought, inter alia, under section 36 of the Investment Company Act . . .

*Jurisdiction*

Before coming to the merits we consider briefly the district court's jurisdiction. Defendants contest vigorously plaintiff's claims that the Investment Company Act establishes a general federal common law of fiduciary obligation, or that she has a valid claim, by way of pendent jurisdiction, under Massachusetts corporate law. We reach neither of these questions, since we see no way in which they would change the result. Defendants do not seriously dispute that the Act impliedly authorizes the courts to grant civil recovery if their conduct fell within the scope of the phrase "gross misconduct or gross abuse of trust" contained in section 36 of the Act [7] . . . . . Our finding of a private right of action is in accord with the majority of the courts that have reached this question. . . .

*The Duty To Recapture*

The brief filed on behalf of Management, Crosby and the two Johnsons states, "The court found that it was the directors' common business judgment that encouraging sales would promote a net cash inflow and growth of the Fund beneficial to the shareholders." Calling this a "policy decision to promote sales" the brief added that the court found that the directors believed that Fund's awards of give-ups to brokers who sold its shares to the public enhanced its sales. Management's implication, which in oral argument it emphasized to the point of affirmation, was that, if recapture was in fact practical, the directors still had a right to choose between recapture of the give-ups for Fund's direct benefit, and awarding them to brokers for its indirect benefit. We hold, however, that if recovery was freely available to Fund, the directors had no such choice.

Fund's charter required that upon sale of its shares it receive their full asset value. The obvious purpose was to prevent the value of the existing shareholders' interest in the assets from being diminished by the addition of further participants. If Fund receives the asset value of new

---

[5]    Plaintiff also complains of the use of "reciprocals," a practice by which Fund, at Management's direction, awarded some of its portfolio business to particular brokers in proportion to their success in selling Fund shares to the public. On the district court's unexcepted-to findings that the execution of Fund's portfolio business was always satisfactory we do not see how reciprocals are involved on this appeal. Whereas furthering sales of its own shares may not have warranted an expense to Fund, reciprocals, as such, cost it nothing. We see no reason to reject the SEC's conclusion that awarding reciprocals even to brokers who have done nothing to benefit the funds is unobjectionable if it "does not in any way operate as a detriment to the funds and if the funds have themselves derived as much as they can from these benefits." Securities & Exchange Comm'n, Report of Special Study of Securities Markets, H.R. Doc. No. 95, 88th Cong., 1st Sess. pt. 4 at 214. This is not to say that granting reciprocals in some particular instance may not conflict with the duty to recapture. See post.

[7]    This section has since been amended [in 1970, see section 36(b) of the 1940 Act] in part to make explicit certain private rights of action. [Before 1970, the section read in relevant part: "If the Commission's allegations of such gross misconduct or gross abuse of trust are established, the court shall enjoin such person from acting in such capacity or capacities either permanently or for such period of time as it in its discretion shall deem appropriate".]

shares, but at the same time rewards the selling broker with give-ups that it has a right to recapture for itself, then the net income Fund receives from the process of selling a share is less than asset value. The existing shareholders have contributed -- by paying more than otherwise necessary on Fund's portfolio transactions -- to the cost of the sale, which was supposed to have been borne by the new member alone. We cannot, therefore, consider absolving the defendants, if we find that they have violated any duty owed the Fund, by finding that directing give-ups to brokers benefitted Fund by stimulating sales of its shares. Such application violated its charter if it would have been practicable to obtain the give-ups for the direct benefit of its treasury.

Management counsel ultimately conceded this during oral argument. We have dwelt upon it to show that the concession was correct. This is not, of course, to say that the court was not justified in finding that it was beneficial to existing shareholders to promote sales of Fund's shares, as well as being beneficial to Management and to Crosby. It is merely that, by the terms of the charter, Fund cannot use free money, or credit, to pay brokers for sales. Sales are Crosby's business. Whether, during the period covered by the complaint, it was practical for Fund to recover commissions for its direct use is another matter.

### Broker Affiliation

There are a number of methods of mutual fund operation. In general, as has been pointed out, management is placed in the hands of an independent entity. Beyond that, some funds sell their participating shares through a captive sales force and others, including Fund, through independent brokers. Some conduct their portfolio business through the same entity that furnishes them with investment advice, while many, like Fund, use independent brokers. There are basic, fundamental differences in the operational problems, and risks to the fund, resulting from the use of affiliated, versus independent, brokers for portfolio transactions. Some of these are dealt with in detail in the district court's comprehensive opinion. We see no purpose in further elaboration. Suffice it to say that a change from independent brokerage to an affiliated broker is not a matter to be lightly undertaken.

It is in this vein that we must see plaintiff's contention that Fund should have decided to have an affiliated broker since recapture could have been effected by having Crosby, or some new subsidiary of Management, become a broker member of an exchange. Plaintiff puts this point with something less than full clarity. Insofar as a fund has a broker affiliate which acts as its executing broker, no question of give-ups arises at all; the issue is the possibility of recapture of the affiliate's profits. It is true that if the broker-affiliate was not used as the fund's exclusive trader, there would in addition be the possibility of using the affiliate to recover give-ups resulting from trading through other houses, and recapturing these as well. It is only too clear, as the court found, that the unaffiliated directors had noted the general risks attendant upon a brokerage operation, especially the risk of loss of best execution, and they had long decided against it. The court found, on adequate evidence, that there were sound business reasons for this decision. We agree; the directors had no duty to pursue plaintiff's suggested course of action, and without their doing so, recapture was not freely available. Plaintiff knew of Fund's practice when she bought her shares; she could have chosen a fund that did have an affiliated broker. . . .

### NASD Recapture

We turn, accordingly, to plaintiff's second major claim, that without the necessity of a broker affiliate, or changing Crosby's methods of operations, give-ups could have been channeled to Crosby -- already eligible to receive them -- to be applied against Management's advisory fee, a process that has been described as indirect recapture.

Six of the seven regional exchanges permitted members of the National Association of Securities Dealers (NASD) who were not exchange members, either by joining the exchange as special members, or even without the formality of any membership, to receive customer-directed give-ups.   Crosby was a member of NASD.  Plaintiff asserts that Crosby, without making any changes in its structure or any basic commitments, was or could have become qualified to receive give-ups on these exchanges, and that Fund could have directed such receipts, having agreed with Management to set them off against its advisory fee. [11]  Management responds that if Fund had so directed, Crosby's crediting Fund would have violated the anti-rebate rules of the exchanges, and hence would not have been permitted.  To this plaintiff replies that by 1965 the Pacific Exchange was allowing funds to recapture brokerage commissions from their broker-affiliates via setoffs against advisory fees owed to management, and that there was no reason to expect that it would draw a distinction, under its anti-rebate rule, against similar recapture of commissions funnelled from independent brokers to NASD members connected with Fund; that Management failed to investigate, or even to inform the unaffiliated directors of the possibility of this indirect recapture; that in 1967 the Philadelphia-Baltimore-Washington Exchange (PBW) did permit a fund to recapture its give-ups through NASD membership of its adviser-underwriters; and that in 1968, when Management finally pursued this subject, a second exchange, Pacific, agreed to essentially this procedure.  The balance of this opinion deals with this subject.

*Management's Duty of Disclosure*

Plaintiff's argument criticizing the Management defendants for not effecting NASD recapture is based on her finding implicit in the Investment Company Act the familiar general principles governing fiduciaries in the area of self-dealing.  We do not denigrate these principles, though we need hold relevant only their expression through the federally imposed standard under section 36, which may vary from the state common law.  We believe, however, that the Act imposes a more fundamental and pervasive requirement where, because of the structure of investment trusts, self-dealing is not the exception but, so far as management is concerned, the order of the day.  One of the primary reasons for Congress' enactment of the Investment Company Act was its finding that,

> "the national public interest and the interest of investors are adversely affected * * * (2) when investment companies are organized, operated, managed * * * in the interest of directors, officers, investment advisers * * * underwriters * * * rather than in the interest of all classes of such companies' security holders. * * *" [Section 1(b) of the 1940 Act.]

Unlike an ordinary trust, or a business, management's normal activities are frequently touched with self-interest, as the example of give-ups, universally used, and benefitting management at least as much as fund shareholders, clearly shows.  Management defendants admit that they gained from the give-up practice, while asserting that Fund also benefitted from the resulting growth.  To the extent that they, or the court in finding for them without finding full

---

[11]   Indeed since Crosby would have done nothing to earn them, under section 17(e) of the Act, Management could not lawfully have kept such money. . . .

disclosure, imply that their self-interest could not influence the decisions to be made on behalf of Fund, Congress had an answer. It responded to this problem by enacting a mandatory provision for unaffiliated, that is, independent, watchdog directors.

Whatever may be the duty of disclosure owed to ordinary corporate directors, we think the conclusion unavoidable that Management defendants were under a duty of full disclosure of information to these unaffiliated directors in every area where there was even a possible conflict of interest between their interests and the interests of the fund. This duty could not be put more clearly than was stated by the SEC in 1965.

"The Investment Company Act's requirement as to unaffiliated directors, if its purposes are not to be subverted, carries with it the obligation on the part of the affiliated directors, and the investment adviser itself, to insure that unaffiliated directors are furnished with sufficient information so as to enable them to participate effectively in the management of the investment company."

Except where it may be fairly assumed that every unaffiliated director will have such knowledge, effective communication is called for. And, in testing that assumption, it must be borne in mind that they are not full time employees of the fund and it may be-- as with Fund's unaffiliated directors-- that neither their activities nor their experience are primarily connected with the special and often technical problems of fund operation. If management does not keep these directors informed they will not be in a position to exercise the independent judgment that Congress clearly intended. The only question can be whether the matter is one that could be thought to be of possible significance.

*Management's Failure To Disclose*

The district court found untrue plaintiff's claim that Management "consistently kept from the directors any of the information which might have aroused them from their inaction." This finding is supportable only in the sense that the concealment was not "consistent." In any other sense it is plainly erroneous as to NASD recapture in the light of the knowledge Management concededly possessed which could well have aroused the unaffiliated directors. As will be developed, the inescapable fact is that Management defendants did, for an extended period of time, keep to themselves possibly, we would say probably, stimulating information.

In June 1965, two representatives of the SEC, Silver and Eisenberg, conducted an inquiry of Fund representatives, trading on the Detroit Stock Exchange and Off-Board Trading by Exchange Members. Sullivan, together with Hamilton, another officer of Management, and Belash, a law partner of Loring, attended. In the course of the proceedings Silver suggested that Crosby, though not an exchange member, could receive give-ups through its NASD membership which could then be set off against the advisory fee. Hamilton responded that directing any give-ups to Crosby would conflict with Illinois blue sky laws, thus affecting Fund's sales there. Silver replied that the Illinois rule was obviously designed to prevent underwriters from benefitting at the expense of the fund, and asked whether Illinois would object if the give-ups were applied to credit Fund. Sullivan in disregard of the charter obligation not to use money or credits that were available to Fund to support sales of its shares, stated that the change would irritate dealers who had been receiving give-ups and have a consequent bad effect upon sales. Silver inquired whether the need to compete with the funds that had joined the Pacific exchange, and were reducing brokerage commissions that way, might change their view of the economics of the situation, which we interpret as a suggestion that Fund's asset loss of recapturable give-ups might have a more adverse effect on sales than would the loss of rewards for dealers.  The SEC had already indicated in its 1963 Special Study, n. 5, ante, that the principal beneficiaries of fund-paid portfolio commissions are not the funds, but the advisers and underwriters.  What was new was the suggestion of how, in fact, the interests of Fund could be better served.  The suggestion by Silver should clearly have imparted to Management the idea that its benefit could now conflict with Fund's interest — and should, in turn, have made these defendants sensitive to the need for passing the suggestion along to the unaffiliated directors.  However, as the court found, this was not done.  Nor was anything else done.

In September 1966, three SEC representatives, Rotberg, Eisenberg and Archie conducted further SEC inquiries, this time entitled Commission Rate Structure.  The same Management representatives attended.  There was a general discussion of NASD recapture of give-ups. [12] Rotberg suggested, inter alia, that Fund should recapture through Crosby.  Sullivan and Belash again mentioned the depressing effect upon sales.  It was added that such conduct would conflict with Crosby's contract, and it was again stated that it raised problems under Illinois blue-sky laws.  Rotberg pointedly asked what Fund had done since the staff's same suggestions had been made at the previous proceeding.  The Fund representatives replied, "Nothing," explicitly adhering to the position that Fund needed the friendship of the small brokers more than it needed the money.  No one suggested the possible illegality of recapture under the anti-rebate rules upon which all defendants now rely.

Again, although by this time the conflict was clearly laid out, the court found that nothing was reported by the Management defendants to the unaffiliated directors.  In their brief the Management defendants say, seemingly to imply that no communication was necessary, that they "investigated the substance of these questions," and concluded that nothing could be done.  "Investigation" seems a palpable exaggeration of what was done.  All the record shows is that they discussed it among themselves.

In sum, we can only conclude that the Management defendants saw a question, that they knew it to be in an area where there was a conflict between their personal interests and the direct interests of the Fund treasury, and that they did not inform the unaffiliated directors or submit it to their consideration. . . .

*Illegality of Recapture*

Turning to defendants' asserted excuses for any failure to disclose, we commence with their single most important point, as it would be a short answer to plaintiff's NASD recapture claim if defendants could support the district court's findings and rulings as to its illegality.  The district court held,

"Insofar as it is a question of fact, this court finds that any scheme involving [Fund's] use of its underwriter Crosby as a recipient of a give-up on the understanding that Crosby's

---

[12]  Management defendants seek to suggest that the 1965 SEC proceedings, having Detroit in their title, raised no questions applicable or relevant to any other exchange.  We do not think, in the light of the content, that it was reasonable for Management to see no broader implication in the discussion recounted above.  In any event, no argument can be made that the 1966 questioning was so restricted.

parent would give (Fund) a credit against charges for investment advisory services is manifestly a rebate within the meaning of the anti-rebate constitutions and rules of the NYSE and other exchanges."

"Inasmuch as an anti-rebate rule is the type of stock exchange rule which has the force of law and is binding alike upon members and customers of the exchange. . . , all recapture devices which are contrary to the anti- rebate provisions of exchange constitutions are illegal." 316 F.Supp. at 57.

. . . . The district court, analyzing the issue as an original question, dismissed as irrelevant the wide-spread, accepted use of give-ups, despite its conclusion that they are also rebates, by saying that "a customer-directed give-up which was not used to establish a credit for a customer is no precedent for a customer directed give-up which does establish such a credit." Recapture, it said, has "the evil consequence of giving back to the customer a dollar credit traceable directly or indirectly to the commission he paid." The fact that there may be some logic in this analysis does not mean that it is correct. The very fact that one type of rebate was uniformly tolerated by the exchanges despite their antirebate rules in itself shows that logic alone cannot supply the answer. The controlling answer must be found in how the exchanges, who were the rule-makers, themselves translated their rules. We have seen that the Pacific and PBW Exchanges, when confronted with proposals for recapture, chose to permit it. We do not accept the district court's disregard of that fact, based on its pronouncement that these exchanges were simply mistaken in doing so. . . . The district court perceived a distinction between recapturing give-ups for the benefit of the customer and its underwriter in terms of selling its shares, and recapturing to pay the fee of the adviser who had generated the transaction from which the give-up arose. Accepting that, we could not think it arbitrary, in view of the common factors shared by these two kinds of rebates, for an exchange to say that the distinction did not compel a difference in result. We reject the district court's ruling that the decision was illegal. . . .

*Liability*

Enough has been said to show that Management defendants were not guilty of mere negligence. They knew . . . that the possibility of recapture was a serious and unresolved issue in the industry. They also knew that it was an issue that involved a potential conflict between their interests and the interests of Fund's shareholders. Their failure to disclose the information available to them to the unaffiliated directors was the result of neither inadvertence nor misapprehension of the facts. Among the abuses enumerated in section 1(b) of the Act, quoted ante, is the operation of investment companies in the interest of advisers, underwriters, and other affiliated persons rather than that of the shareholders. By intentionally pursuing a course of non-disclosure these defendants made the effective functioning of the mechanism protecting Fund from their overreaching impossible. We do not believe that Congress intended that the SEC and the federal courts should be powerless to deal with this kind of conduct, or should excuse it on facts such as those disclosed in the case at bar. . . . Such a construction of the Act would be inconsistent with Congress' direction in section 1(b) that the provisions of the Act be interpreted in accordance with its purpose to "mitigate and, so far as is feasible, to eliminate the conditions enumerated in this section." To hold otherwise would render the benefits Congress sought to obtain through the provisions for unaffiliated directors merely precatory, rather than positive. We therefore conclude that the Management defendants were guilty of gross misconduct within the meaning of the Act in failing to disclose the possibility of NASD recapture to the unaffiliated directors. The two individual management defendants, and the Management corporations, must be held liable for damages under section 36.

On the other hand, the unaffiliated directors, with the possible exception of McKenzie, who is not a defendant here, have not been shown to have had any knowledge of the possibility of NASD recapture. Nor did they have any personal conflicting interest which should have sharpened their attention. Plaintiff has not shown that they violated any duty to discover and explore the issue on their own; recapture was a new problem, and they were entitled to rely on the Management defendants, who devoted full time to the investment industry, to advise them of its emergence. While the unaffiliated directors are not free of all obligations to consider matters on their own, we see no basis for holding them in this case. . . .

### Comments and Questions

1. The *Moses* decision primarily concerns the fiduciary obligations of mutual funds, investment advisers, and investment company directors. The opinion does, however, also explore a related structural limitation on mutual funds. In the section of the decision titled "The Duty to Recapture," the court considers whether the practices in question might have violated a requirement that the fund sell its shares for their "full asset value." What is the source of that requirement? What is its scope? Compare section 22 of the 1940 Act. How does this requirement differ from the fiduciary duties discussed elsewhere in the opinion?

2. As indicated in footnote 7 of the *Moses* opinion, Congress amended section 36 in 1970 to create an express right of action. The content of fiduciary obligations imposed in the newer version of the section differs from the one at issue in the *Moses* case. For one thing, the current version of the section has two subsections (a) and (b), which impose different standards of conduct and establish different procedures for enforcement. Would Moses have been decided differently under the current version of section 36? Under which subsection would the case have been litigated?

### Problem 13-3

Management, Inc., has for many years been the adviser to a large and very successful stock fund. Given its prominence in the investment community, Management Inc. is routinely invited to purchase stock in initial public offerings of promising new companies. Typically, these stock offerings perform very well. If Management chooses to invest in these stocks, must the investment be made through its large stock funds, which hold the bulk of the assets under its management, or could Management create a new IPO fund to take advantage of these opportunities?

# Tannenbaum v. Zeller
### 552 F.2d 402 (2d Cir.), *cert. denied*, 434 U.S. 934 (1977)

FREDERICK van PELT BRYAN, District Judge:

The plaintiff in this derivative action is a shareholder of Chemical Fund Inc., a mutual fund (the Fund). She sued on behalf of the Fund against the Fund's investment adviser, F. Eberstadt & Co., Managers and Distributors, Inc., its parent company, F. Eberstadt & Co., Inc., and Robert G. Zeller, a principal of the Fund, its investment adviser, and the parent company, for alleged unlawful failure to recapture portfolio brokerage commissions for the benefit of the Fund and for alleged inadequate disclosure of the Fund's brokerage practices to Fund shareholders. . . .

The appeal presents troublesome questions concerning the duties of investment advisers and directors of mutual funds with respect to recapture of portfolio brokerage commissions for the benefit of the fund. . . .

## II.

Chemical Fund, Inc., a Delaware corporation, is an open-end, diversified investment company or mutual fund registered with the SEC under the Investment Company Act of 1940. Its investment objective is to attain growth of capital and income through investment in companies specializing in certain aspects of the sciences. . . .

The Fund's investment adviser or manager and the distributor of its shares is, and has been for many years, F. Eberstadt & Co., Managers & Distributors, Inc. (M&D), a Delaware corporation. Pursuant to a written advisory contract, M&D makes investment advisory recommendations to the Fund's board of directors, and, subject to the approval of the board, manages the business and affairs of the Fund. It also furnishes the Fund with office space and ordinary clerical and bookkeeping services. As is customary in the industry, the compensation paid by the Fund to M&D for its services as the Fund's manager is based upon a percentage of the Fund's net assets, with an incentive adjustment for the Fund's investment performance. At all relevant times M&D has been a member of the NASD.

Pursuant to a written distribution contract with the Fund, M&D arranges for the sale of Fund shares to the public through independent securities dealers at a price equal to net asset value plus a sales charge or commission. Under the terms of the distribution agreement, M&D retains less than a quarter of the sales charge and allows the balance to dealers who sell Fund shares.

The parties have stipulated that at all times since at least January 1, 1965, when plaintiff's allegations commence, a majority of the Fund's board of directors have been neither "affiliated" nor "interested" persons within the meaning of the Investment Company Act. These unaffiliated or disinterested Fund directors were characterized by Judge Carter as men of repute in business and the professions.

The defendant F. Eberstadt & Co. Inc. (Eberstadt), M&D's parent company, originally a partnership but later a Delaware corporation, is and has been since 1962 a member firm of the NYSE and a member of the NASD. Eberstadt later became a member of the American Stock Exchange as well.

Robert G. Zeller, the only individual defendant served, is vice-chairman of the Fund's board of directors, vice-chairman of M&D's board, and chairman of the board and chief executive officer of Eberstadt.

Except in unusual circumstances, whenever the Fund wishes to purchase or sell securities for its portfolio it is necessary for M&D to select a broker to execute the transaction or to deal directly with a dealer who owns or wishes to purchase the particular securities being purchased or sold. Total brokerage commissions paid in connection with such portfolio transactions on the NYSE (on which 80% of the transactions were executed), the American Stock Exchange, and regional exchanges ranged from $339,860 in 1965 to $1,291,735 in 1973.

The parties have stipulated that, in selecting brokers for the execution of portfolio transactions, M&D's primary concern has always been securing the best price and quality of execution available to the Fund, i. e., the best execution. Only when two or more executing brokers could provide equal price and quality of execution were other criteria considered in the selection of brokers.

Until July 15, 1973, the criteria employed in selecting a broker were the broker's sales of Fund shares to the public and the usefulness of research and statistical services which it provided to the Fund through M&D. After July 15, 1973, as previously indicated, an NASD rule, binding on both M&D and Eberstadt as members, eliminated sale of Fund shares as a qualifying or disqualifying factor in the selection of executing brokers.

The brokerage commissions paid by the Fund when the sale of shares was a criterion for selecting an executing broker fluctuated from $271,910 in 1965 to $462,613 in 1970. The commissions paid by the Fund when research and statistical services provided were criteria for selecting an executing broker fluctuated from $40,977 in 1965 to $91,662 in 1970. During 1971 and 1972 over 98% of the Fund's portfolio brokerage in each year was allocated as "reciprocals" to brokers who either sold Fund shares or supplied statistical and research information.

As we have seen, prior to December 5, 1968, it was common practice for a mutual fund or its manager to direct executing brokers on the NYSE and other national securities exchanges to "give-up" part of their commissions to other exchange members who had sold shares to the public or who had provided useful research or statistical material, but who had not participated in any way in the execution of the transaction on the exchange. . . .

The NYSE permitted member firms who served as investment advisers to credit against the investment advisory fee some portion of the commissions earned by the member firm for the execution of portfolio transactions on behalf of the investment advisory client. Accordingly, the NYSE would have permitted M&D to credit against the management fee payable to it by the Fund some portion of any brokerage commissions earned by its parent Eberstadt in the execution of the Fund's portfolio transactions and, prior to the time when give-ups were abolished, a portion of any give-ups received by Eberstadt with respect to Fund brokerage business. Prior to December 5, 1968 such recapture would not have required participation by Eberstadt in the execution of portfolio transactions. After December 5, 1968, when give-ups were abolished, recapture was still available although then, appellant asserts, participation by either Eberstadt or M&D in portfolio transactions would have been necessary.

Well aware of this possibility of recapture, the board of directors of the Fund, with the concurrence of the unaffiliated and non-interested directors, consistently directed that Eberstadt not act as broker in the execution of Fund portfolio transactions nor receive give-ups from other brokers in connection with Fund portfolio transactions. . . .

### III.

On this appeal appellant contends (1) that the failure to recapture violated the Fund's advisory and distribution contracts with M&D; (2) that the failure to recapture violated the Fund's certificate of incorporation; (3) that the defendants breached their fiduciary duties to the Fund in their dealings with the independent directors regarding recapture; and (4) that the defendants violated the disclosure provisions of the securities laws by failing to keep the shareholders of the Fund properly informed as to the recapture problem. We will address these contentions seriatim.

### A.

A key contention of appellant is that by allocating brokerage commissions and give-ups to reward dealers for selling shares and providing the Fund with research and statistical information, albeit at the direction of the independent directors on the Fund's board, the defendants violated the management and distribution contracts with the Fund. Appellant argues that, under these agreements, M&D was obligated to pay all the expenses relating to the promotion and sale of Fund shares and to provide research and statistical services to the Fund at its own expense. Through its allocation of the Fund asset of brokerage, appellant asserts, M&D profited at the expense of the Fund to the extent that it was able to avoid using its own funds to purchase sales promotion, research, and statistical services needed to discharge its contractual obligations. Appellant relies heavily on this allegation of self-dealing to support her other claims of breach of fiduciary duty and inadequate disclosure.

Appellees contend that both parties to the management and distribution agreements at all times contemplated that brokerage would be allocated by the investment adviser to obtain sales promotion, research, and statistical services. They claim that this understanding was in accordance with the generally prevailing method of business in the industry, and that this usage added implicit terms to the management and distribution contracts. . . .

The management and distribution agreements are silent on the subject of allocation of excess portfolio commissions. Since the industry usage of brokerage is not inconsistent with the pertinent provisions of the agreements, evidence as to its existence and the parties' awareness of it during negotiations was properly admitted to clarify the intentions of the parties. . . .

The uncontradicted testimony of defendant Zeller was that the amount of compensation awarded to M&D under the distribution contract "was arrived at by a negotiation process in light of all of the circumstances, including the services which the adviser got from outside sources." One of the "circumstances" he specified was the "known industry facts." He also testified that, while there was no explicit provision in the advisory contract which gave M&D the right to use a portion of brokerage commissions to reward firms that assisted it in providing research, such a provision "was implicit in the negotiation of the management fee." Zeller characterized the Fund's use of give-ups as "simply part of the brokerage practices of the times."

In response to a question concerning the compensation paid M&D under its management contract for research and statistical services, Dr. Roger F. Murray, an independent director of the Fund, testified as follows:

The amount we were paying them was for what they could do, and they could not be an expert in all fields, and if they didn't have the benefit of those give- ups or commission business to use for getting outside additional facilities we would have had to raise their fee and make . . . arrange for them to buy them, because we were convinced it was essential to the performance of the fund that that kind of exposure to other ideas get into the decision-making process of the fund.

He stated that while no explicit contractual provision authorized such use of brokerage, it was "fully understood that that would be done," and was made "explicit and clear in the prospectus and in the proxy statements. . . ." The record fully supports this assertion. . . .

### B.

Appellant's next argument can be disposed of briefly. Relying on *Moses v. Burgin*, [445 F.2d 369 (1st Cir.), cert. denied, 404 U.S. 994 (1971)] she contends that defendants' allocation of commissions to compensate dealers for sales promotion and research violated an express provision of the Fund's certificate of incorporation that requires it to receive not less than "net asset value" for each share. . . .

In *Fogel* [v. Chestnutt, 533 F.2d 731 (2d Cir. 1975), cert. denied, 429 U.S. 824 (1976)] Judge Friendly rejected this reasoning and held that

[A]lthough the argument is not without force, we think it presses too far. The term "net asset value" is one of art in the mutual fund industry and is elaborately defined in the certificate of incorporation. The objective of the charter provision was to prevent dilution of per share net asset value by the issuance of new shares at a discount; defendants' failure to recapture part of the commissions on portfolio transactions does not result in such dilution. Plaintiffs' real complaint is not that new shareholders did not pay net asset value but that the Adviser, for selfish motives, refrained from handling portfolio transactions in a manner that would have diverted a portion of the commissions to itself, with an attendant decrease in the advisory fee in substance a charge of breach of a fiduciary duty resulting in corporate waste.

533 F.2d at 744-45.

His holding is equally applicable in the case at bar and disposes of this contention of the appellant.

### C.

Appellant next contends that the conduct of the defendants in implementing the Fund's decision to forego recapture constituted a breach of fiduciary duty under both the Investment Company Act and common law. To resolve this issue, we must determine whether the Investment Company Act imposed on the Fund and the persons who controlled it an absolute duty to recapture excess brokerage commissions, and, if not, whether the decision to forego recapture here is justifiable as a proper exercise of the informed discretion reposed in the board of directors of a mutual fund under the Act.

Section 36 of the Investment Company Act of 1940, which prohibited "gross misconduct or gross abuse of trust," and "breach of fiduciary duty involving personal misconduct" as amended in 1970, established a federal standard of fiduciary duty in dealings between a mutual fund and its adviser. . . . In its original form, this section authorized SEC injunctive actions and, by implication, private damage actions by investors against fiduciaries who failed to meet its standards. The remedial 1970 amendment of the section added a subsection (b) which explicitly granted a private right of action to recover unreasonable compensation paid by a fund to its investment adviser. Congress did not intend this modification to abrogate the private action already recognized under the Act for other types of breach of fiduciary duty. *See Fogel v. Chestnutt, supra; Moses v. Burgin*, supra, at 373, 373 n.7, 384; S.Rep.No.184, 91st Cong., 1st Sess. 16 (1969), U.S.Code Cong. & Admin.News 1970, p. 4897; H.R.Rep.No.1382, 91st Cong., 2d Sess. 38 (1970). *But see Monheit v. Carter*, 376 F.Supp. 334, 342 (S.D.N.Y.1974). Consequently, appellant's claim of breach of duty under the Act is properly before the court.

We have found nothing in the structure or legislative history of the Investment Company Act which indicates that Congress meant to remove the question of how best to use the brokerage generated by portfolio transactions from the informed discretion of the independent members of a mutual fund's board of directors. Nor do the opinions in *Fogel* and *Moses* suggest that the Act compelled recapture of commissions for the Fund's direct cash benefit as a matter of law.

It is true that, in response to the management's argument that even if recapture were practical the directors still had a right to choose between recapturing of give-ups for the fund's direct benefit and awarding them to brokers for its indirect benefit, the Moses court stated that "if recovery was freely available to [the fund], the directors had no such choice." 445 F.2d at 374. This conclusion, however, was based solely on the First Circuit's interpretation of that fund's charter as mandating recapture, *see supra* at 415- 416, and not upon the fiduciary obligations imposed under the Investment Company Act. When the question of the fiduciary duty of the investment adviser under the Act was addressed in *Moses* and *Fogel*, the inquiry of both courts was into the adequacy of the disclosure of the possibilities of recapture by the managers to the independent directors of the mutual fund. Plainly, such full and effective disclosure was required so that the independent directors could exercise informed discretion on the question of recapture vel non, thus performing the watchdog function envisaged for them by Congress.[22] *See, e. g., Moses v. Burgin, supra*, at 383; *Fogel v. Chestnutt, supra*, at 749-50. The violation of section 36 perceived in both cases resulted from management's failure to disclose sufficiently to the independent directors the possibilities of recapture, and not from the breach of an absolute duty to recapture imposed by the Act.

---

[22]    We note that after observing that "a change from independent brokerage to an affiliated broker is not a matter to be lightly undertaken," 445 F.2d at 374, the *Moses* court stated that sound business reasons supported the judgment of the fund's directors that portfolio transactions should not be executed through an affiliated broker. 445 F.2d at 375. *See also Schlusselberg v. Colonial Management Associates, Inc.*, 389 F.Supp. 733, 737 (D.Mass.1974). The *Moses* court also rejected the contention that it was unlawful to allocate "reciprocals" to unaffiliated brokers "in proportion to their success in selling . . . shares to the public," so long as the mutual fund obtained best execution. 445 F.2d at 372 n. 5.

While we thus conclude that the Investment Company Act did not remove the recapture decision from the discretion of the Fund's board of directors,[23] such discretion is by no means unrestrained. As previously mentioned, independent directors can perform their function under the Act only when they exercise informed discretion, and the responsibility for keeping the independent directors informed lies with the management, i. e., the investment adviser and interested directors. This responsibility is particularly pressing when the matter in question is one on which the interests of the management and the mutual fund may be at odds . . . .

Thus the decision to forego recapture here did not violate the fiduciary obligations of either the Fund's adviser or directors under section 36 of the Investment Company Act if the independent directors (1) were not dominated or unduly influenced by the investment adviser; (2) were fully informed by the adviser and interested directors of the possibility of recapture and the alternative uses of brokerage; and (3) fully aware of this information, reached a reasonable business decision to forego recapture after a thorough review of all relevant factors . . . .

[After an extensive review of the record, the court concluded as follows:]

The evidence demonstrates that the independent directors separately considered the subject, investigated it by way of their subcommittees, and arrived at their own conclusion that recapture should not be undertaken. This was a well-qualified board and its determinations did not merely rubber- stamp the recommendations of M&D. We conclude that the independent directors were not dominated or unduly influenced by the investment adviser. . . .

The record demonstrates that M&D promptly brought every administrative, judicial, and legislative development pertaining to recapture to the attention of the Fund's board, including its independent directors. Such communication was "full" and "effective" under the *Moses* test which governs disclosures by management to the fund when the interests of the two may conflict. The independent directors were fully aware early in the game that recapture was possible by having Eberstadt either execute portfolio transactions or receive give-ups, or by resort to a regional exchange technique, and we conclude that the second prong of the applicable test — that the independent directors were fully informed by the adviser and the interested directors of the possibility of recapture and the alternative uses of brokerage — has been met. . . .

There remains the question of whether, under the standards laid down by Judge Friendly in *Fogel*, the independent directors reached a reasonable business judgment to forego recapture after being informed of all relevant factors and thoroughly reviewing them.

There were four principal business reasons which convinced the independent directors to forego recapture.  These reasons were (1) that recapture would have involved the Fund in conflicts of interest in fact and in appearance; (2) recapture would have an adverse impact on the sale of the Fund's shares; (3) it was in the best interests of the Fund to allocate brokerage for research; and (4) imminent changes in the structure of the securities industry made it unwise to change the Fund's long-standing brokerage policies against recapture.

---

[23]    In her supplemental brief, appellant somewhat surprisingly states that

it has never been plaintiff's contention that Section 36 (or Section 36(a), as amended) removes the question of recapture *as a matter of statutory law* from the ambit of directors' discretion.

The directors' view that recapture would have involved the Fund in conflicts of interest in fact and in appearance was based on several factors. It was feared that shareholders would suspect churning if the Fund used an affiliated broker to recapture and that consistent use of Eberstadt to execute portfolio transactions might permit other investors to anticipate Fund investment decisions. There was also concern that best execution would suffer if an affiliate were used as executing broker.

While the prospects of suspected churning and anticipation by others of Fund investment decisions were remote, they were not unreasonable apprehensions. Moreover, there was a real possibility that the obligation of obtaining the best execution might be jeopardized through close affiliation between a broker- dealer and the investment company, and that possibility alone could warrant ruling out such a method of recapture. We note also that concern with eliminating any unnecessary appearance of conflicts of interest in an area already "fraught" with them, is not an unreasonable supplementary business consideration.

The directors also feared that recapture would have an adverse effect on the sale of the Fund's shares. The question of how large a fund should become by increasing its sales is highly debatable. . . . [C]ompetitive considerations relative to sales might argue against recapture. Such considerations were stronger in the case of funds which, like Chemical Fund, had relatively low rates of portfolio turnover and thus little brokerage available for distribution as sales incentives in the first place. In addition, the directors felt that proceeds from new sales were needed to avoid untimely portfolio liquidations and that, since there are economies of scale in managing a portfolio, an increase in the size of the fund would decrease the management costs per dollar. The board's conclusion that recapture might decrease the sale of shares and eventually harm the Fund's performance was reasonable.

The directors' judgment to continue the existing practice of allocating brokerage to obtain additional research was also reasonable. That general practice was confirmed in the Policy Statement of the SEC on the Future Structure of the Securities Market (February 2, 1972), 37 Fed.Reg. 5286, 5290. See also SEC Securities Exchange Act Release 9598 (May 9, 1972), containing an interpretation of the Future Structure policy statement on this point. Moreover, section 28(e)(1) of the Securities Exchange Act of 1934, which was added by the Securities Act amendments of 1975, permits an investment adviser to cause an account to pay a broker an amount of commission for effecting a securities transaction in excess of the commission another broker might have charged, as long as the adviser determines in good faith that the commission was reasonable in relation to the value of both the brokerage and research services provided by such broker.

Finally, the view of the directors that imminent changes in the structure of the industry made it unwise to change the Fund's brokerage policies may not be entitled to much weight. Nevertheless, in the light of the many and often contradictory administrative, legislative and judicial pronouncements on the subject of recapture, this is a factor to be taken into account when evaluating the reasonableness of the business judgment reached by the directors — which they recognized as a very close question.

The independent directors also sought the advice of counsel on the recapture question. It is true that such advice was not given by wholly disinterested counsel since Sullivan & Cromwell represented M&D and Eberstadt as well as the Fund itself. Thus, "it would have been . . . better to have the investigation of recapture methods and their legal consequences performed by disinterested counsel furnished to the independent directors." . . . . Here, however, counsel correctly advised the independent directors as to the applicable law and the necessity for reaching a reasonable business judgment on the recapture question. The fact that counsel were not disinterested does not vitiate the reasonableness of the judgment which the independent directors reached here. . . .

In its amicus brief, the SEC, although critical of some of the reasons advanced for the decision not to recapture, concluded that the reasons considered in the aggregate supported the directors' decision. Among the reasons which the SEC considered valid were the desirability of obtaining additional research, the possibly adverse effect of adopting a recapture policy on sales and on portfolio performance, and the requirement of obtaining the best execution.

It should be borne in mind that the question here is not whether, as a matter of hindsight, the determination of the independent directors was correct. The question is whether the decisions by these directors to forego recapture were reasonable considered at the time and under the circumstances in which they were reached.

We conclude that the *Fogel* test governing the determination of the independent directors not to recapture was satisfied in this case. There was full disclosure by the Fund's adviser as to the possibilities of recapture and the methods available to accomplish it. All material dealing with the question was placed before the independent directors and fully considered by them. They were correctly advised by counsel as to the applicable legal standards. They carefully weighed the relative advantages and disadvantages of recapture and the economic pros and cons involved. Their decision to forego recapture was a reasonable business judgment.

Since all three prongs of the applicable test have been met, we agree . . . that the decision to forego recapture did not violate the fiduciary obligations of either the Fund's adviser or its interested directors under section 36 of the Investment Company Act, and affirm his holding to that effect.

### D.

Appellants' final contention is that the court below erred in not holding M&D, Eberstadt and Zeller liable to the Fund for the issuance to its shareholders of false and misleading proxy statements and prospectuses. . . .

It is charged that proxy statements issued to the Fund's shareholders omitted to state material facts as to the opportunities to recapture portfolio brokerage commissions for the benefit of the Fund, the methods available for such recapture, and the board's decisions to forego recapture. The material facts so omitted, says the appellant, were necessary in order to make the proxy statements not false and misleading within the meaning of SEC rule 14a-9, as made applicable to investment companies.

The question of the adequacy of the information furnished to shareholders in proxy statements is not disposed of by our holding that the defendants did not breach their fiduciary duties relative to the decisions of the independent directors to forego recapture. The management of an investment company also is obliged under rule 14a-9 to furnish its shareholders with all information necessary to enable them to make an informed judgment on questions concerning investment contracts presented to them at annual meetings. . . .

In 1966, 1970, 1971, 1972, and 1973, new investment advisory contracts with M&D or renewals or amendments of existing contracts were submitted for approval by the Fund's shareholders at annual meetings pursuant to section 15(a) of the Act. The shareholders also had the statutory right at any time to terminate the current advisory contract or seek its renegotiation under section 15(a)(3). . . .    In all the years from 1966 to 1974, inclusive, the proxy statements issued for the annual shareholders meetings contained statements concerning the M&D management contract and the Fund's portfolio brokerage practices. Directors of the Fund were also elected by the shareholders annually. . . .

During the years from 1965 to 1971, inclusive, the proxy statements issued to the shareholders made no reference to the fact that brokerage commissions were recapturable, the methods available to effect recapture, the board's periodic decisions to forego recapture, or the board's reasons for so deciding. While each of these proxy statements contained a description of the Fund's existing portfolio brokerage practices, the shareholders were not informed of the alternatives to these practices. Specifically, the 1966, 1967 and 1968 proxy statements, while stating the amount of brokerage allocated to promote sales and obtain additional research and statistical material and the intention to continue these practices, made no allusion to the alternative of recapture for the Fund's benefit by directing give-ups to Eberstadt or otherwise, the board's rejection of these alternatives, and its reasons for rejecting them. The addition in the 1969, 1970 and 1971 proxy statements of a reference to the Fund's intention not to do portfolio business through Eberstadt did not explain the significance of this fact or even mention that recapture for the benefit of the Fund was an available alternative.

The opportunity for recapture and the methods by which it could be accomplished bore directly on the management agreement and what action the shareholders would take respecting it. The disclosure of the recapture alternatives was necessary in order for the shareholders to make an informed decision on whether or not to approve the new management contracts or whether or not to continue or renegotiate the current ones.

We have already held that the management and distribution agreements contemplated the allocation of brokerage by M&D to secure sales, additional research, and statistical services, and that the shareholders were informed of this in proxy statements. The shareholders should also have been informed that by approving these agreements they were foregoing an opportunity to effect recapture and thus lower advisory fees — even if, as management contends, such fees might eventually have to be adjusted to give M&D additional funds to secure the services needed to maintain the Fund's performance which would no longer be obtained by allocating brokerage.

We do not go so far as to hold that every possible alternative to a particular policy must be spelled out in a proxy statement. . . . . We recognize that such a rule would indeed tend to defeat the purposes of the proxy rules by bury[ing] the shareholder in an avalanche of trivial information a result that is hardly conducive to informed decisionmaking. . . . .

But, in our view, the same considerations of clear conflict of interest between the adviser and the Fund which required management to supply the independent directors with full information concerning the recapture question so that they could reach an informed judgment on the subject also mandated disclosure to the shareholders of the recapture alternatives and the board's decisions thereon.

Management recognized that the decision to forego available recapture opportunities was a significant and controversial one which involved substantial amounts of money. We have already seen the care taken to assure that this decision was legally permissible and the product of a carefully considered exercise of business judgment by a fully informed group of independent directors. We have also noted management's acknowledgment that the decision reached was "the closest kind of business decision." Yet, despite the repeated and extensive disclosures to the independent directors about recapture, the subject was never presented to the shareholders until 1972. This contravened the policy of the Investment Company Act as declared in its preamble, rendered ineffectual the shareholders' approval of the management agreements, and deprived the shareholders of their right to terminate or seek renegotiation of the agreements under section 15(a)(3) of the Act.

Under the circumstances here, disclosure of the fact that there were recapture opportunities which the Board had chosen to forego would have altered significantly the total mix of information available to a reasonable investor. There was a substantial likelihood that such disclosure would have assumed actual significance in a reasonable investor's deliberations concerning the management agreements. We view the omissions of any statements as to the recapture alternatives as "so obviously important to an investor, that reasonable minds cannot differ on the question of materiality."

The proxy statements for 1972, 1973 and 1974 are in a different posture. While it failed to detail the available recapture techniques and the board's prior consideration of the issue, the 1972 proxy statement raised the possibility of recapture in its discussion of the proposed amendment to the Fund's certificate of incorporation, and Judge Carter concluded that it was not false and misleading.

After viewing the facts omitted in the 1972 proxy statement against the disclosures that were made, . . . we cannot say that there was such a substantial likelihood that a reasonable shareholder would have considered these omissions either important in deciding how to vote or as so significantly altering the "total mix" of information available that the district judge's finding that they were not material was erroneous. We reach the same conclusion with respect to the 1973 and 1974 proxy statements, which came after the stockholders had been put on notice as to the possibility of recapture and approved the certificate amendment explicitly providing for board control over allocation of brokerage omissions.

We hold that the proxy statements for the annual meetings in the years 1967, 1968, 1969, 1970 and 1971 were false and misleading under rule 14a-9 because of the omission of material facts. We therefore reverse the holding of the court below that the proxy statements for these years did not violate the disclosure provisions of the federal securities laws. Responsibility for such omissions begins with the February 7, 1967 proxy statement since it is clear from the record that by then management and the independent directors had sufficient time to consider and react to [contemporaneous developments] and make appropriate disclosures to the shareholders.

The case is remanded to the district court for determination of what damages, if any, were caused to the Fund by the proxy statements we have held to be in violation of rule 14a-9.

## Comments and Questions

1. How does the holding in *Tannenbaum* differ from the *Moses* decision? To what extent does the second decision enhance the protection of mutual fund investors?

2. Both the *Moses* and *Tannenbaum* decisions discussed charter provisions requiring that shares be sold at a fund's net asset value. The two decisions viewed these charter provisions somewhat differently. What were the differences? Rather than relying on the open-ended legal standards at issue in these cases, would it be better simply to require investment companies to clarify in their corporate charters their intended practices with respect to brokerage allocation and similar issues? Is the approach taken in the *Moses* and *Tannenbaum* decisions a more effective means of regulating conflicts?

3. At the beginning of subsection III.C of the *Tannenbaum* decision, the court justifies its inference of an implied right of action under section 36(a) of the 1940 Act, even though the 1970 Amendments to the Act created an express right of action only under subsection 36(b). Most, though not all, federal courts have been similarly liberal in recognizing implied rights of action under various provisions of the 1940 Act on the grounds that these rights of action have a long legal pedigree and that various congressional reports have recognized their importance in protecting fund shareholders. See Strougo v. Scudder, Stevens & Clark, Inc., 964 F. Supp. 783, 796-98 (S.D.N.Y. 1997) (collecting authorities on this point). Is this a valid basis for judicial recognition of a federal cause of action?

4. The *Tannenbaum* decision also refers in passing to section 28(e) of the 1934 Act, which Congress enacted in 1975. That provision was enacted in response to the brokerage allocation cases, and establishes statutory standards for so-called soft dollar practices. How do the legal duties established under this provision compare to the standards developed in the *Moses* and *Tannenbaum* cases?

### Problem 13-4

Value Advisers, Inc. (VAI), serves as investment advisor for several large mutual funds. In connection with a recent review of advisory operations, VAI is considering employing a new brokerage firm, Research Dealers Corp. ("RDC") to execute most of the purchases and sales of portfolio securities for VAI's mutual funds. The commissions that RDC charges for effecting these transactions is ten percent higher than the commissions charged by the brokerage firm VAI currently uses. RDC will, however, also provide RDC weekly research reports about investment opportunities in emerging stock markets around the world. One of VAI's funds specializes in investments of this source, and VAI believes that the RDC research services will substantially enhance that fund's performance. Can VAI engage RDC under these circumstances? What if RDC were to provide VAI a set of personal computers that could be used to analyze the RDC reports?

## B. Transfer of Advisory Contracts

As the preceding materials explore, investment advisers are fiduciaries with respect to the investment companies they serve. The relationship between advisers and investment companies is regulated by both the specific statutory guidelines of the Investment Company Act (e.g., sections 15 and 18), as well as background norms of fiduciary responsibility. In this respect, the regulation of investment advisers is similar to the regime governing broker-dealers. As was the case with broker-dealers, difficult questions of interpretation arise when the adviser/fiduciary takes an action that complies with all express statutory provisions but arguably runs afoul of background fiduciary norms.

The Rosenfeld v. Black case presents an illustration of precisely this problem. As you read through the decision, consider why courts at equity developed this principle for regulating the sale of fiduciary offices. Do the same policy considerations apply in the context of modern investment companies? Would you foresee any costs in retaining an equitable remedy in this context? Finally, can you think of a better way to regulate the problem at issue in this case? As the note following the Rosenfeld case reveals, Congress revisited the problem in 1975 and adopted section 15(f) of the 1940 Act. How would you rate that solution to the problem?

## Rosenfeld v. Black
### 445 F.2d 1337 (2d Cir. 1971), *cert. denied*, 409 U.S. 802 (1972)

FRIENDLY, Chief Judge:

The appeal here is by plaintiffs, stockholders in what was The Lazard Fund, Inc. ("the Fund"), a mutual fund organized in 1958 and registered under the Investment Company Act of 1940 ("the Act"). Their complaints, brought in the District Court for the Southern District of New York, sought, *inter alia*, an accounting of profits allegedly realized by Lazard Freres ("Lazard"), the organizer and investment adviser of the Fund, when, in 1967, it ceased to be the adviser, and was replaced by Moody's Advisors & Distributors, Inc. ("Moody's A & D"), a wholly-owned subsidiary of Moody's Investors Service, Inc., which in turn was a wholly-owned subsidiary of Dun & Bradstreet, Inc. ("D & B"). The district court granted defendants' motion for summary judgment. The appeal raises an important question with respect to the obligations of an investment adviser that wishes to terminate its services to an investment company.

### I.

As noted, Lazard, a highly reputed investment banking firm, had organized the Fund in 1958. The initial offering was of 8,500,000 shares at a price to the public of $15 per share.[1]

---

[1]   The issue was underwritten, with the proceeds realized by the Fund being $13.875 per share. Lazard was the underwriter with respect to 4,500,000 shares. Apparently a considerable portion of these was placed with customers of the firm.

Although originally organized as a closed-end investment company, the terms of the initial public offering made the Fund "open-end" within § 5(a)(1) of the Act in the sense that the shares were redeemable, at a charge of 1% Of the net asset value of the shares tendered for redemption. The Fund employed Lazard as investment adviser. The advisory contract, which conformed to the requirements of § 15(a) of the Act and was renewed on one occasion with directors' and thereafter with stockholders' approval, provided for quarterly fees which, translated to an annual basis, amounted to 1/2 of 1% on the first $100,000,000 of the Fund's average daily net assets, 3/8 of 1% on the next $50,000,000, and 1/4 of 1% on any excess over $150,000,000. In return, Lazard was obligated not only to advise the Fund in respect of investments but also to provide necessary office facilities and personnel including corporate officers; its compensation was to be reduced by any amounts up to $50,000 per year paid by the Fund to members of its board of directors, executive committee or consultants.

The principal moving affidavit, by a Lazard partner, set forth the following: In contrast to most open-end investment companies, the Fund did not engage in a continuous public offering of its shares. The shrinkage attendant upon redemptions unaccompanied by sales was expected to be counteracted by an additional offering. However, developments in the mutual fund industry accelerated the shrinkage to such an extent that it would not likely be offset by such an offering. By the time of the events here in question, the number of shares had decreased to 5,304,711 and net assets had declined to some $85,000,000. In light of this, Lazard concluded that the best interests of the Fund's stockholders would be served if the Fund were to engage in a continuous offering of its shares and institute various new investment plans and programs of the type provided by competing funds. However, it would have been contrary to Lazard's traditional policies and mode of operation to create the organization needed to that end. In 1966, when Lazard learned that Moody's Investors Service, Inc., which managed more than $4 billion worth of investments for customers as investment adviser, was considering the possibility of entering the mutual fund area, it felt that an ideal solution to the Fund's problem might be in sight.

With the knowledge and approval of the Fund's directors, Lazard approached D & B. The result was a series of agreements. One provided for the "merger" of the Fund into Moody's Capital Fund, which Moody's Investors Service would organize with a capital of $100,000 in cash and Government securities. Each share of the Lazard Fund was exchangeable for one share of the Capital Fund having the same net asset value as one share of the Lazard Fund, and the shares of the Capital Fund owned by Moody's Investors Service prior to merger would also be converted into shares of the surviving corporation having the same net asset value as the shares issued to Lazard Fund stockholders. The Capital Fund would employ Moody's A & D both as investment adviser, on substantially the same terms previously provided with respect to Lazard, and as exclusive agent for the sale of Capital Fund stock at net asset value, plus a scale of sales charges payable to Moody's A & D. Approval of the merger by the Fund's stockholders would constitute approval of the new advisory contract between Capital Fund and Moody's A & D. Thus, as a result of the proposed transactions, the Fund would evolve into an open-end company which offered special investment services and engaged in continuous offering of its shares through the Moody's A & D distributor.

The aspect of the Lazard-D & B negotiations most important for our purposes was an agreement dated April 5, 1967 between Lazard and D & B, which was to become effective upon the effective date of the merger if the advisory contract between Capital Fund and Moody's A &

D were approved at that time. The proxy statement sent to stockholders of the Fund described this as follows:

Agreement between Dun & Bradstreet, Inc. and Lazard Freres & Co.

Dun & Bradstreet, Inc. of which Moody's Investors is a wholly-owned subsidiary has entered into an agreement with Lazard Freres & Co., investment adviser of the Corporation, to take effect upon the consummation of the merger, pursuant to which Lazard Freres & Co. has agreed for a period of five years from the effectiveness of the merger not (a) to become associated, either in a management or advisory capacity, with another investment company subject to registration under the Investment Company Act of 1940; (b) to permit the use of the name "Lazard", or any combination including such name, by any such investment company or investment company manager or adviser; and (c) to act as principal distributor for any open-end investment company making a continuous offering of its shares, and which is subject to registration under the Investment Company Act of 1940.

Lazard Freres & Co. has also agreed for a period of five years from the effectiveness of the merger unless otherwise specified (a) to make available Mr. Hettinger (or others) for the purpose of (1) reviewing and advising with respect to European economic and monetary conditions and (2) serving as a director of Moody's Capital Fund and/or Moody's Fund, Inc.; (b) to consult for a transitional period not in excess of one year with respect to the administrative operations of Moody's Capital Fund; (c) to use its best efforts to induce certain persons presently performing services for the Corporation to similarly perform for Moody's Capital Fund; and (d) to make available certain research reports and analyses prepared by them during the existence of the Corporation.

As consideration for such agreements, Dun & Bradstreet, Inc. will deliver to Lazard Freres & Co. 75,000 shares of its common stock, par value $1 per share. The 75,000 shares will be placed in escrow by Lazard Freres & Co. to secure performance of its obligations set forth in the first paragraph of this subsection and, subject to such performance, will be released at the rate of 10,000 shares annually for the next four years with the remaining 35,000 shares to be released at the end of the fifth year. Cash dividends will not be paid on such shares as from time to time remain unreleased from escrow, but such shares may be voted by Lazard Freres & Co. while they are subject to the escrow.

Plaintiffs allege, and defendants do not dispute, that D & B stock was selling over the counter at more than $37 per share at the time the contract was signed, although it had been selling at a lower price earlier during the negotiating period.

On April 6, 1967, the Fund sent to stockholders a letter, a notice of special meeting of stockholders, a proxy and a proxy statement. The notice stated the chief business of the meeting to be approval of the merger of the Fund with Moody's Capital Fund and consequent adoption of the advisory contract between Capital Fund and Moody's A & D. While the stockholders were told of the agreement between Lazard and D & B in the manner already set forth, they were not asked to approve it. The letter, signed by Mr. Hettinger, a partner of Lazard and president of the Fund, informed the stockholders that the Fund's board of directors [4] recommended approval of

---

[4] The Fund had eight directors. Two of them were Lazard partners; another was a senior partner in Lazard's counsel; all had been selected by Lazard. The meeting at which the merger was approved was attended by only five directors, including the three listed above. An outside director telephoned his approval during the meeting and still another had cabled his approval. The two Lazard partners abstained from voting. . . .

the merger largely because it would cure the disadvantages which the Fund suffered by not engaging in continuous offering of its shares and by not making available special investment services. The proxy statement also recited that Lazard held of record 2,066,310 shares, constituting some 39% of the capital stock of the Fund, although none of these were owned beneficially. . . .

Plaintiffs' case was predicated on a contention that the 75,000 shares of D & B ultimately deliverable to Lazard were not in fact issued solely in consideration of the four undertakings summarized in the quotation from the Proxy Statement but in large part for Lazard's assistance in bringing about the merger and the consequent appointment of Moody's A & D as investment adviser, with the profits anticipated therefrom. Defendants argued that plaintiffs had failed to adduce sufficient evidence on this to resist their motion for summary judgment. While regarding plaintiffs' contrary position as "so extremely thin, in the face of solid proof sustaining defendants' position, that upon a trial we would probably be forced to set aside a verdict in plaintiffs' favor," the judge did not place his decision on that ground. Rather, referring to the provision of § 15(a) of the Investment Company Act whereby any assignment of an advisory contract automatically terminates it, he held that "Where (as here) a majority of the stockholders approve a new advisory contract, as they are empowered to do by § 15(a), the management's conduct in arranging such a substitution does not violate the Act, regardless how it is labeled." In so holding the judge relied heavily on SEC v. Insurance Securities, Inc., 254 F.2d 642 (9 Cir.), cert. denied, 358 U.S. 823 (1958), for the proposition that "the evil toward which the Act is directed is the transfer of control without consent of the shareholders * * * not the money received by the assignors of service contracts."

II.

We start from one of the "well-established principles of equity," recognized in *Insurance Securities* itself, *supra*, 254 F.2d at 650, "that a personal trustee, corporate officer or director, or other person standing in a fiduciary relationship with another, may not sell or transfer such office for personal gain." There are ample authorities to support this proposition. . . . The reason for the rule is plain. A fiduciary endeavoring to influence the selection of a successor must do so with an eye single to the best interests of the beneficiaries. Experience has taught that, no matter how high-minded a particular fiduciary may be, the only certain way to insure full compliance with that duty is to eliminate any possibility of personal gain.

Postponing the question of the effect of specific provisions of the Investment Company Act, we see no reason to doubt that, on the facts of this case, Lazard in its position as investment adviser came within the scope of this principle. In describing the far less intimate role of the publisher of an investment advisory bulletin, the Supreme Court quoted with approval Professor Loss' reference to "the delicate fiduciary nature of an investment advisory relationship." SEC v. Capital Gains Research Bureau, 375 U.S. 180, 191 (1963), citing 2 Loss, Securities Regulation 1412 (2d ed. 1961). Lazard could hardly deny the existence of a fiduciary relationship if stockholders of the Fund had alleged, for example, that the firm had taken for its own account an opportunity that should have been made available to the Fund, even though § 17(e) does not specifically prohibit this. While "to say that a man is a fiduciary only begins analysis," SEC v. Chenery Corp., 318 U.S. 80, 85-86 (1943) (Frankfurter, J.), we would see no reason why the "well-established principle of equity" forbidding realization of profit for effecting the turn-over of corporate or other fiduciary office should not apply to the investment adviser of a mutual fund. See Notes, Protecting the Interests of Mutual-Fund Investors in Sales of Management-Corporation Control, 68 Yale L.J. 113, 121-28 (1958); 63 Colum.L.Rev. 153, 154-55 (1963). Lazard's influence with the Fund's stockholders can scarcely be questioned. Lazard had organized the Fund, and people had bought shares in it because of their trust and confidence in Lazard. All the Fund's personnel were furnished by Lazard. Unless the pattern differed from that of the industry, Lazard effectively managed the Fund's investments, despite the ultimate authority of the directors, quite as a trustee would do. If Lazard did not wish to continue as adviser and chose to recommend a successor and assist in the latter's installation, it was obliged to forego personal gain from the change of office, no matter how deeply or rightly it was convinced it had made the best possible choice. It is wholly immaterial that the prospect of receiving future management fees if it had continued as an adviser would have been an asset of Lazard rather than of the Fund; the same would be true of a trustee's right to receive future commissions or a corporate president's right to receive future salary and other benefits. Even ratification by the beneficiaries would not save a fiduciary from accountability for any amounts realized in dictating or influencing the choice of a successor unless this was secured with notice that the beneficiaries were entitled to the profit if they wished, . . . and it is questionable whether even such ratification by a majority of the beneficiaries could bind others or the Fund itself. Quite apart from the question hereafter discussed whether the proxy statement was misleading as to the terms of the Lazard-D & B agreement, it is clear in any event that the Fund's stockholders were never asked to — and did not — ratify it.

It is understandable that, under "the morals of the marketplace," Lazard should see no reason why, having selected a competent adviser willing to serve on the same terms Lazard had done, it should not receive what the new incumbent was willing to pay for the opportunity. But equity imposes a higher standard. It is fitting to repeat Chief Judge Cardozo's familiar words, "Many forms of conduct permissible in a workaday world for those acting at arm's length, are forbidden to those bound by fiduciary ties * * *. Not honesty alone, but the punctilio of an honor the most sensitive, is then the standard of behavior. As to this there has developed a tradition that is unbending and inveterate." Meinhard v. Salmon, 249 N.Y. 458, 464, 164 N.E. 545, 546 (1928).

### III.

It is argued that, however all this might otherwise be, a different result is demanded because Lazard's advisory contract necessarily terminated under § 15(a) (4) of the Investment Company Act and that, pursuant to § 15(a), the stockholders of the Fund authorized a new contract with Moody's A & D, allegedly on full disclosure, an issue we will discuss below.

Insofar as the argument hinges merely on the statutory nonassignability of the contract with the consequent inference that there was no advisory office that Lazard could sell or transfer, it proves too much. The same could be said of an alleged sale of corporate office or directorship or, in the absence of appropriate provisions in the dispositive instrument, of an executor's or trustee's position. The role of Lazard, an organizer of the Fund and its practical control of the proxy machinery used to recommend the approval of Moody's A & D as new adviser, made it quite as active and influential as a corporate president who recommends a successor to his board of directors, or a trustee who puts the name of a successor before a judge. Indeed, the very fact of nonassignability demonstrates that any payment made to the outgoing adviser by his successor in these circumstances over and above the value of any continuing services represents consideration not for lawful assignment of the contract — which is prohibited — but primarily for the use of influence in securing stockholder approval of the successor who expects to profit from the post. While it is true that the advisory contract is not conceptually an asset of the Fund, it is equally true that the expectation of profits under that contract is not an asset which, under the Act, the adviser can assign outright. Hence, if plaintiffs are correct in asserting that Lazard's few covenants were only a minor part of the consideration for D & B's payment to Lazard, Lazard and D & B must have assumed that the outgoing adviser was in a position to help effect the transfer of his office and that his efforts in so doing were worth valuable consideration.

The more serious contention is that §§ 15(a), (c) and (d) constitute a policy determination by Congress that compliance with those provisions was to be the exclusive protection to an investment company when there is a change in advisory office. We cannot accept that view on the facts of this case. In § 1(b) of the Act, after noting abuses that had been disclosed with respect to investment companies, including the management of such companies in the interest of investment advisers and the transfer of control or management without the consent of the security holders, Congress declared:

> that the policy and purposes of this title, in accordance with which the provisions of this title shall be interpreted, are to mitigate and, so far as is feasible, to eliminate the conditions enumerated in this section which adversely affect the national public interest and the interest of investors.

The purpose of § 15 was to furnish the added protection of approval of a new adviser by a majority of the stockholders,[11] not to withdraw safeguards already afforded by equity. As has been said, "Section 15(a)(4) is directed at transfers of control without shareholder consent, as distinct from profiteering on a transfer of fiduciary office. Hence, the section on its face hardly compels the conclusion that it is the exclusive antidote for such conduct." See Note, 68 Yale L.J., *supra*, at 131.

That alone might suffice to require reversal here, since any argument that simple failure of § 15 to supplant the rule of equity leaves plaintiffs with only a state-created claim would be answered by the fact that their contentions with respect to the inadequacy of the proxy statement, hereafter considered, afford a sufficient basis for pendent federal jurisdiction. However, we do not rest our decision on that ground. We believe rather that the statute not merely did not withdraw safeguards equity had previously provided but impliedly incorporated them. We held in Brown v. Bullock, 294 F.2d 415, 421 (2 Cir. 1961), that in requiring annual approval of

---

[11]    When, as here, a new adviser is appointed, it is clear that 15(a) requires stockholder approval. Although question has been raised whether the alternative of approval "by a majority of the directors who are not parties to such contract or agreement or affiliated persons of any such party," 15(c), is sufficient for "reinstatement" of a contract terminated by a change in control of the advisor, 2(a)(4), see Note, Protecting the Interests of Mutual Fund Investors in Sales of Management-Corporation Control, supra, 68 Yale L.J. 116 fn. 9 (1958), we think a negative answer to be rather clearly dictated. Congress has decreed that a change in control terminates the contract, so that the fund would be dealing with a new party in fact even though not in form. The policy behind 15(a) would thus seem to require that the new contract be approved by the fund's shareholders. See Jennings & Marsh, Securities Regulation 1246 (2d ed. 1968).

investment advisory contracts by directors (or, alternatively, by stockholders) Congress meant to prescribe a uniform federal standard of directorial responsibility. It is wholly consistent with that view to say that when Congress required stockholder approval of a contract with a new investment adviser, it intended that the retiring adviser's use of the proxy machinery to procure appointment of the new adviser must conform to the standards of abnegation of personal gain that equity had long imposed. When Congress, in § 15(a), required shareholder approval of any new advisory contract, it must have meant an approval uninfluenced by any improper motivations on the part of the outgoing adviser- fiduciary. If lured by the possibility of profit, the retiring adviser might recommend a successor who was less qualified or more expensive than other candidates, and who might be on the lookout for ways to recoup his "succession fee" at the expense of the Fund. See Note, supra, 68 Yale L.J. at 128. There is thus every reason for believing that Congress meant to adopt the established prophylactic rule. Just as it is unimaginable that, with respect to the responsibility of directors of investment companies, Congress would have been content "if a particular state of incorporation should be satisfied with lower standards of fiduciary responsibility for directors than those prevailing generally," see 294 F.2d at 421, it is similarly unthinkable that if a particular state had chosen not to recognize the rule of equity here in question Congress would have sanctioned an investment adviser's profiting from using his influence in securing stockholder approval of the appointment of a successor. Indeed, on defendants' view of the law, even disclosure would not be required in such a case, although they assert it was made here, since the profit acquired by the retiring adviser would not be material.

This brings us to the *Insurance Securities* case, *supra*, 254 F.2d 642. The SEC there unsuccessfully attacked a transaction whereby controlling stockholders of a service company which acted as sponsor, depositor, investment adviser and principal underwriter of an investment company sold their stock to a new controlling group at a price twenty-five times its net asset value, and the stockholders of the investment company then approved new contracts with the service company. The actual holding can be readily distinguished since the SEC was proceeding under § 36 of the Act. This authorized the Commission to bring suit for "gross misconduct or gross abuse of trust" and provided that if the court found the Commission's allegations to be established, it should enjoin the person found guilty from acting in its prior capacity either permanently or for such period as the court deemed appropriate. Words and remedies such as these were clearly addressed to highly reprehensible conduct, see Los Angeles Trust Deed & Mortgage Exchange v. SEC, 264 F.2d 199, 210 (9 Cir. 1959), cert. denied, 366 U.S. 919 (1961); we would not dream of suggesting, much less holding, that Lazard's actions were so culpable. However, there are passages in the opinion suggesting that in the court's view none of the excess of the price received by the controlling stockholders over the book value of their stock would be recoverable under any circumstances by stockholders of the investment company. Accord, Krieger v. Anderson, 40 Del.Ch. 363, 182 A.2d 907 (Del.Sup.Ct.1962). While we do not find it necessary at this time to determine whether the difference between a transaction such as that here before us and the sale of a controlling block in a corporate adviser at a price reflecting the expectation of profits under a renewed contract with the corporation which the sellers were to aid in procuring, is sufficiently substantial to warrant a different result in this latter case, we should not wish to be understood as accepting these views.[12]

## IV.

Appellees also rely on the history of the recent amendment to the Investment Company Act, 84 Stat. 1413 (1970). In the Investment Company Report, after stating that "[t]he manager of a mutual fund is unquestionably in a fiduciary relationship to it," and that "consequently, the transfer of that relationship for a price has some elements of the sale of a fiduciary office [which was] strictly prohibited at common law because of the conflicts of interest which are involved," the Report added that "certain of the protective provisions of the Act have had the somewhat ironical, and presumably unintended, effect of diluting the protections provided by common law principles of fiduciary responsibility." P. 151. The Report continued that "by reason of the automatic termination provisions in the event of assignment and the requirement that shareholders approve the new arrangements, it can be argued, as was successfully done in SEC v. Insurance Securities, Inc., that there is no sale of the fiduciary office, since that office automatically terminates and a new one is created with stockholder approval." Pp. 151-52. It went on to say that "[h]owever unrealistic this conclusion may appear in the light of the ability of the retiring management to use the proxy machinery to insure the installation of its self-chosen successors, application of the strict common-law principle might well be unfair insofar as it denies to the retiring management any compensation for the elements of value in the relationship which they may have built up over the years" and "could also be harmful to the Fund, since existing management might be reluctant to surrender that relationship and to provide the Fund with new and possibly more effective management."[14] Arguing that "there is presently no adequate remedy

---

[12]    Some difficulties in applying the principle prohibiting profit in the transfer of the advisory office to the sale of controlling stock in a corporate investment adviser are mentioned in Jaretzki, The Investment Company Act: Problems Relating to Investment Advisory Contracts, 45 Va.L.Rev. 1023, 1030-34 (1959). Since our decision does not rest on § 36 of the Act, as it then stood, many of these criticisms would be inapposite even if we were dealing with the sale of stock situation. Similarly, to the extent that our decision rests on a prophylactic rationale -- removing the temptation for the outgoing adviser to use his influence to recommend a successor, one of whose qualifications is willingness to compensate the retiring adviser for his help-- most of the author's other criticisms also miss the mark. The *Insurance Securities* decision is criticized in Note, Protecting the Interests of Mutual-Fund Investors in Sales of Management-Corporation Control, supra, 68 Yale L.J. at 121-33, which, however, argues that the amount of unjust enrichment may be less when the same adviser is expected to continue, id. at 130. Krieger v. Anderson, 40 Del.Ch. 363, 182 A.2d 907 (Del.Sup.Ct.1962), which followed *Insurance Securities*, is criticized in 63 Colum.L.Rev. 153 (1963).

[14]    It is hard to accept the implication that it is solely up to the adviser to decide whether he will retire from that position in favor of a more effective manager. Section 15(a)(2) has long provided that an advisory contract must be approved annually by the fund's board of directors or stockholders, and 15(a)(3) gives the fund's directors and stockholders the right to terminate the advisory contract without penalty upon sixty days' notice to the adviser. While, in a practical sense, the fact that the adviser ordinarily dominates the fund and its directors lessens the value of these provisions, still the fund's directors are amenable to suit if they discharge their annual approval function in a merely perfunctory fashion. See Brown v. Bullock, *supra*, 294 F.2d at 420-421. And the 1970 amendment of 15(c) makes more stringent the requirements of director approval. Annual advisory contract renewals now *must*

in the Act" since the Commission "must rely primarily at present on its authority to seek an injunction under section 36 of the act upon the ground that, in arranging the succession, management or directors have been 'guilty' of 'gross misconduct or gross abuse of trust,'" a stigma which the courts "might be extremely reluctant" to place upon businessmen "merely because the terms of succession appear unfair," it urged Congress to amend the Act to prohibit a transfer of an advisory contract or the sale of a controlling block in an adviser, "if the sale, or any express or implied understanding in connection with the sale, is likely to impose additional burdens on the investment company or to limit its freedom of future action." P. 152. The bill enacted by Congress did not carry out this recommendation.

Appellees would have us draw two inferences from this episode. One is that the SEC has acceded to the view that the prohibition against receiving compensation for the sale of a fiduciary office is inapplicable to a situation where the retiring adviser of an investment company profits from influencing the designation of a successor. The passages we have quoted demonstrate that if there was any such acceptance, it was a reluctant one, believed, erroneously in our view, to be compelled by the Ninth Circuit's decision in *Insurance Securities*. That case, as we have pointed out, dealt only with the Commission's powers under § 36 as it then stood. The SEC's belief that the unamended Act did not adequately protect fund shareholders against sales of the management organization rested upon a realistic assessment of its own power under § 36 but what we deem an unjustifiably defeatist view of private equitable actions, which the Report apparently did not consider. Although we respect the SEC's interpretation of the statutes it administers, the ultimate responsibility for construction lies with the courts.

The second and even more important inference we are asked to draw is that, by failing to adopt the SEC's proposal, Congress indicated an intention to exclude all remedies other than termination of the old contract and the need for stockholder approval of the new one, even if such approval was obtained by an adviser who was realizing a profit. We have been cited to nothing in the committee reports, in the floor debates, or even in the hearings that casts light on the failure to enact the proposal, or shows that the SEC seriously pressed it. As is well known, the SEC had other, and more important, fish to fry. Congress could well have thought it had handled the problem created by the *Insurance Securities* decision by expanding the SEC's powers under § 36 so that, instead of having to allege that a defendant had been "guilty * * * of gross misconduct or gross abuse or trust," the Commission need now allege only that he has engaged or is about to engage "in any act or practice constituting a breach of fiduciary duty involving personal

---

receive approval of a majority of disinterested directors casting their votes in person at a meeting specially called for that purpose. Hence, the directors can no longer avoid responsibility for approving a disadvantageous advisory contract by leaving the approval to a majority of the outstanding shares. Moreover, the amended section enjoins upon the directors a duty "to request and evaluate * * * such information as may reasonably be necessary to evaluate the terms of any contract whereby a person undertakes regularly to serve or act as investment adviser." Hence, in a situation like that at bar, if Lazard was convinced that its unwillingness to engage in continuous sales was detrimental to the Fund, and the independent directors believed this, they would have an affirmative responsibility to seek out a successor.

misconduct." [15] While a new § 36(b) expressly declares that "the investment adviser of a registered investment company shall be deemed to have a fiduciary duty with respect to the receipt of compensation for services, or of payments of a material nature, paid by such registered investment company, or by the security holders thereof, to such investment adviser or any affiliated person of such investment advisor," the context makes plain that Congress did not mean this to be the only fiduciary duty of investment advisers.

## V.

We come finally to appellants' contention that, regardless of the issues thus far discussed, they were entitled to relief because the portion of the proxy statement quoted above did not fairly summarize the agreement between Lazard and D & B. Two somewhat related criticisms are made. The first is a claim that in truth and fact the 75,000 shares of D $& B referred to in the third paragraph were not being delivered to Lazard solely "as consideration for" the agreements of Lazard listed in the two preceding paragraphs but rather were to be given, at least in part, for Lazard's influencing the Fund's stockholders to assent to the merger and the consequent employment of Moody's A & D as investment adviser. Contrary to the district court's assumption, we do not believe that nothing more was involved here than an alleged misstatement of Lazard's "true motive." Lazard's motive — obtaining 75,000 D & B shares — was never contested. The disputed issue is what consideration Lazard was furnishing for that stock, only the various covenants recited in the proxy statement or also the use of its influence in securing stockholder approval. . . . . [W]e believe appellants' contentions here raised a factual issue which should not have been determined on a motion for summary judgment.

The second criticism is that the reference to 75,000 D & B shares "par value $1 per share" not only gave the stockholders no conception of how much Lazard was obtaining but tended to mislead them. While sophisticated investors could have ascertained the price at which D & B was selling over-the-counter from the New York Times or the Wall Street Journal or, for that matter, by calling their brokers, many would not know, or think, of these possibilities. Moreover, although a lawyer or a sophisticated investor would realize the lack of significance in a statement of $1 par value, which the Fund's shares themselves had, a court could find that not all shareholders would do so. Hence . . . the failure to give the Fund's shareholders some notion that Lazard was obtaining a very substantial sum from D & B, as could so easily have been done, might well be considered to constitute an omission to state a material fact "necessary in order to make the statements therein not false or misleading," Rule 14a-9. . . . If summary judgment had not been granted here, the plaintiffs might have shown that in light of the character and distribution of the Fund's shareholders, the omission to give some indication of the true value of

---

[15]    The amendment also changed the remedial provision so that instead of being limited to enjoining a person from acting in his former capacity, the court might "award such injunctive or other relief against such person as may be reasonable and appropriate in the circumstances, having due regard to the protection of investors and to the effectuation of the policies declared in section 1(b) of this title." Congress recognized that "The highly punitive overtones of the existing section, together with the injunctive penalty, seriously impairs the ability of the courts to deal flexibly and adequately with wrongdoing by certain affiliated persons of investment companies." S.Rep. No. 91-184, 91st Cong. 2d Sess., p. 36 (1970) printed in 3 U.S.Code Cong., & Adm. News 4931.

the D &B shares, after disclosing the nominal par value, was misleading. And we do not entertain the district court's substantial doubt as to the materiality of this information, for even though Lazard was receiving the payment from D & B, not from the Fund, the Fund's stockholders might have hesitated to approve the merger and advisory contract terms if they were told that D & B was willing to pay so large a sum to have the transactions consummated. . . .

The order granting defendants' motion for summary judgment is reversed and the cause is remanded for further proceedings not inconsistent with this opinion.

## Comments and Questions

1. Judge Friendly, the author of the *Rosenfeld* opinion, was among the most able American jurists of the last half century. Notice his discussion of the relationship between traditional fiduciary principles and the statutory obligations of section 15 of the 1940 Act. Do you agree with Judge Friendly that compliance with the explicit requirements of section 15 should not constituted a complete defense for the defendants in this case? Would today's Supreme Court agree with his approach?

2. Wholly apart from its merits as a matter of statutory interpretation, does the decision in *Rosenfeld* diminish the incentives for advisory firms to establish new investment companies? See James K. Sterrett, *Reward for Mutual Fund Sponsor Entrepreneurial Risk*, 58 CORNELL L. REV. 195 (1973).

3. In response to the *Rosenfeld* decision, Congress in 1975 added section 15(f) to the 1940 Act. Does section 15(f) codify the Rosenfeld decision or does it impose a new legal standard in this area? Is section 15(f) an appropriate and effective solution?

*Problem 3-5*

ICM is a major computer manufacturer that several years ago established — through an investment advisory subsidiary — a group of indexed mutual funds for its employees. (Indexed funds limit their investments to a broad group of companies, such as the S&P 500, in order to match general market performance.) Many employees have chosen to invest in these funds, and the funds now have approximately $200 million of assets. Several months ago, ICM's top management decided to refocus corporate efforts on core lines of business, and has instructed all divisions to divest themselves of peripheral activities. The firm's mutual funds are now area slated for immediate divestiture.

After preliminary discussions with several fund complexes, ICM has completed negotiations with Fleece Bancorp., a large bank holding company that is attempting to expand its mutual fund operations. Fleece has proposed that the ICM indexed funds be merged into Fleece indexed funds with similar investment strategies as the ICM funds. In return for the proposed merger, Fleece is willing to pay ICM a fee of $14 million.

At the last minute, ICM received a competing proposal from Avant Guard, Inc., an investment adviser that first developed indexed funds and that operates the country's largest indexed funds. Avant Guard has proposed to ICM that Avant Guard should take over the ICM funds. Although it is not willing to make ICM any payment for the funds, Avant Guard has stressed that its management fees for index fund — less than 0.50 % of invested assets a year — are the lowest in the country. Avant Guard has also pointed out that Fleece's management fees on indexed funds — over 1.20 % of invested funds — exceed the industry's average. Moreover, Fleece has only been advising index funds for a few years, and therefore lacks an established record in the field. Fleece is aware of Avant Guard's competing offer and has emphasized that shareholders in its mutual funds get good service.

How would you advise ICM?

## C. Oversight of Advisory Fees

One of the most important functions of investment company directors is their role in reviewing and approving advisory fees. Directors' performance of this task has been a common subject of litigation over the past few years. As you review the following case, consider how likely it is for plaintiffs to prevail in this sort of litigation. How helpful are independent directors likely to be in controlling advisory fees? How important is it that directors actively police advisory fees?

The following cases considers this question in the context of Merrill Lynch's CMA program, which was the subject the Oregon Attorney General's opinion discussed earlier in this chapter.

### Krinsk v. Fund Asset Management, Inc.
875 F.2d 404 (2d Cir. 1989), *cert. denied*, 443 U.S. 919 (1989)

MINER, Circuit Judge:

Plaintiff-appellant Jeffrey Krinsk is a shareholder in the CMA Money Fund ("Fund"), which is one component of the Cash Management Account program ("CMA program"), a financial services package offered by Merrill Lynch, Pierce, Fenner & Smith Inc. ("MLPF&S"). He brought this action derivatively on behalf of the Fund against the Fund itself and those MLPF&S-related entities responsible for administering and servicing the Fund. In his amended complaint, Krinsk pleaded violations of sections 12(b), 15(a), 20(a) and 36(b) of the Investment Company Act of 1940 ("Act") . . . . Krinsk alleges a breach of fiduciary duty in that the fees paid by the Fund and its shareholders are excessive; attacks the 12b-1 distribution plan as being improper; and contends that a proxy statement of the Fund was false and misleading in regard to defendants' profitability and in comparing fees of the Fund with those of another fund. . . .

*The CMA Program and the Fund*

The CMA program was introduced by MLPF&S in 1977 and has been widely imitated since that time. It consists of a bundle of financial services administered through a central asset account that combines (1) a securities trading account, (2) a savings vehicle, consisting of one of three money market funds (one of which is the Fund) or an insured savings account, (3) a VISA debit card, (4) check-writing privileges and (5) a detailed monthly statement. The focal point of the CMA program is the securities account, which generates substantial revenue for MLPF&S. The program links the securities account to the savings vehicle through a "sweep" feature that automatically transfers idle cash into the savings vehicle--credit balances of $1,000 or more are transferred into savings the day after receipt; balances of less than $1,000 are swept weekly. An initial deposit of $20,000 is required to open a CMA program account, but a minimum balance thereafter need not be maintained.

The subject of this lawsuit, the Fund, is a no-load, diversified, open-ended investment company and thus subject to provisions of the Act. The Fund is the largest registered money market mutual fund, with approximately $19 billion in assets and over 850,000 shareholders as of January 1987. Investors in the Fund hold their investment as shares, on which dividends are declared and reinvested daily. Participation in the CMA program is required in order to invest in the Fund. Participants in the program, however, are not required to invest in the Fund and instead may designate one of the other savings vehicles as their primary savings account.

Other components of the CMA program--the VISA debit card and check writing privileges--are linked to the savings vehicle and securities account, providing immediate access to money in the Fund and to margin credit. Thus, when a customer's check or VISA transaction clears, the debt is first paid out of any free credit balance, then out of the Fund or other savings vehicle and, finally, from the margin loan value in the securities account.

MLPF&S, the sponsor of the CMA program, is the largest securities firm in the United States. It acts as a distributor for the Fund and services the individual CMA program accounts. The day-to-day management of the Fund is performed by Merrill Lynch Asset Management, Inc. ("MLAM"), which serves as investment adviser to approximately forty to fifty mutual funds as well as to institutional and individual investors. Both MLPF&S and MLAM are owned by Merrill Lynch & Co., Inc. ("ML&Co."). The Fund's investment adviser is Fund Asset Management, Inc. ("FAM"), a wholly-owned subsidiary of MLAM. These companies--MLPF&S, MLAM, ML&Co. and FAM (collectively "Merrill Lynch")--are the defendants-appellees in this action along with the Fund.

To service the accounts, MLPF&S employs financial consultants, who act as its sales representatives to investors. Supporting the financial consultants are sales assistants, an extensive "back office" operation and the services of other Merrill Lynch affiliates and subsidiaries.

Direct compensation for services and management comes from three fees: (1) a $65 annual service fee paid by each CMA program participant to MLPF&S; (2) an investment advisory fee paid by the Fund to FAM based on the Fund's asset level; and (3) payments made by the Fund to MLPF&S pursuant to a 12b-1 plan, under which the payments are passed on almost entirely to the financial consultants.

Although all program participants are obliged to pay the service fee, approximately 25% of them do not invest in the Fund. The second fee, the advisory fee, is based on a schedule of declining percentages as assets increase beyond certain breakpoints: 0.5% of the average daily value of net assets under $500 million, 0.425% of that amount between $500 million and $1 billion, and 0.375% of that amount in excess of $1 billion. The third fee, paid pursuant to the 12b-1 plan, is based on a distribution each month at an annual rate of 12.5 basis points (0.125% of the Fund's assets), which MLPF&S passes through to the financial consultants, save for 1 basis point that it pays to sales management and up to .50 of a basis point retained for administrative costs of the program.

The Fund is governed by a Board of Trustees, comprised of one affiliated trustee and six independent trustees. The unaffiliated trustees have joined the Board at the invitation of Merrill Lynch, and each acts as a trustee or director of one or more of Merrill Lynch's other mutual funds. The Board oversees the investments and administration of the Fund, and evaluates the advisory fee annually and the 12b-1 plan quarterly. The district court found, and the parties do not dispute, that the trustees were at all times fully informed on matters relevant to the issues underlying this litigation.

The investment advisory fees of the Fund have been approved by the shareholders. In July of 1984, defendants mailed to the shareholders a proxy statement, one of the principal purposes of which was to obtain shareholder approval of the continuance of the investment-advisory fee agreement. The proxy statement set forth the three-tier schedule of the Fund's advisory fee. It listed also all the other investment companies for which FAM and MLAM act as investment advisers. The list included two columns, indicating for each of the listed companies its "Rate" and "First Breakpoint." The first of the listed money market funds was Merrill Lynch's Ready Asset Trust ("RAT"), with a listed rate of 0.5% and first breakpoint at $500 million, the same percentage and breakpoint as the Fund. The statement failed to indicate, however, the relevant differences between the RAT and the Fund--that RAT had no service fee (as opposed to the then-$50 annual charge for participation in the Fund's program) and had seven breakpoints (as opposed to the Fund's three). Also omitted in the statement was the fact that the annual rate of the advisory fee of the RAT effectively was 0.34% as opposed to 0.38% for the Fund.

*The District Court Proceedings*

Krinsk brought this action derivatively on behalf of the Fund against the Merrill Lynch defendants and the Fund . . . [and] alleged that: (1) FAM and MLPF&S breached their fiduciary duties to the Fund by taking excessive fees, in violation of section 36(b) of the Act; (2) the distribution agreement and plan entered into and continued by the Fund violates section 12(b) of the Act, and Securities and Exchange Commission ("SEC") Rule 12b-1; (3) the annual service fee required for all program participants is not authorized by a written advisory agreement, as required by section 15(a) of the Act; and (4) the Fund's 1984 proxy statement was materially false and misleading in omitting relevant differences between the RAT and the Fund, thus violating section 20(a) of the Act. . . .

## DISCUSSION

*1. Section 36(b)*

Section 36(b) of the Act places on the investment adviser of a registered investment company a fiduciary duty with respect to the receipt of compensation for services paid by the investment company or by the securities holders. Krinsk contends that the trustees neglected this duty by taking excessive fees from the Fund. He notes that lower fees are paid by the RAT fund, which is the second largest investment company affiliated with Merrill Lynch and the only fund comparable in size to the CMA Fund. He observes that despite the Fund's enormous growth, there has been no decrease in the advisory fee rate since 1979, and the rate never has been scaled down beyond the $1 billion breakpoint. He highlights as well the indirect benefits that Merrill Lynch derives from the CMA program: "non-fee-based" revenues and expenses generated from other services integral to the program, such as securities trading and margin interest; and "fall-out" benefits, such as profits made by a Merrill Lynch subsidiary from trading with the Fund.

Krinsk proposes that the trustees had a duty to negotiate for the Fund the "best deal" possible. However, the standard to apply in determining whether compensation for managing a mutual fund violates the fiduciary duty imposed by section 36(b) is "whether the fee schedule represents a charge within the range of what would have been negotiated at arm's-length in the light of all of the surrounding circumstances." *Gartenberg v. Merrill Lynch Asset Management, Inc.*, 694 F.2d 923, 928 (2d Cir.1982), *cert. denied*, 461 U.S. 906 (1983) ("*Gartenberg I* "). To violate section 36(b), "the adviser-manager must charge a fee that is so disproportionately large that it bears no reasonable relationship to the services rendered." Id.

The following factors are to be considered in applying this standard: (a) the nature and quality of services provided to fund shareholders; (b) the profitability of the fund to the adviser-manager; (c) fall-out benefits; (d) economies of scale; (e) comparative fee structures; and (f) the independence and conscientiousness of the trustees. See id. at 929-30. These factors, considered below *seriatim*, all weigh in favor of Merrill Lynch.

A. Nature and Quality of Services

Krinsk does not dispute that the services provided by Merrill Lynch have been only of the highest quality. From 1984 to 1986, the Fund had the third best performance out of 56 prime money funds, with an annual rate of return of 8.4% as compared to the industry average of 8%. During the same years, the Fund ranked second among the nine money market funds associated with central asset accounts.

Krinsk suggests that, because the Fund invested in high-risk items that generally are more profitable, the Fund's performance should be analyzed on a "risk-adjusted" basis. According to Krinsk, the Fund's performance would be below average when adjusted to compensate for the risk. Krinsk's expert conceded, however, that neither the SEC nor the money market industry has adopted "risk adjusted performance" as an industry standard. The district court was unwilling to impose on Merrill Lynch a performance standard "yet to be accepted" by the SEC. The court thus did not err in rejecting that standard.

Krinsk contends also that the Fund's performance is artificially high because the $65 annual CMA program fee was not included as a Fund expense when calculating the Fund's yield. The district court did not err in rejecting this argument. The fee is not paid by the Fund, but by all the participants in the program regardless of whether they invest in the Fund. Furthermore, Merrill Lynch presented evidence, apparently uncontradicted by Krinsk, that leading industry publications exclude such annual program fees in their computation of yields and expense ratios. The expert witness for Merrill Lynch also testified he knew of no money market fund that refers to such charges when reporting to the SEC the yields and expense ratios.

### B. Profitability to Merrill Lynch

Krinsk claims that the Fund is highly profitable to Merrill Lynch, and more profitable than Merrill Lynch admits because costs attributed to the Fund should be attributed to the CMA program. Krinsk further suggests that "excessive profitability alone should suffice to support a finding of unreasonableness." He cites to no case in support of this proposition, however, and in fact courts "must look to *all* the costs and benefits associated with the Fund," *Gartenberg v. Merrill Lynch Asset Management, Inc.*, 740 F.2d 190, 194 (2d Cir.1984) ("*Gartenberg II* ").

Because the Fund is an integral part of the CMA program, it is difficult to calculate the revenues and expenses associated with the Fund apart from those associated with the other aspects of the CMA program. Merrill Lynch's accounting firm and expert at trial, Peat Marwick Mitchell & Co. ("PMM"), therefore developed a "fee-based" analysis, which subtracted fee costs from fee revenues in an effort to determine the profits derived by Merrill Lynch from the Fund. The fee revenues of the study include the CMA program participation fee, the advisory fee and VISA fees; the fee costs include, for example, portfolio management costs, the costs of operations and systems functions (including the sweep and checking/VISA functions), and administrative costs. Defendants introduced at trial an additional study, which they themselves prepared, that was similar to the PMM study. Krinsk had no independent profitability study prepared, but criticized the PMM and Merrill Lynch studies. The district court accepted none of the studies in full, recognizing that "[c]osts within the CMA program must be properly allocated in any profitability study lest the Fund subsidize the costs of Merrill Lynch's commission-generating activities," The court therefore made its own determinations as to costs and profitability. We agree with those determinations:

#### (1) 12-b1 Plan Fees

The 12-b1 plan fees, as stated above, are monthly distributions to MLPF&S personnel based on the net assets in the Fund. The plan was instituted as an incentive to spur the sale of Fund shares and to stimulate improved shareholder service. These fees are paid through MLPF&S directly to its employees, except for deductions for management and administration, and are not recorded on any of defendants' audited financial statements.

The district court treated these fees in the same way as did PMM, namely, as a wash, offset by the cost of payments to the personnel. Krinsk, however, argues that because, in his view, the plan did not achieve its stated purpose--the sale of fund shares--the fees should be counted as revenue to MLPF&S with no offsetting expenses. Since the district court found that Krinsk "failed to demonstrate that the 12b-1 payments have not contributed to the growth of the Fund," and Krinsk's own expert conceded that considering the 12b-1 payments as a fee-based cost was "within the realm of reason," we cannot say that the court's treatment of those fees was "clearly erroneous," *Gartenberg II*, 740 F.2d at 192.

#### (2) Other Costs

Krinsk attacks numerous aspects of the PMM study and the district court's findings as to systems costs, overhead, declines and overrides, CMA marketing and the allocation of certain costs to the securities side as opposed to the Fund side. Determination of these matters, involving extensive analysis of factual data, is best left to the discretion of the district court, which held a two-week trial to resolve the factual questions. There is ample evidence to support the district court's findings on these issues, and Krinsk does not advance any convincing argument that the district court erred.

### (3) Measure of Profitability

Krinsk disputes Merrill Lynch's measure of profitability and offers instead a "return on equity" analysis utilizing a "Dupont formula." The application of the formula was flawed, however, by a speculative approach and lack of crucial figures.[4] Krinsk offers also a "yardstick" analysis that compares the return on equity of the Fund with the return from other segments of the financial services industry, such as banks, insurance companies and companies dealing with stocks and bonds. According to this formula, the Fund reaps a lower return because its fee-based activities are relatively stable. Not accounted for in this formula, however, is the Fund's connection to the CMA program, which provides a variety of financial services. Moreover, the yardstick formula would reduce the Fund's advisory fee to a level far below that of any other mutual fund. The unreasonable result of applying this formula casts suspicion on the formula itself. We therefore cannot fault the district court for rejecting Krinsk's theories and crediting the testimony of Merrill Lynch's expert.

### C. Fall-out Benefits

Krinsk argues that fall-out benefits should include all securities commission and margin revenues from CMA accounts, even if the benefits would have come to Merrill Lynch absent the existence of the Fund (or the CMA program). The district court rejected this definition as too broad. In *Gartenberg II*, a suit attacking Merrill Lynch's RAT fund, Judge Pollack characterized fall-out benefits as the "commissions received by [MLPF&S] that would not have been earned *but for* the fact that [MLPF&S] was able to solicit [RAT fund] shareholders." 573 F.Supp. 1293, 1313 (S.D.N.Y.1983) (emphasis added), *aff'd*, 740 F.2d 190 (2d Cir.1984). Krinsk urges rejection of that approach, noting that our Circuit does not require "but for" causation for costs to be offset with income from "voluntary" float benefits and free credit balances. *See Gartenberg II*, 740 F.2d at 194. However, float benefits and free credit balances are generated directly by the money market fund and cannot be characterized as fall-out revenue. *See* 573 F.Supp. at 1312-13.

### D. Economies of Scale

Krinsk alleges that Merrill Lynch's expenses, in terms of a percentage of fee-based revenues, have declined as a result of the Fund's asset growth. He argues that the Fund should receive the benefit of this economy of scale. The district court noted, however, that the fact that "expenses ... declined at a time when the Fund size grew ... does not establish that such decline was necessarily due to economies of scale." . . . . Rather, to show economies of scale, plaintiff bore the burden of proving that the per unit cost of performing Fund transactions decreased as the number of transactions increased. *See Gartenberg I*, 528 F.Supp. 1038, 1055 (S.D.N.Y.1981), *aff'd*, 694 F.2d 923 (2d Cir.1982), *cert. denied*, 461 U.S. 906 (1983). Krinsk

---

[4]    The "Dupont formula" calculates return on equity by multiplying profit margin by asset turnover by leverage. Krinsk's expert lacked the asset turnover and leverage figures for the Fund or the CMA Program, and used instead figures for ML&Co.

offered no such evidence. Merrill Lynch, in contrast, offered evidence that the per unit costs for most money market funds generally do not decrease as a fund grows. As the Merrill Lynch view is not unreasonable, *see id.* (per unit cost of providing shareholder services remained relatively stable), we cannot say the district erred in finding that Krinsk failed to sustain his burden of proof.

### E. Comparative Expense Ratios and Advisory Fees

The district court found that the Fund's expense ratio and advisory fee are not only consistent with the industry norms, but have been among the lowest of any mutual fund in the industry. Krinsk does not dispute these findings, but instead argues that a general comparison of fees is of limited use. Indeed, we have cautioned against providing much weight to this type of comparison. *See Gartenberg I,* 694 F.2d at 929. According to Krinsk, the only viable comparison of fees would be to a fund comparable in size to the CMA Fund, and the only such fund is Merrill Lynch's RAT. That fund has an effective advisory fee that is 10% less than the CMA advisory fee. Unlike the CMA Fund, however, the RAT is a stand-alone fund, where the investors do not derive the many benefits of the central asset account.

Additionally, the district court allowed Merrill Lynch to exclude the service fee from the computation of the Fund's yield. Krinsk argues that it is inconsistent to consider benefits arising from the program components that are ancillary to the Fund to allow a higher fee, and yet not attribute that fee as a cost to the Fund. Where a money market fund is embedded in a central asset account, the apportionment of the costs and benefits is, as the district court recognized, "an art rather than a science." . . . . Since the fee under consideration is paid by non-shareholders of the Fund as well as shareholders, we are not prepared to say that the district court erred in allowing Merrill Lynch to exclude the fee from the computation of yield.

### F. Trustees' Approval

The expertise of the trustees, whether they are fully informed, and the extent of care and conscientiousness with which they perform their duties are among the most important factors to be examined in evaluating the reasonableness of compensation under section 36(b). *See Gartenberg I,* 694 F.2d at 930. Krinsk cannot dispute the district court's finding that the trustees were qualified and well-informed. Krinsk, however, attacks the independence and deliberations of the trustees, alleging that they did not act at arm's length, did not conclude that the 12b-1 plan would benefit shareholders before voting for it, did not consider profitability to Merrill Lynch, and were more concerned about the CMA program than the Fund of which they were the trustees. He notes, for instance, that the trustees did not fine-tune the advisory fee, as there is no breakpoint beyond $1 billion in the advisory fee schedule.

The evidence amply supports a finding that the trustees were independent and exercised care in their deliberations. For example, when the trustees were not satisfied with the profitability study Merrill Lynch prepared, they required the study to be redone. The trustees also did not violate their fiduciary duties in approving the 12b-1 incentive fee; in fact, the fee seems to have benefitted the shareholders. As a result of the creation of competing bank funds, the CMA Fund had lost approximately 25% of its assets in 1982. The 12b-1 fee was adopted to counteract this erosion of assets. By providing an incentive for the sale of shares, the 12b-1 plan created a positive cash flow for the Fund, enabling the manager to improve the Fund's performance. That the plan has had the added effect of raising morale of MLPF&S financial consultants and consequently improving the quality of services to existing Fund shareholders is no reason to deem the plan, or the motives of the trustees, improper. *Cf. Meyer v. Oppenheimer Management Corp.*, 764 F.2d 76, 84-85 (2d Cir.1985), *on remand*, 707 F.Supp. 1394 (S.D.N.Y.1988). Accordingly, the district court did not err in finding that the trustees were independent and that they deliberated conscientiously.

*2. Section 12(b)*

Section 12(b) mandates that an investment company acting as a distributor of its own securities comply with the rules and regulations promulgated thereunder by the SEC. Sectin 12(b) of the Investment Company Act of 1940. Under Rule 12b-1, the investment company directors are held to the fiduciary standards of section 36 when they consider whether to implement or continue a distribution plan, such as the 12b-1 plan at issue here. Rule 12b-1 under the 1940 Act.

Krinsk complains that the Fund's 12b-1 plan violates section 12(b) and SEC Rule 12b-1 in that the amounts paid by the Fund are based on the entire asset base regardless of whether any additional shares are sold. This claim, however, is a reincarnation of his "excessive fee" argument, and thus is indistinguishable from the section 36(b) claim, which encompassed the 12b-1 plan.[5] To allow this claim, which is cognizable under section 36(b), to be brought under section 12(b) would be to allow circumvention of the following specific procedural limitations of section 36(b), *see Tarlov v. Paine Webber Cashfund, Inc.*, 559 F.Supp. 429, 437 (D.Conn.1983): damages may be recovered only against the recipient of the compensation, are limited to the amount of compensation, and may not be recovered for any period prior to one year before the commencement of the action, see section 36(b)(3) of the Investment Company Ac of 1940. The district court did not err in finding that this circumvention would be impermissible.

*3. Section 15(a)*

Section 15(a) of the Act provides that no one may serve as investment adviser to a fund "except pursuant to a written contract" that "precisely describes all compensation to be paid thereunder." Section 15(a) of the Investment Company Act of 1940. Krinsk alleges that Merrill Lynch violated this section because the $65 CMA program participation fee is not mentioned in a written agreement between the Fund and MLAM.

The first defect in Krinsk's claim is, as the district court noted, that Krinsk did not and cannot allege that the fee is advisory compensation. It is paid not to MLAM or the FAM, but to MLPF&S for program services. In *Gartenberg I*, Judge Pollack dismissed a similar section 15(a) claim against MLPF&S on the ground that MLPF&S was not an investment adviser. See 528 F.Supp. at 1066. Likewise, the fee here is paid to MLPF&S, which is not the investment adviser.

---

[5]     Krinsk does not allege that the plan fails to conform with the mechanical requirements of Rule 12b-1(b), a claim that might be a section 12(b) action independent of an action under section 36(b). *See Meyer*, 764 F.2d at 85. Had Krinsk raised such a claim, we might be forced to reach the issue whether there exists generally a private right of action under section 12(b), *see id.*, in light of the fact that the section, unlike section 36(b), contains no words expressly providing for a private right of action. We leave that issue, however, for another day.

The second reason the claim fails is that it is not the proper subject of a derivative action. The fee is paid by the individual participants, not the Fund. Because the fee "flow[s] directly from the investor ...[,] the investor ... is the proper party to assert this action, not the Fund, nor the plaintiff shareholder on behalf of the Fund," *Cohen v. Fund Asset Management, Inc.*, [1981-1982 Transfer Binder] Fed.Sec.L.Rep. (CCH) P 98,433, at 92,571-92,572 (S.D.N.Y. Mar. 31, 1980).

### 4. Proxy Statement under Section 20(a)

Section 20(a) and Rule 20a-1 thereunder forbid solicitation of proxies containing any materially false or misleading statement or omission. Section 20(a) of the Investment Company Act of 1940; Rule 20a-1(a) under the 1940 Act (incorporating the restrictions of SEC Rules governing section 14(a) of the Securities Exchange Act of 1934. The plaintiff must establish that "there is a substantial likelihood that a reasonable shareholder would consider [the omitted fact] important in deciding how to vote," *TSC Industries, Inc. v. Northway, Inc.*, 426 U.S. 438, 449 (1976); *see Schuyt v. Rowe Price Prime Reserve Fund, Inc.*, 663 F.Supp. 962, 989-90 (S.D.N.Y.) (adopting Northway rule to claim under Section 20(a)), *aff'd*, 835 F.2d 45 (2d Cir.1987) (per curiam), *cert. denied*, 108 S.Ct. 1594 (1988).

The district court dismissed this claim following trial, apparently agreeing with Merrill Lynch that because the CMA Fund and the RAT are so different, comparisons would confuse rather than assist an investor, and that the omission was immaterial. We agree. The proxy statement listed the "First Breakpoint" and, in so doing, alerted the reader that there could be other breakpoints. In no way does the statement imply that these other breakpoints, if existing, would be the same. In fact, the reader would not assume from the face of the statement that for any given fund there are other breakpoints at all, as there are forty-two funds of various sizes listed under the column and some lack any breakpoint. Also, the statement cautioned that "investors seeking solely to invest cash in a money fund ... should consider as a more suitable investment other money funds." Finally, the RAT fees were readily available, for instance, on the RAT proxy statements. This claim properly was dismissed. . . .

## Comments and Questions

1. The *Gartenberg* decisions, applied in the *Krinsk* case, have been widely followed in section 36(b) litigation. How often would you expect plaintiffs to prevail under this standard? If they do prevail, what remedy does section 36(b) provide? Is that remedy adequate?

2. A portion of the *Krinsk* decision deals with Rule 12b-1 fees. These are fees that mutual funds pay broker-dealers for the cost of distributing fund shares. These fees are authorized under rule 12b-1. What procedural protections does rule 12b-1 impose? Are these safeguards adequate to ensure that excessive fund resources will not be used to pay for fund distribution expenses? How does rule 12b-1 relate to the cases you have read so far in this section of the casebook?

3. Underlying cases such as *Gartenberg* and *Krinsk* is a question whether the fees charge mutual fund shareholders are, in some sense, too high. From time to time, industry

analysts and government officials have expressed concern over the level of mutual fund fees. See, e.g., *Levitt Tells Senate Appropriations Panel Concern About Mutual Fund Fee Structure*, BNA Securities Law Daily, Mar. 20, 1997. The primary source of such concerns is the fact that mutual fund fees, as a percentage of assets invested, have not unambiguously declined in recent years, notwithstanding the fact that the industry has grown dramatically and would appear likely to enjoy substantial economies of scale. Defenders of the mutual fund fees note that the industry is highly competitive and that this competition imposes substantial pressure on fees. Industry representatives also cite cases such as *Krinsk* as evidence that that private litigants have been generally unsuccessful in proving the existence of excessive fees. What are the relative strength of these arguments? How should we determine if mutual fund fees are too high?

### Problem 13-6

Advisers Unlimited (AU) is a registered investment adviser that specializes in helping its customers assemble investment portfolios of no-load mutual funds. AU charges its clients an annual fee based on the total amount of assets in their portfolios; AU does not serve as a broker or dealer for its client's investments. Fido Management, a leading mutual fund advisory firm, approaches AU and offers to pay AU a fee for recommending AU clients to invest in Fido-advised funds. The fee will equal an annual payment of 0.10 % of all AU client investments in Fido-advised funds. Can AU accept this offer?

------

Rule 12b-1, like sections 10(a) and 15(f) of the 1940 Act, relies on independent directors to look out for the interests of investment company shareholders. As you read the following article, consider whether that reliance is well-founded.1.35

## The Dog that Rarely Bites
### Forbes, Oct. 2, 1989, at 210

Mutual fund directors are meant to look out for shareholders' interests, making sure that returns are healthy and expenses are low. Which doesn't go a long way to explain fashion designer Pauline Trigere's presence on the board of 22 Oppenheimer funds. Her qualifications for the job? "Oh, my beauty," quips French-born Trigere, 86, in her husky, heavily accented English. Trigere attends eight meetings a year for three hours or so apiece. Oppenheimer won't reveal Trigere's individual take, but, looking at public documents, Forbes estimates that it is close to $50,000 a year, or about $2,000 an hour. Those costs are picked up by the funds' shareholders.

Trigere is not the only celebrity on Wall Street. Browse through some mutual fund prospectuses and you may notice such directors as former President Gerald Ford, astronaut Alan Shepard, basketball star Oscar Robertson and Mrs. Lloyd Bentsen Jr., wife of the senator.

What exactly do these directors discuss at their meetings? "I think in general that these boards act pretty much as other corporate boards in that they approve general concepts," explains Alan Shepard, the first man ever to play lunar golf. "We try to deal in general terms and let the officers of the company do their job." Ah, that must mean the directors discuss the general direction of the market and leave the stock picking to the lowly fund managers. So where does Shepard expect the market to go from here? "You can say that the admiral passed on that."

Some funds actually have strict rules preventing directors from helping with investment advice of any kind, which is probably just as well since many of the directors are picked more for their name value than for their investment credentials. At Value Line, for example, the funds are on a kind of autopilot -- they're managed strictly according to the Value Line ranking system.

Which wouldn't seem to leave the directors a heck of a lot to do. They could, of course, look out for investors' interests in the matter of the fund's fee structure. Maybe they do at the Value Line family which is free of those noxious 12b-1 fees -- advertising and marketing costs that the sponsor bills to fund shareholders. But in many other funds the directors cheerfully endorse such costly fees.

The Securities & Exchange Commission in 1980 permitted funds -- with directors' approval -- to assess 12b-1 fees, under the ostensible logic that better marketing would mean more assets and more assets would lower expense ratios for existing shareholders. That the logic is less than compelling is evidenced by the fact that funds aren't rushing to withdraw their 12b-1 fees even after the fund reaches enormous size.

Former President Gerald Ford and his fellow directors of the IDS funds have approved 12b-1 levies on all of the 26 funds. For this, shareholders pay him director fees totaling $56,000 a year. Here's what Ford has to say on the 12b-1 question: "I think that it is controversial, but we will find a way to live with it."

Oscar ("Big O") Robertson, the former NBA guard and currently a director for the Midwest Income Trust, hasn't contested the 12b-1 assessed on the two fund portfolios in the trust. Says Robertson: "I think that fees are fees and have to be paid. Certain organizations need fees to keep themselves going." Others, however, don't seem to have that need, and investors might do well to stick with those without the thirst for 12b-1.

So what exactly is the role of the director? Explains 76-year old Oppenheimer director Leo Cherne, who is best known as the chairman of the International Rescue Committee, "I see the role of the director fundamentally, in a changing world, as representing the interests of the shareholders. Sort of a watchdog."

Cherne says he barks a lot. "I would say that I cannot recall a meeting at which I have not expressed myself actively and, I would like to think, importantly." Has he ever growled about the 12b-1 fees that Oppenheimer charges on 12 of its funds? "I have no opinion on that," he says tactfully. But, if he truly represents shareholders, shouldn't he have?

Elsewhere in the corporate world a series of lawsuits and some well-publicized scandals have made most corporate boards a lot more assertive than they used to be. Boards sometimes overrule management on policy and have ever been known to chuck out managements. But little of this assertiveness seems to have filtered through to the mutual fund industry.

There are many factors an investor should consider before choosing a mutual fund.  The number of famous names on the board of directors is definitely not one of them.

———————

Should the regulation of independent directors be tightened?  Should the SEC develop testing obligations comparable to those required or registered broker-dealers?  Who should control the nomination of independent directors? Should we be concerned if the same board of directors oversees all of the funds in a large fund complex?  Should we be concerned if that board invariably renews the management contract of an affiliated advisers?  Should boards be expected to shop around for alternative advisers from time to time?

## D.  Board Control of 1940 Act Litigation

As this section has explored in several different context, directors and particularly independent directors are central to the 1940 Act's regulatory structure.  The statute mandates that a certain percentage of investment company directors be independent and then assigns to them the responsibility to oversee a number of operating policies where the interests of management and shareholders are likely to be at odds.  The election of directors is assigned to shareholders, and the proxy rules are intended to insure that those elections are based on materially complete and accurate information.  In addition, directors are potentially subject to liability under the 1940 Act.  The board, however, also has a role in policing some litigation against directors, as the following case illustrates.  (The substantive bases of the claims in this case are complex, and are explored in greater detail in subsection 3.B of this chapter; for the time being, focus your attention the court's discussion of the role of the board.)

## Strougo v. Scudder, Stevens & Clark, Inc.
### 964 F.Supp. 783 (S.D.N.Y. 1997)

In this action alleging violations of the Investment Company Act of 1940, as amended (the "ICA"), and breach of fiduciary duty under the common law, defendants Scudder, Stevens & Clark, Inc. ("Scudder"), Juris Padegs ("Padegs"), Nicholas Bratt ("Bratt"), Edmond Villani ("Villani"), Edgar Fiedler ("Fiedler"), Wilson Nolen ("Nolen"), Roberto Teixeira Da Costa ("Da Costa"), Ronaldo A. Da Frota Nogueira ("Nogueira"), and nominal defendant the Brazil Fund ("the Fund"), have moved to dismiss the complaint of Robert Strougo ("Strougo") . . . pursuant to Fed.R.Civ.P. 23.1 . . . .

### Parties

Strougo purchased 1,000 shares of the Fund on January 11, 1993, and has held shares continuously thereafter.

The Fund, a nominal defendant in this action, is a Maryland corporation whose principal executive office is located in New York, New York. The Fund is a non- diversified, closed-end investment company that invests in the securities of Brazilian companies. Shares in the Fund trade on the New York Stock Exchange.

Scudder is a Delaware corporation whose principal offices are located in New York, New York. Scudder serves as investment advisor to and manager of the Fund. It is a registered investment advisor under the Investment Advisers Act of 1940, as amended.

Padegs is chairman of the board and a director of the Fund. He is also a managing director of Scudder and serves on both Scudder's board and the boards of other funds managed by Scudder.

Bratt is president and a director of the Fund. Bratt is also a managing director of Scudder and serves on the boards of other funds managed by Scudder.

Villani is a director of the Fund. He is also president and managing director of Scudder and serves on both Scudder's board and the boards of other funds managed by Scudder.

Scudder, Padegs, Bratt and Villani will be referred to as the "Scudder Defendants."

Fiedler is a director of the Fund and serves on the boards of seven other funds managed by Scudder. He received $30,003 in compensation for serving on boards of funds managed by Scudder and accrued $366,075 in deferred compensation for service on two Scudder funds.

Nolen is a director of the Fund. He also serves on the boards of fourteen other funds managed by Scudder. Nolen's aggregate compensation for service on these boards was $132,023 in 1994.

Nogueira is a director and resident Brazilian director of the Fund. He serves on the boards of three other funds managed by Scudder. Nogueira's aggregate compensation for serving on these boards was $54,997 in 1994.

Da Costa is a director and resident Brazilian director of the Fund. Da Costa was compensated $13,868 for serving on the Fund's board in 1994. . . .

### The Facts

This action arises from the 1995 decision by the board of directors of the Brazil Fund, a closed-end investment company incorporated under Maryland law and traded on the New York Stock Exchange, to increase the Fund's capital by offering the Fund's existing shareholders rights to purchase additional shares of newly issued stock (the "Rights Offering"). Strougo asserts that Scudder and each of the directors of the Fund breached their respective fiduciary duties of loyalty and due care as a result of the development and implementation of the Rights Offering.

Scudder created the Brazil Fund in 1988. The Fund is a non-diversified, closed-end investment company registered under the Investment Company Act of 1940 (the "ICA") that invests almost exclusively in securities of Brazilian companies. Certain of the Fund's directors serve as executive officers of Scudder and receive substantial compensation from Scudder. A majority of the remaining directors of the Fund serve as directors of other closed-end funds affiliated with Scudder. Defendant Fiedler serves on the boards of eight funds managed by Scudder and received or accrued approximately $400,000 as a result of such directorships during

1994. Defendant Nolen serves on the boards of fifteen funds managed by Scudder and received $132,023 in 1994 as a result thereof. Defendant Nogueira serves on the boards of four funds managed by Scudder and received $54,997 in 1994 as a result thereof.

Unlike a traditional mutual fund in which investors purchase and redeem shares directly from and with the mutual fund, a closed-end fund has a fixed number of shares and (after the initial public offering) investors may only purchase shares from an existing shareholder through a stock exchange on which such shares are listed. Thus, shares in a closed-end fund are traded exactly like the shares of any other publicly-owned corporation. By contrast with an "open- end" mutual fund, in which the number of shares is not fixed and investors can purchase or redeem shares at current net asset value ("NAV") (calculated by dividing the fund's total assets by the number of shares outstanding), a closed-end fund has a fixed number of shares that originally were sold in a public offering. Per-share trading prices may be at either a premium or a discount to NAV, but more often are at a discount.

Because closed-end funds operate with a fixed number of shares, they have limited options for obtaining capital to make new investments. Once a fund's initial capital has been fully invested, new investments generally can be made only if the fund sells existing portfolio holdings. Other options for raising capital include secondary public offerings at net asset value, or rights offerings to current investors at or below NAV.

Scudder is paid a fee equal to a percentage of the Fund's net assets. From December 1994 through November 1995, the Fund's net assets declined significantly, dropping to $271 million on November 16, 1995, from $377 million on December 31, 1994. As the Fund's net assets materially declined, so did Scudder's fee.

As a result of the decline in net assets, as well as in Scudder's fees, Strougo alleges that defendants decided to raise additional capital to increase the Fund's net assets, and thereby restore Scudder's annual compensation. On October 13, 1995, defendants announced that the Fund would conduct the Rights Offering, whereby the Fund would issue transferable rights to its shareholders. Each Fund shareholder received one right for each share held; three rights entitled the holder to purchase an additional share at the "Subscription Price" of $15.75. The rights were transferrable; that is, if the shareholders did not wish to exercise their rights to purchase additional shares, they were entitled to sell the rights to any purchaser. The rights expired on December 15, 1995.

The Subscription Price was 30.19% below the Fund's NAV and resulted in per share NAV being reduced by $1.88. This $1.88 per share dilution was accompanied by a contemporaneous decline in the market price of the Fund's shares. The price of the Fund's stock declined, dropping $2.125 per share from $25.125 the day before the Rights Offering was announced to $23.25 one week later. Strougo alleges that as a result of the "coercive" Rights Offering, plaintiff and the other shareholders of the Fund, as well as the Fund itself, suffered harm in the form of market and dilution damages. The Complaint alleges that Rights Offerings "cause a loss to existing shareholders" because they "dilute the pro rata holdings of ... stock held by the fund allocable to existing shares [, and] because investment banking fees and other transactional costs are incurred by the closed-end fund." Moreover, Strougo alleges that the market value of the Fund's shares was depressed below what it would have been had the Rights Offering not been made.

The Complaint alleges six separate claims. . . . Claims V and VI, also brought derivatively on behalf of the Fund, but pursuant to Fed.R.Civ.P. 23.1, and against all defendants except the fund, allege breaches of fiduciary duty owed to the Fund. Claim V is brought pursuant to ICA Section 36(a) and Claim VI is brought pursuant to the common law.

Claims II, III, and IV are brought as direct class claims pursuant to Fed.R.Civ.P. 23, on behalf of a putative class consisting of Fund shareholders during the period October 13, 1995, to December 15, 1995. Claim II is brought against all defendants (except nominal defendant the Fund) for breaches of their ICA Section 36(a) fiduciary duties owed to the fund's shareholders. Claim IV is brought against all defendants (except nominal defendant the Fund) for breaches of their common law fiduciary duties owed to the Fund's shareholders. Claim III is brought against the Scudder defendants and alleges control person liability pursuant to ICA Section 48.

With respect to Claims V and VI, which are derivative in nature, the Complaint alleges that demand would be futile for the following reasons: (1) the board participated or acquiesced in the alleged wrongful acts or intentionally or recklessly failed to inform themselves of the harms and benefits associated with the Rights Offering; (2) a majority of board members are "controlled by or financially dependent" on Scudder, by virtue of their compensation for sitting on the boards of other Scudder funds; (3) because the entire board was responsible for the wrongful acts, the directors cannot independently determine whether a suit should be brought against themselves; (4) the wrongful acts constituted a waste of the Fund's assets, which is unprotected by the business judgment rule; (5) the wrongful acts constituted violations of federal securities law and fiduciary duties, which are not protected by the business judgment rule; and (6) the Fund's directors' and officers' insurance coverage would be voided if the Fund commenced proceedings against the directors.

## Discussion

### The Class Claims Will Be Dismissed As Derivative

Claim II purports to assert a direct class action claim for breach of fiduciary duty pursuant to Section 36(a), while Claim IV directly asserts breach of fiduciary duty under Maryland common law. However, these claims cannot be maintained by Strougo as direct claims because they allege injury to the Fund, and any harm to Strougo is derivative in nature. Therefore, these claims may be brought only by the corporation, or on its behalf in a shareholder derivative claim.

To determine whether a claim brought under the ICA is direct or derivative, a court must look to the law of the state in which the fund was incorporated. Kamen v. Kemper Fin. Servs., 500 U.S. 90, 97-99 (1991) (holding that non-conflicting state law governs federal rules of decision under the ICA). As the Fund is a Maryland corporation, Maryland law governs the rules of decision. Maryland law directs courts to look to the nature of the wrongs alleged in the complaint to determine whether a complaint states a direct or an individual cause of action. James J. Hanks, Jr., Maryland Corporation Law § 7.21(b) (1990 & 1995-1 Suppl.) (collecting cases).

Under Maryland law,

[i]t is a general rule that an action at law to recover damages to a corporation can be brought only in the name of the corporation itself acting through its directors, and not by an individual

stockholder, though the injury may incidentally result in diminishing or destroying the value of the stock.... Generally, therefore, a stockholder cannot maintain an action at law against an officer or director of the corporation to recover damages for fraud, embezzlement, or other breach of trust which depreciated the capital stock.... Where directors commit a breach of trust, they are liable to the corporation, not to its creditors or stockholders ..."

Waller v. Waller, 187 Md. 185, 189-90, 49 A.2d 449, 452 (1946).

Where the injury falls equally on all shareholders and no special relationship between the plaintiff and the defendant might create a duty other than that owed to the corporation, there is no direct cause of action in a shareholder. Olesh v. Dreyfus Corp., No. CV 94-1664, 1995 WL 500491, * 7 (E.D.N.Y. Aug.8, 1995).

The Complaint here alleges an undifferentiated harm suffered by all shareholders deriving from asserted harm to the Fund. The purported class consists of:

all persons who owned shares in the Fund at any time between October 13, 1995 (the date the Fund first publicly announced the rights offering) and December 15, 1995 (the date the rights expired), and who sustained damages as a result thereby.

The charge that all shareholders were harmed in the same fashion by the same capital-raising exercise states a derivative, not a direct claim.

The assertion that plaintiffs were injured as a result of the increased transaction costs and increased management fees that the Rights Offering brought about for the Fund is, on its face, a claim that all shareholders suffered because the Fund suffered by paying costs that it should not have had to pay. This claim too, is derivative. See Olesh, 1995 WL 500491 at *7 (claim of injuries from increased fees derivative because fees imposed on funds, not shareholders directly).

Plaintiff's claims of dilution and of loss of share value similarly spring from a single course of conduct by the defendants toward all shareholders, which is asserted to have adversely affected the Fund's overall capitalization. These claims accordingly are derivative in nature as well, and consequently can only be brought by the Fund on behalf of all shareholders. See, e.g., Waller, 49 A.2d at 452 ("A cause of action for injury to the property of a corporation or for impairment or destruction of its business *is in the corporation*, and such an injury, *although it may diminish the value of the capital stock*, is not primarily or necessarily a damage to the stockholder, and hence the stockholder's derivative right can be asserted only through the corporation.") (emphasis added); accord Kramer v. Western Pac. Indus., Inc., 546 A.2d 348, 353 (Del.1988) ("[W]here a plaintiff shareholder claims that the value of his stock will deteriorate and that the value of his proportionate share of stock will be decreased as a result of alleged director mismanagement, his cause of action is derivative in nature") (citations omitted).

A complaint that, like this one, alleges no injury to shareholders distinct from diminution of share value does not state a cause of action that can be brought directly in a class action. See Olesh, 1995 WL 500491 at *6 (limiting plaintiffs to derivative action under § 36(a)); Waller, 49 A.2d at 452-53; see also Hanks, Maryland Corporation Law, § 7.21[c], at 264; accord Arent v. Distribution Sciences, Inc., 975 F.2d 1370, 1374 (8th Cir.1992).

Moreover, Strougo's allegations in this case are expressly based on asserted breaches of fiduciary duty. Such claims of breach of duty by directors and other fiduciaries of a corporation generally are regarded as derivative rather than direct, since the duty is owed to the corporation and its shareholders as a whole, and the impact of a breach is felt by the corporation. See, e.g., O'Donnell v. Sardegna, 336 Md. 18, 646 A.2d 398, 402-03 (1994) (plaintiffs whose claims included breach of fiduciary duty held limited to derivative action); Olesh, 1995 WL 500491 at *7 (actions for breach of fiduciary duty generally derivative in nature), citing Robert C. Clark, Corporate Law § 15.9 (1986) ("The kinds of suits that are derivative in nature include most cases based on breach of the fiduciary duties of care and loyalty. These include, for example, suits based on ... gross negligence [and] basic self-dealing"); see also Litman v. Prudential-Bache Properties, Inc., 611 A.2d 12, 15-16 (Del.Ch.1992); Lochhead v. Alacano, 662 F.Supp. 230, 231-32 (D.Utah 1987) (Lochhead I ) (under majority rule, fiduciary duties run only from directors to corporation, not to individual shareholders).

Two recent cases considering efforts to assert direct class action claims for breach of fiduciary duty under Section 36(a) and the common law with respect to rights offerings are instructive. In In re Nuveen Fund Litig., 855 F.Supp. 950 (N.D.Ill.1994) (Nuveen I ), the Court dismissed direct claims challenging rights offerings by two closed-end funds (the "Nuveen Funds") and declared that the suit would have to be pursued as a derivative one. Applying Minnesota law, the Court explained:

> Plaintiffs' alleged injuries are not distinct from the alleged injuries to all the Nuveen funds' shareholders. The defendants' actions were the same with respect to all the shareholders. Plaintiffs allege that all the ... shareholders were harmed because the offerings caused the Nuveen funds' per- share value to decline and the fees paid by the ... funds to cover the costs of the offerings (underwriting and advisory services) have siphoned money out of the ... funds to defendants. An injury shared by all the shareholders of a corporation cannot be personal to each shareholder.

Id. at 954.

Similarly, in King v. Douglas, Civ.No. H-96-1033, slip op., 1996 WL 907734 (S.D.Tx. Dec. 23, 1996), the Court dismissed the plaintiffs' direct claims challenging a rights offering under Section 36(a). The Court reasoned that allegations of reduced NAV and market value and dilution in the value of existing shareholders' interests did not state a direct claim because the alleged actions "affect all shareholders equally, proportionate to each shareholder's ownership interest." Slip op. at 41.

Strougo, however, contends that his injury is separate and distinct from any injury to the Fund. If the injury to the shareholder is separate and distinct from any injury suffered either directly by the corporation or derivatively by the stockholder because of the injury to the corporation, a shareholder will have a direct cause of action. Hanks, Maryland Corporation Law, § 7.21[b] at 263-64. This will be the case, for example, where the corporation or the board violates a duty owed directly to a shareholder as an individual, rather than as a shareholder. See Olesh, 1995 WL 500491 at *7 (action is derivative unless "special relationship" exists between shareholder and defendant that might create duty other than that owed to corporation); Empire Life Ins. Co. v. Valdak Corp., 468 F.2d 330, 334-36 (5th Cir.1972) (shareholder who pledged securities to defendant and then acted to diminish the value of the securities permitted to sue directly because defendant pledgee owed direct legal duty to plaintiff as pledgor not to diminish collateral); Chase Nat'l Bank v. Sayles, 30 F.2d 178, 183 (D.R.I.1927) (direct suit permitted where "independent fiduciary relation" existed between plaintiff shareholder and defendant officer, because defendant was plaintiff's agent).

Strougo here has made no allegation that he or the class of shareholders he purports to represent has any independent or special relationship to the defendants other than that of shareholder of the Fund.  As a result, there is no direct cause of action resulting from the breach of a special relationship.

Strougo, however, contends that the Complaint demonstrates that although all shareholders were affected by the Rights Offering, they were not all affected equally, and thus there is a special injury permitting a direct action.  For example, Strougo contends that those who did not exercise their rights were affected differently from those who did.  Thus, he contends, the injury to shareholders is distinct from the injury to the corporation.

However, the fact that a shareholder might be differently affected by a rights offering based on his own election whether or not to exercise rights given equally to all shareholders does not make his injury distinct from injury to the corporation.  So long as the defendants' action toward all shareholders was the same, and any disproportionate effect was the result of the various shareholders' responses to the action, the shareholders have no direct action.  See Nuveen I, 855 F.Supp. at 955 (dilution in shareholders' proportionate voting rights not basis for direct action, where proportionate rights changed because some shareholders exercised rights where others did not;  defendants' actions were same as to all);  King, slip op. at 41 ("Plaintiffs' allegations that the effect on shareholders' voting rights will be disproportional because some will exercise their rights and purchase new additional stock while others [will not] must ... fail as a basis for a direct claim....  Defendants' actions were the same as to all shareholders and did not disproportionately create the change in ownership or ultimately in voting rights;  the shareholders chose whether to participate or not.")

Strougo cites a number of cases that purportedly support the proposition that dilution of share value creates a direct cause of action in the shareholder. However, the cases cited involved situations in which one class or group of stockholders benefitted at the expense of another class of shareholders, who were then permitted to sue directly.  In Alleghany Corp. v. Breswick & Co., 353 U.S. 151, 160 (1957), for example, minority common stockholders had standing to bring a direct suit when the corporation issued preferred stock that would be convertible into common stock, which would effectively dilute the minority common stockholders' equity, but not the equity of the existing preferred stockholders, who could increase their common stock ownership, while the common stockholders could not.

A number of the other cases cited by Strougo involved similar circumstances in which majority or otherwise controlling shareholders inflicted special injuries that fell only on minority shareholders.  For example, in Lochhead v. Alacano, 697 F.Supp. 406, 411-13 (D.Utah 1988) (Lochhead II ), minority shareholders had standing to bring a direct suit when the directors and majority shareholders approved a stock option plan that disproportionately benefitted them, at the expense of minority shareholders.  See also Swanson v. American Consumer Indus., Inc., 415 F.2d 1326, 1332 (7th Cir.1969) (permitting minority shareholders fraudulently induced to forego appraisal rights to sue directly, because principal shareholder wasted assets of company for own benefit);  Bennett v. Breuil Petroleum Corp., 99 A.2d 236, 239 (Del.Ch.1953) (director and minority shareholder permitted to sue directly where majority allegedly "deliberately caused the stock to be issued to impair plaintiff's interest and to force him out of the corporation").

Unlike the plaintiffs in these cases, Strougo has not alleged that he is a minority shareholder whose ownership interest was diluted disproportionately to that of majority shareholders. All shareholders here were treated equally and could prevent disproportionate dilution by exercising their rights to purchase the newly issued shares.

Accordingly, Claims II and IV will be dismissed.

### The Derivative Claims Under Section 36(a) & Maryland Law

#### A. Exhaustion of Intracorporate Remedies

The defendants contend that the derivative claims under Section 36(a) and the common law of Maryland should be dismissed for failure to allege with particularity, as required by Fed.R.Civ.P. 23.1, the reasons he has not made a demand on the Fund's directors and shareholders prior to instituting this action.

As the Fund is a Maryland corporation, Maryland law governs whether demand is required and the conditions that will excuse demand. See Kamen, 500 U.S. at 101-09; see also Langner v. Brown, 913 F.Supp. 260, 265 (S.D.N.Y.1996); Olesh, 1995 WL 500491 at *8. As a matter of federal law, Fed.R.Civ.P. 23.1 itself requires that the grounds for excusing demand under state law be pleaded with particularity. See Grill v. Hoblitzell, 771 F.Supp. 709, 710 n. 2 (D.Md.1991), citing Kamen, 500 U.S. at 109 n. 10.

Under Maryland law, courts ordinarily "will not entertain a derivative suit by a stockholder on behalf of a corporation until it appears that the intra-corporate remedies have been unsuccessfully pursued by the complaining stockholder." Parish v. Maryland & Virginia Milk Producers Ass'n. Inc., 250 Md. 24, 242 A.2d 512, 544 (1968). This means that, in general, the stockholder must make a demand for remedial action on the corporation itself, first by application to the directors, and then by application to the body of the stockholders. id., citing Eisler v. Eastern States Corp., 182 Md. 329, 35 A.2d 118, 119 (1943).

However, prior demand on the directors and shareholders is excused when it would be futile. Parish, 242 A.2d at 544. The futility exception is to be applied in a practical, common-sense manner. Id. at 544-45.

#### 1. Demand on Directors

Strougo's principal argument for excusing demand against the directors is that six of the Brazil Fund's seven directors have disqualifying financial and professional interests as a result of their paid service on the boards of other Scudder-managed funds, such that they could not impartially consider a demand or impartially prosecute this action against Scudder or themselves.

Under Maryland law, demand is excused where the directors are "dominated and controlled" by persons alleged to be guilty of the misconduct charged in the complaint. See Grill, 771 F.Supp. at 711; see also Rales v. Blasband, 634 A.2d 927, 936 (Del.1993) (under Delaware law, to establish lack of independence excusing demand, plaintiff must show that directors are "beholden" to interested party or so under interested party's influence that discretion is "sterilized").

Padegs, Bratt and Villani, who are all employed directly by Scudder, are concededly "interested" in the Rights Offering. However, the defendants contend that the remaining board members, Fiedler, Nolen, Nogueira and Da Costa, are "independent" of Scudder, and therefore are able evaluate a demand and prosecute any action on behalf of the Fund. They contend that the receipt of director's fees and service on the boards of multiple funds managed by Scudder are insufficient to render these defendants "interested" in the transaction.

Ordinarily, allegations that directors receive fees for their services are not sufficient to demonstrate demand futility. See Kamen v. Kemper Financial Services, 939 F.2d 458, 460 (7th Cir.1991) (applying Maryland law). If the opposite were true, the futility exception would swallow the demand rule, since most corporate directors receive remuneration for their service. Id.

Similarly, allegations of business relationships among directors are generally insufficient to overcome the presumption of independence enjoyed by corporate directors. See Id. (fact that independent directors come to board on recommendation of corporate insiders does not excused demand); Grill, 771 F.Supp. at 712 (vague assertions that "personal relationships" among directors make it unlikely that board would authorize suit against current or former members insufficient to excuse demand); see also Langner, 913 F.Supp. at 266 (under Delaware law, cross-directorships insufficient to create "interest" excusing demand).

Here, however, Strougo has alleged not only that the purportedly independent directors receive remuneration for their service on the Brazil Fund, but that three of the four -- Fiedler, Nolen and Nogueira -- receive substantial remuneration from their service on the boards of other mutual funds managed by Scudder. He characterizes Fiedler, Nolen and Nogueira as Scudder's "house directors," essentially as interested in benefitting Scudder (at the potential expense of fund shareholders) as Scudder's own employees.

In Olesh, the district court for the Eastern District of New York held that demand upon the directors was futile because the complaint sought a determination that the directors were "interested" by virtue of their receipt of directors fees for sitting on multiple boards managed by a single advisor. 1995 WL 500491 at *8-9. Olesh involved a merger that, under the ICA, required the approval of 75% of the non-interested directors of the fund. The court reasoned that demand was futile under these circumstances because, in order for the merger to be approved, the purportedly disinterested directors would have to be replaced if the suit were successful. Thus, the directors' interests in retaining their remuneration and positions were directly at odds with instituting a suit that might ultimately deprive them of these benefits. Id. at *9.[2]

Although Olesh is distinguishable on the grounds that the suit there would pose a more direct threat to the directors' board positions and remuneration than the present suit would present to the directors of the Brazil Fund, Olesh provides some support for the proposition that holding multiple paid directorships of funds managed by the same advisor can compromise a director's

---

[2]    In dictum, the court also stated that demand would not be excused by allegations that the directors' "close business ties" to the fund advisor spoiled their independence. Id. at *8-9. However, the court engaged in no explicit discussion of whether the allegations that paid service on the boards of multiple funds managed by the advisor would be sufficient to call into question the directors' independence from the advisor.

independence from the advisor sufficiently to excuse demand under some circumstances. See also, Rales, 634 A.2d at 936-37 (court excused demand because of "reasonable doubt" as to independence of board members who were employed by corporations of which the alleged wrongdoers were directors or majority stock-holders).

The leading commentator on Maryland Corporation Law has stated that demand should not be excused "so long as there are two directors whose involvement in the facts underlying the claim is not so great as to call into question their compliance with the standard of conduct of Section 2-405.1" of the Maryland Corporations and Associations Code. Hanks, Maryland Corporation Law, § 7.21[c] at 269 (1994-1 Suppl.). Section 2-405.1(a) provides that a director shall perform his or her duties "in good faith," "in a manner he reasonably believes to be in the best interests of the corporation" and "with the care that an ordinarily prudent person in a like position would use under similar circumstances." These statutory provisions are Maryland's codification of the fiduciary duties of a director. "Good faith" is "the absence of any desire to obtain a personal benefit or a benefit for some person other than the corporation." Hanks, Maryland Corp. Law, § 6.6[b] at 163 (1992 Suppl.).

Here, the fact that all but one of the directors who approved the Rights offering received substantial compensation from funds managed by Scudder, and the allegation that, in approving the rights offering, these directors put the interests of Scudder in increasing their advisor's fees before the interests of the Fund and its shareholders "call into question" whether there was a desire on the part of the directors to benefit Scudder, rather than the Fund, in order to please Scudder to retain their lucrative directorships. In Maryland, two is the minimum number of directors necessary to form a committee to consider a demand. Hanks, Maryland Corporation Law, § 7.21[c] at 269, n. 173 (1994-1 Suppl.). Because only one of the directors does not serve on multiple Scudder boards, the Board could not appoint a committee of sufficiently disinterested directors to consider a demand by a shareholder to institute litigation, and thus demand would be futile.

The defendants contend that imposing a rule that would effectively eliminate multiple directorships in complexes of funds managed by a single advisor is inappropriate for several reasons. First, they contend that such practices are common and provide substantial benefits to investors, such as reduced costs and the ability of directors to use their knowledge gained from one fund in the service of others. Moreover, they contend, the ICA's definitions of an "interested person" do not include a limitation on directorships of multiple funds in a fund complex. Similarly, the SEC has not prohibited such multiple directorships, but merely required their disclosure in proxy materials. See Amendments to Proxy Rules for Registered Investment Companies, 57 S.E.C. Dock.2019, 2025 & n. 26 (Oct. 13, 1994) ("receipt of substantial amount of compensation from a fund complex is not necessarily determinative of the director's independence").

Although multiple directorships are not necessarily determinative of a director's independence, either under the statute or the SEC's interpretations, where, as here, a director's actions are alleged to establish that he or she may be acting in the interests of the advisor, the receipt of substantial remuneration from a fund complex does call into question the director's independence from the manager of that complex. Moreover, the rule would not eliminate multiple directorships. It would require only that a sufficient number of directors without such multiple directorships serve on a board so that a litigation committee could be convened to consider proposed litigation.

Accordingly, demand on the board of directors is excused as futile.

## 2. Demand on Shareholders

As set forth above, Maryland law requires demand on shareholders or allegations of why such demand was not made. See Parish, 242 A.2d at 545; Grill, 771 F.Supp. at 713 n. 5. Although the Complaint does not explicitly identify the allegations that excuse shareholder demand, the allegations as a whole are sufficient to excuse demand in this case.

It should be noted that no Maryland case has based a dismissal solely on failure to make demand on shareholders, and the shareholder demand rule has been widely criticized. See Hanks, Maryland Corporation Law, § 7.21 [d]. Stockholders are generally poorly equipped to make a determination whether to sue, since they lack the information available to directors and "are prone to approve the managers' acts reflexively." Kamen, 939 F.2d at 462 (discussing Maryland law). As a result, demand on shareholders is rarely necessary. Id.

Demand on a corporation's shareholders has been held to be futile where the shareholders would have to direct the corporation's directors to sue themselves. In Zimmerman v. Bell, 585 F.Supp. 512 (D.Md.1984), an action alleging breach of fiduciary duty against directors under Maryland law, the court held that shareholder demand was excused. The court stated:

> Although a practical solution to this problem (when all of the members of a corporation's board of directors are alleged wrong-doers named as defendants) would be for the shareholders to authorize the demanding plaintiff to prosecute a derivative suit on the corporation's behalf, such a remedy is not sanctioned by Maryland law. Given the fact that the shareholders would either have to order the directors to maintain the action against themselves, or to remove the present board and replace it with one that could maintain the suit against the former directors, it is readily apparent that there is no reason to require the plaintiffs here to have made a demand on the stockholders. See Oldfield v. Alston, 77 F.R.D. 735, 742 (N.D.Ga.1978) (applying Maryland Law).

Id. at 516.

As in Zimmerman, the shareholders here would be asking the defendants to sue themselves or would have to replace the present board with one that could prosecute the suit. Accordingly, demand on the shareholders is excused.

## Comments and Question

1. Why is it that the plaintiff's claims in this case, which arose primarily under the 1934 Act, turned on procedural requirements of Maryland corporate law? See Kamen v. Kemper Financial Services., 500 U.S. 90, 97-99 (1991).

2. What is the relationship between the holding of this case and the requirement of section 10(a) of the 1940 Act that no more than 60 percent of the directors of registered investment companies be interested persons. See section 2(a)(19) of the 1940 Act.

3. As a matter of regulatory policy, what degree of control should directors have over litigation of this sort? To what extent is your response to this question affected by

the fact that the SEC also has jurisdiction over cases of this sort? How relevant is it that shareholders can protect themselves by selling their shares? How concerned are you about the amount of compensation that the independent directors earned in this case? If compensation of this sort is problematic, should the SEC set limits on the amount of compensation independent directors receive? Would such limitations enhance shareholder protections, or would they detract from the quality of individuals willing to serve on investment company boards?

# Section 3.  Regulation of Disclosure

An important supplement to the legal regime of portfolio restrictions and fiduciary duties described in the preceding pages is the mandatory disclosure rules on which the 1940 Act is built. Like other public corporations in the United States, investment companies must comply with the Securities Act of 1933 and the Securities Exchange Act of 1934. In brief, these statutes demand that investors receive detailed prospectuses before they may purchase shares of investment companies, as well as annual reports, proxy statements, and other occasional disclosures on a periodic basis. The SEC has developed extensive regulations designed to ensure that these official disclosure documents include extensive and reliable information about the past performance and future prospects of investment companies. In addition, the SEC in conjunction with the NASD supervises the content of less formal publications, such as advertisements and other promotional materials. Material misstatements in disclosure documents expose issuers and affiliated parties to SEC and SRO enforcement actions as well as civil liability under a variety of private rights of action.

Disclosure regimes of the sort built into investment company regulation present numerous challenges for regulatory authorities. How much information should be required in these documents? What kind of information? When do the costs and complexities of additional information outweigh the information's usefulness? When can authorities rely on independent services (such as Morningstar and Lipper) to police the performance of investment companies? When should abbreviated disclosure be permitted? If disclosure presents a truly viable regulatory mechanism, should we eliminate (or at least soften) fiduciary standards and other rules imposed under the 1940 Act? The following two sets of readings present these questions in two contexts. Subsection A concerns the question of what should be included in disclosure documents for investment companies. Subsection B addresses special disclosure issues that have arisen in the context of closed-end investment companies.

## A. The Content of Disclosure Documents

The first reading is an SEC concept release on the measurement of risk. As explained in passing in the release, the SEC has been working for a number of years on improving the quality of SEC disclosure documents. Through the late 1980s and early 1990s, the staff expended considerable efforts on enhancing performance disclosure in investment company selling materials. The staff sought to achieve both accurate and consistent disclosure requirements regarding past rates of return and yields. In addition to enhancing the quality of individual disclosure documents, these reforms were intended to facilitate comparisons between competing investment companies. As the following release explores, however, performance data by itself is at best incomplete and potentially misleading. One of the fundamental tenets of financial economics is that return and risk are correlated. In recognition of this fact, the Commission embarked upon the following effort to enhance disclosure on the risk side of the risk-return equation.

## Concept Release on Improving Descriptions of Risk
### 60 Fed. Reg. 17,172 (Apr. 4, 1995)

Today the SEC is continuing its efforts to enhance the information that investors in funds receive to assist them in making an informed investment decision. In recent years, the SEC has taken significant steps designed to improve the understandability and comparability of fund disclosure of performance and expenses. [1] The SEC is now requesting comment on how to improve risk disclosure for investment companies, including ways to increase the comparability of disclosure about funds' risk levels through quantitative measures or other means.

Under existing SEC rules, a fund is required to discuss in its prospectus the principal risk factors associated with investing in the fund. [3] Funds typically describe the risks of investing in

---

[1]    See, e.g., Disclosure of Mutual Fund Performance and Portfolio Managers, Investment Company Act of 1940 ("Investment Company Act") Rel. No. 19382 (Apr. 6, 1993) [58 FR 19050 (Apr. 12, 1993)] (requiring mutual fund prospectuses or annual reports to discuss performance and provide line graph comparing fund performance to that of an appropriate market index over the last ten fiscal years; financial highlights table of prospectus revised to include total return information and generally to provide investors with information showing the performance of funds on a per share basis); Registration Form for Closed-End Management Investment Companies, Investment Company Act Rel. No. 19115 (Nov. 20, 1992) [57 FR 56826, 56829 (Dec. 1, 1992)] (improvements to financial highlights table for closed-end funds; fee table providing standard format for expense information required in closed-end fund prospectuses); Advertising by Investment Companies, Investment Company Act Rel. No. 16245 (Feb. 2, 1988) [53 FR 3868 (Feb. 10, 1988)] [hereinafter "Rel. 16245"] (mutual fund advertisements and sales literature containing performance data required to include uniformly computed performance data); Consolidated Disclosure of Mutual Fund Expenses, Investment Company Act Rel. No. 16244 (Feb. 1, 1988) [53 FR 3192 (Feb. 4, 1988)] (fee table required in mutual fund prospectuses).

[3]    Risk factors include those peculiar to the fund and those that apply generally to funds with similar investment policies and objectives or, in the case of closed-end funds, similar capital structures

the fund by describing the risks of particular investment policies that the fund may use and investments that the fund may make. [4] Lengthy and highly technical descriptions of permissible policies and investments that are often used in meeting existing requirements may make it difficult for investors to understand the total risk level of a fund.  The SEC staff has found that funds typically provide only the most general information on the risk level of the fund taken as a whole and has encouraged funds to modify their existing disclosure to enhance investor understanding of risks.  The SEC believes that it is now appropriate to explore whether SEC disclosure requirements should be revised in order to improve the communication of fund risks to investors and increase the likelihood that investors will readily grasp the risks of investing in a particular fund before they invest.

Several factors make it important that the SEC explore better ways of explaining fund risks to investors.  First, average Americans are placing increasing reliance on funds to meet important financial needs, such as retirement and college expenses. Understanding the risks of various investment products is one of the most important ingredients in creating an overall investment strategy or portfolio to meet these financial needs.  Second, new ways of describing risks may improve investor understanding of the risks associated with the use by some funds of increasingly complex instruments, such as derivatives. Third, the number and types of funds have proliferated, increasing fund investors' need for information that will help them to compare and contrast alternatives. . . . .

## I. The Goals of Risk Disclosure

The SEC's goal is to improve disclosure of fund risks so that investors will have the information they need to understand the risk of any particular fund investment.  The best means for achieving this aim may depend, in part, on the specific goals of risk disclosure.  The SEC therefore requests comment on the specific goals of risk disclosure, including the matters raised below.

The SEC asks persons submitting comments to define, as precisely as possible, what "risks" should be disclosed to investors.  To what extent are investors concerned with the likelihood that they will lose principal, that their return will not exceed a specified benchmark (such as the Standard & Poor's ("S&P") 500), or with the variability of their returns (or the volatility of the value of their investment) over time? How should the relationship between risk and an investor's time horizon shape the disclosure that is provided to investors? For example, is the same risk information useful to an investor with an investment time horizon of less than one year and to an investor with an investment time horizon of twenty years?  How can the disclosure of risk help investors answer the fundamental questions--Is this investment suitable for me? If I

---

or trading markets. . . .

[4]     See Form N-1A, Item 4(a)(ii) (requires concise description of mutual fund investment objectives and policies and brief discussion of how the fund proposes to achieve such objectives, including description of the securities in which the fund will invest and special investment practices or techniques that will be employed); Form N-1A, Item 4(b) (requires discussion of types of investments, policies, and practices that will not constitute the "principal portfolio emphasis" of a mutual fund, but which place more than 5% of the fund's net assets at risk) . . . .

have diversified my investments, how does this particular fund fit into my diversification strategy?

Comments are requested on the nature of risk comparisons that are useful to investors. For example, should risk disclosure facilitate comparison among a broad range of investment options, such as between funds and other investment products? Or is it sufficient to facilitate comparisons among all funds and fund types, both equity and fixed income? Or among all equity funds, on the one hand, and all fixed income funds, on the other? Or only within groups of funds with similar investment objectives and policies, such as short-term government bond funds?

Is improved disclosure of risks equally important for equity, fixed income, and balanced or asset allocation funds? Do recent derivatives-related losses by some fixed income funds, and the apparently greater use of derivatives by fixed income funds, suggest that the need for improved disclosure of risks is greater for fixed income funds? In light of the substantive limits on permitted money market fund investments, should risk disclosure requirements for money market funds be different from those applicable to other funds?

Comments are also requested on the degree of detail regarding fund risk that ideally would be communicated to investors. In meeting existing disclosure requirements, funds often describe the purposes of using particular types of instruments and the risks associated with each type, but typically provide only the most general information on the risk level of the fund taken as a whole. Should disclosure convey the risks of each particular type of instrument held by a fund, the risks of broader classes of instruments (for instance, derivatives as a group), the risks of the fund's portfolio as a whole, or some combination of the foregoing? Should the focus of disclosure be shifted from the characteristics of particular securities to the nature of the investment management services offered, including the objectives of a fund manager and the associated risks and rewards? Do investors need to understand separately the different types of risk, such as market, credit, legal, and operational risks, or is it the aggregate effect of different types of risk that is important to an investment decision?

## II. Narrative and Non-Narrative Risk Disclosure Options

The SEC currently requires fund prospectuses to include narrative descriptions of risk, and the SEC is interested in the potential for improving risk disclosure through changes to the narrative disclosure requirements and the use of non-narrative forms of disclosure. . . .

At present, a number of funds voluntarily supplement narrative descriptions of risk through means such as quantitative measures, graphs, tables, and other pictorial representations. . . .Another method used is a line graph that shows relative risk and return levels for the fund and some benchmark, such as Treasury bills or a market index such as the S&P 500. Another method is a bar graph that shows consistency of returns for the fund and a market index (as measured by monthly rates of return over the life of the fund). Finally, some fund families use pictures to show the relative risks of the various funds within the family.

The SEC believes that quantitative measures, graphs, tables, and other pictorial representations may assist investors in understanding and comparing funds. The SEC currently requires disclosure of quantitative information in tabular form in the areas of fund performance and expenses. Recently, the SEC adopted rules that require graphic depictions of information to facilitate investor understanding of fund performance. The SEC now requests comment on the relative merits and usefulness of various formats for investment company risk disclosure, including quantitative measures, graphs, tables, and other pictorial representations. To what extent should these methods be used to supplement, or replace, current narrative risk disclosure?

## III.  Quantitative Measures of Risk

### A. Specific Historical Quantitative Measures of
### Risk and Risk-Adjusted Performance

Historical measures of risk and risk-adjusted performance are generally calculated from past portfolio returns and, in some cases, past market returns. There are two broad classes of historical risk measures, referred to in this Release as total risk measures and market risk measures. In addition, there is a third class of measures, risk-adjusted measures of performance. (Unless the context indicates otherwise, risk-adjusted measures of performance are included in "quantitative risk measures" and similar terms and phrases used in this Release.) These three classes of measures are described below, and examples of each are provided. Comments are requested on the relative advantages and disadvantages of the three classes of measures and of specific measures within each class.

### 1. Measures of Total Risk

Total risk measures, including standard deviation and semi-variance, quantify the total variability of a portfolio's returns around, or below, its average return.

- Standard Deviation of Total Return. The risk associated with a portfolio can be viewed as the volatility of its returns, measured by the standard deviation of those returns. [5] For example, a fund's historical risk could be measured by computing the standard deviation of its monthly total returns over some prior period, such as the past three years. The larger the standard deviation of monthly total returns, the more volatile, i.e., spread out around the fund's average monthly total return, the fund's monthly total returns have been over the prior period. Standard deviation of total return can be calculated for funds with different objectives, ranging from equity funds to fixed income funds to balanced funds, and can be measured over different time frames. For example, a fund could calculate standard deviation of monthly returns over the prior three years or yearly returns over the prior ten years.

- Semi-variance. Standard deviation measures both "good" and "bad" outcomes, i.e., the variability of returns both above and below the average return. To the individual investor, however, risk may be synonymous with "bad" outcomes. Semi-variance, which can be used to measure the variability of returns below the average return, reflects this view of risk. A fund with a larger semi-variance has returns that are more spread out below the average return.

---

[5]    William F. Sharpe, Gordon J. Alexander, and Jeffery V. Bailey, Investments 178 (5th ed. 1995) [hereinafter "Sharpe, Alexander, & Bailey"]. If the returns earned by a portfolio are "normally" distributed, that is, in the shape of a bell curve, approximately 95% of the actual returns will fall within two standard deviations of the average return. . . . For example, for a fund with an average monthly return of 1% and a standard deviation of 4%, 95% of the fund's monthly returns would fall between -7% (1%- (2 x 4%)) and + 9% (1%+ (2 x 4%)) if the returns were "normally" distributed. . . .

## 2. Measures of Market Risk

Individual securities, and portfolios of securities, are generally subject to two sources of risk: (i) Risk attributable to firm-specific factors, including research and development, marketing, and quality of management; and (ii) risk attributable to general economic conditions, including the inflation rate, interest rates, and exchange rates. According to academic literature in Finance, firm-specific risk can be reduced or eliminated through portfolio diversification, but the risk attributable to general economic conditions, so- called "market risk," cannot be eliminated through diversification. Unlike standard deviation and variance, which measure portfolio risk from both sources, the measures described in this section are measures of market risk. The SEC requests comment on whether, given that most fund portfolios are diversified, it is appropriate to focus on market risk when measuring fund risks.

- Beta. Beta measures the sensitivity of a security's, or portfolio's, return to the market's return. The market's beta is by definition equal to 1. Portfolios with betas greater than 1 are more volatile than the market, and portfolios with betas less than 1 are less volatile than the market. For example, if a portfolio has a beta of 2, a 10% market return would result in a 20% portfolio return, and a 10% market loss would result in a 20% portfolio loss (excluding the effects of any firm-specific risk that has not been eliminated through diversification).

The calculation of a fund's historical beta requires the selection of a benchmark market index, and persons supporting the use of beta are asked to address how the benchmark should be selected and whether a single benchmark should be used for all funds. If a single benchmark should be selected, what should it be? If a single benchmark is not used, how should the lack of comparability of betas for funds using different benchmarks be addressed? Beta is generally used in connection with equity securities, and persons submitting comments are asked to address whether or not the use of beta should be limited to equity funds.

- Duration. Duration is a measure of the price sensitivity of a bond, or bond portfolio, to interest rate changes. There are different types of duration, and persons supporting the use of duration are asked to be specific regarding the duration measure that they support. Would so-called "modified duration," which can be interpreted as the percentage change in the price of a bond, or bond portfolio, for a 100 basis point change in yield, be particularly useful?

The use of duration has several limitations, and persons submitting comments are asked to address each of these. First, duration is only meaningful for bonds and portfolios of bonds and therefore cannot be used to measure the risk of equity funds and has limited applicability to balanced funds. Second, duration measures interest rate risk only and not other risks to which bonds are subject, e.g., credit risks and, in the case of non-dollar denominated bonds, currency risks. Third, duration is difficult to calculate precisely for bonds with prepayment options, e.g., mortgage-backed securities, because the calculation requires assumptions about prepayment rates. Fourth, bond value changes resulting from interest rate changes are sometimes poorly predicted by duration.

The SEC staff takes the position that, for a fund with a name or investment objective that refers to the maturity of the fund's portfolio, such as "short-term" or "long-term," the dollar-weighted average portfolio maturity of the portfolio must reflect that characterization. The SEC requests comment on whether, separate and apart from duration's potential use as a quantitative risk measure, a fund's name or investment objective that refers to the maturity of its portfolio should be required to be consistent with the fund's duration.

### 3. Risk-Adjusted Measures of Performance

Risk-adjusted measures of performance were developed in the 1960s to compare the quality of investment management. Three widely-used risk-adjusted measures are:

- Sharpe Ratio. Also known as the Reward-to-Variability Ratio, this is the ratio of a fund's average return in excess of the risk-free rate of return ("average excess return") to the standard deviation of the fund's excess returns. It measures the returns earned in excess of those that could have been earned on a riskless investment per unit of total risk assumed.

- Treynor Ratio. Also known as the Reward-to-Volatility Ratio, this is the ratio of a fund's average excess return to the fund's beta. It measures the returns earned in excess of those that could have been earned on a riskless investment per unit of market risk assumed. Unlike the Sharpe Ratio, the Treynor Ratio uses market risk (beta), rather than total risk (standard deviation), as the measure of risk.

- Jensen's Alpha. This is the difference between a fund's actual returns and those that could have been earned on a benchmark portfolio with the same amount of market risk, i.e., the same beta, as the portfolio. Jensen's Alpha measures the ability of active management to increase returns above those that are purely a reward for bearing market risk.

### B. General Issues

### 1. Benefits of Quantitative Risk Measures

Would quantitative risk measures, including risk-adjusted measures of performance, help investors to evaluate historical performance and investment management expertise? The SEC requires that fund prospectuses include standardized return information, even though past returns are not necessarily indicative of future returns. Persons submitting comments are asked to address whether quantitative disclosure of the risk level incurred to produce stated returns may provide investors with a better tool to understand past fund performance and management. Historical data could, for example, help investors distinguish among funds that have achieved comparable rates of return with significantly different levels of risk. Would it be helpful to investors for funds to present one or more risk measures together with fund performance data in the financial highlights table? Would a risk measure that covers the same periods currently required for reporting total returns in the financial highlights table in fund prospectuses or in mutual fund advertisements be useful to investors?

Would quantitative risk measures be useful to investors as indicators or guides to future fund risk levels, enhancing investors' ability to compare risks assumed by investing in different funds? The SEC requests any research related to the degree of correlation between historical measures of a fund's risk and expected future levels of risk.

### 2. Risk Measures Currently Used by Investment Companies

The SEC requests comment on whether quantitative risk measures that are currently used by investment companies for internal purposes, such as portfolio management, evaluation or compensation of portfolio managers, and reports by management to the board of directors, could be adapted for disclosure purposes. This approach could have two potential advantages: first, the measures currently used by investment companies presumably have been determined to be the most useful by fund managers, who are in the best position to understand and analyze fund risk; and, second, use of these measures for disclosure purposes should impose relatively small additional costs on funds. The SEC therefore requests that persons submitting comments identify which quantitative risk measures funds use internally and for what purposes.

The SEC also asks persons submitting comments to discuss the extent to which quantitative risk measures used by investment companies for internal purposes would be useful to investors. If such measures would not be useful to investors, why not? How might internal measures be adapted to avoid or overcome these problems?

### 3. Investor Understanding of Quantitative Risk Measures

Persons submitting comments are asked to discuss the difficulties that investors would face in properly interpreting various quantitative risk measures, such as understanding what aspects of risk are measured, the limits on predictive utility of risk measures, and the importance of investment time horizon in determining how much risk to assume. Are the difficulties significantly greater than those associated with the proper interpretation of yield and return figures? Is there a potential problem of investor over-reliance on quantitative risk measures, and, if so, what could be done to protect against such over-reliance?

Comments are also requested regarding which quantitative risk measures would be easiest for investors to use properly and how quantitative measures can be made more understandable to investors. One possibility is to provide some form of interpretation of raw numbers. For example, standard deviations could be divided by the standard deviation for some benchmark such as the S&P 500. Another possibility is to convert raw numbers into a classification scale, such as one to ten or "very low" to "very high" risk. Another possibility would be to represent the level of fund volatility graphically, rather than through computation of standard deviation. Would it be helpful, for example, if funds were required to include a bar graph showing total returns for each of the last 10 years to provide investors a picture of the extent to which annual returns varied over that period and the frequency with which the returns were negative or below some benchmark? . . . .

### 4. Historical Measures v. Portfolio-Based Measures v. Risk Objectives

There are three approaches to the use of quantitative risk measures: historical, portfolio-based, and risk objectives or targets.

The simple historical approach to quantitative risk measures is outlined in section III.A., above. This method generally uses actual past returns of a fund to compute a measure of risk for the fund. An alternative is a portfolio-based computation, which calculates a portfolio risk measure based on the particular securities in the portfolio as of a specified measurement date. This method, too, is historical in that the computation (i) uses the portfolio composition as of a specified measurement date, and (ii) the computation is based on historical behavior of the securities in the portfolio.

There are at least two important limitations of using portfolio-based measures for fund disclosure: first, a fund may be invested in newly introduced financial instruments that have little or no history, and for which historical behavior must be estimated, and, second, portfolio-based measures, which are derived from portfolio composition on one particular date, may be less representative of the risk of a managed portfolio over time than a simple historical measure derived from fund returns over a period of time.

The SEC seeks comment on whether the SEC should require funds generally to disclose portfolio-based risk measures.

The SEC also asks for comments on whether such measures could be useful for new funds that do not have sufficient operating history to make use of a simple historical measure meaningful, funds that change their investment objectives or policies, funds that change investment advisers or portfolio managers, or merged funds comprised of different funds with different operating histories and different past risk levels.

Another approach to risk measures is requiring funds to announce risk objectives or targets. Any of the risk and risk-adjusted performance measures could be used by funds in this manner. For example, a fund could announce its intention to follow a strategy that would yield a standard deviation of 10%-12% per year, a beta of 1.50-1.75 with respect to the S&P 500, or a duration of 7-9 years. Comments are requested regarding the relative merits of this approach as compared to the simple historical and portfolio-based approaches. Persons submitting comments are asked to address specifically the relative merits for funds with significant operating histories, new funds, funds that change their investment objectives or policies, funds that change investment advisers or portfolio managers, or merged funds comprised of different funds with different operating histories and different past risk levels. Persons supporting the use of simple historical measures by relatively new funds, funds that change their investment objectives or policies or their investment advisers or portfolio managers, or merged funds are also asked to address whether narrative disclosure should be required to explain the limits on the usefulness of the disclosure resulting from the funds' circumstances.

### 5. Computation Issues

Comments are requested on the following issues related to computation of quantitative risk measures and on any other relevant computation issues. What length of fund operating history is required to make particular historical risk measures useful? What requirements should be imposed on funds without this operating history? For example, if 18 months of operations are required to calculate a meaningful standard deviation figure, should funds that have been operating for less than 18 months be required to disclose the standard deviation of an appropriate market index or peer group of funds and explain any differences they expect between the fund's standard deviation and that of the index or peer group?

For risk measures that require the use of a benchmark market index, what issues, if any, are associated with the selection of an appropriate benchmark? How should the SEC address the need to use assumptions to calculate certain risk measures, such as the prepayment assumptions that may be required to calculate duration? Can various quantitative risk measures be manipulated and how do the various measures differ in their susceptibility to manipulation? How can the potential for such manipulation be reduced or eliminated? For instance, is there some combination of risk measures the SEC could require that would not be susceptible to simultaneous manipulation?

Persons submitting comments are also asked to describe as specifically as possible the computation method they would recommend for any quantitative risk measure they favor. For example, persons favoring standard deviation should specify whether monthly returns, quarterly returns, or returns over some other periods should be used. As another example, persons favoring beta should describe the benchmark or benchmarks that should be used. Persons submitting comments are also asked to discuss the benefits and limitations associated with their recommended method of computation.

### 6. Effects on Portfolio Management

The SEC recognizes that requiring disclosure of a quantitative risk measure may affect portfolio management, e.g., causing fund managers to adopt more conservative investment strategies. Comments are requested regarding whether, and how, disclosure of a quantitative risk measure might influence portfolio management and evaluating the associated benefits and detriments.

### 7. Third Party Providers of Quantitative Risk Information

The financial press and other third parties currently disseminate some quantitative information regarding fund risks. The available information includes measures such as those described in section III.A., including standard deviation, beta, and duration.[46] In addition, some organizations disseminate fund performance ratings that take risk into account [47] or fund risk ratings. [48] This data is made available either through reports and other documents published by the organizations that collect and calculate the measures or through periodicals and newspapers covering financial issues.

The SEC asks persons submitting comments to address the SEC's role with respect to disclosure of quantitative risk information in light of the availability of fund risk information from the financial press and other third parties. Is there, for example, helpful risk information that third party providers do not make available? Would SEC-required disclosure be important to ensure that all investors have access to some quantitative risk information and to help educate investors about the importance of such information? Would SEC-required disclosure be important to facilitate comparability among funds by ensuring that standardized quantitative risk information will be available for all funds? Would SEC-required disclosure of a quantitative risk measure be helpful wherever historic returns are reported to indicate to investors the risks incurred to generate those returns?

---

[46] See, e.g., CDA/Wiesenberger, Mutual Funds Update, Dec. 31, 1994; Morningstar Mutual Funds, Dec. 9, 1994; The Value Line Mutual Fund Survey, Part 2, Ratings & Reports, Feb. 21, 1995. Value Line also ranks mutual funds in five risk categories, based on historical standard deviation. How to Use The Value Line Mutual Fund Survey, A Subscriber's Guide (1994), at 4- 5.

[47] See, e.g., Business Week, Feb. 14, 1994, at 78-79; Forbes, Aug. 29, 1994, at 174; CDA/Wiesenberger, Investment Companies Yearbook 1994 441 (1994); Morningstar Mutual Fund Performance Report, Jan. 1995, at 3; How to Use The Value Line Mutual Fund Survey, A Subscriber's Guide (1994), at 4-5.

[48] These ratings are based on an analysis of factors such as currency, interest rate, liquidity, and mortgage prepayment risks; hedging; leverage; and the use of derivatives. See "Bond Fund Risks Revealed," Fitch Research Special Report, Oct. 17, 1994, at 1; Gary Arne, Standard & Poor's, CreditReview, Jan. 16, 1995, at 12.

Persons submitting comments are also asked to address whether the SEC should take any steps to facilitate the provision of fund risk information by the financial press and other third parties. For example, should the SEC require more frequent disclosure of fund portfolio holdings or more detailed descriptions of fund portfolio holdings to facilitate third party risk analyses? If so, what information should the SEC require funds to make available and with what frequency? The SEC is currently authorized to require funds to file with the SEC "such information * * * as the SEC may require, on a semi-annual or quarterly basis, to keep reasonably current the information and documents contained in the [funds' Investment Company Act of 1940] registration statement[s] * * *." [49] Persons submitting comments are asked to address whether statutory amendments would be required to implement any recommendations they make in response to this paragraph.

Last year, the SEC requested comment regarding whether it should encourage or require disclosure of third party fund risk ratings in prospectuses, sales literature, and advertisements.[50] Persons who wish to address that issue in the context of today's broad inquiry into improved risk disclosure are invited to do so.

## IV. Narrative Disclosure Options

The SEC asks for comment on the usefulness to investors of narrative risk disclosure currently found in prospectuses. The SEC also asks persons submitting comments to describe ways of improving narrative risk disclosure that will not increase, and may reduce, technical information that may be of limited utility to investors. For example, should prospectus disclosure focus on the broad investment strategies of a fund rather than the particular investments used to implement the strategy?

Can disclosure of fund risks be improved through increased focus on the policies and investments actually used by a fund as opposed to all permissible policies and investments? For example, should a fund describe the policies and investments that have been used during some prior period, such as the preceding year, or that the fund intends to use during some future period, such as the following year, and simply list the other permitted policies and investments? Or should funds be required to provide a table or grid that indicates whether, and the extent to which, the policies and investments authorized to be used were used during some prior period, such as the preceding year? If a fund intends to alter the mix of policies and investments, should it be required to describe the projected change? In addressing the questions of this paragraph, persons submitting comments should consider the possibilities of placing various information in the prospectus, annual report, and statement of additional information. For example, should the prospectus focus on the policies and investments the fund has actually made and that it may make in the reasonably foreseeable future, with the complete list of permissible investments and policies to be disclosed in the statement of additional information? As another example, should periodic reports be enhanced to include more information about what policies and investments the fund has, in fact, pursued and what risks were actually taken?

---

[49]    Investment Company Act § 30(b).

[50]    Nationally Recognized Statistical Rating Organizations, Securities Act Rel. No. 7085 (Aug. 31, 1994) [59 FR 46314 (Sept. 7, 1994)]. . . .

Can risks be accurately depicted through narrative disclosure apart from technical descriptions of particular types of investments? Would investors find it useful for funds to provide in their prospectuses a summary of the risk characteristics of the portfolio as a whole either in lieu of or in addition to disclosure of the characteristics of particular types of permissible investments? If a risk summary would be useful, what risks should it address? For example, should the SEC require a fund that invests a specified level, e.g., 5% or 10% or 25%, of its net assets in a particular manner, e.g., securities of non-U.S. companies, to discuss the related risks, e.g., exchange rate fluctuations?

A mutual fund's Management's Discussion of Fund Performance ("Management's Discussion"), contained in the prospectus or annual report, is currently required to discuss the factors, including the market conditions and the investment techniques and strategies, that materially affected the fund's performance during the previous fiscal year. The SEC requests comments regarding whether narrative risk disclosure can be improved through amendments to the requirements for the Management's Discussion. Should the SEC, for example, explicitly require the Management's Discussion to address the risks assumed during the previous fiscal year and the effects of those risks on fund performance? Should the requirement for the Management's Discussion be extended to money market funds? If the Management's Discussion is a useful vehicle for risk disclosure, how should disclosure be accomplished for closed-end funds, which are not subject to the Management's Discussion requirements?

## V. Self-Assessment of Risk

Another alternative upon which the SEC seeks comment is self-assessment by funds of their aggregate risk level. One approach might be to describe where the fund fits on a risk scale from low risk, for instance, a money market fund, to moderate risk, for instance, a growth and income fund investing in S&P 500 stocks and high quality bonds, to high risk, for instance, an emerging market fund. Some fund complexes currently place various funds within the complex on a risk scale, and the SEC requests comment on whether such an approach would be useful for comparing funds from different complexes. If risk self-assessment is used, should the SEC create a standard scale? Persons supporting an SEC-created scale are asked to describe specifically what that scale should be, with particular attention to designing the scale to promote a high degree of uniformity in funds' self-assessments. Persons who favor a self-assessment approach but not an SEC-created scale are asked to address how the approach will foster meaningful investor comparisons among funds.

Comments are also requested on whether funds should be required to provide self-assessments of their exposures to various types of risk, with the results presented in chart or table format. Bond funds, for example, might rate their interest rate risk, credit risk, prepayment risk, and currency risk on a scale of low to medium to high.

## VI. Risk Management Procedures

The disclosure options described in this Release have focused on improved disclosure of the level of risk incurred by a fund. Persons submitting comments are also asked to consider whether disclosure of fund risk management procedures should be required. Such disclosure could be narrative. For example, should funds be required to disclose the extent and nature of involvement by the board of directors in the risk management process? As another example, should funds describe the "stress-testing" they do to determine how the portfolio will behave in various market conditions? Alternately, such disclosure could be quantitative in format. For example, if the SEC requires disclosure of a quantitative risk objective or target, funds could be required to disclose the funds' actual risk level in subsequent periods and compare it with the previously-provided objective or target and explain the reasons for divergence.

## VII.  Liability Issues

Persons submitting comments are asked to address the appropriate scope of, and limits on, the liability of funds, investment advisers, and others for various risk disclosures. Persons submitting comments should specify any forms of risk disclosure that they believe raise particularly significant liability concerns, explain the concerns, and suggest means for mitigating the concerns.

## Comments and Questions

1.  What approach would you advise the SEC take with respect to risk disclosure for mutual funds?

2.  An interesting aspect of this concept release is the SEC's willingness to consider multiple approaches to the problem of risk regulation. Principally, the concept release explored disclosure-oriented solutions to the problem in an effort to find the proper balance between technical completeness and consumer comprehension. Note, however, that the release also outlines alternative solutions, including reliance on third-party information suppliers, director oversight, and liability rules. Do these other approaches offer more promising solutions to risk-regulation in mutual funds?

3.  In our study of depository institutions, we considered another fairly recent regulatory effort to regulate risk in financial intermediaries: risk-based capital requirements. How do the solutions discussed in this concept release compare to that regulatory regime? Could bank regulators learn something from the SEC on this score? Or do the banking agencies have a better framework for dealing with risk?

———————

Since promulgating its concept release on risk disclosure, Commission has pursued its efforts to improve the quality of risk disclosure through a series of related initiatives. In 1995 and 1996, the staff issued several no-action letters authorizing "profile" or abbreviated prospectuses, which included several experiments in risk disclosure. In addition, the Commission and several trade groups undertook a number of studies to learn more about how consumers actually use and understand disclosure documents. Following these initiatives, the commission issued the following proposal.

## Proposed Amendment to Mutual Fund Registration Form
### 62 Fed. Reg. 10,898-01 (Mar. 10, 1997)

The Securities and Exchange Commission ("Commission") is proposing for comment amendments to Form N-1A, the registration form used by open-end management investment companies ("funds") to register under the Investment Company Act of 1940 ("Investment Company Act") and to offer their shares under the Securities Act of 1933. . . .

### I. Introduction and Executive Summary

Over the last decade, the fund industry has experienced enormous growth both in total assets and in the number of funds. Today, fund assets exceed the deposits of commercial banks.[4] Coincident with the explosive growth of fund investments, the business operations of many funds have become increasingly complex as funds seek to offer investors new investment options and a wider variety of shareholder services. These factors, combined with new and more sophisticated fund investments, have resulted in fund prospectuses that often include long and complicated disclosure, as funds explain their operations, investments, and services to investors.

Many have criticized fund prospectuses, finding them unintelligible, tedious, and legalistic. Although the prospectus remains the most complete source of information about a fund, technical and unnecessarily lengthy prospectus disclosure often obscures important information relating to a fund investment and does not serve the information needs of the majority of fund investors.[6] As millions of Americans have turned to funds as an investment vehicle of choice, investors need to be provided with clear and comprehensible information that will help them evaluate and compare fund investments.

The Commission is committed to improving the disclosure provided to fund investors and is proposing two major initiatives to meet this objective. First, the Commission is proposing changes to fund disclosure requirements in an effort to focus prospectus disclosure on essential information about a particular fund that would assist an investor in deciding whether to invest in that fund.[9] Second, in a companion release, the Commission is proposing a new rule to permit

---

[4]     Compare ICI, Trends in Mutual Fund Investing: November 1996 at 3 (Dec. 1996) (ICI News No. ICI-96-107) (fund net assets exceeded $3.5 trillion as of Nov. 1996) with 82 Fed. Res. Bull. 12, table 1.21, at A13 (1996) (commercial bank deposits were approximately $2.5 trillion as of Sept. 1996).

[6]     A 1995 survey conducted on behalf of the Commission and the Office of the Comptroller of the Currency ("OCC") found that, although fund investors consulted the prospectus more than any other source of information about the fund they bought, they considered the prospectus only the fifth-best source of information, behind employer-provided written materials, financial publications, family or friends, and brokers. Report on the OCC/SEC Survey of Mutual Fund Investors 12-13 (June 26, 1996). See also ICI, The Profile Prospectus: An Assessment by Mutual Fund Shareholders 4 (1996) ("ICI Profile Survey") (about half of fund shareholders surveyed had not consulted a prospectus before making a fund investment).

[9]     As part of the improvements to prospectus disclosure, the Commission is proposing a new rule intended to address certain broad categories of investment company names that are likely to mislead

investors to buy fund shares based on a fund profile (the "profile") that would provide a summary of key information about a fund, including the fund's investment objectives, strategies, risks, performance, and fees. Under this proposal, investors would receive the fund's prospectus upon request or no later than with delivery of the purchase confirmation.

These two initiatives are intended to improve fund disclosure by requiring prospectuses to focus on information central to investment decisions, to provide new disclosure options for investors, and to enhance the comparability of information about funds. Taken together, the proposals seek to promote more effective communication of information about funds without reducing the amount of information available to investors.

As part of its commitment to give investors improved disclosure documents, the Commission recently proposed rule amendments to require the use of plain English principles in drafting prospectuses and to provide other guidance on improving the readability of prospectuses.[11] The Commission intends that the plain English initiatives serve as the standard for all disclosure documents, and the plain English proposals are an important counterpart of the proposed fund disclosure initiatives. If adopted, the plain English requirements would apply to fund prospectuses and the profile.

The Commission's efforts to improve fund disclosure are long-standing. In 1983, the Commission introduced an innovative approach to prospectus disclosure by adopting a two-part disclosure format. Under this format, the Commission intended that a fund would provide investors with a simplified prospectus designed to contain essential information about the fund that assists an investor in making an investment decision. The Commission contemplated that more extensive information and detailed discussions of matters included in the prospectus would be available in a Statement of Additional Information ("SAI") that investors could obtain upon request. In adopting this new format, the Commission's goal was to provide investors with more useful information in "a prospectus that is substantially shorter and simpler, so that the prospectus clearly discloses the fundamental characteristics of the particular investment company. . . ."

Since 1983, the Commission has adopted a number of other initiatives to improve fund disclosure, including a uniform fee table and a requirement for management's discussion of fund performance ("MDFP"). While these changes have provided investors with clear and helpful information about fund expenses and performance, they were not intended to address overall

---

investors about an investment company's investments and risks. The new rule would require funds and other registered investment companies with names suggesting a particular investment emphasis to invest at least 80% of their assets in the type of investment suggested by their name.

[11]    Securities Act Release No. 7380 (Jan. 14, 1997) (62 FR 3152) ("Plain English Release'). In conjunction with these proposals, the Commission's Office of Investor Assistance has issued a draft of A Plain English Handbook: How to Create Clear SEC Disclosure Documents to explain the plain English principles of the proposed amendments and other techniques for preparing clear disclosure documents. See also "Plain English: A Work in Progress," Remarks by Isaac C. Hunt, Commissioner, SEC, before the First Annual Institute on Mergers and Acquisition: Corporate, Tax, Securities, and Related Aspects, Key Biscayne, Fla. (Feb. 6, 1997).

prospectus disclosure requirements. The Commission has concluded that a comprehensive review and revision of fund disclosure requirements is necessary to improve the information provided in fund prospectuses.

The Commission's consideration of disclosure issues has included evaluating the use of the profile as a standardized, summary disclosure document. The Commission, with the cooperation of the Investment Company Institute ("ICI") and several large fund groups, conducted a pilot program permitting funds to use profiles ("pilot profiles") together with their prospectuses.[16] The pilot profiles (like the profile proposed today) contain a summary of key information about the fund. The program's purpose was to determine whether investors found the pilot profiles helpful in making investment decisions. Focus groups conducted on the Commission's behalf ("Focus Groups") responded very positively to the profile concept. Fund investors participating in a survey sponsored by the ICI also strongly favored the pilot profiles.

In another recent initiative, the Commission issued a release requesting comment on ways to improve risk disclosure and comparability of fund risk levels ("Risk Concept Release").[18] The Commission received over 3,700 comment letters, mostly from individual investors. Commenters confirmed the importance of risk disclosure to investors when evaluating and comparing funds and highlighted the need to improve prospectus disclosure of fund risks. In particular, commenters indicated that current risk disclosure is difficult to understand and does not fully convey to investors the risks associated with an investment in a fund.

The Commission remains committed to the same goals articulated in adopting Form N-1A. The initiatives proposed today are intended to further these goals and achieve clear and concise disclosure that would assist fund investors in making investment decisions. . . .

## II. Discussion

Release Organization. The revised Form would retain the overall structure of current Form N-1A. To make the proposed requirements of revised Form N-1A easy to follow and to highlight the proposed changes, this release addresses revised Items in the order that they would appear in the Form. While some Items in proposed Part A (the prospectus) would not be changed (except for technical revisions to improve clarity), other Items would be new or extensively revised. Certain disclosure currently required in the prospectus would be moved to Part B (the SAI), where the information would continue to be available to investors and others who are interested in the information.

---

[16] See Investment Company Institute (pub. avail. July 31, 1995) ("1995 Profile Letter"). The Division of Investment Management (the "Division") has permitted the pilot program, with some modifications, to continue for another year. See Investment Company Institute (pub. avail. July 29, 1996) ("1996 Profile Letter"). The Division also has permitted variable annuity registrants to use "variable annuity profiles" together with their prospectuses. National Association for Variable Annuities (pub. avail. June 4, 1996).

[18] Investment Company Act Release No. 20974 (Mar. 29, 1995) (60 FR 17172).

A. Part A -- Information in the Prospectus

1. Item 1 -- Front and Back Cover Pages

Form N-1A requires certain information to appear on the outside front cover page of a fund's prospectus. In an effort to "unclutter" the prospectus cover page and avoid repeating information contained in the proposed risk/return summary at the beginning of the prospectus, the proposed amendments would simplify the disclosure currently required on the front cover page and require certain information to be included on the outside back cover page.

The front cover page would be required to include a fund's name. The front cover page also would include the disclaimer about the Commission's approval of the securities being offered and the accuracy and adequacy of the information included in the prospectus. The wording of the disclaimer would be simplified and the disclaimer would no longer be required to be in large capital letters and bold-faced type.

The proposed amendments would not require cover page disclosure that would repeat information required to be disclosed in the proposed risk/return summary. This information would include the identification of the type of fund offered (or a brief statement of the fund's investment objectives) and certain disclosure required for money market funds. The proposed amendments also would no longer require a fund to provide statements that the prospectus sets forth concise information about the fund that a prospective investor ought to know before investing and should be retained for future reference. These statements do not appear to be particularly helpful to investors.

The proposed amendments would consolidate disclosure regarding the availability of additional information about a fund on the back cover page of the fund's prospectus. The back cover page would include disclosure about the availability and date of the SAI, which would be revised to require a telephone number that investors could use to obtain the SAI without charge. To ensure prompt delivery of the SAI to those investors who request it, a new Instruction would require a fund to send the SAI within 3 days of the receipt of a request. The back cover page would include information (if applicable) regarding the incorporation by reference of a fund's SAI or financial information from the annual report into the prospectus and disclosure that other information about the fund has been filed with, and is available from, the Commission.[40] The back cover page also would include disclosure about how a shareholder can make inquires about the fund.

2. Item 2 -- Risk/Return Summary: Investments, Risks, and Performance

The proposed amendments would require at the beginning of every prospectus a risk/return summary that would provide key information about a fund's investment objectives, principal strategies, risks, performance, and fees. This information would be required to appear in a specific sequence and to be presented in a question-and-answer format. The proposed question-

---

[40]    The disclosure would be revised to indicate, among other things, that information about the fund (including the SAI) is available on the Commission's Internet Web site. Currently, only funds that disseminate prospectuses electronically are required to provide disclosure about the Commission's Web site. See Investment Company Act Release No. 21946 (May 9, 1996) (61 FR 24652).

and-answer format, frequently used by many funds, is intended to help communicate the required information effectively. The Commission requests comment on this format and whether funds instead should be permitted to choose the type of heading for the prescribed disclosure topics.

The risk/return summary, like the profile, is intended to respond to investors' strong preference for summary information about a fund in a standardized format.[43] Since the profile would be optional, the proposed risk/return summary in the prospectus would provide all investors with key information about a fund in a standardized, easily accessible place that could be used to evaluate and compare fund investments.

a. Investment Objectives and Principal Strategies

The proposed amendments would require a fund to disclose in the risk/return summary its investment objectives and to summarize, based on the information provided in the prospectus, how the fund intends to achieve those objectives. The summary would be required to identify the fund's principal investment strategies, including the particular types of securities in which the fund invests or will invest principally, and any policy of the fund to concentrate in an industry or group of industries.

A fund also would be required to inform investors about the availability of additional information about the fund's investments in the fund's shareholder reports. Fund annual reports typically include the MDFP, which discusses a fund's strategies that materially affected the fund's performance during the most recent fiscal year. The Division's review of and experience with MDFP disclosure indicates that the annual report may be a valuable resource for investors. The proposed amendments would require the risk/return summary to contain disclosure to the following effect:

Additional information about the fund's investments is available in the fund's annual and semi-annual reports to shareholders. In particular, the fund's annual report discusses the relevant market conditions and investment strategies used by the fund's investment adviser that materially affected the fund's performance during the last fiscal year. You may obtain these reports at no cost by calling _____.[47]

The proposed amendments would require this disclosure to appear in the context of information about a fund's investments. The Commission requests comment on this approach. For example, would disclosure about the availability of additional information about the fund

---

[43]   Focus Group participants, for example, expressed strong support for summary information in a standardized format. In addition, in connection with the profile initiative, many individual investors have written to the Commission about the need for concise, summary information relating to a fund. See also Profile Prospectuses: An Idea Whose Time Has Come, Mutual Funds Magazine, Aug. 1996, at 11. In keeping with the goal of providing key information in a standardized summary, proposed General Instruction C.2(b) would not permit a fund to include in the risk/return summary information that is not required or otherwise permitted.

[47]   If applicable, a fund could indicate that its annual and semi-annual reports are available on its Internet site or by E-mail. In addition, a fund that provides its MDFP in the prospectus or a money market fund (which is not required to prepare a MDFP) would omit the second sentence of this disclosure.

(e.g., the fund's shareholder reports, SAI, or any other information) be more helpful to investors if the disclosure was presented under a separate caption in the risk/return summary or on the back cover page of the prospectus? Should this disclosure include an explanation about the various types of information available to investors?

### b. Risks

Narrative Risk Disclosure.  The proposed amendments would require a fund to summarize the principal risks of investing in the fund based on the information provided in the prospectus. More than 75% of the individual investors commenting on the Risk Concept Release specifically favored requiring a risk summary in fund prospectuses. This disclosure would be required to focus on the risks to which the fund's particular portfolio as a whole is subject and the circumstances reasonably likely to affect adversely the fund's net asset value, yield, and total return. The risk section of the risk/return summary also would include disclosure about the risk of losing money and identify the types of investors for whom the fund may be an appropriate or inappropriate investment (based on, for example, an investor's risk tolerance and time horizon).[50] A fund, at its option, could discuss in the risk section the potential rewards of investing in the fund as long as the discussion provides a balanced presentation of the fund's risks and rewards.[51]

Special Risk Disclosure Requirements.  Certain types of funds are required to provide special disclosure on the cover page of their prospectuses.  Form N-1A requires a money market fund to disclose on the cover page of its prospectus that an investment in the fund is neither insured nor guaranteed by the U.S. Government, and that there can be no assurance that the fund will be able to maintain a stable net asset value of $1.00 per share. The Form requires a tax-exempt money market fund that concentrates its investments in a particular state (a "single state money market fund") to disclose that the fund may invest a significant percentage of its assets in a single issuer and that investing in the fund may be riskier than investing in other types of money market funds.  The disclosure required for all money market funds is intended to alert investors that investing in a money market fund is not without risk. [The disclosure required for single state money market funds seeks to inform investors about the particular risks associated with a single state money market fund and to distinguish these funds from other money market funds.   In addition, a fund that is advised by or sold through a bank is required to disclose on the cover page of its prospectus that the fund's shares are not deposits or obligations of, nor guaranteed or endorsed by, the bank, and that the shares are not insured by the Federal Deposit Insurance

---

[50]     Information about whether a fund is appropriate for particular types of investors is designed to help investors evaluate and compare funds based on their investment goals and individual circumstances.  In the pilot profiles, this information is presented under a separate caption relating to the appropriateness of an investment for certain investors.  Because this information is closely related to the risks of investing in a fund, the proposed amendments would integrate this disclosure into the risk section of the risk/return summary.

[51]     The 1996 Profile Letter, in contrast, permits disclosure about the rewards of investing in a fund only if presented separately from disclosure about the fund's risks.  1996 Profile Letter, supra note 16, at 2.

Corporation ("FDIC") or any other government agency. This disclosure is intended to alert investors that funds advised by or sold through banks are not federally insured.[57] . . . .

Risk/Return Bar Chart and Table.  The proposed amendments would require a bar chart showing a fund's annual returns for each of the last 10 calendar years and a table comparing the fund's average annual returns for the last one, five, and ten fiscal years to those of a broad-based securities market index. The bar chart would illustrate graphically a fund's past risks by showing changes in the fund's returns over time.  The information in the table would enable investors to evaluate a fund's performance and risks relative to "the market." Over 75% of individual investors responding to the Risk Concept Release favored a bar chart presentation of fund risks.[61]  Focus Group participants found both a bar chart and tabular presentation of fund performance helpful in evaluating and comparing fund investments, particularly when the table included return information for a broad-based index.

The proposed amendments would require the bar chart and table to be included in the risk section of the risk/return summary under a subheading that refers to both risk and performance.[62] To help investors use the information in the bar chart and table, the proposed amendments would require a fund to explain how the information illustrates the fund's risks and performance.

An example of the risk/return bar chart and table is set forth below:

---

[57]   See Division Bank Letter, supra note 56.  See also Testimony of Ricki Helfer, Chairman, FDIC, on FDIC Survey of Nondeposit Investment Sales at FDIC-Insured Institutions Before the Subcomm. on Capital Markets, Securities, and Government Sponsored Enterprises of the House Comm. on Banking and Financial Services, 104th Cong., 2d Sess. (June 26, 1996) (citing surveys in October 1995 and April 1996 indicating that approximately one-third of bank customers either thought that, or did not know whether, funds sold through banks were insured).

[61]   Risk Concept Release, supra note 18.  See also ICI Risk Survey, supra note 26, at 21, 37 (51% of survey participants indicated they were very confident about using a bar chart to compare the risks of different funds and 49% of survey participants indicated they were very confident in using a bar chart to assess the risks of a single fund).  In addition, all commenters responding to the Commission's initiative to simplify money market fund prospectuses supported the proposal to replace the financial highlights information in money market fund prospectuses with a ten-year bar chart reflecting a money market fund's returns.  See Summary of Comment Letters on Proposed Amendments to the Rules Regulating Money Market Fund Prospectuses Made in Response to Investment Company Act Release No. 21216, at 2 (File No. S7-21-95) ("Money Market Prospectus Comment Summary").

[62]   The 1996 Profile Letter, in contrast, requires the bar chart and table to appear under a caption relating to a fund's past performance.  1996 Profile Letter, supra note 16, at 2.

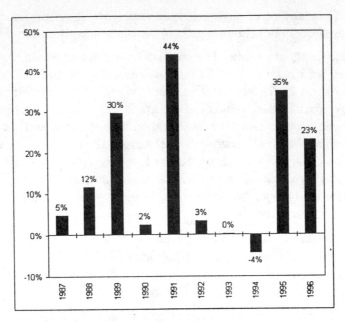

An example of the risk/return bar chart

Bar Chart Return Information.[63]  The proposed amendments would require the bar chart to reflect annual returns for a fund's last 10 calendar years.[64]  Requiring calendar year returns is intended to help investors compare the risks of different funds over similar time periods.

A fund would calculate the annual returns in the bar chart by using the same method required for calculating annual returns in the financial highlights information included in fund prospectuses. Like the returns in the financial highlights information, the returns in the bar chart would not reflect sales loads.  Sales loads can be accurately and fairly reflected in return

---

[63]    Funds generally file Form N-1A electronically on the Commission's electronic data gathering analysis and retrieval system ("EDGAR").  Although EDGAR currently does not reproduce graphic images like the bar chart, the EDGAR rules require a fair and accurate narrative description or tabular presentation in the place of any omitted material.  Rule 304(a) of Regulation S-T (17 CFR 232.304(a)). The Commission anticipates future modifications that would permit EDGAR to reflect graphic images on electronically-filed documents.

[64]    A fund also would be required to present the corresponding numerical return next to each bar. The proposed amendments would require a fund to have at least one calendar year of returns before including the bar chart. A fund that includes a single bar in the bar chart or a fund that does not include the bar chart because the fund does not have annual returns for a full calendar year would be required to modify, as appropriate, the narrative explanation accompanying the bar chart and table (e.g., by stating that the information shows the fund's risks and performance by comparing the fund's performance to a broad measure of market performance).  The proposed amendments would require the bar chart of a fund in operation for fewer than 10 years to include annual returns for the life of the fund.

information of the type contained in the table by deducting sales loads at the beginning (or end) of particular periods from a hypothetical initial fund investment.[65]  Reflecting sales loads in the bar chart, however, may be impracticable.  In addition, reflecting the payment of sales loads may be less important in the bar chart than in the table, since the bar chart is intended primarily to depict fund risks graphically.  The proposed amendments would require a fund that charges sales loads to disclose that sales loads are not reflected in the bar chart and that if the loads were included, returns would be less than those shown.

The Commission requests comment on the proposed bar chart.  In particular, the Commission requests comment whether the bar chart communicates information about fund risks effectively or whether the bar chart has limitations that detract from its usefulness.[68]  The Commission requests comment whether the bar chart should include return information for additional or different time periods.  For example, should the bar chart reflect return information for shorter time periods (e.g., calendar quarters) or longer time periods (e.g., for the life of the fund when more than 10 years)?  The Commission also requests comment whether the return information in the bar chart should include sales loads and, specifically, how sales loads could be accurately and fairly reflected.

Bar Chart Presentation for More than One Fund.  The proposed amendments would not limit the number of funds for which return information could be included in a single bar chart.  While the proposed approach would give funds flexibility in preparing the bar chart, including return information in a single bar chart for a number of funds could make the graphic presentation of the bar chart complex and difficult to follow.[69]  Bar charts included in the pilot profiles reflect information for only one fund.[70]  In addition, Focus Group participants found prototype bar charts that included information for 6 funds (i.e., 6 bars per year) to be confusing.  The Commission requests comment whether the number of funds that could be included in a single bar chart should be limited to one fund or to some other number of funds (e.g., 2, 4, or no more than 6 funds).  This approach could enhance the clarity of the bar chart presentation.  Limiting the number of funds that could be included in a single bar chart, however, could require a prospectus offering several funds to include more than one chart, which, in turn, could complicate bar chart disclosure and lengthen the prospectus.

---

[65]  As a consequence, the fund's average annual returns in the table would reflect the payment of sales loads (if any).

[68]  See, e.g., Remarks by Steven M.H. Wallman, Commissioner, SEC, before the ICI's 1995 Investment Company Directors Conference and New Directors Workshop, Washington, DC. (Sept. 22, 1995) (discussing circumstances when a bar chart's presentation of fund risks may be confusing to investors, such as when bar charts use different scales).

[69]  See, e.g., Remarks by Steven M.H. Wallman, Commissioner, SEC, before the ICI's 1995 Investment Company Directors Conference and New Directors Workshop, Washington, DC. (Sept. 22, 1995) (discussing circumstances when a bar chart's presentation of fund risks may be confusing to investors, such as when bar charts use different scales).

[70]  See 1995 Profile Letter, supra note 16 (permitting the pilot profiles to include disclosure for a single fund or series of a fund).

Multiple Class Funds.  In contrast to the proposed approach with respect to the bar chart presentation for funds, the proposed amendments would require a multiple class fund to include annual return information in the bar chart for only one class. Unlike individual funds, classes represent interests in the same investment portfolio, and the returns of each class differ only to the extent the classes do not have the same expenses.  Including return information for all classes appears to be unnecessary to illustrate the risks of investing in the fund.  In addition, the proposed amendments would require the table accompanying the bar chart to provide return information for each class so that investors would be able to identify and compare the performance of the classes offered in the prospectus.

The proposed amendments would require the bar chart to reflect annual return information for the class offered in the prospectus that has returns for the longest period over the last 10 years. This approach is intended to provide the greatest amount of information about changes in the fund's returns.  When two or more classes have returns for at least 10 years or returns for the same period but fewer than 10 years, the fund would be required to provide annual returns for the class with the greatest net assets as of the end of the most recent calendar year.  Focusing on the class with the greatest net assets is intended to provide returns in the bar chart for a "representative" class offered in the prospectus.

The proposed requirements may result in including returns in the bar chart for a class that has lower annual operating expenses (and better performance) than other classes offered in the prospectus. The Commission considered several other approaches, including requiring a fund to show returns in the bar chart for the class with the highest annual operating expenses.  The Commission has not proposed these alternatives because they would make the bar chart requirements too complex and difficult to apply.  In addition, the bar chart primarily is designed to show graphically the risks of investing in a fund and not the costs of investing in the fund.  The Commission requests comment whether the bar chart presentation for multiple class funds should be limited to one class.  If so, should the selection of the class be made on a basis other than that proposed?

Tabular Presentation of Fund and Index Returns.  The proposed amendments would require the table accompanying the bar chart to present the fund's average annual returns for the last one, five, and ten fiscal years (or for the life of the fund, if shorter) and to compare that information to the returns of a broad-based securities market index.[73] Requiring comparative return information for a broad-based securities market index would provide investors with a basis for evaluating a fund's performance and risks relative to the market.  The proposed approach also would be consistent with the line graph presentation of fund performance required in MDFP disclosure.

---

[73]    A fund's average annual returns would be calculated using the same method required to calculate fund performance included in advertisements, which reflects the payment of sales loads and recurring shareholder account fees. . . .   Consistent with the preparation of the MDFP line graph, if a fund has not had the same adviser for the last 10 years, the fund would be permitted to begin the bar chart and performance information in the table on the date the new adviser began to provide advisory services to the fund so long as certain conditions are met.

| Average Annual Total Returns (for the periods ending December 31, 1996) | Past One Year | Past 5 Years | Past 10 Years |
|---|---|---|---|
| XYZ Stock Fund | 23.2% | 11.5% | 15% |
| S & P 500 | 20.26% | 12.87% | 12.58% |

Consistent with the requirements for preparing the MDFP line graph, the proposed amendments would allow a fund to include return information for other indexes, including a "peer group" index of comparable funds.[74] Focus Group participants indicated that comparing fund returns to a broad-based securities market index and a peer group index could be useful in evaluating and comparing fund investments.[76]

The Commission believes that a comparison of a fund's performance to a broad-based securities market index can assist investors in evaluating the risk of a fund investment. The proposed amendments would include this information in the table accompanying the bar chart to minimize the complexity of the graphic presentation of a fund's risks and returns. The Commission recognizes that other presentations could improve fund risk disclosure and requests comment on alternative approaches. Specifically, the Commission requests comment on requiring the annual returns of a broad-based securities market index (and any optional peer group or other index) to appear in the bar chart instead of the table. By providing investors with a graphic illustration of the relationship between the returns of the fund and the index(es), this approach could help investors evaluate the comparative risk of the fund and the index(es). Including additional bars or lines for index comparisons in the bar chart, however, could complicate the chart (especially if the chart included return information for more than one fund) and make it difficult for investors to follow.

As an alternative to, or in addition to the bar chart, the Commission requests comment on requiring a fund to show its highest and lowest annual returns (or "range" of returns) over a ten-year or other period compared with the same information for a broad-based market index (and any optional peer group or other index). This information, which could be presented as a separate

---

[74]   If an additional index is included, the fund would be required to discuss the additional index in the narrative explanation accompanying the bar chart and table. . . .

[76]   Other commenters have suggested different ways to provide comparative return information. See Letter from John C. Bogle, Chairman of the Board, The Vanguard Group, to Jonathan G. Katz, Secretary, SEC, at 3 (July 28, 1995) (File No. S7-10-95) (recommending disclosure of fund and market index returns on a quarterly basis over a 10-year period); Letter from Daniel Pierce, Chairman of Board, Scudder, Stevens & Clark, Inc., to Jonathan G. Katz, Secretary, SEC, at 2 (July 28, 1995) (recommending that a fund's returns be compared to both a benchmark index (e.g., the S&P 500) and a risk-free measure (e.g., the yield on 3-month U.S. Treasury bills)) . . . .

table or included in the proposed table showing a fund's average annual returns, could help investors assess fund risks.

## Comments and Questions

1. What do you think of the Commission's proposed approach to risk disclosure? How does it compare to your own reaction to the concept release?

2. The SEC's proposal discusses in passing a companion release on "fund profiles," summary documents of one or two pages that would including key information about a fund's investment strategies, risks, performance, and fees in a concise, standardized form. Investors could purchase fund shares based solely on a review of a fund profile, but would receive a full prospectus with the confirmation of purchase, usually delivered several days after the date of the investment. See SEC Proposed New Disclosure Option for Open-End Management Investment Companies, Release No. 33-7399, 1997 WL 87359 (Feb. 27, 1997). Do you think the profile prospectus is a good idea? If so, was the staff correct in imposing the limits it did on the profile's use. Should investors be permitted to purchase mutual fund shares without receiving a complete fund prospectus? Is it realistic to expect investors to read a full prospectus once they have obtained a profile outlining the highlights of that prospectus? Is the level of risk information included in the profile prospectus adequate?

### Problem 13-7

Suppose the SEC adopts its rule authorized fund profiles and suppose further that Complex Advisers distributes a profile for its Major Stock Fund, including bar graphs and tables similar to those illustrated in the preceding release. Based solely on a review of the fund profile, John Smith invests $10,000 in the Major Stock Fund. Three months later, the Dow Jones industrial average drops 2000 points, and a quarter of the Major Stock Fund shareholders seek to redeem their shares. At the time of these withdrawals, Major Stock Fund's assets were fully invested in the stock market. (That is, its cash reserves were very low; much lower, in fact, that those of most other funds.) This lack of liquidity forced the fund to liquidate a substantial number of its stock holdings. Shortly thereafter, the market recovered the 2000 points lost in the crash. John Smith did not sell his shares in the aftermath of the crash, but he did incur substantial capital gain taxes as a result of the forced sales. In addition, he suspects that the NAV calculations at the end of each day during the course of the crash were too high, thereby entitling withdrawing shareholders to a disproportionate large share of fund assets. The fund profile Smith received included no disclosures regarding the fund's low level of liquidity nor did it explain, in any detail, the impact that a market crash could have on fund shareholders. (The fund prospectus and other public documents did present a complete statement of the fund's cash reserves, which did not change materially between the date of Smith's investment and the time of the crash.) From whom, if anyone, can Smith seek recovery for his losses?

## B. Disclosure Problems in Closed-End Companies

We now turn our attention to additional disclosure issues involving closed-end investments companies. Here we consider two readings. The first is an excerpt from an SEC proposal to change the disclosure requirement for closed-end investment companies., along with a separate statement of Commissioner (now Stanford Law Professor) Grundfest exploring some of the issues underlying the proposal. The second reading is a recent case challenging the quality of disclosures in a closed-end company sponsored by a well-known fund family.

## Proposed Amendments to Registration Form for Closed-end Management Investment Companies
## 53 Fed. Reg. 32,993-01 (Aug. 11, 1989)

Form N-2 is the registration form used by closed-end funds to register as investment companies under the 1940 Act and to register their securities under the 1933 Act. Unlike open-end management investment companies ("mutual funds"), closed-end funds do not issue redeemable securities or continuously offer their shares to the public. Rather, a closed-end fund issues, in a traditional underwritten offering, a fixed number of shares that are subsequently traded on a securities exchange or in the over-the-counter market at a price determined by the market, which typically is lower than the share's net asset value. Another distinction between closed-end funds and mutual funds is that the 1940 Act permits a closed-end fund to issue senior securities consisting of one class of preferred stock and one class of debt. However, a closed-end fund is much like a mutual fund in that it offers to investors an opportunity to invest in a professionally managed portfolio of securities. Therefore, closed-end funds usually serve as investment vehicles for individual investors who do not have the expertise or resources to assemble and manage a diversified investment portfolio. . . . .

[T]he Commission is proposing to require prominent disclosure on the cover of a prospectus used during an initial offering stating that the Registrant's securities have no history of public trading, and describing the tendency of closed-end funds frequently to trade in the secondary market at a price below net asset value and their offering price and the risk of loss this creates for those investors purchasing shares in the initial offering. A study recently completed by the Commission's Office of Economic Analysis demonstrates that a substantial decrease in the value of shares quite often occurs shortly after the initial offering. While some of the decrease is due to the sales load, there appears to be, in many instances, a further reduction in share value below net asset value that cannot be explained by the sales load. The significance of this decrease and the likelihood of its occurrence shortly after an initial offering of closed-end fund shares makes this material information that an investor would want to know before investing.

Comment is requested on whether funds should be permitted to develop appropriate disclosure describing the risks associated with closed-end fund discounts, as contemplated by the proposed item, or whether the Commission should require specific disclosure in the form of a prescribed legend describing the discount phenomenon and, if so, what the prescribed legend should be. Commenters are asked to weigh the advantages and disadvantages of a standardized legend with those of providing some flexibility to funds in this area. If funds are permitted to develop their own disclosure, they must, of course, describe the frequency of closed-end fund discounts in a non-misleading manner. Disclosure creating the impression that closed-end fund shares are as likely to trade at a premium as at a discount would not be adequate. Comment also is requested on whether disclosure of the type proposed would sufficiently inform investors of the risks associated with closed-end fund discounts or whether additional, or different requirements should be prescribed and, if so, what those requirements should be. For example, to further investor understanding of the discount from the offering price attributable to underwriting commissions, should consideration also be given to requiring that confirmations for sales of securities of closed-end funds in the initial offering disclose these amounts as sales loads.

The Commission recognizes that prospectus disclosure may not be useful to persons who make a decision to purchase prior to receiving a prospectus. Accordingly, the Commission requests comment with respect to current industry practice by brokers in disclosing the discount risk to customers. In addition, how should brokers consider the discount risk in making determinations whether to solicit or otherwise recommend closed-end funds See Hanly v. SEC, 415 F.2d 589, 597 (2d Cir. 1969) (broker-dealer "cannot recommend a security unless there is an adequate and reasonable basis for such recommendation"). What effect, if any, would prominent prospectus disclosure have on brokers' sales practices with respect to closed-end funds? What is the responsibility of brokers who sell closed-end funds to disclose the discount risk to their customers? Finally, comment is requested on whether the discount disclosure requirements for closed-end bond funds should be different from those for equity funds. [31] . . . .

Separate Statement of Commissioner Grundfest

Among the recommendations proposed for comment is the suggestion that the Commission require the addition of a "warning label" to prospectuses for some or all closed-end fund initial public offerings ("IPOs"). This notion raises intriguing questions about the probable effectiveness of cautionary legends in initial public offerings of closed-end funds. In particular, if investors rely predominantly on the recommendation of brokers when making the decision to purchase shares of a closed-end fund IPO, then the addition of a cautionary legend may not change observed behavior unless the legend also changes broker behavior.

But will broker behavior change? That question is not addressed in the Commission's release. A careful consideration of that issue requires an analysis of the process by which closed-end fund IPOs are sold, and it is to that process that I now turn.

---

[31]    The study found that bond funds trade at a negligible discount after 120 trading days. Id. However, one expert has found that bond funds have, over the past ten years, traded at a discount of 3.96%. See Herzfeld, The People's Choice: Money Still Pouring In to Closed-End Funds, Barron's, May 16, 1988, at 55. The Commission is proposing to require the disclosure on the cover of all closed-end fund prospectuses, including bond funds, since there is an immediate decrease in the value of an investor's investment.

The observation that closed-end domestic equity funds tend to trade at a discount from net asset value is hardly new.[3]  The academic literature is replete with studies that document the pervasiveness and persistence of these discounts.[4]  The popular press has also frequently informed the public that shares of closed-end domestic equity funds tend to trade at substantial discounts.[5]

Viewed from this perspective, the major contribution of the Office of Economic Analysis' recent study of closed-end funds is not to discover that closed-end domestic equity funds trade at a discount.  We already know that.  Instead, the contribution of the OEA study is to document the path followed by the prices of recently offered closed-end domestic equity fund shares as they decline from their initial offering price, which reflects net asset value plus a sales load, to their aftermarket price, which reflects a discount from net asset value.  The OEA Study, which is based on data drawn from 1985-1987 market experience, finds that after 24 weeks closed-end domestic equity funds trade, on average, at a discount of approximately ten percent.  Beyond this point, there appears to be no systematic change in the size of the discount on closed-end domestic equity funds.

This large body of empirical evidence raises some intriguing questions about the IPO market for closed-end domestic equity funds.  In particular, if an investor has a choice between purchasing shares of a closed-end domestic equity fund in its IPO and purchasing shares of the same fund in the aftermarket, the aftermarket purchase is clearly preferable.  The reason for this conclusion is simple:  if a closed-end fund is a good investment at an offering price of, say, $10.50, then it is that much of a better buy in the aftermarket at a price of $9.00 where the same shares are soon trading at a discount from net asset value.[6]

This observation suggests, however, that no new closed-end domestic equity funds could ever successfully bc brought to market because no one would ever want to purchase shares of those funds in the IPO. Investors would, instead, prefer to acquire those same shares in the

---

[3]     This separate statement focuses solely on discounts observed among closed-end domestic equity funds because the available evidence suggests that these discounts are more pronounced and systematic than discounts observed in connection with other closed-end funds. See The Post-Offering Price Performance of Closed-End Funds, Study by the Office of Economic Analysis, Securities and Exchange Commission, at 4, 11-12, 14-15, 27-28   (July 21, 1989) (hereafter cited as "OEA Study").

[4]     For example, Kraakman, Taking Discounts Seriously:  The Implications of "Discounted" Share Prices as an Acquisition Motive, 88 Col. L. Rev. 891, 903 n.39 (1988) . . . .

[5]     See Closed-End Funds' Crop Thins Out, Wall St. J., Apr. 28, 1989, at C1- C2;  Closed-End Funds are Easy Targets.  N.Y. Times, Apr. 14, 1989, at D6;  Five-Month Fizzles -- What Lots of Closed-End IPOs Are, Barrons, Aug. 8, 1988, at 21-22;  Patience, Sir, Forbes, Nov. 2, 1987, at 81.

[6]     Of course, this assumes that the net asset value of the fund does not increase so quickly that the investor winds up earning a profit even after the fund trades at a discount.  Given the magnitude of discounts and the probability of such significant run-ups in net asset value during the immediate aftermarket, the assumption implicit in the text seems quite reasonable.

secondary market where a discount prevails.[7]  This characterization of the market obviously does not accurately describe reality because we in fact observe successful IPOs of closed-end funds that rapidly and systematically trade to significant discounts.

One possible explanation for the successful marketing of closed-end fund IPOs is that fully informed investors believe that each new fund is sufficiently different from its predecessors that it will not trade to a discount even though its predecessors have.  This explanation, which relies on the systematic triumph of hope over experience, seems sufficiently implausible that it can readily be dismissed as an explanation of the behavior of fully informed, rational investors.

A second and probably more accurate explanation for the successful initial public offering of closed-end domestic equity funds relies on the observation that investors can be divided into two categories that, for want of a better label, can be called "smart enough" and "not smart enough."[8]  Investors who are "smart enough" know that initial public offerings of closed- end domestic equity funds quickly trade to a discount.  These investors never purchase in the IPO.  Investors who are "not smart enough" are unaware of the prevalence of closed-end fund discounts and, unless specifically warned, can be persuaded to purchase shares of a closed-end equity fund in an initial public offering.

It should be emphasized that investors who, for purposes of this analysis, fall into the "not smart enough" category can be extraordinarily intelligent, indeed, brilliant in other endeavors.  For example, a professor of engineering who is well versed in the solution of partial differential equations that are far beyond the comprehension of the average stockbroker can be totally oblivious of the empirical evidence that closed-end domestic equity fund IPOs quickly trade to a discount.  Life is complicated and nobody can know everything.

In this context, an IPO of an equity fund can succeed if investors who are  "not smart enough" can be persuaded to purchase all the shares offered in the IPO.  Indeed, compounding this problem is the fact that brokers who sell closed- end domestic equity fund shares earn greater compensation than brokers who sell the same number of fund shares in the aftermarket.[9]  If a

---

[7]    Put another way, the public offering of a closed-end domestic equity fund's shares is analogous to a back-end loaded two-tier offer.  The front-end is composed of the higher priced IPO shares.  The back-end is composed of the lower priced aftermarket shares.  Because rational, fully informed investors have no incentive to participate in the front-end of such offers, back-end loaded two-tier offers cannot succeed in markets composed of rational, fully informed investors.

[8]    The finance literature contains several examples of models in which some investors are better informed than others. See, e.g., Black, Noise, 41 J. Fin. 529 (1986);  De Long, Shleifer, Summers & Waldmann, The Size and Incidence of the Losses From Noise Trading, 44 J. Fin. 681 (1989).

[9]    "Fund specialists say brokers can make $200 on a typical $10,000 closed- end offering, compared with $75 for a similar fund already trading in the secondary market." Caution Urged for Closed-End Fund Investors, Wall St. J., March 22, 1988, at 37.  See also Burnt Offerings:  Closed-End Funds Bring No Blessings to Shareholders, Barrons, Aug. 10, 1987, at 6-7, 32-26.

Because a broker's income is higher if he sells a fund's shares in the IPO than in the

broker is willing to put his interest in commission income ahead of his client's best financial interests, then such a broker might recommend a closed-end IPO purchase to a client who is "not smart enough." Such agency problems are hardly rare in our modern economy.[10]

Interestingly, the available data tend to support a characterization of the closed-end IPO market as one characterized by a subpopulation of investors who are "not smart enough." It seems that institutional investors, whose funds are typically managed by market professionals, tend to avoid closed-end fund IPOs.[11] Thus, institutional investors may tend to be "smart enough" to avoid closed-end domestic equity fund IPOs while the population of investors who are "not smart enough" is drawn from the ranks of retail investors.

Data from January 1988 through May 1989, a period subsequent to that studied in the OEA Report, indicate a marked decline in the volume of closed-end fund IPOs. During that period, of the 77 closed-end funds offered in the U.S., 65 (84.4 percent) were bond funds, 7 (9.1 percent) were foreign stock funds, and only 5 (6.5 percent) were domestic equity funds.[12] The five domestic equity closed-end funds declined in value by approximately 9.45 percent after 120 trading days. These data suggest that the market may have learned that closed-end domestic equity funds tend not to be profitable IPO investments and that the number of those funds brought to market has therefore declined.

This analysis raises some interesting questions about the conduct of brokers who recommend closed-end domestic equity fund IPOs to their customers. Suppose a broker fails to explain to a customer that, rather than buying shares in a closed-end domestic equity fund IPO, the investor would be better off buying shares of the same fund in the aftermarket. Is such a failure unobjectionable because the quantity and quality of the evidence regarding discounts provides an insufficient basis for making such a recommendation? If so, how does the quantity and quality of the closed-end discount evidence compare with information upon which brokers

---

aftermarket, viewed from the broker's selfish perspective, an IPO of a closed-end domestic equity fund is a front-end loaded two-tier transaction. A rational, self-interested broker thus has every incentive to suggest that his clients invest in a closed-end domestic equity fund IPO unless the broker fears the adverse consequences that may follow when the clients complain that the fund is trading at a discount.

[10]    An agency problem arises whenever a person (a principal) hires someone else (an agent) to make a decision and the agent's incentives differ from the principal's. In this case, the agency problem arises, in part, because the closed-end domestic equity fund IPO is back-end loaded from the investor's (principal's) perspective and front-end loaded from the brokers (agent's) perspective. See generally Jensen & Meckling, The Theory of the Firm: Managerial Behavior Agency Costs and Ownership Structure, 3 J. Fin. Econ. 305 (1976); Ross, The Economic Theory of Agency: The Principal's Problem, 63 Amer. Econ. Rev. 134 (1973); Spence & Zeckhauser, Insurance, Information, and Individual Action, 61 Amer. Econ. Rev. 119 (1971).

[11]    OEA Study, at 23-25.

[12]    Office of the Chief Economist, Memorandum from Kathleen Weiss to Kenneth Lehn and David Malmquist, Closed-End Fund Study Update, June 20, 1989 (copy placed in public file no. S7-21-89).

rely when making other recommendations? What quantity and quality evidence should then be required as a basis for a recommendation?

Assuming that the evidence regarding discounts is credible, and recognizing that not every broker can know every fact about every product he recommends, could a failure to advise a customer to purchase in the aftermarket rather than in the IPO be supported on the basis that a broker could not reasonably be expected to know about the prevalence of discounts? The argument in support of this proposition must be that the level of skill and care expected of a broker does not rise to the level at which a customer reasonably should expect the broker to be aware of the substantial probability that the closed-end fund IPO shares will trade at a discount. If one accepts this argument, how knowledgeable should a customer expect a broker to be about specific investment recommendations made to that customer? How does this standard of care relate to the advice that brokers generally provide to clients?

Put a bit differently, if brokers can legitimately rely on evidence of past positive performance of a category of securities as a basis for a recommendation in selling an IPO, to what extent should brokers be expected to take into account equivalently credible evidence of past negative performance of a category of securities before making such a recommendation? For example, consider a situation in which the evidence of the positive performance history of a category of securities is as powerful as the evidence regarding discounts following IPO closed-end domestic equity fund offerings. If brokers are permitted to rely on evidence of past positive performance should they be expected to give equal weight to equally powerful evidence of past negative performance?

Further, if it is correct that no rational, fully informed investor would purchase closed-end domestic equity fund shares in an IPO, how can a broker recommend such a purchase? Is it because the broker is not sufficiently informed? Or, is it because the broker's incentive is different from the customer's and the logical choice from the broker's perspective is not the logical choice from the customer's perspective? After all, the broker earns substantially more by selling the shares in the IPO than by selling the same shares in the aftermarket. In that case, how does the broker's recommendation benefit the customer? Does the presence of such a potential conflict alter the degree of care that one expects the broker to exercise in connection with a recommendation? Does it alter the information that the broker should convey to his customer before making a recommendation? Does it alter the degree of confidence that retail customers should have in broker recommendations?

Finally, how do these observations relate to the proposed requirement that prospectuses contain cautionary legends about closed-end fund IPOs? Will such a legend change broker behavior in recommending closed-end fund IPOs? Should such a legend change broker behavior in recommending closed-end fund IPOs?

### Questions and Comments

1. How would you answer the questions that Commissioner Grundfest poses at the end of his statement and particularly his final questions about the proper content and function of mandatory disclosure for problems of this sort?

2. To what extent should the Commission be concerned with "anomalies" such as the observed discounts in closed-end fund shares?

---

# In re Nuveen Fund Litigation
## 1996 WL 328006 (N.D.Ill. June 11, 1996)

MANNING, District Judge.

This matter comes before the court on objections by defendants John Nuveen & Company, Inc. ("Nuveen"), Nuveen Advisory Corporation ("Advisor"), Richard J. Franke, and Donald E. Sveen to Magistrate Judge Edward E. Bobrick's report and recommendation proposing that the court deny their motion to dismiss. . . .

Plaintiffs bring this derivative suit on behalf of all persons who owned shares of the Nuveen Municipal Value Fund, Inc. ("NUV Fund") or the Nuveen Premium Income Municipal Fund, Inc. ("NPI Fund") on November 6, 1993. Plaintiffs allege that the issuance of new shares of stock in the NUV Fund and NPI Fund ("Funds") violated the Funds' respective articles of incorporation, diluted plaintiffs' interests in the Funds and was made only for the purpose of generating fees for the Funds' investment adviser and its controlling parent corporation. Plaintiffs bring this Complaint in twelve counts: Counts I through VII and XII allege claims for sales of shares under fair value, acts ultra vires, and illegal distribution of rights, all in violation of Minnesota state law; Counts VIII through XI allege violations of the Investment Company Act of 1940 ("ICA"). Defendants include the Funds' unaffiliated directors, the Funds' investment advisor, Nuveen Advisory Corporation ("Advisor"), the Funds' inside directors, Richard J. Franke and Donald E. Sveen, the Advisor's controlling parent corporation, John Nuveen & Company, Inc. ("Nuveen"), the officers for both the Funds and the Advisor, James J. Wesolowski and Larry W. Martin, and the Funds' outside counsel, Michael Meyer.

### BACKGROUND

Nuveen is a multi-million dollar investment banking and investment advisory firm whose growth was, and is dependent on its ability to continually create and market new closed-end funds. Closed-end bond funds, unlike open-end funds, generally do not issue new shares after their initial offering; expansion is usually through the gradual increase in the value of the underlying portfolio. The NUV and NPI funds are both closed-end, diversified management investment companies registered under the ICA in the state of Minnesota.

Nuveen's closed-end municipal bond funds account for at least 75% of Nuveen's business. Nuveen profits on the closed-end funds in two ways: (1) underwriting fees for new funds and (2) management fees based on a percentage of the assets managed by the Advisor, its wholly-owned subsidiary. In the recent past, Nuveen has been able to sustain growth by creating and marketing an average of one new, closed-end fund a month. Plaintiffs claim that Nuveen's future growth through the creation of new closed-end funds has been threatened by market saturation, declining investor interest, and high bond prices. By the fall of 1993, Nuveen's performance had stagnated along with the closed-end bond fund market. Earnings fell below analysts' projections, Nuveen's stock was downgraded, and industry publications noted the slowdown. Due to the impact of the downturn, plaintiffs allege that the Funds resorted to raising capital from the shareholders of its existing Nuveen funds through rights offerings.

On November 8, 1993, the Funds announced the offering of rights to new shares enabling Funds' shareholders to purchase additional shares ("Rights Offerings"). Specifically, the Rights Offerings allowed each NUV or NPI funds shareholder to purchase one additional share for every three shares already owned. Thus, each Fund could have increased its outstanding shares by up to 33%. According to plaintiffs, the Rights Offerings were instituted for Nuveen's benefit rather than for the benefit of the Funds' shareholders. They claim that Nuveen directly benefited from the Offerings by receiving substantial underwriting fees and indirectly benefited from the Offerings because the Advisor would receive significantly greater management fees due to the Funds' increased assets under Advisor's management. Plaintiffs submit that the shareholders were harmed rather than benefited as a result. The price for the new shares was set at:

> the lesser of (A) the net asset value per common share as of the date of the expiration of the offering ("pricing date") or (B) 95% of the average of the last reported sale prices of a common share on the New York Stock Exchange on the pricing date and the four (4) preceding business days.

Plaintiffs explain that defendants knew or should have known that this pricing structure guaranteed that the new shares would be sold at a price below both the Funds' per share net asset value ("NAV"). Plaintiffs allege that analysis presented to the directors predicted that the announcement of the Offerings placed a downward pressure on the trading price for the Nuveen funds' shares in the weeks before the final price was determined. Plaintiffs also contend that the challenged offerings were designed to give the Funds' shareholders a "Hobson's Choice" among three alternatives, each of which caused the shareholders harm: (1) invest more money in the Funds and minimize their NAV dilution; (2) refrain from investing more money and suffer dilution from the addition of new shares and the deduction of underwriting fees; or (3) sell their shares in an intentionally depressed market and suffer losses.

The Complaint calls into question several aspects of the Offerings. First, plaintiffs claim the Offerings were ultra vires because the Funds' articles of incorporation expressly prohibit the sale of shares below NAV. Given the formula for pricing the shares, plaintiffs claim that the Offerings were designed to occur at less than NAV. Second, plaintiffs claim that the Offerings resulted in a waste of corporate assets. According to the Complaint, the Advisor's analysis indicated that the Offerings would not produce even marginal benefits to the Funds' performance. In fact, the Complaint alleges that the directors expected, or should have expected, that the Offerings would worsen the Funds' long-term performance. In addition, the Complaint alleges that the Advisor's predictions explicitly presumed that the Offerings would occur at NAV even though the Advisor and directors knew, or should have known, that the Offerings would occur below NAV.

Third, plaintiffs allege that the Funds employed false and misleading prospectuses in connection with the Offerings. The Complaint alleges that prospectuses failed to disclose that the Rights Offerings constituted an "interest-rate-gamble" as any rise in interest rates would worsen the Funds' performance in relationship to if the Offerings never took place. Plaintiffs assert that the prospectuses did not even suggest the effect rising interest rates would have on the Funds. Plaintiffs also allege that the prospectuses misrepresented that the Offerings would create long-term benefits to the Funds, even though the Advisor's financial analysis indicated that the best-case scenario would be that the Funds' performance would not be worsened by the Offerings. The Complaint also alleges that the directors were self-interested and biased in conducting the Rights Offerings.

In considering the Offerings, the directors relied solely on information and analysis from Nuveen and the Advisor. Of the Funds' seven directors, two have significant relationships with Nuveen and cannot be considered independent in regard to the Offerings in this case. Of the remaining five directors, two have stated in attached depositions that they would not entertain the possibility that information from Nuveen or the Advisor would reflect bias or self-interest.

Nuveen, the Advisor, Franke and Sveen ("Nuveen Defendants") move to dismiss plaintiffs' counts under federal law, and the remaining state counts for lack of jurisdiction. Count VIII is brought under ICA § 34(b), and alleges that defendants violated the ICA through their use of false and materially misleading statements in the offering prospectuses. Count IX alleges that the directors and Advisor breached their fiduciary duties in violation of ICA § 36(a). . . . Count XI, brought under ICA § 36(b), seeks to recover underwriting and management fees that Nuveen and the Advisor realized from the Rights Offerings.

In their motion, defendants first argue that there is no private cause of action under § 34(b) and § 36(a). Assuming arguendo, however, that these causes of action do exist, defendants contend that the Complaint fails to allege the elements of claims under those sections. Defendants also argue that ICA § 23(b)(1), authorized the Offerings at issue. Finally, defendants submit that the plaintiffs' allegations do not state a cause of action under § 36(b).

## DISCUSSION

I. Private Causes of Action under the ICA.

Defendants first object that Magistrate Judge Bobrick incorrectly implied private rights of action under § 36(a) and § 34(b) of the Investment Company Act ("ICA"). . . .

Although defendants correctly assert that "a strong presumption exists against the creation of [ ] implied rights of action," West Allis Memorial Hosp., Inc. v. Bowen, 852 F.2d 251, 254 (7th Cir.1988), this presumption does not require an explicit statement of congressional intent in the text or legislative history. See Community & Economic Deve. Ass'n v. Suburban Cook County, 770 F.2d 662, 664 (7th Cir.1985). Cases cited by defendants reveal that "the failure of Congress expressly to consider a private remedy is not inevitably inconsistent with an intent on its part to make such a remedy available." Id. (quoting Transamerica Mortgage Advisors, Inc. v. Lewis, 444 U.S. 11, 18 (1979)). The decisive question is whether Congress intended to provide such a right in enacting the statute. West Allis, 852 F.2d at 255. Such congressional intent is inferred from the language and structure of the statute, its legislative history, as well as by whether such a cause of action would be consistent with the statute's underlying scheme. Spicer v. Chicago Bd. of Options Exchange, Inc., 977 F.2d 255, 258 (7th Cir.1992).

Defendants first argue that the Supreme Court's refusal to imply a private right for damages under the fiduciary rights created by § 206 of the Investment Advisor Act ("IAA") precludes the court from implying a private action under similar provisions in the ICA. See Transamerica, 444 U.S. 11. In Transamerica, however, the court relied in large part upon the fact that Congress had consciously omitted references to "actions at law" or "liability" from the IAA's jurisdictional provisions, reflecting an intent to not provide private causes of action under the IAA. Id. at 24-25, at 249. In contrast, the ICA grants jurisdiction in "all suits in equity and actions at law brought to enforce any liability or duty created by ... regulations or orders thereunder." Furthermore, ICA § 1(b) explicitly directs the courts to interpret its provisions to "mitigate and, so far as is feasible, to eliminate the conditions enumerated in this section which adversely affect the national public interest and the interest of investors."

More importantly, subsequent legislative history arising from amendments to the ICA indicates that Congress contemplated that the courts should imply private causes of action. Federal courts have widely implied private causes of action under the ICA for over thirty years. See, e.g., Lessler v. Little, 857 F.2d 866 (1st Cir.1988), cert. denied, 489 U.S. 1016 (1989); Bancroft Convertible Fund, Inc. v. Zico Inv. Holdings, 825 F.2d 731, 734 n. 1 (3d Cir.1987); Fogel v. Chestnutt, 668 F.2d 100, 110-11 (2d Cir.1981) (recounting precedent implying private right under ICA § 36). Even though the Congress has revisited the ICA three times since courts began to imply such causes of action, it has never indicated its dissatisfaction with this practice. See Merrill Lynch, Pierce, Fenner & Smith, Inc. v. Curran, 456 U.S. 353, 380-81 (1982).

Defendants respond that congressional silence or inaction does not provide evidence of congressional approval of an implied right. See Central Bank v. First Interstate Bank, 114 S.Ct. 1439, 1453 (1994). However, when Congress amended the ICA through the Small Business Investment Incentive Act of 1980, the House Committee reported:

> The rationale for implying private rights of action under the securities laws beyond those actions expressly provided for had been well articulated by the Supreme Court when it observed that implied rights of action allowing shareholders to sue to remedy their losses would significantly assist the congressional goal of promoting fair corporate suffrage. But in recent years, the Supreme Court has turned its focus toward a strict construction of statutory language and expressed intent.

> The Committee wishes to make plain that it expects the courts to imply private rights of action under this legislation, where the plaintiff falls within the class protected by the statutory provision in question. Such a right would be consistent with and further Congress' intent in enacting that provision, and where such action would not improperly occupy an area traditionally a concern of state law. In appropriate instances, for example, breaches of fiduciary duty involving personal misconduct should be remedied under Section 36(a) of the Investment Company Act. With respect to business development companies, the Committee contemplates suits by shareholders as well as by the Commission, since these are the persons the provision is designed to protect, and such private rights of action will assist in carrying out the remedial purposes of Section 36.

H.R.Rep. No. 1341, 96th Cong., 2d Sess. 28-29 (1980), reprinted in 1980 U.S.C.C.A.N. 4800, 4810-11 (footnotes omitted). The court finds that this enthusiastic expression of intent provides more than mere silence or legislative inaction.

The defendants protest that the interpretation that one Congress applies to an earlier statute is of limited relevance in determining the meaning of an unamended section of a statute.  Central Bank, 114 S.Ct. at 1452.  However, as the magistrate judge noted, Central Bank was concerned with the scope of conduct prohibited by a statute, and did not directly address the question of implying private causes of action.  In addition, Central Bank rejected the plaintiffs' arguments that Securities and Exchange Act of 1934 § 10(b) included aiding and abetting liability based upon oblique references to such liability in later reports by congressional committees.  Central Bank, 114 S.Ct. at 1452;  see also Aaron v. SEC, 446 U.S. 680, 695 n. 11 (1980) (finding irrelevant to requirement of scienter under SEA § 10(b) subsequent legislative history that never directly addressed issue).  In contrast, the above cited reference to implied private rights of action under the ICA is anything but oblique, particularly in regards to ICA § 36(a).  In the course of considering substantial changes to the ICA, the report reveals that the House Committee determined the required changes to the ICA with implied private rights of action in mind.

Most importantly, defendants ignore Congress' amendment of ICA § 36 in 1970.  By enacting the separate provision of ICA § 36(b), Congress provided shareholders with a direct cause of action in order to correct the limited effectiveness of the original provision.  See Fogel, 668 F.2d 111-112.  Congress also retained the previous fiduciary duty under ICA § 36(a), only altering the language to strengthen the standard of care imposed and to provide the courts with greater remedial flexibility.  S.R.Rep. No. 91-184, 91st Cong., 1st Sess. 16, reprinted in 1970 U.S.C.C.A.N. 4897, 4931 (hereinafter "Senate Report ").  As the Second Circuit has persuasively explained, the legislative history behind this amendment does not indicate any intent on the part of Congress to eliminate the private right of action previously recognized under § 36.  Id.  Rather, the Senate Report attendant to this amendment explicitly directed that the creation of a private right of action under 36(b) "should not be read by implication to affect subsection (a)."  Senate Report at 4911.  The court agrees with the magistrate judge's interpretation of these comments as indicating a congressional intent to leave the state of implied remedies under subsection § 36(a) as they were.

Accordingly, the court accepts Magistrate Judge Bobrick's recommendation to imply private rights of action under ICA § 34(b) and ICA § 36(a).

II. Plaintiffs' Claim under ICA § 34(b).

Defendants object to the magistrate judge's recommendation that Count VIII of the Complaint states a claim under ICA § 34(b).  In Count VIII, plaintiffs allege that the defendants violated § 34(b) through misrepresentations and material omissions in the prospectuses used for the Rights Offerings.  Specifically, the Complaint asserts that the prospectuses (1) failed to disclose that the Rights Offerings depended upon stable or lowering interest rates merely to permit the Funds to break even, (2) misrepresented that the Funds would obtain long-term benefits in performance from the Rights Offerings, and (3) failed to disclose that NAV dilution from the Rights Offerings would potentially worsen the Funds' performance so that investors would not obtain NAV benefits for several years.  In his report, Magistrate Judge Bobrick concluded that these pleadings adequately allege a material misrepresentation and omission under § 34(b).  In addition, the magistrate judge recommended that, in contrast to § 10(b) of the Securities and Exchange Act of 1934 ("SEA"), § 34(b) does not require a plaintiff to demonstrate that the alleged violation caused his asserted injury.

Defendants first argue that the Complaint fails to allege a material omission because the asserted omitted information only constitutes public, non-firm specific information. See Wielgos v. Commonwealth Edison Co., 892 F.2d 509, 515 (7th Cir.1989) (Securities and Exchange Act imposes no duty to release public non-firm specific information); see also In re RAC Mortgage Inv. Corp. Sec. Litig., 765 F.Supp. 860, 864 (D.Md.1991) (no duty to disclose basic economic principles of interest rates). Although defendants present a compelling argument that the securities laws did not require them to disclose the consequences of rising interest rates for the Funds, their objection fails to dispose of all the plaintiffs' allegations. The Complaint charges that the defendants' own internal analysis clearly revealed that the Rights Offerings would not benefit the Funds' financial performance. Furthermore, in light of the price structure, the Complaint asserts that defendants knew or should have known that the Rights Offerings would actually harm the Funds' performance. Such information is neither public nor non-firm specific.

Defendants respond that they were not required to characterize the consequences of the Rights Offerings as long as the prospectuses did not misrepresent or omit the actual terms of the transaction. See Issen v. GSC Enterprises, Inc., 508 F.Supp. 1278, 1290 (N.D.Ill.1981). As a general matter, the securities laws do not require disclosure of internal projections or predictions of the outcome of a transaction. See id. But the attached prospectuses reveal general statements representing that the Fund's Board of Directors had determined that the Rights Offerings would provide long term benefits for the Funds' financial performance that would outweigh any of the dilutive consequences for NAV, dividends or non-participating shareholders. The Complaint alleges that the Advisor's analysis directly contradicted these statements. General statements of opinion may be actionable where they may be objectively verifiable and the defendant had no reasonable basis in the opinion. See Wright v. IBM Corp., 796 F.Supp. 1120, 1125 (N.D.Ill.1992); In re Apple Computers Sec. Litig., 886 F.2d 1109, 1113 (9th Cir.1989). Assuming the plaintiffs' allegations as true, the prospectuses' assertions give rise to a potential material misrepresentation. It is uncertain whether plaintiffs can substantiate their allegations. However, a motion to dismiss does not impose this burden on the plaintiffs. The court cannot conclude that reasonable minds would not differ as to whether the alleged misrepresentations and omissions would be material to a reasonable investor. See TSC Industries, Inc. v. Northway, Inc., 426 U.S. 438, 449 (1976).

Defendants also argue that the magistrate judge incorrectly recommended that § 34(b) does not require the element of causation. Defendants contend that a private right of action under § 34(b) would require the same elements as required under SEA § 10(b). For their part, the plaintiffs propose that a claim under § 34(b) does not require causation because, in contrast to SEA § 10(b), § 34(b) does not require proof of a "manipulative or deceptive device": § 34(b) does not require proof of fraud. Rather, plaintiffs compare § 34(b) to SA § 11, § 12(2) and SEA § 14(a). Although the court rejects the contention that § 34(b) requires the same elements of SEA § 10(b), the court finds that causation is a required element of a private claim under § 34(b).

Securities Act of 1933 ("SA") § 11 and § 12(2) are part of an express civil liability scheme that effectively employs the purchasers of securities in the effort to regulate misstatements made in the offering or sale of securities. See Nielsen v. Greenwood, 849 F.Supp. 1233, 1251-55 (N.D.Ill.1994). Each of these provisions provides explicit instructions and, consequently, limits on computing damages arising from an alleged breach.[4]  In contrast, the text of § 34(b) does not provide any presumed damages or injury arising from a violation.  Without such presumed and designated damages, it is inappropriate to permit potential claimants to raise a claim without alleging that he suffered an injury proximately caused by the alleged misstatement.

In contrast to plaintiffs' argument, a private claim under SEA § 14(a) requires proof of causation.  SEA § 14(a) and Rule 14a-9 prohibit misrepresentations and material omissions in any proxy statement.  Because SEA § 14(a) does not focus on fraud, a mere material misstatement in a distributed proxy statement constitutes a violation.  See Mills v. Electric Auto-Lite Co., 396 U.S. 375, 383  (1970).  Furthermore, in light of the policy interests behind SEA 14(a) and the difficulties of demonstrating third parties' reliance, courts will presume that a misrepresentation or material omission in a proxy statement affected the outcome of the proxy vote.  See id. at 384-85, at 621-22.  However, to obtain redress in court, a private claimant must still demonstrate that he suffered an injury that was proximately caused by the alleged misstatement.  See Issen, 522 F.Supp. at 396 (claim under SEA § 14(a) requires that plaintiff establish causal relationship between asserted violation and injury).  For instance, if the defendant can demonstrate that the alleged misstatement was not an essential link in the success of the proxy vote, then the claim must be dismissed.  See Virginia Bankshares, Inc. v. Sandberg, 501 U.S. 1083 (1991).

However, as under SEA § 14(a), a private claimant under § 34(b) need not demonstrate their personal reliance on the alleged misstatement.  Because SEA § 10(b) prohibits "any manipulative or deceptive device" "in connection with the purchase or sale of any security," the elements of a private claim under SEA 10(b) are modeled upon the common law action of deceit.  See Huddleston v. Herman & MacLean, 640 F.2d 534, 547 (5th Cir.1981), aff'd in part and rev'd in part on other grounds, 459 U.S. 375 (1983).  Consequently, courts generally require a SEA § 10(b) claimant to demonstrate either actual or constructive personal reliance on the alleged misstatement as a necessary component of establishing causation.  Basic Incorp. v. Levinson, 485 U.S. 224, 243 (1988).  But nothing in the text of § 34(b) reflects a similar element of fraud.  As under SEA § 14(a), the mere material misstatement executed in a covered document constitutes a violation of § 34(b).  Also like SEA § 14(a), § 34(b) does not "prohibit[] unlawful conduct in connection with a particular activity."  See Cowin v. Bresler, 741 F.2d 410, 427 (D.C.Cir.1984) (finding that a private claim under SEA 14(a) does not require proof of personal reliance).  Rather than regulate only the sale or transfer of securities, § 34(b) is part of the ICA's general regulatory scheme intended to protect the investment company and its shareholders from the danger of self-dealing of management or other insiders that is particularly acute in the mutual fund industry.  See Burks v. Lasker, 441 U.S. 471, 481-84 (1979);  see also Cowin, 741 F.2d at 427 (SEA 14(a)'s goal to "protect a shareholder's investment from self-serving designs of those at odds with the best interests of the corporation" indicates that a private claim does not require reliance).  Accordingly, the court finds that a private claim under § 34(b) does not require the plaintiff to demonstrate personal reliance upon the alleged misstatement.

---

[4]    In fact, causation remains relevant to a claim under SA § 11. Even if a claimant demonstrates materiality, a defendant may still escape liability for damages to the extent that he establishes that other market factors in fact caused the claimant's injury.

Because there is not such a requirement, the Complaint adequately pleads proximate causation. In order to demonstrate loss causation under the securities laws, a plaintiff must show that a misrepresentation or material omission was a substantial factor in causing the plaintiffs' asserted injury. Herzfeld v. Laventhol, Krekstein, Horwath & Horwath, 540 F.2d 27, 33 (2d Cir.1976). As the Complaint presents a derivative suit, the alleged instant injury arises from damages flowing directly to the corporation in the form of its impaired financial performance. In such a claim, neither the plaintiff shareholders' reliance nor the Funds' reliance is at issue. Instead, causation arises from the fellow shareholders' reliance on the alleged misstatements in deciding to participate in the Rights Offerings. Loss causation derives from the common law tort concept of proximate causation. Manufacturers Hanover Trust Co. v. Drysdale Sec. Corp., 801 F.2d 13, 20 (2d Cir.1986), cert. denied, 479 U.S. 1066 (1986). Accordingly, central to loss causation is the question whether the alleged injury was a reasonably foreseeable result of the purported misstatement. Id. at 20-21. In light of the pleadings, it is reasonable to infer that the defendants foresaw and, in fact, expected that the purported misstatement would stimulate participation in the Rights Offerings. From the allegations that the defendants knew or should have known that the Offerings would not benefit the Funds' performance, it is also reasonable to infer that the defendants could reasonably foresee the alleged injury. Consequently, the defendants' motion to dismiss Count VIII is denied.

III. Cause of Action under ICA § 36(a).

A. Implications of ICA § 23(b)(1).

Defendants object that plaintiffs' claim that a rights offering for less than net asset value may constitute a breach of fiduciary duty under ICA § 36(a) would render the exemption under ICA § 23(b)(1) superfluous. ICA § 23(b) states in pertinent part that:

> No registered closed-end company shall sell any common stock of which it is the issuer at a price below the current net asset value ... except (1) in connection with an offering to the holders of one or more classes of its capital stock.

Defendants argue that this language reflects Congress' conclusion that an offering below net asset value that is limited to current shareholders poses no substantial risk to those current shareholders. Defendants contend that such a price structure for a rights offering, if limited to current shareholders, cannot violate the duty of fiduciary care imposed by ICA § 36(a). Consequently, defendants argue that the Report's recommendation that the Rights Offerings may have violated ICA § 36(a) contradicts the plain meaning of ICA § 23(b)(1) and renders it s     u     p     e     r     f     l     u     o     u     s     .

The court rejects the defendants' position. ICA § 23(b)(1) expressly exempts a rights offerings restricted to current shareholders from the blanket prohibition of ICA § 23(b) against rights offerings at below net asset value. As defendants argue, this subsection implies that the decision to offer new shares at below net asset value to current shareholders does not necessarily violate the ICA under § 23(b). However, it does not imply that such a price structure may not violate the ICA's other constraints. The defendants concede that § 23(b)(1) does not provide a safe harbor for offerings to existing shareholders, but insinuate that it sanctions a price structure below net asset value as long as the shares are only offered to current shareholders. Magistrate Judge Bobrick correctly rejected this proposition. § 23(b) provides a general prohibition against below net asset value offerings. The plain language of § 23(b)(1) only states that offerings limited to current shareholders are not necessarily invalid. It does indicate that limiting below net asset value offerings to current shareholders guarantees that the directors' approval of that price structure satisfied other fiduciary duties to existing shareholders. Cf. Meyer v. Oppenheimer Management Corporation, 764 F.2d 76, 82-83 (2d Cir.1985) (rejecting directors' assertion that ICA § 36(b)'s fiduciary duties have no application to setting of fees under a Rule 12b-1 plan).

As Magistrate Judge Bobrick explained, the Complaint alleges harm beyond the inherent immediate dilution arising from an offering at below net asset value. The pleadings also allege that the price structure of the Rights Offerings harmed both the short and long term performance of the Funds. Furthermore, the Complaint specifically pleads that, in light of the Funds' financial position and the current economic context, the Rights Offerings could only injure the Funds' financial performance. Finally, the Complaint alleges that the Advisor proposed these transactions solely to generate fees for itself regardless of the consequences to the Funds. Whether plaintiffs can substantiate these accusations is uncertain. However, the Complaint alleges misconduct beyond merely pricing an offering for a closed-end fund at below net asset value.

B. Personal Misconduct.

Defendants also object that ICA § 36(a) does not provide a cause of action for actions by a corporation or an entire board of directors. § 36(a) holds the directors, officers and investment adviser of an investment company liable for a "breach of fiduciary duty involving personal misconduct." Section 36(a) of the Investment Company Act of 1940. Defendants argue that the legislative history surrounding the enactment of § 36(a) demonstrates that the modifying phrase, "involving personal misconduct," was intended only to limit the fiduciary duty under the subsection to reach only individual acts of dishonesty.

Congress adopted the ICA primarily to address the unique problems of investment adviser self-dealing in the investment fund industry. Daily Income Fund, Inc. v. Fox, 464 F.2d 523, 536, 104 S.Ct. 831, 838 (1984). Unlike most companies, an investment company is " 'mere shell,' a pool of assets consisting mostly of portfolio securities" that belong to the company's shareholders. Tannenbaum v. Zeller, 552 F.2d 402, 405 (2d Cir.1977). The investment adviser who creates the fund manages, operates and supervises most every aspect of the company. Id. This adviser is an independent entity, whose pecuniary interests may often come into conflict with those of its investment companies and their shareholders. Id. at 405-06. Because of the adviser's control over its funds, the danger of self-dealing is particularly acute. Burks, 441 U.S. at 481. To address this danger of self-dealing, the ICA imposes a number of structural and disclosure requirements on those who control investment companies. Tannenbaum, 552 F.2d at 406. However, the ICA primarily relies upon the unaffiliated directors of the investment company to assume the role of "independent watchdog" for the shareholders' interests. Id.

In 1970, Congress amended the ICA, and particularly § 36, in response to its failure to adequately regulate the investment adviser's influence and control over its investment company and their board of directors. See Burks, 483 U.S. at 483-84. Prior to 1970, § 36 imposed a general standard of "gross misconduct or gross abuse of trust" on the conduct of directors and investment advisers in exercising their control over their investment company. Decisions applying this "gross misconduct" standard involved some sort of element of self-dealing; the defendant engaged in a course of conduct or refrained from conduct for its own interests and at the expense of the investment company.  See, e.g., Fogel v. Chestnutt, 533 F.2d 731, 750 (2d Cir.1979) (applying prior standard);  Tannenbaum v. Zeller, 552 F.2d at 406.  Congress eliminated the "gross misconduct" because the standard of proof of serious wrongdoing it imposed on plaintiffs was more onerous than Congress thought appropriate.  Senate Report at 4931.  In its place, Congress adopted the more traditional standard of "fiduciary duty".  Predictably, the investment industry opposed this imposition arguing that it would permit suits based upon mere disagreements with the business judgment and investment decisions of the directors and advisers of mutual funds.  See S. 1695, 90th Cong., 1st Sess. § 20 (1967), reprinted in Mutual Fund Legislation of 1967: Hearings on S. 1659 before the Senate Comm. on Banking and Currency, 90th Cong., 1st Sess.Pt. 2 (1967).  In its place, the investment industry proposed a less onerous standard that would assure that the new § 36 only reach acts of personal dishonesty.  Id.  Ultimately, Congress enacted the current language.

As an initial matter, even if the court were to accept that § 36(a) only reached acts of personal dishonesty, the Complaint adequately alleges a cause of action against Nuveen, the Advisor and the directors affiliated with those defendants, Richard J. Franke and Donald E. Sveen.  Plaintiffs allege that Nuveen and the Advisor proposed the Rights Offerings, despite their knowledge that it would not benefit the Funds, in order to generate fees for itself.  Defendants fail to explain how withholding information on the propriety of a transaction in order to benefit from that transaction would not constitute dishonesty.  The fact that the Advisor revealed its general pecuniary interest in the transaction does not answer the charge that the Advisor provided only a partial analysis and dishonest advice.  Moreover, Congress did not adopt the language of "personal dishonesty" advanced by the investment industry and used in the banking statutes .[5]  Instead, Congress adopted the novel term of "personal misconduct."  In light of the purpose of the amendments to strengthen the ICA, the court interprets this language to refer to misconduct that involves self-dealing by investment company or other insiders.  Plaintiffs' allegations that the Advisor imposed the Rights Offerings for its own benefit at the expense of the Funds are precisely the type of self-dealing contemplated by § 36(a).[6]

Because § 36(a) reaches only actions "involving personal misconduct", defendants argue that the subsection cannot prohibit a defendants' misconduct taken in as group action instead of in an individual capacity.  Therefore, defendants contend that the directors cannot be held accountable under § 36(a) for their approval of the Rights Offerings.  First, the court finds that it would be illogical to presume that "personal misconduct" cannot refer to conduct by a corporate

---

[5]    Not only does "dishonesty" never appear in § 36(a), but the term also does not appear anywhere in the Senate Banking Committee's report explaining the 1970 amendments.  See Senate Report.

[6]    Similarly, the Complaint adequately pleads a cause of action under § 36(a) against defendants Franke and Sveen.  The Complaint reveals that these directors are affiliated with Nuveen and Advisor and, as a legal matter, are not considered independent.  Because the Complaint adequately pleads that these defendants are beholden to Nuveen and the Advisor, it also adequately pleads that their approval of the Rights Offerings constituted a breach of their duty of loyalty to the shareholders.  See Cede & Co. v. Technocolor, Inc., 634 A.2d 345, 363 (Del.1993).

body. The investment adviser, usually an independent corporation, is specifically listed as one of the parties bound by the subsection. See, e.g., Fogel v. Chestnutt, 668 F.2d 100 (affirming § 36(a) judgment against investment adviser). Regardless, a director's breach of his fiduciary duty through his participation in a board vote still may constitute an individual act.

Defendants protest that the duty under § 36(a) cannot reach all misconduct governed under a traditional fiduciary duty. Otherwise, the modifying language of "involving personal misconduct" would be superfluous. See Ratzlaf v. United States, 114 S.Ct. 655, 659 (1994) (statutory language should not be treated as surplusage). In addition, the Senate Banking Committee reiterated the investment industry's concerns when it stated that § 36(a) is not intended to provide a basis for "a general revision of the practices or structures of the investment company industry." See Senate Report at 4931. As defendants argue, this language indicates that Congress did not intend that § 36(a) reach all breaches of due care.

However, the Committee also noted that "[i]n appropriate cases, nonfeasance of duty or abdication of responsibility would constitute a breach of fiduciary duty involving personal misconduct." Id. Congress enacted the ICA in order to insure against the investment adviser using its position of power to further its self-interest at the expense of the investment company it manages. In amending the ICA, Congress imposed the role of "independent watchdog" upon the unaffiliated directors to supervise the investment adviser's management of the funds and prevent adviser self-dealing. Burks, 441 U.S. at 483-84. Consequently, the court finds that § 36(a) contemplates allegations of a director's gross neglect of his responsibility to supervise and inform himself of the investment adviser's management of the fund.[7] The instant Complaint alleges that the Funds' directors blindly relied upon the Advisor's analysis and recommendations and thereby permitted the Advisor to impose a transaction for its own benefit at the cost of the Funds. Therefore, it alleges that the directors abdicated their responsibility to protect the shareholders' interests from the Advisor's self-dealing. Such allegations plead a "breach of fiduciary duty involving personal misconduct." Consequently, the court adopts the magistrate judge's recommendation and denies defendants' motion to dismiss Count IX in respect to all defendants.

---

[7] When Congress amended the ICA in 1980, the House Committee applied a similar interpretation to § 36(a) in its report to Congress:

[t]he Committee believes that the type of misconduct covered by [§ 36(a) ], as it applies to Business Development Companies, extends to personal misconduct evidenced by misfeasance or nonfeasance in carrying out legal responsibilities as well as self-dealing and other examples of unjust enrichment.

Thus, the conduct of Business Development Company directors, in failing to engage in reasonable inquiry or supervision and thereby allowing other business development company affiliates to engage in improper or prohibited conduct, such as the misappropriation of company assets, falls well within the scope of section 36(a).

H.Rep. 96-1341, 96th Cong., 2d Sess., reprinted in 1980 U.S.C.C.A.N. 4800, 4808 (footnote omitted). The Committee indicated that this interpretation of "personal misconduct" was consistent with breath of coverage intended under the 1970 amendment. See id. at n. 3.

IV. ICA § 36(b).

Defendants object to Magistrate Judge Bobrick's recommendation that the Complaint states a cause of action under ICA § 36(b). § 36(b) provides investment company shareholders with a direct cause of action against the company's investment adviser for its breach of fiduciary duty with "respect to the receipt of compensation for services." In contrast to the plaintiffs' other claims against Nuveen and the Advisor, their claim under § 36(b) is not derivative. Defendants assert that this easier access is due to the narrow scope of the provision: § 36(b) only permits challenges to the fee arrangement between the investment adviser and the investment company.

In his report, Magistrate Judge Bobrick concluded that § 36(b) contemplates a claim that accuses an investment adviser of imposing a transaction on the investment company only to generate fees for itself. For the reasons stated below, the court rejects Magistrate Judge Bobrick's recommendation and finds that the Complaint fails to state a claim under § 36.

To determine whether ICA 36(b) proscribes the alleged conduct, the court first looks to the language of the statute. Fox, 464 U.S. at 534. 36(b) imposes a fiduciary duty on an investment company' adviser "with respect to the receipt of compensation for services" that the company has "paid" and provides a cause of action by either the Securities and Exchange Commission ("SEC") "or by a security holder of such registered investment company on behalf of such company" for a breach of such duty. This language indicates a standard of care that only runs to the terms and receipt of compensation and not one that broadly governs an investment adviser's performance. See Freidlob v Trustees of the Alpine Mut. Fund Trust, 905 F.Supp. 843, (D.Col.1995) ("This subsection does not expressly authorize the SEC or a security holder to bring an action challenging a fiduciary's general performance of duties.") Rather, by limiting this duty to "the receipt of compensation for services", § 36(b) creates a standard of care governing the relationship between the management fees that the adviser charges and the services that it provides.

As the magistrate judge explained, Congress originally adopted the ICA out of concern for the inherent conflict of interest and potential for abuse in the relationship between an investment adviser and the investment companies that it manages. See Fox, 464 U.S. at 536. In addition to imposing structural and disclosure requirements, the ICA relied upon the unaffiliated director to assume the role of "independent watchdog" over the investment adviser. Tannenbaum, 552 F.2d at 406. As noted, the original ICA § 36 imposed a fiduciary duty on both directors and the investment adviser providing liability for "gross misconduct or gross abuse of trust" against the investment company. In the face of continuing abuses, primarily due to the investment adviser's inordinate influence over their investment companies' directors, Congress amended the ICA in 1970. From this history of the ICA and the 1970 amendments, the magistrate judge concluded that § 36(b)'s direct cause of action encompasses allegations that investment advice or transactions were imposed merely in order to generate fees for the investment adviser.

However, Congress designed subsection § 36(b) to specifically address the failure of the previous ICA § 36 to "provide any mechanism by which the fairness of management contracts could be tested in court." See Senate Report at 4901. In amending the original § 36, Congress created two distinct subsections. Through each provision, Congress sought to enhance the standard of care for those in control of investment companies by imposing a "fiduciary duty" rather than merely prohibiting "gross misconduct". § 36(a) continued to impose a general standard of care on the exercise of control over an investment company. § 36(b), however, provided "an unusual cause of action ... [that] ... differs significantly from those traditionally asserted in shareholder derivative suits." Fox, 464 U.S. at 535. Most notably, § 36(b) provided shareholders with an express cause of action against the investment adviser that by-passed demand on the directors. Id. In shareholder suits under the previous § 36, the demand requirement proved an insurmountable barrier to challenges to the fee contracts in light of the presumption of validity that those contracts enjoyed when ratified by the unaffiliated directors. See Fox, 464 U.S. at 537 (noting SEC conclusion that shareholder suits were ineffective in challenging the reasonableness of adviser fees because of the legal standards courts applied to those fees). In its report to Congress, the SEC explained that "even the requirement that all of the directors of an externally managed investment company be persons unaffiliated with the company's adviser-underwriter [will] not be an effective check on advisory fees and other forms of management compensation." H.R.Rep. No. 2337, 89th Cong., 2d Sess. 147 (1966). Thus, it was unrealistic to rely upon the directors to adequately enforce or negotiate the terms of the investment company's direct contract with the adviser. Id. In light of the investment company directors' particular ineffectiveness in direct "dealings between the fund and its investment adviser," Congress provided a direct cause of action for shareholders against the investment adviser. See Fox, 464 U.S. at 537. In sum, Congress enacted § 36(b) in order to address a narrow area of concern: the negotiation and enforcement of payment arrangements between the investment adviser and its fund.

Accordingly, every court addressing a § 36(b) claim has required the plaintiff to demonstrate that the compensation or payment received by the investment adviser was disproportionate to the services rendered. See, e.g., Kalish v. Franklin Advisers, Inc., 928 F.2d 590, 592 (2d Cir.), cert. denied, 502 U.S. 818 (1991); Meyer v. Oppenheimer Management Corp., 895 F.2d 861, 866 (2d Cir.1990); Grossman v. Johnson, 674 F.2d 115, 119 (1st. Cir.1982); see also Barnett v. Van Kampen Merritt Inc., 1993 U.S.Dist. LEXIS 3936 (N.D.Ill. March 26, 1993). In light of this legislative history, the courts considered whether the fee "represents a charge within the range of what would have been negotiated at arm's length in the light of all surrounding circumstances." Gartenberg v. Merrill Lynch Asset Managaement, Inc., 694 F.2d 923, 928 (2d Cir.1982), cert. denied, 461 U.S. 906 (1983); see also Kamen v. Kemper Fin. Services, Inc., 908 F.2d 1338, 1339-40 (7th Cir.1990), rev'd on other grounds, 500 U.S. 90 (1991) (§ 36(b) requires courts "to decide whether the fees charged by investment advisers are 'excessive' ") (citation omitted). While these cases did not expressly delineate the limitations on such a claim, each clearly focused on the terms of the fee arrangement in order to discern if a violation of § 36(b) had occurred.[9]

---

[9] The Second Circuit has interpreted § 36(b) to provide a cause of action against an investment adviser for inadequate disclosure of information regarding the fee arrangement. Galfand v. Chestnutt Corp., 545 F.2d 807, 811-12 (2d Cir.1976), aff'd, 573 F.2d 1290 (2d Cir.1977). In Galfand, however, the investment adviser withheld information concerning the approval of alterations to the terms of the fee arrangement with the fund. See id. at 811-14. Thus, the cause of action focused on the adviser's ability to dominate the board and win approval of the fee arrangement, not the adviser's ability to obtain approval of an investment or transaction.

Plaintiffs argue that § 36(b)(3) provides for damages up to "the amount of compensation or payments received from such investment company" by the defendant between the violation and the time of suit. Plaintiffs claim that such an allowance is meaningless if the provision provides only a limited claim for fees charged in excess of the services rendered. But this damages cap simply recognizes that possibility that an investment adviser may attempt to extract fees while essentially providing no services, at all.

Such was the case in Potomac Capital Markets v. Prudential-Bache, 726 F.Supp. 87, 94 (S.D.N.Y.1989), on which plaintiffs rely for the proposition that a shareholder may raise a suit under § 36(b) for receiving a fee for a challenged transaction. However, the allegations in Potomac are inapposite to plaintiffs' instant claim. In Potomac, shareholders raised several counts, including a claim under ICA § 36(b), against the investment adviser to their mutual funds arising from the decision to liquidate the funds' investment portfolios. Id. at 87-88. While the shareholders also attacked the liquidation under other provisions of the ICA, their § 36(b) claim challenged neither the propriety of the liquidation nor the investment adviser's underlying motive for the liquidation. Id. at 94. Rather, the shareholders' § 36(b) claim rested on the investment adviser's receipt and retention of fees paid on the subsequently liquidated assets. Id. The adviser continued to collect management fees for cash that merely sat in accounts. The legality of the liquidation, itself, was irrelevant to the merits of this claim.

Plaintiffs' instant § 36(b) claim, in contrast, relies upon their challenge to the propriety of the Rights Offerings. The plaintiffs neither assert that the Advisor failed to provide any services in relation to the Rights Offerings nor contend that the Advisor has not actively managed the securities obtained from the capital obtained thereunder. Instead, plaintiffs claim that the Advisor devised the Rights Offerings in order to generate fees for itself regardless of the harmful consequences for the Funds. Although plaintiffs allege that the Advisor withheld information from the Funds' directors, this information did not relate directly to receipt of compensation or the terms of the fee arrangement. Cf. Galfand, 545 F.2d at 811-12. Plaintiffs allege that the Advisor withheld information and analysis of the Rights Offerings' likely financial consequences for the Funds. In the opinion of the court, such allegations raise a cause of action under the rubric of ICA § 36(a)'s prohibition of personal misconduct by an investment advisor.

Consequently, the court respectfully rejects Magistrate Judge Bobrick's recommendation that the Complaint alleges a cause of action under ICA § 36(b). While § 36(b) may regulate more than the mere terms of the fee arrangement between the investment adviser and the investment company, the court does not believe that it regulates the propriety of the transactions for which fees are paid. Rather, § 36(b) only imposes a direct fiduciary duty on the investment adviser with "respect to the receipt of compensation or payment for services." It requires that the investment adviser not charge disproportionate fees for the services it provides, that it actually provides the services for which it obtains fees, and that it not withhold information regarding the compensation agreement. However, the text and legislative history of the provision indicate that it does not provide a cause of action challenging the propriety of an investment adviser's financial counsel. Because the Complaint does not challenge the fee arrangement between the Advisor and the Funds, but only challenges the underlying transaction, the defendants' motion to dismiss Count XI is granted.

CONCLUSION

For the reasons set forth above, the court accepts Magistrate Judge Bobrick's report and recommendation except as to the defendants' motion to dismiss Count XI of the plaintiffs' Complaint. It is hereby ordered that defendants motion to dismiss is denied as to Counts VIII and IX and granted as to Counts X and XI.

### Questions and Comments

1. Note the court's discussion of implied rights of action under the 1940 Act. Is it compelling?

2. The *Nuveen* case also explores the causal link that plaintiffs must establish to prevail in this case. Is the standard appropriate?

3. Is this a case about non-disclosure or a fiduciary breach? Or both? What is the difference?

————

*Problem 13-8*

Investco is a mutual fund organized under the laws of the state of Ames. The president of the advisory firm that manages Investco apparently has close ties to the Governor of the State of Ames, and, according to press accounts, has been using Investco assets to purchase large quantities of Ames bonds, which the credit agencies recently down-graded. Shareholders of Investco want to file a claim under section 36(a) of the 1940 Act. Under Ames corporate law, derivative shareholder actions must be preceded by a demand on the board of directors. Must the shareholders make such a demand on the Investco board? Would the shareholders be better advised to bring the suit under section 36(b)?

## Section 4. Structural Restraints Under the 1940 Act

In addition to the fiduciary obligations and disclosure rules we have considered in the preceding sections of this chapter, the 1940 Act also imposes a considerable number of structural restraints on investment companies. For example, section 18 of the 1940 Act prohibits mutual funds from issuing any class of senior security and imposes lesser, though still stringent limitations, on leverage in closed-end companies. The function of these prohibitions is to simplify the capital structure of investment companies and prevent the sort of abuses and losses that leveraged investment caused in the 1930s. Congress could, of course, have chosen to deal with the risks associated with leverage through disclosure rules and fiduciary obligations. Instead, however, it chose structural restraints.

In this final section of Chapter Four, we explore several other illustrations of structural restraints in the 1940 Act. In each area we consider, alternative regulatory structures are possible. As you read through these materials, consider whether mandatory restrictions as opposed to other regulatory regimes are the best choice for these problems.

## A. Anti-Conflict Rules Under the 1940 Act

Among the most important of the 1940 Act's structural restraints are section 17's prohibitions regarding transactions between investment companies and various affiliated parties. Section 17 was intended to preclude the kinds of abusive insider transactions that SEC investigations uncovered in the 1930s. Functionally, section 17's restrictions are similar to section 23A and 23B of the Federal Reserve Act, which impose comparable restrictions for depository institutions. See Chapter Three, Section 3.F. The parameters of section 17, however, are more complex, and the SEC has broad latitude to issue orders and rules exempting certain transactions from these prohibitions. For example, section 17(a) establishes a broad prohibition on transactions between investment companies and affiliated persons. Rule 17a-7 creates an exception to this broad prohibition by establishing procedures whereby investment companies in the same complex can buy and sell securities from each other. Similarly, section 17(b) regulates situations in which investments companies and affiliated persons are joint participants in the same transactions.

For the most the SEC is responsible for enforcing section 17's restrictions. The Commission can used administrative procedures to sanction entities that violate section 17's prohibitions. See, e.g., SEC v. Talley Industries, Inc., 399 F.2d 396 (2d Cir. 1968), *cert. denied*, 393 U.S. 1035 (1969).; cf. Lessler v. Little, 857 F.2d 866 (1st Cir. 1988) (recognizing a private implied right of action for violations of section 17). As the following case illustrates, however, criminal sanctions also have a role in policing these rules.

## United States v. Ostrander
### 999 F.2d 27 (2d Cir. 1993)

WINTER, Circuit Judge:

Patricia Ostrander was charged with two counts of accepting unlawful "compensation" or a "thing of value" from a source other than her employer in connection with the performance of her duties as a portfolio manager, see section 17(e) of the 1940 Act . . . and one count of failing to report a personal investment to her employer, see section 17(j) of the 1940 Act; Rule 17j-1. After an eight-day trial, the jury convicted Ostrander on all three counts. Judge Owen sentenced her to concurrent terms of two months' imprisonment. . . .

### BACKGROUND

Most of the pertinent events occurred during 1985 and 1986. When all permissible inferences are drawn in favor of the government, the evidence showed the following. Ostrander was a portfolio manager for Fidelity Management Research and Fidelity Management Trust Company (collectively "Fidelity"), investment advisers registered with the Securities and

Exchange Commission, from 1970 to 1987. As a manager of Fidelity's funds, Ostrander purchased hundreds of millions of dollars worth of securities from Drexel Burnham Lambert, Inc. ("Drexel").

During early 1985, Kohlberg Kravis Roberts & Co. ("KKR"), a firm specializing in leveraged-buyouts ("LBOs"), decided upon an LBO of Storer Communications, Inc. ("Storer"). KKR hired Drexel to underwrite the securities for the financial transactions. The publicly offered securities included zero coupon bonds, debenture bonds paying fifteen percent per annum, and preferred stock. The preferred stock "paid-in-kind", meaning that it paid dividends of preferred stock rather than cash. It was the most junior of the securities and the most difficult of the securities to sell.

In addition to these publicly offered securities, 67,840,000 warrants were created. Their holders were entitled to exchange each warrant for one share of common stock in the Storer holding company at an exercise price of $2.05. The warrants represented thirty-two percent of the Storer holding company's common stock. They were described as "equity sweeteners" or "equity kickers" because they were designed to assist in the sale of the debentures and preferred stock. Drexel thus told KKR that they would be offered for private sale only to those institutions who had purchased zero coupon bonds, debentures, or preferred stock. This intent also was stated in the prospectus. Thereafter, the head of Drexel's High Yield Bond Department, Michael Milken, falsely indicated to KKR that the warrant price was too high and that potential bond or stock purchasers were "balking" at a price of fourteen cents per warrant. The warrants then were sold for seven cents each and offered only to a few select investors, including Drexel employees. Many of these Drexel employees kept the warrants in partnerships, one of which was MacPherson Investment Partners L.P.

On behalf of Fidelity, Ostrander attended a Drexel roadshow on October 28, 1985. She agreed to purchase for Fidelity Storer securities issued pursuant to the LBO. On December 5, 1985, KKR executed the Storer LBO. On behalf of Fidelity, Ostrander purchased $10 million of the zero coupon bonds, $26 million of the preferred stock (ten percent of the preferred stock offering), and $59 million of the fifteen percent senior subordinated debentures.

During late December 1985, Drexel's Michael Milken offered Ostrander the opportunity to invest her personal funds in MacPherson Investment Partners L.P., a partnership holding some of the Storer warrants. She was not alone. Sixty-five percent of MacPherson was owned by fiduciaries for institutions that purchased other securities issued in the Storer LBO. Ostrander invested $13,200 in MacPherson (paying approximately nine cents per warrant) during January 1986. When purchased, the warrants were highly speculative, and no witnesses were able to value them even as of late December 1985. KKR sold Storer's stations and cable systems at the top of the market in 1987 and 1988 and realized a profit that surpassed prior expectations. The value of Ostrander's $13,200 investment grew to roughly $750,000.

On October 11, 1991, Ostrander was indicted on three counts. Count One charged her with accepting unlawful compensation in connection with her purchases or sales of securities for registered investment companies that she managed as an affiliated person in violation of [section 17(e) of the 1940 Act] . . . . The third count charged that Ostrander, an access person, failed to report the securities at issue to her employer, a registered investment advisory company, as required by [section 17(j) of the 1940 Act] and Rule 17j-1(c).

The jury convicted her on all counts. Judge Owen sentenced Ostrander to concurrent terms of two months' imprisonment and to a $100,000 fine.

## DISCUSSION

Ostrander challenges the trial court's instruction that the "opportunity" to purchase the warrants might constitute a violation of Section 17(e) . . . even though there was no proof that the warrants were purchased at a price below their market value. The challenged instruction is set out in full in the margin.[1]

Specifically, Ostrander argues that Counts One and Two require proof of receipt of "compensation" or a "thing of value" for a price less than its market value. She argues that the judge charged on a faulty legal theory in stating that "you [jurors] need not concern yourself with finding [the warrants'] precise value in the marketplace." We disagree.

In *United States v. Deutsch*, 451 F.2d 98 (2d Cir.1971), *cert. denied*, 404 U.S. 1019 (1972), the case upon which Ostrander primarily relies, we upheld a trial court's definition of the term compensation as a "benefit or thing of value [including] being granted an opportunity to purchase securities at a discounted price." *Id.* at 114. Our holding that this kind of benefit was included among "things of value" did not limit that definition to securities sold at a discount. In fact, the panel stated that the instructions "were more favorable" to Deutsch than necessary. Id. at 115. "He was entitled to an instruction merely that the jury could not convict without being

---

[1]    The challenged instruction stated:

Compensation is anything of benefit or anything of value, whether directly or indirectly received. It may take several forms and is not limited to money or tangible things with an identifiable commercial price tag.

To prove that compensation was received the government must prove that what Mrs. Ostrander received constituted something of value at the time she received it. You need not concern yourselves with finding a precise value in the marketplace. But you may look to the value the recipient here, Mrs. Ostrander, placed on the thing at the time she received it. In other words, the value of something can well be judged and set by the desire of that recipient to have the thing and depends upon that individual and all the circumstances surrounding its receipt.

On this issue you may consider whether or not the defendant herself attached a value to the opportunity to purchase MacPherson and, if she did, whether the value she placed on it was materially above the price being asked to pay for it. Here the defendant contends that MacPherson ... had all of the attendant risks and therefore was not a thing of value as defined. The government, on the other hand, contends that the mere opportunity to invest in MacPherson was itself compensation or a thing of value because the MacPherson interests were by their nature scarce or available to only a few individuals....

It is sufficient that the government prove that the compensation at issue here, namely, the opportunity to invest in MacPherson, was connected to the sale of securities to the funds she managed or, in other words, that it was given and received by her in appreciation of past or in anticipation of future conduct by her.

persuaded beyond a reasonable doubt that the agreement to buy [the note] was made with the knowledge that it constituted something of value." *Id.*

Nor do other cases require that the "thing of value" received be shown to have been transferred at a discount somehow calculated. In *United States v. Williams*, 705 F.2d 603 (2d Cir.), *cert. denied*, 464 U.S. 1007 (1983), we upheld an instruction that the jury should disregard the stock's "worth in the commercial world." *Id.* at 623; *see also United States v. Crozier*, 987 F.2d 893, 901-02 (2d Cir.1993); *United States v. Blitz*, 533 F.2d 1329, 1344, 1345 (2d Cir.), *cert. denied*, 429 U.S. 819 (1976) (construing "thing of value" under Section 17(e) of the Investment Companies Act to include loans repaid with interest); *United States v. Roth*, 333 F.2d 450, 453 (2d Cir.1964) (upholding instruction that jury must "find more than a loan [and] substantial monetary benefit or thing of value" because, "if anything, [it was] *too favorable* to defendants") (emphasis added), *cert. denied*, 380 U.S. 942 (1965).

These decisions take a common sense view of Section 17(e). . . . Under th[is] statute[], it is enough if the item received was regarded as a benefit by the recipient, whether or not others might have taken a different view of its value. Based on the evidence before it, the jury could reasonably conclude that Ostrander regarded the opportunity to purchase the warrants as a benefit. This opportunity was carefully limited by Milken to selected persons, including himself, other Drexel employees, firms, and fiduciaries for institutions that had purchased securities in the Storer LBO. There was no market price set by public trading in which all were free to engage, and the opportunity to purchase the warrants was at Milken's whim and at a price set by him. Ostrander's claim that the legal theory underlying her conviction would criminalize transactions in heavily traded securities at open market prices is simply wrong. Such transactions are not benefits within the meaning of the statutes because the purchaser obtains nothing unavailable elsewhere at the same price. Such a transaction cannot influence a fiduciary's decisionmaking. Although Ostrander got no guarantee of profit, she did get an opportunity offered only to a few that she clearly believed to be a good buy. That is a thing of value, or so a jury might find.

Without irony, she also contends that the warrants had no value and that the judge erred by instructing the jury to "look to the value [she] placed on the thing at the time she received it." We disagree. First, the warrants had value, if for no other reason because numerous investment professionals, including Drexel employees and fiduciaries for investors, were willing to, and did, purchase them. *See Williams*, 705 F.2d at 623. Indeed, the "they-had-no-value" argument rings particularly hollow from one who actually paid value and then made a profit of nearly $750,000 on an investment of $13,200. Second, the instruction was proper according to our decision in Williams, which upheld an instruction "to focus on the value that the defendants subjectively attached to the items received." *Id.*

The jury might easily have found that the warrants were compensation for her past and future purchases of securities from Drexel for Fidelity. She had purchased on behalf of Fidelity large blocs of the securities offered in the LBO, including ten percent of the preferred, the most difficult securities of the package to sell. We are unpersuaded by her argument that, because she purchased no Storer bonds after agreeing to buy the warrants, the jury could not as a matter of law find a connection to her purchase of the Storer securities or to potential future purchases from Drexel of securities in other companies.[2]

Ostrander also challenges the admission of evidence concerning two conversations that purportedly are inadmissible hearsay. The first conversation occurred between Michael Milken and Ted Ammon, a general partner from KKR. During the telephone conversation, Milken told Ammon that potential bond or preferred stock buyers were "balking" because the warrants were too expensive. This conversation induced Ammon to agree to reduce the initial offering price for the warrants from fourteen to seven cents. Because this evidence was not offered by the government to prove the truth of its contents, it was not hearsay. *See* Fed.R.Evid. 801(c). The evidence was intended to show that Milken had made such statements and persuaded KKR to authorize a drop in price, not that the contents of the statements were true. Indeed, Milken's statements were false and were offered to show only that he successfully induced Storer to reduce the price and, by implication, that he believed the warrants, which he intended to appropriate for himself, co-workers and other selected purchasers, were of value.

Craig Cogut, a witness, testified about the second conversation. He stated that he had overheard Michael Milken's brother Lowell tell Milken "words to the effect that you better get moving selling the preferred or we are going to be long a whole lot of it," a statement with which Michael did not disagree. This statement reflected the state of mind of each brother that the preferred was a hard sell, *see* Fed.R.Evid. 803(3), a fact that was relevant to their motive to pay compensation to Ostrander.

Finally, Ostrander argues that Count III does not allege a crime. Count III charged that she had violated section 17(j) and Rule 17j-1 by failing to report her MacPherson investment to Fidelity. Section 17(j) of the Investment Companies Act states in pertinent part:

> It shall be unlawful [for a person in Ostrander's position] to engage in any act, practice, or course of business in connection with the purchase or sale, directly or indirectly, by such person of any security held or to be acquired by such registered investment company in contravention of such rules and regulations as the Commission may adopt to define, and prescribe means reasonably necessary to prevent, such acts, practices, or courses of business as are fraudulent, deceptive or manipulative.

Rule 17j-1(c)(1), promulgated pursuant to Section 17(j), states in pertinent part:

> Every [portfolio manager for] a registered investment company ... shall report to such investment company, ... [the date of a purchase or sale of a security, the price, and the broker] with respect to transactions in any security in which such access person has, or by reason of such transaction acquires, any direct or indirect beneficial ownership....

---

[2]    Because we reject Ostrander's theory that the payment of a fair market value for the warrants was a defense, we need not consider her two related arguments: (i) she was deprived of presenting her defense that she did not know that the warrants may have been sold below their market value; if the law does not recognize a legal argument as a valid defense, the court has no duty to instruct the jury on that argument; (ii) the government lacked sufficient evidence that the warrants were sold below their actual value; that is not an element of the crime and thus need not be proven.

Both the statutory provision and the regulation may be enforced through criminal proceedings. [Section 49 of the 1940 Act.]

Ostrander does not dispute that she failed to inform Fidelity of her MacPherson investment, thus violating a company rule as well as Section 270.17j-1(c)(1). Rather, she argues that Section 17(j) applies only to securities "held or to be acquired" by Fidelity. Because Fidelity never held an interest in MacPherson, she concludes, she was under no duty to report. The argument is entirely frivolous. Any payment to a portfolio manager intended to induce the purchase of a firm's securities on behalf of an investment company easily qualifies as a "fraudulent, deceptive or manipulative" act "in connection with" the investment company's acquisition of securities, whether or not the payment consists of an opportunity to purchase securities in a different firm. Moreover, Section 17(e) expressly invites the Commission to flesh out its general prohibitions by regulation. The regulation in question, which requires portfolio managers to report to their companies their interests in various securities, is a prophylactic measure reasonably related to the enforcement of Section 17(j). *See United States v. Chestman*, 947 F.2d 551, 556-63 (2d Cir. 1991). Ostrander's failure to report her interest in MacPherson was thus a crime.

Affirmed.

## Comments and Questions

1. Was it appropriate to initiate a criminal prosecution against Patricia Ostrander? Were other, lesser sanctions available? When should criminal as opposed to civil, administrative, or market sanctions be imposed?

2. As the *Ostrander* case explores, there are both statutory (section 17(j)) and regulatory (rule 17j-1) rules governing personal trading of personnel associated with investment companies. Transactions, such as the ones underlying the Ostrander prosecution, prompted some industry analysts to criticize existing restrictions on personal trading as too lax. Responding to these criticisms, the Investment Company Institute, a trade association, formed an advisory group to review industry practices in the area. In a report released in May of 1994, the group revealed that "[m]ost, if not all" investment companies had adopted codes of conduct regarding personal investing that "far exceeds the requirements of current law." The group also rejected proposals for an absolute ban on personal investing on the grounds that market forces could effectively police abuse in this area and that a prohibition "would arbitrarily and unfairly foreclose" many individual employees from engaging in "wholly legitimate and appropriate investment opportunities," thus creating "substantial and needless disincentives to the continued service of these talented individuals in the industry." The advisory group recommended instead a series of more modest restrictions on personal trading, plus enhanced compliance procedures. In a substantive proposal, the Commission has recommended a number of amendments to rule 17j-1 that are generally consistent with the advisory group's recommendations and focus on enhanced disclosure and oversight as opposed to a broad prohibition on personal trading. See SEC Release 33-7212 (Sept. 8, 1995). Do you agree with this regulatory approach?

*Problem 13-9*

Daniel Shere was the portfolio manager for the Janes Fund. Early one morning, Shere received and rejected an offer to purchase on behalf of the fund a block of thinly traded securities at a price of $17 per share. Later in the day, Shere received a second offer to purchase the same securities at a price of $17 ½ per share. Reasoning that it would be a deviation from the fund's normal investment practices to purchase and sell securities in a single day, Shere did not attempt to match up the two offers on behalf of the fund. When he got home at night, however, he did contact both counter-parties, and executed matching purchases and sales for a block of 10,000 shares, earning himself a gross profit of fifty cents a share. Shere has been making matching trades of this sort for his own account since he was in high school. Did he violate the law by engaging in arbitraging the two offers here?

## B. Portfolio Restrictions for Money Market Mutual Funds

Our final reading in this chapter concerns special structural restrictions on a subclass of investment companies — money market mutual funds. Such funds were at the heart of the Merrill Lynch CMA program we have encountered several times already in this chapter.

## Final Amendments Revising Rules Regulating Money Market Funds
### 56 Fed Reg 8113 (Feb. 27, 1991)

The Securities and Exchange Commission ("Commission") is adopting several amendments to rules and forms affecting money market funds, including rule 2a-7 under the Investment Company Act of 1940 ("1940 Act"). . . . Rule 2a-7 is used by most money market funds to maintain a stable net asset value of $1.00 per share.

The Commission is adopting amendments to rule 2a-7 to require a money market fund to: (1) Limit its investment in the securities of any one issuer to no more than five percent of fund assets, measured at the time of purchase (the "five percent diversification test"), except for certain investments held for not more than three business days; (2) limit its investment in securities which are "Second Tier Securities" to no more than five percent of fund assets, with investment in the Second Tier Securities of any one issuer being limited to the greater of one percent of fund assets or one million dollars; and (3) limit investments to securities that are determined to have "minimal credit risks" and are "Eligible Securities." "Eligible Securities" are defined as securities rated by the Requisite NRSROs in one of the two highest short-term rating categories and comparable unrated securities. "Second Tier Securities" are Eligible Securities that are not "First Tier Securities." "First Tier Securities" are defined as securities which are rated by at least two nationally recognized statistical rating organizations ("NRSROs")[1] or by the only NRSRO that has rated the security (the "Requisite NRSROs") in the highest short-term rating category, or comparable unrated securities.

The amendments also (1) Limit fund investments to securities with a remaining maturity of not more than thirteen months (except that money market funds that do not use the amortized cost method of valuation may invest in U.S. Government securities that have a remaining maturity of not more than twenty-five months);  (2) require a fund to maintain a dollar-weighted average portfolio maturity of not more than ninety days;  (3) require a fund, in the event that a portfolio security goes into default or the rating of a portfolio security is downgraded so that it is no longer an Eligible Security, and in certain other circumstances, to reassess promptly whether the security presents minimal credit risks, determine whether continuing to hold the security is in the best interest of the fund, and record such actions in fund records;  and (4) require a fund to notify the Commission if it holds defaulted securities which amount to one-half of one percent or more of fund assets.  Finally, the amendments to rule 2a-7 make it unlawful for any registered investment company to use the term "money market" in its name or hold itself out as a "money market fund" unless it meets the risk limiting conditions of the rule.  Funds that hold themselves out as distributing income that is exempt from regular federal income tax ("tax exempt funds") are exempted from the five percent diversification test for First Tier Securities, the five percent limit on investments in Second Tier Securities and the one percent limit on investments in the Second Tier Securities of any one issuer.

The Commission is also adopting amendments to rule 482 under the Securities Act of 1933, rule 34b-1 under the 1940 Act, and Forms N-1A, N-3, and N-4 under the 1933 and 1940 Acts to:  (1) Require the cover page of money market fund prospectuses, and fund advertisements and sales literature, to disclose prominently that an investment in a money market fund is neither insured nor guaranteed by the U.S. Government and that there is no assurance that the fund will be able to maintain a stable per share net asset value; and (2) revise the definition of a "money market fund" for purposes of those funds eligible to quote a seven-day yield in advertisements and sales literature to include only those funds that meet the risk-limiting conditions. . . . .

### Background

On July 17, 1990, the Commission proposed amendments to rules and forms under the 1933 Act and the 1940 Act affecting money market funds, including rule 2a-7 under the 1940 Act. [2]

---

[1]     The term "nationally recognized statistical rating organization" is used in the Commission's uniform net capital rule (17 CFR 240.15c3- 1(c)(2)(vi) (E), (F) and (H).  The Commission's Division of Market Regulation responds to requests for NRSRO designation through no-action letters.  Currently, the Division of Market Regulation has designated five NRSROs:  Duff and Phelps, Inc. ("D&P"), Fitch Investors Services, Inc. ("Fitch"), Moody's Investors Service Inc. (Moody's"), Standard & Poor's Corp. ("S&P"), and, with respect to debt issued by banks, bank holding companies, United Kingdom building societies, broker-dealers and broker dealers' parent companies, and bank-supported debt, IBCA Limited and its affiliate, IBCA Inc. ("IBCA").

[2]     Investment Company Act Rel. No. 17589 (July 17, 1990) (55 FR 30239 (July 25, 1990)) (the "Proposing Release").  Money market funds are open-end management investment companies investing

Rule 2a-7 permits money market funds to maintain a stable price per share, [3] through the use of the amortized cost method of valuation [4] and the penny-rounding method of pricing. [5]    But for rule 2a-7, section 2(a)(41) of the 1940 Act, together with rules 2a-4 and 22c-1 under the 1940 Act (17 CFR 270.2a-4 and 270.22c-1), would require a money market fund to calculate its current net asset value per share by valuing portfolio securities for which market quotations are readily available at market value, and other securities and assets at fair value as determined in good faith by the board of directors ("mark-to-market"). [6]

Rule 2a-7 was adopted in 1983. [7]    It contains a number of conditions designed to reduce the likelihood that the net asset value of a money market fund as determined by the amortized cost method will deviate materially from its net asset value as determined by the mark-to-market

---

in short-term debt instruments. There are currently 710 money market funds with over $536 billion in assets in approximately 21.3 million shareholder accounts.  IBC/Donoghue's Money Fund Report, (Feb. 8, 1991) (the "Money Fund Report").  Data derived from the Money Fund Report is as of February 5, 1991.  The information with respect to shareholder accounts is derived from the Investment Company Institute Mutual Fund Factbook 102 (30th ed. 1990). . . . .

[3]    Most money market funds maintain a stable price of $1.00 per share.  The stable $1.00 price has encouraged investors to view money market funds as an alternative to bank deposit and checking accounts, even though money market funds lack federal deposit insurance.

[4]    Under the amortized cost method, portfolio securities are valued by reference to their acquisition cost as adjusted for amortization of premium or accretion of discount.  The definition of the term "amortized cost method" has been amended to substitute the term "accretion" for "accumulation" in order to reflect current finance and accounting terminology.  Paragraph (a)(1) of rule 2a-7, as amended.

[5]    Share price is determined under the penny rounding method by valuing securities at market value, fair value, or amortized cost (as described in note 6 and accompanying test, infra) and rounding the per share net asset value to the nearest cent on a share value of a dollar, as opposed to the nearest one tenth of one cent.  Paragraph (a)(11) of rule 2a-7, as amended. See also Investment Company Act Rel. No. 13380 (July 11, 1983) (48 FR 32555 (July 18, 1983)) (hereinafter, "Release 13380") at n. 6, and Investment Company Act Rel. No. 12206 (Feb. 1, 1982) (47 FR 5428 (Feb. 5, 1982)) (hereinafter, "Release 12206") at n. 5.

[6]    The Commission has adopted an interpretive position permitting open-end investment companies that hold a significant amount of debt securities to use the cost amortization method of valuation with respect to debt securities that mature in sixty days or less unless the particular circumstances dictate otherwise (i.e., due to the impairment of the creditworthiness of an issuer). Investment Company Act Rel. No. 9786 (May 31, 1977) (42 FR 28999 (June 7, 1977)) (hereinafter, "Release 9786").

[7]    Rule 2a-7 was proposed in Release 12206, supra note 5, and adopted in Release 13380, supra note 5.  Since its adoption, rule 2a-7 has been amended only once, in 1986, to permit money market funds to acquire put options and standby commitments.  See Investment Company Act Rel. No. 14983 (Mar. 12, 1986) (51 FR 9773 (Mar. 21, 1986)) (hereinafter, "Release 14983").

method. [8] The rule also requires a fund's board of directors to take promptly such action as it deems appropriate to eliminate or reduce to the extent reasonably practicable any deviation between a fund's amortized cost and its mark-to-market value if the deviation could result in material dilution or unfair results to investors. [9] Currently, money market funds that rely on rule 2a-7 can invest only in "high quality" debt securities, i.e., securities rated in one of the top two quality categories by any NRSRO. [10] Funds using the rule are prohibited from investing in instruments with a maturity of greater than one year and from maintaining a dollar-weighted average portfolio maturity that exceeds 120 days. [11] The rule's conditions have had the effect of maintaining the quality of securities held by money market funds, thus reducing the likelihood that a fund will hold securities that will substantially decline in value and that a fund will break a dollar.

As discussed in the Proposing Release, the Commission decided to reexamine the conditions contained in rule 2a-7 in light of developments in the commercial paper market since the rule was adopted. [12] In June 1989 and March 1990, several money market funds held commercial paper of issuers that defaulted. The shareholders of these money market funds were not adversely affected only because each fund's investment adviser (or an affiliate) purchased the defaulted paper from the fund at its amortized cost or principal amount.

The Commission proposed amendments to rule 2a-7 that would have required a money market fund to limit fund investments in securities that had received less than the highest rating from any NRSRO to five percent of fund assets (the "five percent quality test"). Investment in any single lower-rated issuer would have been limited to one percent of fund assets (the "one percent diversification test"). [13] The amendments would have reduced the maximum permitted

---

[8]    If the net asset value of a fund, as determined by the mark-to-market method of pricing, were to drop significantly below the net asset value as determined by the amortized cost method, investors who redeemed their investments would receive more than their pro rata share of the fund's assets, the interests of other shareholders would be diluted, and purchasing investors would pay too much for their shares.

[9]    The board is required to consider promptly what action should be initiated where the deviation between the amortized cost and the mark-to- market value exceeds one half of one percent, including whether to reduce the share price to less than $1.00 ("breaking a dollar").

[10]    The rule limits money market fund investment to these securities because they are subject to less credit risk than lower quality securities, and are therefore less likely to decrease in value while they are held by the fund.

[11]    These conditions limit fund exposure to the risk that the quality of a security might decline over time or that market interest rates would rise, resulting in a decline in the value of the portfolio securities.

[12]    See the Proposing Release, supra note 2, at nn. 15 through 20, and accompanying text.

[13]    These securities were referred to in the Proposing Release as "Securities Not Having the Highest Rating." Rule 2a-7, as amended, refers to securities that are subject to the adopted investment limitations as "Second Tier Securities." While the basis for identifying a Second Tier Security is

dollar-weighted average portfolio maturity to ninety days. The amendments would also have required money market funds to disclose to investors that investment in the fund is not federally insured or guaranteed. The proposal had two principal purposes: to provide additional safeguards to reduce the likelihood that a money market fund would have to break a dollar, and to increase investor awareness that investments in a money market fund are not "risk free." . . .

## Discussion

A. Preliminary Matters

Rule 2a-7 limits a money market fund to investing in securities that its board of directors determines present "minimal credit risks" and that are "high quality" as defined in the rule. [17] While the amendments revise the definition of high quality, they do not revise the requirement that a money market funds' board of directors (or its delegate) evaluate the creditworthiness of the issuer of any portfolio security and any entity providing a credit enhancement for a portfolio security. Possession of a certain rating by a NRSRO is not a "safe harbor." Where the security is rated, having the requisite NRSRO rating is a necessary but not sufficient condition for investing in the security and cannot be the sole factor considered in determining whether a security has minimal credit risks. To underscore this point, a parenthetical has been added to the rule stating that the determination of whether an instrument presents minimal credit risks "must be based on factors pertaining to credit quality in addition to the rating assigned * * * by a NRSRO." [18]

The extensiveness of the evaluation will vary with the type and maturity of the security involved and the board's (or its delegate's) familiarity with the issuer of the security. For example, little credit analysis of a Government security would be expected. A different analysis may be appropriate for a security with a remaining maturity of seven days than for one of the same issuer with a remaining maturity of one year. In a letter dated May 8, 1990, the Division of Investment Management provided guidance on elements of a minimal credit risk analysis. [19] As stated in the May 8 Letter and reiterated in the Proposing Release, these elements are only

---

somewhat different from the proposed test for Securities Not Having the Highest Rating, for ease of reference the term Second Tier Securities is also used in this Release to refer to securities that under the amendments as proposed would have been Securities Not Having the Highest Rating.

[17]    The rule as originally adopted used the term "high quality." The Proposing Release used the term "Eligible Quality." Rule 2a-7, as amended, uses the term "Eligible Security." See note 15, supra.

The board generally can delegate to the fund's investment adviser the responsibility for determining that individual portfolio securities present minimal credit risks, but only under guidelines established by the board. In certain instances, these determinations must be expressly approved or ratified by the board (and not its delegate). See section II.F. of this Release, infra.

[18]    Paragraph (c)(3) of rule 2a-7, as amended.

[19]    Letter to Registrants (pub. avail. May 8, 1990) (hereinafter, the "May 8 Letter").

examples.  The focus of any minimal credit risk analysis must be on those elements that indicate the capacity of the issuer to meet its short-term debt obligations.

The amendments adopted in this Release place additional restrictions on money market funds in selecting portfolio securities, including commercial paper.  The Commission believes these amendments are necessary to ensure that money market funds meet investors' expectations for safety, soundness and convenience by maximizing the likelihood that these funds will be able to maintain a stable net asset value under the pricing procedures they are permitted to use.  Rule 2a-7 and the amendments adopted today were developed in response to the characteristics of a specific type of registered investment company with a specific type of share pricing standard.  The Commission wishes to emphasize that the amendments are not intended to limit the ability of investment companies not holding themselves out as money market funds to invest in lower-rated securities, including lower-rated commercial paper.  Nor are the amendments intended to suggest that these investment limitations are necessarily appropriate for any other types of investment vehicles.

B. Portfolio Quality and Diversification

1. Five Percent Diversification Test

Most money market funds taking advantage of the exemptions provided by rule 2a-7 are "diversified" investment companies within the meaning of section 5(b)(1) of the 1940 Act. [20] Section 5(b)(1) provides that a diversified investment company, with respect to seventy-five percent of its assets, may not invest more than five percent of its assets in securities of any issuer, other than cash, cash items, Government securities, [21] and securities of other investment companies. [22]  The remaining twenty-five percent of the fund's assets (the "twenty-five percent basket") may be invested in any manner.  The Commission proposed to amend rule 2a-7 to limit any money market fund (except a tax exempt fund) to investing no more than five percent of its total assets [23] in the securities -- except Government securities -- of any one issuer.  The effect of this proposal would be to eliminate the twenty-five percent basket.

Most commenters, including most mutual fund commenters, supported the proposed five percent diversification test as appropriate for a money market fund and indicated that, despite the

---

[20]   Several tax exempt funds which concentrate in the obligations of state and local governments are not diversified within the meaning of section 5(b)(1).  As discussed infra, the new diversification requirements of the rule are not being applied to tax exempt funds at this time.  See paragraph (c)(4)(i) of rule 2a-7, as amended.

[21]   The term "Government security" is defined in section 2(a)(16) of the 1940 Act.  Paragraph (a)(8) of rule 2a-7, as amended, incorporates this definition.

[22]   Section 5(b)(1) also prohibits diversified funds, with respect to seventy-five percent of their assets, from investing in securities that comprise more than 10% of the outstanding voting securities of an issuer.

[23]   "Total Assets" is defined in paragraph (a)(18) of rule 2a-7, as amended, to mean, with respect to a fund using the amortized cost method, the total amortized cost of its assets, and with respect to any other money market fund, the total market-based value of its assets.

flexibility provided by section 5(b)(1) with respect to the twenty-five percent basket, in practice, most taxable money market funds limit their investment in non-U.S. Government issuers to approximately five percent or less of total assets. The Commission has decided to adopt the five percent diversification test as proposed, with a provision designed to permit funds to make certain temporary investments in excess of the five percent limit, and with the clarifications noted below. [24] . . . .

### 2. Diversification and Quality Test for Second Tier Securities

The Commission proposed to prohibit a taxable money market fund from investing more than five percent of its total assets in Second Tier Securities, with investment in the Second Tier Securities of any one issuer being limited to no more than one percent of total assets. [34] In proposing these limitations the Commission stated that, in light of recent experiences of money market funds, a substantial investment in these securities may create an inappropriate risk for funds seeking to maintain a stable price per share. While most commenters representing the mutual fund industry supported or did not oppose these limitations on Second Tier Securities (or suggested additional limitations), all of the commercial paper dealers and issuers of Second Tier Securities that commented on the proposals strongly opposed them. [35]

The Commission requested comment on the possibility of excluding money market funds aimed at institutional investers from the risk-limiting conditions of rule 2a-7. Comment was divided, and the Commission has decided not to create such an exemption at this time. The Commission is concerned that, if an institutional fund were to break a dollar, there might be a loss of confidence in the money market fund industry. An institutional investor exception is being considered in the Division of Investment Management's current study of the Investment Company Act. See Investment Company Act Rel. No. 17534 (June 15, 1990) (55 FR 25322 (June 21, 1990)).

Commenters opposing the proposal argued that these diversification and quality tests would raise the borrowing costs of second tier issuers by reducing the amount of their short-term paper bought by money market funds, and expressed concern that many funds, especially smaller funds, would not invest in any Second Tier Securities. Several of these commenters also argued that the Commission's concerns over the creditworthiness of second tier issuers were misplaced. These commenters urged the Commission to rely instead on increased prospectus disclosure concerning

---

[24]    Paragraph (c)(4)(i)(A) of rule 2a-7, as amended. For purposes of the diverisfication and quality tests, subsidiaries and parent companies are treated as separate issuers. In the case of banks having more than one branch, all branches are treated as the same issuer.

[34]    In each case compliance with the limitations would be determined at the time of acquisition.

[35]    The proposed exemption of tax exempt funds from the five percent diversification and Second Tier Security tests was generally supported by commenters, who stated that these funds often would have difficulties meeting the tests due to the limited number of tax exempt issuers in certain markets. Paragraph (c)(4)(i) of rule 2a-7, as amended, adopts the exemption. The definition of tax exempt fund has been amended to clarify that it includes a fund that distributes income exempt from "regular" federal income tax. See paragraph (a)(17) of rule 2a-7, as amended. A fund that distributes income that is subject to the alternative minimum tax would therefore be considered a tax exempt fund for this purpose.

the risks posed when a money market fund invests in a substantial amount of Second Tier Securities. Many commenters also argued that the proposed limitations would discourage funds from performing independent credit research, since the benefits of research are often realized by investment in lower-rated securities that fund managers conclude have minimal credit risks. Commenters asserted also that the one percent diversification test would not permit a fund to make a sufficient investment in any one issuer of Second Tier Securities to justify the level of credit analysis that would be required to determine that the investment presented minimal credit risks. Commenters also noted that, because commercial paper is usually sold in minimum denominations of one million dollars, the one percent diversification test would preclude smaller money market funds from investing in Second Tier Securities.

In contrast, the Investment Company Institute ("ICI") and substantially all of the individual investor commenters urged the Commission to prohibit money market funds from investing in any Second Tier Securities. [36] The ICI argued that "past experience indicates that [Second Tier Securities] may undergo rapid deterioration and therefore may involve risks inappropriate for funds seeking to maintain a stable net asset value." Commenters favoring the Second Tier Security tests noted that a few funds with riskier investment policies breaking a dollar might lead to a loss of investor confidence in the entire money market industry. The ICI asserted that "in determining the quality standards for money market fund portfolio securities the exclusive focus must be on the protection of money market fund shareholders, who seek safety by investing in funds whose objective is the maintenance of a stable net asset value."

The Commission continues to believe that the recent history of defaults in the commercial paper market and the extent to which these defaults have affected funds warrant taking measures to assure that investors' expectations of the relative safety of investment companies holding themselves out as money market funds continue to be met. Almost all money market funds attempt to maintain a stable net asset value, and this policy is understood by investors to imply a high level of investor safety. Investors have come to equate investments in these funds to "money." Because holding money does not entail any credit risks, the credit risks to which holders of money market shares are exposed should be minimized to the lowest level practicable. [37]

After considering the comments received and after weighing the increased risks and benefits of allowing money market funds to invest a greater percentage of their assets in Second Tier Securities, the Commission has decided to adopt the Second Tier Security tests substantially as proposed, with one change to the one percent diversification test. As amended, rule 2a-7 limits money market fund investment in Second Tier Securities to no more than five percent of fund

---

[36]    The ICI, however, urged the Commission to permit money market funds to invest up to ten percent of their assets in split rated paper (i.e., paper that had received the highest rating from at least one NRSRO, but not from other NRSROs rating the paper), with investment in any split rated issuer being limited to three percent of fund assets. See discussion of the treatment of split rated paper in section II.B.3 of this Release, infra.

[37]    In addition, these limitations are necessary in order to assure that shareholders of funds using the amortized cost of penny rounding method will not suffer any dilution of the value of their investment. See note 8, supra.

assets. [38]  Paragraph (c)(4)(i)(B) of rule 2a-7, as amended, limits the amount a money market fund may invest in the Second Tier Securities of a single issuer to the greater of one percent of the fund's total assets or one million dollars.  The alternative one million dollar test is intended to allow smaller money market funds to invest in Second Tier Securities. [39]  The three day safe harbor discussed above applies only to First Tier Securities and thus it would not permit a fund to exceed the diversification limits for Second Tier Securities.

As explained in the Proposing Release, compliance with the five percent diversification and Second Tier Security tests is measured at the time the fund purchases the security.  Thus a fund would not be required subsequently to dispose of a security because of a change in the percentage of fund assets the security represents or in the fund's overall investment in Second Tier Securities. [40]  In addition, to facilitate determining compliance with the Second Tier Security tests, rule 2a-7, as amended, specifies that in calculating the percentage of fund assets invested in Second Tier Securities, a fund should only include securities that were Second Tier Securities at the time they were acquired (at original purchase or at any subsequent roll-over) and need not take into account rating changes subsequent to the acquisition of the security. [41] . . . .

C. Maturity of Portfolio Securities

1. Ninety-Day Dollar Weighted Average Maturity

The Commission is adopting proposed rule amendments to require a money market fund to maintain a dollar weighted average portfolio maturity of not more than ninety days, as opposed

---

[38]    Paragraph (c)(4)(i)(B)(2) of rule 2a-7, amended.  Paragraph (a)(14) of rule 2a-7, as amended, defines a Second Tier Security as any Eligible Security that is not a "First Tier Security," Paragraph (a)(6) of rule 2a-7, as amended, defines a First Tier Security as a security that is rated by the "Requisite NRSROs" in the highest rating category, or if unrated, which is of comparable quality.  See, section II.B.3 of this Release, infra, discussing the definition of the term "Requisite NRSROs," and its effect on split rated securities.

[39]    The five percent diversification and five percent quality tests would still apply, and thus a fund could not purchase one million dollars of Second Tier Securities if it would result, immediately after the purchase of the securities, in the fund having more than five percent of its total assets invested either in securities of that issuer or in Second Tier Securities.

[40]    Paragraph (c)(4)(i) of rule 2a-7, as amended.

[41]    Thus, a fund would not be required to "drop" a First Tier Security into the five percent Second Tier Security "basket" due to a downgrade.  Paragraph (c)(4)(i)(B) of rule 2a-7, as amended.  However, a fund board of directors (or its delegate) will be required to assess promptly whether a security which has ceased to be a First Tier Security presents minimal credit risks and cause the fund to take such action as is determined to be in the best interest of the fund.  See note 70 and accompanying text, infra, and paragraph (c)(5)(i) of rule 2a-7, as amended.  If the security is no longer a Second Tier Security because of a rating downgrade, it must be disposed of unless the board of directors determines that holding it is in the fund's best interest.  See section II.E.1 of this Release, infra, and paragraph (c)(5)(ii) of rule 2a-7, as amended.

to the 120 days now permitted. [49] The change will decrease the exposure of money market fund investors to interest rate risk.

Most commenters supported the change. These commenters stated that almost all funds already limit their maturities to an even greater extent than the amendments would require. [50] As explained in the Proposing Release, the ninety-day limit is a maximum. [51] A money market fund must maintain a dollar-weighted average portfolio maturity appropriate to its objective of maintaining a stable net asset value or price per share. [52] Thus, in delegating portfolio management responsibilities to the fund's investment adviser, the board should adopt guidelines with respect to portfolio maturity designed to assure that this objective is met.

2. Extension of Maximum Maturity Period for Any Security

The proposed amendments would have extended the current limit on the maximum remaining maturity of any portfolio security from one year [53] to two years. Most commenters addressing this issue criticized this proposal as inconsistent with other changes proposed by the Commission. Commenters stated that a two-year maximum would increase the exposure of funds to both credit risk and interest rate risk. One commenter supported the proposed extension, arguing that, in the context of the ninety-day average limit, increasing maximum allowed maturities would have little effect on the overall risk exposure of a fund while allowing it to enhance yield. Several commenters stated that if the Commission was concerned by the degree of risk involved in increasing the permitted maturity period of securities, it could limit purchases of longer maturity instruments to Government securities. In view of the increased credit risks of securities with longer maturities, the Commission has decided to limit investment in securities

---

[49]   Paragraph (c)(2)(iii) of rule 2a-7, as amended.

[50]   As of February 5, 1991 the average portfolio maturity of taxable money market funds was 53 days and the average maturity of tax exempt funds was 50 days. See the Money Fund Report, supra, note 2. One commenter noted that the danger that a long portfolio maturity might cause a fund to break a dollar has been demonstrated. In 1987, municipal money market instruments fluctuated by 240 basis points over a sixty day period, a fluctuation large enough to cause a fund with a ninety-day average dollar weighted average maturity to break a dollar. The commenter suggested that the maximum portfolio maturity be reduced to sixty days. However, the Commission believes that a ninety day period should provide money market fund investors with additional safeguards without unduly limiting the flexibility of money market funds to adjust fund maturities to levels that are appropriate in view of market conditions.

[51]   See the Proposing Release, supra note 2, at n. 61.

[52]   See paragraph (c)(2) of rule 2a-7, as amended.

[53]   The current rule defines one year as 365 days, but provides that in the case of an instrument that was issued as a one year instrument, but has up to 375 days until maturity, one year means 375 days. This provision was designed to accommodate certain government agency securities that have this characteristic. See Release 13380, supra note 5, at n. 13.

with longer maturities to Government securities. [54]   However, since the value of Government securities with a remaining maturity in excess of thirteen months may be subject to price fluctuations due to changes in interest rates (which could result in significant deviations between amortized cost and market values), rule 2a-7, as amended, permits their purchase only by a money market fund that uses market-based values in calculating its net asset value (including funds that rely on Release 9786 to value portfolio securities). [55]

With respect to securities other than Government securities, as suggested by several commenters, the rule extends the maximum permitted maturity of individual securities to thirteen months. This change has been made in order to accommodate funds purchasing annual tender bonds, and securities on a when- issued or delayed delivery basis. These securities often are not delivered for a period of up to one month after the purchaser has made a commitment to purchase them. Since the purchaser must "book" the security on the day it agrees to purchase it, the maturity period begins on that day. The revised rule allows funds to invest in securities with a remaining maturity of no more than thirteen months (397 days). [57]

### 3. Variable Rate Demand Instruments

Many commenters objected to the provision of the current rule that the remaining maturity of a variable rate instrument with a demand feature be deemed equal to the longer of (i) the period remaining until the next interest readjustment or (ii) the period remaining until the principal amount can be recovered through demand. Several commenters urged the Commission to revise the standard to provide that the maturity period is the shorter of the two periods. One commenter recommended that the maturity period simply be made equal to the period remaining until the next interest readjustment, ignoring any demand feature.

The current treatment of variable rate instruments derives from a concern that measuring maturity only from interest rate readjustments does not reflect the risk that the quality of a variable rate instrument might decline. [58] Therefore, retaining the current approach continues to be appropriate generally. . . .

### F. Portfolio Management Responsibilities

---

[54]    Paragraph (c)(2) of rule 2a-7, as amended. In order to accommodate Government securities purchased on a delayed delivery or when issued basis as discussed infra, paragraph (c)(2)(ii) provides that a fund not using the amortized cost method may invest in a Government security with a remaining maturity of 762 calendar days (25 months). In addition, funds may invest in Government securities that have final maturities in excess of twenty-five months provided that the interest rate is adjusted at least every twenty- five months. See paragraph (d)(1) of rule 2a-7, as amended.

[55]    See note 6, supra.

[57]    Paragraph (c)(2)(i) of rule 2a-7, as amended.

[58]    See Release 13380, supra note 5, at n. 27. The Commission also believed that variable rate demand notes might not be readily marketable. The term "Variable Rate Instrument" is defined in paragraph (a)(21) or rule 2a-7, as amended.

On several occasions the Commission has stated that the portfolio management requirements imposed by rule 2a-7 may be delegated by the board of directors to the fund's investment adviser, provided that the board retains sufficient oversight. [77] In response to commenter concern over the scope of the board's responsibility, new paragraph (e) of rule 2a-7 clarifies the responsibilities of the board to guide and monitor the investment adviser when the board delegates responsibilities for portfolio determinations. The paragraph states that the board may delegate to the investment adviser or an officer of the fund all of the responsibilities it has under the rule other than the determination that the fund should maintain a stable net asset value (paragraph (c)(1)), the establishment of amortized cost method procedures to achieve this objective (paragraphs (c)(6)(i) and (c)(6)(ii)), certain determinations with respect to Second Tier Securities, Unrated Securities, and certain securities that have been downgraded by NRSROs (paragraphs (c)(5)(i)(B) and (c)(5)(ii)), and in connection with the pennyrounding method of pricing, and duty to supervise the delegate (paragraph (c)(7)). In addition, credit risk determinations with respect to Unrated Securities and securities that have been rated by only one NRSRO must be approved or ratified by the fund's board of directors. [78] The requirements of paragraph (e) are substantially consistent with previously stated Commission positions concerning the circumstances under which the board may delegate its responsibilities. [79]

## G. Investment Companies Holding Themselves Out as Money Market Funds

The Commission is adopting, substantially as proposed, a new paragraph (b) to rule 2a-7 to make it unlawful for a registered investment company to (1) adopt "money market" or similar terms as part of its name or title, or the name or title of any redeemable security of which it is the issuer, or (2) hold itself out to investors as a money market fund, or the equivalent of a money market fund, unless the company meets the risk-limiting conditions of paragraphs (c)(2) (maturity), (c)(3) (quality) and (c)(4) (diversification) of rule 2a-7, as amended. [80]

---

[77] See, e.g., Release 13380, supra note 5, and the Proposing Release, supra note 2.

[78] Paragraph (c)(3) of rule 2a-7, as amended. It would not be necessary to convene the board of directors every time the fund acquires such a security. The board of directors could establish an approved list of securities, provided that it periodically makes the requisite credit risk determinations with respect to the securities on the list. In addition, the adviser could acquire a security in accordance with guidelines established by the board, but the board would have to ratify the acquisition at its next meeting.

[79] . . . . Written copies of the guidelines established by the board in delegating portfolio management responsibilities must be maintained by the fund. Paragraph (c)(8) of rule 2a-7, as amended.

[80] An investment company holding itself out as a money market fund would not be required to use the amortized cost method of valuation or the penny- rounding method of pricing. Nor would the rule require a fund that does not meet the risk-limiting conditions of the rule to change its investment policies. The rule would only require such a fund to meet the risk-limiting conditions of the rule if it continues to hold itself out as a money market fund.

The prohibition on using the term "money market" in the name of a security has been limited to redeemable securities. Paragraph (b) of rule 2a-7, as amended. . . . .

A fund that determines not to comply with the risk-limiting conditions of rule 2a-7, as amended, will be required to change its name to the extent it includes the term "money market" or similar terms. Pursuant to paragraph (b) of the rule, as amended, a fund which invests in short-term instruments but which does not wish to hold itself out as a money market fund may call itself any name that would accurately convey its character without being misleading. [81]

One commenter argued that the Commission lacked rulemaking authority under section 38(a) of the Act to adopt paragraph (b). The Commission disagrees. Section 34(b) of the Act makes it unlawful for any person to make any untrue statement of a material fact in any document filed with the Commission or transmitted pursuant to the Act, or the keeping of which is required by section 31(a) of the Act, or to omit to state any fact necessary in order to prevent the statements made therein, in light of the circumstances under which they were made, from being materially misleading. Through sections 9(b) and 42 of the Act, the Commission has the authority to enforce these prohibitions. Section 38(a) provides that the Commission has the authority to adopt rules and regulations "as are necessary or appropriate to the exercise of the powers conferred upon the Commission elsewhere in this title." [82] The Commission believes that this is ample authority to adopt a rule interpreting the application of section 34(b) to specific circumstances. [83] In addition, to the extent that paragraph (b) affects the registration statements of money market funds, section 8(b) of the Act provides the Commission authority to prescribe the form of registration statements by adopting such rules as are necessary or appropriate in the public interest or for the protection of investors. [84]

---

[81]    The rule amendments adopt a significantly more restrictive view of the term money market fund than currently permitted by Guide 1 to Form N-1A, which states that if a registrant has a name indicating that it is a money market fund, it should have investment policies requiring investment of at least 80% of its assets in debt securities maturing in thirteen months or less. The Commission does not believe that funds previously relying on the staff guideline have misled investors. However, the Division of Investment Management is withdrawing this portion of Guide 1 effective on the date the amendments to rule 2a-7 become effective.

[82]    Section 38(a) of the Act provides that: The Commission shall have the authority from time to time to make, issue, amend and rescind such rules and regulations and such orders as are necessary or appropriate to the exercise of the powers conferred upon the Commission elsewhere in this title, including rules and regulations defining accounting, technical, and trade terms used in this title, and prescribing the form or forms in which information required in registration statements, applications, and reports to the Commission shall be set forth. For the purposes of its rules or regulations the Commission may classify persons, securities, and other matters within its jurisdiction and prescribe different requirements for different classes of persons, securities, or matters.

[83]    See, e.g., rule 34b-1 under the Act. Contrary to the commenter's assertion, the plain language of section 38(a) does not differ in substance from provisions of the other securities acts that grant the Commission authority to adopt rules necessary and appropriate to implement provisions of those acts. See, e.g., section 19(a) of the 1933 Act; section 23(a)(1) of the 1934 Act.

[84]    If, as the commenter argued, section 38(a) only "elaborates on" authority specifically granted by sections of the Act such as sections 6(c), 17(d) or 17(e), the portion of section 38(a) that grants the Commission authority to adopt "such rules and regulations and orders as are necessary or appropriate

As discussed in the Proposing Release, fund marketing and disclosure documents have encouraged investor expectations that money market funds are secure investments. [85] These expectations are reflected in the risk- limiting conditions of rule 2a-7 that are today being amended. The Commission believes that there is a significant danger of misleading investors if an investment company holds itself out as a money market fund when it engages in investment strategies not consistent with the risk-limiting conditions of rule 2a-7. It is therefore necessary and appropriate in the public interest and for the protection of investors for the Commission to adopt a new paragraph (b) of rule 2a-7 prohibiting an investment company from holding itself out as a "money market fund" unless it meets the risk-limiting conditions of rule 2a-7.

## H. Money Market Fund Prospectus Disclosure

The proposed amendments to Forms N-1A and N-3 require that cover page of a money market fund prospectus to disclose prominently (i) that the shares of the money market fund are neither insured nor guaranteed by the U.S. Government and (ii) that there is no assurance that the fund will be able to maintain a stable net asset value of $1.00 per share. The proposal was widely supported by commenters and is being adopted substantially as proposed. [86]

Several commenters urged that the prescribed legend appear in money market fund sales literature and advertisements. In view of the important role that advertising and sales literature play in marketing money market funds, the Commission has adopted this suggestion.

## I. Funds Eligible to Quote Seven-Day Yields

The Commission is adopting the proposed amendment to rule 482 under the 1933 Act to prohibit funds that do not meet the risk-limiting conditions stated in rule 2a-7 from quoting a seven-day yield figure. These funds, which under rule 2a-7, as amended, may not hold themselves out as money market funds, are treated as other types of mutual funds that quote thirty-day yield figures accompanied by total return figures. While money market funds that follow the risk-limiting provisions of rule 2a-7 are unlikely to incur capital losses or gains, the

---

to the exercise of powers conveyed elsewhere in this title * * *" would be superfluous because the authority specifically granted by the cited sections requires no "elaboration." See Sutherland Stat. Const. s 46.06 (4th Ed.) ("A statute should be construed so that effect is given to all its provisions, so that no part will be inoperative or superfluous, void or insignificant, and so that one section will not destroy another unless the provision is the result of obvious mistake or error." (citations omitted)).

[85] See, e.g., Money Market Funds: A Part of Every Financial Plan (publication of the Investment Company Institute), a pamphlet prepared by the major investment company trade association for distribution to the general public.

[86] Several technical revisions have been made. As proposed, the statement must disclose that the "securities of the fund are neither insured nor guaranteed by the U.S. Government." This has been changed to "an investment in the fund is neither insured nor guaranteed * * *" to reduce the likelihood that a reader would be confused between the securities issued by the fund and its portfolio securities. Second, a parenthetical has been added to the second part of the legend to take into account funds that stabilize their net asset value at a price other than $1.00. Third, an instruction has been added to permit a money market fund not stabilizing its net asset value to omit the second part of the legend. Finally, as proposed, the amendments require that the legend be "prominent" but do not require certain type size.

same may not hold true for funds not following the risk-limiting provisions. These funds, therefore, must also provide total return figures to investors which reflect the effect of capital losses or gains. . . . .

## Comments and Questions

1. Are the SEC's restrictions on money market mutual funds necessary? What costs do they impose? How do they compare to the investment restrictions imposed on FDIC insured banks in the United States? Given the strictness of these rules, are fiduciary safeguards also necessary for money market mutual funds?

2. Who decides whether any particular investment qualifies as a money market mutual fund investment? What is the role of the Nationally Recognized Statistical Rating Organizations (NRSROs) defined in the first footnote of the release? Is it appropriate for the SEC to rely on NRSROs in this way? Are there risks to such reliance? For a good introduction to NRSROs, see Amy K. Rhodes, *The Role of the SEC in the Regulation of Rating Agencies: Well-Placed Reliance or Free-Market Interference?*, 20 SETON HALL LEGIS. J. 293 (1996).

### Problem 13-10

Hammie Mae is a federal agency charged with supplying credit to the U.S. entertainment industry. To fund its operations, Hammie Mae regularly issues bonds in the capital markets. Given its association with the federal government, Hannie Mae has an AAA credit rating, the highest possible level. At the suggesting of its investment bankers, Hammie Mae has decided to issue a new class of variable rate notes — TOPHATS — which will pay an interest rate that varies every six months. At each adjustment date, the interest rate on TOPHATS will be reset to equal whatever rate comparable rated federal instrumentalities are at the time paying on six month notes. To prevent abrupt changes in its interest costs, however, rates on TOPHATS will not change by more than 1.00 % at each adjustment date. Can a money market fund buy TOPHATS under rule 2a-7?

### Problem 13-11

Revisit Problem 4-14 in Chapter Four. If Horizon attempts to engage in the proposed transaction, what issues, if any, arise under the 1940 Act?

# CHAPTER FOURTEEN

# INNOVATIONS IN INSURANCE PRODUCTS

A recurring theme in this book has been attention to the lines that define the scope of regulatory jurisdictions. In many respects, our legal structure divides financial institutions into three basic groups: depository institutions, insurance companies, and securities firms (broadly defined to include investment companies). Within each sector, different legal rules apply and a different combination of regulatory authorities exert jurisdiction. The formal divisions do not, however, prevent individual firms from attempting (often successfully) to breach these jurisdictional boundaries. As we have seen in earlier sections of the book, banks have long offered stand-by letters of credit and even debt cancellation contracts that look a lot like specialized forms of insurance contracts. Insurance companies such as Executive Life have developed Guaranteed Investment Contracts ("GIC") that are functionally equivalent to interest-bearing deposits. And securities firms such as Merrill Lynch have put together products such as the cash-management account that compete directly with traditional checking accounts, while bank trust departments offer many services that securities firms have traditionally offered their customers.

In prior readings, we have considered these inter-sector conflicts in the context of definitional provisions, trying to determine which regulatory authority should supervise the activity in question or whether the activity was in fact authorized for the entity proposing to offer it. In this part of the book, we consider competitive aspects of these inter-sector forays as well as more general policy concerns. Perhaps the most prominent example of this phenomenon has been the efforts of depository institutions to offer various kinds of securities services to their customers. This topic, which entails among other things careful interpretation of the Glass-Steagall Act, is the subject of the next chapter. Before addressing those issues, however, we will consider another, earlier example of inter-industry combat: efforts by insurance companies dating back to the 1950s to compete with the securities industry in offering pooled investment vehicles (that is, to offer functional equivalents to investment companies). In the final chapter of the book we will consider the on-going competition between depository institutions and insurance companies.

As you read through these final chapters, there are a number of underlying questions to keep in mind. Why do financial institutions spend so much time and effort trying to cross sector lines? Is it simply the quest for additional profits? Or, do our regulatory structures create incentives for inter-industry expansion? Whatever the reason for inter-industry expansion, how should our legal system deal with the phenomenon? When should it be prohibited? When, if ever, should it be encouraged? To the extent that we are going to tolerate inter-industry expansion, should we impose any organizational restraints on the manner in which it is effected? For example, should a single corporate entity be allowed to offer depository services and also engage in insurance activities? Should we strive for intra-corporate separation — that is, separate legal entities for each basic financial function? If we are going to require separate entities, should these bear any particular relationship to each other — that is, parent-subsidiary, commonly-controlled affiliates, or some other structure? What are the costs of permitting or prohibiting inter-sector competition?

## Section 1: Variable Products Under Other Legal Regimes

Variable insurance products represent one of the initial grounds of inter-sectoral competition in the financial services industry. The following excerpt explains the history behind this development as well as the differences between variable products and traditional insurance.

### Robert C. Pozen, Financial Institutions 551-55 (1978)

During the 1950s, insurance companies developed variable annuities. In the typical form of variable annuity, annuitants pay in premiums of fixed amounts at periodic intervals during their working life. After making deductions for managerial fees and other expenses, the insurance company invests the premiums from all annuitants in common stock and other equity securities. For each premium paid in by annuitants, the insurance company credits their accounts with a specific number of "accumulation units." The value of each "accumulation unit" is determined by dividing the total value of the company's investments by the total number of outstanding "accumulation units." Upon retirement, annuitants usually have two choices: 1) they may obtain one lump sum payment for their "accumulation units" as valued at the date of their retirement; or 2) they may receive for the rest of their lives periodic payments that will vary according to the value of the company's equity investments. Thus, unlike fixed annuities, variable annuities do not guarantee annuitants periodic payments of predetermined amounts during their retirement years. Instead of such guarantees, variable annuities permit annuitants to share in the investment experience of the insurance company during the pay-in and/or pay-out periods.

During the 1970s, insurance companies developed variable life insurance. In the typical form of variable life insurance, the policyholders pay in premiums of fixed amounts at periodic intervals throughout their remaining lives. After making deductions for managerial fees and other expenses, the insurance company invests the premiums from policyholders in common stocks and other equity investments. When policyholders die, their beneficiaries receive at least a minimum amount of death benefits guaranteed in the original insurance contract. Beneficiaries may also receive an additional amount because of the equity investments made by the insurance company for the benefit of variable life insurance policyholders. This additional amount of death benefits will depend on the market value of these equity investments at the death of the policyholder. Thus, unlike regular life insurance, variable life guarantees the beneficiaries of policyholders only a portion of their death benefits at a predetermined rate. But variable life insurance does give these beneficiaries the right to share in the rise or fall of the stock portfolio held by the insurance company.

To purchase equity securities for variable annuities and variable life insurance polices, insurance companies were obliged to circumvent the restrictions on their investments imposed by state laws. State laws severely restrict both the quantity and quality of investments by insurance companies. In New York, for example, the common stock investments of life insurance companies may not exceed the lesser of 10% of admitted assets or 100% of surplus. N.Y.Ins.Law § 81-13(c) (McKinney Supp.1976). Nor may a life insurance company invest in the common stock of any corporation unless corporate earnings over the last seven years would have been sufficient to pay annual dividends of at least 4% on par or stated value. Id. at § 81-13(a). Moreover, New York State has traditionally required that out-of-state insurance companies licensed to do business in New York comply in substance with the state's investment restrictions to assure that insurance companies would be capable of paying the predetermined amounts of death benefits and retirement benefits in traditional life insurance policies and fixed annuities. But these restrictions were incompatible with the concepts of variable annuities and variable life policies as hedges against inflation through large investments in common stock.

Therefore, insurance companies funded variable annuities and variable life policies through "separate accounts," as opposed to "general accounts" for the investments of the insurance companies. Under state law, a "separate account" is an entity distinct form the insurance company for accounting purposes—i.e., "income gains and losses, whether or not realized, from assets allocated to a separate account shall, in accordance with the applicable agreement or agreements, be credited to or charged against such account without regard to other income, gains or losses of the insurer." N.Y.Ins.Law § 227-1(a) (McKinney Supp.1976). Yet the assets in a separate account are owned by the insurance company under state law. Id. at § 227-1(j). If separate accounts meet all the requirements of state law, they are exempted from most of the severe restrictions on investments applicable to insurance companies. See, e.g., id. at § 227-1(b). An insurance company may maintain one or many separate accounts. A separate account may invest the premiums of only one client or commingle the premiums of many clients. One of the prime uses of separate accounts is the funding of pension plans. By placing pension contributions in separate accounts, insurance companies can compete with mutual funds and bank trust departments, which may invest pension contributions in common stocks. In 1970, Congress exempted separate accounts maintained by insurance companies for qualified pension plans from the registration requirements of the federal securities laws. See section 3(a)(2) of the 1933 Securities Act and section 3(c)(11) of the Investment Company Act.

The advent of variable annuities, variable life policies, and separate accounts raises many complex questions about the regulation of the insurance industry. If insurance companies are selling products with investment as well as insurance features, should these hybrid products be exempted from the Securities Act of 1933? If insurance companies fund these new products through separate accounts with heavy investments in common stocks, should these separate accounts be treated as investment companies? If insurance companies are competing with mutual funds and commercial banks for investments in common stock, should all three financial institutions be subject to the same regulatory scheme? On the other hand, since the McCarran-Ferguson Act establishes a strong presumption for state regulation of the insurance business, how can insurance companies be regulated in the same manner as national banks and mutual funds?

To understand the differences between variable annuities and fixed annuities, we must analyze the three types of risk involved in such annuities. First is mortality risk—the chance that annuitants will live longer than expected after the specified age of retirement. This is an important risk in all annuities since the insurance company is obliged to make periodic payments to annuitants throughout their retired lives. To protect against mortality risk, insurance companies set their premium and benefit schedules according to detailed mortality tables. These tables predict the average age at which each category of annuitants is likely to die. Since insurance companies provide annuities to a large number of people, the overall mortality experience among annuitants is likely to approximate the averages in mortality tables. Since the predictions in the mortality tables are not always accurate, however, insurance companies deduct a small percentage from each premium to provide reserves against mortality risk. If these reserves are insufficient to absorb large discrepancies between the mortality tables and the actual experience of annuitants, the insurance company must bear the loss.

Second is expense risk. In fixed annuities, the insurance company guarantees a certain level of benefits to annuitants during their retirement years. To generate the income needed to pay these benefits, the insurance company invests the premiums of annuitants in various securities. In theory, if these investments do not generate enough income to meet benefit commitments, the insurance company suffers a loss. In practice, the investment risk of the insurance company in fixed annuities is quite low. Because of state laws, insurance companies must invest mainly in fixed-income securities, like corporate bonds and first mortgages, with stable but low returns relative to common stocks. Thus, in setting benefit levels for annuitants, insurance companies can be fairly certain about the expected return from the investment of premiums.

In the purest form of variable annuities, the insurance company does not guarantee any level of benefits and does not therefore assume any investment risk. In such variable annuities, the level of benefits paid out to annuitants depends on the performance of their premiums invested through a separate account. Since a separate account is not bound by the severe restrictions on investments applicable to insurance companies, the assets in a separate account may be heavily invested in common stocks. As compared to the conservative investments mandated for insurance companies, common stocks are characterized by high risks and high returns. If the common stock held by the separate account appreciates in value, the annuitants receive relatively large benefits. If the stock holdings of the separate account decline in value, then annuitants receive relatively small benefits. In short, annuitants assume the investment risk in variable annuities, but they enjoy the possibility of high returns through capital appreciation.

---

Almost as soon as the insurance industry unveiled these new variable products in the 1950s, controversy arose over which regulatory authorities would exercise control over their sale to the public. In particular, the courts were called upon to consider whether variable annuities and other similar products should fall under the supervision of the Securities and Exchange Commission. The litigation was ultimately resolved in the Supreme Court:

# Securities & Exchange Commission v. VALIC
## 359 U.S. 65 (1959)

Mr. Justice DOUGLAS delivered the opinion of the Court.

We start with a reluctance to disturb the state regulatory schemes that are in actual effect, either by displacing them or by superimposing federal requirements on transactions that are tailored to meet state requirements. When the States speak in the field of 'insurance,' they speak with the authority of a long tradition. For the regulation of 'insurance,' though within the ambit of federal power (United States v. South-Eastern Underwriters' Ass'n, 322 U.S. 533), has traditionally been under the control of the States.

We deal, however, with federal statutes where the words 'insurance' and 'annuity' are federal terms. Congress was legislating concerning a concept which had taken on its coloration and meaning largely from state law, from state practice, from state usage. Some States deny these 'annuity' contracts any status as 'insurance.' Others accept them under their 'insurance' statutes. It is apparent that there is no uniformity in the rulings of the States on the nature of these 'annuity' contracts. In any event how the States may have ruled is not decisive. For, as we have said, the meaning of 'insurance' or 'annuity' under these Federal Acts is a federal question.

While all the States regulate 'annuities' under their 'insurance' laws, traditionally and customarily they have been fixed annuities, offering the annuitant specified and definite amounts beginning with a certain year of his or her life. The standards for investment of funds underlying these annuities have been conservative. The variable annuity introduced two new features. First, premiums collected are invested to a greater degree in common stocks and other equities. Second, benefit payments vary with the success of the investment policy. The first variable annuity apparently appeared in this country about 1952 when New York created the College Retirement Equities Fund to provide annuities for teachers. It came into existence as a result of a search for a device that would avoid paying annuitants in depreciated dollars. The theory was that returns from investments in common stocks would over the long run tend to compensate for the mounting inflation. The holder of a variable annuity cannot look forward to a fixed monthly or yearly amount in his advancing years. It may be greater or less, depending on the wisdom of the investment policy. In some respects the variable annuity has the characteristics of the fixed and conventional annuity: payments are made periodically; they continue until the annuitant's death or in case other options are chosen until the end of a fixed term or until the death of the last of two persons; payments are made both from principal and income; and the amounts vary according to the age and sex of the annuitant. Moreover, actuarially both the fixed-dollar annuity and the variable annuity are calculated by identical principles. Each issuer assumes the risk of mortality from the moment the contract is issued. That risk is an actuarial prognostication that a certain number of annuitants will survive to specified ages. Even if a substantial number live beyond their predicted demise, the company issuing the annuity--whether it be fixed or variable--is obligated to make the annuity payments on the basis of the mortality prediction reflected in the contract. This is the mortality risk assumed both by respondents and by those who issue fixed annuities. It is this feature, common to both, that respondents stress when they urge that this is basically an insurance device.

The difficulty is that, absent some guarantee of fixed income, the variable annuity places all the investment risks on the annuitant, none on the company. The holder gets only a pro rata share of what the portfolio of equity interests reflects--which may be a lot, a little, or nothing. We realize that life insurance is an evolving institution. Common knowledge tells us that the forms have greatly changed even in a generation. And we would not undertake to freeze the concepts of 'insurance' or 'annuity' into the mold they fitted when these Federal Acts were passed. But we conclude that the concept of 'insurance' involves some investment risk-taking on the part of the company. The risk of mortality, assumed here, gives these variable annuities an aspect of insurance. Yet it is apparent, not real; superficial, not substantial. In hard reality the issuer of a variable annuity that has no element of a fixed return assumes no true risk in the insurance sense. It is no answer to say that the risk of declining returns in times of depression is the reciprocal of the fixed-dollar annuitant's risk of loss of purchasing power when prices are high and gain of purchasing power when they are low. We deal with a more conventional concept of risk-bearing when we speak of 'insurance.' For in common understanding 'insurance' involves a guarantee that at least some fraction of the benefits will be payable in fixed amounts. . . . The companies that issue these annuities take the risk of failure. But they guarantee nothing to the annuitant except an interest in a portfolio of common stocks or other equities -- an interest that has a ceiling but no floor. There is no true underwriting of risks, the one earmark of insurance as it has commonly been conceived of in popular understanding and usage.

Mr. Justice BRENNAN, with whom Mr. Justice STEWART joins, concurring.

I join the opinion and judgment of the Court. However, there are additional reasons which lead me to the Court's result, and since the nature of this case lends it to rather extended treatment, I will express these reasons separately.

First. The facts of this case are quite complex, but the basic problem involved is much more simple. I will try to point it up before developing the details of the sort of contracts sold by the respondents. It is one of the coverage of two Acts of Congress which concentrated on applying specific forms of regulatory controls to the various ways in which organizations get and administer other people's money--the Securities Act of 1933 and the Investment Company Act of 1940. These Acts were specifically drawn to exclude any 'insurance policy' and any 'annuity contract' (Securities Act § 3(a)(8)) and any 'insurance company' (Investment Company Act s 3(a)(3)) from their coverage. These exclusions were to take effect where the issuer of the policy or contract was subject to the supervision of the state 'insurance commissioner, bank commissioner, or any agency or officer performing like functions' (Securities Act § 3(a)(8)) or where a company classifiable as an 'insurance company' was 'subject to supervision by the insurance commissioner or a similar official or agency of a State' (Investment Company Act § 2(a) (17)). The exclusions left these contracts and companies to the sole control of such state officials. Except for these exclusions, there is little doubt that these contracts and the companies issuing them would be subject to the Federal Acts.

Why these exclusions? They could not have been made out of some general desire on the part of Congress to avoid any concurrent regulation by both the Federal Government and the States of investments or companies subject to the two Acts. On the contrary, § 18 of the Securities Act and § 50 of the Investment Company Act preserve generally the jurisdiction of state officials over their subject matter; the former in terms of 'the jurisdiction of the securities commission (or any agency or office performing like functions) of any State' and the latter in terms of 'the jurisdiction of any other commission, board, agency, or officer of * * * any State or political subdivision.' Conversely, of course, however adequately State Securities Commissioners might regulate an investment, it was not for that reason to be freed from federal regulation. Concurrent regulation, then, was contemplated by the Acts as a quite generally prevailing matter. Nor is it rational to assume that Congress thought that *any* business whatsoever regulated by a specific class of officials, the State Insurance Commissioners, would be for that reason so perfectly conducted and regulated that all the protections of the Federal Acts would be unnecessary. This approach of personally selective deference to the state administrators is hardly to be attributed to Congress. The point must have been that there then was a form of 'investment' known as insurance (including 'annuity contracts') which did not present very squarely the sort of problems that the Securities Act and the Investment Company Act were devised to deal with, and which were, in many details, subject to a form of state regulation of a sort which made the federal regulation even less relevant.

At this time, of course, the sort of 'variable annuity' contract with which we are concerned in this case did not exist. When Congress made the exclusions provided for in the Acts, it did not make them with the 'variable annuity' contract before it. Of course, the point is not that if the insurance industry seeks to retain its exemption, it must limit itself to the forms of policies and contracts in effect in 1933 and 1940. But if a brand-new form of investment arrangement emerges which is labeled 'insurance' or 'annuity' by its promoters, the functional distinction that Congress set up in 1933 and 1940 must be examined to test whether the contract falls within the sort of investment form that Congress was then willing to leave exclusively to the State Insurance Commissioners. In that inquiry, an analysis of the regulatory and protective purposes of the Federal Acts and of state insurance regulation as it then existed becomes relevant.

At the core of the 1933 Act are the requirements of a registration statement and prospectus to be used in connection with the issuance of 'securities'--that term being very broadly defined. Detailed schedules, set forth in the Act, list the material that the registration statement and the prospectus are to contain. The emphasis is on disclosure; the philosophy of the Act is that full disclosure of the details of the enterprise in which the investor is to put has money should be made so that he can intelligently appraise the risks involved.

The regulation of life insurance and annuities by the States proceeded, and still proceeds, on entirely different principles. It seems as paternalistic as the Securities Act of 1933 was keyed to free, informed choice. Prescribed contract clauses are ordained legislatively or administratively. Solvency and the adequacy of reserves to meet the company's obligations are supervised by the establishment of permissible categories of investments and through official examination. The system does not depend on disclosure to the public, and, once given this form of regulation and the nature of the 'product,' it might be difficult in the case of the traditional life insurance or annuity contract to see what the purpose of it would be.

This congressional division of regulatory functions is rational and purposeful in the case of a traditional life insurance or annuity policy, where the obligations of the company were measured in fixed-dollar terms and where the investor could not be said, in any meaningful sense, to be a sharer in the investment experience of the company. In fact, one of the basic premises of state regulation would appear to be that in one sense the investor in an annuity or life insurance company *not* become a direct sharer in the company's investment experience; that his investment in the policy or contract be sufficiently protected to prevent this. But the situation changes where the coin of the company's obligation is not money but is rather the present condition of its investment portfolio. To this extent, the historic functions of state insurance regulation become meaningless. Prescribed limitations on investment and examination of solvency and reserves become perfectly circular to the extent that there is no obligation to pay except in terms measured by one's portfolio. But beyond controlling corporate solvency and the adequacy of reserves, and maintaining observance of the legal list of investments, the state plans of regulation do not go in regulating investment policy. Where the nature of the obligation assumed is such, the federally protected interests in disclosure to the investor of the nature of the corporation to whom he is asked to entrust his money and the purposes for which it is to be used become obvious and real. The contract between the investor and the organization no longer squares with the sort of contract in regard to which Congress in 1933 thought its 'disclosure' statute was unnecessary. . . .

This is not to say that because subjection of the contracts in question here to federal regulation is desirable, it has in fact been accomplished; but one must apply a test in terms of the purposes of the Federal Acts as a guide to interpreting the scope of an exemption from their coverage for 'insurance.' . . . When Congress passed the Securities Act of 1933 and the Investment Company Act of 1940, no State Insurance Commissioner was, incident to his duties in regulating insurance companies, engaged in the sort of regulation, outlined above as provided in the Federal Acts, that Congress thought would be appropriate for the protection of people entrusting their money to others to be invested on an equity basis. There is no reason to suppose that Congress intended to make an exemption of forms of investment to which its regulatory scheme was very relevant in favor of a form of state regulation which would not be relevant to them at all.

Second. Much bewilderment could be engendered by this case if the issue were whether the contracts in question were 'really' insurance or 'really' securities--one or the other. It is rather meaningless to view the problem as one of pigeonholing these contracts in one category or the other. Obviously they have elements of conventional insurance, even apart from the fixed-dollar term life insurance and the disability waiver of premium insurance sold with some of these contracts (both of which are quite incidental to the main undertaking). They patently contain a significant annuity feature (unless one defines an annuity as a contract necessarily providing fixed-sum payments), and the granting of annuities has been considered part of the business of life insurance. Of course, some urge that even the traditional annuity has few 'insurance' features and is basically a form of investment. . . . But the point is that, even though these contracts contain, for what they are worth, features of traditional annuity contracts, administering them also involves a very substantial and in fact predominant element of the business of an investment company, and that in a way totally foreign to the business of a traditional life insurance and annuity company, as traditionally regulated by state law. This is what leads to the conclusion that it is not within the intent of the 1933 and 1940 statutes to exempt them. . . .

Mr. Justice HARLAN, whom Mr. Justice FRANKFURTER, Mr. Justice CLARK and Mr. Justice WHITTAKER join, dissenting.

. . . . Admittedly the variable annuity was not in the picture when the Securities and Investment Company Acts were passed. It is a new development combining both substantial insurance and securities features in an experiment designed to accommodate annuity insurance coverage to contingencies of the present day economic climate. This, however, should not be allowed to obscure the fact that Congress intended when it enacted these statutes to leave the future regulation of the business of insurance wholly with the States. This intent, repeatedly expressed in a history of which the Securities and Investment Company Acts were only a part, in my view demands that *bona fide* experiments in the insurance field, even though a particular development may also have securities aspects, be classed within the federal exemption of insurance, and not within the federal regulation of securities. Certainly these statutes breathe no notion of concurrent regulation by the SEC and state insurance authorities. The fact that they do not serves to reinforce the view that the congressional exemption of insurance was but another manifestation of the historic federal policy leaving regulation of the business of insurance exclusively to the States.

It is asserted that state regulation, as it existed when the Securities and Investment Company Acts were passed, was inadequate to protect annuitants against the risks inherent in the variable annuity and that therefore such contracts should be considered within the orbit of SEC regulation. The Court is agreed that we should not 'freeze' the concept of insurance as it then existed. By the same token we should not proceed on the assumption that the thrust of state regulation is frozen. As the insurance business develops new concepts the States adjust and develop their controls. This is in the tradition of state regulation and federal abstention. If the innovation of federal control is nevertheless to be desired, it is for the Congress, not this Court, to effect.

## Comments and Questions

1. How does Justice Douglas's opinion for the majority of the Court differ from the perspective of the concurring opinion of Justice Brennan? Which is the better view? What is the basis of Justice Harlan's dissent? Is it well founded?

2. Although the opinions in the VALIC case focus most of their attention on Securities Act of 1933, the Court also ruled that the Investment Company Act of 1940 governed the contracts in question. The decision, however, involved an insurance company dedicated exclusively to the business of issuing variable annuity products, and thus left open the question whether the 1940 Act would also apply to an insurance company that was primarily engaged in traditional insurance operations but that also offered a relatively small number of variable annuity products. That issue was addressed in the following decision of the Third Circuit.

## Prudential Insurance Co. v. Securities and Exchange Commission
### 326 F.2d 383 (3d Cir.), *cert. denied*, 377 U.S. 953 (1964)

STALEY, Circuit Judge.

The narrow but provocative question posed by this case is whether the Investment Company Act of 1940 applies to the Investment Fund resulting from the sale of variable annuity contracts to members of the public by The Prudential Insurance Company of America. The Securities and Exchange Commission answered this question in the affirmative, rejecting the view of Prudential that the Act exempts such a program because the contracts are offered and sold by an insurance company. . . . . .

Though there are variations in the form of the variable annuities which Prudential proposes to sell, their salient characteristics are not disputed and their nature has been concisely summarized by the Commission in its opinion in this case:

'In substance, the variable annuity contracts which Prudential proposes to sell to individuals provide that the purchaser will make monthly purchase payments of fixed amounts over a period of years (the 'pay-in' period), the proceeds of which, after certain deductions, will be invested in a portfolio of securities. The purchaser will be credited monthly with 'units' representing his proportionate interest in this fund. The value of these units will fluctuate, essentially depending upon the investment results of the fund. During the annuity, or 'pay-out' period, Prudential guarantees that the purchaser will receive in cash the varying value of a fixed number of units as monthly annuity payments.

'Specifically the payments made by the purchasers will be placed in a 'Variable Contract Account' which will be managed by Prudential and be subdivided into two accounts. The first, the 'Investment Fund' account, will have its assets invested primarily in common stocks and will constitute the fund in which the purchasers hold units; this account will be dedicated solely to the variable annuity contract holders and its assets will not be subject to claims of any other contract or policyholder of the company. The second, the 'Other Assets' account, an administration account, will receive the amounts deducted from the purchase payments to cover administration expenses, sales commissions, and certain taxes, and to provide a surplus or reserve for the obligations to purchasers contained in the contracts. Transfers will be made periodically from the Other Assets account to the Investment Fund account to meet the contractual requirements that the assets of the latter be equal to the company's existing obligations under the variable contracts. Any excess over the amounts estimated to be needed for the foregoing purposes may be declared as so-called 'dividends' which will provide additional fund units or cash payments for the contract holders; it will also be available to support the guarantees on contracts administered by Prudential's other operations. Any deficiency resulting from lower mortality than assumed, for example, will be met out of the general surplus of Prudential.

'During the pay-in period a purchaser will have the right to terminate the contract and receive the value of all units credited to his account, less certain termination charges. If a purchaser should die during the pay-in period, the contract is automatically terminated and his beneficiary is paid the greater of (i) the value of all units credited to the purchaser's account or (ii) an amount equal to the total of all purchase payments made.

'Absent death or redemption, the pay-in period normally runs for at least 15 years. Thereafter, during the pay-out period, the variable annuitant is entitled to receive each month the current value of a fixed number of units determined at the end of the pay-in period. This number of units is calculated on the basis of the number of units accumulated by the purchaser during the pay-in period, an assumed annual investment increment of 2 1/2% from dividend and interest income, and actuarial computations which take into account the length of the pay-out period anticipated in light of the age and sex of the purchaser and any co-annuitant. The value of the variable unit during the pay-in and pay-out periods will be determined at the end of each month and will reflect the changes in the market value of the securities in the Investment Fund account, realized gains and losses, and dividend or interest income. Deductions will be made for investment advisory and other expenses in an amount equal to 0.6% Per annum of the value of the fund's assets and for taxes.'

Prudential concedes that such contracts have been held to be 'securities' within the meaning of the Securities Act of 1933, Securities and Exchange Commission v. Variable Annuity Life Insurance Co. (hereinafter called 'VALIC'), 359 U.S. 65 (1959), and it is willing to register them under that Act. Prudential argues, however, that the Investment Company Act of 1940 specifically excludes insurance companies from its scope. The Commission acknowledged that Prudential is excluded from the Act, but held that the fund created by the sale of the contracts, which is to be used for investment purposes, gives rise to a separate investment company within the coverage of the statute. The Commission concluded that Prudential is not itself an investment company but is the creator of one, and proposes to be its investment adviser and principal underwriter.

In this court, Prudential, premising its argument on the insurance company exclusion, asserts that this construction of the statute is inordinately complicated, abstruse, and without basis in law. It asserts that the statute is plain and forecloses Commission jurisdiction in this case. However, since it is conceded that Prudential is excluded from the Act, the issue is narrowed to the question of whether the Commission made a permissible interpretation in concluding that the variable annuity program results in the creation of a separate, non-exempt investment company.

Of course, in resolving this issue we start with the premise that securities legislation must be broadly construed in order to insure the investing public a full measure of protection. . . . The parties agree that the statutory definitions contained in the Investment Company Act of 1940 are cast in broad terms. The critical term is 'company', which, so far as relevant to our discussion, is defined as 'a trust, a fund, or any organized group of persons whether incorporated or not.' Section 2(a)(8) of the 1940 Act.

The Commission determined that the variable annuity contracts constitute the purchasers an 'organized group of persons'; that they create a 'trust' held by Prudential for these purchasers; and, more importantly, that the separate Investment Fund resulting from the sale of the variable annuity contracts is a 'fund' within the statutory definition. Based upon this last decisive holding, the Commission then concluded that the Investment Fund is the 'issuer' of the variable annuity securities, and that it is an 'investment company' subject to the Act.

On this score Prudential argues that the Act regulates only identifiable business entities with some sort of internal organization, and that it is the only such entity involved in this program. Thus, it is asserted that the purchasers cannot be described as an 'organized group of persons'; that the plan has no elements of a common-law trust; and that the 'fund' referred to in the Act means a mutual fund or any other similar entity, but not Prudential's Investment Fund. But, as Mr. Justice Brennan has cogently observed, the regulatory provisions of the Act 'are of particular relevance to situations where the investor is committing his funds to the hands of others on an equity basis, with the view that the funds will be invested in securities and his fortunes will depend on the success of the investment.' VALIC, 359 U.S. at 79 (concurring opinion). Furthermore, a study of the legislative history of the Act shows that Congress intentionally drafted the statutory definitions in general terms in order to control such situations regardless of the legal form or structure of the investment enterprise.

Initially, it must be noted that the Committee reports of both the House and the Senate state that the legislation was drafted principally on the basis of reports submitted by the Securities and Exchange Commission following an extensive study of investment trusts and investment companies undertaken at the direction of Congress. H.R.Rep.No.2639, 76th Cong., 3rd Sess. 5-6 (1940); S.Rep.No. 1775, 76th Cong., 3rd Sess. 1, 5 (1940). The Act itself contains a similar acknowledgment. 15 U.S.C. § 80a-1. The significance of such reports in ascertaining the intent of Congress in enacting securities legislation was recently underscored by the Supreme Court in Securities and Exchange Commission v. Capital Gains Research Bureau, Inc., 375 U.S. 180 (1963).

Among the various types of investment companies referred to in the exhaustive report of the Commission were those involving 'an agency relationship between the individual contributors to the fund and the management upon whom they confer substantially a power of attorney to act as agent in the investment of the moneys contributed. *The group of individual investors is not a legal entity* but rather constitutes in essence a combination of distinct individual interests.' (Emphasis supplied.) H.R.Doc.No.707, 75th Cong., 3rd Sess. 24 (1939). Additionally, the report made specific reference to an investment company known as the 'Alexander Fund' which it described as 'merely a descriptive name given to the commingled funds of numerous investors who employed W. Wallace Alexander as their agent to invest such funds.' Id. at 46. Similarly, in describing the nature of the investment enterprises which Congress was seeking to control, the House Report quotes from the testimony of Commissioner Healy who stated that 'Essentially these organizations are large liquid pools of the public's savings entrusted to managements to be invested.' H.R.Rep.No.2639, 76th Cong., 3rd Sess. 6 (1940).

In these circumstances we reject Prudential's argument that the broad statutory phrase 'a trust, a fund, or any organized group of persons whether incorporated or not' refers only to recognizable business entities. On the contrary, the legislative history compels the conclusion that Prudential's Investment Fund is a 'fund' as that term is used in the statute. As we have previously seen, the Investment Fund is a completely segregated account, devoted to investing in securities. The cash for these investments is derived from payments made by the purchaser of the variable annuity contract. Though the proceeds of the fund are held for the sole benefit of the annuitant, it is this fund, and no other entity, in which he has an interest. Thus, the fund is separable from the insurance company which, as the Supreme Court noted in VALIC, 'guarantee(s) nothing to the annuitant except an interest in a portfolio of common stocks or other equities-- an interest that has a ceiling but no floor.' 359 U.S. at 72. The restricted interest of the annuitant is perhaps best expressed in the Court's pithy observation that he 'gets only a *pro rata* share of what the portfolio of equity interests reflects-- which may be a lot, a little, or nothing.' 359 U.S. at 71.

It follows from this that the Investment Fund, and not Prudential, is the 'issuer' of these securities for the purposes of the Investment Company Act of 1940. As the Commission observed, 'Prudential would in fact be the writer of the *contracts* — the insurance and annuity promises and the obligation to set up the investment fund. But the investment fund, the 'company' to which the investment interests relate, is the 'issuer' of those interests.'

One of the principal arguments of Prudential in favor of exclusion is that the existence of adequate state regulation was the basis for the exemption of insurance companies. But this line of argument was conclusively rejected by the Supreme Court in VALIC for the reason that variable annuities are 'securities' and involve considerations of investment not present in the conventional contract of insurance. Prudential attempts to distinguish VALIC on the grounds that the company there involved was not, on the basis of the Court's decision, primarily or predominantly engaged in the business of writing insurance. But regardless of the merits of this distinction, that case holds unequivocally that adequate state regulation of insurance is immaterial when variable annuity contracts are being considered under a Federal statute.

Prudential also asserts that the specific exemption provided for the common trust funds of banks shows that regulation under the Act was imposed on an institutional rather than on a functional basis. It is pointed out that this exemption is provided in addition to the general exemption for banks. Prudential declares that such common trust funds are functionally indistinguishable from investment companies, but were excluded from the Act 'because they were in fact part of the banking business and intended to be covered by the broad exemption for banks.' We think that this specific exemption leads to the opposite conclusion, for as the Commission reasoned:

'* * * Obviously, if as Prudential argues, the exemption of banks and insurance companies had been intended to include an exemption of funds set up by such companies, there would have been no need to provide for the additional specific exemption of funds set up by banks. Congress thus viewed such funds, even though usually maintained as departments of the bank, as separate from the banking business. It rested this exemption on the special considerations that the funds were used for bona fide fiduciary purposes rather than as a medium for general public investment and had only a limited impact in the investment fund picture.'

Considerations of logic and policy provide further support for our conclusion. The Investment Company Act of 1940 contains significant safeguards for the protection of those who, like the purchasers of variable annuities, invest in 'securities.' These safeguards, characterized by the Commission as insuring 'corporate democracy,' include disclosure of investment policy and operating practices, and the regulation of fees, trading practices, and changes in investment policy. See VALIC, 359 U.S. at 79. The mere fact that the investment program in the case at bar is under the aegis of an insurance company ought not to negate compliance with these controls in the absence of compelling circumstances. We find no such circumstances here.

We have considered the other contentions advanced by Prudential, but find that they are merely variations on its insurance company exclusion argument and have been fully disposed of by the Commission.

## Comments and Questions

1. To demonstrate that Prudential Investment Fund was an investment company for purposes of the 1940 Act, the SEC developed what has come to be known as the "ectoplasm" theory of investment companies. That theory allows the Commission to apply the restrictions of the Investment Company Act to separate accounts inside of insurance companies. Is this interpretation consistent with the definitional provisions of the 1940 Act? Does the 1940 Act also apply to separate accounts that banks maintain for common trust funds? See section 3(c)(3) of the 1940 Act.

2. The *VALIC* and *Prudential* decisions authorized the SEC to regulate variable insurance products. Implementing that authority has presented the Commission's staff with numerous complexities. Consider, for example, the differences in regulatory philosophy between the 1940 Act and insurance company regulation. Insurance regulation consists of a large number of mandatory rules that govern the structure of an insurance company's balance sheet — imposing restrictions on investments and requiring specific amounts of capital reserves. The 1940 Act, in contrast, allows investment companies considerable freedom in choosing investments, and relies primarily on extensive disclosure rules and fiduciary obligations supplemented with strict regulation of transactions with affiliated parties. How can these restrictions be superimposed on the same entity? In particular, how should the 1940 Act's prohibited transaction rule apply to the relationship between a separate account and the insurance company of which it is a part? For an interesting SEC staff report on 1940 Act regulation of variable insurance products and several recommendations for reform, see PROTECTING INVESTORS: A HALF-CENTURY OF INVESTMENT COMPANY REGULATION ch. 10 (May 1992).

---

In the years since the *VALIC* and *Prudential* decisions were handed down, variable annuity products have grown in popularity. Over the years, the insurance industry has attempted to design variable insurance products that would escape regulation under the federal securities laws. The following problem illustrates one such effort, which came in the form of a no-action request to the SEC staff. How should the SEC respond to this request?

*Problem 14-1*

Following the failure of Executive Life Insurance Company in the early 1990s, the insurance industry began to encounter difficulties marketing guaranteed insurance contracts (GICs). To assuage concerns of consumers, the Traveling Assurance Company (TAC) designed a new annuity product that would be linked to a separate account containing a pool of assets designed to match the company's contractual commitments on GICs. So, for example, if the company issued $100 million of GICs offering a five percent rate of interest, it would place $100 million of securities yielding at least the same rate of interest in corresponding separate accounts.

Pursuant to a newly-enacted provision of insurance law in the state in which TAC is incorporated, these separate accounts would only be available for claims of holders of corresponding GICs. Other TAC creditors could not make claims on assets in these separate accounts. If, however, the assets in the separate accounts were insufficient to repay holders of the corresponding GICs, these holders could make a claim for the shortfall on TAC's general accounts.

TAC seeks confirmation from the SEC staff that it need not register these separate accounts as investment companies under the 1940 Act. How should the SEC proceed? See The Travelers T-Mark Annuity, SEC No-Action Letter, 1993 WL 173769 (avail. May 13, 1993), withdrawn, The Equitable Life Assurance Society of the United States, SEC No-Action Letter, 1995 WL 771389 (avail. Dec. 22, 1995).

---

The preceding materials explored the application of the federal securities laws to variable insurance products issued by traditional insurance companies. A similar dispute has arisen over the application of securities laws to another specialized form of insurance product: private pension plans. As explored above in section 3 of Chapter Eight, employee benefit plans in the United States are governed by a separate regulatory structure: the Employee Retirement Income Security At of 1974, as amended (ERISA). In the following decision, the Supreme Court was called upon to determine the extent to which the federal securities laws apply to ERISA-regulated retirement benefit plans.

## International Brotherhood of Teamsters v. Daniels
### 439 U.S. 551 (1979)

Mr. Justice POWELL delivered the opinion of the Court.

This case presents the question whether a noncontributory, compulsory pension plan constitutes a "security" within the meaning of the Securities Act of 1933 and the Securities Exchange Act of 1934 (Securities Acts).

I

In 1954 multiemployer collective bargaining between Local 705 of the International Brotherhood of Teamsters, Chauffeurs, Warehousemen, and Helpers of America and Chicago trucking firms produced a pension plan for employees represented by the Local. The plan was compulsory and noncontributory. Employees had no choice as to participation in the plan, and did not have the option of demanding that the employer's contribution be paid directly to them as a substitute for pension eligibility. The employees paid nothing to the plan themselves.

The collective-bargaining agreement initially set employer contributions to the Pension Trust Fund at $2 a week for each man-week of covered employment.[2] The Board of Trustees of the Fund, a body composed of an equal number of employer and union representatives, was given sole authority to set the level of benefits but had no control over the amount of required employer contributions. Initially, eligible employees received $75 a month in benefits upon retirement. Subsequent collective-bargaining agreements called for greater employer contributions, which in turn led to higher benefit payments for retirees. At the time respondent brought suit, employers contributed $21.50 per employee man-week and pension payments ranged from $425 to $525 a month depending on age at retirement.[3] In order to receive a pension an employee was required to have 20 years of continuous service, including time worked before the start of the plan.

The meaning of "continuous service" is at the center of this dispute. Respondent began working as a truckdriver in the Chicago area in 1950, and joined Local 705 the following year. When the plan first went into effect, respondent automatically received 5 years' credit toward the 20-year service requirement because of his earlier work experience. He retired in 1973 and applied to the plan's administrator for a pension. The administrator determined that respondent was ineligible because of a break in service between December 1960 and July 1961. Respondent appealed the decision to the trustees, who affirmed. Respondent then asked the trustees to waive the continuous-service rule as it applied to him. After the trustees refused to waive the rule, respondent brought suit in federal court against the International Union (Teamsters), Local 705 (Local), and Louis Peick, a trustee of the Fund.

Respondent's complaint alleged that the Teamsters, the Local, and Peick misrepresented and omitted to state material facts with respect to the value of a covered employee's interest in the pension plan. Count I of the complaint charged that these misstatements and omissions constituted a fraud in connection with the sale of a security in violation of § 10(b) of the Securities Exchange Act of 1934, and the Securities and Exchange Commission's Rule 10b-5. Count II charged that the same conduct amounted to a violation of § 17(a) of the Securities Act of 1933. Other counts alleged violations of various labor law and common-law duties. . . .

The petitioners moved to dismiss the first two counts of the complaint on the ground that respondent had no cause of action under the Securities Acts. The District Court denied the motion. 410 F.Supp. 541 (ND Ill.1976). It held that respondent's interest in the Pension Fund constituted a security within the meaning of § 2(1) of the Securities Act, and § 3(a)(10) of the Securities Exchange Act, because the plan created an "investment contract" as that term had been

---

[2]    Contributions were tied to the number of employees rather than the amount of work performed. For example, payments had to be made even for weeks where an employee was on leave of absence, disabled, or working for only a fraction of the week. Conversely, employers did not have to increase their contribution for weeks in which an employee worked overtime or on a holiday.

[3]    Because the Fund made the same payments to each employee who qualified for a pension and retired at the same age, rather than establishing an individual account for each employee tied to the amount of employer contributions attributable to his period of service, the plan provided a "defined benefit." See ERISA § 3(35).

interpreted in SEC v. W. J. Howey Co., 328 U.S. 293, 66 S.Ct. 1100, 90 L.Ed. 1244 (1946).[7] It also determined that there had been a "sale" of this interest to respondent within the meaning of § 2(3) of the Securities Act, as amended, and § 3(a)(14) of the Securities Exchange Act.[8] It believed respondent voluntarily gave value for his interest in the plan, because he had voted on collective-bargaining agreements that chose employer contributions to the Fund instead of other wages or benefits.

The order denying the motion to dismiss was certified for appeal pursuant to 28 U.S.C. § 1292(b), and the Court of Appeals for the Seventh Circuit affirmed. 561 F.2d 1223 (1977). Relying on its perception of the economic realities of pension plans and various actions of Congress and the SEC with respect to such plans, the court ruled that respondent's interest in the Pension Fund was a "security." According to the court, a "sale" took place either when respondent ratified a collective-bargaining agreement embodying the Fund or when he accepted or retained covered employment instead of seeking other work. The court did not believe the subsequent enactment of the Employee Retirement Income Security Act of 1974 (ERISA) affected the application of the Securities Acts to pension plans, as the requirements and purposes of ERISA were perceived to be different from those of the Securities Acts.[10]

II

. . . . In spite of the substantial use of employee pension plans at the time they were enacted, neither § 2(1) of the Securities Act nor § 3(a)(10) of the Securities Exchange Act, which defines the term "security" in considerable detail and with numerous examples, refers to pension

---

[7]    Section 2(1) of the Securities Act, as amended, 15 U.S.C. § 77b(1), defines a "security" as

"any note, stock, treasury stock, bond, debenture, evidence of indebtedness, certificate of interest or participation in any profit- sharing agreement, collateral-trust certificate, preorganization certificate or subscription, transferable share, investment contract, voting-trust certificate, certificate of deposit for a security, fractional undivided interest in oil, gas, or other mineral rights, or, in general, any interest or instrument commonly known as a 'security,' or any certificate of interest or participation in, temporary or interim certificate for, receipt for, guarantee of, or warrant or right to subscribe to or purchase, any of the foregoing."

The definition of a "security" in § 3(a)(10) of the Securities Exchange Act is virtually identical and, for the purposes of this case, the coverage of the two Acts may be regarded as the same. . . .

[8]    Section 2(3) of the Securities Act provides, in pertinent part, that "[t]he term 'sale' or 'sell' shall include every contract of sale or disposition of a security or interest in a security, for value." Section 3(a)(14) of the Securities Exchange Act states that "[t]he terms 'sale' and 'sell' each include any contract to sell or otherwise dispose of." Although the latter definition does not refer expressly to a disposition for value, the court below did not decide whether the Securities Exchange Act nevertheless impliedly incorporated the Securities Act definition, cf. n. 7, supra, as in its view respondent did give value for his interest in the pension plan. In light of our disposition of the question whether respondent's interest was a "security," we need not decide whether the meaning of "sale" under the Securities Exchange Act is any different from its meaning under the Securities Act.

[10]    Respondent did not have any cause of action under ERISA itself, as that Act took effect after he had retired.

plans of any type.  Acknowledging this omission in the statutes, respondent contends that an employee's interest in a pension plan is an "investment contract," an instrument which is included in the statutory definitions of a security.

To determine whether a particular financial relationship constitutes an investment contract, "[t]he test is whether the scheme involves an investment of money in a common enterprise with profits to come solely from the efforts of others."  Howey, 328 U.S., at 301, 66 S.Ct., at 1104.  This test is to be applied in light of "the substance--the economic realities of the transaction--rather than the names that may have been employed by the parties."  United Housing Foundation, Inc. v. Forman, 421 U.S. 837, 851-852 (1975).  Cf. SEC v. Variable Annuity Life Ins. Co., 359 U.S. 65, 80 (1959) (BRENNAN, J., concurring) ("[O]ne must apply a test in terms of the purposes of the Federal Acts . . .").  Looking separately at each element of the Howey test, it is apparent that an employee's participation in a noncontributory, compulsory pension plan such as the Teamsters' does not comport with the commonly held understanding of an investment contract.

## A. Investment of Money

An employee who participates in a noncontributory, compulsory pension plan by definition makes no payment into the pension fund.  He only accepts employment, one of the conditions of which is eligibility for a possible benefit on retirement.  Respondent contends, however, that he has "invested" in the Pension Fund by permitting part of his compensation from his employer to take the form of a deferred pension benefit.  By allowing his employer to pay money into the Fund, and by contributing his labor to his employer in return for these payments, respondent asserts he has made the kind of investment which the Securities Acts were intended to regulate.

In order to determine whether respondent invested in the Fund by accepting and remaining in covered employment, it is necessary to look at the entire transaction through which he obtained a chance to receive pension benefits.  In every decision of this Court recognizing the presence of a "security" under the Securities Acts, the person found to have been an investor chose to give up a specific consideration in return for a separable financial interest with the characteristics of a security.  See SEC v. United Benefit Life Ins. Co., 387 U.S. 202 (1967) (portion of premium paid for variable component of mixed variable- and fixed-annuity contract); Variable Annuity Life Ins. Co., supra (premium paid for variable-annuity contract); Howey, supra (money paid for purchase, maintenance, and harvesting of orange grove); SEC v. C. M. Joiner Leasing Corp., 320 U.S. 344 (1943) (money paid for land and oil exploration).  Even in those cases where the interest acquired had intermingled security and nonsecurity aspects, the interest obtained had "to a very substantial degree elements of investment contracts . . . ." Variable Annuity Life Ins. Co., supra, 359 U.S., at 91 (BRENNAN, J., concurring).  In every case the purchaser gave up some tangible and definable consideration in return for an interest that had substantially the characteristics of a security.

In a pension plan such as this one, by contrast, the purported investment is a relatively insignificant part of an employee's total and indivisible compensation package.  No portion of an employee's compensation other than the potential pension benefits has any of the characteristics of a security, yet these noninvestment interests cannot be segregated from the possible pension benefits. Only in the most abstract sense may it be said that an employee "exchanges" some portion of his labor in return for these possible benefits.[12] He surrenders his labor as a whole, and in return receives a compensation package that is substantially devoid of aspects resembling a security. His decision to accept and retain covered employment may have only an attenuated relationship, if any, to perceived investment possibilities of a future pension. Looking at the economic realities, it seems clear that an employee is selling his labor primarily to obtain a livelihood, not making an investment.

Respondent also argues that employer contributions on his behalf constituted his investment into the Fund. But it is inaccurate to describe these payments as having been "on behalf" of any employee. The trust agreement used employee man-weeks as a convenient way to measure an employer's overall obligation to the Fund, not as a means of measuring the employer's obligation to any particular employee. Indeed, there was no fixed relationship between contributions to the Fund and an employee's potential benefits. A pension plan with "defined benefits," such as the Local's, does not tie a qualifying employee's benefits to the time he has worked. See n. 3, supra. One who has engaged in covered employment for 20 years will receive the same benefits as a person who has worked for 40, even though the latter has worked twice as long and induced a substantially larger employer contribution. Again, it ignores the economic realities to equate employer contributions with an investment by the employee.

### B. Expectation of Profits From a Common Enterprise

As we observed in Forman, the "touchstone" of the Howey test "is the presence of an investment in a common venture premised on a reasonable expectation of profits to be derived from the entrepreneurial or managerial efforts of others." 421 U.S., at 852. The Court of Appeals believed that Daniel's expectation of profit derived from the Fund's successful management and investment of its assets. To the extent pension benefits exceeded employer contributions and depended on earnings from the assets, it was thought they contained a profit element. The Fund's trustees provided the managerial efforts which produced this profit element.

As in other parts of its analysis, the court below found an expectation of profit in the pension plan only by focusing on one of its less important aspects to the exclusion of its more significant elements. It is true that the Fund, like other holders of large assets, depends to some extent on earnings from its assets. In the case of a pension fund, however, a far larger portion of its income comes from employer contributions, a source in no way dependent on the efforts of the Fund's managers. The Local 705 Fund, for example, earned a total of $31 million through investment of its assets between February 1955 and January 1977. During this same period employer contributions totaled $153 million. Not only does the greater share of a pension plan's income ordinarily come from new contributions, but unlike most entrepreneurs who manage other people's money, a plan usually can count on increased employer contributions, over which the plan itself has no control, to cover shortfalls in earnings.

---

[12]    This is not to say that a person's "investment," in order to meet the definition of an investment contract, must take the form of cash only, rather than of goods and services. See Forman, supra, 421 U.S., at 852 n. 16.

The importance of asset earnings in relation to the other benefits received from employment is diminished further by the fact that where a plan has substantial preconditions to vesting, the principal barrier to an individual employee's realization of pension benefits is not the financial health of the fund. Rather, it is his own ability to meet the fund's eligibility requirements. Thus, even if it were proper to describe the benefits as a "profit" returned on some hypothetical investment by the employee, this profit would depend primarily on the employee's efforts to meet the vesting requirements, rather than the fund's investment success. When viewed in light of the total compensation package an employee must receive in order to be eligible for pension benefits, it becomes clear that the possibility of participating in a plan's asset earnings "is far too speculative and insubstantial to bring the entire transaction within the Securities Acts," Forman, 421 U.S., at 856.

### III

The court below believed that its construction of the term "security" was compelled not only by the perceived resemblance of a pension plan to an investment contract but also by various actions of Congress and the SEC with regard to the Securities Acts. In reaching this conclusion, the court gave great weight to the SEC's explanation of these events, an explanation which for the most part the SEC repeats here. Our own review of the record leads us to believe that this reliance on the SEC's interpretation of these legislative and administrative actions was not justified.

### A. Actions of Congress

The SEC in its amicus curiae brief refers to several actions of Congress said to evidence an understanding that pension plans are securities. A close look at each instance, however, reveals only that Congress might have believed certain kinds of pension plans, radically different from the one at issue here, came within the coverage of the Securities Acts. There is no evidence that Congress at any time thought noncontributory plans similar to the one before us were subject to federal regulation as securities.

[One] action cited was the rejection by Congress in 1934 of an amendment to the Securities Act that would have exempted employee stock investment and stock option plans from the Act's registration requirements.[17] The amendment passed the Senate but was eliminated in conference. The legislative history of the defeated proposal indicates it was intended to cover plans under which employees contributed their own funds to a segregated investment account on which a return was realized. . . . In rejecting the amendment, Congress revealed a concern that certain interests having the characteristics of a security not be excluded from Securities Act protection simply because investors realized their return in the form of retirement benefits. At

---

[17]   The amendment would have added the following language to § 4(1) of the Securities Act:

"As used in this paragraph, the term 'public offering' shall not be deemed to include an offering made solely to employees by an issuer or by its affiliates in connection with a bona fide plan for the payment of extra compensation or stock investment plan for the exclusive benefit of such employees." 78 Cong.Rec. 8708 (1934).

no time however, did Congress indicate that pension benefits in and of themselves gave a transaction the characteristics of a security. . . . .

## B. SEC Interpretation

The court below believed, and it now is argued to us, that almost from its inception the SEC has regarded pension plans as falling within the scope of the Securities Acts. We are asked to defer to what is seen as a longstanding interpretation of these statutes by the agency responsible for their administration. But there are limits, grounded in the language, purpose, and history of the particular statute, on how far an agency properly may go in its interpretative role. Although these limits are not always easy to discern, it is clear here that the SEC's position is neither longstanding nor even arguably within the outer limits of its authority to interpret these Acts.

As we have demonstrated above, the type of pension plan at issue in this case bears no resemblance to the kind of financial interests the Securities Acts were designed to regulate. Further, the SEC's present position is flatly contradicted by its past actions. Until the instant litigation arose, the public record reveals no evidence that the SEC had ever considered the Securities Acts to be applicable to noncontributory pension plans. In 1941, the SEC first articulated the position that voluntary, contributory plans had investment characteristics that rendered them "securities" under the Acts. At the same time, however, the SEC recognized that noncontributory plans were not covered by the Securities Acts because such plans did not involve a "sale" within the meaning of the statutes. . . . .

In an attempt to reconcile these interpretations of the Securities Acts with its present stand, the SEC now augments its past position with two additional propositions. First, it is argued, noncontributory plans are "securities" even where a "sale" is not involved. Second, the previous concession that noncontributory plans do not involve a "sale" was meant to apply only to the registration and reporting requirements of the Securities Acts; for purposes of the antifraud provisions, a "sale" is involved. As for the first proposition, we observe that none of the SEC opinions, reports, or testimony cited to us address the question. As for the second, the record is unambiguously to the contrary. Both in its 1941 statements and repeatedly since then, the SEC has declared that its "no sale" position applied to the Securities Acts as a whole. . . . As far as we are aware, at no time before this case arose did the SEC intimate that the antifraud provisions of the Securities Acts nevertheless applied to noncontributory pension plans.

## IV

If any further evidence were needed to demonstrate that pension plans of the type involved are not subject to the Securities Acts, the enactment of ERISA in 1974, 88 Stat. 829, would put the matter to rest. Unlike the Securities Acts, ERISA deals expressly and in detail with pension plans. ERISA requires pension plans to disclose specified information to employees in a specified manner, see ERISA §§ 101-111, in contrast to the indefinite and uncertain disclosure obligations imposed by the antifraud provisions of the Securities Acts . . . . Further, ERISA regulates the substantive terms of pension plans, setting standards for plan funding and limits on the eligibility requirements an employee must meet. For example, with respect to the underlying issue in this case--whether respondent served long enough to receive a pension--§ 203(a) of ERISA now sets the minimum level of benefits an employee must receive after accruing specified years of service, and § 203(b), governs continuous-service requirements. Thus, if respondent had retired after § 203 took effect, the Fund would have been required to pay him at least a partial pension. The Securities Acts, on the other hand, do not purport to set the substantive terms of financial transactions.

The existence of this comprehensive legislation governing the use and terms of employee pension plans severely undercuts all arguments for extending the Securities Acts to noncontributory, compulsory pension plans. Congress believed that it was filling a regulatory void when it enacted ERISA, a belief which the SEC actively encouraged. Not only is the extension of the Securities Acts by the court below unsupported by the language and history of those Acts, but in light of ERISA it serves no general purpose. . . . Whatever benefits employees might derive from the effect of the Securities Acts are now provided in more definite form through ERISA.

## Comments and Questions

1. In the *Daniels* decision, the Court applied the *Howey* test to determine whether the pension plan in question constituted an investment contract for purposes of federal securities laws. What are the elements of that test? Does it differ from the standard the court applied twenty years earlier in its VALIC decision? In what·other contexts have we seen this test applied?

2. In Part IV of the *Daniels* decision, the Court relied on the fact that in ERISA Congress had developed an alternative regulatory structure for protecting pension beneficiaries. How does the regulatory structure of ERISA differ from that provided by the federal securities laws? Would Mr. Daniels have been assured of adequate retirement income had the federal securities laws applied in this context?

3. As the Part III of the *Daniels* decision chronicles, the SEC's position with respect to pension plans has evolved over time. The Commission has, for example, distinguished between contributory and non-contributory pension plans — a distinction based on whether the employer or the employee transfers funds to the plan. The Commission has also argued that in certain contexts the anti-fraud provisions of the federal securities laws (in particular, rule 10b-5 promulgated under the 1934 Act) should apply to the accrual of pension benefits even though the registration requirements of the 1933 Act (that is, mandatory disclosure and prospectus delivery requirements) should not. Putting aside their statutory basis, do these distinctions makes sense as a matter of policy?

4. The pension at issue in Daniels was a defined benefit plan, under which participants were promised a certain benefit (that is, an annuity) upon retirement. When the Daniels case was decided, defined benefit plans were the most common form of pension in the United States. Since then, defined contribution plans have become increasingly popular. Under defined contribution plans, pension contributions are allocated to individual accounts, and each employee's retirement benefit depends upon the performance of that employee's account. In many defined contribution plans, employees have substantial control over the manner in which their accounts are invested. ERISA has special rules governing the regulation of these self-directed accounts. See Section 404(c)(1)

of ERISA. Under the *Daniels* decision, do the federal securities laws extend to self-directed, defined contribution plans? For an overview of the SEC's views on these issues and a summary of legislative and regulatory developments since the *Daniels* decision, see SEC STAFF REPORT, PROTECTING INVESTORS: A HALF-CENTURY OF INVESTMENT COMPANY REGULATION ch. 3 (May 1992).

---

The *Daniels* case and the notes that followed concerned the question whether additional regulatory structures should extend the pension plan participants. The Court in that case ruled that in many contexts ERISA's protection would be exclusive. But how far should this exclusivity extend? This question is of particular importance in the treatment of pension plan assets. Under section 3(21) of ERISA, anyone who "exercises any discretionary authority or discretionary control" over pension plan assets is an ERISA fiduciary and subject to an elaborate system of prudential constraints and enforcement provisions. See, e.g., section 404(a) of ERISA. But what happens if pension plan assets are invested in a mutual fund or a insurance company or a bank trust department? Does an intermediary also become subject to ERISA's fiduciary rules if it accepts responsibility for investing pension plan assets? In some contexts, ERISA provides express exception from the application of its fiduciary rules. See section 401(b)(1) (involving assets of investment companies registered under the 1940 Act). Elsewhere, the jurisdictional boundaries are less clear, as the following case illustrates:

## Associates in Adolescent Psychiatry v. Home Life Insurance Co.
### 941 F.2d 561 (7th Cir. 1991), *cert. denied*, 502 U.S. 1099 (1992)

EASTERBROOK, Circuit Judge.

Associates in Adolescent Psychiatry, S.C., its owner, Marvin P. Schwarz, and his wife (collectively "AAP"), bought a variable annuity and seek relief against Home Life Insurance Company, a Rhode Island bank, and various accountants and lawyers involved in the process. They present claims under the securities acts [and] ERISA. . . .

A defined benefit plan promises specified levels of benefits on retirement. The employer may set aside amounts actuarially necessary to fund these future payments. In 1977 Schwarz began looking into the possibility of establishing a defined benefit plan for AAP, the professional corporation through which he rendered psychiatric services. Professional corporations often serve principally as sources of tax benefits. Contributions made by an employer are deductible as ordinary and necessary business expenses. I.R.C. § 404(a). As the deduction is limited to the amount necessary to keep the plan fully funded, § 404(a)(1)(A), it may be advantageous to purchase instruments with low stated rates of return. The lower the nominal return, the more the plan needs to remain fully funded, and consequently the higher the permissible deduction. If the investment actually earns more than the stated rate of return, permissible contributions (and deductions) in future years are lower, but the taxpayers have enjoyed benefits in the interim.

Home Life offered Dr. Schwarz a defined benefit plan that allowed for greater annual contributions, and hence greater deductions, than other plans he had seen. Home Life achieved this by using a "Flexible Annuity", an instrument with a relatively low guaranteed rate of return. Sums invested in the Flexible Annuity accumulate earnings at an annual guaranteed rate plus a variable excess rate. The Flexible Annuity that AAP ultimately purchased guaranteed a return of 7% during the first year, 6% for the next two years, 5% for the following two years, and 4% thereafter. The variable rate, referred to in the contract as the "annual dividend", is defined as the "excess, if any, of the interest credited to the Participant's Accumulated Account Value over the interest calculated at the Minimum Interest Rate." The contract provides further that "the interest rate ... applicable to all funds held under this contract [will be] declared annually by the Board of Directors of [Home Life]".

Home Life wished to sell its Flexible Annuity throughout the country but did not want to submit the product for regulatory approval in every state. To accomplish both objectives Home Life entered into an agreement with Rhode Island Hospital Trust National Bank (HTNB) establishing a "Qualified Corporate Plan Trust". This trust is the sole buyer of Flexible Annuities, so Home Life had only to do what was necessary to qualify its offering in Rhode Island, provided that insurance regulators in other states did not balk. Home Life sells the Flexible Annuity to employers as a group annuity contract. An employer, as the sponsor of the defined benefit plan, sends contributions to Home Life, which wires these amounts to HTNB. The bank, as trustee of the corporate plan trust, uses the money to buy a Flexible Annuity from Home Life. The triple-transfer arrangement (employer to Home Life to HTNB to Home Life) entails some delay. HTNB wires funds to Home Life only on Mondays, so it enjoys the float on money received during the preceding week. Home Life credits employers' accounts as soon as it receives their funds, so it bears the cost of the float. Each employee designated as a beneficiary under the plan must sign an agreement enrolling in the trust; the employee receives a certificate memorializing his participation. Each beneficiary receives annual statements from Home Life of the amounts accumulated by virtue of the employer's contributions and the earnings allocated according to the terms of the Flexible Annuity.

The Employee Retirement Income Security Act (ERISA) requires that plan assets be held in trust. ERISA § 403(a). Home Life gave AAP documents establishing a plan trust, naming the two Schwarzes as trustees. Dr. and Mrs. Schwarz executed these documents in July 1977. At the same time, they signed a participation agreement listing them as "Plan Investment Managers". The participation agreement provided that AAP was to fund the plan with two financial instruments: whole life insurance policies and the Flexible Annuity. AAP made payments under the terms of the Home Life products until 1980. During this period interest rates skyrocketed. Home Life's "excess rate", derived from the return on the insurer's entire portfolio of assets (which was locked into long-term projects), lagged well behind the returns available from short-term investments such as money market funds. This shortfall eclipsed the tax advantages of the plan. AAP regretted its choice and brought this action.

. . . We have no doubt that the Flexible Annuity is an "investment contract" and so comes within the broad definitional clauses of the [federal securities] statutes. See Reves v. Ernst

& Young, 494 U.S. 56, 64 (1990);  United Housing Foundation, Inc. v. Forman, 421 U.S. 837, 852 (1975);  SEC v. W.J. Howey Co., 328 U.S. 293, 298-99 (1946);  Chicago Mercantile Exchange v. SEC, 883 F.2d 537, 545 (7th Cir.1989).  Yet almost all insurance and annuity products are securities, broadly understood, because they entail entrusting money to the hands of others in pursuit of appreciation.  The Securities Act of 1933 partitions investments between the world of securities regulation and insurance regulation via § 3(a)(8), which exempts "[a]ny insurance or endowment policy or annuity contract or optional annuity contract, issued by a corporation subject to [state regulation]".  AAP conceded at oral argument that the whole life policies come within this exemption.  Home Life argues that its Flexible Annuity also falls within § 3(a)(8), and the district court agreed.

Both the district court and the parties devoted substantial energy to the SEC's Rule 151, which establishes a "safe harbor" for some variable annuities.  Only persons who rely on a regulation may claim the benefit of its safe harbor.  Section 19(a) of the 1933 Act.  Rule 151 became effective on June 4, 1986;  Home Life introduced the first version of the Flexible Annuity in 1975;  AAP purchased its Flexible Annuity in 1977.  The SEC's rules may facilitate understanding of statutory law, see Otto v. Variable Annuity Life Insurance Co., 814 F.2d 1127, 1133 (7th Cir.1986), but the technical details of Rule 151 do not affect the disposition of this case, which we decide under 3(a)(8).

An ordinary annuity is a promise to pay fixed amounts of money beginning at a time specified in the contract.  The seller funds its performance by a combination of the purchase price and income earned by investing that sum.  Sellers of annuities invest the receipts in diversified portfolios.   All annuities therefore are pooled investment vehicles, but fixed annuities are characterized by a particular division of risk:  the buyer obtains a payment stream reflecting assumptions about how well the portfolio will do, and the seller reaps the reward (suffers a loss) if the investments do better (worse).  Annuities sometimes contain an element of insurance:  they may, for example, promise a monthly payment from retirement until death, so that the total payments are larger the longer the purchaser survives.  The seller then bears both investment and insurance risks.  For simplicity we disregard the insurance component of annuities (although the Flexible Annuity has such an insurance component).

Traditional annuities in which the exact (monthly or total) amounts to be paid to the purchaser are fixed are not responsive to inflation.  This makes them unattractive to investors who cannot otherwise protect themselves against variation in the value of money.  Fixed annuities carry relatively low (implicit) rates of return even in an inflation-free economy, because underwriters cannot readily hedge against changes in the economy-wide rate of return.  If the issuer has promised payments that imply a 4% annual return, a decline in the return of its portfolio below this figure produces bankruptcy.  In order to reduce the bankruptcy risk, an issuer makes conservative assumptions about the return to investment.  Conservative assumptions yield low returns--which in turn make annuities less attractive compared with, say, mutual funds that deliver to investors the entire return of the portfolio.

The variable annuity responds to both of these problems.  Instead of providing fixed payments, the variable annuity contract promises a modest guaranteed return (one low enough to curtail the bankruptcy risk) plus an additional amount to be determined in the future.  Some variable annuities tie the level of return to a publicly-reported index--the inflation rate, for example. Another form of the variable annuity contract ties the amount the purchaser receives to the rate of return that the insurer earns on its investment portfolio. Although the purchaser of this type of variable annuity shares in the success of the insurer's investment portfolio, he also bears the risk of a disappointing performance.

No annuity transfers all of the risk to the seller. Any fixed annuity places on the buyer the risk that the seller's portfolio will perform too poorly to finance the promised payments. Section 3(a)(8) therefore necessarily exempts annuities that leave purchasers with some investment risk. If on the other hand a seller just pins the label "annuity" on a mutual fund, in which the buyer bears all of the risk, § 3(a)(8) is inapplicable. SEC v. Variable Annuity Life Insurance Co., 359 U.S. 65 (1959), holds that a contract providing for variable payments based on the investors' stakes in a special investment portfolio is not an "annuity contract". The Court reasoned that because there was no guarantee of any return, the entire investment risk was borne by the purchaser of the annuity. Where there is no transfer of risk, the exemption does not apply. Id. at 71-73. SEC v. United Benefit Life Insurance Co., 387 U.S. 202 (1967), extended "no" to "slight", holding that § 3(a)(8) does not apply to an instrument permitting purchasers to share in the performance of an investment portfolio with a guaranteed but low minimum rate of return. These guaranteed rates were well below what would be provided in a conventional annuity, so that the purchaser relied on the investment skills of the issuer to maintain earnings in excess of the contractual minimum. The Court thought that the dominant aspect of the instrument was that the seller acted as an "investment agency". Id. at 208.

How much risk is too much? The Court's opinions do not say, and the parties to our case debate the question vigorously. Our own decisions recognize that a minimal guarantee will not do the trick. Peoria Union Stockyards Co. v. Pennsylvania Mutual Life Insurance Co., 698 F.2d 320 (7th Cir.1983), considered a contract providing that funds contributed by the purchaser would accumulate earnings at a modest guaranteed rate plus a pro rata share of the insurer's "divisible surplus", the amount earned on the insurer's general portfolio of investments. Relying on both VALIC and United Benefit, we held that Penn Mutual had sold its investment expertise and not an annuity; by leaving the bulk of the investment risk with the buyer, Penn Mutual disqualified the instrument from exemption under § 3(a)(8). See also Otto, 814 F.2d at 1140-42 (§ 3(a)(8) inapplicable when issuer has total control, after the fact, over the excess rate).

At first blush our case appears parallel to Peoria Union. AAP's contributions accumulated interest at the guaranteed minimum rates, plus the "excess" interest that Home Life's board of directors declared annually. This "excess", the parties agree, was derived from the rate of return Home Life earned on its general investment portfolio. Home Life stresses that by putting its entire portfolio behind the Flexible Annuity it reduced the buyers' risks-- true enough, but equally true in Peoria Union and, for that matter, in any large mutual fund. A large, well-diversified portfolio has a small bankruptcy risk, but § 3(a)(8) does not carve out of the securities laws all investments that are safe in this sense. Many investments have negligible bankruptcy risk but are still securities. Compare Reves with Marine Bank v. Weaver, 455 U.S. 551 (1982).

Yet one feature of the Flexible Annuity makes it look more like a fixed annuity than did the instruments in Peoria Union and Otto. In both of these cases (as in VALIC and United Benefit) the buyer paid money; the seller held it for a time, after which it announced the rate of interest to be credited. The ex ante uncertainty about that rate made the "annuity" look like a mutual fund, with the seller supplying only investment advice. Home Life, by contrast, announced the annual interest rate in advance. At the beginning of each policy year Home Life would declare a rate of return for the coming year. The terms of the Flexible Annuity left the purchaser free (a) to withdraw all funds and invest them elsewhere, if dissatisfied with the rate; (b) to leave the funds with Home Life and add nothing to them; and (c) to make additional purchases. AAP knew what rate of return it would earn for the next year not only before it made its initial contribution but also prior to deciding to "roll over" its investment each year thereafter. Had it found the declared rate unsatisfactory, it was free under the terms of the contract to take its money and go elsewhere. The Flexible Annuity, then, resembled nothing so much as a series of fixed annuities, each one year in duration, with the purchaser having an option to renew. That the return is fixed for such a short period does not make the instrument less an annuity.

AAP points out that if it had taken out its money during the first four years of the contract it would have incurred a withdrawal penalty. This front- end load covering sales and administrative expense did nothing to throw *investment risk* on the investor. (The same holds for any tax burden that might have befallen AAP had it demanded its money back.) AAP also argues that the Flexible Annuity provides no guarantee at all, that Home Life was free to change the interest rates at any time. Otto deemed such a reserved power fatal to the use of § 3(a)(8).

Although the group annuity contract issued to AAP states that the interest rate for contributions under the contract will be "declared annually by the Board of Directors", it does not expressly deny Home Life authority to modify the rate more than once a year. AAP submits that Home Life may alter interest rates at its discretion. In support of this claim, AAP points to the depositions of two of Home Life's officers describing how the Board of Directors arrived at the annual rate, and to a series of internal memoranda detailing the process by which the firm established interest rates for certain years. These documents show that Home Life did not assume a great deal of risk by guaranteeing an annual rate of return in advance: the declared rate was based on the performance of Home Life's portfolio over the past year, and only about 6% of the value of the portfolio was reinvested annually. The depositions and memoranda do not show, however, that Home Life varied during any year the interest rate for funds paid in prior to the declaration, or that it believed it had the authority to do so. In the early 1980s, when rates of return on other investments fluctuated rapidly, Home Life did begin to change more than once a year the rate of interest it would credit on *new* money. The rate declared on new funds was guaranteed through the remainder of the calendar year, but the changes in this rate did not affect the return on funds that had already been paid to Home Life in reliance on an earlier announcement. So far as this record reveals, then, Home Life neither claimed nor exercised the power to change rates after accepting funds, the power that spoiled the exemption in Otto, 814 F.2d at 1140-41.

The contract provides that interest rates are to be "declared annually" by Home Life's board of directors. This language most naturally means that the interest rates for amounts paid over to Home Life cannot be altered more than once per year. As the district court observed, this is how Home Life operated the Flexible Annuity program, and AAP has pointed to nothing in the voluminous record that suggests anything to the contrary. We therefore agree with the district court that Home Life's Flexible Annuities do not place excessive investment risk on the purchaser and consequently are annuities. (State regulation is essential to the exemption under § 3(a)(8); Home Life is regulated in many states, and Rhode Island in particular regulated the Flexible Annuity. Nothing in § 3(a)(8) equates regulation with formal approval, so we make nothing of its absence.)

Next we take up AAP's claims under ERISA. AAP believes that Home Life, HTNB, and others involved in the preparation and sale of the group annuity contract violated their fiduciary duties under § 404 of ERISA by failing to reveal that HTNB would reap the benefits of the float in the triple-transfer system employed to leave HTNB as the formal purchaser. Defendants reply that they are not fiduciaries under ERISA ...

HTNB is a trustee, but not the trustee of an ERISA *plan* established by an employer and therefore not a "named fiduciary" under ERISA. § 403(a). The ERISA plan is the one established by AAP. (Only a plan established by an "employer" is an ERISA plan. ERISA § 3(2)(A).) AAP's plan names the Schwarzes, not any of the defendants, as trustees. Even without being named, a person is a fiduciary with respect to an ERISA plan to the extent: "(i) he exercises any discretionary authority or discretionary control respecting management of such plan or exercises any authority or control respecting management or disposition of its assets, ... or, (iii) he has any discretionary authority ... in the administration of such plan." ERISA § 3(21). See Forys v. United Food & Commercial Worker's International Union, 829 F.2d 603 (7th Cir.1987). AAP argues that Home Life and HTNB are fiduciaries because they controlled the assets of premiums paid for life insurance. Home Life has complete control over the composition of this portfolio and need not manage it to prefer pension claimants over the interests of insureds.

AAP argues that the defined benefit plan's assets included an equity interest in this investment portfolio to the extent of AAP's accumulated contributions and earnings, and consequently that Home Life's discretionary authority over these investments gives rise to a fiduciary duty. Yet § 401(b)(2) of ERISA provides that where a plan purchases a "guaranteed benefit policy" from an insurer, the assets of the plan include that policy but not an interest in any assets of the insurer. A "guaranteed benefit policy" is an "insurance policy or contract ... [that] provides for benefits the amount of which is guaranteed by the insurer." ERISA § 401(b)(2)(B). We agree with the district court's conclusion that the Flexible Annuity is a guaranteed benefit policy because Home Life not only set fixed annual rates but also backed its promise with its full assets. It is difficult to see how an instrument could be an "annuity" for purposes of the securities laws and not be a "guaranteed benefit policy" for purposes of ERISA. Our discussion in Part II therefore establishes that Home Life was not holding its entire investment portfolio as AAP's fiduciary. . . .

## Comments and Questions

1. How persuasive is the court's treatment of the securities law issue here? Does the fact that the insurance company announces its guaranteed rate of return at the beginning of each calendar year mean that the insurance company retains substantial investment risk? Is it likely that the plan will withdraw its funds in response to a low rate? Are insurance regulations adequate in this context? Or would a disclosure based regime of regulation make more sense?

2. As the AAP case illustrates, private pension plans have been an important market for variable annuity products. In the AAP case, the plaintiffs also attempted to obtain relief under ERISA's fiduciary rules. The court also rejected these claims, relying on an exception from ERISA's fiduciary rules for guaranteed investment contracts. The scope of this exception has been the subject of some controversy over the past ten years, and in John Hancock Mutual Life Insurance Co. v. Harris Trust & Savings Bank, 114 S. Ct. 517 (1993), the Supreme Court ruled that an insurance contract similar to the one at issue in AAP was not protected by that exception. The following release summarizes subsequent developments:

# Department of Labor, Pension and Welfare Benefits Administration Proposed Rule on Clarification of Application of ERISA to Insurance Company General Accounts
## 61 Fed. Reg. 59845 (Nov. 25, 1996)

### A. Background

Life insurance companies issue a variety of group contracts for use in connection with employee pension benefit plans, some of which provide benefits the amount of which is guaranteed, some of which provide benefits that may fluctuate with the investment performance of the insurance company, and some of which offer elements of both. Under section 401(b)(2) of ERISA, if an insurance company issues a``guaranteed benefit policy'' to a plan, the assets of the plan are deemed to include the policy, but do not solely by reason of the issuance of the policy, include any of the assets of the insurance company. Section 401(b)(2)(B) defines the term ``guaranteed benefit policy'' to mean an insurance policy or contract to the extent that such policy or contract provides for benefits the amount of which is guaranteed by the insurer. In addition, in paragraph (b) of ERISA Interpretive Bulletin 75-2, 29 CFR 2509.75-2 (1975), the Department stated that if an insurance company issues a contract or policy of insurance to a plan and places the consideration for such contract or policy in its general asset account, the assets in such account shall not be considered to be plan assets.[18]

On December 13, 1993, the Supreme Court rendered its decision in John Hancock Mutual Life Insurance Co. v. Harris Trust & Savings Bank, 114 S. Ct. 517 (1993) (Harris Trust) which interpreted the meaning of``guaranteed benefit policy''. In its decision, the Court held that a contract qualifies as a guaranteed benefit policy only to the extent it allocates investment risk to the insurer:

[w]e hold that to determine whether a contract qualifies as a guaranteed benefit policy, each component of the contract bears examination. A component fits within the guaranteed benefit policy exclusion only if it allocates investment risk to the insurer. Such an allocation is present when the

---

[18]   Paragraph (b) of 29 C.F.R. 2509.75-2 was removed effective July 1, 1996. 61 FR 33847, 33849 (July 1, 1996).

insurer provides a genuine guarantee of an aggregate amount of benefits payable to retirement plan participants and their beneficiaries.

Accordingly, under the Supreme Court's decision, an insurer's general account includes plan assets to the extent it contains funds which are attributable to any nonguaranteed components of contracts with employee benefit plans. Because John Hancock's contract provided for a return that varied with the insurer's investment performance, the Court concluded that John Hancock held plan assets, and was, therefore, a fiduciary with respect to the management and disposition of those assets. Under the reasoning of the Court's decision, a broad range of activities involving insurance company general accounts are subject to ERISA's fiduciary standards.

Because of the retroactive effect of the Supreme Court decision, numerous transaction engaged in by insurance company general accounts may have violated ERISA's prohibited transaction and general fiduciary responsibility provisions. The insurance industry believed that, absent legislative or administrative action, it would be subject to significant additional litigation and potential liability with respect to the operation of its general accounts.

If the underlying assets of a general account include plan assets, persons who have engaged in transactions with such general account may be viewed as parties in interest under section 3(14) of ERISA and disqualified persons under section 4975 of the Code, including fiduciaries with respect to plans which have interests as contractholders in the general account. For example, insurance companies are a source of loans for smaller and mid-sized companies. Many of these companies have party in interest relationships with plans that have purchased general account contracts. Application of the prohibited transaction rules to the general account of an insurance company as a result of the Harris Trust decision could call such loans into question under ERISA. Lastly, the underlying assets of an entity in which a general account acquired an equity interest may include plan assets as a result of the Harris Trust decision.

On March 25, 1994, the American Council of Life Insurance (ACLI) submitted an application for a class exemption from certain of the restrictions of sections 406 and 407 of ERISA and from certain excise taxes imposed by section 4975 (a) and (b) of the Code. The ACLI requested broad exemptive relief for transactions which included the following: all internal operations of general accounts, all investment transactions involving general account assets, including transactions with parties in interest with respect to plans that have purchased general account contracts, and the purchase by the general account of securities issued by, and real property leased to, employers of employees covered by plans that have purchased general account contracts.

On August 22, 1994, the Department published a notice of proposed Class Exemption for Certain Transactions Involving Insurance Company General Accounts. (59 FR 43134). Although the ACLI requested exemptive relief for activities in connection with the internal operation of general accounts, the Department determined that it did not have sufficient information regarding the operation of such accounts to make the findings required by section 408(a) of ERISA. Accordingly, the proposed class exemption did not provide relief for transactions involving the internal operation of an insurance company general account. The final exemption (Prohibited Transaction Exemption [PTE] 95-60, 60 FR 35925) was published in the Federal Register on July 12, 1995.

B. Public Law 104-188

In response to the Supreme Court decision in Harris Trust, Congress amended section 401 of ERISA by adding a new subsection 401(c) which clarifies the application of ERISA to insurance company general accounts. Pub. L. 104-188, Sec. 1460. This statutory provision requires that the Department, not later than June 30, 1997, issue proposed regulations providing guidance for the purpose of determining, in cases where an insurer issues one or more policies (supported by the assets of the insurer's general account) to or for the benefit of an employee benefit plan, which assets held by the insurer (other than plan assets held in its separate accounts) constitute plan assets for purposes of part 4 of Title I and section 4975 of the Code and to provide guidance with respect to the application of Title I to an insurer's general account assets. The proposed regulations must be subject to public notice and comment until September 30, 1997, and final regulations shall be issued not later than December 31, 1997.

The regulations will only apply to those general account policies which are issued by an insurer on or before December 31, 1998. In the case of such policies, the regulations will take effect at the end of the 18 month period following the date the regulations become final. Pub. L. 104-188, however, authorizes the Secretary to issue additional regulations designed to prevent avoidance of the regulations described above. These additional regulations, if issued, may have an earlier effective date.

The Department must ensure that the regulations issued under Pub. L. 104-188 are administratively feasible, and protect the interests and rights of the plan and of its participants and beneficiaries. In addition, the regulations must require, in connection with any policy (other than a guaranteed benefit policy) issued by an insurer to or for the benefit of an employee benefit plan, that: (1) an independent plan fiduciary authorize the purchase of the policy (unless the purchase is exempt under ERISA section 408(b)(5)); (2) the insurer provide information on an annual basis to policyholders (as prescribed in such regulations) disclosing the methods by which any income and expenses of the insurer's general account are allocated to the policy and the actual return to the plan under the policy and such other financial information as the Department determines is appropriate; (3) the insurer disclose to the plan fiduciary the extent to which alternative arrangements supported by the assets of the insurer's separate accounts are available, whether there is a right under the policy to transfer funds to a separate account and the terms governing any such right, and the extent to which support by assets of the insurer's general account and support by assets of the insurer's separate accounts might pose differing risks to the plan; and (4) the insurer must manage general account assets prudently, taking into account all obligations supported by such general account.

Compliance with the regulations issued by the Department will be deemed compliance by such insurer with sections 404, 406 and 407 of ERISA. In addition, under this statutory provision, no person will be liable under part 4 of Title I or Code section 4975 for conduct which occurred before the date which is 18 months following the issuance of the final regulation on the basis of a claim that the assets of an insurer (other than plan assets held in a separate account) constitute plan assets. The limitation on liability is subject to three exceptions: (1) the Department may circumscribe this limitation on liability in regulations intended to prevent avoidance of the regulations which it is required to issue under the statutory amendment; (2) the Department may bring actions pursuant to paragraph (2) or (5) of section 502(a) for breaches of fiduciary responsibilities which also constitute violations of Federal or State criminal law; and (3) civil actions commenced before November 7, 1995 are exempt from the amendment's coverage.

## Issues Under Consideration

The Department is publishing this notice to provide interested persons with an opportunity to submit information and comments which will be considered by the Department in developing the regulations mandated by Pub. L. 104-188.

In order to assist interested parties in responding, this notice contains a list of specific questions designed to elicit information that the Department believes would be especially helpful in developing a notice of proposed rulemaking. The questions developed by the Department may not address all issues relevant to the development of the regulation. Therefore, the Department further invites interested parties to submit comments on other matters that they believe are pertinent to the Department's consideration of the regulation.

## Annual Disclosures

(1) What information relating to the financial soundness of an insurer do plan fiduciaries currently rely upon in selecting an insurer?

(2) Should additional information be required to be disclosed to plan fiduciaries prior to selecting an insurer? What would be the cost of supplying this information? To what extent would these costs be passed on to the contractholders?

(3) What annual information would plan fiduciaries find helpful in evaluating the appropriateness of an existing general account contract?

(4) Is there any information which should be disclosed more frequently than annually? Should this information be provided or available upon request?

(5) Do insurers currently disclose to potential contractholders the availability of alternative insurance arrangements supported by separate accounts, the right to transfer funds under a general account contract to a separate account, and the terms governing any such right?

(6) In general, what are the comparative risks and benefits of general account contracts vis-a-vis separate account contracts?

(7) To what extent, and in what format, should insurers be required to disclose information concerning the following: (a) The expenses allocated to the contract and the basis for the allocation; (b) The investment income allocated to the contract and the basis for the allocation; (c) The mortality or morbidity experience attributed to the contract and the basis for the attribution; (d) The allocation of any other aspect of the insurance company's financial performance which has an impact on the contract's return, and the basis for the allocation; (e) The timing of the allocation of expenses, investment income, mortality or morbidity experience, and of any other factors affecting the contract's return; (f) Any charges or provisions attributable to the contract for risks or profits, and the basis for the charges or provisions; (g) Comparative data concerning the return, expenses, investment income, profit and risk charges attributable to other contracts, and an explanation of any disparities; (h) The particular investment income allocation methodology or methodologies employed by the insurer, and any departures from the general methodologies in the actual allocation of investment income to the contract; (i) Financial or

familial relationships or transactions between (1) the insurer, its officers, or directors, and (2) the plan, the plan sponsor, or plan fiduciaries; and (j) Financial transactions between the insurer and any person or entity in which the insurer, its officers, or directors have a financial interest or familial relationship. Do different formats have different cost implications? Which items are costly to produce, or involve confidential or proprietary information? What professional skills are required to prepare the required information?

(8) Should the insurer be required to retain documentation supporting the required disclosures, and to make the supporting documentation available to the Secretary of Labor, plan sponsors, plan fiduciaries, or plan participants and beneficiaries? To what extent are these documents retained as part of current business practice? What are the estimated costs of retaining and producing these documents to the appropriate parties?

(9) How should the insurer calculate the actual return to the plan for purposes of any disclosure requirement? In particular, (a) Should the insurer be required to take into account any market value adjustments, termination expense adjustments, withdrawal charges, or surrender charges in stating the contract's return?  (b) Should the regulations permit different approaches for calculating the rate of return for contracts requiring the issuance of annuities as opposed to those in which benefit payments are made without the issuance of an annuity? (c) Should the regulations require that dividends that are anticipated or declared buy not yet paid, be included in determining the contract's return? (d) To what extent should the regulations permit the return to be reported on a gross basis (i.e., before expenses or charges)?

(10) Under what circumstances would regulations requiring disclosure of the contractholder's return apply to general account contracts before the end of the 18 month period following the issuance of the final regulations?

Market Value Adjustments Upon Termination of General Account Contracts

(1) In what ways is discretion exercised by insurers under general account contracts in imposing market value adjustments or in determining the amount of such adjustments?

(2) What standards should the Department adopt to assure that market value adjustments reflect market conditions at the time of contract termination?

(3) Should the Department require general account contracts to set forth in ``plain English" the method for calculating market value adjustments that can be objectively verified by the contractholder pursuant to standards set forth in the contract? In this regard, should the Department require that the method used for calculating market value adjustments only use parameters that can be independently verified by the contractholder?

(4) Should the Department limit or forbid the imposition of termination expense adjustments, withdrawal charges, or surrender charges pursuant to general account contracts?

(5) Under what circumstances should regulations regarding market value adjustments and other termination charges be applicable to general account contracts prior to the end of the 18 month period following the issuance of the final regulations?

### Comments and Questions

1. Why did the Hancock decision generate such strong reaction on the part of the insurance industry?  Why didn't the industry just bring itself into compliance with the requirements of ERISA?  What regulatory philosophy underlies Pub. L. No. 104-188?  Should ERISA fiduciary be required to review specific information before investing funds with an insurance company?

2.  Section 3(a)(8) of the Securities Act of 1933 provides an exemption from federal securities laws for certain insurance products.  How does ERISA's exemption for guaranteed benefit policies compare to the section 3(a)(8) exemption?  Should the contours of the two exemptions be the same?  If not, how should they differ?

# Section 2.  Futures and Options

Financial futures and options offer investors mechanisms for hedging (and speculating upon) certain kinds of risk.  As such, these markets provide what might be characterized as a specialized form of insurance.  This section reviews the evolution of the regulation of these markets in the United States, and also several important jurisdictional issues that have led to litigation over the past decade. In particular, two jurisdictional boundaries are explored: the line between SEC and CFTC jurisdiction over formal trading markets, and, second, the authority of the CFTC to police off-exchange transactions in products, such as derivatives, that are functionally similar to futures.

Introductory background for this section comes from a brief that the U.S. Solicitor General's Office prepared for a recent case before the Supreme Court.  Central to the case was the difference between options and futures, and that distinction is highlighted in the excerpt.  The reading, however, also provides useful background on the evolution of the regulation of commodities trading in the United States.  As you read through these materials consider how the substance of commodities regulation compares to other regulatory structures we have considered.  What features are familiar?  What is new?  What explains the differences in structure?

## Brief of the Commodities Future Trading Commission
### Dunn v. CFTC, No. 95-1181 (U.S. Aug. 30, 1996)

### The History Of Commodity Futures And Options Regulation

The concept of a "commodity future" originated in the needs of farmers and their customers to fix the price of agricultural products before harvest and delivery.  Those parties found it useful to engage in the sale of a commodity before it was ready for market by agreeing to terms for future delivery at a specified price.  The growth of that practice led to the organization of commodity exchanges, which employ standard contracts and rules for trading.  The exchanges not only provide price discovery and hedging functions for commodity producers and processors, but they also provide speculative opportunities for investors.

1. Initial regulation of futures and options trading. In 1848, when the Chicago Board of Trade was founded as the first American commodity exchange, traders engaged primarily in the purchase and sale of "futures" contracts, which obligate the seller to deliver a commodity, and the buyer to pay for it, on a specified future date. See Jerry W. Markham, The History of Commodity Futures Trading and Its Regulation 4 (1987). By 1865, commodities traders were also engaged in the purchase and sale of "options" contracts (also known as "privileges," "indemnities," "puts," and "calls"), which granted the option holder the unilateral temporary right, but not the obligation, to purchase or sell a commodity at a specified price. Id. at 8-9. Although futures and options bear important similarities, they have always been recognized as distinctly different transactions, both as a matter of law and as a matter of practical consequence. See, e.g., 1 Timothy J. Snider, Regulation of the Commodities Futures and Options Markets §§ 7.01-7.02, 10.11-10.13 (2d ed. 1995); Robert C. Lower, The Regulation of Commodity Options, 1978 Duke L.J. 1095, 1096 nn. 2 & 3.

During the late 19th and early 20th centuries, farmers and other members of the general public came to question the integrity of the commodity markets. They complained that speculation in commodity futures and options resulted in devastating price swings, particularly when exchange participants attempted to "corner" the market in particular commodities. See Markham, supra, at 5-7, 10-11. They also criticized certain off-exchange practices, including the operation of "bucket shops," which enticed individuals to place bets on commodity price movements. Id. at 9-10, 11. Proponents of reform frequently identified options trading as a particular source of abuse. Many farmers and grain dealers considered options as simply gambling contracts that were unnecessary to the functioning of the marketplace. 1 Snider, supra, at § 7.03; Markham, supra, at 8-9; Lower, supra, 1978 Duke L.J. at 1097-1101.

The outbreak of World War I led to rampant commodity speculation and ultimately prompted Congress to enact the Futures Trading Act of 1921, ch. 86, 42 Stat. 187. See Markham, supra, at 10-12. Congress attempted to curb price manipulation and bucketing by imposing a prohibitive tax on grain futures unless they were traded on government licensed boards of trade, known as "contract market[s]," that met prescribed governmental standards. § 4, 42 Stat. 187. In addition, Congress proposed a prohibitive tax on all grain options. § 3, 42 Stat. 187. That provision reflected the sentiment, expressed in congressional hearings, that options were simply "gambling" transactions. See, e.g., Future Trading In Grain: Hearings on H.R. 5676 Before the Senate Comm. on Agriculture and Forestry, 67th Cong., 1st Sess. 60-63, 180 (1921); see also id. at 84 (noting that the "national trades" favored prohibiting privileges).

This Court ruled that the provisions of the Futures Act of 1921 that placed a tax on futures transactions conducted outside of a contract market were an unconstitutional exercise of the taxing power. See Hill v. Wallace, 259 U.S. 44 (1922). In response, Congress enacted the Grain Futures Act of 1922, ch. 369, 42 Stat. 998, which relied on the Commerce Clause to prohibit futures transactions outside of a licensed contract market. The Court rejected a challenge to the constitutionality of that legislation, Board of Trade of Chicago v. Olsen, 262 U.S. 1 (1923), and the federal government began to conduct regulatory oversight of the futures markets, Markham, supra, at 14- 21. Questions remained, however, over the constitutionality of the surviving provisions of the Futures Trading Act of 1921, not at issue in Hill, that placed a prohibitory tax on options. See 259 U.S. at 71. The Court eventually invalidated the options tax. Trusler v. Crooks, 269 U.S. 475 (1926). As a result, trading in options resumed. See Markham, supra, at 20; Lower, supra, 1978 Duke L.J. at 1100-1101.

2. The Commodity Exchange Act of 1936. Following the stock market crash of 1929, the market for wheat and other grains began to weaken. In 1932, speculative trading led to a calamitous collapse in wheat prices, and President Roosevelt called for expanded regulatory controls over the commodity markets. See 1 Snider, supra, at § 7.03; Markam, supra, at 22-25; Lower, supra, 1978 Duke L.J. at 1101. In response, Congress enacted the Commodity Exchange Act of 1936(CEA), ch. 545, 49 Stat. 1491. Congress adopted the CEA to "insure fair practice and honest dealing on the commodity exchanges, and to provide a measure of control over those forms of speculative activity which too often demoralize the markets to the injury of producers and consumers and the exchanges themselves." H.R. Rep. No. 421, 74th Cong., 1st Sess. 1 (1935).

Congress enacted the CEA as an amended version of the Grain Futures Act. See § 1, 49 Stat. 1491. Congress defined the term "commodity" to include specifically enumerated agricultural products, including grains, butter, eggs, potatoes, rice, and cotton, see §§ 2-3, 49 Stat. 1491, and it continued to allow trading of futures contracts in those commodities in the controlled environment of a federally-designated "contract market," see §§ 4-5, 49 Stat. 1492. Congress subjected those markets, however, to more exacting registration and regulatory requirements, which were administered by the Department of Agriculture's Commodity Exchange Authority. Congress also prohibited specific trading practices that were believed to contribute to excessive speculation, price instability, market manipulation, or fraud. See §§ 4-9, 49 Stat. 1492-1501; see generally Markham, supra, at 27-34.

Congress specifically outlawed trading in options. See § 5, 49 Stat. 1494 (adding Section 4c). Many persons, including Members of Congress, believed that options trading encouraged inappropriate speculation and played a significant role in the wheat market's collapse. See Lower, supra, 1978 Duke L.J. at 1101 & n. 23; see also, e.g., 78 Cong. Rec. 10,449 (1934) (Rep.Gilchrist) (denouncing options as "purely gambling transactions" that "prevent the producer from getting an honest price"). In the face of concerns that options "lent themselves to cheating or fraudulent practices," 80 Cong. Rec. 6162 (1936), Congress enacted an outright ban on the trading of options in the enumerated commodities. That ban effectively brought an end to commodity option trading in the United States for the next 35 years. See 1 Snider, supra, at § 7.03; Lower, supra, 1978 Duke L.J. at 1098, 1101-1102.

3. The Commodity Futures Trading Commission Act of 1974. During the decades following the enactment of the CEA, the commodity markets grew in both size and complexity as world-wide trade developed in new and previously unregulated commodities. See, e.g., Markham, supra, at 35-59. Congress responded to the evolution in the commodity markets in 1968 by extending the coverage of the CEA. See Act of Feb. 19, 1968, Pub. L. No. 90-258, 82 Stat. 26. But six years later, Congress concluded that more significant changes were needed, and it enacted the Commodity Futures Trading Commission Act of 1974 (CFTC Act), Pub. L. No. 93-463, 88 Stat. 1389. See S. Rep. No. 1131, supra, at 18-19. The CFTC Act comprehensively overhauled and expanded the CEA, which is codified as amended at 7 U.S.C. 1 et seq. The

CFTC Act also created the CFTC as a new federal agency devoted to commodity futures and options regulation. See generally Markham, supra, at 60-72. Two general considerations of the CFTC Act are particularly pertinent to this case.

First, Congress greatly expanded the scope of federal commodity regulation. Since the enactment of the CEA in 1936, world markets had developed for new commodities, such as coffee, sugar, and precious metals, which were not regulated under the CEA. In the face of that development, Congress redefined the term "commodity" to include not only previously enumerated commodities, but also virtually "all other goods and articles * * * and all services, rights, and interests in which contracts for future delivery are presently or in the future dealt in." 7 U.S.C. 1a(3). Congress also gave the CFTC correspondingly broad regulatory power over trading in those commodities. Subject to certain important exceptions (including the Treasury Amendment, discussed below), Congress gave the CFTC "exclusive jurisdiction" with respect to "accounts, agreements * * *, and transactions involving contracts of sale of a commodity for future delivery." 7 U.S.C. 2(i). See generally S. Rep. No. 1131, supra, at 23-24, 31; H.R. Conf. Rep. No. 1383, 93d Cong., 2d Sess. 35- 36 (1974).

Second, Congress retained the CEA's ban on trading of options involving the previously-regulated agricultural commodities, 7 U.S.C. 6c(a)(B) (1976), but it left open the possibility of an options market in the new commodities. Congress acted cautiously in light of the American experience during the early 1970s, when several new forms of unregulated options in those commodities (which were known as "London," "naked," and "dealer" options) first appeared. See Lower, supra, 1978 Duke L.J. at 1102-1109. Although some of those options provided legitimate investment opportunities, others resulted in largescale losses and highly publicized instances of fraud. Ibid. Congress consequently concluded that options involving newly regulated commodities should be allowed only in accordance with CFTC rules, regulations, and orders. 7 U.S.C. 6c(b) (1976). See generally S. Rep. No. 1131, supra, at 26, 41-42; H.R. Conf. Rep. No. 1383, supra, at 40. Congress gave the CFTC authority to permit or prohibit options trading in the newly regulated commodities. See 1 Snider, supra, at §§ 7.03-7.04; Markham, supra, at 66; Lower, supra, 1978 Duke L.J. at 1111.

4. The CFTC's regulation of options. Upon commencing operations in 1975, the CFTC began to examine whether option transactions in "new" commodities should be permitted. The CFTC initially promulgated interim rules that allowed the off-exchange offer and sale of such options under certain circumstances. See 41 Fed. Reg. 7774 (1976); id. at 44,560; id. at 51,808. Those rules did not allow trading of options on United States exchanges. Id. at 51,808. See 1 Snider, supra, at § 7.04.

By 1978, the Commission concluded that "the offer and sale of commodity options has for some time been and remains permeated with fraud and other illegal or unsound practices notwithstanding a substantial investment of the Commission's resources in attempting to regulate rather than prohibit option trading." 43 Fed. Reg. 16,153, 16,155 (1978). It therefore adopted regulations prohibiting the domestic sale of most commodity options after June 1, 1978. Id. at 16,161; 17 C.F.R. 32.11 (1982). The regulations did, however, permit sales to continue in certain "trade options," which are purchased for commercial purposes relating to the commodity and are not marketed to the general public. See 17 C.F.R. 32.4(a) and 32.11(b) (1982); 1 Snider, supra, at § 7.14 (describing trade options). The Commission also permitted existing companies that dealt in the actual commodity to continue marketing of so-called "dealer options" under detailed conditions. 43 Fed. Reg. 52,467 (1978). See 1 Snider, supra, at §§ 7.05-7.06, 7.14.

Congress, which was then considering other amendments to the CEA, endorsed the CFTC's assessment by adopting a statutory ban on the marketing of options in the newly regulated non-agricultural commodities. See Futures Trading Act of 1978, Pub. L. No. 95-405, § 3, 92 Stat. 867. Like the CFTC, Congress included an exception for dealer and trade options, and it authorized the CFTC to develop a program, subject to congressional approval, for exchange-traded options. Ibid., codified at 7 U.S.C. 6c(c)-(e) (Supp. II 1978); see S. Rep. No. 850, 95th Cong., 2d Sess. 14 (1978).

In 1981, the CFTC announced a three year "pilot program" for trading of options on futures contracts on exchanges designated as contract markets. 46 Fed. Reg. 54,570 (1981). Congress authorized the CFTC to extend the pilot program to agricultural commodities, see Futures Trading Act of 1982, Pub. L. No. 97-444, Tit. II § 206, 96 Stat. 2301, and the CFTC correspondingly expanded the program, see 47 Fed. Reg. 56,996 (1982). In 1984, the CFTC increased the number of options a particular contract market could offer. 49 Fed. Reg. 33,641 (1984). The CFTC ended the pilot program two years later by adopting final regulations allowing exchange-traded commodity options. 51 Fed. Reg. 27,529 (1986). See Futures Trading Act of 1986, Pub. L. No. 99-641, § 102, 100 Stat. 3557; see generally 1 Snider, supra, at ss 3.01-3.02.

Since that time, Congress has made other revisions to the CEA. See Futures Trading Practices Act of 1992, Pub. L. No. 102-546, 106 Stat. 3590; CFTC Reauthorization Act of 1995, Pub. L. No. 104-9, 109 Stat. 154. The 1992 Amendments are particularly significant because they grant the CFTC broad exemptive authority, similar to that contained in Section 6c respecting options, respecting other transactions that are subject to CEA regulation. See § 502(a)(2), 106 Stat. 3629; 7 U.S.C. 6(c) and (d). That exemption authority gives the CFTC additional flexibility to exempt appropriate agreements, contracts, and transactions from CEA requirements. See, e.g., 17 C.F.R. 35.2 (the so-called swaps exemption).

---

# Chicago Mercantile Exchange v. Securities Exchange Commission
883 F.2d 537 (7th Cir. 1989), *cert. denied*, 496 U.S. 936 (1990)

EASTERBROOK, Circuit Judge.

The Commodity Futures Trading Commission has authority to regulate trading of futures contracts (including futures on securities) and options on futures contracts. The Securities and Exchange Commission has authority to regulate trading of securities and options on securities. If an instrument is both a security and a futures contract, the CFTC is the sole regulator because "the Commission shall have exclusive jurisdiction with respect to ... transactions involving ... contracts of sale (and options on such contracts) for future delivery of a group or index of securities (or any interest therein or based upon the value thereof)", 7 U.S.C. § 2a(ii). See also 7 U.S.C. § 2 ("the Commission shall have exclusive jurisdiction, except to the extent otherwise provided in section 2a of this title"); Chicago Board of Trade v. SEC, 677 F.2d 1137 (7th Cir.), vacated as moot, 459 U.S. 1026 (1982) (GNMA Options ). If, however, the instrument is both a futures contract and an option on a security, then the SEC is the sole regulator because "the [CFTC] shall have no jurisdiction to designate a board of trade as a contract market for any transaction whereby any party to such transaction acquires any put, call, or other option on one or more securities ... including any group or index of such securities, or any interest therein or based on the value thereof." 7 U.S.C. § 2a(i).

The CFTC regulates futures and options on futures; the SEC regulates securities and options on securities; jurisdiction never overlaps. Problem: The statute does not define either "contracts ... for future delivery" or "option"--although it says that " 'future delivery' ... shall not include any sale of any cash commodity for deferred shipment or delivery". See Lester G. Telser, Futures and Actual Markets: How They Are Related, 59 J. Business S5 (1986). Each of these terms has a paradigm, but newfangled instruments may have aspects of each of the prototypes. Our case is about such an instrument, the index participation (IP). We must decide whether tetrahedrons belong in square or round holes.

## I

Index participations are contracts of indefinite duration based on the value of a basket (index) of securities. The seller of an IP (called the "short" because the writer need not own the securities) promises to pay the buyer the value of the index as measured on a "cash-out day". Any index, such as the Standard & Poor's 500, can be used. The buyer pays for the IP in cash on the date of sale and may borrow part of the price (use margin) on the same terms the Federal Reserve sets for stock--currently 50%. The exchange designates a conversion ratio between the index and the IP, so that (say) each IP unit entitles the holder on cash-out day to the value of the index times 100. Until cash-out the IP may trade on the exchange just like any other instrument. At the end of each quarter the short must pay the buyer (the "long") a sum approximating the value of dividends the stocks in the index have paid during the quarter. From the perspective of the long, then, an IP has properties similar to those of a closed-end mutual fund holding a value-weighted portfolio of the securities in the index: the IPs last indefinitely, pay dividends, and may be traded freely; on cash-out day the IP briefly becomes open-end, and the investor can withdraw cash without making a trade in the market.

Things differ from the short's perspective. Unlike the proprietor of a mutual fund, the short need not own the securities in the index; it will own them (equivalently, a long futures contract based on the same index) only to reduce risk. The short receives the long's cash but must post margin equal to 150% of the value of the IP, similar to the margin required for a short sale of stock. The short sees the IP as a speculative or hedging instrument scarcely distinguishable from a futures contract that terminates on the cash-out day, plus an option held by the long to roll over the contract to the next cash-out date. Cash-out days for an IP generally are the third Friday of March, June, September, and December, the expiration dates of the principal stock-index futures contracts, making the link even more apparent.

Longs and shorts do not deal directly with each other. After the parties agree on the price, the Options Clearing Corporation (OCC) issues the IP to the long, receiving the cash; at the same time the OCC pays the short and "acquires" the short's obligation to pay at cash-out time. OCC guarantees the short's obligations to the long, to secure which it holds the short's 150% margin.

As the quarter progresses the short must pony up cash to cover dividend-equivalent obligations. When a long exercises the cash-out privilege, the OCC chooses a short at random to make the payment. Any link between the original buyer and seller of an IP thus does not extend beyond the formation of the instrument; after that instant, each person's rights and obligations run to the OCC exclusively. This arrangement also permits either party to close its position by making an offsetting transaction. If the seller of an IP buys an identical contract in the market, the OCC cancels the two on its books.

The Philadelphia Stock Exchange asked the SEC in February 1988 for permission to trade IPs. The American Stock Exchange and the Chicago Board Options Exchange later filed proposals of their own. Each exchange's IP differs slightly from the others. Philadelphia's IP, called a "Cash Index Participation", allows the long to exercise the cash-out privilege on any business day, at a discount of 0.5% from the value of the index. (The long may cash out on a quarterly date without penalty.) The AMEX's IP, called the "Equity Index Participation", permits the long to cash out quarterly for money or shares of stock in a ratio matching the index. Holders of 500 or more EIP trading units based on the S & P 500 index (each the equivalent of 100 multiples of that index) may exercise the right to receive securities, and they must pay a "delivery charge" to be established by the AMEX. Writers of EIPs may volunteer to deliver stock; if not enough do, a "physical delivery facilitator" at the AMEX will buy stock in the market, using money provided by the shorts whose positions have been liquidated. The CBOE's product, the "Value of Index Participation", has a semi-annual rather than quarterly cash- out date. CBOE's wrinkle is that the short as well as the long may cash out, by tendering the value of the index on the cash-out date. If shorts seeking to close their positions exceed the number of longs who want cash, the OCC will choose additional long positions at random to pay off.

The three stock exchanges and the OCC asked the SEC to allow them to trade these varieties of IP. Each contended that the SEC has exclusive jurisdiction because IPs are securities and not futures contracts. The AMEX added that in its view an IP is an option on securities, activating the savings clause of § 2a(i). The Chicago Board of Trade and the Chicago Mercantile Exchange, supported by the CFTC, asked the SEC to deny the requests. Each futures market, and the CFTC, argued that IPs are futures and not securities, so that the CFTC's jurisdiction is exclusive under 7 U.S.C. §§ 2 and 2a(ii). Complicating the picture, the Investment Company Institute argued that if IPs are securities and not futures, the OCC is an "investment company", offering a product combining features of closed-end and open-end mutual funds, and must register under the Investment Company Act of 1940, 15 U.S.C. §§ 80a-1 to 80a-64.

On April 11, 1989, the SEC granted the exchanges' requests. Release No. 34- 26709, 54 Fed.Reg. 15280 (1989). At the same time, its Division of Market Regulation, acting with delegated authority, allowed the OCC to change its rules so that it could issue, settle, and clear IPs. Release No. 34-26713, 54 Fed.Reg. 15575 (1989). The SEC concluded that IPs are "stock" within the meaning of § 3(a)(10) of the Securities Exchange Act of 1934, 15 U.S.C. § 78c(a)(10). IPs are negotiable, pay dividends, may appreciate in value, and may be hypothecated; the only attribute of stock missing from IPs is voting rights, which the SEC thought unimportant. 54 Fed.Reg. at 15285-86. If not stock, the SEC concluded, IPs are "certificates of interest or participation in" stock, another of the instruments defined as "securities" in § 3(a)(10). See 54 Fed.Reg. at 15286. Next the SEC found that IPs are not "futures", id. at 15286-89, because they lack two features the SEC thought essential: "futurity" and "bilateral obligation". "Futurity" means that value is set in the future, while as the SEC observed the buyer of an IP pays a price fixed at the time of sale; "bilateral obligation" means that the contract is executory on both sides until expiration or settlement, while the long on an IP performs at the time of purchase, leaving only the short with executory obligations. The SEC went on to say, id. at 15289-90, that the OCC need not register under the Investment Company Act because there is no "issuer" within the meaning of § 3(a)(1) of that statute, 15 U.S.C. § 80a-3(a)(1). Concluding that IPs may serve as substitutes for "program trading", provide "an additional layer of liquidity to the market", and afford "an alternative vehicle for retail customers to invest in 'the market' ", 54 Fed.Reg. at 15290, the SEC allowed the exchanges to proceed with their plans. We denied the futures markets' request for a stay but accelerated the hearing of the case on the merits. IPs have been trading on the three exchanges since May. . . . .

### III

### A

A futures contract, roughly speaking, is a fungible promise to buy or sell a particular commodity at a fixed date in the future. Futures contracts are fungible because they have standard terms and each side's obligations are guaranteed by a clearing house. Contracts are entered into without prepayment, although the markets and clearing house will set margin to protect their own interests. Trading occurs in "the contract", not in the commodity. Most futures contracts may be performed by delivery of the commodity (wheat, silver, oil, etc.). Some (those based on financial instruments such as T-bills or on the value of an index of stocks) do not allow delivery. Unless the parties cancel their obligations by buying or selling offsetting positions, the long must pay the price stated in the contract (e.g., $1.00 per gallon for 1,000 gallons of orange juice) and the short must deliver; usually, however, they settle in cash, with the payment based on changes in the market. If the market price, say, rose to $1.50 per gallon, the short would pay $500 (50 cents per gallon); if the price fell, the long would pay. The extent to which the settlement price of a commodity futures contract tracks changes in the price of the cash commodity depends on the size and balance of the open positions in "the contract" near the settlement date. When the contract involves financial instruments, though, the price is fixed by mechanical computation from the instruments on which the contracts are based. . . . .

A security, roughly speaking, is an undivided interest in a common venture the value of which is subject to uncertainty. Usually this means a claim to the assets and profits of an "issuer". Shares of stock entitle their holders to receive dividends and payments on liquidation (or a change in corporate form), see Landreth Timber Co. v. Landreth, 471 U.S. 681 (1985); bonds and other debt instruments promise interest plus a balloon payment of principal at the end. Unusual interests such as rights in orange groves still may be "securities" if they represent a pro rata share of a variable pool of earnings. SEC v. W.J. Howey Co., 328 U.S. 293 (1946).

Securities usually arise out of capital formation and aggregation (entrusting funds to an entrepreneur), while futures are means of hedging, speculation, and price revelation without transfer of capital. So one could think of the distinction between the jurisdiction of the SEC and that of the CFTC as the difference between regulating capital formation and regulating hedging. Congress conceived the role of the CFTC in that way when it created the agency in 1974 to assume functions that had been performed by the Department of Agriculture but which were no longer thought appropriate for that Department as futures markets expanded beyond commodities into financial instruments. See GNMA Options for a recap of the history. Unfortunately, the distinction between capital formation and hedging falls apart when it comes time to allocate the regulation of options.

A call option is a promise by the writer to deliver the underlying instrument at a price fixed in advance (the "strike price") if the option is exercised within a set time. The buyer pays a price (the "premium") in advance for the opportunity; the writer may or may not own the instrument he promises to deliver. Call options are written "out of the money"--that is, the exercise price exceeds the market price at the outset. The writer will make money if by the time the option expires the market price is less than the strike price plus the premium (plus the interest earned on the premium in the interim); the buyer of the option hopes that the market price will rise above the strike price by enough to cover the premium, the time value of money, and the transactions costs of executing the option. Options play valuable roles in price-discovery, and they also allow the parties to adjust the net riskiness of their portfolios. Writers of call options reduce the risk they bear if the market falls while limiting gains if the market rises; buyers hope for large proportional gains if the market rises while accepting the likelihood that the options will turn out to be worthless. Options are side deals among investors, which do not augment an entrepreneur's coffers (except to the extent greater liquidity and opportunities to adjust risk increase social marginal propensity to invest). Dwight M. Jaffee, The Impact of Financial Futures and Options on Capital Formation, 4 J. Futures Markets 417 (1984). Unlike financial and index futures, options call for delivery of the underlying instrument--be it a share of stock or a futures contract.

The SEC consistently has taken the position that options on securities should be regulated as securities. For some years the CFTC maintained that options on securities should be regulated as futures because options are extrinsic to capital formation and because it is almost always possible to devise an option with the same economic attributes as a futures contract (and the reverse). Matters came to a head in 1980, when both agencies asserted jurisdiction over options on securities based on pools of notes. The Government National Mortgage Association (GNMA) sold pass-through certificates representing proceeds of mortgage notes, and persons started writing options on them to allow hedging against movements in interest rates. The SEC observed that options written on securities are securities under § 3(a)(10) of the '34 Act; indeed the SEC contended that because options are securities it should regulate all options. The CFTC countered that options on financial instruments are futures under § 4c(b) of the CEA, 7 U.S.C. § 6c(b), and added that because its jurisdiction is exclusive, it is the sole lawful regulator. When the SEC allowed stock exchanges to start trading GNMA options, the futures markets sought review in this court and the CFTC howled bloody murder.

While the case was pending, the agencies reached a pact, which the SEC calls the Shad-Johnson Agreement and the CFTC calls the Johnson-Shad Agreement. (John Shad was the SEC's Chairman at the time, and Phillip Johnson the CFTC's.) This Accord (as we shall call it to avoid offending either agency) provided that jurisdiction over options follows jurisdiction over the things on which the options are written. So the SEC received jurisdiction of options on securities, while the CFTC got jurisdiction of options on futures contracts. Things were not quite done, though, because we held in GNMA Options that the agencies could not alter their jurisdiction by mutual agreement. 677 F.2d at 1142 n. 8. Starting from the proposition that options on GNMAs are both securities and futures, we held that the CFTC's jurisdiction is exclusive in light of 7 U.S.C. §§ 2 and 2a.

Congress then enacted the Accord almost verbatim, producing the explicit reference to options in § 3(a)(10) of the '34 Act, the SEC savings clause in § 2a(i) of the CEA, and a small change in 7 U.S.C. § 6n to implement an understanding about pools. The legislature thought that this Accord would resolve things and restore a regime in which the SEC supervises capital formation and the CFTC hedging. See S.Rep. No. 97-384, 97th Cong., 2d Sess. 21-24 (1982); H.R.Rep. No. 97-565, 97th Cong., 2d Sess., Part I at 38-40 (1982), U.S.Code Cong. & Admin.News 1982, p. 3871; H.R.Rep. No. 97-626, 97th Cong., 2d Sess., Part II at 3 (1982), U.S.Code Cong. & Admin.News 1982, p. 2780; 128 Cong.Rec. 24910 (1982) (Rep. De La Garza). . . .

The legislation implementing the Accord left in place the premise on which GNMA Options was founded: if an instrument is *both* a security and a futures contract, then the CFTC's jurisdiction is exclusive. Section 2a(ii) has no other possible meaning. Like many an agreement resolving a spat, the Accord addressed a symptom rather than the problem. Options are only one among many instruments that can have attributes of futures contracts as well as securities. Financial markets work best when they offer every possible combination of risk and return--a condition financial economists call "spanning"--so that investors can construct a portfolio to each need and taste. Exchanges and professional investors therefore continually devise financial products to fill unoccupied niches. See Dennis W. Carlton, Futures Markets: Their Purpose, Their History, Their Growth, Their Successes and Failures, 4 J. Futures Markets 237 (1984); William L. Silber, Innovation, Competition and New Contract Design in Futures Markets, 1 J. Futures Markets 123 (1981). These products are valuable to the extent that they do *not* match the attributes of instruments already available. New products, offering a new risk-return mixture, are designed to depart from today's models.

Which means that the dispute of 1980-82 about options will be played out--is being played out--about each new instrument. Today's case repeats the conflict. Other novel instruments are being handled by regulation. For example, on July 17, 1989, the CFTC adopted rules exempting from its regulation certain hybrid instruments combining equity or debt with payments based on the price of commodities. 17 C.F.R. Part 34, 54 Fed.Reg. 30684 (1989). Only merger of the agencies or functional separation in the statute can avoid continual conflict. Functional separation is hard to achieve (new instruments will appear at any border). The SEC favors merger; it has asked Congress repeatedly for jurisdiction over all products (including stock-index and financial futures) based on securities, which would relegate the CFTC to its original role as superintendent of commodities futures. The CFTC has so far defended its position, in part with the argument that multiple regulatory bodies allow greater competition and experimentation--a new product can reach market if either agency approves the variant within its domain. See Daniel R. Fischel, Regulatory Conflict and Entry Regulation of New Futures Contracts, 59 J. Business S85 (1986); Ronald W. Anderson, The Regulation of Futures Contracts Innovations in the United States, 4 J. Futures Markets 297 (1984).

Unless Congress changes the allocation of jurisdiction between the agencies, the question a court must resolve is the same as in GNMA Options: is the instrument a futures contract? If yes, then the CFTC's jurisdiction is exclusive, unless it is also an option on a security, in which case the SEC's jurisdiction is exclusive. So long as an instrument is a futures contract (and not an option), whether it is also a "security" is neither here nor there. Still, if IPs really are "stock" they almost certainly are not "futures contracts", so the inquiries aren't so distinct as the statutes imply.

B

From the perspective of the long, IPs look like an interest in a portfolio of stock. IPs last indefinitely (except for the chance that a long may be cashed out involuntarily on the CBOE), may be sold like stock or used to secure margin and other loans, change in value with the market, and pay dividends. IPs lack other common attributes of stock: they do not confer voting rights and are not "certificated"; owners of IPs receive dividend- equivalent payments quarterly, not when the firms pay dividends. We need not debate whether these differences come to anything, for they pale beside the larger difficulties in calling IPs "stock". The greatest is that IPs are not stock *in* anything. There isn't an issuer--which the SEC emphasized when concluding that the Investment Company Act is inapplicable, 54 Fed.Reg. at 15289-90. Stock is an equity interest in an issuer, the residual claim to the profits of a venture. United Housing Foundation, Inc. v. Forman, 421 U.S. 837 (1975). Landreth rejected the "sale-of-business doctrine" because the owner of 100% of the equity interest in a firm still owns "stock".[19] Purchasers of IPs don't own equity, directly or indirectly; they don't have a claim to the proceeds and liquidating distribution of a business; there isn't an underlying pool of assets; there is only a "short" on the other side. The absence of an issuer--IPs don't carry votes because they don't have anything to do with equity--tells all. There is no common venture, not even the commonality represented by a mutual fund (which reinvests in real stock and creates the risk that the stakeholder will join Robert Vesco with the kitty).

IPs do not fit comfortably into any of the other pigeonholes of § 3(a)(10). A "certificate of interest or participation in ... any of the foregoing" securities is a security too, but IPs do not represent an "interest or participation" in the stocks in the index; they are based on the value *of* stock without creating a legal interest *in* stock. Perhaps the closest match is the language, part of the Accord in 1982, covering a "privilege on any security ... or group or index of securities (including any interest therein *or based on the value thereof*)". Then there's the catch-all: "in general, any instrument commonly known as a 'security' ". IPs convey privileges based on the value of an index, and what is "commonly known as a security" changes as new instruments come into use. So there is a basis for drawing IPs within § 3(a)(10), even though they do not duplicate a recognized category. See also, e.g., SEC v. United Benefit Life Insurance Co., 387 U.S. 202 (1967).

---

[19]    Attributes such as transferrability, appreciation, and votes are useful to distinguish "real stock" from pieces of paper labeled "stock" that do not convey the ordinary interests of equity. Landreth, 471 U.S. at 686. Such documents had been issued in Forman as part of a residential co-op development. Transferrability and the like are not talismans, however, but only ways to identify equity claims. Much real "stock" does not trade or appreciate in value, because it is covered by buy-sell agreements. (Closely held firms often provide that stock may be sold only to the firm, and then at a formula price.) It is nonetheless stock, as Landreth holds, because it is a real equity claim to a business.

Although the SEC found IPs to be securities by looking at the promises made *to* the longs, the CFTC found them to be futures by virtue of the promises made *by* the shorts, a perspective implied by the CEA's references to "contracts ... for future delivery"--emphasizing the shorts' obligation. Shorts on IPs make the same pledge as shorts on stock-index futures contracts: to pay the value of an index on a prescribed day (the expiration date for the futures contract, the cash-out date for the IP). The short owes this obligation to the clearing house rather than to the long. IPs may be settled by buying or selling an offsetting obligation, after which the clearing house cancels the two on the books, just as with futures contracts. Shorts on IPs must put up more margin than shorts on futures contracts and must make dividend-equivalent payments, but the CFTC did not find these differences any more dispositive than the SEC found the IPs' lack of voting rights. Shorts also face an obligation of indefinite duration on the Philadelphia and AMEX IPs, but the CFTC and the futures markets treat this as no more than a prepaid rollover privilege.

Despite the congruence of futures and IPs on the short side, the SEC and the stock exchanges say that both "futurity" and "bilateralism" are missing. According to the SEC, IPs lack "futurity" because an IP is the "present obligation to pay current value". And IPs are not bilateral because the long performs in full by paying up front, although in a futures contract both sides must perform on settlement or expiration.

With respect to bilateralism, the SEC's point is inescapable. With respect to futurity, the SEC is wrong. IPs are no more a "present obligation to pay current value" than are futures contracts. The holder of either an IP or a stock-index futures contract may go to market and trade it; the price necessarily tracks current value. Neither the long on an IP nor the long on a futures contract can compel the short to *pay* current value, however.[20] Both the futures contract and the IP are settled quarterly (the same dates for both kinds of instrument, except for the CBOE's omission of two of the four dates). The short's obligation is to pay the value of the index *on that date* --which lies in the future to the same extent as the settlement date of any futures contract. Even from the long's point of view, IP and futures contract ultimately look the same. The long pays up front for the IP, but the long on a futures contract *promises* up front to make a defined payment on the settlement date; the difference in the timing of the payment does not affect the fact that valuation comes at the defined future date.

So the IP has futurity but not bilateralism. It looks like a futures contract to the short-- except that it is of indefinite duration, carries a dividend-equivalent obligation, and requires higher margin. It looks like a mutual fund to the long — except that it has no voting rights, does not represent any interest in an underlying pool of stock, and may be settled by executing an offsetting transaction. Fact is, it is no less a future than it is a security, and no more. It just doesn't fit. Which is the whole point. It isn't supposed to be just like something else; the IP was designed as a novel instrument so that it could offer attributes previously missing in the market.

---

[20]    The daily cash-out-at-a-penalty feature of the Philadelphia's IP may oblige the short to pay "current" value less 0.5%, but none of the parties to the case suggests that the Philadelphia's product should be treated differently on this account. We therefore do not pursue it. Similarly, we bypass the delivery option in the AMEX IP and the short's opportunity to get out of the CBOE IP, both of which make IPs look more like futures.

The only thing of which we are sure is that an IP is not an option on a security. The AMEX contends that it is a prepaid option, with a premium equal to the full value and an exercise price of zero. The SEC did not accept this contention, writing:

> [W]hile IPs contain some characteristics of stock index options (e.g., the issuance and clearance and settlement features of IPs are analogous to those of stock index options), the Commission believes that IPs predominantly have the attributes of a portfolio of common stock.

54 Fed.Reg. at 15286 n. 57. The only "characteristics of stock index options" that either the AMEX or the SEC identified are those introduced by the presence of a clearing house-- characteristics that the IP shares with stock-index futures to the last detail. Unless we were to say that all futures are also options (they aren't), these features do not make IPs options. The very features that the SEC emphasizes to show that IPs are securities--indefinite duration, payment up front in cash, dividend equivalency, and so on--show that IPs cannot be options. Options are written out of the money, limited in time, and establish a careful balance among premium, strike price, and duration; the writer retains dividends. IPs possess none of these distinguishing features. As the AMEX defines an "option", someone who buys an automobile for cash and drives it away really has obtained an option with a high premium, zero strike price, perpetual duration, and 100% probability of exercise. Words are useful only to the extent they distinguish some things from others; symbols that comprise everything mean nothing. IPs are not options.

C

Having concluded that neither the '34 Act nor the CEA addresses the status of IPs in a straightforward way, the logical thing to do is to defer to the agency's resolution of the problem. Chevron U.S.A. Inc. v. Natural Resources Defense Council, Inc., 467 U.S. 837 (1984). But which agency? Each claims to be exercising its discretion; each claims entitlement to deference on a subject within its domain.

Although cases frequently say that courts should defer to the judgment of the responsible agency whenever the statute is ambiguous as applied to a subject, e.g., NLRB v. Hearst Publications, Inc., 322 U.S. 111 (1944), this is something of an oversimplification. Ambiguity does not necessarily dictate whether the court or the agency has the dispositive word. Many's the statute that drops a half-resolved dispute in the lap of the courts even though one or more agencies exercise jurisdiction. Think of the anti-trust laws, which courts freely construe even though both the Antitrust Division of the Department of Justice and the Federal Trade Commission may lay claim to greater expertise. When a statute has gaps and uncertainties--the status of all rules--the anterior question is: who is charged with filling the gaps? Often statutes delegate comprehensive powers to agencies, and the meaning of the law is that agencies shall solve novel problems as they arise. Solutions may involve complex and unanticipated adjustments. Courts can be more confident that power has been delegated than that any particular exercise is "right". Deference to the agency's conclusion follows naturally from such a determination, for what Congress wanted to obtain is the judgment of the agency--Congress delegates precisely because it cannot foresee and resolve all problems. See Chevron, 467 U.S. at 843-45; Young v. Community Nutrition Institute, 476 U.S. 974, 981-84 (1986); Homemakers North Shore, Inc. v. Bowen, 832 F.2d 408, 411-12 (7th Cir.1987); Henry P. Monaghan, Marbury and the Administrative State, 83 Colum.L.Rev. 1 (1983). When the agency is the addressee of the statutory command, it takes the leading part in giving structure to the statute; when the court is the addressee, it has the principal role.

When two agencies claim to be the addressees, though, this allocation breaks down. Perhaps a court could say that because the agencies disagree, neither is entitled to deference. Yet disagreement doesn't make the court the recipient of interpretive powers. One or the other agency is still in charge. Courts readily could accept both the SEC's application of the '34 Act to IPs and the CFTC's application of the CEA. Our difficulty is not any logical conundrum in deferring to both agencies when they disagree. It is instead that a dispute about the agencies' jurisdiction is a zero-sum game because of the exclusivity clauses in the CEA.

Any distinction between action under delegated powers and fixing the scope of delegation will break down at the edges, and some recent cases suggest that a court should not try to draw such a line in the first place--one of them concerning the scope of the CFTC's powers. CFTC v. Schor, 478 U.S. 833, 844-46 (1986); see also Mississippi Power & Light Co. v. Mississippi ex rel. Moore, 487 U.S. 354 (1988) (Scalia, J., concurring); CSX Transportation v. United States, 867 F.2d 1439, 1445 (D.C.Cir.1989) (Edwards, J., dissenting) (suggesting that Chevron disallows inquiry into the extent of delegation, although that should be the right question). But even if unambiguous delegation is not a necessary condition of deference, it is an important ingredient in the formula, else it becomes impossible to distinguish statutes such as the Sherman Act from those such as the Clean Air Act, or to conceive where the boundary between court and commission falls. Delegation to agencies is not without its costs to the separation of powers; holding agencies within their delegated scope is an important task in maintaining constitutional structure.

Difficulties in establishing the competence of the agencies and the judicial branch do not influence the outcome of this case, however. We may assume without deciding that even in this jurisdictional dispute, each agency is entitled to leeway in applying its own statute to Ips.

D

If each agency's interpretation of its own statute is entitled to some deference, then the IP is both a security and a futures contract. It has some attributes of both, and all attributes of neither, as we have laid out in excessive detail. Neither characterization can be called wrong.

The only element of financial futures contracts that is missing is "bilateralism". Yet bilateralism is not essential to a futures contract. CFTC v. Co Petro Marketing Group, Inc., 680 F.2d 573 (9th Cir.1982), held that a contract that imposes performance obligations only on the short may be a futures contract. Co Petro sold interests in gasoline that were designed to look like forward contracts, which under the CEA are not futures contracts. Buyers put down deposits to obtain Co Petro's promise to deliver gasoline on future dates. These contracts could not be traded on any market, but Co Petro promised to pay the investor in cash if the market price should rise (that is, the investor could sell the contract back to Co Petro). The investor risked no more than 95% of his deposit; if the price of gasoline fell, the investor's position would be closed. Thus buyers of Co Petro's contracts performed fully on the date they posted the deposit; thereafter only Co Petro had obligations. Despite that, and despite the fact that the contracts were illiquid, the court of appeals concluded that they were futures contracts because their value depended entirely on the price of the commodity at their expiration date, and they were not formed in contemplation of physical delivery.

The SEC brushes off Co Petro and similar cases in district courts as based on the principle that once it smells sulfur (Co Petro may have been a bucket shop), either agency may protect the investor. No such principle may be found in the '34 Act or the CEA, however. An instrument either is or is not a futures contract. If it is, the CFTC has jurisdiction; if it is not, the CFTC lacks jurisdiction; if the CFTC has jurisdiction, its power is exclusive. The SEC's position entails the proposition that if Co Petro Marketing Group, Inc., had approached the CFTC after losing in the Ninth Circuit and applied for permission to trade its gasoline contracts as futures, the CFTC would have had to say no, *on the ground that the contracts are not "contracts ... for future delivery "* under the CEA. That can't be right.

Perhaps this point will be clearer if we ask what would have happened if the CBOT and CME had approached the CFTC in 1987 (before the Philadelphia Stock Exchange filed its proposal with the SEC) seeking permission to trade IPs. When we asked the SEC's Solicitor during oral argument whether the CFTC could have granted such an application, he said yes-- largely on the ground that granting the application would have introduced a new product with benefits for investors. When we persisted with the question whether the CFTC could grant the identical application, filed by the CBOT and CME in 1989 (after the SEC's decision), the Solicitor said no, on the ground that by 1989 the SEC had asserted jurisdiction. Yet this principle of first-come-first-served finds no support in the '34 Act or the CEA. Either IPs are futures contracts or they aren't. If they are futures contracts, then the CFTC could have approved their trading in 1987 (as the Solicitor agreed); if IPs were futures in 1987, they are futures today, and the CFTC still may approve their trading. But if the CFTC may approve their trading because they are futures contracts, then the CFTC's jurisdiction is exclusive.

Doubtless such a decision gives the futures markets the opportunity to block competition from an innovative financial product. The SEC's order, and its brief in this court, casts much of the argument in the form: "The IP is a desirable product; the futures markets have not proposed to trade IPs; if IPs are futures then the CFTC's jurisdiction is exclusive and IPs won't exist, which would be regrettable; therefore IPs are not futures." Everything works until the "therefore". Whether IPs are futures can't depend on who first proposed to trade them, or on whether anyone does. We doubt the premise of the SEC's argument as well as its conclusion, for *if* IPs are useful to investors, then someone will offer them--if not the CBOT and CME, then a market in New York, or Kansas City, or Tokyo. The CBOT and CME will be compelled to follow or they will lose business. There are too many futures exchanges to suppose that a conspiracy could suppress a beneficial financial instrument, cf. Matsushita Electric Industrial Co. v. Zenith Radio Corp., 475 U.S. 574, 590 (1986). But whether or not a futures market will seek to trade a financial product does not change the nature of that product, and both the '34 Act and the CEA define coverage by the attributes of the *instrument* rather than by the identity of those who own or trade it. This is the central message of Landreth, which at the SEC's urging rejected the "sale of business doctrine" precisely because that doctrine disregarded the characteristics of the financial instrument in order to go straight to the question whether certain persons needed the protection of the law--that is to say, whether coverage was a good idea.

From time to time, the Supreme Court has looked to the purposes of the '34 Act to define "securities", usually with a view to enlarging the definition. (The exception is Marine Bank v. Weaver, 455 U.S. 551 (1982).) With the SEC urging it on, the Court has drawn in orange groves covered by joint harvesting contracts, W.J. Howey, leaseholds in land near oil wells, SEC v. C.M. Joiner Leasing Corp., 320 U.S. 344 (1943), and other unusual instruments that have some (but far from all) attributes of conventional securities. Obviously the SEC does not ask us to abandon this approach--for itself. It demands, however, that we apply strictissimi juris to the CEA, to hold that only an instrument with *every* attribute of a conventional futures contract may be one. Why? If the interpretive approach is proper for the securities acts, it is no less proper for the futures acts. It has been employed under both statutes--not only in Co Petro but also in redefining futures contracts to omit the delivery obligation. Recall the statutory scope of the CEA: contracts "for future delivery". Commodity futures contracts may be settled by delivery; financial futures contracts are settled exclusively in cash. One might have thought the prospect of "future delivery" the sine qua non of a "futures" contract. Yet no one, not even the SEC, doubts that a contract may be a futures contract even though it provides for cash settlement. If delivery is not essential, then the "traditional" elements of futures contracts are not invariable ingredients of the CFTC's jurisdiction.

Perhaps the SEC wants us to put a thumb on the scales, enlarging the category "securities" while shrinking the category "futures" because of the exclusivity clauses in the CEA: if both categories expand, then the SEC's jurisdiction shrinks. We do not conceive it our function, however, to invent counterweights to statutes; judges should be interpreters rather than sappers and miners. As we said in GNMA Options, 677 F.2d at 1161, "[o]ur task should not reflect a value judgment as to which of the competing agencies is best equipped to regulate these [products]."

To the extent instrumental arguments influence the coverage of the laws, they do not necessarily cut for the SEC. The futures markets' reply brief invites us to imagine a "Wheat Index Participation" (WIP) having the same characteristics as the IP except that it is based on an index of wheat prices rather than of stock prices. The buyer would pay cash for the WIP and be able to trade it freely; on a date identical to the expiry of the wheat futures contracts, the writer could be required to pay cash measured by the value of the wheat index. According to the SEC, such an instrument would not be a futures contract because it would lack both futurity and bilateralism (and we would agree on the latter point). So the CFTC could not allow it to be traded, no matter how valuable participants in the market might find it. On the other hand, the WIP certainly would not be "stock" and probably would not meet the criteria for being a "security" of any kind. So the SEC could not allow it to be traded on stock exchanges (anyway, the WIP would be a duck out of water on the AMEX!). We could escape from such silliness by reaching the logical conclusion that a WIP would be a futures contract. Yet if the WIP is a futures contract, it is hard to avoid the conclusion that the IP is one, too.

## Comments and Questions

1. The *Chicago Merchant Exchange* case entailed a jurisdictional dispute between the SEC and the CFTC over which agency or agencies should be empowered to authorize trading in a new financial product. How did the court go about deciding which agency's view should prevail?

2. How would you have characterized the financial product at issue in this case?

### Problem 14-2

After extensive marketing research, Sandlot Insurance Company ("SIC") has determined that many of its customers are interested in investing in the stock market, but would also like some assurance that they will achieve some minimum level of return. To satisfy this demand, SIC proposes to create a new variable annuity product with a guaranteed real rate of return of one percent. Funds invested in this product will be placed in a separate account composed exclusively of a portfolio of stock designed to match the performance of the S&P-500 stock index. In years in which S&P-500 stocks yield less than one percent real rate of return, SIC would contribute to the account the amount of the shortfall. In years in which the S&P-500 yield more than one percent, annuity contract holders will accrue the benefit, up to a maximum real annual rate of return of nine percent. Yields above nine percent will be distributed to SIC on an annual basis.

Investors will be charged an annual fee for participating in this new account. SIC's Vice President of Finance has concluded that the accounts should be profitable for the company, and that it can cover any risks associated with the accounts by establishing offsetting long and short positions through market-traded indices based on the SP500.

What legal issues, if any, does this product present?

---

## Brief of the Commodities Futures Trading Commission
### Dunn v. CFTC, No. 95-1181 (U.S. Aug. 30, 1996)

#### Regulation Of Foreign Currency Futures And Options

At the time that Congress was considering the CFTC Act of 1974, an off-exchange market had developed for trade in foreign currency futures. See S. Rep. No. 1131, supra, at 94 (Appendix III); City of New York Bar Ass'n Comm. on Futures Regulation, The Evolving Regulatory Framework For Foreign Currency Trading (1986). That market grew out of privately negotiated transactions between commercial banks, multi-national corporations, and sophisticated investors who entered into those transactions for both commercial hedging and speculative purposes. Id. at 3. Congress responded to the existence of that market by including within the CFTC Act a provision currently known as the Treasury Amendment to the CEA.

1. The Treasury Amendment. The Treasury Amendment originated in concerns expressed in a July 30, 1974, letter from the Department of the Treasury's Acting General Counsel to the Chairman of the Senate Committee on Agriculture and Forestry. See S. Rep. No. 1131, supra, at 49-51 (reproduced at App. B, infra, 10a-14a). The Acting General Counsel warned that, as a result of the proposal to expand the CEA definition of the term "commodity" through the CFTC Act, financial instruments such as foreign currency futures and government securities futures, which were then traded among banks and other sophisticated institutions, could become subject to new and unnecessary regulation. Ibid.

The Treasury Department suggested that the pending legislation include additional language that would expressly exclude from regulation transactions in foreign currency and other specified financial instruments. See S. Rep. No. 1131, supra, at 50-51. Congress responded by incorporating the Department's proposed statutory language, except as to "puts and calls on securities." The Treasury Amendment provides in pertinent part:

> Nothing in this chapter shall be deemed to govern or in any way be applicable to transactions in foreign currency, * * * unless such transactions involve the sale thereof for future delivery conducted on a board of trade.

7 U.S.C. 2(ii). At the time that the Treasury Department proposed the Treasury Amendment, it made specific reference to the foreign currency futures market. See S. Rep. No. 1131, supra, at 49-51. But the Treasury Department made no mention of any market in foreign currency options. That market did not develop until some time later in the 1970s, when banks began trading foreign currency options on a commercial scale. See Comm. on Futures Regulation, supra, at 18, 23.

2. The SEC/CFTC Accord. Following the enactment of the CFTC Act, both national securities exchanges and futures exchanges sought to market and trade in new financial products, which led to questions concerning the CFTC's jurisdiction. Of particular relevance here, the Chicago Board of Trade and the Securities and Exchange Commission (SEC) became involved in a dispute over whether the SEC or the CFTC had jurisdiction to regulate options in mortgage-backed debt securities guaranteed by the Government National Mortgage Association (GNMA). See Board of Trade of Chicago v. SEC, 677 F.2d 1137 (7th Cir.), vacated as moot, 459 U.S. 1026 (1982).

The Board of Trade litigation was ultimately rendered moot by an inter-agency agreement between the SEC and the CFTC, sometimes referred to as the "Shad/Johnson" or "SEC/CFTC" Accord, which defined with greater precision the division of regulatory authority between the SEC and the CFTC respecting options on financial instruments. See Joint Explanatory Statement of the Commodity Futures Trading Commission, and the Securities and Exchange Commission, reprinted in [1980-1982 Transfer Binder] Comm. Fur. L. Rep. (CCH) p 21,332 (Feb. 2, 1982). Of particular significance here, the legislation implementing the Accord provides that the SEC shall exercise jurisdiction over the trading of foreign currency options on United States securities exchanges, but leaves unaffected the CFTC's authority over foreign currency options traded in other markets. See Act of Oct. 13, 1982, Pub. L. No. 97-303, 96 Stat. 1409, codified at 15 U.S.C. 77(b)(1), 78c(a)(10), 78i(g), 80a-2(a)(36), and 80b- 2(a)(18) (1982); Futures Trading Act of 1982, Pub. L. No. 97-444, Tit. I, § 102, 96 Stat. 2296, codified at 7 U.S.C. 6c(f) (1982). The Senate Report accompanying the latter Act states: The trading of options on foreign currencies will be regulated by both agencies; the SEC will regulate these options when they are traded on a national securities exchange, the CFTC will regulate them when they are traded other than on a national securities exchange. S. Rep. No. 384, 97th Cong., 2d Sess. 22 (1982). See also H.R. Rep. No. 565, 97th Cong., 2d Sess., Pt. 1, at 39 (1982) (CFTC has jurisdiction over all "[o]ptions directly on foreign curencies"); see generally 1 Snider, supra, at § 10.24.

3. The ABT and Salomon Forex Litigation.  In the late 1970s, the CFTC began to encounter situations in which unscrupulous promoters fraudulently marketed foreign currency futures and options to the general public.  In 1979, the CFTC brought an enforcement action against an entity organized by Arthur Economou called the American Board of Trade (ABT).  CFTC v. American Board of Trade (ABT), 473 F. Supp. 1177 (S.D.N.Y.1979), aff'd, 803 F.2d 1242 (2d Cir.1986). ABT claimed to provide "an exchange and marketplace" for certain commodity options transactions, including foreign currency options.  803 F.2d at 1244.  The CFTC charged that those unlicensed activities were unlawful under the CEA.  Among its defenses, ABT asserted that the Treasury Amendment excluded its foreign currency option transactions from regulation under the CEA.

The district court rejected ABT's arguments, entered a judgment enjoining ABT from engaging in options transactions, and ordered ABT to reimburse injured customers.  803 F.2d at 1244-1246.  The Second Circuit affirmed the district court's decision, specifically rejecting ABT's Treasury Amendment defense.  The court of appeals agreed with the district court that "an option to buy or sell foreign currency is not a purchase or sale of the currency itself and hence is not a transaction 'in' that currency, but at most is one that relates to the currency."  803 F.2d at 1248 (citing 473 F. Supp. at 1182).  Having found that ABT's options were not "transactions in foreign currency" for purposes of the Treasury Amendment, the court of appeals discerned no need to determine whether ABT's transactions fell within the Treasury Amendment's "board of trade" proviso.  Ibid.

Several years later, litigation arose that again raised questions over the meaning of the Treasury Amendment.  Salomon Forex, Inc. v. Tauber, 795 F. Supp. 768 (E.D.Va.1992), aff'd, 8 F.3d 966 (4th Cir.1993), cert. denied, 114 S. Ct. 1540 (1994).  The Tauber litigation grew out of a private debt collection dispute.  A foreign currency brokerage company, Salomon Forex, brought a diversity suit in federal district court to enforce a trading debt against a sophisticated foreign currency trader, Dr. Laszlo Tauber.  The trader principally argued that the debts were unenforceable because they arose from off-exchange futures and options transactions that were not conducted in compliance with the CEA. He contended that the Treasury Amendment exempted from CEA regulation only "spot" and "cash forward" foreign currency transactions, in which the parties anticipate actual delivery of the commodity.  See 1 Snider, supra, at ss 9.01, 10.04, 10.16.

The district court ruled that the trading debts were enforceable because the Treasury Amendment's reference to "transactions in foreign currency" exempted off-exchange foreign currency futures and options from CEA regulation.  See 795 F. Supp. at 773.  The Fourth Circuit affirmed, reasoning that the "broad and unqualified" phrase "transactions in foreign currency" reaches "all transactions in which foreign currencies are the subject matter, including options." 8 F.3d at 975.  The Fourth Circuit distinguished the Second Circuit's decision in ABT on the basis that the ABT case involved a foreign currency options transaction conducted by "unsophisticated private individuals buying on an organized exchange." Id. at 977-978.

### [Introduction to the Dunn Litigation]

On April 8, 1994, the CFTC filed a complaint in federal district court charging [William C. Dunn and Delta Consultants, Inc. (as well as two additional corporate defendants, Delta Options Ltd. and Nopkine Co., Ltd.)] with fraud in connection with commodity option transactions, in violation of 7 U.S.C. 6c(b) and 17 C.F.R. 32.9. The complaint alleged that Dunn and each corporation had made misrepresentations to existing and prospective customers concerning the likelihood of profit and loss associated with trading commodity options and the true status of their invested funds. The options identified in the complaint consisted of various foreign currencies (Japanese yen, Australian dollars, German marks, British pounds, Canadian dollars, and Swiss francs) that are subject to futures trading on United States contract markets. . . .

. . . . The CFTC moved the district court to appoint a temporary equity receiver to locate, preserve, and control all four defendants' property for the benefit of customers. That request was based primarily upon the serious allegations of fraudulent conduct, the apparent disappearance of more than $180 million of customers' funds, and the defendants' apparent transfer of a large sum of money from the United States to Switzerland in late 1993. On June 23, 1994, the district court granted the request for appointment of a temporary receiver. . . . . The court of appeals affirmed the district court's appointment of a temporary receiver. . . .

---

## Dunn v. Commodity Futures Trading Commission
### 117 S.Ct. 913 (Feb. 25, 1997)

Justice STEVENS delivered the opinion of the Court.

The question presented is whether Congress has authorized the Commodity Futures Trading Commission (CFTC or Commission) to regulate "off-exchange" trading in options to buy or sell foreign currency.

### I

The CFTC brought this action in 1994, alleging that, beginning in 1992, petitioners solicited investments in and operated a fraudulent scheme in violation of the Commodity Exchange Act (CEA), 7 U.S.C. § 1 et seq., and CFTC regulations. See 7 U.S.C. § 6c(b); 17 CFR § 32.9 (1996).[2] The CFTC's complaint, affidavits, and declarations submitted to the

---

[2] The statute provides: "No person shall offer to enter into, enter into or confirm the execution of, any transaction involving any commodity regulated under this chapter which is of the character of, or is commonly known to the trade as, an 'option' ... contrary to any rule, regulation, or order of the Commission prohibiting any such transaction or allowing any such transaction under such terms and conditions as the Commission may prescribe." 7 U.S.C. § 6c(b). The regulations at issue here further

District Court indicate that customers were told their funds would be invested using complex strategies involving options to purchase or sell various foreign currencies. App. 8. Petitioners apparently did in fact engage in many such transactions. Ibid.; 58 F.3d 50, 51 (C.A.2 1995). To do so, they contracted directly with international banks and others without making use of any regulated exchange or board of trade. In the parlance of the business, petitioners traded in the "off-exchange" or "over-the-counter" (OTC) market.[3] Ibid. No options were ever sold directly to petitioners' customers. However, their positions were tracked through internal accounts, and investors were provided weekly reports showing the putative status of their holdings. Petitioners and their customers suffered heavy losses. Id., at 51-52. Subsequently, the CFTC commenced these proceedings.

Rejecting petitioners' defense that off-exchange transactions in foreign currency options are exempt from the CEA, the District Court appointed a temporary receiver to take control of their property for the benefit of their customers. . . . [T]he Court of Appeals affirmed.

## II

The outcome of this case is dictated by the so-called "Treasury Amendment" to the CEA. 88 Stat. 1395, 7 U.S.C. § 2(ii). We have previously reviewed the history of the CEA and generally described how it authorizes the CFTC to regulate the "volatile and esoteric" market in futures contracts in fungible commodities. See Merrill Lynch, Pierce, Fenner & Smith, Inc. v. Curran, 456 U.S. 353, 356, 357-367 (1982). As a part of the 1974 amendments that created the CFTC and dramatically expanded the coverage of the statute to include nonagricultural commodities "in which contracts for future delivery are presently or in the future dealt in," see 88 Stat. 1395, 7 U.S.C. § 2 (1970 ed., Supp. IV), Congress enacted the following exemption, which has come to be known as the "Treasury Amendment":

> "Nothing in this chapter shall be deemed to govern or in any way be applicable to *transactions in foreign currency*, security warrants, security rights, resales of installment loan contracts, repurchase options, government securities, or mortgages and mortgage purchase commitments, unless such transactions involve the sale thereof for future delivery conducted on a board of trade."
> 7 U.S.C. § 2(ii) (emphasis added)

---

make it unlawful "for any person directly or indirectly ... [t]o cheat or defraud or attempt to cheat or defraud any other person; ... [t]o make or cause to be made to any other person any false report or statement thereof or cause to be entered for any person any false record thereof; ... [or] [t]o deceive or attempt to deceive any other person by any means whatsoever ... in or in connection with an offer to enter into, the entry into, or the confirmation of the execution of, any commodity option transaction." 17 CFR § 32.9 (1996).

[3]    We are informed by amici that participants in the "highly evolved, sophisticated" OTC foreign currency markets include "commercial and investment banks ... foreign exchange dealers and brokerage companies, corporations, money managers (including pension, mutual fund and commodity pool managers), commodity trading advisors, insurance companies, governments and central banks." Brief for Foreign Exchange Committee et al. as Amici Curiae 8. These markets serve a variety of functions, including providing ready access to foreign currency for international transactions, and allowing businesses to hedge against the risk of exchange rate movements. Id., at 8-9.

The narrow issue that we must decide is whether the italicized phrase ("transactions in foreign currency") includes transactions in options to buy or sell foreign currency. An option, as the term is understood in the trade, is a transaction in which the buyer purchases from the seller for consideration the right, but not the obligation, to buy or sell an agreed amount of a commodity at a set rate at any time prior to the option's expiration. . . .

### III

"[A]bsent any 'indication that doing so would frustrate Congress's clear intention or yield patent absurdity, our obligation is to apply the statute as Congress wrote it.' " Hubbard v. United States, 115 S.Ct. 1754, 1759 (1995) (quoting BFP v. Resolution Trust Corporation, 511 U.S. 531, 570 (1994) (SOUTER, J., dissenting)). The CFTC argues, and the Court of Appeals held, that an option is not itself a transaction "in" foreign currency, but rather is just a contract right to engage in such a transaction at a future date. Brief for Respondent 30-31; 58 F.3d, at 53. Hence, the Commission submits that the term "transactions in foreign currency" includes only the "actual exercise of an option (i.e., the actual purchase or sale of foreign currency)" but not the purchase or sale of an option itself. Brief for Respondent 31. That reading of the text seems quite unnatural to us, and we decline to adopt it.

The more normal reading of the key phrase encompasses all transactions in which foreign currency is the fungible good whose fluctuating market price provides the motive for trading. The CFTC's interpretation violates the ordinary meaning of the key word "in," which is usually thought to be "synonymous with [the] expressions 'in regard to,' 'respecting,' [and] 'with respect to.' " Black's Law Dictionary 758 (6th ed.1990); see Babbitt v. Sweet Home Chapter, Communities for Great Ore., 115 S.Ct. 2407, 2412-2413 (1995). There can be no question that the purchase or sale of a foreign currency option is a transaction "respecting" foreign currency. We think it equally plain as a matter of ordinary meaning that such an option is a transaction "in" foreign currency for purposes of the Treasury Amendment.

Indeed, adopting the Commission's reading would deprive the exemption of the principal effect Congress intended. The CFTC acknowledges that futures contracts fall squarely within the Treasury Amendment's exemption, Brief for Respondent 30, and there is no question that the exemption of off-exchange foreign currency futures from CFTC regulation was one of Congress' primary goals.[8] Yet on the CFTC's reasoning the exemption's application to futures contracts could not be sustained.

---

[8] The amendment was enacted on the suggestion of the Treasury Department at the time of a dramatic expansion in the scope of federal commodities regulation. The Department expressed concerns in a letter to the relevant congressional committee that this development might lead, inter alia, to the unintended regulation of the offexchange market in foreign currency futures. See S.Rep. No. 93-1131, pp. 50-51 (1974) ("The Department feels strongly that foreign currency futures trading, other than on organized exchanges, should not be regulated by the new agency") (letter of Donald Ritger, Acting General Counsel). The Treasury Amendment, which tracks almost verbatim the language proposed by the Department, cf. id., at 51, was included in the legislation to respond to these concerns. Id., at 23. The CFTC is therefore plainly correct to reject the suggestion of its amici that the Treasury Amendment's exemption be construed not to include futures contracts within its coverage. See Brief for Chicago Mercantile Exchange as Amicus Curiae 17-18; Brief for Board of Trade of City of Chicago as Amicus Curiae 10.

A futures contract is no more a transaction "in" foreign currency as the Commission understands the term than an option. The Commission argues that because a futures contract creates a legal obligation to purchase or sell currency on a particular date, it is somehow more clearly a transaction "in" the underlying currencies than an option, which generates only the right to engage in a transaction. Brief for Respondent 30-32. This reasoning is wholly unpersuasive. No currency changes hands at the time a futures contract is made. And, the existence of a futures contract does not guarantee that currency will actually be exchanged. Indeed, the Commission concedes that, in most cases, futures contracts are "extinguished before delivery by entry into an offsetting futures contract." Id., at 30 (citing 1 T. Snider, Regulation of the Commodities Futures and Options Markets § 2.05 (2d ed.1995) (hereinafter Snider)); see also Munn & Garcia 414. Adopting the CFTC's reading would therefore place both futures and options outside the exemption, in clear contravention of Congress' intent.

Furthermore, this interpretation would leave the Treasury Amendment's exemption for "transactions in foreign currency" without any significant effect at all, because it would limit the scope of the exemption to "forward contracts" (agreements that anticipate the actual delivery of a commodity on a specified future date) and "spot transactions" (agreements for purchase and sale of commodities that anticipate near-term delivery).[9] Both are transactions "in" a commodity as the CFTC would have us understand the term. But neither type of transaction for any commodity was subject to intensive regulation under the CEA at the time of the Treasury Amendment's passage. See 7 U.S.C. § 2 (1970 ed., Supp. IV) ("term 'future delivery,' as used in this chapter, shall not include any sale of any cash commodity for deferred shipment or delivery"); Snider § 9.01; J. Markham, The History of Commodity Futures Trading and Its Regulation 201-203 (1987). Our reading of the exemption is therefore also consonant with the doctrine that legislative enactments should not be construed to render their provisions mere surplusage. See Babbitt, 115 S.Ct., at 2413, (noting "reluctance to treat statutory terms as surplusage"); Mountain States Telephone & Telegraph Co. v. Pueblo of Santa Ana, 472 U.S. 237, 249 (1985).

Finally, including options in the exemption is consistent with Congress' purpose in enacting the Treasury Amendment. Although at the time the Treasury Amendment was drafted a thriving off-exchange market in foreign currency futures was in place, the closely related options market at issue here had not yet developed. See City of New York Bar Association Committee on Futures Regulation, The Evolving Regulatory Framework for Foreign Currency Trading 18, 23 (1986). The CFTC therefore suggests that Congress could not have intended to exempt foreign currency options from the CEA's coverage. Brief for Respondent 41-42. The legislative history strongly suggests to the contrary that Congress' broad purpose in enacting the Treasury Amendment was to provide a general exemption from CFTC regulation for sophisticated off-exchange foreign currency trading, which had previously developed entirely free from supervision under the commodities laws.

In explaining the Treasury Amendment, the Senate Committee Report notes in broad terms that the amendment "provides that inter-bank trading of foreign currencies and specified financial

---

[9]    See Snider § 9.01 (defining "spot transactions" and "forward contracts").

instruments is not subject to Commission regulation." S.Rep. No. 93-1131, 93rd Cong. 2nd Sess. 6 (1974) U.S.Code Cong. & Admin.News 1974, pp. 5843, 5848. Elsewhere, the Report again explains in general terms--without making reference to any distinction between options and futures--that the legislation:

> "included an amendment to clarify that the provisions of the bill are not applicable to trading in foreign currencies and enumerated financial instruments unless such trading is conducted on a formally organized futures exchange. A great deal of the trading in foreign currency in the United States is carried out through an informal network of banks and tellers. The Committee believes that this market is more properly supervised by the bank regulatory agencies and that, therefore, regulation under this legislation is unnecessary." Id., at 23.

Similarly, the Treasury Department submitted to the Chairman of the relevant Senate Committee a letter that was the original source of the Treasury Amendment. While focusing on the need to exempt the foreign currency futures market from CFTC regulation, the letter points out that the "participants in this market are sophisticated and informed institutions," and "the [CFTC] would clearly not have the expertise to regulate a complex banking function and would confuse an already highly regulated business sector." Id., at 50 (letter of Donald Ritger, Acting General Counsel). The Department further explained that "new regulatory limitations and restrictions could have an adverse impact on the usefulness and efficiency of foreign exchange markets for traders and investors." Ibid.

Although the OTC market for foreign currency options had not yet developed in 1974, the reasons underlying the Treasury Department's express desire at that time to exempt off-exchange commodity futures trading from CFTC regulation apply with equal force to options today. Foreign currency options and futures are now traded in the same off-exchange markets, by the same entities, for quite similar purposes. See Brief for Foreign Exchange Committee et al. as Amici Curiae 19. Contrary to the Commission's suggestion, we therefore think the purposes underlying the Treasury Amendment are most properly fulfilled by giving effect to the plain meaning of the language as Congress enacted it.

The CFTC rejoins that the Treasury Amendment should be construed in the light of Congress' history of regulating options more strictly than futures. See Snider §§ 7.03-7.04; Brief for Respondent 38-39. The Commission submits that this distinction was motivated by the view that options lend themselves more readily to fraudulent schemes than futures contracts. Hence, the CFTC argues that Congress would have acted reasonably and consistently with prior practice had it regulated commodities differently from options. While that may be true, we give only slight credence to these general historical considerations, which are unsupported by statutory language, or any evidence evocative of the particular concerns focused on by the legislators who enacted the Treasury Amendment. We think the history of the Treasury Amendment suggests-- contrary to the CFTC's view--that it was intended to take all transactions relating to foreign currency not conducted on a board of trade outside of the CEA's ambit. This interpretation is consistent with the fact that, prior to the enactment of the CEA in 1974, foreign currency trading had been entirely unregulated under the commodities laws.

Our interpretation is also consonant with the history of evolving congressional regulation in this area. That history has been one of successively broadening the coverage of regulation by the addition of more and more commodities to the applicable legislation. It seems quite natural in this context to read the Treasury Amendment's exemption of transactions in foreign currencies as a complete exclusion of that commodity from the regulatory scheme, except, of course, to the extent that the proviso for transactions "conducted on a board of trade" qualifies that exclusion. See 7 U.S.C. § 2(ii).

## IV

To buttress its reading of the statute, the CFTC argues that elsewhere in the CEA Congress referred to transactions "involving" a particular commodity to describe options or used other "more encompassing terminology," rather than what we are told is the narrower term transactions "in" the commodity, which was reserved for futures, spot transactions, and forward contracts. Brief for Respondent 30-33. Not only do we think it unlikely that Congress would adopt such a subtle method of drawing important distinctions, there is little to suggest that it did so.

Congress' use of these terms has been far from consistent. Most strikingly, the use of the word "involving" in the Treasury Amendment itself completely eviscerates the force of the Commission's argument. After setting forth exemptions for, inter alia, "transactions in foreign currency," the Amendment contains a proviso sweeping back into the statute's coverage "such transactions *involv[ing]* the sale thereof for future delivery conducted on a board of trade." 7 U.S.C. § 2(ii) (emphasis added). As we have already noted, the CFTC agrees that futures contracts are a subset of "transactions in foreign currency." The Commission further submits that the proviso uses the word "involve" to make the exemption inapplicable to those futures contracts that are conducted on a board of trade. This contradicts the "in" versus "involving" distinction. We would expect on the Commission's reasoning that this provision would refer to "transactions in futures." The use of the term "involving" instead, within the very amendment that respondent claims embraces this distinction, weighs heavily against the view that any such distinction was intended by Congress.[12]

---

[12] Similarly, the statute refers at one point to "[t]ransactions *in* commodities *involving* the sale thereof for future delivery ... and known as 'futures.' " 7 U.S.C. § 5 (emphasis added). Had Congress meant to maintain the Commission's distinction, we would not have expected the Legislature to use the words "in" and "involving" loosely in the same sentence to refer to futures, which the CFTC informs us are transactions "in" (but not "involving") foreign currency. Similarly, the statute refers elsewhere to "transaction[s] *in an option* on foreign currency." § 6c(f) (emphasis added). If Congress had spoken in the manner the CFTC suggests, that provision would instead use the phrase "transactions *involving* an option."

The statute's general jurisdictional provision also fails to maintain the distinction the Commission presses. The CEA provides that the CFTC "shall have exclusive jurisdiction ... with respect to accounts, agreements (including any transaction which is of the character of, or is commonly known to the trade as, an 'option' ... ), and transactions *involving* contracts of sale of a commodity for future delivery." § 2(i) (emphasis added). The Commission submits that this language gives the CFTC regulatory authority over options on futures contracts, see Snider § 10.11, and argues that the use of the word "involving" is therefore in keeping with its interpretation of the statutory scheme. See Brief for Respondent 32. But § 2(i) provides the CFTC with exclusive jurisdiction over far more. Among other things, it explicitly grants jurisdiction over any "transactio[n] *involving* contracts of sale of a commodity for future delivery," plainly meaning at a minimum ordinary futures contracts, which the Commission

The CFTC argues further that the proviso properly understood aids its cause. The proviso sweeps back into the CFTC's jurisdiction otherwise exempt "transactions in foreign currency" that "involve the sale thereof for future delivery" and are "conducted on a board of trade." Since the proviso refers to futures without mentioning options, the Commission submits that the exemption itself should be read only to cover futures because Congress cannot reasonably have intended to regulate exchange trading in foreign currency futures without also regulating exchange trading in such options. We agree that Congress intended no such anomaly. But we are satisfied that the anomaly is best avoided by reading the proviso broadly rather than reading the exemption narrowly.

The proviso's language fairly accommodates inclusion of both options and futures. To fall within the proviso, a transaction must "*involve* the sale [of foreign currency] for future delivery." § 2(ii) (emphasis added). Because options convey the right to buy or sell foreign currency at some future time prior to their expiration, they are transactions "involv[ing]" or related to the sale of foreign currency for future delivery. Thus, both futures and options are covered by both the exemption and the proviso. While that may not be the only possible reading of the literal text, and we do not intend to suggest that a similar construction would be required with respect to other provisions of the CEA, our interpretation is faithful to the "contemporary legal context" in which the Treasury Amendment was drafted. Cannon v. University of Chicago, 441 U.S. 677, 699 (1979); see also Massachusetts v. Morash, 490 U.S. 107, 115 (1989) (noting that " 'in expounding a statute, we [are] not ... guided by a single sentence or member of a sentence, but look to the provisions of the whole law, and to its object and policy' ") (quoting Pilot Life Ins. Co. v. Dedeaux, 481 U.S. 41, 51 (1987)).

Finally, the CFTC calls our attention to statements in the legislative history of a 1982 amendment to the CEA,[13] indicating that the drafters of that amendment believed that the CFTC had the authority to regulate foreign currency options "when they are traded other than on a national securities exchange." See S.Rep. No. 97-384, p. 22 (1982). Those statements, at best, might be described as "legislative dicta" because the 1982 amendment itself merely resolved a conflict between the Securities Exchange Commission and the CFTC concerning their respective authority to regulate transactions on an exchange. See Snider § 10.24. The amendment made no change in the law applicable to off-exchange trading. Although the "dicta" is consistent with the position that the CFTC advocates, it sheds no light on the intent of the authors of the Treasury Amendment that had been adopted eight years earlier. See, e.g., Mackey v. Lanier Collection Agency & Service, Inc., 486 U.S. 825, 839-840 (1988).

V

Underlying the statutory construction question before us, we recognize that there is an important public policy dispute--with substantial arguments favoring each side. Petitioners, their amici, and the Treasury Department, argue that if off-exchange foreign currency options are not treated as exempt from CEA regulation, the increased costs associated with unnecessary regulation of the highly sophisticated OTC foreign currency markets might well drive this

---

otherwise insists are transactions "in" commodities.

[13] Futures Trading Act of 1982, Tit. I, § 102, 96 Stat. 2296, 7 U.S.C. § 6c(f).

business out of the United States. The Commission responds that to the extent limited exemptions from regulation are necessary, it will provide them, but argues that options are particularly susceptible to fraud and abuse if not carefully policed. Brief for Respondent 26, 49. As the Commission properly acknowledges, however, these are arguments best addressed to the Congress, not the courts. See United States v. Rutherford, 442 U.S. 544, 555 (1979). Lacking the expertise or authority to assess these important competing claims, we note only that "a literal construction of the statute" does not "yiel[d] results so manifestly unreasonable that they could not fairly be attributed to congressional design." Ibid.

The judgment of the Court of Appeals is reversed, and the case is remanded for further proceedings consistent with this opinion.

## Comments and Questions

1. The *Dunn* case involved an over-the-counter or OTC product — that is, an instrument not routinely traded on a regulated exchange. The transaction was permissible only if it fell within the "Treasury Amendment" of the CEA. What defines the boundaries of this exception? For example, suppose two individuals entered into the following transaction: Individual A pays individual B several thousand dollars. In return, Individual B promises to pay Individual A a certain sum of money if the English pound increases in value against the U.S. dollar by more than five percent at the end of six months. If the pound does not increase in value by this amount, Individual B would not have any obligation to Individual A. What if Individual A made similar contracts with a number of friends and acquaintances? What if Individual A advertised his willingness to enter into such contracts in a newspaper? What if Individual A offered to enter into a similar contract based on price movements in the pork bellies?

2. The authority of the CFTC to police over-the-counter derivatives markets has been a hotly contested issues over the past fifteen years. In the 1980s, there was considerable uncertainty over the CFTC authority in this area, particularly for derivatives not clearly covered by the Treasury Amendment. Through a series of regulatory and legislative initiatives in the late 1980s and early 1990's, the CFTC and Congress sanctioned the development of a robust derivative marketplace in the United States. For a lucid overview of these developments, see Roberta Romano, *The Regulation of Derivative Securities*, 55 MD. L. REV. 1, 55-65 (1996). See also Henry T.C. Hu, *Misunderstood Derivatives: The causes of Informational Failure and the Promise of Regulatory Incrementalism*, 102 YALE L.J. 1047 (1993) (exploring the justifications for and problems with the regulation of OTC derivatives). In 1998, the CFTC surprised many in the derivatives industry by issuing a concept release, suggesting that the Commission was considering changes in its approach to the regulations of OTC derivatives.

The Commission has been engaged in a comprehensive regulatory reform effort designed to update the agency's oversight of both exchange and off-exchange markets. As part of this process, the Commission believes that it is appropriate to reexamine its regulatory approach to the OTC derivatives market taking into account developments since 1993. The purpose of this release is to solicit comments on whether the regulatory structure applicable to OTC derivatives under the Commission's regulations should be modified in any way in light of recent developments in the marketplace and to generate information and data to assist the Commission in assessing this issue.

The market has continued to grow and to evolve in the past five years. As indicated above, volume has increased dramatically. New end-users of varying levels of sophistication have begun to participate in this market. Products have proliferated, with some products becoming increasingly standardized. Systems for centralized execution and clearing are being proposed.

The Commission hopes that the public comments filed in response to this release will constitute an important source of relevant data and analysis that will assist it in determining how best to maintain adequate regulatory safeguards without impairing the ability of the OTC derivatives market to continue to grow and the ability of U.S. entities to remain competitive in the global financial marketplace. The Commission has no preconceived result in mind. . . . .

The Commission is open both to evidence in support of broadening its exemptions and to evidence indicating a need for additional safeguards. Serious consideration will be given to the views of all interested parties before regulatory changes, if any, are proposed. In evaluating the comments and ultimately deciding on its course of action, the Commission will, of course, also engage in its own research and analysis. Any proposed changes will be carefully designed to avoid unduly burdensome or duplicative regulation that might adversely affect the continued vitality of the market and will be published for public comment. Moreover, any changes which impose new regulatory obligations or restrictions will be applied prospectively only.

CFTC Concept Release on Over-The-Counter Derivatives, 63 Fed. Reg. 26,114-01 (May 12, 1998). Notwithstanding the tentative tone of the CFTC's release, its publication proposed an intense reaction from the derivatives industry and other regulatory authorities. See, e.g., *Critics of CFTC's OTC Concept Release Propose Stopgap Bill to Preserve Status Quo*, BNA Securities Law Daily, June 9, 1998. What do others find so threatening about the CFTC's recent initiative?

3. Jurisdiction over OTC derivatives has also been a subject of interest to the SEC. A number of U.S. securities firms are active participants in this marketplace. Often these firms operate their OTC derivatives activities through affiliates located outside of the United States. In December of 1997, the Securities and Exchange Commission proposed a voluntary, alternative regulatory regime for U.S. broker-dealers engaged primarily in privately-negotiated OTC derivatives transactions. See Proposed Rule on OTC Derivatives Dealers, 62 Fed. Reg. 67,940 (Dec. 30, 1997). This proposal, known in the industry as "Broker-Dealer Lite,"was intended to encourage U.S. securities firms to repatriate their OTC derivative operations. The CFTC filed a comment objecting to the proposal on the grounds that the SEC lacks jurisdiction over most OTC derivatives products, that the CFTC was the more appropriate source of supervision in this area, and that the Commission was planning to issue a concept release (mentioned in the preceding note) in the near future. See Letter from Jane A. Webb, Secretary of the CFTC, to

Jonathan G. Katz, Secretary of the SEC (May 19, 1998) <http://www.sec.gov/rules/proposed/s73097/webb2.htm>. In light of this jurisdictional dispute, consider the following problem:

*Problem 14-3*

Bankers National Bank is a leading dealer of interest rate swaps. Interest rates swaps are contracts based on some notional amount (say, a million dollars) over a certain period of time (say two years), in which one party agrees to make interest payments based on some fixed rate of interest (say, seven percent), and the second party agrees to make interest payments based on some floating rate of interest (say, the London Interbank Overnight Rate). Which party profits from an interest rate swap depends one whether the floating rate rises above or falls below its fixed rate. Every year, Bankers National Bank enters into hundreds of interest rate swaps with different customers. In general, the bank tries to balance its positions, so that if it loses money on a fixed-rate position it has an offsetting gain on a floating-rate position.

Last year, Bankers National Bank entered into an unusually complicated swap with the Stallmark Stationery Company, a medium-sized commercial firm. Unexpected market fluctuations caused Stallmark to lose several million dollars on the swap. The company alleged that Bankers National Bank had not fully disclosed the terms of the swap nor had it revealed the bank's internal analyses of how the swap would perform in periods of extreme volatility.

Both the CFTC and the SEC have instituted investigations into the transactions. Do either of these agencies have jurisdiction over this transaction?

# CHAPTER FIFTEEN

# DEPOSITORY INSTITUTIONS IN THE SECURITIES BUSINESS

The Glass-Steagall Act is one of the best known pieces of financial legislation in American history. Adopted in 1933 at the height of the Great Depression, the Act was designed to separate banking from securities activities. And for many decades, it did precisely that. Since the 1970's, however, the line between the banking and securities industry has gradually, but increasingly, blurred. Perhaps the most interesting aspect of this development is not that it has occurred, but that it has occurred almost entirely without legislative participation. Through a combination of judicial decision and regulatory initiatives, banks have gained access to almost every subsector of the securities industry. Though still hampered by many vestiges of the Glass-Steagall Act and other regulatory restrictions, depository institutions are now major participants in the securities industry.

This chapter summarizes the key legal events underlying this revolution in bank powers. As you read this chapter, ask yourself how these changes took place. Twenty-five years ago — when popular sentiment and judicial precedent supported a strict interpretation of the Glass-Steagall Act — it appeared unlikely that depository institutions would be permitted to engage in even modest securities activities. The notion that such activities might be undertaken without express congressional support would have been inconceivable. How did all this change? Was the change legitimate? Was it good public policy?

For an excellent and detailed analysis of this area of the law, see MELANIE L. FEIN, SECURITIES ACTIVITIES OF BANKS (2d ed. 1998).

## Section 1.  Background on the Glass-Steagall Act

Banking and securities activities have not always been considered distinct or unrelated lines of business. In fact, persons engaged in either or both activities often call themselves "bankers." Nevertheless, enterprises usually came to emphasize one or the other activity, and since 1933 the Glass-Steagall Act has largely mandated their separation. But exactly what activities have been separated? What are the traditional definitions of "commercial banking" and "investment banking" that identify the predominant standard activities of banks and securities firms throughout their history in the United States?  The Glass-Steagall Act essentially defines commercial banking as deposit taking—"the business of receiving deposits subject to check or to repayment upon presentation of a passbook, certificate of deposit, or other evidence of debt, or upon request of the depositor. . . . " 12 U.S.C. § 378.  In addition to the monetary function of deposit taking, banks also engage in a credit function—making loans.  The Glass-Steagall Act defines investment banking as "the business of issuing, underwriting, selling, or distributing, at wholesale or retail, or through syndicate participation, stocks, bonds, debentures, notes or other securities . . . ."  The distinction from commercial banking seems to be that the investment (deposit) here is of a more permanent nature, as is the credit extension in the form of stocks or bonds.  Also, the deposit is a special deposit, made for a particular purpose, not a general deposit.  Consequently, the relationship with the customer is more agency than debtor-creditor.

There are four major sections in the Glass-Steagall Act that affect banking and securities relations.  Two of these provisions, sections 16 and 21 of the Act (codified at 12 U.S.C. §§ 24(Seventh), 378) address the activities of depository institutions. Section 16, which was enacted as an amendment to the National Banking Act, states: the "business of dealing in securities and stock by [a national bank] shall be limited to purchasing and selling such securities and stock without recourse, solely upon the order, and for the account of, customers, and in no case for [its] own account, and [a national bank] shall not underwrite any issue of securities or stock."  The section then goes on to provide that national banks may underwrite certain government securities, particularly general obligation government securities.  Thus section 16 of the Glass-Steagall Act  generally provides that a member bank may act as agent (broker) for its customers, but may not underwrite corporate debt or equity securities, or buy equities for its own account.  As we know from Chapter Three, national banks may invest in investment securities for their own account, with some limitations.  (By way of 12 U.S.C. § 335, section 16 of the Glass-Steagall Act also applies to state chartered member banks.)

Section 21 of the Glass-Steagall Act reinforces section 16 by making it a criminal offense for any organization engaged in a securities underwriting business to engage at the same time in the business of receiving deposits.  To a certain extent this section is a reciprocal of section 16, in that it prohibits securities firms from taking deposits just as section 16 prohibits member banks from underwriting securities.  But section 21 goes further because it extends the section 16 underwriting prohibitions to state chartered non-member banks.  Finally, while it is at times difficult to read the two sections together, it has been judicially determined that section 21 does not prohibit the activities specifically authorized by section 16.

Sections 20 and 32 of the Glass-Steagall Act (codified at 12 U.S.C. § 377 and § 78) expand the Act's prohibitions beyond the corporate boundaries of depository institutions and imposes statutory limits on certain bank affiliates and other related entities.  In particular, section 20 provides that no member bank may be affiliated with any organization "engaged principally in the issue, flotation, underwriting, public sale, or distribution at wholesale or retail or through syndicate participation of stock, bonds, debentures, notes or other securities . . . ."  Section 32 imposes similar restrictions on management interlocks by stating that no officer, director, employee or partner of any organization engaged primarily in the securities business or any individual so engaged, "shall serve at the same time as an officer, director, or employee of any member bank . . . . "  Together sections 20 and 32 supplement — at least for member banks — the restrictions that the Bank Holding Company Act imposes on bank affiliation.  See Chapter Four.

For roughly fifty years, these four provisions of the Glass-Steagall Act imposed a formidable boundary between commercial and investment banking.  On occasion, as in the following case, banks attempt to work around these constraints, but for the most part their efforts were futile.  The following decision of the Supreme Court is illustrative of the era.

## Investment Co. Institute v. Camp
### 401 U.S. 617 (1971)

MR. JUSTICE STEWART delivered the opinion of the Court.

The issue before us is whether the Comptroller of the Currency may, consistently with the banking laws, authorize a national bank to offer its customers the opportunity to invest in a stock fund created and maintained by the bank.  Before 1963 national banks were prohibited by administrative regulation from offering this service.  The Board of Governors of the Federal Reserve System, which until 1962 had regulatory jurisdiction over all the trust activities of national banks, allowed the collective investment of trust assets only for "the investment of funds held for true fiduciary purposes."  The applicable regulation, Regulation F, specified that "the operation of such Common Trust Funds as investment trusts for other than strictly fiduciary purposes is hereby prohibited."  The Board consistently ruled that it was improper for a bank to use "a Common Trust Fund as an investment trust attracting money seeking investment alone and to embark upon what would be in effect the sale of participations in a Common Trust Fund to the public as investments."  26 Fed.Reserve Bull. 393 (1940) . . . .

In 1962 Congress transferred jurisdiction over most of the trust activities of national banks from the Board of Governors of the Federal Reserve System to the Comptroller of the Currency, without modifying any provision of substantive law.  The Comptroller thereupon solicited suggestions for improving the regulations applicable to trust activities.  Subsequently, new regulations were proposed which expressly authorized the collective investment of monies delivered to the bank for investment management, so-called managing agency accounts.  These proposed regulations were officially promulgated in 1963 with changes not material here.  In 1965 the First National City Bank of New York submitted for the Comptroller's approval a plan for the collective investment of managing agency accounts.  The Comptroller promptly approved the plan, and it is now in operation.  This plan, which departs in some respects from the plan envisaged by the Comptroller's Regulation, is expected, the briefs tell us, to be a model for other banks which decide to offer their customers a collective investment service.

Under the plan the bank customer tenders between $10,000 and $500,000 to the bank, together with an authorization making the bank the customer's managing agent.  The customer's investment is added to the fund, and a written evidence of participation is issued which expresses in "units of participation" the customer's proportionate interest in fund assets.  Units of participation are freely redeemable, and transferable to anyone who has executed a managing agency agreement with the bank. The fund is registered as an investment company under the Investment Company Act of 1940. The bank is the underwriter of the fund's units of participation within the meaning of that Act. The fund has filed a registration statement pursuant to the Securities Act of 1933. The fund is supervised by a five-member committee elected annually by the participants pursuant to the Investment Company Act of 1940. The Securities Exchange Commission has exempted the fund from the Investment Company Act to the extent that a majority of this committee may be affiliated with the bank, and it is expected that a majority always will be officers in the bank's trust and investment division. The actual custody and investment of fund assets is carried out by the bank as investment advisor pursuant to a management agreement. Although the Investment Company Act requires that this management agreement be approved annually by the committee, including a majority of the unaffiliated members, or by the participants, it is expected that the bank will continue to be investment advisor.

. . . The petitioners contend that a purchase of stock by a bank's investment fund is a purchase of stock by a bank for its own account in violation of [sections 16 and 21] of the Glass-Steagall Act and] that the creation and operation of an investment fund by a bank which offers to its customers the opportunity to purchase an interest in the fund's assets constitutes the issuing, underwriting, selling, or distributing of securities or stocks in violation of these sections.

The questions raised by the petitioners are novel and substantial. National Banks were granted trust powers in 1913. Federal Reserve Act, § 11, 38 Stat. 261. The first common trust fund was organized in 1927, and such funds were expressly authorized by the Federal Reserve Board by Regulation F promulgated in 1937. . . . For at least a generation, therefore, there has been no reason to doubt that a national bank can, consistently with the banking laws, commingle trust funds on the one hand, and act as a managing agent on the other. No provision of the banking law suggests that it is improper for a national bank to pool trust assets, or to act as a managing agent for individual customers, or to purchase stock for the account of its customers. But the union of these powers gives birth to an investment fund whose activities are of a different character. The differences between the investment fund that the Comptroller has authorized and a conventional open-end mutual fund are subtle at best, and it is undisputed that this bank investment fund finds itself in direct competition with the mutual fund industry. One would suppose that the business of a mutual fund consists of buying stock "for its own account" and of "issuing" and "selling" "stock" or "other securities" evidencing an undivided and redeemable interest in the assets of the fund. On their face, §§ 16 and 21 of the Glass-Steagall Act appear clearly to prohibit this activity by national banks.

But we cannot come lightly to the conclusion that the Comptroller has authorized activity that violates the banking laws. . . .

The difficulty here is that the Comptroller adopted no expressly articulated position at the administrative level as to the meaning and impact of the provisions of §§ 16 and 21 as they affect bank investment funds. The Comptroller promulgated Regulation 9 without opinion or accompanying statement. His subsequent report to Congress did not advert to the prohibitions of the Glass-Steagall Act. . . . Quite obviously the Comptroller should not grant new authority to national banks until he is satisfied that the exercise of this authority will not violate the intent of the banking laws. If he faces such questions only after he has acted, there is substantial danger that the momentum generated by initial approval may seriously impair the enforcement of the banking laws that Congress enacted.

## IV

There is no dispute that one of the objectives of the Glass-Steagall Act was to prohibit commercial banks, banks that receive deposits subject to repayment, lend money, discount and negotiate promissory notes and the like, from going into the investment banking business.  Many commercial banks were indirectly engaged in the investment banking business when the Act was passed in 1933.  Even before the passage of the Act it was generally believed that it was improper for a commercial bank to engage in investment banking directly.  But in 1908 banks began the practice of establishing security affiliates that engaged in, *inter alia*, the business of floating bond issues and, less frequently, underwriting stock issues.  The Glass-Steagall Act confirmed that national banks could not engage in investment banking directly, and in addition made affiliation with an organization so engaged illegal.  One effect of the Act was to abolish the security affiliates of commercial banks.

It is apparent from the legislative history of the Act why Congress felt that this drastic step was necessary.  The failure of the Bank of United States in 1930 was widely attributed to that bank's activities with respect to its numerous securities affiliates.  Moreover, Congress was concerned that commercial banks in general and member banks of the Federal Reserve System in particular had both aggravated and been damaged by stock market decline partly because of their direct and indirect involvement in the trading and ownership of speculative securities.  The Glass-Steagall Act reflected a determination that policies of competition, convenience, or expertise which might otherwise support the entry of commercial banks into the investment banking business were outweighed by the "hazards" and "financial dangers" that arise when commercial banks engage in the activities proscribed by the Act.

The hazards that Congress had in mind were not limited to the obvious danger that a bank might invest its own assets in frozen or otherwise imprudent stock or security investments.  For often securities affiliates had operated without direct access to the assets of the bank.  This was because securities affiliates had frequently been established with capital paid in by the bank's stockholders, or by the public, or through the allocation of a legal dividend on bank stock for this purpose.  The legislative history of the Glass-Steagall Act shows that Congress also had in mind and repeatedly focused on the more subtle hazards that arise when a commercial bank goes beyond the business of acting as fiduciary or managing agent and enters the investment banking business either directly or by establishing an affiliate to hold and sell particular investments.  This course places new promotional and other pressures on the bank which in turn create new temptations.  For example, pressures are created because the bank and the affiliate are closely associated in the public mind, and should the affiliate fare badly, public confidence in the bank might be impaired.  And since public confidence is essential to the solvency of a bank, there might exist a natural temptation to shore up the affiliate through unsound loans or other aid.  Moreover, the pressure to sell a particular investment and to make the affiliate successful might create a risk that the bank would make its credit facilities more freely available to those companies in whose stock or securities the affiliate has invested or become otherwise involved.  Congress feared that banks might even go so far as to make unsound loans to such companies.  In any event, it was thought that the bank's salesman's interest might impair its ability to function as an impartial source of credit.

Congress was also concerned that bank depositors might suffer losses on investments, that they purchased in reliance on the relationship between the bank and its affiliate. This loss of customer good-will might "become an important handicap to a bank during a major period of security market deflation." More broadly, Congress feared that the promotional needs of investment banking might lead commercial banks to lend their reputation for prudence and restraint to the enterprise of selling particular stocks and securities, and that this could not be done without that reputation being undercut by the risks necessarily incident to the investment banking business. There was also perceived the danger that when commercial banks were subject to the promotional demands of investment banking, they might be tempted to make loans to customers with the expectation that the loan would facilitate the purchase of stocks and securities. There was evidence before Congress that loans for investment written by commercial banks had done much to feed the speculative fever of the late 1920's. Senator Glass made it plain that it was "the fixed purpose of Congress" not to see the facilities of commercial banking diverted into speculative operations by the aggressive and promotional character of the investment banking business.

Another potential hazard that very much concerned Congress arose from the plain conflict between the promotional interest of the investment banker and the obligation of the commercial banker to render disinterested investment advice. . . . Congress had before it evidence that security affiliates might be driven to unload excessive holdings through the trust department of the sponsor bank. Some witnesses at the hearings expressed the view that this practice constituted self-dealing in violation of the trustee's obligation of loyalty, and indeed that it would be improper for a bank's trust department to purchase anything from the bank's securities affiliate.

In sum, Congress acted to keep commercial banks out of the investment banking business largely because it believed that the promotional incentives of investment banking and the investment banker's pecuniary stake in the success of particular investment opportunities was destructive of prudent and disinterested commercial banking and of public confidence in the commercial banking system. . . . .

V

The language that Congress chose to achieve this purpose includes the prohibitions of § 16 that a national bank "shall not underwrite any issue of securities or stock" and shall not purchase "for its own account . . . any shares of stock of any corporation," and the prohibition of § 21 against engaging in "the business of issuing, underwriting, selling, or distributing . . . stocks, bonds, debentures, notes, or other securities." In this litigation the Comptroller takes the position that the operation of a bank investment fund is consistent with these provisions, because participating interests in such a fund are not "securities" within the meaning of the Act. It is argued that a bank investment fund simply makes available to the small investor the benefit of investment management by a bank trust department which would otherwise be available only to large investors, and that the operation of an investment fund creates no problems that are not present whenever a bank invests in securities for the account of customers.

But there is nothing in the phrasing of either § 16 or § 21 that suggests a narrow reading of the word "securities." To the contrary, the breadth of the term is implicit in the fact that the antecedent statutory language encompasses not only equity securities but also securities representing debt. And certainly there is nothing in the language of these provisions to suggest that the sale of an interest in the business of buying, holding, and selling stocks for investment is to be distinguished from the sale of an interest in a commercial or industrial enterprise.

Indeed, there is direct evidence that Congress specifically contemplated that the word "security" includes an interest in an investment fund. . . .

But in any event, we are persuaded that the purposes for which Congress enacted the Glass-Steagall Act leave no room for the conclusion that a participation in a bank investment fund is not a "security" within the meaning of the Act. From the perspective of competition, convenience, and expertise, there are arguments to be made in support of allowing commercial banks to enter the investment banking business. But Congress determined that the hazards outlined above made it necessary to prohibit this activity to commercial banks. Those same hazards are clearly present when a bank undertakes to operate an investment fund.

A bank that operates an investment fund has a particular investment to sell. It is not a matter of indifference to the bank whether the customer buys an interest in the fund or makes some other investment. If its customers cannot be persuaded to invest in the bank's investment fund, the bank will lose their investment business and the fee which that business would have brought in. *** When interests in the fund were redeemed, the bank would be effectively faced with the choice of selling stocks from the fund's portfolio or of selling new participations to cover redemptions. The bank might have a pecuniary incentive to choose the latter course in order to avoid the cost of stock transactions undertaken solely for redemption purposes.

Promotional incentives might also be created by the circumstance that the bank's fund would be in direct competition with mutual funds that, from the point of view of the investor, offered an investment opportunity comparable to that offered by the bank. The bank would want to be in a position to show to the prospective customer that its fund was more attractive than the mutual funds offered by others. The bank would have a salesman's stake in the performance of the fund, for if the fund were less successful than the competition the bank would lose business and the resulting fees.

A bank that operated an investment fund woud necessarily put its reputation and facilities squarely behind that fund and the investment opportunity that the fund offered. The investments of the fund might be conservative or speculative, but in any event the success or failure of the fund would be a matter of public record. Imprudent or unsuccessful managment of the bank's investment fund could bring about a perhaps unjustified loss of public confidence in the bank itself. If imprudent management should place the fund in distress, a bank might find itself under pressure to rescue the fund through measures inconsistent with sound banking.

The promotional and other pressures incidental to the operation of an investment fund, in other words, involve the same kinds of potential abuses that Congress intended to guard against when it legislated against bank security affiliates. It is not the slightest reflection on the integrity of the mutual fund industry to say that the traditions of that industry are not necessarily the conservative traditions of commercial banking. The needs and interests of a mutual fund enterprise more nearly approximate those of securities underwriting, the activity in which bank security affiliates were primarily engaged. When a bank puts itself in competition with mutual funds, the bank must make an accommodation to the kind of ground rules that Congress firmly concluded could not be prudently mixed with the business of commercial banking.

And there are other potential hazards of the kind of Congress sought to eliminate with the passage of the Glass-Steagall Act. The bank's stake in the investment fund might distort its credit decisions or lead to unsound loans to the companies in which the fund had invested. The bank might exploit its confidential relationship with its commercial and industrial creditors for the benefit of the fund. The bank might undertake, directly or indirectly, to make its credit facilities available to the fund or to render other aid to the fund inconsistent with the best interests of the bank's depositors. The bank might make loans to facilitate the purchase of interests in the fund. The bank might divert talent and resources from its commercial banking operation to the promotion of the fund. Moreover, because the bank would have a stake in a customer's making a particular investment decision—the decision to invest in the bank's investment fund—the customer might doubt the motivation behind the bank's recommendation that he make such an investment. If the fund investment should turn out badly there would be a danger that the bank would lose the good-will of those customers who had invested in the fund. It might be unlikely that disenchantment would go so far as to threaten the solvency of the bank. But because banks are dependent on the confidence of their customers, the risk would not be unreal. . . .

VI

The Glass-Steagall Act was a prophylactic measure directed against conditions that the experience of the 1920s showed to be great potentials for abuse. The literal terms of that Act clearly prevent what the Comptroller has sought to authorize here. Because the potential hazards and abuses that flow from a bank's entry into the mutual investment business are the same basic hazards and abuses that Congress intended to eliminate almost 40 years ago, we cannot but apply the terms of the federal statute as they were written. We conclude that the operation of an investment fund of the kind approved by the Comptroller involves a bank in the underwriting, issuing, selling, and distributing of securities in violation of §§ 16 and 21 of the Glass-Steagall Act. . . .

Justice BLACKMUN, dissenting.

The Court's opinion and judgments here, it seems to me, are based more on what is deemed to be appropriate and desirable national banking *policy* than on what is a necessary judicial construction of the Glass-Steagall Act of almost four decades ago. It is a far different thing to be persuaded that it is wise policy to keep national banks out of the business of operating mutual investment funds, despite the safeguards that the Comptroller of the Currency and the Securities and Exchange Commission have provided, than it is to be persuaded that existing and somewhat ancient legislation requires that result. Policy considerations are for the Congress and not for this Court.

I recognize and am fully aware of the factors and of the economic considerations that led to the enactment of the Glass-Steagall Act. The second and third decades of this century are not the happiest chapter in the history of American banking. Deep national concerns emerged from the distressful experiences of those years and from the sad ends to which certain banking practices of that time had led the industry. But those then-prevailing conditions, the legislative history, and the remedy Congress provided, prompt me to conclude that what was proscribed was the involvement and activity of a national bank in investment, as contrasted with commercial, banking, in underwriting and issuing, and in acquiring speculative securities for its own account. These were the banking sins of that time.

The propriety, however, of a national bank's acting, when not in contravention of state or local law, as an inter vivos or testamentary trustee, as an executor or administrator, as a guardian or committee, as a custodian and, indeed, as an agent for the individual customer's securities and funds . . . is not, and could not be, questioned by the petitioners here or by the Court. This being so, there is, for me, an element of illogic in the ready admission by all concerned, on the one hand, that a national bank has the power to manage, by way of a common trust arrangement, those funds that it holds as fiduciary in the technical sense, and to administer separate agency accounts, and in the rejection, on the other hand, of the propriety of the bank's placing agency assets into a mutual investment fund. The Court draws its decisional line between the two. I find it impossible to locate any statutory root for that line drawing. To use the Glass-Steagall Act as a tool for that distinction is, I think, a fundamental misconception of the statute.

Accordingly, I am not convinced that the Congress, by that Act or otherwise, as yet has proscribed the banking endeavors under challenge here by competitors in a highly competitive field. None of the judges of the Court of Appeals was so convinced, and neither was the Comptroller of the Currency whose expertise the Court concedes. I would leave to Congress the privilege of now prohibiting such national bank activity if that is its intent and desire.

In Parts IV and V of its opinion the Court outlines hazards that are present when a bank indulges in specified activities. The Court then states, in the last paragraph of Part V, that those hazards are not present when a bank undertakes to purchase stock for individual customers or to commingle assets held in its several fiduciary capacities, and the like. I must disagree. It seems to me that exactly the same hazards are indeed present. A bank offers its fiduciary services in an atmosphere of vigorous competition. One need only observe the current and continuous advertising of claimed fiduciary skills to know that this is so and that the business is one for profit. In the fiduciary area a bank is engaged in direct competition with other investment concepts and with non-banking fiduciaries. Failure or misadventure of a single trust may constitute a threat to public confidence among the bank's other trust beneficiaries, prospective trustors, and even the commercial activities of the bank itself. It has an inevitable adverse effect upon the bank's fulfillment of what is fashionably described today as its 'full service.'

Thus I feel that the Court overstates its case when it seeks to diminish the significance of these hazards in the fiduciary area as contrasted with mutual fund operation. After all, we deal here with something akin to the traditional banking function and with a device that makes available for the small investor what is already available for the large investor by way of the individual agency account.

What the Court decries in the investment fund is the combination of three banking operations, each concededly permissible: acting as agent for the customer, purchasing for that customer, and pooling assets. It is said that 'the union of these powers' gives birth to something 'of a different character' and is statutorily prohibited. I doubt that those three powers, each allowed by the controlling statutes, somehow operate in combination to produce something forbidden by those same controlling statutes, and I doubt that the unitization is something more than or something different from the mere sum of its parts and that it thereby expands to achieve offensiveness under the Glass-Steagall Act.

## Comments and Questions

1.   Would the same result obtain in ICI v. Camp if the bank had been state-chartered?  What if the activity had been operated out of a subsidiary of a state-chartered bank?

2.  ICI v. Camp is, in certain respects, analogous to the *VALIC* decision reproduced in Chapter Fourteen.  There, an insurance company attempted to offer an insurance-company-sponsored alternative to mutual funds.  Here, the banking industry was trying to offer a bank-sponsored substitute.  Having learned the lesson of *VALIC*, however, the bank sponsor here acceded to SEC regulation, obtaining various exemptions from inconsistent requirements of the 1940 Act.  Could the bank sponsor have claimed a complete exemption from the federal securities laws?  See section 3(a)(3) of the 1940 Act (exempting "any common trust fund or similar fund maintained by a bank exclusively for the collective investment and reinvestment of moneys contributed thereto by the bank in its capacity as a trustee, executor, administrator, or guardian"); see also section 3(a)(2) of the 1933 Act.

3.   In the *Camp* decision, the banking industry, with the acquiescence of the Comptroller of the Currency, structured the proposed product as an extension of trust powers.  Although a majority of the Court rejected this characterization — ruling instead that the proposal entailed the impermissible underwriting of securities — Justice Blackmun viewed the proposal as substantially similar to traditional trust functions.  Who was right?  Is there a clear line between trust functions and securities underwriting?

4.  For subsequent interpretations of the Glass-Steagall Act, one of the most important aspects of the Camp decision was the "subtle hazards" analysis of Part IV of the majority opinion. As we will see, later courts have expended considerable effort determining whether other proposed activities present any or all of these hazards.  What is the statutory basis of subtle hazard analysis? Is it a sound approach from a policy perspective?

5.  An important element of *Camp* and of other contemporaneous interpretations of the Glass-Steagall Act was a shared understanding that securities affiliations of banks in the 1920s and 1930s contributed substantially to the problems of the  banking industry during the Great Depression.  More recent academic studies have questioned the historical basis of this interpretation.  Would it matter if economic historians were to conclude definitively that the *Camp* Court and the Congress of 1993  misunderstood the causes of  bank failures of the Great Depression?  To what extent should courts or regulatory agencies consider such insights in interpreting statutes such as the Glass-Steagall Act?

---

In many respects, the *Camp* decision represented the high-water mark of Glass-Steagall interpretation.  For more than a decade, the decision presented a formidable barrier to banking industry efforts to enter the securities business.  The balance of this chapter chronicles the multifaceted counter offensive that the banking industry mounted

against this barrier in the 1980s. As you read through these materials, consider the following questions: Is *Camp* still good law?  To the extent it has been overruled, who overruled it, and when?

## Section 2.  Brokerage Activities

As we explored in Chapter Eleven, 1975 was a watershed year for the U.S. securities industry in that it marked the end of the era of fixed commissions for NYSE securities. The deregulation of commissions prompted the emergence of a new breed of securities firm: the discount brokerage house specializing in low-cost execution services with little or no ancillary research and advisory services.  One of the most successful of these new firms was Charles Schwab & Co.

In March 1982, BankAmerica Corp., a large bank holding company, sought Federal Reserve Board approval to acquire Schwab as a holding company affiliate.  The Board approved the application the following year, and the Securities Industry Associate (SIA) challenged the Board's action as a violation of both the Bank Holding Company Act and the Glass-Steagall Act.  In Securities Industry Association  v. Board of Governors, 468 U.S. 207 (1984) ("Schwab"), the Supreme Court unanimously upheld the Board's order. In discussing the challenge under the Bank Holding Company Act, the Court wrote:

> Relying on record evidence and its own banking expertise, the Board articulated the ways in which the brokerage activities provided by Schwab were similar to banking. The Board found that banks currently offer, as an accommodation to their customers, brokerage services that are virtually identical to the services offered by Schwab. Moreover, the Board cited a 1977 study by the Securities and Exchange Commission that found that
>
>> "bank trust department trading desks, at least at the largest banks, perform the same functions, utilize the same execution techniques, employ personnel with the same general training and expertise, and use the same facilities ... that brokers do."
>
> [T]he Board concluded that the use by banks of "sophisticated techniques and resources" to execute purchase and sell orders for the account of their customers was sufficiently widespread to justify a finding that banks generally are equipped to offer the type of retail brokerage services provided by Schwab. On the basis of these findings, the Board held that a securities brokerage business that is "essentially confined to the purchase and sale of securities for the account of third parties, and without the provision of investment advice to the purchaser or seller" is "closely related" to banking . . .

Id. at 211-12.  Continuing its discussion of the closely-related test, the Court found support for the Board's decision in the limitations on the prohibitions that the Glass-Steagall Act imposes directly on banks:

> Banks long have arranged the purchase and sale of securities as an accommodation to their customers. Congress expressly endorsed this traditional banking service in 1933. Section 16 of the Glass-Steagall Act authorizes banks to continue the practice of "purchasing and selling ... securities and stock without recourse, solely upon the order, and for the account of, customers, and in no case for [their] own account[s]." . . . [T]he brokerage services that

Schwab performs for its customers are not significantly different from those that banks, under the authority of § 16, have been performing for their own customers for years. [The Board's decision here] expressly limits the securities brokerage services in which a bank may engage "to buying and selling securities solely as agent for the account of customers" and does not authorize "securities underwriting or dealing or investment advice or research services."

Id. at 215.

The Court then addressed the provision of the Glass-Steagall Act that was directly applicable to the transaction in question: section 20, which prohibits member banks from affiliating with firms "engaged principally in the issue, flotation, underwriting, public sale, or distribution at wholesale or retail or through syndicate participation of stocks, bonds, debentures, notes, or other securities "

SIA concedes that Schwab is not engaged in the "issue, flotation, underwriting, ... or distribution" of securities. It argues, however, that the term "public sale" of securities as used in § 20 applies to Schwab's brokerage business. . . .

"Public sale" is used in conjunction with the terms "issue," "flotation," "underwriting," and "distribution" of securities. None of these terms has any relevance to the brokerage business at issue in this case. Schwab does not engage in issuing or floating the sale of securities, and the terms "underwriting" and "distribution" traditionally apply to a function distinctly different from that of a securities broker.  An underwriter normally acts as principal whereas a broker executes orders for the purchase or sale of securities solely as agent. Under the "familiar principle of statutory construction that words grouped in a list should be given related meaning," . . . , the term "public sale" in § 20 should be read to refer to the underwriting activity described by the terms that surround it, and to exclude the type of retail brokerage business in which Schwab principally is engaged.

Id. at 217-18. Upon completion of its interpretation of the statutory language of section 20, the Court continued as follows:

Congressional concern over the underwriting activities of bank affiliates included both the fear that bank funds would be lost in speculative investments and the suspicion that the more "subtle hazards" associated with underwriting would encourage unsound banking practices. None of the more "subtle hazards" of underwriting identified in Camp is implicated by the brokerage activities at issue here. Because Schwab trades only as agent, its assets are not subject to the vagaries of the securities markets. Moreover, Schwab's profits depend solely on the volume of shares it trades and not on the purchase or sale of particular securities. Thus, BankAmerica has no "salesman's stake" in the securities Schwab trades. It cannot increase Schwab's profitability by having its bank affiliate extend credit to issuers of particular securities, nor by encouraging the bank affiliate improperly to favor particular securities in the management of depositors' assets. Finally, the fact that § 16 of the Glass-Steagall Act allows banks to engage directly in the kind of brokerage services at issue here, to accommodate its customers, suggests that the activity was not the sort that concerned Congress in its effort to secure the Nation's banks from the risks of the securities market.

Id. at 215.

The Supreme Court's *Schwab* decision opened the doors for banks to establish discount brokerage operations in either holding company affiliates (as BankAmerica had done) or as operating units with banks themselves. When banking organizations chose to pursue the latter course, an important and distinct legal question arose: Would the SEC have jurisdiction to regulate brokerage activities located within banks? That question is addressed in the following case:

## American Bankers Association v. Securities and Exchange Commission
### 804 F.2d 739 (D.C. Cir. 1986)

WALD, Chief Judge:

This appeal involves the single critical question of whether the Securities and Exchange Commission (SEC) has authority under the Securities Exchange Act of 1934 (1934 Act) to regulate banks as "broker-dealers." After instituting notice and comment rulemaking procedures, the SEC adopted Rule 3b-9 which requires banks engaging in the securities brokerage business for profit to register as broker-dealers under the 1934 Act. . . .

In this action, the American Bankers Association (ABA) seeks a declaratory judgment that Rule 3b-9 is invalid under the 1934 Act and an injunction prohibiting the SEC from enforcing the Rule against its member banks. . . .

### I. BACKGROUND OF THE SEC'S DECISION TO REGULATE BANKS

The current controversy arises over fifty years after Congress passed the Securities Exchange Act because of a change in the administrative interpretation of the Banking Act of 1933, commonly referred to as the Glass-Steagall Act. . . .

In 1936, the Comptroller construed the Glass-Steagall Act to limit brokerage activities by national banks to purchase and sale transactions for "actual customers of the bank, which customer relationship exists independently and apart from the particular transaction in which the bank buys or sells upon the order and for the account of such 'customer.'" 1 Bulletin of the Comptroller of the Currency para. 36 (October 26, 1936). The Comptroller also ruled that a national bank "is not authorized to retain any commission, rebate, or discount obtained from others in purchasing for a customer [securities or stock] unless it does not exceed the cost of handling the transaction." Id. para. 10. The Comptroller justified limiting the charge for brokering a customer's securities or stock on the grounds that the purpose of § 16 of the Glass-Steagall Act was "to prevent national banks from engaging in the brokerage business for profit." Id. Thus, under the Comptroller's original interpretation of the Glass-Steagall Act, a national bank could engage in brokerage activities only as "an accommodation agent" for the convenience of existing customers of the bank's traditional banking services. Id. para. 35. For example, a bank could purchase or sell securities for a trust account that it managed, but it could not make any money on its trades for that account.

This original administrative construction of the Glass-Steagall Act has been dismantled piecemeal over the last fifty years. First, in 1957, the Comptroller repudiated the requirement that national banks receive no profit from the brokerage transactions that they perform for the convenience of their customers. See Digest of Opinions of the Comptroller of the Currency para. 220A (August 1957 Edition) (quoted in [1973-1978 Transfer Binder]Fed. Banking L. Rep. (CCH) P96,272 at 81,357). Nevertheless, at that time, the Comptroller retained the notion that banks could not perform "functions [that] would amount to engaging in the brokerage . . . business . . . beyond the permissible scope of limited accommodation services." Id. Moreover, the Comptroller in 1957 explicitly reiterated its earlier requirement that bank brokerage services "must be limited to actual customers of the bank -- that is, the customer relationship must exist independently of the particular securities transaction." Id.

Then, in 1974, the Comptroller interpreted Glass-Steagall to allow banks to offer and advertise computer-assisted stock purchasing services. . . . Answering the argument that these services, and in particular, dissemination of advertising about them, controverted the concept of "limited accommodation services," the Comptroller noted that "the 'accommodation' concept is not contained in the statute." Id. at 81,360. Because, however, the automatic investment service was limited to customers of the bank's checking accounts, the Comptroller did not explicitly address whether bank could offer and advertise brokerage services for nonbanking customers.

Finally, in 1982, the Comptroller abandoned its interpretation that § 16 of the Glass-Steagall Act limited bank brokerage activities to customers of traditional banking services by allowing a national bank to establish a subsidiary to offer retail discount brokerage services, to banking and nonbanking customers alike, at branch offices of the bank. . . . The Comptroller has subsequently made clear that its new interpretation of § 16 applies to the brokerage activities of a bank itself in addition to those of a bank subsidiary. . . .

The SEC never attempted to apply its broker-dealer regulations to banks that engaged in profitless accommodation transactions. Nor did the SEC attempt to regulate banks as broker-dealers after either the 1957 or the 1974 revisions in the Comptroller's interpretation. The dramatic surge of banks into the discount brokerage business, resulting from the post-1980 administrative reinterpretations of Glass-Steagall, however, prompted the SEC to subject banks engaging in brokerage business to the same broker-dealer regulation as nonbank brokers.[6]

Thus, in 1985, the SEC issued Rule 3b-9. The Rule regulates as a broker-dealer a bank that either "publicly solicits brokerage business for which it receives transaction-related compensation" or "receives transaction-related compensation for providing brokerage services for trust, managing agency or other accounts to which the bank provides advice." 17 C.F.R. § 240.3b-9(a)(1)(2) (1986). The Rule goes on to define "transaction-related compensation" to "mean monetary profit to the bank in excess of cost recovery for providing brokerage execution services." Id. § 240.3b-9(d). In other words, the SEC Rule does not reach banks which engage only in the profitless accommodation brokerage service permitted by the Comptroller's original

---

[6]    In 1977 (after the Comptroller's 1974 reinterpretation but before the 1980s reinterpretations), the SEC knew of only a single bank that engaged in profit-seeking, nonaccommodation brokerage business comparable to nonbank brokers. See Reports on Bank Securities Activities of the Securities and Exchange Commission for the Senate Comm. on Banking, Housing, and Urban Affairs, 95th Cong., 1st Sess. 86, 97-98 (Comm. Print 1977). In contrast, by December 1983 the ABA itself stated that there were as many as 1,000 banks engaging in discount retail brokerage services and that the number was growing rapidly. Administrative Record at 41.

1936 ruling. But it does cover banks that seek profit from their brokerage business, whether that business was generated from public solicitation or from their existing banking customers.[7]

Rule 3b-9 proceeds on the premise that regulatory authority should be divided among government agencies according to the different financial functions performed by the regulated entity, and not according to the species of financial institution it is (as defined by its charter or even its *primary* function). While this regulatory philosophy enjoys favor in many circles and has received the endorsement of a special task force established to conduct a comprehensive evaluation of federal financial regulation,[8] it is, unfortunately, not the approach taken by the 73rd Congress, which enacted the Securities Exchange Act of 1934. . . .

## II. THE 1934 ACT DEFINITIONS OF "BROKER," "DEALER," AND "BANK"

### A. The Statutory Language

Section 3 of the 1934 Act excludes banks from the statutory definitions of "broker" and "dealer." The Act states that "the term 'broker ' means any person engaging in the business of effecting transactions in securities for the account of others, *but does not include a bank*." Section 3(a)(4) of the 1934 Act (emphasis supplied). Similarly, the statute states that "the term 'dealer' means any person engaged in the business of buying or selling securities for his own account . . . *but does not include a bank* . . . ." Section 3(a)(5) of the 1934 Act (emphasis supplied).

In order to subject banks engaging in profit-seeking brokerage business to broker-dealer regulation, the SEC had to draft Rule 3b-9 to redefine the term "bank." It did so by excluding banks engaging in brokerage business for profit from the meaning of "bank" in §§ 3(a)(4) and (5) of the 1934 Act, thus recapturing such banks into the statutory definition of "broker" and "dealer." Thus Rule 3b-9 reads, in relevant part:

---

[7]   In addition to requiring banks to register with the SEC as broker-dealers, Rule 3b-9 would subject banks to additional specific regulations. First, under current SEC rules, persons associated with broker-dealers must pass SEC examinations before they can sell securities or become involved in the management of a securities firm. See 50 Fed. Reg. 28,385, 28,387. Second, the 1934 Exchange Act itself imposes on broker-dealers an affirmative duty to adequately supervise its employees in order to prevent violations of federal securities laws. Id. at 28,388. Third, the SEC has adopted rules prohibiting broker-dealers from engaging in abusive sales practices, such as "churning" customer accounts in order to increase brokerage commissions. Id. at 28,388, 28,390. Fourth, broker-dealers must comply with specific guidelines concerning the content and review of advertisements. Id. at 28,388. Fifth, the SEC administers periodic examinations and inspections of broker-dealers as part of its supervisory authority to ensure compliance with the securities laws. Id. Sixth, brokers are required by statute to become members of the Securities Investor Protection Corporation, an entity with potentially conflicting authority with the Federal Deposit Insurance Corporation which now regulates banks. See Appellant's Brief at 37-38; Administrative Record at 521-22. Finally, the SEC sets capital requirements for broker-dealers, which allegedly could conflict with the capital requirements set for banks by appropriate banking regulators. See Appellees' Brief at 61 n.76.

[8]   See Blue Print for Reform: Report of the Task Group on Regulation of Financial Services 39-41 (1984) ("The Bush Report") (recommending a "mix of institutional and functional regulatory programs").

The term "bank" as used in the definition of "broker" and "dealer" in sections 3(a)(4) and (5) of the Act does not include a bank that: (1) Publicly solicits brokerage business for which it receives a transaction-related compensation . . .; (2) Directly or indirectly receives transaction-related compensation for providing brokerage services for trust, managing agency, or other accounts to which the bank provides advice . . . .

17 C.F.R. § 240.3b-9(a)(1)-(2) (1986).[9]

A crucial problem with the SEC's new rule defining "bank," however, is that the 1934 Act already contains a definition of the term "bank." Indeed, the Act's definition of "bank" immediately follows its definitions of "broker" and "dealer."

The term "bank" means (A) a banking institution organized under the laws of the United States, (B) a member bank of the Federal Reserve System, (C) any other banking institution, whether incorporated or not, doing business under the laws of any State or of the United States, a substantial portion of the business of which consists of receiving deposits or exercising fiduciary powers similar to those permitted to national banks under section 11(k) of the Federal Reserve Act, as amended, and which is supervised and examined by State or Federal authority having supervision over banks and which is not operated for the purpose of evading the provisions of this chapter . . . .

Section 3(a)(6). This definition notably does not contain any exception for a bank that "publicly solicits brokerage business for which it receives transaction-related compensation" or that "directly or indirectly receives transaction-related compensation for providing brokerage service for . . . accounts to which the bank provides advice." In sum, the statutory definition of bank contains no exception for banks engaging in brokerage activities for profit; there is no ambiguity or imprecision on this point. As far as the statutory definition of bank is concerned, then, Rule 3b-9 directly conflicts with the language of the 1934 Act.

## B. Congressional Intent

The manner in which Congress defined "broker," "dealer," and "bank" in the 1934 Act reflects a purposeful decision on its part that the SEC should not have oversight jurisdiction with respect to banks, because banks were already subject to a complex scheme of administrative regulation at the federal and state level. In the 1934 Act, Congress defined "bank" essentially as an institution subject to at least one of several existing banking regulators: the federal Comptroller of the Currency (for all nationally chartered banks), the Board of Governors of the Federal Reserve System (for all member banks), or any other "State or Federal authority having

---

[9]    Rule 3b-9 exempts a bank that publicly solicits brokerage business from broker-dealer regulation if the bank itself does not perform the brokerage services but instead contracts with a registered broker-dealer to perform the brokerage services. Similarly, a bank receiving commissions for brokerage services for its trust accounts need not register as a broker-dealer if "the bank executes the transactions through a registered broker-dealer and . . . each account independently chooses the broker-dealer through which execution is effected." 17 C.F.R. § 240.3b-9(a)(2)(i) (1986). Rule 3b-9, however, also requires a bank to register with the SEC as a broker-dealer if it "deals in . . . securities," id. § 240.3b-9(a)(3), even though § 16 of the Glass-Steagall Act provides that a national bank "may purchase for its own account investment securities under such limitations and restrictions as the Comptroller of the Currency may by regulation prescribe." 12 U.S.C. § 24 (Seventh). Rule 3b-9 also exempts from SEC broker-dealer regulation a bank that effects each year no more than 1,000 transactions of the type that would bring the bank within the Rule. Id. § 240.3b-9(b)(2).

supervision over banks." Thus, the exemption from SEC broker-dealer regulation is available only to banking institutions regulated by some other government authority.

### 1. Evidence of Congress' Intent Not to Impose Additional Government Supervision Upon Banks

Relevant legislative history confirms that Congress intended to preclude SEC regulation of institutions meeting the statutory definition of "bank" in order to avoid duplicative regulation. The Senate Committee Report accompanying S. 3420 stated that most of the definitions in the bill were "self-explanatory." S. Rep. No. 792, 73d Cong., 2d Sess. 14 (1934). Nevertheless, the Report did comment on the definitions of "broker," and "dealer," definitions the Committee considered to be "the most important . . . since many of the provisions of the act apply only to members of exchanges and brokers and dealers who do business through them." Id. Expressly recognizing, then, that institutions excluded from the definitions of "broker" and "dealer" would not be subject to many of the Act's important regulatory provisions, the Report unambiguously stated that "banks are expressly exempted from the definitions of 'broker' and 'dealer.'" Id. Finally, in summarizing the definition of "bank," the Report highlights its critical essence as including "any . . . bank performing normal banking functions, which is subject to supervision and examination by State and Federal authorities." Id. The necessary implication of the Senate Report was that any bank already subject to administrative oversight need not be subjected to the new regulatory regime that the bill established for nonbank brokers and dealers.

In 1934, nonbank stockbrokers and securities traders, unlike banks, were not subject to any nationwide, systematic regulation or oversight by federal or state government authorities. The purpose of the 1934 Act was to bring *these* previously unregulated participants in financial markets under a regime of government supervision and examination analogous to that which the Glass-Steagall Act had already mandated for banks. Indeed, one purpose of the 1934 Act's regulation of securities exchanges and broker-dealers was to protect America's banking system.[14] Pre-1929 overextended margin accounts and unwise extensions of credit to brokers by banks had contributed to bank failures: financially precarious banks often could not collect on the loans made to brokers for margin purchases by the brokers' customers.[15] As a result, some of the 1934

---

[14]   Among the reasons for legislation enumerated in § 2 of the Securities Exchange Act, Congress specifically cited the need "to protect and make more effective the national banking system and the Federal Reserve System."

[15]   The Senate Report states in detail:

> The evidence submitted to the committee by experts on the staff of the Federal Reserve Board has indicated that uncontrolled speculation on security markets was an important cause of the credit inflation which led to the collapse of 1929 and the subsequent depression.  Banks diverted their credit from agriculture, commerce and industry to the stock market, where it contributed to the over-expansion of big enterprises, largely engaged in interstate commerce. Corporations took advantage of the abnormal demand for securities by raising new capital, which was not necessary for plant expansion, but which they loaned in the call-money market, thus encouraging further speculation.  When the crash finally came, brokers' loans were called, causing greater depreciation in the value of securities, including those held in bank portfolios. This contributed largely to the widespread bank failures, which imperiled the national banking structure. . . .

Act's most significant provisions regulate margin lending by brokers and control the credit that brokers can receive from banks. . . . Because these banking-related provisions implicated the stability of the banking system, the 1934 Act entrusted the Board of Governors of the Federal Reserve System with their administration. Although Congress decided to delegate the supervision and examination of exchanges and broker-dealers to a new agency, there is no indication that in 1934 Congress wanted this new agency, created for a particular specialization, to regulate the banks.[16]

To the contrary, there is much evidence in the Act's legislative history that Congress decided to exempt banks from the broker-dealer jurisdiction of the SEC because they were already subject to systematic government oversight. The original House and Senate bills did not expressly exclude banks from the definitions of "broker" and "dealer." At the hearings, a prominent New York banker, William Potter, Chairman of the Guaranty Trust Company, complained before the Senate Committee on Banking and Currency that the definitions of "broker" and "dealer," as they then stood, would cover some securities services already being performed by banks:

> Banks of this country do not confine their activities solely to banking. . . . A very large proportion of the people of this country turn to their bankers for advice with respect to their investments and the purchase and sale of securities.
>
> Furthermore, banks are called upon constantly to act as the agent of others in the care and custody of securities, the placing of orders for their purchase and sale and in the completion of such transactions, including the receipt or delivery of securities against payment or receipt of the purchase price, and in the safe transmittal of such securities. Many people are utterly unfamiliar with the manner in which such transactions should be carried on . . . and turn to the bankers in recognition of their experience and expertise in such matters. . . .

Stock Exchange Practices: Hearings Before the Senate Comm. on Banking and Currency, Part 15, 73d Cong., 1st Sess. 7222 (1934) [hereinafter cited as "Senate Hearings"]. After describing how banks engaged in activities that fit the then definitions of "broker" and "dealer," Potter went on to advocate that banks should nevertheless not be subjected to the new regulation proposed for nonbank brokers and dealers:

> Permit me to indulge in a further general observation. It seems to me that the regulation of the banks, so far as the National Government is concerned, should be confined to the Comptroller of the Currency, the Federal Reserve Board, and other agencies within the Federal Reserve System. I doubt the wisdom of divided responsibility with respect to such matters, and it seems to me obvious that

---

S. Rep. No. 792, 73d Cong., 2d Sess. 3 (1934).

[16]    Congress considered two alternatives before it decided to create the SEC. One plan was to have all the provisions of the statute administered by the Board of Governors. 78 Cong. Rec. 8162 (1934). The other proposal was that the Board of Governors should administer only those provisions affecting banks and banking, and that the Federal Trade Commission should administer the exchanges and broker-dealers. Id. Congress rejected these alternatives because it did not want existing agencies directly involved with the oversight of exchanges and broker-dealers. Congress wanted a new commission to handle this specialty, but Congress also limited the new commission to this specialty; Congress did not intend the new commission to involve itself with the Federal Reserve System. See id. at 8161-63.

the banks should not be subjected to the jurisdiction of two arms of the Government whose purposes and policies might at times conflict.

Id. Potter then specifically recommended that the bill be amended to exclude banks from the definition of "broker" and "dealer": "I submit that these definitions should be changed, or that some specific statement should be made that banks are not included in such definition." Id.

At this point Ferdinand Pecora, the counsel to the Senate Committee and a draftsman of the 1934 Act, interrupted to say that he agreed that the bill should not include banks within the definitions of "broker" and "dealer." Id. When the bill was reported out of the Senate Committee, it contained the new clauses excluding banks from the "broker" and "dealer" definitions, as well as a definition of "bank." The House version, ultimately enacted into law, was similarly amended in Committee to exclude banks from the definition of "broker" and "dealer" and to add a definition of "bank." . . . .

Since the 1934 Act, Congress has repeatedly exempted banks from the jurisdiction of the SEC, and defined banks in precisely the same way. In 1940, when Congress enacted the Investment Company and Investment Advisers Acts, Congress repeated the same bank exemption from the definitions of "broker" and "dealer," and also from the crucial definitions of "investment company" and "investment adviser" in these Acts. . . . . Moreover, in these Acts, Congress again defined banks in terms of the government agencies that regulated them. . . . Thus, the definitions in the 1934 Act are but one part of a consistent congressional policy of keeping oversight of the banking system separate from the SEC's oversight of the securities trading and investment industries.

2. The Special Problem Posed by the Changing Interpretation of the Glass-Steagall Act

The SEC contends that when Congress exempted banks from SEC broker-dealer regulation in 1934, it was acting under the impression that the Glass-Steagall Act of 1933 precluded banks from brokering securities for a profit or for nonbanking customers. As evidence of this congressional understanding, the SEC points to the testimony of Thomas Corcoran before both the House and Senate Committees that considered the legislation. Corcoran, at the time, was counsel to the Reconstruction Finance Corporation, and an active participant in the drafting of the 1934 Act. Corcoran, too, argued vigorously that the original bill should be amended to exempt banks from broker-dealer regulation. In making his point to the Senate Committee, Corcoran referred extensively to his reading of the Glass-Steagall Act as barring retail brokerage activities by banks:

Of course under the Glass-Steagall bill a bank can no longer peddle securities at retail. It can do two things: it can buy securities for its own account, for its own investment; and it can act as agent to transmit to a broker an order to purchase or sell securities, given to it by one of the bank's customers.

Certainly we had no conception when we drafted the language of this bill that it would be said that if a bank bought securities for its bond account, or merely transmitted, for a service charge, an order from a customer to a broker (because very often customers of banks do not know whom to go to for brokerage service), that operations of that kind on the part of a bank constituted transacting a business in securities.

And I might say that if there is any difficulty with that language, or any conception that it does cover a bank, acting as banks may act under the Glass-Steagall Act, then the language should be changed so that banks so acting are not within the scope of the language. . . .

Senate Hearings, supra, at 6470.

Similarly, in his testimony before the House Committee, Corcoran pleaded, "the bill needs to be clarified, so that a bank which just acts for you in passing on an order to a broker . . . does not come within that sort of provision," referring specifically to the bill's restrictions on borrowing by brokers. Stock Exchange Regulation: Hearings on H.R. 7852 and H.R. 8270 Before the House Comm. on Interstate and Foreign Commerce, 73d Cong., 2d Sess. 86 (1934). When asked by Representative Edward Kenney why banks should be exempted from these control-of-credit provisions, Corcoran responded: "Because there are plenty of other limitations on the banks. A bank cannot normally go in the business, like a broker, of dealing in securities." When the Congressman interrupted to protest that banks do act like a broker, Corcoran answered, "They are not allowed to do those things any longer, under the Glass-Steagall bill." Id. Pressing Corcoran again on exactly what business banks were excluded from, the Congressman was sidestepped: "You may be able to answer that better than I can," said Corcoran. Id.

The SEC uses the Corcoran testimony to make the following argument: Congress, in enacting the 1934 Act, adopted Corcoran's understanding that the Glass-Steagall Act precluded banks from engaging in brokerage activities for nonbanking customers. If it turns out that the Glass-Steagall Act in fact does not preclude these activities, then it follows that the SEC must be allowed to advance congressional intent by regulating these new retail brokerage activities of banks. It is not an illogical argument, but it does raise basic issues about the role of courts in construing legislation.

Initially, we emphasize that we do not and need not rule today whether, in fact, the Glass-Steagall Act permits a bank, as opposed to a nonbanking subsidiary of a bank or a bank holding company, to engage in discount brokerage services for members of the general public who do not use the bank's banking services . . . .

We will assume that Corcoran was incorrect in telling the 1934 Congress that the Glass-Steagall Act precluded banks from acting like other brokers. It still does not necessarily follow that we should attribute Corcoran's erroneous belief to Congress. A court must assure itself of strong evidence of congressional misapprehension before it goes on to decide what Congress would have done, if Congress had known the "truth." Indeed, there is a legitimate question whether a court should ever engage in such surrogate behavior. Here, the conclusion that Congress misinterpreted its own statute, enacted only a year before, in a crucial jurisdictional matter, requires a stronger evidentiary base than the SEC has offered. The end of the exchange between Corcoran and Representative Kenney suggests that Corcoran himself may have been less than totally sure about the effect of Glass-Steagall, since even he ultimately deferred to the legislators' greater familiarity with Glass-Steagall's scope. Corcoran's testimony as a whole may also reasonably be read as an advocate's argument that however Glass-Steagall limits banks, they should be exempted from the definitions of "broker" and "dealer." This interpretation of Corcoran's testimony would line up with the earlier recounted dialogue between Pecora, the Senate Committee counsel, and Potter, the New York banker, see supra, as further evidence that

Congress' primary reason for exempting banks from SEC broker-dealer regulation was that banks were already extensively regulated by other federal and state agencies.

The SEC, however, calls our attention to the fact that Corcoran's interpretation of the Glass-Steagall Act as precluding profit brokerage echoed that of the then Comptroller of the Currency, an official enforcer of the Act. Actually the Comptroller's first official interpretation of the Glass-Steagall Act did not occur until after Congress passed the 1934 Exchange Act. But even if we credit the SEC's argument that it corroborates some common understanding among significant outside participants in the process that the Act limited banks to accommodation brokerage transactions, we are still hesitant to conclude without more direct evidence from congressional sources themselves, i.e., reports or member statements, that Congress itself not only misunderstood the thrust of its own Glass-Steagall offspring, but proceeded to enact further legislation based primarily on that misconception.

Finally, even if we did accept the SEC's assumption that Congress, when enacting the Securities Exchange Act in 1934, acted on an erroneous premise that Glass-Steagall precluded retail bank brokerage activities, SEC's Rule 3b-9 still could not stand. Yet another assumption is essential to its validity: that if Congress had only known how the Comptroller and the courts were going to interpret the Glass-Steagall Act, Congress would not have exempted banks from the SEC's broker-dealer regulation. There is absolutely no evidence in the legislative history supporting (or negating) this assumption. It is entirely possible -- though admittedly speculative -- that had Congress anticipated a more liberal interpretation of the Glass-Steagall Act, it would still have decided to leave banks in the hands of bank regulators alone, so as not to subject banks to the double-whammy of additional federal oversight. The contrary prediction may be just as plausible -- and just as speculative. It comes down to this: It is not the job of courts to play the game of "what if" in predicting congressional reactions to hypothetical circumstances. Absent an express delegation to the SEC to take account of future changes in banking practices and/or banking regulatory activities, we must give effect to the unambiguous language of the statute itself. . . . Our review of the legislative history of the 1934 Act does reveal some ambiguities in it -- but these ambiguities cannot serve to erode the unambiguous language of the Act. There is no clear congressional intent to direct otherwise. . . . .

## CONCLUSION

. . . Rule 3b-9, whatever its beneficial purpose or the regulatory need for some such authority, . . . represents an attempt by one federal agency to reallocate, on its own initiative, the regulatory responsibilities Congress has purposefully divided among several different agencies. It is tantamount to one of the regulatory players unilaterally changing the rules of the game. The SEC by itself cannot extend its jurisdiction over institutions expressly entrusted to the oversight of the Comptroller, the Board of Governors, the FDIC, and others.

Given the dramatic changes in the nature of financial institutions and market practices in the last fifty years, Congress might do well to undertake a comprehensive reexamination of the Glass-Steagall Act and the Securities Acts. Indeed, it might well determine from such a reexamination that banks should be allowed to engage in brokerage business like any other broker, but that banks should be regulated by the SEC like any other broker. Until that day, however, the SEC operates under the limited authority of the 1934 Act and must refrain from regulating banks as broker-dealers. The judgment of the District Court is reversed.

## Questions and Comments

1. The *ABA v. SEC* case presented a classic confrontation between two regulatory philosophies: functional regulation and entity regulation. Under functional regulation, championed in this case by the SEC, the same regulatory authority supervises an activity no matter what kind of legal entity engages in the activity. Under entity regulation, the legal status of the entity offering the service determines which agency will provide supervisory oversight. Consider, for a moment, the relative advantages of each approach. On the one hand, functional regulation assures a consumer the same supervisory protections wherever the consumer chooses to obtain a financial service. On the other hand, functional regulation requires legal entities to operate under the requirements of two or more regulatory agencies. Supervisory requirements may be redundant and potentially even contradictory. Entity regulation has the advantage of allowing entities to work under fewer different regulatory authorities, but may force regulatory agencies to oversee activities they do not fully understand.

2. In the case of bank securities activities of the sort the rule 3b-9 was designed to reach, the federal banking agencies eventually developed guidelines for banks offering brokerage services. See, e.g., Interagency Statement on Retail Sales of Nondeposit Investment Products (Feb. 15, 1994). Are ad hoc accommodations of this sort likely to be inferior to the SEC's more established regulatory systems that we studied in Chapter Ten? Or is it useful for the SEC to have a regulatory competitor in the field of securities regulation? Would it make more sense to apply SEC regulatory standards to banks that engage in securities activities, but to leave enforcement in the hands of traditional bank regulators?

2. At roughly the same time as the ABA v. SEC case was being litigated, a separate question arose over where a national bank could conduct discount brokerage operations. Were national banks limited by the McFadden Act's restrictions on branching — that is, governed by state branching rules — or could a national bank establish offices offering discount brokerage services without regard to local limitations on branching? See sections 36 & 81 of the National Bank Act. See also Clarke v. Securities Industry Association, 479 U.S. 388 (1987).

### Problem 15-1

Congress has, from time to time, considered whether to amend the 1934 Act to grant the SEC jurisdiction over the securities activities of banks. Assume that you are a member of a congressional committee charged with fashioning such an amendment. How would you advise the committee to address the following issues:

a. Should SEC jurisdiction extend to banks that engage in only a *de minimis* amount of securities activities each year? Or should the Commission use the same standard in determining when a bank becomes a broker or dealer that it uses when it considers whether any other entity constitutes a broker or dealer? If banks are to be granted some sort of *de minimis* exception, how should that exception be structured? Fewer than 100 transactions per year? No more than a dozen customers? A dollar limit?

b. Should there be an exemption to deal with bank trust activities? As discussed in Justice Blackmun's dissent in the *Camp* case, bank trust departments routinely invest trust assets in various kinds of securities, including pooled investment vehicles for small accounts? Should these activities be exempt from SEC regulation?

c. Various other activities conducted by banks might also be characterized as securities activities. Consider, for example, a bank that routinely sells loan participations to other investors. What about banks that deal in interest rate and foreign currency swaps?

d. How should the amendment deal with financial products developed in the future? What if bank regulators and the SEC disagree over whether a new product constitutes a security? How should such disagreements be resolved?

e. Assuming some banks become subject to SEC broker-dealer regulation, should any special accommodations be made in the application of these regulations in the context of banks? In particular, how should the SEC's net capital rules apply to banks? See Chapter Ten, Section 4. What modifications, if any, should be made to the SEC's disclosure rules in light of the confidentiality that has traditionally surrounded bank examination procedures? Should, for example, banks engaged in securities activities be required to disclose what would otherwise be confidential information about pending enforcement actions by bank regulators? Should the SEC be required to take into account traditional concerns about the solvency of banks?

f. To the extent you find conflicts between bank and broker-dealer regulation to be substantial, would it make more sense to require banking organizations to locate their securities activities in separate corporate entities that can be regulated the same way as other broker-dealers? Should all bank securities activities be pushed out in this manner or only those activities that surpass some threshold? What threshold?

---

Another important arena of competition between commercial banks and securities firms has been the market for commercial paper — high-quality short-term notes traditionally sold by only a relatively small number of the country's largest and most reputable firms. As the following excerpt reveals, the structure of the commercial paper market began to change in the 1970s:

Many large, financially sound nonfinancial corporations have relied primarily on the commercial paper market for short-term funds during the prolonged business expansion of the late 1970's. This important new development in short-term corporate finance has occurred largely at the expense of the money-center banks in New York and other major financial centers. According to our analysis, this development stems from the unavoidably higher costs of bank as compared to paper-market credit, as well as the relatively low value of the intermediation "services" which banks can provide to potential commercial-paper borrowers.

Thus, the observed trend represents an improvement in the efficiency of the U.S. financial system. . . .

This development has several important policy implications. Commercial-paper issuers almost always include the most financially sound firms in the economy, and their reduced use of bank loans thus implies greater riskiness of bank-loan portfolios. The probable permanence of this phenomenon should interest bank regulators in setting capital-adequacy standards. . . . [T]he switch to commercial paper by many prime-rated bank loan customers reinforces the postwar trend toward greater bank exposure to financial-market risk caused by the decline in capital cushions and holdings of low-risk financial investments.

John P. Judd, *Competition Between the Commercial Paper Market and Commercial Banks*, Economic Review, Federal Reserve Bank of San Francisco, Winter 1978, at 39.

In response to this trend, the banking industry sought to win back lost business by entering the commercial paper market as underwriters. For many years, national bank had been allowed to purchase commercial paper as investment securities for their own account, and, industry representatives argued, the Glass-Steagall Act should not preclude them from underwriting the sale of those instruments to other investors. The Federal Reserve Board accepted this argument, reasoning that commercial paper more closely resembles a commercial loan than an investment transaction and is not, therefore, a security for purposes of the Glass-Steagall Act. The securities industry challenged this interpretation, and ultimately the Supreme Court resolved the question by rejecting the Board's analysis:

"The authority to discount [that is, purchase] commercial paper is very different from the authority to underwrite it. The former places banks in their traditional role as a prudent lender. The latter places a commercial bank in the role of an investment banker, which is precisely what Congress ought to prohibit in the [Glass Steagall] Act. . . .

"The fact that commercial banks properly are free to acquire commercial paper for their own account implies not that commercial paper is not a "security," but simply that the process of extending credit by "discounting" commercial paper is not part of the "business of dealing" in securities."

See Securities Industry Association v. Board of Governors, 460 U.S. 137, 158 & n.11 (1984) ("Bankers Trust I"). Faced with a loss in the country's highest court, the banking industry and the Federal Reserve Board were left to seek other avenues for bank entrance into the commercial paper market.

# Securities Industry Association v. Board of Governors ("Bankers Trust II")
807 F.2d 1052 (D.C. Cir. 1986), *cert. denied,* 483 U.S. 1005 (1987)

BORK, Circuit Judge:

I.

"Commercial paper" comprises unsecured, large denomination promissory notes written with maturities of less than nine months to supply the current capital needs of corporate issuers. In privately negotiated transactions, issuers typically place commercial paper with large, financially sophisticated institutional investors (such as insurance companies or pension funds).

Bankers Trust acts as an advisor and agent to commercial paper issuers by advising each issuer of the interest rates and maturities that institutional investors are likely to accept, by soliciting prospective purchasers for commercial paper the client decides to issue, and by placing the issue with the purchasers. Bankers Trust does not make any general advertisement or solicitation regarding any issue it is seeking to place, and does not place any issues with individuals or the general public.

Bankers Trust receives a commission for its services based upon a percentage of the issuer's total outstanding commercial paper during a one-year period. To ensure that it acts solely as an agent without an independent financial stake in the success of issues it places, which would clearly involve it in investment banking, Bankers Trust does not purchase or repurchase for its own account, inventory overnight, or take any ownership interest in any commercial paper it places. Nor does Bankers Trust any longer make loans on or collateralize loans with the paper it places (a practice it formerly followed when necessary to remedy any deficiency in placement of an issue).

This appeal is the latest installment in a dispute that began in 1979 when the Securities Industry Association ("SIA"), a trade association of underwriters, brokers, and securities dealers, petitioned the Board of Governors for a ruling that it was unlawful for Bankers Trust and other commercial banks to sell commercial paper issued by unrelated entities. The Board ruled against the SIA, but ultimately the Supreme Court, disagreeing with the Board of Governors, held that commercial paper is included within the category of "notes or other securities" addressed by the Banking Act of 1933, commonly known as the Glass-Steagall Act, and remanded the case for a determination of an unresolved issue: whether Bankers Trust's placement of commercial paper constituted the "underwriting" or "business of issuing, underwriting, selling or distributing" that the Act prohibits. Securities Indus. Ass'n v. Board of Governors of the Fed. Reserve Sys., 468 U.S. 137, 160 n. 12 (1984) (*SIA* ).

Upon remand, the Board of Governors found that Bankers Trust's placement of commercial paper constituted the "selling" of a security without recourse and solely upon the order and for the account of customers, a practice permitted by section 16 of the Act, 12 U.S.C. § 24 (Seventh) (1982). Federal Reserve System, Statement Concerning Applicability of the Glass-Steagall Act to the Commercial Paper Activities of Bankers Trust Company (June 4, 1985) ("Board Statement"), Joint Appendix ("J.A.") at 195. The district court reviewed the Board's decision on the petition of the SIA and granted SIA summary judgment, holding that Bankers

Trust's activities involved the "underwriting" and "distributing" prohibited by section 21(a)(1) of the Act, 12 U.S.C. § 378(a)(1) (1982). Securities Indus. Ass'n v. Board of Governors of the Fed. Reserve Sys., 627 F.Supp. 695 (D.D.C.1986). This appeal followed.

## II.

In reviewing the Board's decision, we owe the agency's determination "the greatest deference." Board of Governors of the Fed. Reserve Sys. v. Investment Co. Inst., 450 U.S. 46, 56 (1981) (*ICI* ); *accord* Securities Indus. Ass'n v. Board of Governors of the Fed. Reserve Sys., 468 U.S. 207, 217 (1984) (*Schwab*) (giving Board "substantial deference"); *see also* Board of Governors of the Fed. Reserve Sys. v. Agnew, 329 U.S. 441, 450 (1947) (Rutledge, J., concurring) ("[The Board's] specialized experience gives [it] an advantage judges cannot possibly have, not only in dealing with the problems raised for [its] discretion by the system's working, but also in ascertaining the meaning Congress had in mind in prescribing the standards by which [the Board] should administer it."). This principle is not contradicted by *SIA*, 468 U.S. at 143–44 (according only "little deference"), or Investment Co. Inst. v. Camp, 401 U.S. 617, 626–28 (1971) (*Camp* ) (rejecting a deferential approach).

In the latter cases, the agency involved failed to present the Court with anything to which to defer. In *Camp*, Justice Stewart, writing for the majority, noted that "courts should give great weight to any reasonable construction of a regulatory statute adopted by the agency charged with the enforcement of that statute," 401 U.S. at 626–27, but said the "difficulty" was that the Comptroller of the Currency had promulgated the challenged regulation "without opinion or accompanying statement," *id.* at 627. Without the benefit of any "expressly articulated position at the administrative level," the Court refused to defer to the agency's position, reasoning that "[i]t is the administrative official and not appellate counsel who possesses the expertise that can enlighten and rationalize the search for the meaning and intent of Congress." *Id.* at 628.

In *SIA*, the Board had provided an opinion explaining its view of whether commercial paper constituted "securities" for purposes of the Glass-Steagall Act but failed to analyze the legislative purposes behind the Act. Because of this omission, the Court gave "little deference" to the Board's position that its interpretation ran afoul of none of the purposes of the Act. 468 U.S. at 143–44. The Court at the same time observed generally that because "[t]he Board is the agency responsible for federal regulation of the national banking system, ... its interpretation of a federal banking statute is entitled to substantial deference." *Id.* at 142.

In the present case, as in *ICI* and *Schwab*, the Board has comprehensively addressed the language, history, and purposes of the Act that bear on whether commercial banks should be able to place commercial paper. We consequently owe the Board's determination "substantial deference" or "significant weight," and we must look to *Chevron U.S.A. Inc. v. NRDC*, 467 U.S. 837 (1984), to guide our application of such principles of review. *See Investment Co. Inst. v. Conover*, 790 F.2d 925, 932 (D.C.Cir.1986). Since Congress has not clearly addressed the question of whether activities such as those conducted by Bankers Trust fall within the prohibitions of the Act, we must examine whether the agency, in filling the statutory gap left by Congress, has acted reasonably. *Chevron*, 467 U.S. at 843–45

## III.

The question in this case involves the interplay of sections 16 and 21 of the Glass-Steagall Act. These provisions implement what the Supreme Court has described as the Act's "general purpose of separating as completely as possible commercial from investment banking," *ICI,* 450 U.S. at 70 . . . .

. . . Because no one disputes that Bankers Trust constitutes a commercial bank within the meaning of these sections, we must determine, first, if the Board has reasonably concluded that the commercial paper placement activities of Bankers Trust fall within the permissive language of section 16. To determine this, we must look at the question of what the statute means by "underwrite," for underwriting not only triggers section 21's prohibitions but also defeats section 16's permissive effect. We must, in contrast, address the meaning of section 21's terms "issuing, ... selling, or distributing" only if section 16 is inapplicable. In other words, section 21 cannot be read to prohibit what section 16 permits. *See ICI,* 450 U.S. at 63 (section 21 not intended to bar banking practices permitted by section 16) . . . Therefore, if we find that the Board acted reasonably in concluding that section 16 permits Bankers Trust's activities, that is the end of our analysis. . . .

## IV.

We believe that the Board's determination is reasonable. The Board found that Bankers Trust's activities fell within section 16's requirement that "[t]he business of dealing in securities and stock by the [bank] shall be limited to purchasing and selling such securities and stock without recourse, solely upon the order, and for the account of, customers, and in no case for its own account, and the [bank] shall not underwrite any issue of securities or stock." 12 U.S.C. § 24 (Seventh) (1982). While the district court did not dispute the Board's finding that Bankers Trust's activities "fit neatly within the literal language of section 16's permissive phrase," and relied instead on an analysis of the legislative purposes of the Act to reverse the Board's holding, *see Securities Indus. Ass'n v. Board of Governors,* 627 F.Supp. at 701–02, SIA vigorously disputes on several grounds the conclusion that the bank's activities come within the permissive language of that section. We take up these arguments in turn . . . .

SIA . . . contends that the Board erred in concluding that the activities of Bankers Trust are "upon the order *** of *** customers," claiming that Congress imposed this restriction to make it clear that banks could perform the transactions permitted by section 16 only as an accommodation to the existing customers of the bank. In support of this proposition, SIA relies almost exclusively on the Supreme Court's recent opinion in *Schwab,* in which SIA unsuccessfully challenged a bank holding company's retail brokerage operations under section 20 of the Glass-Steagall Act. . . . In approving the retail brokerage operation, run by a non-bank affiliate of the bank holding company as an accommodation to the affiliate's customers, the Court relied in part on the fact that section 16 "allows banks to engage directly in the kind of [retail] brokerage activities at issue here, to accommodate [their] customers." 468 U.S. at 221. SIA suggests that this statement amounted to an interpretation of section 16 requiring banks to provide securities services under the relevant language only as an accommodation to the bank's preexisting customers. This argument misses the mark. While the Court did state that section 16 permitted retail brokerage as an accommodation to customers of the bank's other services, it specifically left open the question whether such securities brokerage, if more broadly available, would still satisfy that provision. *Id.* at 219 n. 20. Thus, the Court did not, as we must, decide whether section 16 allows the placement of securities only as an accommodation to existing customers of other bank services.

While the meaning of "upon the order *** of *** customers" is decidedly ambiguous, we defer, as *Chevron* requires, to the Board's reasonable conclusion that section 16 should not be given such a narrow reading. The Board below correctly observed that "[n]othing in the literal terms of section 16 requires a preexisting customer relationship." Board Statement at 16, J.A. at 210. According to SIA, however, the legislative history makes it clear that Congress had such a relationship in mind when it included the language "upon the order, and for the account of, customers." In support of its thesis, SIA directs us to a remark in the committee reports that the purpose of section 16 was to permit "[n]ational banks *** to purchase and sell investment securities for their customers to the same extent as heretofore." S.Rep. No. 77, 73d Cong., 1st Sess. 16 (1933); H.R.Rep. No. 150, 73d Cong., 1st Sess. 3 (1933). Because the Supreme Court in *Schwab* stated that "[b]anks long have arranged the purchase and sale of securities as an accommodation to their customers," and that section 16, read in conjunction with the above-cited legislative history, "expressly endorsed this traditional banking service," 468 U.S. at 215, SIA contends that section 16 was intended *only* to permit such services as had been traditionally performed as an accommodation to preexisting customers of the bank.

SIA again reads too much into *Schwab*. Congress, in enacting section 16, may well have intended to endorse traditional banking services as they existed before 1933. This does not mean, however, that section 16 permits the transactions covered by its language *only* to the extent that identical transactions occurred prior to the enactment of Glass-Steagall. Since nothing in the language or legislative history of section 16 even remotely suggests that the Act meant to freeze particular functions in place as of 1933, we decline to read that meaning into the Act.

Moreover, the history of commercial banking shows that, prior to the Glass-Steagall Act, banks offered the securities brokerage services at stake in *Schwab* both to existing customers and to persons with no preexisting relationship to the banks. *See* Securities Indus. Ass'n v. Comptroller of the Currency, 577 F.Supp. 252, 255 (D.D.C.1983), *aff'd per curiam*, 758 F.2d 739, 740 (D.C.Cir.1985) (affirmed "generally for the reasons stated" by district court), *cert. denied*, 474 U.S. 1054 (1986); *see also* Greenfield v. Clarence Sav. Bank, 5 S.W.2d 708, 708–09 (Mo.Ct.App.1928) (transaction in which plaintiff, having no account with the bank, "went there with the sole purpose of purchasing bonds as an investment"); Smith, *Stock Market Service Comes High*, Am.Bankers A.J. 965 (Apr. 1929) (bank will "buy and sell securities for its customers and the public in general"). Thus, we may not construe "upon the order ... of ... customers" to require a preexisting relationship between the bank and the user of the services permitted under section 16, since Congress intended that language to ratify banking practices that served at least some persons without any relationship to the bank except as "customers" of the services permitted by section 16.

Despite the conclusion that section 16 requires no preexisting customer relationship as a matter of law, we still must inquire whether the Board reasonably concluded that Bankers Trust places commercial paper solely on the order of the issuer. The Board stated that "[a]ccording to Bankers Trust's submission, the issuer, not the bank, decides whether to raise funds by issuing commercial paper and, if so, in what amount." Board Statement at 15–16, J.A. at 209–10. The

Board concluded that this meant that "the bank places commercial paper solely on the request and on the order of its customer, the commercial paper issuer." *Id.* at 18, J.A. at 212. SIA counters that the bank solicits the business of issuers and gives financial advice about the terms and timing of the potential issue of commercial paper. Neither point upsets the Board's conclusion.

SIA offers no support for its claim that Bankers Trust recruits or solicits the business of issuers beyond the assertion that the bank "touts" its placement services in advertisements. "Touting" is not enough to render the Board's conclusion unreasonable. Although the bank may generally solicit customers for its placement services by making it known that such services are available, either in the so-called "tombstone ads" or in more general advertisements (for example, "What do you get when you combine an investment bank with a commercial bank? Bankers Trust Company."), any given placement of commercial paper still takes place solely on the order of the customer. We illustrate by analogy. The Supreme Court in *Schwab* stated that section 16 permitted banks to engage in retail brokerage operations at least as to their own customers. Even if we assume that a bank makes its retail brokerage operations available only to its depositors, it still must find some way to let them know that these services are available. It would strain credibility to assert that the circulation of a brochure or the running of an advertisement to publicize the availability of these services would mean that the brokerage services performed are now barred since no longer performed solely upon the order of the customer.

Nor are we convinced that the rendering of financial advice itself removes Bankers Trust's placements from the category of transactions made solely upon the order of customers. Nothing in section 16 suggests that the bank may not advise issuers who have decided that they may or do want to raise money by issuing commercial paper. If a customer asks the advice of Bankers Trust but makes its own decision about whether and in what amount to issue commercial paper, the transaction is made solely on the order of that customer. Consider, by contrast, a case in which an investment bank decides that the market is favorable to the refinancing of a bond issue or the conversion of debt to equity and initiates discussions with its customer leading up to the eventual transaction. In such a situation, the initiative of the investment banker itself creates the very demand for the particular transaction. This is a far cry from the type of passive advice that Bankers Trust renders after the issuer has decided that it needs to raise capital and must only decide the best way to do it. Indeed, the legislative history provides support for just this distinction, evincing a concern about bankers who found it "necessary *** to seek for customers to become makers of issues of securities when the needs of those customers for long-term money were not very pressing." 75 Cong.Rec. 9911 (1932) (remarks of Sen. Bulkley). We cannot conclude that the Board acted unreasonably in deciding that the danger identified by Senator Bulkley does not characterize the financial advice rendered by Bankers Trust.

SIA also argues that, because section 16 applies both to "purchasing and selling" of securities, the solicitation of buyers of commercial paper by Bankers Trust means that its activities are not "upon the order *** of *** customers." This argument is meritless. Since Bankers Trust acts as sales agent for the issuer, it is clearly engaged in "selling" securities for its customers and necessarily finds and solicits buyers for those securities, buyers who may be customers of other bank services. This does not mean, however, that Bankers Trust is "purchasing" securities for those investors who buy the paper. The buyers decide upon and make their own purchases, while Bankers Trust has an explicit policy against purchasing for any account that it manages, advises, or serves as trustee—the only accounts for which the bank would even have the authority to make such purchases.

Moreover, no sensible construction of the statute could say that otherwise permissible selling activities cannot involve the solicitation of buyers. The seller's very purpose in engaging a selling agent and paying a commission is to acquire that agent's superior ability to place the product with buyers. If placement of the product with buyers did not require any solicitation of buyers, no rational business would pay another firm to do what it could without cost to itself: passively wait for orders. This construction of "upon the order *** of *** customers," therefore, would lead to the absurd statutory result of allowing a seller-agent relationship to arise only in circumstances that not only would never actually exist but that also would strip the relationship itself of its purpose. The Board's rejection of such a construction appears eminently reasonable.
. . .

The final assault on the Board's conclusion that the activities of Bankers Trust fit within the terms of section 16 suggests that these activities amount to "underwriting" and thus divest Bankers Trust of its exemption. Although the Act and its legislative history are barren of any definition of the term "underwriting," the parties and the district court have spent much effort considering whether the term "underwriting" includes agency, as well as principal, transactions, and whether what is commonly called "best efforts" underwriting, in which the selling group assumes none of the risk of its failure fully to distribute the issue, amounts to statutory underwriting for purposes of the exemption. These efforts were needless, since we find that the Board reasonably concluded that an "underwriting" defeats the section 16 exemption only if it includes a public offering; private placements therefore do not for this purpose constitute statutory "underwriting." The Board's reliance on the distinction between public offerings and private placements is reasonable because the distinction derives support from congressional intent embodied in contemporaneous securities legislation and reasonably relates to concerns that the Glass-Steagall Act sought to meet.

1. *Contemporaneous Securities Legislation*—The Glass-Steagall Act nowhere defines "underwriting," and the legislative history contains nothing to clarify the term. When in *SIA* the Supreme Court reviewed the case we now consider on remand, similar ambiguity surrounded the definition of the terms "security" and "note." The Court in *SIA* made it very plain that the meaning of a term in other legislation passed roughly at the same time as the Glass-Steagall Act with the shared purpose of restoring confidence in the nation's financial markets provided "considerable evidence" of the "ordinary meaning" Congress attached to the same term in the Glass-Steagall Act itself. *SIA*, 468 U.S. at 150. The statutes to which the Court resorted in discerning congressional understanding of the term "security" were the Securities Act of 1933, the Securities Exchange Act of 1934, and the Public Utility Holding Company Act of 1935.. *SIA*, 468 U.S. at 150. In each of these statutes, the sweeping definition of "security" encompasses commercial paper; the Court accordingly found that when Congress meant to exempt commercial paper from the strictures of one of these statutes, it expressly so provided. *Id.* at 150–51. Congress, the Court concluded, understood "that, unless modified, the use of the term 'security' encompasse[d] [commercial paper]." *Id.* at 151.

Only the Securities Act of 1933 defines the term "underwriter" (although the Securities Exchange Act of 1934 provides useful evidence on the meaning of that term as used in the

Securities Act). While the evidence of the ordinary congressional cognizance of the term "underwrite" or "underwriter" thus comes from only one piece of similar legislation, that legislation, the Securities Act of 1933, is the closest to Glass-Steagall in time and purpose of the various statutes relied on in *SIA*. The Securities Act and the Glass-Steagall Act were signed into law within three weeks of each other and both statutes were among the legislative reforms that marked President Roosevelt's first hundred days in office. Thus, while the precise purposes of the Securities Act and the Glass-Steagall Act may differ, both emerged from the same effort to restructure the American financial markets; absent any contrary indication, we must consider Congress' understanding of the financial terms it used in one statute highly relevant to discovering the meaning attached to similar but ambiguous terms in the other. With that rule in mind, we turn to the Securities Act of 1933.

SIA contends that the significance of the Securities Act for this case is that it provides an express exemption from registration for "transactions by an issuer not involving any public offering." Section 4(2) of the 1933 Act. SIA asserts that this exemption demonstrates Congress' ability knowingly to provide an exemption from statutory requirements for private offerings; Congress' failure so to provide in section 16 of the Glass-Steagall Act means that the Board acted unreasonably when by interpreting the term "underwrite" it effectively read such a private offering into the Act. This point would have considerable force, except that the history of the Securities Act's exemption betrays SIA's argument and, in fact, establishes the converse—that Congress did understand the concept of underwriting to connote involvement in a public offering of securities.

The Securities Act in section 2(11) defines an "underwriter" as "any person who has purchased from an issuer with a view to, or offers or sells for an issuer in connection with, the distribution of any security, or participates or has a direct or indirect participation in any such undertaking, or participates or has a direct participation in the direct or indirect underwriting of any such undertaking." An "underwriter" thus cannot exist unless a "distribution" exists.

As originally introduced in the House bill that was to become the Securities Act of 1933, the exemption relied on by SIA applied to "transactions by an issuer not with or through an underwriter." *See* H.R. 5480, 73d Cong., 1st Sess. § 4(1) (1933). The House Committee added to this language the phrase "and not involving any public offering." H.R.Rep. No. 85, 73d Cong., 1st Sess. 1 (1933). While the deliberate inclusion of both "not with or through an underwriter" and "not involving a public offering" would ordinarily support the conclusion that Congress viewed the coverage of the two phrases as being different, other legislative history shows that, in fact, both phrases had the same coverage. In interpreting the statute contemporaneously with its passage, the Federal Trade Commission, the agency originally charged with administering the securities laws, observed that a statutory "distribution" necessarily involved a "public offering," thus making it clear that one could not be an "underwriter" in the absence of a public offering. *See* H.R.Conf.Rep. No. 1838, 73d Cong., 2d Sess. 41 (1934). Acknowledging the correctness of the Commission's interpretation, the same Congress that had passed the Securities Act of 1933 eliminated as "superfluous" the language "not with or through an underwriter" when it amended the Securities Act in Title II of the Securities Exchange Act of 1934. *Id.; see* ch. 404, § 203(a)(1), 48 Stat. 881, 906 (1934); *see also* 1 L. Loss, *Securities Regulation* 551 & n. 307 (2d ed.1961) (distribution "more or less synonymous with" public offering). While by no means conclusive, this history offers support for the reasonableness of the Board's view that Congress understood "underwriting" (and, for that matter, "distribution") of securities to connote a public offering, and that the private offerings of commercial paper effected by Bankers Trust do not come within the Glass-Steagall Act's meaning of "underwriting." At the least, it refutes SIA's contention that the Securities Act undercuts the Board's conclusion in this regard. . . .

The Board's responsibility in this case was to arrive at a reasonable determination of what should constitute a private offering under the Glass-Steagall Act. The Board found Bankers Trust's activities to constitute a private offering because (1) the bank "places commercial paper by separately contacting large financial and non-financial institutions," (2) the bank "does not place commercial paper with any individuals," (3) "the maximum number of offerees and purchasers of commercial paper placed by the bank in any given case is relatively limited," (4) the bank "makes no general solicitation or advertisement to the public" with respect to the placement of particular paper (though it does advertise its activities in business publications to publicize its availability as an agent to issuers), and (5) "the commercial paper placed with the bank's assistance is issued in very large average minimum denominations, which are not a likely investment of the general public." Board Statement at 29–30, J.A. at 223–24. Such considerations properly determine what distinguishes a private from a public offering of securities; we shall shortly see that they also have a strong relationship to one of the principal concerns that animated the Glass-Steagall Act.

2. *Legislative Purposes*—As the Supreme Court has amply documented, the legislative history of the Glass-Steagall Act shows that, besides "the obvious risk that a bank could lose money by imprudent investment of its funds in speculative securities," Congress sought to address " 'the more subtle hazards that arise when a commercial bank goes beyond the business of acting as fiduciary or managing agent and enters the investment banking business.' " *SIA,* 468 U.S. at 145 (quoting *Camp,* 401 U.S. at 630). The hazards identified by the Court included danger to the impartiality of the bank as a dispenser of financial advice. For example, "Congress concluded that it was unrealistic to expect a banker to give impartial advice about [whether and how best to issue equity or debt securities] if he stands to realize a profit from the underwriting or distribution of securities." *SIA,* 468 U.S. at 146 (citing 75 Cong.Rec. 9912 (1932) (remarks of Sen. Bulkley)). Moreover, the Court pointed to congressional fears that commercial-bank involvement in investment banking might lead to the use of a bank's credit facilities to "shore up a company whose securities the bank sought to distribute" or to facilitate the purchase of securities of the bank's commercial customers. *See id.* at 146–47. Congress, in sum, did not believe that bankers could act as proper fiduciaries if faced with the "pressures" of "involvement in the distribution of securities." *Id.* at 146.

Congress recognized that these pressures largely resulted from the heavy fixed costs incurred by commercial banks in running investment banking operations. In the period immediately preceding the financial collapse that precipitated the enactment of Glass-Steagall, the distribution of an issue of securities took place through an elaborate syndication involving various tiers of purchase, banking, and selling groups managed by an originating banker who handled the negotiations with the issuer. *See* 1 L. Loss, *Securities Regulation* 164–66 (2d ed.1961). The precise details of the distribution process, as it then existed, are not important for our purposes. What is important is that "a large number of the leading originators of securities, particularly the security affiliates of commercial banks," developed "large selling organizations" in this period. Gourrich, *Investment Banking Methods Prior to and Since the Securities Act of 1933,* 4 Law & Contemp.Probs. 44, 49 (1937). Indeed, the "bank affiliates were particularly active in constructing substantial retail organizations" to distribute the securities to which they had committed themselves as originators or members of a purchase group. *Id.* at 48 n. 8.

Congress was well aware of these developments. The heavy overhead incurred by banks to carry these large retail operations caused much of the congressional concern about "subtle hazards" that animated the sponsors of the Glass-Steagall Act. As one of the principal sponsors stated:

> In order to be efficient a securities department had to be developed; it had to have salesmen; and it had to have correspondent connections with smaller banks throughout the territory tributary to the great bank. Organizations were developed with great enthusiasm and efficiency. The distribution of the great security issues needed for the development of the country was facilitated, and the country developed. But the sales departments were subject to fixed expenses which could not be reduced without the danger of so disrupting the organization as to put the institution at a disadvantage in competition with rival institutions. These expenses would turn the operation very quickly from a profit to a loss if there were not sufficient originations and underwritings to keep the sales departments busy.
>
> It was necessary in some cases to seek for customers to become makers of issues of securities when the needs of those customers for long-term money were not very pressing. Can any banker, imbued with the consciousness that his bond-sales department is, because of lack of securities for sale, losing money and at the same time losing its morale, be a fair and impartial judge as to the necessity and soundness for a new security issue which he knows he can readily distribute through channels which have been expensive to develop but which presently stand ready to absorb the proposed security issue and yield a handsome profit on the transaction?
>
> It is easy to see why the security business was overdeveloped and why the bankers' clients and country bank correspondents were overloaded with a mass of investments many of which have proved most unfortunate.

75 Cong.Rev. 9911 (1932) (remarks of Sen. Bulkley).

The distinction between public and private offerings meshes well with the congressional goal of eliminating the "subtle hazards" of conflicts of interest and abuse of fiduciary relationships in banking. Senator Bulkley's remarks show a concern with the development of a vast selling apparatus necessary to participate in the distribution of "great security issues needed for the development of the country" and mirror the unchallenged evidence in the literature that banks in the early twentieth century were building that type of large selling organization.

In light of the specific congressional focus on the large fixed costs that accompanied retail participation in public distributions, it seems highly plausible that one line Congress might have drawn in adopting the permissive language of section 16 of the Glass-Steagall Act was at the point of public offering, a line which could well explain the prohibition against underwriting. While regular involvement in private offerings of securities undoubtedly produces some fixed costs and some attendant pressures, it seems reasonable to think that Congress might have found these relatively minor expenses acceptable when compared with the much heavier fixed burden of having a far-flung retail network to distribute securities to the public. Although implementation of this distinction through the prohibition of commercial-bank underwriting would not address all the "subtle hazards" with which Congress was concerned (for example, it would do nothing to meet the fear that a bank would sell securities for an issuer to help the issuer repay loans to the bank), the prohibition of underwriting is only one of the limitations that section 16 imposes on banks that desire to deal in securities. We believe that the distinction between public and private offerings as drawn by the Board reasonably interprets the prohibition of underwriting and reasonably relates to the elimination of some of those hazards.

## V.

While SIA has not met its burden of refuting the reasonableness of the Board's conclusion that Bankers Trust's activities fit within the literal terms of section 16, SIA mounts a final, sweeping challenge to the reasonableness of the Board's interpretation of the Act. SIA asks the court to analyze the activities approved by the Board to determine whether they pose the "subtle hazards" that the Act seeks to eliminate. The district court relied on the potential for these hazards to conclude that, while the activities of Bankers Trust come within the literal terms of section 16, those terms should be construed narrowly to exclude an otherwise permissible arrangement that frustrates the policies of the Act. In other words, although the language and history of the specific provisions support the reasonableness of the Board's construction of those provisions, the Board might nonetheless be obligated to adopt a different construction if the background policies of the Act as interpreted by the Supreme Court in cases like *Camp* and *SIA* conflict with that construction and render it unreasonable. . . .

We believe that the district court erred in concluding that the private placement of commercial paper by Bankers Trust creates the kind of "subtle hazards" that would require the Board to construe section 16 narrowly to exclude that activity. Since the Supreme Court has already undertaken a "subtle hazards" analysis with respect to commercial paper, albeit without the benefit of the Board's analysis of that issue, we know precisely the concerns the Court has identified in this area. What we must decide is whether the practices of Bankers Trust at issue here sufficiently differ from those in the last round of this litigation to justify concluding that the hazards identified are no longer present, or whether the Board has presented new considerations that were not before the Court in *SIA* and that meet the concerns expressed by the Court.

Initially, it bears noting that the most obvious hazard reached by the Act—the investment of bank funds in speculative securities—is not at issue in this case. Bankers Trust does not purchase the commercial paper of its customers; it does not inventory the paper overnight; and it makes no loans to provide financing to an issuer when an offering of paper falls short of its goal. Nothing in Bankers Trust's services puts its own resources at risk.

This takes us directly to the "subtle hazards" analysis, which catalogues the various conflicts of interest and dangers that may result from a commercial bank's dealing in "particular" securities. The first set of potential conflicts involves the bank in its role as a lender, raising the dual specter of the bank's making loans to the issuer (to ensure the success of its issue) or to the purchasers of commercial paper placed by the bank. *SIA*, 468 U.S. at 146–47, 156–57. The Board's analysis adequately answers those concerns.

To avoid any danger of making unsound loans to an issuer, Bankers Trust has, since the Supreme Court decided *SIA*, adopted a policy of providing no back-up credit or guarantees to facilitate the acceptance of commercial paper; any line of credit now granted to an issuer must have "substantially different timing, terms, conditions and maturities from the commercial paper being placed." Board Statement at 40, J.A. at 234. *SIA* does not dispute the salutary nature of this change, but argues that the Board's reliance on such representations amounts to "regulation" in a statute that Congress meant to operate through "flat prohibitions." This argument is without merit. The Glass-Steagall Act does impose a system of flat "prohibitions" and "prophylactic" measures, *see SIA,* 468 U.S. at 147–48, 157, but this cannot obviate the need to examine particular factual situations to determine on which side of the prohibitory line they fall. Although the Act may seek to prevent even "potential" conflicts, *see ICI,* 401 U.S. at 637–38, this does not foreclose the Board from deciding that the realities of a situation make even the potential for conflict substantially unlikely. Bankers Trust has made representations about the conduct of its loan department that seem to meet the congressional concerns identified by the Supreme Court; it is perfectly appropriate for the Board to credit the bank's new policies. Moreover, we do not believe that the Board's assumption that Bankers Trust will keep adequate records to substantiate its contentions transforms the Board's decision into an instance of "regulation." If a member of the industry were to file charges with the Board, claiming that Bankers Trust was not adhering to its stated policies, the availability of Bankers Trust's records would facilitate the Board's investigation of that charge. It is in no way an impermissible "regulation" to require Bankers Trust to keep adequate records.

The Board has also advanced an argument not considered by the Court in *SIA* to explain why the arrangement adopted by Bankers Trust will not lead to the lending of money to "shore up" customers of the bank's commercial paper service. The Board points out that the profit from the placement of commercial paper is small, amounting to a commission on the order of one-eighth of one percent of the total amount of the issuer's commercial paper, computed on an annualized basis. The rewards from these commissions are so small compared to the cost of the loans the bank would have to write to make an unsound issuer's paper more attractive to the market that writing such loans would not be worth the risk. Board Statement at 40–41, J.A. at 234–35. A judgment such as this, that the economic realities of the financial marketplace would preclude banks from making loans to shore up troubled issuers, is precisely the kind of exercise of delegated expertise that deserves our full deference.

The Board has also concluded that there is no appreciable risk of the bank's placing commercial paper to enable a debtor of the bank to repay its loans. The Board's opinion reasons that an issuer unable to repay bank loans will probably be unable to raise money in the commercial paper market in any case; Bankers Trust furthermore has adopted a policy of not providing letters of credit or guarantee arrangements to make such paper more attractive. Board Statement at 44, J.A. at 238. Moreover, the antifraud provisions of the securities laws would compel the disclosure of the intended use of the proceeds to satisfy a potentially bad debt owed to the bank, providing an obvious disincentive to such a transaction. *Id.* Finally, empirical evidence indicates that the proceeds of private placements by banks have not been used to pay off any loans involving a material risk of nonpayment. *Id.* at 45, J.A. at 239. The Board's findings as to these factors, which the *SIA* Court apparently did not consider, are reasonable and accordingly receive our deference.

As for the second "subtle hazard," the possibility of the bank's making self-interested loans to finance the purchase of commercial paper it helps issue, the Board provides a persuasive argument, again not before the Supreme Court in *SIA*, that no such hazard arises here. Turning again to an analysis of financial markets, the Board asserts that it is wholly impractical for a commercial bank to make such loans because the yields on commercial paper are generally lower than the interest rates the loans would have to bear. Board Statement at 41 n. 39, J.A. at 235 n.

39.  In the absence of any evidence that this conclusion is wrong, the Board is again entitled to our deference.

Another category of concerns involves the bank's role as a disinterested financial advisor to its customers.  First, there is the potential that the bank will give unsound financial advice to the issuer in order to reap the profits from placement of the issuer's commercial paper.  *See SIA*, 468 U.S. at 146.  The Board found any such risk to be insignificant because the profit from such placements is so low that the bank has no incentive to offer deliberately unsound advice.  Board Statement at 46, J.A. at 240.  This rationale, not considered by the Supreme Court, seems consistent with the notion that much of the concern with banks' giving self-interested advice was based on the banks' need to meet the fixed costs of far-flung distribution networks.  *See supra* pp. 1065–1066.  When the rewards and incentives are lower, the potential benefits from rendering unsound and self-interested advice seem likely to be outweighed by the damage to the bank's reputation and goodwill that would arise from giving bad advice.  The Board's conclusion that bad advice will not result from the scheme at issue here is rational.

The role of disinterested financial advisor to depositors presents different concerns.  Congress feared that depositors purchasing securities through their bank might lose confidence in their bank if an issuer using the bank's securities services defaulted on their securities.  *SIA*, 468 U.S. at 155–56.  Although Bankers Trust has prevented any conflict of interest concerning any account managed or advised by the bank or its affiliates or for any account in the bank's trust department by adopting a flat rule that it will purchase none of the commercial paper it places for these accounts, Board Statement at 45, J.A. at 239, Bankers Trust does otherwise place commercial paper with its depositors.  The Board argues that because the depositors who purchase commercial paper are large, sophisticated business institutions, they would be unlikely to blame their bank for what really amounts to their own error in judgment, while any harm to the bank that did result would not affect its public reputation.  *Id.* at 42–43, J.A. at 236–37.  Though this assessment seems entirely realistic, the Supreme Court in *SIA* clearly rejected these arguments, stating that the Act makes no distinctions on the basis of financial expertise and that the loss of confidence of a few large depositors might, in fact, prove "especially severe."  *SIA*, 468 U.S. at 156, 159  While the Board also argues that an empirical study has indicated no harm to the reputation of commercial banks from their private placements of securities, Board Statement at 42, J.A. at 236, nowhere does the Board's analysis indicate that the study specifically addressed the effect of issuer defaults on depositor/purchaser confidence in commercial banks.

We believe, however, that despite the existence of this one "subtle hazard," we must still affirm the Board.  There are several reasons for that conclusion.  First, the "subtle hazards" addressed in *Camp* and returned to in *ICI, Schwab,* and *SIA* have never alone caused the Supreme Court to hold that Glass-Steagall permits or prohibits any particular banking practice.  Rather, analysis of the hazards in those cases simply reinforced the Court's conclusion that, as a matter of statutory interpretation, Glass-Steagall permitted or prohibited the questioned practice.  Moreover, the Court has concluded that "subtle hazards" counsel prohibition of a banking practice only when the practice gave rise to each and every one of the hazards.  *See SIA*, 468 U.S. at 154–59.  *Camp*, 401 U.S. at 630–34, 636–38.  Nor must a hazard be "totally obliterated" to permit a banking practice—avoidance of the hazard "to a large extent" suffices.  *See ICI*, 450 U.S. at 67 n. 39.  Finally, our conclusion is reinforced by our view that the "subtle hazards" analysis as a whole is a specific instance of the *Chevron* principle that requires our deference to an agency's reasonable construction of its statute's ambiguities, *see Investment Co. Inst. v. Conover*, 790 F.2d 925, 931–33, 935–36. (D.C.Cir.1986) (applying *Chevron* to agency interpretation of Glass-Steagall), since an agency's statutory interpretation that impairs one of the statute's purposes but not others may surely nonetheless be reasonable. (Indeed, the binding force of the Supreme Court's "subtle hazards" analysis in *SIA* is unclear, since, as we have already noted, *supra* p. 1056, the Board failed to offer the Court any rationale concerning those hazards to which the Court could defer. . . . We think, in short, that the Board reasonably concluded not only that Bankers Trust's placements of commercial paper meet the literal requirements of section 16, but also that those placements are consistent with the panoply of the Act's purposes.

## Comments and Questions

1. The legal issue before the court of appeals was whether Bankers Trust's proposed activities constituted the sale of securities "solely upon the order, and for the account of, customers." Thus, the case was reminiscent of the matter before the Supreme Court in the 1984 *Schwab* case. Both decisions involved agency, as opposed to principal, activities. Formalities aside, are the two proposed activities really that similar?

2. In part V of his opinion, Judge Bork applies the so-called subtle hazard analysis that the Supreme Court first developed in its 1971 *Camp* decision. Has he applied the analysis properly in this case? What is the relationship between this portion of the decision and the more traditional statutory interpretation Judge Bork undertakes earlier?

3. In this case, Bankers Trust had agreed not to offer credit enhancements — such as guarantees or standby letters of credit — for the securities being sold in these transactions. Suppose Bankers Trust wished to offer this additional service in the future. Could it do so? Would it need either regulatory approval or statutory authorization?

4. In the *Bankers Trust II* case, the Federal Reserve Board's decision was afforded considerable deference, in contrast to several earlier Glass-Steagall precedents. What factors go into determining whether deference is or is not shown? Judge Bork emphasizes the reasonableness of the Board's interpretation and the failure of the SIA to meet the burden of refuting the reasonableness of the Board's conclusions. One might call this approach a dialogue standard. If the agency provides a reasoned elaboration of its interpretation, then the agency's position is treated as presumptively correct, much as in a dialogue conversation the reasoning of one party on a topic is accepted as correct unless the other party to the conversation can provide a reasoned elaboration which would persuade an impartial listener of the correctness of the rebuttal. Is this an appropriate or a problematic posture for a court to adopt? If you were a member of Congress, would you endorse this approach?

*Problem 15-2*

As the Bankers Trust decision discusses, section 4(2) of the 1933 Act exempts from registration under the 1933 Act "transactions not involving a public offering"—commonly referred to as private placements. In Regulation D, the SEC has interpreted this exemption to allow issuers to sell securities to an unlimited number of accredited investors (a terms that includes any individual with a net worth of more than $1 million) and also to up to 35 non-accredited investors, provided certain disclosure and other standards are met.

a.  Could Bankers Trust privately place limited-partnership interests in real estate projects, as long as the sales were limited to retirees with more than a $1 million of assets in their retirement accounts and otherwise complied with Regulation D?

b.  Could it also place these interests with up to 35 less-wealthy widows and widowers as long as Regulation D's disclosure and other requirements were satisfied?

*Problem 15-3*

Return to Problem 15-1 and consider whether SEC broker-dealer regulation of bank securities activities should include an exemption for the sort of private placement activities the *Bankers Trust II* case sanctions?

# Section 3.  Advisory Services & Related Activities

In the preceding section, we considered the authority of depository institutions to engage in brokerage or other agency activities.  Now, we turn to advisory services.  Advice is something that depository institutions have traditionally afforded their customers. In Board of Governors v. Investment Company Institute, 450 U.S. 46 (1981), the Supreme Court acquiesced in an expansion of traditional advisory powers by upholding a Federal Reserve Board order allowing a bank holding company to act as an investment adviser to a closed-end investment company.   The Court's ruling, however, was limited and emphasized the limited role of the adviser and the fact that closed-end companies, unlike typical mutual funds, do not continuously engage in the issuance and repurchase of their shares. The case thus left open the question under what circumstances, if any, banking organizations could combine advisory services and other securities services.

# SIA v. Board of Governors (National Westminster)
## 821 F.2d 810 (D.C. Cir. 1987), *cert. denied* 484 U.S. 1005 (1988)

BORK, Circuit Judge:

Section 20 of the Glass–Steagall Act prohibits the affiliation of member banks of the Federal Reserve System with corporations "engaged principally in the issue, flotation, underwriting, public sale, or distribution" of securities. The issue here is whether the Board of Governors of the Federal Reserve System reasonably concluded that the combined provision of securities brokerage services and investment advice by a member bank's affiliate does not implicate section 20's prohibition of the "public sale" of securities. . . .

I.

In August 1985, National Westminster Bank PLC and its subsidiary NatWest Holdings, Inc. (collectively "NatWest") submitted an application to the Board pursuant to section 4(c)(8) of the Bank Holding Company Act of 1956, as amended, for permission to provide investment advice and securities brokerage services to institutional customers through a newly formed subsidiary, County Services Corporation ("CSC").[3]

As proposed by NatWest, CSC's brokerage services would be restricted to buying and selling securities solely as agent for the account of customers. CSC would execute transactions only at the request of its customers and would not exercise any discretion with respect to a customer's account. CSC would not act as principal or as underwriter and would not bear any financial risk with respect to any security it brokers or recommends. Generally, CSC would receive all of its compensation, including that for investment advice, in the fees for securities transactions it executes for customers. CSC would charge separate fees for investment advice and brokerage services upon request of a customer.

---

[3]    Specifically, NatWest sought approval for CSC to engage in the following activities:

(1) provide "portfolio investment advice to Institutional Customers," a term defined to include a bank, insurance company or corporation "with assets exceeding $5,000,000 that regularly invests in the types of securities as to which investment advice is given, or that regularly engages in transactions in securities; ... an employee benefit plan with assets exceeding $5,000,000 ...; and a natural person whose individual net worth ... at the time of receipt of the investment advice or brokerage services exceeds $5,000,000."

(2) provide "securities brokerage services, related securities credit activities pursuant to the Board's Regulation T, and incidental activities such as offering custodial services and cash management services, in each case for Institutional Customers, and in each case under circumstances where the securities brokerage services are restricted to buying and selling securities solely as agent for the account of such Customers;"

(3) furnish "general economic information and advice, general economic statistical forecasting services and industry studies to Institutional Customers; and"

(4) serve "as investment advisor (as defined in Section 2(a)(20) of the Investment Company Act of 1940) to investment companies registered under that Act."

NatWest's application also provided that CSC would hold itself out as a corporate entity separate and distinct from NatWest and would have its own assets, liabilities, books and records. NatWest and CSC would not share customer or depositor lists or confidential information.[4]

In an order dated June 13, 1986, the Board approved the application. *National Westminster Bank PLC,* 72 Fed.Res.Bull. 584 (1986). The Board determined first that CSC's proposed activities are closely related to banking and that the proposal may reasonably be expected to result in public benefits that outweigh possible adverse effects so that the activities are a "proper incident" to banking within the meaning of section 4(c)(8) of the Bank Holding Company Act. *Id.* at 584–91. The Board then concluded that NatWest's acquisition of CSC would not violate the Glass–Steagall Act because the combination of investment advice and execution services does "not constitute a 'public sale' of securities for purposes of sections 20 and 32 of the ... Act." *Id.* at 592.[5] The Securities Industry Association ("SIA") a trade association

---

[4]    While the application was pending, the Board sought and received further commitments from NatWest regarding its relationship with CSC and regarding CSC's proposed activities:

"1. The Subsidiary will not transmit its investment advisory research or recommendations to the commercial lending department of any member of the NatWest group. (This is not intended, of course, to preclude the publication or dissemination of the Subsidiary's research or recommendations to potential Institutional Customers (as defined in the Application) generally.)"

"2. In any brokerage transaction performed by the Subsidiary where the counterparty (as principal) is a member of the NatWest group, NatWest will disclose this fact to the brokerage customer and obtain specific consent from the customer for such transaction."

"3. No director of the Subsidiary will also be a director of either NatWest PLC, National Westminster Bank USA, N.A. ("*NatWest USA* ") or any subsidiary of NatWest USA. It is anticipated, however, that certain directors of the Subsidiary may also be directors of other subsidiaries of NatWest PLC."

"4. No officer of the Subsidiary will also serve as an officer of either NatWest PLC, NatWest USA or any subsidiary of NatWest USA. In addition, no officer of the Subsidiary engaged in providing investment advisory or securities brokerage services will also provide such services for, on behalf of or with respect to any other member of the NatWest group. As noted in the Application (at 9), the Subsidiary will be maintained, and will hold itself out to the public, as a separate and distinct corporate entity, and will conduct its business separate from the other members of the NatWest group."

"5. The Subsidiary will not refer its customers who desire to purchase securities on credit to any Affiliate."

"6. There will be no established program by which an Affiliate will extend credit for securities purchases to the Subsidiary's customers."

"7. As set forth in the Application (at 60), the Subsidiary is seeking approval to engage in securities credit activities pursuant to the Board's Regulation T and, accordingly, is expected to have its own margin account/lending ability, with normal associated powers."

---

[5]    Those non-bank activities found by the Board to be "closely related to banking" and thus permissible activities for bank holding companies are listed in the Board's Regulation Y. . . . At the time of NatWest's application, Regulation Y provided that a bank holding company could at as an

of underwriters, brokers and securities dealers, then petitioned for review of the Board's decision. SIA challenges only the Board's determination that provision of the proposed services would not violate section 20 of the Glass–Steagall Act.

## II.

Because the Board engaged in a comprehensive review of the language and legislative history of section 20, and provided a detailed and reasoned explanation for its conclusion that the proposed activities do not fall within that provision's prohibitions, its decision is entitled to "substantial deference." *Securities Indus. Ass'n v. Board of Governors of the Fed. Reserve Sys.,* 807 F.2d 1052, 1056 (D.C.Cir.1986) (*"Bankers Trust II "*), *cert. denied,* 483 U.S. 1005 (1987); *see Securities Indus. Ass'n v. Board of Governors of the Fed. Reserve Sys.,* 468 U.S. 207, 217 (1984); *Board of Governors of the Fed. Reserve Sys. v. Investment Co. Inst.,* 450 U.S. 46, 56 (1981). Since Congress has not addressed the issue of whether the combined provision of brokerage services and investment advice is a "public sale" within the meaning of section 20, we must uphold the Board's interpretation if it is a reasonable construction of the statute. . . .

In determining the meaning of section 20 of the Act, which prohibits member bank affiliation with any corporation "engaged principally in the issue, flotation, underwriting, public sale, or distribution" of securities, we are not without guidance. In *Securities Indus. Ass'n v. Board of Governors of the Fed. Reserve Sys.,* 468 U.S. 207 (1984) (*"Schwab "*), the Supreme Court addressed the issue of whether the provision of "discount" brokerage services—the provision of execution services without investment advice—violated section 20 and concluded that the term "public sale" must be read in conjunction with the terms surrounding it. The Court then held that discount brokerage did not fall within the term "public sale":

> None of the[ ] terms [in section 20] has any relevance to the brokerage business at issue in this case. Schwab does not engage in issuing or floating the sale of securities, and the terms "underwriting" and "distribution" traditionally apply to a function distinctly different from that of a securities broker. An underwriter normally acts as principal whereas a broker executes orders for the purchase or sale of securities solely as agent.

468 U.S. at 217–18 (footnotes omitted). The Court thus upheld the Board's determination that "the business of purchasing or selling securities upon the unsolicited order of, and as agent for, a particular customer does not constitute the 'public sale' of securities for purposes of section 20," *id.* at 221 (internal quotation omitted). The Court did not reach the question presented in this petition of whether the combined provision of brokerage services and investment advice is the "public sale" of securities.

The Court has, however, addressed the question of whether the independent provision of investment advice violates the prohibitions in the Act. In *Board of Governors of the Fed. Reserve Sys. v. Investment Co. Inst.,* 450 U.S. 46 (1981) (*"ICI "*), the Court held that "[t]he management of a customer's investment portfolio—even when the manager has the power to sell securities owned by the customer—is not the kind of selling activity Congress contemplated when

---

investment advisor . . . . This provision was upheld by the Supreme Court in Board of Governors v. Investment Co. Inst., 450 U.S. 35 (1981). . . .

it enacted § 21," *id.* at 63, because when the advisor acts in this situation it is "for the account of its customer—not for its own account." *Id.* at 66 n. 37.[6]

Thus, because the Court has upheld against Glass–Steagall challenges the independent provision of CSC's proposed services, the only issue presented here is whether the combined provision of investment advice and securities brokerage services transforms these separately permissible activities into a "public sale" within the meaning of section 20. The Board concluded that they did not because

> [i]n providing investment advice in connection with the execution of securities transactions, CSC would act solely as agent for its customers and would not act as a principal (*i.e.,* with its own funds) in buying and selling securities. CSC would not, like many securities firms, make a market in securities with its own funds. Nor would CSC offer securities to the public as agent for the issuer of securities.

72 Fed.Res.Bull. at 592 (footnote omitted). We believe that this is a reasonable interpretation of the term "public sale" as defined by the Court in *Schwab.* The addition of investment advice to brokerage activities does not implicate any of the activities which the *Schwab* Court described as traditionally associated with underwriting.

As was the case in *Schwab,* CSC will have no relationship with the issuer other than that related to the execution of transactions as agent for the customer. CSC will not purchase the issuer's securities for sale to the public, *see Schwab,* 468 U.S. at 217–18 n. 17, but instead will "execute[ ] orders for the purchase or sale of securities solely as agent." *See id.* at 218. Nor will CSC act as agent for the issuer as a "best efforts" underwriter. *See id.* at 217–18 n. 17. The proposed activities in this case, for purposes of determining the scope of the term "public sale," are simply indistinguishable from the activities described in *Schwab.*

The sole distinction cited by SIA is that CSC will also provide investment advice. We cannot understand, however, why this should transform the proposed activities into the public sale of securities. *See Bankers Trust II,* 807 F.2d at 1061 (rejecting contention that rendering financial advice itself removes a bank's placement activities from the category of transactions made "solely upon the order of a customer"). While it is true that the provision of investment advice may be another attribute common to underwriters, this does not necessarily mean that it transforms the activities into those of underwriters. The critical attributes of underwriters, as defined in *Schwab,* are that they either purchase securities from the issuer or act as the agent of the issuer. 468 U.S. at 217–18. The provision of investment advice does not alter the fact that CSC will not engage in either of these activities.

This interpretation of the Act is also consistent with the Court's decision in *ICI.* The Court there specifically held that the provision of investment advice by a non-bank subsidiary, even when coupled with the power to sell the securities owned by the customer, was not "selling"

---

6    There is no reason to believe that the Court's holding with respect to § 21, which prohibits any entity "engaged in the business of ... selling" securities from receiving deposits, would not be equally applicable to the "public sale" provision in § 20. In fact, the Supreme Court has specifically noted that "a less stringent standard should apply to determine whether a holding company has violated section 20 than is applied to a determination of whether a bank has violated sections 16 and 21." *ICI,* 450 U.S. at 61 n. 26.

within the meaning of section 21. 450 U.S. at 63. The Court based its decision in part on the finding that Congress could not have intended in section 21 to require banks to abandon the traditional practice of managing investment accounts in a fiduciary capacity or as an agent for an individual. *Id.* The Court described these practices earlier in the opinion as follows:

> The services of an investment adviser are not significantly different from the traditional fiduciary functions of banks. The principal activity of an investment adviser is to manage the investment portfolio of its advisee—to invest and reinvest the funds of the client. Banks have engaged in that sort of activity for decades. As executor, trustee, or managing agent of funds committed to its custody, a bank regularly buys and sells securities for its customers. Bank trust departments manage employee benefits trusts, institutional and corporate agency accounts, and personal trust and agency accounts.

*Id.* at 55; *see also Schwab*, 468 U.S. at 212 n. 8 ("banks often execute purchase and sell orders for securities that are not traded on an exchange without an intervening broker. To this extent they perform the same services as a retail broker"). The activities described by the Court in *ICI* are similar to those proposed by CSC. In each case the bank, or bank affiliate, offers investment advice and provides for the execution of the purchase or sale of securities for the customer. One difference between the services proposed here and those addressed by the Court in *ICI* is that the bank in *ICI* also had discretionary authority with respect to the customer's account and CSC will be permitted to execute a transaction only upon the request of a customer. This distinction, of course, cuts against the argument that CSC's services are a "public sale." The discretionary authority of the bank in *ICI* rendered it arguably more like a principal than the mere agent of a customer.

The second distinction, which was raised by SIA during oral argument, is that the bank in *ICI* rendered advice only to its existing customers whereas CSC will provide services for any "Institutional Customer." *See supra* note 3. SIA argues that this distinction renders CSC's proposed services a "public sale" because it will place CSC in a better position to manipulate the market through the purchase and sale of securities. This conclusion does not follow from its premise. A bank with existing large institutional customers, and with discretionary management authority over the customer's accounts, would seem to be in a better position than CSC to affect the market through the purchase or sale of securities.

SIA has not raised a serious challenge to the Board's finding that CSC's proposed activities do not fall within the literal meaning of "public sale" as interpreted by the Court in *Schwab*. SIA relies primarily on the definition of "sale" in the *American Heritage Dictionary* (1970 ed.), which includes to "promote," for its argument that the provision of investment advice transforms the brokerage services into a sale. *See* Reply Brief for Petitioner Securities Industry Association at 1–2 & n. 2. While a dictionary definition may be useful for a number of purposes, it cannot override a more specific meaning given by the statutory context in which a word resides. The Supreme Court in *Schwab* held that the term "public sale" must be read in conjunction with the underwriting activities surrounding it in the Act and the definition so derived is the one the Board is bound to apply.

### III.

SIA's primary challenge to the Board's order is that CSC's proposed activities implicate the "subtle hazards" that led Congress to pass the Act and thus must be deemed to be included in the term "public sale." We find, however, that the legislative history, from which the Supreme Court has gleaned these "subtle hazards," confirms the Board's interpretation of section 20.

In *Investment Co. Institute v. Camp,* 401 U.S. 617 (1971), the Supreme Court held that the operation by a bank of a mutual fund which was the equivalent of an open-end investment company was prohibited by the language of sections 16 and 21 of the Act. *Id.* at 625, 639. The Court went on, however, to address the legislative history and the policies underlying the Act and concluded that "[t]he hazards that Congress had in mind were not limited to the obvious danger that a bank might invest its own assets in frozen or otherwise imprudent stock or security investments." *Id.* at 630. The Court found that "Congress also had in mind and repeatedly focused on the more subtle hazards that arise when a commercial bank goes beyond the business of acting as fiduciary or managing agent and enters the investment banking business either directly or by establishing an affiliate to hold and sell particular investments." *Id.*

As later summarized by the Court, the subtle hazards identified in *Camp* were these:

> The Court recognized that because the bank and its affiliate would be closely associated in the public mind, public confidence in the bank might be impaired if the affiliate performed poorly. Further, depositors of the bank might lose money on investments purchased in reliance on the relationship between the bank and its affiliate. The pressure on banks to prevent this loss of public confidence could induce the bank to make unsound loans to the affiliate or to companies in whose stock the affiliate has invested. Moreover, the association between the commercial and investment bank could result in the commercial bank's reputation for prudence and restraint being attributed, without justification, to an enterprise selling stocks and securities. Furthermore, promotional considerations might induce banks to make loans to customers to be used for the purchase of stocks and might impair the ability of the commercial banker to render disinterested advice.

*ICI,* 450 U.S. at 66–67 n. 38.

In *Schwab,* also decided after *Camp,* the Court again addressed the legislative history of the Act and concluded "that Congress enacted § 20 to prohibit the affiliation of commercial banks with entities that were engaged principally in 'activities such as underwriting.' " 468 U.S. at 219, *quoting ICI,* 450 U.S. at 64. The Court reaffirmed the finding in *Camp* that "[c]ongressional concern over the underwriting activities of bank affiliates included both the fear that bank funds would be lost in speculative investments and the suspicion that the more 'subtle hazards' associated with underwriting would encourage unsound banking practices," 468 U.S. at 220, but the opinion limited this finding by concluding that "all" of the "subtle hazards" identified by Congress "are attributable to the promotional pressures that arise from affiliation with entities that purchase and sell investments on their own account." *Id.* at 220 n. 23.

The Court then held that the provision of discount brokerage services does not implicate any of the "subtle hazards" identified by Congress:

> Because Schwab trades only as agent, its assets are not subject to the vagaries of the securities markets. Moreover, Schwab's profits depend solely on the volume of shares it trades and not on the purchase or sale of particular securities. Thus, [the bank] has no "salesman's stake" in the securities Schwab trades. It cannot increase Schwab's profitability by having its bank affiliate extend credit to issuers of particular securities, nor by encouraging the bank affiliate improperly to favor particular securities in the management of depositors' assets.

468 U.S. at 220–21.

As an initial matter, we do not believe that any discussion of "subtle hazards" is necessary here because it is clear that CSC will not "hold and sell particular investments," *see Camp*, 401 U.S. at 630, or "purchase and sell [securities] on [its] own account," *see Schwab*, 468 U.S. at 220 n. 23 —the circumstances the Supreme Court has stated give rise to these "subtle hazards." Further, each of the negative findings in *Schwab* is equally applicable to CSC's proposed services. CSC will not invest its own funds, or those of NatWest, but will act only as agent for the customer. Because CSC will receive a commission only on transactions it executes, regardless of whether CSC advised the customer to purchase the security or whether the customer followed that advice, its profits will depend "solely on the volume of shares it trades and not on the sale of particular securities." Therefore, because CSC has no interest in the sale of a particular security, NatWest has no "salesman's stake" in the particular security and the "subtle hazards" identified in *Camp* are not implicated.

SIA argues that NatWest will have a "salesman's stake" in the securities CSC may advise its customers to purchase because "CSC will actively promote trades in specific securities and will generate profits based upon its success in convincing customers to purchase or sell those particular securities[:] [w]hen CSC recommends and sells a particular security, CSC acquires an interest in the performance of that security and derivatively, in the financial condition of the issuer." Brief for Petitioner Securities Industry Association at 12–13.

As an initial matter, we do not understand the reasoning underlying SIA's "subtle hazards" analysis. CSC will not have any financial interest in the sale of a particular security. CSC will have no relationship with any issuer and will receive a commission on any sale or purchase it executes for a customer. If CSC advises a customer to buy Company X's securities but the customer would prefer to buy Company Z's securities, then CSC clearly would not have an incentive to sell Company X's securities. CSC would be indifferent because it would receive its brokerage fee either way. Thus, CSC's financial incentive relates solely to the *number* of shares it trades and not to any particular security. Further, as noted by NatWest, since CSC will in reality recommend only a small percentage of securities traded, "CSC can hope to operate profitably only if the vast majority of transactions that it brokers involve securities as to which it has made no investment recommendation at all." Brief for Intervenors–Respondents National Westminster Bank PLC and NatWest Holdings, Inc. at 5. Thus, SIA's argument that CSC will have the ability "to influence in *which* securities the customers will trade, with a prospect of increased income as a result," Reply Brief for Petitioner Securities Industry Association at 6, is incorrect.

Although we believe that the decision in *Schwab* is dispositive with respect to the nonexistence of any "subtle hazards" arising from CSC's proposed services, we also find that SIA has not identified any "subtle hazard" which would require the Board to reject NatWest's application. Most of the alleged hazards raised by SIA have been addressed by the Supreme Court and rejected as not within the category of activity Congress sought to prohibit under the Act in the absence of an interest in a particular security.

SIA argues that NatWest might make unsound loans to issuers of securities CSC recommends, that CSC might recommend securities issued by bank customers who have or seek loans from the bank, and that NatWest may lose its reputation for "prudence and restraint" if a depositor follows CSC's advice and the security performs poorly. *See* Brief for Petitioner

Securities Industry Association at 12–13. These same potential hazards might flow from the provision of investment advice, which was nonetheless upheld by the Court in *ICI*. We cannot determine how the CSC's provision of execution services will add to the potential for these hazards, and thus we remain bound by the Court's analysis in *ICI*. A contrary holding, that the potential for these hazards is sufficient to render an activity unlawful, would render all investment advisory activities, including those traditionally performed by bank trust departments, unlawful. We agree with the Court's reasoning in *ICI*, and conclude that Congress could not have intended to render unlawful a significant part of a bank's fiduciary activities through section 20 of the Act. *See ICI*, 450 U.S. at 63; *see also Investment Co. Inst. v. Conover*, 790 F.2d at 931.

We also believe that the Board's conclusion that these hazards are not likely to develop given the realities of the brokerage industry and the commitments made by NatWest is entitled to substantial deference. *See Bankers Trust II*, 807 F.2d at 1067 (Board is not foreclosed from "deciding that the realities of a situation make even the potential for conflict substantially unlikely").

The Board found "no significant potential for loss of confidence in an affiliate bank as a result of [the] proposal, given the strict operational separation proposed, ... the fact that the public and bank depositors should understand that CSC would not commit its funds to any specific investments, and that depositor lists would not be transmitted from an affiliated bank to CSC." 72 Fed.Res.Bull. at 595. The Board also noted that the potential for loss of depositor confidence exists whenever a bank gives investment advice. *Id.* at 589.

The Board also found that there was no "significant potential" that CSC would recommend particular securities of customers so that the proceeds could be used to pay existing loans because CSC's advice will most likely relate to securities traded in the secondary market and federal securities laws require disclosure of the intended use of the proceeds from newly issued securities and because NatWest will not disclose information to CSC regarding loans to customers. 72 Fed.Res.Bull. at 590, 595.

Finally, the Board did not find that there was any significant possibility that NatWest would extend unsound loans to issuers whose securities CSC had recommended because "the expected benefit of such conduct would likely be outweighed by the potential losses resulting from the bad loans, and ... information relating to the particular recommendations made by CSC would not be provided to NatWest affiliates." 72 Fed.Res.Bull. at 595.

SIA does not challenge the substance of these reasoned determinations but instead argues that the Board's analysis is flawed because it cannot rely on any of the commitments made by NatWest in its "subtle hazards" analysis. SIA argues that if the Board recognizes any potential hazard, the activity must be prohibited without regard to any arrangement which would prevent its occurrence. By relying on these commitments, SIA argues, the Board again engaged in the practice rejected by the Supreme Court in *Securities Indus. Ass'n v. Board of Governors of the Fed. Reserve Sys.*, 468 U.S. 137 (1984) ("*Bankers Trust I* "), of " 'effectively convert[ing] a portion of the Act's broad prohibition into a system of administrative regulation.' " Brief for Petitioner Securities Industry Association at 19, *quoting Bankers Trust I*, 468 U.S. at 153.

We recently rejected this flawed interpretation of *Bankers Trust I*. In *Bankers Trust II*, we held that although "[t]he Glass–Steagall Act does impose a system of flat 'prohibitions' and 'prophylactic' measures, ... this cannot obviate the need to examine particular factual situations to determine on which side of the prohibitory line they fall." 807 F.2d at 1067. Here, the Board has not attempted to save by continuing regulatory oversight [over] a proposed activity that falls within the literal language of the statute. *See Bankers Trust I,* 468 U.S. at 153. Instead, the Board has reviewed the "realities of a situation," *Bankers Trust II,* 807 F.2d at 1067, has determined that the activities do not fall within the literal language of the statute, and has "impos[ed] restrictions designed to assure that the activity is insulated from that associated with investment banking." 72 Fed.Res.Bull. at 595 (footnote omitted). This practice has been approved by the Supreme Court, *see ICI,* 450 U.S. at 66–67 ("none of these 'more subtle hazards' would be present were a bank to act as an investment adviser . . . subject to the restrictions imposed by the Board"), and we will not disturb it here.

## Comments and Questions

1. After the *National Westminster* decision, the Federal Reserve broadened the definition of "institutional customer" to encompass individuals with a net worth in excess of one million dollars, and also permitted bank holding companies to provide investment advice to retail customers, to share customer lists with affiliates, to have certain officer and director interlocks within the BHC subsidiaries, and to crossmarket certain services. Are these subsequent actions consistent with the logic of the decision?

2. Aside from underwriting securities, after the *National Westminster* decision what is left of the Glass–Steagall barrier between commercial and investment banking? What of the supposed policies underlying the Glass-Steagall Act? Does the decision effectively transfer the apparent general prohibitions of Glass–Steagall into a network of administrative regulation?

3. Does the combination of services raise serious questions similar to those considered in *Camp?* A discount broker such as Schwab does not appear to have a promotional interest in particular securities because it offers only discount brokerage services. But where the entity also advises persons about which securities to purchase, the entity does have an interest as to the future success of the price of the recommended stock, even though bank capital is not directly at risk. Customer satisfaction is based not only on the immediate execution of the brokerage, but also on the future success of the security. It would seem that after *National Westminster* a bank could readily offer a complete securities service, including security safekeeping, cash management, and portfolio performance measurement. The account could incorporate a cash management account similar to those offered by the major brokerage houses. The bank thus could charge both an investment advisory fee based on the value of the assets under management, as well as a brokerage fee for the actual securities transactions.

4. Under *National Westminster* and related authority, banks may offer investment advisory services to a wide range of customers. How should bank advisers be regulated when they choose to enter this line of business? As we saw in Chapter Ten, Section 3, the United States has a specialized regulatory system for policing advisory services: the Investment Advisers Act of 1940. That Act, however, has an exemption for "banks and bank holding companies." See section 2(a)(11)(A) of the Investment Advisers Act.

Banking organizations that qualify for this exemption are not, however, freed from supplemental supervision. The banking regulatory agencies have developed guidelines requiring banks that engage in certain advisory services to obtain fiduciary licenses, see, e.g. 12 C.F.R. § 9.2(g) (1998), thus ensuring advisory customers a minimum level of protections. Where else have we seen banking agencies create such alternative regulatory structures?

*Problem 15-4*

Universal National Bank has for many years offered discount brokerage services to its clients. Following regulatory developments in the area, the bank has supplemented its basic brokerage service with advisory services for qualified customers. Now it would like to offer margin loans for its customers. Under what terms, if any, are margin loans permissible? See section 23A and 23B of the Federal Reserve Act, as amended, 12 U.S.C. §§ 371c, 371c-1 (1998). What if the securities were acquired from an affiliate of Universal National Bank? What if Universal National Bank acquired the securities as a riskless principal – that is, in a principal transactions entered solely for the purposes of supplying a customer's order?

---

The *National Westminster* decision and its progeny established the proposition that banks (and presumably bank holding companies) can offer their customers a substantial amount of advice in connection with the acquisition of securities. But what if that advice is offered not to individual investors, but to a group of individuals investing together in a mutual fund? Bank-sponsored mutual funds were what the Supreme Court had disallowed in the Camp decision. But was there a way around the *Camp* barrier?

## In re First Union National Bank
### OCC Interpretive Letter No. 403 (Dec. 9, 1987)

This is in response to your letter dated March 30, 1987, notifying us of the intent of First Union National Bank of North Carolina (the Bank) to establish a de novo operating subsidiary, First Union Securities Corporation (the Subsidiary). The Subsidiary will provide brokerage services and investment advice to retail and institutional customers. . . .

#### The Bank's Proposal

Our understanding of the Bank's proposal is based upon the Bank's notification letter, a legal memorandum provided by Bank counsel, and conversations between Bank counsel and Deborah Katz, an attorney in the Legal Advisory Services Division of this Office.

The Subsidiary's brokerage services will include related securities credit activities (margin accounts) and other related activities such as custodian services and individual retirement accounts. It will also provide investment advice consisting of both general and specific or personalized advice with respect to the appropriateness of particular investments for a customer's individual investment requirements. The investment advice will include advice generated by the Company's own research department, research generated by an affiliated company (such as the Capital Management Group of First Union National Bank of North Carolina) or by unrelated third parties.

The Subsidiary will make recommendations to customers from a broad range of secondary market securities and collective investment securities products including mutual funds and UITs [unit investment trusts, a form of investment company]. In its capacity as investment advisor and broker, the Subsidiary proposes to advise a mutual fund and to simultaneously offer investment advice and purchase fund shares on the order and for the account of its customers. The Subsidiary will insure that all appropriate disclosures mandated by the federal securities laws are made in connection with these activities.

Where the Subsidiary offers advice regarding mutual fund shares and UIT interests, the Subsidiary will provide information to its customers indicating that, while particular funds and UITs may be recommended or suggested as investments, such funds and UITs are sponsored by third parties independent of the Subsidiary, the Bank, and affiliates thereof. The information will also state that such shares or interest are not endorsed or guaranteed by, and do not constitute obligations of, the Subsidiary, the Bank, or its affiliates. It will further state that the mutual fund shares and UIT interests are not insured by the Federal Deposit Insurance Corporation.

The Subsidiary will not manage customer accounts on a discretionary basis and the customer will always make the final decision on the purchase or sale of securities. The Subsidiary will not engage in the underwriting of securities, will not deal in securities, and will not purchase securities for its own account except to the extent that national banks are permitted to do so under applicable law. The Subsidiary will register as a broker-dealer under the Securities Exchange Act of 1934 and as an investment adviser under the Investment Advisers Act of 1940.

The principal office of the Subsidiary will be located in Charlotte, North Carolina, in the main office complex of First Union National Bank of North Carolina. Additional offices of the Subsidiary may be opened throughout the United States.

## Discussion

In our opinion, all of the Subsidiary's proposed activities are permissible for national banks and their operating subsidiaries under the National Bank Act and the Glass–Steagall Act. Indeed, the Bank's proposal is within the scope of activities which have been previously considered and found permissible by this Office, other regulatory agencies, or the courts.

It is well established that national banks and their subsidiaries may perform brokerage services for their customers under Section 16 of the Glass–Steagall Act. *See, e.g., Securities Industry Association v. Comptroller of the Currency*, 577 F.Supp. 252 (D.D.C.1983), *aff'd per curiam*, 758 F.2d 739 (D.C.Cir.1985), *cert. denied*, 106 S.Ct. 790 (1986) (brokerage issue), *rev'd*, 479 U.S. 388 (1987) (branching issue) (Security Pacific). *See also Securities Industry Association v. Board of Governors of the Federal Reserve System*, 468 U.S. 207 (1984) (*Schwab*) (bank holding companies).

Similarly, the Office has also determined that the provision of investment advice is permissible for national banks. *See, e.g., Decision of the Comptroller of the Currency Concerning an Application by American National Bank of Austin, Texas, to Establish an Operating Subsidiary to Provide Investment Advice* (September 2, 1983), *reprinted in* Fed.Banking L.Rep. (CCH) ¶ 99,732, *suit filed, Securities Industry Association v. Conover*, No. 83–3581 (D.D.C. November 30, 1983) (*American National Decision* ) (extensive analysis and authorities); OCC Letter No. 367 (August 19, 1986), *reprinted in* Fed.Banking L.Rep. (CCH) ¶ 85,537. Moreover, the provision of investment advice also has been found permissible under the Glass–Steagall Act in the context of activities by bank holding company affiliates of member banks. *See Board of Governors of the Federal Reserve System v. Investment Company Institute*, 450 U.S. 46 (1981).

The combination of investment advisory, planning, or information services and brokerage services in related subsidiaries, or in the same subsidiary, has also been previously approved by the Office. *See, e.g., American National Decision, supra* (related subsidiaries, full range of investment advisory services, including specific advice, institutional or retail customers); OCC Letter No. 360 (April 16, 1986), *reprinted in* Fed.Banking L.Rep. ¶ 85,530 (same subsidiary, general research information and advice, institutional customers); OCC Letter No. 370 (April 16, 1986), *reprinted in* Fed.Banking L.Rep. (CCH) ¶ 85,540 (same subsidiary, includes specific advice, retail customers). The staff has also taken a no-objection position with regard to the provision of a financial planning service and brokerage services within the bank. *See* OCC No-action Letter No. 85–1 (July 30, 1985), *reprinted in* Fed.Banking L.Rep. (CCH) ¶ 84,001. The Federal Reserve Board similarly has approved the combination of investment advisory services and securities brokerage in a single company for bank holding company affiliates of member banks. *See* National Westminster Approval Order, 72 Fed.Res.Bull. 584 (June 13, 1986). This order was recently upheld by the D.C. Circuit Court which ruled that the combined provision of securities brokerage services and investment advice by a member bank's affiliate does not transform these separately permissible activities into a "public sale" of securities prohibited by Section 20 of the Glass–Steagall Act. *See Securities Industry Association v. Board of Governors of the Federal Reserve System*, No. 86–1412, slip op. at 10 (D.C.Cir. July 7, 1987).

Moreover, another recent case has considered and approved a bank's provision of both advisory services and agency transaction services under Section 16 of the Glass–Steagall Act, although in a different context. *See Securities Industry Association v. Board of Governors of the Federal Reserve System*, 807 F.2d 1052 (D.C.Cir.1986) (Bankers Trust). In that case, the bank both advised issuers of commercial paper regarding structure and terms and then assisted the issuers, as agent, in privately placing the commercial paper. The court expressly rejected the argument that the combination with advice transformed the bank's agency transactional activity (*i.e.,* selling the commercial paper as agent for the issuer) into an activity prohibited by the Glass–Steagall Act; instead the court held such activity was squarely permitted under section 16 of the Act. *Bankers Trust*, 807 F.2d at 1061. We believe this analysis also supports the permissibility of the combined provision of investment advice and brokerage service.

As noted above, the Subsidiary will offer investment advice to a mutual fund and simultaneously provide investment advice and brokerage services to its customers. The Subsidiary may recommend, purchase or sell shares of the mutual fund for which it will act as investment advisor. In our opinion, the contemporaneous provision of these services is a permissible activity under the national banking laws, including the Glass–Steagall Act. The disclosures required by the federal securities laws and regulations, which govern such transactions, will provide customers with sufficient information to alleviate any concerns relating to conflicts of interest. *See Bankers Trust*, 807 F.2d at 1067; *see generally Securities Industry Association v. Board of Governors of the Federal Reserve System*, No. 86–1412, slip op. at 19 (hazards not likely to develop given realities of brokerage industry and commitments made by the bank).

Although there is obviously no "affiliation" within the meaning of Section 20 or 32 of the Glass–Steagall Act between the Subsidiary and the mutual fund which it will advise, *see* 12 U.S.C. § 221a, the Subsidiary would be considered an affiliate of the investment company it advises for the purposes of Section 23A of the Federal Reserve Act. *See* 12 U.S.C. § 371c(b)(1)(D). This statute defines a covered transaction to include "the acceptance of securities issued by the affiliate as collateral security for a loan or extension of credit to any person or company." 12 U.S.C. § 371c(b)(7)(D). Where the Subsidiary allows its customers to purchase on margin shares of the mutual fund for which it acts as investment advisor, such margin lending will be deemed a covered transaction. If the Subsidiary chooses to engage in margin lending with respect to the mutual fund shares described above, it will have to comply with the pertinent limitations and requirements of 12 U.S.C. § 371c.

You state that the principal office of the Subsidiary will be located in the main office complex of the Bank; however additional offices of the Subsidiary may be opened throughout the United States. In our opinion, the Subsidiary's proposed activities do not include the types of business for which a branch license is required under 12 U.S.C. § 36(f), and therefore the bank may offer them at locations other than its branches.

In a recent case, the Supreme Court affirmed the Office's decision that a national bank could offer discount brokerage at non-branch locations because discount brokerage did not involve the three types of core banking business enumerated in section 36(f) or an activity similar to the enumerated types. *See Security Pacific*, supra. The Office also has previously taken the position that the provision of investment advice is likewise not an activity requiring a branch license under section 36(f) because it too is not one of the three enumerated activities. *See* Letter from Michael Patriarca, Deputy Comptroller (March 28, 1985). The recent case in the related area of discount brokerage is supportive of that analysis. Thus, the Subsidiary's proposed activities may be offered at locations other than approved branches.

Where the Subsidiary is engaged in margin lending for customers, please note that the Bank and Subsidiary must take appropriate steps to ensure this activity is conducted in compliance with 12 U.S.C. § 36. *See, e.g.,* 12 C.F.R. § 7.7380.

## Comments and Questions

1. What is the difference between the activities authorized with respect to mutual fund products made available to customers in accordance with the interpretive letter and those prohibited in the *Camp* case? Is it fair to say that the bank may actively advertise mutual funds that the bank is involved with as the investment adviser? May the bank

advise people to buy the fund? Is the distinction that someone else is technically "distributing" the fund, i.e., there is a third party underwriter/distributor? What if the distributor subcontracts with an affiliate of the bank holding company to provide administrative and record-keeping support for the distribution process?

2. The *First Union* letter and the precedents upon which it relied paved the way for substantial banking involvement in the mutual fund industry. Perhaps most prominent illustration of this trend was Mellon's 1993 acquisition of the Dreyfus family of mutual funds. See Mellon Bank Corp., 79 Fed Res. Bull. 626 (June 1993). Even before that transaction took place, however, banking organizations had made substantial inroads in this market. Consider the following account, written shortly after the Mellon-Dreyfus transaction took place:

Depository institutions can break into the mutual fund market in two ways. First, they can sell already-established, non-banking mutual funds (known as non-proprietary funds) through their institution. For many small depository institutions, selling non-proprietary mutual funds is the easiest way to satisfy the needs of their customers interested in investment products. Banks may sell these funds through their own employees, through the employees of a broker-dealer affiliate, or through a networking arrangement with an unaffiliated broker-dealer whose employees conduct business in the banks' offices.

Second, banks can also offer proprietary funds – funds that a bank or affiliate advisers. Large banks have not been timid in offering such funds even though this strategy requires a concerted effort among different entities to organize the mutual funds and attract assets. As interest rates have fallen in over the last few years and the financial services industry has become more competitive, many banks have seized the opportunity to derive stable fee income from the mutual fund business while satisfying their depositors' investment needs

During the past five years, bank-advised mutual funds have grown from 213 portfolios with $35.4 billion in assets and to a 1,017 portfolios with $181.1 billion in assets. Thus, and in the five years prior to 1993, bank-advised mutual funds increased from two percent to 11 percent of all mutual fund assets.

See Jane E. Willis, *Banks and Mutual Funds, A Functional Approach to Reform*, 1 COLUM. BUS. L. REV. 221, 222-23 (1995). For a detailed treatment of the regulatory safeguards that federal banking agencies have promulgated to govern the manner in which banking organizations market bank-advised mutual funds, see MELANIE L. FEIN, ET AL., MUTUAL FUND ACTIVITIES OF BANKS (1998). Are these developments consistent with *Camp*?

# Section 4. Underwriting and Dealing

As explored in the preceding two sections, banking organizations have succeeded in gaining regulatory approval to undertake a wide range of agency and advisory services for their customers. The only remaining sector of the securities business untouched by these precedents was the direct purchase and sale of securities, as either underwriter or dealer. We now explore the extent to which banking organizations have penetrated this final market.

## Security Industry Association  v. Board of Governors ("Citicorp, et al.")
### 839 F.2d 47 (2d Cir.), *cert. denied*, 486 U.S. 1059 (1988)

CARDAMONE, Circuit Judge:

We review on this appeal those provisions of the Banking Act of 1933 that separated the commercial and investment banking industries and are known as the Glass–Steagall Act. . . . Demand for divorcing banking and securities activities followed in the wake of the stock market crash of 1929, which occurred, it was said, because a mountain of credit rested on only a molehill of cash. The actions of the Federal Reserve Board that we review today allow commercial and investment banking to compete in a narrow market, and to that extent dismantle the wall of separation installed between them by the Glass–Steagall Act. Whether Santayana's notion that those who will not learn from the past are condemned to repeat it fairly characterizes the consequences of the Board's action is not for us to say. Our task is to review the Glass–Steagall Act, the legislative history that surrounded its enactment, and its prior judicial construction to determine whether the Board reasonably interpreted the Act's often ambiguous terms.

The Securities Industry Association (SIA) and seven bank holding companies petition for review of six related orders of the Board of Governors of the Federal Reserve System (Board). The orders approved the bank holding companies' applications to utilize subsidiaries as the vehicle by which they can underwrite and deal in certain securities. The Board determined that the approved activities would not run afoul of § 20 of the Glass–Steagall Act, which proscribes affiliations of banks—here, the holding companies' member bank subsidiaries—with entities that are "engaged principally" in underwriting and dealing in securities. At the same time, the Board limited the scope of the approved activities. The decisions allowing bank subsidiaries to engage in securities transactions and the limitations that were imposed are the focus of the petitions seeking review. For the reasons set forth below, we deny the petitions for review save for the bank holding companies' cross-petition for review that seeks to eliminate the market share limitation.

BACKGROUND

*I The Board's Orders*

On April 30, 1987 the Board approved the applications of Citicorp, J.P. Morgan & Co., Inc., and Bankers Trust New York Corp. to engage in limited securities activities through wholly-owned subsidiaries. 73 Fed.Reserve Bull. 473 (1987). At the time of the applications, the subsidiaries were engaged entirely in underwriting and dealing in U.S. government and agency securities and those of state and municipal governments. The holding companies sought to extend their subsidiaries' activities to underwriting and dealing in municipal revenue bonds, mortgage related securities, consumer receivables related securities, and commercial paper. With the exception of the consumer receivables, on which decision was deferred because of an insufficient record, the Board approved the applications by a vote of three to two. Limitations on the scope of the activities more restrictive than those initially proposed by the holding companies—to be discussed more fully below—were imposed. . . .

SIA, a trade association representing securities brokers, dealers, and underwriters, petitioned for review of the April 30th and May 18th orders, arguing that the approved activities would violate § 20 of the Glass–Steagall Act. The holding companies cross-petitioned challenging the Board imposed limitations. We granted a stay of the orders on May 19, 1987 pending this expedited appeal.

## II  The Board's Analysis

The bank holding companies' applications were made pursuant to § 4(c)(8) of the Bank Holding Company Act of 1956, which allows a bank holding company to acquire the "shares of any company the activities of which the Board ... has determined ... to be so closely related to banking ... as to be a proper incident thereto." 12 U.S.C. § 1843(c)(8) (1982). The determination that the approved securities activities are closely related to banking is not contested on this appeal. Rather, since the Board's discretion under § 4(c)(8) is limited by the Glass–Steagall Act, cf. *Board of Governors of Fed. Reserve Sys. v. Investment Co. Inst.*, 450 U.S. 46, 76–77 (1981) (*ICI* ), the principal issue before the Board was whether the approval of the activities would contravene that Act.

Section 20 of the Glass–Steagall Act forbids a member bank of the Federal Reserve System from affiliating with an organization "engaged principally" in, *inter alia,* underwriting or dealing in securities. 12 U.S.C. § 377 (1982). Bank holding companies have been allowed since 1978—without a court challenge by SIA—to acquire or form subsidiaries that underwrite and deal in securities representing obligations of the United States and of states and their political subdivisions. *See, e.g., United Bancorp,* 64 Fed.Reserve Bull. 222 (1978); *see also* 12 C.F.R. § 225.25(b)(16) (1987) (regulation permitting such activity). Section 16 of the Glass–Steagall Act expressly permits banks themselves to underwrite and deal in these governmental securities, known as "bank-eligible securities." 12 U.S.C. § 24 (Seventh) (1982 & Supp. IV 1986).

Given the authorization in § 16 for banks to engage in bank-eligible securities activities, the Board concluded that Congress did not aim in § 20 to proscribe bank affiliates from engaging in the same activities. 73 Fed.Reserve Bull. at 478–81. It reasoned that it would be anomalous not to permit the bank's subsidiary to engage in the activities lawfully permitted the bank. That illogical result necessarily follows if bank-eligible securities are defined as "securities" under § 20 because that section prohibits a member bank from being affiliated with an organization "engaged principally" in securities dealing. Hence, according to the Board, "securities" cannot logically mean bank-eligible securities. "Securities" in § 20 must therefore only refer to those types of securities that under § 16 banks cannot themselves deal in or underwrite, known as "bank-ineligible securities." The activities approved in the orders at issue on this appeal—underwriting and dealing in municipal revenue bonds, mortgage related securities, and commercial paper—cannot be conducted by a member bank and are therefore bank-ineligible securities activities.

Establishing as a predicate that the proscription in § 20 extends only to bank-ineligible securities, the Board turned to the question of when an affiliate is "engaged principally" in such activity. Relying on its order in *Bankers Trust New York Corp.*, 73 Fed.Reserve Bull. 138 (1987), the Board held that the term "engaged principally" means any substantial activity. 73 Fed.Reserve Bull. at 482. It then concluded that subsidiaries would not be engaged substantially in bank-ineligible activities if no more than five to ten percent of their total gross revenues was derived from such activities over a two-year period, and if the activities in connection with *each* type of bank-ineligible security did not constitute more than five to ten percent of the market for that particular security. *Id.* at 485–86. The Board then proceeded to approve gross revenue and market share levels at five percent—the low end of the acceptable range—but stated that it would review the five percent limitations within a year after the implementation of its orders. The applicants wanted, of course, to engage in higher levels of activity.

On review, SIA argues that the Board erroneously construed the Glass–Steagall Act by construing the word "securities" in § 20 not to include bank-eligible securities. In other words, SIA contends that § 20 limits both bank-eligible *and* bank-ineligible security activities by a member bank affiliate. SIA also objects to the Board's construction of "engaged principally." The bank holding companies urge us to adopt the Board's construction of § 20 with regard to "securities", but argue, at the same time, that the Glass–Steagall Act mandates that the Board allow a higher level of bank-ineligible activity than that approved. . . .

[T]he first question is whether § 20 is ambiguous.

The Board readily concedes that the term "securities" in § 20 could be read to include not only those securities that banks are expressly permitted to underwrite or deal in, that is, bank-eligible securities, but also those that banks are not entitled to underwrite or deal in, that is, bank-ineligible securities. Unlike § 16—which expressly distinguishes bank-eligible from bank-ineligible securities—§ 20 does not distinguish the terms. Hence, at least on the surface § 20 would appear to refer to both kinds of securities.

But a closer examination of Glass–Steagall leads us to reject this conclusion. In the first place, the Act makes three different references to the term "securities." Section 16 distinguishes bank-eligible from bank-ineligible securities. 12 U.S.C. § 24 (Seventh) (1982 & Supp. IV 1986). Repealed § 19(e), discussed *infra* note 4, referred to "securities *of any sort.*" 48 Stat. at 188 (emphasis added). And §§ 20 and 32 refer simply to "securities." 12 U.S.C. § 377 (1982) (§ 20); 48 Stat. at 194 (codified as amended at 12 U.S.C. § 78 (1982)) (§ 32). That Congress chose three distinctively different ways to describe securities raises a red flag that cautions against declaring that the meaning of that term in § 20 is clear.

Further support for the proposition that § 20 is uncertain is provided by the subsequent amendment to § 21 of Glass–Steagall. Section 21 originally did not expressly exempt bank-eligible securities as did § 16. A 1935 amendment made it plain that § 21 did not prevent that which § 16 permitted. *See* Banking Act of 1935, Pub.L. No. 74–305, § 303, 49 Stat. 684, 707. The significance of this to the issue of § 20's ambiguity is that the amendment was only intended to *clarify* existing law, *see, e.g.,* H.R.Rep. No. 742, 74th Cong., 1st Sess. 16 (1935); S.Rep. No. 1260, 73d Cong., 2d Sess. 2 (1934); *Securities Indus. Ass'n v. Board of Governors of the Fed. Reserve Sys.*, 807 F.2d 1052, 1057–58 (D.C.Cir.1986) (*Bankers Trust II* ), *cert. denied*, 483 U.S. 1005 (1987), and did not purport to effect any substantive change. But, if the 1935 amendment was not intended to alter the substance of § 21, it follows that the Congress that enacted Glass–Steagall did not invariably make an explicit distinction between bank-eligible and bank-ineligible securities, even when it aimed to distinguish them from one another. Based on this, we can conclude with some confidence that Congress' reference in § 20 to "securities" is ambiguous, and undertake to decide whether the Board's interpretation of securities in § 20 is reasonable and therefore entitled to deference.

Of course, "deference is not to be a device that emasculates the significance of judicial review." *Securities Indus. Ass'n v. Board of Governors of the Fed. Reserve Sys.*, 468 U.S. 137, 142–43  (1984) (*Bankers Trust I* ).  One factor militating against deference to the Board's definition of securities is its failure to address an apparent contradiction, discussed below, between its interpretation of § 20 and its prior view of § 32. This failure implicates two factors that courts take into consideration in deciding whether to accord deference to an administrative agency charged with implementing a statute: first, "the thoroughness, validity, and consistency of an agency's reasoning," *Federal Election Comm'n v. Democratic Senatorial Campaign Comm.*, 454 U.S. 27, 37 (1981), and, second, the consistency of the agency's present interpretation with its earlier pronouncements, *Morton v. Ruiz*, 415 U.S. 199, 237 (1974); *Skidmore v. Swift & Co.*, 323 U.S. 134, 140 (1944).

The Board should have examined § 32 in its analysis of § 20 because—as the Supreme Court has indicated—"§§ 32 and 20 contain identical language, were enacted for similar purposes, and are part of the same statute." *Securities Indus. Ass'n v. Board of Governors of the Fed. Reserve Sys.*, 468 U.S. 207, 219 (1984) (*Schwab* ).  Thus, an established interpretation of the language of one section is important in interpreting the language of the other. *See id.*  In that respect, the Board's 120–page opinion is deficient.

The Board's earlier view of § 32 suggests that bank-eligible securities were *included* within the term "securities" in § 32.  In 1936 the Board exempted from § 32 individuals dealing in or underwriting "bonds, notes, certificates of indebtedness, and Treasury bills of the United States."  22 Fed.Reserve Bull. 51, 52 (1936).  As SIA argues, this suggests that the Board understood that bank-eligible securities were covered by § 32, because there was otherwise no need to exempt from § 32 individuals involved in those securities activities.  At oral argument the Board's response to SIA's contention was that it had merely failed to explain its reasoning for the exemption, and that granting the exemption from the prohibitions of § 32 was done only for purposes of clarity.

This could be a plausible explanation, but in this instance we think it is not.  Although in its current form Regulation R does exempt from § 32 individuals engaged in any securities activity permitted to banks under § 16, *see* 12 C.F.R. § 218.2 (1987), the exemption, as originally enacted, did not exempt *all* forms of bank-eligible securities, but only the obligations of the United States.  Omitted from exemption were the general obligations of the States or their political subdivisions. *See* 22 Fed.Reserve Bull. at 52.  From this it is obvious that the Board did not read § 32 as excluding *ab initio* all bank-eligible securities, but rather that it exercised the authority granted it by Congress under § 32—authority not granted in § 20—to create a narrow exemption for individuals dealing in United States government obligations.  In addition, in a footnote to the 1936 regulation, the Board enumerated instances in which the terms of § 32 did not apply. *See* 22 Fed.Reserve Bull. at 51 n. 1. Plainly, the Board knew how to say when § 32 did not apply to a certain activity, and how to state that a certain activity was subject to § 32, but was nevertheless *exempted* pursuant to the Board under its statutory authority.

The Board's orders on appeal here are not instances where the Board failed to adopt an expressly articulated position on the meaning of § 20. *Cf. Investment Co. Inst. v. Camp*, 401 U.S. 617, 627–28 (1971) (*Camp* ). Nonetheless, its failure to address—in what is an otherwise comprehensive and reasoned decision—the significance of its prior interpretation of § 32 counsels against granting it full deference. Our own review of the history of the Glass–Steagall Act leads us nonetheless to conclude that construing § 20 as not encompassing activities by bank affiliates in bank-eligible securities is essential if Congress' purpose in enacting § 20 is to be effectuated.

DISCUSSION

The two principal issues presented to this court are the Board's constructions of the terms "securities" and "engaged principally" under § 20 of the Glass–Steagall Act. The proper interpretation of § 20 is an issue of first impression and necessitates a comprehensive examination of both the relevant legislation and the events surrounding its enactment. . . .

*II The Meaning of "Securities" in § 20*

When called upon to interpret the Glass-Steagall Act, judges "face a virtually insurmountable burden due to the vast dichotomy between the ostensible legislative intent and the actual motivations of Congress." *Glass-Steagall Dilemma, supra*, at 1-2. Divining the aim of Congress in enacting § 20 is particularly formidable because the issue of the proper relationship between commercial banks and their affiliates caused considerable disagreement among legislators and experts who participated in the development of what became the Banking Act of 1933. *See generally Perkins, The Divorce of Commercial and Investment Banking: A History*, 88 Banking L.J. 483, 505-12 (1971) [hereinafter *Banking Divorce* ]. Consequently, we approach the subject first by examining the legislative history of § 20, analyzing the Congressional compromise that resulted in the enactment of § 20, and then by looking at prior judicial construction of the Act.

A. Legislative History

1. Envisioning § 20--Congress' Purpose

The Act's legislative history reflects the notion that the underlying cause of the stock market crash in 1929 and subsequent bank insolvencies came about from the excessive use of bank credit to speculate in the stock market. *See* S.Rep. No. 77, 73d Cong., 1st Sess. 3-9 (1933) [hereinafter *1933 Senate Report*]; *see also* 75 Cong.Rec. 9883-84 (1932) (remarks of Sen. Glass) (criticizing transformation of the Federal Reserve System from a commercial banking system into one used for "stock-market speculative operations"). Bank affiliates were identified as a major factor in the overextension of credit for security loans. *See 1933 Senate Report, supra*, at 9-10.

Congress' concern was not limited solely to how securities affiliates contributed to the excesses in bank credit; its apprehension was far more fundamental and structural. Senator Bulkley, for example, repeatedly stressed that the debate over affiliates should not obscure "[t]he important and underlying question [of] whether banking institutions receiving commercial and savings deposits ought to be permitted at all to engage in the investment-security business." 75 Cong.Rec. 9910 (1932). He argued that "[t]he existence of security affiliates is a mere incident to this question," id., and reiterated that "the real question is not whether . . . banks shall be permitted to have investment-security affiliates but rather whether they should be permitted to engage in the investment-security business in any manner at all, through affiliates or otherwise," id. at 9911.

Two large problems attendant upon the involvement of a commercial bank in investment banking--either on its own or through use of an affiliate--were identified by Congress. The first was "the danger of banks using bank assets in imprudent securities investments." *ICI*, 450 U.S. at 66; *see also Camp*, 401 U.S. at 630. The second "focused on the more subtle hazards that arise when a commercial bank goes beyond the business of acting as fiduciary or managing agent and enters the investment banking business either directly or by establishing an affiliate to hold and sell particular investments." *Camp*, 401 U.S. at 630. . . .

Sections 16 and 21 effectively barred commercial banks from *direct* engagement in investment banking, with the notable exception of government securities. Yet even before the 1929 crash, direct involvement by a bank had been considered "improper," *see Camp*, 401 U.S. at 629, but bank affiliates had developed as the medium for commercial banks' *indirect* entry into investment banking, *see id.* Even though the stock market debacle laid bare the dangers arising from the activities of securities affiliates, opinion was divided on how best to mitigate those dangers.

No one argued that the affiliate system had not been abused in the past, *see, e.g., 1931 Hearings, supra*, at 298-99 (remarks of Charles E. Mitchell, Chairman, National City Bank of New York). Experts believed that an adequate check on such abuse was to establish rigorous examination requirements for affiliates, which had remained largely unregulated before 1929. *See, e.g., id.* at 117 (testimony of J.H. Case, Chairman, Board of Directors of the Federal Reserve Bank of New York); *id.* at 192 (testimony of A.H. Wiggin, Chairman of the Governing Board, Chase National Bank); *id.* at 364 (testimony of O.D. Young, Chairman of the Board, General Electric Co.); *id.* at 405 (testimony of M.W. Traylor, Chairman of the Board, First National Bank of Chicago). Others thought that if the slate were wiped clean, affiliates should not be legal, but that in 1933 a complete divorce between commercial and investment banking was not feasible given the established role of affiliates in the banking system. *See, e.g., id.* at 22 (testimony of J. Pole, Comptroller of the Currency); *id.* at 38-39 (testimony of G.L. Harrison, Governor, Federal Reserve Bank of New York); *id.* at 148 (testimony of A.C. Miller, Member, Federal Reserve Board).

Some advocated complete separation of the commercial and investment banking industries. See, e.g., id. at 231 (testimony of B.W. Trafford, Vice Chairman, First National Bank of Boston). Senator Glass--an adherent of this view--was of the opinion that a "complete separation" was both warranted and capable of being accomplished. *E.g., Operation of the National and Federal Reserve Banking Systems, Hearings on S.4115 Before the Senate Comm. on Banking and Currency*, 72d Cong., 1st Sess. 42, 267 (1932) (remarks of Sen. Glass) [hereinafter 1932 Hearings ]. Senator Glass' views are significant, of course, because of his role in drafting and shaping the Banking Act of 1933, a portion of which bears his name. . . . Yet, despite the Senator's goal of complete separation, the Senate took a less drastic step.

Acknowledging that "[i]t has been suggested ... that the affiliate system be simply 'abolished,' " the Senate rejected this as impossible and stated that its goals toward regulating affiliates were to (1) separate "*as far as possible* " member banks from affiliates of all kinds; (2) limit advances or loans from parent to affiliate; and (3) install satisfactory examination requirements for affiliates. *1933 Senate Report, supra,* at 10 (emphasis added).

### 2. Construing § 20--Congress' Compromise

Section 20 was Congress' solution to the problem of affiliates and establishes the boundary separating banks from their security affiliates. While § 21 prohibits firms "engaged" in investment banking activities from accepting deposits, § 20 prohibits commercial bank affiliation with firms "engaged principally" in underwriting and dealing in securities. The inference following from this different terminology is obvious: § 20 applies a "less stringent standard" than the absolute bar between commercial and investment banking laid down by §§ 16 and 21. *ICI*, 450 U.S. at 60 n. 26. Nor can the difference in terminology be attributed to oversight. Section 21 originally contained the term "engaged principally." In offering the amendment that deleted "principally," Senator Bulkley argued that "[i]t has become apparent that at least some of the great investment houses are engaged in so many forms of business that there is some doubt as to whether the investment business is the principal one." 77 Cong.Rec. 4180 (1933). Given that one of the leading advocates of Glass-Steagall recognized that "engaged" connoted a stricter standard than "engaged principally," it is inconceivable that the latter term could remain in § 20 by sheer happenstance. Thus, while the original impetus behind the Glass-Steagall bill on the floor of Congress may have been to sever completely the commercial and investment banking industries, it fell short of that goal--a victim of legislative compromise.

Legislative history also supports the view that § 20's use of the word "securities" did not imply a complete separation between commercial and investment banking. A colloquy between Senators Glass and Long is illuminating:

MR LONG. I have been told that the Senator has said that he did not think this bill would prohibit the handling of Government and State bonds by the Federal reserve banks, that the Senator's provision against affiliates handling bonds was not intended to affect the handling of Government and State bonds.

MR. GLASS. They are expressly excluded from the terms of the bill.

MR. LONG. As to both affiliates and the banks?

MR. GLASS. As to affiliates? We are trying to abolish the affiliates in a period of years.

MR. LONG. The Senator has no objection, has he, to an affiliate handling them if they handle nothing but the Government and State Bonds under supervision, the same supervision the banks are given?

MR. GLASS. I am objecting to affiliates altogether. I am objecting to a national banking institution setting up a back-door arrangement by which it may engage in a business which the national bank act denies it the privilege of doing. If investment banking is a profitable business, who does not know that such business will be set up as a separate institution, not using the money and prestige and facilities of a national bank and its deposits to engage in investment activities? I want to make it impossible hereafter to have the portfolios of commercial banks filled with useless speculative securities, so that when stringency comes upon the country these banks may not respond to the requirements of commerce. That is what is the matter with the country to-day, and it is because this bill would avert a repetition of that disaster that intense and bitter opposition has been organized against it.

76 Cong.Rec. 2000 (1933). Senator Glass' aspiration to divorce completely commercial banks from their security affiliates was never attained: § 20 only prohibits affiliation with firms that are "engaged principally" in forbidden investment activity. SIA urges from the above colloquy that Senator Glass objected to affiliates' handling even securities that banks themselves could underwrite under the proposed legislation and that the Senator's view carried the day in § 20 as enacted. On the contrary, we believe Senator Glass' response to Senator Long indicates that he was primarily concerned with "back-door" arrangements between banks and their security affiliates that permitted affiliates to engage in the securities business denied by law to the bank itself. Senator Glass' reservation did not encompass affiliate activity in a business that § 16 grants to a bank "the privilege of doing."

Further, Senator Long's initial query indicates that the issue of whether affiliates ought to be able to engage in bank-eligible activities to the same extent as banks themselves was not dormant during the debates. Thus, Senator Long commented that those who had opposed some provisions in the bill "have seen some virtue in it. I particularly refer to the divorcing of the affiliates, except in so far as they handle municipal and Government bonds and securities." 76 Cong.Rec. 2274 (1933). To make certain affiliates had the same right to deal in government obligations, Senator Long had printed and circulated an amendment to the Glass-Steagall bill to that effect. Proposed Amend. to S. 4412, 72d Cong., 2d Sess. (Jan. 10, 1933). Despite Senator Long's repeated insistence that § 20 would not preclude bank-eligible activities by an affiliate, this amendment was never formally raised in debate. The Banking Act of 1933 became law five months later, on June 16, 1933, and it can be plausibly urged that the bill finally agreed upon and enacted into law made his amendment unnecessary. Recognizing the power of Senator Long's position, SIA argues that statements and actions taken during debate are not entitled to much weight. . . . A look at subsequent events in this case illustrates the soundness of that rule. In 1935, just two years after his strong rhetoric in the Banking Act debate, Senator Glass himself supported a proposed amendment to that law granting to commercial banks the right to underwrite securities. 79 Cong.Rec. 11,827 (1935). So much for not having "the portfolios of commercial banks filled with useless securities."

Thus, it seems eminently reasonable to conclude from Senator Glass' response to Senator Long, as well as other evidence in the legislative history, that Congress' concern was primarily with bank affiliate activities in bank-ineligible securities. Bank affiliates often "devote[d] themselves ... to perilous underwriting operations, stock speculation, and maintaining a market for the banks' own stock often largely with the resources of the parent bank." *1933 Senate Report, supra,* at 10. According to Senator Glass, "[w]hat the committee had foremost in its thought was to exclude from commercial banking all investment securities except those of an undoubted character that would be surely liquidated; and for that reason we made an exception [in § 16] of United States securities and of the general liabilities of States and subdivisions of States." 76 Cong.Rec. 2092 (1933). Given that Glass–Steagall was a means to sever commercial banking only from more speculative, "perilous" investment activities, in which bank-eligible activities were not included, an interpretation of "securities" in § 20 that excludes bank-eligible securities from its reach is entirely consistent with Congress' aim.

The history of security affiliates in the United States also supports this view. Many banks formed security affiliates in order to handle the sale of government bonds used to finance World War I. B. Klebaner, *Commercial Banking in the United States: A History* 109–10 (1974); *Banking Divorce, supra,* at 490–91; *see also 1932 Hearings, supra,* at 29 (testimony of A.M. Pope, President, Investment Bankers' Ass'n of Am.). Banks were "expected" to aid the government in distributing war loans and were "encouraged" to aid potential investors by lending them the purchase price of government bonds. *Banking Divorce, supra,* at 491. It was not until the 1920's that affiliates began to expand into private debt and equity securities activities in response to the demands of the public and business. *See id.* at 493–96; *see also* 77 Cong.Rec. 3835 (1933) (remarks of Rep. Steagall) ("Our great banking system was diverted from its original purposes into investment activities, and its service devoted to speculation and international high finance."); 75 Cong.Rec. 9904–05 (1932) (remarks of Sen. Walcott) (businesses began to finance their requirements by sale of securities rather than by borrowing; growth of affiliates was "the outgrowth of the willingness of public to buy readily and without very much inquiry"). It was not the affiliate system as a concept that worried Congress, but the affiliate system as it had developed. The evil that Congress intended to attack was bank involvement in speculative securities, that is, bank-ineligible securities. We cannot attribute to Congress a purpose to limit *all* securities activities when it consistently made clear that it was only concerned with *one type.*
. . . .

In light of these principles, the Court's subtle hazards analysis does not preclude the Board's construction of § 20. As noted, Congress was not concerned with affiliation *per se,* but rather with the dangers attendant upon the entry of commercial banks into the investment banking field either directly or indirectly. Yet even after acknowledging these perils, Congress allowed banks to underwrite and deal in bank-eligible securities under § 16, making it plain therefore that it believed the risks were not so great when banks dealt in these securities. As Senator Bulkley stressed, whether or not a bank chooses to engage in these activities itself or through an affiliate is relatively unimportant compared to the question of whether a bank should engage in them at all. Since banks are allowed under § 16 to underwrite and deal in government obligations without limitation, it would be incongruous for § 20 to prohibit banks from affiliating with entities that are merely "engaged principally" in those same activities.

Further, the Supreme Court observed that "[i]n both the Glass–Steagall Act itself and in the Bank Holding Company Act, Congress indicated that a bank affiliate may engage in activities that would be impermissible for the bank itself." *ICI,* 450 U.S. at 64. Similarly, in *Schwab* the Court commented that "the fact that § 16 of the Glass–Steagall Act allows banks to engage directly in [a service] suggests that the activity was not the sort that concerned Congress in its effort to secure the Nation's banks from the risks of the securities market." 468 U.S. at 221. The same principle necessarily applies here. As we recently stated, "the latitude the Act grants bank holding companies partially to engage in activities such as underwriting, which implicate the Act's policies whether conducted by banks or by bank holding companies, suggests that bank holding companies can, under the Act, be allowed principally to engage in activities which pose the dangers the Act addressed only when conducted by banks." *Securities Indus. Ass'n v. Board of Governors of the Fed. Reserve Sys.,* 716 F.2d 92, 100 (2d Cir.1983), *aff'd, Schwab,* 468 U.S. 207 (1984). Because underwriting and dealing in government securities pose no hazards to banks themselves, *a fortiori* bank affiliates should be able principally to engage in the same activity.

In sum, the Board's construction of Glass–Steagall is not only reasonable, but dictated by a thorough examination of the legislative history of Glass–Steagall and of the hazards that Congress sought to prevent when enacting § 20. We hold that it was not Congress' purpose in § 20 to preclude a bank affiliate from engaging in the same activities to the same extent as a member bank and we uphold the Board's determination that the reference in § 20 to "securities" does not encompass those securities which § 16 allows banks themselves to underwrite.

### III  "Engaged Principally"

We now turn to the Board's determination of when a security affiliate is "engaged principally" in activities covered by § 20. In their applications the bank holding companies sought to comply with the "engaged principally" standard of § 20 by proposing limitations on their underwriting and dealing in bank-ineligible securities. J.P. Morgan & Co., for example, proposed that its bank-ineligible securities activities would not exceed during any rolling two-year period 15 percent of its total business. J.P. Morgan & Co. Proposal, 50 Fed.Reg. 41,025 (1985). It proposed a combination of accounting tests to measure its compliance with the 15 percent limitation. The other companies proposed total volume limits of ten to 15 percent of their total business.

The Board rejected these proposals. Following the analysis set forth in its *Bankers Trust* order, 73 Fed.Reserve Bull. 138 (1987), the Board concluded that "engaged principally" in § 20 denotes any "substantial" bank-ineligible activity. *See* 73 Fed.Reserve Bull. at 482. Measured quantitatively, the Board stated that an affiliate would not be principally or substantially engaged in bank-ineligible activities if: (1) the gross revenue from § 20 activities did not exceed five to ten percent of the affiliate's total gross revenues (gross revenue limitation or gross revenue test); and (2) the affiliate's activities in connection with *each* particular type of ineligible security did not account for more than five to ten percent of the total amount of that type of security underwritten domestically by all firms (or, with commercial paper, the average amount of dealer-placed commercial paper outstanding) during the previous calendar year (market share limitation or market share test). Applying this measure to the applications before it, the Board selected the lower five percent figure for both gross revenue and market share limitations. It recognized that this was a "conservative approach," but stated that it would review the limitations within one year of the implementation of its orders. 73 Fed.Reserve Bull. at 485.

The bank holding companies petition for review of this interpretation of "engaged principally." First, they argue that the Board's view contravenes Supreme Court precedent. Second, they contend that the limitation is inconsistent with the language, structure, and legislative intent of the Glass–Steagall Act. Finally, cross-petitioner Security Pacific Corporation argues that the Board erred in adopting an inflexible percentage test instead of approaching each affiliate's application on a case-by-case basis.

The term "engaged principally" is intrinsically ambiguous. As discussed above, we must uphold the Board's interpretation if it is reasonable. Unlike the facts presented on the issue of the scope of § 20, the Board's position here does not contradict its prior interpretations. Accordingly, we defer to the Board's construction of § 20.

*A. Agnew*

The Board found that "principally" in § 20 means "substantially." The banks urge that in *Board of Governors of the Fed. Reserve Sys. v. Agnew,* 329 U.S. 441 (1947), the Supreme Court decided that "principally" means something more than substantially, and therefore that the Board's decision conflicts with *Agnew.*

In *Agnew* the Board issued an order that required the removal of directors of a national bank because of their affiliation with a company which, in the Board's view, was "primarily engaged" in underwriting securities as prohibited by § 32 of the Act. The United States Court of Appeals for the District of Columbia reversed the Board and held that a company is not "primarily engaged" in underwriting unless the activity is its chief or principal activity—one exceeding 50 percent of the company's business. *See Agnew,* 153 F.2d 785, 790–91 (D.C.Cir.1946). The Court of Appeals rejected the Board's argument that "primarily" in § 32 could mean "substantially" or "importantly."

The Supreme Court reversed, holding that "primarily" in § 32 meant "substantially." 329 U.S. at 446. In support of that conclusion, the Court noted that Congress used three different terms in the Glass–Steagall Act to describe underwriting firms: (1) those merely *"engaged "* in underwriting (§ 21); (2) those *"primarily engaged "* in underwriting (§ 32); and (3) those *"engaged principally "* in underwriting (§ 20). 329 U.S. at 448. It then concluded that "[t]he inference seems reasonable to us that Congress by the words it chose marked a distinction which we should not obliterate by reading 'primarily' to mean 'principally'." *Id.* Because the Board has found that a gross income level of ten percent of covered activities will trigger § 32, *see* Staff Opinion 3–939, 1 Fed.Reserve Reg.Serv. 389 (Dec. 14, 1981), the holding companies argue that "principally" under § 20 mandates approval of a higher level of activity, and that their proposed ten to 15 percent limitations were well within that level.

The statements in *Agnew* regarding the meaning of "principally" are not dispositive in the instant case. For one thing the meaning of § 20 was not before the Supreme Court in that case. *See Cohens v. Virginia,* 19 U.S. (6 Wheat.) 264, 398 (1821). Further, the statements concerning § 20 are not essential to its holding that "primarily" means "substantially." *See Kastigar v. United States,* 406 U.S. 441, 454–55 (1972). The main focus of the Court's analysis is on definitions of "primary," *see* 329 U.S. at 446, and on the perils Congress sought to check by enacting § 32, *id.* at 447. In fact, the brief discussion of § 20 is used to demonstrate that "[t]here is other intrinsic evidence in the Banking Act of 1933 to support our conclusion [on the meaning of "primary"]." *Id.* Hence, we read *Agnew* as holding only that "primarily engaged" in § 32 means any "substantial activity."

### B. *"Substantially"*

The Board's construction of "engaged principally" as denoting any substantial activity is reasonable. We do not conclude that because "engaged principally" in § 20 and "primarily engaged" in § 32 both denote "substantial activity" that the two terms are therefore synonymous. Substantiality is an amorphous qualitative concept that has many quantitative definitional manifestations, *see The Shorter Oxford English Dictionary* 2172 (3d ed. 1973), which vary with the context in which the term is used. Hence, the *Agnew* dicta that "engaged principally" and "primarily engaged" do not necessarily mean the same thing, *see* 329 U.S. at 448–49, is not entirely circumscribed by the Board's interpretation. In fact, the same considerations that compelled the Court in *Agnew* to conclude that "primarily" in § 32 means "substantially" apply equally—if not more forcefully—here.

The Supreme Court in *Agnew* rejected a reading that "primarily" meant "chief" or "leading" because the concerns that Congress addressed in enacting § 32 do not vanish if the firm's underwriting activities are 49 percent rather than 51 percent. *See* 329 U.S. at 447. In both situations, "a bank director interested in the underwriting business may use his influence in the bank to involve it or its customers in securities which his underwriting house has in its portfolio or has committed itself to take." *Id.* The banks' argument essentially adopts the Court of Appeals holding in *Agnew,* that is, "principally" means "chief" or "first." But the same reasoning that guided the Supreme Court guides us. The worries envisioned by bank affiliation with securities firms do not disappear simply because the activity is less than 50 percent of a firm's business.

An example illuminates how equating "principally" in § 20 with "chief" or "first" begets the dangers foreseen by Congress. Such an interpretation would allow a member bank to become affiliated with any large integrated securities firm. One commentator has pointed out that reading "principally" as "chief" would allow a bank to be affiliated with Merrill Lynch & Co., Inc., one of the nation's largest investment bankers. *See* Plotkin, *What Meaning Does Glass–Steagall Have for Today's Financial World?*, 95 Banking L.J. 404, 414–16 (1977). It cannot be supposed that the Congress that enacted Glass–Steagall would have intended that § 20 not prohibit such affiliations. This is not to say that "principally" cannot in some contexts mean "chief" or "first," but rather that in § 20 the term must be given a definition that is both sensible *and* in harmony with legislative purpose.

Moreover, the logic of the holding companies' position is that "principally" in § 20 is a directly quantitative, not a qualitative, term. "Substantially," on the other hand, reflects the qualitative aspects of "principally." When Congress wanted to use a quantitative test in the Banking Act of 1933, it knew how to do it. *See* § 2(b), (c), 48 Stat. at 162–63 (definition of affiliate); § 13, 48 Stat. at 183 (collateral requirements for loans to affiliates); § 16 (Seventh), 48 Stat. at 185 (limitations on banks' purchase of securities for own account), § 19(b), 48 Stat. at 187 (level of assets for holding company affiliates to be maintained free of any liens); § 19(c), 48 Stat. at 187 (shareholders' liability determination). Because in § 20 Congress departed from a quantitative approach, the argument that a qualitative test should be controlling is all the more compelling.

SIA and ICI advance several arguments against the Board's interpretation of "principally." They assert that "engaged principally" in § 20 at least covers any firm "formed for the purpose of" underwriting securities, relying on the Supreme Court's statement in *ICI* regarding repealed § 19(e) that "[a]ll companies formed for the purpose of issuing or underwriting securities would surely meet the 'engaged principally' test." 450 U.S. at 70 n. 43. Concededly, the subsidiaries here were formed for the purpose of engaging in securities activities.

Yet, this argument is unpersuasive too. The Court's statement in *ICI* is dicta and seems to indicate nothing more remarkable than that a company formed for the purpose of underwriting securities most likely would be expected to be engaged principally in that activity. Further, since § 20 does not restrict bank-eligible securities activities, SIA and ICI arguably miss the point. Companies formed for the purpose of dealing in bank-eligible securities would not fall within the prohibitions of § 20. . . .

Alternatively, SIA claims that Congress intended that § 20 bar underwriting or dealing activities that constitute a "regular" or "integral" part of the affiliate's business, as opposed to "incidental" or "occasional" activities. The activities that concerned Congress did not necessarily arise only with the frequency of their repetition. In any event, the Board's interpretation of "principally" as any "substantial" activity adequately addresses any apprehension arising from the frequency or integral nature of an activity.

The final argument raised by SIA is that because the Board's interpretation of "engaged principally" necessitates regulation, it *a fortiori* contravenes the Glass–Steagall Act. It is true that "Congress rejected a regulatory approach when it drafted the statute." *Bankers Trust I,* 468 U.S. at 153. The Board's interpretation is one that attempts to walk the line that Congress laid down. The mere necessity of "regulation" in carrying out Glass–Steagall's "prohibitions" is insufficient to justify rejection of an otherwise reasonable interpretation of the Act. *Cf. Bankers Trust II,* 807 F.2d at 1067 ("The Glass–Steagall Act does impose a system of flat 'prohibitions' and 'prophylactic' measures, but this cannot obviate the need to examine particular factual situations to determine on which side of the prohibitory line they fall.").

Consequently, the Board's view of "engaged principally" as meaning any substantial activity is reasonable and consistent with Congressional purpose.

### C. Gross Revenue Limitation

The Board determined that substantial activity, measured quantitatively, constituted five to ten percent of an affiliate's gross revenues over a two-year period. 73 Fed.Reserve Bull. at 485. It set the approved level of activity at the five percent end of this range, but stated its intent to review this level within a year after the order's effective date. *Id.*

One troublesome facet of the Board's ruling is that "engaged principally" in § 20 is equally restrictive as—if not *more* restrictive than—"primarily engaged" in § 32. The Board has stated that if a firm's prohibited activities constitute less than ten percent of its gross business, *see* Staff Opinion 3–939, 1 Fed.Reserve Reg.Serv. 389 (Dec. 14, 1981), or amount to less than ten million dollars regardless of the percentage figure, *see* Board Letter 3–896, 1 Fed.Reserve Reg.Serv. 367 (May 22, 1959), the firm is not "primarily engaged" in such activities under § 32. By placing the permissible level of § 20 activity currently at only five percent of gross revenues—and never more than ten percent—the Board is employing, at least for the present, a more restrictive gross revenue test for § 20 than for § 32.

This initially seems to contradict the Supreme Court's indication that §§ 32 and 20 should be interpreted consistently. *See Schwab,* 468 U.S. at 219 (the term "public sale" should be interpreted consistently because "§§ 32 and 20 contain identical language, were enacted for similar purposes, and are part of the same statute."). But with regard to "engaged principally" versus "primarily engaged," §§ 20 and 32 differ; accordingly, there is justification for interpreting them slightly differently.

The legislative history also supports the conclusion that the Board's stringent quantitative interpretation of § 20 is reasonable. What became § 20 was proposed by Eugene Meyer, a governor of the Federal Reserve Board, as a *substitute* for the section which eventually became § 32, *see 1932 Hearings, supra,* at 387–88, because he believed that the language in the predecessor to § 32—in relevant respects identical to § 32—was overbroad and that it would therefore be ineffectual. *See id.* at 387. Meyer commented on the "difficulties in the way of accomplishing a complete divorce of member banks from their affiliates arising from the fact that a law intended for that purpose is likely to be susceptible of evasion or else to apply to many cases to which it is not intended to apply," *id.* at 388, and tentatively suggested substituting what is now § 20 for what is now § 32. It defies logic that § 20 should be interpreted *less* restrictively than § 32, based on Meyer's comments that § 20 was intended to be *more* restrictive than § 32.

Further support for a stricter interpretation of § 20 than of § 32 is derived from the fact that the dangers resulting from affiliation are arguably greater than those resulting only from personnel interlocks. The public associates a member bank and its affiliate because of their common ownership and often similar names. The potential for the public to associate the misfortunes of the affiliate with the bank is far greater than the association of firms with personnel interlocks, which are generally unknown to the public.

Given these considerations, we defer to the Board's determination that § 20 allows an affiliate to engage in bank-ineligible securities activities so long as those activities do not exceed five to ten percent of the affiliate's gross revenue. This range is both reasonable and consistent with the statute. Because of the Board's expertise we also defer to its decision to set the gross revenue limitation at five percent.

### D. Market Share Limitation

The Board's second limitation on the subsidiaries' bank-ineligible securities activities provides that the subsidiaries' involvement in *each* activity may not exceed a five percent share of the total market for that activity. It reasoned that it has employed a market share limitation in determining whether a firm is "primarily engaged" in securities activities within the meaning of § 32. 73 Fed.Reserve Bull. at 484. The Board stated that "the fact that an affiliate would be a major force in a particular securities market would be an evidentiary factor suggesting that the affiliate is 'engaged principally' in underwriting securities." *Id.* It also concluded that a sales volume test—currently employed under its interpretation of § 32—would be subject to manipulation and that a market share test "would provide a useful and objective proxy for sales volume." *Id.* It was concerned that sales volume could be easily inflated by use of repurchase and reverse repurchase agreements for government securities—a common practice among government securities dealers—or by "churning." *Id.*

The bank holding companies argue that neither § 20 nor the legislative history of the Glass–Steagall Act provides a basis for the Board's market share test. They assert that § 20 mandates an inquiry only into activities *within* a subsidiary rather than one into the size of the subsidiary's activity in relation to the market as a whole. A market share test, they claim, is intended *sub silentio* to promote competition rather than to protect against the hazards of affiliation envisioned by Congress.

The Board's justifications for imposing a market share limitation are not persuasive. It cites only two instances in which it has relied on market share data under § 32. One citation is to a 1947 internal letter from the Board to the Federal Reserve Bank of New York. The second citation is to a 1948 letter now included in a compilation of Board interpretations of Regulation R. *See* Fed.Reserve Reg.Serv. ¶ 3–895 (1948). The 1948 interpretative letter apparently was intended as a guide for future decisions.

It is true that § 32 implicitly delegates to the Board the power to determine when a firm is "primarily engaged" in securities activities, in the same way that § 20 implicitly delegates the power to determine when a firm is "engaged principally" in securities activities. Yet Congress chose to grant the Board power to exempt individuals from § 32, but did not grant it similar power in § 20. Since Congress expressly granted the Board different regulatory power in § 32 than in § 20, it does not at all follow that the Board's power to define the meaning of § 20 is coextensive with its power under § 32. Thus, the Board's reliance on § 32 is not dispositive.

We discern no support in § 20 for the Board's market share limitation. In the legislative history there is evidence that before the enactment of Glass–Steagall, banks and bank affiliates had acquired an increasingly large share of securities activity in relation to investment banks. *See* W. Peach, *The Security Affiliates of National Banks* 108–10 (1941). For example, between 1927 and 1930 the percentage share of commercial banks in origination of bond issues more than doubled. *Id.* at 109. This increasing market share of commercial banks in traditional investment banking activities was not unknown to Congress. *See 1931 Hearings, supra,* at 299 (testimony of C.E. Mitchell, Chairman, National City Bank of New York) (presenting data). But, the fact that this was brought to Congress's attention and that Congress did not directly address it is, if anything, a strong indication that Congress was not concerned about market share. Rather, by using the term "engaged principally," Congress indicated that its principal anxiety was over the perceived risk to bank solvency resulting from their over-involvement in securities activity. A market share limitation simply does not further reduce this congressional worry.

In addition, the Board has not proven on the record before us that a market share limitation is an objective proxy for a sales volume test. The Board makes no claim that the Act empowers it to limit the power of bank affiliates to compete in the securities markets open to them. Consequently, the banks' cross-petition to eliminate the market share limitation is granted.

. . . .

## Comments and Questions

1. Like many other cases interpreting the Glass-Steagall Act, the *Citicorp* decision required the court to balance, on the one hand, an arguably ambiguous statutory provision drafted by a New Deal Congress clearly hostile to affiliations between commercial and investment banking with, on the other hand, a contemporaneous administrative agency's carefully constructed order sanctioning an incremental expansion of bank powers. Did the court here balance these factors appropriately? Could the 1933 Congress have intended this result? Are that Congress's intentions relevant? Does it matter that Congress in the 1980s on numerous occasions considered but failed to enact reform of the Glass-Steagall Act?

2. Note the approach of the SIA. Essentially, the group ignored the BHCA issues of closely related and proper incident. Rather, it essentially went back to the idea latent in the 1971 *Camp* decision that the intent of Congress was to keep bank affiliates completely separated from investment banking, because the purpose was not only safety and soundness, but also what might be termed economic neutrality. Thus, the SIA argued,

the fact that there is no great risk to the bank or its depositors ought not to be sufficient. How did the court dispose of this argument?

3. The *Citicorp, et al.* court rejected the Board's market share test as beyond the Board's discretion because, according to the court, the test has no basis in section 20. Do you agree? The court acknowledges that the interpretation of both "primarily engaged" and "engaged principally" may be interpreted by the Board to mean "any substantial activity." Yet when the court gets to the discussion of the market share limitation it says that absolute size is irrelevant to defining "any substantial activity." As a consequence, it is possible for a money center bank to be the largest investment banker in a particular field, and for the money center banks to be among the largest investment banks generally. Why is it not possible to call a multi-billion dollar activity a substantial activity? Why is the Board unreasonable on the market share test, yet reasonable on the revenue share test?

4. The banking industry's victory in the *Citicorp, et al.* case was simply a foot in the door. Over the next decade, the Federal Reserve Board gradually liberalized its interpretation of section 20 on three separate fronts:

*Bank-ineligible Securities Activities* : In the order challenged in the *Citicorp* case, the Board sanctioned underwriting and dealing in only three types of securities: commercial paper, municipal revenue bonds, and mortgage-backed securities. Shortly thereafter, the Board added consumer receivable-backed securities, and by 1989 added corporate debt and equity securities for qualified applicants. Subsequently, the Board has approved various other incidental securities activities.

*Stringency of Firewalls*: The Board's initial section 20 orders included substantial firewalls, requiring among other things the separate capitalization of section 20 affiliates, physical segregation of section 20 activities, special restrictions on extensions of credit to securities affiliates and their customers, and prohibitions on management interlocks, joint marketing and other coordination of business activities. Over time, the Board has largely eliminated these restrictions, preferring to rely instead on existing bank regulations, such as sections 23A and 23B of the Federal Reserve Act, as amended, and otherwise applicable laws, such as federal securities and anti-trust laws.

*Percentage of Gross Revenues*: Finally, the Board has gradually raised the percentage of revenues that section 20 affiliates can derive from bank-ineligible securities activities. First the percentage was raised to ten percent of gross revenues, and then in 1996 it was upped to twenty-five percent.

For the most part, the Board's reinterpretations of section 20 have not been subject to judicial scrutiny. Are they consistent with the relevant precedents in this area? For a comprehensive review of the evolution of section 20, see MELANIE L. FEIN, SECURITIES ACTIVITIES OF BANKS at §§ 9.03-9.05 (2d ed. 1998).

5. By the late 1990s, the restrictions of section 20 were sufficiently liberalized the major banks were capable of acquiring substantial investments companies and absorbing underwriting and dealing activities into section 20 affiliates. In 1997, for example, Bankers Trust acquired Alex Brown, a major regional underwriter, and shortly thereafter, Bank of

American acquired Robertson, Stephens & Co, another substantial securities firm. These and subsequent transactions constitute the culmination of a process begun with the *Citicorp, et al.* decision.

6.    Even after the Board's subsequent interpretations, section 20 affiliates have remained limited in the percentage of gross revenues they can derive from bank-ineligible securities activities. Occasionally, financial modernization proposals include similar recommendations for affiliations between banks and commercial firms. For instance, in 1997, the Clinton Treasury Department proposed that bank holding companies be permitted to engage in a limited amount of commercial activities so long as no more than a fixed percentage — for example, ten percent — of a holding company's gross revenues derive from commercial activities. While there is logic to this approach — if an activity is questionable, it is better to have a little than a lot of it — do gross revenue tests have unintended, perhaps undesirable consequences? Consider the following problem.

*Problem 15-5*

MidWest Bancorp, is a regional bank holding company, that has traditionally specialized in commercial lending to small- and medium-sized businesses. It is considering the acquisition of Central Securities, a regional securities firms that often serves as lead underwriter for initial public offerings of local firms. The acquisition would allow MidWest to offer its corporate customers access to both commercial lending and capital markets. Unfortunately, preliminary analysis indicates that fifty percent of Central Securities' gross revenues come from bank-ineligible activities. MidWest is considering the following ways of dealing with the problem. Which, if any, would be effective solutions?

a. MidWest currently conducts certain discount brokerage, investment advisory, fiduciary activities within its principal banking subsidiary; these activities could be transferred to a newly-created section 20 affiliate into which Central Securities could be merged.

b.    MidWest also privately places commercial paper for some of its larger corporate customers; these private placement activities could be moved to the section 20 affiliate.

c. MidWest could modify its pricing strategy for corporate customers that will receive both commercial loans from MidWest and investment banking services from the new section 20 affiliate; in effect decreasing the affiliate's gross revenues from underwriting and increasing the organization's return on lending. Alternatively, it could make some accounting adjustments to increase the return on its section 20 affiliate's bank permissible activities.

d.    Although MidWest had not otherwise planned to enter the business of dealing in U.S. government securities, it could explore the possibility of acquiring an existing government securities dealer and then merge that entity into its newly form section 20 affiliate.

*Problem 15-6*

Imagine you are on the staff of the Senate Banking Committee. Pending before the committee is a bill that would repeal section 20 and 32 of the Glass-Steagall Act and amend the Bank Holding Company Act to allow well-capitalized and well-managed bank holding companies to engage in a full range of financial services, including securities underwriting and dealing. The Committee chair has asked for your thoughts on the following questions:

a. To what extent is it necessary for Congress to address this controversial issue in light of the evolution of the Federal Reserve Board's section 20 orders over the past ten years and the fact that some bank holding companies now appear capable of acquiring substantial securities firms?

b. Is there any way for the committee to resolve the debate between the proponents of Glass-Steagall reform, who argue that combination of commercial and investment banking activities strengthen banks and enhances consumer welfare, and the critics of reform who see the same combination as risky to bank solvency and detrimental to capital market competitiveness?

c. Is there any evidence that the committee should examine from either the experience of section 20 affiliates operating over the past decade or the experience of securities affiliates of banks in other countries that might shed light on this debate?

d. At this stage, what are the likely political (and fund-raising) implications of repealing the Glass-Steagall Act? In other words, who wins and loses from Glass-Steagall reform?

---

A final question regarding securities underwriting and dealing is the extent to which banks themselves can engage in these activities. The place where this issue has arisen most prominently has been in the securitization of financial assets — that is the process by which a group of financial assets (typically loans) are placed in a separate legal entity, typically a special-purpose trust or corporation, and then interests in that entity are sold into the capital markets. Under federal securities laws, interests in securitized loan pools are generally considered to be securities, and asset securitizations are routinely registered under the 1933 Act. But does a bank engage in impermissible securities underwriting — and hence run afoul the Glass-Steagall Act — when it "securitizes" a pool of loans?

# Securities Industry Association v. Clarke
## 885 F.2d 1034 (2d Cir. 1989), *cert. denied*, 493 U.S. 1070 (1990)

MESKILL, Circuit Judge:

Plaintiff-appellee Securities Industry Association (SIA) brought the instant action in the United States District Court for the Southern District of New York, Duffy, J. SIA's suit challenged a decision of Robert L. Clarke, the Comptroller of the Currency (the Comptroller). The Comptroller determined that the sale of mortgage pass-through certificates by intervenor-defendant-appellant Security Pacific National Bank (SPN Bank) was not in violation of those sections of the Banking Act of 1933, ch. 89, Pub.L. No. 73–66, 48 Stat. 162 (1933) (codified as amended in scattered sections of 12 U.S.C.), commonly referred to as the Glass–Steagall Act. *See Securities Industry Ass'n v. Board of Governors*, 839 F.2d 47, 54–56 (2d Cir.), *cert. denied*, 486 U.S. 1059 (1988) (*Citicorp*). The district court granted SIA's Fed.R.Civ.P. 56 motion for summary judgment, rejecting the statutory analysis of the Comptroller's decision. *Securities Industry Ass'n v. Clarke*, 703 F.Supp. 256 (S.D.N.Y.1988).
. . .

## BACKGROUND

### A. Mortgage Pass–Through Certificates

Mortgage pass-through certificates are used by banks as a mechanism for selling mortgage loans. A number of mortgage loans previously originated by a bank are placed in a pool. The bank then transfers the pool to a trust. In exchange for the pool, the trustee transfers to the bank pass-through certificates. These certificates represent fractional undivided interests in the pool of mortgage loans. The certificates may then be sold publicly or privately.

After sale of the certificates, the mortgage loans are often serviced by the originator-bank. In such a case, the bank collects the loan payments and "passes through" the principal and interest on a pro rata basis to the certificate holders. In doing so, the bank may deduct service or other fees.

Use of this mechanism has important benefits for banks, benefits that have resulted in its increasing popularity and use. Because residential mortgage loans typically are of long duration, banks traditionally have bought and sold the loans to facilitate management of their assets and liabilities. Use of the pass-through certificate mechanism makes the sale of these loans easier. Individual loans do not have to be sold separately, and buyers may find it more efficient and less risky to purchase interests in a pool of mortgages instead of single mortgages.

### B. The January 23, 1987 Offering of SPN Bank

A Prospectus and Prospectus Supplement dated January 23, 1987 described the offering of approximately $194 million of Security Pacific Mortgage Pass–Through Certificates, Series 1987–B.

The Prospectus provided for the creation of a pool consisting of conventional, fixed-rate residential mortgage loans. "Each Mortgage Loan [would] be selected by [SPN Bank] for inclusion in the Mortgage Pool from among those originated by [SPN Bank] in the ordinary course of [SPN Bank's] lending activities as carried on in its offices in California." Certain characteristics of the mortgages to be selected were specified.

The Prospectus provided that, at the time of issuance of the series, "[SPN Bank] will assign the Mortgage Loans in the Mortgage Pool evidenced by that series to the Trustee.... The Trustee will, concurrently with such assignment, authenticate and deliver Certificates evidencing such series to [SPN Bank] in exchange for the Mortgage Loans." The freely transferable certificates would represent fractional undivided interests in the Trust Fund.

Limited credit support for the issue was to be provided either by (1) an irrevocable letter of credit issued by SPN Bank, (2) a limited guaranty issued by an entity other than SPN Bank, or (3) third-party mortgage insurance purchased by SPN Bank in its role as servicer of the mortgage loans. If SPN Bank provided its own letter of credit, the coverage was to be no more than ten percent of the initial aggregate principal balance of the mortgage pool. Any risk of delinquency or default not covered by these mechanisms of credit support would be borne by the certificate holders.

The Prospectus provided for distribution of the certificates by any of three methods: "1. By negotiated firm commitment underwriting and public reoffering by underwriters; 2. By placements by [SPN Bank] with institutional investors through agents; and 3. By direct placements by [SPN Bank] with institutional investors."

After the sale of the certificates, SPN Bank was to continue to service the mortgage loans on behalf of the certificate holders for a contractually specified fee. As part of its ongoing responsibilities, SPN Bank would "monthly distribute[ ] to certificate holders the payments received from the mortgagors (net of its servicing fee) based on their pro rata interest in the mortgage loans."

The Prospectus Supplement for Series 1987–B described various characteristics of the mortgages selected for inclusion in the pool for that particular issue. The Supplement also specified that the trustee was to be Union Bank, a California bank. Credit support was to be provided by SPN Bank's parent, Security Pacific Corporation, in the form of a limited guaranty of no more than ten percent of the aggregate principal balance of the mortgage loans. With respect to distribution of this issue, the Supplement provided, in pertinent part:

> Subject to the terms and conditions of [an] Underwriting Agreement ... among [SPN Bank, its parent Security Pacific Corporation and Kidder, Peabody & Co., Inc.], under which [SPN Bank] and Kidder Peabody ... will act as [the U]nderwriters ..., the Certificates are being purchased from [SPN Bank] by the Underwriters upon issuance. Distribution of the Certificates is being made by the Underwriters from time to time in negotiated transactions or otherwise at varying prices to be determined at the time of sale.

On February 23, 1987, the sale of certificates for Series 1987–B closed and the certificates were delivered to their purchasers. . . . .

## DISCUSSION

. . . . "Demand for divorcing banking and securities activities followed in the wake of the stock market crash of 1929." *Citicorp*, 839 F.2d at 49. Desiring to protect bank depositors after widespread bank closings, Congress enacted the Glass–Steagall Act. *See [Board of Governors v. Investment Co. Inst.*, 450 U.S. 46, 61 (1981) *(ICI )]*. "The Act responded to the opinion, widely expressed at the time, that much of the financial difficulty experienced by banks could be traced to their involvement in investment-banking activities both directly and through security affiliates." *Bankers Trust I,* 468 U.S. at 144. As the Supreme Court has explained, Congress endeavored to eliminate not only the obvious hazards associated with banks' participation in the inherently risky securities business, but also the "subtle hazards" arising from participation in both banking and investment activity. *See id.* at 145–47; *Camp,* 401 U.S. at 630–34.

By responding to the problem by means of the Glass–Steagall Act, Congress decided upon a "broad structural approach." *See Bankers Trust I,* 468 U.S. at 147. "Through flat prohibitions, the Act sought to 'separat[e] as completely as possible commercial from investment banking.' " *Id.* (quoting *ICI,* 450 U.S. at 70).

"Sections 16 and 21 of the Act are the principal provisions that demarcate the line separating commercial and investment banking." *Id.* at 148; *see also Citicorp,* 839 F.2d at 54 (describing §§ 16, 20, 21 and 32 as the " 'Maginot Line' of the financial world") (citations omitted). The Supreme Court has indicated that sections 16 and 21 "seek to draw the same line." *Bankers Trust I,* 468 U.S. at 149; *see also Citicorp,* 839 F.2d at 55. . . . .

In addition to these "line-drawing" sections of the Glass–Steagall Act, also of importance here is 12 U.S.C. § 371(a) (1982), which was amended by the Garn–St Germain Depository Institutions Act of 1982, Pub.L. No. 97–320, Title IV, § 403(a), 96 Stat. 1469, 1510, to provide that "[a]ny national banking association may make, arrange, purchase or sell loans or extensions of credit secured by liens on interests in real estate, subject to such terms, conditions, and limitations as may be prescribed by the Comptroller of the Currency by order, rule, or regulation."

### D. The Comptroller's Decision

As it is the decision of the Comptroller that is at issue here, we review that decision in some detail.

### 1. Sale of Mortgages Is Permitted

In considering the legality of the SPN Bank transaction under federal banking laws, the Comptroller began his analysis by examining the national bank's authority to sell its mortgage loans generally. In concluding that national banks have such authority, the Comptroller relied on three bases. First, since the enactment of the National Bank Act in 1864, national banks have had the express power to "carry on the business of banking ... by ... negotiating promissory notes ... and other evidences of debt." 12 U.S.C. § 24 (Seventh). Second, the Supreme Court long ago concluded that the sale of mortgages is within the incidental powers of national banks. *See First National Bank v. City of Hartford,* 273 U.S. 548, 560 (1927). Finally, under 12 U.S.C. § 371(a), national banks are permitted to "make, arrange, purchase or sell loans or extensions of credit secured by liens on interests in real estate." The Comptroller concluded that "it is clearly established that national banks may sell their mortgage assets under the express authority of 12 U.S.C. §§ 24 (Seventh) and 371(a)."

*2. Use of the Pass–Through Certificate Mechanism To Sell Mortgages Is Either an Express or an Incidental Banking Power*

Having determined that SPN Bank had the express power to sell its mortgage loans, the Comptroller concluded "[t]he fact that the negotiation and sale may be accomplished through the creation and sale by a bank of participation certificates, an activity which [the OCC] long has approved, does not alter in any respect the substance of the transaction, nor its permissibility under the national banking laws."

The Comptroller justified permitting use of the pass-through certificate mechanism on two grounds. First, he considered use of the mechanism as simply a new way of performing the old job of selling bank assets. He cited the Ninth Circuit's admonition that "the powers of national banks must be construed so as to permit the use of new ways of conducting the very old business of banking." *M & M Leasing Corp. v. Seattle First Nat'l Bank*, 563 F.2d 1377, 1382 (9th Cir.1977), *cert. denied*, 436 U.S. 956 (1978). He concluded that the transaction at issue here "represents nothing more than the negotiation of evidences of debt and the sale of real estate loans, which is expressly authorized under 12 U.S.C. §§ 24 (Seventh) and 371(a)."

Alternatively, the Comptroller concluded that use of the pass-through certificate mechanism to sell mortgages is an "incidental power[ ]" of SPN Bank. *See* 12 U.S.C. § 24 (Seventh). In *Arnold Tours, Inc. v. Camp*, 472 F.2d 427, 432 (1st Cir.1972), the First Circuit examined several Supreme Court decisions and concluded from them that

> a national bank's activity is authorized as an incidental power, "necessary to carry on the business of banking," within the meaning of 12 U.S.C. § 24, Seventh, if it is convenient or useful in connection with the performance of one of the bank's established activities pursuant to its express powers under the National Bank Act. If this connection between an incidental activity and an express power does not exist, the activity is not authorized as an incidental power.

The Comptroller noted the OCC's position that the "convenient [and] useful" test of *Arnold Tours* is overly restrictive of the powers of national banks. Nevertheless, the Comptroller concluded that sale of the pass-through certificates satisfied even the *Arnold Tours* test. Emphasizing the increased marketability of mortgages packaged in the form of pools, the Comptroller said "the process of pooling bank assets and selling certificates representing interests therein can be 'convenient [and] useful' to a bank's ability to sell its assets." That is, because the pass-through certificate mechanism is a "convenient [and] useful" means for carrying out the express power of selling mortgages, SPN Bank's sale of the certificates falls within the "incidental powers" of the national bank under 12 U.S.C. § 24 (Seventh). *See M & M Leasing*, 563 F.2d at 1382–83.

The Comptroller thus concluded that

> whether [SPN] Bank's use of the mortgage-backed pass-through certificate is viewed as a new way of selling bank assets or as an activity incidental to an authorized banking practice, we are satisfied that the issuance and sale of participation interests in pooled bank mortgage assets is permitted under 12 U.S.C. § 24 (Seventh).

*3. The Prohibitions and Concerns of the Glass–Steagall Act Are Not Implicated*

The Comptroller then stated that "[b]ecause the sale of bank assets through this medium is authorized under the national banking laws, the prohibitions of the Glass–Steagall Act are inapplicable to this transaction." Nevertheless, the Comptroller went on to argue that, even if the Glass–Steagall prohibitions were to be applied, they would not forbid this transaction.

First, the Comptroller found that SPN Bank's program did not involve "securities" within the meaning of the Glass–Steagall Act. The Comptroller noted that SPN Bank's registration of the offering with the Securities and Exchange Commission (SEC) did not mean that the certificates were "securities" for purposes of the Glass–Steagall Act. *See Investment Co. Inst. v. Clarke,* 630 F.Supp. 593, 594 n. 2 (D.Conn.), *aff'd,* 789 F.2d 175 (2d Cir.) (per curiam), *cert. denied,* 479 U.S. 940 (1986); *see also Conover,* 790 F.2d at 933. The Comptroller wrote:

> Th[e OCC] has previously considered pass-through certificates representing undivided interests in pooled bank assets to be legally transparent for purposes of the Glass–Steagall analysis. In other words, because the certificateholders have essentially the same rights, liabilities, and risks as if they were the owners of the underlying assets, the certificates are considered to be substantially the same as those assets.... To the extent that the participation certificates represent "investment opportunities", the opportunity being offered is, in substance, no different than the opportunity of investment in the underlying loans which banks are clearly authorized to sell.

The means used to pool and package the sale of the mortgages was thus thought not to transform the transaction into a sale of "securities." Finally, the Comptroller reinforced his interpretation of the term "securities" by referring to his finding that the "subtle hazards" identified by the Supreme Court as motivating the Glass–Steagall Act were not implicated by this transaction. *See infra.*

The Comptroller next concluded that even if the mortgage pass-through certificates are considered "securities" for purposes of the Glass–Steagall Act, the Act was still not violated here because SPN Bank's activities did not fall within the meaning of "dealing" or "underwriting" securities, as prohibited by section 16. In concluding that SPN Bank was not "dealing" or "underwriting" here, the Comptroller said:

> An issuer that merely participates in the initial placement of its own securities with investors, and does not subsequently engage in the business of repurchasing those securities, does not thereby enter into the "business of underwriting" nor does it become involved in the "business of dealing." In this regard, we underscore the point that the activity in question is, in substance, a sale of [SPN] Bank's assets. [SPN] Bank is not in this transaction purchasing and selling securities of other issuers but, rather, is participating in the placement of certificates representing interests in its own assets.

(footnotes omitted).

The Comptroller followed up on his section 16 analysis by recognizing that because SPN Bank's "activities are permissible under Section 16, there is no need to conduct any inquiry under Section 21 of the Act." He nevertheless concluded that if it were applied, section 21 would not prohibit the activity at issue here. In so finding, the Comptroller again emphasized that this transaction essentially involved only SPN Bank's sale of its own assets. Further, the Comptroller relied on the specific proviso in section 21 stating that "nothing in this paragraph shall be construed as affecting in any way such right as any bank ... may otherwise possess to sell, without recourse or agreement to repurchase, obligations evidencing loans on real estate."

The Comptroller concluded by considering the purposes of the Glass–Steagall Act, finding that they were not implicated here. He first noted that the most obvious risks associated with banks participating in the securities business, *see Camp,* 401 U.S. at 630, were not present here because "[a]t no time will [SPN] Bank's resources be committed to any securities investment whatsoever, since the program involves only the sale of bank assets."

Turning to the "subtle hazards" identified by the Supreme Court, *see Bankers Trust I,* 468 U.S. at 145–47; *Camp,* 401 U.S. at 630–34, the Comptroller first noted that SPN Bank's program "does not involve the marketing of bank customers' securities." Under these circumstances, he found, "the conflicts of interest identified by the Supreme Court ... are simply not at issue." Because the bank has no "promotional interest" in customers' securities, it will not be tempted to make unsound loans to improve the success of the securities offerings. "Similarly, there is no possibility that the Bank might improperly advise its customers on how and when to issue securities in order to profit from the distribution process or to use the proceeds in obtaining repayment on outstanding loans."

The Comptroller next turned to the possibility that SPN Bank would offer limited credit support for the offering. He noted that the Prospectus provided that such credit support could only be, at a maximum, ten percent of the aggregate principal balance. He noted that in the absence of the sale of the mortgage loans, SPN Bank would retain 100 percent of the associated credit risk. In light of this, he found it "difficult to conceive how a decision to provide credit support for no more than 10% of the initial aggregate principal balance of a pool comprised of these same assets could be the product of 'unsound' lending practices."

The Comptroller rejected the argument that permitting use of the pass-through certificate mechanism would affect the soundness of SPN Bank's mortgage lending practices. He concluded:

> We think it extremely unlikely that a bank would engage in unsafe mortgage lending practices simply because of the possibility that the resulting mortgage loans might thereafter be placed in a pool and sold in certificate form. In this regard, at the time of origination, it will generally not be possible for the Bank to know whether a particular loan will be suitable for subsequent inclusion in a public offering. In addition, the Bank would have difficulty marketing the Certificates if the underlying mortgages were themselves unsound investments because the federal securities laws require full disclosure of all material facts concerning the Certificates and the offering. In short, the Bank does not stand to profit by making unsound loans with the intent of remarketing them to uninformed purchasers.

Finally, the Comptroller found that SPN Bank's program would not likely result in its making unsound loans to its own depositors so as to finance sale of the certificates. "[S]ince [SPN] Bank's objective is to sell the mortgage loans, it would hardly make economic sense for it to replace these assets with unsound loans acquired in the process." The Comptroller found such a scenario equally irrational from the point of view of the depositor. Because service charges would be deducted from the "pass-through" payments, it would not make sense, the Comptroller thought, for the depositor to obtain a loan at a higher commercial rate so as to invest in the certificates.

*E. The Comptroller Correctly Determined That SPN Bank's Sale of the Certificates Was Within the "Business of Banking" and Therefore Did Not Violate the Glass–Steagall Act*

As our review of the Comptroller's decision indicates, under his interpretation of the Glass–Steagall Act, the conclusion that SPN Bank's activity was authorized by the banking laws was sufficient to resolve the dispute. That is, once the Comptroller concluded that SPN Bank's activity was encompassed by its power "to carry on the business of banking," 12 U.S.C. § 24

(Seventh), he found it unnecessary to consider the application of the Glass–Steagall prohibition on national banks' "underwrit[ing] securities," *id.* The district court appeared to accept this reading of the banking laws, *see* 703 F.Supp. at 258 ("the Comptroller's analysis could end at this point, having determined that the offering of mortgage-backed securities is within SPN Bank's power under the national banking laws"), although, as we demonstrate below, the court's reasoning and resolution were not consistent with it.

We find support for the Comptroller's interpretation of section 16 in *Bankers Trust I,* 468 U.S. at 158 n. 11. In that case, the Supreme Court considered a bank's efforts to enter the business of selling third-party commercial paper. *Id.* at 139. The Court held that the commercial paper was a "security" within the meaning of the Glass–Steagall Act, thereby rejecting a decision of the Board of Governors of the Federal Reserve Board. In the course of reaching this result, the Court rejected an argument made by the Board based on a provision in section 16 permitting a bank to "purchase for its own account investment securities." 12 U.S.C. § 24 (Seventh). The Board argued that if commercial paper were considered a "security" under the Glass–Steagall Act, then banks would not be permitted to purchase commercial paper for their own accounts. The Board argued that because banks had long purchased commercial paper for their own accounts with no suggestion of illegality, "the practice cannot be reconciled with § 16 unless commercial paper is not deemed a 'security.' " *Bankers Trust I,* 468 U.S. at 158 n. 11.

Of crucial significance here is the Court's reasoning in rejecting the Board's argument. Justice Blackmun, writing for the Court, said

> we find the Board's argument unpersuasive because it rests on the faulty premise that the process of acquiring commercial paper necessarily constitutes "the business of dealing" in securities. The underlying source of authority for national banks to conduct business is the first sentence of § 16, which originated as § 8 of the National Bank Act of 1864, ch. 106, 13 Stat. 101. That provision grants national banks the authority to exercise "all such incidental powers as shall be necessary to carry on the business of banking" and enumerates five constituent powers that constitute "the business of banking." One of those powers is "discounting and negotiating promissory notes." 12 U.S.C. § 24 Seventh. The Board appears to concede that the authority for national banks to acquire commercial paper is grounded in this authorization to discount promissory notes.... *The subsequent prohibition on engaging in "[t]he business of dealing in securities" does not affect this authority; while the Glass–Steagall Act does not define the term "business of dealing" in securities, the term clearly does not include the activity of "discounting" promissory notes because that activity is defined to be a part of the "business of banking."* In short, the fact that commercial banks properly are free to acquire commercial paper for their own account implies not that commercial paper is not a "security," but simply that the process of extending credit by "discounting" commercial paper is not part of the "business of dealing" in securities.

*Id.* (emphasis added). The three dissenting Justices rejected this argument. *Id.* at 167 n. 8 (O'Connor, J., dissenting).

We think the distinction drawn by the Court between the "business of banking" and the "business of dealing" under section 16 supports the Comptroller's approach to the issue presented in this case. The Court's reading of section 16 of the Glass–Steagall Act establishes the threshold question as whether the challenged activity of SPN Bank constitutes "the business of banking" or, instead, the "business of dealing in securities and stock." *See* 12 U.S.C. § 24 (Seventh). Activity that falls within the "business of banking" is not subject to the restrictions the latter part of section 16 places on a bank's "business of dealing in securities and stock." Thus, the issues concerning the definitions of "securities" and "underwriting" only become relevant if the activity constitutes the "business of dealing in securities and stock." If the activity constitutes the "business of banking," then the Glass–Steagall Act prohibitions SIA claims are violated here do not apply.

The Comptroller correctly concluded that SPN Bank has the express power under the national banking laws to sell its mortgage loans. In 1982, Congress amended 12 U.S.C. § 371(a) to provide that "[a]ny national banking association may make, arrange, purchase or sell loans or extensions of credit secured by liens on interests in real estate, subject to such terms, conditions, and limitations as may be prescribed by the Comptroller of the Currency by order, rule, or regulation." Legislative history indicates that the amendment was intended to "simplif[y] the real estate lending authority of national banks by deleting rigid statutory requirements. Section 403 [which amended 12 U.S.C. § 371] is intended to provide national banks with the ability to engage in more creative and flexible financing, and to become stronger participants in the home financing market." S.Rep. No. 536, 97th Cong., 2nd Sess. 27 (1982), *reprinted in* 1982 U.S.Code Cong. & Admin.News 3054, 3081; *see also id.* at 60, 1982 U.S.Code Cong. & Admin.News at 3114.

We need not consider the extent, nature or bases of national banks' powers to sell mortgages before this amendment, as we have no difficulty concluding that the amended 12 U.S.C. § 371(a) supports the Comptroller's conclusion that SPN Bank has the express power to sell its mortgage loans.

In determining that the use of mortgage pass-through certificates to sell mortgage loans fell within SPN Bank's "incidental powers" under 12 U.S.C. § 24 (Seventh), the Comptroller turned to the test adopted in *Arnold Tours*, 472 F.2d at 432. There, the First Circuit framed the inquiry as follows: in order to be authorized under section 16's "incidental powers" provision, a national bank's activity must be "convenient [and] useful in connection with the performance of one of the bank's established activities pursuant to its express powers under the National Bank Act." *Id.*

Although he applied the test of *Arnold Tours,* the Comptroller argued that that test is unnecessarily restrictive of the powers of national banks. The Comptroller argued that several of the Supreme Court decisions relied on by the First Circuit in *Arnold Tours* in fact indicate that more flexible standards have been used. . . . We have no need to address the Comptroller's position that the *Arnold Tours* test is overly restrictive, as we believe that the proper test is no more restrictive than *Arnold Tours* and we agree with the Comptroller that SPN Bank's activities here satisfied even the *Arnold Tours* test.

We have little difficulty concluding that SPN Bank's use of the pass-through certificate mechanism is "convenient [and] useful in connection with the performance of" its power to sell its mortgage loans. *See Arnold Tours,* 472 F.2d at 432. Indeed, SIA does not appear to argue otherwise. The pass-through certificate mechanism permits the bank to offer purchasers an interest in a pool of mortgage loans, rather than just single mortgage loans. The popularity of the mechanism confirms what seems apparent, that many investors who might be wary of the risk of investing in a single mortgage loan will be willing to invest in a pool of loans. With the increased marketability that pass-through certificates make possible comes increased liquidity, an important benefit as banks face the task of funding long term mortgage loans with short term deposits. We thus conclude that the Comptroller's view that SPN Bank's "incidental powers" authorized its activity in the transaction at issue here was reasonable.

The Comptroller properly recognized that once he determined that SPN Bank's activity was authorized under section 16, he did not need to analyze the transaction under section 21. "[S]ection 21 cannot be read to prohibit what section 16 permits.... Therefore, if we find that the [Comptroller] acted reasonably in concluding that section 16 permits [SPN Bank's] activities, that is the end of our analysis." *See Securities Industry Ass'n v. Board of Governors,* 807 F.2d 1052, 1057 (D.C.Cir.1986), *cert. denied,* 483 U.S. 1005  (1987) (*Bankers Trust II* ).  This is so because section 21 "was not intended to require banks to abandon an accepted banking practice that was subjected to regulation under § 16." *ICI,* 450 U.S. at 63; *see also Bankers Trust I,* 468 U.S. at 149 ("§ 16 and § 21 seek to draw the same line").

The language of section 21 supports this approach.  The section imposes restrictions on those "engaged in the business of issuing, underwriting, selling, or distributing ... stocks, bonds, debentures, notes, or other securities." 12 U.S.C. § 378(a)(1).  The section then contains two provisos.  The first is that the section "shall not prohibit national banks ... from dealing in, underwriting, purchasing, and selling investment securities, or issuing securities, to the extent permitted to national banking associations by the provisions of section 24 of this title [section 16 of the Glass–Steagall Act]." *Id.*  The second proviso states that "nothing in this paragraph shall be construed as affecting in any way such right as any bank ... may otherwise possess to sell, without recourse or agreement to repurchase, obligations evidencing loans on real estate." *Id.*  The provisos, added as amendments in 1935, *see* Banking Act of 1935, Pub.L. No. 74–305, ch. 614, tit. III, § 303(a), 49 Stat. 684, 707, clarify the relationship between sections 16 and 21 and support the Comptroller's view that section 21 cannot be read to prohibit SPN Bank's activity, as it is permitted by section 16. *See Bankers Trust II,* 807 F.2d at 1057–58; *see also Citicorp,* 839 F.2d at 56, 60–61.  That is to say, even if SPN Bank's activity here were to be considered "underwriting ... securities," section 21 would not prohibit such activity if it were permitted under section 16, as we have found it to be. . . . .

## Comments and Questions

1. Have we come full circle in determining what activities are permissible for banks and bank holding companies, to the question of what is meant by the phrase, "the business of banking"?  Who should answer this question?  Bank regulatory officials?  The courts? The SEC?  Incidentally, recall problem 15-1.  If we move towards a system of functional regulation, should banks be allowed an exemption for their asset securitization programs?

2. Does the court permit banks (and also bank holding companies?) to act as underwriters, without limit, of all mortgage-backed securities, a market that comprises hundreds of billions of dollars a year in new offerings?  Does the court permit a bank that wishes to be active in exercising the permitted powers to become an underwriter of all forms of consumer and commercial loans, even loans purchased from other banks?  With respect to a section 20 affiliate of a bank holding company, should the underwriting of mortgage-backed pass-through certificates not count toward the now ten percent ineligible securities level, but rather be counted as eligible securities activity?

3. Will a Glass-Steagall analysis ever occur if the asset is initially created by a bank loan transaction? Consider whether the decision would authorize a national bank to make a 25–year loan to a corporation, and then sell undivided interests in the loan in the form of corporate bonds. Would this activity be within the "lending" and "discounting" activities authorized by section 24(7)?

# CHAPTER SIXTEEN

# DEPOSITORY INSTITUTIONS IN INSURANCE

In this final chapter, we consider the on-going competition between depository institutions and insurance companies. This is a topic we have touched upon in prior readings. The *Taylor* case, from Chapter Seven, section 1, concerned the authority of national banks to issue insurance-like debt cancellation contracts. The *Citicorp (Family Guardian)* decision discussed in Chapter Four, section 4 , involved the application of the Bank Holding Company Act's insurance provisions to bank subsidiaries. And, section 303 of FDICIA — codified at 12 U.S.C. § 1831a(b), (d)(2) — limited the practical significance of the *Citicorp (Family Guardian)* decision by imposing new statutory restrictions on the ability of FDIC-insured state chartered institutions and their subsidiaries to engage in insurance underwriting (i.e., principal) activities not permissible for national banks.

Prior readings, however, left open a number of questions. Precisely what sort of insurance activities can national banks undertake? Are these activities limited to the insurance agency activities authorized by section 92 of the National Bank Act? Or may national banks (and therefore state-chartered banks as well if authorized by local laws) also undertake some insurance underwriting activities? What, in any event, is the scope of the insurance agency activities that section 92 provides? To the extent that national banks can engage in some insurance activities, what power, if any, do the state insurance authorities have to oversee those activities? These questions are the subject matter of this chapter.

## Section 1.  Background

Traditionally — that is to say, two decades ago — financial intermediaries generally did not combine insurance products with deposit-taking services. There were, however, several notable exceptions to this proposition. For example, prior to the enactment of the Bank Holding Company Act of 1956, the Transamerica Insurance Company developed an extensive network of banking affiliates, which the conglomerate subsequently had to divest. On the banking side, there were also pockets of permissible affiliation. Since 1916, section 92 of the National Bank Act had allowed:

> In addition to the powers now vested by law in national banking associations organized under the laws of the United States any such association located and doing business in any place the population of which does not exceed 5,000 inhabitants, as shown by the last preceding decennial census, may, under such rules and regulations as may be prescribed by the Comptroller of the Currency, act as the agent for any fire, life, or other insurance company authorized by the authorities of the State in which said bank is located to do business in said State, by soliciting and selling insurance and collecting premiums on policies issued by such company;  and may receive for services so rendered such fees or commissions as may be

agreed upon between the said association and the insurance company for which it may act as agent: Provided, however, That no such bank shall in any case assume or guarantee the payment of any premium on insurance policies issued through its agency by its principal: And provided further, That the bank shall not guarantee the truth of any statement made by an assured in filing his application for insurance.

A number of state-chartered banks enjoyed similar or even broader insurance powers.

Beginning in the 1970s, insurance companies initiated a number of incursions into the depository institution field. One of the earliest efforts was the development of guaranteed investment contracts (which we considered in some detail in Chapter Seven, section 3, in connection with the ELIC insolvency). GICs are functionally similar to bank certificates of deposit. Starting in the 1980s, the industry began a more direct attack Firms such as Prudential, John Hancock and the Travelers Corporation, established non-bank banks, before that loophole was closed with the passage of the Competitive Equality Banking Act of 1987. Then, because federal law does not limit the activities of unitary savings and loan holding companies, many insurance companies attempted to enter the depository field by acquiring savings and loan subsidiaries. For example, in 1988 The Home Group — a major New York-based property and casualty insurer — acquired the FSLIC-insured Cartaret Savings Bank, one of the country's largest thrifts. Shortly thereafter, Prudential added to its stable of depository-institution subsidiaries by acquiring an insolvent thrift in Georgia. See *Prudential Gets Approval to Buy An Ailing Thrift*, Wall St. J., Aug. 8. 1989, at A2. Throughout the 1990's, insurance companies have increasingly used thrift acquisitions as a vehicle for competing with depository institutions.

Partially in response to these incursions from the insurance industry and partially for independent business reasons, depository institutions have been engaging in their own counter offensive throughout this same period. Their efforts have led to numerous pitched battles, fought not just before regulatory agencies and federal courts, but also in the halls of Congress and the pages of the national press. The result has been a mass of confusing and conflicting precedents and statutes. As you read over the following materials, pay particular attention to the corporate entity that provides the insurance product at issue. Whether the provider is a bank, a bank subsidiary, or a bank holding company affiliate turns out to be highly relevant. Why are formalities so important in this field? Would a functional approach to regulation be preferable? What would a functional approach look like?

Early efforts on the part of depository institutions to gain access to the insurance industry were straightforward: banks sought confirmation from their regulatory supervisors that insurance activities were a permissible extension of bank powers. Responding to such an initiative in 1963, Comptroller of the Currency Saxon issued a ruling interpreting 12 U.S.C. § 24(Seventh) to grant national banks the "authority to act as an agent in the issuance of insurance which is incident to banking transactions." Trade groups for independent insurance agents were quick to challenge the ruling, and, in Saxon v. Georgia Association of Independent Insurance Agents, 399 F.2d 1010 (5th Cir. 1968), obtained a widely followed judicial victory. The *Saxon* court struck down the Comptroller's interpretative ruling on the following grounds:

In interpreting the meaning of one provision of an act it is proper that all other provisions in pari materia should also be considered. So, in construing the general authority contained in Section 24(7) we must give equal consideration to Section 92 as it specifically deals with the power of national banks to act as insurance agents, and when the general language in Section 24(7) dealing with 'incidental' powers is construed in conjunction with the specific grant in Section 92 it is clear that application for the *expressio unius est exclusio alterius* rule requires the construction that national banks have no power to act as insurance agents in cities of over 5,000 population. . . . Since Congress dealt specifically with the insurance agency power in Section 92, the *expressio unius* rule negates the existence of any other power to act as an insurance agent under the general provisions of Section 24(7).

Id. at 1013-14; see also American Land Title Association v. Clarke, 968 F.2d 150 (2d Cir. 1992) (striking down on similar grounds OCC approval of title insurance agency), *cert. denied*, 508 U.S. 971 (1993).

With decisions such as *Saxon* preventing national banks from expanding into the insurance business, the banking industry turned to holding company affiliates as an alternative path for new insurance authority. For several years, this maneuver proved a modestly successful strategy. Faced with a series of applications under section 4(c)(8) of the Bank Holding Company Act, the Federal Reserve Board promulgated amendments to Regulation Y defining the following insurance activities to be closely related to the business of banking:

[A]cting as insurance agent or broker in offices at which the holding companies . . . [is] otherwise engaged in business . . . with respect to the following types of insurance:

(i) Any insurance for the holding company and its subsidiaries;

(ii) Any insurance that (a) is directly related to an extension of credit by a bank . . ., or (b) is directly related to the provision of other financial services by a bank . . . or (c) is otherwise sold as a matter of convenience to the purchases, so long as the premium income from sales . . . does not constitute a significant portion of the aggregate insurance premium income of the holding company . . .

(iii) Any insurance sold in a community that (a) has a population not exceeding 5,000, or (b) the holding company demonstrates has inadequate insurance agency facilities.

12 C.F.R. § 225.4(a)(9) (1976) (repealed). While court challenges invalidated certain components of this regulation, see, e.g., Alabama Association of Insurance Agents v. Board of Governors, 533 F.2d 224 (5th Cir. 1976) (invalidating, inter alia, bank holding company sale of insurance as a matter of convenience to customers), *on rehearing*, 558 F.2d 729 (1977), *cert. denied*, 435 U.S. 904 (1978), the Federal Reserve Board did succeed in providing bank holding companies a limited and potentially expandable path into the insurance business.

In 1982, however, representatives of the insurance industry launched a counter-attack in Congress. Title VI of the Garn-St Germain Depository Institutions Act of 1982, Pub. L. No. 97-320, 96 Stat. 1469, amended section 4(c)(8) of the Banking Holding

Company Act to clarify that "it is not closely related to the business of managing or controlling banks for a bank holding company to provide insurance as a principal, agent, or broker" except for eight, relatively narrow exceptions currently codified at 12 U.S.C. § 1843(c)(8)(A)-(G). The result of this amendment to the Bank Holding Company Act was to stymie the banking industry's heretofore successful effort to gain a toehold in the insurance field through the use of bank holding company affiliates.

The balance of this chapter chronicles the banking industry's gradual recovery from the setbacks of the *Saxon* decision and passage of the Garn-St Germain Act. Before turning to those materials, consider for a moment what advice you could have given a bank holding company client in the mid-1980s if the client had still wanted to offer its customers insurance products beyond those authorized by the limited exceptions of 12 U.S.C. § 1843(c)(8)(A)-(G).

## Section 2.  Expansion through State-Chartered Banks

The following decision represents one of the industry's first responses to the Garn-St Germain Act. Is this strategy familiar? Look back to Chapter Two for a similar, albeit more successful, effort of the same holding company in South Dakota.

### In re Citicorp ("American State Bank of Rapid City")
### 71 Fed. Res. Bull. 789 (Oct. 1985)

Citicorp, New York, New York, a registered bank holding company within the meaning of the Bank Holding Company Act (the 'BHC Act') has applied for Board approval under section 3 of the Act to acquire all of the shares of American State Bank of Rapid City ('Bank'), Rapid City, South Dakota. In connection with this application, Citicorp has specifically requested the Board's approval to engage through Bank in underwriting life insurance, accident and health insurance and annuities, and to act as agent or broker for the sale of all lines of insurance on a nationwide basis.. . . . [1]

South Dakota law specifically provides that an out-of-state bank holding company may acquire a single existing state chartered bank in South Dakota. S.D. Codified Laws Ann. § 51-16-40(b) (1984). South Dakota law also permits all banks chartered under the laws of South Dakota to engage, either directly or through subsidiaries, in all facets of the insurance business. S.D.

---

[1]    Comments in opposition to the proposed transaction and a request for a formal hearing were made on behalf of the American Council of Life Insurance, the American Insurance Association, the National Association of Independent Insurers, and the Alliance of American Insurers. The Board also received comments urging denial of this application from the National Association of Insurance Commissioners; from the Mortgage Insurance Companies of America; and from the Independent Insurance Agents of America, the National Association of Casualty and Surety Agents, the National Association of Surety Bond Producers, the National Association of Professional Insurance Agents, and the National Association of Life Underwriters.

Codified Laws Ann. § 51-18-30 (1984). Under South Dakota law, however, a South Dakota bank acquired by an out-of-state bank holding company is prohibited from expanding or acquiring new banking offices or remote service units by merger, acquisition or de novo and is required to conduct its insurance activities in South Dakota in a manner and at a location that is not likely to attract customers from the general public in South Dakota to the substantial detriment of existing insurance companies, brokers and agents in the state. S.D. Codified Laws Ann. § 51-16-41 (1984). In addition, a de novo South Dakota bank acquired by an out-of-state bank holding company is limited to operating a single banking office in South Dakota and is required to conduct its banking business in South Dakota at a location and in a manner so that it is not likely to attract customers from the general public in South Dakota to the substantial detriment of existing banks in the state. Id. South Dakota banks owned by South Dakota bank holding companies are not subject to the same limitations or restrictions as apply to state banks owned by out-of-state bank holding companies, and may, for example, establish branches statewide.

This application was originally submitted to the Board in June 1983, and included a proposal by Citicorp that contemplated engaging in insurance activities without limitation. On January 6, 1984, the Board suspended processing of the application at the request of Citicorp, noting that the application raised significant legal questions concerning the applicability of the Bank Holding Company Act to state chartered holding company banks and their nonbank subsidiaries, as well as concerning the compatibility of the proposed insurance activities with the provisions of the Act prohibiting bank holding companies from engaging in certain insurance activities. The Board expressed its 'tentative judgment that it could not approve the proposed bank acquisitions in view of present law and expressions of Congressional intent, subject to any further consideration by the Congress.'

Citicorp requested that the Board reactivate processing of its application on February 20, 1985. Citicorp proposes to conduct a wide variety of insurance activities through Bank, including underwriting general life and other types of insurance and acting as agent or broker for all types of insurance unrelated to extensions of credit. While Citicorp states that it has not yet determined the full range of insurance activities that it will conduct through Bank and has further stated that it will not underwrite property and casualty insurance without prior Board approval, Citicorp has stated that it expects to conduct insurance activities through Bank 'to the fullest extent possible.'[2] Citicorp expects to conduct these general insurance activities throughout the United States.

While this application has been filed under section 3 of the Act (governing the acquisition of banks), the Board does not believe that approval of such an application would be warranted where the proposal would result in a violation or evasion of the nonbanking provisions of section 4 of the Act.[3] Section 4 of the Act prohibits a bank holding company from engaging in any

---

[2]     Citicorp has indicated that it wishes to conduct insurance activities through separately incorporated nonbank subsidiaries of Bank. If the Board concludes that the Act prohibits the conduct of the activity through nonbank subsidiaries of Bank, however, Citicorp has stated it will conduct the insurance activities through separate divisions of Bank.

[3]     The Board is authorized under section 5(b) of the Act, indeed in certain circumstances required, to deny proposals that represent a clear evasion of the purposes of the Act, even if the proposal

activity other than banking or managing or controlling banks and activities determined by the Board to be closely related to banking and a proper incident thereto under section 4(c)(8) of the Act. In addition, section 4 of the Act prohibits a bank holding company from acquiring or retaining direct or indirect ownership or control of voting shares of any company that is not a bank, unless the company engages in an activity closely related to banking (or is otherwise exempt under the Act). In 1982, Congress, in Title VI of the Garn-St Germain Depository Institutions Act of 1982, amended section 4(c)(8) of the Act to provide specifically that insurance activities, with certain exceptions not relevant here, are not closely related to banking, thereby precluding the Board from authorizing bank holding companies to conduct these activities.

The Board believes that the record in this case demonstrates that the primary, if not sole, purpose of the proposed acquisition is to permit Citicorp to engage through Bank in various insurance activities that are impermissible for bank holding companies under section 4 of the Act. The Board has considered that the South Dakota statute itself has the effect of enabling out-of-state bank holding companies to evade the nonbanking insurance provisions of the Act. The South Dakota statute allows out-of-state bank holding companies to acquire South Dakota banks, but simultaneously sharply limits the ability of any state bank acquired by an out-of-state bank holding company to conduct a banking business in South Dakota by prohibiting these out-of-state owned banks from expanding their banking offices in any way.

In furtherance of the state's objective of permitting out-of-state holding companies to engage in the insurance business outside South Dakota while restricting banking activities within that state, the South Dakota statute places an even more stringent restriction on de novo banks acquired by out-of- state bank holding companies. The statute limits their banking business to a single office and requires that banking activities be conducted at a location and in a manner that is 'not likely to attract customers from the general public in the state to the substantial detriment of existing banks in the state.' S.D. Codified Laws Ann. § 51-16-41.

While an out-of-state bank holding company is significantly limited in its ability to conduct a banking business in South Dakota once it acquires a South Dakota bank, the out-of-state bank holding company is permitted to use the South Dakota bank franchise to conduct insurance activities nationwide without any limitation (other than that it restrict its insurance activities within South Dakota itself to avoid competing with South Dakota firms). It is that grant of broad insurance powers, which are otherwise prohibited to bank holding companies, that replaces the opportunity to conduct a banking business in South Dakota as the incentive to attract out-of-state bank holding companies to acquire South Dakota banks. This incentive--crucial to the success of the South Dakota statute's aim of attracting out-of-state bank holding companies as a means of increasing tax revenues and jobs in South Dakota--exists only because insurance activities are expressly prohibited for bank holding companies under the BHC Act.

The Preamble to the South Dakota statute explicitly recognizes that the statute is intended to secure employment and revenue for the state by enabling out-of-state bank holding companies

---

technically conforms to the terms of the Act. . . . The U.S. Supreme Court has recognized the authority of the Board to impose restrictions on holding company banks to prevent evasion of the nonbanking provisions of the Act. See Board of Governors v. Investment Company Institute, 450 U.S. 46, 60 n.25 (1981).

to take advantage of 'a unique opportunity' afforded by national laws. As demonstrated, this opportunity is the ability to use a South Dakota bank franchise to conduct insurance activities prohibited to bank holding companies. Thus, the effectiveness of the South Dakota statute to achieve its purpose is premised upon its ability to enable bank holding companies to evade the provisions of the BHC Act.

In these circumstances, it is important to note that Bank will serve primarily as an insurance subsidiary of Citicorp and will conduct relatively insignificant banking activities.[4] While Citicorp has not provided any financial projections regarding the insurance or banking activities it will conduct through Bank, Citicorp has stated that it will conduct insurance activities 'to the fullest extent possible' and on a nationwide basis. In this regard, Citicorp has committed to the South Dakota Banking Commissioner to devote approximately $2.5 million to a facility in Rapid City and to employ a minimum of 100-125 additional persons for the purpose of conducting insurance or other nonbanking activities. These plans illustrate that Citicorp contemplates devoting significant resources to conducting a broad range of insurance activities through Bank.

The Board believes, based upon the foregoing commitments and Citicorp's stated intention of conducting insurance activities 'to the fullest extent possible,' that the resources required to conduct an insurance business as proposed by Citicorp are beyond the capacity of the Bank itself (with $17.5 million in total assets and about 28 full time employees as of March 31, 1985) and that in this situation the bank is acting as a proxy for Citicorp. Moreover, it appears that the activities Citicorp will conduct through Bank will be preponderantly insurance activities prohibited under the Act and not banking activities.[5]

While the potential scope and volume of Bank's insurance activities are not limited, the prohibition imposed on Bank's ability to expand into new banking markets or to open new locations to accommodate growth in the Rapid City market clearly indicates that the banking activities of Bank will be insignificant relative to its contemplated nationwide insurance activities. Under the South Dakota statute, Bank would be limited to its two existing offices and one additional approved but not yet open office in the Rapid City market and--unlike other banks in the state--could not open additional branches either de novo or through acquisition or merger.

The Board also notes that the great preponderance of insurance activities proposed for Bank raises a substantial question whether Citicorp's activities, after consummation of the proposal, will be limited to those permitted to bank holding companies under the terms of section 4 of the Act. Under that section, the activities of bank holding companies are limited to 'banking' or 'managing and controlling banks' and activities that the Board determines are closely related to banking. The broad range of insurance activities involved in this case are regulated as insurance and have been expressly determined by Congress to be not closely related to banking.

---

[4] Under the South Dakota statute, Bank and its insurance subsidiaries must be licensed and supervised by the South Dakota Department of Insurance as well as the state insurance departments in each state in which Bank conducts its insurance activities.

[5] The Board would be prepared to entertain an application by Citicorp to acquire Bank that was limited to engaging in banking activities in South Dakota.

On this basis, these activities do not appear to fall within the scope of either 'banking' or 'closely related to banking' activities permissible for bank holding companies under section 4 of the Act. In this regard, the Board notes that the South Dakota statute itself makes a sharp distinction between 'banking' and the 'insurance' activities authorized.

In this situation, the Board concludes that the acquisition of Bank is in reality an acquisition for the purposes of permitting Citicorp to engage in insurance activities prohibited for bank holding companies under section 4 of the BHC Act and the Bank is simply a device to accomplish this objective. Accordingly, the Board has determined that the proposal constitutes an evasion of section 4 of the Act and section 225.22(d)(2) of Regulation Y and that Board approval is therefore precluded.

For the foregoing reasons, the Board hereby denies the application.

Concurring Statement of Governor Rice

I concur in the Board's decision that this application represents an attempt to evade the provisions of the Bank Holding Company Act that prohibit bank holding companies from engaging in most insurance activities. In addition, I wish to emphasize that the nonbanking prohibitions of the Act apply to investments made by bank holding companies, even when those investments are made through a subsidiary bank. Moreover, I believe that the terms, structure, legislative history and purpose of the Act make clear that a bank holding company may not avoid the nonbanking restrictions of the Act by conducting these activities through a subsidiary bank. . . .

Concurring Statement of Governor Seger

This application raises the important question of the extent to which a state bank within a bank holding company system may conduct activities authorized for the bank under state law. While I agree with the Board that denial of this case is appropriate because of the nature of the Citicorp proposal and certain provisions of the South Dakota statute, I wish to emphasize that I do not object to proposals under which a state bank engages in activities authorized by the state for its banks provided those activities may be conducted within the state without restriction. I believe that states should be authorized to delineate the types of activities that banks may engage in within their borders. Indeed, one of the virtues of the dual banking system is that it allows the states to serve as laboratories for the development and expansion of banking services and activities within their boundaries. . . .

## Comments and Questions

1. Why was Citicorp successful in its efforts to establish a credit-card bank in 1981 (See Chapter Two, section 3), but unsuccessful in this case only four years later?

2. This Citicorp order was one of the first prominent cases to explore the question of whether the limitations of the Bank Holding Company Act — and particularly prohibitions on insurance activities enacted in Title VI of the Garn-St Germain Act — apply to banks and subsidiaries of banks. Note how the two concurring statements deal with this issue. Whose view did the Second Circuit adopt their views in the *Citicorp (Family Guardian)* decision? See Chapter Four, section 4.C. To what extent has Congress accepted

their perspective? See 12 U.S.C. § 1831a. To what extent do the OCC's new regulation for operating subsidiaries reflect their perspective? See 12 C.F.R. § 5.34.

# Section 3. Expansion through National Banks

An alternative path to expanded insurance powers for depository institutions has been the creative interpretation of existing bank powers. As discussed above, decisions such as the *Saxon* case established implicit limitations on the direct authority of national banks to engage in additional insurance activities. As the following cases explore, however, those implicit limitations have not proved insurmountable. For one thing, *Saxon* and related cases did not have direct application to state-chartered banks. In theory, state-chartered banks were free to engage in insurance activities, provided appropriate state authorities approved the activities and no Bank Holding Company Act problems of the sort discussed in the *In re Citicorp ("American State Bank of Rapid City")* order arose. See Independent Insurance Agents of America (IIAA) v. Board of Governors, 890 F.2d 1275 (2d Cir. 1989), *cert. denied*, 498 U.S. 810 (1990). In 1991, however, Congress limited the authority of state-chartered institutions (and their subsidiaries) to engage in any significant insurance underwriting, thus restricting them to only insurance agency functions. See 12 U.S.C. § 1831a. The next cases explore the efforts of national banks to keep pace with their state-chartered counterparts, notwithstanding the *Saxon* line.

## A. Section 92 Powers

## Independent Insurance Agents of America v. Ludwig
### 997 F.2d 958 (D.C. Cir. 1993)

Buckley, Circuit Judge:

In 1963, the Comptroller ruled that section 92 [of the National Bank Act, enacted in 1916,] permits the branch of a national bank located in a community with a population of 5,000 or under ("small town") to sell insurance even though its principal office is located in a larger community. This policy is codified at 12 C.F.R. § 7.7100 (1993).

The present controversy has its genesis in an opinion issued in 1983 by Debra A. Chong, an attorney in the Comptroller's San Francisco office. In response to a letter from a Commerce Department official, she asserted that a small-town bank could sell insurance "without geographic restriction to the community [in which] it is located," though whether sales could be made across state lines was "an unsettled issue." In 1984, the United States National Bank of Oregon ("the Bank"), a subsidiary of U.S. Bancorp, proposed to sell insurance from its branch in Banks, Oregon, population 489, "to customers of U.S. Bank and others." The Bank said that its proposal relied on section 92 and the Chong letter. In reply, the Comptroller told the Bank not to proceed until "this Office communicates in writing that it has no objection." See 12 C.F.R. § 5.34(d)(1). The Comptroller then undertook a review of the policy set forth in the Chong letter.

In 1986, the agency endorsed the Chong position and approved the Bank's proposal. A letter from Judith A. Walter, the Senior Deputy Comptroller for National Operations, explained:

> Based on our analysis of the relevant legal precedent, we have concluded that Ms. Chong correctly determined that a national bank or its branch which is located in a place of 5,000 or under population may sell insurance to existing and potential customers located anywhere. In other words, while the bank or bank branch must be located in a small town, it can sell insurance to persons and businesses located outside that town.

As bases for this conclusion, the official discussed the statute, its legislative history, principles of statutory construction, and the regulation allowing branch banks to sell insurance from small towns.

## DISCUSSION

Appellants challenge the Comptroller's action as contrary to congressional intent, contrary to the Comptroller's prior interpretations of section 92, and contrary to the parallel provisions of the Bank Holding Company Act. We discuss these arguments in turn.

A. Interpretation of Section 92

The precise question before us is whether section 92 places any limitations on the geographical scope of the insurance business that may be conducted by a national bank located in a community having a population of 5,000 or under. It is not relevant, for this purpose, that the bank in question is a subsidiary of a major banking corporation.

In examining the Comptroller's interpretation of the National Bank Act, we apply the principles set forth in Chevron U.S.A. Inc. v. NRDC, 467 U.S. 837, 842-45 (1984). We start by searching for an "unambiguously expressed intent of Congress," id. at 843, that addresses the "precise question at issue," id. at 843 n.9. If we find such an intent, "that is the end of the matter"; we must enforce it. Id. at 842. If we do not, we must defer to the agency's interpretation so long as it is permissible. Id. at 843; see also K Mart Corp. v. Cartier, Inc., 486 U.S. 281, 292 (1988) (court must defer if agency construction "not in conflict with the plain language of the statute"). Appellants argue that Congress specifically intended to restrict the insurance sales geographically. In the alternative, they submit that although Congress had no specific intent on the matter, the Comptroller's interpretation is unreasonable.

In our quest for congressional intent, we begin, as always, with the words of the statute. See Mead Corp. v. Tilley, 490 U.S. 714, 722 (1989). Section 92 provides that a national bank located and doing business in a community having a population of not more than 5,000 may "act as the agent for any ... insurance company ... by soliciting and selling insurance and collecting premiums." 12 U.S.C.S. § 92. These words evince no unambiguous command that the banks may sell insurance only to local townspeople.

The statutory structure is even less helpful to appellants. As originally enacted, section 92 also permitted banks in small towns to "act as the broker or agent for others in making or procuring loans on real estate *located within one hundred miles* of the place in which said bank may be located." 12 U.S.C.S. § 92 (1978) (emphasis added). As Judge Pratt noted, this provision indicates that "Congress knew how to impose geographic restrictions when it wanted to." 736 F.

Supp. at 1168; see INS v. Cardoza-Fonseca, 480 U.S. 421, 432 (1987). Congress subsequently repealed the loan-brokering provision, see Pub. L. No. 97-320, § 403(b), 96 Stat. 1511 (1982), but that repeal did not purport to affect the provisions at issue here; they continue to be governed by the 1916 congressional intent.

As the words and structure do not reflect an unambiguous intent on the issue, we may consult legislative history. See Burlington N. R.R. v. Oklahoma Tax Comm'n, 481 U.S. 454, 461 (1987) (stating that "legislative history can be a legitimate guide to a statutory purpose obscured by ambiguity"). The only "history" appellants are able to offer is a letter from the then-Comptroller, J. Skelton Williams, to the Chairman of the Senate Banking and Currency Committee, which the Chairman entered in the Congressional Record. 53 Cong. Rec. S11,001 (1916), cited in Saxon v. Georgia Ass'n of Indep. Ins. Agents, 399 F.2d 1010, 1015-16 (5th Cir. 1968).

In that letter, Mr. Williams observed that many banks in small towns had failed and others had been "tempted to exact excessive and in some cases grossly usurious rates." 53 Cong. Rec. at S11,001. To give the struggling banks "additional sources of revenue and [to] place them in a position where they could better compete with local State banks and trust companies," he recommended allowing national banks in towns with a population of 3,000 or under to sell insurance and to broker real estate loans. Id. He stressed that the new powers should be limited to small-town banks, which would be unlikely to "trespass upon outside business naturally belonging to others." Id. He added:

> I think it would be unwise and therefore undesirable to confer this privilege generally upon banks in large cities where the legitimate business of banking affords ample scope for the energies of trained and expert bankers. I think it would be unfortunate if any movement should be made in the direction of placing the banks of the country in the category of department stores. The business is one requiring training, skill, and application, and I think that the profession of banking would suffer if there should be a departure from the principles which should govern and have heretofore governed.

Id. As enacted, the amendments used a population cut-off of 5,000 rather than 3,000.

We agree with appellants that U.S. Bancorp, with its more than $ 7 billion in assets, is not the sort of struggling "country bank" whose plight troubled Mr. Williams. He and any members of Congress who were influenced by his letter might well have been dismayed if they had foreseen a multi-billion-dollar holding company selling insurance nationwide through the small-town branch of a subsidiary bank. But we cannot assume that Mr. Williams' letter was read, much less relied upon, by the majorities in Congress who enacted section 92. Cf. Murphy v. Empire of Am., FSA, 746 F.2d 931, 935 (2d Cir. 1984) (isolated remarks on floor of Congress "are entitled to little or no weight"). Thus, we accord it only limited deference.

In sum, we find nothing in this history to suggest an unambiguous congressional intent on the precise question at issue. Furthermore, it is not our job to divine how legislators would have responded to hypotheticals, see American Bankers Ass'n v. SEC, 804 F.2d 739, 749 (D.C. Cir. 1986) --particularly where the question is as unknowable as the reaction of 1916 legislators to a world of microchips, communication satellites, fax machines, direct mail and telephone solicitation, and all the other technologies and techniques that now enable a nationwide business to be conducted from any hamlet. We decline appellants' invitation to recast the statute to fit contemporary circumstances; when time and technology open up a loophole, it is up to Congress to decide whether it should be plugged, and how.

As we have found no specific congressional intent to restrict the geographical reach of the insurance sales authorized by section 92, we turn to the second prong of Chevron: whether the challenged interpretation represented "a permissible construction of the statute." 467 U.S. at 843. In appellants' view, the Comptroller's action fails this lenient test by "interpreting the limited exception contained in Section 92 so broadly as to destroy the National Bank Act's overarching policy against permitting national banks to engage in the sale of insurance and other commercial activities not incidental to the business of banking."

We see no need, however, to canvass the landscape of banking regulation. The Fifty-third Congress expressly permitted small town banks to sell insurance, and the Comptroller has concluded that it did not impose a geographic limit on the insurance business they are allowed to conduct. To overturn the Comptroller's construction, we would have to conclude that it is "so inconsistent" with a "sufficiently clear" statutory policy as to demonstrate that "Congress' clear intent has been violated." Investment Co. Inst. v. Conover, 790 F.2d 925, 935 (D.C. Cir. 1986) (internal quotation marks and citation omitted). We find no basis for doing so. And, to the extent that subsequent developments have threatened to cause the section 92 exception to swallow any rules, the "solution," if there is to be one, lies with Congress, not the courts.

If, as appellants claim, there has indeed been a departure from the "overarching policy" of the NBA, it had its genesis decades before the Comptroller approved the Bank's proposal. In 1963, the Comptroller permitted small-town branch banks to sell insurance. See 36 Fed. Reg. 17,000, at 17,015 (1971) (publishing 1963 ruling). No longer did section 92 aid only the "small national banks" about which Mr. Williams had written, 53 Cong. Rec. at S11,001; now, heavily capitalized corporations with faraway headquarters could share its benefits, including those deriving from technological innovations undreamed of in the early years of this century. This appears to be the crucial step away from the constraints on the activities of major banks that Congress may well have intended. Judge Pratt, however, ruled that laches prevented appellants from challenging the 1963 regulation, see 736 F. Supp. at 1165 n.11, and they do not appeal that ruling.

Finally, appellants note that the Comptroller's Chief Counsel asserted in a 1987 speech that "the business of banking is the business of providing financial services--and insurance is one of them." J.A. 162. Appellants maintain that this speech exposes the Comptroller's order here as "an effort to subvert the core policies sub silentio in pursuit of a covert deregulatory agenda." Brief for Appellants at 31. The district court, however, refused to consider the speech as a supplemental exhibit, and termed it "a post hoc commentary" of no relevance. 736 F. Supp. at 1163 n.4. In our view, the speech is hardly a smoking gun, and the evidentiary ruling was well within the court's capacious discretion. See United States v. Dakins, 872 F.2d 1061, 1063 (D.C. Cir. 1989).

B. Deviation from Prior Policy

"Divergence from agency precedent demands an explanation." Hall v. McLaughlin, 864 F.2d 868, 872 (D.C. Cir. 1989). As evidence of inconsistent prior policies, appellants proffer six unpublished letters from the Comptroller's office that are dated between 1963 and 1986. They were released to appellants under the Freedom of Information Act, with the recipients' names and addresses blacked out.

We need not determine whether these letters conflict with the Comptroller's current interpretation because, like "most decisions in most federal agencies," they "have no effect as precedents." 4 K. Davis, Administrative Law Treatise § 20:9, at 31 (2d ed. 1983). In "the real world of agency practice," informal unpublished letters "should not engender reliance." Malkan FM Assocs. v. FCC, 935 F.2d 1313, 1319 (D.C. Cir. 1991); cf. USAA Fed. Savings Bank v. McLaughlin, 849 F.2d 1505, 1509 (D.C. Cir. 1988) (finding agency action not yet final based partly upon "the informality of the communication (an unpublished letter to a particular individual responding to a specific inquiry)"); New York Stock Exch., Inc. v. Bloom, 562 F.2d 736, 741 (D.C. Cir. 1977) (finding informal advisory letter from Comptroller's office not ripe for review). The Comptroller may well have assumed that section 92 imposed some geographic limit, but, as he never set forth that assumption in a binding statement, his current interpretation of section 92 does not deviate from prior policy.

C. Bank Holding Company Act

Appellants base two arguments on the 1982 amendment to the Bank Holding Company Act ("BHCA"), which permits any subsidiary of a bank holding company to sell insurance in a place with a population of 5,000 or under. See 12 U.S.C. § 1843(c)(8)(C). Congress evidently intended that the provision parallel section 92, see S. Rep. No. 536, 97th Cong. 2d Sess. 38 (1982), and the Federal Reserve Board has interpreted it as limiting the insurance activities to areas with fewer than 5,000 people and "other areas of less than 5,000 adjacent" to them, 51 Fed. Reg. 30,201, at 36,206 (1986).

Appellants assert that the 1982 BHCA amendment, as interpreted by the Federal Reserve Board, illuminates the intent of the 1916 Congress. The problems with this argument are multiple. As Judge Pratt noted, "the two provisions were enacted over sixty-five years apart and deal with two different types of banking institutions, each subject to a distinct set of laws and regulations administered by separate agencies." 736 F. Supp. at 1171. Moreover, an act of Congress in 1982 can shed no light on the intent of Congress in 1916. See Russello v. United States, 464 U.S. 16, 26 (1983). . . .

## Comments and Questions

1. What is the significance of the Court's decision in the *Ludwig* decision? Are there any limits on the authority of national banks to establish offices in small towns and then developing national marketing programs? For example, suppose a large national bank established an insurance agency in a branch located in a town of less than 5,000, and then the agency launched a national insurance marketing program and contracted with holding company affiliates to provide advertising support, direct mail marketing, telemarketing services, and other types of back office services. If personnel located at the branch office undertook to oversee and supervise all affiliate services and if all client records were located at the branch office, would this arrangement be permissible? What if hard copies of client records were stored elsewhere, but electronic copies were maintained at the branch office? See Letter from Julie L. Williams, Chief Counsel, OCC, to Robert L.

Andersen, Esq., First Union Corporation (Nov. 4, 1996) (OCC Interpretive Letter No. 753).

2. Section 92 of the National Bank Act has been a much litigated provision in recent years. Earlier in this proceeding, the District of Columbia Circuit reached the surprising conclusion that the provision had been accidentally repealed through a drafting error in 1918. See Independent Insurance Agents of America v. Clarke, 955 F.2d 731 (D.C. Cir. 1992). That decision caused a mild sensation in the banking industry until both the applicant bank and the Comptroller sought review in the Supreme Court, which concluded that the provision survived notwithstanding the scrivener's mistake. See United States National Bank of Oregon v. Independent Insurance Agents of America, 508 U.S. 439 (1993). Was the Supreme Court's decision a victory for the banking industry?

## B. Insurance as an Incidental Banking Power

The *Independent Insurance Agents of America v. Ludwig* decision offered national banks one important entree into the insurance business. The next case represents an effort to build on that success.

## Nationsbank v. VALIC
### 513 U.S. 251 (1995)

Justice GINSBURG delivered the opinion of the Court.

These consolidated cases present the question whether national banks may serve as agents in the sale of annuities. The Comptroller of the Currency, charged by Congress with superintendence of national banks, determined that federal law permits such annuity sales as a service to bank customers. Specifically, the Comptroller considered the sales at issue "incidental" to "the business of banking" under the National Bank Act, Rev. Stat. § 5136, as amended, 12 U.S.C. § 24 Seventh (1988 ed. and Supp. V). The Comptroller further concluded that annuities are not "insurance" within the meaning of § 92; that provision, by expressly authorizing banks in towns of no more than 5,000 people to sell insurance, arguably implies that banks in larger towns may not sell insurance. . . .

I

Petitioner NationsBank of North Carolina, N. A., a national bank based in Charlotte, and its brokerage subsidiary sought permission from the Comptroller of the Currency, pursuant to 12 CFR § 5.34 (1994), for the brokerage subsidiary to act as an agent in the sale of annuities. Annuities are contracts under which the purchaser makes one or more premium payments to the issuer in exchange for a series of payments, which continue either for a fixed period or for the life of the purchaser or a designated beneficiary. When a purchaser invests in a "variable" annuity, the purchaser's money is invested in a designated way and payments to the purchaser vary with investment performance. In a classic "fixed" annuity, in contrast, payments do not vary. Under the contracts NationsBank proposed to sell, purchasers could direct their payments to a variable, fixed, or hybrid account, and would be allowed periodically to modify their choice. The issuers would be various insurance companies. See Letter from J. Michael Shepherd, Senior Deputy Comptroller, to Robert M. Kurucza (Mar. 21, 1990) (Comptroller's Letter).

The Comptroller granted NationsBank's application. He concluded that national banks have authority to broker annuities within "the business of banking" under 12 U.S.C. § 24 Seventh. He further concluded that § 92, addressing insurance sales by banks in towns with no more than 5,000 people, did not impede his approval; for purposes of that provision, the Comptroller explained, annuities do not rank as "insurance." See Comptroller's Letter 41a-47a.

Respondent Variable Annuity Life Insurance Co. (VALIC), which sells annuities, challenged the Comptroller's decision. . . . Relying on its decision in Saxon v. Georgia Assn. of Independent Ins. Agents, Inc., 399 F.2d 1010 (1968), the Fifth Circuit first held that § 92 bars banks not located in small towns from selling insurance, and then rejected the Comptroller's view that annuities are not insurance for purposes of § 92. See 998 F.2d, at 1298-1302.

## II.

### A

In authorizing NationsBank to broker annuities, the Comptroller invokes the "power [of banks] to broker a wide variety of financial investment instruments," Comptroller's Letter 38a, which the Comptroller considers "part of [banks'] traditional role as financial intermediaries," ibid., and therefore an "incidental power . . . necessary to carry on the business of banking." 12 U.S.C. § 24 Seventh; see also Interpretive Letter No. 494 (Dec. 20, 1989) (discussing features of financial investment instruments brokerage that bring this activity within the "business of banking") (cited in Comptroller's Letter 38a). The Comptroller construes the § 24 Seventh authorization of "incidental powers . . . necessary to carry on the business of banking" as an independent grant of authority; he reads the specific powers set forth thereafter as exemplary, not exclusive.

VALIC argues that the Comptroller's interpretation is contrary to the clear intent of Congress because the banking power on which the Comptroller relies--"brokering financial investment instruments"--is not specified in § 24 Seventh. According to VALIC, the five specific activities listed in § 24 Seventh after the words "business of banking" are exclusive--banks are confined to these five activities and to endeavors incidental thereto. Id., at 35-36. VALIC thus attributes no independent significance to the words "business of banking." We think the Comptroller better comprehends the Act's terms.

The second sentence of § 24 Seventh, in limiting banks' "dealing in securities," presupposes that banks have authority not circumscribed by the five specifically listed activities. Congress' insertion of the limitation decades after the Act's initial adoption makes sense only if banks already *had* authority to deal in securities, authority presumably encompassed within the "business of banking" language which dates from 1863. VALIC argues, however, that the limitation was imposed by the Glass-Steagall Act of 1933, and that the power Glass-Steagall presupposed was specifically granted in the McFadden Act of 1927. While the statute's current wording derives from the Glass-Steagall Act, see Act of June 16, 1933, ch. 89, § 16, 48 Stat. 184, the earlier McFadden Act does not bolster VALIC's case, for that Act, *too*, limited an activity already part of the business national banks did. See Act of Feb. 25, 1927, § 2(b), 44 Stat.

1226 ("*Provided*, That the business of buying and selling investment securities shall hereinafter be limited to buying and selling without recourse . . . ."); see also Clarke v. Securities Industry Assn., supra, at 407-408 (even before the McFadden Act, banks conducted securities transactions on a widespread basis); 2 F. Redlich, The Molding of American Banking: Men and Ideas, pt. 2, pp. 389-393 (1951) (describing securities activities of prominent early national banks).[2]

### B

As we have just explained, the Comptroller determined, in accord with the legislature's intent, that "the business of banking" described in § 24 Seventh covers brokerage of financial investment instruments, and is not confined to the examples specifically enumerated. He then reasonably concluded that the authority to sell annuities qualifies as part of, or incidental to, the business of banking. National banks, the Comptroller observed, are authorized to serve as agents for their customers in the purchase and sale of various financial investment instruments, Comptroller's Letter 38a,[3] and annuities are widely recognized as just such investment products. See D. Shapiro & T. Streiff, Annuities 7 (1992) (in contrast to life insurance, "annuities . . . are primarily investment products"); 1 J. Appleman & J. Appleman, Insurance Law & Practice § 84, p. 295 (1981) ("Annuity contracts must . . . be recognized as investments rather than as insurance.").

By making an initial payment in exchange for a future income stream, the customer is deferring consumption, setting aside money for retirement, future expenses, or a rainy day. For her, an annuity is like putting money in a bank account, a debt instrument, or a mutual fund. Offering bank accounts and acting as agent in the sale of debt instruments and mutual funds are familiar parts of the business of banking. See, e.g., Securities Industry Assn. v. Board of Governors, FRS, 468 U.S. 207, 215 (1984) ("Banks long have arranged the purchase and sale of securities as an accommodation to their customers."); First Nat. Bank of Hartford v. Hartford, 273 U.S. 548, 559-560 (1927) (banks have authority to sell mortgages and other debt instruments they have originated or acquired by discount).

In sum, modern annuities, though more sophisticated than the standard savings bank deposits of old, answer essentially the same need. By providing customers with the opportunity to invest in one or more annuity options, banks are essentially offering financial investment instruments of the kind congressional authorization permits them to broker. Hence, the Comptroller reasonably typed the permission NationsBank sought as an "incidental power . . . necessary to carry on the business of banking."[4]

---

[2]   We expressly hold that the "business of banking" is not limited to the enumerated powers in § 24 Seventh and that the Comptroller therefore has discretion to authorize activities beyond those specifically enumerated. The exercise of the Comptroller's discretion, however, must be kept within reasonable bounds. Ventures distant from dealing in financial investment instruments--for example, operating a general travel agency--may exceed those bounds.

[3]   The Comptroller referred to Interpretive Letter No. 494 (Dec. 20, 1989) (approving brokerage of agricultural, oil, and metals futures).

[4]   Assuring that the brokerage in question would not deviate from traditional bank practices, the Comptroller specified that NationsBank "will act only as agent, . . . will not have a principal stake in

### III.

### A

In the alternative, VALIC argues that 12 U.S.C. § 92 (1988 ed., Supp. V) bars NationsBank from selling annuities as agent. . . . The parties disagree about whether § 92, by negative implication, precludes national banks located in places more populous than 5,000 from selling insurance. We do not reach this question because we accept the Comptroller's view that, for the purpose at hand, annuities are properly classified as investments, not "insurance."

Again, VALIC contends that the Comptroller's determination is contrary to the plain intent of Congress, or else is unreasonable. In support of its position that annuities are insurance, VALIC notes first that annuities traditionally have been sold by insurance companies. But the sale of a product by an insurance company does not inevitably render the product insurance. For example, insurance companies have long offered loans on the security of life insurance, see 3 Appleman & Appleman, Insurance Law and Practice § 1731, at 562 (1967), but a loan does not thereby become insurance.

VALIC further asserts that most States have regulated annuities as insurance and that Congress intended to define insurance under § 92 by reference to state law. Treatment of annuities under state law, however, is contextual. States generally classify annuities as insurance when defining the powers of insurance companies and state insurance regulators. See, e.g., 998 F.2d, at 1300, n. 2 (citing statutes). But in diverse settings, States have resisted lump classification of annuities as insurance. See, e.g., In re New York State Assn. of Life Underwriters, Inc. v. New York State Banking Dept., 83 N.Y.2d 353, 363, 632 N.E.2d 876, 881 (1994) (rejecting "assertion that annuities are insurance which [state-chartered] banks are not authorized to sell," even though state insurance law "includes 'annuities' in its description of 'kinds of insurance authorized'"); In re Estate of Rhodes, 197 Misc. 232, 237, 94 N.Y.S.2d 406, 411 (Surr. Ct. 1949) (annuity contracts do not qualify for New York estate tax exemption applicable to insurance); Commonwealth v. Metropolitan Life Ins. Co., 254 Pa. 510, 513-516, 98 A. 1072, 1073 (1916) (annuities are not insurance for purposes of tax that insurance companies pay on insurance premiums received within the State); State ex rel. Equitable Life Assurance Soc. of United States v. Ham, 54 Wyo. 148, 159, 88 P.2d 484, 488 (1939) (same).

As our decisions underscore, a characterization fitting in certain contexts may be unsuitable in others. See, e.g., Atlantic Cleaners & Dyers, Inc. v. United States, 286 U.S. 427, 433 (1932) ("meaning [of words] well may vary to meet the purposes of the law"; courts properly give words "the meaning which the legislature intended [they] should have in each instance"); cf. Cook, "Substance" and "Procedure" in the Conflict of Laws, 42 Yale L. J. 333, 337 (1933) ("The tendency to assume that a word which appears in two or more legal rules, and so in connection with more than one purpose, has and should have precisely the same scope in all of them, runs all through legal discussions. It has all the tenacity of original sin and must constantly be guarded against."). Moreover, the federal banking law does not plainly require automatic reference to state law here. The Comptroller has concluded that the federal regime is best served by classifying annuities according to their functional characteristics. Congress has not ruled out that course, see

---

annuity contracts and therefore will incur no interest rate or actuarial risks." Comptroller's Letter 48a.

Chevron, 467 U.S., at 842; courts, therefore, have no cause to dictate to the Comptroller the state law constraint VALIC espouses.

VALIC further argues that annuities functionally resemble life insurance because some annuities place mortality risk on the parties. Under a classic fixed annuity, the purchaser pays a sum certain and, in exchange, the issuer makes periodic payments throughout, but not beyond, the life of the purchaser. In pricing such annuities, issuers rely on actuarial assumptions about how long purchasers will live.

While cognizant of this similarity between annuities and insurance, the Comptroller points out that mortality risk is a less salient characteristic of contemporary products. Many annuities currently available, both fixed and variable, do not feature a life term. Instead they provide for payments over a term of years; if the purchaser dies before the term ends, the balance is paid to the purchaser's estate. Moreover, the presence of mortality risk does not necessarily qualify an investment as "insurance" under § 92. For example, VALIC recognizes that a life interest in real property is not insurance, although it imposes a mortality risk on the purchaser. Tr. of Oral Arg. 42. Some conventional debt instruments similarly impose mortality risk. See Note, Reverse Annuity Mortgages and the Due-on-Sale Clause, 32 Stan. L. Rev. 143, 145-151 (1979).

B

VALIC also charges the Comptroller with inconsistency. As evidence, VALIC refers to a 1978 letter from a member of the Comptroller's staff describing annuity investments as insurance arrangements. See Letter from Charles F. Byrd, Assistant Director, Legal Advisory Services Division, Office of the Comptroller of the Currency (June 16, 1978) (Byrd Letter). We note, initially, that the proposal disfavored in the 1978 letter did not clearly involve a bank selling annuities as an agent, rather than as a principal. See Byrd Letter 1a ("The bank would purchase a group annuity policy from an insurer and then sell annuity contracts as investments in trust accounts."). Furthermore, unlike the Comptroller's letter to NationsBank here, the 1978 letter does not purport to represent the Comptroller's position. Compare Byrd Letter 1a ("It is my opinion . . . ") with Comptroller's Letter 35a ("The OCC's legal position on this issue was announced in a [prior 1990 letter]. Since I find neither policy nor supervisory reasons to object to this proposal, the Subsidiary may proceed."). Finally, any change in the Comptroller's position might reduce, but would not eliminate, the deference we owe his reasoned determinations. See Good Samaritan Hospital v. Shalala, 508 U.S.    (1993) (slip op., at 14) (quoting NLRB v. Iron Workers, 434 U.S. 335, 351 (1978)).

The Comptroller's classification of annuities, based on the tax deferral and investment features that distinguish them from insurance, in short, is at least reasonable. See Comptroller's Letter 44a. A key feature of insurance is that it indemnifies loss. See Black's Law Dictionary 802 (6th ed. 1990) (first definition of insurance is "contract whereby, for a stipulated consideration, one party undertakes to compensate the other for loss on a specified subject by specified perils"). As the Comptroller observes, annuities serve an important investment purpose and are functionally similar to other investments that banks typically sell. See supra, at 7-8. And though fixed annuities more closely resemble insurance than do variable annuities, fixed annuities too have significant investment features and are functionally similar to debt instruments. See ibid.

Moreover, mindful that fixed annuities are often packaged with variable annuities, the Comptroller reasonably chose to classify the two together.

\* \* \*

We respect as reasonable the Comptroller's conclusion that brokerage of annuities is an "incidental power . . . necessary to carry on the business of banking." We further defer to the Comptroller's reasonable determination that 12 U.S.C. § 92 is not implicated because annuities are not insurance within the meaning of that section. Accordingly, the judgment of the Court of Appeals for the Fifth Circuit is reversed.

## Comments and Questions

1. The respondent in this case was also a party to SEC v. VALIC, 359 U.S. 65 (1959), a decision we considered in Chapter Fourteen. In the prior decision, the company failed to persuade the Supreme Court that variable annuities should be considered solely an insurance product for purposes of the federal securities laws. Here, the company was unable to persuade the Court that the product had sufficient insurance characteristics to implicate the implicit prohibitions of *Saxon* and related cases. Was the Court in this later case correct in overlooking the insurance characteristics of fixed and variable annuities?

2. After this decision, suppose a national bank proposed to offer its clients a retirement CD, under which a customer would deposit a minimum of $5000 and choose a maturity date at least a year in the future (usually an expected date of retirement). Suppose further that at maturity the customer would be entitled to withdraw two thirds of the account balance, and the rest would be paid out as a monthly annuity. Could the Comptroller of the Currency authorize such an activity? See OCC Interpretive Letter No. 649, 1994 Fed Banking L. Rep. (CCH) ¶ 83,556 (May 12, 1994). Could the Federal Reserve Board authorize a bank holding company to market such products? Could the Federal Reserve Board authorize a bank holding company to a financial service firm with extensive insurance underwriting operations? How? See *Fed Approves Citicorp-Travelers Merger; Surprisingly Few Conditions Put on Deal,* Wall St. Jr., Sept. 24, 1998.

4. In both the *Ludwig* and *VALIC* decisions, federal courts showed substantial deference to the Comptroller's interpretations of law. In light of these judicial victories is it appropriate for the OCC and its legal staff to advance innovative, even aggressive interpretations of the National Bank Act? Or should the agency limit itself to its best guess of what Congress intended when a particular provision was adopted? Which approach was the agency following in *Ludwig* and *VALIC?*

### *Problem 16-1*

Representatives of the insurance industry, among others, have been critical of the Comptroller of the Currency's support of bank insurance powers. Pending before Congress are several proposals to constrain the OCC in this area in the future. If you were on the staff of the Senate Banking Committee, would you support any of these proposals?

a.  An amendment instructing courts to defer to state insurance regulators and not the OCC in determining whether insurance activities were authorized activities for national banks.

b.  An amendment instructing courts to make de novo determinations of all issues relating to bank insurance powers, deferring to neither the OCC nor state insurance regulators.

c.  The creation of a National Council on Financial Services — including the heads of the federal banking agencies, chairs of the SEC and CFTC, representatives of state insurance regulators, and the Secretary of the Treasury — to resolve inter-sector disputes involving banking, insurance, and securities.

## Section 4. State Authority Over Bank Insurance

A final issue to consider is the authority of state insurance regulators to impose state insurance regulations on bank insurance activities.  This has been a simmering issue for a number of years.  Back in the 1980s, the Pennsylvania insurance commissioner succeeded in blocking Ford Motor's efforts to own thrift subsidiaries at the same time the company controlled insurance affiliates licensed to do business in the Commonwealth.  The Commissioner persuaded the Third Circuit that such an arrangement violated anti-affiliation provisions in the Pennsylvania insurance statute that prohibited depository institutions from affiliating with insurance companies in the jurisdiction.  See Ford Motor Co. v. Insurance Commissioner, 874 F.2d 926 (1989).  The following case presents a similar challenge to a national bank seeking to capitalize on the D.C. Circuit's *Independent Insurance Agents of America v. Ludwig* decision.

### Barnett Bank v. Nelson
### 517 U.S. 570 (1996)

Justice BREYER delivered the opinion of the Court.

The question in this case is whether a federal statute that permits national banks to sell insurance in small towns pre-empts a state statute that forbids them to do so.  To answer this question, we must consider both ordinary pre-emption principles, and also a special federal anti-pre-emption rule, which provides that a federal statute will *not* pre-empt a state statute enacted "for the purpose of regulating the business of insurance"-- *unless* the federal statute *"specifically relates to the business of insurance."*  McCarran-Ferguson Act, 15 U.S.C. § 1012(b) (emphasis added). . . .

I

In 1916 Congress enacted a federal statute that says that certain national banks "may" sell insurance in small towns.  It provides in relevant part:

"In addition to the powers now vested by law in national [banks] organized under the laws of the United States *any such [bank]* located and doing business in any place [with a population] ... [of not more than] five thousand ... may, under such rules and regulations as *may* be prescribed by the Comptroller of the Currency, *act as the agent for any fire, life, or other insurance company* authorized by the authorities of the State ... to do business [there], ... by soliciting and selling insurance ... Provided, however, That no such bank shall ... guarantee the payment of any premium ... And provided further, That the bank shall not guarantee the truth of any statement made by an assured [when applying] ... for insurance." Act of Sept. 7, 1916 (Federal Statute), 39 Stat. 753, 12 U.S.C. § 92 (emphases changed).

In 1974 Florida enacted a statute that prohibits certain banks from selling most kinds of insurance. It says: "No [Florida licensed] insurance agent ... who is associated with, ... owned or controlled by ... a financial institution shall engage in insurance agency activities...." Fla. Stat. Ann. § 626.988(2) (Supp.1996) (State Statute). The term "financial institution" includes "any bank ... [except for a] bank which is not a subsidiary or affiliate of a bank holding company and is located in a city having a population of less than 5,000 ...." § 626.988(1)(a). Thus, the State Statute says, in essence, that banks cannot sell insurance in Florida--except that an *unaffiliated* small town bank (i.e., a bank that is not affiliated with a bank holding company) may sell insurance in a small town. Ibid.

In October 1993 petitioner Barnett Bank, an "affiliate[d]" national bank which does business through a branch in a small Florida town, bought a Florida licensed insurance agency. The Florida State Insurance Commissioner, pointing to the State Statute, (and noting that the unaffiliated small town bank exception did not apply), ordered Barnett's insurance agency to stop selling the prohibited forms of insurance. Barnett, claiming that the Federal Statute pre-empted the State Statute, then filed this action for declaratory and injunctive relief in federal court.

The District Court held that the Federal Statute did not pre-empt the State Statute, but only because of the special insurance-related federal anti-pre-emption rule. The McCarran-Ferguson Act, which creates that rule, says: "No act of Congress shall be construed to invalidate, impair, or supersede any law enacted by any State for the purpose of regulating the business of insurance, or which imposes a fee or tax upon such business, unless such Act specifically relates to the business of insurance...." McCarran-Ferguson Act (or Act), § 2(b), 59 Stat. 34, 15 U.S.C. § 1012(b).

The District Court decided both (1) that the Federal Statute did not fall within the McCarran-Ferguson Act's exception because it did not "specifically relat[e] to the business of insurance"; and (2) that the State Statute was a "law enacted ... for the purpose of regulating the business of insurance." Barnett Banks of Marion County, N.A. v. Gallagher, 839 F.Supp. 835, 840-841, 843 (M.D.Fla.1993) (internal quotation marks omitted). Consequently, the McCarran-Ferguson Act, in the District Court's view, instructs courts not to "constru[e]" the Federal Statute "to invalidate" the State Statute. 15 U.S.C. § 1012(b). The Eleventh Circuit Court of Appeals, for similar reasons, agreed that the Federal Statute did not pre-empt the State Statute. Barnett Bank of Marion County, N.A. v. Gallagher, 43 F.3d 631, 634-637 (1995).

We granted certiorari due to uncertainty among lower courts about the pre- emptive effect of this Federal Statute. See Owensboro Nat. Bank v. Stephens, 44 F.3d 388 (C.A.6 1994) (pre-emption of Kentucky statute that prevents national banks from selling insurance in small towns); First Advantage Ins., Inc. v. Green, 652 So.2d 562 (La.Ct.App.), rev. den., 654 So.2d 331 (1995) (no pre-emption). We now reverse the Eleventh Circuit.

## II

We shall put the McCarran-Ferguson Act's special anti-pre-emption rule to the side for the moment, and begin by asking whether, in the absence of that rule, we should construe the Federal Statute to pre-empt the State Statute. This question is basically one of congressional intent. Did Congress, in enacting the Federal Statute, intend to exercise its constitutionally delegated authority to set aside the laws of a State? If so, the Supremacy Clause requires courts to follow federal, not state, law. U.S. Const., Art. VI, cl. 2; see California Fed. Sav. & Loan Assn. v. Guerra, 479 U.S. 272, 280-281 (1987) (reviewing pre-emption doctrine).

Sometimes courts, when facing the pre-emption question, find language in the federal statute that reveals an explicit congressional intent to pre-empt state law. E.g., Jones v. Rath Packing Co., 430 U.S. 519, 525, 530-531 (1977). More often, explicit pre-emption language does not appear, or does not directly answer the question. In that event, courts must consider whether the federal statute's "structure and purpose," or nonspecific statutory language, nonetheless reveal a clear, but implicit, pre-emptive intent. Id., at 525; Fidelity Fed. Sav. & Loan Assn. v. de la Cuesta, 458 U.S. 141, 152-153 (1982). A federal statute, for example, may create a scheme of federal regulation "so pervasive as to make reasonable the inference that Congress left no room for the States to supplement it." Rice v. Santa Fe Elevator Corp., 331 U.S. 218, 230 (1947). Alternatively, federal law may be in "irreconcilable conflict" with state law. Rice v. Norman Williams Co., 458 U.S. 654, 659 (1982). Compliance with both statutes, for example, may be a "physical impossibility," Florida Lime & Avocado Growers, Inc. v. Paul, 373 U.S. 132, 142-143 (1963); or, the state law may "stan[d] as an obstacle to the accomplishment and execution of the full purposes and objectives of Congress." Hines v. Davidowitz, 312 U.S. 52, 67 (1941).

In this case we must ask whether or not the Federal and State Statutes are in "irreconcilable conflict." The two statutes do not impose directly conflicting duties on national banks--as they would, for example, if the federal law said, "you must sell insurance," while the state law said, "you may not." Nonetheless, the Federal Statute authorizes national banks to engage in activities that the State Statute expressly forbids. Thus, the State's prohibition of those activities would seem to "stan[d] as an obstacle to the accomplishment" of one of the Federal Statute's purposes--unless, of course, that federal purpose is to grant the bank only a very *limited* permission, that is, permission to sell insurance *to the extent that state law also grants permission to do so.*

That is what the State of Florida and its supporting amici argue. They say that the Federal Statute grants national banks a permission that is limited to circumstances where state law is not to the contrary. In their view, the Federal Statute removes only federal legal obstacles, not state legal obstacles, to the sale of insurance by national banks. But we do not find this, or the State's related, ordinary pre-emption arguments convincing.

For one thing, the Federal Statute's language suggests a broad, not a limited, permission. That language says, without relevant qualification, that national banks "may ... act as the agent" for insurance sales. 12 U.S.C. § 92. It specifically refers to "rules and regulations" that will govern such sales, while citing as their source not state law, but the federal Comptroller of the Currency. Ibid. It also specifically refers to state regulation, while limiting that reference to licensing--not of banks or insurance agents, but of the insurance companies whose policies the bank, as insurance agent, will sell. Ibid.

For another thing, the Federal Statute says that its grant of authority to sell insurance is an "addition to the *powers* now vested by law in national [banks]." Ibid. (emphasis added). In using the word "powers," the statute chooses a legal concept that, in the context of national bank legislation, has a history. That history is one of interpreting grants of both enumerated and incidental "powers" to national banks as grants of authority not normally limited by, but rather ordinarily pre-empting, contrary state law. See, e.g., First Nat. Bank of San Jose v. California, 262 U.S. 366, 368-369 (1923) (national banks' "power" to receive deposits pre-empts contrary state escheat law); Easton v. Iowa, 188 U.S. 220, 229-230, (1903) (national banking system normally "independent, so far as powers conferred are concerned, of state legislation"); cf. Waite v. Dowley, 94 U.S. 527, 533 (1876) ("[W]here there exists a concurrent right of legislation in the States and in Congress, and the latter has exercised its power, there remains in the States no authority to legislate on the same matter").

Thus, this Court, in a case quite similar to this one, held that a federal statute permitting, but not requiring, national banks to receive savings deposits, pre-empts a state statute prohibiting certain state and national banks from using the word "savings" in their advertising. Franklin Nat. Bank v. New York, 347 U.S. 373, 375-379 (1954) (Federal Reserve Act provision that national banks "may continue ... to receive ... savings deposits" read as "declaratory of the right of a national bank to enter into or remain in that type of business"). See also de la Cuesta, supra, at 154-159 (1982) (federal regulation permitting, but not requiring, national banks to include in mortgage contracts a debt accelerating "due on sale" clause, pre-empts a state law forbidding the use of such a clause); cf. Lawrence County v. Lead-Deadwood School Dist. No. 40-1, 469 U.S. 256 (1985) (federal statute providing that local government units "may" expend federal funds for any governmental purpose pre-empts state law restricting their expenditure).

In defining the pre-emptive scope of statutes and regulations granting a power to national banks, these cases take the view that normally Congress would not want States to forbid, or to impair significantly, the exercise of a power that Congress explicitly granted. To say this is not to deprive States of the power to regulate national banks, where (unlike here) doing so does not prevent or significantly interfere with the national bank's exercise of its powers. See, e.g., Anderson Nat. Bank v. Luckett, 321 U.S. 233, 247-252 (1944) (state statute administering abandoned deposit accounts did not "unlawful[ly] encroac[h] on the rights and privileges of national banks"); McClellan v. Chipman, 164 U.S. 347, 358 (1896) (application to national banks of state statute forbidding certain real estate transfers by insolvent transferees would not "destro[y] or hampe[r]" national banks' functions); National Bank v. Commonwealth, 76 U.S. (9 Wall.) 353, 362 (1869) (national banks subject to state law that does not "interfere with, or impair [national banks'] efficiency in performing the functions by which they are designed to serve [the Federal] Government").

Nor do these cases control the interpretation of federal banking statutes that accompany a grant of an explicit power with an explicit statement that the exercise of that power is subject to state law. See, e.g., 12 U.S.C. § 36(c) (McFadden Act) (authorizing national banks to operate branches, but only where state law authorizes state banks to do so); § 92(a) (Comptroller of Currency may grant fiduciary powers "by special permit to national banks applying therefor, when not in contravention of State or local law"). Not surprisingly, this Court has interpreted those explicit provisions to mean what they say. See, e.g., First Nat. Bank in Plant City v. Dickinson, 396 U.S. 122, 131 (1969) (under McFadden Act, state branching restrictions apply to national banks); First Nat. Bank of Logan v. Walker Bank & Trust Co., 385 U.S. 252, 260-261 (1966) (same); see also Van Allen v. Assessors, 70 U.S.(3 Wall.) 573, 586 (1865) (enforcing 1864 amendments to National Bank Act expressly authorizing state taxation of national bank shares).

But, as we pointed out, supra, at 1108-1109, where Congress has not expressly conditioned the grant of "power" upon a grant of state permission, the Court has ordinarily found that no such condition applies. In Franklin Nat. Bank, the Court made this point explicit. It held that Congress did not intend to subject national banks' power to local restrictions, because the federal power-granting statute there in question contained "no indication that Congress [so] intended ... as it has done *by express language* in several other instances." 347 U.S., at 378, and n. 7 (emphasis added) (collecting examples).

The Federal Statute before us, as in Franklin Nat. Bank, explicitly grants a national bank an authorization, permission, or power. And, as in Franklin Nat. Bank, it contains no "indication" that Congress intended to subject that power to local restriction. Thus, the Court's discussion in Franklin Nat. Bank, the holding of that case, and the other precedent we have cited above, strongly argue for a similar interpretation here--a broad interpretation of the word "may" that does not condition federal permission upon that of the State.

Finally, Florida and its supporters challenge this interpretation by arguing that special circumstances surrounding the enactment of the Federal Statute nonetheless demonstrate Congress' intent to grant only a limited permission (subject to State approval). They point to a letter to Congress written by the Comptroller of the Currency in 1916. The Comptroller attached a draft of what became the Federal Statute, and the letter explains to Congress why the Comptroller wants Congress to enact his proposal. The letter says that, since 1900, many small town national banks had failed; that some States had authorized small town state banks to sell insurance; that providing small town national banks with authority to sell insurance would help them financially; and that doing so would also improve their competitive position vis-a-vis state banks. The relevant language in the letter (somewhat abridged) reads as follows:

"[Since 1900, of 3,084 small national banks, 438] have either failed or gone into liquidation.... [T]here are many banks located in [small towns] ... where the small deposits which the banks receive may make it somewhat difficult [to earn] ... a satisfactory return.... "For some time I have been giving careful consideration to the question as to how the powers of these small national banks might be enlarged so as to provide them with additional sources of revenue and place them in a position where they could better compete with local State banks and trust companies which are sometimes authorized under the law to do a class of business not strictly that of commercial banking.... "[The federal banking laws, while granting national banks certain "incidental powers," do not give them] either expressly nor by necessary implication the power to act as agents for insurance companies .
. . .

"My investigations lead me respectfully to recommend to Congress an amendment to the national-bank act by which national banks located in [small towns] ... may be permitted to act as agents for insurance companies.... "It seems desirable from the standpoint of public policy and banking efficiency that this authority should be limited to banks in small communities. This additional income will strengthen them and increase their ability to make a fair return. . . . "I think it would be unwise and therefore undesirable to confer this privilege generally upon banks in large cities where the legitimate business of banking affords ample scope for the energies of trained and expert bankers. . . . "I inclose . . . a draft . . . designed to empower national banks located in [small] towns . . . under such regulations and restrictions as may from time to time be approved and promulgated by the Comptroller of the Currency, to act as agents for the placing of insurance policies. . . ." 53 Cong. Rec. 11001 (1916) (Letter from Comptroller Williams to the Chairman of the Senate Bank and Currency Committee).

Assuming for argument's sake that this letter is relevant, and in response to the arguments of Florida and its supporters, we point out that the letter does not significantly advance their cause. Although the letter mentions that enlarging the powers of small national banks will help them "better compete with local State banks," it primarily focuses upon small town national banks' need for added revenue--an objective met by a broad insurance-selling authority that is not limited by state law. The letter refers to limitations that *federal* regulation might impose, but it says nothing about limitations imposed by *state* regulation or *state* law. The letter makes clear that authority to sell insurance in small towns is an added "incidental power" of a national bank--a term that, in light of this Court's then-existing cases, suggested freedom from conflicting state regulation. See Easton, 188 U.S., at 229-230; First Nat. Bank, 262 U.S., at 368-369. The letter sets forth as potential objections to the proposal, (or to its extension to larger national banks), concerns about distracting banking management or inhibiting the development of banking expertise--not concerns related to state regulatory control.

We have found nothing elsewhere in the Federal Statute's background or history that significantly supports the State's arguments. And as far as we are aware, the Comptroller's subsequent interpretation of the Federal Statute does not suggest that the statute provides only a limited authority subject to similar state approval. Cf. 12 CFR § 7.7100 (1995); OCC Interpretive Letter No. 366, CCH Fed. Banking L. Rep. P 85,536, p. 77,833 (1986).

In light of these considerations, we conclude that the Federal Statute means to grant small town national banks authority to sell insurance, whether or not a State grants its own state banks or national banks similar approval. Were we to apply ordinary legal principles of pre-emption, the federal law would pre- empt that of the State.

III

We now must decide whether ordinary legal principles of pre-emption, or the special McCarran-Ferguson Act anti-pre-emption rule, governs this case. The lower courts held that the McCarran-Ferguson Act's special anti-pre-emption rule applies, and instructs courts not to "construe" the Federal Statute to "invalidate, impair, or supersede" that of the State. 15 U.S.C. § 1012(b). By its terms, however, the Act does not apply when the conflicting federal statute "*specifically relates to the business of insurance.*" Ibid. (emphasis added). In our view, the Federal Statute in this case "specifically relates to the business of insurance"--therefore the McCarran-Ferguson Act's special anti- pre-emption rule does not apply.

Our conclusion rests upon the McCarran-Ferguson Act's language and purpose, taken together. Consider the language--"specifically relates to the business of insurance." In ordinary English, a statute that says that banks may act as insurance agents, and that the Comptroller of the Currency may regulate their insurance-related activities, "*relates*" to the insurance business. The word "relates" is highly general, and this Court has interpreted it broadly in other pre-emption contexts. See, e.g., Pilot Life Ins. Co. v. Dedeaux, 481 U.S. 41, 47 (1987) (words " 'relate to' " have " 'broad common-sense meaning, such that a state law "relate[s] to" a benefit plan "... if it has a connection with or reference to such a plan" ' ") (quoting Metropolitan Life Ins. Co. v. Massachusetts, 471 U.S. 724, 739 (1985), and Shaw v. Delta Air Lines Inc., 463 U.S. 85, 97 (1983)); Morales v. Trans World Airlines, Inc., 504 U.S. 374, 383-384 (1992) (interpreting similarly the words " 'relating to' " in the Airline Deregulation Act).

More importantly, in ordinary English, this statute "*specifically*" relates to the insurance business. "Specifically" can mean "explicitly, particularly, [or] definitely," Black's Law Dictionary 1398 (6th ed.1990), thereby contrasting a *specific* reference with an *implicit* reference made by more general language to a broader topic. The general words "business activity," for example, will sometimes include, and thereby implicitly refer, to insurance; the particular words "finance, banking, and insurance" make that reference explicitly *and specifically.*

Finally, using ordinary English, one would say that this statute specifically relates to the "*business of insurance.*" The statute explicitly grants national banks permission to "act as the agent for any fire, life, or other insurance company," to "solici[t] and sel[l] insurance," to "collec[t] premiums," and to "receive for services so rendered ... fees or commissions," subject to Comptroller regulation. 12 U.S.C. § 92. It also sets forth certain specific rules prohibiting banks from guaranteeing the "payment of any premium on insurance policies issued through its agency ..." and the "truth of any statement made by an assured in filing his application for insurance." Ibid. The statute thereby not only focuses directly upon industry-specific selling practices, but also affects the relation of insured to insurer and the spreading of risk--matters that this Court, in other contexts, has placed at the core of the McCarran-Ferguson Act's concern. See Union Labor Life Ins. Co. v. Pireno, 458 U.S. 119, 129 (1982) (citing Group Life & Health Ins. Co. v. Royal Drug Co., 440 U.S. 205 (1979); see also Department of Treasury v. Fabe, 508 U.S. 491, 502-504 (1993).

Consider, too, the McCarran-Ferguson Act's basic purposes. The Act sets forth two mutually reinforcing purposes in its first section, namely that "continued regulation and taxation by the several States of the business of insurance is in the public interest," and that "*silence* on the part of the Congress shall not be construed to impose any barrier to the regulation or taxation of such business by the several States." 15 U.S.C. § 1011 (emphasis added). The latter phrase, particularly the word "silence," indicates that the Act does not seek to insulate state insurance regulation from the reach of all federal law. Rather, it seeks to protect state regulation primarily against *inadvertent* federal intrusion--say, through enactment of a federal statute that describes an affected activity in broad, general terms, of which the insurance business happens to comprise one part.

The circumstances surrounding enactment of the McCarran-Ferguson Act suggest the same. Just prior to the law's enactment, this Court, in United States v. South-Eastern Underwriters Assn., 322 U.S. 533 (1944), held that a federal antitrust law, the Sherman Act, applied to the business of insurance. The Sherman Act's highly general language said nothing specifically about insurance. See 15 U.S.C. § 1 (forbidding every "contract, combination ... or conspiracy, in restraint of trade or commerce among the several States"). The Sherman Act applied only to activities in or affecting interstate commerce.  Hopkins v. United States, 171 U.S. 578, 586 (1898).  Many lawyers and insurance professionals had previously thought, (relying, in part, on this Court's opinion in Paul v. Virginia, 75 U.S.(8 Wall.) 168, 183 (1868), and other cases), that the issuance of an insurance policy was not a "transaction of commerce," and therefore fell outside the Sherman Act's scope.  South-Eastern Underwriters told those professionals that they were wrong about interstate commerce, and that the Sherman Act did apply.  And South-Eastern Underwriters' principle meant, consequently, that other generally phrased congressional statutes might also apply to the issuance of insurance policies, thereby interfering with state regulation of insurance in similarly unanticipated ways.

In reaction to South-Eastern Underwriters, Congress "moved quickly," enacting McCarran-Ferguson "to restore the supremacy of the States in the realm of insurance regulation." Fabe, supra, at 500.  But the circumstances we have just described mean that "*restor[ation]*" of "supremacy" basically required setting aside the unanticipated effects of South-Eastern Underwriters, and cautiously avoiding similar unanticipated interference with state regulation in the future.  It did not require avoiding federal pre-emption by future federal statutes that indicate, through their "specific relat [ion]" to insurance, that Congress had focused upon the insurance industry, and therefore, in all likelihood, consciously intended to exert upon the insurance industry whatever pre-emptive force accompanied its law.  See also, e.g., insofar as relevant, 91 Cong. Rec. 483 (1945) (statement of Sen. O'Mahoney, floor manager of the Act, that the Act was intended to be "a sort of catch-all provision to take into consideration other acts of Congress which might affect the insurance industry, but of which we did not have knowledge at the time"); ibid. (similar statement of Sen. Ferguson).

The language of the Federal Statute before us is not general.  It refers specifically to insurance.  Its state regulatory implications are not surprising, nor do we believe them inadvertent.  See Part II, supra. Consequently, considerations of purpose, as well as of language, indicate that the Federal Statute falls within the scope of the McCarran- Ferguson's "specifically relates" exception to its anti-pre-emption rule.  Cf. John Hancock Mut. Life Ins. Co. v. Harris Trust & Sav. Bank, 114 S.Ct. 517, 525 (1993) (adopting the United States' view that language in the Employee Retirement Income Security Act of 1974 defining a "guaranteed benefit policy" as a certain kind of "insurance" policy, "obviously and specifically relates to the business of insurance") (internal quotation marks omitted).

We shall mention briefly why we are not convinced by several of the parties' remaining arguments.  Florida says that the Federal Statute "specifically relates" to banking, not to insurance.  But, a statute may specifically relate to more than one thing.  Just as an ordinance forbidding dogs in city parks specifically relates to dogs and to parks, so a statute permitting banks to sell insurance can specifically relate to banks and to insurance.  Neither the McCarran-Ferguson Act's language, nor its purpose, requires the Federal Statute to relate *predominantly* to insurance.  To the contrary, specific detailed references to the insurance industry in proposed legislation normally will achieve the McCarran-Ferguson Act's objectives, for they will call the proposed legislation to the attention of interested parties, and thereby normally guarantee, should the proposal become law, that Congress will have focused upon its insurance-related effects.

An amicus argues that our interpretation would give the Act "little meaning," because "whenever a state statute 'regulates' the business of insurance, any conflicting federal statute necessarily will 'specifically relate' to the insurance business." We disagree. Many federal statutes with potentially pre-emptive effect, such as the bankruptcy statutes, use general language that does not appear to "specifically relate" to insurance; and where those statutes conflict with state law that was enacted "for the purpose of regulating the business of insurance," the McCarran-Ferguson Act's anti-pre-emption rule will apply. See generally Fabe, 508 U.S., at 501 (noting the parties' agreement that federal bankruptcy priority rules, although conflicting with state law, do not "specifically relate" to the business of insurance.)

The lower courts argued that the Federal Statute's 1916 date of enactment was significant, because Congress would have then believed that state insurance regulation was beyond its "Commerce Clause" power to affect. The lower courts apparently thought that Congress therefore could not have intended the Federal Statute to pre-empt contrary state law. The short answer to this claim is that there is no reason to think that Congress believed state insurance regulation beyond its constitutional powers to affect--insofar as Congress exercised those powers to create, to empower, or to regulate, national banks. See McCulloch v. Maryland, 17 U.S.(4 Wheat.) 316, (1819); Farmers' and Mechanics' Nat. Bank v. Dearing, 91 U.S. 29, 33 (1875); see also, e.g., Easton v. Iowa, 188 U.S., at 238. We have explained, see Part II, supra, why we conclude that Congress indeed *did* intend the Federal Statute to pre-empt conflicting state law.

Finally, Florida points to language in Fabe, which states that the McCarran-Ferguson Act "imposes what is, in effect, a clear-statement rule" that forbids pre-emption "unless a federal statute specifically requires otherwise." 508 U.S., at 507. Florida believes that this statement in Fabe means that the Federal Statute would have to use the words "state law is pre-empted," or the like, in order to fall within the McCarran-Ferguson Act exception. We do not believe, however, that Fabe imposes any such requirement. Rather, the quoted language in Fabe was a general description of the Act's effect. It simply pointed to the existence of the clause at issue here--the exception for federal statutes that "specifically relat[e] to the business of insurance." But it did not purport authoritatively to interpret the "specifically relates" clause. That matter was not at issue in Fabe. We therefore believe that Fabe does not require us to reach a different result here.

## Comments and Questions

1. As it turns out, the Comptroller of the Currency did authorize a national bank to offer the Retirement CD outlined in the questions following the *VALIC* decision. Does the *Barnett Bank* decision ensure that a national bank could not be barred from offering such a product in a state with an anti-affiliation statute like Florida's? See American Deposit Corp. v. Schacht, 84 F.3d 834 (7th Cir.), *cert. denied*, 117 S.Ct. 185 (1996).

2. Suppose a state-chartered bank from a jurisdiction that allows its institutions broad insurance agency powers established a branch in a neighbor state with an anti-affiliation statute. Could the bank conduct insurance agency activities in its new branch?

3. After the *Barnett Bank* case, do state insurance regulators have any authority over national banks? How much? Who will resolve disagreements over this jurisdiction? Who

should?  For the Comptroller's initial views on the matter, see OCC Advisory Letter 96-8 (Oct. 8, 1996).  Is it reasonable to superimpose state insurance regulation on a national bank?  Would it be significantly more difficult to coordinate the two regulatory structures if national banks also engaged in substantial amounts of insurance underwriting?  How did Delaware deal with overlapping jurisdiction in the *Citicorp (Family Guardian)* decision?  How were similar problem resolved when banks began to undertake securities activities?

4.  Suppose Florida amended its Blue Sky laws to establish new approval procedures designed to police the fairness of variable annuity products, and then the state securities commissioner attempted to use this new power as a basis for reviewing the terms and pricing of all annuities sold through the Barnett Banks. Would this be a lawful exercise of power?

*Problem 16-2*

Under Texas insurance law, all agents selling annuities are required to obtain a licence from the Texas Insurance Department.  Licenses are only available to individuals or corporations organized under Texas law.  In addition, for a corporation to be licensed as an insurance agent for annuities in Texas, each of its officers, directors, and shareholders must be individually licensed as an agent.  To what extent, if at all, does this law apply to national banks selling annuities in Texas?

# Index

---

**References are to pages.**

---

1143